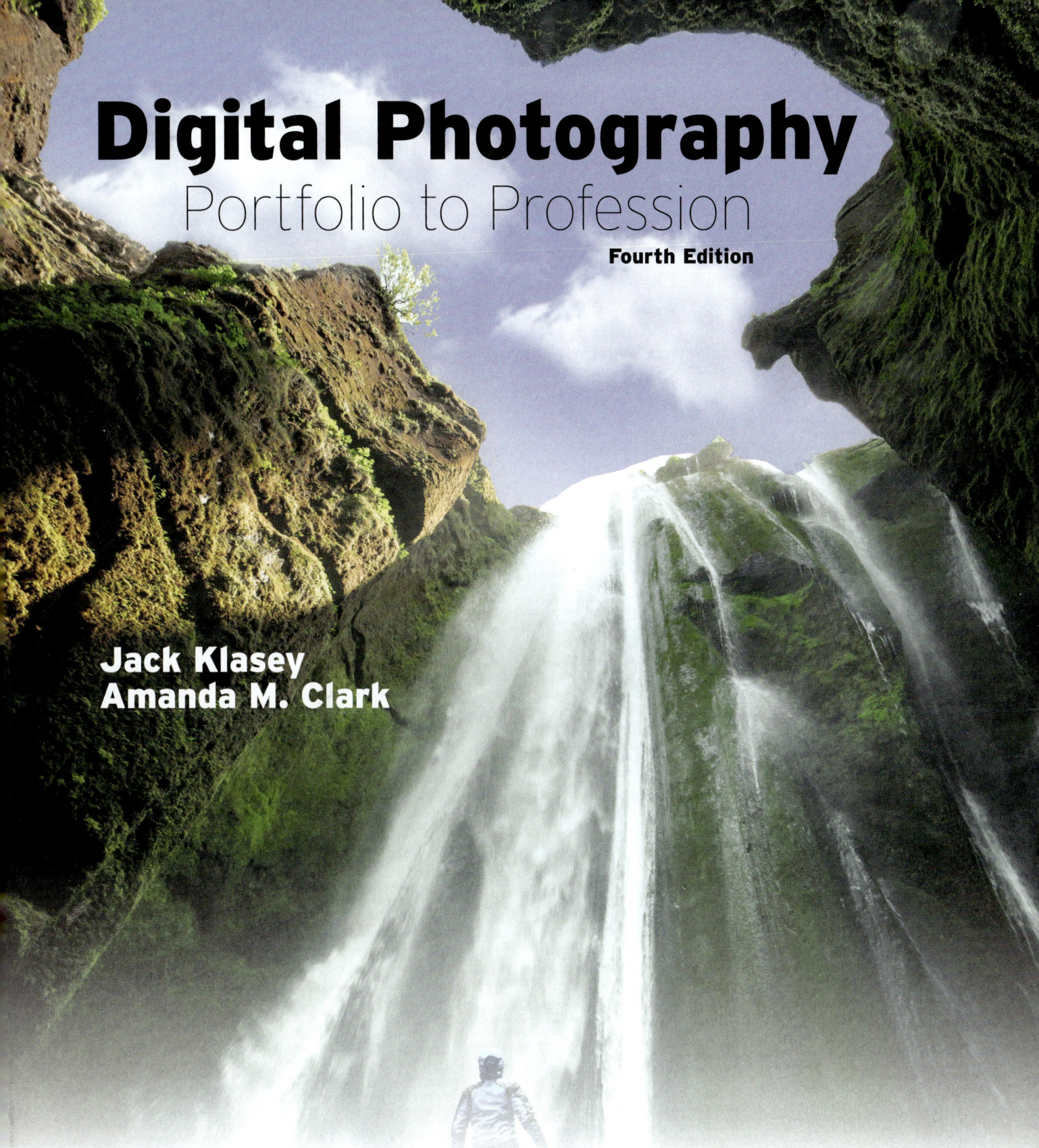

Digital Photography
Portfolio to Profession
Fourth Edition

Jack Klasey
Amanda M. Clark

Publisher
The Goodheart-Willcox Company, Inc.
Tinley Park, IL
www.g-w.com

Copyright © 2024
by
The Goodheart-Willcox Company, Inc.

Previous editions copyright 2017, 2012, 2002

All rights reserved. No part of this work may be reproduced, stored, or transmitted in any form or by any electronic or mechanical means, including information storage and retrieval systems, without the prior written permission of
The Goodheart-Willcox Company, Inc.

ISBN 978-1-63776-709-2

1 2 3 4 5 6 7 8 9 – 24 – 28 27 26 25 24 23

The Goodheart-Willcox Company, Inc. Brand Disclaimer: Brand names, company names, and illustrations for products and services included in this text are provided for educational purposes only and do not represent or imply endorsement or recommendation by the author or the publisher.

The Goodheart-Willcox Company, Inc. Safety Notice: The reader is expressly advised to carefully read, understand, and apply all safety precautions and warnings described in this book or that might also be indicated in undertaking the activities and exercises described herein to minimize risk of personal injury or injury to others. Common sense and good judgment should also be exercised and applied to help avoid all potential hazards. The reader should always refer to the appropriate manufacturer's technical information, directions, and recommendations; then proceed with care to follow specific equipment operating instructions. The reader should understand these notices and cautions are not exhaustive.

The publisher makes no warranty or representation whatsoever, either expressed or implied, including but not limited to equipment, procedures, and applications described or referred to herein, their quality, performance, merchantability, or fitness for a particular purpose. The publisher assumes no responsibility for any changes, errors, or omissions in this book. The publisher specifically disclaims any liability whatsoever, including any direct, indirect, incidental, consequential, special, or exemplary damages resulting, in whole or in part, from the reader's use or reliance upon the information, instructions, procedures, warnings, cautions, applications, or other matter contained in this book. The publisher assumes no responsibility for the activities of the reader.

The Goodheart-Willcox Company, Inc. Internet Disclaimer: The Internet resources and listings in this Goodheart-Willcox Publisher product are provided solely as a convenience to you. These resources and listings were reviewed at the time of publication to provide you with accurate, safe, and appropriate information. Goodheart-Willcox Publisher has no control over the referenced websites and, due to the dynamic nature of the Internet, is not responsible or liable for the content, products, or performance of links to other websites or resources. Goodheart-Willcox Publisher makes no representation, either expressed or implied, regarding the content of these websites, and such references do not constitute an endorsement or recommendation of the information or content presented. It is your responsibility to take all protective measures to guard against inappropriate content, viruses, or other destructive elements.

Adobe Disclaimer: Adobe Illustrator, InDesign, Lightroom, and Photoshop are registered trademarks of Adobe Incorporated.

Image Credits. Front cover: Smit/Shutterstock.com; Section opener: Rostizna/Shutterstock.com; Essential Question icon: ydecosta/Shutterstock.com; Portfolio Assignment, Procedure, and Real-World Photography feature icons: leosapiens/Shutterstock.com

Printed in Canada

Preface

Digital Photography: Portfolio to Profession is designed to provide beginning photographers with a blend of theory and practice that builds a solid foundation of photographic skills. The fourth edition of this textbook added "digital" to the title to reflect changes in the industry and to emphasize a digital-first approach. The content has been extensively revised to reflect the fact that digital imaging is accepted as the standard method of photography today. Mobile photography is also recognized as a category of photography.

To organize this vast subject, *Digital Photography: Portfolio to Profession* is presented in five major sections:
- Chapters 1 through 3 introduce you to the world of photography.
- Chapters 4 through 8 cover the basics of camera operation and the important concepts a photographer must understand before taking a picture (such as types of lenses and image capture media).
- Chapters 9 through 11 demonstrate how to create great photos through the elements of composition, effective lighting, and proper exposure.
- Chapters 12 through 16 explore various types of photography and how the nuances among the different types require slightly different approaches.
- Chapters 17 through 21 focus on postprocessing your images, including how to import, edit, and display your final photographs.

Each section concludes with a project that provides hands-on activities to help students practice the major concepts they have learned in each chapter. The goal is to create a thorough, well-rounded experience for students who are eager to start taking their own photographs and maintaining a portfolio.

While the continuing development of digital cameras, smartphones, and related software provides photographers with ever-improving and more convenient tools, the basic skill of photography will always be essential to the effective use of those tools. The photographer's need to produce a meaningful photograph that is well composed, properly lighted, and correctly exposed is constant.

About the Authors

Jack Klasey is the author of multiple books and is currently at work on a fourth. Mr. Klasey has several decades of experience in various areas of technical and educational communication as a writer, photographer, and editor. In addition to authoring books, he has done photographic illustrations for a number of publications and has developed dozens of audiovisual programs in the education and technical training fields.

Amanda M. Clark is a high school teacher at Southeast High School in Bradenton, Florida, where she is responsible for writing and managing her own curriculum for the five television production courses she teaches. Each course is part of the program known as SETV (Southeast TV). Ms. Clark is also Faculty Advisor and Director of Television for the SETV club, which live streams school sporting events, awards ceremonies, and other special projects that have gained national recognition. As part of the program, students compete in various events in SkillsUSA. Her students have earned more than 15 state championship titles and 8 national championship titles. Ms. Clark also advises the Technology Student Association (TSA) chapter at Southeast High School. She serves on the Florida TSA State Board of Directors, where she was recognized nationally as the High School Advisor of the Year for the state of Florida. In addition, Ms. Clark serves on the Florida Department of Education committee that oversees the standards for both the Digital Video Production and Television Production courses across the state. She earned her bachelor's degree in Telecommunications from the University of Florida and her master's degree in Digital Video and Design from the University of South Florida. Prior to joining education, Ms. Clark had some professional experience as a news producer and an anchor for NPR's *Morning Edition* in Gainesville, Florida. Most recently, Ms. Clark coauthored the fifth edition of ***Video: Digital Communication & Production***. Her work included restructuring the original text, adding new and relevant chapters, and incorporating section projects to create a capstone project for students.

Reviewers

The author and publisher wish to thank the following industry and teaching professionals for their valuable input into the development of *Digital Photography: Portfolio to Profession*.

Izehi Agboaye
Arlington ISD
Arlington, TX

John Bordeau
Kankakee Community College
Kankakee, IL

Enrique Crosby
Mexia High School
Mexia, TX

Batavia Domingue-Yost
Community Christian School
Stockbridge, GA

Wesley G. Force
Valdosta High School/Valdosta
  State University
Valdosta, GA

Aaron Jackson
United Technologies Center
Bangor, ME

Karen James
Maypearl High School
Maypearl, TX

Elizabeth Karp
Riverwood High School
Atlanta, GA

Christine Keyser-Fanick
John Paul Stevens High School
San Antonio, TX

Gregory Lewis
Washoe County SD-Region 2
Reno, NV

Steve Picklesimer
Smyrna High School
Smyrna, TN

Becky Raffalovich
Phoenix High School/Gwinnett
  County Public Schools
Lawrenceville, GA

Rodney Ragsdale
Coffee High School
Douglas, GA

Thomas Robinson
South San Francisco High
  School
South San Francisco, CA

Antonia Seltzer
Del Valle High School
El Paso, TX

Madelyn Troutner
E2CCB Hewes Educational
  Center
Ashville, NY

Acknowledgments

The author and publisher would like to thank the following companies, organizations, and individuals for their contribution of resource material, images, or other support in the development of ***Digital Photography: Portfolio to Profession.***

Better Light, Inc.
Bogen
Bogen Kata
Bonnie Knight/Kankakee Camera Club
Christy Clark
Clayton Pratt
Cokin Filters
Delkin Devices
Eastman Kodak Company
Foveon, Inc.
FUJIFILM North America Corporation, 2015
Glory Klasey
Gossen
Image Group Photography, LLC
Istabilizer
Jack O.P. Klasey
Jeep and Wrangler, registered trademarks of FCA US LLC
Justus Hayes/Shoes on Wires/shoesonwires.com
Kankakee County Museum archives
Katie Gorham
Kirk Enterprises
Kodak
Kodak Alaris
Larry Morris
Lensbaby
Lensbaby Photo by Ben Hutchison
Leonard Rue Enterprises
Lexar
Library of Congress
LPA Design photo by Zachary Gauthier
Manfrotto
Manfrotto/Kata
Metz
National Aeronautics and Space Administration
National Archives and Records Administration
Nikon, Inc., Melville, New York
NOAA/Harald Richter
Nokia
Olympus America, Inc.
Panasonic
Paul C. Buff, Inc.
Pelican
Phase One
Phase One photo by Alexander Flemming
Polaroid Corporation
Porter's Camera Store
Rollei Fototechnic
SanDisk
Seal/Bienfang
Sekonic
Siemens
Sinar Bron Imaging
Smith-Victor Corporation
Stroboframe
SUNWAYFOTO
Suzanne M. Silagi
Vivitar

New to This Edition

The following changes were made to the fourth edition of *Digital Photography: Portfolio to Profession* to strengthen the integrated learning solution and to remain current with industry standards and trends:

- New Chapter 10, *Improving Lighting*, was added to discuss how lighting affects a final image to emphasize the importance of proper lighting.
- New Chapter 16, *Mobile Photography*, was added to discuss shooting images with a smartphone and using the native camera app to address growing smartphone photography.
- New Chapter 21, *Mobile Postprocessing*, was added to discuss editing photos on the go using a smartphone to address growing smartphone postprocessing.
- The text was divided into five sections, with a hands-on project at the end of each section that includes the major concepts from each chapter.
- There is a heavier focus on digital-first content to reflect changes in the industry. There is also a greater focus on using newer technology (such as taking pictures on a smartphone and storing files on cloud-based software).
- Updated end-of-chapter questions reflect a more robust Instructional Learning Solution to assess multiple levels of learning: Know and Understand, Apply and Analyze, Critical Thinking, Suggested Activities, and Communicating about Photography.
- Added a Real-World Photography feature to provide examples of photography applications in the real world and in the industry.
- Added a new video library to the supplement package for digital users. Tutorial videos help reinforce important concepts, such as composition, handling a camera, and setting up projects in Adobe Photoshop and Lightroom. A short assessment is included for each video to ensure students understood the video.

The fourth edition also added a coauthor, Amanda M. Clark. Ms. Clark teaches high school television production in Florida and is Faculty Advisor and Director of Television for her school's TV club. Her students compete in SkillsUSA and have earned a number of impressive titles over the years. Ms. Clark also serves on the Florida TSA State Board of Directors, where she has been recognized nationally as the High School Advisor of the Year for the state of Florida. Having a coauthor who teaches today's high school students is highly beneficial. She knows what appeals to them, understands the current technology that is used, and is aware of the requirements instructors must meet in various digital photography courses. Ms. Clark also coauthored the fifth edition of *Video: Digital Communication & Production*.

Precision Exams by YouScience Certification

Goodheart-Willcox is pleased to partner with YouScience to correlate *Digital Photography: Portfolio to Profession* with their *Commercial Photography I* and *Commercial Photography II* certification standards. Students who pass the exam and performance portion of the exam can earn a Career Skills certification. Precision Exams by YouScience and Career Skills Exams were created in partnership with industry and subject matter experts to align real-world job skills with marketplace demands. Students can showcase their skills and knowledge with industry-recognized certifications—and build outstanding résumés to stand out from the crowd!

And for teachers, Precision Exams by YouScience provides:
- Access to a library of Career Skills Exams, including pre- and post-assessments for all 16 National Career Clusters
- Suite of on-demand reporting to measure program and student academic growth
- Easy-to-use, 100% online administration

To see how *Digital Photography: Portfolio to Profession* correlates to Precision Exams by YouScience standards, visit the Correlations tab at www.g-w.com/digital-photography-2024. For more information about Precision Exams by YouScience, visit www.youscience.com/certifications/career-clusters/.

michaeljung/Shutterstock.com

Features of the Textbook

The instructional design includes student-focused learning tools to help students succeed. This visual guide highlights the features designed for the textbook.

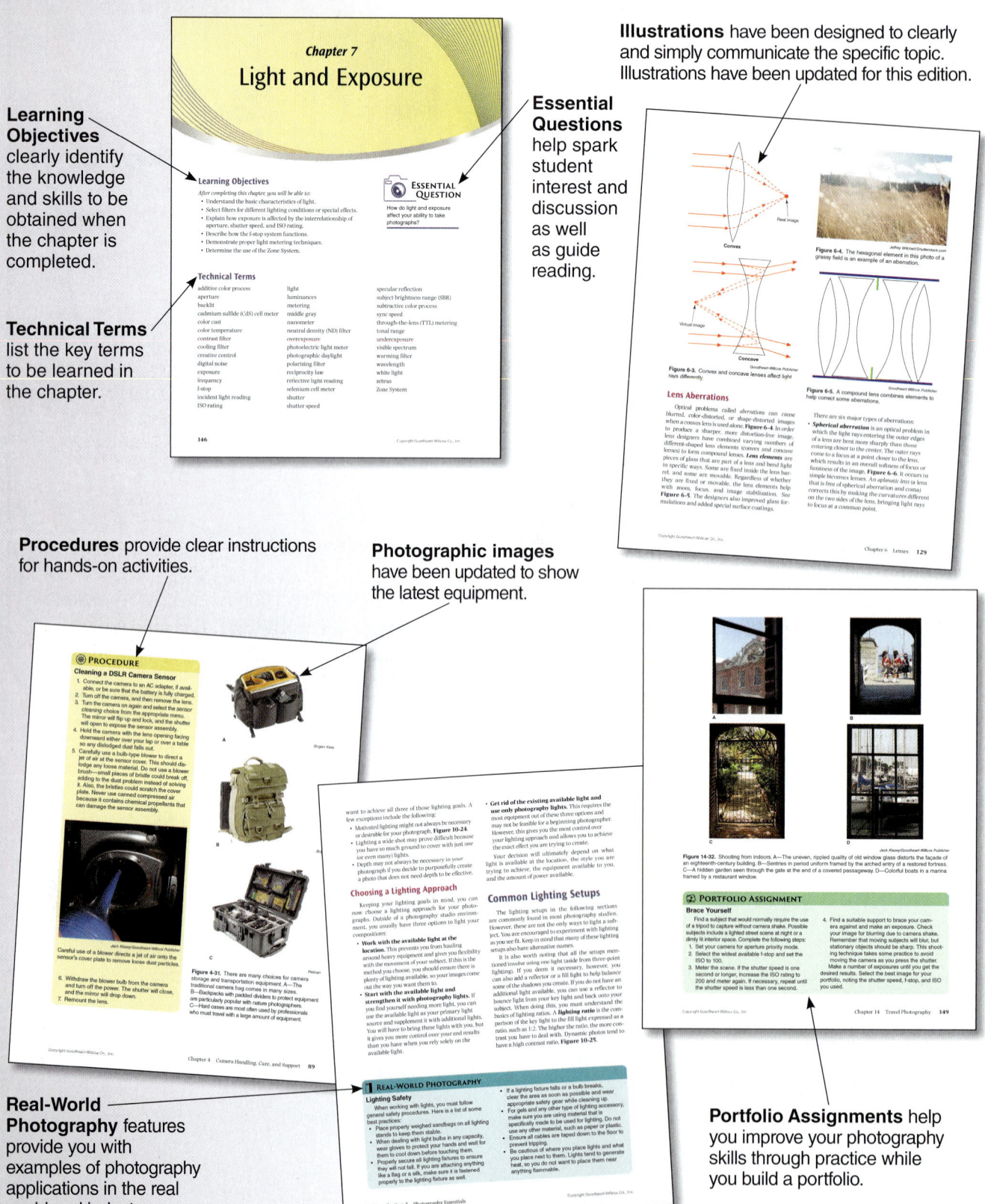

Learning Objectives clearly identify the knowledge and skills to be obtained when the chapter is completed.

Technical Terms list the key terms to be learned in the chapter.

Essential Questions help spark student interest and discussion as well as guide reading.

Illustrations have been designed to clearly and simply communicate the specific topic. Illustrations have been updated for this edition.

Procedures provide clear instructions for hands-on activities.

Photographic images have been updated to show the latest equipment.

Real-World Photography features provide you with examples of photography applications in the real world and industry.

Portfolio Assignments help you improve your photography skills through practice while you build a portfolio.

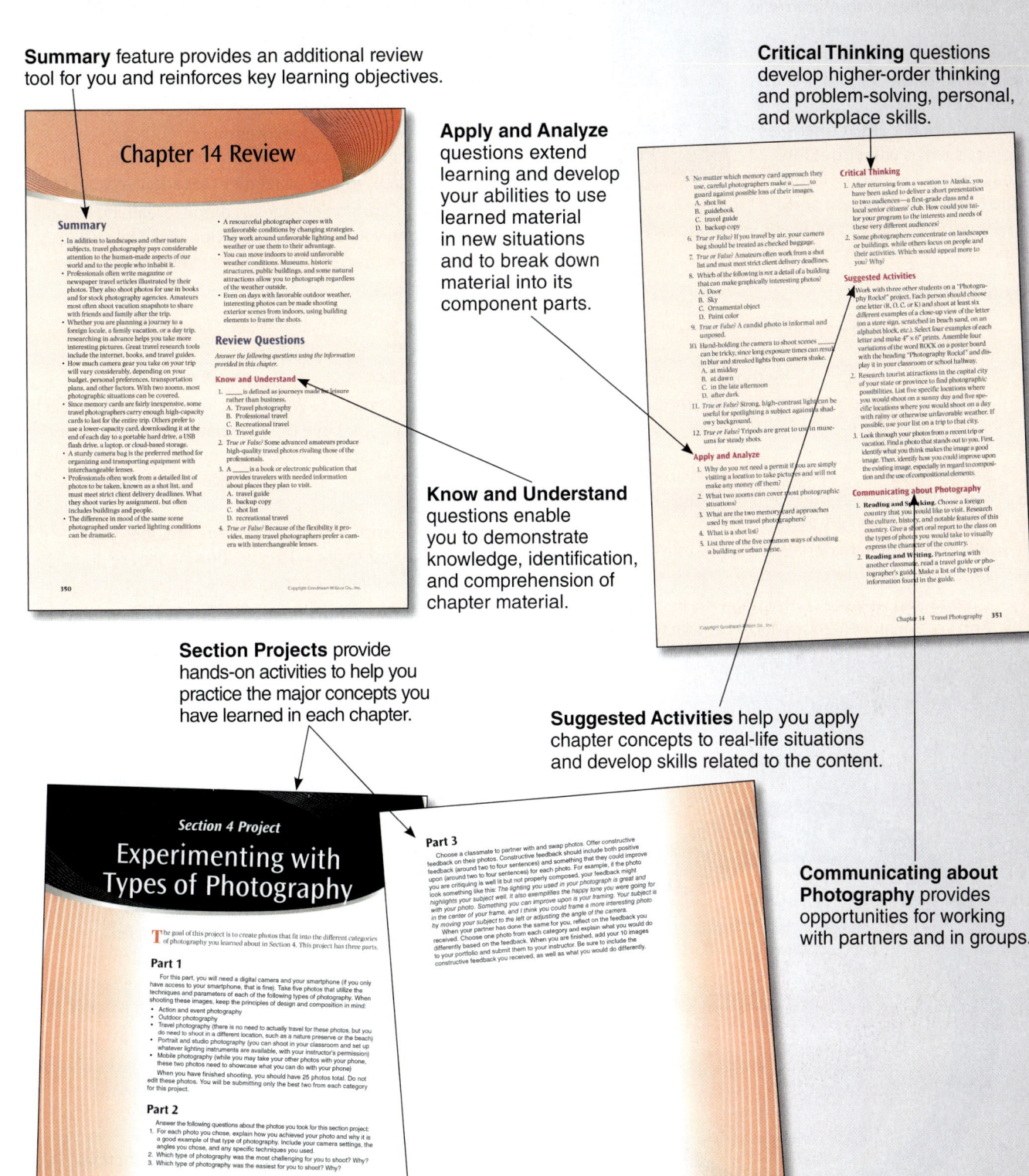

TOOLS FOR STUDENT AND INSTRUCTOR SUCCESS

Student Tools

Student Text

Digital Photography: Portfolio to Profession is intended for beginning photographers and is a blend of theory and practice that builds a solid foundation of photographic skills. It discusses topics such as what goes into making a good photograph, the types of equipment and methods involved in various types of photography, and how to edit photos.

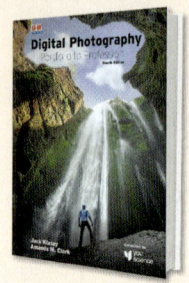

Lab Workbook

- Hands-on practice includes questions and activities.
- Organized to follow the textbook lessons to help students achieve key learning outcomes.

Online Learning Suite

- Online student text and lab workbook, along with rich supplemental content, brings digital learning to the classroom.
- All instructional materials are accessible at home, at school, or on the go.
- Companion website containing e-flash cards and vocabulary exercises allows interaction with content to create opportunities to increase achievement.

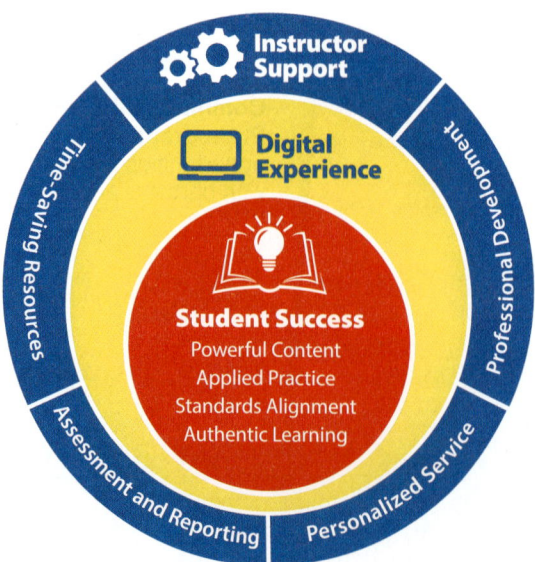

Instructor Tools

LMS Integration

Integrate Goodheart-Willcox content within your Learning Management System for a seamless user experience for both you and your students. EduHub LMS–ready content in Common Cartridge® format facilitates single sign-on integration and gives you control of student enrollment and data. With a Common Cartridge integration, you can access the LMS features and tools you are accustomed to using and G-W course resources in one convenient location—your LMS.

G-W Common Cartridge provides a complete learning package for you and your students. The included digital resources help your students remain engaged and learn effectively:

- **Digital Textbook**
- Online **Lab Workbook content**
- **Tutorial Videos**
- **Drill and Practice** vocabulary activities

When you incorporate G-W content into your courses via Common Cartridge, you have the flexibility to customize and structure the content to meet the educational needs of your students. You may also choose to add your own content to the course.

For instructors, the Common Cartridge includes the Online Instructor Resources. QTI® question banks are available within the Online Instructor Resources for import into your LMS. These prebuilt assessments help you measure student knowledge and track results in your LMS gradebook. Questions and tests can be customized to meet your assessment needs.

Online Instructor Resources

- The **Instructor Resources** provide instructors with time-saving preparation tools such as answer keys, editable lesson plans, and other teaching aids.
- **Instructor's Presentations for PowerPoint®** are fully customizable, richly illustrated slides that help you teach and visually reinforce the key concepts from each chapter.
- Administer and manage assessments to meet your classroom needs using **Assessment Software with Question Banks**, which include hundreds of matching, completion, multiple choice, and short answer questions to assess student knowledge of the content in each chapter.

See www.g-w.com/digital-photography-2024 for a list of all available resources.

Professional Development

- Expert content specialists
- Research-based pedagogy and instructional practices
- Options for virtual and in-person professional development

Brief Contents

Section 1 — The World of Photography
1. Our Visual World 4
2. From Pinholes to Pixels 24
3. Professional Photography 44

Section 2 — Understanding Camera Basics
4. Camera Handling, Care, and Support 72
5. The Camera System 106
6. Lenses 126
7. Light and Exposure 146
8. Digital Image Capture Media 178

Section 3 — Photography Essentials
9. Making a Picture 196
10. Improving Lighting 222
11. Making Exposure Decisions 244

Section 4 — Types of Photography
12. Action and Event Photography 270
13. Outdoor Photography 300
14. Travel Photography 332
15. Portrait and Studio Photography 352
16. Mobile Photography 378

Section 5 — Postprocessing
17. Importing Images 406
18. Digital Postprocessing Basics 424
19. Advanced Digital Postprocessing Techniques 466
20. The Finishing Touches 502
21. Mobile Postprocessing 524

Appendix: Film Basics and Safety 560

Contents

Section 1
The World of Photography

Chapter 1
Our Visual World 4
   Introduction to Our Visual World 6
   Photography Is Everywhere 6
   Photographic Career Opportunities 10
   Learning to See 15
   Building Your Portfolio 19

Chapter 2
From Pinholes to Pixels. 24
   Introduction to From Pinholes to Pixels. 26
   The Birth of Photography 26
   Introduction of Roll Film 30
   Color Photography 32
   The Growth of Digital Photography 34
   The Future of Photography 36

Chapter 3
Professional Photography 44
   Introduction to Professional Photography . . . 46
   What Is Professional Photography? 46
   How to Enter the Professional
      Photography Field 47
   Setting Up Your Business 49
   Operating Your Business 52
   Building Your Business 56
   Working with Clients, Employees,
      and Independent Contractors 60
   Growing Professionally 62
   Section 1 Project 68

Section 2
Understanding Camera Basics

Chapter 4
**Camera Handling, Care,
and Support 72**
   Introduction to Camera Handling, Care,
      and Support 74
   Learning about Your Camera 74
   Physical Care of Your Camera 85
   Camera Carrying Methods 90
   Camera Support Methods 91

Chapter 5
The Camera System 106
   Introduction to the Camera System 108
   Viewing/Focusing System 108
   Light Control System 112
   Image Receiver System 115
   Camera Varieties 117

Chapter 6
Lenses 126
   Introduction to Lenses 128
   How a Lens Works 128
   Camera Lens Types 135

Chapter 7
Light and Exposure 146
   Introduction to Light and Exposure 148
   Basic Light Theory 148
   Controlling Light with Filters 153
   Controlling Exposure 160
   Measuring Light 163
   The Zone System 169

Chapter 8
Digital Image Capture Media ... 178
- Introduction to Digital Image Capture Media ... 180
- Image Capture—Digital vs. Film ... 180
- The Digital Imaging Process ... 181
- Section 2 Project ... 192

Section 3
Photography Essentials

Chapter 9
Making a Picture ... 196
- Introduction to Making a Picture ... 198
- "Taking" a Picture vs. "Making" a Picture ... 198
- Composition Considerations ... 200
- Creating Visual Effects While Shooting ... 214

Chapter 10
Improving Lighting ... 222
- Introduction to Improving Lighting ... 224
- The Importance of Lighting ... 224
- Introduction to Lights ... 230
- Lighting Design ... 232
- Common Lighting Setups ... 234

Chapter 11
Making Exposure Decisions ... 244
- Introduction to Making Exposure Decisions ... 246
- Proper Exposure ... 246
- Determining Exposure ... 248
- Correcting Exposure Problems ... 249
- Equivalent Exposures ... 251
- Capturing the Light ... 257
- Section 3 Project ... 266

Section 4
Types of Photography

Chapter 12
Action and Event Photography ... 270
- Introduction to Action and Event Photography ... 272
- Stopping Motion ... 272
- Focus Techniques ... 276
- Blurring for Visual Interest ... 277
- Photojournalism ... 278
- Working with Flash ... 288

Chapter 13
Outdoor Photography ... 300
- Introduction to Outdoor Photography ... 302
- Landscape Photography ... 302
- Water Photography ... 315
- Animal Photography ... 318
- Close-Up Photography ... 322

Chapter 14
Travel Photography ... 332
- Introduction to Travel Photography ... 334
- Traveling with a Camera ... 334
- What Will You Shoot? ... 337
- When Will You Shoot? ... 343

Chapter 15
Portrait and Studio Photography ... 352
- Introduction to Portrait and Studio Photography ... 354
- Types of Portrait Photography ... 354
- Working with Ambient Light ... 356
- Working with Studio Lighting ... 357

Chapter 16
Mobile Photography 378
- Introduction to Mobile Photography 380
- What Is Mobile Photography? 380
- Mobile Camera Controls 380
- Traditional Camera Controls 383
- Native Camera Apps vs. Third-Party Photography Applications 388
- Tips and Tricks for Shooting with a Phone . . . 391
- Section 4 Project 402

Section 5
Postprocessing

Chapter 17
Importing Images 406
- Introduction to Importing Images 408
- Importing Methods from a Camera. 408
- Other Importing Methods. 410
- Copyright and the Photographer. 412
- Image Management. 414

Chapter 18
Digital Postprocessing Basics . . . 424
- Introduction to Digital Postprocessing Basics 426
- Digital vs. Traditional Postprocessing 426
- Image Editing Software. 427

Chapter 19
Advanced Digital Postprocessing Techniques 466
- Introduction to Advanced Digital Postprocessing Techniques 468
- Ethical Conduct and Image Manipulation. . . 468
- Selecting Parts of Images 468
- Combining Images. 479
- Applying Transformations and Filters 490
- Adding Color to a Monochrome Image 495

Chapter 20
The Finishing Touches. 502
- Introduction to the Finishing Touches. 504
- Electronic Display 504
- Making Prints. 506
- Print Mounting and Matting 511

Chapter 21
Mobile Postprocessing 524
- Introduction to Mobile Postprocessing. 526
- What Is Mobile Postprocessing? 526
- Posting to Social Media. 552
- Printing Mobile Photos 553
- Section 5 Project 558

Appendix: Film Basics and Safety 560

Glossary 564

Index 581

Feature Contents

Procedure

Experimenting with Composition	17
Changing Lenses	86
Cleaning a DSLR Camera Sensor	89
Working with Reflectors	225
Using Screens	226
Finding the Hyperfocal Distance	256
Using Image Editing Software	429
Using Curves to Alter Contrast	448
Correcting a Color Cast	450
Converting to Monochrome with a Black & White Adjustment Layer	456
Eliminating a Spot Using the Clone Stamp Tool	459
Using the Quick Selection Tool	474
Making Scrap Pixels More Visible to Simplify Cleanup	478
Creating a Layer Mask	484
Creating Irregular Borders	488
Creating a Clipping Mask That Fills Type with an Image	489
Correcting a Tilted Horizon	491
Using the Lens Blur Filter to Reduce Depth of Field	494
Creating a Vector Image	496
Exporting for Presentation	550

Real-World Photography

Famous Photographers	14
Subject Choice	56
Boosting Your Photography Business Online	59
What's in Your Photography Bag?	88
Lens Prices	138
Smartphone Effects and Filters	158
Maintaining a Memory Card	185
Lighting Safety	234
Smartphone Flash	291
Posing	355
Photography Studio Safety	365
Controlling Lighting with a Phone Camera	386
Photography Internships	391
Shooting for Social Media	396
Adobe Lightroom vs. Adobe Photoshop	409
Copyright Ownership	413
Contact Sheets	416
Respecting Intellectual Property in Editing	427
Adobe Lightroom Develop Module	432
Exporting from Lightroom	505
Mobile Postprocessing Tips	552
Ethical Implications of Editing Photos	552

Portfolio Assignment

Exploring a Subject	20
Shake It Up!	122
Extract a Detail	141
Backlit Subject	172
Extracting Images	218
Selecting a Mood	239
Minus and Plus	261
Stop It!	295
Photographer's Choice	327
Brace Yourself!	349
Finding the Right Ratio	373
Smartphone Photography	397
Monochrome Conversion	462
Edit It!	498
Framing and Matting	519
On-the-Go Edits	554

Section 1
The World of Photography

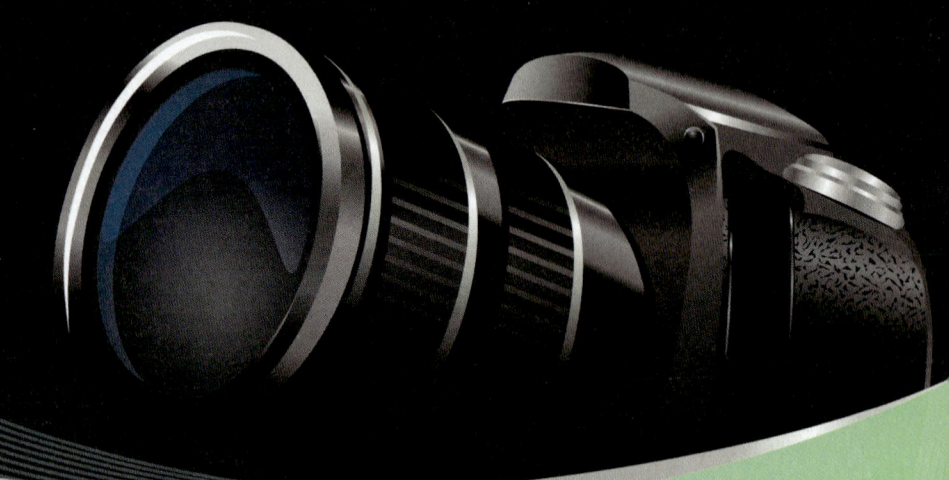

Chapter 1 Our Visual World
Chapter 2 From Pinholes to Pixels
Chapter 3 Professional Photography

Photography is a visual medium designed to capture and document brief moments in time. Whether you want to take photographs professionally or just make your social media photos look nicer, there are numerous ways to communicate through photos. Regardless of how or why you decide to take photographs, this book will guide you through techniques, principles, and technology to help you develop the skills you need to be a successful photographer.

This book is divided into five sections, and each section covers a different component of photography. Section 1 is a general overview of the world of photography. Chapter 1 is an introductory chapter that describes various types of photography. It also briefly discusses how to take your own photos.

In Chapter 2, you will see how photography originated and how it has evolved over time. This chapter also examines the differences between film-based photography and digital photography.

Finally, Chapter 3 will introduce you to the professional photography industry. It will also provide you with an overview of what it takes to start and operate a photography business.

Andrekart Photography/Shutterstock.com

Chapter 1
Our Visual World

Learning Objectives

After completing this chapter, you will be able to:
- Discuss the significance of photography in our visual society.
- Explain the six most common types of photography.
- Identify major photographic career opportunities.
- Describe the basic skills important to succeeding as a professional photographer.
- Understand what it means to "see" a photograph.
- Create a portfolio for use as a career tool.

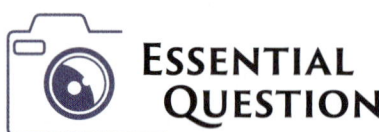

Essential Question

Why is photography important in today's society?

Technical Terms

abstractionism
composition
documentation
frame
freelancer
photography
photojournalist
portfolio
portrait photography
product photography
professional photographer

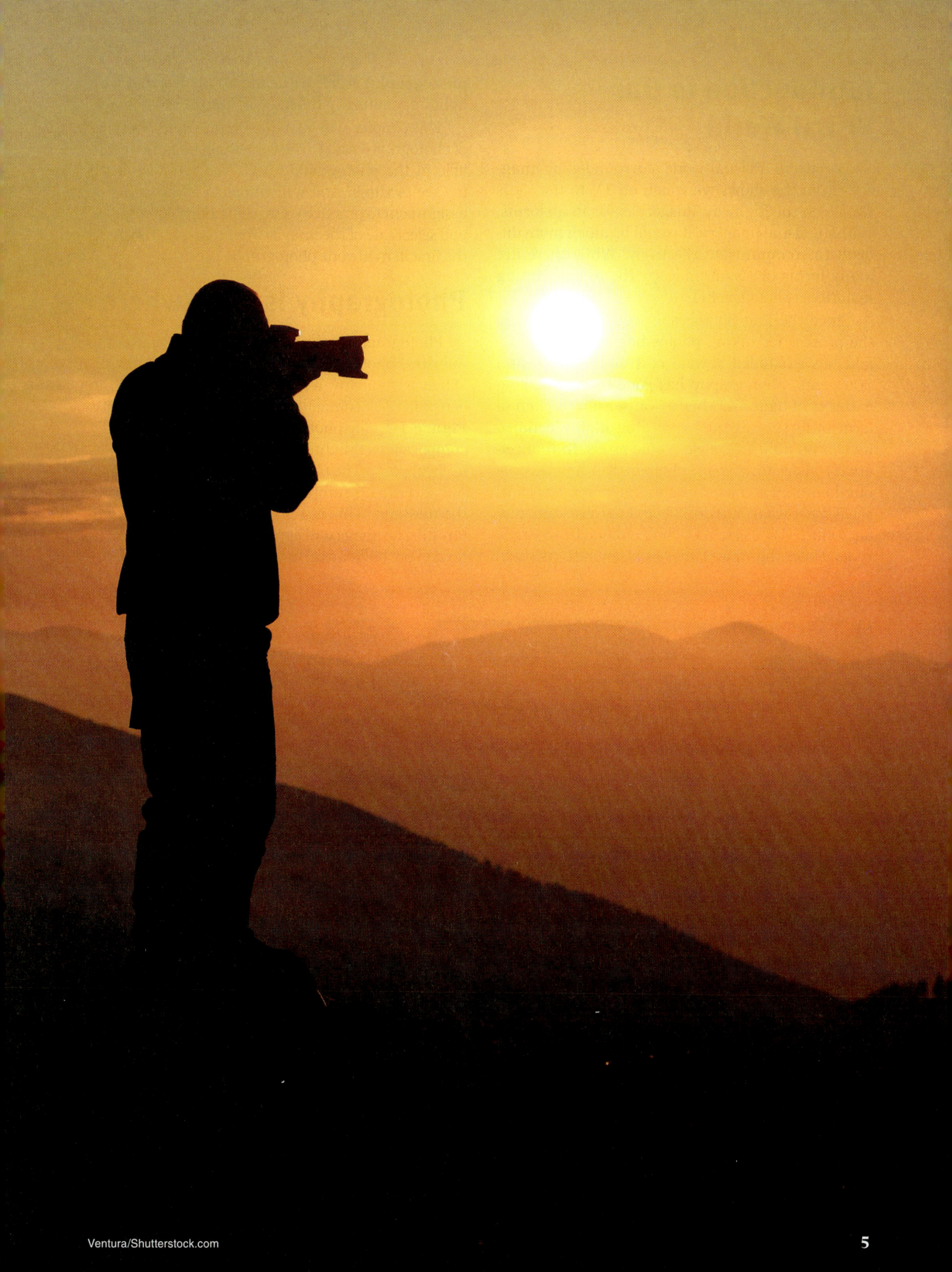
Ventura/Shutterstock.com

Introduction to Our Visual World

We live in a visual world, surrounded by imagery. From the shows we watch on TV to the signs we see on the highway, imagery exists in all forms. Without visual imagery, it would be much more difficult to communicate effectively. While there are many forms of visual imagery, the overwhelming majority is photographic.

Since the first photograph was taken in 1826, the process for taking photos has become simpler and has expanded beyond portraits. In less than 200 years, photography has gone from capturing patterns of light and shadow on sensitized pitch (a form of tar) to digitally recording highly detailed images on an array of electronic pixels. In that relatively short time span, photography has become our dominant means of visual expression. The word *photography* was coined in 1839 by English astronomer Sir John F. W. Herschel, who combined the Greek roots *photos* (light) and *graphos* (drawing). As such, *photography* is defined as the act of "drawing with light," or capturing reflected light to form an image.

This chapter will introduce you to different types of photography and to the career opportunities available in the photographic field. You will also learn to "see pictures" and will complete a photographic assignment to practice your seeing skills. Finally, you will select one of the images from that assignment as the first item in your photography portfolio.

Photography Is Everywhere

Photography really is everywhere. No matter the industry, photography is involved to some degree. When a company wants to introduce an item to consumers, a compelling photograph is a priority, **Figure 1-1**. The photograph is typically a carefully composed, well-lighted picture with the product as its focal point. The photo becomes the centerpiece of the advertising campaign by wordlessly conveying the message "This is a great product—you have to buy it!" The image will appear in many different contexts—on billboards, in magazine and newspaper

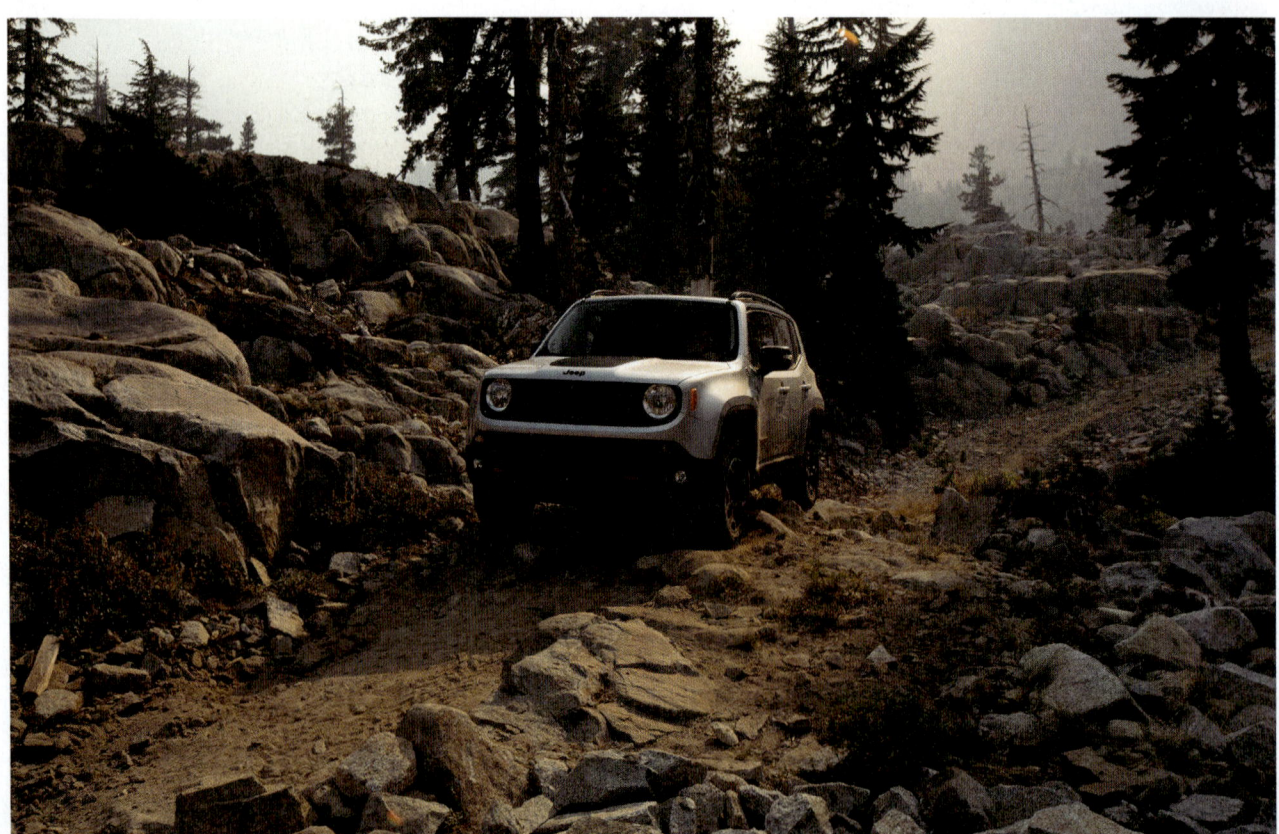

Jeep and Wrangler are registered trademarks of FCA US LLC

Figure 1-1. Photographing this vehicle in a rugged, natural setting is designed to appeal to adventurous car buyers.

advertisements, in television commercials, on packaging and point-of-purchase displays, and on websites and social media. There are multiple types of photography, but this chapter will discuss six of the most common types. (You will also find that almost every type of photography can fit into one of these six groups.)

Product Photography

Photographs of products for advertising and packaging are a major use of photographic illustration. ***Product photography***, also known as *advertising photography*, is photography that involves taking pictures of products in a way that makes them stand out to consumers in order to drive sales. Product photography provides a livelihood for a large number of professional photographers who specialize in such areas as food, automobiles, clothing, or health and fitness equipment, **Figure 1-2**. The rapid growth of the internet, online shopping, and social media has created new opportunities for studios specializing in product photography. In addition to photos aimed at consumers, a large volume of product photography is done each year to sell products to business clients, **Figure 1-3**.

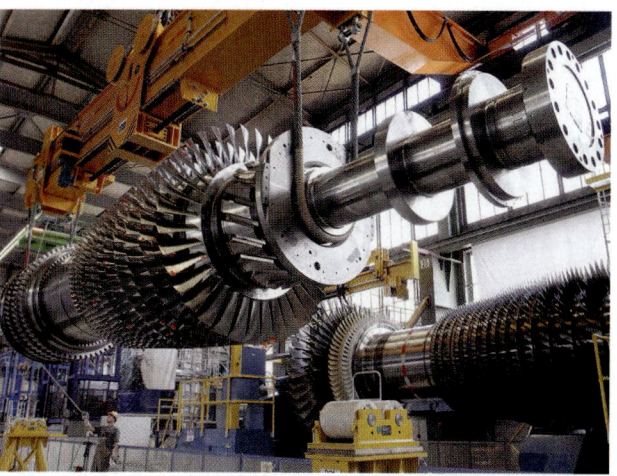

www.siemens.com/press

Figure 1-3. Industrial and commercial firms use photographic illustrations of products, such as this turbine for electrical power generation, to reach potential customers.

Some traditional forms of product photography are billboards and ads in magazines and newspapers. However, these traditional forms have limitations, especially regarding reach (how many people will see it). Social media has the ability to reach a much wider audience, so many companies and brands have taken advantage of various online platforms. Despite the differences between them (such as the presentation of the product and the language used to sell the product), there are many similarities between product photography for social media and traditional product photography. The main similarity is that companies are still selling a product.

Portrait Photography

Portrait photography, also known as *portraiture*, is photography of individuals or groups of people. Like product photography, portraiture is a major activity for professional photographers. Large communities have dozens or even hundreds of photographers who create portraits on either a full-time or part-time basis. Even small towns typically have a portrait studio. Many families "sit" for professionally taken portraits to document growth and relive memories. The early years of childhood and major milestones, such as high school and college graduation, account for a large share of portrait photography, **Figure 1-4**. Many professional photographers also contract with schools and organizations to produce individual or group photos.

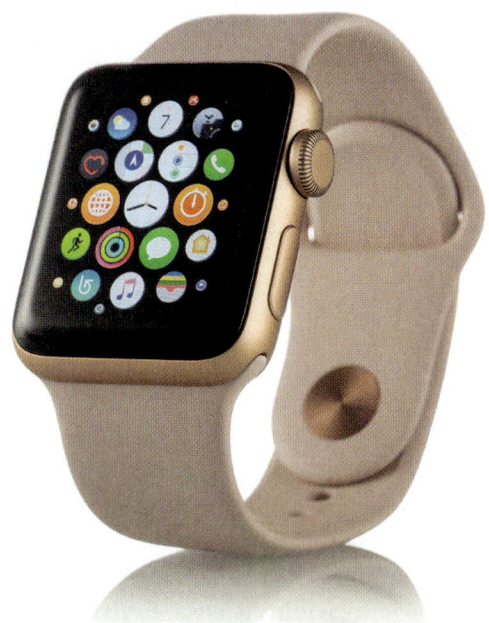

Oleg GawriloFF/Shutterstock.com

Figure 1-2. This image of an Apple Watch® was created for use in advertisements aimed at people interested in tracking their fitness habits.

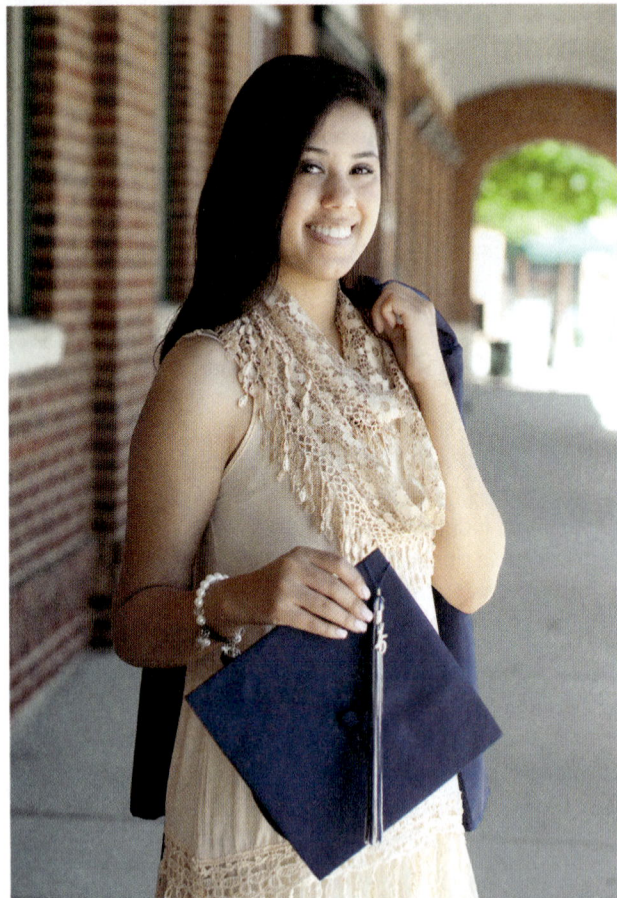

tammykayphoto/Shutterstock.com

Figure 1-4. Portraits are popular with high school and college seniors.

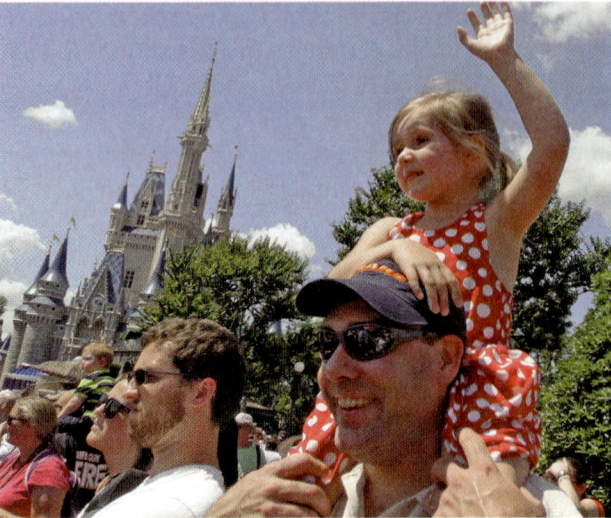

Katie Gorham

Figure 1-5. Snapshots are taken by the millions each year to document important family events, such as vacations, birthday parties, graduations, and weddings.

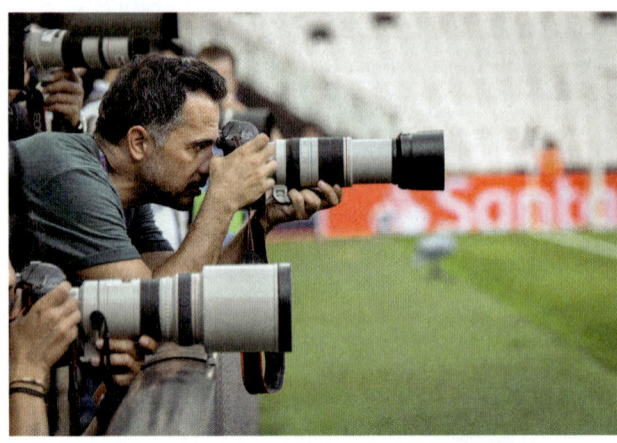

Vlad1988/Shutterstock.com

Figure 1-6. Photojournalists often cover various sporting events.

Documentation

In a sense, all forms of photography can be classified as **documentation**, or photography that records what a photographer saw, such as a scene, event, person, or object. Each of these photographs records a bit of history that has meaning to the photographer, **Figure 1-5**. The entire consumer photographic industry is built on the public's fascination with recording people and events.

A major area of documentation is photographic illustration for use in newspapers, magazines, and digital media to tell a story. **Photojournalists** are photographers who produce still pictures or videos for use in various forms of print and digital media. They produce thousands of still pictures and many hours of video each day to meet the demand for news ranging from political developments and international conflicts to fires, auto accidents, and sporting events, **Figure 1-6**. Photojournalists can also capture people, emotions, action, or something extraordinary for use in a story.

At times, journalistic photos go far beyond being mere record shots. Some become iconic, summing up the emotions or events of a particular period. For example, astronaut Neil Armstrong's 1969 photo of Edwin Aldrin Jr. walking on the moon not only records a moment in history, but also carries associations with the changes in American society resulting from the Space Race with Russia, **Figure 1-7**.

Beyond breaking news, a great deal of photography is needed to illustrate informational articles in newspapers and magazines. While such photos may be produced by a publication's staff photographers, this area represents a significant opportunity for freelancers. **Freelancers** are self-employed photographers,

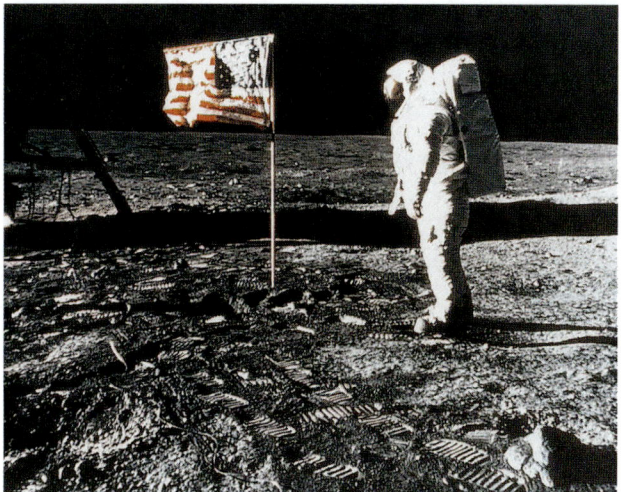

National Aeronautics and Space Administration

Figure 1-7. This iconic photograph of Edwin Aldrin Jr. walking on the moon encapsulated the Space Race between the United States and Russia.

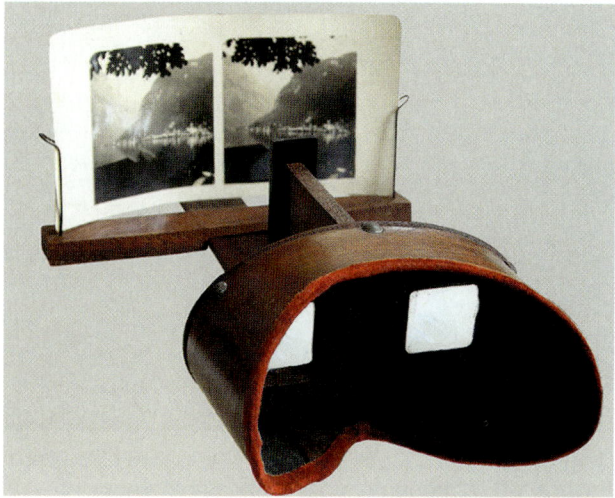

Pattarapong Kumlert/Shutterstock.com

Figure 1-8. The stereoscope allowed viewers to see a three-dimensional image by using pairs of identical photographs side by side.

especially those without a physical studio, who actively seek business from many sources and take on various types of photographic assignments. Freelance photographers have the flexibility to set their own hours and take on assignments that are the most interesting to them and suit their style or vision. Some freelancers start in high school by taking photos of their friends for senior pictures or other events, such as high school graduations and weddings. Being a freelance photographer is also an option for people who have another job. By freelancing, you can work when you have extra time and earn additional income.

Photography as Entertainment

Photography as entertainment has been around nearly as long as we have had the ability to take photographs. The first form of photographic entertainment to achieve wide popularity was the stereoscope, invented during the 1860s. It was a handheld device used to view pairs of identical photographs, giving the viewer the illusion of depth or three-dimensional space. The stereoscope introduced viewers to natural wonders and exciting locations they had never seen before, **Figure 1-8**.

Television and movies, two of today's dominant forms of entertainment, convey their messages through moving photographic images. While some *cinematographers* (people who primarily record movies) and *videographers* (people who primarily record television and events) work exclusively with moving images, many professional photographers offer both still and motion image capture. This is because DSLR cameras (a popular tool for many photographers) have the ability to capture both still and moving images.

In addition to television and movies, social media has become an outlet for photographers to showcase their work. Instagram is photography-focused and showcases everything from informal, day-in-the-life snapshots to highly stylized photography. Being able to easily access and post these photos has led to millions of people turning to Instagram and other photography apps for some form of entertainment.

Scientific and Technical Photography

In the scientific realm, photography is a useful investigative tool for dealing with subjects as small as molecules and as large as entire galaxies. Scanning electron microscopes allow scientists to investigate the structure of the very building blocks of matter. At the other end of the scale, astronomers use photography as an aid to forming theories on the development of the universe, **Figure 1-9**.

Since specialized equipment and knowledge is needed for most scientific and technical photographic work, this field presents limited opportunities for professional photographers. However, those with corporate clients in medical, pharmaceutical, and other science-related fields may be called upon to handle photo assignments in those areas.

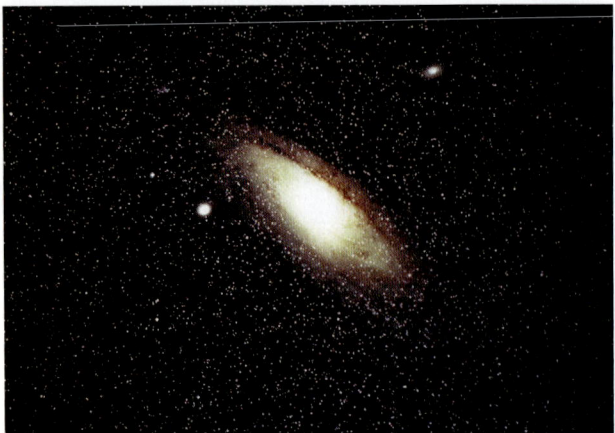

National Aeronautics and Space Administration

Figure 1-9. Astronomers often take photographs of space with specialized equipment to learn more about the universe and develop theories on how it came to be.

Photography as Art

The use of the photograph as a form of artistic expression and the continuing debate over whether photography is art or craft dates back almost to the beginning of photography. The earliest practitioners were most concerned with merely obtaining a recognizable and permanent image. For a time, photography was used as an imitation of painting. It then evolved into what was termed *naturalistic photography*, which did not attempt to mimic the look of a painted image. A later development was the growth of **abstractionism**, a school of photographic thought that places strong emphasis on forms and their relationships, **Figure 1-10**.

The advent of digital image manipulation has opened new avenues of expression for the photographer. With appropriate computer software, processes such as combining, abstracting, distorting, emphasizing, texturizing, and recoloring image elements can be used to realize the photographer's vision, **Figure 1-11**.

Photographic Career Opportunities

Some photographers can earn a living as strictly fine art practitioners whose works are sold to collectors, galleries, and museums, but that is relatively difficult. Additionally, not all people who are interested in a career in photography want to sell their work to galleries or museums. If you are not interested in that route but still want to pursue a career in photography, you should consider professional photography.

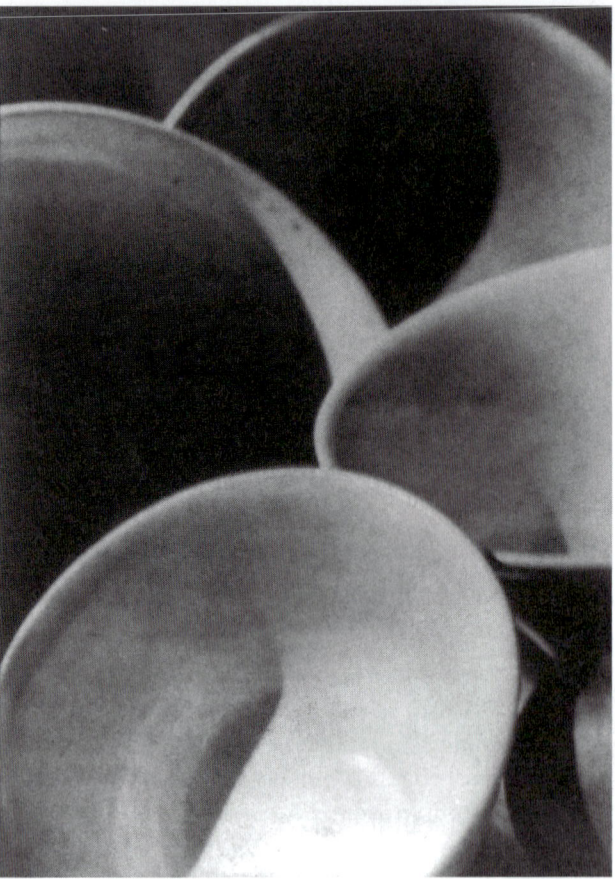

Courtesy of the Library of Congress

Figure 1-10. In this 1917 abstract study, photographer Paul Strand explored the interplay of light and shadow on four white bowls.

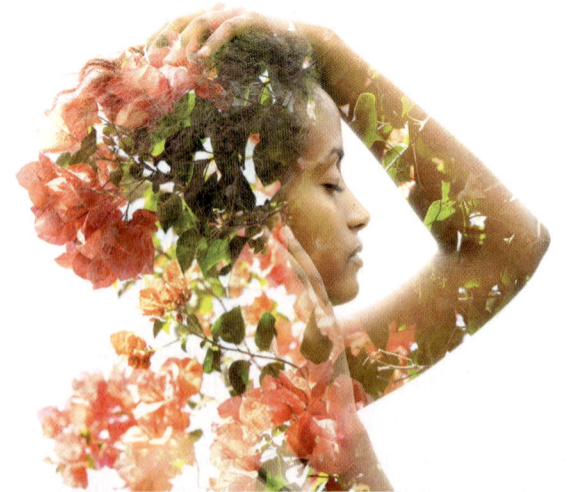

LUMEZIA.com/Shutterstock.com

Figure 1-11. By combining and manipulating images, a photographer can lead the viewer to see a subject in new ways.

Professional photography, also referred to as *commercial photography*, is an occupation in which photographic skills are used to create images in exchange for payment. That simple definition covers a broad area ranging from capturing historic news events to taking glamorous fashion shots to shooting portraits for athletic programs, **Figure 1-12**.

The Professional Photography Field

Professional photographers make all or most of their living from photographic work. Jobs in this field can be divided into two broad groups: salaried and self-employed. Statistics show that about two-thirds of the workers classified as photographers are self-employed, and about half of those self-employed photographers operate their business on a part-time basis. A typical part-time photographer might do wedding photography on weekends while working at another job during the week.

Salaried photographers often work for large companies, such as manufacturing firms or studios specializing in advertising or industrial photography, **Figure 1-13**. They may also work for institutions, such as universities, government agencies, or national organizations like trade associations or nonprofit organizations. Once a major employer of photographers, newspapers and newsgathering organizations have reduced their salaried staffs significantly. However, this reduction has created opportunities for self-employed photographers willing to work on an assignment-by-assignment basis.

A majority of self-employed photographers own and operate photo studios doing primarily portraiture, wedding photography, and similar community-based work. As mentioned previously, freelancers are self-employed photographers, but they do not operate a physical studio. They actively seek business from many sources and take on assignments of various types, from weddings and organization events to high school or college senior portraits to breaking news stories.

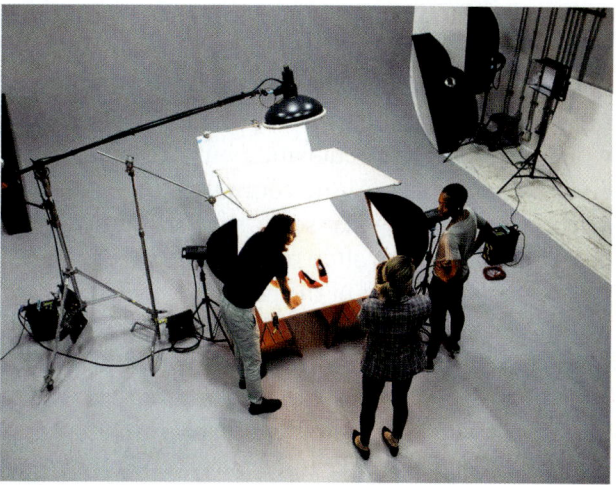

Rawpixel.com/Shutterstock.com

Figure 1-13. These professional photographers work for a studio that specializes in product photography. This type of photography can often use complex lighting setups.

Photographic Career Requirements

Some areas of professional photography require a college or technical school degree in photography, but many photographers begin their careers with only a high school diploma. A degree is usually needed to gain entry to corporations or

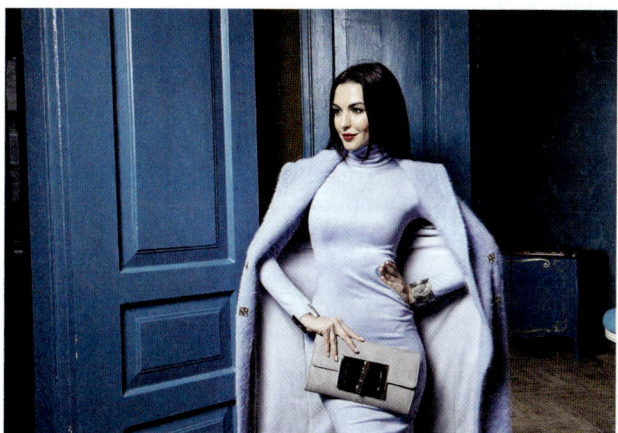

indira's work/Shutterstock.com

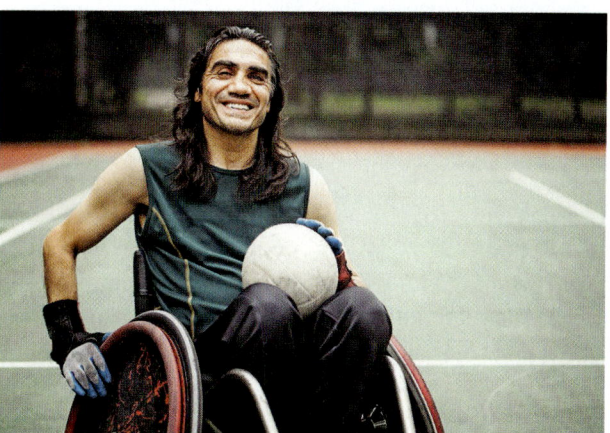

Mila Supinskaya Glashchenko/Shutterstock.com

Figure 1-12. Professional photographers are hired for a wide range of projects, including fashion shoots and taking portraits of athletes.

organizations offering full-time salaried positions. Photographic studios or photo service companies, such as those doing advertising or product photography, are usually more open to hiring candidates who have less formal education but a strong portfolio of creative work. Many community colleges and larger universities offer some sort of photography degree. Colleges also often require that you complete an internship as part of the program, which can be a great way to get started in the photography world. A quick online search should guide you to schools in your area that offer a photography program. If you are having a hard time finding a program at a community college or larger university, you can always look for art schools that offer a photography degree.

One traditional entry route into professional photography is to be hired as a professional photographer's assistant. Assistants perform many of the routine tasks of organizing equipment and materials for a shoot, whether in studio or on location, **Figure 1-14**. Working as an assistant provides many learning opportunities. A talented assistant may progress to doing actual photography work within the organization, or they may eventually begin an independent career.

Artistic ability and well-developed photographic skills are basic requirements for successfully entering the professional photography field. Additionally, there are many personal qualities and positive work behaviors you must have in order to be employable. Photographers must show a great deal of professionalism in every situation, such as dressing appropriately and speaking to others with care and respect. Being dependable is especially paramount in professional photography. Clients must be able to depend on you to take high-quality photos and deliver them on time. Having a positive attitude is also essential. Staying positive in stressful situations can help you and your team solve any problems and complete the task at hand.

It is also important to have people skills and a business-oriented attitude. A photographer must relate well to people since they are in constant contact with others while working. For example, a portrait photographer must be able to help their client relax and act naturally when the shutter clicks. A fashion photographer on a complex, high-budget shoot must motivate a team to work together smoothly and efficiently.

The ability to communicate information clearly and openly to clients, assistants, and fellow professionals is vital. Listening carefully to what others are communicating is also critical. Misunderstandings cause mistakes that cost money and time. In some cases, failure to communicate clearly can lead to serious injury, such as an industrial assignment being carried out in hazardous conditions.

Business skills are also very important to a photographer. When used effectively, they help them stay in business. When ignored or used inconsistently, they usually result in business failure. To be successful, a photographer must reach out to potential clients through advertising and marketing activities. With the popularity of social media, many photographers opt to market their services through platforms like Instagram and Facebook, **Figure 1-15**. Successful photographers also apply interpersonal and customer service skills to deliver high-quality finished projects on time and within budget and promptly bill the customer for the work. The skills and abilities required to develop and succeed in a professional photography operation are covered in greater detail in Chapter 3, *Professional Photography*.

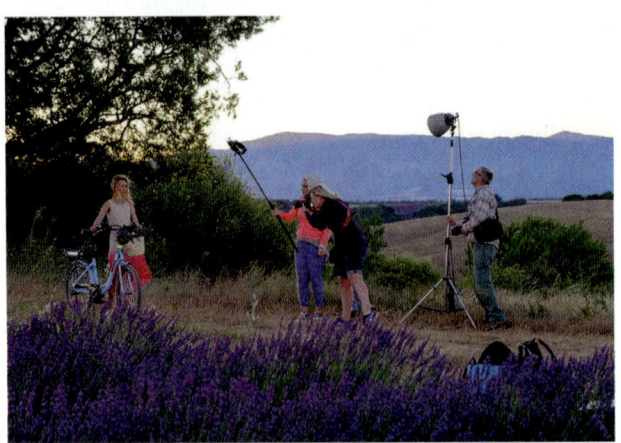

Anton Gvozdikov/Shutterstock.com

Figure 1-14. On a location shoot, photography assistants often help the photographer with lighting.

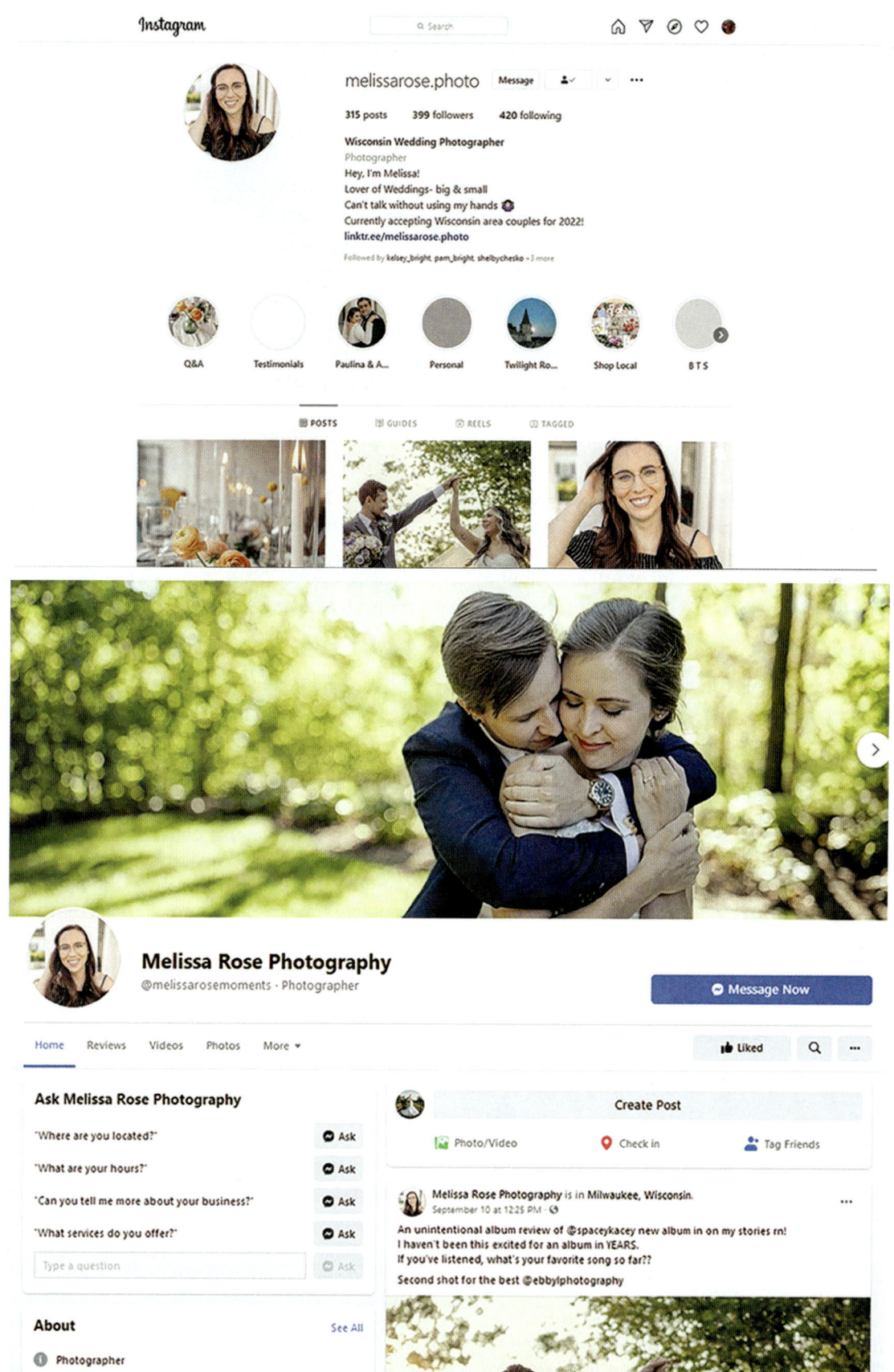

Melissa Rose Photography

Figure 1-15. Social media is an important tool for showcasing a photographer's work and communicating with potential customers.

Chapter 1　Our Visual World

REAL-WORLD PHOTOGRAPHY

Famous Photographers

There are many well-known photographers who often serve as the standard for their specific area of expertise. The following are just a few examples of famous photographers and their impact on the industry. They may even provide you with some inspiration:

- **Annie Leibovitz** is an American portrait photographer known for her celebrity portraiture. She often uses intimate settings and poses in her work. Leibovitz has taken photos of John Lennon, Dolly Parton, Michael Jackson, the Obama family, and Queen Elizabeth II. She is the first woman to have a feature exhibition at the National Portrait Gallery in Washington, D.C. Leibovitz was also declared a Living Legend by the Library of Congress. Her work can be found in the collections of the Art Institute of Chicago, the Museum of Modern Art in New York City, the Los Angeles County Museum of Art, and other well-known museums.

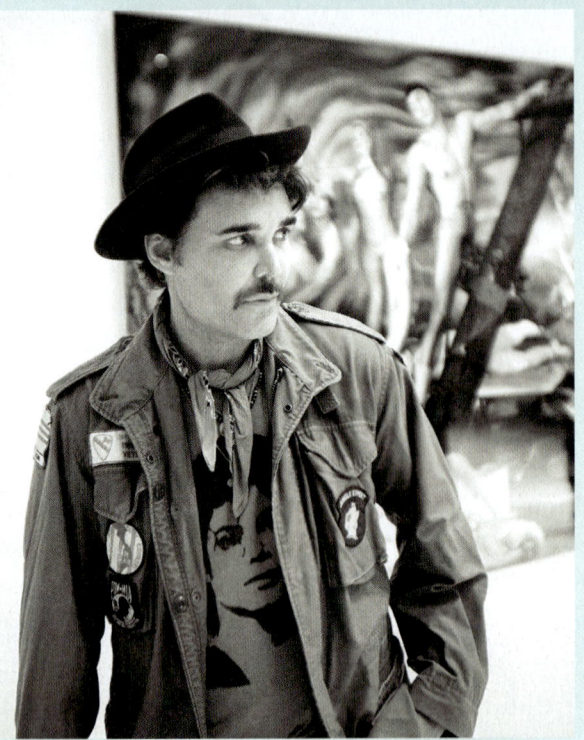

Daniele Pisani/Shutterstock.com

David LaChapelle has worked with numerous high-profile celebrities.

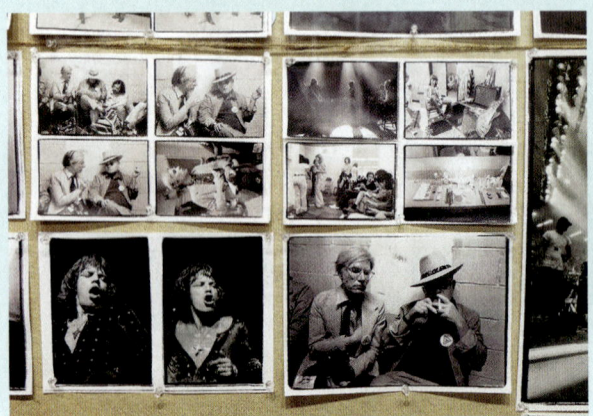

Tetiana Tuchyk/Shutterstock.com

Annie Leibovitz is best known for her portraits of celebrities.

- **David LaChapelle** is an American commercial and fine art photographer known for his ability to include art history and social messages in his work. He is also a music video director and film director. He was even hired by Andy Warhol when he was 17 years old. LaChapelle's images have appeared on the covers and pages of several magazines, including *Vogue Paris*, *Vogue Italia*, *Rolling Stone*, and *GQ*. He has worked with Elton John, Christina Aguilera, Whitney Houston, Hozier, Britney Spears, Lizzo, Travis Scott, and more.

- **Dana Scruggs** is a photographer and art director. She published *SCRUGGS Magazine* early in her career so that she could create editorial and creative content that matched her vision. After working for some time as a freelance photographer, ESPN reached out to have her shoot their famous Body Issue. She became the first Black female photographer to shoot an athlete for the Body Issue, and she later became the first Black person to photograph the cover of *Rolling Stone*. She has shot for *Vanity Fair*, *TIME*, *Rolling Stone*, Glossier, Apple, Nike, and more. Some of the famous people she has photographed include Simone Biles, Stacey Abrams, Issa Rae, Ty Dolla Sign, Janelle Monáe, and Megan Rapinoe.

- **Groana Melendez** is a lens-based artist who was born in Brooklyn, New York. She was raised between New York City and Santo Domingo, Dominican Republic. Her family immigrated to the US in the late 1970s to pursue the "American Dream." This inspired Melendez to learn more about her family and build a connection with them through her photography. She often takes portraits of her relatives in the spaces where they live and spend their lives, building her own relationship with her family. Through her photography, Melendez aims to explore issues revolving around class, familial relationships, and her own heritage. She graduated from Syracuse University and had her first solo show in the New York Public Library. Melendez has also been published in *Nueva Luz* and *Latina Magazine*.

Learning to See

For a photographer, *seeing* is a specialized skill, something far different from the way most people look at the world around them. A nonphotographer standing at the rim of the Grand Canyon will likely take snapshots (informal photographs that are taken rather quickly) of the overall scene, some posed photos of companions with the canyon as the background, and perhaps a selfie. A photographer, on the other hand, will see and capture subjects like patterns of light and shadow on formations, the colors and textures of the rock layers and vegetation, and a line of hikers on a distant trail.

Seeing in the photographic sense involves awareness of the relationship of masses and colors, the emotional content of the scene, the play of light and shadow, and meaning that goes beyond the obvious. For example, while a tourist might marvel over a spectacular sunset, a photographer is more likely to turn their back to the sun to capture the warm evening light on an old barn or a rock formation, **Figure 1-16**. Where others see an unsightly auto graveyard, a photographer may see hundreds of subjects to photograph, such as patterns, relationships, and isolated details.

Selecting a Photograph

Selecting a subject to photograph depends on many factors, but the first is personal interest. You must recognize a possible subject for photography and then decide that you want to photograph it. How to select a subject for your photograph properly is discussed in more depth in Chapter 9, *Making a Picture*. You might want to photograph a given subject for a wide variety of reasons:

- It is a simple and straightforward record to show others that you have been somewhere, such as Disney World or a rock concert. Most snapshots fall into this category.
- It is a subject that you have been conditioned to photograph, such as a parade, a birthday party, a bed of colorful spring flowers, or a city skyline, **Figure 1-17**. Our constant exposure to visual media trains us to think of what a suitable subject is and how it should be photographed.
- It engages your emotions. You may be awed by the stark beauty of a desert landscape, unnerved by the ominousness of an abandoned building, or delighted by the energetic play of children, **Figure 1-18**.
- It appeals to you aesthetically because of its shapes, colors, composition, or visual impact.
- It can be a means of stating your political, moral, or social views. For example, in the late nineteenth century, published photographs of very young factory workers led to the passage of child labor laws. See **Figure 1-19**.

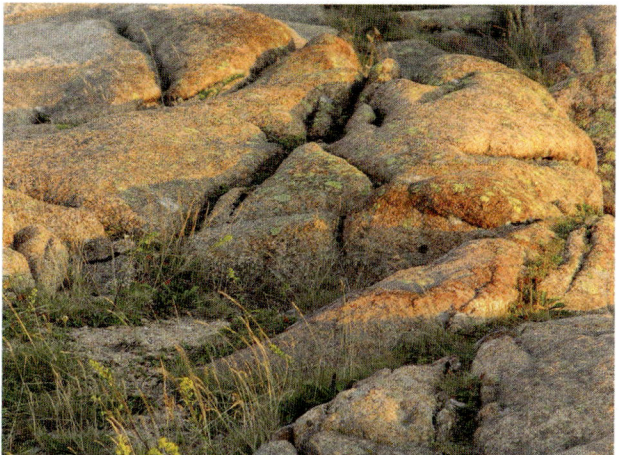

Jack Klasey/Goodheart-Willcox Publisher

Figure 1-16. The golden light of the setting sun bathing a rock formation on Mount Washington in Maine's Acadia National Park makes for an interesting photograph.

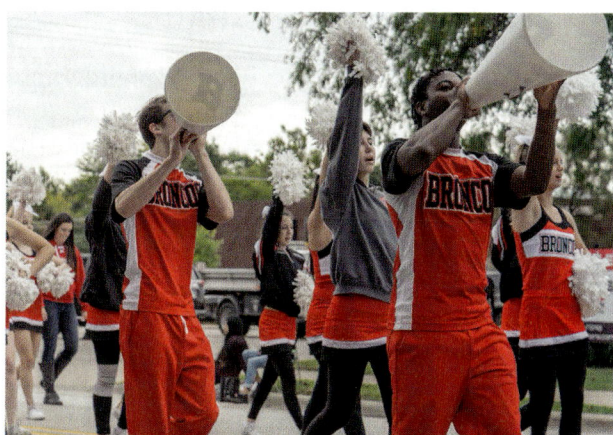

Kristen Prahl/Shutterstock.com

Figure 1-17. Cheerleaders are popular subjects for snapshots at parades.

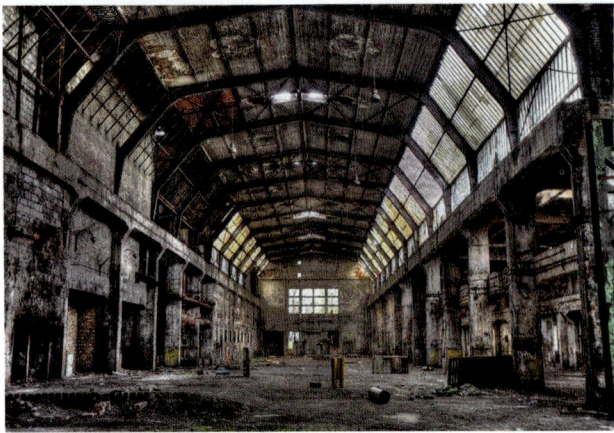

Lukasz Pawel Szczepanski/Shutterstock.com

Figure 1-18. Debris and broken windows in an abandoned building can generate an emotional response in viewers.

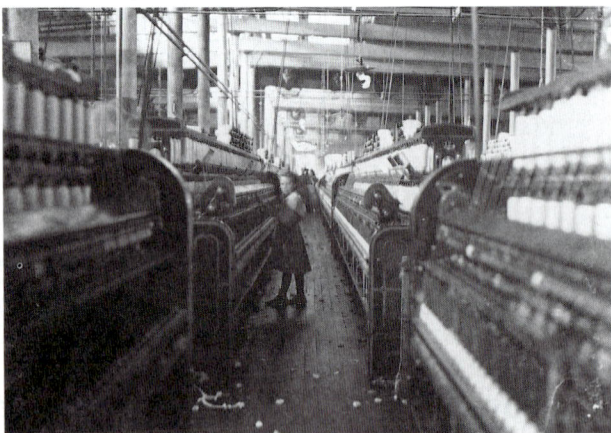

Courtesy of the Library of Congress

Figure 1-19. Photographer Lewis W. Hine documented the exploitation of children. This photograph from 1908 shows a very young girl working as a spinner in a South Carolina textile mill.

Composing a Photograph

Once you decide *what* you want to photograph, you must next decide *how* to photograph it. Too often, our first impression of a scene becomes the viewpoint from which we capture it—a standing, eye-level, horizontal view. See **Figure 1-20.** That first-impression image is not the only possible way to capture a subject and often is not the most effective or most pleasing way of photographing it. Experienced photographers look at a subject from different angles and distances, **Figure 1-21.** They may return at different hours of the day, or even different seasons, to see the subject under various lighting or weather conditions.

Cameras capture images within a four-sided space known as the frame. The ***frame*** is defined as the working space within which a picture is composed.

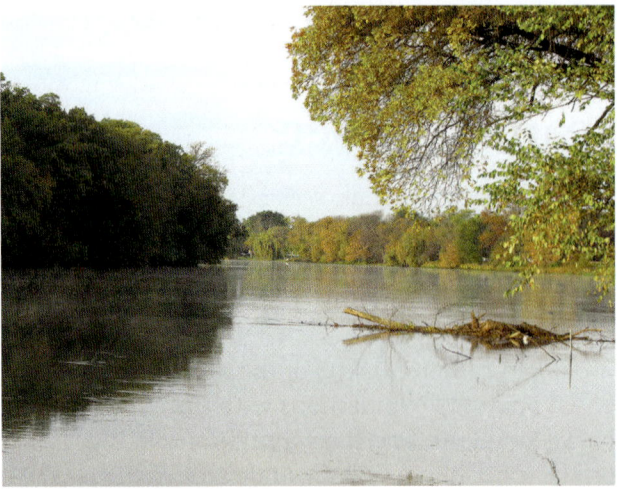

Jack Klasey/Goodheart-Willcox Publisher

Figure 1-20. The most common photographic approach is a horizontal image taken from a standing, eye-level position.

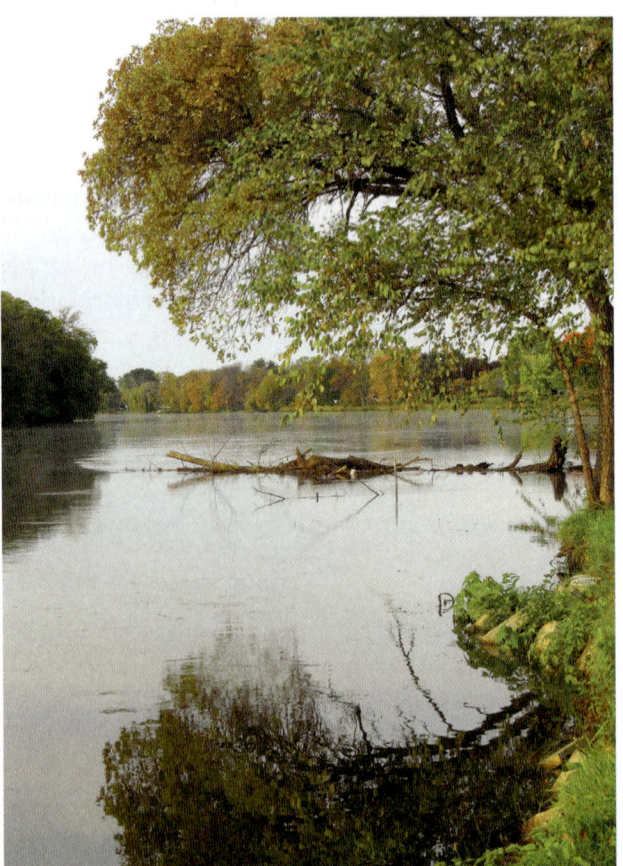

Jack Klasey/Goodheart-Willcox Publisher

Figure 1-21. This image captures the scene from **Figure 1-20** in a different way. The vertical image was taken from a greater distance and a lower angle.

The arrangement of visual elements, such as shapes, colors, and textures, within that frame form the photograph's **composition**. The two broadest categories of composition are *horizontal framing* (landscape format) and *vertical framing* (portrait format). These topics are covered more thoroughly in Chapter 9. As illustrated in **Figure 1-20** and **Figure 1-21**, photographing the same subject in both formats results in images with distinctly different impressions. Professional photographers whose work is intended for use in magazines and books typically strive for dramatic vertical shots to be used as cover illustrations. Professional photographers whose work is intended for double-page spreads in magazines or various forms of display (like in a museum or gallery) often strive for dramatic horizontal shots.

Composition is governed by various design principles, such as pattern, simplicity, order, balance, and emphasis. Design principles and their application are covered in detail in Chapter 9. The following are a few examples:

- **Pattern.** A repetition of elements within the frame. The repetition may present a feeling of rhythm. See **Figure 1-22**.
- **Balance.** The arrangement of major visual elements within the frame. Balance may be symmetrical (formal) or asymmetrical (informal). See **Figure 1-23**.
- **Emphasis.** The relative prominence of the most important visual element. The element may be larger, closer, lighter, or more vivid in color. See **Figure 1-24**.

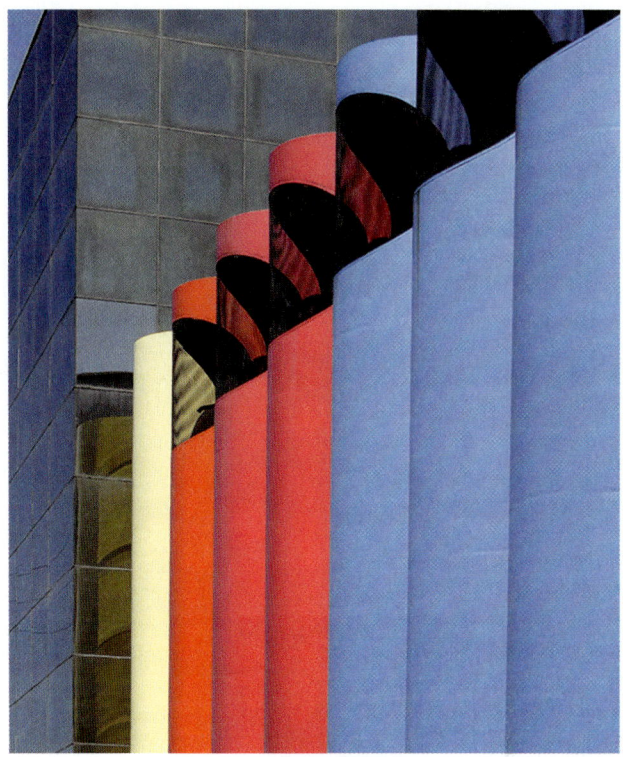

Jack Klasey/Goodheart-Willcox Publisher

Figure 1-22. This colorful array of ventilation pipes forms a striking pattern with a strong rhythm.

- **Simplicity.** The elimination of unnecessary visual elements within the frame. This reduces the number of elements a viewer must identify. See **Figure 1-25**.
- **Order.** The organization of visual elements within the frame. Order helps make information in the frame easier for the viewer to understand. See **Figure 1-26**.

PROCEDURE

Experimenting with Composition

In order to take good photos, you must be comfortable with composition. For this activity, you will need either a digital camera with a viewfinder or a smartphone. You will also need someone in your class to be your subject.

Complete the following tasks using the lines of the viewfinder grid. If you turn on your camera or open your camera app and do not see a grid, you must enable it in your device's settings. You should complete each task twice (once for a horizontal photo and once for a vertical photo):

1. Place your subject in between the two middle lines of the grid to center them. Once they are centered, take a photo.
2. Line up the center of your subject with the leftmost line of the grid. Once they are in line, take a photo.
3. Line up the center of your subject with the rightmost line of the grid. Once they are in line, take a photo.

These guiding lines will help you when you are first starting out on your photography journey. Over time, you may become comfortable enough to take photos without them, but even the most experienced photographers will still use a grid to help them achieve the best shots possible.

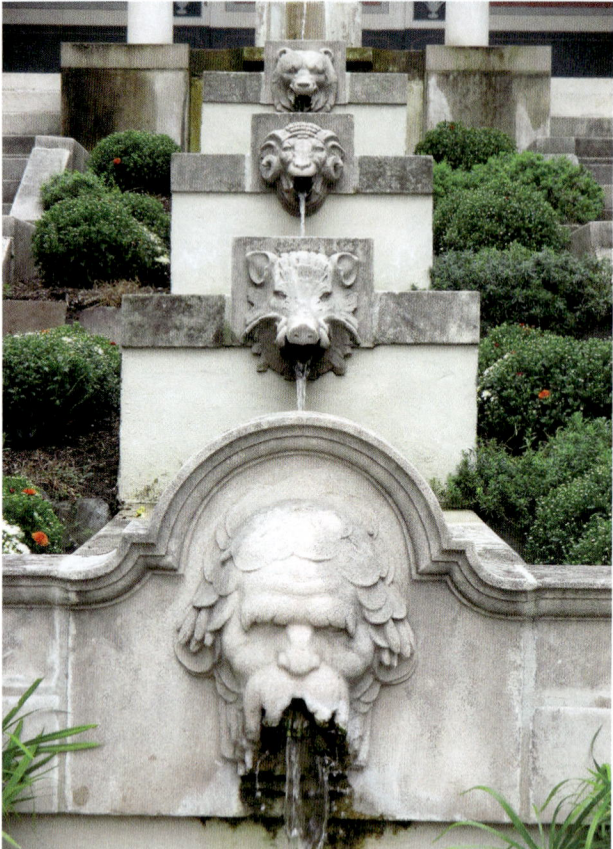 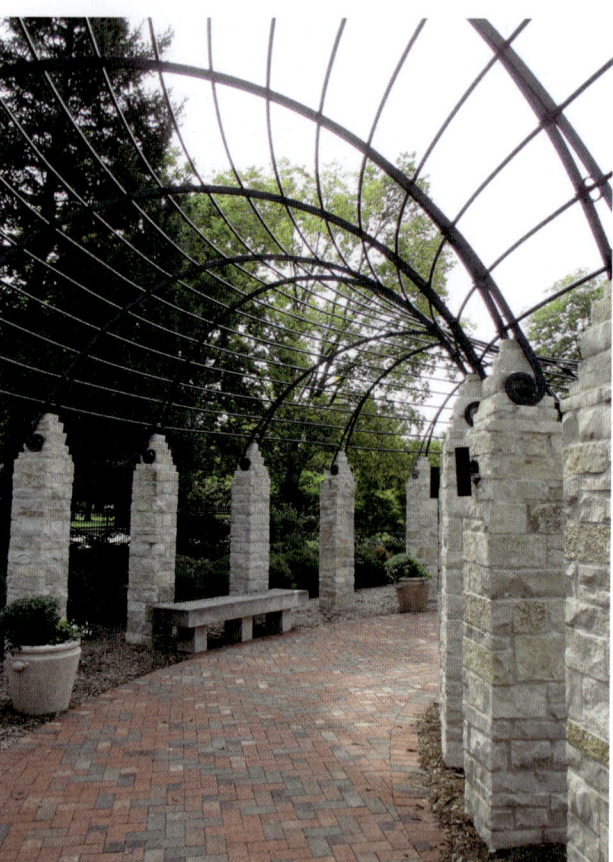

Jack Klasey/Goodheart-Willcox Publisher

Figure 1-23. A composition may exhibit symmetrical or asymmetrical balance. The image on the left demonstrates symmetrical balance, while the image on the right demonstrates asymmetrical balance.

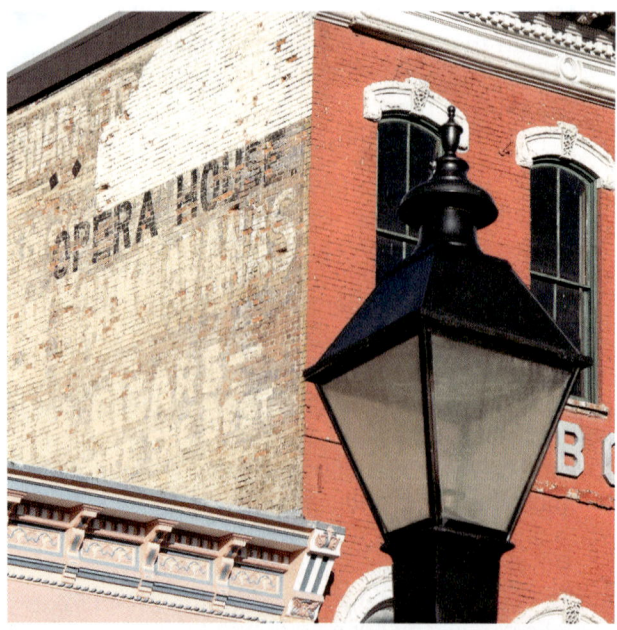 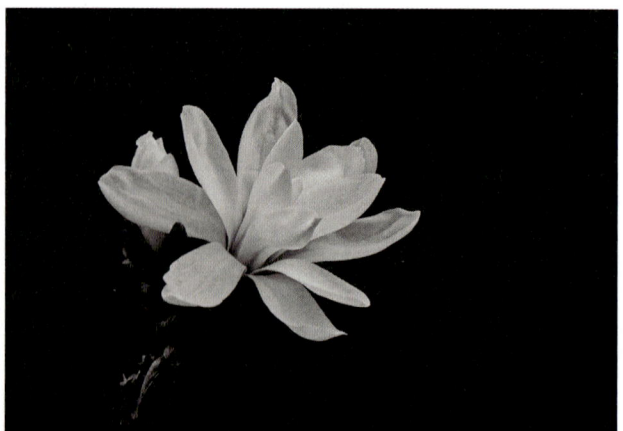

Jack Klasey/Goodheart-Willcox Publisher

Figure 1-24. The size, shape, and dark color of the foreground gaslight fixture establish it as the most important visual element in this image.

SwedishStockPhotos/Shutterstock.com

Figure 1-25. Simplicity allows the viewer to focus on the main subject (in this case, a flower) without being distracted by other elements.

Building Your Portfolio

As an aspiring photographer, you will want to develop a **portfolio**, which is a physical or digital collection of a photographer's best work. It is essential for a photographer because it is used to show potential clients or employers their skills and abilities. This text provides various photographic assignments that will produce one or more images to add to your portfolio. The assignments reflect different photographic skills or types of photography, resulting in a variety of images in your portfolio.

As you complete each assignment, add the best image from that activity to your portfolio. As you pursue your development as a photographer after completing this class, you will add more samples of your work to the portfolio. You will also replace some images with better examples as your skill level increases. Your portfolio will become an important tool as you pursue a career in photography.

Physical Portfolio

Physical portfolios vary in size and content. One common type is a three-ring binder with individual clear sleeves that allow prints to be seen clearly while protecting them from damage and fingerprints. It also allows prints to be easily rearranged, added, or removed. Another common type is a printed book. A

Bojsha/Shutterstock.com

Figure 1-26. The order of the berries makes what is in the frame easier for your viewers to understand.

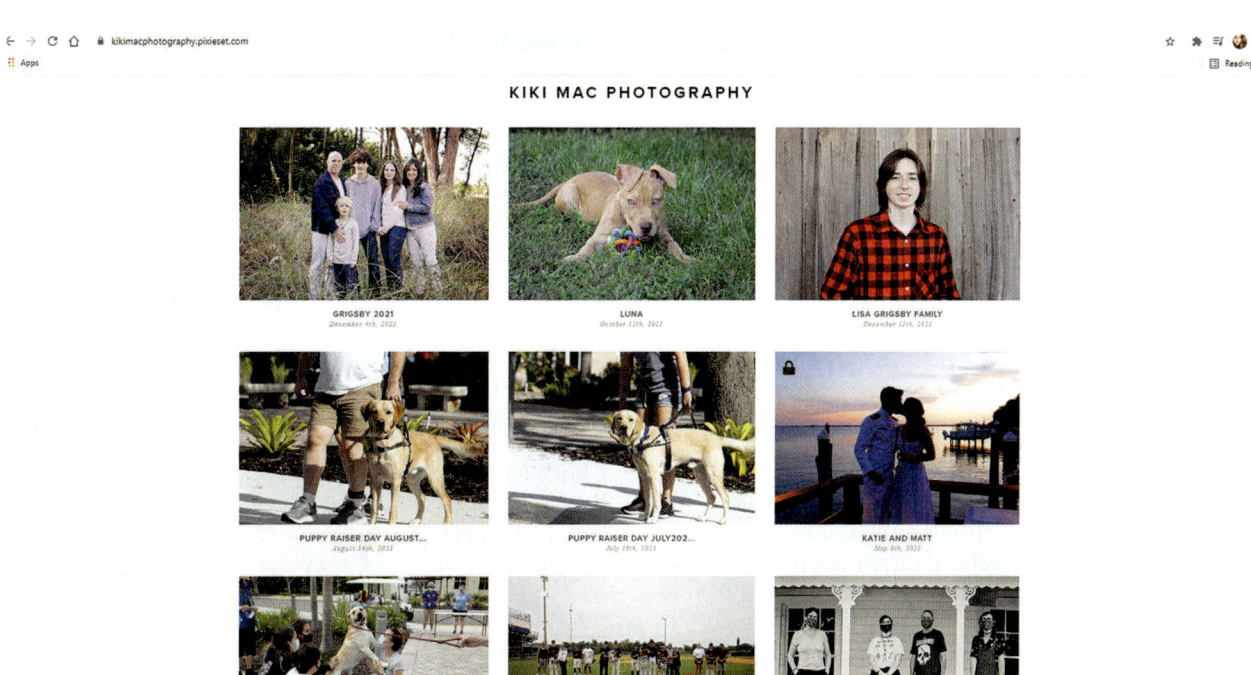

Christy Clark

Figure 1-27. There are numerous websites designed to host your photography portfolio.

book portfolio looks very professional and sleek. However, there are some drawbacks. Photos are not easily rearranged, added, or removed, so if you need to update your portfolio, you will have to print a new book.

Digital Portfolio

Digital portfolios are becoming more prevalent for several reasons. One reason is that they are easily accessible from nearly anywhere. Having your portfolio online allows you to show someone your work by simply pulling it up on your phone or by sending them a link to access it at their convenience. Digital portfolios also do not require you to spend money to print high-quality physical copies of your photos, and you do not run the risk of losing a digital portfolio like you do with a physical portfolio.

There are many websites designed to host your photography portfolio, such as Pixieset and SmugMug, **Figure 1-27**. Beginning photographers may be hesitant to spend money on hosting their portfolios on a website, so they may choose to post their portfolios to an Instagram account or other social media platform. Every photographer has their own preference, and you will need to find what works best for you.

Portfolio Assignment

Exploring a Subject

A good way to practice seeing photographically is to select a simple subject and photograph it as many different ways as you can visualize. This exploration of a subject helps you improve your creativity and seek unusual ways to look at what you are photographing.

Example A shows some of the many ways of photographing a common object—a fire hydrant. Although only 10 photos are shown, the photographer shot more than 30 different images in about 15 minutes.

For this activity, choose a subject that you feel is interesting and can be photographed in a number of ways. You may choose an inanimate object, such as a piece of playground equipment or a car, or a living subject, such as a person or a pet. The options are virtually limitless. The only requirement is that all the images should feature the exact same subject, not individual examples of the same *kind* of subject.

When you have completed the assignment, examine each image critically. Reject those with obvious defects, such as being out of focus or including some distracting element you did not notice when you took the picture. Select two or three of your best images. For each of these, ask yourself the following questions:
- What makes this image more interesting than the others?
- Why would someone want to hang a print of this photo on a wall, share it on social media, or display it on a smartphone or computer screen?
- What does this image tell the viewer about the subject?

The answers to these questions should help you decide which images are your best shots, or the ones that are most successful at capturing your subject. If you are keeping a physical portfolio, send your photos to a printing service and print them to your instructor's specifications. If you are keeping a digital portfolio, save a copy of your photos in a designated place, like a folder in your photos app or a folder in a cloud service like Microsoft OneDrive. If your instructor does not specify what type of portfolio to keep, create your portfolio digitally.

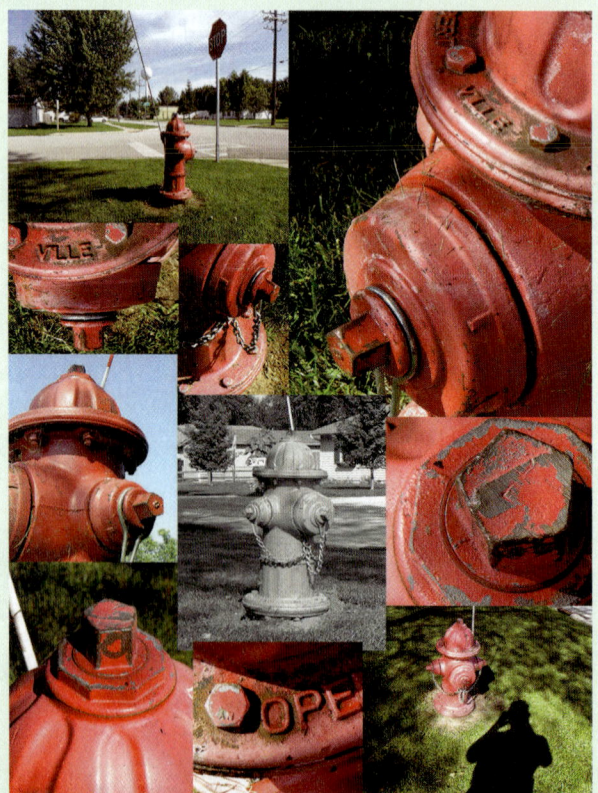

Jack Klasey/Goodheart-Willcox Publisher

Example A. Ten views of a fire hydrant.

Chapter 1 Review

Summary

- While there are many forms of visual imagery, the overwhelming majority is photographic.
- Product photography is photography of products for advertising and packaging. The photographs may be aimed at consumers or business clients.
- Portrait photography is photography of individuals or groups of people. It is a major activity for professional photographers.
- Documentation is photography that records what a photographer saw, such as a scene, event, person, or object. A major area of documentation is photographic illustration for use in newspapers, magazines, and digital media.
- Photography as entertainment has been around nearly as long as we have had the ability to take photographs. Television, movies, and social media are popular outlets for photographers to showcase their work.
- In the scientific realm, photography is a useful investigative tool. Specialized equipment and knowledge is needed for this kind of photographic work.
- The use of the photograph as a form of artistic expression and the continuing debate over whether photography is art or craft dates back almost to the beginning of photography.
- Professional photography is an occupation in which photographic skills are used to create images in exchange for payment. Jobs in this field can be divided into two broad groups: salaried and self-employed.
- Some areas of professional photography require a college or technical school degree in photography, but many photographers begin their careers with only a high school diploma. There are also other basic requirements, such as artistic ability and business skills.
- Seeing is a specialized skill for a photographer. It involves awareness of the relationship of masses and colors, the emotional content of the scene, the play of light and shadow, and meaning that goes beyond the obvious. Major components of seeing include selecting a subject and composition.
- A portfolio is a physical or digital collection of a photographer's best work. It is essential for a photographer because it is used to show potential clients or employers their skills and abilities.

Review Questions

Answer the following questions using the information provided in this chapter.

Know and Understand

1. _____ is the act of "drawing with light," or capturing reflected light to form an image.
   A. Composition
   B. Photography
   C. Abstractionism
   D. Documentation
2. *True or False?* A large volume of product photography is done each year to sell products to business clients.
3. The early years of childhood and major milestones account for a large share of _____ photography.
   A. product
   B. scientific
   C. technical
   D. portrait
4. *True or False?* In a sense, all photography can be classified as documentation.

5. _____ are photographers who produce still pictures or videos for use in various forms of print and digital media.
   A. Cinematographers
   B. Freelancers
   C. Photojournalists
   D. Videographers

6. *True or False?* Cinematographers primarily record events.

7. Since specialized equipment and knowledge is needed for most _____ photographic work, this field presents limited opportunities for professional photographers.
   A. scientific
   B. journalistic
   C. freelance
   D. portrait

8. A school of photographic thought that places strong emphasis on forms and relationships is known as _____.
   A. documentation
   B. composition
   C. photojournalism
   D. abstractionism

9. *True or False?* Professional photographers make all or most of their living from photographic work.

10. _____ perform many of the routine tasks of organizing equipment and materials for a shoot, whether in studio or on location.
    A. Photojournalists
    B. Assistants
    C. Freelancers
    D. Videographers

11. Selecting a subject to photograph depends on many factors, but the first is _____.
    A. size
    B. color
    C. personal interest
    D. location

12. *True or False?* One of the broadest categories of composition is diagonal framing.

13. Which of the following is *not* a design principle?
    A. Balance
    B. Subject
    C. Emphasis
    D. Pattern

14. A _____ should highlight a photographer's best work.
    A. portfolio
    B. composition
    C. portrait
    D. documentation

Apply and Analyze

1. How is a photograph used in advertising to persuade consumers to purchase a product?
2. What is the difference between a salaried professional photographer and a self-employed professional photographer?
3. Describe three basic skills that are necessary to succeed as a professional photographer.
4. What has trained us to think of what a suitable subject might be, and how it should be photographed?
5. What is a portfolio, and why is it important?

Critical Thinking

1. Imagine you are asked to create a photo that illustrates the emotion of loneliness for a class project. How would you convey this emotion photographically?
2. Think about how your interests and your personality relate to the different types of photography you read about in this chapter. Does one or more of them seem to be a good match for you? Why or why not?

Suggested Activities

1. Use the information in this chapter to do one of the following:
   A. Write a short proposal to your instructor describing the creation of a fundraising calendar using photographs taken by class members.
   B. Create an online help-wanted ad for a photography assistant, describing needed skills. The ad should be fewer than 50 words.
   C. Compose a direct message to send to members of your photography class, proposing the formation of a school photography club.

2. Use a smartphone, tablet, or laptop to browse internet "job boards," such as LinkedIn or Indeed.com, to find advertisements for photographic employment. Try to identify which geographic areas provide the largest numbers of job opportunities. Write a short report with your findings.

Communicating about Photography

1. **Speaking.** Working with a partner, debate the topic of whether photography is art or craft. You should gather information in support of either the argument that photography is art or that it is craft. Use definitions and descriptions from this chapter to support your side of the debate and to clarify word meanings as necessary. Use the internet to research various opinions on this topic. Present you and your partner's final argument to your class.

2. **Listening.** As classmates deliver their presentations, listen carefully to their arguments. Take notes on important points and write down any questions that occur to you. After they have presented, ask questions to obtain additional information or clarification from your classmates as necessary.

Chapter 2
From Pinholes to Pixels

Learning Objectives

After completing this chapter, you will be able to:
- Describe the birth of photography and the various methods developed to attain a permanent photographic image.
- Explain the significance of Eastman's roll-film camera in making photography a popular activity.
- Understand the impact of color photography on the history of photography.
- Summarize the growth of digital photography.
- Discuss the future roles of both film-based and digital methods.

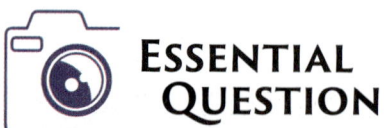

Essential Question

How has the rise of digital photography shaped how we interact with and view the world?

Technical Terms

ambrotype
Autochrome process
calotype
camera lucida
camera obscura
camera phone
cellulose nitrate
collodion
daguerreotype
developing-out paper
digital back
digital photography
dry plate process
ferrotype
fixing
latent image
negative
negative/positive system
photogram
Polaroid process
positive
printing-out paper
prosumer
tintype
wet-plate collodion process

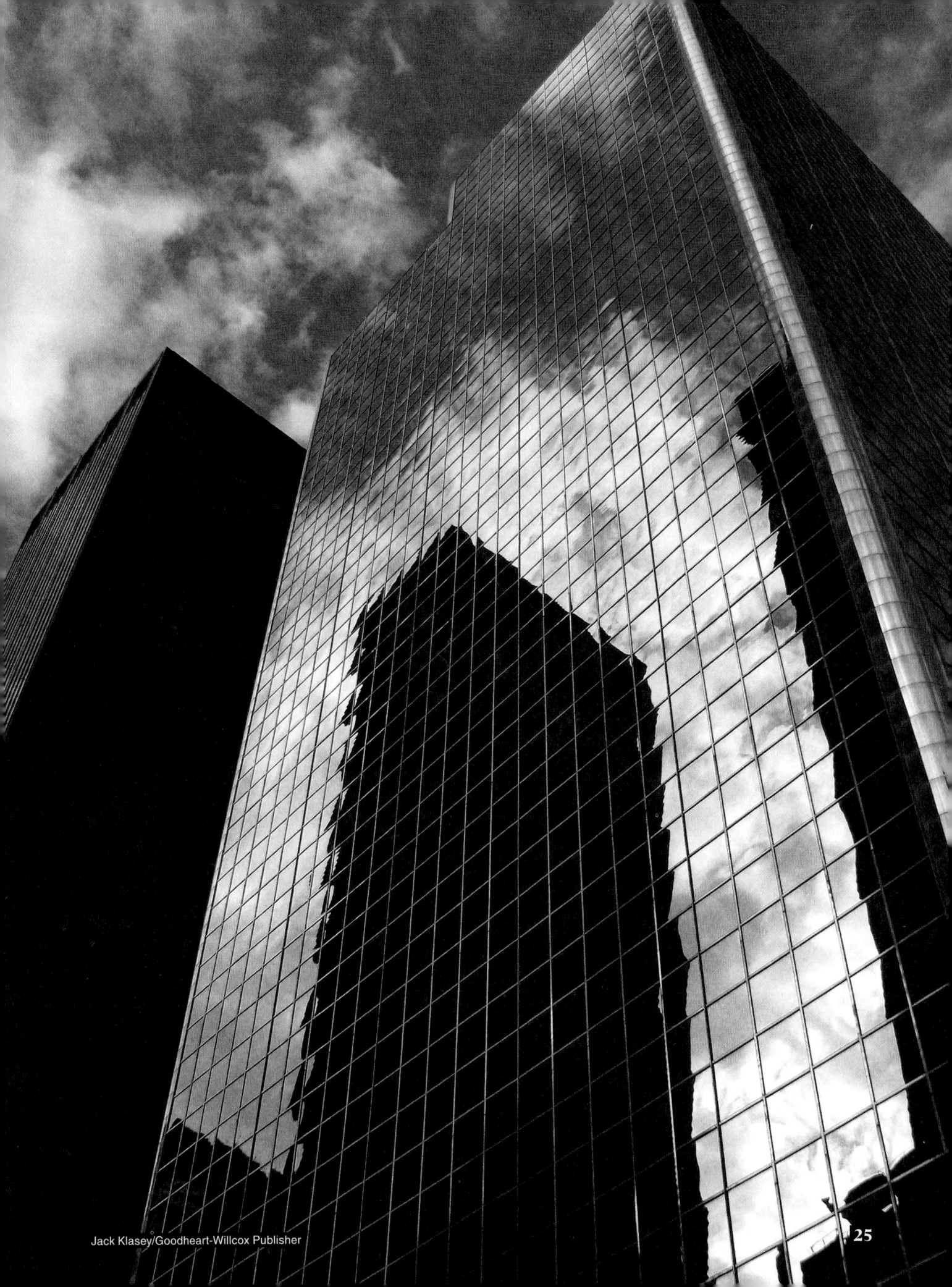
Jack Klasey/Goodheart-Willcox Publisher

Introduction to From Pinholes to Pixels

For years, instructors have used the experience of making and photographing with a pinhole camera as an introduction for beginning photography classes. The simple device, constructed from a light-tight cardboard box, has a tiny covered opening in one wall and a sheet of film or photographic paper attached to the opposite wall.

The basic principle of the pinhole camera is that light rays reflected from a subject pass through the tiny opening and form an exact, though inverted, image on the other side, **Figure 2-1**. The pinhole principle was known as early as the fifth century BCE in China, but it did not have a practical application until the 1500s, when the camera obscura came into use. **Camera obscura**, meaning *dark chamber* or *dark room*, is an enclosed space with a pinhole opening on one side through which an image of the scene outside is projected onto a movable screen or wall. By working from an actual room or a room-sized box or tent, an artist could bring the projected image into focus and trace it onto a piece of paper or canvas. The tracings would later form the basis for a painting.

A simple lens eventually replaced the pinhole, providing a brighter and sharper image. By the 1700s, the "dark room" had shrunk to the size of a large tabletop box. An Englishman, William Hyde Wollaston, did away with the box in the early 1800s when he invented the **camera lucida**, a tracing aid consisting of a prism mounted on a stand that projects a scene at a right angle onto a piece of paper. The device was placed above a sheet of drawing paper, and

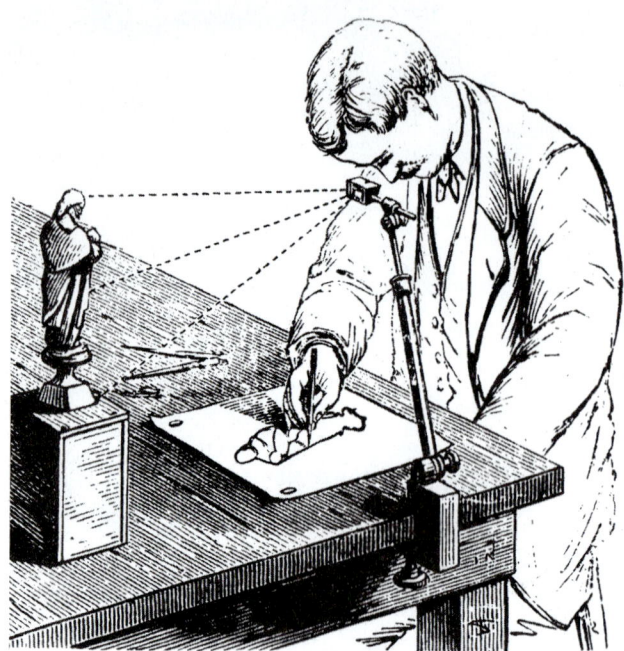

Goodheart-Willcox Publisher

Figure 2-2. The camera lucida was a tracing aid that allowed artists to trace the projected scene onto a sheet of paper.

the scene in front of the camera lucida was projected onto the paper so an artist could trace it, **Figure 2-2**.

However, neither of these methods involved photographic principles. They could not make a picture in permanent form, like a modern camera records a scene on film or electronic media. Although they may seem rudimentary today, the creation of these methods helped drive the birth of photography as we know it.

The Birth of Photography

When the recording medium (film) and the recording device (camera) came together, photography was born. The first important step toward a recording medium came in 1727, when Johann Heinrich Schulze observed that certain silver compounds darkened when exposed to light. The stencil-like images formed this way were not permanent, however.

More than 70 years later, in 1802, English scientists Thomas Wedgwood and Humphry Davy applied a silver chloride solution to paper, placed opaque objects on it, and exposed the paper to light. Their images were not permanent either, but the method led to the photographic form known as the **photogram**, a stencil-like photographic image created by placing opaque objects on treated paper that is then exposed to light, **Figure 2-3**.

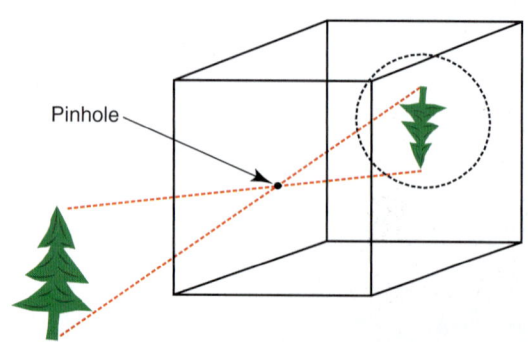

Goodheart-Willcox Publisher

Figure 2-1. Rays of light entering a darkened space through a tiny opening form an image that is inverted in relation to the actual scene. Photographs of surprisingly good quality can be taken with a pinhole camera, which is based on the principle shown in this illustration.

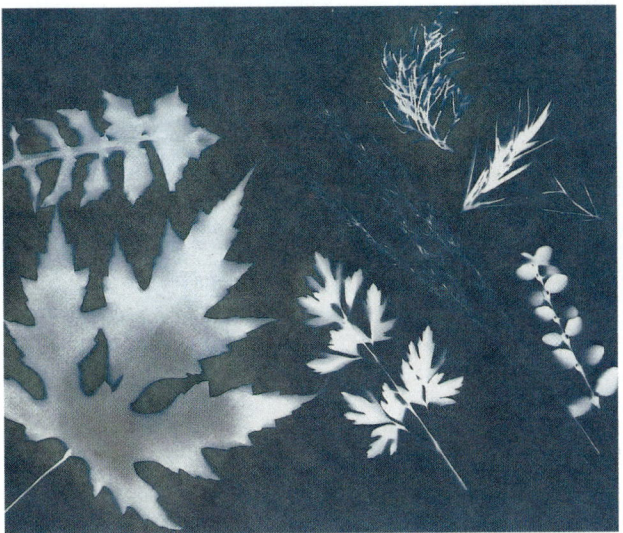

Goodheart-Willcox Publisher

Figure 2-3. Opaque objects placed on a sensitized material form stencil-like images when the material is exposed to light. The resulting picture is called a *photogram*.

The final element that made Daguerre's method a practical means of photography was fixing the image. *Fixing* was the chemical process of treating a developed photographic image to prevent further darkening of the silver by exposure to light. In late 1839, the English astronomer John Herschel found that hyposulfite of soda, or hypo, would make photographic images permanent. Now called sodium thiosulfate, hypo fixed the image by dissolving the unexposed silver on the plate's surface.

Word of Daguerre's success in producing permanent photographic images reached the scientific world in 1839. That year, a joint meeting of the French Academy of Sciences and the Academy of Fine Arts heard a detailed description of how a daguerreotype was made. A *daguerreotype* was the first widely available form of permanent photography, in which the image was recorded on a silver plate. A few months later, a small handbook written by Daguerre was on the market, and daguerreotypes were being made in a number of countries. See **Figure 2-4**.

The First Permanent Image

Joseph Nicéphore Niépce, a French experimenter, created a permanent photographic image in 1826. He coated a pewter metal plate with a light gray layer of bitumen of Judea, a type of tar. Using a camera with a simple lens, he made an eight-hour exposure of the scene outside the window of his home.

The light-sensitive bitumen of Judea hardened in proportion to the amount of light striking it. A solvent was used to process the exposed plate. In shadow areas with little or no exposure, the bitumen dissolved completely, revealing the dark surface of the pewter. Highlight areas—those exposed to the most light—resisted the action of the solvent, remaining light gray. Varying degrees of exposure provided the middle tones. Niépce's image was permanent—it remained unchanged when further exposed to light. He later refined his process by using silver plates and was able to reveal the bright metal for highlight areas.

Niépce died in 1833, but his business partner, Louis Jacques Mandé Daguerre, continued to perfect the process. In 1835, Daguerre found that a silver plate made light-receptive by iodine fumes and then exposed in the camera held an invisible latent image. A *latent image* is defined as a photographic image that does not develop (become visible) until exposed to developing chemicals.

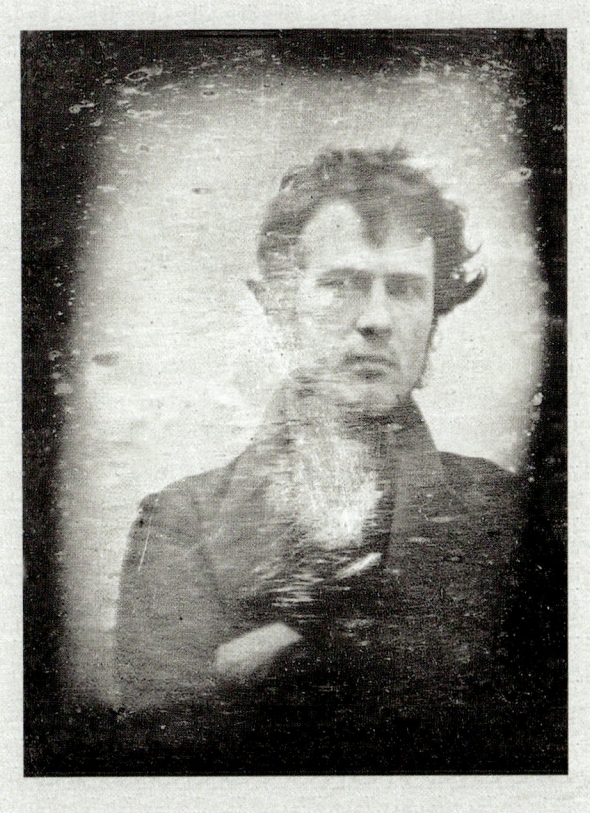

Courtesy of the Library of Congress

Figure 2-4. This self-portrait of Robert Cornelius of Philadelphia was made in 1839, only months after Daguerre's process was described in detail for the first time. It is one of the first daguerreotype images made in the United States.

At first, portrait subjects had to sit perfectly still for long exposures of up to 20 minutes. In 1840, however, a new camera lens was introduced that reduced exposures to a much more practical length of a minute or less. The lens was designed by Hungarian mathematician Josef Petzval. Once sitting time was drastically reduced, daguerreotype portrait studios became common.

Each daguerreotype image was unique. The only way to obtain an additional copy was to photograph the original subject again. Eventually, the daguerreotype was supplanted by the more flexible negative/positive system (chemical-based photographic printing).

Discovery of the Negative

In the early 1830s, English scientist William Henry Fox Talbot began experimenting with methods to make permanent images. Rather than metal plates, Fox Talbot used paper that he coated with silver compounds. In 1835, he captured a detailed image of his home's leaded glass window on paper that had been coated first with a solution of common salt, then with silver nitrate. Following a long exposure, a visible image appeared on the sensitized paper. A photographic paper on which an image appears without the use of a chemical developer, as in this case, is called **printing-out paper**. The photographic paper used today for prints made from film is known as **developing-out paper**, since the latent image must be brought out with a chemical developer.

Fox Talbot's process produced **negatives**, which are images made on film that are reversed in light, shade, tone, and orientation (left-to-right). He created the **negative/positive system**, the basis of chemical-based photographic printing, in which the original is a negative image that can be used to print any number of duplicate positive images. A **positive** image is an image that shows the light, shade, tone, and orientation as it appears in the original scene. See **Figure 2-5**. The original negative image can be placed atop another sensitized sheet, and that sandwich can then be exposed to strong light. The resulting print is a positive version, with both tones and orientation matching the photographed scene.

By discovering and refining the negative/positive system, Fox Talbot altered the direction taken by photography. Instead of being limited to one-at-a-time images, photographers could now make as many copies as they wished from each negative.

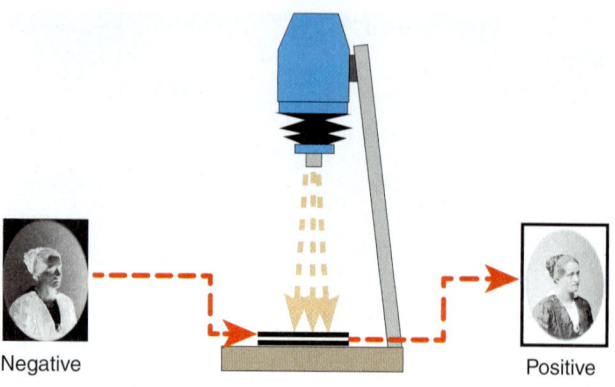

Goodheart-Willcox Publisher

Figure 2-5. In the negative/positive system, the original image (negative) is placed against a sheet of sensitized paper and exposed to a light source. After chemical development, a same-size contact print (positive) results. Later, it became possible to expose enlarged copies called *projection prints*.

Fox Talbot next devised the **calotype**, an early version of the negative/positive system that used treated paper as the negative material. The calotype (later renamed the *talbotype*) process was used in 1844 to produce Fox Talbot's *The Pencil of Nature*, the first book illustrated with photographs. The 24 photographs were individually printed and adhered to the pages.

Plate-Based Photography

By 1848, a method of adhering a light-sensitive albumen (egg white) coating to a sheet of glass was found by Abel Niépce de Saint-Victor in France. The clear and smooth glass base of the negative permitted making prints that rivaled the daguerreotype.

An improved coating process using **collodion** (a viscous liquid that dries to form a clear, tough layer) was devised in England by Frederick Scott Archer in 1851. The **wet-plate collodion process**, a photographic system in which a glass plate was coated with a liquid emulsion (a light-sensitive colloid used to coat photographic paper and film) and then exposed and developed while the emulsion was still wet, quickly drove both the daguerreotype and the talbotype out of the marketplace.

The wet-plate method required a cumbersome series of steps to prepare, expose, and develop the plate. The collodion, mixed with iodide, was flowed onto the surface of a carefully cleaned sheet of glass. Once the collodion became tacky, the plate was plunged into a silver nitrate solution to make it light-sensitive. From this point until the negative was developed and fixed, the photographer had to work in darkness or under dim red or orange light since emulsions of that time were not sensitive to red light.

Because the sensitivity of the emulsion would be lost if it were allowed to dry, the plate had to be exposed quickly. It was placed in a holder covered with an opaque lid, called a dark slide, and inserted in an already positioned and focused camera. The dark slide was removed and the camera shutter opened. After an exposure of up to 15 seconds, the plate was quickly taken to the darkroom and developed in an open tray. After fixing and washing, the plate was air-dried in a rack.

Wet-plate collodion photography typically required at least two people—the photographer to set up and operate the camera and an assistant to prepare and develop plates. For location photography, a wagon or tent that could be made light-tight to handle the development of the plates was needed. See **Figure 2-6**.

Collodion also made possible the ambrotype and ferrotype processes. The **ambrotype** was a glass negative placed over a black backing material that changed the appearance of the negative into a positive so it resembled a daguerreotype. **Ferrotype** was the formal name for the popular **tintype** process, in which a wet collodion emulsion was applied to a thin iron plate that had been painted with a black or brown enamel, **Figure 2-7**. This process was used for quick and inexpensive portraiture. Exposure and processing resulted in a positive-appearing image because of the dark background material. The ferrotype process was widely used in the United States from 1855 until well into the twentieth century.

The invention of the dry plate process in 1871 freed the photographer from the need to prepare plates. The **dry plate process** was a photographic system in which a glass plate was coated with a gelatin-based photosensitive emulsion. A British physician, Richard Leach Maddox, discovered that gelatin could be substituted for collodion when coating glass plates. Gelatin emulsions remained light-sensitive after drying, so plates could be prepared and stored for months before being exposed. After exposure, development could be delayed until convenient.

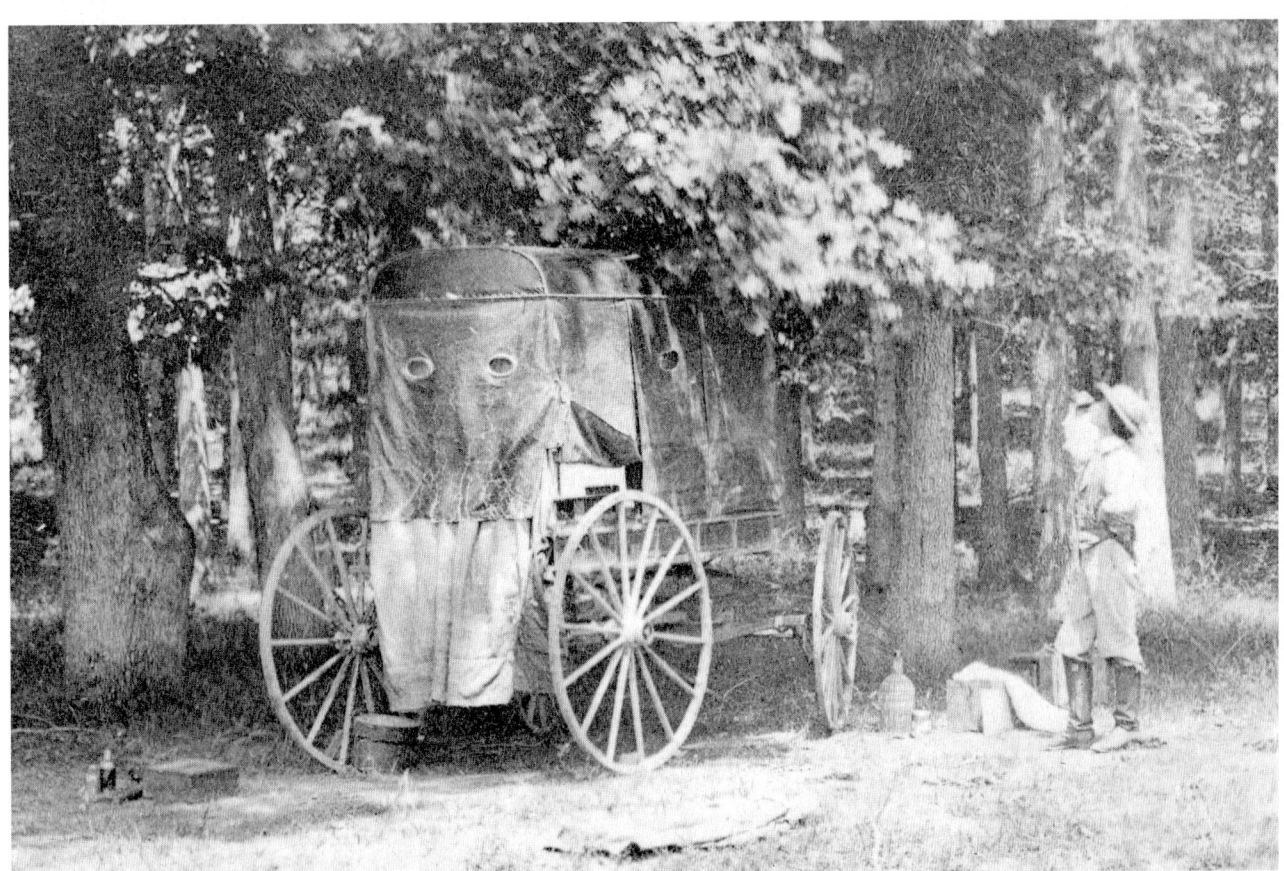

Courtesy of the Library of Congress

Figure 2-6. This portable darkroom wagon, parked near the Manassas battlefield in Virginia, was used by Timothy O'Sullivan, one of Mathew Brady's staff of Civil War photographers. The photo was taken July 4, 1862.

Commercial production of dry plates began in England in 1876. In the United States, John Carbutt of Philadelphia began offering them in 1879, and George Eastman founded his Dry Plate Company in 1880. See **Figure 2-8**. The convenience of using dry plates soon ended the general use of the wet-plate method.

Introduction of Roll Film

The dry plate was a major step toward making photography available to a wider audience. The new plates still required access to a darkroom for developing and printing and retained the drawbacks of the glass support—fragility, bulk, and weight. These problems were resolved in the late 1880s when films consisting of gelatin emulsions adhered to a flexible, transparent base came onto the market.

Truly widespread acceptance of photography as a hobby occurred in 1888, when George Eastman patented and began marketing the first self-contained camera to use roll film, **Figure 2-9**. The box-type camera was simple to operate—the user pulled a string to cock the shutter, pressed a button to release it, and then turned a key-like knob to advance to the next frame. Sealed inside the camera was a roll of gelatin-emulsion film sufficient for 100 exposures, each 2 1/2″ in diameter, **Figure 2-10**.

Eastman's self-contained Kodak system eliminated the need for a darkroom. It also made

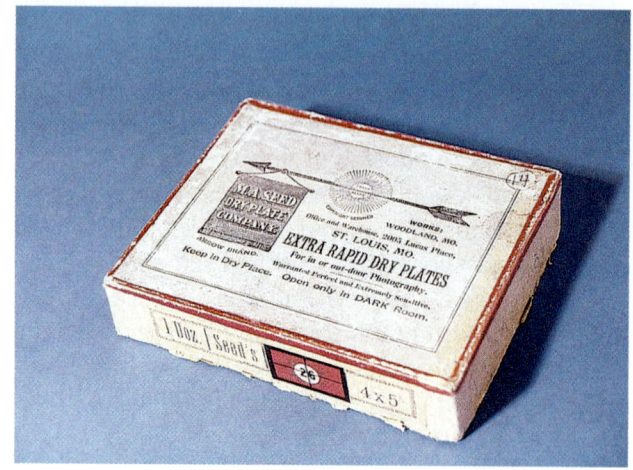

Goodheart-Willcox Publisher

Figure 2-8. The invention of the dry plate process allowed photographers to carry a ready-to-use supply of plates rather than having to prepare each plate just before exposure.

photography more accessible by decreasing the need for technical knowledge of developing photographs as well as the need to have an extensive amount of photography supplies to develop those photographs. When all the film was exposed, the entire camera was sent back to the company. For a $10 fee, the film was developed and printed, and a new roll was loaded into the camera. The camera, negatives, and prints were returned to the photographer.

Eastman's earliest roll film consisted of a gelatin emulsion applied to a paper backing. Within a

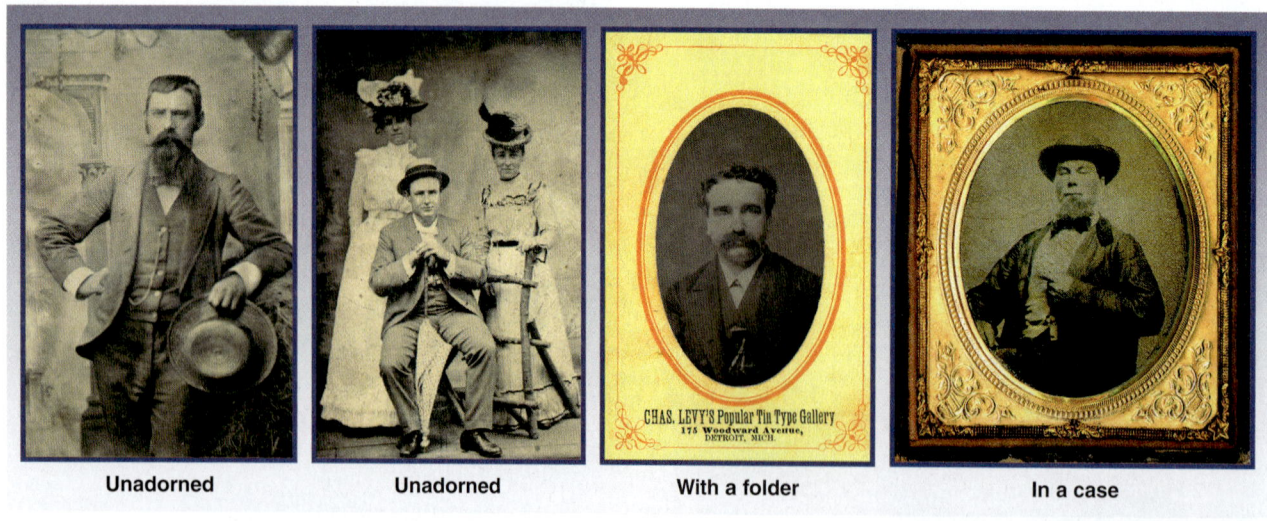

Goodheart-Willcox Publisher

Figure 2-7. The low cost of the tintype made it popular as "the people's photograph." A completed tintype may have been presented to the customer in unadorned form, like the first two examples. However, it was often placed in a printed paper folder advertising the photographer's studio. Some tintypes were packaged in a wood and leather case to emulate a daguerreotype. The case at far right is missing its lid.

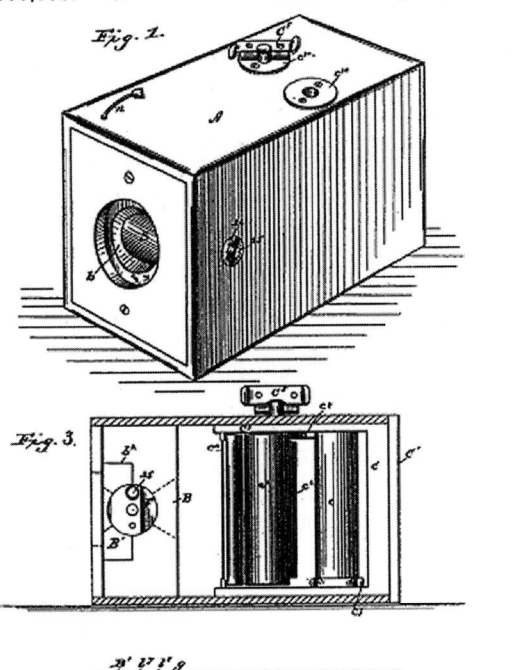

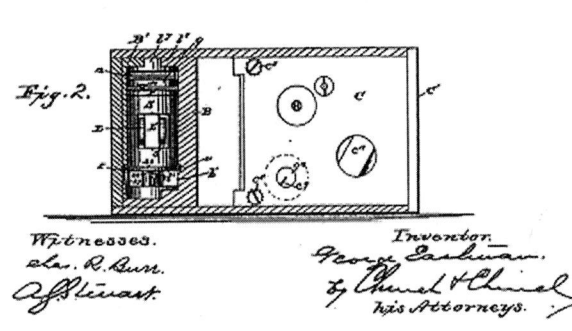

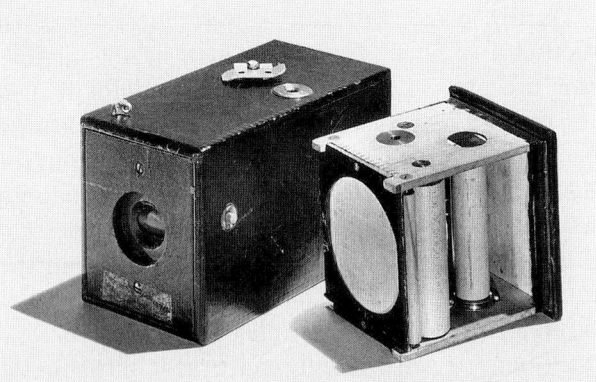

A

B

US Patent Office; Eastman Kodak Company

Figure 2-9. The simple-to-use roll-film camera made photography a popular pastime. A—George Eastman's 1888 patent application. B—The camera.

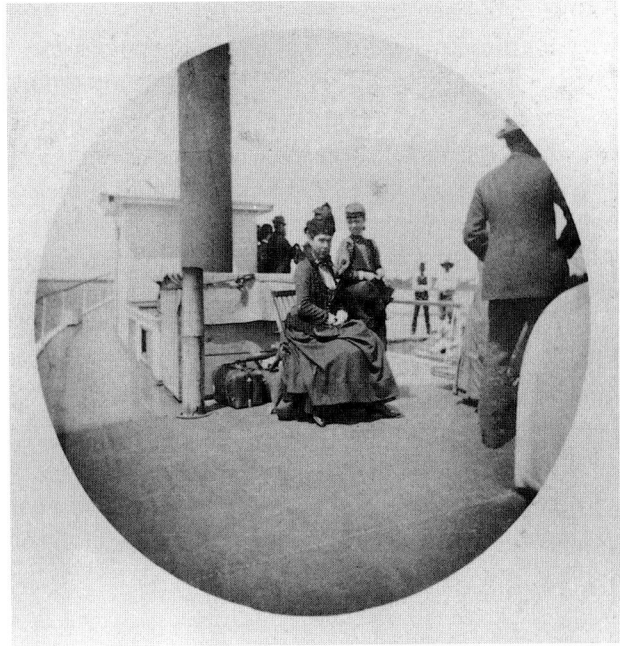

Courtesy of the Library of Congress

Figure 2-10. Eastman's slogan "You press the button, we do the rest" set the direction that the consumer photographic industry would take. The Kodak camera produced up to 100 small circular prints. This snapshot of two people on a boat deck in Florida was taken in 1889.

year of introducing the roll-film camera, Eastman adopted a simpler and better system—the light-sensitive material was coated onto a backing of clear cellulose nitrate rather than the paper support. **Cellulose nitrate**, also known as *celluloid*, was a highly flammable plastic used as the clear base for early roll films, later replaced by the more stable cellulose acetate. With the exception of changes in the type of plastic material used for the base, the roll form devised by George Eastman remains the standard for film-based still photography and motion pictures.

In fact, the motion picture industry owes its existence to Eastman's film. The strong, flexible, transparent base for the light-sensitive emulsion made possible Thomas Edison's development of the first motion picture camera in 1891. Interestingly, the film that evolved as the standard for motion pictures—35 millimeters in width and perforated with holes to accept the drive sprockets of the movie camera—did not become widely used for still photography until many years later.

In 1914, machinist Oskar Barnack of the German optical firm of Ernst Leitz and Co. built a still camera that could be used with the 35 mm film format. The film was loaded into a small, light-tight metal cassette and rewound into that container when all frames had been exposed. By 1924, the Leitz firm was manufacturing and marketing Barnack's camera under the name Leica, which it still bears today.

For many years after the Leica's introduction, the use of 35 mm cameras was known as *miniature photography*. See **Figure 2-11**. These small cameras appealed primarily to the adventurous person who was already involved with photography. As more and more 35 mm cameras came on the market, they began to be purchased as primary photo equipment, **Figure 2-12**. Most of these 35 mm cameras were *rangefinders*, or devices used to measure distances between the photographer and a still object.

Single-lens reflex (SLR) cameras with interchangeable lenses became more widely available in the late 1950s and 1960s. Their flexibility, light weight, and ability to take photographs under almost any conditions greatly accelerated the trend toward 35 mm. Other formats, such as disc film, 126 and 110 Instamatic films, and the Advanced Photo System (APS) were introduced, but eventually faded away or declined to form only a tiny portion of the film market.

Part of the success of 35 mm photography was due to the growth of its support system. Overnight film processing, once considered an extra-cost rush option, was superseded by the explosive growth of one-hour processing minilabs in shopping centers and retail stores. Those same sites now offer service for prints made from digital media.

Color Photography

While black-and-white photography was being developed and refined in the mid-to-late nineteenth century, some experimenters were also working to achieve photography in full color. The first practical system of color photography, the **Autochrome process**, was introduced in 1907. Brothers Louis and Auguste Lumière of France found that applying fine grains of potato starch to a plate, then coating the plate with an emulsion, made it possible to produce a colored image. The starch grains were dyed three different colors—cyan, magenta, and yellow—and then thoroughly mixed. The starch powder was dusted in a thin layer onto a transparent plate covered with wet varnish. A second coat of varnish and another layer of powder were added, and then very finely ground charcoal was applied to fill any spaces between the starch grains. A light-sensitive emulsion was coated over the top starch layer.

During exposure, the starch layers worked together as a filter to condition light by the additive color process. To reach the emulsion, light had to pass through the colored starch grains. Light passing through a yellow grain and then a cyan grain (or vice versa) produced green, cyan and magenta yielded blue, and magenta and yellow made red. After development, the plate was viewed from the emulsion side, so light passed through both the starch grains and the emulsion to the eye. The result was a surprisingly natural-looking color image, **Figure 2-13**.

Like the daguerreotype, each Autochrome image was one of a kind. Despite this limitation, the process was used extensively until the mid-1930s. Additive color processes, such as Autochrome, were

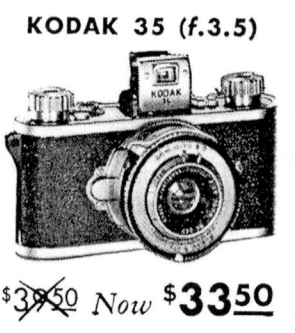

Goodheart-Willcox Publisher

Figure 2-11. Fifteen years after their introduction, 35 mm cameras were still referred to as "miniature cameras," as shown in this portion of a 1939 Kodak advertisement.

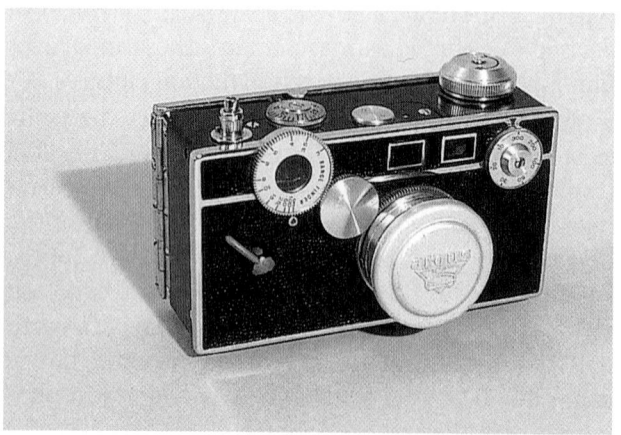

Jack Klasey/Goodheart-Willcox Publisher

Figure 2-12. The 1939 Argus C-3 camera introduced many people to "miniature photography." The camera's size, shape, and 1 1/2 pound weight earned it the descriptive nickname "The Brick."

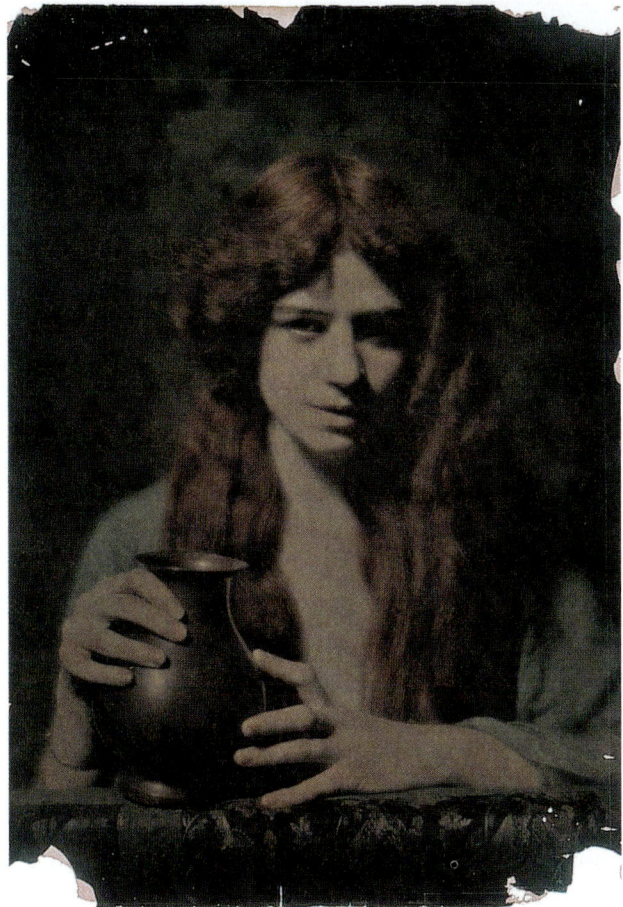

Courtesy of the Library of Congress

Figure 2-13. This Autochrome portrait of a woman with red hair was made by San Francisco photographer Arnold Genthe in the early 1900s.

made obsolete by the introduction of *Kodachrome*, a subtractive color film, in 1935. *Kodacolor*, the first color negative film using the subtractive color process, was introduced in 1942.

In the subtractive color process, dyes block specific colors from the white light that is used to view the image. For example, a cyan dye absorbs red light and passes blue and green, a magenta dye absorbs green and passes blue and red, and a yellow dye absorbs blue and passes red and green. The subtractive color process eliminated the complex mechanical masking (blocking) involved in additive color processes.

"Instant" Photography— The Polaroid Process

Photographers have always been eager to see the results of their efforts as quickly as possible. A unique system introduced in 1947 by American inventor Edwin H. Land allowed the photographer to view a fully developed picture only one minute after exposure, **Figure 2-14**. The *Polaroid process* achieved this rapid development time by incorporating a small packet of chemicals in each sheet of film. After exposure, the sheet passed through a set of rollers while being ejected from the camera. Roller pressure broke open the packet of chemicals and spread the mixture evenly over the film surface. At the end of the development period, a cover sheet was peeled off the film, revealing the finished photograph, **Figure 2-15**.

A color version was marketed beginning in the early 1960s. The Polaroid SX-70 film system, introduced in 1972, allowed the photographer to watch the picture develop, with no need to remove and discard a cover sheet.

The Polaroid process never achieved the widespread acceptance of conventional film-based photography and saw its market segment greatly eroded by digital cameras. In 2008, Polaroid announced that it was ceasing production of all its instant film products because of the lack of interest in the instant film market. However, in recent years, there has

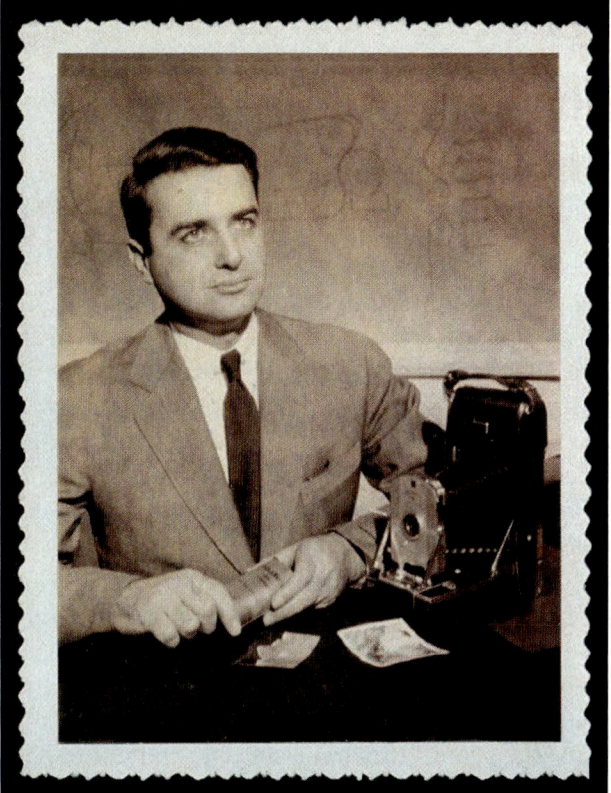

Courtesy of the Polaroid Corporation archives

Figure 2-14. Edwin H. Land's 1947 Polaroid camera system made possible, for the first time, an immediate assessment of photo results.

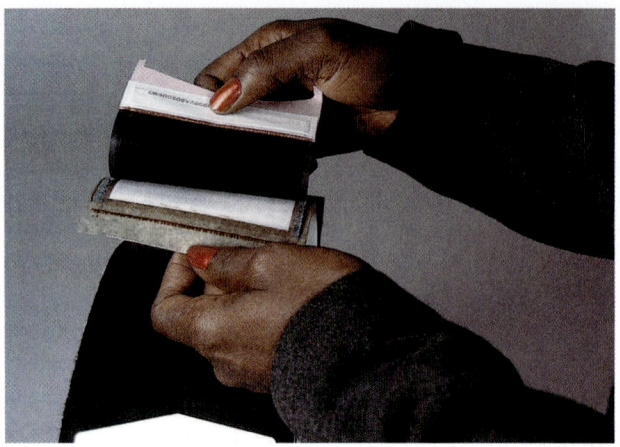

Goodheart-Willcox Publisher

Figure 2-15. A cover sheet must be peeled off Polaroid film to reveal the developed image.

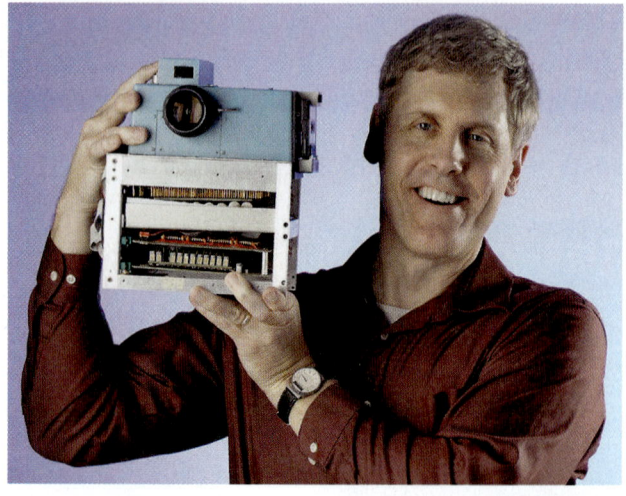

Eastman Kodak Company

Figure 2-16. Steve Sasson displaying his prototype electronic camera.

been a resurgence of interest in instant film, particularly among younger generations. This renewed interest prompted Polaroid to make a comeback in 2017. Their new cameras are rechargeable, can autofocus, and even have an app to use with a smartphone. There are also comparable instant films, in both color and black-and-white versions, available from Fujifilm and other instant film companies.

The Growth of Digital Photography

Digital photography is the process of using electronic devices to capture, create, edit, and share digital images. Although photography without film seemed to burst on the public's consciousness in the late 1990s, it dates back to 1975. Steven Sasson, an Eastman Kodak engineer, developed and demonstrated a prototype camera that captured images electronically. The camera weighed eight pounds and took 23 seconds to capture a low-resolution black-and-white image, **Figure 2-16**.

In 1984, Canon introduced a prototype "electronic still camera" that recorded an analog signal. The first commercially available electronic camera, the Canon RC-701, was offered for sale in 1986 and was used almost exclusively by photojournalists. Two years later, the first electronic camera offered to consumers reached the marketplace. Cameras that recorded images in digital form became available in 1990, but their high cost and the low resolution of images made the market slow to develop.

Digital photography using large format cameras (cameras that expose individual sheets of film, most commonly in 4″ × 5″ or 8″ × 10″ sizes) was being done in the studios of catalog and advertising photographers by the early 1990s, which helped it become a serious competitor to film. Also available to photographers were **digital backs**, which are digital capture devices attached to a camera in place of a traditional film holder that allows a camera designed to use film to take digital photographs. They are often used with medium format cameras (cameras that use 2 1/4″ wide roll film but produce negatives in different formats) or large format cameras. These digital cameras and backs could be used only for photos of stationary objects, since scanning required exposures that often were measured in minutes. The very large arrays (arrangements of image sensors in a digital camera) provided a high-quality image rivaling and even exceeding the resolution of traditional film. See **Figure 2-17**. Later, digital backs that could capture an image in a single, shorter exposure were developed for both large format and medium format cameras, **Figure 2-18**.

Photojournalists and other photographers working with live subjects needed a camera that could capture an image instantly. They also needed a camera that was flexible and portable, a means of viewing the captured image to evaluate composition and exposure, and some form of in-camera storage of completed images. The digital camera would have to retain most of the attributes of the 35 mm film camera while providing the highly desirable feature of instantly visible results. Those requirements also

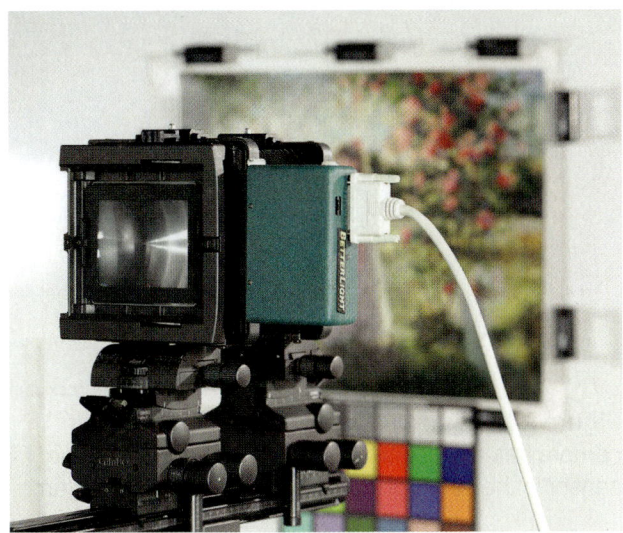

Better Light, Inc.

Figure 2-17. Developed to produce extremely high-resolution captures for applications such as fine art reproductions, this 416 MP digital back is being used on a 4″ × 5″ studio camera.

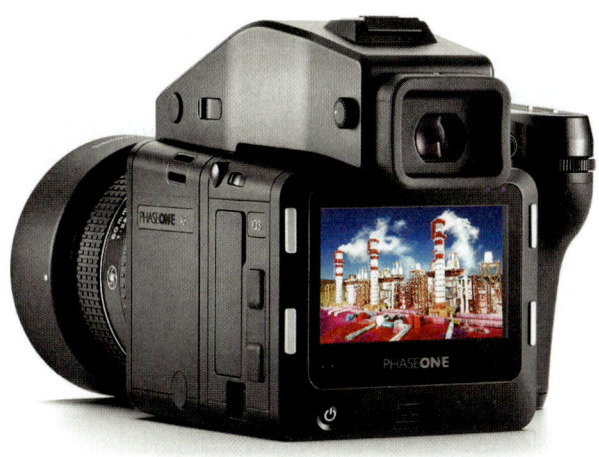

Phase One

Figure 2-18. This digital back, mounted on a Phase One medium format camera body, has an 80 MP sensor.

filled, a card can be removed from the camera and a new one inserted. Some computers have built-in card readers, but for those that do not have one, a card reader that plugs into the computer allows images stored on a memory card to be transferred rapidly to computer memory. See **Figure 2-19**. Most early cards could hold a small number of high-resolution (large) images or a larger number of images at a lower resolution. Today, there are cards available that can store thousands of high-resolution images.

Early digital cameras for professional use consisted of an array and associated electronic components combined with an existing professional-level 35 mm SLR. By the early 2000s, camera companies were developing and marketing expensive SLR cameras specifically designed for digital capture rather than film cameras adapted to use a digital array. In August 2003, Canon introduced the EOS Digital Rebel, a 6.3 megapixel (6.3 MP) SLR priced at under $1,000, making a digital SLR (DSLR) relatively affordable to many advanced amateurs. See **Figure 2-20**. Other major camera and electronics manufacturers quickly introduced SLR models aimed at the advanced amateur market, often called the ***prosumer*** (blending of the terms *professional* and *consumer*) market, a marketing term used to identify cameras that bridge the gap between amateur and professional equipment.

The surge in consumer acceptance of digital cameras paralleled the great expansion of home computer use and the explosive growth of the internet in the late 1990s. Dozens of digital cameras designed for consumer use became available. These cameras varied widely in capabilities and price, appealing to different market segments. Most were the digital equivalent of the 35 mm "point-and-shoot" snapshot camera—focus, aperture, and shutter speed all would be the key to making digital photography accepted in the consumer market.

A method of viewing the completed image became available in 1995, when electronics-maker Casio introduced a digital camera with a small liquid crystal display (LCD). Today, the LCD on many digital cameras acts as the viewfinder (a screen on or attached to a camera that shows the field of view of the lens) for composing the picture as well as a means of reviewing the captured image.

Image storage cards, also known as memory cards, are the equivalent of "digital film." When

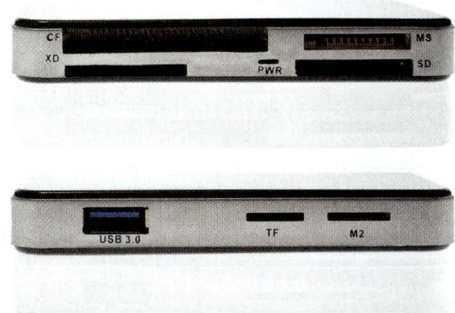

JGA/Shutterstock.com

Figure 2-19. This card reader is able to accept several types of memory cards.

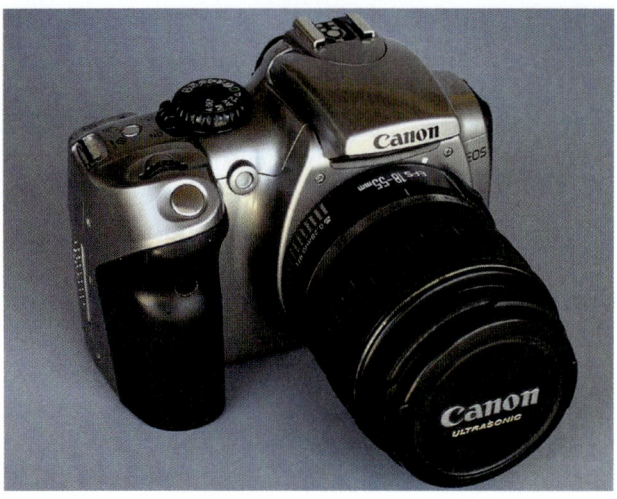

Jack Klasey/Goodheart-Willcox Publisher

Figure 2-20. The Canon EOS Digital Rebel was the first prosumer camera.

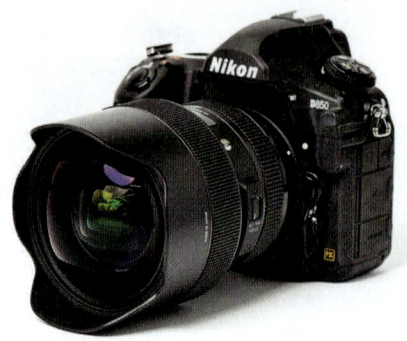

SAVIKUTTY VARGHESE/Shutterstock.com

Figure 2-22. The Nikon D850 professional digital camera has a 45.7 MP full-frame sensor. A full-frame sensor is the same physical size as a 35 mm film frame.

were automatically set by the camera's electronics. More sophisticated models allowed the photographer to manually set exposure controls.

For a time in the early 2000s, cameras with 3-megapixel (3 MP) sensors were state of the art for consumers. The pixel count quickly escalated, however, and by 2015, even many low-priced point-and-shoot (compact camera) models offered 16 MP sensors, **Figure 2-21**. More sophisticated advanced compact cameras and prosumer SLRs typically have sensors in the 16 MP–20 MP range. Professional-level SLRs have sensors as large as 36 MP. Those with full-frame sensors have lower pixel counts since their individual pixels are larger, **Figure 2-22**. Virtually all of today's digital cameras are capable of producing printed images that approach or exceed the quality of those made with conventional film. Digital camera sensors and other camera systems are explained more thoroughly in Chapter 5, *The Camera System*.

Camera Phones

Japanese electronics companies began incorporating photo capability in their cell phones in the early 2000s, and by 2004, camera phones were available in the United States. A *camera phone* is a cell phone that includes a photographic device. Although early cell phone cameras had only 1 MP or 2 MP sensors, most smartphone cameras today have between 8 MP and 16 MP sensors, **Figure 2-23**. For example, most iPhone® cameras have 12 MP sensors. Smartphones have large touch screens and combine the functions of a cell phone, camera, and web browser. Users can download and use many available apps to not only take photos but edit them as well. With each new iteration of smartphone, the quality of the camera increases. Phones are now built with cameras that have more megapixels and more lenses. In some instances, smartphone cameras surpass traditional cameras in terms of quality. Smartphones are also much more accessible to most people than digital cameras are.

The Future of Photography

When digital photography became affordable for the consumer in the mid-to-late 1990s, most experts predicted the new medium would gradually become competitive with film, and someday even surpass it in popularity. However, the pace of change was so rapid that it could be called a revolution. According to statistics from the Camera & Imaging Products Association, between 2002 and 2003, worldwide shipments of digital cameras increased from 24.5 million to nearly 44.5 million, while traditional film cameras dropped from 23.6 million to 16.3 million.

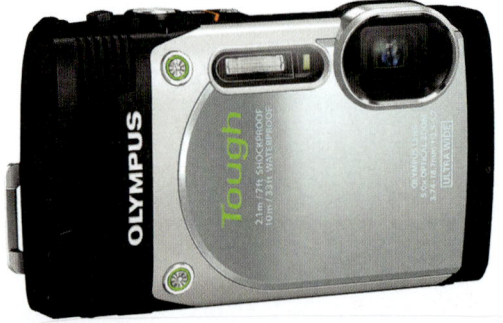

Olympus America, Inc.

Figure 2-21. This 16 MP point-and-shoot camera has a 3.74 mm to 18.7 mm zoom lens and is small enough to carry in a pocket or bag.

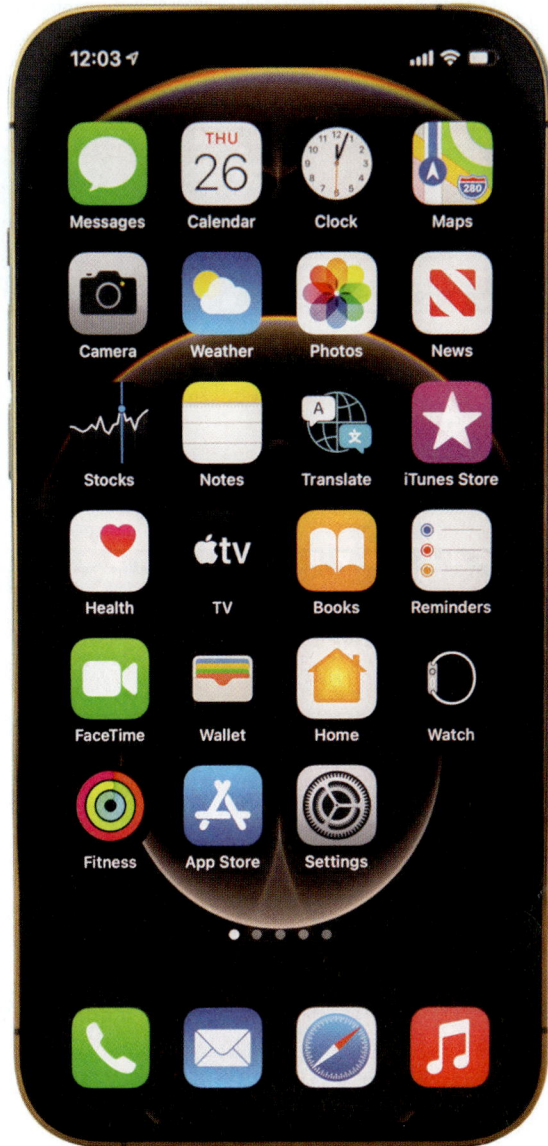

DenPhotos/Shutterstock.com

Figure 2-23. A 12 MP camera is used in this Apple® iPhone® 12 Pro Max.

By 2010, digital camera shipments reached their peak, with 121.5 million units shipped, while film camera shipments had dropped well below 1 million units. Since then, the pace of digital camera shipment has slowed steadily as the market became saturated and the shift to smartphones continued.

Factors that contributed to the digital revolution include increased picture quality, rapidly declining camera prices, and the ability to view the captured image immediately. However, possibly the most significant factor was the development of a large number of sites for quickly and inexpensively making prints from digital files. According to the Photo Marketing Association, a trade group that monitors the photographic field, the trend in printing shows steady movement toward retail store and internet printing and away from producing prints at home. Since 1996, when the first digital labs were introduced to retailers, digital processing has spread to virtually every drugstore and major discount store. Most even offer the photographer the convenience of uploading the files through their website or app, then picking up prints at the store an hour later. This overcame what had been a perceived limit to digital photography's growth—the cost and time needed to make prints at home. Some companies, such as Shutterfly, allow you to have your photos printed and shipped directly to you.

With the ease of sharing images offered by smartphones, more and more people are choosing to display their photos on social media rather than making prints. An estimated 350 million photos are uploaded daily to Facebook, and another 95 million to Instagram.

Will Film-Based Photography Survive?

Digital image capture has become almost universal among advertising and commercial photographers, and it has achieved wide acceptance by the general public. However, a significant number of serious amateurs and professionals dedicated to fine art photography can be expected to remain with film-based methods as a creative tool. The process of capturing the image on film and producing it with traditional darkroom practices allows the artist to present a subject in a manner very different from the same subject captured and presented by digital methods. The evolution of film-based photography from a broad popular form of expression to a narrow fine art specialization seems likely to continue.

Photographers who choose to work with traditional film-based methods will find their equipment and material choices increasingly limited and their costs steadily increasing. Major camera manufacturers have either eliminated or severely cut back production of film cameras. Photographic supplies, particularly film and printing papers, have become more expensive and less readily available. In the face of steadily declining demand, fewer once-popular films and papers will be available. Dedicated film photographers, however, will overcome such equipment and materials limitations, using their skills and experience to continue producing high-quality images.

Milestones in Photography

1500s: Camera obscura first used as aid for artists.
1727: Schulze discovers that certain silver compounds darken when exposed to light.

Niépce records the first permanent photographic image.

Fox Talbot captures a photographic image on a paper base coated with a light-sensitive silver chloride solution.

Daguerre discovers that a sensitized silver plate would capture a latent image that could then be made visible by development.

The Petzval lens greatly reduced sitting times for photographic portraits. Basic principles of portrait photography are developed by Adamson and Hill.

| 1500s–1727 | 1826 | 1834 | 1835 | 1840 |

Kodachrome film invented by Godowsky and Mannes.

Electronic flash invented by Edgerton.

Barnack develops the prototype of the 35 mm still camera.

Lumière brothers invent the first practical color photographic method, the Autochrome process.

Panchromatic film emulsions introduced.

| 1935 | 1931 | 1914 | 1907 | 1904 |

1942 — Kodacolor, the first subtractive-process color print film, is introduced.

1946 — Ektachrome, the first color film capable of being processed by the photographer, is marketed.

First autofocus point-and-shoot camera marketed by Konica.

First modern-style drones created in Israel.

| 1947 | 1963 | 1976 | 1978 | 1980s | 1984 |

Land devises the Polaroid instant photography system.

Instamatic cameras and 126-size film are introduced.

Canon introduces the first 35 mm camera with a built-in microprocessor. Inkjet printer developed.

The first digital camera (electronic still camera) used to photograph opening of summer Olympic Games.

Kodak ceases production of infrared film.

12 MP cameras become common in smartphones.

| 2017 | 2016 | 2011 | 2009 | 2008 | 2007 |

Polaroid returns to the market after increased interest in instant film.

Revolutionary "light field" camera announced; will allow focus changes after exposure is made and eliminate need for flash.

Kodak announces the end of production for Kodachrome, its oldest transparency film (invented in 1935).

Polaroid announces that it will cease production of instant film products due to consumer switch to digital photography. Sony announces 25 MP full-frame sensor.

1844	The first book illustrated with photographs is published.
1851	Archer develops the wet-plate collodion process.
1855	Ferrotype (tintype) process introduced.
1860	First surviving aerial photograph taken in Boston.
1861	Maxwell describes and demonstrates the additive color process.
1871	Maddox devises the gelatin-based dry-plate process.
1873	Vogel introduces orthochromatic film emulsion, responsive to both blue and green light.
1880	Eastman Dry Plate Company founded in Rochester, New York.
1888	Eastman introduces the trade name Kodak; begins marketing the first roll-film camera.
1889	Eastman introduces the first commercial roll film to use a transparent base.
1890	Hurter and Driffield publish research on exposure measurement and emulsion sensitivity (the basis of the "characteristic curve").
1891	Edison develops the first motion picture camera, using a film format devised by Eastman.
1900	Eastman Kodak introduces the "Brownie," the first mass-marketed camera.
1986	Minolta introduces Maxxum 9000, the first professional autofocus camera; Kodak develops the first megapixel sensor.
1987	Single-use cameras introduced by both Fuji and Kodak.
1990	Adobe Photoshop image editing software introduced for Apple® computers. Photo CD system developed by Kodak.
1994	First optical-stabilized lens introduced by Nikon.
1995	Casio unveils first digital camera with an LCD screen. First image-stabilized lens introduced by Canon.
1996	The Advanced Photo System is introduced.
1997	First known publicly shared picture taken with a cell phone.
1999	First consumer-level 3-megapixel digital cameras offered.
2000	Nikon and Canon introduce professional-level digital SLR cameras. Sharp markets first camera phone in Japan.
2002	Hewlett Packard begins selling printers equipped with memory card slots (for direct printing). Canon develops the first market-successful full-frame DSLR.
2003	Digital cameras begin to outsell film cameras. First prosumer digital SLR cameras reach the market.
2004	Kodak stops producing film cameras in the US. Epson develops the first true consumer mirrorless camera, the Epson R-D1.
2005	Canon introduces the EOS 5D, first full-frame digital SLR priced for the prosumer market. AgfaPhoto ends production of consumer films and files for bankruptcy.
2006	Nikon announces it will cease production of film cameras except for two professional models. Konica Minolta exits camera and film business. Live preview feature for digital SLRs introduced by Olympus.

Chapter 2　From Pinholes to Pixels

Chapter 2 Review

Summary

- The basic principle of the pinhole camera is that light rays reflected from a subject pass through the tiny opening and form an exact, though inverted, image on the other side. A simple lens eventually replaced the pinhole, providing a brighter and sharper image.
- When the recording medium (film) and the recording device (camera) came together, photography was born. The first images were not permanent, but the method English scientists Thomas Wedgwood and Humphry Davy developed in 1802 led to the photographic form known as the photogram.
- French experimenter Joseph Nicéphore Niépce created a permanent photographic image in 1826. Louis Jacques Mandé Daguerre perfected the process, and in 1839, his success in producing permanent photographic images, called daguerreotypes, reached the scientific world.
- In the early 1830s, English scientist William Henry Fox Talbot began experimenting with methods to make permanent images. His process produced negatives, and he created the negative/positive system, the basis of chemical-based photographic printing.
- By 1848, a method of adhering a light-sensitive albumen coating to a sheet of glass was found by Abel Niépce de Saint-Victor in France. An improved coating process using collodion was devised in England by Frederick Scott Archer in 1851, and the wet-plate collodion process was developed.
- Collodion also made possible the ambrotype and ferrotype processes. The ferrotype process was widely used in the United States from 1855 until well into the twentieth century.
- The invention of the dry plate process in 1871 freed the photographer from the need to prepare plates. The convenience of using dry plates soon ended the general use of the wet-plate method.
- Truly widespread acceptance of photography as a hobby occurred in 1888, when George Eastman patented and began marketing the first self-contained camera to use roll film. His Kodak system eliminated the need for a darkroom.
- In 1914, machinist Oskar Barnack of the German optical firm of Ernst Leitz and Co. built a still camera that could be used with the 35 mm film format. As more and more 35 mm cameras came on the market, they began to be purchased as primary photo equipment.
- While black-and-white photography was being developed and refined in the mid-to-late nineteenth century, some experimenters were also working to achieve photography in full color. Brothers Louis and Auguste Lumière of France introduced the Autochrome process in 1907.
- The Polaroid process was introduced in 1947 by American inventor Edwin H. Land. It allowed the photographer to view a fully developed picture only one minute after exposure. A color version was marketed in the early 1960s.
- Digital photography dates to 1975, when Steven Sasson, an Eastman Kodak engineer, developed and demonstrated a prototype camera that captured images electronically.
- The Canon RC-701, the first commercially available electronic camera, was offered for sale in 1986 and was used almost exclusively by photojournalists. Two years later, the first electronic camera offered to consumers reached the marketplace.

- By the early 2000s, camera companies were developing and marketing expensive SLR cameras specifically designed for digital capture rather than film cameras adapted to use a digital array. The surge in consumer acceptance of digital cameras paralleled the great expansion of home computer use and the explosive growth of the internet in the late 1990s.
- Japanese electronics companies began incorporating photo capability in their cell phones in the early 2000s, and by 2004, camera phones were available in the United States.
- When digital photography became affordable for the consumer in the mid-to-late 1990s, it first became competitive with film and eventually surpassed it in popularity. Today, smartphones have become even more popular than digital cameras.
- The evolution of film-based photography from a broad popular form of expression to a narrow fine art specialization seems likely to continue.

Review Questions

Answer the following questions using the information provided in this chapter.

Know and Understand

1. *True or False?* Camera lucida means dark chamber or dark room.
2. A stencil-like photographic image created by placing opaque objects on treated paper that is then exposed to light is called a _____.
   A. latent image
   B. photogram
   C. tintype
   D. calotype
3. *True or False?* A daguerreotype was the first widely available form of permanent photography.
4. *True or False?* Printing-out paper requires a chemical developer to bring out the latent image.
5. The _____ was an early version of the negative/positive system that used treated paper as the negative material.
   A. daguerreotype
   B. calotype
   C. ambrotype
   D. talbotype
6. The _____ process quickly drove both the daguerreotype and talbotype out of the marketplace.
   A. tintype
   B. dry plate
   C. Polaroid
   D. wet-plate collodion
7. *True or False?* The ambrotype was a glass negative placed over a black backing material that changed the appearance of the negative into a positive so it resembled a daguerreotype.
8. The _____ process was a photographic system in which a glass plate was coated with a gelatin-based photosensitive emulsion.
   A. dry plate
   B. wet-plate collodion
   C. tintype
   D. Autochrome
9. Truly widespread acceptance of photography as a hobby occurred in 1888, when George Eastman patented and began marketing the first self-contained camera to use _____.
   A. collodion
   B. developing-out paper
   C. roll film
   D. negatives
10. The _____ process was the first practical system of color photography.
    A. Kodachrome
    B. wet-plate collodion
    C. Autochrome
    D. Polaroid
11. The _____ process allowed the photographer to view a fully developed picture only one minute after exposure.
    A. Polaroid
    B. tintype
    C. dry plate
    D. Autochrome
12. *True or False?* Photography without film dates back to 1975.
13. A(n) _____ is the equivalent of "digital film."
    A. digital back
    B. photogram
    C. image storage card
    D. calotype

14. _____ is a marketing term used to identify cameras that bridge the gap between amateur and professional equipment.
    A. Daguerreotype
    B. Camera obscura
    C. Digital back
    D. Prosumer
15. Most sophisticated advanced compact cameras and prosumer SLRs typically have sensors in the _____ range.
    A. 3 MP–12 MP
    B. 12 MP–16 MP
    C. 16 MP–20 MP
    D. 20 MP–36 MP
16. *True or False?* Camera phones were available in the United States in 2000.
17. Which of the following is *not* a factor that contributed to the digital photography revolution?
    A. Increased picture quality
    B. Size of the camera
    C. Rapidly declining camera prices
    D. The ability to view the captured image immediately
18. Which of the following is *not* true of film-based photography today?
    A. Film and printing papers have become less readily available.
    B. Film-based photography is considered a narrow fine art specialization.
    C. Film-based photography has achieved wide acceptance by the general public.
    D. The cost of film-based equipment and material choices is increasing steadily.

Apply and Analyze

1. How did the negative/positive system alter the direction of photography?
2. Why did the plate have to be exposed quickly during the wet-plate collodion process?
3. In what decade did digital photography first become a serious competitor to film?
4. What was the significance of the 6.3 MP EOS Digital Rebel SLR marketed by Canon in late 2003?
5. What might be considered the most significant factor in making the digital revolution possible?

Critical Thinking

1. In 1888, George Eastman patented and began marketing the first self-contained camera to use roll film. Why do you think the Eastman camera led to truly widespread acceptance of photography as a hobby?
2. Introduced in 1947, the Polaroid photographic process made it possible to take a photo and have a developed print in about one minute. In 2008, the Polaroid Corporation stopped producing instant film products and cameras, but in 2017, they made a comeback due to the increased popularity of instant film among younger generations. Why do you think there was a sudden resurgence in interest among younger generations?

Suggested Activities

1. Locate a photographer (professional or amateur) who is still shooting film. Your instructor might be able to direct you to such a person, or you could contact your community photography club or local photo studios. Interview the photographer about their reasons for continuing to do film-based photography. Ask what challenges and benefits it presents compared to digital photography. Write a report to present to your class or record a video of the interview with your smartphone.
2. Chemicals employed in some early photographic processes, such as the mercury fumes used in creating daguerreotypes, were very dangerous. Using internet and library resources, research early photographic processes and make a list of the chemical hazards you find.

Communicating about Photography

1. **Speaking and Reading.** With a group of classmates, make a list of at least 20 words that begin with "photo." Photo comes from the Greek root *photos* (light). You can use the text glossary, a dictionary, and online sources. With your group, discuss the meaning of each word and use each word in a sentence.

2. **Reading and Speaking.** Select a milestone in the Milestones in Photography graphic that focuses on a type of camera, such as 1900 or 1947. Research the type of camera and the impact it had on the photography industry. Explain the milestone to the class using visuals, such as a PowerPoint presentation. Show examples of images taken with the camera in your milestone and explain how the image is indicative of the camera and/or era.

Chapter 3
Professional Photography

Learning Objectives

After completing this chapter, you will be able to:

- Define professional photography.
- Determine the skills and career preparation needed to enter the professional photography field.
- Describe the four different forms of business organization.
- Identify several different ways of financing a new photography business.
- Explain the importance to a photographer of retaining all rights to an image.
- Compare various methods of marketing a photography business.
- Recognize social skills needed to work effectively with clients and with fellow professionals.
- Explain the importance of continuing education in the professional photography field.

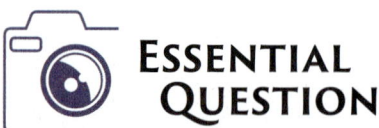

Essential Question

How will an understanding of professional photography practices help you in your photography career?

Technical Terms

business plan
contract
corporation
e-commerce capability
entrepreneurship
intellectual property
internship
invoice
limited liability company (LLC)
marketing
mass marketing
partnership
photography assistant
professional photography
profit
release
sole proprietor
targeted marketing

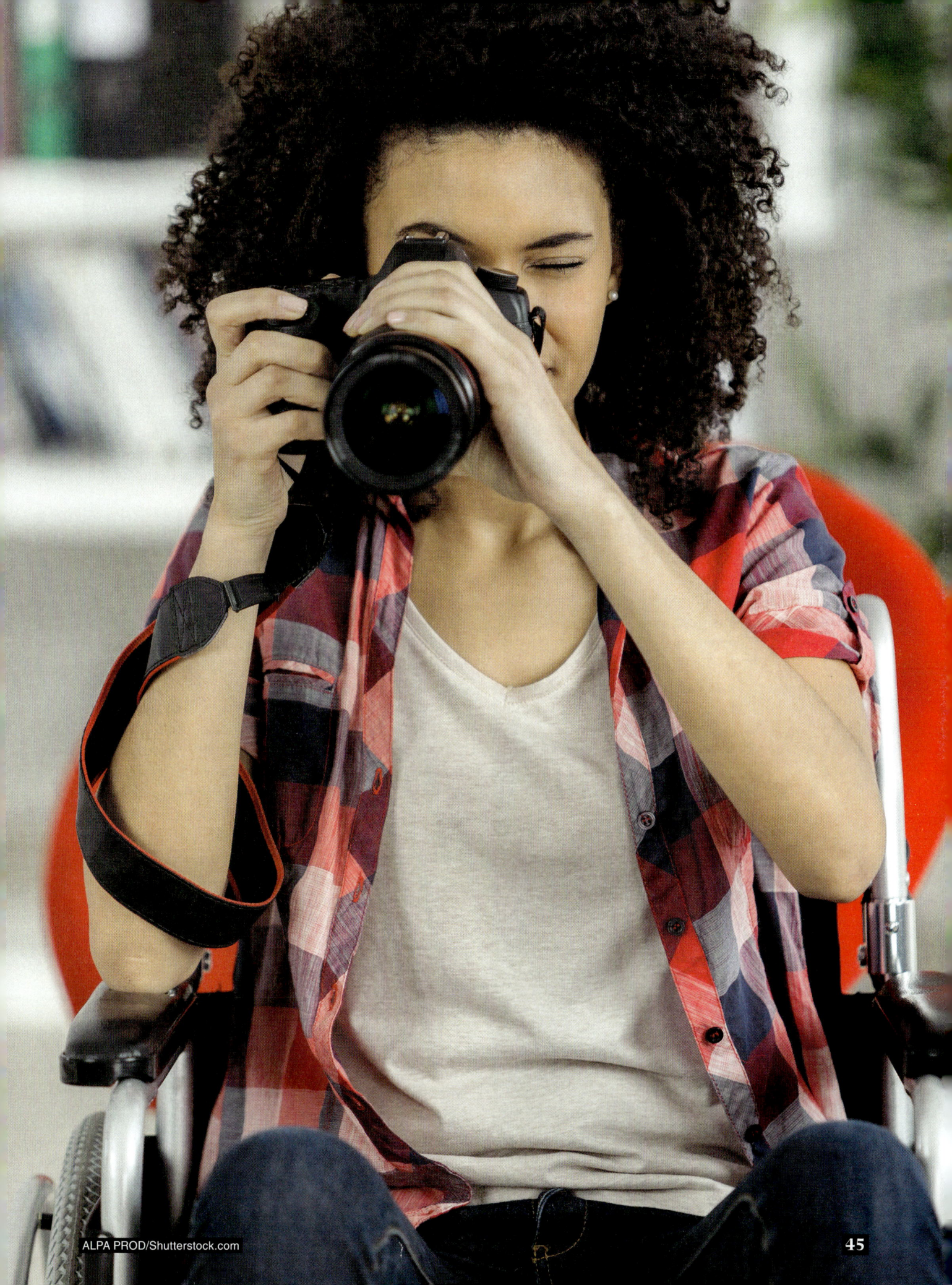

Introduction to Professional Photography

Ansel Adams is one of the most widely recognized names in photography, **Figure 3-1**. His dramatic images of scenes in the American West brought him fame as a fine-art photographer. However, for most of his career, his major source of income was professional photography. Adams sold family portraits, advertising and publicity photos for industrial and utility companies, and illustrations for books and magazine articles. See **Figure 3-2**. Although income from selling his landscape images grew steadily from the time he began selling them in the late 1920s, he depended on professional photography assignments until the 1970s.

Programs in most colleges and technical schools focus primarily on the artistic and technical aspects of photography. Their aim is to provide students with the photographic skills and abilities needed to produce good images. To be successful, however, an aspiring photographer also must develop business and social skills. This chapter is designed to help you learn about the business side of photography, including areas such as getting a job in the field, starting and operating your own photographic business, and working with clients, employees, and independent contractors.

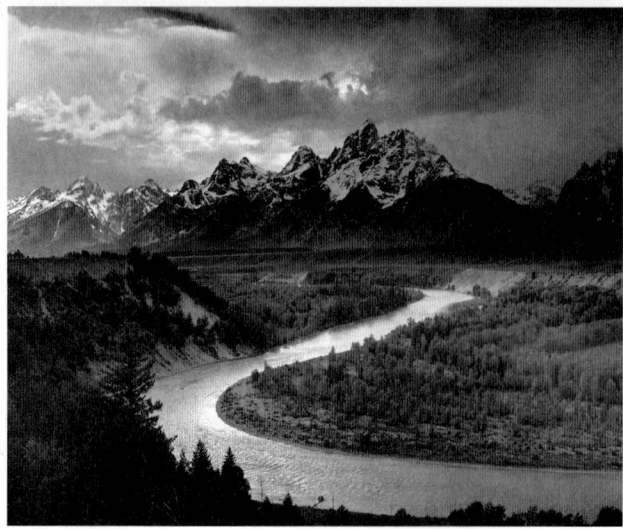

National Archives and Records Administration

Figure 3-2. Adams' image *The Tetons and the Snake River* was made in 1942 as part of a commissioned project to photograph scenes in national parks for the US Department of the Interior.

What Is Professional Photography?

As noted in Chapter 1, *Our Visual World*, ***professional photography*** is an occupation in which photographic skills are used to create images in exchange for payment. While that definition applies to the fairly small number of photographers who make a living from selling their fine-art prints, it usually describes someone who works in the fields of portraiture, advertising/product photography, or photojournalism. The term *commercial photography* is sometimes used interchangeably with *professional photography*, but this textbook uses professional photography exclusively.

Professional photography as we know it became prevalent in the mid-1800s. Up until then, photography was seen as a luxury. The development of the first Kodak camera made photography more accessible and helped create the intersection of advertisement and photography. In 1920, roughly 15% of advertisements used photographs, and by 1930, that number increased to 80%. With every new advancement in the photography industry, it became easier and easier for people to make professional photography a full-time (or part-time) career.

About one-third of all professional photographers work in salaried positions with publications, corporations, government agencies, or studios.

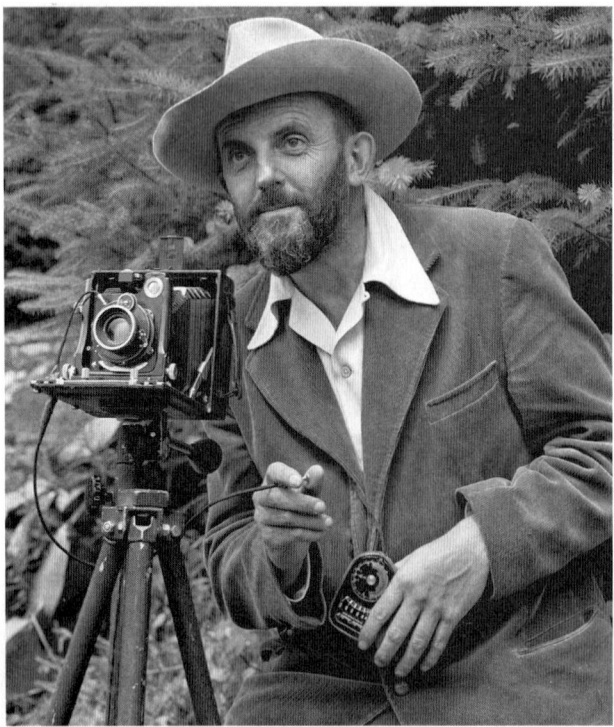

Photo by J. Malcolm Greaney [Public domain], via Wikimedia Commons

Figure 3-1. Ansel Adams shooting on location in about 1947.

The remaining two-thirds are self-employed individuals who have started independent businesses. These businesses range from specialized single-person operations, such as freelance news photography and studios doing only weddings or portraits, to companies with several employees handling assignments as varied as school pictures, event coverage, product photography, and industrial/corporate assignments, **Figure 3-3**. Professional photography has taken on a new life over the last several years as the way we market products has changed. It is easy to see old product photography and judge it as out of fashion, or even cheesy, but product photography is still prevalent. It is simply the style that has evolved.

How to Enter the Professional Photography Field

There are a number of paths to employment in professional photography. Jobs in a photographic organization typically require formal education, practical experience, or a combination of the two. While some successful photographers began their careers in entry-level jobs requiring few or no photographic skills, they are a rarity today.

The most common type of career preparation is formal education at a traditional college or university, a community college, a specialized technical school, or an online institution. College or university programs leading to a four-year degree provide a broad education that includes both training in photographic skills and classes in the humanities. Strong emphasis is placed on the artistic aspects of photography.

Community colleges and technical schools (both classroom-oriented and online) offer two-year or shorter programs, with primary emphasis devoted to learning photographic skills. Some of these programs include classes to prepare students for running a photography business. See **Figure 3-4**.

An important benefit offered by some educational programs is the opportunity to work in a photographic business as an intern. An ***internship*** is a position that provides a student or trainee experience in a working environment, such as a newspaper, a corporate photo department, or a portrait studio. Internships typically last a school semester or several summer months. In addition to gaining experience in a working environment, participating in an internship program provides many benefits. It can often be done for academic credit, and it may be paid (though it can also be unpaid). Furthermore, making a good impression while serving as an intern may lead to a job offer upon graduation.

Working as a Photography Assistant

For many graduates, the next step in developing a career is seeking work as a ***photography assistant***, or a person who aids a photographer with a variety of tasks in the studio and on location. Depending mostly on the size of the community, an assistant may be an employee of a single studio or company, or they may be an independent contractor working

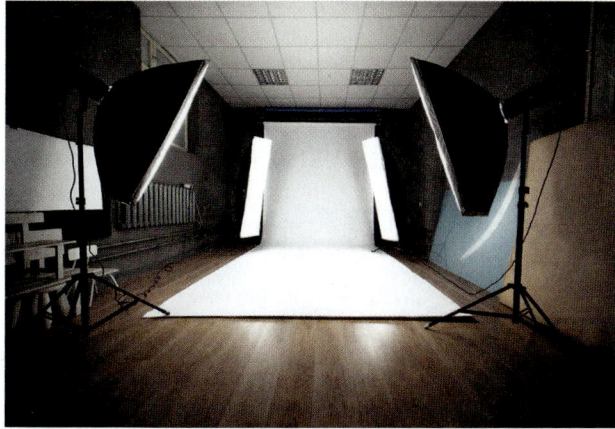

Vasilyev Alexandr/Shutterstock.com

Figure 3-3. Photography businesses can serve a wide variety of clients. This setup uses a backdrop and four softbox lights, which are flexible enough to be used in various scenarios.

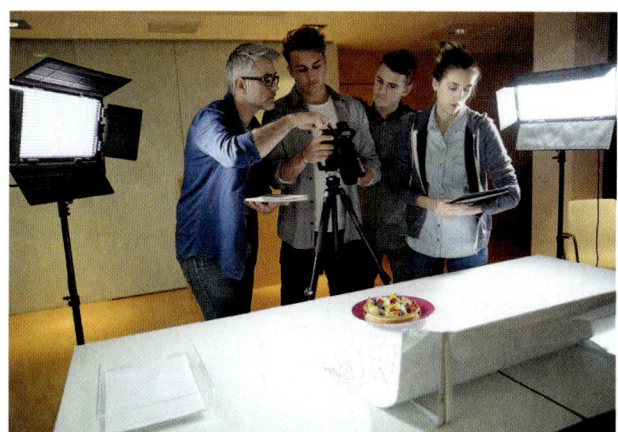

goodluz/Shutterstock.com

Figure 3-4. Community colleges offer two-year programs in a variety of photographic areas.

on assignments for different photographers. In larger markets, such as New York or Los Angeles, most assistants work on a job-by-job basis. One day they may be helping on a product photo session at a studio, and the next day they might be on location for a fashion shoot with a different photographer.

Although most assistants will not be (at least initially) shooting photographs, they must have well-developed photographic skills. A thorough knowledge of lighting is important because an assistant usually sets up and adjusts lighting equipment to the photographer's specifications. An assistant may also sit in for a model while light readings and color temperature readings are made, or they may assist with lighting for the shoot, **Figure 3-5**.

An assistant is also expected to perform many duties that do not deal exclusively with the art of photography but rather the business side of photography. These might include answering the studio telephone, arranging catering for a daylong location shoot, and picking up clients at the airport. Since they will often be working closely with clients, models, and others involved in the photography process, an assistant must have good people skills.

Working as an assistant provides a great deal of practical experience in the different aspects of the professional photography business. Experience as an assistant could result in promotion to a photographer's duties with the studio, being hired as a photographer by another studio, or launching your own photography business.

Entrepreneurship

Many photographers, as well as people in other fields, have a goal of working for themselves. The process of starting a business is called *entrepreneurship*. There are several approaches to starting your own photography business. Keep in mind that these are somewhat traditional photography businesses and do not outline the only approaches to creating a successful business.

Many entrepreneurs begin doing professional photography on a part-time basis while relying on a full-time job for regular income. They typically seek assignments that can be done on evenings and weekends. Since few part-time professionals have access to studio space, they most often contract to do weddings or similar celebrations, youth team photography, and informal portraiture, often in outdoor settings, **Figure 3-6**.

Operating a part-time photography business poses less financial risk and needs a smaller amount of capital than setting up a full-time operation, but it still requires a sound business approach. For example, you must realistically identify your business costs before pricing your work. If income is not greater than expenses, your business will not survive, and you will not make any money from your venture.

Another means of becoming a business owner is to go into partnership with a photographer who has an established business. This method requires financial capital because you are buying a share of the business. It also requires strong photography skills and a good reputation. Some business owners take on a partner as a means of expanding and improving their business, and others may be looking forward to retirement and see the new partner as a potential successor.

Instead of buying a share of a business, you can purchase a going business outright (a going business is one that is financially stable enough to

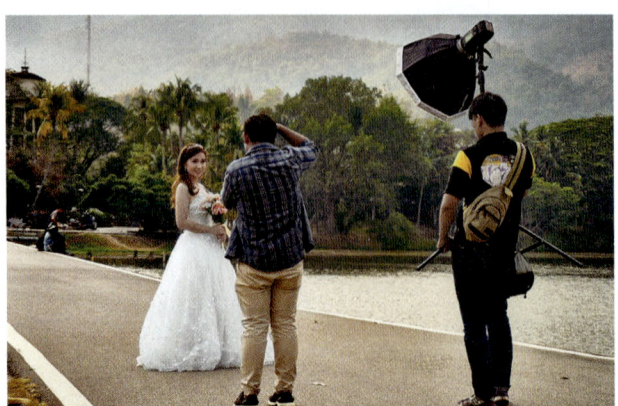

Kirill Smirnov/Shutterstock.com

Figure 3-5. On a wedding shoot, a photography assistant might help the photographer with lighting.

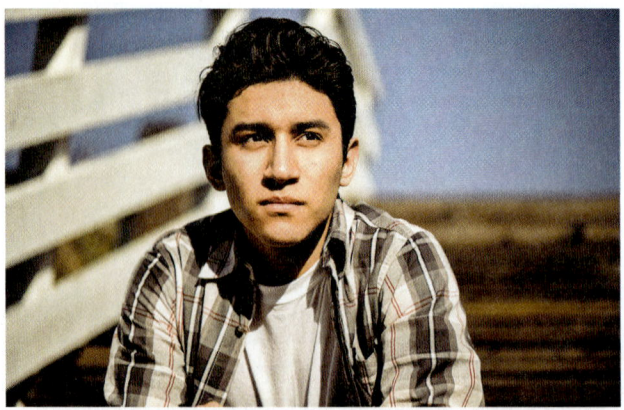

Manuela Durson/Shutterstock.com

Figure 3-6. Many part-time professional photographers devote their weekends to shooting portraiture.

continue business for the foreseeable future). This method requires a considerable investment, but it provides you with an established customer base, a known business name, and a fully equipped business location.

Creating a new full-time business of your own is often the most expensive and riskiest approach. You will need a good credit record and enough financial capital to acquire and equip your office/studio and to cover operating expenses until you begin making a profit. You will also need to devote considerable time and money to attracting and keeping paying clients. While this path is the most difficult to follow, many choose it because it provides opportunity for considerable personal satisfaction and financial success.

Setting Up Your Business

When breaking into the photography industry, there are quite a few options. Whether you start in high school, college, or after, there are many ways to start a career in photography. One option is to form your own business. The first step you must take when setting up a business is to determine which form of organization to use. There are four basic business types: sole proprietorship, partnership, corporation, and limited liability company (LLC).

Each form of organization has its advantages and disadvantages. Your specific needs and interests will determine the type you choose. The four business types are described in the following sections. Remember that these are all options for professional photographers. If you are looking to start your own business while in high school, you will need to take different steps.

Sole Proprietorship

The federal government defines a **sole proprietor** as a person who owns an unincorporated business by themselves. The owner of a sole proprietorship typically performs all the work needed to earn the business' income and pays all the expenses of operating the business. Any profit from the business belongs to the proprietor, but if it fails to make a profit, the proprietor is responsible for the unpaid debts.

As a sole proprietor, you must play many different roles beyond creating the photographs. You are the company's bookkeeper, purchasing agent, sales/marketing/advertising person, equipment manager, and even janitor.

Many sole proprietorships begin as, and remain, one-person businesses. Owners of such businesses are content to earn a sufficient living without the extra responsibility of hiring employees. They may bring in assistants or other photographers as independent contractors for specific assignments as needed. Other sole proprietors actively pursue expansion of their business, adding employees and facilities as needed to serve their customers. Even though a business might have dozens of employees and operate in several locations, it is still a sole proprietorship if it has only a single owner.

Partnership

In a **partnership**, two or more individuals join together to operate a business. Each of the partners contributes something to the business, such as capital, property, labor, or skills. The partners share the profits or losses. This is the route often followed by newspaper photographers and other salaried workers moving into self-employment. A partnership agreement should specify what each partner will bring to the business and what share of the business each will own.

For example, in a two-person partnership, one partner might be contributing business skills and most of the operating capital needed, while the other partner has the photography skills, equipment, and a studio location, **Figure 3-7**. Depending on the relative value of their contributions, the partners might decide on equal ownership shares or different percentages, such as 60/40 or 70/30.

Sometimes, a partnership consists of a general partner and one or more silent partners. The general

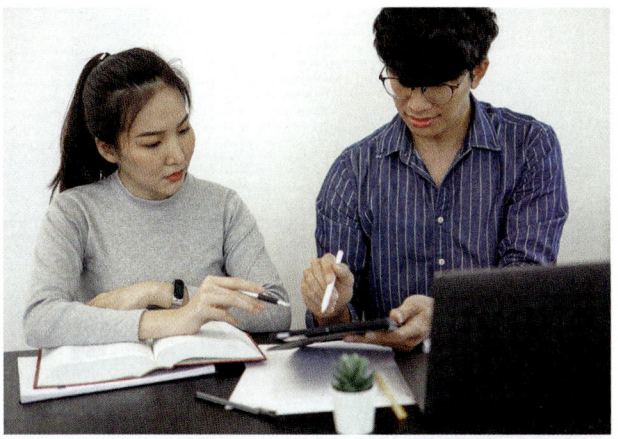

Indypendenz/Shutterstock.com

Figure 3-7. Business partners often bring different skills to the organization.

partner operates the business, while the silent partner's involvement is primarily financial. The silent partner provides all or most of the money needed to set up and operate the business and usually has the largest ownership share. Silent partners typically are not involved in the day-to-day operation of the business.

Corporation

A *corporation* is a form of business organization in which investors or shareholders purchase ownership in the form of shares of stock. There may be only a few investors, each holding a large number of the total shares, or many investors, each holding a small number of shares. The investors elect a board of directors, which in turn appoints or hires the people who operate the corporation.

For example, imagine a photographer decides to form a corporation to operate their studio business, **Figure 3-8**. The photographer and several family members each purchase shares of stock in the new corporation. The shareholders elect a board of directors from among themselves. The directors, in turn, appoint the photographer as the corporation's chief operating officer or president.

The major advantage of a corporation is *limited liability*. If the business fails, individual shareholders are not responsible for the debt. Only the corporation's assets can be used to pay creditors. It is worth noting that photographers forming a corporation is relatively rare.

Limited Liability Company (LLC)

A ***limited liability company (LLC)*** is a hybrid form of business organization that combines some of the advantages of a corporation with some of the advantages of a sole proprietorship or a partnership. An LLC may be owned by a single individual or by two or more individuals or organizations (such as corporations or other LLCs). The owners are described as "members" and share in the company's profits or losses. Like sole proprietors or partners, the members report business income and/or losses

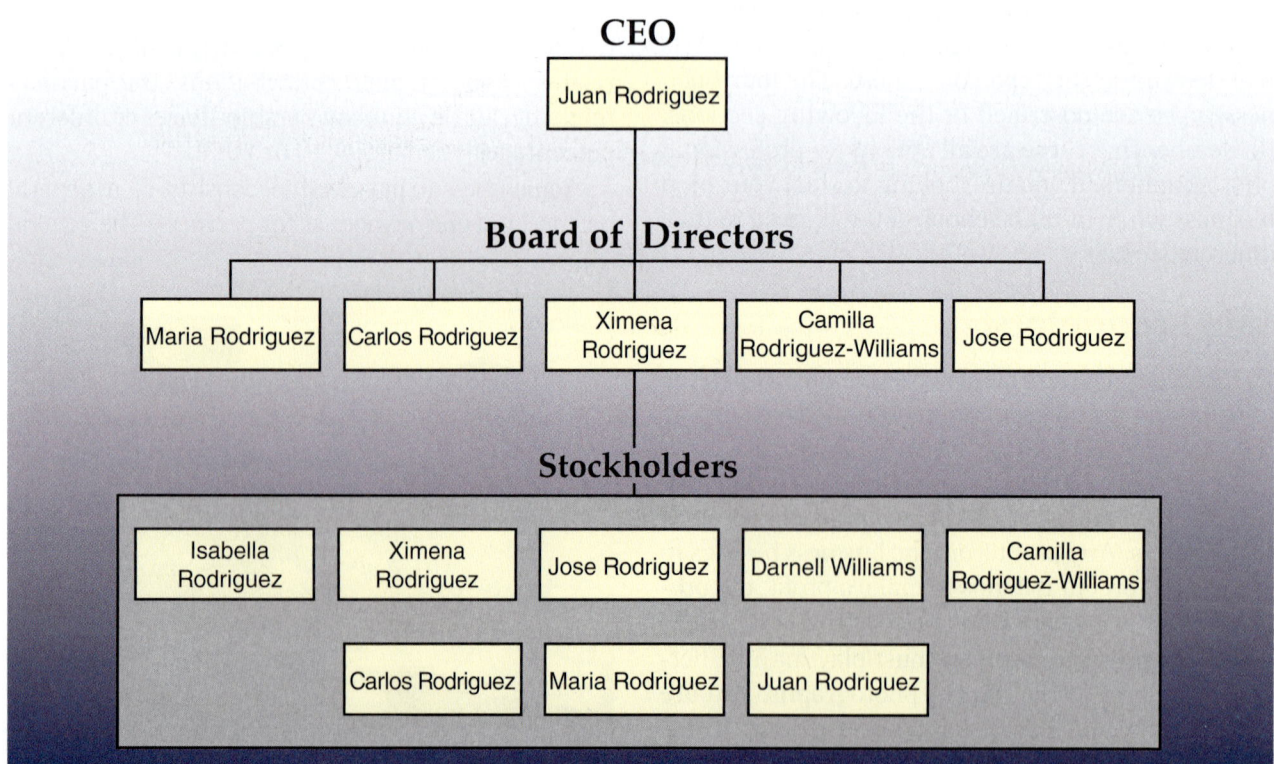

Goodheart-Willcox Publisher

Figure 3-8. An example of a photography business organized as a corporation.

on their personal tax returns. However, like corporate stockholders, they are not liable for the LLC's debts if the company fails. Only company assets can be used to settle with creditors.

Limited liability and tax advantages have made the LLC form of organization a favorite for photographers and other professionals. This is one of the most common options for photographers to create their own businesses, and creating an LLC is relatively straightforward.

Finding Your Business Niche

What kind of photography will your business offer? What market segment (niche) will you serve? Some photographers specialize in a single area, such as portrait work, fashion, or entertainment. Others restrict their work to several related areas, such as school and team photography or product photography for clients in a particular industrial category. Still others develop a mix of clients in different areas, such as weddings, portraits, and institutional.

Deciding on your business niche is a process that combines your personal interests and skills with information gathered through market research. That research is a key element of the business plan you will develop before seeking funding to start your business. Researching your market will take into account several factors, including the following:

- Size of your community or trade area
- Your area's economic and population characteristics
- The number and sizes of established professional photography businesses
- The types of photography done by businesses in your area
- Purchasing patterns (for example, do people typically buy from local businesses, or do they tend to go to a nearby large city to make purchases?)

As part of your research, look for unserved or underserved areas of the market. For example, you may find that while local youth baseball and softball leagues all have contracted with photographers, no one is doing group and individual portraits for dance studios, gymnastics schools, or competitive swimming programs, **Figure 3-9**. You might also find a number of small businesses in your area are in need of someone to take promotional photos for social media or their business website. If you determine that they would be interested in photography services, you have identified an area with potential clients.

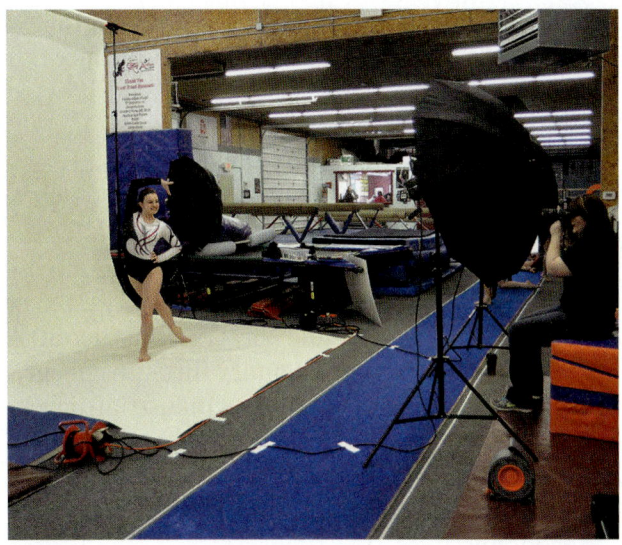

A

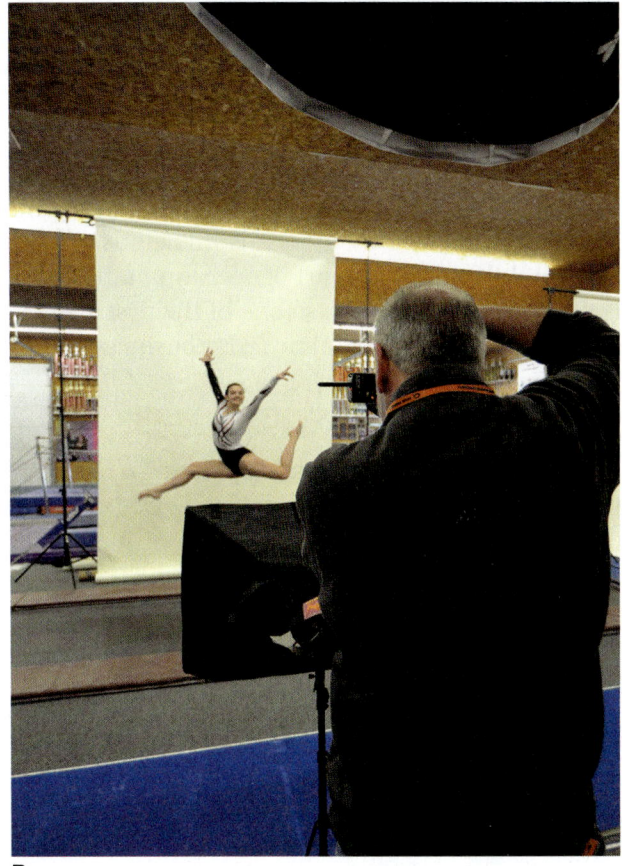

B

Image Group Photography, LLC

Figure 3-9. Photographing gymnastics school students. A—Posed portrait. B—Action portrait.

The size and location of the community where you open your business may be a limiting factor in the type of photography you plan to do. In a small- to medium-size community located far from a major city, it could be difficult to succeed in a business specializing in high fashion or food photography. Being in or near cities like New York, Chicago, Los Angeles, Atlanta, Miami, or Dallas would provide many more opportunities in such fields.

While many photography businesses successfully pursue a specialty, others find a mix of photography types and clients helps them to stay in business and prosper. For instance, at one successful studio in a medium-size Midwestern city, 30% of the work is in weddings and portraits, another 30% is school photography (elementary through college), and the remaining 40% is a mix of industrial, advertising, event, and institutional assignments. The variety of photography work is a great advantage because it helps the studio survive fluctuations in the economy.

Operating Your Business

To start a business, you have to spend money. To stay in business, you must spend money as well, but you also have to bring in more money than you spend. The amount of money left after paying all the expenses for a business is known as *profit*, **Figure 3-10**. A major part of operating a business is dealing with finances, so one of the first steps is understanding how to finance your business.

Financing the Business

As mentioned, starting and operating a business takes money. How much money is required depends on several factors:

- Will the business be operated from your home, or will office/studio space have to be purchased or rented?
- Will you need to replace, upgrade, or add to your current photographic equipment?
- How much money must be available to pay for business licenses and fees, insurance, taxes, and other business expenses?
- Will you have an income source to pay living expenses (rent, utilities, car payment, etc.) until the business starts generating cash flow?

Answering these questions will help you determine how much money you need to make to run your business successfully. This will then help you determine whether a part-time or full-time business is right for you.

Starting a Part-Time Business

If you begin your photography business on a part-time basis, you will most likely not need to rent or buy studio space because most work will be done on location. While you may already have the basic equipment, you will probably have to upgrade to better-quality lenses or add tools such as a portable lighting kit. If you plan to rent photo equipment for specific needs, you must be sure to include that in your expenses. A realistic calculation of what you will need to meet business expenses is critical. To pay your living expenses during the start-up period of your business, you need an income source. A paycheck from other employment, savings or investments, a loan from a financial institution, or support from a parent or guardian, a partner, or other individual would be required.

Starting a Full-Time Business

Starting a full-time business from scratch multiplies your financial needs. Acquiring, preparing, and equipping a studio/office location is a major expense, especially if you will be providing a complete range of services (shooting, postproduction, and printing). See **Figure 3-11**. Compared to a part-time investment, a larger and more sophisticated array of equipment will be needed. Insurance and other business costs will also increase. A more extensive, and thus expensive, marketing effort will be necessary to bring in enough business to pay the increased costs. An employee, possibly part-time, may have to be hired to staff the business while you are busy shooting.

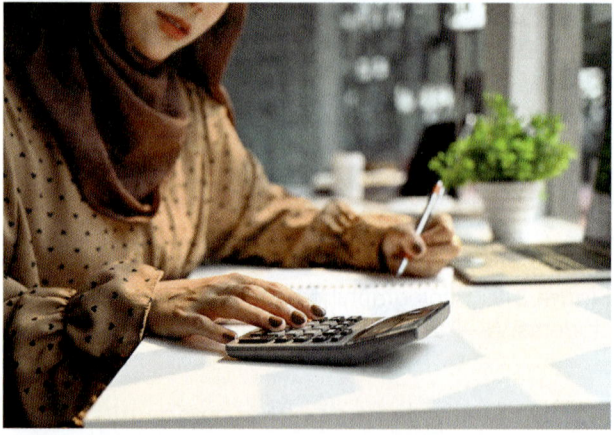

Mr. Whiskey/Shutterstock.com

Figure 3-10. To make a profit, your business must have more income than expenses.

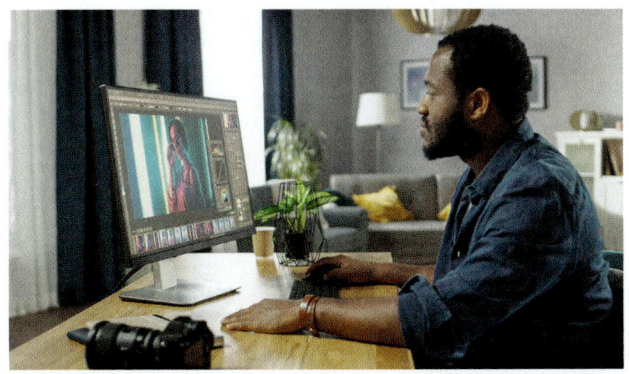

Gorodenkoff/Shutterstock.com

Figure 3-11. Postproduction services are an important part of a commercial photography business.

Seeking Funding

Where will you find the money needed to become a partner in an existing photography business or to start your own? Before you look for financing, you must determine how much money you will need.

The US Small Business Administration recommends that you carefully estimate the costs of doing business for the first months of operation. These include *one-time costs* (such as a sign in front of the building) and *ongoing costs*, or *operating costs*.

Ongoing costs fall into two categories: *fixed expenses* and *variable expenses*. Fixed expenses include insurance, utilities, and services with a monthly fee. Variable expenses include business supplies, equipment purchase or rental, services of independent contractors (such as assistants or makeup artists), and shipping costs. Your estimates should include only costs essential to starting the business, such as a professional-level camera system. Optional items, like a high-end music system for your office, should not be part of your estimate.

Once you know how much you will need, you can begin to seek financing. If you are self-funding the start-up from your savings or investments, or you are being financed by family members or close friends, your cost estimate could be all you need. You could also apply for a loan from a financial institution or government program with a business plan. A **business plan** is a document that describes a proposed business in detail and lays out a roadmap for its growth over a period of up to five years. The plan typically includes sections describing the company and the products/services it will offer, an analysis of the market it will serve, sales strategies and marketing plans, detailed information on your estimated costs, and a financial projection of income and expenses for two to five years. Each institution or program has different requirements for what must be included in a business plan, so be sure to check their individual websites to confirm what they need before submitting your plan.

Generating Income

Business income is generated by the sale of services and products. As a professional photographer, you follow a different business model from companies that manufacture and sell many copies of an identical product. Your product (a photograph) is a one-of-a-kind item. Like the works produced by authors, composers, painters, and other artists, your photographs are considered intellectual property. **Intellectual property** is a one-of-a-kind work, such as an artistic or musical work, that is protected by law.

As the creator of a work of art, the law grants you a copyright for a term of your lifetime plus 70 years. You can sell the photograph outright or license many different rights for a fee. For example, reproduction rights for use in a book or magazine might be licensed for a single edition or for a term of years. The license might be only for publication in the United States, in a specified group of countries, or worldwide.

Professional photographers typically retain all rights to their photographs, licensing certain uses to the client. For instance, a manufacturer contracts with a photographer to shoot various people producing products in its factory. The purpose of the project is to create a cover illustration for the company's annual report to shareholders. Following the shoot, the photographer provides low-resolution images electronically for the client to review. Once the desired image is chosen, a high-resolution file suitable for reproduction is sent to the client, along with an invoice.

The invoice includes the photographer's professional service fee for creating the image, expenses such as travel and rental of special equipment, and the licensing fee for reproduction rights. In this example, the licensing fee would allow the client to use the image once on the cover of the annual report. Additional uses of that image, such as a magazine ad or brochure, would be licensed separately with appropriate fees.

The image could be licensed for the exclusive use of the manufacturer, usually for a specific period of time, such as one year. If the license is not exclusive, the photographer can offer the image in other markets, such as stock photography or illustration in a textbook.

By retaining all rights to the images they create, a photographer can generate a continuing income from each assignment. Wedding and portrait photographers typically charge a professional fee that includes shooting and postproduction work, **Figure 3-12**. Most of their income in these areas, however, comes from the sale of packages or individual prints to the client and the client's family and friends.

Some beginning photographers try to generate business by shooting a wedding for a single flat fee that includes a flash drive or online gallery with all the original images, allowing the newlyweds to have their own prints made. By doing so, they are settling for a relatively small one-time payment instead of generating the continuing income needed to establish a successful business.

Photographers with institutional clients, like hospitals or universities, often work on a retainer basis. Under this business arrangement, the institution pays a flat monthly or annual fee to have the photographer's services whenever needed, **Figure 3-13**. Those services might include doing portraits of administrators or faculty members, creating images for promotional materials, or covering a variety of events. Retainers help to provide a steady income for the business.

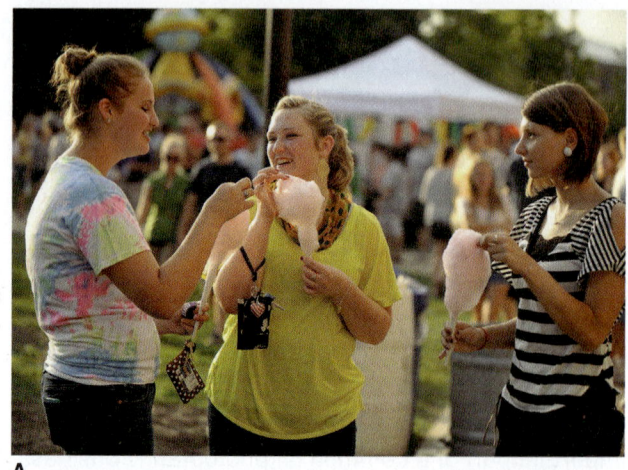

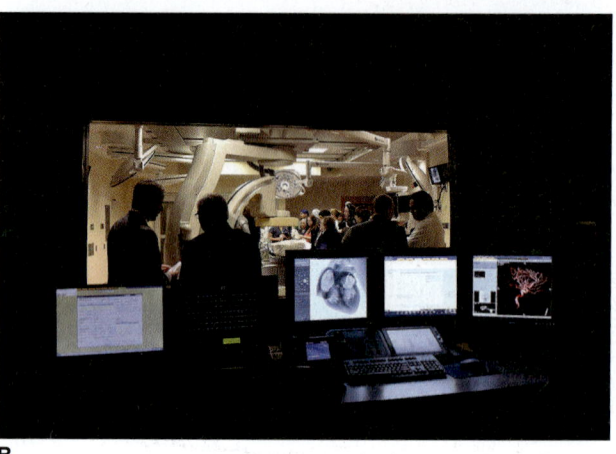

Image Group Photography, LLC

Figure 3-13. Institutional client services. A—Documenting a student social event for a university. B—Providing coverage at an open house for a hospital's new facility.

Another source of regular income is contracting with schools or organizations, such as youth sports programs. Typically, a school would contract with the photographer to produce individual student portraits and group photos each year, **Figure 3-14**. Unlike a retainer, this arrangement does not include a payment by the school. The photographer's income is from the sale of portrait packages to students' families.

Staffing Your Business

Many self-employed photographers operate one-person businesses and have no employees. Certain tasks are contracted to firms or individuals who provide services such as legal work, bookkeeping, and office/studio cleaning. Photography assistants are hired as independent contractors for specific assignments, and postproduction work also may be

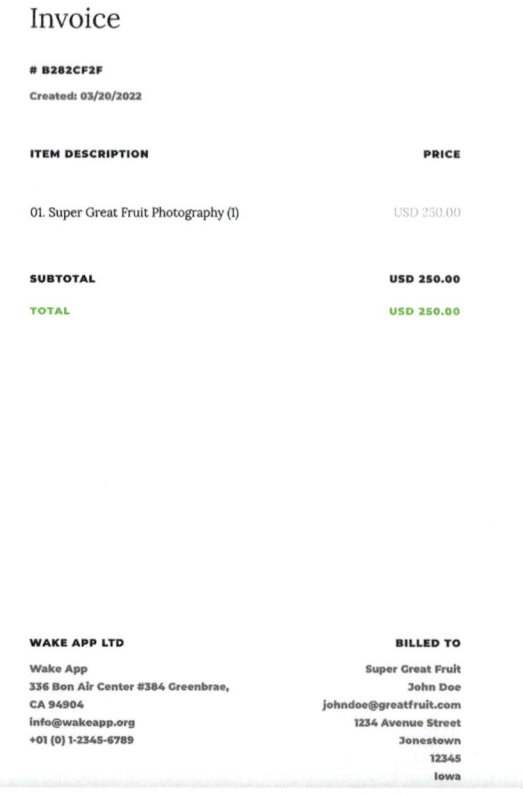

Goodheart-Willcox Publisher

Figure 3-12. An invoice for product photography.

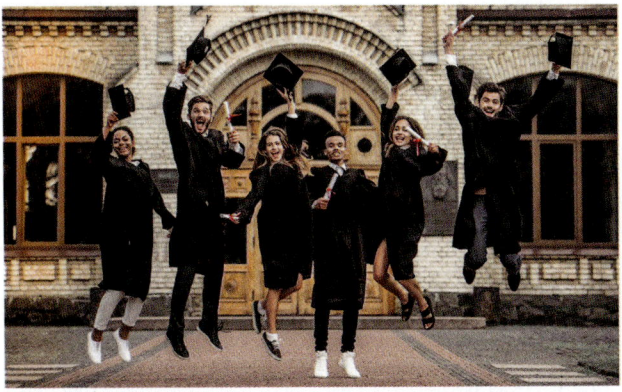

George Rudy/Shutterstock.com

Figure 3-14. Photographers are often contracted to shoot graduation photos.

done by an independent contractor. However, some photographers who are self-employed often take care of these responsibilities themselves.

Growth of the business and demands on the photographer's time are often the major factors in deciding to hire one or more employees. By adding people to handle various business tasks, the photographer is free to perform the primary work of creating images for clients, **Figure 3-15**.

However, that freedom comes at a price in the form of added paperwork and expense. Once a company has at least one employee, it must meet government regulations for matters such as wages and hours of work, working conditions, and safety on the job.

Doing the Paperwork

You may prefer to spend all your time making images, but as a business owner, you must take care of business. That means dealing with many kinds of paperwork—contracts, releases, reports, tax forms, and invoices, to name a few.

Even if your business is only part-time, you should set up a separate bank account for it. Using that account for all business-related deposits and payments helps you keep personal and business finances separate.

Every photographic project, whether a simple studio portrait or a weeklong multiple-location advertising shoot, requires a written contract. A **contract** is a legal document that specifies the responsibilities of both the photographer and the client and spells out every detail of the arrangement.

Sample contracts are available from various sources, but you should work with an attorney who has experience with intellectual property law. The attorney will prepare contracts and other documents that protect your interests and can advise you in matters such as licensing rights.

Another legal document that is often needed is a release. A **release** is a legal document granting permission to include people, places, and objects in a photograph. There are various types of releases, such as model releases, materials releases, and location releases. For your protection, you should have a signed model release for any person who appears in a photograph that might possibly be used in advertising or similar applications, **Figure 3-16**. Releases

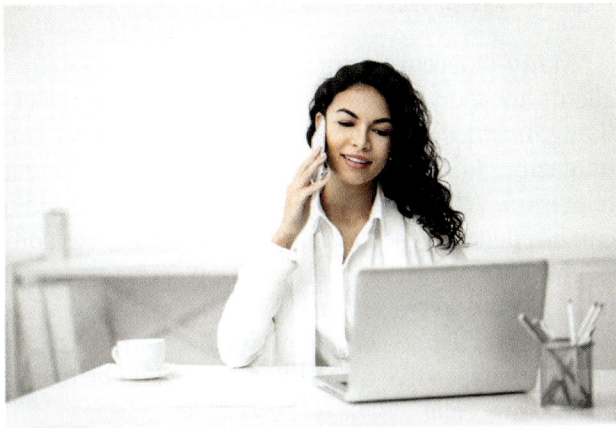

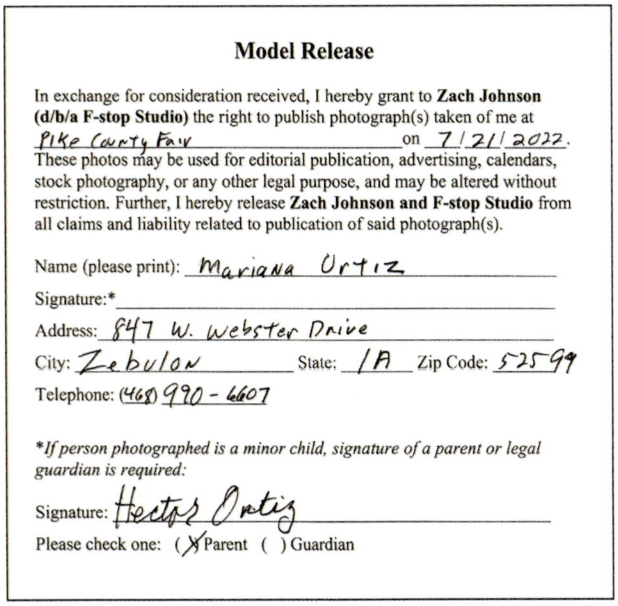

Prostock-studio/Shutterstock.com

Figure 3-15. As a business grows, employees are hired to handle various responsibilities.

Goodheart-Willcox Publisher

Figure 3-16. A signed model release allows you to use the person's photograph in various ways. The "consideration" mentioned could be a print of the photograph or a small monetary sum.

should be signed before your shoot begins. The release gives you the right to use your photograph of that person. If you do not get the proper releases from your subjects, you could be opening yourself up for a lawsuit down the line. The only use that does not require a model release is editorial publication, such as newspapers.

To be paid for your work, you must present an invoice to the client. An *invoice* is a detailed list of the fees for your services and any expenses or other charges, **Figure 3-17**. The invoice should also specify when payment is due (usually 30 days) and may offer a small discount for early payment. A penalty for late payment may also be shown. Invoicing should be done as soon as possible after work is completed so you can be paid promptly.

Money will also flow in the other direction—you have to pay the invoices presented by your suppliers and contractors, bills from utilities and various taxing agencies, and wages for any employees. Some photographers handle all payments themselves, while others employ a bookkeeper or use an outside accounting firm. Almost all photography businesses use an accountant to handle taxes.

 REAL-WORLD PHOTOGRAPHY

Subject Choice

It is incredibly important to be aware of the ethics related to social and legal issues in subject choice (including image appropriateness and cultural sensitivity). As a photographer, it is your duty to ensure all subjects are portrayed in a fair light and any racial or social stereotyping is not reinforced. While there are no laws regulating these principles, photographers have an ethical responsibility to appropriately represent and respect the world around them.

INVOICE

Invoice #	16-00146
Date	March 23, 2022
Terms	2% 10/Net 30 Over 30, add 10% penalty
Name of person	Zach Johnson

Goodheart-Willcox Publisher

Figure 3-17. Typical payment terms on an invoice show a 2% discount for payment in 10 days, or payment in full (net) in 30 days. If payment is not made in 30 days, a 10% penalty is added.

Building Your Business

Across the entire lifespan of your business, a vital activity is the finding, acquiring, and keeping of clients. This activity, called **marketing**, can be defined as everything you do to acquire clients and establish an ongoing relationship with them.

As noted earlier in this chapter, an important first step is marketing research to determine what business niche your company will serve. In other words, you must identify your potential clients. The next step is to develop a plan to attract those clients to your business. For some businesses, like a fast-food restaurant chain, almost every human being is a potential client. For others, such as a studio specializing in pet portraits, there is a much smaller and more specific group of potential clients.

The first type of business uses a mass marketing strategy, while the second uses a targeted marketing strategy, **Figure 3-18**. *Mass marketing* is aimed at a wide range of people. It involves large-scale advertising efforts—heavy use of national television spots and extensive advertising in newspapers and magazines. *Targeted marketing* is much more selective, as it is aimed at a specific group of people. This approach uses local media (radio, television, and print), advertising in local publications, and the advertising feature on social media. Targeted marketing seems to be more beneficial for photographers since it allows them to select the area in which their ads appear, as well as the demographic of the people they are targeting. This allows photographers to reach people who are looking for their services and will hopefully yield more results.

Marketing Methods

Many different methods can be used to attract clients to your business. Traditional media advertising includes print advertising in newspapers and magazines and broadcast commercials on radio and television. While advertising on television and radio can be effective when carefully used, it involves considerable expense. A good solution is using social media to market your business. There are expenses when advertising on social media, but it is not nearly as expensive as a traditional radio or television commercial.

Another traditional method of reaching potential clients is direct mail, in which printed materials are tailored to and delivered to selected people,

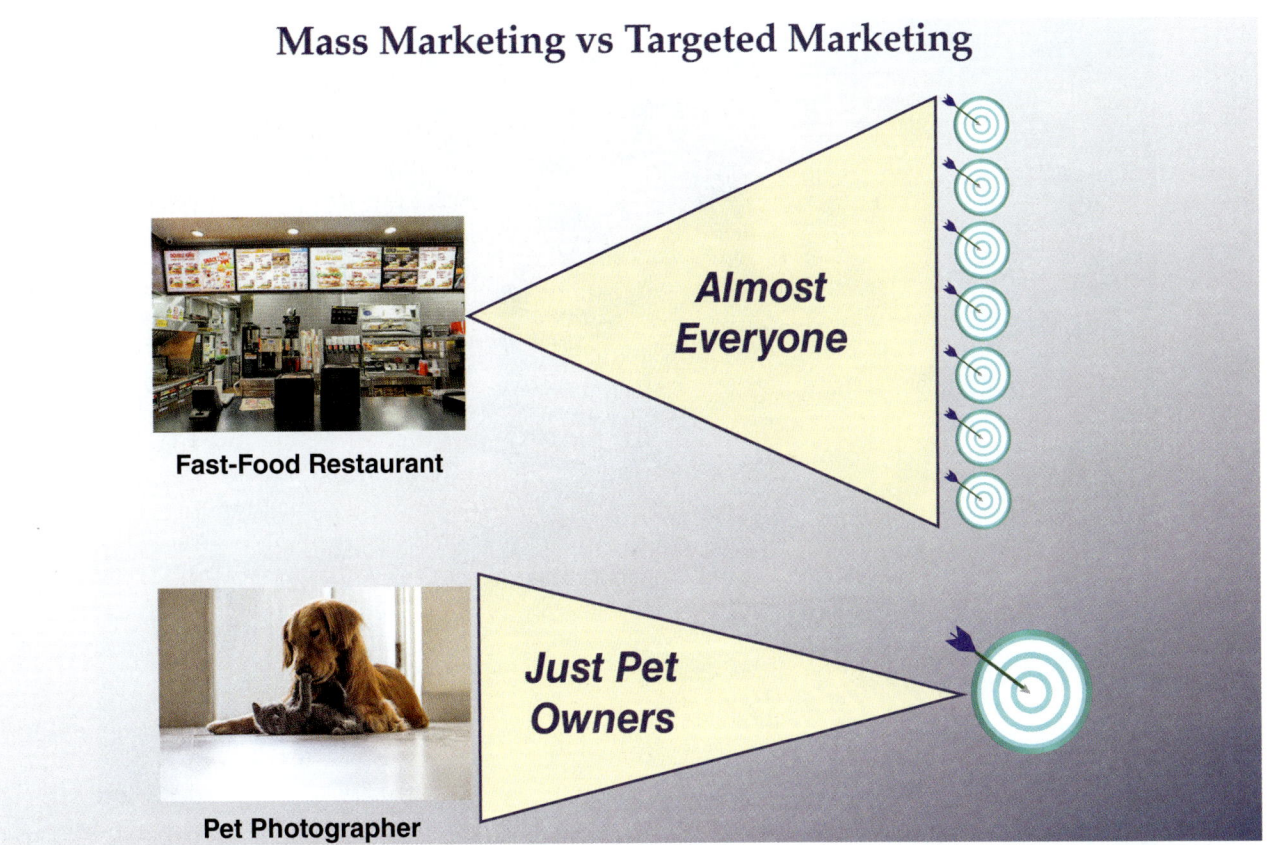

Goodheart-Willcox Publisher
Fast-food restaurant: Sorbis/Shutterstock.com
Dog and cat: Chendongshan/Shutterstock.com

Figure 3-18. Mass marketing is aimed at a broad audience, while targeted marketing is directed to a specific group.

Figure 3-19. Lists of names and addresses of people in particular categories—for example, high school seniors or antique car club members—are rented or purchased for targeted mailings. Even though this method may seem a bit antiquated, it is still effective. However, you should use this method with caution. On occasion, direct mail can come across as junk mail and be tossed in the trash. You do not want to waste your resources, so if you use direct mail, make sure you include links to your social media portfolio or your website for people to see examples of your work.

Participating in events designed to attract certain groups, such as a wedding expo at your local convention center, lets you interact with exactly the people you want to reach. Newspapers and local magazines often produce special editions or sections devoted to a particular topic. An advertisement in one of these targeted publications usually will be more effective than advertising in the regular editions.

Internet and Social Media

The internet and the growth of social media platforms, such as Facebook, LinkedIn, Twitter, Instagram, and TikTok, have opened a whole new set of opportunities for business marketing. Almost every business markets itself online in some way, so it is important that you also utilize these tools to promote your business.

A vital internet tool for a business today is a well-designed, easy-to-navigate website. The website serves as a showcase for your photographic ability and creativity and provides potential clients with needed information about your business. The site's design should make it easy for people to contact you, either by completing a form, sending an email, or calling your telephone number.

Ideally, your website should have ***e-commerce capability***, which is a feature that allows clients to view images and order prints or other products. Many portrait and wedding photographers use this system, eliminating the need for printed proofs.

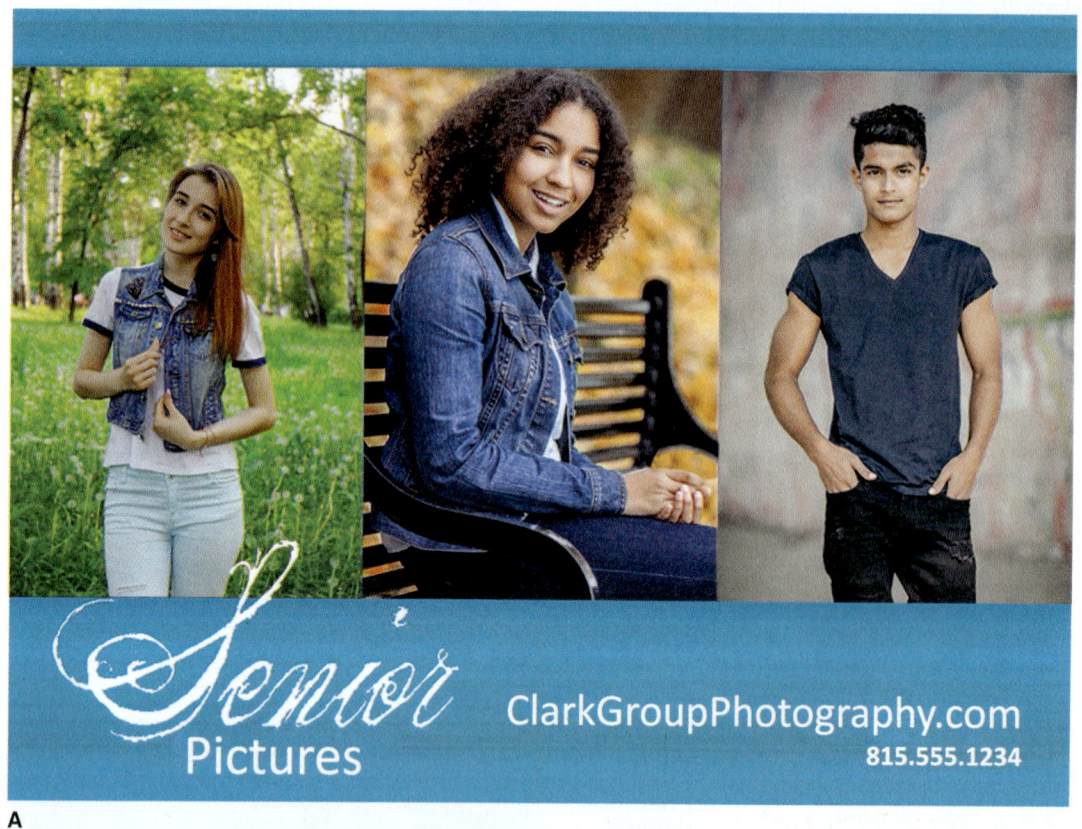

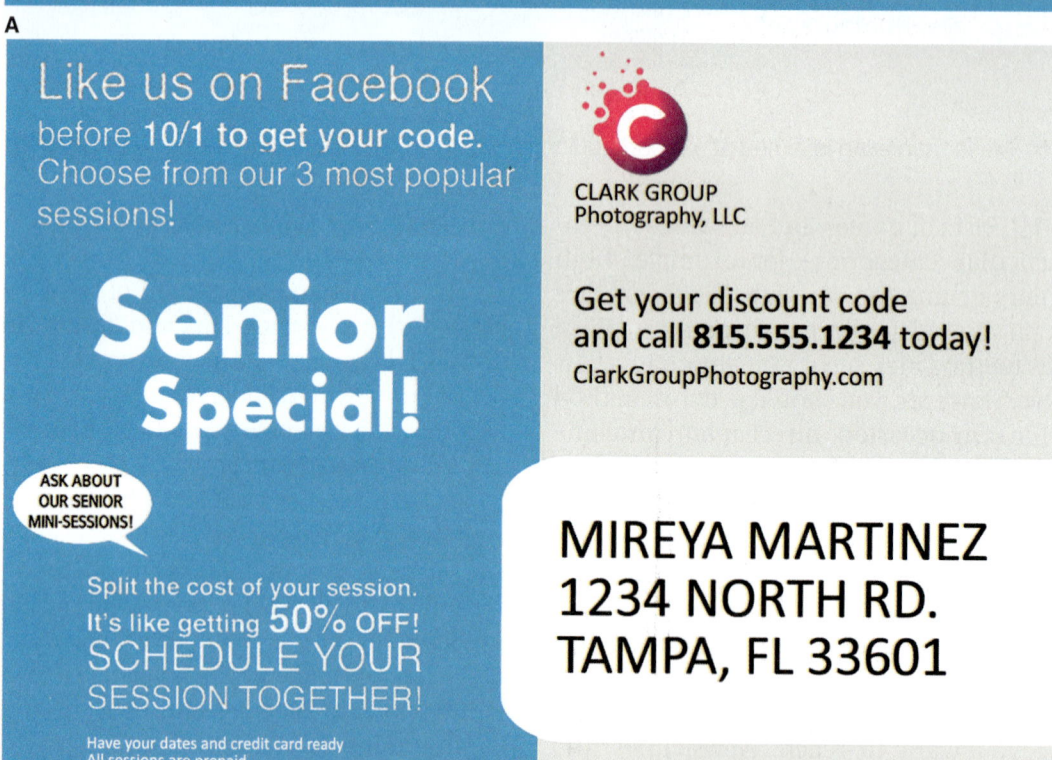

Goodheart-Willcox Publisher
Person on left: Singulyarra/Shutterstock.com
Person in middle: Darren Baker/Shutterstock.com
Person on right: StevenK/Shutterstock.com
Photography company logo: Razvan Ionut Dragomirescu/Shutterstock.com

Figure 3-19. Targeted marketing direct mail piece. A—Front of card. B—Back of card.

After the wedding or portrait session, the images are processed, and the client makes selections. See **Figure 3-20**. The selected images are then posted in a gallery on the studio's website. The client is provided with a password to access the gallery so family and friends can view images, order the desired prints, and pay online, **Figure 3-21**.

Social networking and photo sharing sites provide greater exposure of your work and are a mechanism to draw people to your website through links in your postings. On sites such as Facebook, Flickr, and Instagram, you can build a regular following for your work. Some sites accept paid advertising, and some permit purchase of posted images.

Email can also be used as a marketing tool, especially in developing additional business through your existing client base. Periodic emails can be sent to your client list to advertise special promotions or events, while an electronic newsletter can help you develop good customer relations.

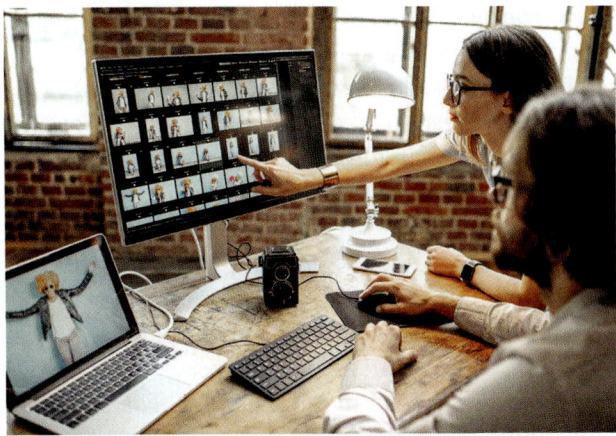

RossHelen/Shutterstock.com

Figure 3-20. Instead of printed proofs, most clients make their photo selections online.

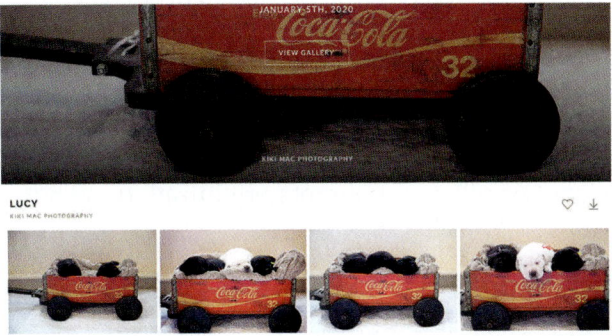

Christy Clark

Figure 3-21. A gallery on a photographer's website allows clients to order and pay for prints.

REAL-WORLD PHOTOGRAPHY

Boosting Your Photography Business Online

A helpful tool for any photographer is using social media to reach out to new potential customers. Since most people have some form of social media, it is a great way to reach a wider audience.

Both Instagram and Facebook allow you to boost posts, or spend money to expand a post's reach, which can potentially increase engagement. The further your post reaches, the greater the number of people who have the opportunity to see your business and become your customers. You even have the ability to monitor how effective your ad is.

Boosting a post is fairly similar across social media platforms. When boosting a post, simply create a post, identify your audience and who you want your post to reach, set your budget, and then select "Boost." Every day your post is up, you can review engagement and make changes to your budget or your range if you so choose. This flexibility makes this form of advertising a good option for many photographers.

Personal Contact

Promoting your business through personal contact is important. Especially when seeking assignments from companies, institutions, and publications, face-to-face meetings are necessary, whether they are done in person or virtually. When you are first in business, many of these meetings will be made on speculation. You hope the investment of your time and effort will result in a promise to consider your services for the next appropriate assignment. Later, you can expect to schedule more meetings on a referral basis, such as when a satisfied client passes on your name as a reliable and creative photography services provider.

Whenever you meet with a potential client, come to the table prepared. Research the company or organization so you can confidently discuss how you would photograph its products or services. If possible, tailor your portfolio to include examples of work in fields like that of the potential client, but avoid images made for their direct competitor.

A good way to become known in the community and develop contacts is to join and be actively involved in organizations like civic clubs, service organizations, and chamber of commerce or similar business-oriented groups. Networking with fellow organization members can provide useful leads for business development. If a local high school offers a photography class, you could make an appearance as a guest speaker to discuss career options. Another form of involvement would be to serve as a mentor for a student interested in becoming a professional photographer.

You can also share your knowledge with others. Teaching a photography class or conducting an educational seminar will not only build recognition for your business, but help you develop relationships that could later lead to paying work. For example, you might join with a local travel agency to offer their customers a free one-hour class on how to take better travel pictures, **Figure 3-22**. Creating a good impression on the attendees would lay the groundwork for future portrait or wedding commissions. Another option is creating a social media account that focuses on providing photography tips. This could create an opportunity for you to showcase your talent while also helping other people.

Photographers are often asked to donate their services, usually to a nonprofit organization, with the idea that it could later lead to paying assignments. While it is usually not a good practice to give away your work, making carefully chosen donations is a form of community involvement. For example, you may choose to support a charitable organization by producing photographs that will further its work. An example might be doing portraits of pets being offered for adoption by your local animal shelter.

You might also donate services that demonstrate your abilities to a potential client group. Golf outings sponsored by charitable organizations typically attract local business and industry leaders as participants. Your donation to the charity could take the form of a commemorative photo of each group made before it tees off. While the group is on the course, the image is processed and placed in a designed template displaying their names, the event title and date, and (of course) your company logo, **Figure 3-23**. As the golfers come off the course, each member receives a copy. Many of these images are likely to be framed and displayed on office walls, where they will serve as a reminder when the person needs photography services.

Working with Clients, Employees, and Independent Contractors

Operating a photography business requires far more than the ability to produce excellent images. You need an understanding of good business practices and the ability to put them to use. You need to efficiently manage time—your own, your

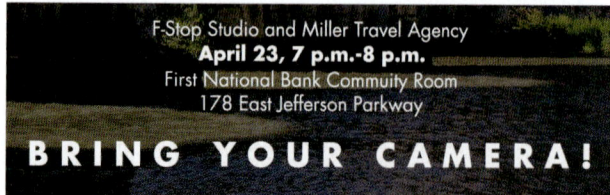

Goodheart-Willcox Publisher
Background image: MaxZh/Shutterstock.com
Figure 3-22. Partnering with another local business can develop leads for future photo bookings.

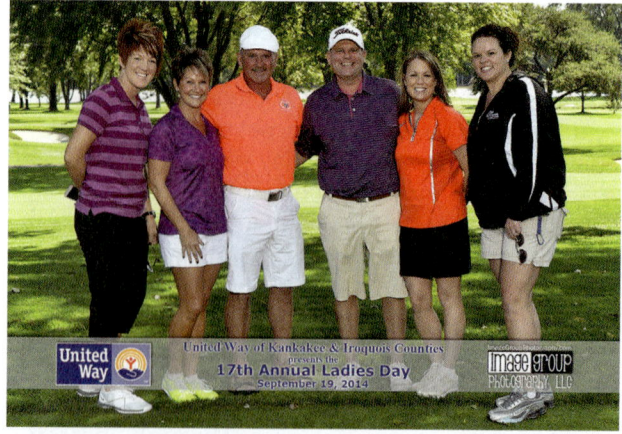

Image Group Photography, LLC
Figure 3-23. Donating your services to a charity event, such as a golf tournament, can attract new clients to your business.

employees', and your clients'. Above all, you need the ability to work effectively with your clients and with employees and the independent contractors who supply needed services.

Successful salespeople work hard at getting their customers to like them. Studies have shown that people are much more likely to make a purchase from someone they find friendly and likeable than from someone to whom they do not relate well. The benefits of being likeable carry over into areas other than sales. For example, likeability is a benefit when developing and leading a project team or working with various agencies and contractors to organize a complex location shoot.

Meeting with Clients

Meetings with clients may be as simple as sitting down with a couple to discuss their wedding plans or as complex as making a formal, detailed audiovisual presentation to advertising agency executives considering you for product photography assignments, **Figure 3-24**. In any meeting with potential clients, you should project confidence and capability, but you also must be open to their ideas or desires.

Your role as a salesperson is not just to talk, but to listen. For instance, the prospective celebrants might indicate that they really like the wedding package that you have presented but seem hesitant to make a decision. While their reluctance might be due to price, it might well be something else. You would have to ask questions and listen carefully to their answers to uncover the true cause of their uneasiness. Once you have identified the problem, you can suggest alternatives that should result in a solution and a signed contract.

Portrait photography has special challenges, since most people are self-conscious and tend to be nervous about "looking good." There may be other negative factors at play—your business-executive client is squeezing the portrait session into a crammed schedule, or the child you are to photograph has a hovering, fussy parent. To create a client-pleasing portrait, you must be able to keep your subjects relaxed and comfortable in front of the camera.

Your approach to keeping your clients comfortable will change based on who you are photographing. For example, you would not handle a prospective wedding couple the same way you would handle parents with an upset newborn or a business executive. Your interpersonal skills will come into play when you are working with a wide range of people, but remember that you should keep it professional regardless of the situation.

Leading a Team

In many photographic situations, you will find yourself working with additional people. Photographing a high school senior in an outdoor setting is often done with the help of a single assistant, but a shoot involving several models or products, either in-studio or on location, may involve a team of assistants. See **Figure 3-25**. Whether simple or complex, these situations call for good use of your social, supervisory, and leadership skills.

Your leadership and team-building skills will be tested when conflicts arise between team members. Resolving such conflicts involves listening carefully to what each person has to say and working to achieve a solution that is fair and acceptable to all parties.

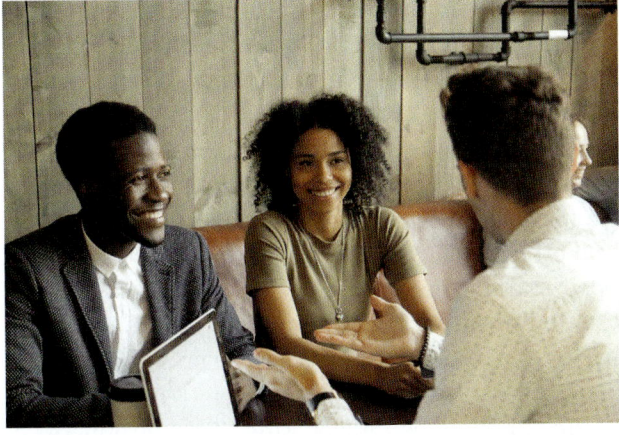

fizkes/Shutterstock.com

Figure 3-24. At the initial meeting with a prospective couple, a wedding photographer describes their services.

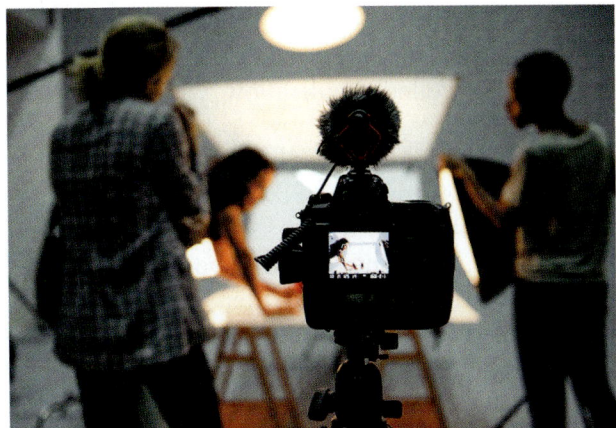

Rawpixel.com/Shutterstock.com

Figure 3-25. More complex shoots require multiple assistants to help with various tasks.

Planning and direction are vital. Whether your team consists of 2 people or 20 people, it is essential to provide members clear communication of what is expected and how each person fits into the plan before conducting a shoot. A preshoot meeting with everyone involved, whether employees or independent contractors, helps ensure that everyone is on the same page. Encourage team members to ask questions and make suggestions where appropriate. A similar meeting when the shoot is completed can provide information useful for future projects.

As you work with various independent contractors, evaluate their skills and personalities to determine which of them you would engage for future assignments. At the same time, of course, they will be evaluating you to decide if they wish to be on your team for future projects.

During the shoot, show respect for members of the team as fellow professionals. Instead of barking orders, make a request, and say "thank you" where appropriate. If someone makes a mistake, correct it and move on. Save any criticism or discussion with the person making the mistake for a later private meeting.

Using such a positive approach will build team morale and help to ensure a successful shoot. At the end of a lengthy or complex shoot, it is a good idea to host a party for everyone involved. A group photo of team members, talent, and client representatives can be made and distributed as a memento.

Growing Professionally

For a professional person, continuing education is a fact of life. It is important to stay up-to-date with new techniques, as well as further develop and refine existing skills. As a professional photographer and a businessperson, you must continue to seek education in a number of areas. Many trade schools and colleges will allow you to enroll in certificate programs to stay up-to-date with the newest trends and processes. You can also attend freestanding seminars, go to seminars at conventions, or participate in workshops. If you attend any of these, it is imperative that you participate by asking questions to help further your knowledge. If you already have a lot of experience, you can volunteer to help at these conferences or even offer to lead a session or seminar yourself. YouTube is also a great place to research new techniques. There are millions of videos online that can help you not only stay current but try new things.

Honing your research skills will also help you grow professionally. Depending on the career path you want to take, you will have to follow certain steps, and those steps can vary depending on your timeline and your end goal. As students, and even as working professionals, it is not expected that you know everything. Being able to determine what actions to take next will help position you in the field better and gain access to opportunities to hone your skills and expand your knowledge. For example, if you are interested in becoming a fashion photographer, it is a good idea to search for a few open positions at fashion houses or fashion magazines. Researching the qualifications you need will help you determine what you still need to acquire before being considered for the position, as well as figure out how you can gain those qualifications.

Staying aware of current practices will help keep you competitive and innovative. Photography is a rapidly growing field, and almost every photographer has a different approach to how they handle photography. Trying new techniques can also help you develop your own personal style, which will help you stand out among other photographers.

Photography Organizations

A broad range of educational programs to improve both business and technical skills are offered to members of professional photography organizations. These organizations also provide members with services such as insurance, event calendars, advocacy on legal issues involving photographers' rights, and searchable databases usable by agencies and companies seeking photographers. Becoming a member of a professional photographic organization will also help you achieve professional growth. Becoming a member can help you build your professional network. You can also take classes offered through the organization to further your skills, **Figure 3-26**.

The American Society of Media Photographers (ASMP) is devoted primarily to the needs of professionals whose photographs are used in magazines and other publications. The organization has developed standardized forms, such as model releases. Continuing business education for members, including live and recorded webinars, is also provided.

American Photographic Artists (APA) was formerly known as Advertising Photographers of America. This organization offers members educational articles on its website, a downloadable

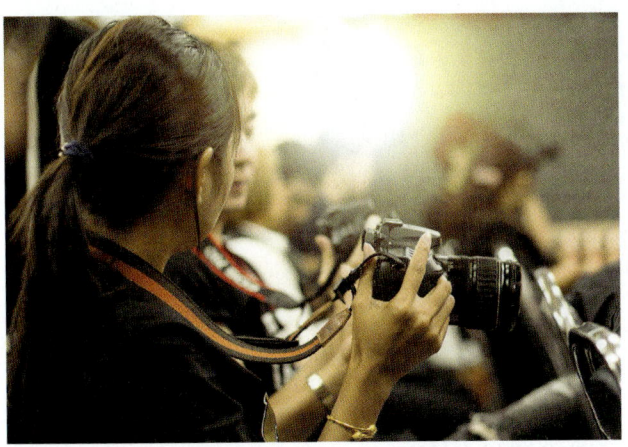
Bignai/Shutterstock.com

Figure 3-26. Professional photographic organizations provide many services for their members, such as classes.

business manual, seminars and workshops, and photo competitions.

With more than 30,000 members, Professional Photographers of America (PPA) is the largest nonprofit photography organization. It was created by and for professional photographers and is devoted primarily to providing protection, education, and resources for wedding, portrait, and studio photographers. PPA has an extensive educational program lineup ranging from workshops and seminars held at various locations around the country to a catalog of more than 1,100 online courses. The organization offers its members an opportunity to become a Certified Professional Photographer. Certification involves passing a detailed written exam and submitting images for review.

Imaging USA, PPA's annual conference and trade show, is one of the largest annual photography conventions and expos in the United States. It offers numerous workshops, classes, and programs presented over a three-day period. Subjects range from business strategies to a variety of photography techniques. The trade show showcases vendors of photographic equipment and accessories, computer hardware and software, and many photo-related services. Imaging USA also features many opportunities for networking and a large photo exhibit showcasing the works of many of PPA's International Photographic Competition participants.

Professional Photography Workshops

In addition to workshops and seminars sponsored by professional organizations, many educational programs are available to photographers. An internet search for "professional photography workshops" results in thousands of listings. Some of these are sponsored by camera manufacturers or equipment sales organizations, but the majority are from individuals or companies that make a business of presenting educational programs. Many of these are one- or two-day workshops held in hotel meeting rooms in various cities, while others are weeklong courses at resorts or other sites that include residence accommodations. Many online programs and courses are also available.

Continuing education should be considered one of the keys to success for a professional photographer. Some companies may also require you to participate in these seminars or workshops as a condition of your employment. Many industries, including photography, make continuing education part of your contract so you can continue to grow and offer new and better services to your clients. John Harrington, author of *Best Business Practices for Photographers*, notes, "All photographers should look to have a plan to regularly learn and grow from the knowledge bases of others."

Chapter 3 Review

Summary

- While it is important to have the photographic skills and abilities to produce good images, an aspiring photographer must also develop good business and social skills.
- Professional photography is an occupation in which photographic skills are used to create images in exchange for payment. About one-third of all professional photographers work in salaried positions with organizations, and the other two-thirds are self-employed and started independent businesses.
- There are a number of paths to employment in professional photography. The most common is formal education at a traditional college, technical school, or online institution.
- For many graduates, the next step in developing a career is seeking work as a photography assistant. Depending mostly on the size of the community, an assistant may be an employee of a single studio or company, or they may be an independent contractor working on assignments for different photographers.
- There are several approaches to starting your own photography business. Some of the more traditional approaches include operating a part-time photography business, going into partnership with a photographer who has an established business, or creating a new full-time business.
- The first step you must take when setting up a business is to determine which form of organization to use. The four basic business types are sole proprietorship, partnership, corporation, and limited liability company (LLC). Each has its advantages and disadvantages.
- Deciding on your business niche is a process that combines your personal interests and skills with information gathered through market research. That research is a key element of the business plan you will develop before seeking funding to start your business.
- To start a business, you have to spend money. To stay in business, you must spend money as well, but you also have to bring in more money than you spend. How much money you need to spend depends on a variety of factors.
- Starting a full-time business from scratch is much more expensive than starting a part-time business.
- Before you look for financing, you must determine how much money you will need. It is recommended to estimate your one-time costs and ongoing costs of doing business for the first months of operation.
- Once you know how much you will need, you can begin to seek financing. If you need to apply for a loan from a financial institution, you will need to develop a business plan.
- Professional photographers typically retain all rights to their photographs, licensing certain uses to the client. By retaining all rights to the images they create, a photographer can generate a continuing income from each assignment.
- As a business owner, you deal with many kinds of paperwork, including contracts, releases, reports, tax forms, and invoices.
- Many self-employed photographers operate one-person businesses and have no employees, while others hire people to handle various business tasks.
- Marketing is an important part of building a business. Two major types of marketing include mass marketing and targeted marketing.
- Many different marketing methods can be used to attract clients to your business, such as advertising on television, radio, a website, or a social media platform.
- Promoting your business through personal contact is important. Whenever you meet with a potential client, come to the table prepared.
- You must be able to work effectively with clients, employees, and independent contractors when operating a photography business.

- It is important to stay up-to-date with new techniques, as well as further develop and refine existing skills. As a professional photographer and a businessperson, you must continue to seek education in a number of areas. There are many trade schools, colleges, photography organizations, and videos to help you stay current.

Review Questions

Answer the following questions using the information provided in this chapter.

Know and Understand

1. *True or False?* In 1920, roughly 80% of advertisements used photographs.
2. *True or False?* About one-third of all professional photographers are self-employed individuals who have started independent businesses.
3. A(n) _____ is a position that provides a student or trainee experience in a working environment, such as a newspaper, a corporate photo department, or a portrait studio.
   A. photography assistant
   B. internship
   C. partnership
   D. sole proprietorship
4. A(n) _____ is a person who aids a photographer with a variety of tasks in the studio and on location.
   A. entrepreneur
   B. sole proprietor
   C. photography assistant
   D. intern
5. *True or False?* The process of starting a business is called entrepreneurship.
6. A(n) _____ is a person who owns an unincorporated business by themselves.
   A. intern
   B. partner
   C. entrepreneur
   D. sole proprietor
7. Which of the following forms of business organization involves two or more individuals joining together to operate a business?
   A. Partnership
   B. Corporation
   C. Sole proprietorship
   D. Limited liability company (LLC)
8. Which of the following forms of business organization is a hybrid of two other forms?
   A. Sole proprietorship
   B. Limited liability company (LLC)
   C. Corporation
   D. Partnership
9. Which of the following is *not* one of the typical factors you must consider when deciding on a business niche?
   A. Size of your community or trade area
   B. The number and sizes of established professional photography businesses
   C. The photographic equipment you currently own
   D. Purchasing patterns
10. *True or False?* The amount of money left after paying all the expenses for a business is known as profit.
11. Which of the following is an example of a fixed expense?
    A. Shipping costs
    B. Insurance
    C. Equipment purchase or rental
    D. Business supplies
12. A(n) _____ is a document that describes a proposed business in detail and lays out a roadmap for its growth over a period of up to five years.
    A. business plan
    B. contract
    C. model release
    D. invoice
13. As the creator of a work of art, the law grants you a copyright for a term of your lifetime plus _____ years.
    A. 50
    B. 60
    C. 70
    D. 80
14. *True or False?* Professional photographers typically retain all rights to their photographs, licensing certain uses to the client.
15. A(n) _____ is a legal document specifying the responsibilities of both the photographer and the client and spells out every detail of the arrangement.
    A. model release
    B. invoice
    C. business plan
    D. contract

16. *True or False?* Targeted marketing involves large-scale advertising efforts, such as heavy use of national television spots and extensive advertising in newspapers and magazines.

17. A vital internet tool for a business today is a well-designed, easy-to-navigate _____.
    A. magazine advertisement
    B. website
    C. email
    D. direct mail

18. Which of the following is a form of community involvement that would best help a student interested in becoming a professional photographer?
    A. Join a civic club
    B. Donate your services to charity
    C. Serve as a mentor
    D. Conduct an educational seminar

19. Making a(n) _____, detailed audiovisual presentation to advertising agency executives considering you for product photography assignments is an example of a complex meeting with clients.
    A. formal
    B. informal
    C. mass marketing
    D. targeted marketing

20. *True or False?* Your approach to keeping your clients comfortable will change based on who you are photographing.

21. Conducting and participating in a(n) _____ meeting with everyone involved, whether employees or independent contractors, helps ensure that everyone is on the same page.
    A. postshoot
    B. formal
    C. preshoot
    D. informal

22. Which of the following professional organizations offers its members an opportunity to become a Certified Professional Photographer?
    A. American Photographic Artists (APA)
    B. Professional Photographers of America (PPA)
    C. American Society of Media Photographers (ASMP)
    D. Imaging USA

Apply and Analyze

1. What are four potential benefits of taking part in a photography internship program?
2. Why is it an advantage for a studio owner to develop a mix of clients from different areas such as portraits, weddings, product photography, event coverage, and institutional work?
3. Why is retaining all rights to their work important for a professional photographer?
4. Why is it essential to communicate with team members clearly before conducting a photo shoot?
5. How can becoming a member of a professional photographic organization help you achieve professional growth?

Critical Thinking

1. Working in the photography field requires good language skills, including the ability to communicate orally with individuals or groups. Teaching a photography class is one example. What are three other examples?
2. On a location shoot, two of your team members disagree on which one of them should perform a particular task. How would you resolve the problem?
3. Explain what is meant by the statement "Your role as a salesperson is not just to talk, but to listen."

Suggested Activities

1. Browse some online career sites, such as Indeed or LinkedIn. What employment ads do you find for careers discussed in this chapter? Choose three careers and identify the requirements listed in the ads for them.
2. Investigate the requirements for opening a small photography business in your area. What licenses would you need? How much financial capital would you need to invest to get the business off the ground? Share your answers with the class.
3. To gain firsthand knowledge of the day-to-day activities of a professional photographer, arrange to job shadow or assist a photographer on an assignment. Give an oral presentation to the class about your experience.

4. Identify a charity or other organization in your community that you might wish to support. Describe three ways in which you could contribute your photographic skills to help the organization.

Communicating about Photography

1. **Speaking and Listening.** Interview a studio photographer or photojournalist. Ask the person to describe a typical day at work. Here are some questions you might ask:
   - What is the work environment like?
   - What are the job duties?
   - What types of people do you work with?
   - What types of equipment do you use?

   Report your findings to the class, giving reasons why you would or would not want to pursue a career similar to that of the person you interviewed.

2. **Writing and Listening.** Working in small groups, compile a list of local nonprofit or charitable organizations. Report to the other students in your group, detailing how a photographer could donate services to the organization you chose and how the donated services would demonstrate photographic abilities to a potential client group.

3. **Speaking and Listening.** Research time-management skills. Then, in small groups, discuss the time-management challenges that could occur in a photography business. One person should create a list of time-management skills needed to complete tasks in a photography business.

Section 1 Project
Exploring Photography

This project will help you become more familiar with photography in general. Part 1 focuses on photography jobs available in your area. The goal is to help you understand the real-world requirements of photographers. Part 2 focuses on examining the works of famous photographers, which is intended to help you develop your photographic "eye."

Part 1

Using an online career site, research different careers available in the photography industry. Search for available careers in your area in the following fields:

- Product photography
- Portrait photography
- News/documentation photography
- Entertainment photography
- Scientific and technical photography

For each field, write down the name of the company, the job title, the requirements listed for each job, the starting salary (if applicable), and any other relevant information. Once you have completed this task for each field, answer the following questions:

1. What job interests you the most? Why?
2. What steps would you need to take in order to be hired for that job? Are there any requirements on the job listing that you do not have? How can you obtain those requirements?

Part 2

Find five examples of professional photography that speak to you. You can start by looking up famous photographers, such as Ansel Adams and Annie Leibovitz, and browse their body of work. This search could also lead to related images by other photographers. When you have five photos that catch your eye, answer the following questions for each:

1. How is the photo composed?
2. What colors are the most prominent in the photo?
3. What techniques does the photographer use to capture the subject?

After answering the questions, identify any overlapping trends. Once you have examined the trends in the photos, take five photos of your own and try to replicate these techniques. Add the photos you take to your portfolio.

Section 2
Understanding Camera Basics

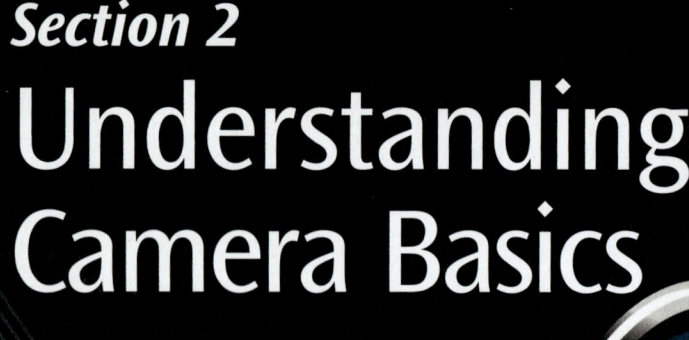

Chapter 4   Camera Handling, Care, and Support
Chapter 5   The Camera System
Chapter 6   Lenses
Chapter 7   Light and Exposure
Chapter 8   Digital Image Capture Media

In Section 1, you learned about the history of photography and careers in the industry. Now that you understand what photography is, you can begin learning how a camera works.

Section 2 will teach you how to identify and use basic camera settings as well as how to use a camera safely. This section covers concepts in general terms as not everyone reading this book will have access to the same equipment. Regardless of the equipment you have, the information in this section is vital for taking great photos.

Chapter 4 will introduce you to some general tips on how to properly handle and care for your camera. This chapter will also discuss common camera controls and how to use them.

In Chapter 5, you will learn about the camera system and how it works. The information in this chapter is crucial because it teaches you how to properly adjust the three major components that affect how an image appears: shutter, aperture, and ISO.

Chapter 6 teaches you about various types of lenses. It provides an overview of the differences among wide, normal, and telephoto lenses in order to help you choose the best lens for what you are photographing.

Chapter 7 delves into light and exposure, both of which can make or break a photo. This chapter will also help you understand the effect of different types of lighting on your image.

Finally, Chapter 8 discusses how to get an image from a camera into a digital format and how it is stored. Understanding what capture devices to use will help you choose the best option for you and your shooting habits.

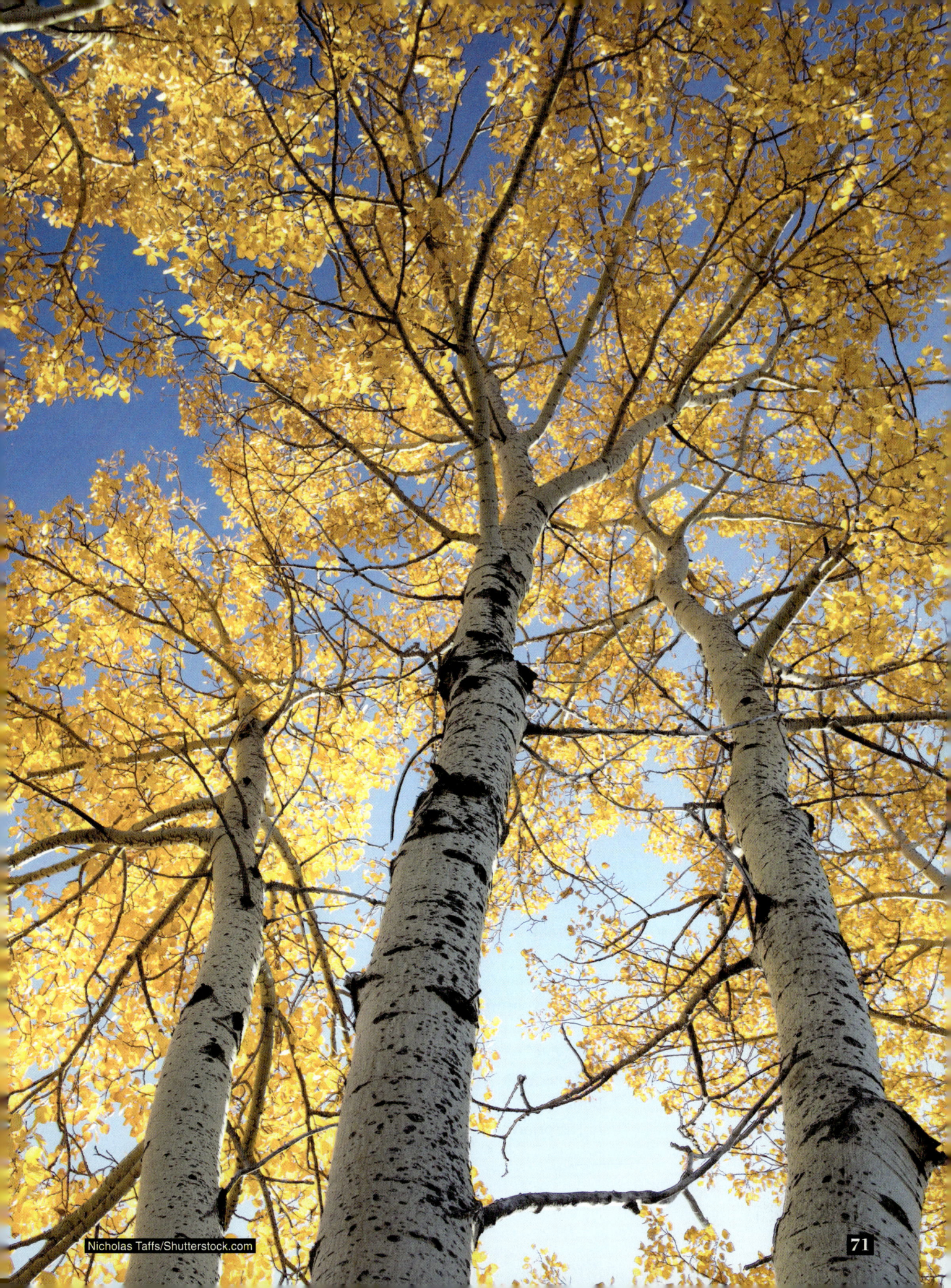

Chapter 4
Camera Handling, Care, and Support

Learning Objectives

After completing this chapter, you will be able to:

- Describe the physical attributes and controls common to most digital cameras.
- Identify the digital controls and features common to most digital cameras.
- Discuss the importance of protecting cameras from environmental dangers, such as water and dust.
- Demonstrate proper procedures for cleaning the camera body, LCD screen, lens, and image sensor.
- Recall different methods of storing and transporting photographic equipment.
- Explain various camera carrying methods that allow for immediate use.
- Describe the proper techniques for supporting different types of cameras.
- Explain the components of and appropriate use of a tripod.

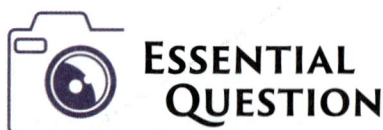

Essential Question

How will understanding the basic functionality of a camera help you when taking a picture?

Technical Terms

Adobe RGB
aperture priority
ball head
burst mode
compression
depth of field
depth of field (DOF) preview
exposure lock
focus lock

histogram
hot shoe
ISO
manual exposure
monopod
pan head
Program AE
shutter lag
shutter priority

snapshot
sRGB
stabilizing systems
tethered shutter release
tripod
ultraviolet (UV) filter
untethered shutter release
viewfinder
white balance

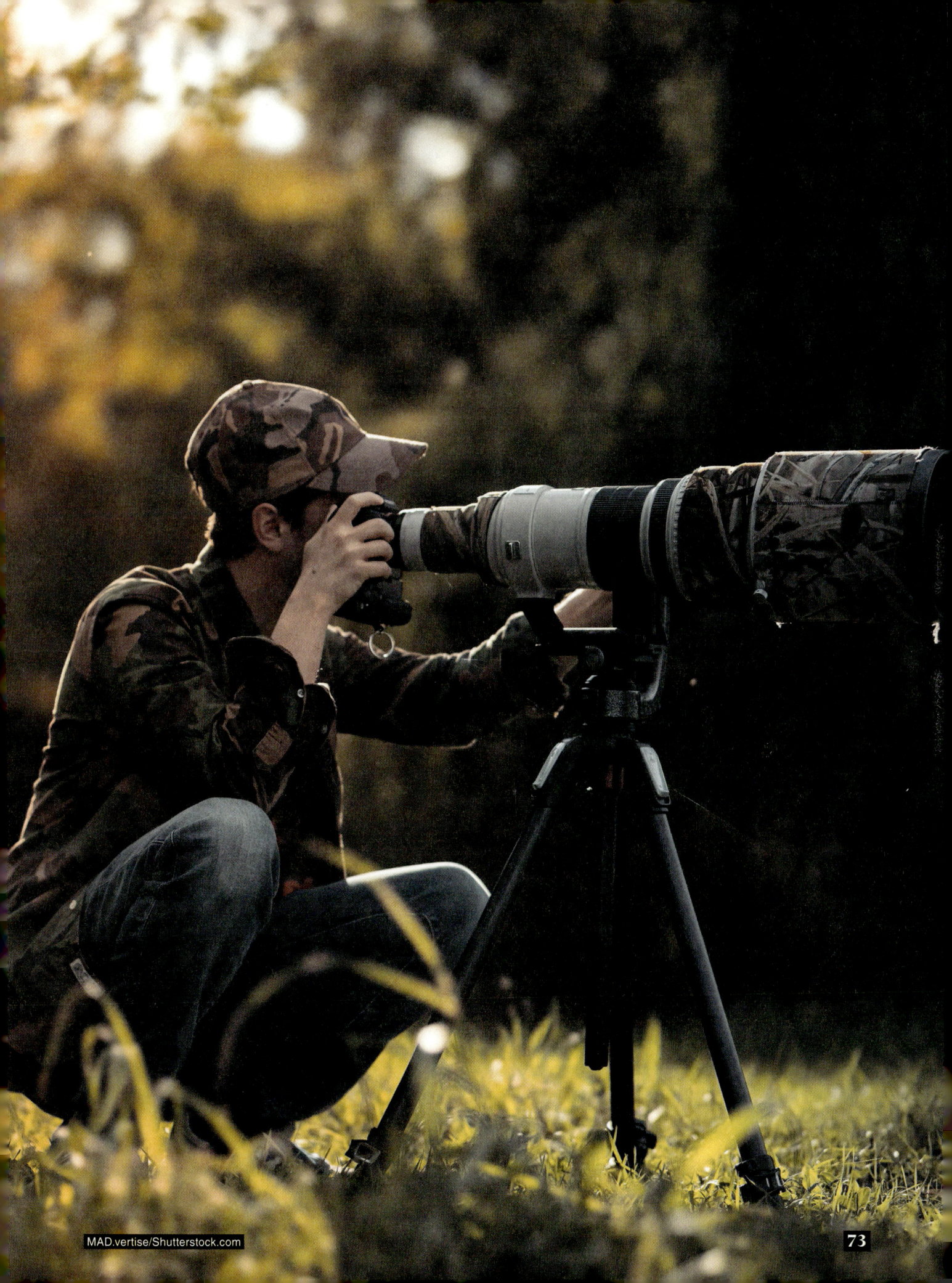

Introduction to Camera Handling, Care, and Support

Imagine that you must drive a car that is unfamiliar to you across town for an important appointment. You start the car and, using the familiar basic controls, you are on your way and on schedule. But what if a storm arises and you have to turn on the headlights and use the windshield wipers? You would probably have to pull over and figure out where the headlight and wiper controls are on this car and how to use them. By the time you do that, you are probably running late for your appointment.

Many people approach a new camera in the same way. They can "point and shoot" using the basic controls, but they are not prepared to handle an unexpected situation. By the time they figure out what to do, the picture opportunity may be lost. Being prepared and knowing how your camera works before you take on a shoot will help you avoid losing those moments.

Learning about Your Camera

Today's cameras are sophisticated pieces of equipment. Most have dozens of controls and features that allow you to make an image successfully in almost any situation. It takes time and effort to learn what those controls and features do, as well as how and when to use them. To move beyond the level of birthday party and vacation *snapshots* (photos taken to record an event, activity, or location, often with a point-and-shoot camera or camera phone), you must take the time to learn about your camera.

Some people learn about a new camera by simply experimenting with various controls, while others virtually memorize the owner's manual before using the camera. In other words, some people are "hands-on" learners, while others learn by studying instructions. A good method is to blend those approaches. First, study the manual on how to use a feature or control, and then use the camera to practice with that control or feature.

Begin on the manual page that displays a drawing or photo of the camera and labels the controls. If your camera does not come with a physical manual (or you lose yours and need to reference it again), you can always search for a digital copy online. Locate each of the labeled controls. The first time you do this, rest the camera on a surface with the lens pointing toward you to make it easier to locate the controls on the front and top of the camera, **Figure 4-1**. Next, turn the camera to point away

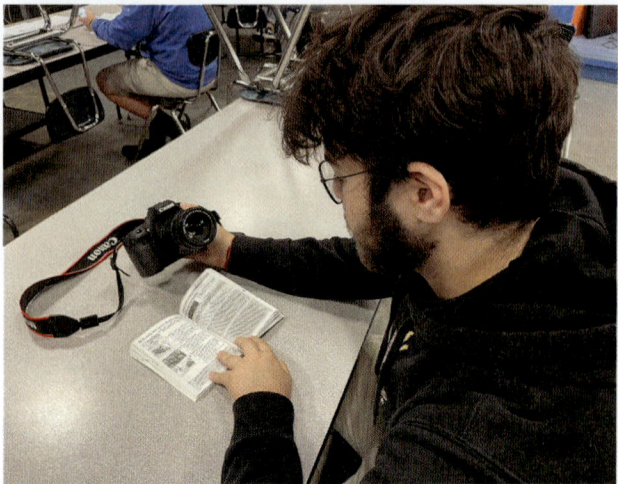

Goodheart-Willcox Publisher

Figure 4-1. Using your manual and camera together is the best way to learn about basic camera controls and features.

from you so you can identify the controls on the back of the camera, **Figure 4-2**. Practice operating, or at least touching, each of the controls on the camera front, top, and back from behind the camera. This builds muscle memory that helps you locate and operate frequently used controls.

Another great tool for learning about your camera is online tutorials. Many of the well-known camera companies (such as Canon and Nikon) have their own video tutorials hosted on their website, but YouTube is a great resource for real-time tutorials. These are helpful because you can pause and rewind for clarification and take notes while you watch. They are also good to follow along with when using your own camera.

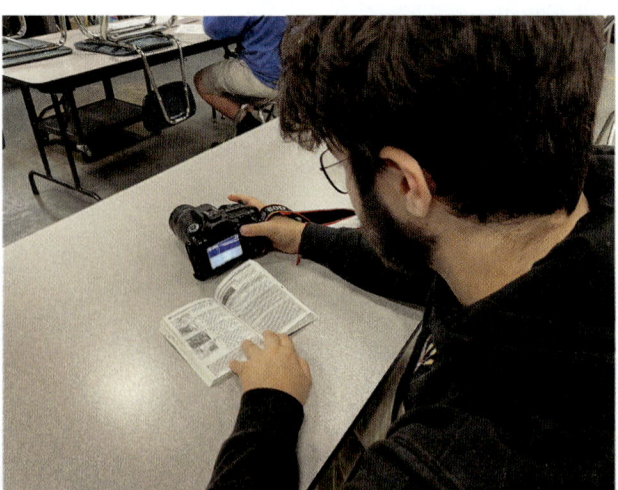

Goodheart-Willcox Publisher

Figure 4-2. Camera controls and their locations are clearly labeled in the owner's manual.

Physical Camera Attributes and Controls

Digital cameras have a number of common features and controls. Not all cameras or all models will have a particular feature or control, but most will. For this reason, the following section describes the physical attributes and controls in general terms.

Power Button/Switch

Many digital cameras have a *power button* or *power switch* that turns the camera on, **Figure 4-3**. Some cameras have this switch wrapped around the shutter release button. On other cameras, it is located elsewhere. If you use multiple cameras, it is important to know where the power button is on each one. If you are unsure where it is, you might miss something at a critical moment in the field.

Shutter Release

The *shutter release*, or *remote release*, on digital cameras is a button located on the top right side of the body. To avoid moving the camera when pressing the shutter button or lever, a shutter release device is often used. There are two types of commonly used shutter releases: *tethered* and *untethered*. **Tethered shutter releases** are wired remote triggers that enable the camera's shutter release. They attach directly to the camera with a cable that plugs into one of the camera's ports, **Figure 4-4**. **Untethered shutter releases** do the same thing, but without cables. They make use of wireless receiver technology, such as Bluetooth, to connect a separate device, like a button or your phone, to the camera to trigger the shutter release, **Figure 4-5**. Tethered shutter releases tend to be faster than untethered shutter releases because they are physically connected to the camera and do not rely on wireless technology to make the camera function. In some instances, untethered releases may have a delay as long as a few seconds.

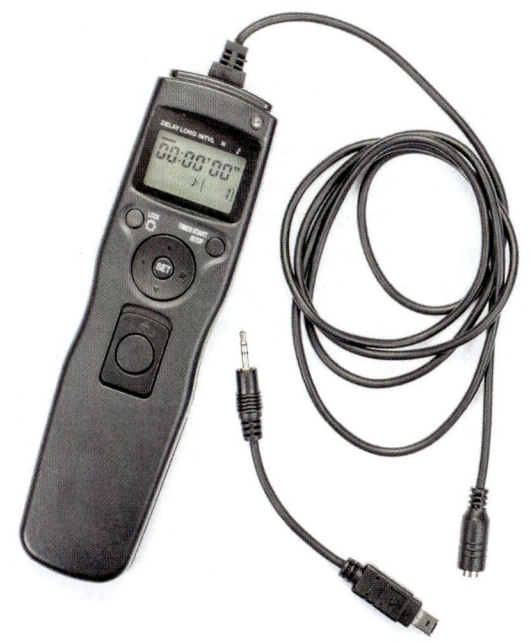

pattara puttiwong/Shutterstock.com

Figure 4-4. A tethered shutter release is attached to your camera with a cable.

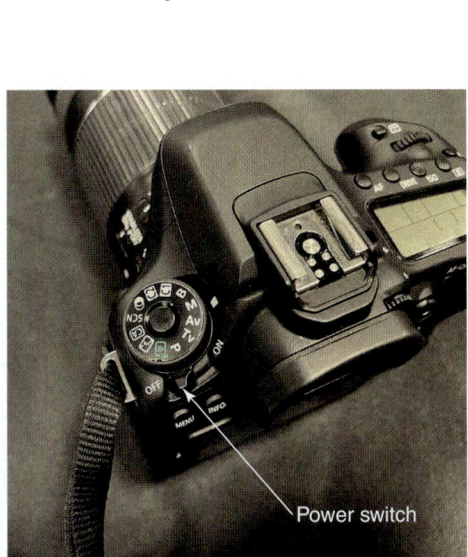

Goodheart-Willcox Publisher

Figure 4-3. The power switch turns the camera on and off.

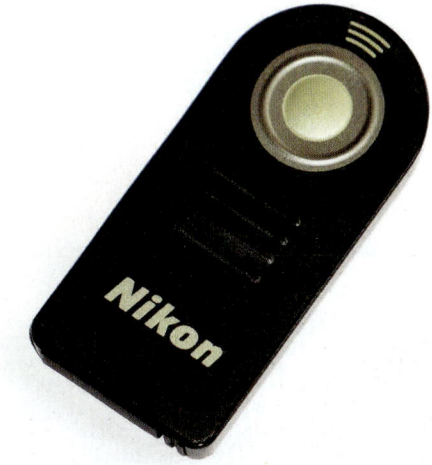

AjayTvm/Shutterstock.com

Figure 4-5. An untethered shutter release does not physically connect to your camera.

If a shutter release device is not available, the camera's self-timer can be used to operate the shutter without causing vibration. When the shutter button is pressed, the timer performs a countdown for a set number of seconds, and then operates the shutter. The delay permits any vibration from pressing the shutter release to die out.

On cameras using autofocus, pressing the shutter button also activates the focusing system. The camera focuses, and then opens the shutter to take the picture. One advantage of this two-step process is the ability to select a focus point that may not be in the center of your picture and lock the focus by pressing the button halfway down. You can then recompose your scene and capture it by pressing the button the rest of the way down. A second advantage is the ability to minimize **shutter lag**, which is a delay between pressing the shutter button and the actual opening of the shutter. Shutter lag is common in some digital cameras, especially compact cameras and older models. It is caused by the slow operation of many autofocus systems. With the two-step method, the already-focused camera opens the shutter more quickly when you press the button all the way down. This is a definite advantage when capturing action subjects.

Viewfinder

The **viewfinder** is a small viewing screen on the back side of a digital camera that allows review of each image immediately after it is exposed, **Figure 4-6**. Most viewfinders are *liquid crystal display (LCD) screens*. A viewfinder allows you to quickly evaluate composition and exposure and determine whether the image is worth keeping or should be reshot. The viewfinder can also display information on camera settings such as shutter speed, aperture, and ISO. A useful feature on some models is an LCD screen that swings out from the camera body. The screen can be positioned to aid in composing pictures taken from various angles. See **Figure 4-7**.

Because of their design, older DSLRs did not permit using the camera-back LCD as a viewfinder. Today, many camera models have a live-view LCD that can be used for composing the image. A DSLR has an additional small LCD display on the top or back side of the camera to show exposure settings, battery status, and other information. On most DSLR models, the camera-back LCD is used strictly for reviewing images.

Although camera controls allow you to zoom in on an image to judge sharpness or examine details, the viewfinder does not allow you to accurately assess whether the image is well exposed. For example, when the viewfinder is viewed under bright lighting conditions, the image can appear overexposed or "washed out." For critical evaluation of exposure, the display can be switched to show a histogram and image information.

Menu Button

The *menu button* allows you to access the camera's internal menu functions on the camera's viewfinder. You can adjust settings here and make other changes to how your camera operates by clicking through

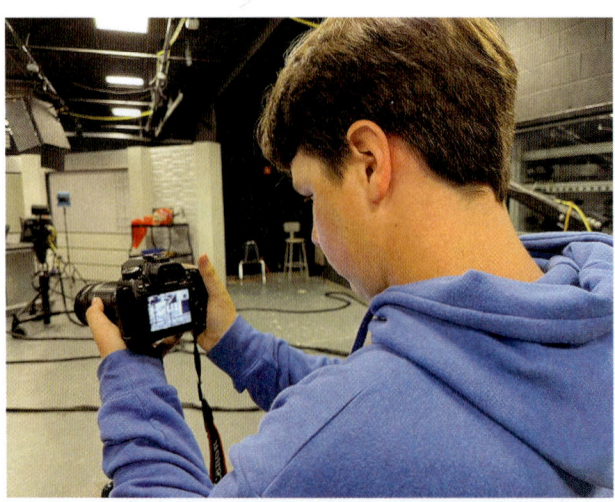

Goodheart-Willcox Publisher

Figure 4-6. After a digital camera makes an exposure, it displays the image on the viewfinder for review.

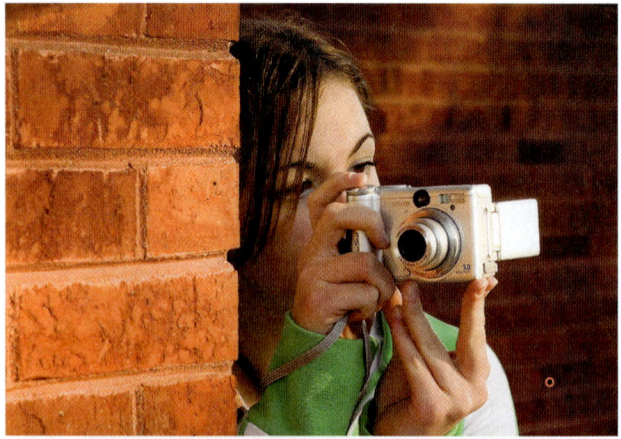

Jack Klasey/Goodheart-Willcox Publisher

Figure 4-7. A pivoting LCD can be used as a viewfinder for situations such as shooting over a crowd, capturing flowers silhouetted against the sky, or even making "around the corner" photographs.

using the *selection dial* or *cross keys*, **Figure 4-8**. Depending on your camera, you will have one or the other. Both allow you to navigate menus and select different values on your camera. On the other hand, some cameras have touch screens, which enable you to navigate any menu using your finger.

View Button

Also referred to as the *play button*, the *view button* allows you to access the images you have taken. Depending on the camera, it will automatically pull up the images taken most recently or allow you to view a gallery of the images you have recorded on the viewfinder.

Erase Button

Just as the name implies, the erase button allows you to erase an image that you have taken. In most instances, your camera will ask for confirmation before permanently deleting the photograph.

Histogram/Exposure Display

A **histogram** is a bar graph that displays all the tonal values of an image, **Figure 4-9**. The graph is composed of 256 bars or columns that represent the number of tones in an 8-bit image. Ranging from pure black at the left to pure white at the right, each bar represents the number of pixels of a specific value in the image. The result is a mountain range appearance with peaks and valleys. Peaks indicate a large number of pixels, while valleys are indicators of few or no pixels.

Learning to read the histogram is the key to evaluating your exposures and making necessary adjustments to obtain the best possible image. This topic is discussed in more depth in Chapter 11, *Making Exposure Decisions*.

On-Board (Built-In) Flash

With the exception of high-end professional models, virtually every camera available today includes an on-board flash, **Figure 4-10**. When shooting in automatic mode, most cameras fire the flash

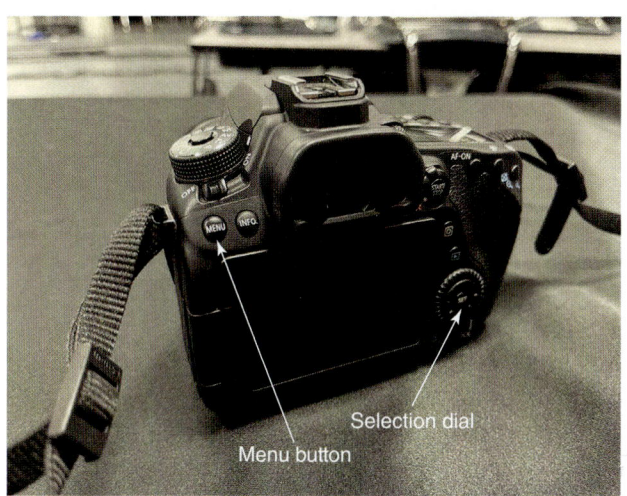

Goodheart-Willcox Publisher

Figure 4-8. After pressing the menu button, the selection dial lets you click through the camera's internal menu and adjust the settings.

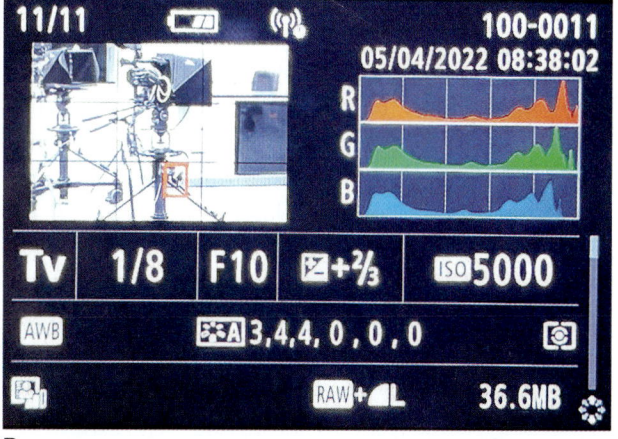

Goodheart-Willcox Publisher

Figure 4-9. A camera's histogram display is an essential tool for the digital photographer. A—The display is a bar graph showing all the tones in the image, allowing you to evaluate exposure and make any needed changes. B—Some cameras allow you to select an additional histogram display that shows the values for each of the three primary colors.

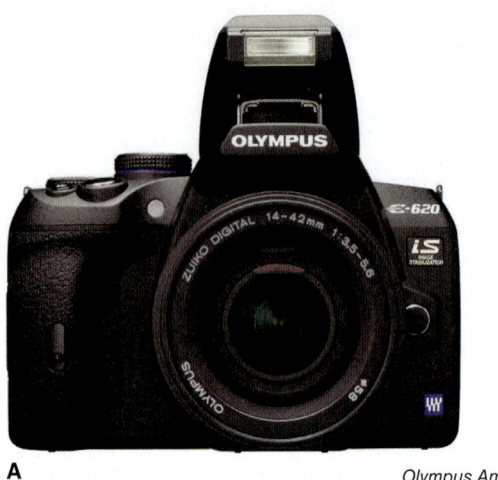

A

Olympus America, Inc.

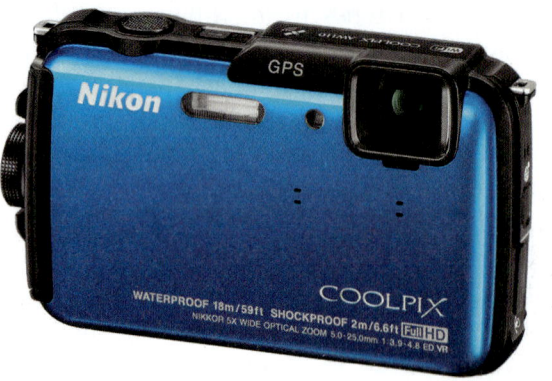

B

Courtesy of Nikon Inc., Melville, New York

Figure 4-10. An on-board flash provides light when needed or desired to capture an image under lower-light conditions. A—Many larger-bodied cameras, such as DSLRs, have a pop-up flash that can be raised when needed. Most also have a hot shoe for mounting a separate flash unit. B—Compact cameras typically have a small flash built into the camera body.

whenever needed. In other situations, the photographer selects when to use the flash. On-board flashes have limited range. Many compact cameras and all interchangeable-lens models have a hot shoe for mounting a more powerful flash unit, **Figure 4-11**. A **hot shoe** is a flash mounting terminal often located on top of a DSLR. Its electrical contacts mate with those on the flash unit, triggering the flash when the shutter release is pressed. Use of a separate flash is described in Chapter 12, *Action and Event Photography*.

Lens Release

The *lens release* is in roughly the same spot for all digital cameras. When this button is pressed, you can release the lens from your camera and either replace it with another lens or store the camera body

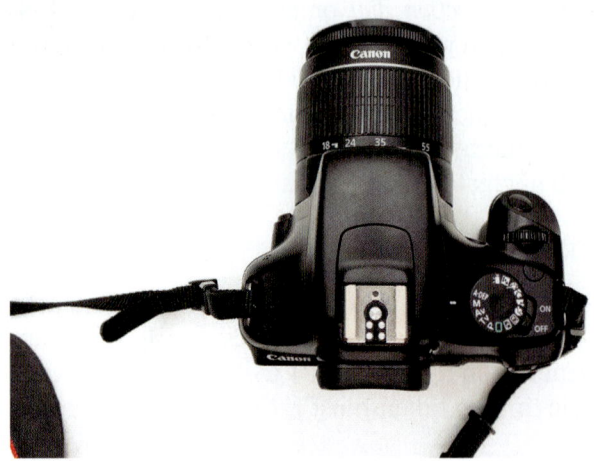

ReaLiia/Shutterstock.com

Figure 4-11. A camera's hot shoe is a bracket that provides a photographer with a way to connect different accessories to the camera, including a separate flash.

and the lens separately. Before you change your lenses, make sure that you turn off your camera and are changing it in a clean area. It is especially important to avoid dusty or sandy areas. The camera's sensor is exposed when swapping out lenses, making it a prime opportunity for dirt and other debris to get into the sensor. If you are removing the lens to store separately from the camera body, make sure you put both the rear cap and the camera body cap in place to avoid damage.

Mode Dial

A *mode dial*, also referred to as a *camera dial*, is a dial used on digital cameras to adjust the camera's mode. Almost all digital cameras support multiple modes that automatically change your camera settings to best fit the situation, such as aperture priority mode, manual mode, action mode, and more. This dial is often located on the top left-hand side of your camera, near the shutter release.

Focus Lock/Exposure Lock

Depending on the type of camera you have, the functions described in the next four sections may be a single button that enables both functions to occur. Review your camera's manual for specifics.

Described in the section on shutter release, ***focus lock***, also known as *AF lock*, is a function that allows the photographer to set and maintain focus on a specific point in a shot and then recompose the shot while holding the focus on the previously selected point. ***Exposure lock***, also known as *AE lock*, works similarly. It allows the photographer to reframe a shot while keeping the current exposure reading the same. Exposure lock is useful for shooting subjects that are backlit and for panoramic photography.

Exposure Lock/Zoom Button

As explained in the previous section, exposure lock allows you to set an exposure and maintain it while you recompose your image and take another photograph. This is only useful in the auto mode of your camera, since other modes will require you to set your exposure manually or have a preset exposure already set.

The zoom function is the second function. It allows you to zoom in on a specific spot in a recorded image so you can get a closer look.

Focus Point Selector/Zoom Button

When enabled, the *focus point selector* lets you choose a point of focus from several points that appear on your camera's display. If you select auto, the camera will make that decision for you and set your focal point.

The second function is similar to the zoom button from the previous section. While that button allows you to zoom in, this one allows you to zoom out of an image if you are reviewing it in your gallery.

Aperture Selector/Exposure Compensation Button

The *aperture selector* allows you to select your aperture by holding it down and using the selection dial or cross keys to select the aperture you want to use.

Exposure compensation lets you adjust the standard exposure that your camera sets. This allows you to make your image darker or brighter and can be used in almost any of the camera's modes. This does not turn off or reset when you turn off your camera, so you must manually reset it when you are done.

Digital Camera Controls and Features

Digital cameras have several digital controls and features accessed through the camera's display. Since camera brands and models can vary considerably, the following section describes these features and controls in general terms.

Exposure Mode Selection

The most basic camera models do not provide any shooting choices. Instead, they are all preset or automatically adjusted. Most cameras, however, offer at least four different exposure modes to choose from. See **Figure 4-12**. These exposure modes are *automatic*, *aperture priority*, *shutter priority*, and *manual*.

Often designated as *AE*, the automatic exposure mode lets the camera make all the decisions. The camera's processor uses readings from the built-in exposure meter to select an aperture/shutter speed combination that provides a properly exposed photograph. *Aperture* is the size of the opening through which light passes to strike the camera's image receiver. *Shutter speed* is the speed at which the camera's shutter closes once the shutter release is pressed. On a film camera, the film speed (ISO) setting is factored into the exposure decision. Digital cameras also factor in the ISO setting but may alter the value to improve the exposure. **ISO** is the camera image receiver's sensitivity to light. Auto exposure is the simplest mode to use and gives acceptable results much of the time. However, it cannot cope with certain kinds of photographic situations, such as backlit subjects or rapid motion.

Some camera models have a Program AE mode to allow limited control. **Program AE** is an exposure mode in which the camera's processor selects exposure settings based on the meter reading, but the photographer can change either the shutter speed or aperture. The processor will then make the appropriate adjustment for a proper exposure.

In **aperture priority** mode, the photographer selects the aperture setting, and the camera sets a shutter speed based on its meter reading. The

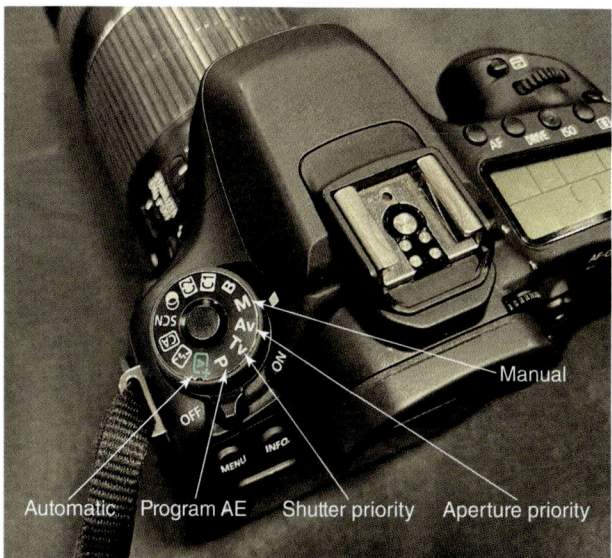

Goodheart-Willcox Publisher

Figure 4-12. The exposure modes commonly found on digital cameras.

advantage of using aperture priority is the ability to control ***depth of field***, which is the distance between the nearest and farthest objects that are in acceptably sharp focus. As aperture size decreases, depth of field increases. Aperture priority is often selected when shooting landscapes. See **Figure 4-13**.

When a moving subject is involved, shutter priority mode is typically selected. ***Shutter priority*** is an exposure mode in which the photographer selects the shutter speed, and the camera chooses an aperture based on its meter reading. Slower shutter speeds that keep the shutter open for longer create longer exposures and capture motion blur. Faster shutter speeds that force the shutter to open and close quickly create shorter exposures and stop motion. See **Figure 4-14**. The effect of the selected

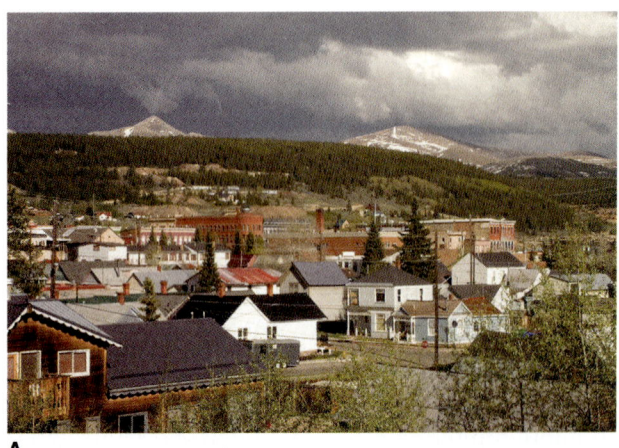
A

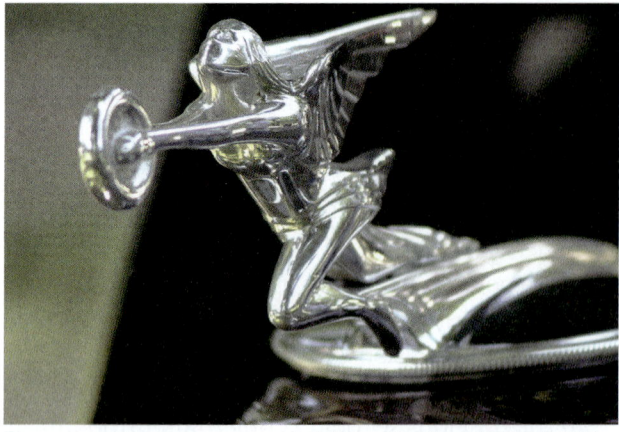
B
Jack Klasey/Goodheart-Willcox Publisher

Figure 4-13. Depth of field increases as aperture decreases. A—In this scenic shot, depth of field is great, with focus sharp from the nearest house to the distant mountains. Aperture is f/20 at 1/60 second using a 50 mm lens. B—A 300 mm telephoto lens and an aperture of f/5.6 at 1/100 second result in very shallow depth of field. Focus is sharp only for the central figure in this photo of an antique automotive hood ornament.

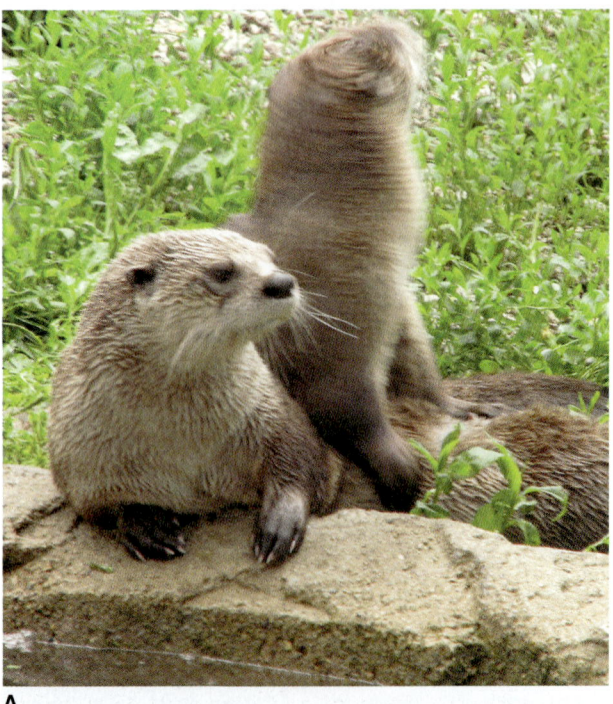
A

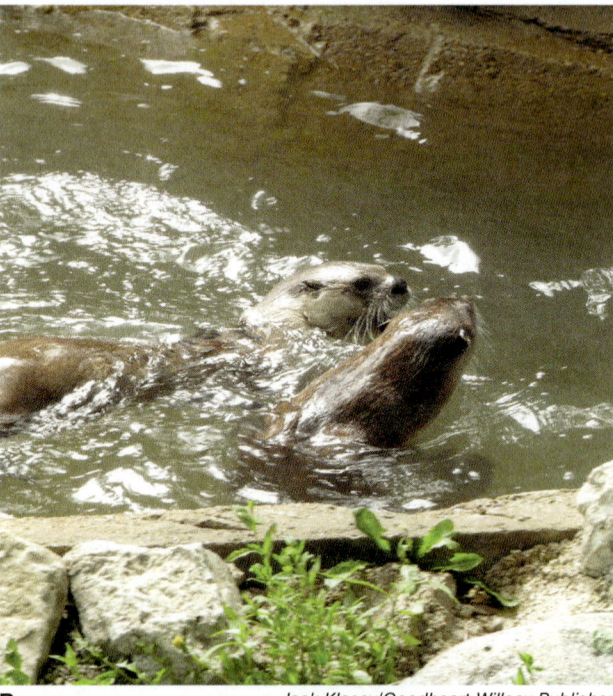
B
Jack Klasey/Goodheart-Willcox Publisher

Figure 4-14. Using shutter priority to control motion blur. A—A relatively slow shutter speed of 1/40 second results in strong motion blur as one of the otters turns rapidly. B—Using a faster shutter speed (1/125 second) freezes the motion of the swimming otters.

shutter speed is relative to the motion involved. A relatively fast shutter speed of 1/250 second freezes a jogger's movement in mid-stride but records a baseball pitcher's 95 mph fastball as a streak. Shutter priority is commonly used for sports photography, the performing arts, and photojournalism.

The manual exposure mode provides the greatest degree of control. **Manual exposure** is an exposure mode in which the photographer chooses the aperture, shutter speed, and ISO. See **Figure 4-15**. To use this mode successfully, you must be thoroughly familiar with the use of equivalent exposures so you can select the proper combination of shutter speed and aperture for the situation, **Figure 4-16**. Equivalent exposures are covered in detail in Chapter 11, *Making Exposure Decisions*.

Many digital cameras allow you to choose an exposure mode that is preset for a particular situation, **Figure 4-17**. The following are some typical preset exposure modes:

- *Portrait*: Portrait mode uses a shallow depth of field to blur the background and focus attention on the subject.
- *Landscape*: Landscape mode is preset for maximum depth of field.
- *Sports/Action*: Sports/action mode selects a fast shutter speed. On some cameras, it also activates a focus tracking feature that helps keep a moving subject in focus.
- *Close-up*: Close-up mode is used at the closest focusing distance of the camera's lens.
- *Night scene*: Night scene mode uses both flash and a slow shutter speed to balance foreground and background exposures.

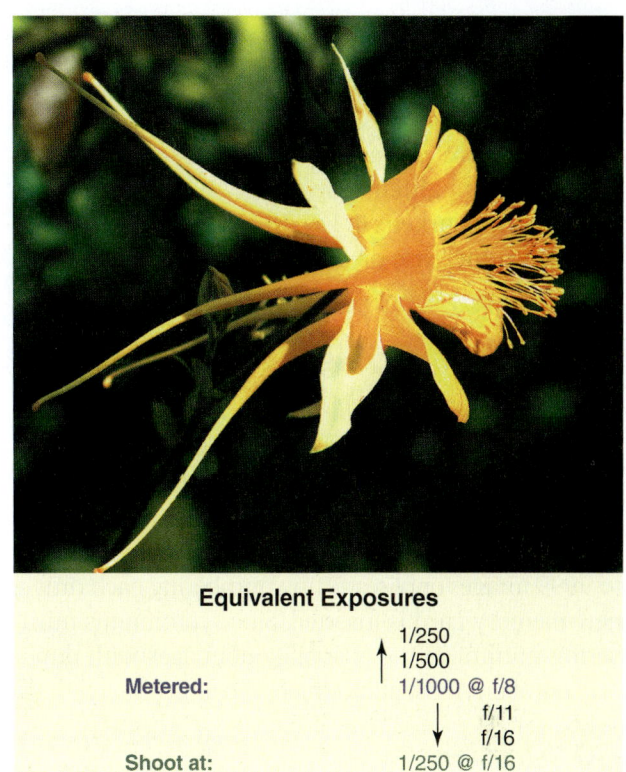

Goodheart-Willcox Publisher

Figure 4-16. Selecting an equivalent exposure. If your meter reading is 1/1000 second at f/8, you can stop down from f/8 to f/16 (two stops) for greater depth of field. This would require a shutter speed two steps slower (1/1000 second to 1/250 second) to obtain an equivalent exposure value.

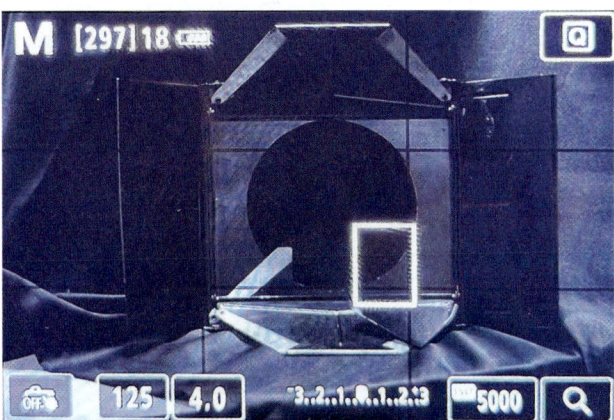

Goodheart-Willcox Publisher

Figure 4-15. Manual mode allows you to separately select an aperture and a shutter speed that result in a correct exposure.

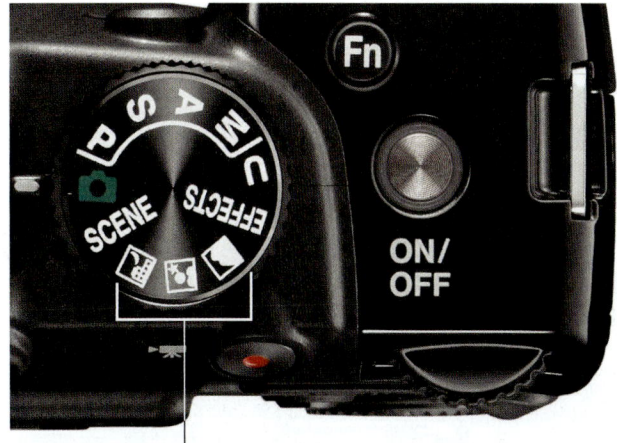

Goodheart-Willcox Publisher

Figure 4-17. Most digital cameras have several preset exposure modes for use in specific situations. They are usually selected by rotating a dial.

Exposure Compensation

Exposure compensation allows you to increase or decrease exposure in shutter priority, aperture priority, or Program AE modes, **Figure 4-18**. Increasing the exposure lightens the image, while decreasing the exposure darkens it. Exposure compensation can provide an increase or decrease in your exposure in small intervals to make gradual adjustments.

Exposure Numbering

Digital images are numbered by the camera's software. Each image is electronically tagged with an identifying number that becomes a part of the file and is usually used as the filename, such as IMG_2237. Most cameras offer a choice of continuous numbering of up to 9999 images or of restarting numbering each time a new memory card is inserted. Since continuous numbering minimizes the possibility of images with duplicate numbers, most photographers choose that method.

ISO Selection

Almost all cameras allow the user to select the sensitivity of the image receiver. The camera's sensitivity to light is expressed as an ISO rating. The higher the ISO rating, the more light allowed into the camera's digital sensor. The lower the ISO rating, the less light allowed into the camera's digital sensor. If you are working with a DSLR and want to select a specific ISO rating, you will most likely see a display of ISO options that you can choose from, **Figure 4-19**. However, be careful when adjusting your ISO. Depending on your environment, image quality declines as the ISO rating increases.

Goodheart-Willcox Publisher

Figure 4-19. On digital cameras, the ISO setting is usually selected from a menu displayed on the viewfinder. Increasing the ISO setting makes the camera's image receiver more sensitive to light, permitting photography under lower-light conditions.

Depth of Field Preview

Found on most DSLRs, the **depth of field (DOF) preview** control is a camera feature that allows the photographer to see what the scene will look like at the desired aperture and assess the actual depth of field. DOF preview is usually activated by pressing a button at the front of the camera near the lens. This adjusts the lens to the desired aperture and helps you adjust how much of your photo is in focus. The scene in the viewfinder will be darker, since less light is entering, but will accurately show the depth of field that will appear in your captured image.

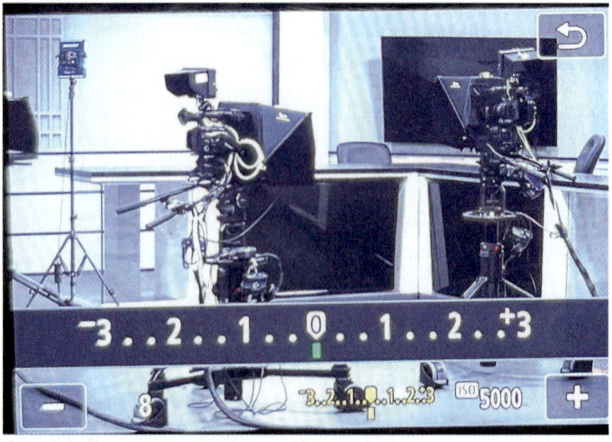
A

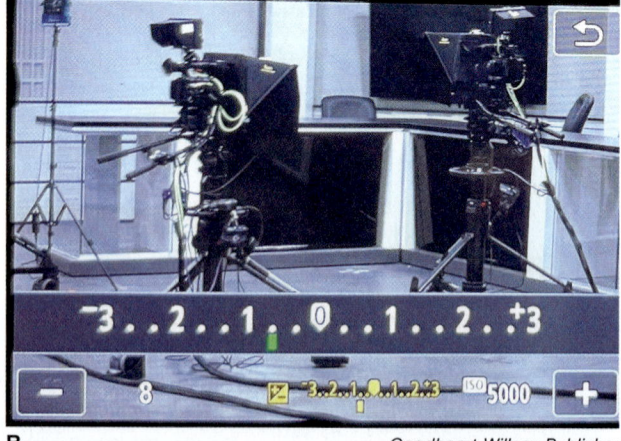
B

Goodheart-Willcox Publisher

Figure 4-18. Exposure compensation. A—The indicator is centered under the 0 point of the scale. The photo will be exposed at the metered values. B—With the indicator moved to the left -1, the exposure will be darker. It will be made at one stop under the metered values.

Burst Mode

For sports and other types of action photography, making a series of exposures in a second or less can allow you to capture the peak of action or to show a sequence of actions, **Figure 4-20**. Almost all digital cameras can operate in a **burst mode**, which is a continuous shooting mode in which the number of possible exposures ranges from two to eight or more per second. The number of possible exposures depends on the camera model.

White Balance

The human eye compensates for the color of light, but a camera does not. To capture and display colors accurately, digital camera users select a white balance. **White balance** is a method of adjusting how the camera sees a white object. By adjusting the camera's response to make a white object *appear* white under specific light conditions, all other colors seen under that lighting will be shown accurately.

Most digital cameras allow you to select automatic white balance (AWB) or one of a number of presets for conditions such as sunlight, shade, tungsten lighting, fluorescent lighting, or flash, **Figure 4-21**. AWB or one of the presets provides good results in most situations.

Image Quality (Resolution/Compression) Settings

Digital cameras can produce images at different quality levels to meet particular photography needs. An image to be used in a book or displayed as an 11″ × 14″ inkjet print has different requirements from a 4″ × 6″ snapshot or an image to be displayed on a web page.

The quality level for JPEG image files is typically described as large, medium, or small, and it is based on the size of the output that can be produced from that file. See **Figure 4-22**. The definition of large, medium, and small, in turn, depends on the camera's resolution. A large quality image from a 12 MP camera is approximately 4000 × 3000 pixels and can produce an excellent inkjet print approximately 9″ × 12″ in size. In contrast, a large quality print from a 6 MP camera is approximately 3000 × 2000 pixels and can produce an excellent 7″ × 10″ print. The medium and small sizes are relative to the large size. For a 12 MP camera, a medium quality would produce a 7″ × 10″ print, and a small quality print would be 4″ × 5.5″.

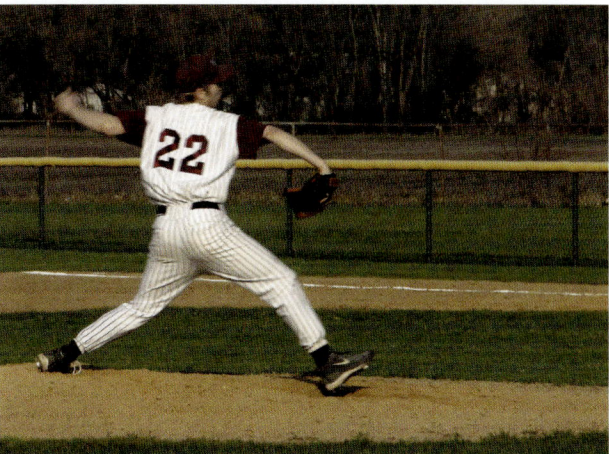
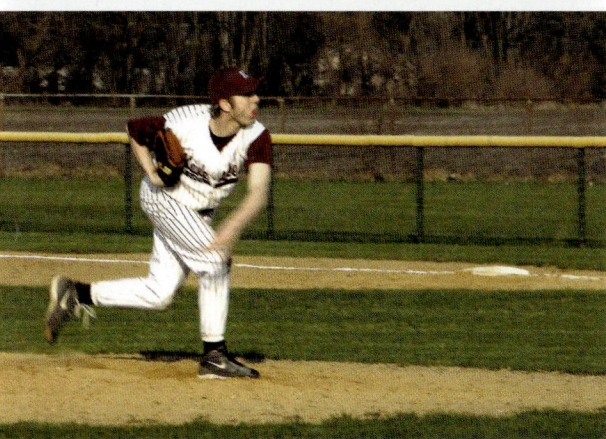
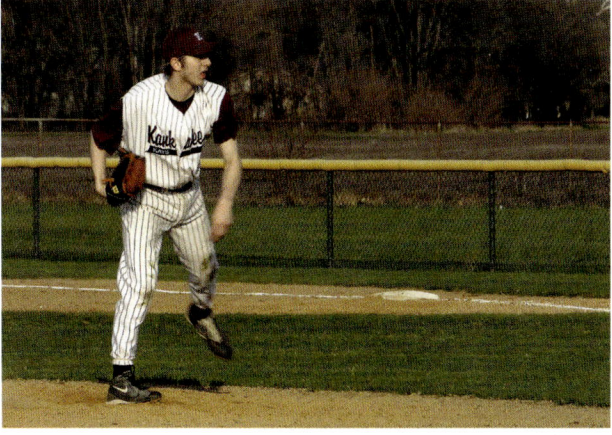

Jack Klasey/Goodheart-Willcox Publisher

Figure 4-20. These three shots of a baseball pitcher's delivery were taken in a span of approximately one second using the camera's continuous shooting (burst) mode.

Compression is the squeezing of an electronic file to reduce its size. The size reduction allows more images to be stored on a memory card, faster copying from camera to computer, and faster transmission via email. Compression of JPEG files is called *lossy*, which means that some image data is discarded in processing. The amount of discarded data

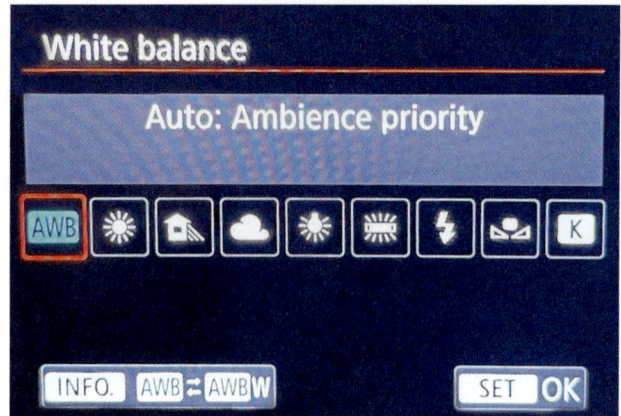

Goodheart-Willcox Publisher

Figure 4-21. Automatic white balance usually provides good results, but some situations call for selecting one of the other preset white balances from the camera's menu.

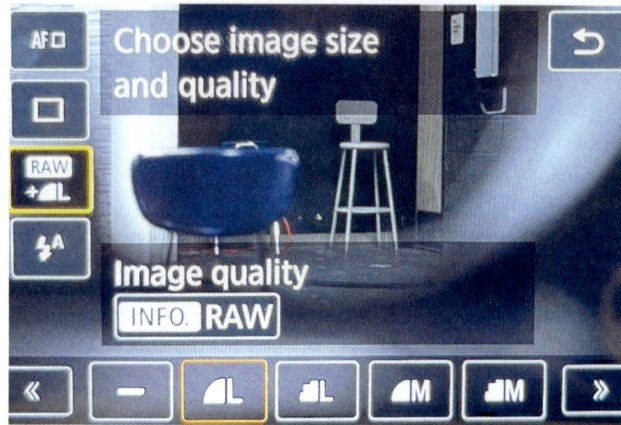

Goodheart-Willcox Publisher

Figure 4-23. Professional digital cameras and some advanced amateur models allow you to choose output of both RAW and JPEG files for greater flexibility.

affects image quality—the more a file is compressed, the greater the data loss. The amount of compression applied to an image file can be selected from a camera menu.

Sophisticated cameras may offer the ability to capture RAW images, **Figure 4-23**. These images include all of the information captured by the camera's sensor and are not compressed or processed in any way. With special computer software, RAW images can be adjusted and then converted to a conventional image file, such as JPEG, TIF, or PNG. Most professional photographers shoot in RAW because it allows them an incredible amount of flexibility during postproduction. The trade-off is that RAW images often take up more storage space on a memory card than non-RAW images. All DSLR cameras have the ability to shoot in RAW. **Figure 4-24** outlines the differences between shooting in RAW and shooting in JPEG.

Color Space Selection

A color space is a specific description of the range, or gamut, of colors that can be provided by a particular device. Most digital cameras capture images in the color space called sRGB. **sRGB** stands for standard Red, Green, Blue, and it is a color space that was defined by the computer industry for consistent display of colors on monitors. The other major RGB color space is **Adobe RGB**, which was developed by the manufacturer of Photoshop and other graphics software.

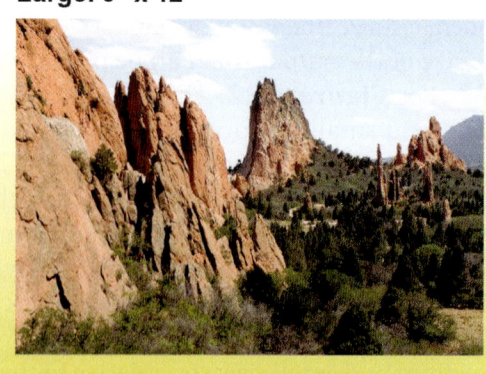

Jack Klasey/Goodheart-Willcox Publisher

Figure 4-22. Relative sizes of high-quality prints that could be made from large, medium, and small JPEG files produced by a 12 MP camera.

Shooting in RAW vs. JPEG	
RAW	JPEG
High-quality image files retain all data	Image files could possibly lose some minor details
Uncompressed file	Compressed file
Not easily shareable without some form of processing	Easily and immediately shareable
Larger file size	Smaller file size

Goodheart-Willcox Publisher

Figure 4-24. A table outlining the differences between shooting in RAW and shooting in JPEG.

If your camera offers both color spaces, the reason for choosing one over the other depends primarily on how the image will be seen. The sRGB color space reproduces more vividly for viewing on a computer monitor. Adobe RGB would be the choice for inkjet printers and traditional printing presses, which use inks that can reproduce the wider gamut of this color space.

Physical Care of Your Camera

Cameras and lenses are precision instruments that can be damaged by rough handling or by exposure to water, dust, sand, or other environmental dangers. Protecting your camera from damage is mostly a matter of common sense. You would not use the camera in a rainstorm without some form of waterproof covering, nor would you set it down in the sand while shooting at the beach.

Wet-Weather Protection

Rainy weather can often allow you to make good photographs. To protect both you and the camera while photographing under rainy conditions, use various forms of shelter, such as a building doorway or porch, a vehicle with the window rolled down, or an umbrella. When conditions are both wet and windy, however, such shelter may not be enough to keep your camera dry.

Better protection is offered by flexible plastic housings that fit over the camera and lens barrel. These housings do not cover the front of the lens because the material would cause distortion of the image. The housings may have cutouts or other provisions for using camera controls. See **Figure 4-25**.

An inexpensive alternative can be made with a large plastic food storage bag and a rubber band. For DSLRs with telephoto lenses, either a one-gallon or two-gallon zip-closure bag is adequate. Cut off one of the bottom corners of the bag to leave a hole approximately the diameter of the lens hood (an additional accessory that attaches to the front of a camera to help protect the lens). Place the camera in the bag with the lens protruding from the hole, then use the rubber band to secure the plastic around or just behind the lens hood. The open end of the bag lets you use the viewfinder and operate camera controls.

A large plastic bag can also serve as emergency protection for your camera. If you are caught in the open when it starts to rain, or you are on a boat or a beach where wind-whipped spray becomes a problem, you can quickly slip the camera into the bag for protection.

If you are caught in a wet situation without protection, shelter the camera as well as you can inside a jacket or other article of clothing. As soon as you are in a dry area, carefully wipe off all visible moisture with a dry cloth or paper towels. If possible, use a hair dryer to evaporate any water that remains in crevices of the camera body and lens. Remember, you and your clothes will recover from water. Your camera may not if it is not properly protected.

Dust Protection

Like water, dust is a major enemy of your camera. Fine particles of dirt or sand can lodge between moving parts and cause costly wear. If ground in by

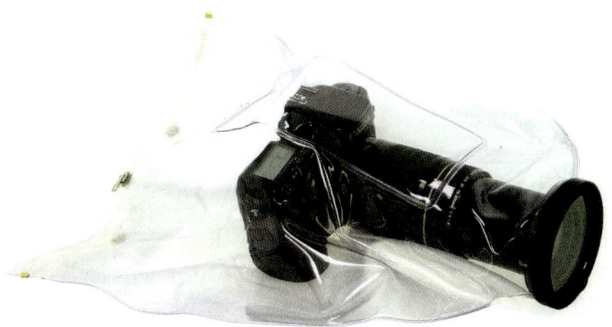

Ewa-marine Gmbh

Figure 4-25. Plastic rain covers protect the camera's delicate electronics from moisture on rainy or snowy days, or when photographing from a boat or canoe. Various sizes are available to accommodate different zoom lens lengths.

improper cleaning methods, particles on the glass surface of a lens leave scratches that diminish optical performance. Dust inside a DSLR camera body can settle on the sensor, resulting in unsightly spots that appear on every image, **Figure 4-26**. Newer camera models use ultrasonic vibration or other methods to shake loose particles off the sensor every time the camera is turned on.

To keep dust out of the camera body, always turn off the camera before changing lenses. If the lens is removed with the camera still switched on, the electrical charge on the sensor will attract dust particles.

When changing a lens in a windy environment, protect the equipment from flying particles by making the change under some form of cover. If possible, move into a building, a vehicle, or other protected area. If such an area is not available, work beneath the cover of a jacket, shirt, or towel draped over your hands. If no other method is available, turn your back to the wind and shelter the operation with your body as much as possible.

> ### PROCEDURE
>
> **Changing Lenses**
>
> 1. Turn off the camera's power switch.
> 2. Hold the camera body with the lens facing downward either over your lap or over a table. This allows any loose dust to fall away when the lens is dismounted and prevents the lens from falling to the ground. Grasp the lens firmly.
> 3. Press the lens release button on the camera body, then rotate and remove the lens from the mount.
> 4. Place a rear lens cap on the lens where it detaches from the camera to keep out dust. Often, you will simply switch the rear cap from the new lens to the one just dismounted.
> 5. Insert the new lens into the mount and rotate it until it is firmly in place.
> 6. Turn on the camera's power again.

Protecting Lens Elements

Most lens elements are inside the lens barrel (tube-shaped housing that holds all the lens components), where they are protected against possible causes of damage. The front element (the piece of the lens that is first to receive light from the scene), however, is exposed to both abrasion damage from dust or sand and physical damage from bumping against hard objects.

An inexpensive form of protection used by many photographers is the ultraviolet (UV) filter. An **ultraviolet (UV) filter**, also called a *haze filter* or *skylight filter*, is a virtually clear filter that is screwed into place on the front of the lens to protect the front lens element from dust, salt spray, and bumps against hard objects, **Figure 4-27**. A damaged UV filter can be replaced easily and at much less cost than the front lens element.

Some photographers claim that a UV filter, even one of good quality, can degrade the quality of the image. Others consider the slight quality loss to be

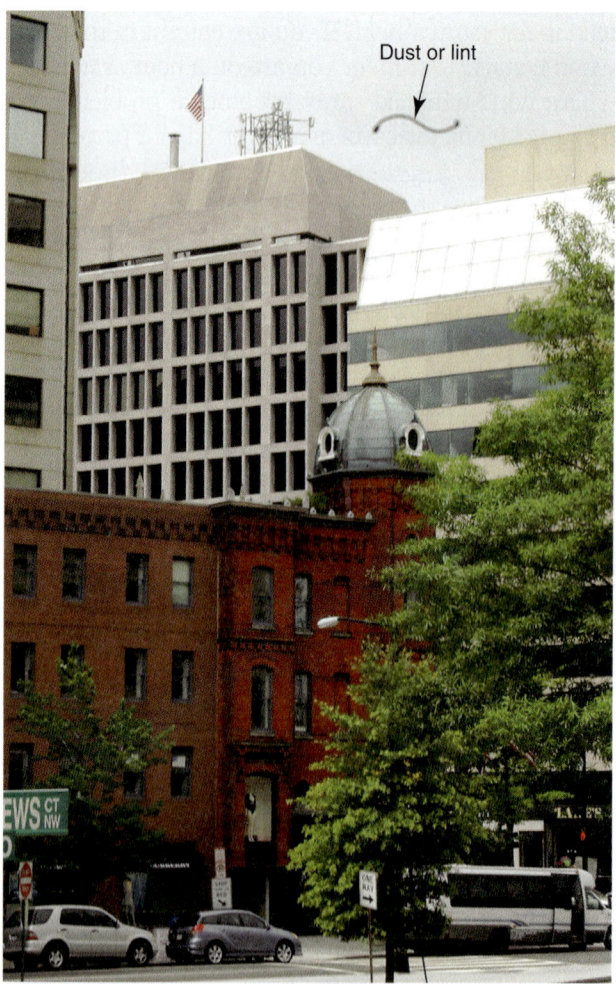

Jack Klasey/Goodheart-Willcox Publisher

Figure 4-26. This S-shaped black object, probably a piece of lint, settled on the camera's sensor. Dust spots are typically not visible on the camera's viewfinder and are detected only when the image is displayed on the larger screen of a computer. Proper lens-changing techniques and regular sensor cleaning will help prevent dust spots.

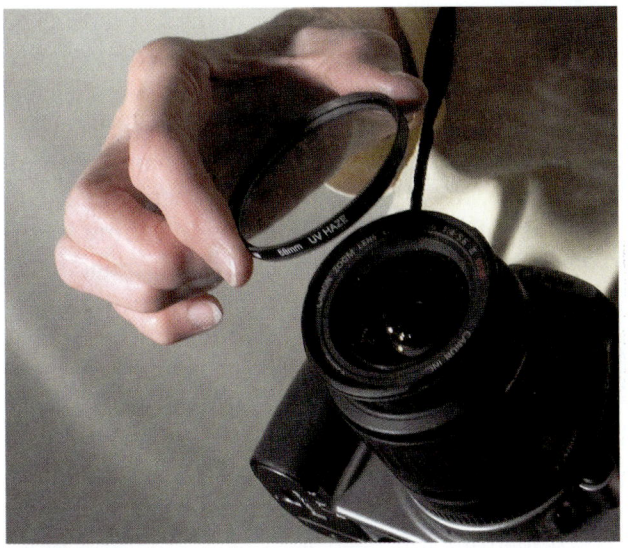

Jack Klasey/Goodheart-Willcox Publisher

Figure 4-27. Mounting a UV filter on a lens protects the coating on the front element and helps to eliminate atmospheric haze in landscape photos.

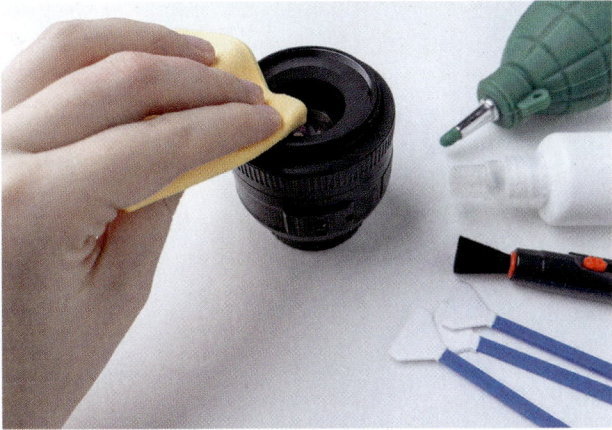

Sergey Hramov/Shutterstock.com

Figure 4-28. Tools used for cleaning a lens or filter include a blower or soft brush for loose dirt and lens cleaning cloths used with a cleaning solution for oily deposits.

offset by the protection the filter provides. A compromise is to leave the filter in place except when actually shooting, although constantly removing and replacing the filter is cumbersome.

Cleaning a Lens or Filter

Frequent lens or filter cleaning is important to maintain optical quality, and proper cleaning methods are vital to preventing damage. See **Figure 4-28**. If a UV filter normally remains on the lens, the front lens element seldom, if ever, needs to be cleaned. However, the filter should be cleaned frequently to minimize its effect on optical quality. When the back element of a lens (the part that attaches to the camera) is accessible, it should be cleaned from time to time.

Cleaning is a two-step process. First, hold the lens facing downward either over your lap or over a table so any loose material falls away, and use a soft brush or squeeze-bulb air blower to clear away any particles. Second, place a drop of lens cleaning solution on a piece of lens cleaning tissue (a soft, lint-free paper), then gently rub the lens in a circular motion. Work outward from the center of the lens to the rim to remove oily deposits such as fingerprints. If left on the lens, fingerprints can permanently etch the surface. Many photographers carry a small microfiber cleaning cloth and use it in place of cleaning solution and tissue. The cloth must be washed regularly to remove particles that can cause scratches.

Camera Body Cleaning and Maintenance

Keeping equipment clean and in good working order is the mark of a skilled professional who shows pride in their work. Keeping equipment clean helps to minimize wear and damage and makes the equipment easier to use.

Cleaning the Camera Body and LCD Screen

Examine the camera body regularly, and use a soft brush to remove dust, grit, or lint from any crevices on the exterior. Pay special attention to areas around openings, such as the lens mount, battery door, or card slots. Be careful when cleaning around the focal plane shutter (type of shutter located in the camera body) since the curtains are easily damaged. To remove dirty deposits on the camera body, use a clean, lint-free cloth slightly moistened with warm water.

Do not clean the LCD screen with liquid materials. Carefully brush or blow away any loose dust, then gently rub the surface with a clean, soft dry cloth, such as a microfiber cloth, **Figure 4-29**. Do not press hard on the LCD surface as this could damage its delicate structure.

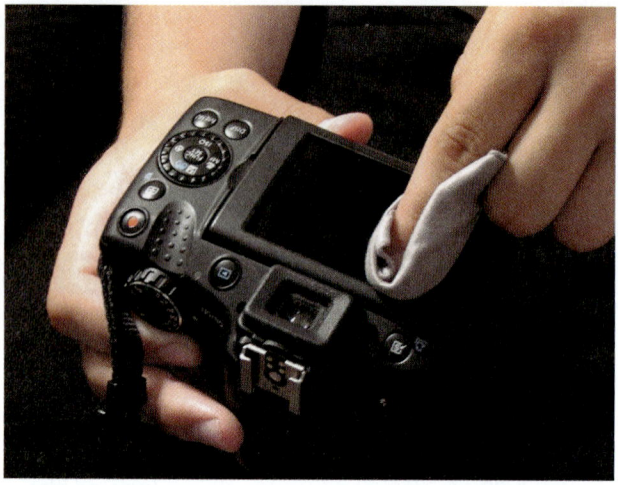

Jack Klasey/Goodheart-Willcox Publisher

Figure 4-29. Gentle wiping with a clean, soft cloth is recommended for cleaning LCD screens and viewfinders.

> ### 📱 REAL-WORLD PHOTOGRAPHY
>
> #### What's in Your Photography Bag?
>
> When it comes to shooting, you need to be prepared. Sometimes camera batteries die, you run out of room on your SD card, the camera gets dirty, or the weather changes. Here are some things that you can keep in your camera bag so you can be prepared for a wide variety of situations:
>
> 1. Extra battery in case your battery dies in the middle of your shoot.
> 2. Spare SD cards in case you run out of storage on the one in your camera.
> 3. Microfiber cloth to gently clean your lens in case of fingerprints or dirt. Lens cleaning wipes can also do the same thing.
> 4. A multitool that will help you in case of any physical issues, like a stuck screw on a tripod plate.
> 5. A waterproof cover (or plastic storage bag) to help cover your camera in case of rain.

Sensor Cleaning

Specks of dust or lint that have settled on the camera's image sensor are most noticeable in image areas of lighter color, such as the sky or clothing. Eliminating the spots from your files by using image editing software is time-consuming and tedious. A better solution is to remove the particles by cleaning the clear cover plate that is placed over the delicate sensor. The recommended procedure for sensor cover cleaning varies among manufacturers. The following procedure lists the general steps involved.

If one or more dark spots are still visible on your images after using the blower, the dust is most likely adhered to the sensor cover. Camera manufacturers discourage any form of cleaning other than use of a blower, often warning that other cleaning methods will void the camera's warranty. Manufacturers recommend having the sensor cleaned by a trained technician. However, products for cleaning adhered particles from the sensor are used by many photographers. The most common is a swab with a very small amount of a solvent that is carefully rubbed across the sensor's cover plate. Single-use individual swabs are sealed in airtight packaging.

To identify the need for sensor cleaning or to check its effectiveness, a special magnifying viewer can be placed over the camera's lens mount opening. This device provides a brightly lit, magnified view of the sensor to reveal the presence of dust particles or other debris. See **Figure 4-30**.

Camera Storage and Transportation

If you plan to take photographs at locations other than your home or studio, you must have some way to transport your equipment. A simple compact camera or even a DSLR with a single zoom lens can be hand-carried or hung around your neck with a camera strap. Most photographers, however, use a bag or case to carry and store equipment, **Figure 4-31**.

The traditional method of storing and carrying photographic equipment is the camera bag. Made

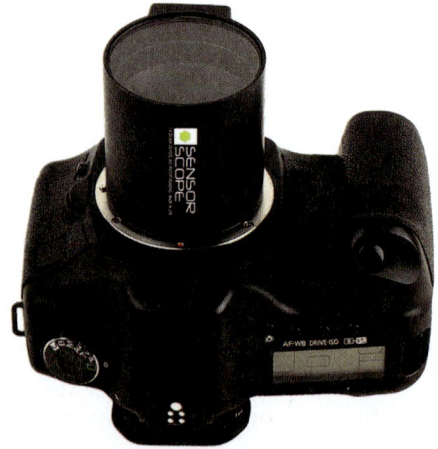

Delkin Devices

Figure 4-30. A magnifying device can be used to inspect the digital camera sensor. This model includes LEDs to illuminate the sensor and show dust particles.

PROCEDURE

Cleaning a DSLR Camera Sensor

1. Connect the camera to an AC adapter, if available, or be sure that the battery is fully charged.
2. Turn off the camera, and then remove the lens.
3. Turn the camera on again and select the *sensor cleaning* choice from the appropriate menu. The mirror will flip up and lock, and the shutter will open to expose the sensor assembly.
4. Hold the camera with the lens opening facing downward either over your lap or over a table so any dislodged dust falls out.
5. Carefully use a bulb-type blower to direct a jet of air at the sensor cover. This should dislodge any loose material. Do not use a blower brush—small pieces of bristle could break off, adding to the dust problem instead of solving it. Also, the bristles could scratch the cover plate. Never use canned compressed air because it contains chemical propellants that can damage the sensor assembly.

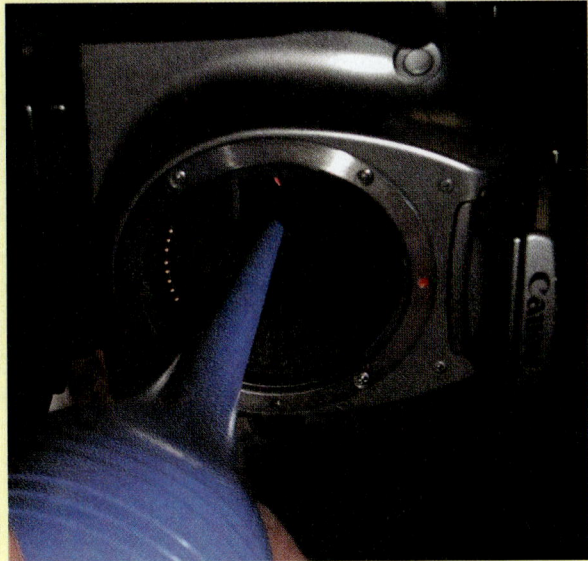

Jack Klasey/Goodheart-Willcox Publisher

Careful use of a blower directs a jet of air onto the sensor's cover plate to remove loose dust particles.

6. Withdraw the blower bulb from the camera and turn off the power. The shutter will close, and the mirror will drop down.
7. Remount the lens.

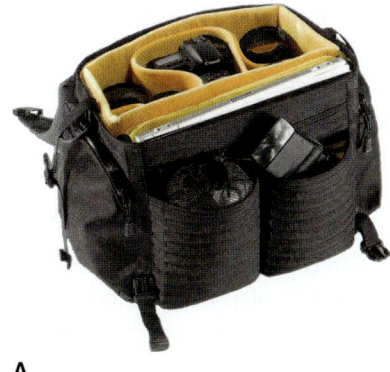

A

Bogen Kata

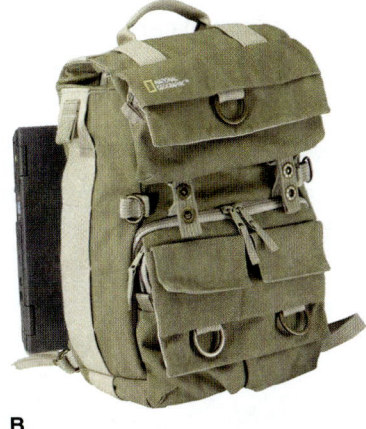

B

Bogen

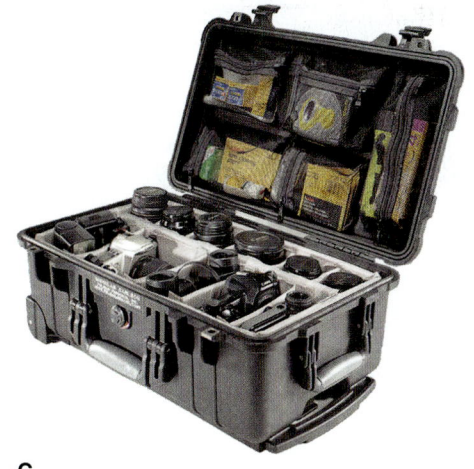

C

Pelican

Figure 4-31. There are many choices for camera storage and transportation equipment. A—The traditional camera bag comes in many sizes. B—Backpacks with padded dividers to protect equipment are particularly popular with nature photographers. C—Hard cases are most often used by professionals who must travel with a large amount of equipment.

of a strong woven material and padded for protection against bumps, most bags have partitions to hold different-sized items, such as lenses and camera bodies. Bags vary in size from small handheld or belt-mounted cases for compact cameras to very large bags capable of holding several camera bodies, a selection of lenses, a flash unit, and various other accessories.

With the growth in active lifestyles and interest in nature photography, the photo backpack has become popular. A backpack allows safe and comfortable transport of camera gear and other items while hiking, climbing, skiing, or bicycling. In areas where equipment theft is a problem, a backpack is less obvious than a traditional camera bag.

The ultimate protection from the elements, or from baggage-handling damage while traveling, is the hard case. Made from high-impact plastics or metal, these cases are sealed against water and dust and have padded interiors to prevent equipment damage.

Camera Carrying Methods

When a photo opportunity suddenly arises, a camera in a bag or backpack is not of much use. For this reason, and for convenience, most people prefer to carry a camera in a way that allows immediate use, **Figure 4-32**.

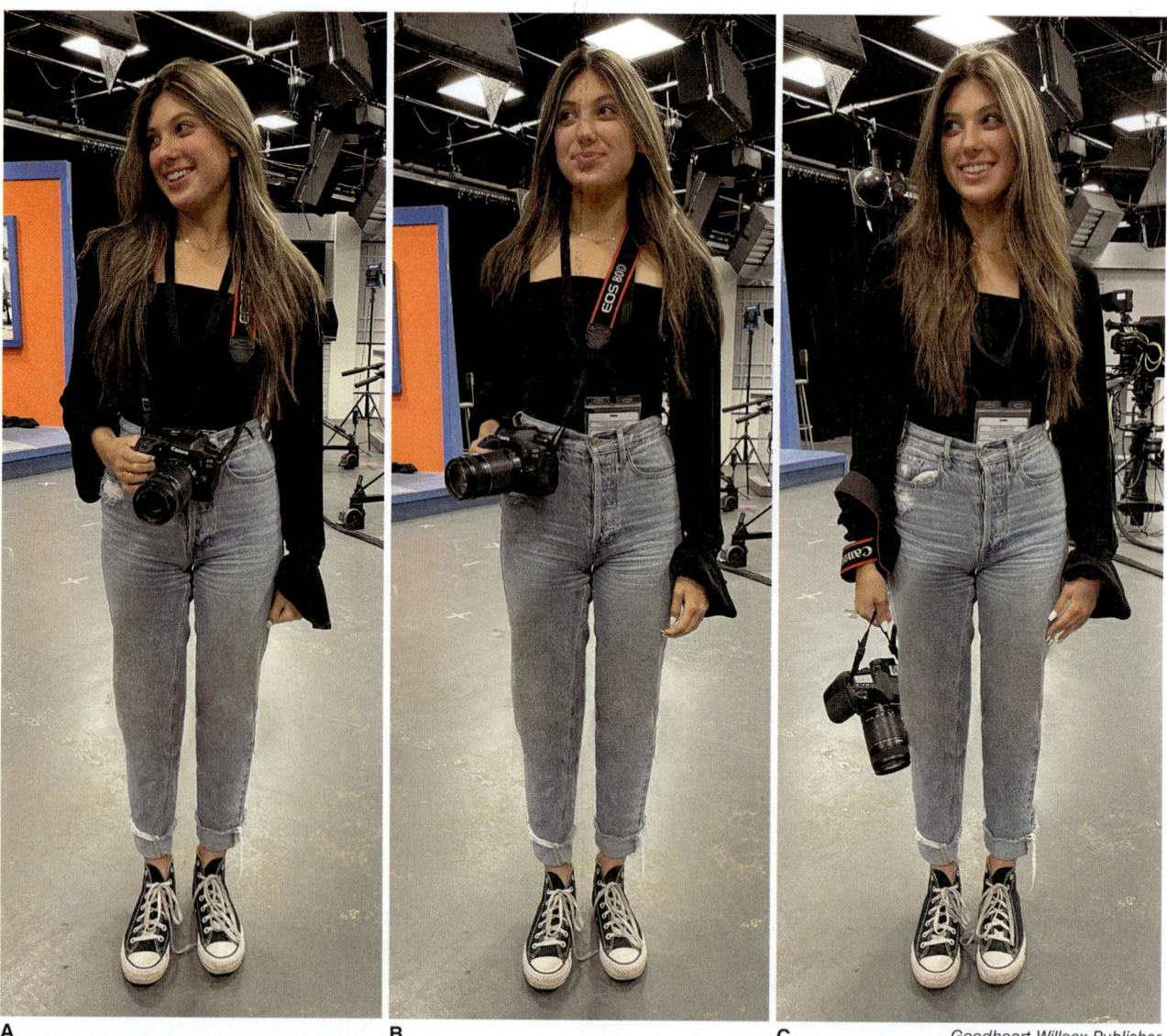

Figure 4-32. Camera carrying methods for a DSLR. A—One way is to have the strap around the neck and the camera in front of the body. B—Another way is to have one arm through the strap, with the camera between the arm and body. C—A final way is to hold the camera in one hand, with the strap looped around the wrist for safety.

DSLRs and similar-size cameras are usually carried with a strap around your neck and the camera resting on the front of your body somewhere between the chest and the waist, **Figure 4-32A**. The camera can be lifted into position quickly for a picture. One drawback to this method (especially with a longer zoom lens attached) is the free-swinging movement of the camera. Some photographers also dislike the constant bouncing of the equipment against their bodies as they walk.

Two variations of the neck strap carry can overcome these problems. In **Figure 4-32B**, your arm is inserted through the strap, so the camera rests between that arm and the side of your body. Arm pressure keeps the camera from bouncing or swinging as you walk. The other variation is to place the strap on one shoulder rather than around your neck and carry the camera between your arm and body. Either variation allows the camera to be brought into shooting position easily.

Used by some photographers who find the neck strap uncomfortable, a less secure method is to carry the camera in one hand, with the strap looped around the wrist, **Figure 4-32C**. This provides some degree of safety if the camera slips out of your hand.

Compact cameras and camera phones are often carried in a pocket, purse, or small case clipped to the belt. If it has a wrist strap, a camera or camera phone can be carried in the hand with a strap used for safety. Allowing a camera to swing free, supported only by the wrist strap, is poor practice because the camera could be damaged by striking a hard object.

Camera Support Methods

Two kinds of blur that can be seen in photographs are those caused by subject motion and those caused by camera movement. Camera support methods and devices are used to avoid blur by holding the camera motionless during the vital period when the shutter is open. That period may range from a fraction of a second to minutes. The camera to be supported might be a tiny point-and-shoot weighing a few ounces or a large studio view camera weighing several pounds.

Hand-Holding a Camera

Poor hand-holding technique is the most common cause of blur due to camera movement. When proper methods are used, the human body can be an effective camera support, allowing photos to be taken at fairly slow shutter speeds.

Effective hand-holding begins with using the correct grip. The camera should be held with both hands in a firm but relaxed grip. Clenching the camera body too tightly is tiring and more likely to make your hands shake. Most professionals recommend holding a DSLR camera as shown in **Figure 4-33**. Use the fingers and palm of your right hand to grip the right end of the camera, leaving the index finger free to press the shutter release.

Cradle the lens with the fingers of your left hand, allowing the left side of the camera's baseplate (bottom) to rest on the heel of your left palm. This provides support for the weight of the camera and allows you to use your fingers to rotate the lens barrel for manual focusing or zooming.

Your head is also part of the camera support system. When the camera is held horizontally, the back should be pressed lightly against your nose and cheek as you look through the viewfinder, **Figure 4-33A**. In the vertical position, your forehead and nose help to hold the camera steady, **Figure 4-33B**.

Proper positioning of your arms and good breath control provide additional steadiness. When holding the camera horizontally, tuck your elbows in against your sides. Like your handgrip on the camera, elbow pressure should be firm but light—pressing too hard can cause you to shake. If you are using the vertical position, only one elbow will be tucked into your side. If you are moving while shooting, such as when following a moving subject, rotate from your waist, not from your shoulders. This will allow for smoother movement, which will help prevent any shakiness in your final photo.

Most people who take photos with a digital compact camera, and some who shoot with DSLRs, use the LCD screen to compose their shots. To see the LCD, the camera must be held a comfortable distance away from the eye, **Figure 4-34**. For steadiness, arm positions should be the same as those used for DSLRs. Compact cameras are often gripped with the thumb and index finger of both hands. Holding the camera one-handed or at arm's length can cause camera shake, although this method is commonly successful when shooting selfies with a camera phone, **Figure 4-35**.

When you are ready to make an exposure with any handheld camera, take a deep breath, then exhale about half of it, otherwise the camera can shake and ruin your image. Press the shutter release with a light, steady movement of your index finger. Jabbing the shutter release with a quick, sharp movement will almost always cause camera blur.

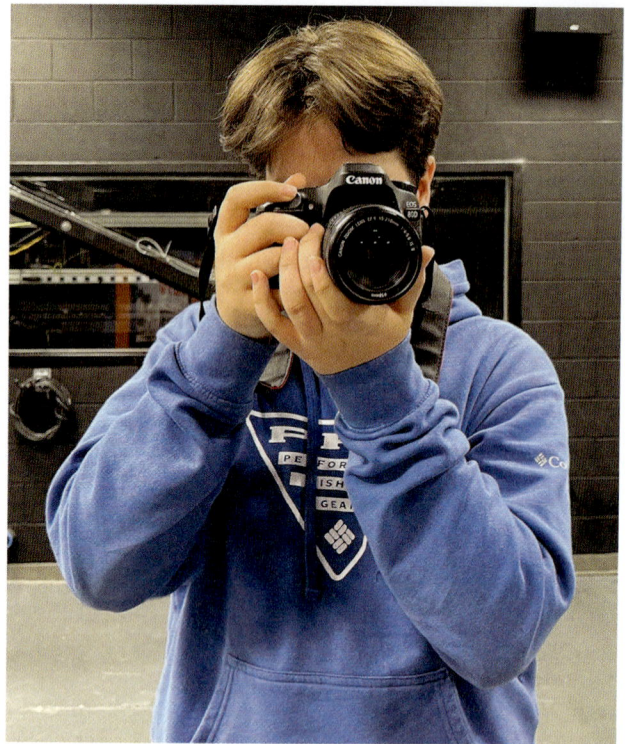

A

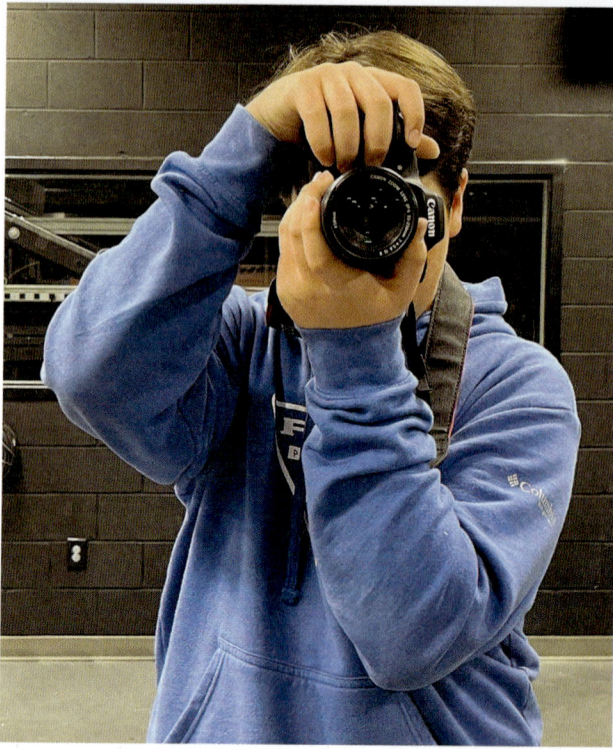

B

Goodheart-Willcox Publisher

Figure 4-33. Holding a DSLR camera. A—A horizontal camera position. B—A vertical camera position.

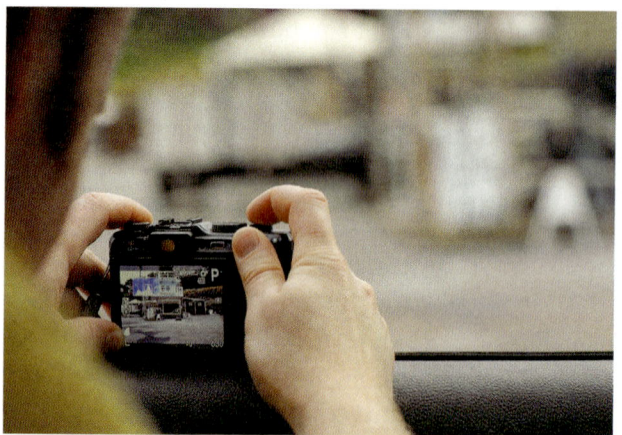

Logoboom/Shutterstock.com

Figure 4-34. Compact camera shooters most often use the LCD as a viewfinder, extending their arms to obtain a good view.

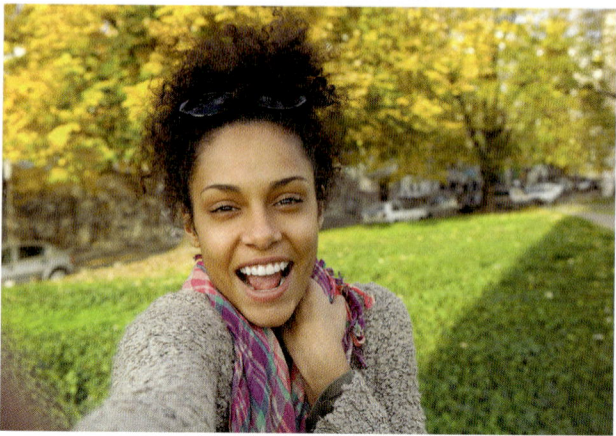

Mimagephotography/Shutterstock.com

Figure 4-35. The popular selfie is typically shot with the camera held in one hand at arm's length. Care must be taken to avoid blurring from camera shake.

At times, you may be taking photos from a sitting, kneeling, or lying position. **Figure 4-36** shows methods of properly supporting the camera when using these positions to achieve more creative camera angles.

In general, keep the camera strap around your neck. This will not only help prevent the camera from falling, as mentioned previously, but it will also provide you with some stability when shooting. For both your protection and the camera's protection, do not remove the strap from around your neck unless absolutely necessary. This is especially important when you are just starting out and becoming accustomed to taking photos.

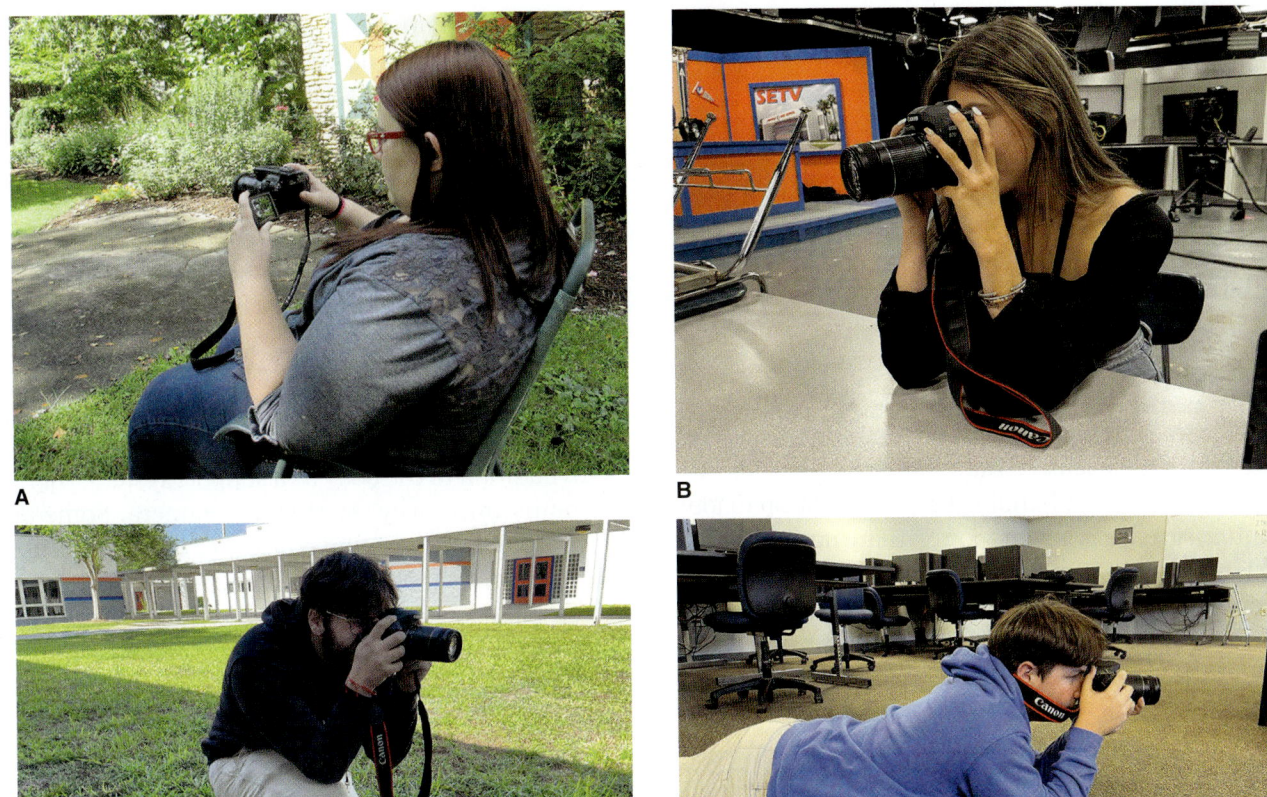

Figure 4-36. Additional methods for steadying a camera. A—Use chair arms for support while sitting. B—Place your elbows on a table or other support surface when sitting, standing, or kneeling. C—Rest one elbow on your thigh when in a kneeling position. D—Use your chest and elbows as the three legs of a tripod when lying on your stomach.

Shutter Speeds for Hand-Holding

The slowest practical shutter speed for most people is 1/30 second. Very few can achieve acceptable results at 1/15 second. Those speeds, however, are with 50 mm or shorter lenses. As focal lengths increase, shutter speeds for hand-holding must become faster. Digital cameras display a flashing "shake warning" in the viewfinder when the speed is too slow for a hand-held exposure.

The denominator, or bottom number, of the shutter speed fraction should be larger than the focal length of the lens to decrease the chance for camera movement. For example, if you are using a 100 mm lens, your shutter speed should be 1/125 second or higher. If you are using a 300 mm lens, shoot at 1/500 second or faster since the 1/500 value is the largest number close to 300. There are both physical and optical reasons for this practice.

Physically, longer focal length lenses extend farther from the camera and are often heavier than short lenses, making them harder to hold steady. Optically, you are dealing with a magnified image of a distant object, so any movement is exaggerated. See **Figure 4-37**. Additionally, the longer your shutter is open, the more likely it is that you will have some camera shake blurring in your final images.

By selecting a shutter speed that is appropriate for the focal length you are using, you improve your chances of overcoming the effects of lens weight and exaggerated movement. The faster shutter speed is a thinner slice of time, capturing the image before movement is detectable.

The introduction of anti-shake or stabilizing systems in digital cameras has made it easier to avoid camera shake when hand-holding. ***Stabilizing systems*** are methods used to control camera shake that causes blurry photos. Some stabilizing systems are

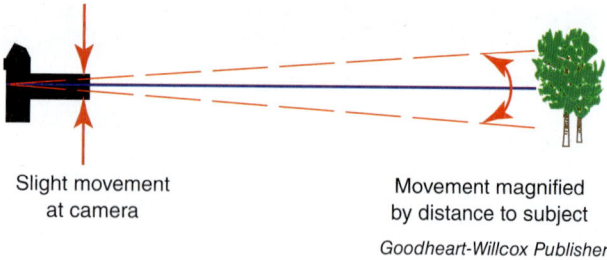

Slight movement at camera

Movement magnified by distance to subject

Goodheart-Willcox Publisher

Figure 4-37. When a telephoto lens is focused on a distant object, the slightest movement of the camera is greatly magnified.

specific to camera bodies, while others are specific to interchangeable lenses. Many cameras are using stabilization to permit handheld exposures at up to four shutter-speed increments lower than normally possible. With stabilization, a shot that would normally require a 1/500 second shutter speed to avoid blur from camera movement might be successfully made at a speed as low as 1/30 second. See **Figure 4-38**.

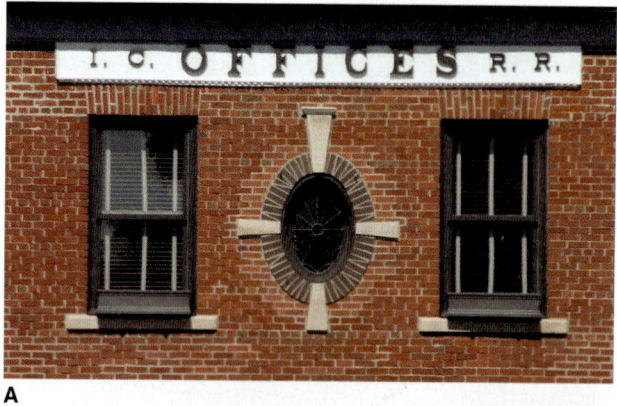

A

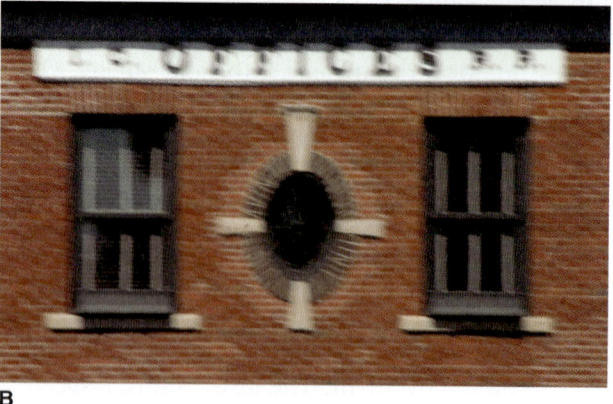

B

Jack Klasey/Goodheart-Willcox Publisher

Figure 4-38. Shots made with and without stabilization. A—This handheld exposure, made at a focal length of 460 mm with a shutter speed of 1/30 second, is very sharp with stabilization. B—Without stabilization, a handheld exposure made at the same settings shows significant blurring from camera shake.

There are two basic approaches to stabilizing images—*lens-shift* and *sensor-shift*. Both systems combat camera shake by detecting movement and making a compensating movement of a lens element or the image sensor in the opposite direction. In effect, this cancels out the unwanted movement. Even with the advantage of a faster shutter speed or anti-shake technology, using proper holding and support techniques are vital to avoid camera movement.

Camera Support Devices and Methods

In addition to the body as a support system, there are many other ways to steady a camera. Some of these provide greater convenience or comfort, while others permit shooting at shutter speeds one or two increments slower than with body support alone.

Monopods

A **monopod** is a one-legged camera support that combines improved camera support with good mobility, especially when using telephoto lenses, **Figure 4-39**. This makes monopods a favorite for those who shoot sports and similar activities. A typical monopod has three to four telescoping sections, allowing it to extend to about 5′ for use and collapse down to about 18″ for storage. All monopods have some device for mounting a camera at the top. Ideally, the mounting device should swivel and tilt to adjust the angle of the camera and be capable of being locked in place.

A monopod works in combination with the photographer's body to provide a firm and steady support. As shown in **Figure 4-40**, by spreading your feet apart slightly and then leaning into a slightly angled monopod, you can create a firm three-point support for the camera. Unlike the more cumbersome tripod, a monopod can be quickly picked up, relocated, and set up again at a different location to follow action.

Shoulder Mounts

Wildlife photographers, especially those whose subjects move rapidly and unpredictably, frequently mount their cameras on a shoulder mount, **Figure 4-41**. Since these photographers typically use lenses of 300 mm and longer, the shoulder mount helps them to better follow their target and steady the camera during exposure.

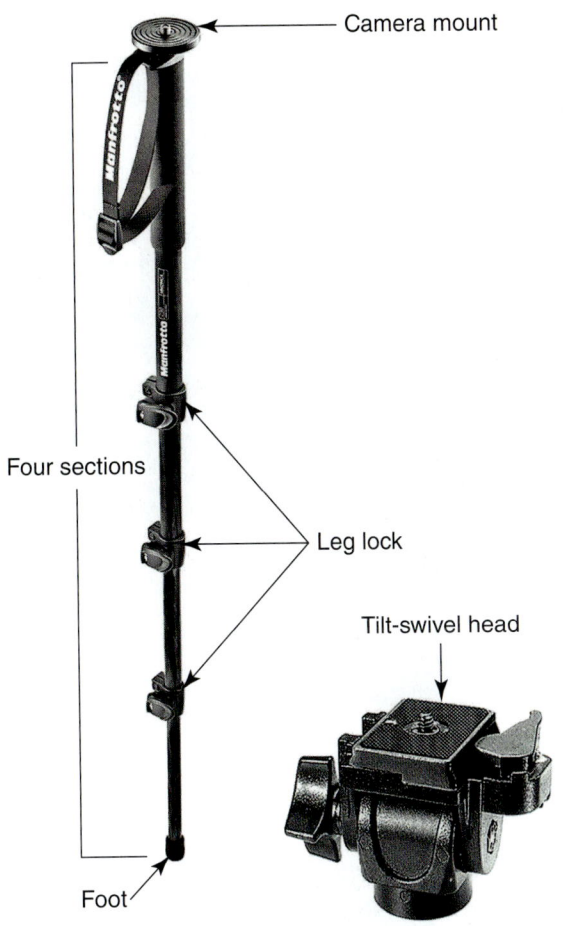

Figure 4-39. This monopod has four telescoping sections. The tilt-swivel head at lower right can be attached to the camera mount for easy leveling of the camera. The head has a quick-release plate and mechanism.

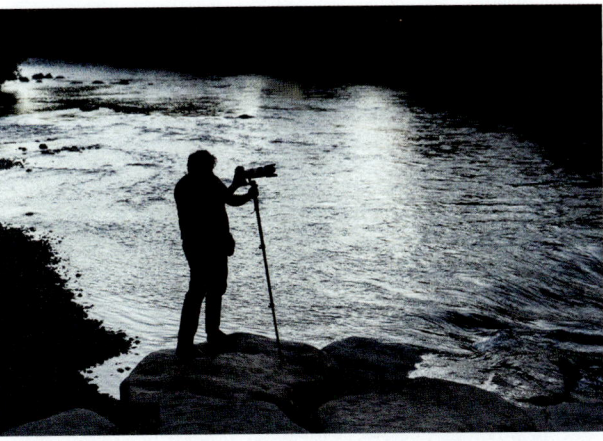

Figure 4-40. By forming a three-point support with the monopod and their two legs, the photographer provides a steady camera platform. This is a particular advantage when using a longer lens, which magnifies unwanted movement.

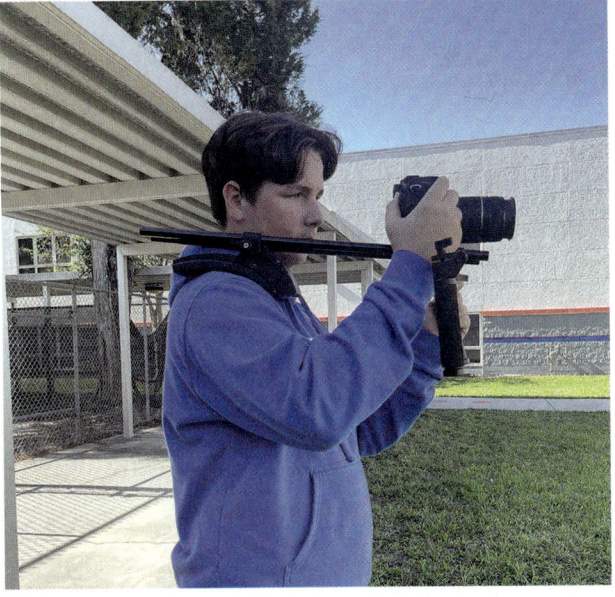

Figure 4-41. When a camera with a heavy telephoto lens is used to photograph birds and similar types of fast-moving subjects, the shoulder mount is a handy accessory.

Clamping Devices

One of the most widely used types of clamping support devices is the vehicle window clamp, **Figure 4-42**. Since wild creatures frequently allow a car or truck to approach them more closely than a human on foot, window clamps are the mount of choice for this type of photography. Before shooting, the vehicle engine must be shut off to eliminate vibration.

Other clamping devices permit mounting a camera on various supports ranging from door edges and chair backs to walls or tables, fence rails, pipes, or tree limbs, **Figure 4-43**. These devices must include some form of camera mount that can be rotated and adjusted for proper leveling.

Beanbags and Onsite Supports

A beanbag is a small pillow-shaped cloth bag filled with dry beans, rice, or similar materials. A beanbag can be placed on a surface, and it can conform to the shape of the camera or lens. The support provided is firm enough that even a time exposure can be made if a shutter release or the camera's

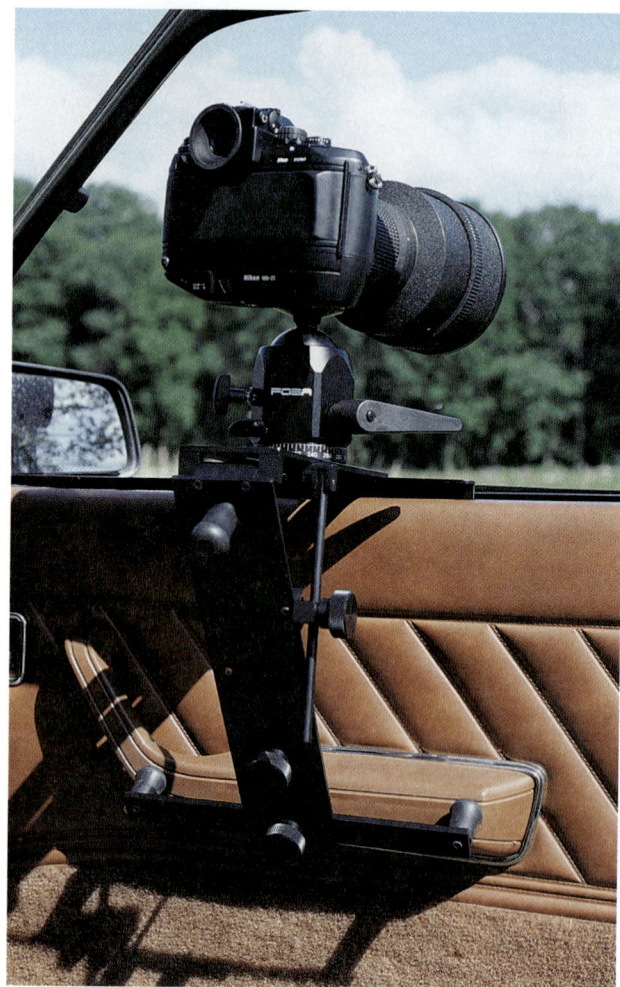

Leonard Rue Enterprises

Figure 4-42. This window clamp, called the Groofwin Pod™, is designed for use as a ground-level camera support, a window clamp, or a support on a car or truck roof for large-animal photography.

self-timer is used to trip the shutter. **Figure 4-44** shows a beanbag, as well as the use of typical onsite supports. These are surfaces that can be used to rest the camera on or against to provide extra support and steadiness.

Tripods

The best type of camera support is a sturdy and well-made tripod. A ***tripod*** is a three-legged camera support in which each leg's length is independently adjustable, allowing it to be firmly set in place on almost any kind of terrain. When mounted atop the tripod, the camera can be adjusted to the desired orientation and locked in position. Exposures of any length can be made with little danger of camera movement. Tripods are manufactured in many sizes, from small tabletop models to large, heavy units suitable only for studio use.

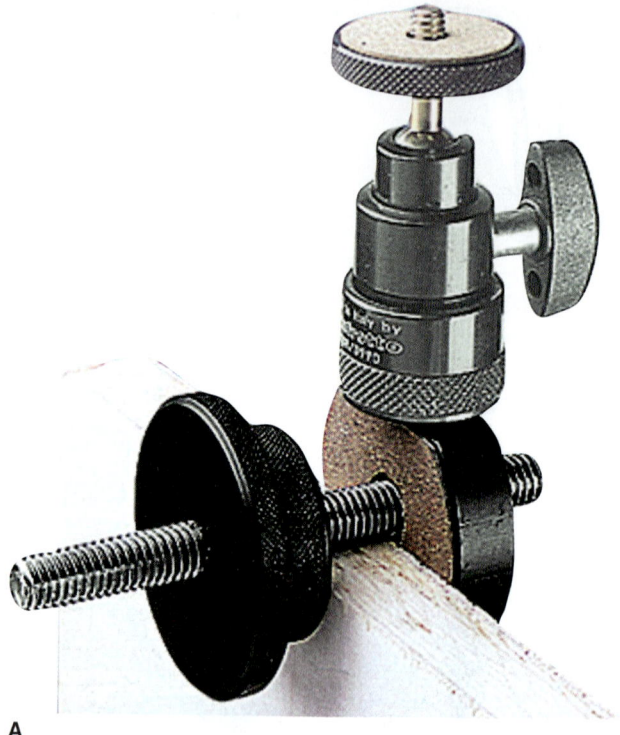

A

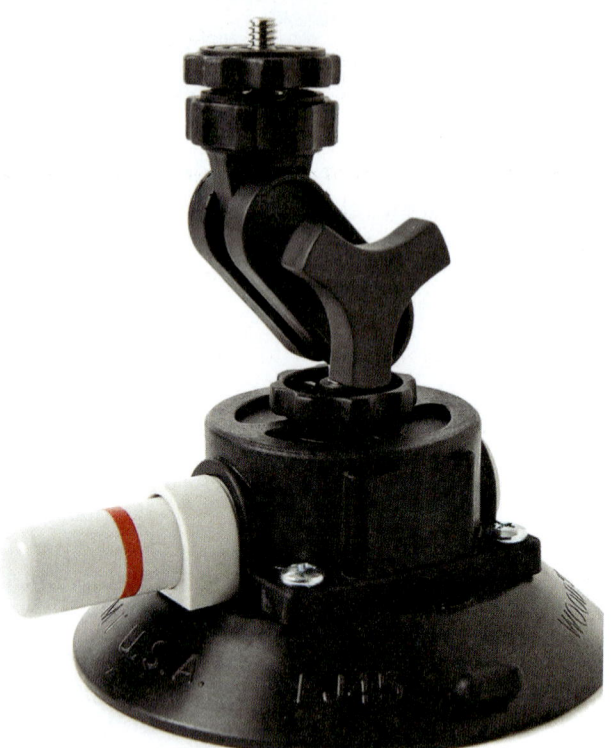

B

Manfrotto; Tether Tools

Figure 4-43. Clamping devices for mounting cameras. A—This clamp with a ball head can be used on chair backs, doors, table edges, or similar surfaces. B—For flat nonporous surfaces, including walls, ceilings, windows, and even vehicle bodies, a vacuum clamp provides strong and secure camera support.

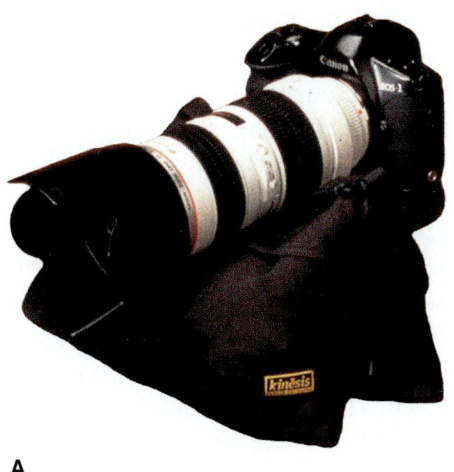

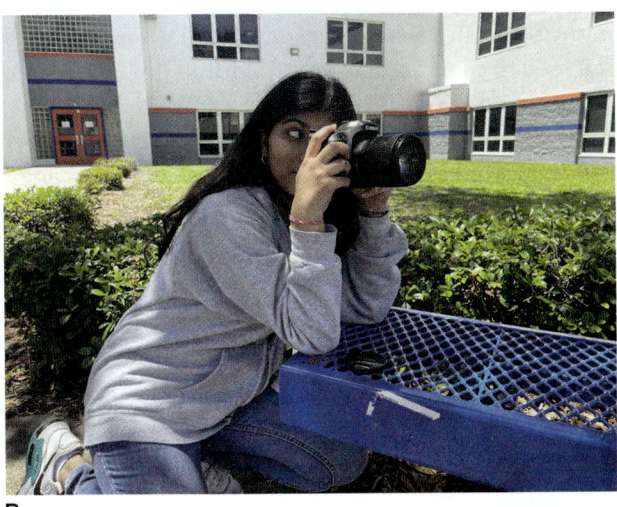

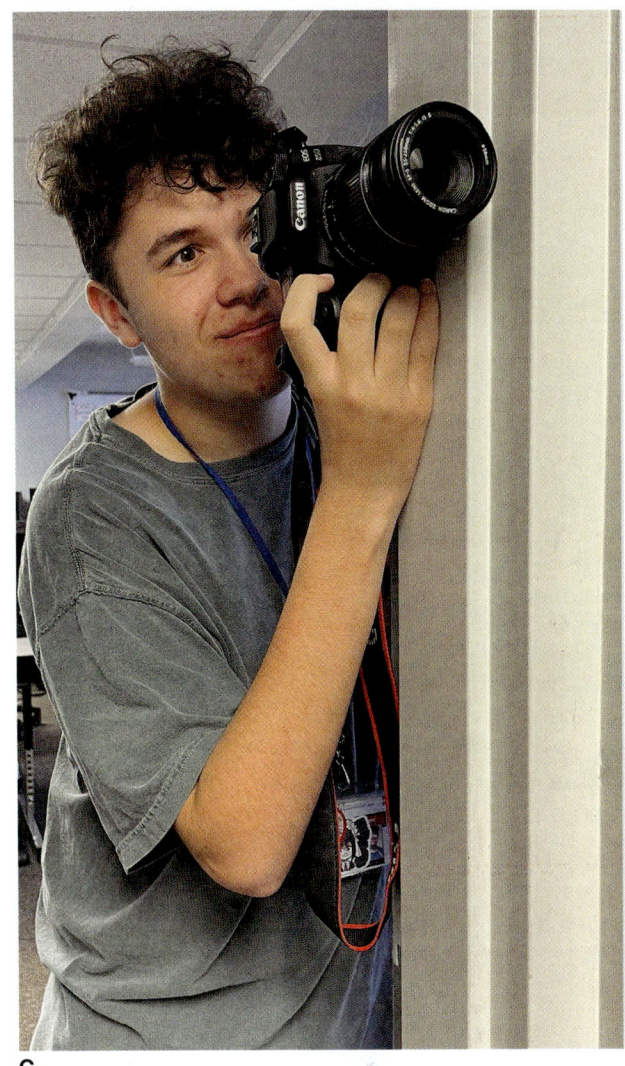

A: Kinesis
B and C: Goodheart-Willcox Publisher

Figure 4-44. Camera support techniques. A—A beanbag filled with beans, polystyrene beads, sand, or water holds a camera steady enough to make a time exposure. B—Resting a camera on a firm surface helps to avoid movement. C—Extra support can be obtained by pressing the camera against a solid structure, such as a post, doorframe, wall, or tree.

Basic components of the tripod are identified in **Figure 4-45**. They consist of the following:

- *Quick-release mechanism*: Part of the tripod head, this mechanism allows rapid dismounting and remounting of the camera.
- *Tripod head*: This is the device that connects the tripod to the camera and allows various degrees of rotation.
- *Center column or centerpost*: This is a vertical shaft used on some tripods that can be extended and locked in place.
- *Leg-locking mechanism*: Each leg section needs one of these to hold it at the desired amount of extension.
- *Telescoping leg sections*: Each leg section can be extended independently.
- *Nonslip feet*: Most feet are rubber for use on smooth or hard surfaces. Some feet can retract to expose spikes for a better grip on soft surfaces.

Traditionally, tripods have been made of aluminum or well-seasoned wood to strike a balance between sturdiness and weight. In recent years, carbon fiber reinforced polymer (CFRP), a material with an excellent strength-to-weight ratio, has become popular.

Tripod Legs

Since photographers have different needs and tastes in tripod heads, better-quality tripods are

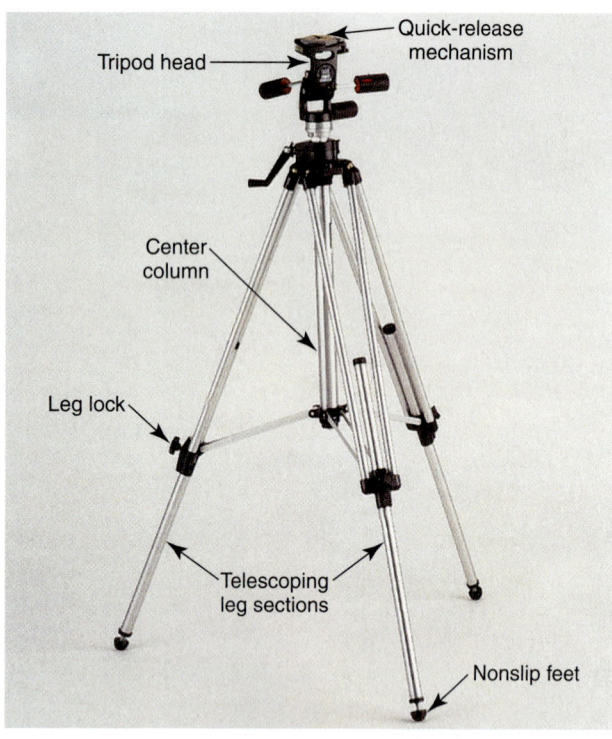

Manfrotto

Figure 4-45. A sturdy tripod is the best camera support available. The basic parts of a tripod are shown here.

typically sold as legs-only, **Figure 4-46**. Although there are several leg patterns, the most common type consists of three or four tubular sections nesting inside each other. The locking mechanism is usually either a lever-type or a collar that is rotated to lock or release the section. When fully closed, legs are usually 18″ to 24″ in length, although some large, heavy-duty tripods may be more than 3′ long when closed. Fully extended, the tripod may be less than 5′ in height, or more than 8′. A practical height for most photographers is between 5 1/2′ and 6′, without the centerpost extended. This height allows the camera to be placed at a comfortable eye-level position.

Tripod Heads

The device attached to the tripod legs to allow mounting and positioning of a camera is typically referred to as a *tripod head*. Depending on the method used for positioning the camera, tripod heads can be classified into one of two general categories—*pan heads* and *ball heads*.

A **pan head** allows you to move the camera in either two or three axes. As shown in **Figure 4-47**, a two-axis head can tilt the camera forward or

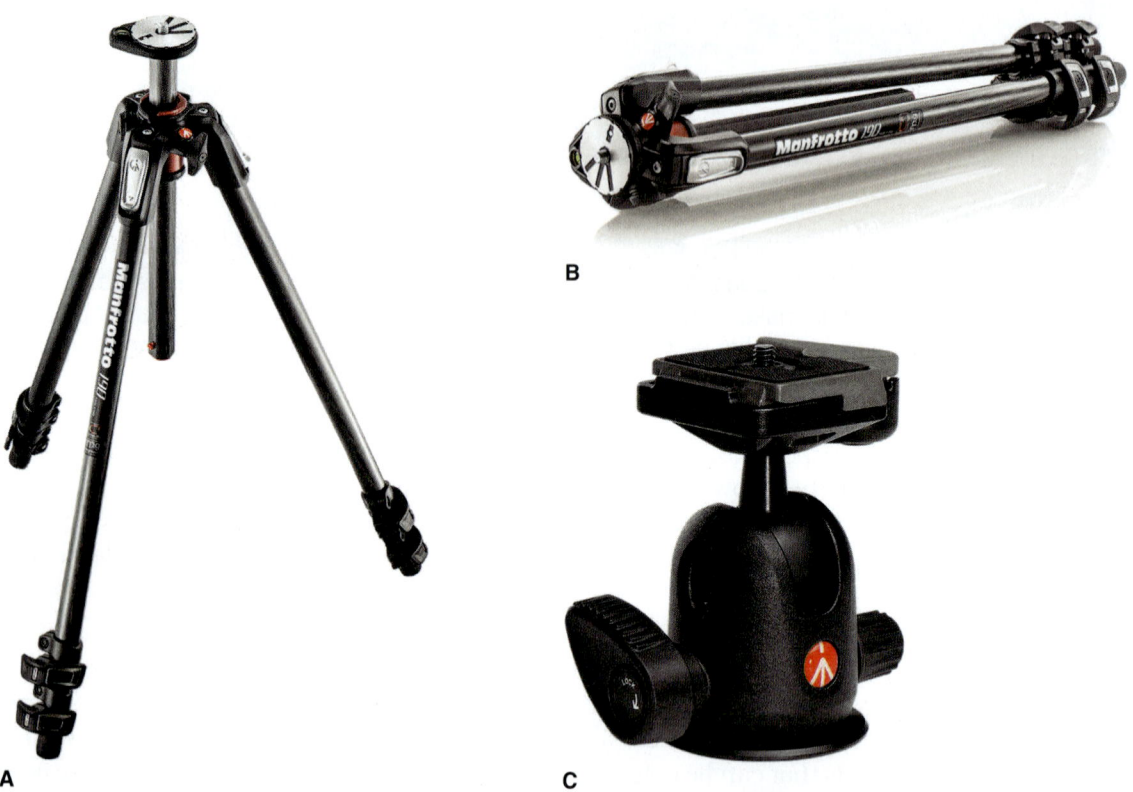

Manfrotto

Figure 4-46. Tripod legs. A—This set of tripod legs is made from strong, lightweight carbon fiber. With the centerpost extended, its height is almost 6′. B—For storage or transportation, the legs can be folded down to only 15″. C—For positioning a camera, a tripod head must be attached to the legs.

backward or pan from side-to-side. A pan-tilt head, or a three-axis head, allows tilting from side to side as well as forward and back. A variation of the pan-tilt head, the gearhead uses gears rotated with cranks or knobs to achieve even greater precision of movement.

Although they provide excellent control of the camera's positioning, pan-tilt heads are rather cumbersome and slow to operate. Many photographers have switched to a **ball head**, which uses a single control to lock the camera in position, **Figure 4-48**. A typical ball head has a camera platform attached to a highly polished metal sphere contained in a housing. When a locking device, such as a lever or knob, is released, the ball can be rotated 360° and tilted through an arc of 180°, providing quick and almost infinitely adjustable positioning.

Quick-release systems built into many tripod heads are convenient for photographers because they allow a camera to be quickly mounted or dismounted without changing any position adjustments. The two components of the quick-release system are a special mounting plate fastened to the camera and a latching mechanism that is attached to the tripod head. See **Figure 4-49**. A lever or spring control on the latching mechanism allows the mounting plate and camera to be quickly installed or released.

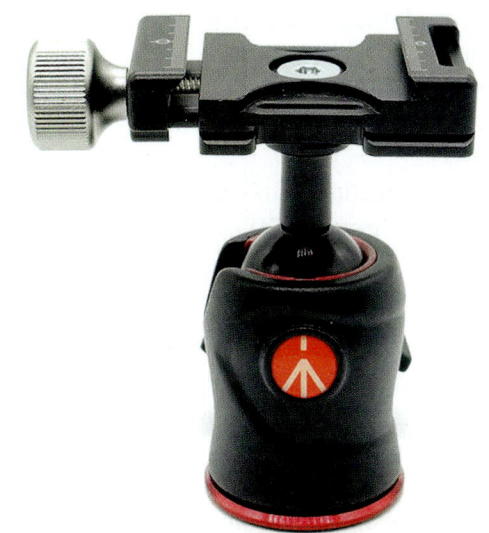

James McDowall/Shutterstock.com

Figure 4-48. A typical ball head camera platform.

Tripod Advantages and Disadvantages

Some photographers make virtually every exposure with a camera mounted on a tripod, while others use tripods rarely, if at all. The type of camera and the type of photography determine whether using a tripod will be an advantage or disadvantage.

Common reasons for using a tripod include the following:

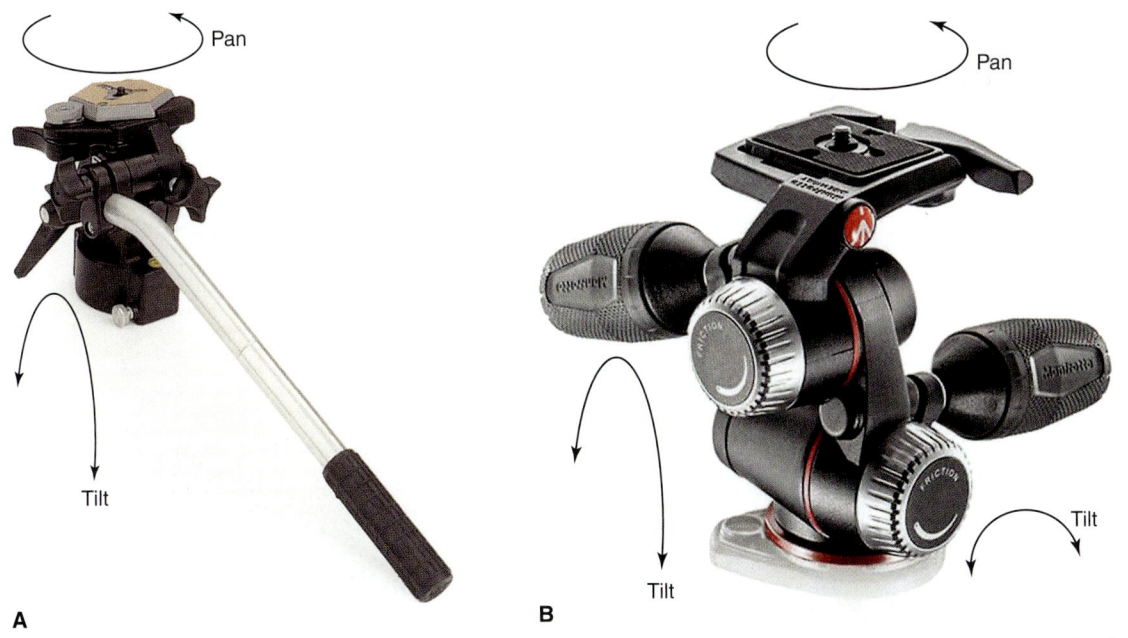

Manfrotto

Figure 4-47. Pan head operation. A—The two-axis head is able to pan (turn) horizontally and tilt forward or backward. Usually, a single handle is used to control movement in both axes. B—The three-axis head can move in a third plane, tilting from side to side. Separate controls are used to adjust and lock each axis.

- Improved image sharpness through elimination of camera shake
- Precise camera positioning for better composition
- Long-exposure capability due to rigid and steady support
- Freeing your hands to shade the lens or hold a reflector, **Figure 4-50**

Common reasons for *not* using a tripod include the following:

- Weight and cumbersome shape, especially when the tripod must be carried some distance
- Time-consuming setup and resulting lack of mobility
- Possible tripping hazard to others in confined areas (many museums ban tripods for this reason)

Choosing a Tripod

Your camera type and the kind of photography you undertake are major factors when choosing a tripod. Consider the following questions when choosing a tripod:

- *How much weight must the tripod support?* A compact digital camera weighs only a few ounces. Most DSLR cameras with a zoom lens attached weigh a pound or more. Many medium format cameras will be in the 4 lb to 6 lb range, while the large format field and studio cameras may weigh as little as 8 lb or more than 20 lb.

- *How much does the tripod weigh?* If you are carrying your tripod any distance at all, its weight can be a major consideration, especially when combined with a heavy camera bag. Aluminum tripods suitable for use in the field typically weigh anywhere from 3 lb to 10 lb, while carbon fiber units with matching capacities will be approximately 30% lighter. For use with a DSLR or medium format equipment, a tripod in the 5 lb to 6 lb range is usually a good choice. It represents a good compromise between sturdiness and weight. The lighter (3 lb–4 lb) tripods are a good choice for photographers who backpack for considerable distances. The trade-off, of course, is that they are not as sturdy.

- *How well made is the tripod?* To provide a solid support for your camera, a tripod must be strong and rigid, even when fully extended. Leg-locking mechanisms should operate smoothly but hold the leg position securely. If the tripod has a centerpost, it should move up and down smoothly, without binding, and lock firmly in position. The tripod should have nonslip feet made of rubber, not plastic. Retractable spikes

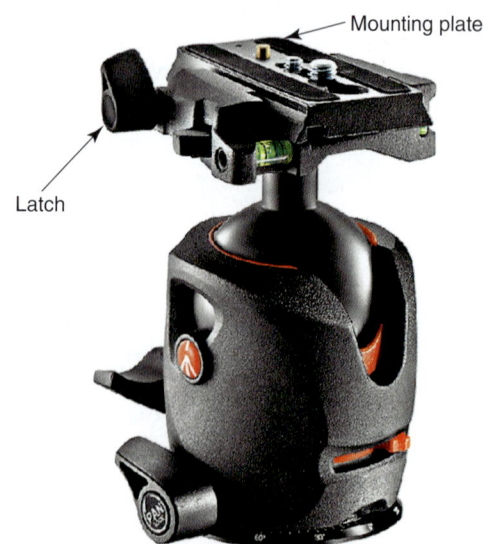

Manfrotto

Figure 4-49. Quick-release systems consist of a mounting plate that attaches to the camera body and fits into a latching mechanism on the tripod head. Some quick-release systems include mounting plates custom-made for use with specific camera models.

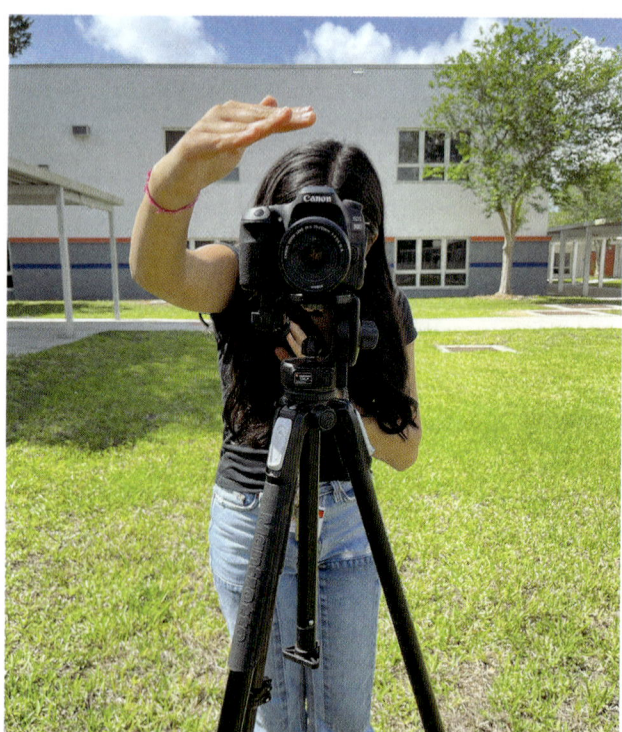

Goodheart-Willcox Publisher

Figure 4-50. Placing the camera on a tripod leaves your hands free for other tasks, such as using a card, hand, or cap to prevent flare from light from falling directly on the lens.

for soft surfaces are a desirable feature. The tripod head should be sturdily made, and all controls should operate smoothly and positively.

Using a Tripod

When setting up a tripod, extend it to full height unless you know you will be shooting from a lower vantage point. Fully extend and lock the bottom leg sections. Follow suit with the middle sections, then spread the legs and stand the tripod on the ground or floor.

Position the legs so one of the three is pointing toward the subject, **Figure 4-51**. This provides you with more working room between the two legs to the rear, and it adds some support and rigidity beneath the extended lens.

Make any necessary leg height or angle adjustments. Try to avoid extending the centerpost more than a few inches—the taller the centerpost extension, the greater the danger of *shutter shock*, or the vibration that comes from a camera's shutter mechanism when it is activated. Adjust the tripod head to properly position the camera and frame the subject. Long, heavy telephoto lenses usually need additional support, such as the special mounting brackets shown in **Figure 4-52**.

For maximum sharpness, eliminate all possible causes of camera movement, even vibrations caused while opening the shutter. If your camera offers mirror lockup, use that feature to eliminate possible vibration caused by the viewing mirror flipping up out of the light path when the shutter release is pressed. Use a shutter release or the camera's self-timer to trip the shutter.

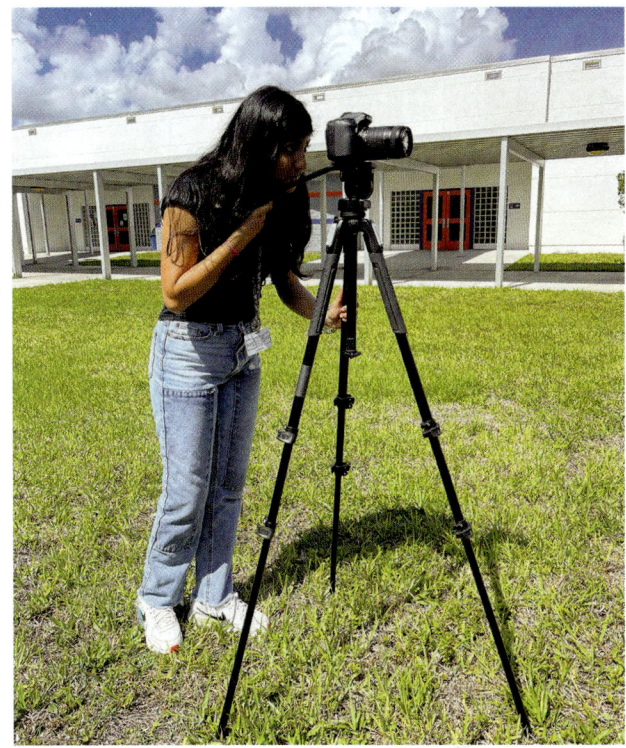

Goodheart-Willcox Publisher

Figure 4-51. When properly set up, a tripod should have one leg pointing toward the subject.

Camera movement can be caused by wind, especially if it comes in intermittent gusts. The classic solution to this problem is to suspend a weight, such as a heavy camera bag, from the tripod to provide greater stability. Some photographers use a container made from canvas or a similar strong fabric and fill it with rocks or sand at the site.

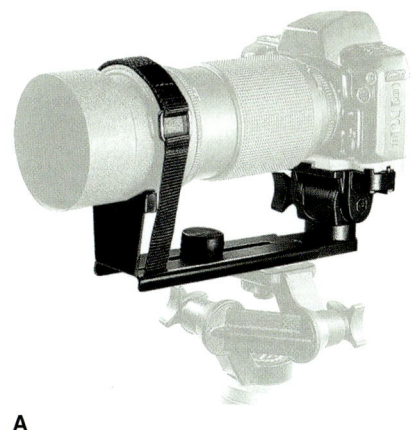

A

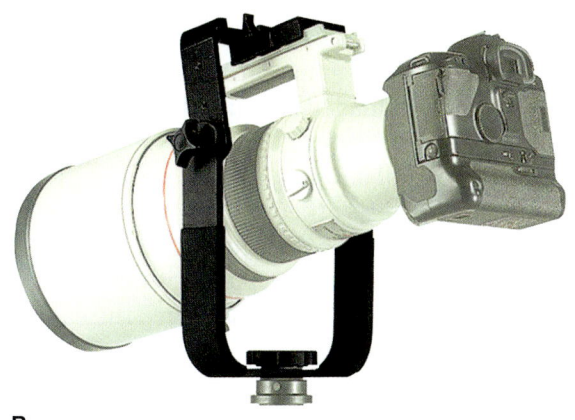

B

Manfrotto

Figure 4-52. Longer telephoto lenses are usually mounted with a tripod collar or some form of bracket to steady them and prevent their weight from placing stress on the camera body's lens mount. A—This mount features a support for the front of the lens and a strap to hold the lens firmly in place. B—This bracket provides adjustable support for a long, heavy lens.

Chapter 4 Review

Summary

- Being prepared and knowing how your camera works before you take on a shoot will help you avoid losing a picture opportunity.
- Some people learn about a new camera by simply experimenting with various controls, while others virtually memorize the owner's manual before using the camera. A good method is to blend both approaches.
- Digital cameras have a number of common physical attributes and controls. Common ones include a power button/switch, shutter release, viewfinder, menu button, view button, erase button, histogram/exposure display, on-board (built-in) flash, lens release, mode dial, focus lock/exposure lock, exposure lock/zoom button, focus point selector/zoom button, and aperture selector/exposure compensation button.
- Digital cameras have several digital controls and features accessed through the camera's display. Common controls and features include exposure mode selection, exposure compensation, exposure numbering, ISO selection, depth of field preview, burst mode, white balance, image quality (resolution/compression) settings, and color space selection.
- Cameras and lenses are precision instruments that can be damaged by rough handling or by exposure to water, dust, sand, or other environmental dangers. There are various methods to protect them from damage.
- Keeping equipment clean helps to minimize wear and damage and makes the equipment easier to use. It is important to keep the camera body, viewfinder, and sensor clean.
- If you plan to take photographs at locations other than your home or studio, you must have some way to transport your equipment, such as a camera bag or backpack.
- DSLRs and similar-size cameras are usually carried with a strap around your neck and the camera resting on the front of your body somewhere between the chest and the waist. Compact cameras and camera phones are often carried in a pocket, purse, or small case clipped to the belt.
- Poor hand-holding technique is the most common cause of blur due to camera movement.
- In addition to the body as a support system, there are many other ways to steady a camera. Some common support systems are monopods, clamping devices, and beanbags.
- A tripod is a three-legged camera support in which each leg's length is independently adjustable, allowing it to be firmly set in place on almost any kind of terrain.
- Since photographers have different needs and tastes in tripod heads, better-quality tripods are typically sold as legs-only.
- The device attached to the tripod legs to allow mounting and positioning of a camera is typically referred to as a tripod head. They can be classified as a pan head or a ball head.
- The type of camera and the type of photography determine whether using a tripod will be an advantage or disadvantage.
- Your camera type and the kind of photography you undertake are major factors when choosing a tripod.
- When setting up a tripod, extend it to full height unless you know you will be shooting from a lower vantage point.

Review Questions

Answer the following questions using the information provided in this chapter.

Know and Understand

1. *True or False?* The best way to learn about a new camera is by simply experimenting with various controls.

2. _____ is a delay between pressing the shutter button and the actual opening of the shutter.
   A. Shutter priority
   B. Tethered shutter release
   C. Shutter lag
   D. Untethered shutter release

3. The _____ allows you to quickly evaluate composition and exposure and determine whether an image is worth keeping or should be reshot.
   A. histogram
   B. exposure compensation
   C. viewfinder
   D. depth of field (DOF) preview

4. *True or False?* The menu button allows you to access the camera's internal menu functions on the camera's viewfinder.

5. *True or False?* In a histogram, peaks indicate a large number of pixels.

6. A(n) _____ is a flash mounting terminal often located on top of a DSLR.
   A. histogram
   B. untethered release
   C. hot shoe
   D. tethered release

7. *True or False?* Focus lock is useful for shooting subjects that are backlit.

8. The advantage of using _____ is the ability to control depth of field.
   A. aperture priority
   B. Program AE
   C. shutter priority
   D. manual exposure

9. _____ is an exposure mode in which the photographer chooses the aperture, shutter speed, and ISO.
   A. Program AE
   B. Aperture priority
   C. Shutter priority
   D. Manual exposure

10. Which of the following is *not* a typical preset exposure mode?
    A. Portrait
    B. Nature
    C. Night scene
    D. Sports

11. *True or False?* Image quality declines as the ISO rating increases.

12. The _____ control is a camera feature that allows the photographer to see what the scene will look like at the desired aperture and assess the actual depth of field.
    A. exposure compensation
    B. depth of field (DOF) preview
    C. ISO
    D. focus lock

13. *True or False?* In a burst mode, the number of possible exposures is the same for all camera models.

14. _____ is a method of adjusting how the camera sees a white object.
    A. Manual exposure
    B. sRGB
    C. Burst mode
    D. White balance

15. *True or False?* Only certain DSLR cameras have the ability to shoot in RAW.

16. The _____ color space reproduces more vividly for viewing on a computer monitor.
    A. Adobe RGB
    B. Program AE
    C. sRGB
    D. burst mode

17. *True or False?* A large plastic bag can serve as emergency protection for your camera from wet weather.

18. *True or False?* To keep dust out of the camera body, always turn the camera on before changing lenses.

19. A(n) _____ is screwed into place on the front of the lens to protect the front lens element from dust, salt spray, and bumps against hard objects.
    A. tethered shutter release
    B. ultraviolet (UV) filter
    C. stabilizing system
    D. untethered shutter release

20. *True or False?* If left on the lens, fingerprints can permanently etch the surface.
21. Specks of dust or lint that have settled on the camera's image sensor are most noticeable in image areas of _____ color.
    A. lighter
    B. darker
    C. neutral
    D. primary
22. When transporting a camera, the ultimate protection from the elements, or from baggage-handling damage while traveling, is the _____.
    A. photo backpack
    B. hard case
    C. camera bag
    D. neck strap
23. *True or False?* Poor hand-holding technique is the most common cause of blur due to camera movement.
24. The denominator of the shutter speed fraction should be _____ the focal length of the lens to decrease the chance for camera movement.
    A. smaller than
    B. larger than
    C. the same as
    D. The denominator does not matter.
25. A _____ is a one-legged camera support that combines improved camera support with good mobility, especially when using telephoto lenses.
    A. tripod
    B. beanbag
    C. shoulder mount
    D. monopod
26. The _____ of a tripod allows rapid dismounting and remounting of the camera.
    A. leg-locking mechanism
    B. quick-release mechanism
    C. centerpost
    D. tripod head
27. *True or False?* A ball head allows you to move the camera in either two or three axes.
28. Which of the following is a common reason for using a tripod?
    A. Time-consuming setup and resulting lack of mobility
    B. Possible tripping hazard to others in confined areas
    C. Freeing your hands to shade the lens or hold a reflector
    D. Weight and cumbersome shape
29. Which of the following is *not* a typical question to consider when choosing a tripod?
    A. How many colors does the tripod come in?
    B. How much weight must the tripod support?
    C. How much does the tripod weigh?
    D. How well made is the tripod?

Apply and Analyze

1. What is the advantage of using aperture priority?
2. Why do most professional photographers shoot in RAW?
3. Why should you always turn off the camera before changing lenses?
4. Explain the two-step process of cleaning a lens.
5. Describe the two variations of the neck strap camera carrying method.
6. What are the two kinds of blur that can be seen in photographs?
7. Name the two basic approaches to stabilizing images.
8. When setting up a tripod, what are the two reasons why you should position the legs so one of the three is pointing toward the subject?

Critical Thinking

1. You are going on a vacation to the seashore, where you will be spending time on the beach, in boats, and doing other activities that could cause damage to your camera. What different hazards might you encounter? What steps could you take to protect your equipment?
2. The exposure compensation feature found on many digital cameras allows you to increase or decrease exposure in the shutter priority, aperture priority, or Program AE exposure modes. It cannot be used in the *automatic* or *manual* exposure modes. Why do you think this feature cannot be used in those modes?

Suggested Activities

1. Using a digital camera, tablet, or smartphone that has a continuous shooting (burst mode) feature, photograph an interesting moving subject, such as a high jumper at a track meet or a skateboarder doing tricks. Review the individual shots and select three of them to show a sequence of motion. Use the slideshow feature to play back the sequence.
2. Plan and deliver to your class a short demonstration on setting up a tripod. Your demonstration should include extending and locking the tripod legs, leveling the tripod, attaching the camera, using the centerpost (if so equipped), and operating the ball head or other camera-mounting device.

Communicating about Photography

1. **Speaking and Writing.** In small groups, discuss the appropriate use of tripods and other camera support equipment. Talk about the advantages and disadvantages of using tripods in various situations. Compile a list of various photographic situations and the best camera support choice for each situation. Present your conclusions to the class.
2. **Speaking and Listening.** In groups of three students, choose a digital camera feature or control, such as the histogram or built-in flash. Explain the feature or control in a presentation to the class using visual aids. Take notes while other students give their presentations. Ask questions about any details that you would like clarified.

Chapter 5
The Camera System

Learning Objectives

After completing this chapter, you will be able to:
- Identify the three interactive systems of the camera.
- Describe various camera viewing methods.
- Understand various camera focusing methods and the differences among them.
- Explain the light control functions of the aperture and shutter.
- Identify the various types of sensors used in digital cameras.
- Recall the characteristics of the major camera types.

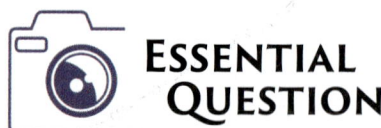

Essential Question

How does knowing the basic systems of a camera help you as a photographer?

Technical Terms

active autofocus
advanced compact digital camera
aperture
APS-C size sensor
camera
camera shake
charge-coupled device (CCD)
compact digital camera
complementary metal oxide semiconductor (CMOS)
electronic viewfinder
focal plane shutter
image receiver system
iris
large format camera
medium format camera
medium format digital camera
mirrorless camera
parallax error
passive autofocus
photosite
pixel
sensor
separate viewfinder
shutter
small format camera
subject blur
through-the-lens viewing system
trilinear array
view camera

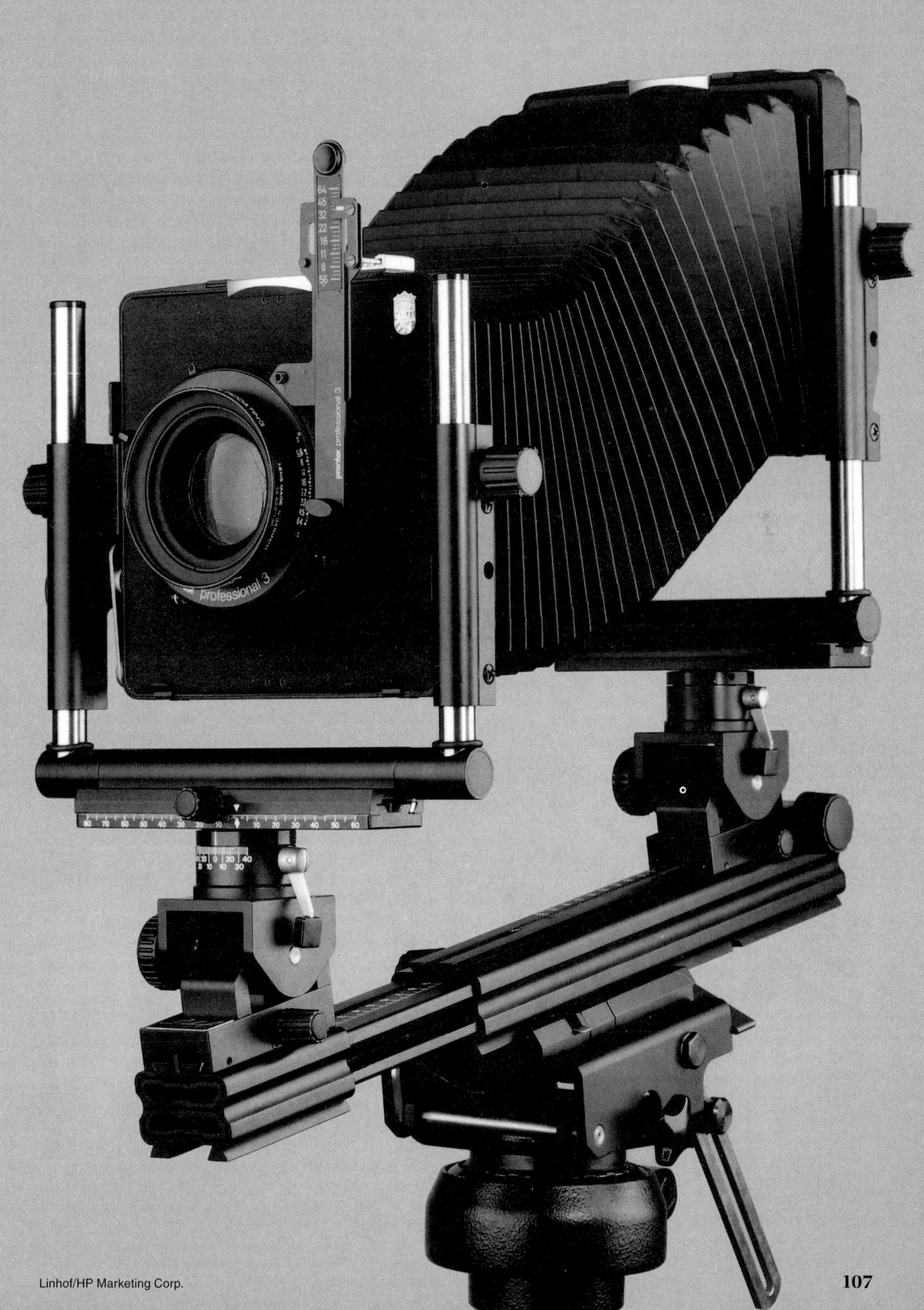

Linhof/HP Marketing Corp.

Introduction to the Camera System

A ***camera*** is a device used to capture a photographic image. In its most basic form, it is a light-tight box with a closable hole at one side and a light-sensitive material on the opposite inside surface. The camera may be simple or highly sophisticated, but it must accomplish one basic task—getting the picture. To do so, the camera must gather the light rays reflected from an object or scene and focus them on the light-sensitive material (film or an electronic sensor). That material, in turn, is affected by the light rays and captures a representation of the scene. Film records the scene as a latent image, while the sensor captures it as a digital pattern of on/off or high/low voltages that can be stored on a magnetic medium. Later, the film image can be developed and fixed for permanence. The stored electronic image can be displayed on a computer screen or printed to paper.

A camera is a device made up of three interacting systems. They are a viewing/focusing system, a light control system, and an image receiver system.

Viewing/Focusing System

When taking pictures, it is important to be able to see what your camera sees. Without the ability to see what you are shooting, it is nearly impossible to make adjustments based on the previous images you took, such as changing the focus or the framing of your shot. Thankfully, most modern cameras offer a built-in system that helps you view and focus your images.

Viewing Methods

Cameras may use a system in which the photographer views a scene or subject through the same lens that is used to take the picture or through a separate viewfinder. The most common form of ***separate viewfinder*** is a small viewing window found on cameras ranging from simple, inexpensive cameras to rangefinder models. It does not present a "through the lens" view of the subject. Another form of separate viewfinder is used on twin-lens reflex (TLR) cameras, which have one lens for viewing and focusing and another for taking the photo. See **Figure 5-1**.

While separate viewfinders work well for many situations, they can cause a problem when you take close-up photos. The problem is called ***parallax error***, and it is a mismatch in what the photographer

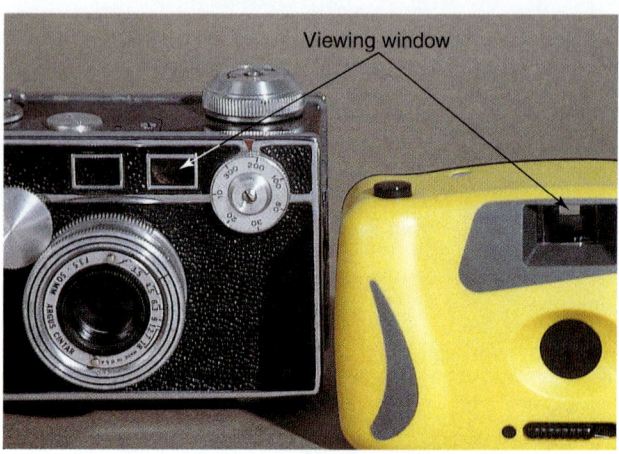

A

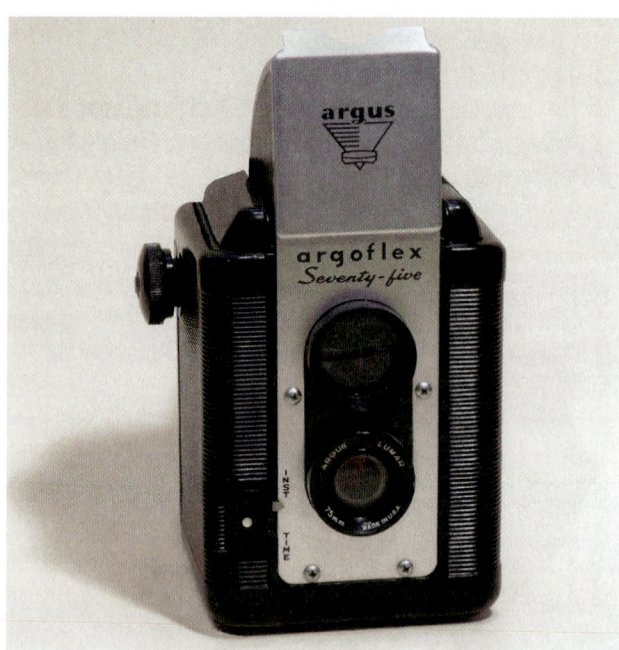

B

Jack Klasey/Goodheart-Willcox Publisher

Figure 5-1. Viewing systems. A—Rangefinder and simple cameras use a separate small viewing window. B—On a twin-lens reflex camera, the viewing lens is above the taking lens.

sees though the viewfinder and what the camera's lens sees, **Figure 5-2**. The slight difference can result in cutting off part of a subject.

On the other hand, a ***through-the-lens viewing system*** is a composing and focusing method in which the viewfinder image is the scene viewed through the camera's taking lens. For the most part, what you see in the viewfinder is the image you will get. Except for some professional models, cameras with through-the-lens viewfinders often show less of the scene than is recorded on the sensor. What you see in the viewfinder may be only 92% to 95% of what the camera records. This might not be critical for most

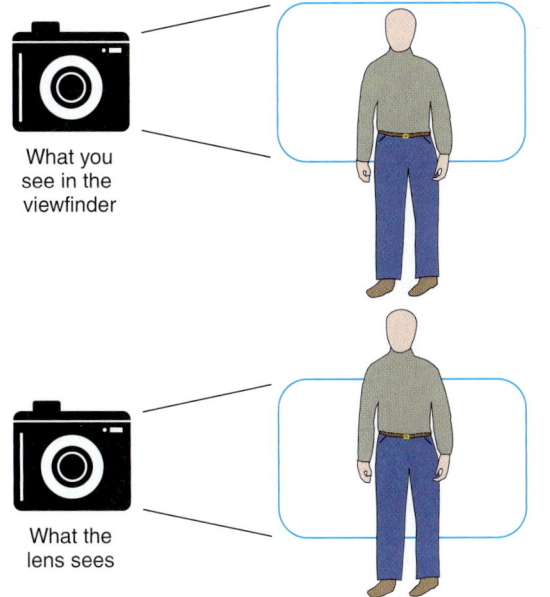

Goodheart-Willcox Publisher

Figure 5-2. Parallax error can cause part of a subject to be lost when taking a close-up photo.

photographs, but it could allow a distracting element to appear at the edge of a carefully composed picture.

Used on some digital cameras, an **electronic viewfinder** is a small LCD screen that shows the image that the camera will produce after receiving information from the camera's sensor. Instead of a mirror to reflect the scene viewed by the lens, the electronic viewfinder makes use of an LCD that shows the image that is processed from the camera's sensor, **Figure 5-3**.

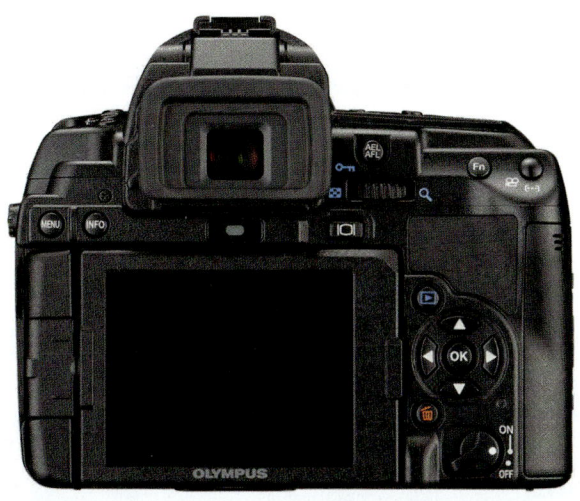

Hayk_Shalunts/Shutterstock.com

Figure 5-3. Located above the LCD screen, a separate electronic viewfinder is found on DSLRs and some advanced compact cameras.

For many digital models, the primary viewfinder is the LCD screen on the back of the camera. The photographer uses the screen to frame the shot and to review the image after it is captured, **Figure 5-4A**. A major shortcoming of the LCD screen as the primary viewfinder is that it tends to be difficult to see in bright sunlight. To overcome this problem, a number of companies have developed hood-like devices that shade the screen to improve visibility, **Figure 5-4B**.

Focusing Methods

Bringing a subject into sharp focus can be done manually or automatically. Manual focus is used on rangefinder and older 35 mm single-lens reflex (SLR) cameras, many medium format cameras, and all large format cameras. It also is an option on many

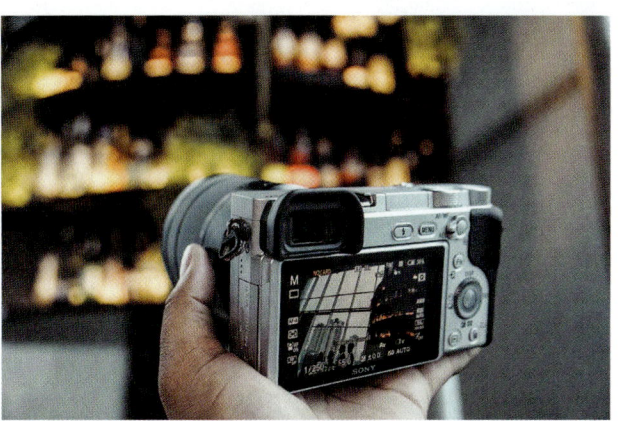

A
Lukmanazis/Shutterstock.com

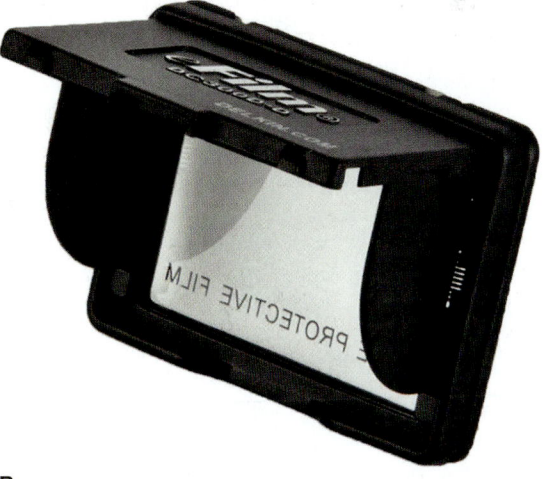

B
Delkin Devices

Figure 5-4. LCD viewing screen. A—Non-SLR digital cameras often use the LCD screen for both composing and reviewing images. B—To shade the camera's LCD screen for better visibility under bright lighting conditions, collapsible hoods are available.

Chapter 5 The Camera System **109**

autofocus cameras. Automatic focus (autofocus) is now available on virtually all digital cameras, DSLRs, most 35 mm film cameras, and some medium format cameras. Cell phone cameras have autofocus features built into them, but you still have the ability to control the focus manually if you need to.

Manual Focusing

To manually focus a through-the-lens DSLR camera, rotate the lens barrel while looking through the viewfinder. As the barrel rotates, the image in the viewfinder becomes either sharper or more diffused (softer). When the image is at maximum sharpness, it is said to be in focus, resulting in a picture that is sharp as well, **Figure 5-5**.

Some cameras have focusing aids to help the photographer judge whether the subject is in focus. The two major types are the split prism and the microprism. Some cameras have one or the other, but many use both, **Figure 5-6**.

Split-prism focusing aids are usually circular and are divided by a horizontal line. As the lens barrel is rotated, the image in the upper and lower halves of the prism shift left or right. When they are aligned, the subject is in focus.

Microprism focusing aids appear as a narrow ring of small diamond-shaped elements surrounding the split prism. They "break up" the image when it is out of focus. As the lens barrel is rotated and the image comes into focus, the image becomes smooth and whole.

Ground Glass Focusing

Ground glass focusing requires the photographer to judge when the image seen in the viewfinder is sharply focused. This makes using a ground glass more open to error than other focusing methods. This method is most common on twin-lens reflex and large format cameras. Some users of 35 mm and medium format cameras prefer a viewfinder with plain ground glass, considering it faster and easier to use than other focusing aids.

Rangefinder Focusing

A number of cameras that have separate viewfinders are of the rangefinder type. The focusing method is similar to split-prism focusing. When the split image comes together, or when overlapped images are perfectly aligned, the subject is in focus, **Figure 5-7**. Compared to DSLRs, rangefinders have a brighter viewfinder image, which is an advantage in low-light situations.

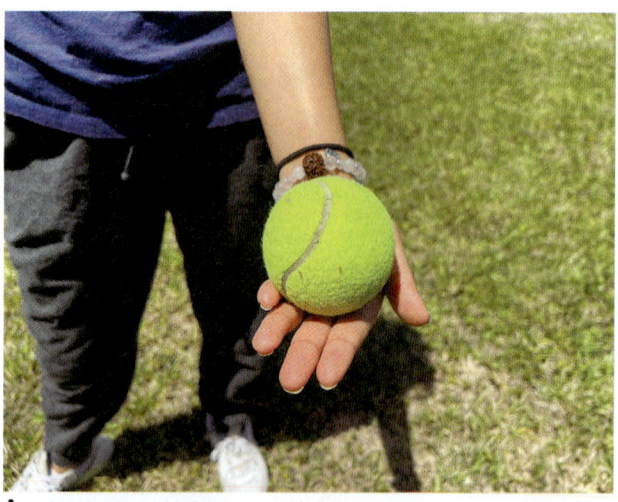
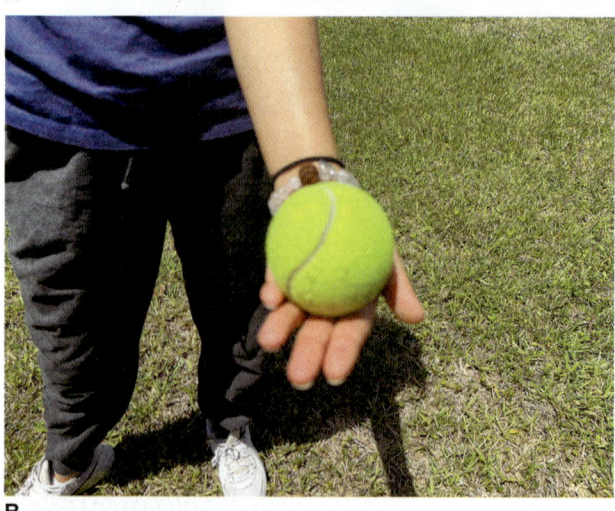

Goodheart-Willcox Publisher

Figure 5-5. Use the viewfinder to determine if a subject is in or out of focus. A—The tennis ball in this image is in focus. B—The tennis ball in this image is out of focus.

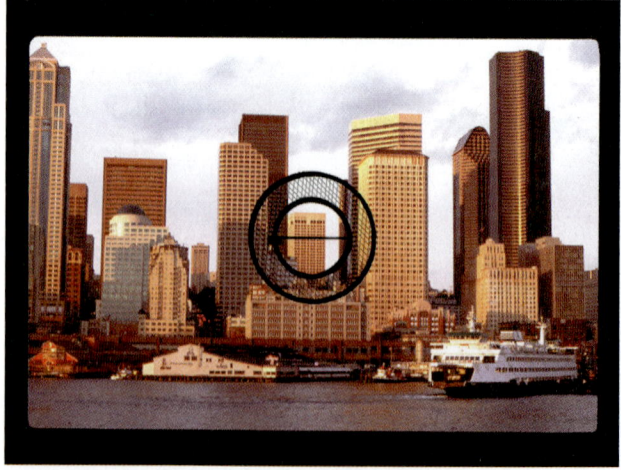

Jack Klasey/Goodheart-Willcox Publisher

Figure 5-6. Cameras with manual focusing often have a split prism surrounded by a microprism.

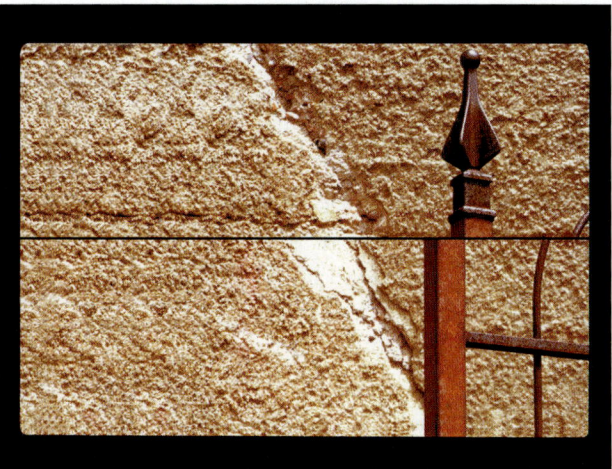

Jack Klasey/Goodheart-Willcox Publisher

Figure 5-7. When the overlapped or split images are aligned perfectly, the rangefinder camera is focused.

Autofocusing

Nearly all cameras today have autofocus capability. Using sensors built into the camera's viewing system, they bring the image into sharp focus before the shutter is released. The two broad categories of autofocus systems are *active* and *passive*.

The term active autofocus is based on the method employed to achieve focus. In an **active autofocus** system, a beam of infrared light is emitted to bounce off the subject, **Figure 5-8**. The system times the interval between the departing and returning burst of light, calculates the distance, and focuses the camera to that distance. Active autofocus is widely used in point-and-shoot digital cameras designed primarily for snapshots and smartphone cameras.

An occasional problem with active autofocus is a noticeable lag between the time the shutter release is pressed to activate the autofocus system and the opening of the shutter. The length of the autofocus lag varies greatly. In some cameras, it may be long enough that the subject has moved out of the frame before the shutter opens.

More sophisticated cameras use various versions of the passive autofocus system. A **passive autofocus** system evaluates incoming light and makes focusing adjustments automatically. This allows it to react much more rapidly than systems that send out a beam and must wait for its return. They use multiple sensors and computer circuitry to achieve focus quickly and precisely under almost any condition. See **Figure 5-9**. The user can select which sensor or combination of sensors should be dominant in focusing under given conditions.

SLR cameras generally use a phase detection autofocus method, which reads changing energy levels as the image is brought into focus. Compact cameras and many of the increasingly popular mirrorless SLR cameras use a contrast-based system, which is the electronic equivalent of split-image focusing.

The ability of computer circuits to make decisions and order actions rapidly led to the development of predictive autofocus. With a fast-moving subject, the system continually calculates speed and direction and makes adjustments to ensure that the focus will be precise at the instant the exposure is made.

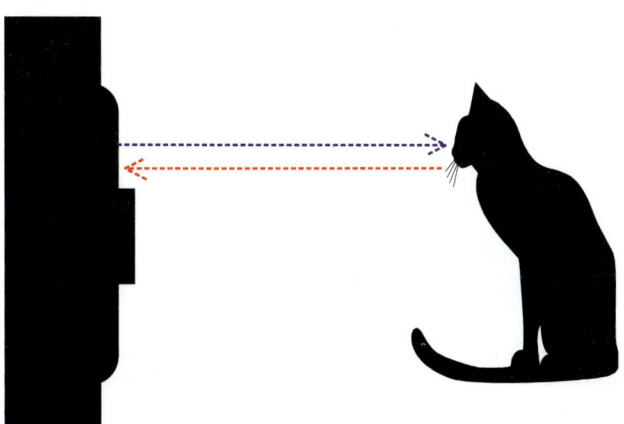

Goodheart-Willcox Publisher

Figure 5-8. In active autofocus, a beam of infrared light is bounced off the subject to establish camera-to-subject distance. The camera then focuses to that distance.

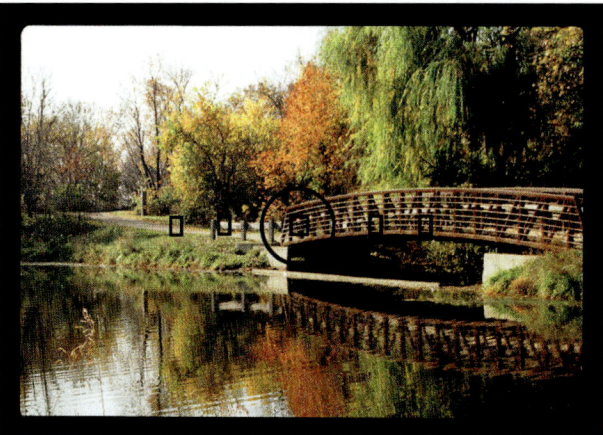

Jack Klasey/Goodheart-Willcox Publisher

Figure 5-9. Multiple sensors are used in the passive autofocus systems of many current camera models. The photographer can select one or more sensors to be dominant for specific situations.

Light Control System

The amount of light reaching the camera's sensor to record an image is governed by the light control system. The two parts of this system are the aperture and the shutter. These two parts function together to regulate how much light strikes the image receiver. The relationship between aperture and shutter speed affects the ability to stop subject motion and dictates how much of a scene will be in sharp focus.

Aperture

The word aperture means *opening*. In photography, the **aperture** is the size of the opening through which light passes to strike the camera's image receiver. The aperture may be fixed or variable, and it can be found in the camera body or the lens assembly. A fixed aperture lens (sometimes referred to as a constant aperture lens) keeps the aperture at the same value regardless of focal length. Some very simple cameras have both a fixed aperture and a fixed-speed shutter. To provide acceptable pictures, they must be used in bright lighting conditions, preferably with subjects that hold still.

Methods for Varying Aperture

There are two basic methods of varying the aperture—a series of different fixed-size openings or an adjustable device that can be opened or closed to provide holes of various sizes. Early box cameras were equipped with a plate that had two or more openings of different sizes. By pivoting or rotating the plate, the photographer moved the desired-size opening into the light path.

An **iris**, also known as a *diaphragm*, is a variable-aperture device consisting of an assembly of thin, overlapping metal blades, **Figure 5-10**. On DSLR cameras, the iris is mounted in the interchangeable lenses rather than in the camera body. On digital cameras, the aperture is set electronically and is selected on the LCD screen or in the viewfinder. See **Figure 5-11**.

Apertures are presented as specific-size openings called *f-stops*. The f-stop system is explained in detail in Chapter 7, *Light and Exposure*.

Aperture and Depth of Field

The size of the aperture has a direct relationship to how much of the picture will be in

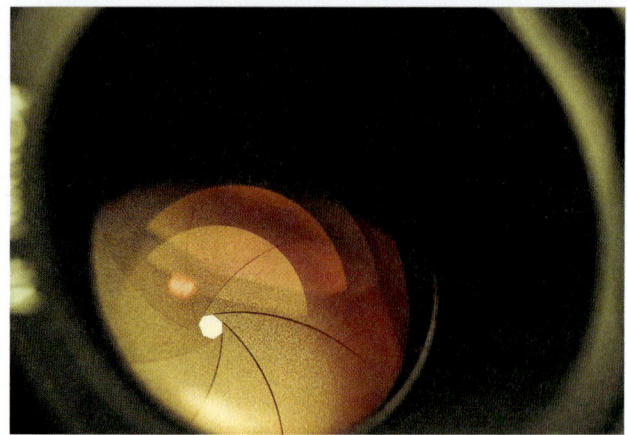

Bushko Oleksandr/Shutterstock.com

Figure 5-10. An iris consists of overlapping metal plates that can form round openings of various sizes.

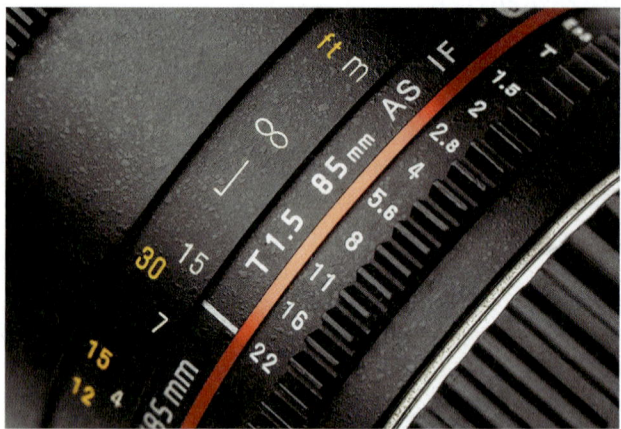

A avi_gamliel/Shutterstock.com

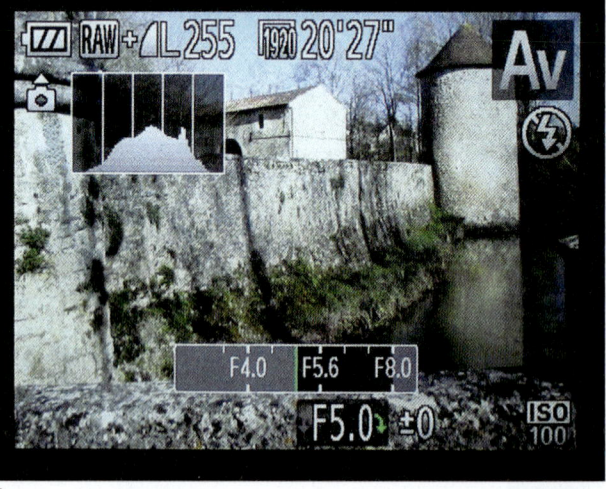

B Jack Klasey/Goodheart-Willcox Publisher

Figure 5-11. Aperture selection. A—An aperture ring on a lens barrel. B—Aperture display on a digital camera LCD screen.

sharp focus. As you learned in Chapter 4, *Camera Handling, Care, and Support*, *depth of field* is the distance between the nearest and farthest objects that are in acceptably sharp focus. Depth of field becomes greater as the aperture size decreases and shrinks as the aperture size increases. See Chapter 11, *Making Exposure Decisions*.

Shutter

A **shutter** is a device that opens and closes to control the flow of light to the camera's image receiver. The shutter acts like a valve, opening and closing to control the flow of light to the image receiver. While the aperture varies the amount of light through changes in size, the shutter regulates light by the length of time it remains open.

Most shutters are mechanical, meaning they physically open and close. Shutters can be divided into two categories based on their location. Between-the-lens shutters are part of the lens assembly. **Focal plane shutters** are located in the camera body, just in front of the image receiver. Between-the-lens shutters are found almost exclusively in older cameras. Focal plane shutters are almost universally used in DSLRs. Some digital cameras use an electronic shutter system that controls the length of time the sensor is actively gathering light.

Between-the-Lens Shutters

Many older film camera designs used a rotating or pivoting disk with a hole in it, **Figure 5-12**. A more complex mechanism, which makes it possible to vary shutter speeds, is called the leaf shutter. In appearance, it is quite similar to the iris used to vary apertures. When the release is pressed, the shutter snaps to the fully open position. At the end of the preset exposure time, it snaps back to the fully closed position.

Focal Plane Shutters

The first focal plane shutters were made with a curtain of thin, tough cloth fastened to two rollers equipped with spring drives. Spring tension was varied to move the narrow slit past the film at different shutter speeds.

Two-piece curtains of flexible metal are used in most cameras to achieve a wide range of shutter speeds. At speeds of 1/60 second or slower, the first curtain typically moves all the way across the sensor before the second curtain begins its travel,

Figure 5-13. The delay between first-curtain and second-curtain movement is the exposure time. For shutter speeds faster than 1/60 second, the curtains are driven independently to form a moving slit of

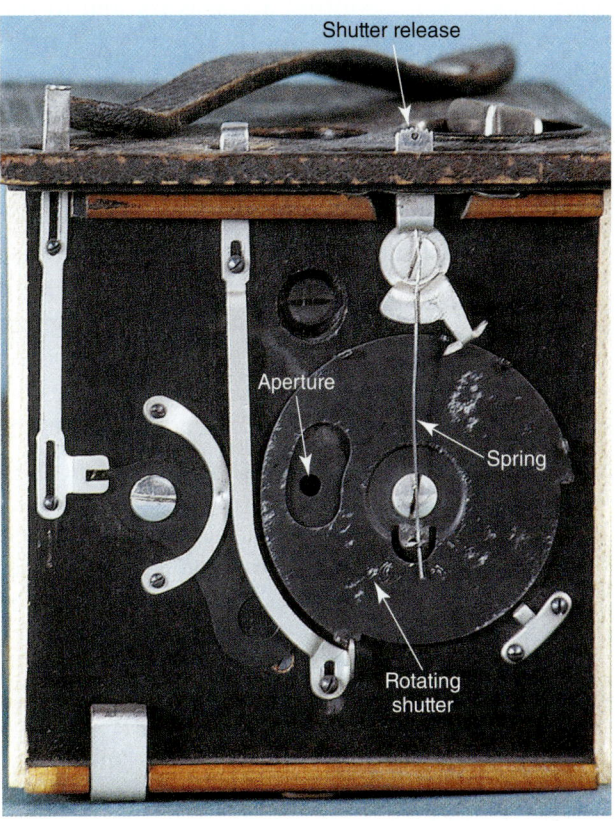

Jack Klasey/Goodheart-Willcox Publisher

Figure 5-12. This early camera had a spring-operated rotating shutter. The camera's outer shell was removed to show the shutter mechanism.

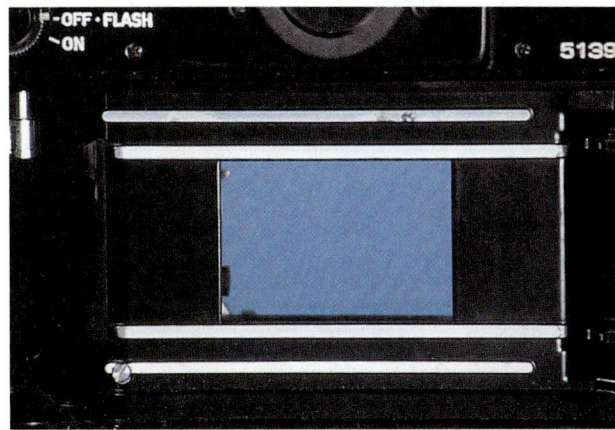

Jack Klasey/Goodheart-Willcox Publisher

Figure 5-13. At a shutter speed of 1/60 second or slower, the first curtain of a focal plane shutter is completely open before the second curtain begins its travel.

the desired width. Depending on camera design, the shutter curtains may travel horizontally or vertically. Most digital cameras with focal plane shutters use the vertical type.

To select the shutter speed on a camera equipped with a focal plane shutter, a dial is rotated to the proper setting, **Figure 5-14**. Alternatively, a button or other control may be pressed until the desired speed is shown on an LCD display. The cameras you use in class will most likely not have a shutter speed dial, so you will have to adjust those settings in your camera's internal settings.

Available shutter speeds vary widely. Older 35 mm cameras generally offered speeds ranging from 1/1000 second to 1 second in length. Newer film and digital models with electronically controlled shutter motors allow exposures as long as 30 seconds and as short as 1/8000 second. Many cameras also have settings to allow longer, manually controlled exposures.

Shutter speeds have a constant relationship, just like the f-stops that are used to indicate aperture. The shutter speed/f-stop relationship is covered in detail in Chapter 7, *Light and Exposure*.

Shutter Speed and Motion Control

Shutter speed is the primary means of controlling camera and subject motion. Blurring of a photograph caused by camera motion is almost always undesirable, while blurring resulting from subject movement has both negative and positive aspects.

Camera shake, or the involuntary movement of a camera during exposure that causes a blurred picture, typically occurs when the camera is handheld at shutter speeds slower than 1/60 second. See **Figure 5-15**. Although bracing against a post or other support allows some photographers to hand-hold successfully at slower shutter speeds, a minimum of 1/60 second is usually recommended. Available on many cameras, image stabilization technology allows hand-holding at lower shutter speeds, **Figure 5-16**.

Subject blur is an out-of-focus condition that occurs when a person or object is moving too fast for the selected shutter speed to stop its motion, **Figure 5-17**. Finding the proper shutter speed to

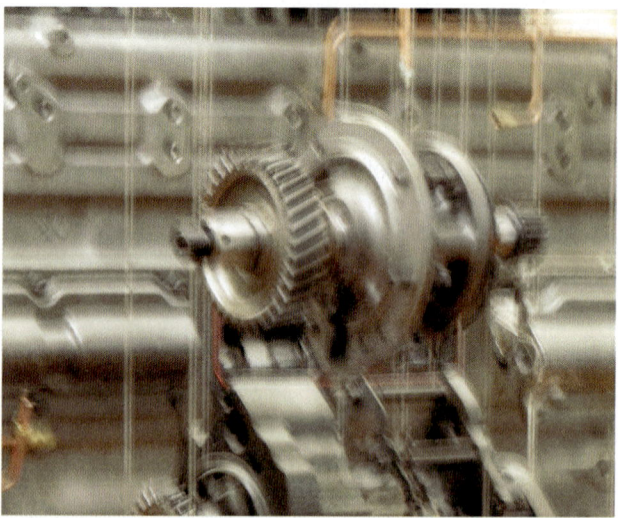

Jack Klasey/Goodheart-Willcox Publisher

Figure 5-15. Blurring due to camera shake is evident in this shot of an "exploded engine" display at a museum.

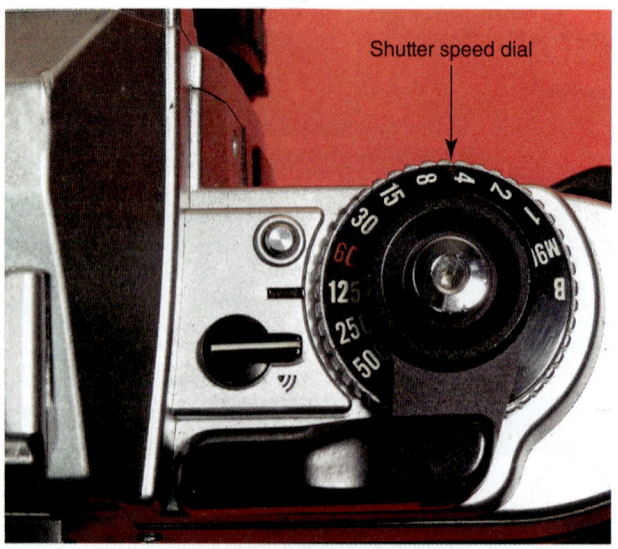

Jack Klasey/Goodheart-Willcox Publisher

Figure 5-14. On a camera with a focal plane shutter, the shutter speed is often selected by rotating a knob or dial.

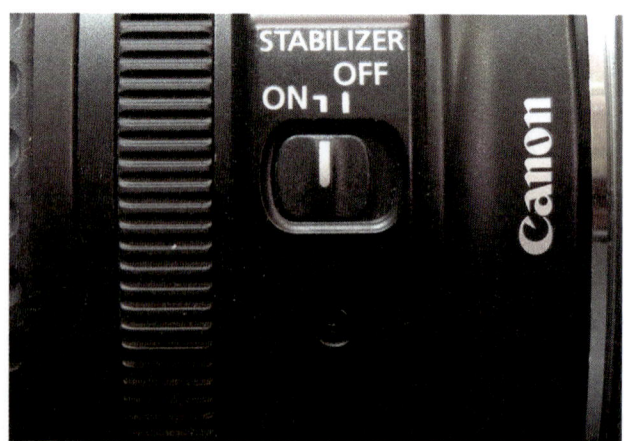

Jack Klasey/Goodheart-Willcox Publisher

Figure 5-16. In this camera system, image stabilization is turned on or off using a switch on the lens.

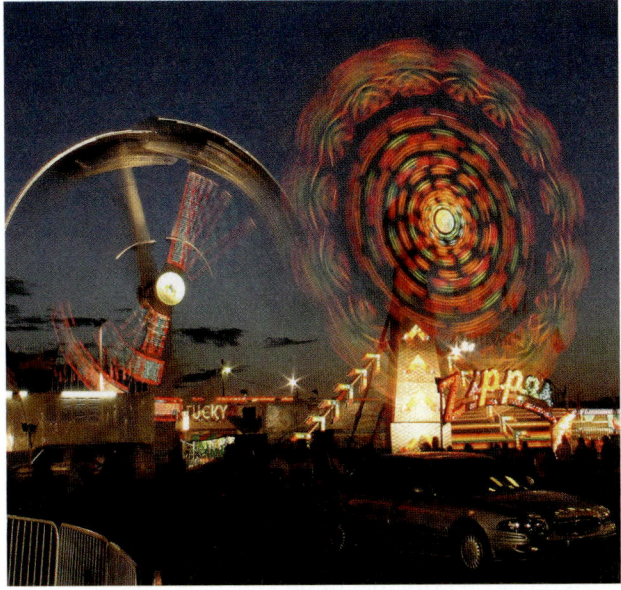

Jack Klasey/Goodheart-Willcox Publisher

Figure 5-17. A subject moving too rapidly for the selected shutter speed will be blurred, while the rest of the picture is sharp. This fairgrounds scene uses intentional subject blur for creative effect.

stop motion or allow a desired degree of blur for a given situation is a matter of experience and experimentation, **Figure 5-18**.

Image Receiver System

The third major camera system is the ***image receiver system***, which is designed to place a light-sensitive medium at the point where light rays converge after passing through the lens. Depending on the camera type, it consists of either film and the means to hold it in place or a digital sensor and related electronic circuits. Since film cameras are not used as commonly today and are mostly used for aesthetic and nostalgic reasons, only digital sensors will be discussed.

Digital Sensor

A ***sensor*** is an array of light-sensitive picture elements, or ***photosites***, that serves as the image receiver in digital cameras. The common term for each individual photosite on a sensor is ***pixel***, which is an abbreviation of the term *picture element*. Pixels are typically arranged in rows to form a grid or area array, **Figure 5-19**. Cameras are often classified by the number of pixels contained in their CCD array. Thus, a camera that has an array of 2000 rows with 3000 pixels per row would have 6 million photosites. The Greek prefix *mega* represents a million, so

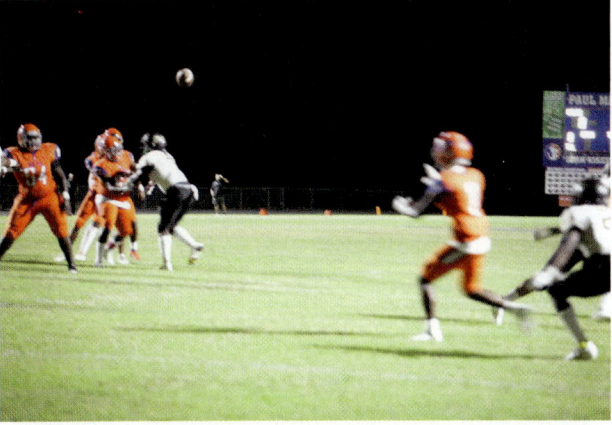

A

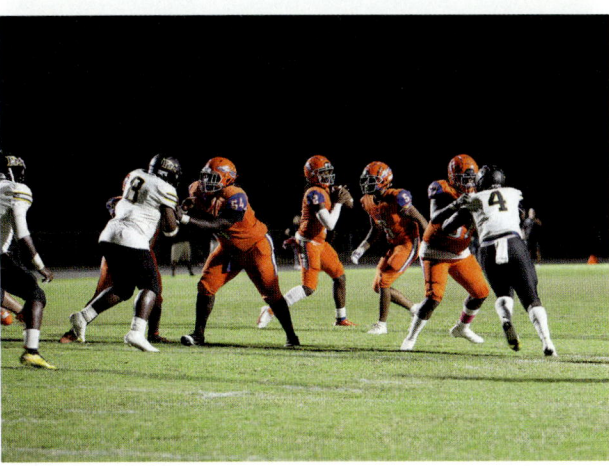

B

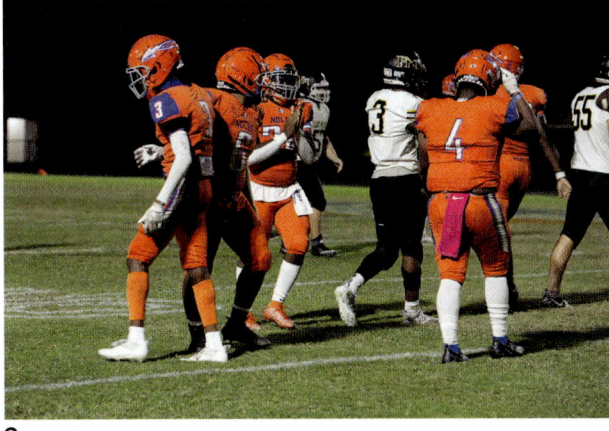

C

Goodheart-Willcox Publisher

Figure 5-18. Shutter speeds affect how your image develops. Notice how movement is clearer with faster shutter speeds. A—Shutter speed of 1/100 second. B—Shutter speed of 1/160 second. C—Shutter speed of 1/200 second.

a camera with 6 million photosites is referred to as a 6-megapixel (6 MP) camera. In most arrays, the individual pixels are square, but some manufacturers use rectangular or even octagonal pixels.

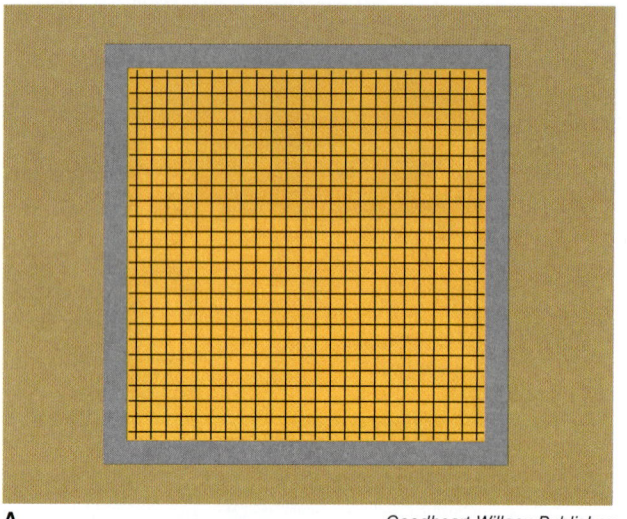
A
Goodheart-Willcox Publisher

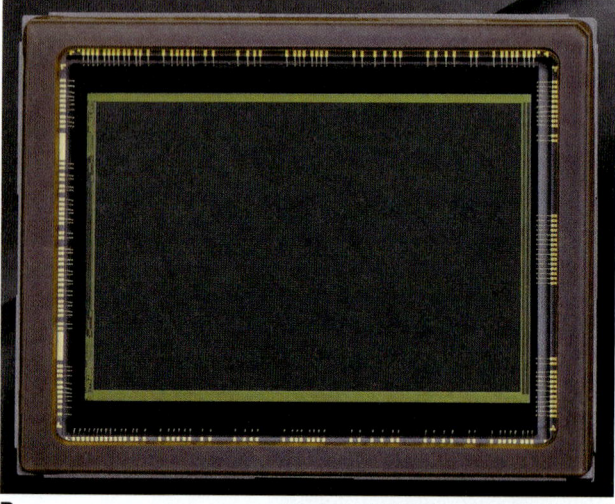
B
Courtesy of Nikon, Inc., Melville, New York

Figure 5-19. A digital camera has an array of millions of tiny sensors known as pixels. A—Pixel size is greatly exaggerated in this diagram of an area digital array. B—This 24.3-million pixel full-frame sensor is used in Nikon's top-of-the-line prosumer digital camera.

Sensor Types

There are two basic types of camera sensors: the charge-coupled device (CCD) and the complementary metal oxide semiconductor (CMOS). A **charge-coupled device (CCD)** is an electronic sensor that has an array of light-sensitive elements that captures images by converting photons to electrons. A **complementary metal oxide semiconductor (CMOS)** is an electronic sensor that converts light into images in a digital camera. These are typically high speed, and they have low sensitivity. Either type is capable of capturing high-quality images. Detailed information on these sensors and how they operate is presented in Chapter 8, *Digital Image Capture Media*.

Sensor Sizes

Although the number of pixels is often thought of as a means of describing sensor size, the true measure of size is the sensor's physical dimensions, **Figure 5-20**. Full-frame 35 mm (24 mm × 36 mm) sensors are expensive to manufacture and are found primarily in professional-level DSLR cameras. These sensors have low-light sensitivity (good pictures can be taken in low light), shallow depth of field, wider dynamic range (the contrast ratio between the brightest and darkest tones in an image), and a zero-crop factor (no part of the image taken is lost to cropping). Most digital compact, mirrorless, and prosumer DSLRs use the smaller **APS-C size sensor**, which is approximately 24 mm × 16 mm. Cameras from Olympus, Panasonic, and Leica employ a still-smaller

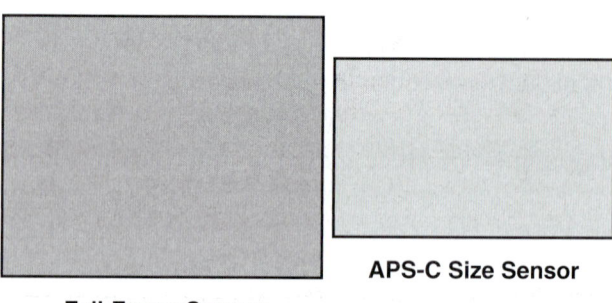
Goodheart-Willcox Publisher

Figure 5-20. The full-frame sensor is about one and one-half times larger than the APS-C size sensor. Sensors used in the Four Thirds System are smaller still.

sensor called the *Four Thirds System*. A micro 4:3 sensor shares the same sensor size and specification with the Four Thirds System, but at a comparatively lower cost. This sensor also has crop magnification. In short, things appear larger than they actually are.

Medium format digital cameras are equipped with sensors similar in size to the frame of 120-size film. The sensors are slightly smaller than the popular 645 (6 cm × 4.5 cm) film format, with resolutions as high as 40 MP. The larger sensor has an increased surface size and physically larger individual pixels, providing higher-quality results. An integrated medium format DSLR is similar in most respects (other than size) to the 35 mm DSLR.

Trilinear Arrays

Studio capture devices called *scanning backs* make use of a **trilinear array**, which is a bar containing three rows of sensors that is moved across the image receiver area, permitting image capture in a single pass. One row of sensors is filtered to capture red wavelengths, one is filtered for green, and one is filtered for blue. This permits image capture in a single pass as the bar is moved in tiny increments by a stepping motor. See **Figure 5-21**. Scanning backs are attached to medium format or large format cameras, capturing images that are the equivalent of the 6 cm × 6 cm or 4″ × 5″ film formats. They are used only with subjects that do not move.

Camera Varieties

Since general-use cameras were introduced in the late 1800s, many different designs have developed. Most are variations in size or complexity on a few basic types. One method of classifying cameras is by their format, or size of image receiver. The traditional format classes are small, medium, and large:

- **Small format cameras** use image receivers ranging from 35 mm size down to small cameras that use 9.5 mm or 16 mm size. See **Figure 5-22**.
- **Medium format cameras** are cameras that have been adapted from medium format film photography. In medium format digital cameras, images are recorded on image receivers larger than 24 mm × 36 mm but smaller than 100 mm × 130 mm, which are considered large format. These medium format cameras have higher-resolution sensors, better low-light capabilities, and a wider dynamic range.

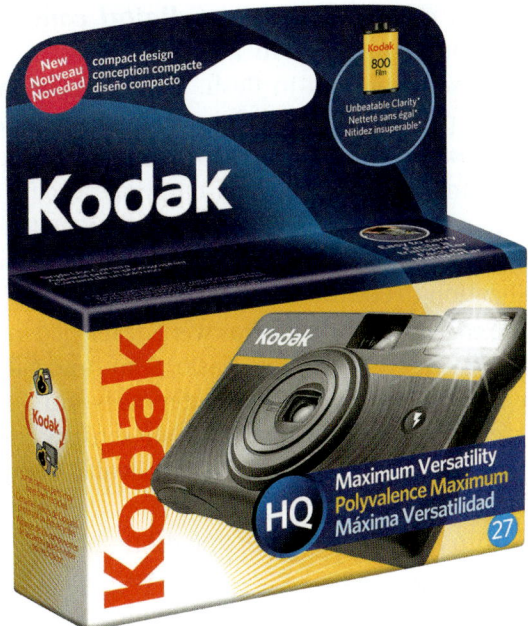

Kodak

Figure 5-22. Single-use cameras are sent to a photography lab to have the film developed.

- **Large format cameras** use film or scanning backs and are recorded on image receivers around 100 mm × 130 mm. As technology continues to improve, there have been advancements in trying to create a large format digital camera, but the main barrier is cost since the sensor would be incredibly expensive to produce. People continue to use large format film cameras because they create photos at a higher resolution than their smaller counterparts.

Simple Cameras

Simple cameras are the least sophisticated in construction. These point-and-shoot units require little of the user other than to frame the desired subject matter in the viewfinder and press the shutter release. Most cameras in this category include camera phones, tablets with cameras, small point-and-shoot cameras, and action cameras. These typically have what are considered basic camera sensors since they are portable, inexpensive, and easy to use for most people.

Virtually every digital camera offers point-and-shoot simplicity. Even the most sophisticated DSLR models have an automatic mode that allows the camera to choose all exposure and focus settings. However, digital cameras can be generally categorized as compact, advanced compact, and interchangeable

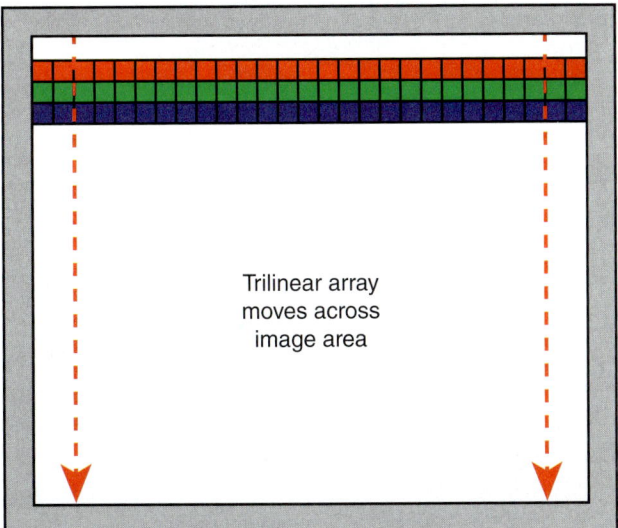

Goodheart-Willcox Publisher

Figure 5-21. Three rows of pixels are typically used in scanning backs. The scanning process requires exposures that are usually minutes in length.

lens (SLR) models. A ***compact digital camera*** is small enough to carry in a pocket, usually with zoom lenses and built-in flash. They are the most common point-and-shoot class of digital cameras. An ***advanced compact digital camera*** has many of the same features as SLR cameras, except for interchangeable lenses. Cameras in this category have extended zoom ranges and often include image stabilization to counteract camera shake.

The earliest digital cameras were developed in the mid-1990s by Apple, Kodak, Casio, Sony, and Nikon. They were simple point-and-shoot models with fixed-focal-length lenses and 1 MP or 2 MP sensors. Memory was small and internal, and removable memory cards were still several years away.

Within a few years, 3 MP and 4 MP models were common, and zoom lenses were becoming standard. By 2015, compact digital cameras typically offered sensors in the 12 MP–16 MP range and were equipped with 4× to 12× optical zoom lenses. See **Figure 5-23**. The term "4×" means that the telephoto end of the zoom range is roughly three times the wide end (an example is a 28 mm lens with a 4× zoom range that would allow you to have the appearance of a 112 mm lens). Most models offer automatic (program), manual, aperture priority, or shutter priority operation, and some have selectable preset modes for situations such as action, night, or portrait photography. All have built-in flash. Most compacts are small enough to carry in a pocket. Ultracompact models are even smaller, often the length and width of a credit card and a thickness of 3/4″ or less.

As mentioned previously, advanced compact digital cameras have most of the same features as SLR cameras, except for interchangeable lenses. Many are categorized as superzooms, with a zoom range of

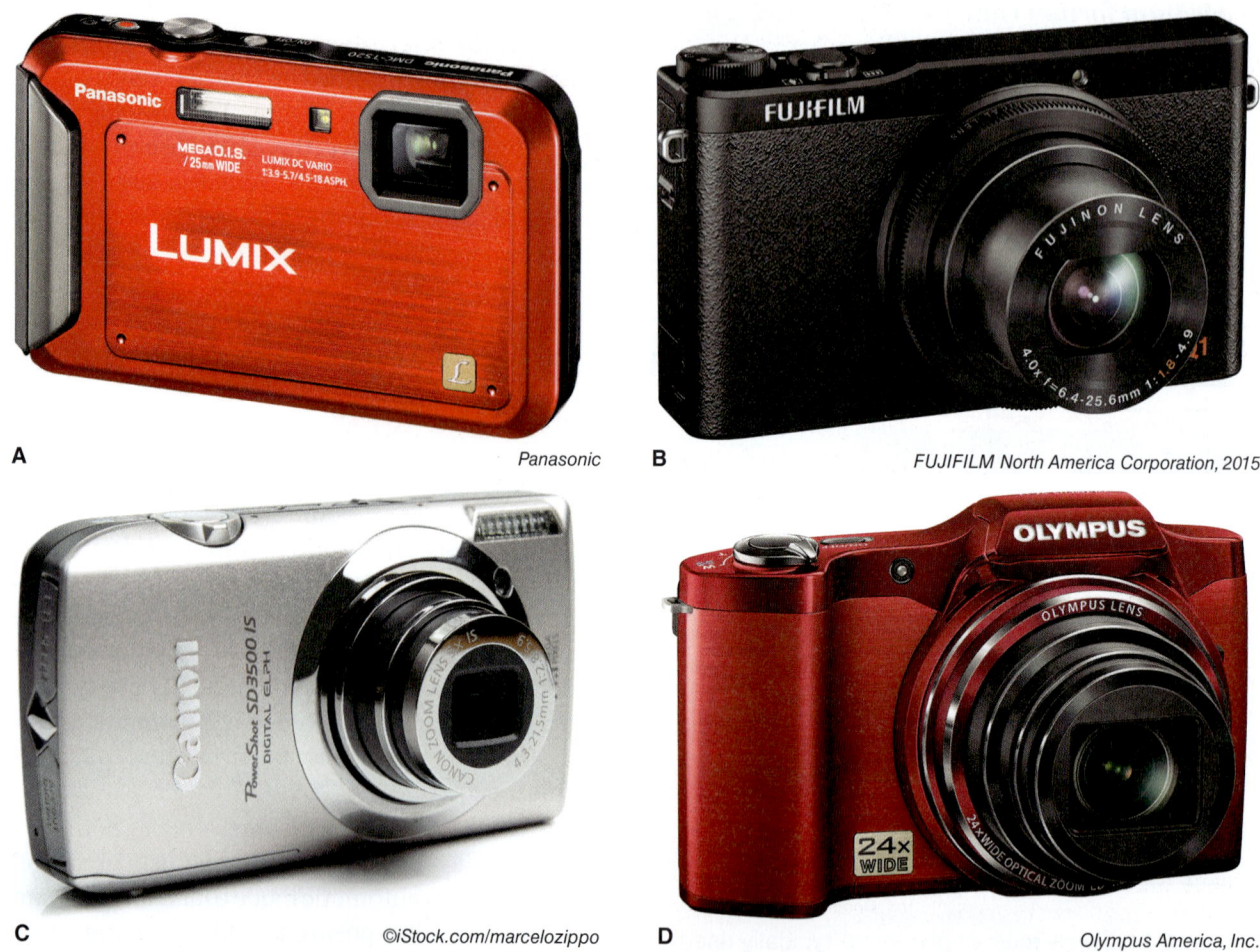

Figure 5-23. Many compact digital cameras on the market today have 12 MP to 16 MP sensors. A—Lumix DMC-TS20. B—XQ1. C—PowerShot ELPH 115. D—Olympus SZ-12.

50× (24 mm–1200 mm) or more, **Figure 5-24**. Most advanced compact digital cameras offer image stabilization to counter camera shake and have both a built-in flash and a hot shoe to accept a separate flash unit.

Cell phone cameras have achieved incredible popularity since being introduced in the early 2000s. Ease of use and the ability to transmit photos to friends instantly have made smartphones nearly universal, **Figure 5-25**.

Cell phone cameras generally have CMOS sensors. Over the last several years, smartphone cameras have drastically improved, and most have cameras that range from 12 MP to 16 MP. Some smartphones even take photos that can be printed at a high resolution and displayed as if they were taken on a much larger camera. **Figure 5-26** was taken on an iPhone® 12 Pro Max and is not edited in any way. Even with recent advancements, resolution and image quality continue to improve. By early 2015, a variety of smartphone models offered 16 MP–20 MP resolution, and at least two phones included extremely high resolution 41 MP cameras, **Figure 5-27**. As each new cell phone generation

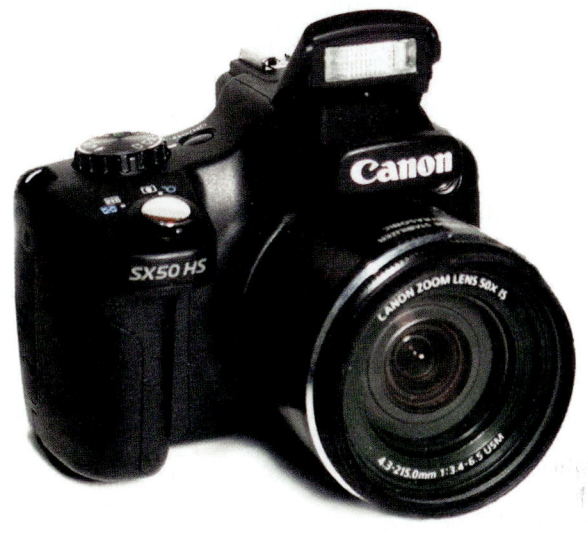

Goodheart-Willcox Publisher

Figure 5-24. Superzoom cameras are a growing segment of the advanced compact digital market.

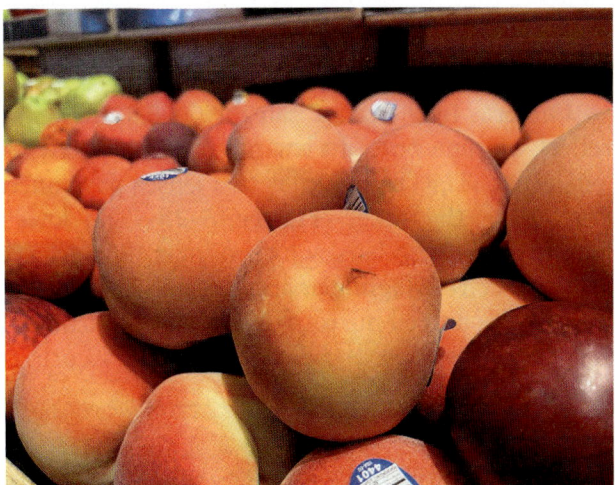

Goodheart-Willcox Publisher

Figure 5-26. This image of fruit in a grocery store was taken on an iPhone® 12 Pro Max and was not edited.

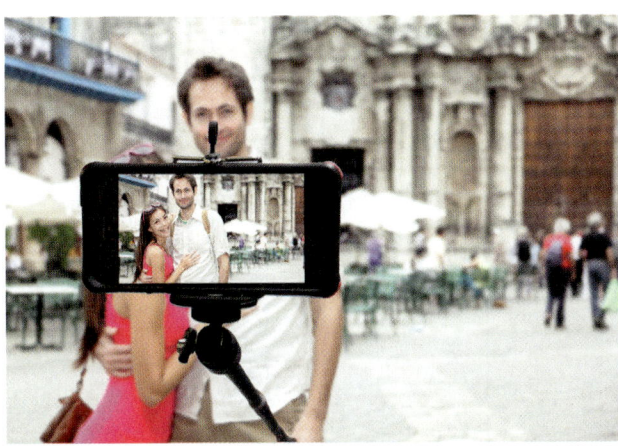

Istabilizer

Figure 5-25. Smartphones are popular because they are small, portable, and easy to use. Resolution and image quality are increasing rapidly, making the smartphone a strong competitor to compact digital models.

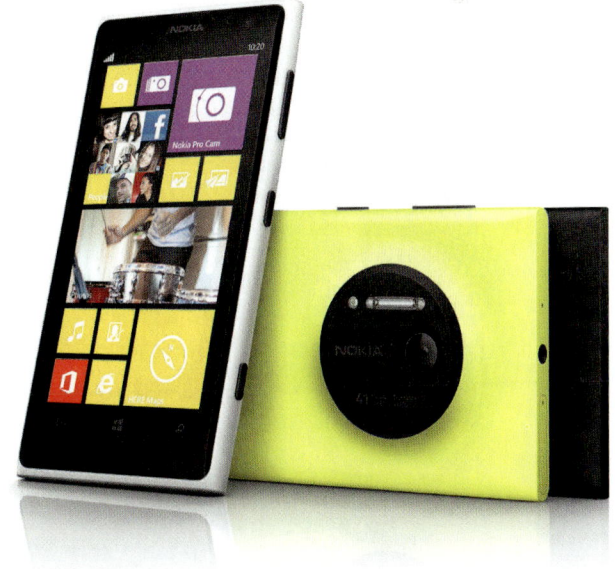

Nokia

Figure 5-27. The camera in a Lumia 1020 smartphone has a 41 MP sensor.

emerges, there are continuous updates to camera hardware and software, allowing photographers to take professional-quality photos using just the device in their hand.

Rangefinder Cameras

Focusing by means of bringing together two overlapping images or two halves of a split image has long been a popular system for cameras. The use of 35 mm film rangefinders declined with the surge in SLR models, but by 2004, the first digital rangefinder model was introduced. In 2013, Leica offered a full-frame 24 MP professional digital rangefinder.

Reflex Cameras

Cameras in the reflex category use a mirror to reflect a scene onto a viewing screen. The twin-lens reflex (TLR) camera has two lenses positioned one above the other, **Figure 5-28**. The lower lens is the taking lens, which admits light to the image receiver. Light passing through the upper lens strikes a fixed mirror set at a 45° angle and is reflected onto a ground glass screen for focusing. The reflected image is large and fairly bright, but it is reversed left-to-right.

The single-lens reflex (SLR) camera for 35 mm film came into wide use in the late 1940s and 1950s. In 1991, the first professional-level digital SLR was introduced. Affordable DSLRs entered the consumer market in 2003. Medium format film SLRs were first used in the 1980s. Digital backs for medium format models were introduced in 2005.

Like the TLR, the SLR uses a mirror to reflect an image onto a viewing screen, but the resemblance ends there. In the SLR camera, the same lens is used for focusing and for taking the picture. Light reflected from the subject passes through the lens, strikes the angled mirror, and is reflected upward onto a screen. The light then passes through a five-sided prism (pentaprism) that corrects the inverted and reversed image for viewing through the eyepiece. See **Figure 5-29**. When the shutter release is pressed, the hinged mirror flips upward, allowing light to reach the film.

Since both viewing and picture-taking are done through the same lens, there is no parallax error

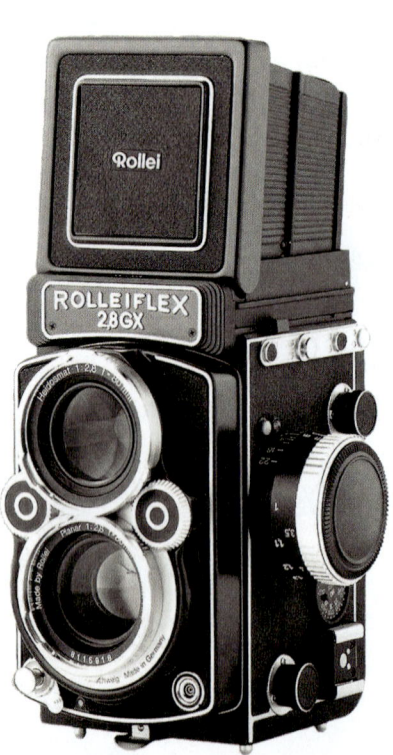

Rollei Fototechnic

Figure 5-28. On twin-lens reflex cameras, viewing and focusing are done using a separate lens above the one that is used to take the photograph.

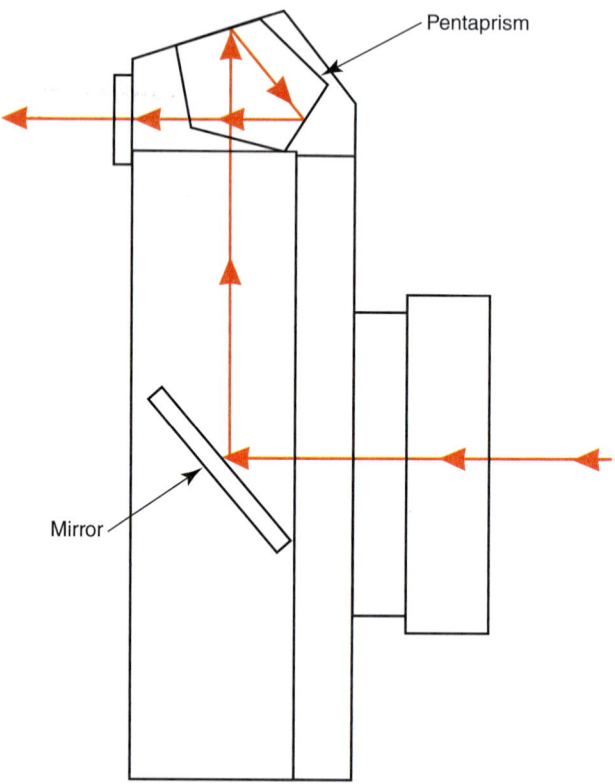

Goodheart-Willcox Publisher

Figure 5-29. In an SLR camera, light entering the lens bounces off an angled mirror, then through a pentaprism to the viewfinder, so the picture can be composed and focused.

with an SLR. This arrangement also permits selective focusing, depth of field (DOF) preview, and easy interchangeability of different focal length lenses. Selective focus and depth of field preview are discussed in more depth in Chapter 9, *Making a Picture*.

Mirrorless Cameras

The mirrorless camera, a relatively new category of interchangeable lens equipment, has seen rapid growth in the marketplace. A **mirrorless camera** is an interchangeable-lens camera that is smaller and lighter than a traditional SLR interchangeable-lens camera because it does away with the mirror assembly and pentaprism, **Figure 5-30**. Mirrorless cameras are also quieter in operation, eliminating the mechanical noise made by pivoting the mirror out of the light path. Although lenses specifically designed for use with mirrorless cameras are increasingly available, older lenses can be used with adaptors.

Sensors on mirrorless cameras vary from the APS-C size common to most compact and prosumer cameras to the full-frame size found on a few high-end models. Most cameras in this category use the LCD screen as both the viewfinder and the review screen.

View Cameras

A **view camera** is a camera that accepts individual sheets of film, uses a ground glass back for composition and focusing, and offers a variety of mechanical adjustments for control of perspective and depth of field. It can be fitted with a scanning back for digital image capture, but the camera itself is typically very large and cumbersome. With older models, the photographer composed and focused the scene on a ground glass viewing surface at the back of the camera. Once this was done, a sensitized glass plate was slipped in place behind the ground glass, and the picture was exposed.

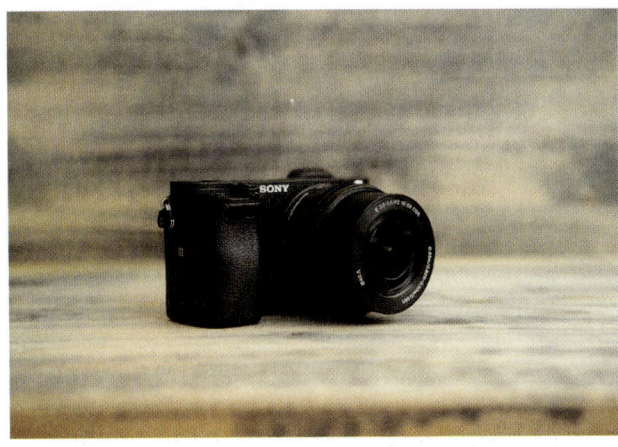

nadtochiy/Shutterstock.com

Figure 5-30. Mirrorless cameras with interchangeable lenses are gaining popularity.

Today's view cameras are constructed generally of metal and plastic. They capture images using film or a digital back rather than a glass plate.

Aside from its awkward size, a drawback of the film-based view camera is the need to use a hood or focusing cloth for proper viewing of the ground glass while focusing. A greater problem is the double inversion of the image on the ground glass—it is both upside-down and reversed left-to-right. Use of a digital back connected by cable to a computer eliminates the double inversion problem. The image from the sensor is processed to appear on the screen in the proper orientation.

PORTFOLIO ASSIGNMENT

Shake It Up!

Camera shake can create some interesting and artistic images. For this assignment, you will purposely create some blurry pictures by experimenting with different shutter speeds.

1. Experiment with different combinations of slow shutter speeds (such as 1/4 second, 1/2 second, and one second) and different motions (such as rapid panning, jiggling up and down, shaking, and jumping up and down). Try at least six different combinations. It is important to note that as shutter speeds decrease, you will get motion even when you try to hold still.
2. Try shooting from a vehicle. The image of a city skyline at night was a one-second exposure taken from the open top deck of a stopped tour bus. See **Example A**. You could also make images from a playground swing, slide, or seesaw.
3. Try shooting with different focal lengths (such as 14 mm–35 mm, 35 mm–85 mm, and 85 mm–135 mm). As lenses become longer, even tiny movements are exaggerated. The portrait of a person in a Paris café was shot from across the street using a 400 mm telephoto with a 1/4 second exposure. See **Example B**.

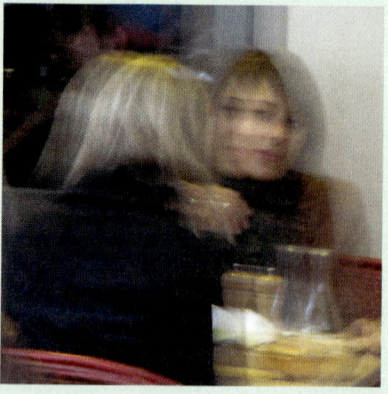

Jack Klasey/Goodheart-Willcox Publisher

Example B. Motion blur in this portrait of a person in a café resulted from use of a long lens.

After reviewing your images, choose the one you feel is the most interesting and creative. Add that image to your digital portfolio. Add a note with the photo's shutter speed, aperture, ISO, focal length, and a brief description of how you achieved the results.

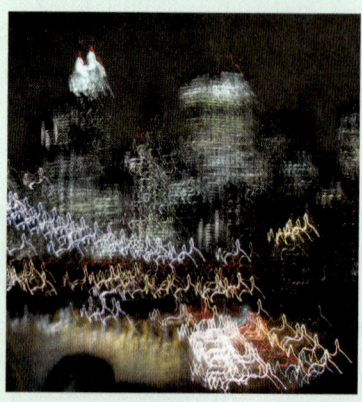

Jack Klasey/Goodheart-Willcox Publisher

Example A. A handheld one-second exposure created this interestingly blurred city skyline.

Chapter 5 Review

Summary

- A camera is a device made up of three interacting systems. They are a viewing/focusing system, a light control system, and an image receiver system.
- When taking pictures, it is important to be able to see what your camera sees. Most modern cameras offer a built-in system that helps you view and focus your images.
- Cameras may use a system in which the photographer views a scene or subject through the same lens that is used to take the picture or through a separate viewfinder. It does not present a "through the lens" view of the subject.
- A through-the-lens viewing system is a composing and focusing method in which the viewfinder image is the scene viewed through the camera's taking lens. For the most part, what you see in the viewfinder is the image you will get.
- Bringing a subject into sharp focus can be done manually or automatically.
- The two major types of focusing aids for manual focus are spilt-prism and microprism. Other focusing aids include ground glass focusing and rangefinder focusing.
- In an active autofocus system, a beam of infrared light is emitted to bounce off the subject. The system times the interval between the departing and returning burst of light, calculates the distance, and focuses the camera to that distance.
- A passive autofocus system evaluates incoming light and makes focusing adjustments automatically. This allows it to react much more rapidly than systems that send out a beam and must wait for its return.
- The two parts of a light control system are the aperture and the shutter. These two parts function together to regulate how much light strikes the image receiver.
- In photography, the aperture is the size of the opening through which light passes to strike the camera's image receiver. The aperture may be fixed or variable, and it can be found in the camera body or the lens assembly.
- The two basic methods of varying the aperture are a series of different fixed-size openings or an adjustable device that can be opened or closed to provide holes of various sizes.
- A shutter is a device that opens and closes to control the flow of light to the camera's image receiver. Between-the-lens shutters are part of the lens assembly. Focal plane shutters are located in the camera body, just in front of the image receiver.
- Shutter speed is the primary means of controlling camera and subject motion. Camera shake is the involuntary movement of a camera during exposure that causes a blurred picture. Subject blur is an out-of-focus condition that occurs when a person or object is moving too fast for the selected shutter speed to stop its motion.
- The third major camera system is the image receiver system, which is designed to place a light-sensitive medium at the point where light rays converge after passing through the lens.
- A sensor is an array of light-sensitive picture elements, or photosites, that serves as the image receiver in digital cameras. The common term for each individual photosite on a sensor is pixel, which is an abbreviation of the term picture element.
- There are two basic types of camera sensors: the charge-coupled device (CCD) and the complementary metal oxide semiconductor (CMOS). Either type is capable of capturing high-quality images.
- Although the number of pixels is often thought of as a means of describing sensor size, the true measure of size is the sensor's physical dimensions.

- Studio capture devices called scanning backs make use of a trilinear array, which is a bar containing three rows of sensors that is moved across the image receiver area, permitting image capture in a single pass.
- One method of classifying cameras is by their format, or size of image receiver. This includes small format, medium format, and large format varieties. Camera types include simple cameras, rangefinder cameras, reflex cameras, mirrorless cameras, and view cameras.

Review Questions

Answer the following questions using the information provided in this chapter.

Know and Understand

1. *True or False?* Separate viewfinders are found on both classic and modern rangefinder cameras.
2. *True or False?* For many digital cameras, the primary viewfinder is the LCD screen on the back of the camera.
3. One of the two major types of manual focusing aids is the _____.
   A. ground glass
   B. split-prism
   C. rangefinder
   D. active autofocus
4. An occasional problem with _____ is a noticeable lag between the time the shutter release is pressed to activate the autofocus system and the opening of the shutter.
   A. passive autofocus
   B. ground glass focusing
   C. active autofocus
   D. microprism focusing aids
5. The _____ is the size of the opening through which light passes to strike the camera's image receiver.
   A. aperture
   B. shutter
   C. iris
   D. depth of field
6. *True or False?* On DSLR cameras, the iris is mounted in the interchangeable lenses rather than in the camera body.
7. *True or False?* Between-the-lens shutters are almost universally used in DSLR cameras.
8. _____ typically occurs when the camera is handheld at shutter speeds slower than 1/60 second.
   A. Subject blur
   B. Parallax error
   C. Passive autofocus
   D. Camera shake
9. A _____ is an array of light-sensitive picture elements that serves as the image receiver in digital cameras.
   A. pixel
   B. trilinear array
   C. sensor
   D. photosite
10. *True or False?* The APS-C size sensor is approximately 24 mm × 36 mm.
11. _____ cameras are the most common point-and-shoot class of digital cameras.
    A. Advanced compact digital
    B. Compact digital
    C. Twin-lens reflex (TLR)
    D. Single-lens reflex (SLR)
12. Most advanced compact digital cameras offer _____ to counter camera shake.
    A. image stabilization
    B. built-in flash
    C. ground glass focusing
    D. interchangeable lenses
13. A _____ camera has two lenses positioned one above the other.
    A. mirrorless
    B. single-lens reflex (SLR)
    C. view
    D. twin-lens reflex (TLR)
14. In a _____ camera, the same lens is used for focusing and for taking the picture.
    A. single-lens reflex (SLR)
    B. twin-lens reflex (TLR)
    C. rangefinder
    D. mirrorless
15. A _____ camera is an interchangeable-lens camera that is smaller and lighter than a traditional SLR interchangeable-lens camera because it does away with the mirror assembly and pentaprism.
    A. rangefinder
    B. twin-lens reflex (TLR)
    C. mirrorless
    D. view

16. A _____ camera can be fitted with a scanning back for digital image capture.
    A. single-lens reflex (SLR)
    B. view
    C. rangefinder
    D. twin-lens reflex (TLR)

Apply and Analyze

1. Define parallax error and explain why it is an issue with cameras that have separate viewfinders.
2. What are the two parts of a camera's light control system?
3. Where is a focal plane shutter located on a camera?
4. What is an image receiver system?
5. Explain how a twin-lens reflex camera works.

Critical Thinking

1. In only about 20 years, the sensors in consumer-level digital cameras have grown from 1 MP to 16 MP or more, while professional large-format cameras have sensors in excess of 400 MP. Is it reasonable to expect this growth trend will continue until there is a camera with a greater-than-1 GP (gigapixel) sensor? Do the math before you decide on an answer.
2. Imagine that a salesperson shows you two new camera models with comparable features. One has an active autofocus system and the other has a passive autofocus system. Which one would you be inclined to buy? Why?

Suggested Activities

1. Survey 20 people—10 teens and 10 people over age 50. Ask them what type and make of camera (point-and-shoot, SLR, smartphone, etc.) they use most often. Also ask why they use that type of camera and whether they would choose a different type the next time they buy a camera. Compile your results for each of the two age groups in a table. Analyze the data and report your conclusions in a short paper.
2. Study the light control system on your camera. Turn on the camera and then look through the camera lens from the front side as you operate the shutter release. You should see a flash of light as the focal plane shutter opens and closes. Set the shutter speed to 1/8 second and watch the focal plane shutter from the back of the camera after you press the shutter release. You should be able to clearly see the operation of the shutter curtains. Experiment with longer and shorter shutter speeds to see the difference in curtain movement. Describe and demonstrate the shutter operation to another student.

Communicating about Photography

1. **Speaking.** Choose two major camera manufacturers and debate the topic of which produces the better products. Divide into two groups. Each group should gather information in support of either the *pro* argument (Brand A is better) or the *con* argument (Brand B is better). You will want to do further research to find expert opinions, costs associated with the camera models, and other relevant information.
2. **Listening.** As classmates deliver their presentations, listen carefully to their arguments. Take notes on important points and write down any questions that occur to you. Later, ask questions to obtain additional information or clarification from your classmates as necessary.

Chapter 6

Lenses

Learning Objectives

After completing this chapter, you will be able to:
- Explain how a lens focuses an image on a sensor.
- Understand how the shape of a lens affects how it works.
- Describe the effects of the six types of lens aberrations.
- Determine the relationship of focal length to image size.
- Explain the multiplier effect on lenses used with most DSLR cameras.
- Recall the characteristics of the various types of lenses.

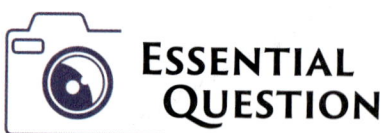

Essential Question

How do lenses enhance your ability to take meaningful photos?

Technical Terms

angle of view
astigmatism
back focus
barrel distortion
chromatic aberration
coma
concave
converge
convex
creative effects lens
curvature of field
digital zoom
distortion

diverge
fish-eye lens
focal length
focal point
front-focusing
lens
lens elements
macro lens
meniscus lens
normal lens
optical zoom
perspective
pincushion distortion

prime lens
refraction
reproduction ratio
retrofocus
spherical aberration
superzoom
teleconverter
telephoto lens
wide-angle lens
zoom lens
zoom range

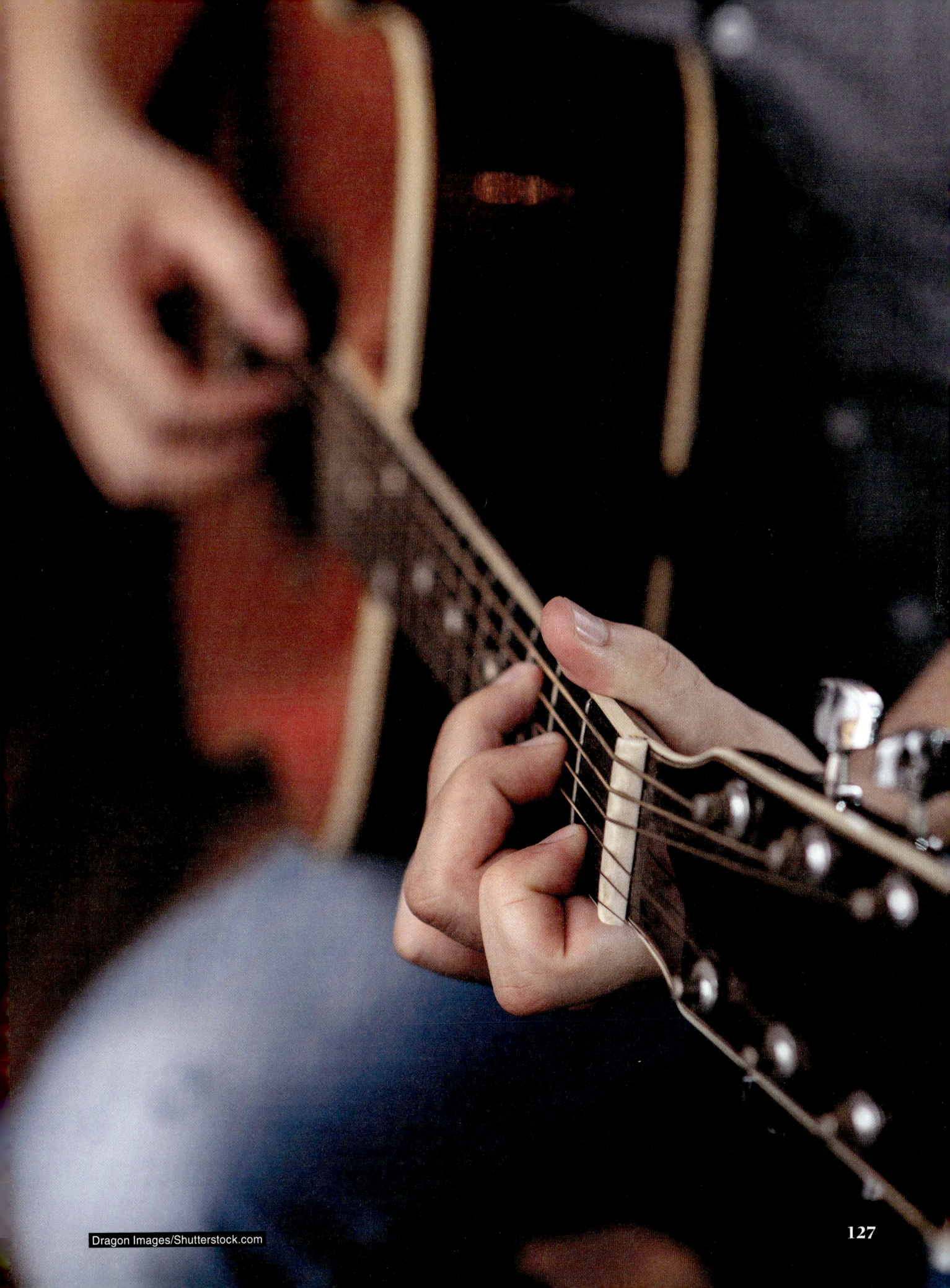

Introduction to Lenses

As a device for making small objects appear larger or distant objects appear closer, the lens has been in use for thousands of years. It was not until the late 1500s and early 1600s, however, that the magnifying power of lenses was put to practical scientific use with the invention of the microscope and the telescope.

In photography, a **lens** is defined as an optical lens or assembly of lenses that work together with a camera body to bring light to a fixed focal point that is processed by the camera to create an image. Photographic applications of the lens began well before the first permanent photographic image was captured by Niépce in about 1826. William Hyde Wollaston, an English scientist and inventor, designed the meniscus lens in 1812. The **meniscus lens** was the first lens developed specifically as a camera lens. It was designed to improve the image projected by the camera obscura. As shown in **Figure 6-1**, the lens had one convex face and one concave face. By changing the shape of the lens, Wollaston was able to project a flatter, less distorted image than the previously used biconvex lens. Learning about the different types of lenses will help you become a better photographer because different lenses have different applications.

How a Lens Works

As mentioned previously, lenses bring light into the camera body where the light can be processed as an image by the camera's sensor. This light is then bent through the process of refraction. **Refraction** is the bending of light rays that takes place in a lens because of the differing densities of glass and air. As shown in **Figure 6-2**, a light ray passing from air into glass changes direction. Because glass is denser than air, it slows the speed of the light ray slightly, causing its path to bend. When the light ray emerges from the other surface of the glass, it again changes speed, and thus direction.

Lens Shapes and Light

Lenses are curved shapes, so the rays of light entering them are bent to different angles by different parts of the curved surface. If the lens shape is **convex** (curved outward), the emerging light rays will **converge**, or come together. If the lens shape is **concave** (curved inward), the rays will **diverge**, or be spread apart. Rays that enter the lens at a 90° angle to its surface pass straight through and are not refracted. A convex lens is also referred to as a positive lens, and a concave lens is also referred to as a negative lens.

Figure 6-3 shows how simple convex and concave lenses affect light. In the convex lens, light rays that enter different areas of the curved surface are bent to converge on the **focal point**, which is the common point at which converging light rays meet. The convex lens produces a real image at its focal point. That image can be seen or captured on film or an electronic sensor.

The concave lens, on the other hand, causes light rays that pass through it to diverge. This lens also forms an image, but on the front side of the lens. This virtual image can be seen only by looking through the lens.

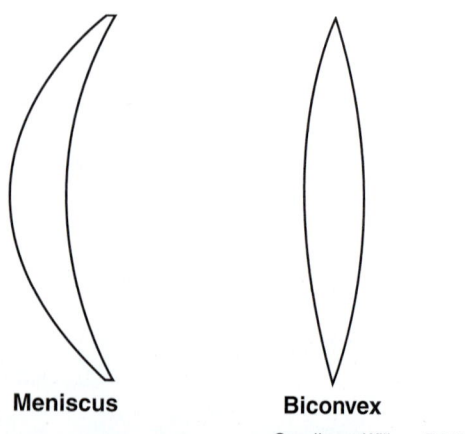

Figure 6-1. A meniscus lens projects a less distorted image than a biconvex lens.

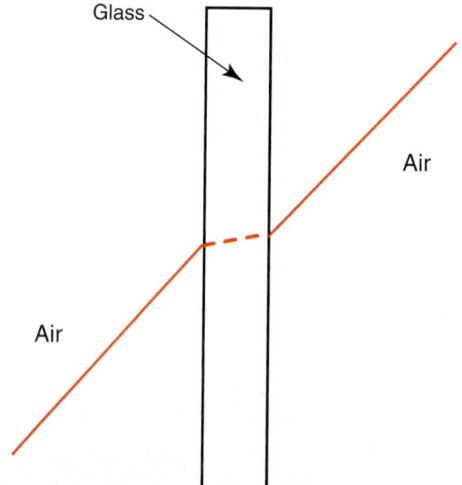

Figure 6-2. Light rays are bent as they pass through materials of different densities, such as glass and air.

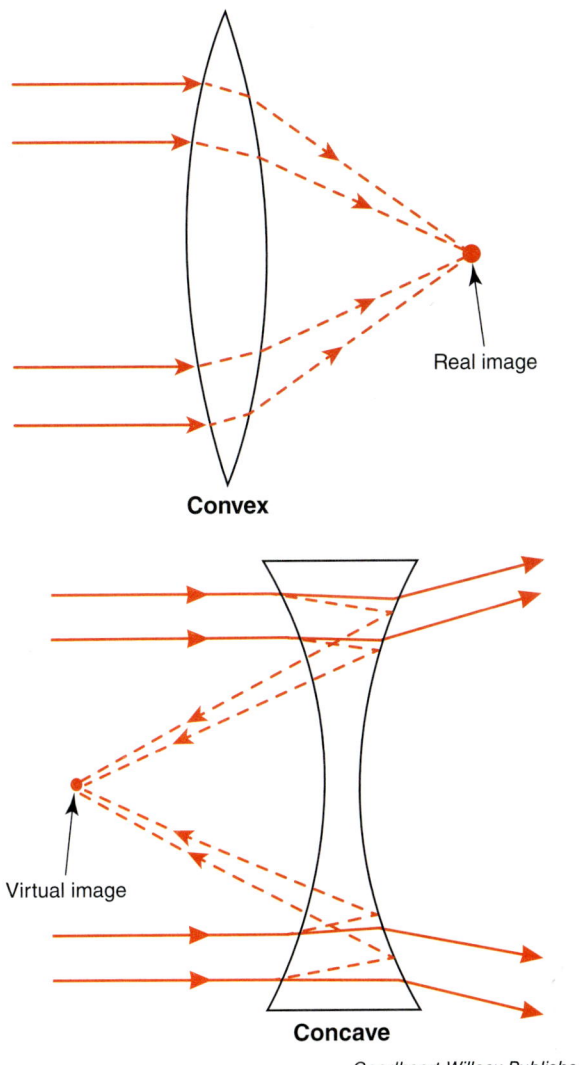

Figure 6-3. Convex and concave lenses affect light rays differently.

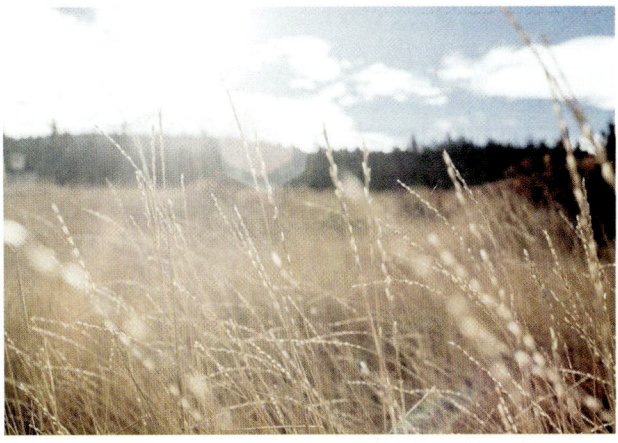

Jeffrey Mitchell/Shutterstock.com

Figure 6-4. The hexagonal element in this photo of a grassy field is an example of an aberration.

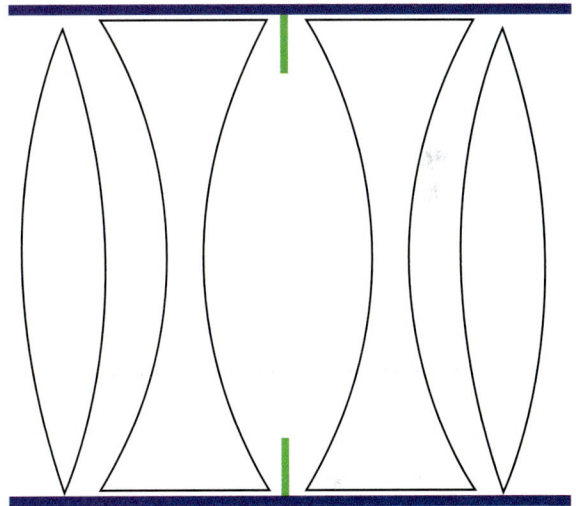

Goodheart-Willcox Publisher

Figure 6-5. A compound lens combines elements to help correct some aberrations.

Lens Aberrations

Optical problems called *aberrations* can cause blurred, color-distorted, or shape-distorted images when a convex lens is used alone, **Figure 6-4**. In order to produce a sharper, more distortion-free image, lens designers have combined varying numbers of different-shaped lens elements (convex and concave lenses) to form compound lenses. **Lens elements** are pieces of glass that are part of a lens and bend light in specific ways. Some are fixed inside the lens barrel, and some are movable. Regardless of whether they are fixed or movable, the lens elements help with zoom, focus, and image stabilization. See **Figure 6-5**. The designers also improved glass formulations and added special surface coatings.

There are six major types of aberrations:

- **Spherical aberration** is an optical problem in which the light rays entering the outer edges of a lens are bent more sharply than those entering closer to the center. The outer rays come to a focus at a point closer to the lens, which results in an overall softness of focus or fuzziness of the image, **Figure 6-6**. It occurs in simple biconvex lenses. An *aplanatic lens* (a lens that is free of spherical aberration and coma) corrects this by making the curvatures different on the two sides of the lens, bringing light rays to focus at a common point.

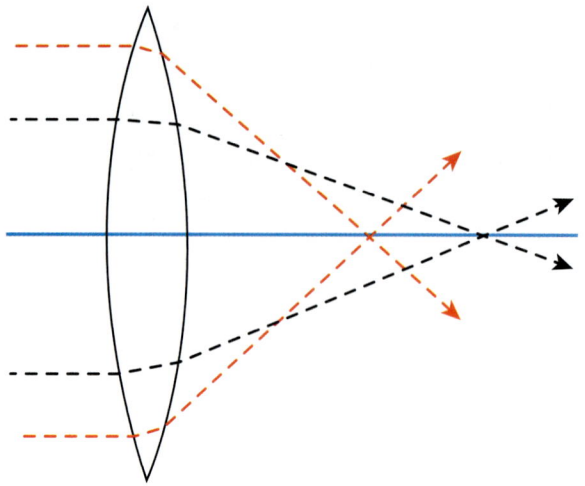

Figure 6-6. In spherical aberration, light rays do not come to a common focal point.

- **Chromatic aberration** is an optical problem in which different wavelengths (colors) of light focus at slightly different distances behind the lens, **Figure 6-7**. It is similar to spherical aberration but involves the different colors of light, which refract differently when passing through a lens. In the 1700s, a convex lens of crown glass and a concave lens made from flint glass were combined to bring the different colors of light to a common focus. An *apochromatic lens* is corrected to provide precise convergence of red, blue, and green wavelengths.
- **Curvature of field** is a failure of light rays to focus at a common point. The projected image is either in focus at the center and out of focus at the edges, or vice versa, depending on which focal point is chosen. The curved surface of the lens causes an image that would be in perfect focus on a matching spherical field. On a flat surface, however, only one portion of the image will be in focus, **Figure 6-8**. This problem is overcome by *aspheric lenses* (those with surfaces that are not a section of a sphere).
- **Astigmatism** is the inability of a lens to bring horizontal and vertical lines of the subject into sharp focus at the same time, **Figure 6-9**. In the 1880s, the development of a new optical glass called *Jena glass* made possible the development of anastigmatic lenses to overcome this problem.
- **Coma** is a lens aberration that occurs when light rays that are not parallel to the lens axis create a series of overlapping circles of decreasing size, **Figure 6-10**. Lenses are corrected for coma by using elements with coma aberrations that cancel each other out.

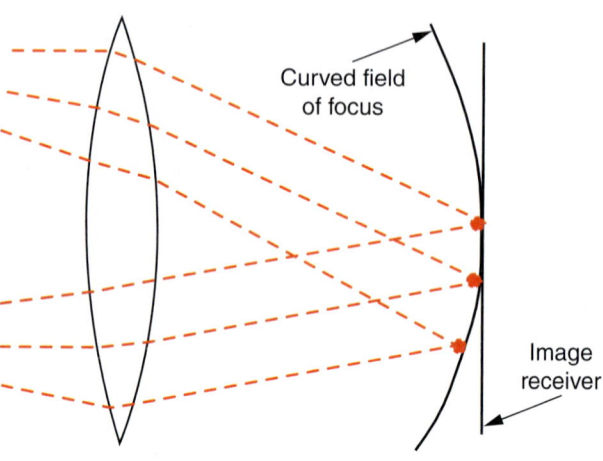

Figure 6-8. When a lens exhibits curvature of field, only one part of the image is in focus.

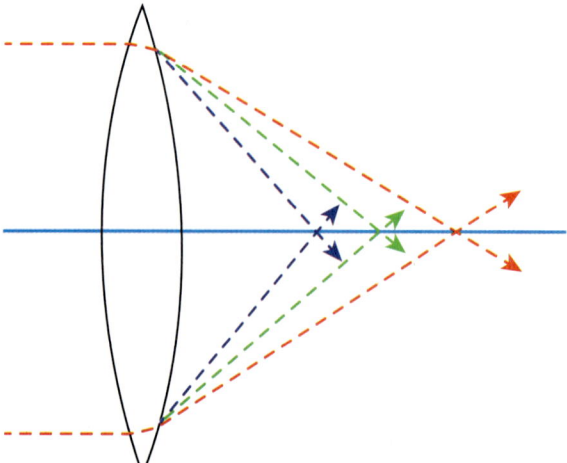

Figure 6-7. The different wavelengths of light are refracted differently in chromatic aberration.

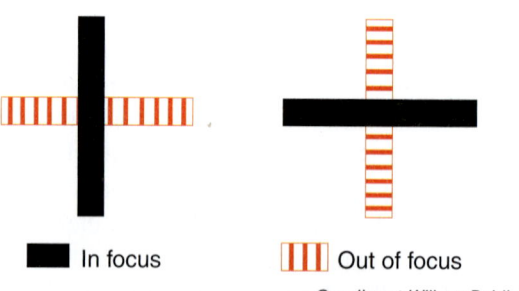

Figure 6-9. Astigmatism makes it impossible to obtain sharp focus on both the horizontal and vertical lines of the subject.

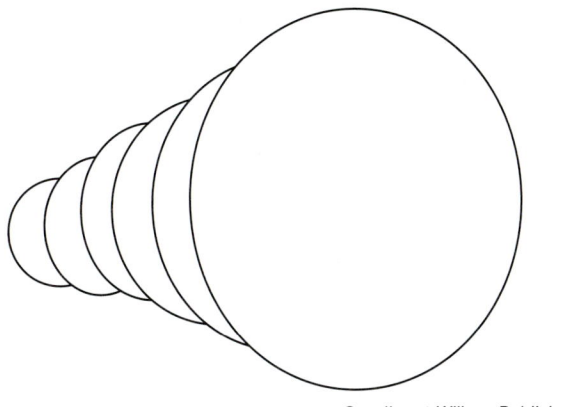

Figure 6-10. Points of light from the edge of an image are distorted into a teardrop (comet) shape in the coma aberration.

- **Distortion** is a change in the shape of a rectangular image projected by a lens. As shown in **Figure 6-11**, the distortion may take the form of outward-bulging sides (**barrel distortion**) or sides that are pushed inward (**pincushion distortion**). A *symmetrical lens*, which consists of two groups of lens elements with the lens diaphragm placed between them, corrects distortion.

Lens Coatings

In addition to refracting light, lenses also *reflect* some light from their surfaces. This reflection of light has two negative effects on lens performance. First, light reflected from the lens is lost and cannot be focused on the image receiver to help make an image. Second, light reflected off multiple surfaces of the lens elements can cause *flare* (lens phenomenon where the light scatters on the camera's sensor) and *ghost images* (reflections of the pentaprism used in the viewfinder). To lessen or eliminate these problems, manufacturers apply nonreflective coatings to lenses.

The loss of light from reflection can be severe. For example, a lens with six elements could have total light transmission cut by almost one-third (about 5% from each uncoated lens surface). This makes the lens slower because it has only about two-thirds the light-gathering power that it should provide.

Problems caused by ghost images and flare can degrade picture quality, **Figure 6-12**. If a bright light source shines directly into the lens, one or more ghost images may appear. Flare may be less immediately noticeable. It may be a mild effect, with colors or shadow values appearing less intense than expected, or it may create a severe washed-out appearance that mimics overexposure.

Coatings were initially applied as a single, extremely thin layer that reduced flare significantly and increased light transmission into the 90% range. Later, multiple coatings with as many as 10 layers raised light transmission levels to as high as 99%.

Focal Length

Focal length is defined as the distance from the optical center of the lens to the point where the light rays converge (the image receiver plane). See **Figure 6-13**. Although focal lengths may be stated in inches or in millimeters, the general practice is to refer to a 50 mm lens rather than a 2-inch lens.

Not too long ago, a photographer typically carried a camera bag filled with as many as a half dozen lenses in a variety of fixed focal lengths. Today's well-equipped photographer can cover a range of focal lengths from wide to telephoto with only two zoom (variable-focus) lenses. **Zoom lenses** are lenses

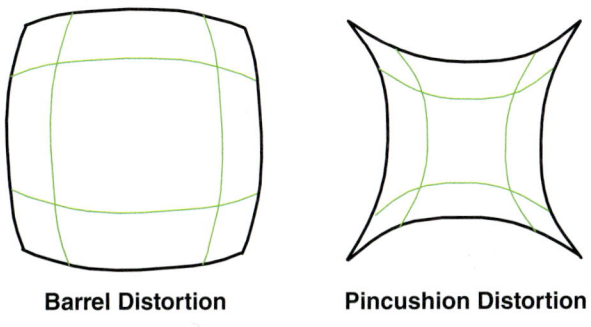

Barrel Distortion   **Pincushion Distortion**

Figure 6-11. This diagram demonstrates two different forms of distortion affecting a rectangular image.

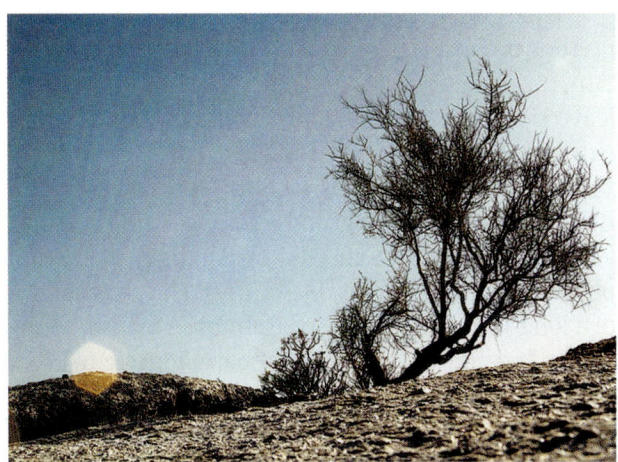

Jack Klasey/Goodheart-Willcox Publisher

Figure 6-12. The sun causing this ghost image is just outside the frame on the upper-right corner.

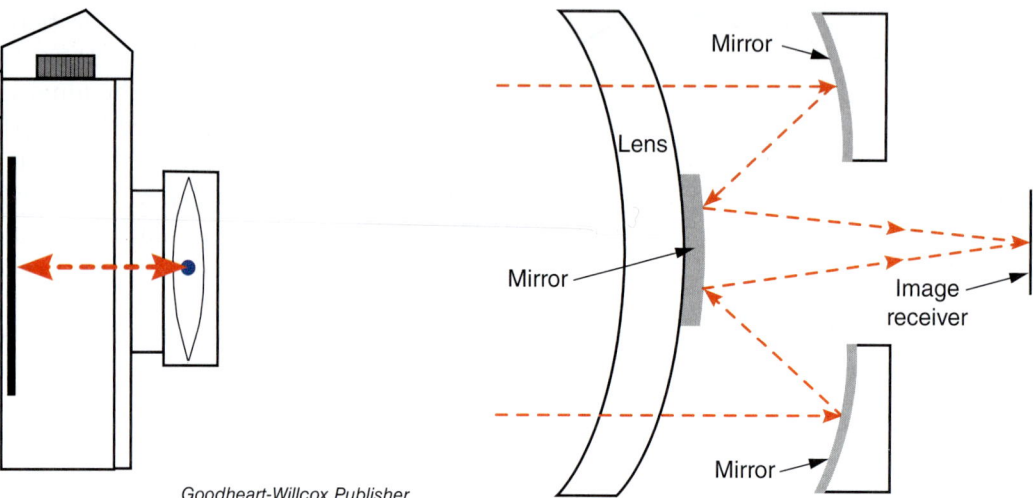

Figure 6-13. Focal length is measured from the optical center of the lens to the plane of the image receiver.

Figure 6-14. Mirrors fold the light path of a long focal length lens to allow a physically shorter lens.

that have variable focal lengths, allowing a photographer to use a range of focal lengths in a single lens. Zoom ranges continue to expand, with 28 mm–300 mm, 80 mm–400 mm, 50 mm–500 mm, 170 mm–500 mm, and even 300 mm–800 mm lenses offered by various manufacturers.

Advanced compact digital cameras include a subcategory referred to as **superzooms**. These small cameras have exceptionally wide zoom ranges, from as wide as 21 mm to as long as 1365 mm. The zoom range and light weight have made superzooms a favorite with travelers.

For many years after they were introduced, zoom lenses were considered optically inferior to **prime lenses**, which are those with a fixed focal length. Advances in materials, manufacturing techniques, and design have made the best zoom lenses of today equivalent to comparable prime lenses.

Lenses with very short or very long focal lengths present problems. If built with the normal construction, a very short-focus lens, such as a 20 mm, would leave no room for the camera mirror. At the other extreme, a conventional 1000 mm lens would be an unmanageable 39 inches (one full meter) in length. By arranging varying groups of convex and concave lenses, designers can shorten or lengthen the actual physical distance traveled by the rays. The physical size of a long-focus lens can also be changed by using mirrors to fold and shorten the light path, **Figure 6-14**.

Focal Length and Image Size

The focal length of the lens directly affects the size of the image projected onto the image receiver, **Figure 6-15**. As the focal length becomes shorter, the light rays are bent at sharper angles, converging a short distance behind the lens and producing a small image. As the focal length becomes longer, the light rays are bent less sharply and converge a greater distance behind the lens, resulting in a larger image.

Directly related to the image size is the **angle of view** of the lens, or how much of an image in front of the camera and its lens will be captured by the camera's sensor, **Figure 6-16**. The image projected by a short-focus lens covers a wide area, with objects in the scene relatively small in relation to the overall view. For example, a 28 mm lens has an angle of view of 65°, compared to the 40° angle of view of a normal 50 mm lens. As the focal length increases, the angle of view becomes progressively narrower. A 100 mm lens has a 20° angle of view—half as wide as the 50 mm. **Figure 6-17** shows the relationship between angle of view and object size for different focal lengths.

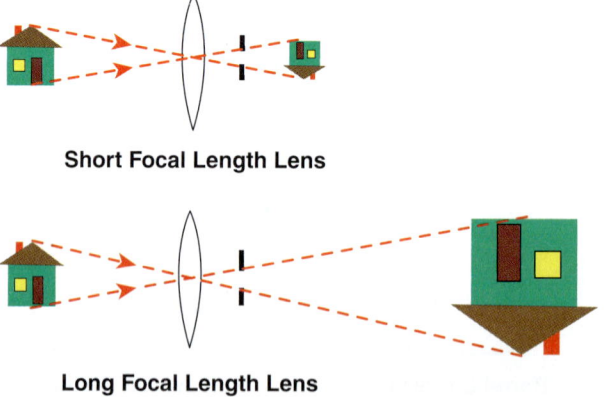

Figure 6-15. Image size at the receiver is directly affected by the focal length of the lens.

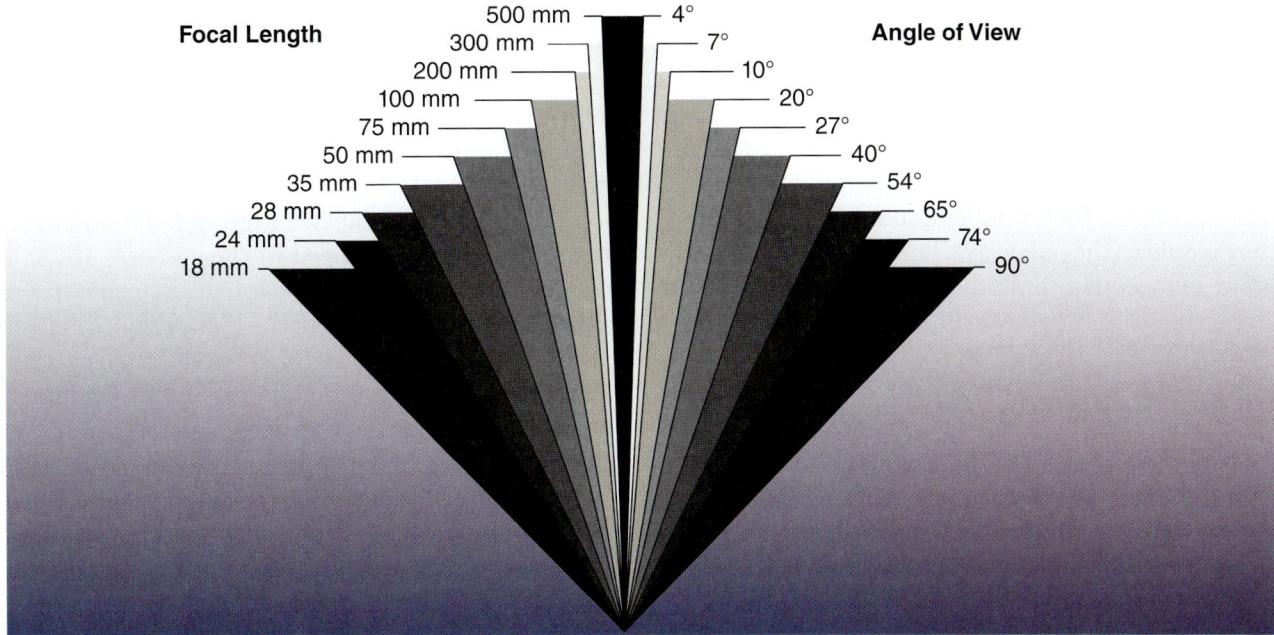

Figure 6-16. This graphic shows the angle of view for a number of common lens focal lengths.

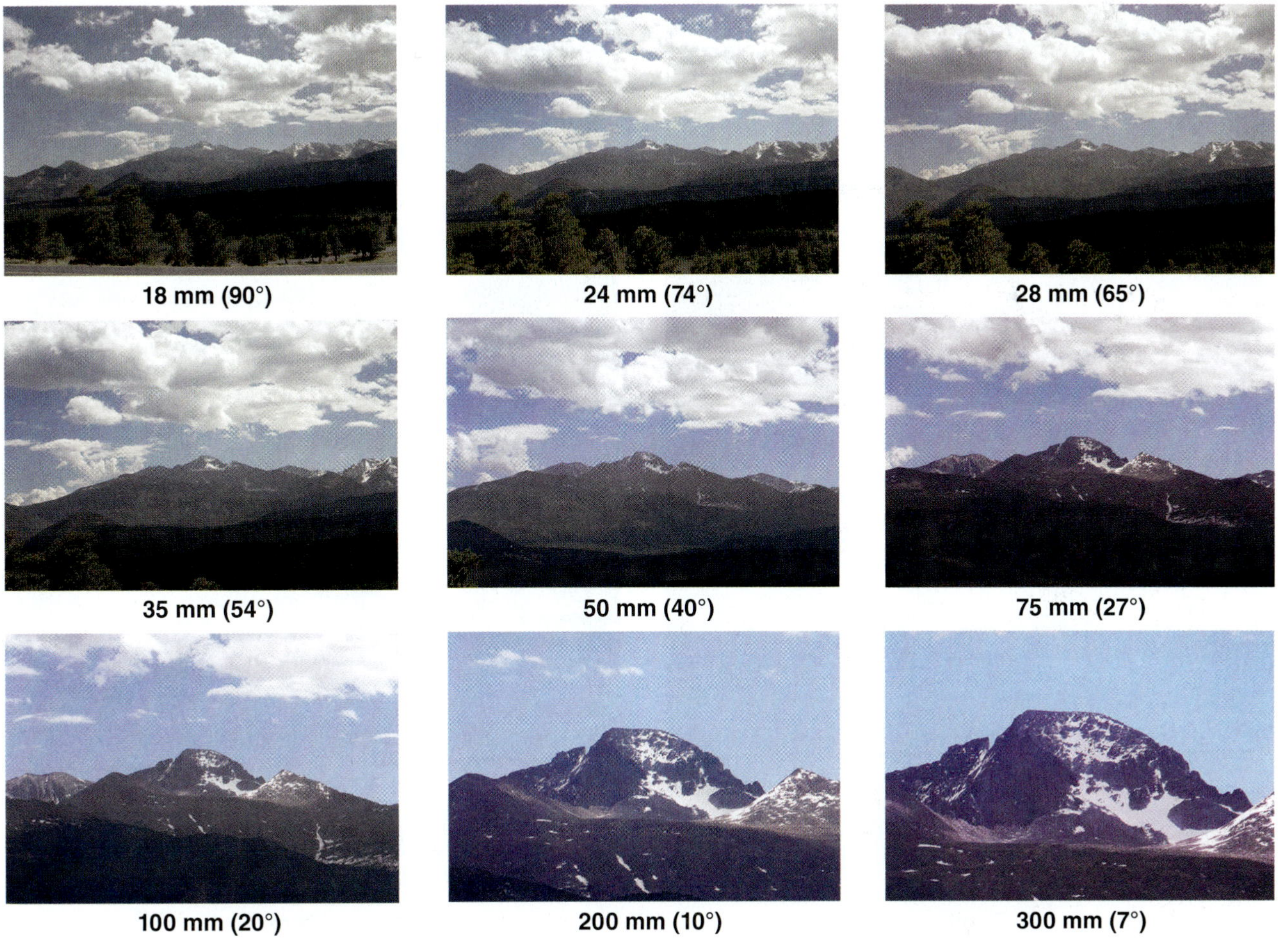

Figure 6-17. As the focal length of a lens increases, angle of view decreases. These nine views were taken using a tripod-mounted camera with only the focal length of the lens changed for each view.

Chapter 6 Lenses

Focal length also affects **perspective**, or the relative size of objects in a scene and how they are aligned. A view made with a 50 mm lens presents near and far objects in a size relationship that is very close to what we are used to seeing in everyday life. A short-focus lens exaggerates depth and width, making objects look smaller and farther apart than they would to the naked eye. Long-focus lenses compress perspective, making distant objects appear larger and closer together, **Figure 6-18**.

Digital Multiplier Effect

Lenses used on most DSLR cameras exhibit what is sometimes called a *multiplier effect*—the focal length appears to increase by approximately 1.5 times. Thus, a 100 mm lens behaves as if it were a 150 mm lens.

In actuality, the focal length of the lens remains the same. A 50 mm lens focuses the image at a point 50 mm (2″) from its optical center, no matter the type of camera on which it is mounted. The image circle projected by the lens onto the image receiver is large enough to cover the 35 mm film frame or a full-size sensor. The smaller APS-C size sensor of most DSLRs is able to capture only a smaller portion of the image circle. See **Figure 6-19**. In effect, the image is being cropped in the camera. Thus, it would be more accurate to refer to it as *cropping effect* rather than multiplier effect. The cropping effect varies from Nikon's factor of 1.5 and Canon's factor of 1.6 to the 2.0 factor (doubling) used by Olympus, Leica, and Panasonic cameras.

More and more lenses are being developed specifically for digital cameras. Designed to project an image circle matched to the APS-C size sensor, these lenses are smaller and lighter than conventional lenses with equivalent wide-angle coverage. They are less expensive to manufacture, making them more affordable.

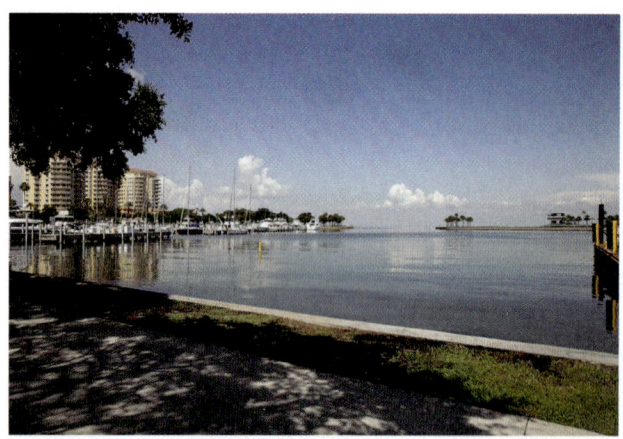
24 mm

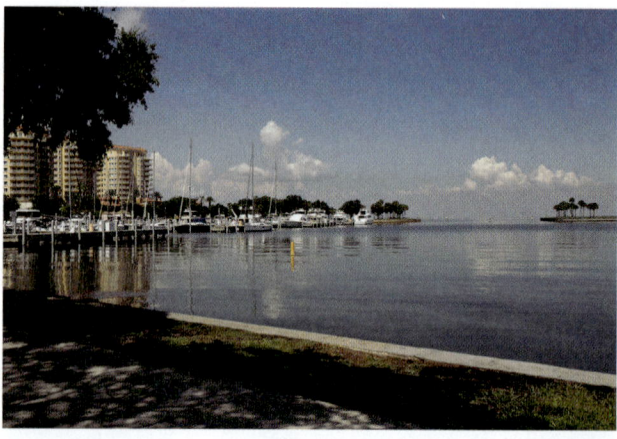
35 mm

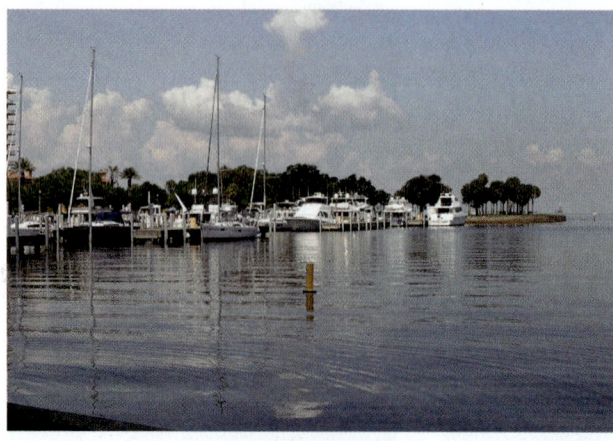
70 mm

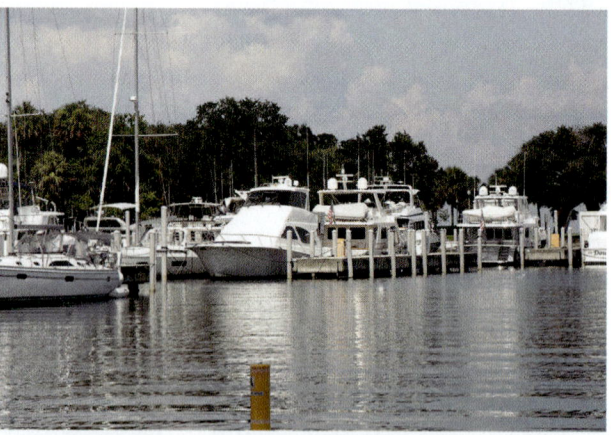
200 mm

Goodheart-Willcox Publisher

Figure 6-18. Compressed perspective. Note how the background objects seem to be made larger and brought closer to the foreground objects.

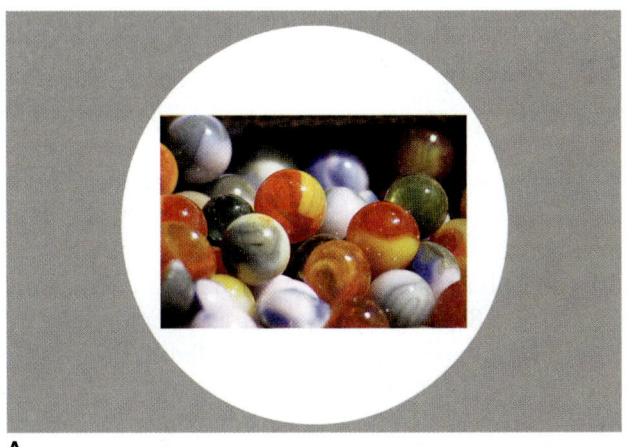
A

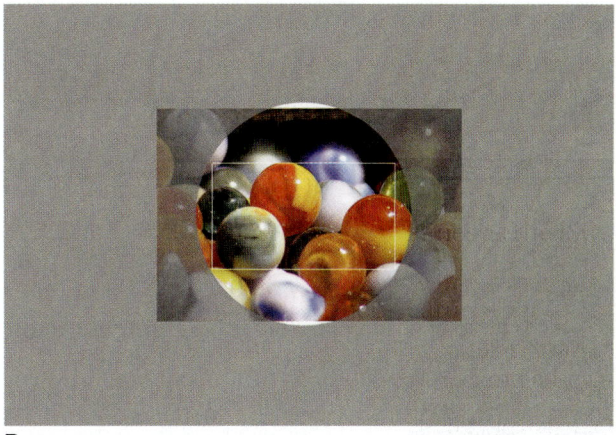
B

Goodheart-Willcox Publisher

Figure 6-19. Multiplier effect of APS-C size sensors. A—Image circle coverage on a full-frame 35 mm sensor. B—Image circle coverage for the same lens on a typical APS-C size sensor.

Camera Lens Types

Prime lenses, or fixed focal length lenses, have traditionally been grouped based on their angle of view. The three categories are normal, wide angle, and telephoto. Zoom lenses cover ranges of focal lengths but can be broadly classified as wide angle or telephoto.

Normal Lenses

The 50 mm lens is usually described as a ***normal lens*** or *standard lens* because it provides an angle of view and a perspective close to that of the unaided human eye. In reality, the focal length that provides the most distortion-free normal view is one that is equal to the diagonal measurement of the image receiver. The diagonal of a full-size sensor is 43 mm, so in theory, 43 mm is the normal focal length. However, normal lens focal lengths typically fall within 50–70 mm. Refer to the bottom left image in **Figure 6-18**.

The smaller APS-C size sensors used in most digital cameras have a diagonal measurement of 34 mm. Taking into account the digital multiplier factor of 1.5, a 24 mm lens would have a focal length of 36 mm (24 × 1.5 = 36). On cameras with these smaller sensors, the conventional 24 mm lens would be normal.

Since the definition of normal is based on the diagonal of the image receiver size, the focal length of the normal lens is different for medium format and large format cameras. **Figure 6-20** is a table showing equivalent focal lengths for various formats.

Wide-Angle Lenses

A lens with an angle of view from about 55° to as much as 180° is considered a ***wide-angle lens***. In terms of focal length, wide-angle lenses are typically between 10 and 35 mm. Refer to the two top images in **Figure 6-18**. Some lenses with an angle of view greater than 100° show considerable barrel distortion. Vertical and horizontal lines are straight when near the center of the image, but they bow

Equivalent Lens Focal Lengths						
	35 mm	APS	6 cm × 6 cm	6 cm × 7 cm	4″ × 5″	8″ × 10″
Wide	28 mm	18 mm	34 mm	60 mm	105 mm	210 mm
Normal	43 mm	28 mm	75 mm	85 mm	150 mm	300 mm
Telephoto	105 mm	65 mm	190 mm	210 mm	370 mm	740 mm

Goodheart-Willcox Publisher

Figure 6-20. Equivalent lens focal lengths for various formats.

outward when located near the image edges. A lens with an angle of view greater than 180° that produces a round image with considerable spherical distortion is called a *fish-eye lens*, **Figure 6-21**. It is important to note that not all wide-angle lenses are fish-eye lenses.

Other lenses with an angle of view of approximately 100° are referred to as *superwide lenses*. These lenses are rectilinear, which means they are corrected for barrel distortion. Straight lines are straight no matter where they fall in the image.

To allow room for the hinged mirror of an SLR camera, most wide-angle lenses are of the **retrofocus** type, **Figure 6-22**. This lens combines negative and positive lens elements to "stretch" the light path within the lens. This provides sufficient **back focus** (the distance from the rear element of the lens to the image receiver) for mirror clearance while maintaining the focal length of the lens.

Telephoto Lenses

A lens with an angle of view roughly 25° or smaller is considered a **telephoto lens**. It also has a longer-than-normal focal length, usually 80 mm and above. Refer to the bottom right image in **Figure 6-18**. Most of the longer lenses made today, especially zoom lenses, use a **front-focusing** design. See **Figure 6-23**. In this type of lens, the front element group has a converging design, and the rear element group has a diverging design. This shortens the light path, making a larger image possible at the focal plane with less physical distance between the front lens element and the image receiver. The point from which the distance to the focal plane is measured has been moved forward into the space in front of the first lens element group.

Zoom Lens

The major attraction of the zoom lens is its variable focal length, which allows the photographer to change composition without physically changing lenses or position. The lens can be zoomed out for a broader view of the scene or zoomed in to focus on a detail quickly and easily. See **Figure 6-24**.

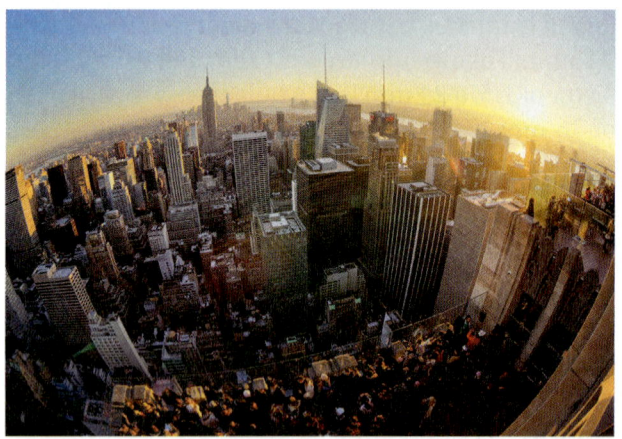

Matej Kastelic/Shutterstock.com

Figure 6-21. This photo of the New York City skyline shows the 180° angle of view and distinctive round shape of an image shot with a fish-eye lens.

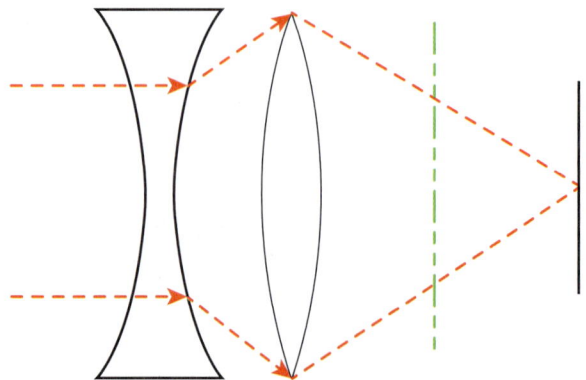

Goodheart-Willcox Publisher

Figure 6-22. A retrofocus lens design moves the point of measurement for focal length (the green dashed line) backward so it is located in midair behind the rear lens element.

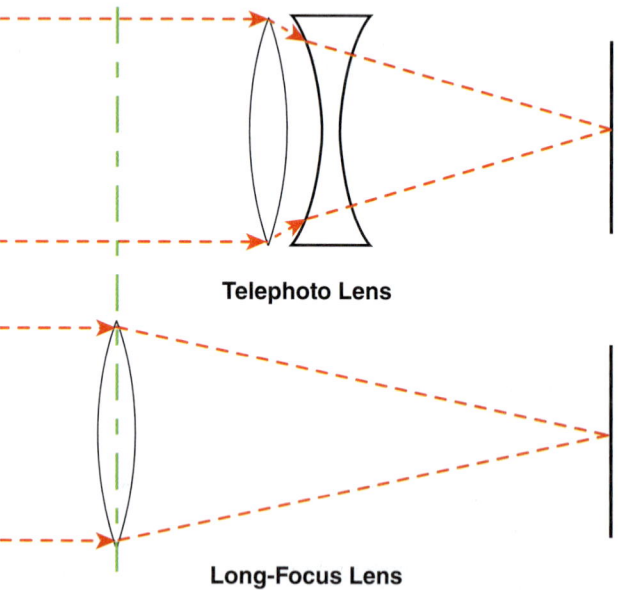

Goodheart-Willcox Publisher

Figure 6-23. The focal length point of measurement (the green dashed line) is shifted forward, out in front of the lens itself, in this front-focusing telephoto lens design.

The zoom lens operates on the principle of lens groups moving varying distances within the housing to provide the different focal lengths. As shown in simplified form in **Figure 6-25**, a negative lens is placed between two positive lenses. As the negative lens moves forward, the focal length of the zoom

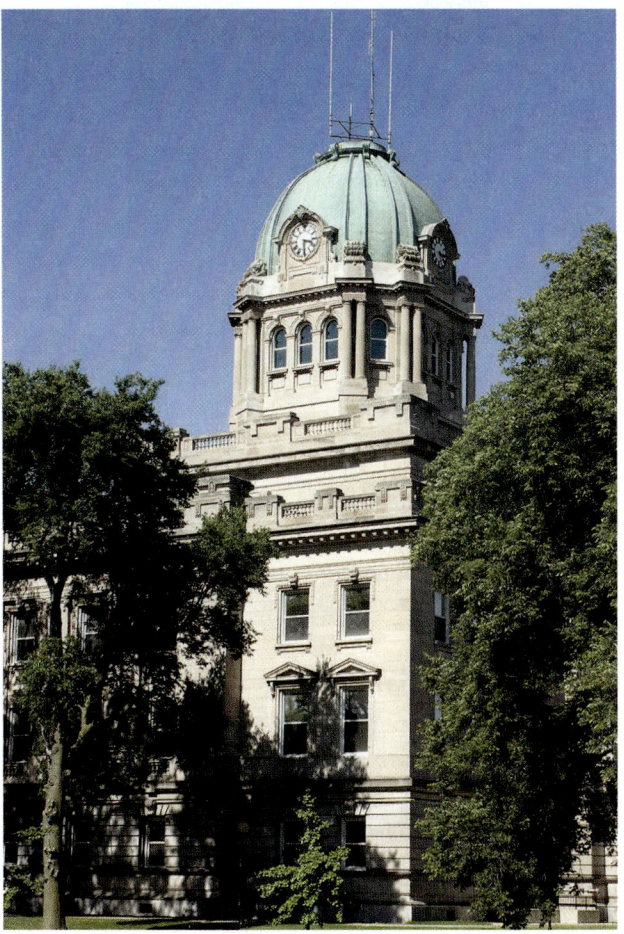
View at 100 mm setting on a zoom lens

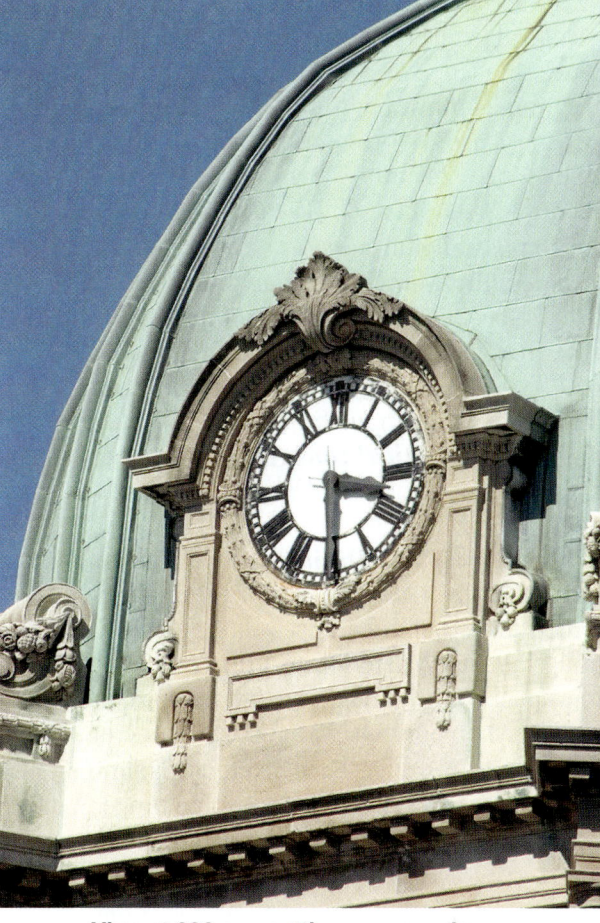
View at 300 mm setting on same lens

Jack Klasey/Goodheart-Willcox Publisher

Figure 6-24. A zoom lens lets the photographer choose an overall view or extract a detail of the scene.

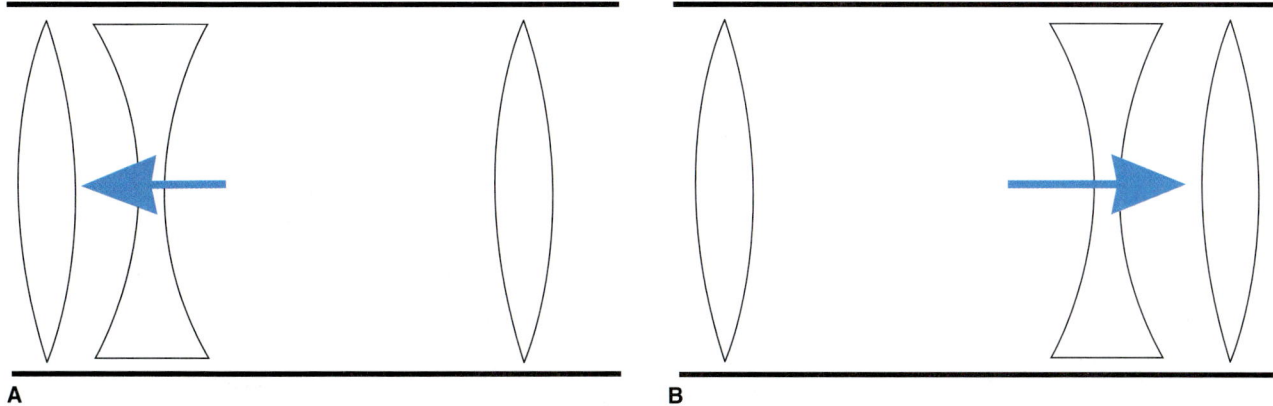

A B

Goodheart-Willcox Publisher

Figure 6-25. Moving groups of lens elements provide the varying focal lengths in a zoom lens. A—Moving the negative element closer to the front positive element shortens the focal length. B—Moving the negative element closer to the rear positive element lengthens the focal length.

lens is shortened. As it moves backward, the focal length becomes longer. A zoom lens uses groups of lens elements, with a number of the groups moving varying distances as the focal length is changed.

The **zoom range**, or classification of a zoom lens by the spread from its shortest focal length to its longest focal length, is expressed as a digit followed by a times sign (such as 3×). Ranges may be as low as 2× (12 mm–24 mm) or as high as 16× (18 mm–300 mm), but most are 3× or 4×. Common zoom ranges for DSLRs are 24 mm–70 mm, 28 mm–300 mm, 70 mm–200 mm, and 200 mm–400 mm.

Compact digital cameras have lenses with shorter focal lengths. Many models are available with zoom ranges between 5× and 8×. Some models have 10×, 16×, or 20× zooms, while a few offer 50× or 65×. When selecting a compact digital camera, it is important to distinguish between optical zoom and digital zoom. **Optical zoom** is a physical camera feature that moves the lens elements to change the angle of view, and thus, image size, without affecting the quality of the image. **Digital zoom** is a digital camera feature that electronically crops the image to smaller dimensions, making it appear larger but causing the image quality to deteriorate, **Figure 6-26**. As a photographer, you should disregard digital zoom specifications when purchasing or using a camera.

Zoom lenses often have different maximum apertures at the two extremes of the zoom range. A difference of 2/3 stop to one full stop is most common (see Chapter 7, *Light and Exposure*, for more information on f-stops). A typical 70 mm–300 mm lens may have a wide-open aperture of f/4 at the 70 mm end and f/5.6

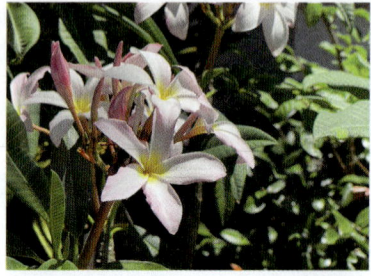
A

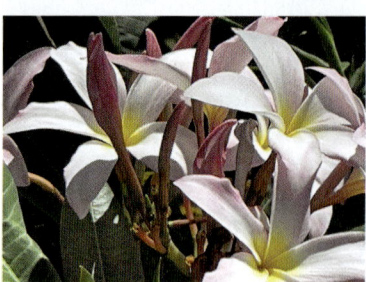
B

Goodheart-Willcox Publisher

Figure 6-26. Difference between optical zoom and digital zoom. Notice how the digital zoom looks distorted and is not as high quality as the optical zoom. A—Optical zoom. B—Digital zoom.

at the 300 mm end. Zoom lenses that feature a constant maximum aperture, often f/2.8 or f/4, are typically more expensive due to their greater complexity. These zoom lenses offer better light-gathering power, allowing the use of faster shutter speeds, especially under dim lighting conditions. As a beginning photographer, you may not have extra money to spend on various lenses. In that case, zoom lenses are great until you figure out what you need in your photography kit.

REAL-WORLD PHOTOGRAPHY

Lens Prices

The price of lenses varies widely. It depends on both the quality of the lens and the type of camera being used. Many factors go into appropriately pricing a lens, including the materials used to make the lens and the type of lens (normal, wide angle, telephoto, etc.). Additionally, each camera company makes its own lenses that are compatible with its cameras. However, you can often find third-party lenses that also work with the camera you have. Using a compatible third-party lens can be a good way to save money, as lenses created by individual camera companies are often more expensive.

The included chart provides information on pricing for normal, wide-angle, and telephoto lenses. Keep in mind that these prices are current at the time of this book's publication, and prices may change at any time. It is also worth noting that the prices are for brand-new lenses and are meant to show the wide range of prices. If you are looking for a higher-quality lens without the price tag, you can always buy them used or refurbished. You can also rent a lens if you need something specific for a short amount of time.

Typical Lens Prices		
Lens Type	Inexpensive	High-End
Normal	$120.00	$12,995.00
Wide Angle	$129.00	$1,789.00
Telephoto	$129.00	$33,699.99

Goodheart-Willcox Publisher

Specialty Lenses

Many photographers carry one or more special-purpose or specialty lenses for use in specific situations. They include teleconverters, macro lenses, tilt-shift lenses, creative effects lenses, and smartphone accessory lenses.

Teleconverter

The focal length of a telephoto lens can be increased by mounting an accessory lens called a **teleconverter** between the camera lens and the camera body. Teleconverters are usually available in two different degrees of magnification. A 2× extender doubles the focal length of the lens, and a 1.4× extender increases focal length by 1.4 times. See **Figure 6-27**.

General-purpose teleconverters are not designed for a specific lens. They are relatively inexpensive, but they may cause a noticeable loss of sharpness and contrast, especially with a zoom lens. A multiple-element teleconverter made specifically for use with a given lens is more expensive but is designed to work together optically with the lens, maintaining image quality.

Macro Lens

Photographing objects so they are larger than life is called *macrophotography*, or *close-up photography*. A **macro lens** (short for *macro-focusing lens*) can focus more closely than a typical lens of the same focal length, providing a larger image of an object on the image receiver. A numeric expression of size relationships, such as 1:4, is known as the **reproduction ratio**. In the ratio, the first number represents the object's size on the image receiver, and the second number represents the actual size. For example, if the actual size of an object is 1/4″ (6.3 mm) and the recorded image is only 1/8″ (3.1 mm), the reproduction ratio is 1:2, or half life-size.

In the past, normal lenses typically only focused close enough to provide a 1:7 or 1:8 reproduction ratio. Today, macro capability built into a number of fixed focal length lenses often provides 1:1 reproduction ratios. Most zoom lenses allow macro focusing only at the long end of their zoom range and provide only a 1:4 reproduction ratio. Close-up photography is described in greater detail in Chapter 13, *Outdoor Photography*.

Tilt-Shift Lens

A tilt-shift lens is a very niche lens. It can be shifted/tilted in relation to the image sensor, which allows it to move in multiple directions. Photographing tall buildings often creates the problem of converging verticals—elements that seem to come together as they recede from the viewer. The convergence is particularly noticeable when the camera must be tilted upward to include the full height of a building.

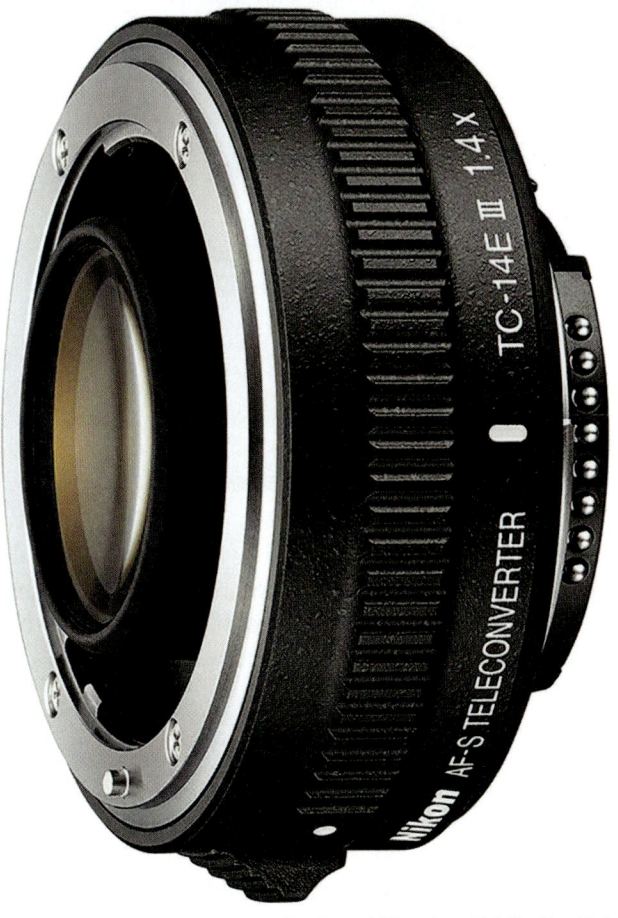

Courtesy of Nikon, Inc., Melville, New York

Figure 6-27. Adding this teleconverter between the camera and lens will increase the focal length of the lens by 1.4 times.

Photographers using large format cameras correct convergence problems with tilt and swing controls. There are two ways to control converging verticals. You can move far enough away from the subject to minimize the convergence, or you can use a special perspective control lens. Moving away or using a lens with a shorter focal length makes the subject smaller, so the camera does not have to be tilted upward. The perspective control or tilt-shift lens permits some of the same corrective adjustments used by large format photographers. See **Figure 6-28**.

Creative Effects Lens

A ***creative effects lens*** is an accessory lens that permits manipulation of the area of sharp focus in an image, **Figure 6-29**. The lens element is housed on a swivel ball and focusing mechanism that can be used to vary the plane of focus, somewhat like the more sophisticated tilt-shift lens, **Figure 6-30**. A variety of specialized lens elements can be mounted on the swivel mechanism for different optical effects.

Smartphone Accessory Lenses

The rapid growth of smartphone photography has created demand for accessory devices to provide improved capabilities, especially extended wide-angle and telephoto ranges. Some devices designed to mount on a phone are fixed or adjustable lenses that fit over the existing camera lens. More

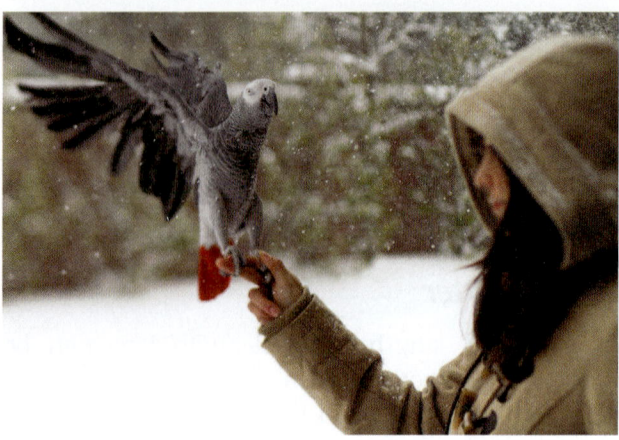

Courtesy of Lensbaby; Photo by Ben Hutchison

Figure 6-29. A creative effects lens permits unusual effects, such as this image with a single sharp plane of focus.

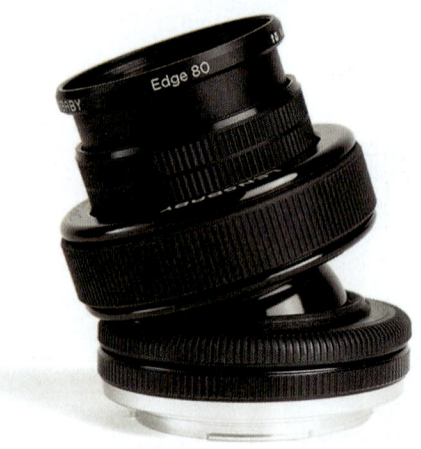

Courtesy of Lensbaby

Figure 6-30. Different lens elements can be mounted on the swivel ball of this creative effects lens system, which is designed to manipulate the plane of focus in an image.

sophisticated are the tiny lens-style cameras that mount on and electronically interface with the phone, **Figure 6-31**. These devices have their own built-in sensor and interchangeable lenses. They use the phone's screen as the viewfinder and the phone's Wi-Fi capability for sharing images online.

As newer smartphone models are released, their cameras become more sophisticated. Many photographers have noted that recent smartphone cameras can rival DSLR cameras in terms of quality, and they may also be a better option for photographers who are on the go and cannot carry much gear. The size of a smartphone is much more compact and easier to travel with than a traditional digital camera and its separate lenses.

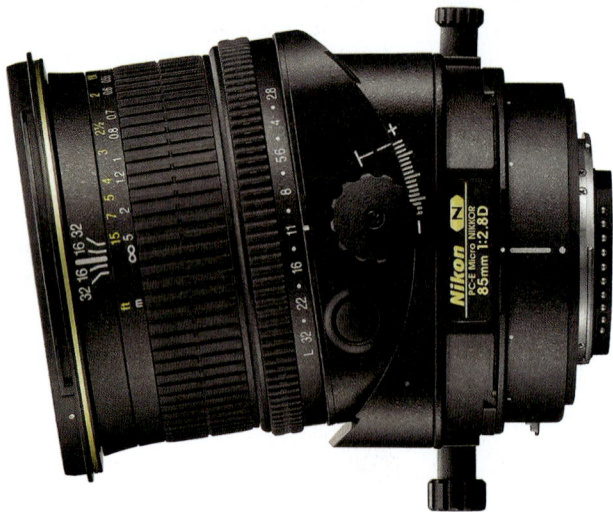

Courtesy of Nikon, Inc., Melville, New York

Figure 6-28. A perspective control lens allows a 35 mm SLR to have some of the correction capabilities usually reserved for large format cameras equipped with tilts and other movements.

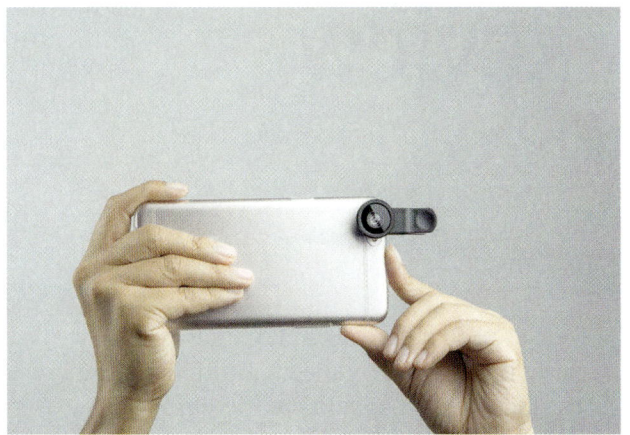

BonNontawat/Shutterstock.com

Figure 6-31. Add-on lens accessories can extend the photography capabilities of a smartphone.

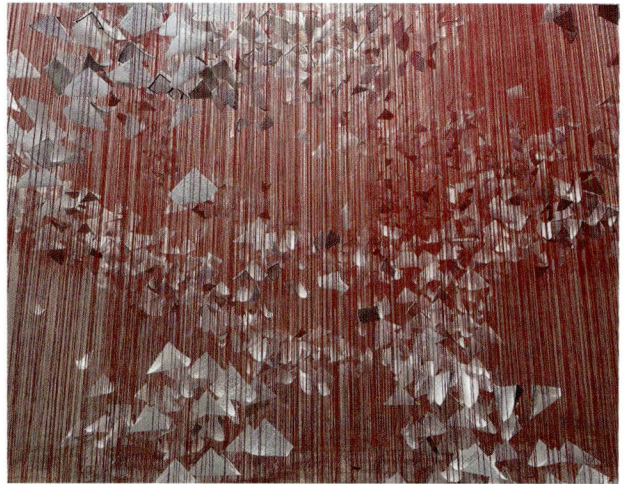

Goodheart-Willcox Publisher

Figure 6-32. This image was taken on a smartphone. Camera quality on phones continues to improve and rival some DSLRs.

For instance, the iPhone® 12 Pro Max comes with three lenses built into the phone itself, as does the Google Pixel 7, **Figure 6-32**. These lenses allow the user flexibility when it comes to taking photographs and are the equivalent of a photographer swapping out lenses with just the push of a button on the device's screen. The native camera apps allow you to switch seamlessly between the lenses, meaning that almost everyone who has a relatively new smartphone has a near-professional-quality camera right in the palm of their hand.

Portfolio Assignment

Extract a Detail

Use your telephoto lens to zoom into a scene and extract (pull out) a visually interesting detail.

1. Select a scene to shoot, such as a nature scene, a street view or crowd, or a building. **Example A** shows a scene and the extracted detail.
2. Using your telephoto lens, spend some time examining different scenes, looking for details you can extract.
3. Shoot several different subjects from the same scene. Take several photos of each subject.

Select the best two images you made for your portfolio.

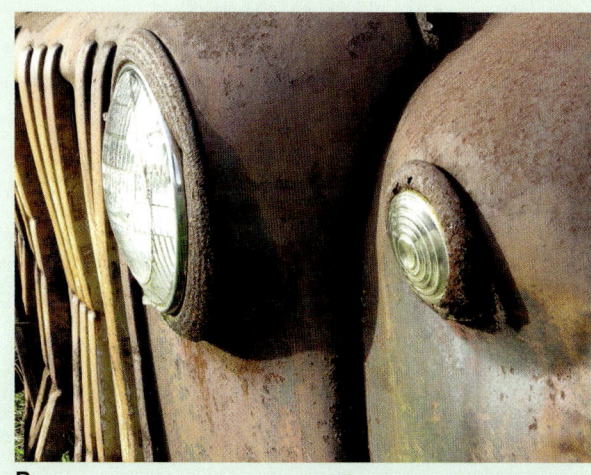

A   B

Jack Klasey/Goodheart-Willcox Publisher

Example A. Extracting a detail. A—Original scene. B—Detail extracted by zooming in.

Chapter 6 Review

Summary

- In photography, a lens is defined as an optical lens or assembly of lenses that work together with a camera body to bring light to a fixed focal point that is processed by the camera to create an image.
- Lenses bring light into the camera body where the light can be processed as an image by the camera's sensor. This light is then bent through the process of refraction.
- Lenses are curved shapes, so the rays of light entering them are bent to different angles by different parts of the curved surface. If the lens shape is convex, the emerging light rays will converge. If the lens shape is concave, the rays will diverge.
- Optical problems called aberrations can cause blurred, color-distorted, or shape-distorted images when a convex lens is used alone. The six major types of aberrations are spherical aberration, chromatic aberration, curvature of field, astigmatism, coma, and distortion.
- To lessen or eliminate issues like loss of light, flare, and ghost images, manufacturers apply nonreflective coatings to lenses.
- Focal length is defined as the distance from the optical center of the lens to the point where the light rays converge (the image receiver plane). Although focal lengths may be stated in inches or in millimeters, the general practice is to refer to a 50 mm lens rather than a 2-inch lens.
- The focal length of the lens directly affects the size of the image projected onto the image receiver. Directly related to the image size is the angle of view of the lens.
- Lenses used on most DSLR cameras exhibit what is sometimes called a multiplier effect—the focal length appears to increase by approximately 1.5 times.
- Fixed focal length lenses have traditionally been grouped based on their angle of view. The three categories are normal, wide angle, and telephoto.
- The 50 mm lens is usually described as a normal lens because it provides an angle of view and a perspective close to that of the unaided human eye. In reality, the focal length that provides the most distortion-free normal view is one that is equal to the diagonal measurement of the image receiver.
- A lens with an angle of view from about 55° to as much as 180° is considered a wide-angle lens. In terms of focal length, wide-angle lenses are typically between 10 and 35 mm.
- A lens with an angle of view roughly 25° or smaller is considered a telephoto lens. Most of the longer lenses made today, especially zoom lenses, use a front-focusing design.
- The major attraction of the zoom lens is its variable focal length, which allows the photographer to change composition without physically changing lenses or position.
- Many photographers carry one or more special-purpose or specialty lenses for use in specific situations. They include teleconverters, macro lenses, tilt-shift lenses, creative effects lenses, and smartphone accessory lenses.
- The focal length of a telephoto lens can be increased by mounting an accessory lens called a teleconverter between the camera lens and the camera body.
- A macro lens (short for macro-focusing lens) can focus more closely than a typical lens of the same focal length, providing a larger image of an object on the image receiver.

- A tilt-shift lens is a very niche lens. It can be shifted/tilted in relation to the image sensor, which allows it to move in multiple directions.
- A creative effects lens is an accessory lens that permits manipulation of the area of sharp focus in an image.
- The rapid growth of smartphone photography has created demand for accessory devices to provide improved capabilities, especially extended wide-angle and telephoto ranges. Many photographers have noted that recent smartphone cameras can rival DSLR cameras in terms of quality, and they may also be a better option for photographers who are on the go and cannot carry much gear.

Review Questions

Answer the following questions using the information provided in this chapter.

Know and Understand

1. *True or False?* The macro lens was the first lens developed specifically as a camera lens.
2. _____ is the bending of light rays that takes place in a lens because of the differing densities of glass and air.
   A. Reflection
   B. Refraction
   C. Astigmatism
   D. Convergence
3. *True or False?* If the lens shape is convex, the emerging light rays will converge.
4. Which of the following lens types was designed to correct the aberration known as curvature of field?
   A. Aspheric
   B. Apochromatic
   C. Symmetrical
   D. Aplanatic
5. Which of the following lens types was designed to correct the aberration known as distortion?
   A. Symmetrical
   B. Apochromatic
   C. Aplanatic
   D. Aspheric
6. *True or False?* To combat reflection issues, manufacturers apply reflective coatings to lenses.
7. _____ is defined as the distance from the optical center of the lens to the point where the light rays converge (the image receiver plane).
   A. Focal point
   B. Selective focus
   C. Back focus
   D. Focal length
8. *True or False?* As the focal length becomes shorter, the light rays are bent at sharper angles, converging a short distance behind the lens and producing a small image.
9. *True or False?* Long-focus lenses compress perspective, making distant objects appear larger and closer together.
10. In what is known as the _____, the focal length appears to increase by approximately 1.5 times.
    A. curvature of field
    B. reproduction ratio
    C. multiplier effect
    D. angle of view
11. *True or False?* The 35 mm lens is usually described as a normal lens because it provides an angle of view and a perspective close to that of the unaided human eye.
12. A lens with an angle of view greater than 180° that produces a round image with considerable spherical distortion is called a _____ lens.
    A. zoom
    B. telephoto
    C. superwide
    D. fish-eye
13. Superwide lenses are rectilinear, which means they are corrected for _____.
    A. coma
    B. barrel distortion
    C. spherical aberration
    D. pincushion distortion
14. *True or False?* Most of the zoom lenses made today use a front-focusing design.

15. _____ electronically crops the image to smaller dimensions, making it appear larger but causing the image quality to deteriorate.
    A. Digital zoom
    B. Superzoom
    C. Optical zoom
    D. Zoom range
16. General-purpose _____ are relatively inexpensive but may cause a noticeable loss of sharpness and contrast.
    A. macro lenses
    B. creative effects lenses
    C. teleconverters
    D. tilt-shift lenses
17. A _____ lens can focus more closely than a typical lens of the same focal length, providing a larger image of an object on the image receiver.
    A. tilt-shift
    B. telephoto
    C. creative effects
    D. macro
18. *True or False?* One of the ways to control converging verticals is moving far enough away from the subject to minimize the convergence.
19. A _____ lens can focus more closely than a typical lens of the same focal length, providing a larger image of an object on the image receiver.
    A. wide-angle
    B. creative effects
    C. fish-eye
    D. telephoto
20. *True or False?* Many photographers have noted that recent smartphone cameras can rival DSLR cameras in terms of quality.

Apply and Analyze

1. What are the two negative effects reflection of light has on lens performance?
2. What is perspective?
3. What does applying retrofocus design to a wide-angle lens do?
4. What are the two degrees of magnification in which teleconverters are usually available?
5. Your macro lens permits you to make close-ups at a magnification of 1:3. If you are making a close-up of a flower that is 3/8″ across, how wide will the flower's image be on your camera's sensor?

Critical Thinking

1. On a digital camera using an APS-C size sensor, a lens may exhibit a multiplier effect that increases its apparent focal length approximately 1.5 times. For example, a 28 mm lens becomes a 42 mm lens, while a 200 mm lens becomes a 300 mm lens. What are the photographic advantages and disadvantages of this multiplier effect?
2. When purchasing a digital camera, should you consider digital zoom a desirable feature? Why or why not?

Suggested Activities

1. The first scientific applications of lenses were the microscope and the telescope. Research the invention and development of either the microscope or the telescope and create a short, illustrated report on your findings.

2. Because of their smaller physical size, the focal lengths of lenses used on compact digital cameras are much shorter than the familiar focal lengths of 35 mm camera lenses. To convert a digital camera focal length to its equivalent 35 mm focal length, multiply by 5.6. To convert 35 mm focal length to digital camera focal length, divide by 5.6. Construct a table showing the digital camera lens equivalents for the following 35 mm lenses—24 mm, 28 mm, 50 mm, 70 mm, 100 mm, 200 mm, 300 mm, 500 mm. Round the numbers up to the nearest tenth.

Communicating about Photography

1. **Speaking.** Choose one of the lens aberrations discussed in this chapter. In your own words, explain the aberration to the class. Talk about the cause and effect of the aberration.

2. **Speaking and Listening.** In small groups, discuss with your classmates—in basic, everyday language—your knowledge of the different types of lenses. Take notes on the observations expressed. Then review the points discussed, factoring in your new knowledge of lens types. Develop a summary of what you have learned about lens types and present it to the class. Use the terms that you have learned in this chapter.

Chapter 7
Light and Exposure

Learning Objectives

After completing this chapter, you will be able to:
- Understand the basic characteristics of light.
- Select filters for different lighting conditions or special effects.
- Explain how exposure is affected by the interrelationship of aperture, shutter speed, and ISO rating.
- Describe how the f-stop system functions.
- Demonstrate proper light metering techniques.
- Determine the use of the Zone System.

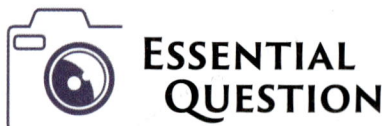

Essential Question
How do light and exposure affect your ability to take photographs?

Technical Terms

additive color process
aperture
backlit
cadmium sulfide (CdS) cell meter
color cast
color temperature
contrast filter
cooling filter
creative control
digital noise
exposure
frequency
f-stop
incident light reading
ISO rating
light
luminances
metering
middle gray
nanometer
neutral density (ND) filter
overexposure
photoelectric light meter
photographic daylight
polarizing filter
reciprocity law
reflective light reading
selenium cell meter
shutter
shutter speed
specular reflection
subject brightness range (SBR)
subtractive color process
sync speed
through-the-lens (TTL) metering
tonal range
underexposure
visible spectrum
warming filter
wavelength
white light
zebras
Zone System

146   Copyright Goodheart-Willcox Co., Inc.

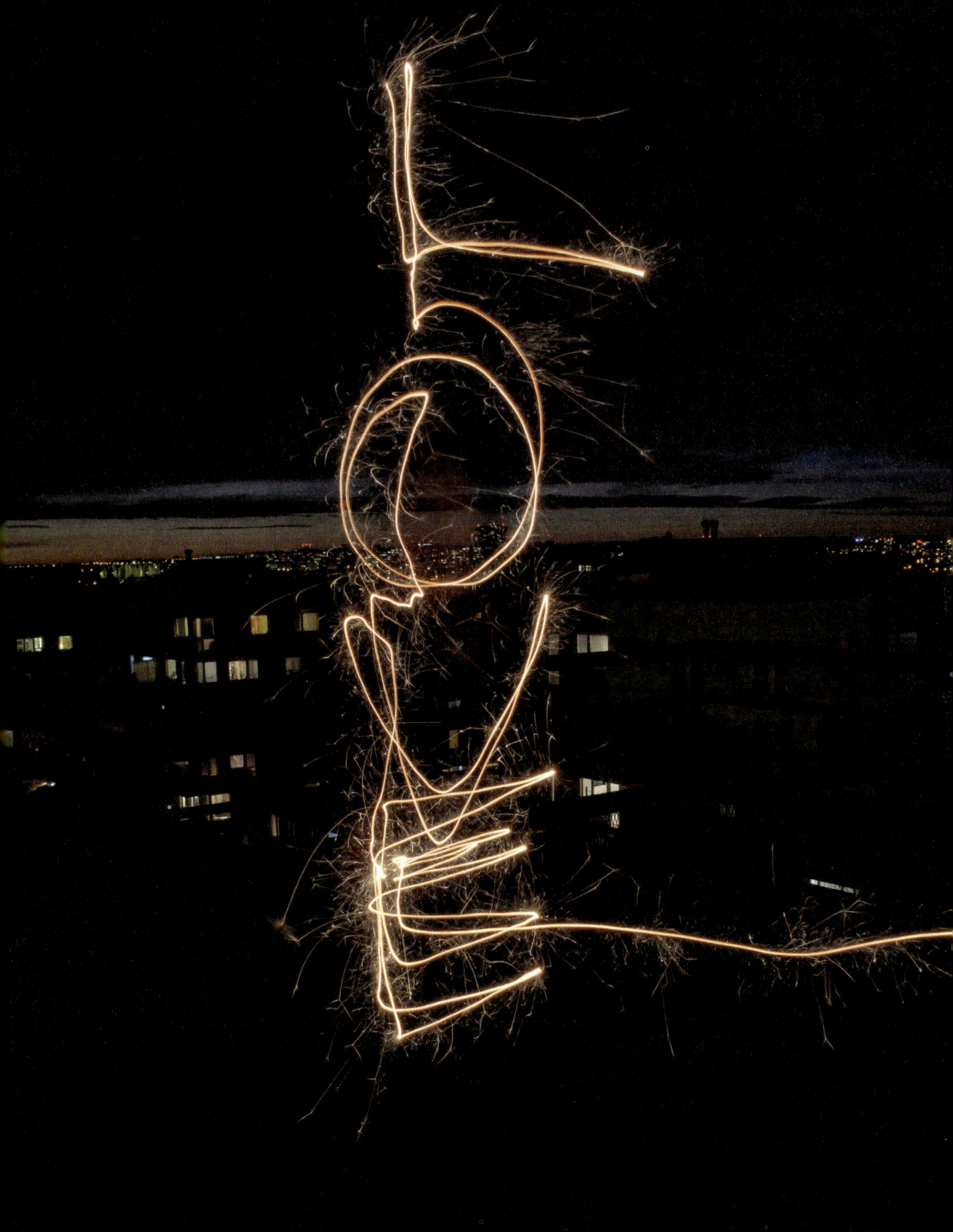

Introduction to Light and Exposure

As you learned in Chapter 1, *Our Visual World*, *photography* is defined as the act of "drawing with light." This description is an appropriate one since light rays entering a digital camera cause electrical changes on an array of electronic sensors. These "light drawings" then can be given permanent form and reproduced for viewing. When it comes to taking photos, it is important to ensure that they are lit and exposed properly. If these elements are not carefully monitored, you risk creating an image that is hard for viewers to process and understand.

Basic Light Theory

Being aware of how light behaves can help you overcome problems and capture the scene as you visualized it. **Light** is a form of electromagnetic radiation, or radiant energy, that is visible to the human eye. The largest natural producer of this radiant energy is the sun. Artificial sources of radiant energy are lamps that produce light through *discharge*, *fluorescent*, *incandescent*, or *electroluminescent* means.

An electronic flash is an example of light emitted by discharge. The flash tube is filled with xenon gas that emits a short and very intense burst of light when a high-voltage electrical discharge takes place inside the tube.

In a fluorescent light source, a discharge of electrical energy causes a gas (usually mercury vapor) to emit ultraviolet radiation. This radiation, in turn, causes a coating inside the glass tube to glow and emit light.

Incandescent light sources consist of a metal element with high electrical resistance inside a sealed glass container or bulb. When an electric current is passed through the element, resistance causes it to heat rapidly to the point where it glows white-hot and emits light.

A light-emitting diode (LED) is an electroluminescent light source. The LED is a semiconductor device that emits light when a suitable voltage is applied to it. LED lights are more energy efficient than incandescent lights and are often considered the most cost-effective.

Movement of Light

Everything we see is a reflection of light bouncing off objects that is then interpreted by our brain. When light is emitted from a source, it radiates (moves away) in straight lines in all directions. The light rays move in the form of a wave, vibrating at right angles to the direction of travel. The waves move away from the source at a speed of 186,000 miles per second. This is why a room appears to instantly fill with light when you press a wall switch—the light quickly bounces off the walls and is then translated by our brain so we can make sense of what is there.

Two characteristics of a light wave can be measured, as shown in **Figure 7-1**. The **wavelength** is the distance from the crest (top) of one wave to the crest of the next. The unit of measure for wavelength is the **nanometer**, which is equal to one-billionth of a meter (0.000000001 m = 1 nm). **Frequency** is a measure of the number of waves (cycles) passing a given point in one second. The unit of measure for frequency is the hertz (one cycle per second = 1 Hz).

Visible Spectrum

The tiny portion of the electromagnetic spectrum that can be seen by the human eye is referred to as the **visible spectrum**. It consists of waves with wavelengths ranging from about 400 nm to about 700 nm. Our eyes see different wavelengths of light as different colors, **Figure 7-2**. Although we may be able to distinguish as many as 100 different colors within the red-to-violet spectrum, the spectrum is traditionally divided into seven colors—red, orange, yellow, green, blue-green, blue, and violet.

The wavelengths for some distance on either side of the visible spectrum are not normally visible to the eye, but they can be recorded on film. Infrared (IR) wavelengths are longer than 700 nm, so they are below red (infra means *below*) on the spectrum. Ultraviolet (beyond violet) wavelengths are shorter than 400 nm. Film can be made sensitive to infrared radiation with special dyes added in manufacture, and it is normally quite sensitive to ultraviolet

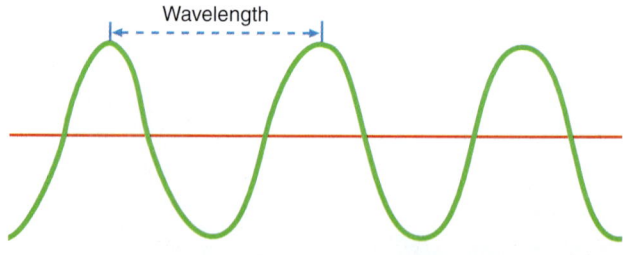

Goodheart-Willcox Publisher

Figure 7-1. Wavelength is measured from one wave crest to the next wave crest. The number of waves passing a point in one second is the frequency.

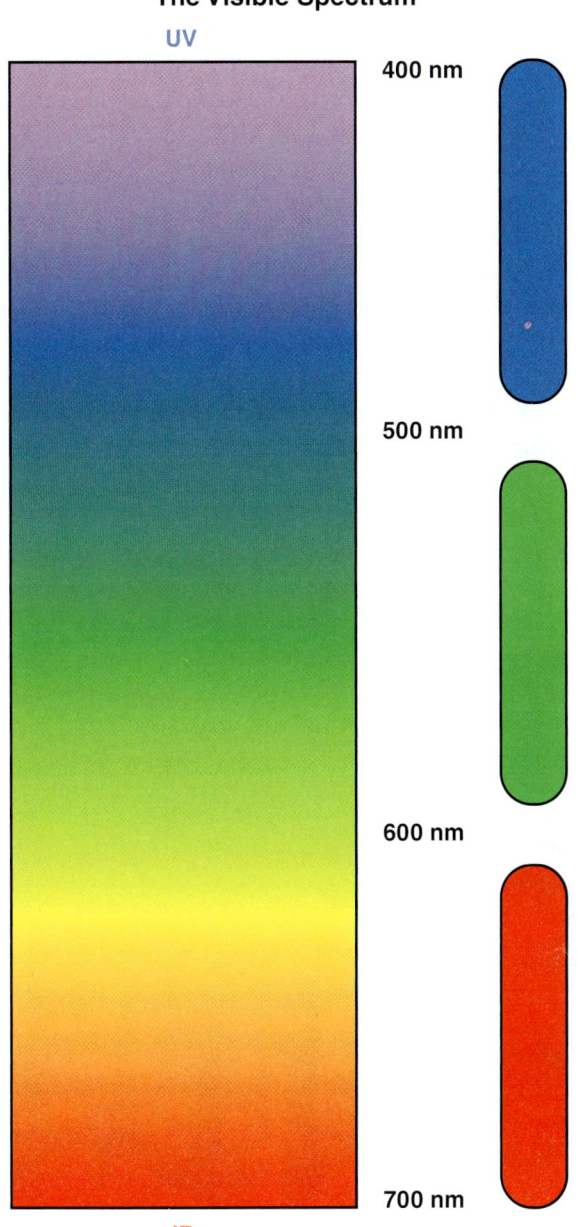

Figure 7-2. The wavelengths from approximately 400 nm to 700 nm make up the visible spectrum. The human eye perceives the different wavelengths as colors.

(UV) wavelengths. Digital camera sensors are infrared-sensitive and are typically covered by a factory-installed filter to balance that sensitivity.

The Color of Light

White light is light composed of red, green, and blue wavelengths in approximately equal proportions. Such a light is produced by the midday sun on a clear and cloudless day. Light has a specific **color temperature**, which is a measurement of the color of light, expressed in units called degrees kelvin (K). The light produced by the midday sun on a clear and cloudless day has a color temperature of 5500 K and is referred to as **photographic daylight**. See **Figure 7-3**.

Although different types of artificial light have different colors, the human vision system adjusts to the differences and sees them as white light. Ordinary incandescent light bulbs emit a light that is heavily balanced toward the red/orange/yellow end of the spectrum, while electronic flash tubes are balanced toward the spectrum's opposite blue/violet end.

In Kelvin scale measurements, lower temperatures are warmer and higher temperatures are colder. This is the opposite of the Fahrenheit and Celsius temperature scales, in which lower temperatures are colder and higher temperatures are warmer.

The color of light is an important factor in selecting the correct white balance for digital image capture. These topics are covered later in this chapter.

Absorption and Reflection of Light

To better understand what happens when light rays strike an object, visualize directing a stream of water from a garden hose at a brick wall, **Figure 7-4**. Some of the water soaks into the brick (is absorbed), but most of it bounces off (is reflected). If you direct the stream at a piece of wooden latticework, some of the water is absorbed and some is reflected. Most of it, though, passes (is transmitted) through the diamond-shaped openings of the lattice.

The amount of light that is absorbed, reflected, or transmitted depends on the material from which

Color Temperature	
Light source	°Kelvin
Candle	1800
100 W tungsten bulb	2900
250 W studio flood lamp	3400
Photographic daylight	5500
Electronic flash	6000
Sky light (overcast)	8000

Goodheart-Willcox Publisher

Figure 7-3. This table outlines some common light sources and their color temperatures, expressed in degrees Kelvin.

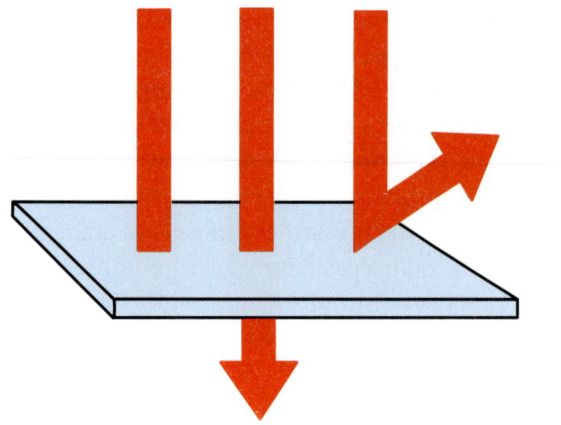

Figure 7-4. Light rays striking a material may be absorbed, transmitted, or reflected.

the object is made, the type of surface finish, and the object's color. Transparent or translucent (milky in color) material reflects very little light. Most of the light is either transmitted or absorbed. Opaque materials do not transmit light. They absorb or reflect light in different proportions, depending on their surface finish. A dull or rough surface absorbs a high percentage of light rays. The reflections from such a surface are diffuse (reflected in many directions). A surface that is smooth and polished reflects a very high percentage of the light. This type of surface reflects rays as bright points of light, which is referred to as **specular reflection**. The rays are reflected in an orderly and concentrated manner. Even materials that transmit most of the light that strikes them, such as glass or water, produce specular reflections from their smooth surfaces. White or light-colored objects reflect light rays readily, while black or dark-colored objects absorb most light rays.

Our perception of an object's color is based on the wavelengths of light that are reflected from that object. When white light strikes the surface of a lime, the red and blue wavelengths are absorbed by the fruit's surface. The green wavelengths are reflected back to the viewer's eye, and the lime is seen as green. The yellow color of a lemon viewed under white light results from the blue wavelengths being absorbed and equal amounts of red and green wavelengths being reflected. See **Figure 7-5**.

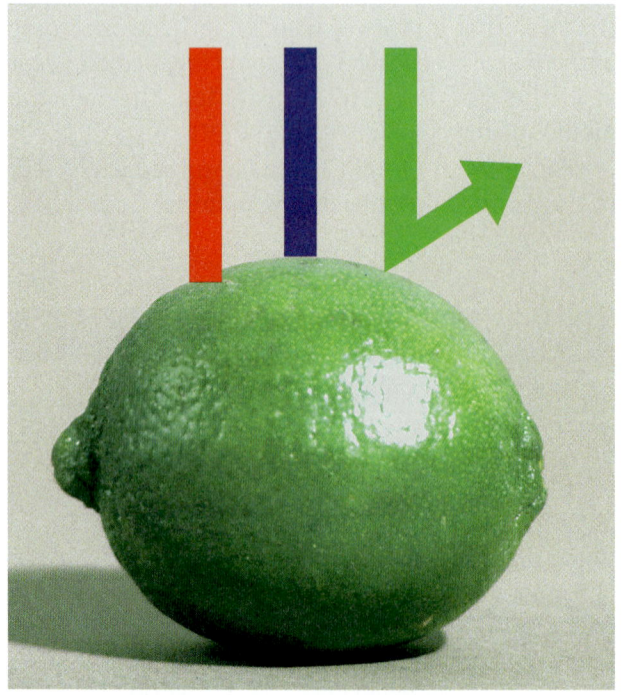

A

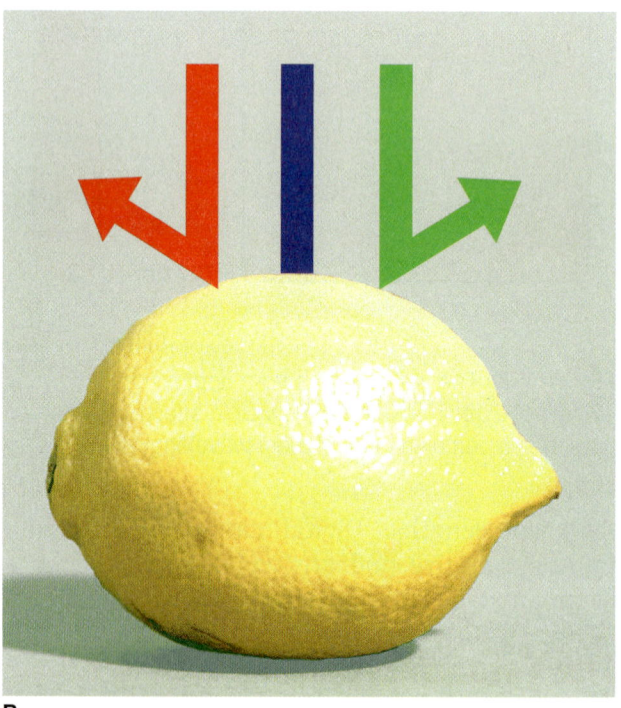

B

Figure 7-5. Color perception. A—Red and blue wavelengths of white light are absorbed by the lime, while green wavelengths are reflected. The lime is seen as green. B—Blue light is absorbed by the lemon's skin, while red and green wavelengths are reflected, providing the yellow color.

Additive and Subtractive Color Processes

Visualize overlapping circles of red, green, and blue light thrown onto a screen by three separate slide projectors, **Figure 7-6**. The center area, where all three circles overlap, has no color, only the white of the screen. Where the red and the blue circles overlap, there is a wedge of magenta. Overlapping blue and green produce a wedge of cyan, while the overlap of green and red creates a yellow wedge.

This is a demonstration of the **additive color process**, which is a color reproduction method used with transmitted light in which the additive primaries (red, blue, and green) interact to create all other colors. You see this process every time you look at a television screen, a computer monitor, or the LCD screen of a digital camera. Older television sets and monitors use cathode ray tube (CRT) screens. The inside surfaces of the screens are covered with rows of tiny phosphorescent dots that glow red, green, or blue when struck by an electron beam. The LCDs on digital cameras and newer TVs and monitors have rows of liquid crystal pixels in red, blue, and green. These pixels light up when turned on by an electronic impulse. In both types of devices, the process results in a glowing full-color image.

Digital cameras capture images using red, blue, or green filters positioned over the individual pixels making up the sensor array. The filters are arranged in a Bayer pattern, **Figure 7-7**. This pattern has twice as many green filters as either red or

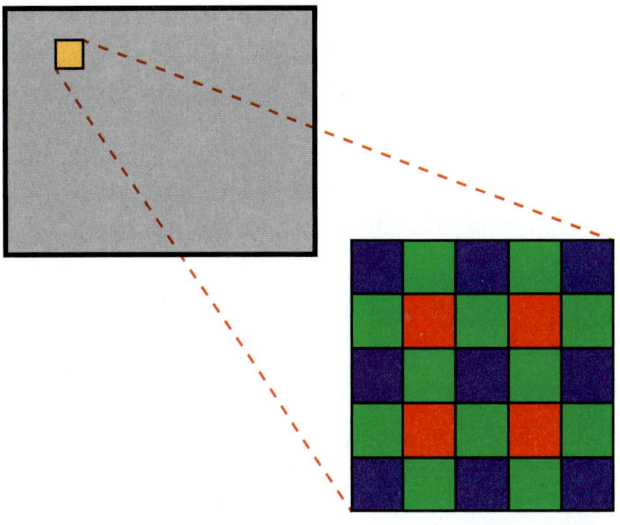

Figure 7-7. A Bayer pattern has twice as many green filters as either red or blue filters.

blue filters because human vision is most sensitive to light in the green portion of the visible spectrum.

Color film photography is based on the subtractive color process. The **subtractive color process** is a color reproduction method used with reflected light in which the subtractive primary colors (cyan, magenta, and yellow) of light subtract or block specific colors from the white light that is used to view an image. Instead of colors combining to create other colors, the subtractive process takes away some colors and allows others to be seen. On a color wheel, the subtractive primaries fall between the additive primaries, **Figure 7-8**. Each of these

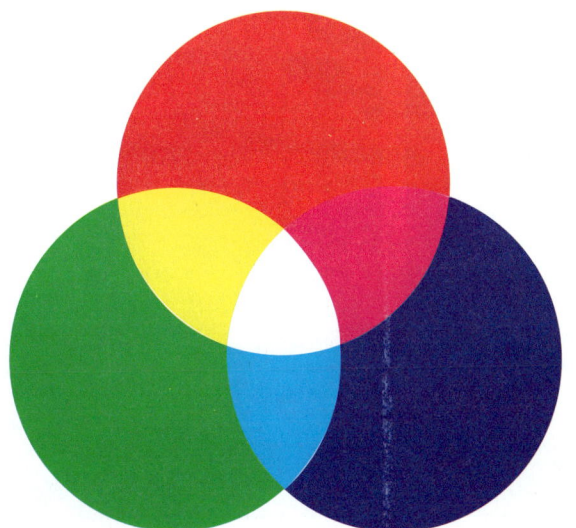

Figure 7-6. Additive colors (red, green, and blue) can be combined in various ways to create any other color.

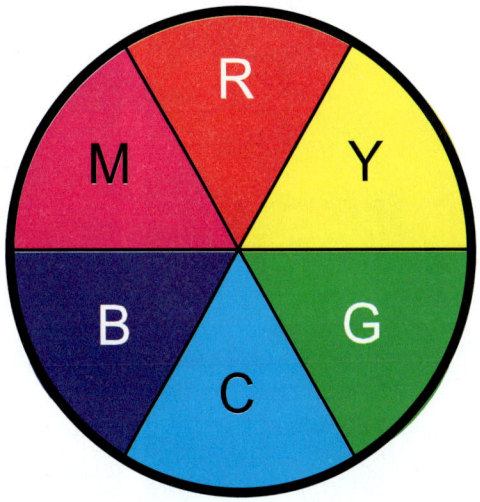

Figure 7-8. On a color wheel, the subtractive primaries (C, M, Y) are located between the additive primaries (R, G, B).

subtractive primaries absorbs the light of its complementary color, which is the color positioned opposite it on the color wheel. The subtractive primary reflects or transmits the colors on either side of its position. Cyan absorbs red light and passes green and blue. Magenta absorbs green light and passes blue and red. Finally, yellow absorbs blue light and passes red and green.

White Balance Considerations

The human vision system automatically compensates for variation in the color temperature of light. This is why when you go outside after spending time inside, things that are white still appear white. However, image receivers interpret color temperature literally—they do not adjust like the human eye to see a range of colors as white.

Digital camera users can compensate for different color temperatures by using the camera's white balance control. The concept of white balance involves selecting a color temperature that renders a white object correctly, so all other colors in the image will be correct. Most cameras offer an automatic white balance setting and settings for specific lighting conditions, such as *Daylight*, *Cloudy*, and *Tungsten*. See **Figure 7-9**. You can set a camera's white balance by using a white card and placing it in front of the lens. The camera will either automatically

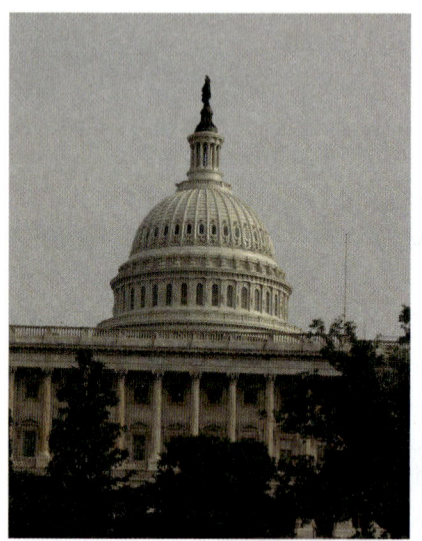
Auto white balance (AWB) setting

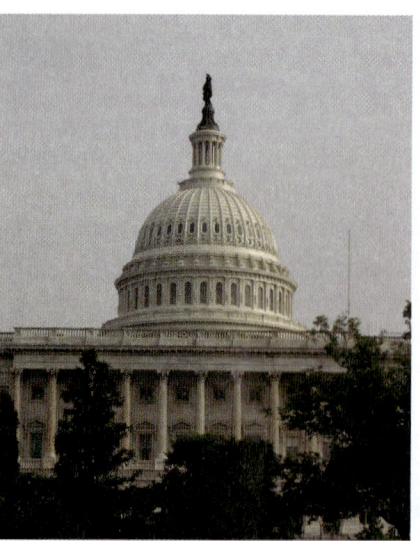
Daylight setting

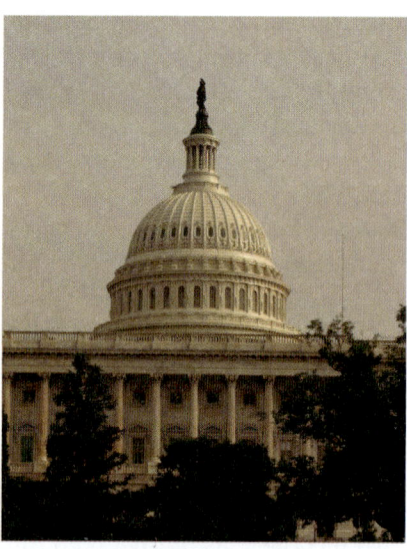
Shade setting

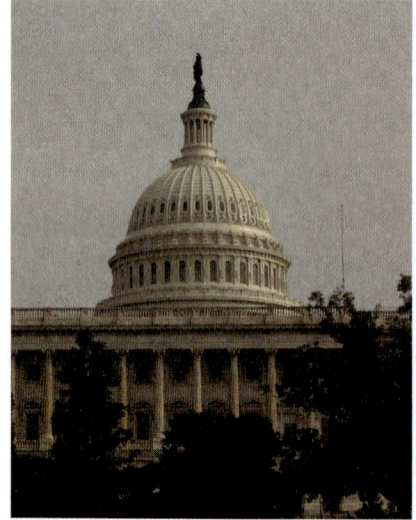
Cloudy setting

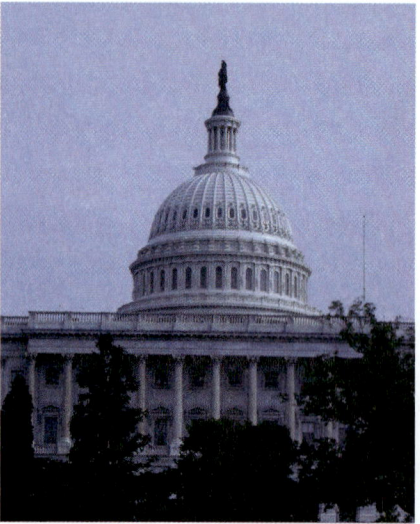
Fluorescent light setting

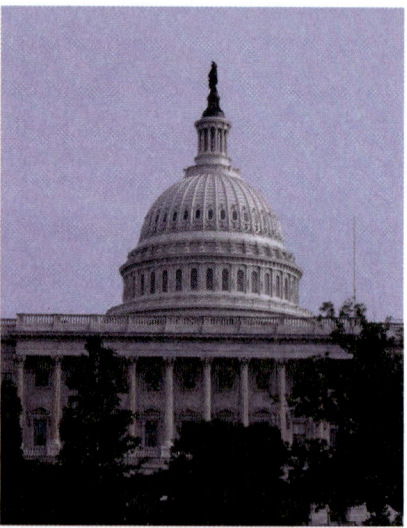
Tungsten light setting

Jack Klasey/Goodheart-Willcox Publisher

Figure 7-9. The effect of different white balance settings is shown in this series of photos of the US Capitol dome.

adjust, or you can use the white balance setting to set the color. Thanks to recent advancements, most cameras will take care of this process for you, but sometimes the color may not be entirely accurate to what your eyes are seeing. It is always worth taking the time to ensure the color is captured accurately to save yourself time in postproduction.

Controlling Light with Filters

As mentioned previously, all photographs are made with reflected light. Light rays from the source bounce off an object and pass through the camera lens to be focused on the image receiver, the same way that our eyes function. How the camera records those reflected rays of light can be controlled to a great extent with filters. Filters come in two basic forms— the round screw-in type that fits over the lens and the square type that is used in a special holder that attaches to the lens, **Figure 7-10**.

Using Filters for Contrast

Contrast filters are made in deep shades of red, green, and blue. Each transmits light of its own color and absorbs light of the other two colors. These filters are used with black-and-white film or with digital cameras that offer a black-and-white shooting mode. If used with color film or a digital camera shooting color, a contrast filter would create an image with a very strong ***color cast***, which is an unwanted color shift across an entire image caused by light temperature or other elements in an image.

Contrast filters help differentiate between colors when they are rendered as gray shades. The effect is to lighten objects of the same color as the filter and darken objects of other colors. Thus, a red filter

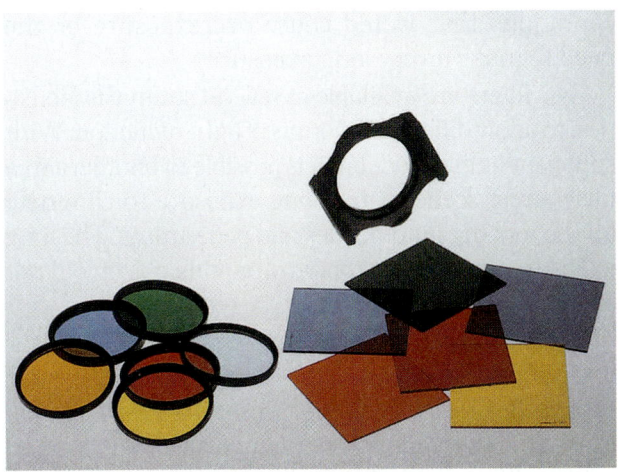

Jack Klasey/Goodheart-Willcox Publisher

Figure 7-10. The two basic forms that filters come in are round and square.

lightens a red object and darkens green and blue objects, **Figure 7-11**. What about objects of other colors? Since colors are combinations of two or all three of the primary colors in different proportions, they are affected according to their makeup.

Digital images captured in color and converted to monochrome (black-and-white) may exhibit the same contrast problems as black-and-white film images. Image processing programs offer tools, such as the Channel Mixer in Photoshop, which can be used to mimic the effects of a contrast filter.

Using Filters to Reduce Light

A ***neutral density (ND) filter*** is a type of filter that attaches to the front of a camera's lens to reduce the quantity of light reaching the image receiver without altering the light's color. An ND filter is most often used to compensate for bright lighting

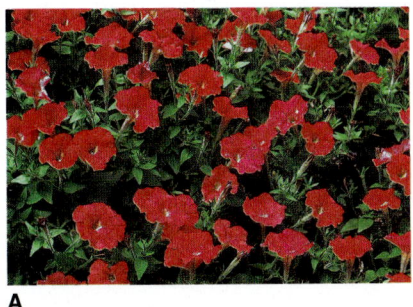
A

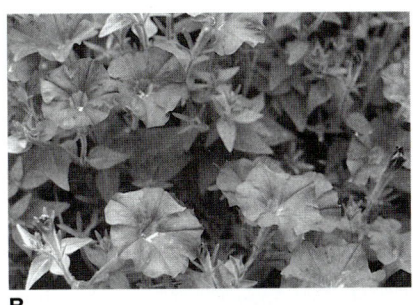
B

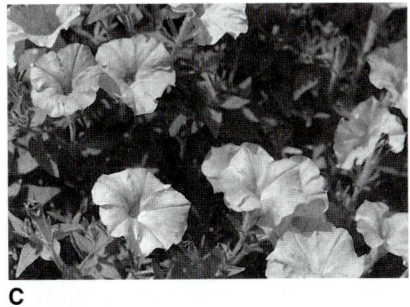
C

Jack Klasey/Goodheart-Willcox Publisher

Figure 7-11. Rendering red and green. A—Red flowers on green leaves, as the human eye would see them. B—A print from panchromatic film, with flowers and leaves rendered almost identical shades of gray. C—A contrast filter lightened the red flowers and darkened the green leaves to separate the two tones.

conditions that would cause overexposure or the need to make a very long exposure.

ND filters are available in several strengths (densities) to allow different amounts of light reduction. With sufficient light reduction, it is possible to photograph a busy street scene with a long exposure to eliminate all the moving automobiles and pedestrians. The long exposure time means that any moving object will not be in the scene long enough to be recorded.

Filters with a density that graduates to a clear background are made in a square or rectangular shape. The *graduated neutral density filter*, or *ND grad*, is used in landscape photography where there is often a large difference in brightness between the sky and the foreground. To balance the exposure of the scene, the filter is slid into its holder with the darker portion at the top. It can then be adjusted so the transition from dark to clear is positioned at the horizon. The camera is set to obtain proper exposure of the foreground area, and the ND filter reduces the sky exposure to avoid overexposure, or burning it out. See **Figure 7-12**. Some high-end digital cameras come with built-in ND filters that you can cycle through using the camera's menu, eliminating the need to carry separate filters with you as part of a camera kit.

Using Filters to Control Reflection and Color Saturation

A **polarizing filter** is a valuable tool. It is used to deepen the color of a blue sky, improve the color saturation of natural objects by reducing glare, and reduce or eliminate reflections from glass, water, and similar surfaces.

Polarization occurs when light is reflected from a shiny surface at an angle of approximately 35°. Light becomes polarized when its waves all vibrate in the same plane rather than vibrating in all directions perpendicular to the line of travel.

A polarizing filter consists of a material in which tiny crystals are all oriented in a single direction. Light striking the filter is either transmitted or blocked, **Figure 7-13**. If the light waves are oriented in the same direction as the crystals, the waves can pass through the filter. If the light waves are oriented at a right angle (90°) to the crystals, transmission is blocked.

Reflections off water, glass, painted finishes, smooth leaves, and similar surfaces can be reduced by a polarizing filter, **Figure 7-14**. As the polarizing filter is rotated to diminish or eliminate the

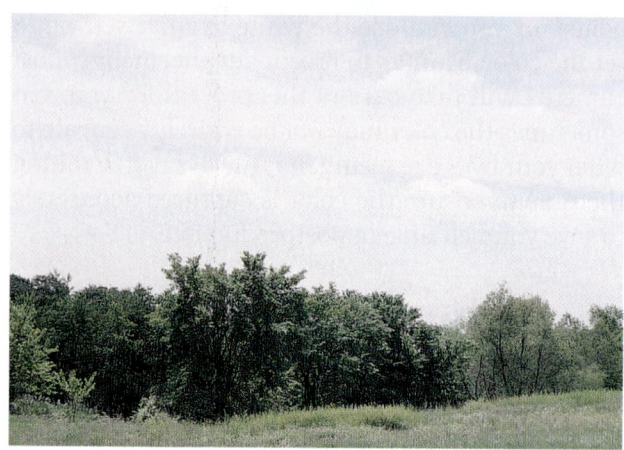
Exposed for the foreground

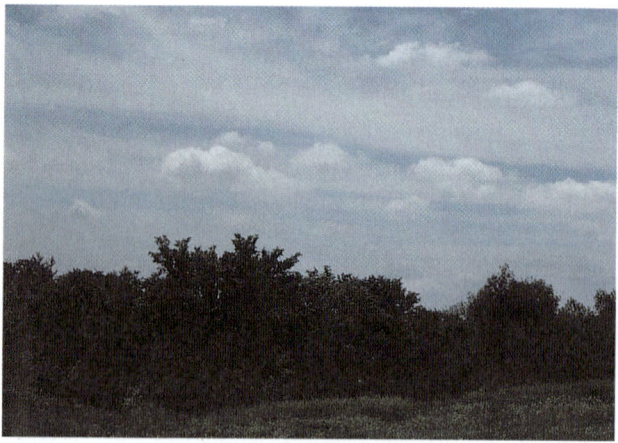
Exposed for the sky

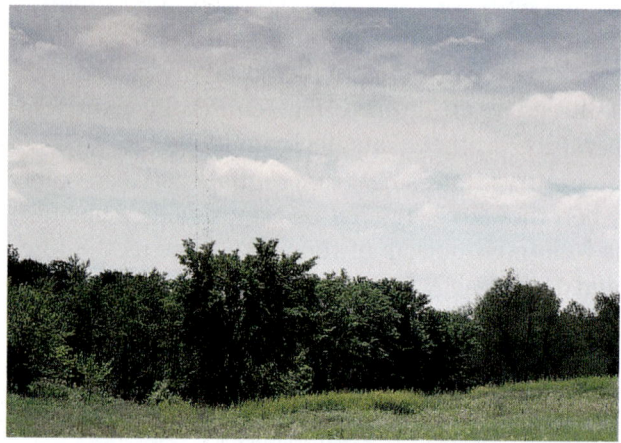
Exposed for the entire scene with a graduated neutral density filter

Jack Klasey/Goodheart-Willcox Publisher

Figure 7-12. Using a graduated neutral density filter helps to properly balance exposure of the foreground and the sky.

reflection, the result can be seen through the camera's viewfinder, permitting you to judge the point of best effect. Light reflected off bright metal surfaces

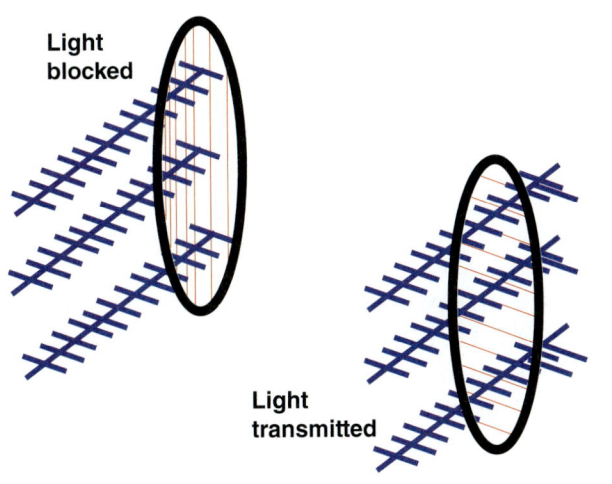

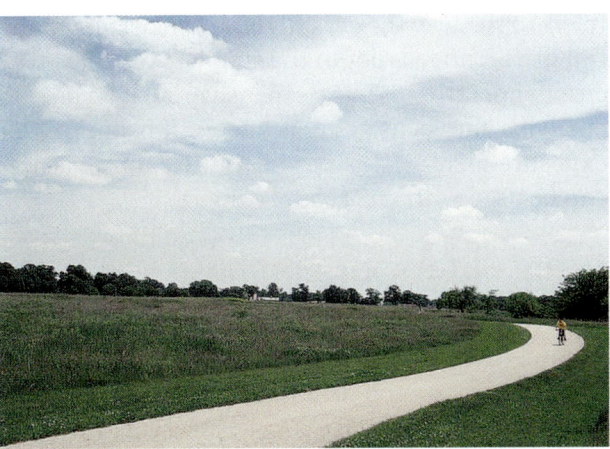

Without a polarizing filter

Figure 7-13. This diagram demonstrates the operation of a polarizing filter.

(specular reflection) is not polarized, so the polarizing filter has no effect.

Darkening of a blue sky is achieved with a polarizing filter because a large percentage of sky light is polarized. Bright light from the sky causes a glare from leaves and other surfaces that mutes or washes out their colors. Many photographers never notice this until they see the stronger, more saturated colors that become visible when using a polarizer to eliminate the glare. A polarizing filter is most effective on a blue sky when the sun is at a right angle to the axis of the camera lens, **Figure 7-15**.

When purchasing a polarizing filter, it is important to buy the type that is compatible with your camera. There are two types—the *linear polarizer* and the *circular polarizer*. A linear polarizer is commonly used with older manual film cameras. It cannot be

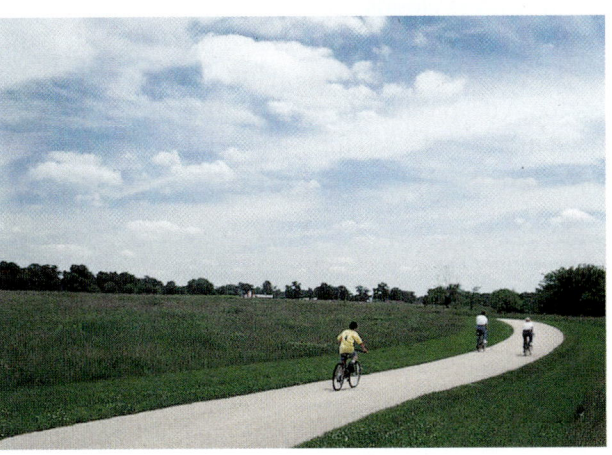

With a polarizing filter

Jack Klasey/Goodheart-Willcox Publisher

Figure 7-15. A polarizing filter darkens the blue of the sky and brings out cloud forms more strongly.

used with autofocus cameras or with those that use a beam splitter as part of their exposure metering system. The word "circular" in circular polarizer

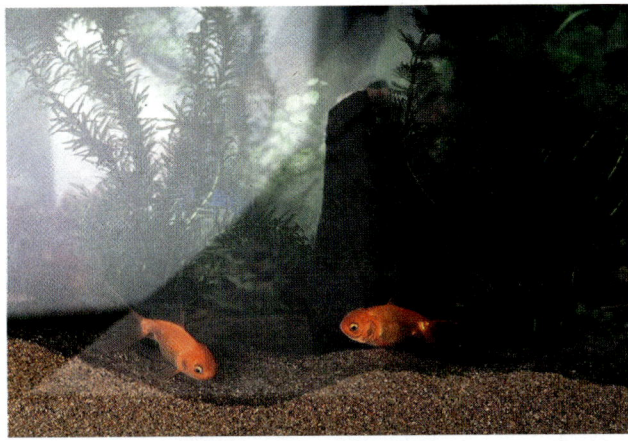

Without a polarizing filter

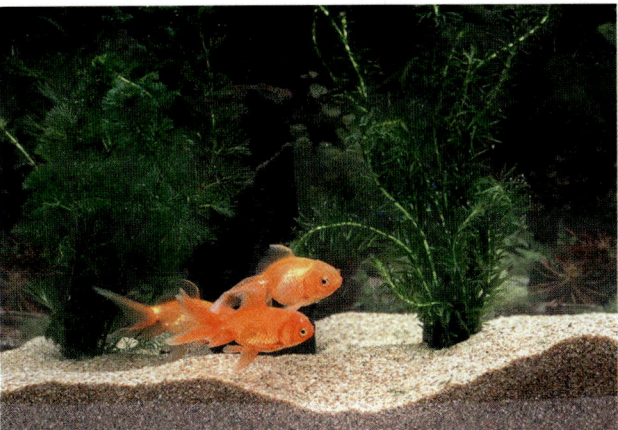

With a polarizing filter

Cokin Filters

Figure 7-14. Glare reflecting from the glass surface of an aquarium is filtered out with a polarizing filter.

Chapter 7 Light and Exposure **155**

refers to the way the crystals of the polarizing material are arranged, not to the shape of the filter. The circular polarizer is more expensive, but it is compatible with autofocus systems and with beam-splitter exposure meters. This means the circular polarizer can be used with any type of camera.

Using Filters for Emphasis

Creative use of filters can emphasize certain colors and deemphasize others. The most frequent use for filters in black-and-white photography is darkening the sky. Because image receivers are sensitive to the blue wavelengths, skies tend to photograph as white. Unless clouds are quite dark, they almost disappear. A yellow filter absorbs some of the blue light, darkening the sky and allowing clouds to stand out better. A deep yellow or orange filter darkens the sky even more, and a red filter gives the strongest effect. See **Figure 7-16**.

When shooting in color, a photographer can correct color balance with filters. If you are shooting in daylight conditions or with an electronic flash that can throw a blue hue, you can use a warming filter to avoid the cold blue cast. A **warming filter** is a yellowish filter that will absorb some of the blue light, warming the scene. Similarly, if you are shooting indoors immediately after shooting outdoors, your images may have a yellow hue to them, **Figure 7-17**. To combat this, you can use a blue filter to counteract the yellowness. Fluorescent lighting may also cause a green cast, and this can be corrected with a magenta filter, **Figure 7-18**.

The automatic white balance setting on a digital camera usually provides well-balanced color results. If a color balance problem is detected while shooting, specific white balance settings can often be used to avoid the problem. Color cast problems

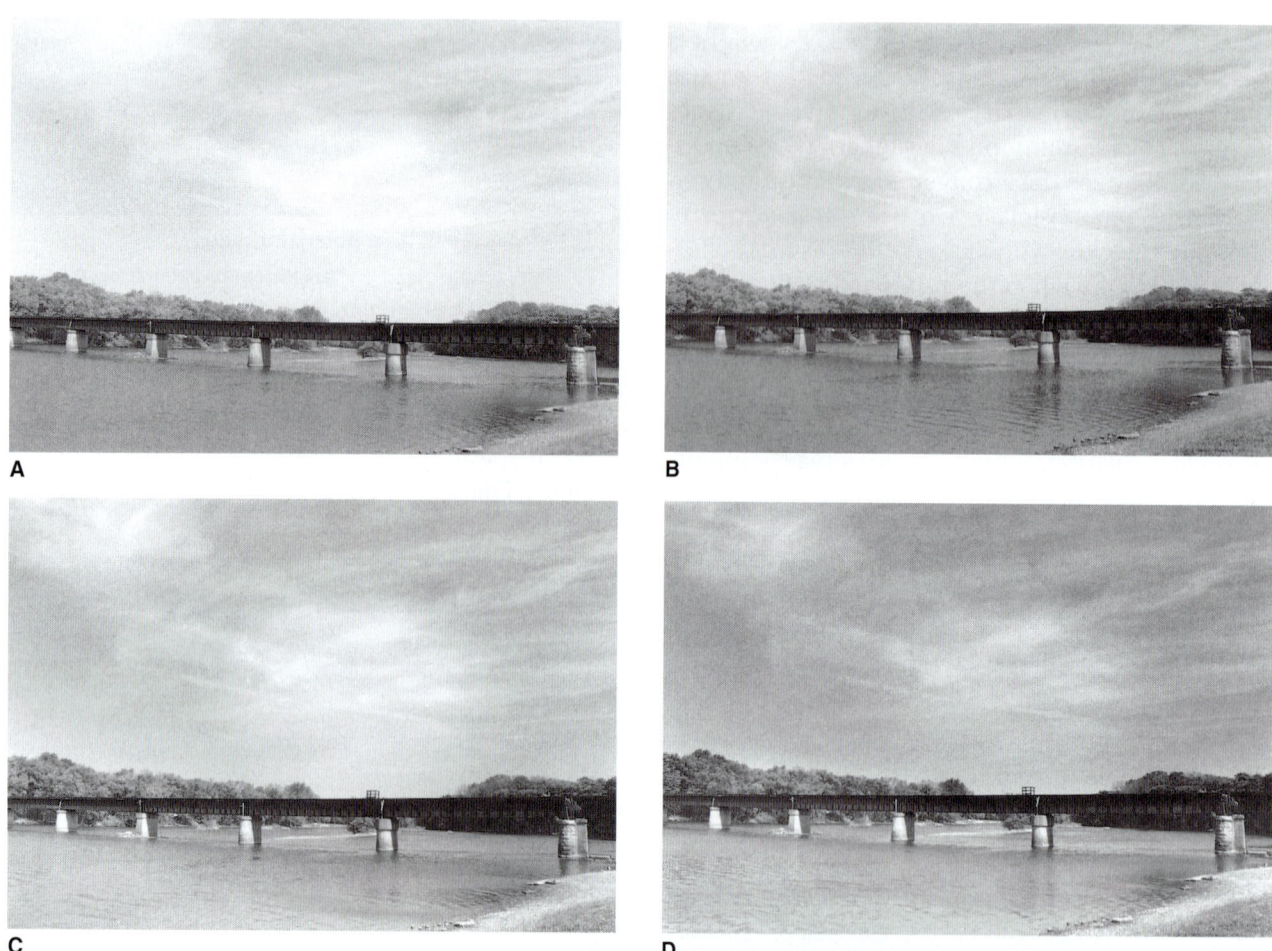

Jack Klasey/Goodheart-Willcox Publisher

Figure 7-16. Using filters to darken the sky. A—No filter. The sky is white and clouds barely visible. B—Yellow filter. The sky is darkened, making clouds more visible. C—Orange filter. The sky is darkened even more, making clouds stand out more strongly. D—Red filter. The most dramatic contrast between dark sky and bright clouds.

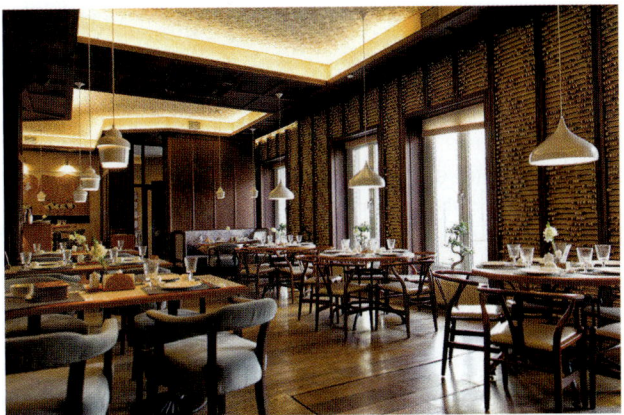

ArtEvent ET/Shutterstock.com

Figure 7-17. Shooting indoors immediately after shooting outdoors can cause your image to have a yellow hue.

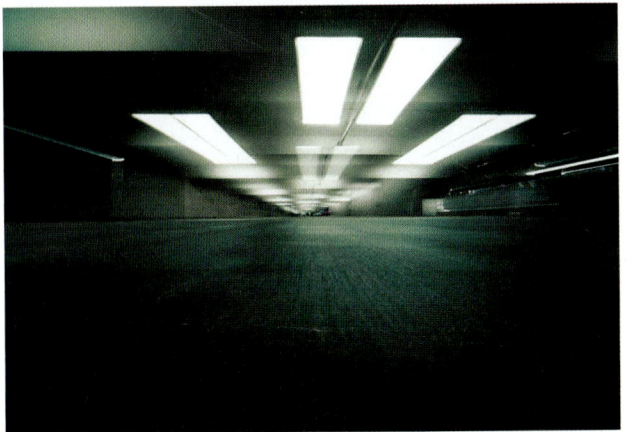

logoboom/Shutterstock.com

Figure 7-18. Fluorescent lighting often produces a green or blue coloration.

can sometimes be corrected or minimized after capture with image processing software.

Using Filters for Special Effects

Filters for achieving special effects are sold in both the round screw-in and square holder types. Special-effects filters can be used to change color in all or part of a scene, or to achieve many other creative variations.

Color-Changing Filters

The same yellow, orange, red, blue, and green filters used with black-and-white photography to improve contrast or separate gray tones can be employed with color photography to give a scene an overall color cast. For example, a desert scene might be exposed through an orange or dark yellow filter, or a seascape shot with a blue filter.

Graduated color, or color-grad, filters are available to add color to part of a scene. A popular color-grad filter is a yellow-orange color that enhances the sky hues when a sunrise or sunset is photographed. The same filter can be inverted to add warmth to a foreground, such as a beach scene, without affecting the color of the sky.

A more subtle use of color filters is to warm or cool a scene. For example, if reflected skylight gives shadow areas a cold, blue appearance, you could put a warming filter on your lens. At the other extreme, you might wish to make the coloration of a campfire scene a bit less yellow. A *cooling filter* is a light blue filter that will achieve the effect you want.

The white balance control of a digital camera can be used to achieve the same effects. To warm the blue tones of a bright, sunlit day, set the white balance to *Shade* or *Cloudy*. The yellow light from a campfire could be tamed with a daylight or electronic flash white balance setting.

Diffusion Filters

For portrait work or other applications, a slightly softened or diffused appearance is often desirable. A photo taken with a diffusion filter appears as if it were shot through a light veiling of fog, **Figure 7-19**. The slight softening of the image helps smooth out small wrinkles and skin imperfections. For years, photographers have created diffusion effects by such means as stretching a piece of sheer black nylon stocking material over the lens or applying a thin smear of petroleum jelly to a UV filter. However, you should avoid potentially damaging a filter or lens and instead use an image processing program to achieve the same effect.

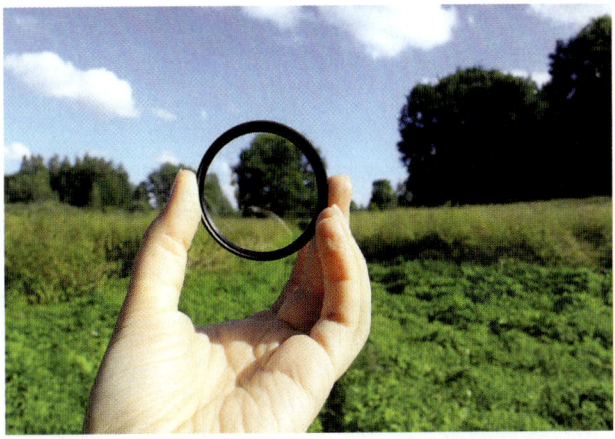

Pictures_for_You/Shutterstock.com

Figure 7-19. A diffusion filter produces an overall softening of an image and is often used for portrait work.

REAL-WORLD PHOTOGRAPHY

Smartphone Effects and Filters

Smartphone cameras are becoming more advanced with each new phone release, and they can even rival some DSLR cameras. While there are some third-party apps that can enhance your phone's native app, there are many features that come as part of a smartphone's camera system. The following is specific to an iPhone®:

- *Portrait mode*: This feature allows you to take photos that have a depth of field effect, meaning that your subject is in focus and the background is blurred. Your phone will guide you to make sure you have the correct amount of distance between the lens and the subject to maximize the depth of field effect.
- *Pano mode*: Pano (short for panorama) mode lets you take photos with the wide-angle lens by slowly moving your device from left to right. This feature comes with a guide bar in the middle to help you move your phone smoothly for seamless panoramic photos.
- *Filters*: Most newer iPhone models come with 10 different filters to choose from. These filters can be applied as you take a photo or after the fact. These filters all have different functions, from increasing contrast to decreasing highlights and more.

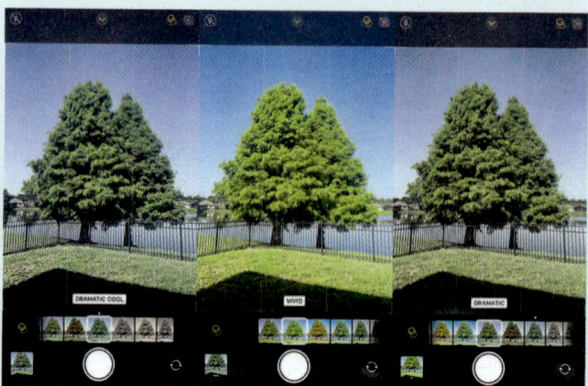

Goodheart-Willcox Publisher

There are numerous filters to choose from to give your images the effect you desire.

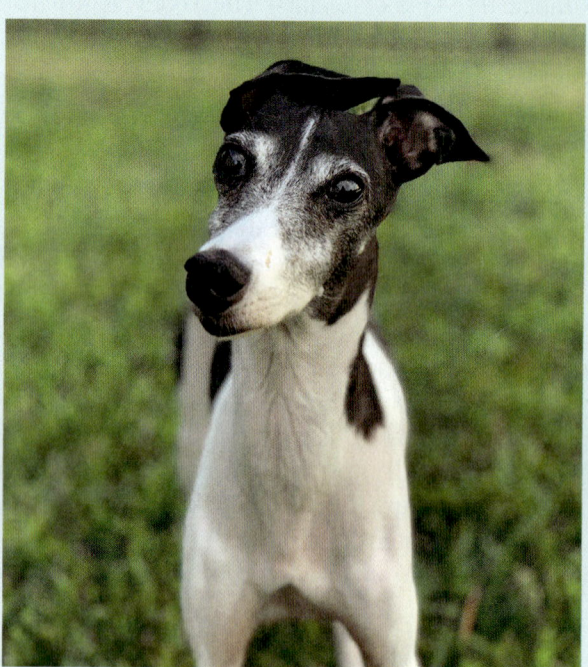

Goodheart-Willcox Publisher

Portrait mode keeps your subject in focus while blurring the background.

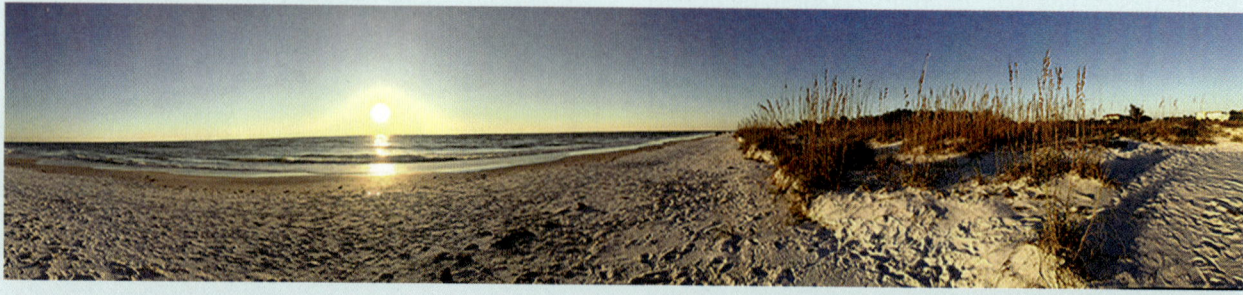

Goodheart-Willcox Publisher

Pano mode allows you to take seamless panoramic photographs.

Image-Modifying Filters

In a strict sense, all filters are image modifiers because their purpose is to change what appears on the image receiver. In this section, however, the term is being used to group filters that have a more pronounced effect on the image. Filter manufacturers offer many varieties, including the following commonly used filters:

- **Star filters.** These filters have a grid of finely etched lines called a *diffraction grating*. The lines cause bright rays to extend from any small, intense light source in the picture. Different gratings will produce "stars" with four, eight, or sixteen rays. See **Figure 7-20**.
- **Multiple-image filters.** Anywhere from two to twenty-five repetitions of the image are displayed. Patterns in which the images are arranged vary with the number of repetitions.
- **Blur filters.** Different degrees and patterns of blurring are offered to provide such effects as motion blur, zoom, rotation, or fog.
- **Double-exposure filter.** This device is an opaque mask that can be rotated to cover half of the lens at a time. In use, the first exposure is made with the mask in position over half the lens area. The mask is then rotated to cover the area first exposed, and the second exposure is made. The result is two nonoverlapping exposures.

Filter Factors

Almost any filter placed on a lens reduces the amount of transmitted light. This loss is called a

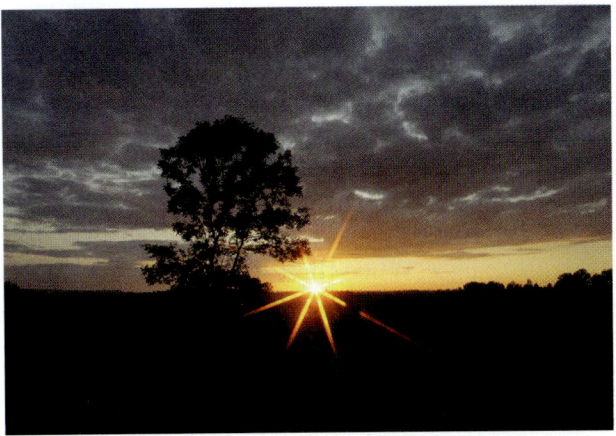

Kurtjurgen/Shutterstock.com

Figure 7-20. Star filters add interest to photos that include bright points of light.

filter factor. The filter factor is important information when exposure must be calculated and set manually for large format and medium format cameras. With DSLR cameras, no adjustments are necessary. The camera's built-in meter takes its reading through the already mounted filter, automatically including the additional exposure required by the filter.

The filter factor is normally stated as a number by which normal exposure must be multiplied to correct for the light loss. Filter factors increase as the filter colors get darker. A UV filter, which is essentially clear glass, has a filter factor of 1. A yellow No. 8 filter has a factor of 2, and the dark red No. 25 filter has a factor of 8. Filter factors for daylight and for tungsten lighting often differ. **Figure 7-21** lists filter factors and exposure compensations for a number of contrast filters.

Filter Factor Adjustments				
Filter	Daylight Factor	Increase f-stop by:	Tungsten Factor	Increase f-stop by:
#6 Light Yellow	1.5	2/3	1.5	2/3
#8 Yellow	2	1	1.5	2/3
#11 Yellow-Green	4	2	3	1 2/3
#15 Deep Yellow	2.5	1 1/3	1.5	2/3
#25 Red	8	3	5	2 1/3
#47 Blue	6	2 2/3	12	3 2/3
#58 Green	6	2 2/3	6	2 2/3

Goodheart-Willcox Publisher

Figure 7-21. This table outlines filter factors and f-stop compensation for contrast filters used with black-and-white film.

Controlling Exposure

Exposure is the amount of light reflected from a scene that reaches the camera's image receiver. Exposure is primarily determined by three interacting factors—aperture, shutter speed, and ISO rating. These three factors are also referred to as the *exposure triangle*. When these are properly balanced, you will get an image that is properly exposed. If one variable changes, one of the others must also change to make sure the correct exposure is maintained.

Most cameras today offer totally automatic exposure control. The in-camera exposure meter reads the scene and sets the proper combination of aperture and shutter speed for the photo. Digital cameras may alter the sensitivity of the sensor (and thus, the effective ISO) as well as the aperture and shutter speed.

Automatic exposure control is useful, but it is important to understand how the factors of aperture, shutter speed, and ISO rating can be altered to affect image appearance. The ability to affect image appearance through choice of shutter speed, aperture, white balance, and other camera settings is called **creative control**. By learning how changing the various factors affects exposure, you will be able to create good photographs in situations where automatic exposure control would produce poor results.

Aperture

As you learned in Chapter 5, *The Camera System*, the **aperture** is the size of the opening through which light passes to strike the camera's image receiver. The *iris*, or *diaphragm*, is a variable-aperture device consisting of an assembly of thin, overlapping metal blades that make the opening larger or smaller. Movement of the iris can be controlled manually or automatically. Some lenses also allow you to have manual control of aperture size. This involves rotating a collar on the lens to one of a series of marked settings (f-stops). On digital cameras, a control on the camera body is used to change aperture size.

The F-Stop System

An **f-stop** is a unit of measure that represents the size of a specific aperture. The standard f-stop designations are f/0.7, f/1, f/1.4, f/2, f/2.8, f/4, f/5.6, f/8, f/11, f/16, f/22, f/32, f/45, and f/64. This system probably creates more confusion among beginners than any other aspect of photography. First, the mix of whole numbers and decimals is hard to remember. Second, as f-stop numbers become larger, the opening (aperture) that they represent becomes smaller.

The f-numbers themselves are calculated by dividing the focal length of the lens by the diameter of the aperture. See **Figure 7-22**. For a 50 mm lens with an aperture of 25 mm, the f-number is 2. For a 50 mm lens with an aperture of 4.5 mm, the f-number is 11. In the first example, the aperture is 1/2 the focal length. In the second example, it is 1/11 the focal length. Thus, an f-stop can be thought of as a fraction— f/2 is an aperture 1/2 the focal length, f/11 is an aperture 1/11 the focal length, and so on.

Aperture Size and Light Transmission

More important than the method of calculating f-stops is the relationship of the stops to each other. In the standard series of f-stops, the area of the iris opening is either halved or doubled from one f-stop to the next, depending on whether the number is larger or smaller. At the same shutter speed, the effect of this is to allow either half as much or twice as much light to reach the image receiver.

Aperture sizes are the reverse of the f-stop numbers. As the numbers get larger, the area of the opening gets smaller, **Figure 7-23**. The opening at f/16 is half as large as the opening at f/11, and the opening at f/22 is half as large as the opening at f/16. Moving in the opposite direction, the opening at f/16 is twice as large as the opening at f/22, and the opening at f/11 is twice as large as the opening at f/16.

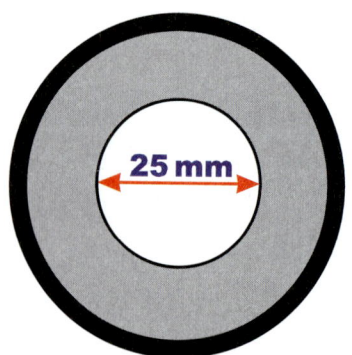

Focal length ÷ Aperture = f/stop
50 mm ÷ 25 mm = f/2
f/2 = 1/2 focal length

Goodheart-Willcox Publisher

Figure 7-22. The f-number of a lens is calculated by dividing the focal length of the lens by the diameter of the aperture.

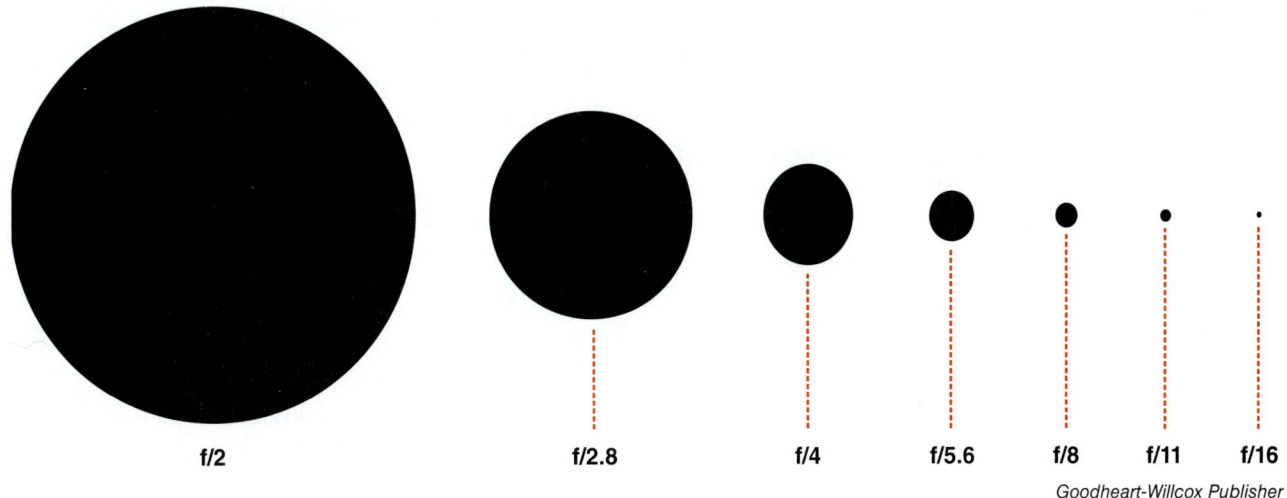

Figure 7-23. F-stop relationships are based on halving or doubling of the aperture area.

Relative Aperture

The sequence of f-stop numbers is the same regardless of the focal length of the lens, but the size of opening that a given stop represents changes with the focal length. This is called *relative aperture*, and it is important in order to obtain consistent photographic results.

A lens with twice the focal length of another lens has an aperture twice as large for a given f-stop. If f/2 represents an aperture of 25 mm on a 50 mm lens (50 ÷ 25 = 2), then f/2 on a 100 mm lens would require an opening of 50 mm (100 ÷ 50 = 2). The difference in aperture compensates for the difference in the intensity of the light reaching the image receiver because of the increased focal length. This is demonstrated in **Figure 7-24**, which shows that both the 50 mm and 100 mm lenses transmit the same amount of light reflected from the subject. The image of the ball projected onto the image receiver by the 100 mm lens is twice as large as the image of the ball from the 50 mm lens. The light reflected from the ball is spread over an area four times as large with the 100 mm lens. The aperture of the 100 mm lens at f/2 is twice the diameter (four times the area) of the same f-stop of the 50 mm lens, so the image receiver receives the same exposure. The apertures are different physical sizes, but they are the same relative size.

Lens Speed

To shoot a speeding motorcycle at noon, you are unlikely to need a fast lens, but to photograph a tortoise at dusk, you probably will. A fast lens has a large maximum aperture, giving it great light-gathering

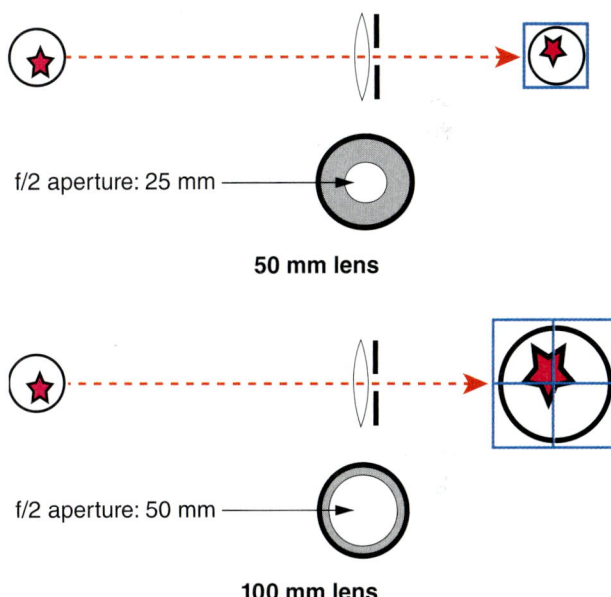

Figure 7-24. Relative aperture. As focal length increases, the aperture also becomes larger for a given f-stop, and vice versa.

power. A fast lens can be "opened up" to allow relatively short exposures in low-light conditions. With the speeding motorcycle at noon, plentiful light allows exposure at smaller apertures. The fading light at dusk, especially with a dark-colored subject like a tortoise, requires a large aperture.

The fastest lenses for DSLRs are typically 50 mm lenses with maximum apertures greater than f/2. On many 50 mm lenses, a fractional stop such as 1.7 or 1.8 (one-third stop faster than f/2) is the maximum, but f/1.4, f/1.2, and even f/0.7 lenses are available.

Zoom lenses typically have a maximum aperture of f/3.5 or f/4 at their shortest focal length and f/4.5 or f/5.6 at the long-focus end. Longer lenses are slower than shorter-focus lenses because greater speed requires larger-diameter irises than are practical for most users. The very large 1200 mm f/5.6 lenses used by professional sports photographers are almost 3′ in length and 8″ in diameter. See **Figure 7-25**.

Shutter Speed

The camera **shutter** is a device that opens and closes to control the flow of light to the camera's image receiver. How long the shutter remains open (in combination with the size of the aperture) is known as **shutter speed**, and it determines how much light reaches the image receiver.

Depending on the type and age of the camera, the range of shutter speeds varies widely. The shutter speeds of older 35 mm film cameras generally range from 1/1000 second to 1 second in length. Newer cameras, both film and digital, are often fully electronic and stretch the range in both directions. They offer exposures as long as 30 seconds and as short as 1/16,000 second. The fastest shutter speed of most models is 1/4000 second. Many also offer T (time) and B (bulb) settings for longer, manually controlled exposures. When the T setting is chosen, the shutter release must be operated once to open the shutter and again to close it. With the B setting, the shutter remains open as long as the shutter release is being pressed. Releasing the pressure closes the shutter.

Like the f-stops that are used to indicate aperture, shutter speeds have a constant relationship. At a given value (for example, 1/60 second), the shutter is open for half as long as the preceding speed (1/30 second) and twice as long as the following speed (1/125 second). This means that the adjoining speeds will admit twice as much or half as much light, respectively, just as adjoining f-stop values admit half as much or twice as much light.

Sync Speed

Sync speed is the fastest speed at which a camera's image sensor can be open to light. This speed is determined by how quickly the camera's shutter curtains move once the flash is triggered. *High speed sync*, occasionally abbreviated *HHS*, lets you use flash at a shutter speed that is higher than 1/200 second. This is considered a normal flash speed on most DSLR cameras and is great for sky exposures.

Other sync speeds include *front curtain sync*, *rear curtain sync*, and *maximum shutter sync speed*. With front curtain sync, the flash firing is synched with the front curtain at the beginning of the photo-taking process. It works great for standard photos. With rear curtain sync, the shutter opens first, then the flash goes off at the end of the exposure as the rear curtain closes. It is good for slow exposures in which you want to create blur. Maximum shutter sync speed is the fastest shutter speed setting on a camera, where both curtains fully expose the camera sensor. It is typically around 1/180 or 1/200 second.

ISO Rating

An **ISO rating** is a numerical designation indicating the light sensitivity of an image receiver, with higher numbers indicating greater sensitivity. The rating is an international standard that was originally developed to ensure consistency in films from different manufacturers. With the development of digital photography, the concept was applied to different levels of sensitivity that could be selected for a camera's sensor.

ISO ratings follow the same pattern as apertures and shutter speeds. Each is twice as sensitive to light as the preceding rating and half as sensitive as the one that follows. The number designations are typically whole numbers that double as they increase (25, 50, 100, 200, 400, 800, 1600). Films are generally available with ISO ratings as high as 3200, but the most widely used are 100, 200, 400, and 800.

Digital cameras may offer a range of ISO equivalents as minimal as 100, 200, and 400 (mostly in the simplest compact models) or as wide as 50 to 6400 in DSLRs. Top-level professional cameras offer

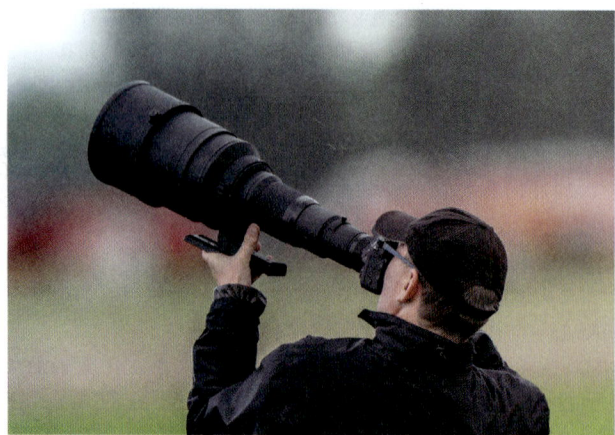

Ryan Fletcher/Shutterstock.com

Figure 7-25. Very long lenses, like this 1200 mm telephoto lens, are relatively slow because of the large aperture required to produce larger f-stops.

equivalents as high as 51,600. Since the sensitivity of the sensor is changed electronically, a camera used in automatic mode may select an ISO anywhere in its full range (for instance, 179 or 3266). When the camera is used in other modes, the photographer selects the desired ISO equivalent from a menu.

Measuring Light

To properly expose a photograph, a means of measuring light is needed to help you make decisions on your camera settings. Virtually all cameras sold today have a built-in light meter that is used to determine and control exposure for automatic operation. The meter also indicates exposure when the camera is operated in the manual mode. Various types of handheld meters can also be used to determine proper exposure, **Figure 7-26**. Photographers working with medium format and large format cameras generally must rely on handheld meters for exposure determination.

How Exposure Meters Measure Light

A ***photoelectric light meter*** uses electrical changes caused by different light intensities to indicate various levels of illumination. These indications, in turn, can be used to determine the exposure needed for a scene. The electrical changes can be either a generated current or a change in resistance. The changes drive a pointer against a scale or provide an LCD (liquid crystal display) readout. Photoelectric meters use either selenium cells or silicon cells. The silicon cell most widely used in meters is the cadmium sulfide (CdS) cell.

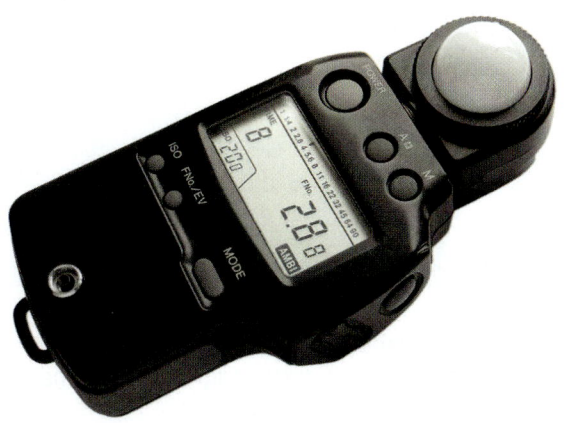

Aleksandr Pobedimskiy/Shutterstock.com

Figure 7-26. Photographers often rely on handheld light meters to measure light readings accurately.

A ***selenium cell meter*** measures photoelectric light and is used to generate or control an electric current. It was once the most common type, but it is used much less frequently today. It has a photoelectric cell that generates a tiny electrical current whenever it is struck by light. The strength of the current generated is directly proportional to the intensity of the light—the stronger the light, the larger the current, and vice versa. The current moves a pointer across a scale to indicate an exposure value. Selenium cell meters do not need a battery to operate.

A ***cadmium sulfide (CdS) cell meter*** measures the electrical resistance caused by light striking the CdS cell. A battery generates a small electrical current through the meter circuit. The intensity of the light striking the cell causes a change in electrical resistance. The increase or decrease in resistance is directly reflected as a change in the current flowing through the circuit. The changing current is translated into exposure values indicated on a scale or a display. A CdS meter provides a more precise reading than a selenium cell meter, especially under low-light conditions.

Meter Displays

Exposure values displayed by a meter may be either indirect or direct. Indirect-reading meters provide an index number that must be related to an f-stop/shutter speed combination, while direct-reading meters give a specific f-stop/shutter speed combination. Older handheld meters usually are the indirect type, with a needle moving over a scale. Newer meters typically provide a direct reading on an LCD. See **Figure 7-27**.

Through-the-lens (TTL) metering is a feature of a camera where the intensity of light reflected from the scene is measured through the camera's lens as opposed to using a separate light meter. It is direct-reading, although the reading is presented in a number of different ways in the viewfinder. Some use blinking LEDs on a scale of shutter speeds or apertures. Others require matching two needles or indicators by changing aperture or shutter speed. Most newer models display both aperture and shutter speed in numerals. Digital compact cameras typically display the information on the LCD screen used to compose and review images. Because of the great variety of systems used, TTL meters will be covered only in general terms. For specific information, consult the owner's manual for your camera.

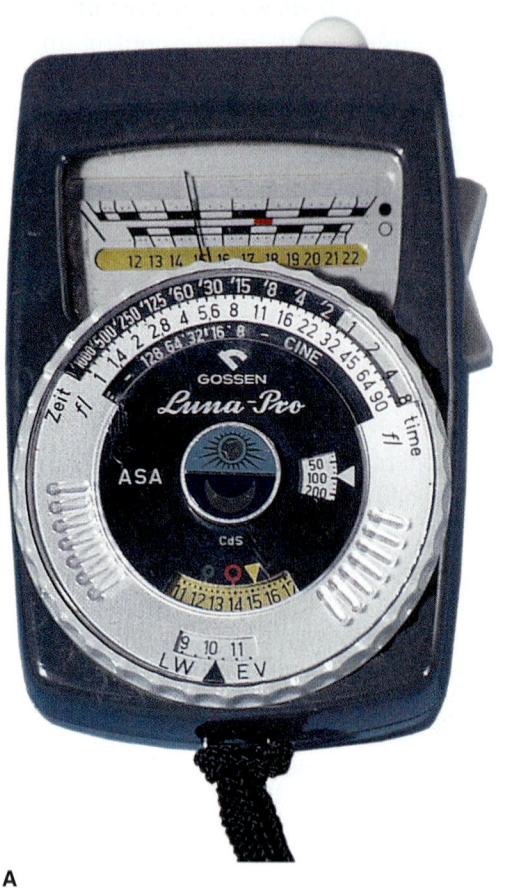

A

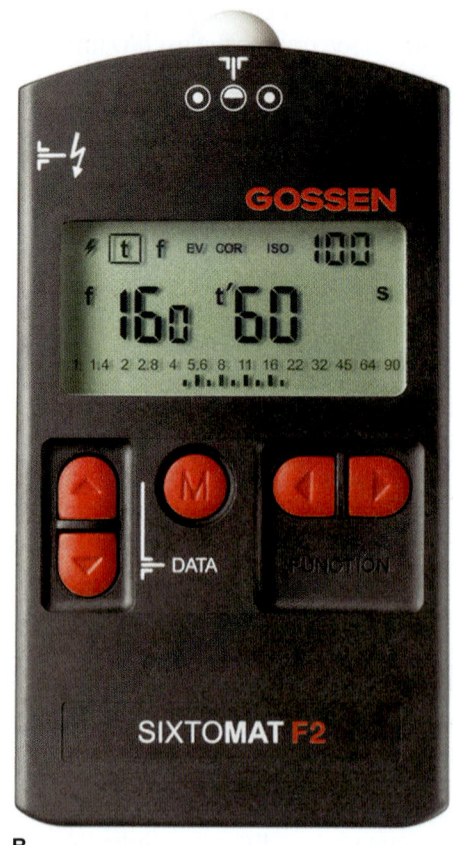

B

Gossen *Manfrotto*

Figure 7-27. Types of meter displays. A—Indirect reading. B—Direct reading.

Types of Meter Readings

In-camera meters can only be used to read reflected light, or light that enters the lens after bouncing off the subject. Handheld meters typically make reflected light readings, but many can also be used to read incident light, which is the light that is falling on the subject.

Reflected light readings are made with the meter facing the subject, and they are usually made from the camera position. To avoid having the meter influenced by adjacent brighter or darker areas, readings are sometimes made close to the most important part of the subject.

Since they measure light falling on the subject, incident light readings are taken from the subject's position, with the meter facing toward the light source. Meters used for incident light readings have a translucent cover over the light-sensitive cell to diffuse the light rays and help produce an average reading. Meters that can be used for both types of readings typically have a translucent plastic dome that can be slid over the cell to read incident light, **Figure 7-28**.

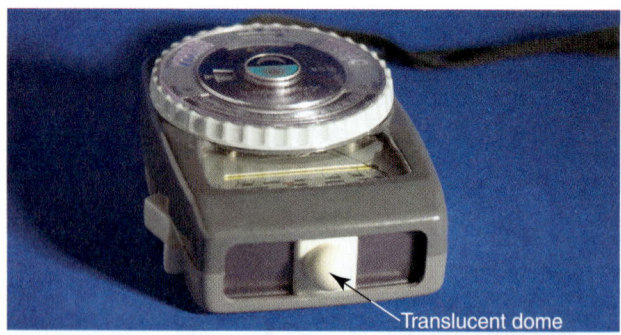

Jack Klasey/Goodheart-Willcox Publisher

Figure 7-28. A translucent dome can be slid over the light-sensitive cell of a reflected light meter to make incident light readings.

Spot meters and flash meters are specialized instruments. A spot meter can take reflected light readings from very tiny areas and distant subjects, **Figure 7-29**. It has an angle of view as narrow as 1°. A typical handheld light meter has an angle of view of 30° to 50°.

Newer cameras often allow selection of various metering patterns, including a spot meter mode. Whether done with a handheld meter or a camera, spot metering allows you to make precise readings to compare light reflected from different areas of the subject.

A flash meter is used to make an accurate reading of the short pulse of bright light produced by electronic flash equipment. Flash meters are used most often for studio photography or special field applications, such as weddings. Depending on the situation, a flash meter can be used to make either an incident or a reflected light reading.

Also available are multifunction handheld models that can be used as an incident meter, reflected light meter, flash meter, or spot meter with zoom capability. Readings are displayed on a large LCD panel, **Figure 7-30**.

Making a Light Reading

Metering is the process of using an in-camera or handheld exposure meter to determine the amount of light being reflected from the subject. To obtain an accurate handheld meter reading, the meter first must be programmed with the ISO rating being used. If the ISO equivalent set in the camera is different from the rating in the meter, exposure will be incorrect. For example, if the meter is programmed for ISO 100, and the camera is set for ISO 400, the meter's recommended settings cause images to be overexposed by two full stops.

For built-in meters in most cameras, this problem does not occur. A digital camera in automatic mode selects the appropriate ISO, shutter speed, and aperture. If the camera is being used in manual, shutter priority, or aperture priority mode, the exposure readings are based on the selected ISO equivalent.

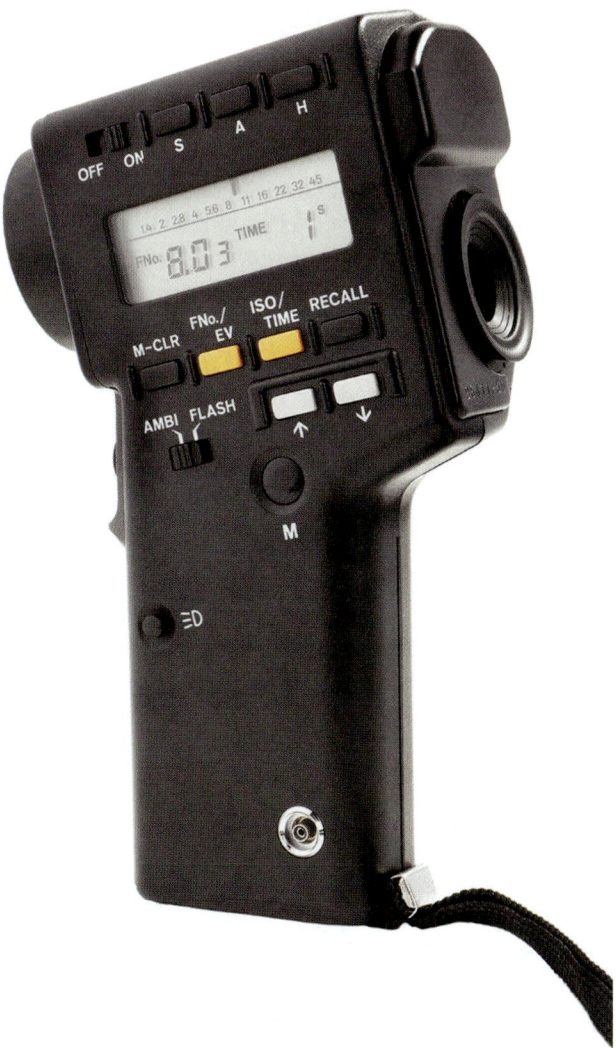

Pieralfonso/Shutterstock.com

Figure 7-29. The spot meter can make reflected light readings from distant subjects or tiny areas of closer subjects.

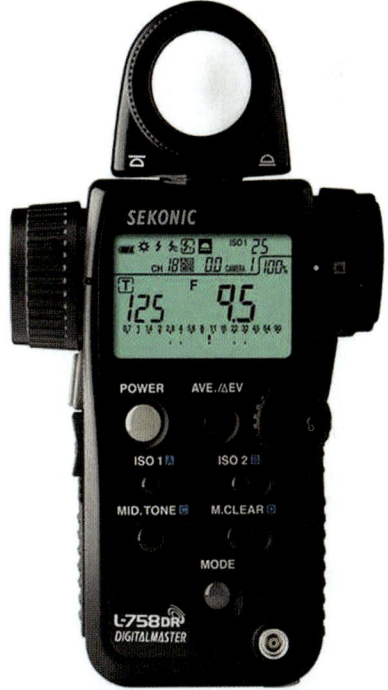

Sekonic

Figure 7-30. A multifunction exposure meter can be used as an incident meter, reflected light meter, flash meter, or spot meter with zoom capability.

Selecting the right areas to meter and the correct methods to obtain consistent and accurate readings are vital to taking well-exposed pictures. The following sections will concentrate on correct use of a handheld meter.

Making Averaged Readings

A **reflective light reading**, or *averaged reading*, is made by pointing the meter at the main subject, **Figure 7-31**. Since a handheld meter has about the same angle of view as a normal lens, it is affected by light that is reflected from the same area that appears in the photo. The scene usually includes a range of tones, from those that reflect a great deal of light (highlights) to those that reflect little or no light (shadows). The meter reading falls somewhere in the middle, averaging out the reflected light. This reading allows the image receiver to properly expose most of the tones present in the scene. Tones also fall on a scale, known as the **tonal range**. This is the spread of tones, from deepest shadows to brightest highlights, represented in a photograph.

An **incident light reading** measures the intensity of the light falling on a subject, and it accomplishes the same purpose for scenes with a wide range of tones. The incident meter is pointed at the light source from the subject's position to measure the light falling on the subject. The photograph is taken by reflected light. The average of that reflected light is equivalent to the incident light reading.

What averaged reflective readings and incident readings actually produce is an exposure value for **middle gray**, which is equivalent to a tone that reflects 18% of the light that falls on it. By properly exposing for the middle gray value, the darker and lighter tones in the scene generally reproduce properly.

When it is important to keep detail in specific shadow or highlight areas, a more precise technique involves the use of two meter readings. First, select the shadow area in which you want to preserve detail and take a meter reading from that area. Next, repeat the process with the selected highlight area, and then find the exposure midway between the two readings. For example, if the shadow reading indicated an exposure of f/4 at 1/60 second, and the highlight reading was f/16 at 1/60 second, the brightness range that you metered would be four stops (f/4, f/5.6, f/8, f/11, f/16), **Figure 7-32**. The midway point in that range is f/8. By using an exposure of f/8 at 1/60 second, you would likely keep the desired detail in the shadow and highlight areas you selected.

Metering Subjects That Are Not Average

When the object or portion of a scene that is metered is much darker or lighter than middle gray, problems can occur. The meter provides an exposure reading that results in a seriously overexposed or underexposed picture. As shown in **Figure 7-33**, exactly following the meter readings taken from the black or the white squares results in pictures that are too dark or too light because the meter always makes a middle gray reading. If a large amount of light is being reflected (as from the white square), the meter adjusts the exposure reading downward to avoid overexposure. **Overexposure** refers to a photo that is very bright due to an excessive amount of light. As a result, the photo is underexposed. In the same way, the meter reacts to the small amount of light reflected from the black square by adjusting the exposure reading upward to prevent underexposure. **Underexposure** refers to a photo that is very dark due to an insufficient amount of light. In this case, the photo will be overexposed.

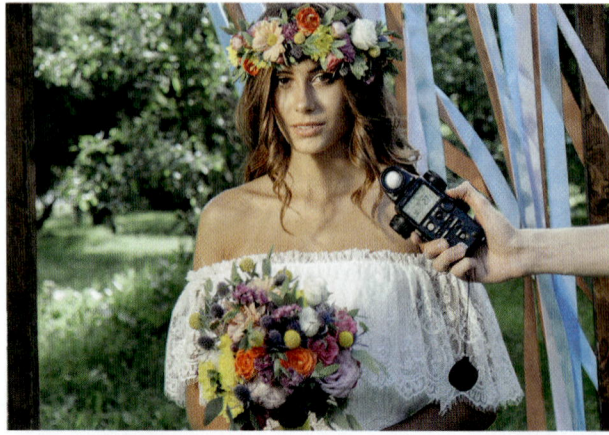

Sharaf Maksumov/Shutterstock.com

Figure 7-31. Pointing the meter at the main subject provides a reflected light reading.

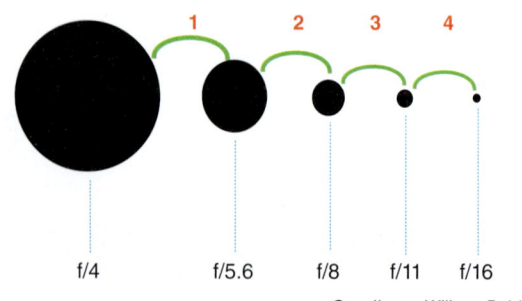

Goodheart-Willcox Publisher

Figure 7-32. A scene with a shadow reading of f/4 and a highlight reading of f/16 has a range of four stops.

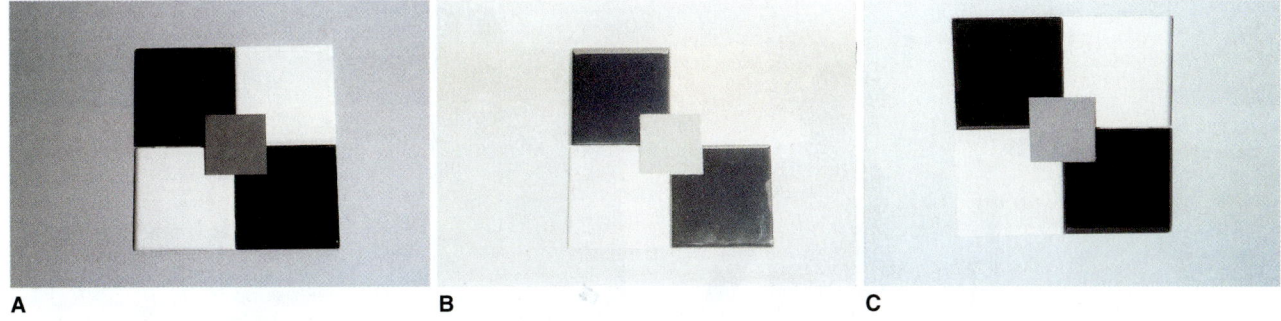

Figure 7-33. The exposure of this scene depends on where the meter reading was taken. A—Reading taken from the white square (underexposed). B—Reading taken from the black square (overexposed). C—Reading taken from the middle gray square (properly exposed).

Compensating for the meter's behavior in such situations is a matter of experience. As a general rule, however, an adjustment of 1 to 1 1/2 stops usually provides a good exposure. For example, when photographing a winter snow scene, open up 1 1/2 stops from the meter's recommended exposure to reproduce the snow as white instead of gray. At the opposite extreme, to make a black cow appear black in a close-up photo, stop down 1 or 1 1/2 stops from the meter's reading.

If you are not careful about where you point the meter, it can produce an incorrect value even when making an overall reading of a scene. A typical situation is a scene in which the subject is **backlit** (has most of the light coming from behind it). As shown in **Figure 7-34**, a meter reading influenced by the bright light underexposes the subject, and it may even create a silhouette. To prevent unplanned silhouettes, move in to take a reading directly from the subject, **Figure 7-35**. If a close-up reading cannot be made, increase your exposure by 1 1/2 stops over the meter reading.

There will also be times when you are shooting your subject and only certain portions of the image are overexposed. Depending on your camera's settings and capabilities, you will see what are referred to as zebras. **Zebras**, also called a *zebra pattern*, are highlight warning indicators that alert you if certain portions of an image are overexposed or blown out, **Figure 7-36**. The name comes from the striped pattern that is applied to areas that are "too hot" for the camera. While this is a helpful tool when taking photos, it does not control exposure. It only gives you a warning as to where a problem area might be. Additionally, zebras are not recorded onto your final image. If you do see zebras in your image, you will need to adjust your exposure down so that less light is hitting your image receiver. Start with small and slow adjustments.

Reading the Meter

Newer handheld meters and in-camera meters display the aperture and shutter speed combination directly on an LCD panel. Older handheld meters, however, typically use an index number that is manually translated into exposure recommendations by moving a dial. As shown in **Figure 7-37**, this type of meter is pointed at the desired subject and a button or switch is pressed to activate the metering circuit. A needle moves against a scale of index numbers to show the strength of the reflected light reaching the meter's photoelectric cell. A dial is then rotated to align an indicator mark with a number matching the

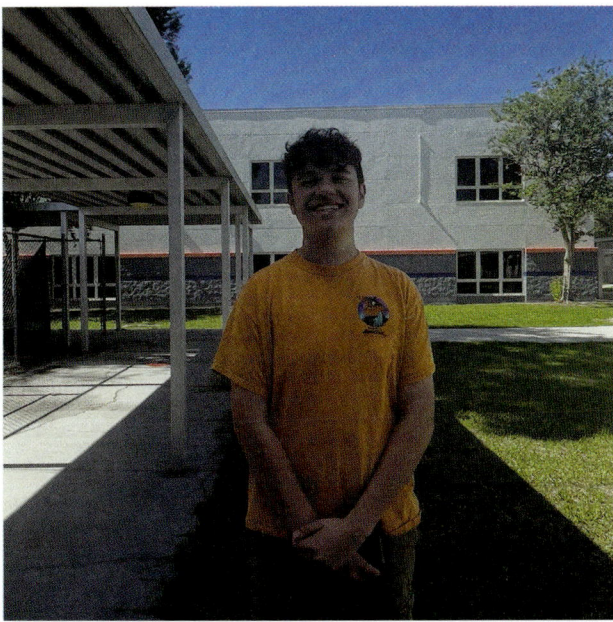

Figure 7-34. Underexposure due to an overall meter reading made when a subject is backlit.

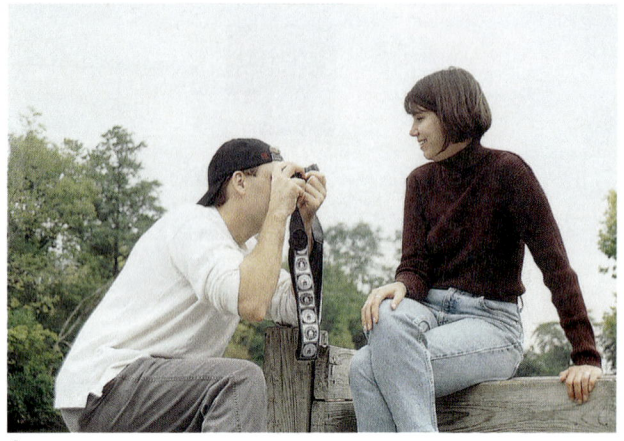

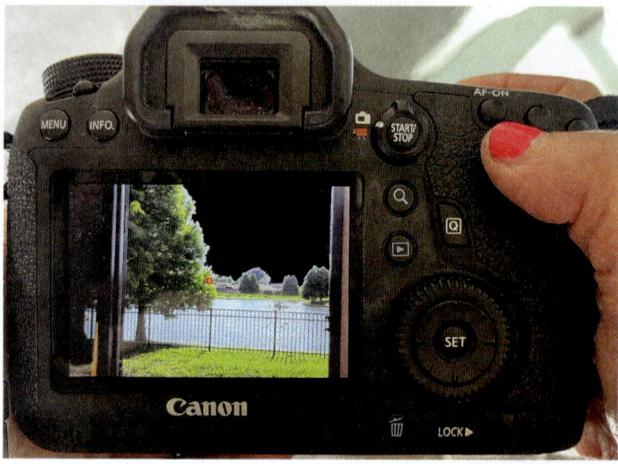

Goodheart-Willcox Publisher

Figure 7-36. Zebras highlight areas of an image that may be overexposed. This specific camera highlights overexposed areas with a block of black.

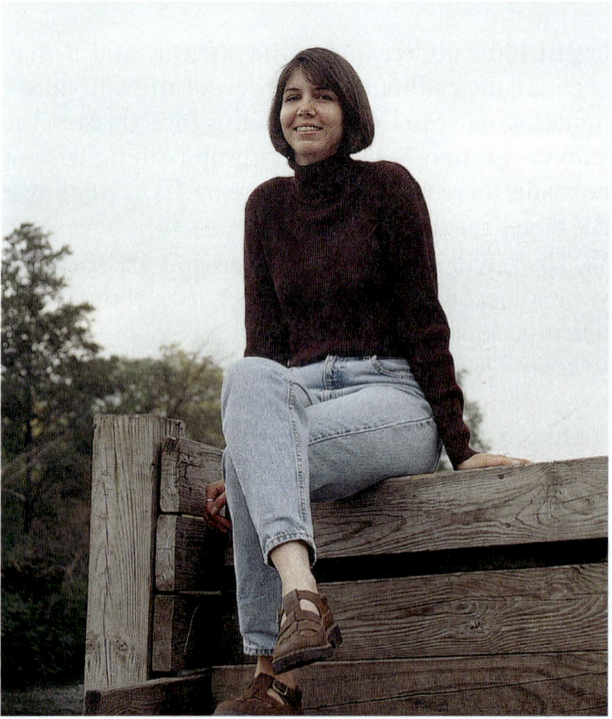

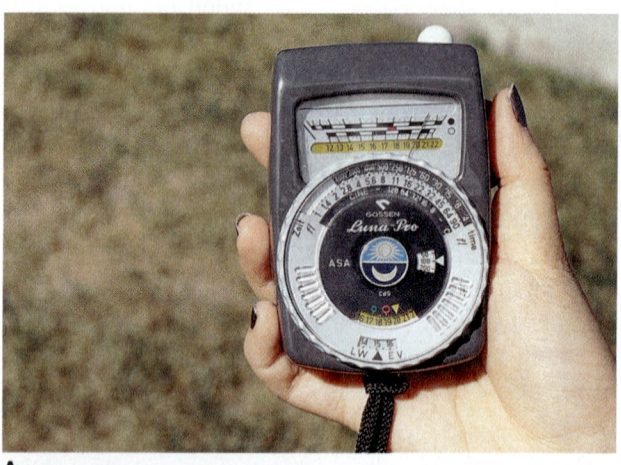

Jack Klasey/Goodheart-Willcox Publisher

Figure 7-35. Moving in close to the subject keeps the meter reading from being influenced by the strong backlight. A—Meter close to the subject. B—Move back to shoot the entire subject.

index number indicated by the needle. This action provides recommended exposures by aligning an f-stop scale with a shutter-speed scale. There are also apps available on smartphones that act as light meters. There are plenty of free options available in your smartphone's app store, and this is a good option while in the beginning stages of your photography journey, **Figure 7-38**.

The combinations presented by the paired f-stop and shutter-speed scales illustrate the ***reciprocity law***,

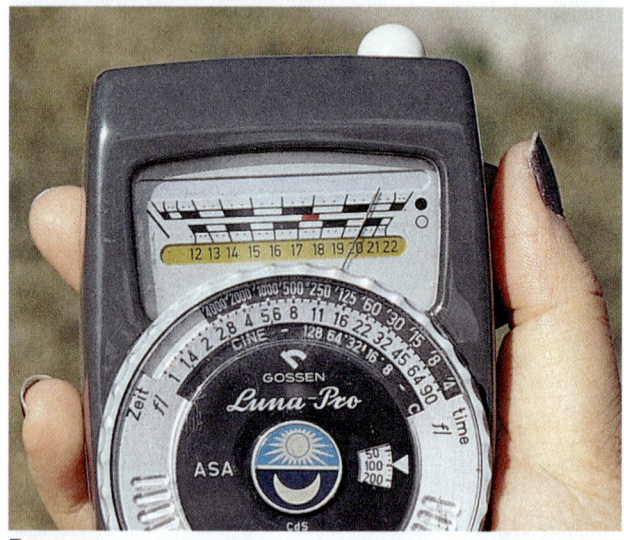

Jack Klasey/Goodheart-Willcox Publisher

Figure 7-37. Using a handheld light meter. A—Making the light reading. B—Reading equivalent exposures directly from the f-stop and shutter speed scales.

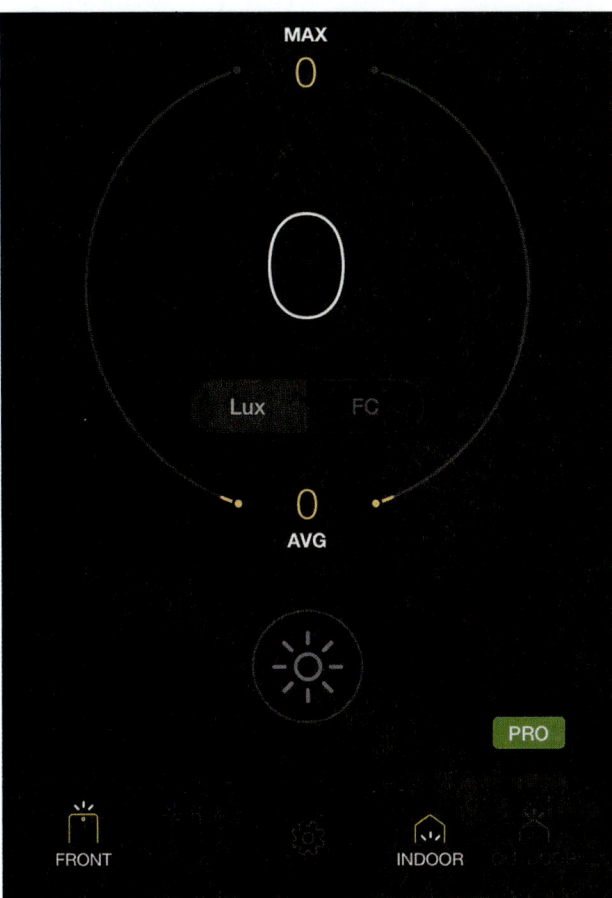

Figure 7-38. Light meter apps are available on smartphones and are good, inexpensive options when just starting out.

which is the theory that a one-stop increase in aperture is equivalent to the shutter duration doubling. Both increase light by one stop. For example, f/5.6 at 1/125 second, f/8 at 1/60 second, and f/11 at 1/30 second result in the same amount of light reaching the image receiver. For this reason, they are known as *equivalent exposures*.

The reciprocity law has its limitations. When very long or very short exposures are made on film, the time/light intensity relationship does not remain constant—longer exposure times or larger apertures are needed. This is known as *reciprocity law failure* or *reciprocity failure*. The reciprocity law typically fails at 1 second and 1/1000 second. Film manufacturers provide information on the changes needed to compensate for reciprocity failure.

Digital camera sensors are not subject to reciprocity law failure. Very long or short exposure times do not require lengthening exposure times or increasing apertures. However, very long exposures do increase **digital noise**, or tiny light-colored spots especially noticeable in shadow areas of an image.

The Zone System

The **Zone System** is a photographic method designed to produce consistent, predictable results through careful control of exposure, film development, and printing. Devised by Ansel Adams and Fred Archer in 1939 for film photography, this system uses a 10-step scale of image values (tones) from pure black to pure white to allow precise description and control. Although its original use was with large format black-and-white sheet film, the Zone System can also be applied to digital photography.

The 10-Step Scale of Values

Adams developed the Zone System to allow photographers to consistently produce a final print that matched their visualization of the scene. Sometimes that final print would be a literal rendering of the scene. At other times, the finished product would have a far different range of tones or contrasts from what the eye had seen. See **Figure 7-39**.

Any photograph can potentially have an almost infinite gradation of tones from absolute black to absolute white. Adams reduced the range to 11 specific tones numbered in Roman numerals. This provided for a progression of 10 steps from the darkest tone (0) to the lightest (X). See **Figure 7-40**.

Adams distinguished between the term *zone* (used to describe exposure) and the term *value* (used to describe the result of that exposure as seen on the negative and print). The zones are equivalent to f-stops and have the same halving and doubling relationship.

Three of the zones have particular importance. Zone V represents the middle of the exposure scale, equivalent to the gray card with its 18% reflectance. Gray cards are cards with a gray scale printed on them to help photographers adjust their exposure and white balance, but they are not used as commonly today as they used to be. Zone III is an exposure that yields a dark (shadow) print value with texture and detail just visible. Zone VIII is an exposure that yields a light (highlight) print value in which texture and detail are just visible.

Unless you are photographing a gray card, any subject that you capture presents a variety of tones, or **luminances** (percentages of reflected light).

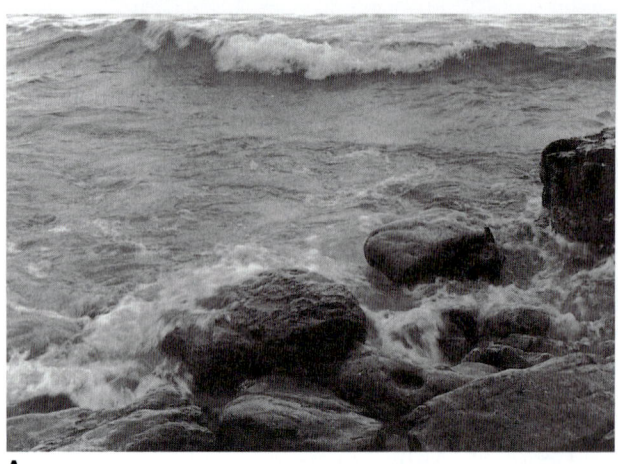 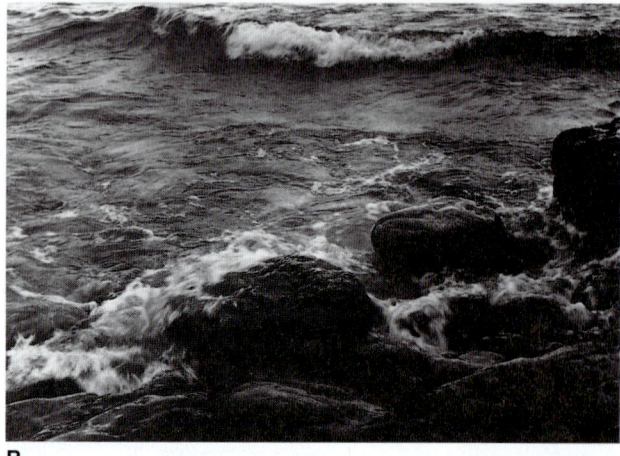

Figure 7-39. Different visualizations. A—A scene that the photographer chose to render as seen. B—The same scene, visualized by the photographer as a much more dramatic, higher-contrast image.

Jack Klasey/Goodheart-Willcox Publisher

The scene is made up of shadows (low-luminance areas), highlights (high-luminance areas), and middle tones (luminances between the extremes). As shown in **Figure 7-41**, these luminances in the subject are reproduced in a photographic print as values correlated with the exposure zones.

An average sunlit outdoor scene typically produces a range of luminances equivalent to nine stops, or Zones I to IX on the scale. Luminances present in the scene, from brightest to darkest, are expressed in stops is known as the **subject brightness range (SBR)** or *dynamic range* of the scene. Some scenes may have a wider SBR, from Zone 0 to X and beyond, but most have a narrower range of three to seven stops. That range of stops may be located anywhere on the scale. A predominantly dark-toned subject with a three-stop range might have values equivalent to Zones II, III, and IV. A light subject with the same range of three stops could have values equivalent to Zones VII, VIII, and IX.

Placing an Exposure Value

Metered values may be shifted up or down the scale to provide an exposure that matches the photographer's visualization of the scene. For example, a significant shadow area in a scene may be selected and a meter reading may be taken. The reading indicates the exposure required to yield a middle gray or Zone V value for that area. If the photographer visualizes that shadow area as dark enough so texture and detail will be just visible in the resulting print (Zone III), the exposure must be adjusted. By giving the scene two stops less exposure, the shadow area is exposed at Zone III instead of Zone V.

This adjustment is called *placing a value*. As a result of selecting the desired exposure, the shadow has been placed on Zone III. Other values in the scene will fall on the remaining Zones within the subject brightness range in relation to the Zone III placement. Thus, a light area that originally would have been a highlight (Zone VII) will now fall on Zone V, and thus be a middle tone. A shadow area that would have been Zone III (shadow with some visible detail) becomes Zone I (featureless black). See **Figure 7-42**.

Using a Simplified Zone System Exposure Method

Strict application of the Zone System to fully control the photographic process is a complex and time-consuming endeavor. Many beginning and intermediate photographers improve their work by applying a simplified form of the Zone System that

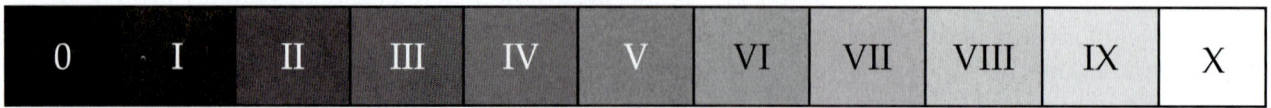

Goodheart-Willcox Publisher

Figure 7-40. The Zone System provides 10 steps of gradation from black to white.

3. Determine processing and paper grade adjustment for best rendition of highlights.

Metering Shadows and Highlights

To identify the subject brightness range of the scene, first meter the darkest shadow area in which you want to retain some detail and texture in the final print. Note the reading. Next, meter the lightest highlight in which you want to retain detail and texture in your print. Note that reading. Both readings should be for the same shutter speed, such as 1/60 second or 1/125 second.

Determine the SBR of the scene by counting the number of stops between the shadow reading and the highlight reading. For example, if the shadow reading is f/4 at 1/60 second and the highlight reading is f/22 at 1/60 second, you have a five-stop range of brightness (4 → 5.6 → 8 → 11 → 16 → 22).

Placing a Zone Value

To achieve a print in which the significant shadow area shows just a trace of detail and texture, place that area on Zone III. Since your meter reading of f/4 at 1/60 second would result in a Zone V value for the shadow, it is necessary to reduce exposure by two stops (and thus two Zones). An exposure of f/8 at 1/60 second would place the shadow area on Zone III.

Since you placed the shadow on Zone III, all other values would be two Zones lower. This means that your highlight value then falls on Zone VIII, exactly where it needs to be so it will show slight texture and detail. An exposure of f/8 at 1/60 second would result in a photo exposed properly to print on normal contrast paper.

Adjusting for Highlights

When the SBR is greater than seven stops, you usually can salvage what would otherwise be blank

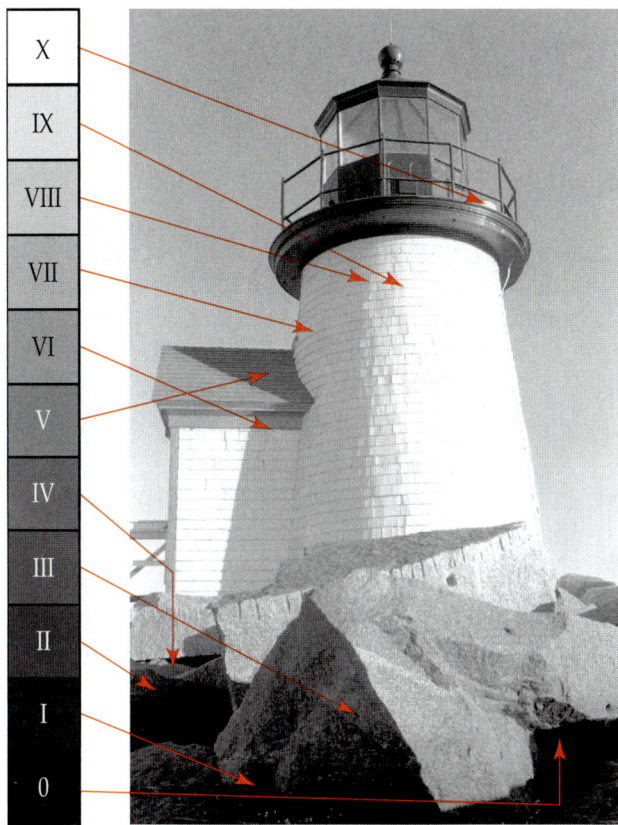

Jack Klasey/Goodheart-Willcox Publisher

Figure 7-41. Values corresponding to the exposure zones can be identified in a photographic print. Each value represents the luminance of a specific area of the subject.

concentrates on better exposure control. It is most applicable to black-and-white photography, but it can also be used to some benefit with color print film. The simplified method consists of three steps:

1. Meter significant shadow and highlight areas of the scene.
2. Adjust the selected shadow reading to place it on the desired Zone.

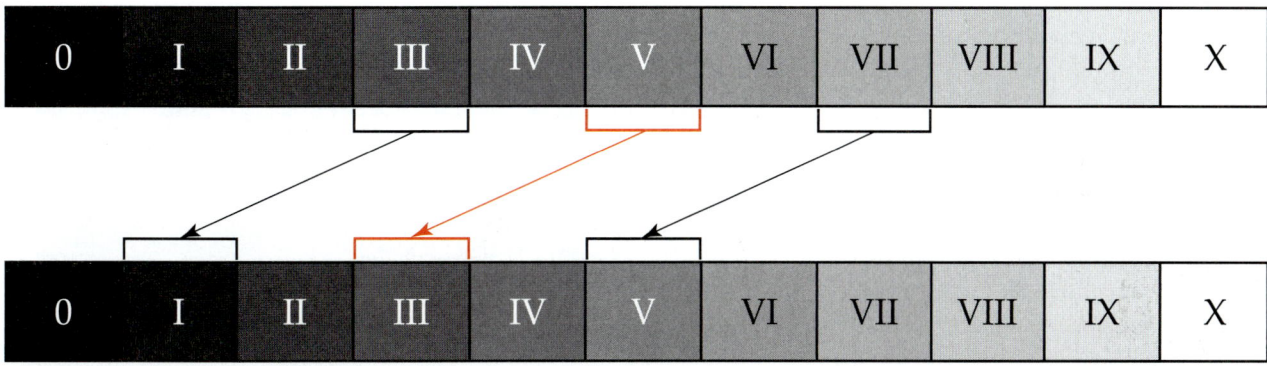

Goodheart-Willcox Publisher

Figure 7-42. When a value in a scene is placed on a specific Zone, all the remaining Zones shift as well.

white highlights by adjusting film development to reduce contrast. If all the frames on a roll were taken under the same high-contrast (wide SBR) conditions, reducing the development time makes the highlight values (dark areas on the negative) less dense than they would be with normal-length development. The reduction in development time prevents the highlights from becoming so dense that no light comes through when making a print. The reduction time for a given situation is usually established by trial and error, but it may be as great as 30%.

Digital Cameras and the Zone System

The simplified Zone System described in the preceding section can be applied to digital photography using the manual shooting mode. However, note that in the simplified Zone System, you do not have control over the image's development, just the exposure. A handheld meter or the camera's built-in metering system can be used to determine exposure values. You would then make a trial exposure and examine the camera's histogram display, **Figure 7-43**. Based on the display, you would increase or decrease exposure as needed.

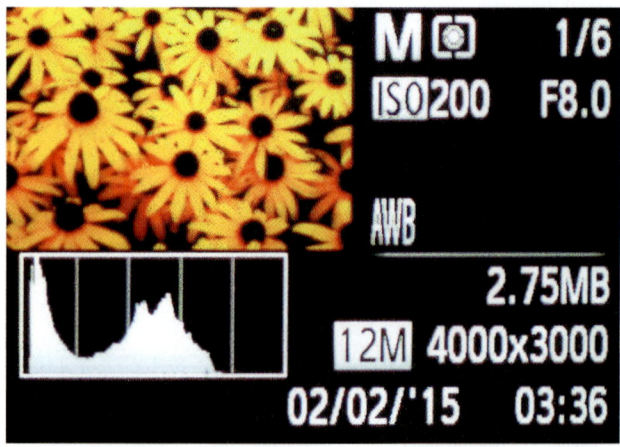

Jack Klasey/Goodheart-Willcox Publisher

Figure 7-43. A camera's histogram display shows the range of tones in the photograph.

PORTFOLIO ASSIGNMENT

Backlit Subject

Find or arrange a strongly backlit subject to practice metering for proper exposure. The subject should be a person or an object in front of a plain, bright background, such as a clear blue sky. The subject should be much less brightly illuminated than the background and should fill only about one-third of the frame. See **Example A**.

Expose the scene in different ways:
1. Meter the background.
2. Meter the overall scene.
3. Meter the subject close-up, then reframe.

Continue shooting and experimenting until you are satisfied with the subject exposure. Add your final image to your portfolio.

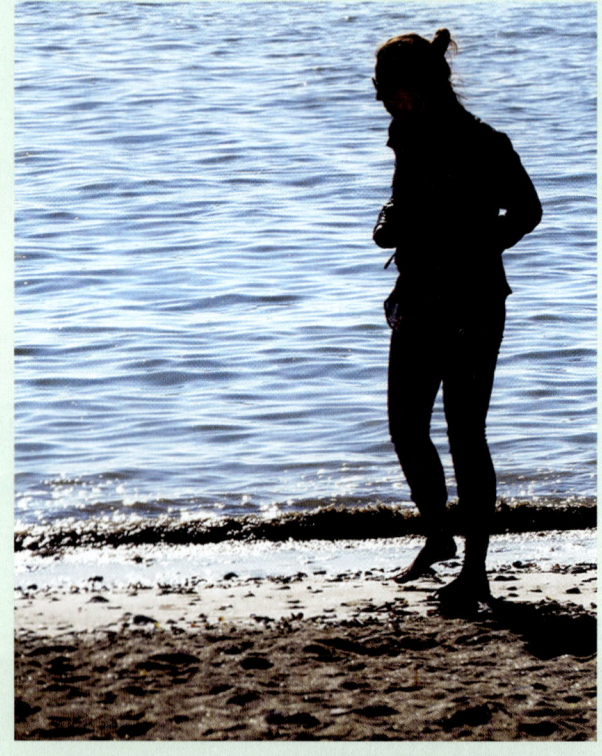

Jack Klasey/Goodheart-Willcox Publisher

Example A. A strongly backlit subject.

Chapter 7 Review

Summary

- When it comes to taking photos, it is important to ensure that they are lit and exposed properly. If these elements are not carefully monitored, you risk creating an image that is hard for viewers to process and understand.
- Being aware of how light behaves can help you overcome problems and capture the scene as you visualized it. Light is a form of electromagnetic radiation, or radiant energy, that is visible to the human eye.
- Everything we see is a reflection of light bouncing off objects that is then interpreted by our brain. When light is emitted from a source, it radiates in straight lines in all directions. The light rays move in the form of a wave, vibrating at right angles to the direction of travel.
- The tiny portion of the electromagnetic spectrum that can be seen by the human eye is referred to as the visible spectrum. It consists of waves with wavelengths ranging from about 400 nm to about 700 nm.
- White light is light composed of red, green, and blue wavelengths in approximately equal proportions. Light also has a specific color temperature, which is a measurement of the color of light, expressed in units called degrees kelvin (K).
- The amount of light that is absorbed, reflected, or transmitted depends on the material from which the object is made, the type of surface finish, and the object's color.
- The additive color process is a color reproduction method used with transmitted light in which the additive primaries (red, blue, and green) interact to create all other colors.
- The subtractive color process is a color reproduction method used with reflected light in which the subtractive primary colors (cyan, magenta, and yellow) of light subtract or block specific colors from the white light that is used to view an image.
- The human vision system automatically compensates for variation in the color temperature of light. Digital camera users can compensate for different color temperatures by using the camera's white balance control.
- How the camera records reflected light can be controlled to a great extent with filters. Various filters include contrast, neutral density (ND), polarizing, special-effects, diffusion, and image-modifying filters.
- Exposure is the amount of light reflected from a scene that reaches the camera's image receiver. Exposure is primarily determined by three interacting factors—aperture, shutter speed, and ISO rating.
- The aperture is the size of the opening through which light passes to strike the camera's image receiver. The aperture is affected by the f-stop system, aperture size and light transmission, relative aperture, and lens speed.

- The camera shutter is a device that opens and closes to control the flow of light to the camera's image receiver. How long the shutter remains open (in combination with the size of the aperture) determines how much light reaches the image receiver.
- An ISO rating is a numerical designation indicating the light sensitivity of an image receiver, with higher numbers indicating greater sensitivity. The rating is an international standard that was originally developed to ensure consistency in films from different manufacturers. With the development of digital photography, the concept was applied to different levels of sensitivity that could be selected for a camera's sensor.
- To properly expose a photograph, a means of measuring light is needed to help you make decisions on your camera settings. While virtually all cameras sold today have a built-in light meter, handheld meters are also used. Handheld meters include photoelectric light meters, selenium cell meters, and cadmium sulfide (CdS) cell meters.
- Exposure values displayed by a meter may be either indirect or direct. Types of meter readings include reflected light readings and incident light readings.
- Selecting the right areas to meter and the correct methods to obtain consistent and accurate readings are vital to taking well-exposed pictures. This includes making averaged readings, metering subjects that are not average, and reading the meter.
- The Zone System is a photographic method designed to produce consistent, predictable results through careful control of exposure, film development, and printing. It was originally developed for film photography but can be applied to digital photography.

Review Questions

Answer the following questions using the information provided in this chapter.

Know and Understand

1. _____ is a form of electromagnetic radiation, or radiant energy, that is visible to the human eye.
   A. Exposure
   B. Light
   C. Specular reflection
   D. Frequency
2. *True or False?* Frequency is a measure of the number of waves (cycles) passing a given point in one second.
3. The tiny portion of the electromagnetic spectrum that can be seen by the human eye is referred to as the _____.
   A. additive color process
   B. subject brightness range (SBR)
   C. wavelength
   D. visible spectrum
4. *True or False?* Color temperature is expressed in units called nanometers.
5. *True or False?* Opaque materials do not transmit light.
6. The _____ is a color reproduction method used with transmitted light in which the additive primaries (red, blue, and green) interact to create all other colors.
   A. subtractive color process
   B. visible spectrum
   C. additive color process
   D. subject brightness range (SBR)
7. *True or False?* Digital cameras can compensate for different color temperatures using white balance control.
8. _____ filters are made in deep shades of red, green, and blue, and each transmits light of its own color and absorbs light of the other two colors.
   A. Polarizing
   B. Neutral density (ND)
   C. Contrast
   D. Diffusion

9. A _____ filter is used to deepen the color of a blue sky, improve the color saturation of natural objects by reducing glare, and reduce or eliminate reflections from glass, water, and similar surfaces.
   A. polarizing
   B. blur
   C. neutral density (ND)
   D. contrast

10. _____ filters are available in several strengths (densities) to allow different amounts of light reduction.
    A. Blur
    B. Diffusion
    C. Polarizing
    D. Neutral density (ND)

11. *True or False?* For portrait work, a slightly softened or diffused appearance is often undesirable.

12. *True or False?* Filter factors decrease as the filter colors get darker.

13. The ability to affect image appearance through choice of shutter speed, aperture, white balance, and other camera settings is called _____.
    A. frequency
    B. creative control
    C. ISO rating
    D. digital noise

14. The size of the opening through which light passes to strike the camera's image receiver is called the _____.
    A. aperture
    B. shutter
    C. ISO rating
    D. iris

15. *True or False?* As f-stop numbers become larger, the opening (aperture) that they represent becomes smaller.

16. *True or False?* As aperture size numbers get larger, the area of the opening gets larger.

17. *True or False?* Apertures can be different physical sizes but the same relative size.

18. The camera _____ is a device that opens and closes to control the flow of light to the camera's image receiver.
    A. f-stop
    B. ISO rating
    C. shutter
    D. aperture

19. A(n) _____ is a numerical designation indicating the light sensitivity of an image receiver, with higher numbers indicating greater sensitivity.
    A. f-stop
    B. ISO rating
    C. specular reflection
    D. incident light reading

20. A _____ meter measures the electrical resistance caused by light striking the CdS cell.
    A. selenium cell
    B. photoelectric
    C. cadmium sulfide (CdS) cell
    D. through-the-lens (TTL)

21. *True or False?* Indirect-reading meters give a specific f-stop/shutter speed combination.

22. *True or False?* Since they measure light falling on the subject, incident light readings are taken from the subject's position, with the meter facing toward the light source.

23. _____ is an exposure value that is equivalent to a tone that reflects 18% of the light that falls on it.
    A. Incident light
    B. Middle gray
    C. Reflective light
    D. Backlit

24. *True or False?* Zebras do not control exposure.

25. Very long exposures increase _____, or tiny light-colored spots especially noticeable in shadow areas of an image.
    A. specular reflection
    B. zebras
    C. color temperature
    D. digital noise

26. The _____ is a photographic method designed to produce consistent, predictable results through careful control of exposure, film development, and printing.
    A. Zone System
    B. additive color process
    C. subject brightness range (SBR)
    D. subtractive color process
27. Luminances present in the scene, from brightest to darkest, expressed in stops is known as the _____ of the scene.
    A. subtractive color process
    B. subject brightness range (SBR)
    C. additive color process
    D. Zone System
28. *True or False?* Adjusting metered values to provide an exposure that matches the photographer's visualization of the scene is called placing a value.

Apply and Analyze

1. By what four means do artificial light sources produce radiant energy?
2. Briefly explain why we perceive a lime as green.
3. Explain how a neutral density (ND) filter makes it possible to eliminate all the automobiles from a photograph of a busy street.
4. Explain why the actual size of a given aperture (such as f/8) is larger for a 200 mm lens than it is for a 28 mm lens. Calculate the physical size of the aperture at f/8 for the two lenses.
5. What is the difference between a reflective light reading and an incident light reading?
6. Identify and describe the three zones with particular significance in the Zone System.

Critical Thinking

1. The Zone System was developed to produce consistent results using film cameras and making prints in a chemical darkroom. Do you think that studying the Zone System has any value for a photographer using a digital camera and making color inkjet prints?
2. Many photographers install an ultraviolet filter in front of their camera's lens. Can you think of reasons both for and against using this filter?

Suggested Activities

1. Explore the effects of a polarizing filter. Determine how its effectiveness is related to the location of the sun and how it can be used to eliminate reflections in glass or water, deepen colors by removing glare, and bring out details in clouds. Use pairs of before and after pictures to illustrate a written report.
2. To better understand how changes in lighting affect exposure, choose a fairly large object (such as a statue or the wall of a storage shed or garage) that will not change position. Set your camera to aperture priority and choose f/8 as the aperture. Meter the object and note the displayed shutter speed. Make readings from the same position at different times of day and under various weather conditions. Keep careful notes of the date, time, weather conditions, and meter reading. Continue for one week, making three to five readings each day. Compile your notes in the form of a table.

Communicating about Photography

1. **Speaking.** Pick a figure in this chapter, such as Figure 7-22 or 7-24. Working with a partner, tell and then retell the important information being conveyed by that figure. Through your collaboration, develop what you and your partner believe is the most interesting description of the importance of the chosen figure. Present your narration to the class.

2. **Writing and Speaking.** Working in a group, brainstorm ideas for creating classroom tools (such as posters, flash cards, and/or games) that will help your classmates learn and remember the different types of filters. Choose the best idea(s), and then delegate responsibilities to group members for constructing the tools and presenting the final products to the class.

Chapter 8
Digital Image Capture Media

Learning Objectives

After completing this chapter, you will be able to:
- Determine the differences between digital image capture and the traditional chemical method of image capture.
- Explain the digital imaging process.
- Describe how bit depth relates to color in an image.
- Recall various digital sensor sizes.
- Understand how various memory cards work.
- Identify common file formats used by digital cameras.
- Recall common post-shoot storage methods.

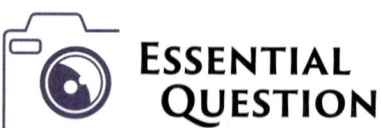

Essential Question

How does choosing the right image capture medium change how you approach taking photos?

Technical Terms

analog signal
area array
bit depth
buffer
card speed
charge-coupled device (CCD)
complementary metal oxide semiconductor (CMOS)

compression
digital signal
file formats
firmware
full-frame
gray levels
HEIC

image file
JPEG
memory card
RAW
solid-state
TIFF

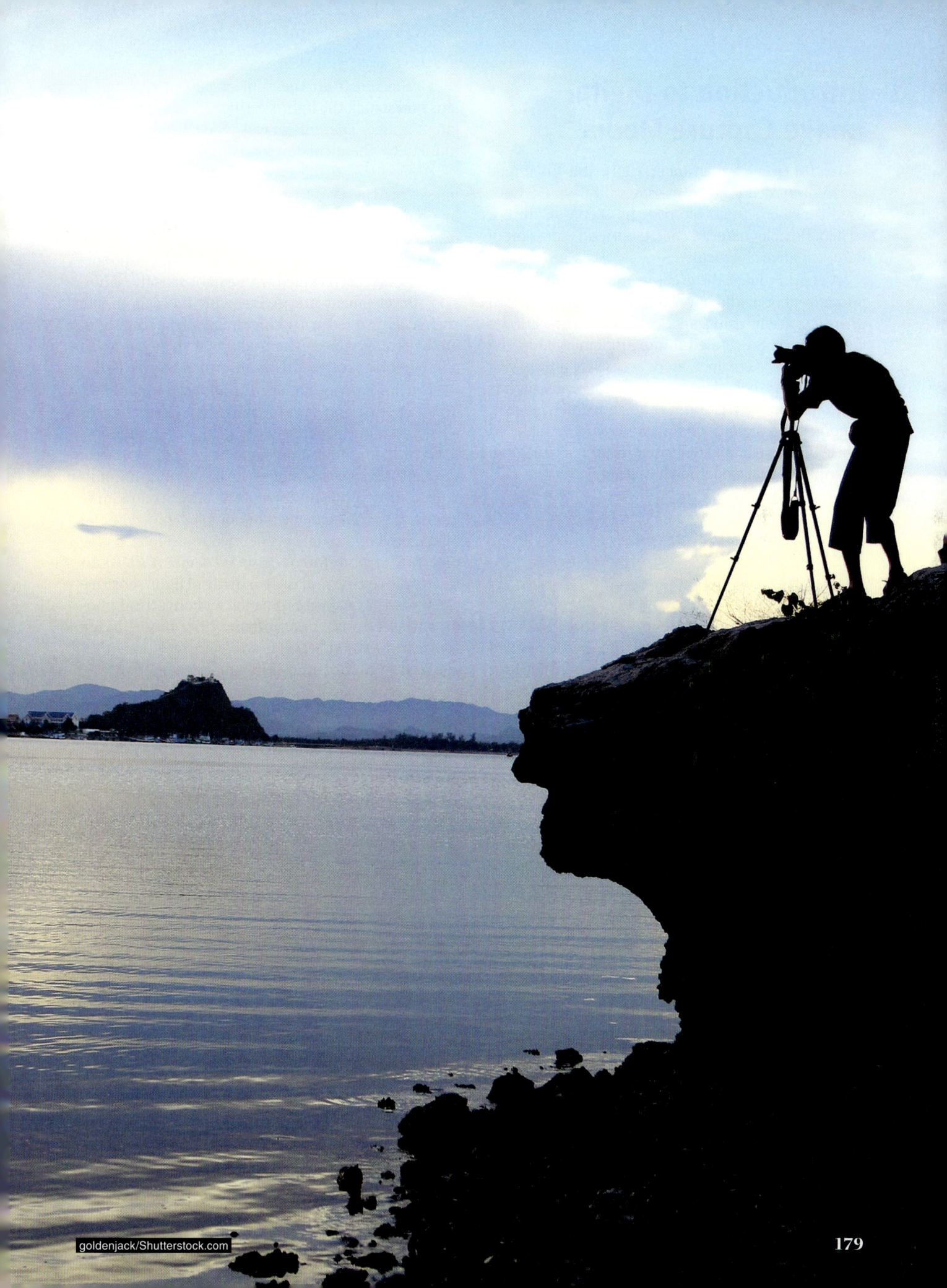

Introduction to Digital Image Capture Media

In 1900, a photographer capturing an image of children sledding on a snowy hill would have used a camera that recorded the scene on film, a strip of flexible material coated with an emulsion of light-sensitive chemicals.

A century later, the great-granddaughter of that photographer would have been more likely to record a similar scene using an electronic array called a *digital sensor*. Since digital imaging emerged in the late 1990s as a cheaper, more accessible alternative to traditional chemical-based photography, it has almost completely captured the consumer market. Among professionals, digital cameras have replaced film equipment for photojournalism, product imaging, portraiture, and wedding photography.

Image Capture— Digital vs. Film

For more than 150 years, photography was an image capture process that involved chemical changes in substances exposed to light. The light rays reflected from the subject passed through a lens and struck the light-sensitive film, imprinting a latent image. That image was made visible and permanent by chemical development and fixing.

Depending on the type of film used, the visible image could be a positive or a negative. As you learned in Chapter 2, *From Pinholes to Pixels*, positive film resulted in a projectable image. Negative film could be used to create positive prints on a paper or plastic surface that had been coated with a light-sensitive emulsion. Development and fixing with the appropriate chemicals resulted in a positive image of the scene originally photographed. The traditional chemical-based photographic process is diagrammed in **Figure 8-1**.

The similarities between traditional and digital image capture end at the camera's image receiver. In a traditional camera, light rays cause a latent image to form in the film emulsion. In a digital camera, the light rays strike image sensors containing millions of tiny photosites, or pixels. The sensors may be charge-coupled devices or complementary metal oxide semiconductors. As defined in Chapter 5, *The Camera System*, a **charge-coupled device (CCD)** is an electronic sensor that has an array of light-sensitive elements that captures images by converting photons to electrons. A **complementary metal oxide semiconductor (CMOS)** is an electronic sensor that converts light into images in a digital camera.

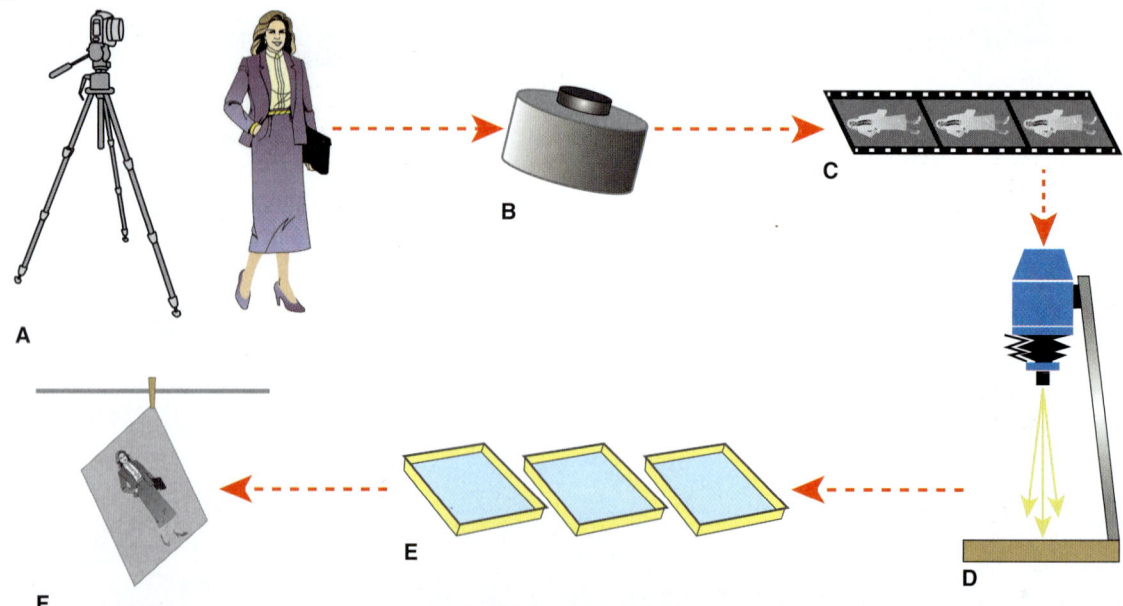

Goodheart-Willcox Publisher

Figure 8-1. The traditional, chemical-based process of capturing an image and creating a finished print has been used for more than 150 years. A—The film is exposed. B—The film negative is developed and fixed. C—The negative is washed and dried. D—The print is made by projection or contact method. E—The print is developed and fixed. F—The print is washed and dried.

Each type of sensor has its advantages. A CCD sensor is more sensitive, especially to lower light levels, and generates less digital noise than a comparable CMOS sensor. A CMOS sensor, on the other hand, is less expensive to manufacture, uses less power (thus draining the camera battery more slowly), and sends information to the camera's processing circuits faster.

Pixels are arranged in rows to form a grid made up of rows and columns of electronic sensors known as an *area array*. A compact digital camera typically has 3200 rows with 5000 pixels per row, yielding a sensor with 16 million pixels. This camera would be referred to as a *16-megapixel camera*. See **Figure 8-2**. When light strikes an individual pixel, a tiny electrical charge is generated. The electrical charge from each pixel is passed on to a processor, or computer chip. The processor converts the charges into an *image file*, which is an individual digital image that can be stored, transferred, or manipulated. Image files can be displayed on the camera's LCD screen; sent to a smartphone, computer, or the internet for viewing; projected onto a screen by a digital projector; or converted to a print on paper.

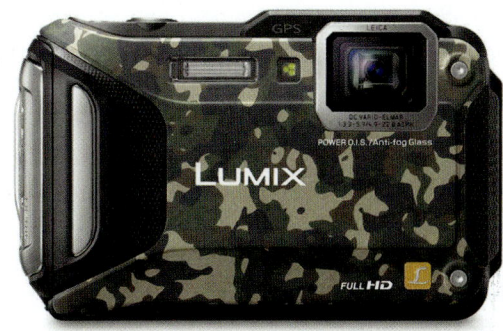

Panasonic

Figure 8-2. This Panasonic Lumix compact camera has a sensor with 16 million pixels.

The Digital Imaging Process

When light rays strike the camera's sensor, the electrical charges generated by each pixel vary in strength based on the brightness of the light. These varying charges are then converted to an *analog signal* (a continuous signal in which the electrical charges vary in strength) for further processing. CCD and CMOS devices handle this step differently. See **Figure 8-3**.

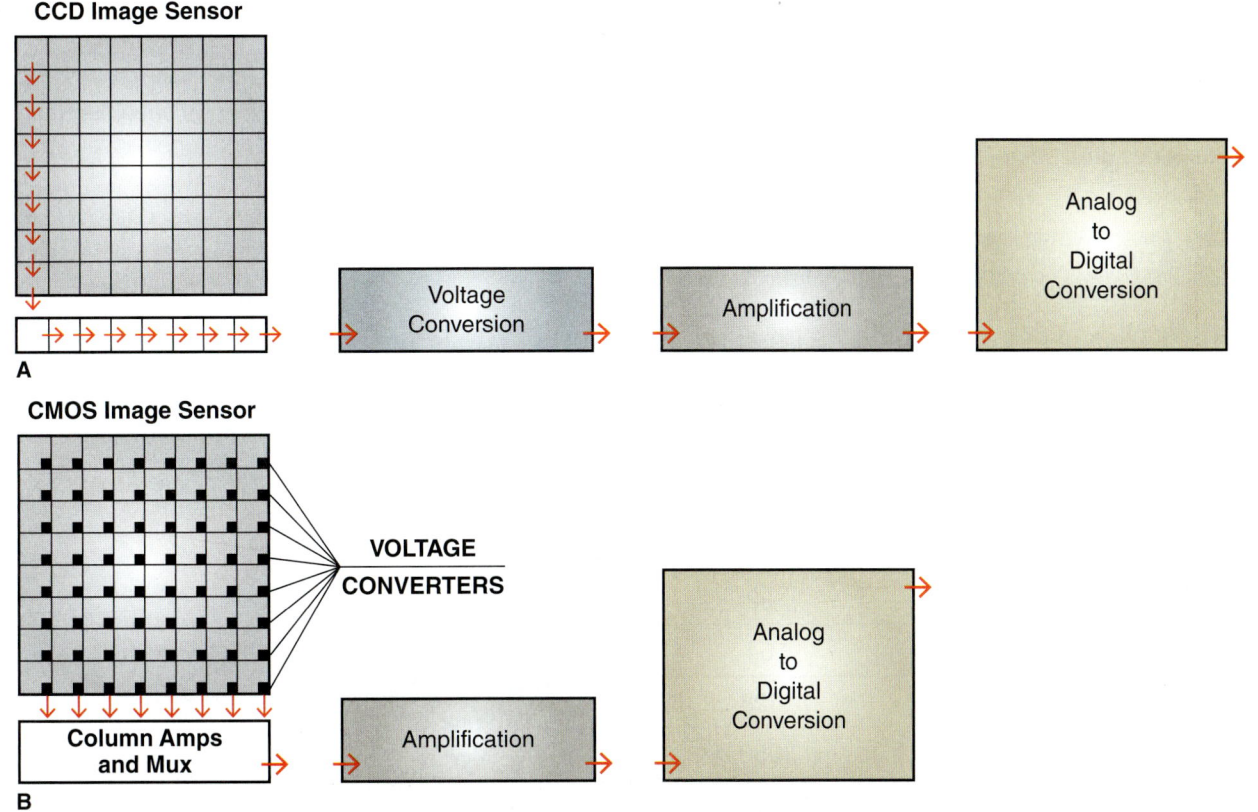

Goodheart-Willcox Publisher

Figure 8-3. CCD and CMOS sensors. A—CCD sensor processing. B—CMOS sensor processing.

In a charge-coupled device, the charges from individual pixels are moved, row-by-row, to a transfer register and converted to voltages. The voltages are passed to an amplifier and then to a converter that changes them from analog to digital values. A ***digital signal*** is a signal in which image information is encoded as a series of on/off states (usually represented by 1 and 0) rather than varying continuously. It is processed by the camera's built-in program or ***firmware***.

Complementary metal oxide semiconductors handle the charges differently. Each pixel has its own circuitry for converting the charge to a voltage and amplifying it. The signal then goes to an analog-to-digital converter (system that converts an image into a digital file for storage on an SD card), where it is then processed by the camera's firmware.

From Gray to Color

Firmware translates the signal from each pixel into a shade of gray. How many ***gray levels***, or distinct steps between pure white and pure black, the camera sees is determined by the pixel's bit depth. ***Bit depth*** is defined as a numeric expression of the number of shades of gray a pixel is capable of displaying.

Bit depth increases exponentially, as shown in **Figure 8-4**. A pixel with a bit depth of 1 distinguishes only white and black, a 2-bit pixel can distinguish four shades of gray, a 3-bit pixel can distinguish eight shades, and so on. A bit depth of 8 (256 shades of gray) is equivalent to the number of gray values in a black-and-white photographic print.

Color information is recorded by filtering the light striking the array to obtain three different grayscale channels. One channel is for green, one is for red, and one is for blue. Each channel typically has a bit depth of 8, so the resulting image has a bit depth of 24 (3×8). Up to 16.7 million different tones of color can be reproduced. See **Figure 8-5**. A 24-bit color depth is considered the minimum for good color reproduction.

The Foveon X3 sensor used in cameras made by Sigma is made up of three layers of pixels—each sensitive to blue, green, or red wavelengths. See **Figure 8-6**. According to the manufacturer, the layered pixel sensor design provides more accurate color, increased sharpness, and faster image processing in the camera.

Bit Depth and Shades of Gray		
Bit Depth	Exponent (Base of 2)	Shades of Gray
1	2^1	2
2	2^2	4
3	2^3	8
4	2^4	16
5	2^5	32
6	2^6	64
7	2^7	128
8	2^8	256

Goodheart-Willcox Publisher

Figure 8-4. Bit depth increases exponentially by powers of two.

Bit Depth for Color Images		
Bit Depth	Exponent (Base of 2)	Shades of Gray
8	2^8	256
16	2^{16}	64,000
24	2^{24}	16.7 million

Goodheart-Willcox Publisher

Figure 8-5. Bit depth for color images becomes much larger because of the three color channels involved.

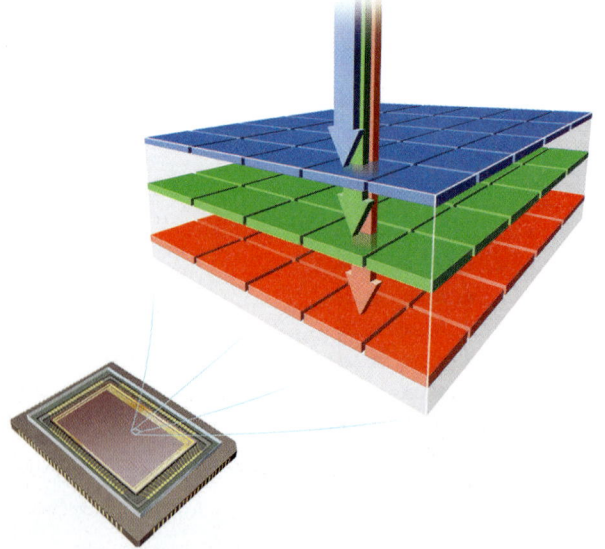

Foveon, Inc.

Figure 8-6. The Foveon X3 sensor has three layers of pixels.

Sensor Sizes

There are a number of different sensors that can be used in digital cameras. **Full-frame** is a term describing digital camera sensors that are 24 mm × 36 mm, corresponding to the 35 mm film frame. See **Figure 8-7**. The most common sensor is the *APS-C size*, which is approximately 24 mm × 16 mm. Many advanced compact and prosumer SLR cameras use this sensor. The *Foveon X3* sensor is somewhat smaller at 21 mm × 14 mm, and the *Four Thirds system* sensor used in Olympus and some other camera brands is smaller still at 17 mm × 13 mm. Introduced in 2008, the *Micro Four Thirds* sensor is the same size, but it is used in mirrorless cameras.

A full-frame sensor does not necessarily contain more pixels than an APS-C size sensor. In fact, there are many compact cameras with a higher megapixel count than some professional full-size sensor models. The major difference is the size of the individual pixels. Full-frame pixels are approximately one-third larger than APS-C size pixels. They gather more light and do not have to be amplified as much before processing, generating less digital noise.

Studio Cameras

Digital capture equipment used for studio work is typically medium format and large format cameras. These cameras may have an area array, usually in the form of a digital back, or a scanning back that functions much like the sensor array of a flatbed scanner.

Most common are medium format cameras capable of being used with either film or a digital back, **Figure 8-8**. As you learned in Chapter 2, a

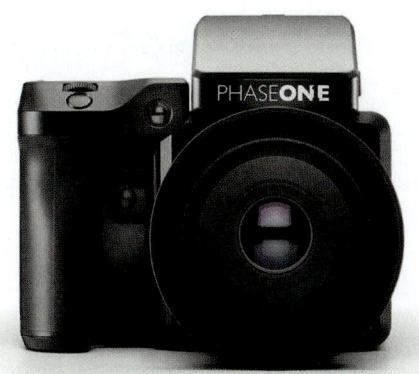

Phase One

Figure 8-8. This medium format camera is equipped with a digital back.

digital back is a capture device attached to the camera in place of a traditional film holder that allows a camera that is designed to use film to take digital photographs. It uses a large sensor, such as 54 mm × 40 mm, that produces an image file as large as 240 MB (megabytes). These cameras are also used for location shooting. They deliver large images of extremely high quality, **Figure 8-9**.

Studio cameras with capture devices called *scanning backs* make use of a trilinear array rather than an area array, **Figure 8-10**. As mentioned in Chapter 5, the trilinear array is a bar containing three rows of sensors that is moved across the image capture area. Operation is much like the movement of the capture element in a flatbed scanner.

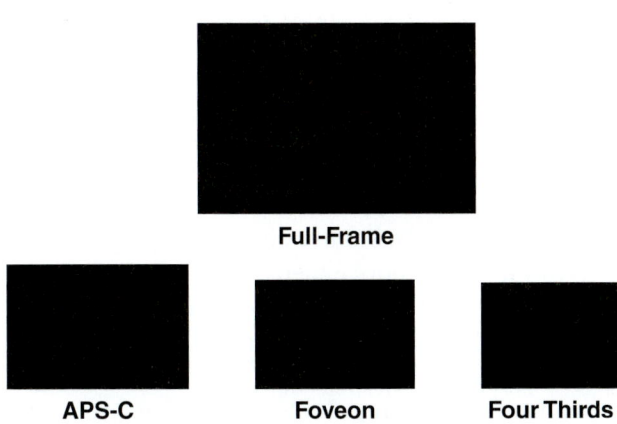

Goodheart-Willcox Publisher

Figure 8-7. Compared to a full-frame sensor, APS-C, Foveon X3, and Four Thirds sensors are much smaller in size.

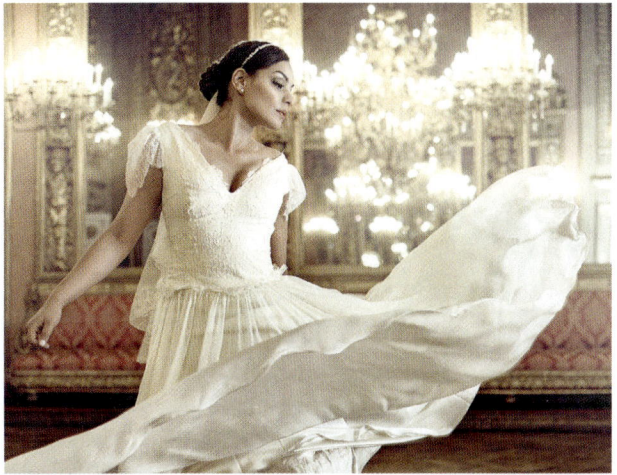

Phase One photo by Alexander Flemming

Figure 8-9. With their large arrays, medium format and large format digital cameras capture very high-quality images. This photo was taken by a camera with an 80 MP sensor.

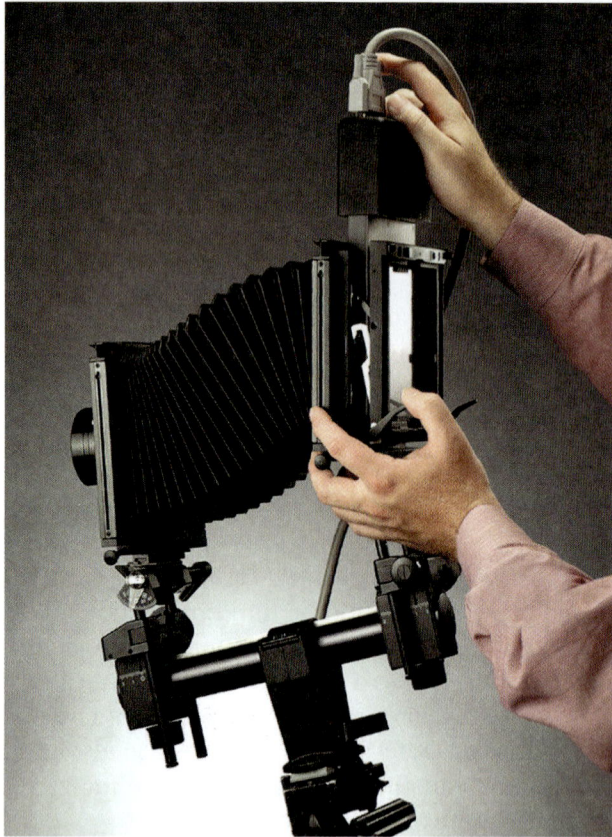

Courtesy of Better Light

Figure 8-10. This studio camera is fit with a scanning back.

Resolutions achieved with scanning backs are very high, but the trade-off is speed. Exposure times with a scanning back often are measured in minutes. The long exposures require a rock-solid camera mount, usually a heavy studio stand, and lighting that is constant in intensity and free from flicker. Digital studio cameras may be connected to a computer for framing and focusing. See **Figure 8-11**.

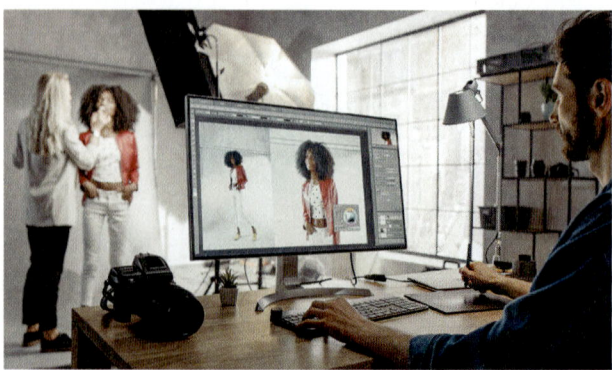

Gorodenkoff/Shutterstock.com

Figure 8-11. Connecting a digital studio camera to a computer works well for framing and focusing.

This arrangement also makes use of the computer's hard drive for image storage.

Image Storage

The earliest digital cameras offered only internal memory, but virtually every camera model today uses some form of removable storage device. Because of increases in camera resolution, and thus file size, a camera's internal memory would quickly fill up with image files without a removable device. Shooting would then have to stop until the files were transferred to a computer.

A **memory card** is a digital storage device used in digital cameras. It can be filled with image files and replaced in the camera with a fresh card so shooting can continue. The contents of the filled card can be transferred to a computer's hard drive, and the device formatted for use again. While the umbrella term is memory card, they are commonly referred to as *SD cards*.

Memory Cards

Most memory cards are **solid-state**, meaning they have no moving parts. The cards vary in physical size and capacity, **Figure 8-12**. Some can be used in many different makes and models of cameras, while others are usable in only a few brands of cameras. The following are examples of common memory cards:

- *CompactFlash (CF) cards* are available in capacities from 512 MB to 512 GB (gigabytes). Once widely used, today they are most common in professional-level DSLRs.
- *Secure Digital (SD) cards* are physically smaller and thinner than CF cards. They are available with capacities from 512 MB to 256 GB. SD cards are the most commonly used memory cards. They are used for compact, advanced compact, and a number of DSLR models.
- *CFexpress cards* are a relatively new memory card format but are considered much faster than their counterparts. They come in three types (Type A, Type B, and Type C) that all offer different speeds, but are different physical sizes. They are also more expensive.
- *SDXC (UHS2)* is short for Secure Digital Extended Capacity card. These cards are small flash memory cards that have a greater storage capacity than a regular SD card. They are compatible with smartphones, digital cameras, camcorders, computers, and even music players. These cards have an extended capacity (hence the name) and can store up to 2 terabytes (TB).

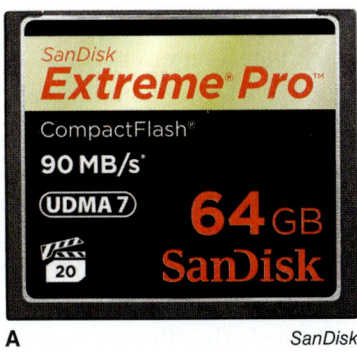
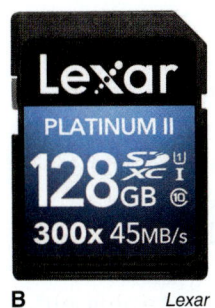
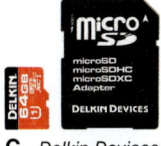

A   SanDisk   B   Lexar   C   Delkin Devices

Figure 8-12. Removable storage devices. A—CompactFlash card. B—Secure Digital card. C—MicroSD card and an adapter that allows it to be used in an SD card slot.

- *SDHC* stands for Secure Digital High-Capacity card. These cards are popular among both photographers and videographers for their fast write speeds and their ability to hold up to 32 GB of data. While regular SD cards may meet your needs for class, most hobby photographers often use SDHC cards because of the amount of photos they store.

Other types of memory include the following:

- *MicroSD cards*, which are about the size of a postage stamp, are available in capacities of 4 GB to 64 GB. They are most commonly used for image storage in camera phones.
- *Memory stick cards* are used primarily in Sony cameras. They are available in 512 MB to 32 GB capacities.
- *Microdrive devices* record information on a tiny hard disc the diameter of a US 25-cent coin. These removable drives are the size of a CF card and can store up to 8 GB of files.
- *Internal storage* is a rare find in modern DSLRs. However, internal storage allows you to take photos on your camera without the need for a memory card. These files are stored on the camera itself, and the photographer then transfers them to other storage, such as a computer or cloud-based storage system.

Solid-state removable storage devices can usually survive extreme conditions and rough handling. Unlike film, they are not affected by airport X-rays. However, they should not be exposed to strong magnetic fields or water.

> ### 📷 REAL-WORLD PHOTOGRAPHY
> #### Maintaining a Memory Card
> Memory cards are a critical part of the photography process. Without them, you would not be able to take photos on your digital camera. It is important that you maintain your memory card properly not only so you can continue using it, but so you do not risk losing your files. The following are some tips for maintaining your memory card:
>
> - **Keep your card dry and avoid heat.** Just like other photography equipment, it is very important to keep your memory card dry and avoid extreme temperatures.
> - **Remove the card after turning off your camera.** While technology has come a long way in the last several years, it is best to remove your memory card from the camera after it is turned off to avoid any potential voltage shocks.
> - **Format your card.** Formatting your memory card for the camera you will be using is important to ensure that the camera can write to the card properly. The process for each camera is different. Formatting wipes your card of all files, so remember to store your files from a previous shoot in a different location (such as an archive or on your computer) to prevent losing them permanently.
> - **Use a computer to delete images.** Using a computer to delete your images will help protect your memory card and ensure your card has a longer life span.
> - **Properly eject cards from your computer.** As with any USB, it is helpful to properly eject your memory card from your computer without pulling it straight out of the computer. This prevents any unnecessary data loss.

Card Capacities

The most important factors in choosing a memory card capacity are the size of the files you will be producing, how long you want to shoot before changing cards, and the speed of the card (card speed is explained more thoroughly in the next section). For example, if you have a 10 MP camera and prefer to shoot RAW files, you would want a card larger than 512 MB; otherwise you would be able to shoot only about 30 images before running out of space. See **Figure 8-13**. At the other extreme, you could shoot almost 1,000 images before filling a 16 GB card.

For most people, the right size card is somewhere in between, especially if they use high-quality JPEG files, as do most nonprofessional photographers. A card size of 2 GB or 4 GB represents a good compromise between capacity and price. Cards larger than 2 GB use a file system called FAT 32 that is readable only by newer cameras. Before purchasing a 4 GB or larger card, check your camera manual to determine if the card and camera are compatible.

Some photographers buy the largest-capacity card they can afford so they can shoot without interruption for long periods. Others take a more cautious approach, preferring to use several smaller-capacity cards, minimizing any potential loss of images due to card failure.

The number of images that fit on a card, as indicated by charts found in most camera manuals, are only an approximation. The actual size of an image, measured in megabytes, varies depending on its content, especially with the JPEG file format. A simple scene with a limited number of tones and details produces a smaller file than a complex scene with a wide range of tones and many details. See **Figure 8-14**.

Storage Card Image Capacities						
File Type	512 MB	1 GB	2 GB	4 GB	8 GB	16 GB
6 MP RAW	65	130	260	520	1040	2080
6 MP JPEG	140	280	560	1120	2240	4480
10 MP RAW	30	60	120	240	480	960
10 MP JPEG	80	160	320	640	1280	2560

Goodheart-Willcox Publisher

Figure 8-13. Approximate image capacities of different-size removable storage cards.

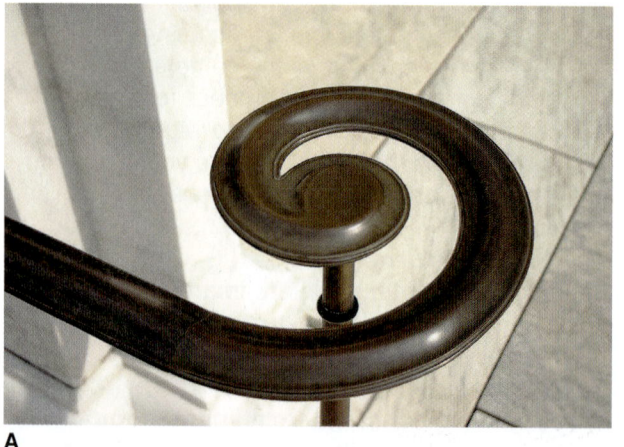
A

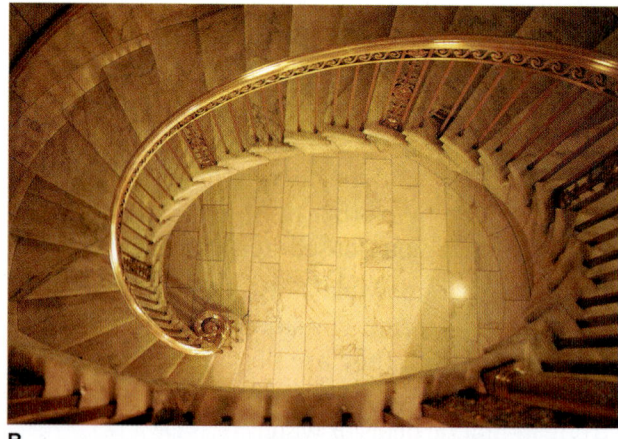
B

Jack Klasey/Goodheart-Willcox Publisher

Figure 8-14. File sizes become larger as the subject becomes more detailed and complex. A—This simple subject has only a few tones. The file size is 1.57 MB. B—This complex subject includes a wide variety of tones. The file size is 3.12 MB.

Card Speed

Card speed is a measure of how rapidly image files can be transferred from a camera to a memory card. A fast card is an advantage in situations where images are being recorded quickly with little pause between exposures, such as sports or news coverage. A digital camera has a **buffer**, which is internal memory that functions as a holding tank for image information that has been processed but not yet transferred to a memory card. Fast-paced shooting may feed image information into the buffer faster than it can be output to the card. If the buffer fills up, the camera does not allow another exposure to be made until buffer space is available.

Card speeds are expressed in "×" terms, based on 1× being equal to a transfer rate of 150 KB per second. Higher numbers, such as 80× or 256×, indicate higher transfer speeds, **Figure 8-15**. For example, a card rated at 1000× would be able to accept a 6 MB image file from the buffer in 0.16 seconds.

A fast card is not an advantage if your camera cannot write (send) information to the card at a high speed. The owner's manual for your camera should provide write speed information on its specifications page.

Image File Sizes

The size of electronic files generated by a digital camera makes file storage and handling an important consideration. For example, a color image captured by a 16 MP camera and saved at the highest resolution (4068 × 3456 pixels) creates a file size of more than 47 MB. File size is computed by multiplying the dimensions in the pixel array (4068 × 3456 = 15,925,248). If the image is black-and-white, this would be its file size. A color image, however, is made up of three channels, each of which is 15,925,248 bytes in size. Adding together the red, green, and blue channel file sizes produces the actual file size of 47,775,744 bytes (47 MB). See **Figure 8-16**.

File Formats

Digital cameras allow files to be saved in a number of different modes or **file formats**. Some of these retain their original size and all the original pixel data. Files may also be compressed. **Compression** is the squeezing of an electronic file to reduce its size. The smaller size takes up less storage space and helps speed up transfer time. However, the files may lose some image information in the process.

Depending on the camera, digital cameras may offer the user one or two file formats, including RAW, JPEG, or TIFF. Each has its advantages and drawbacks:

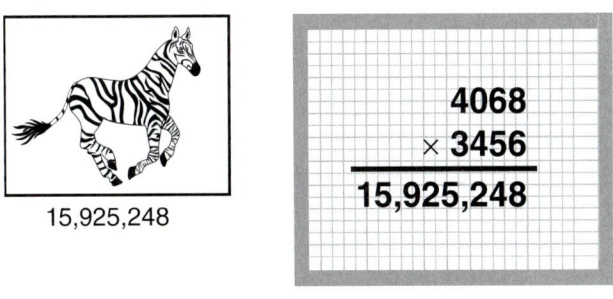

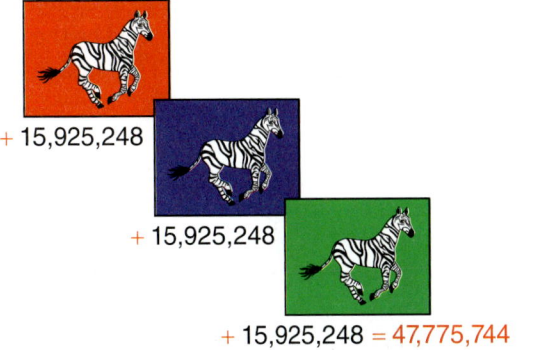

Goodheart-Willcox Publisher

Figure 8-16. At the highest resolution, a digital camera produces a monochrome (black-and-white) image file that is the same as the resolution of the array. A color image file has three times the number of pixels in the array because it consists of three channels (red, green, and blue).

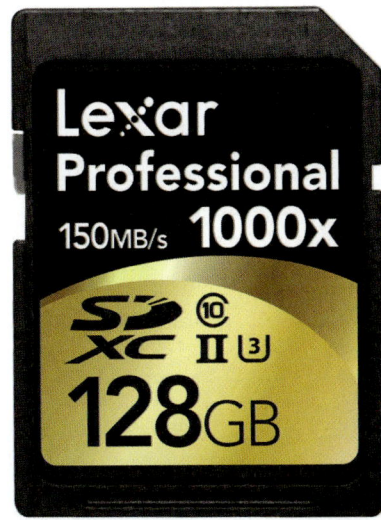

Lexar

Figure 8-15. Card speed is a measure of the rate at which data can be transferred to the memory card from the camera.

- **RAW**: RAW is technically not a file format like JPEG or TIFF. Instead, it is the basic image information captured by the camera's sensor and saved with minimal processing by the camera's computer. It is available on all DSLRs and some advanced compacts. RAW is popular among professionals and advanced amateur photographers. With the proper software, a photographer can adjust many aspects of a RAW image, such as exposure or color temperature, without degrading the image quality. After adjustment, the file is converted to another format, such as TIFF, JPEG, or Adobe Photoshop's proprietary PSD. However, it has two negative aspects—its large file sizes and the need to perform extra operations on the file before it can be further processed with image editing software.
- **JPEG**: The JPEG format, also referred to as *JPG*, is the most common compressed file format and often the only compression choice offered on many cameras. Most smartphone cameras also take photos in this format. The JPEG method of reducing file size is lossy, which means that some image information is discarded in the process of compressing the file. The amount of compression can be small or large. For example, a file from a 16 MP camera saved at the highest quality setting compresses to 3.6 MB. At the lowest quality (most compressed) setting, the file shrinks to 484 KB (kilobytes). When the highest quality is selected, the loss is minimal, but more severe compression can seriously degrade image quality. Additional image information is lost every time a JPEG image is opened and resaved.
- **TIFF**: Short for Tagged Image File Format, TIFF is a file format that retains all the image information through the processing steps performed by the camera's computer. Unlike JPEG, a TIFF image retains all its information because its compression is not lossy, but lossless. Like RAW, TIFF file sizes are large. Unlike RAW, no additional steps are needed before using image editing software.
- **HEIC**: HEIC is Apple's proprietary version of the file format called HEIF, short for High-Efficiency Image File format. HEIC allows images taken on an iPhone® to be stored as a smaller file size while retaining high quality. This format can also include video and audio. Even though it retains high-quality images, there are occasional compatibility issues across devices. However, these file types are easy to convert to the more universally used JPEG.

Post-Shoot Storage

Once you have finished taking photos, it is important to consider how you want to store them. Many photographers choose to do one of three things: store them on the original SD card and continuously purchase new cards, save them in a cloud-based storage system, or store them on an external hard drive, **Figure 8-17**. While the last two options are the most popular, keep in mind that they are not your only options. Whatever method of permanent storage you choose should ensure your images are easily accessible and provide enough space to store all your files. Storing your image files permanently is discussed more thoroughly in Chapter 17, *Importing Images*.

Cloud-Based Storage

Cloud-based storage is one of the most popular methods for storing photos. Storing photos in any cloud-based service has many benefits, including keeping your personal hard drive free of large files, being easily accessible (as long as you have access to the internet), and allowing you to share your files with others. There are also many free and low-cost cloud-based storage options to choose from, making it a good affordable option.

External Hard Drives

External hard drives, sometimes referred to as archives, are another popular method of storing photos after a shoot. Unlike cloud-based storage, you do not have to rely on internet access to view your photos. In essence, external hard drives are very large flash drives. Sizes for external hard drives vary, starting at 10 GB and going all the way up to an 8 TB capacity.

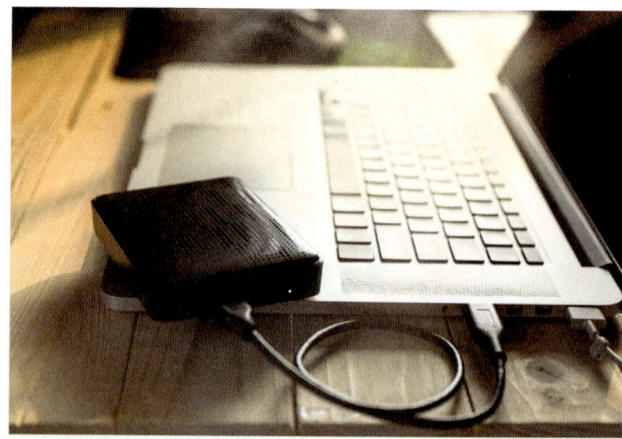

Dourleak/Shutterstock.com

Figure 8-17. Many photographers choose to store their photography files on external hard drives after shooting.

Chapter 8 Review

Summary

- Since digital imaging emerged in the late 1990s as a cheaper, more accessible alternative to traditional chemical-based photography, it has almost completely captured the consumer market.
- The similarities between traditional and digital image capture end at the camera's image receiver. In a traditional camera, light rays cause a latent image to form in the film emulsion. In a digital camera, the light rays strike image sensors containing millions of tiny photosites, or pixels.
- When light rays strike the camera's sensor, the electrical charges generated by each pixel vary in strength based on the brightness of the light. These varying charges are then converted to an analog signal for further processing.
- Firmware translates the signal from each pixel into a shade of gray. How many gray levels the camera sees is determined by the pixel's bit depth.
- There are a number of different sensors that can be used in digital cameras, including full-frame, APS-C size, Foveon X3, Four Thirds system, and Micro Four Thirds sensors.
- Digital capture equipment used for studio work is typically medium format and large format cameras. These cameras may have an area array, usually in the form of a digital back, or a scanning back that functions much like the sensor array of a flatbed scanner.
- The earliest digital cameras offered only internal memory, but virtually every camera model today uses some form of removable storage device.
- A memory card is a digital storage device used in digital cameras. It can be filled with image files and replaced in the camera with a fresh card so shooting can continue. Most are solid-state, meaning they have no moving parts.
- The most important factors in choosing a memory card capacity are the size of the files you will be producing, how long you want to shoot before changing cards, and the speed of the card.
- Card speed is a measure of how rapidly image files can be transferred from a camera to a memory card.
- The size of electronic files generated by a digital camera makes file storage and handling an important consideration.
- Digital cameras allow files to be saved in a number of different modes or file formats. Some of these retain their original size and all the original pixel data, and some may be compressed. Common file formats include RAW, JPEG, TIFF, and HEIC.
- Once you have finished taking photos, it is important to consider how you want to store them. Many photographers choose to either store them on the original SD card and continuously purchase new cards, save them in a cloud-based storage system, or store them on an external hard drive.

Review Questions

Answer the following questions using the information provided in this chapter.

Know and Understand

1. *True or False?* A CCD sensor uses less power than a CMOS sensor.
2. Pixels are arranged in rows to form a grid made up of rows and columns of electronic sensors known as a(n) _____.
   A. trilinear array
   B. image file
   C. area array
   D. solid-state
3. *True or False?* An analog signal is a continuous signal in which the electrical charges vary in strength.

4. _____ is defined as a numeric expression of the number of shades of gray a pixel is capable of displaying.
   A. Firmware
   B. Bit depth
   C. Gray levels
   D. Solid-state

5. *True or False?* An 8-bit color depth is considered the minimum for good color reproduction.

6. *True or False?* Full-frame is a term describing digital camera sensors that are 24 mm × 16 mm.

7. The most common sensor used in digital cameras is the _____.
   A. Micro Four Thirds
   B. full-frame
   C. Four Thirds system
   D. APS-C size

8. Resolutions achieved with scanning backs are very high, but the trade-off is _____.
   A. quality
   B. speed
   C. size
   D. storage

9. A _____ is a digital storage device used in digital cameras.
   A. memory card
   B. trilinear array
   C. buffer
   D. file format

10. *True or False?* Secure Digital (SD) cards are the most commonly used memory cards.

11. _____ are used primarily in Sony cameras and are available in 512 MB to 32 GB capacities.
    A. MicroSD cards
    B. Microdrive devices
    C. Memory stick cards
    D. CompactFlash (CF) cards

12. *True or False?* Solid-state removable storage devices are *not* affected by airport X-rays.

13. *True or False?* A card size of 2 GB or 4 GB represents a good compromise between capacity and price.

14. Card _____ is a measure of how rapidly image files can be transferred from a camera to a memory card.
    A. capacity
    B. speed
    C. size
    D. type

15. *True or False?* RAW is technically *not* a file format.

16. The _____ format is the most common compressed file format and often the only compression choice offered on many cameras.
    A. JPEG
    B. RAW
    C. HEIC
    D. TIFF

17. The _____ format allows images taken on an iPhone to be stored as a smaller file size while retaining high quality.
    A. TIFF
    B. RAW
    C. JPEG
    D. HEIC

18. Which of the following is *not* one of the three most common ways photographers choose to store their photos?
    A. Store them in the camera itself
    B. Store them on the original SD card and continuously purchase new cards
    C. Store them on an external hard drive
    D. Store them in a cloud-based storage system

Apply and Analyze

1. Where do the similarities between traditional and digital image capture end?
2. List the three most important factors in choosing a memory card capacity.
3. When is a fast card an advantage? When is it *not* an advantage?
4. Why is RAW popular among professionals and advanced amateur photographers?
5. Name the two most popular methods of post-shoot storage.

Critical Thinking

1. If you were developing a new camera model intended for first-time camera users, would you use a CCD sensor or a CMOS sensor? Why?
2. Imagine you are buying storage media for a two-week vacation to photograph African wildlife. Would you buy several very-high-capacity cards or a number of smaller-capacity cards that would provide the same total amount of storage? Explain your reasoning.

Suggested Activities

1. Visit an online retailer that sells digital cameras (such as Amazon, B&H Photo and Video, Best Buy, or Adorama) and find three different brands of DSLR camera (such as Nikon, Canon, Panasonic, or Sony). For each camera, list the price, the storage device type, and other specs that could help you decide which camera to purchase.
2. Use your smartphone's native camera app to take photos of a still subject. Take five photos total: one without a filter and four with a built-in filter, utilizing a different filter for each one. Once you have shot all five images, write a list of the visual qualities of each filtered image that differs from the original, unfiltered photo. Present your observations to the class in an oral presentation.

Communicating about Photography

1. **Speaking and Listening.** Divide into groups of four or five students. Each group should choose one of the following topics: file formats, image sensors, or memory cards. Using your textbook as a starting point, research your topic and prepare a report on the different capabilities of the items within the topic. As a group, deliver your presentation to the rest of the class. Take notes while other students give their reports. Ask questions about any details that you would like clarified.
2. **Speaking and Writing.** Prepare a written or oral report comparing and contrasting the different types of file formats.

Section 2 Project
Photography Basics

The goal of this project is to help you become more acquainted and comfortable with your camera, whether it is a digital camera or your smartphone camera.

Part 1

Locate the manual that accompanies the DSLR camera you are using in class. If you do not have a physical copy, search for the manual online (make sure it is the correct one for the camera make and model you are using). Read through the manual and work through various settings, including the following (if you are using a smartphone, search for your specific model online and read about the camera app):

- Exposure
- Shutter speed
- ISO
- Lenses
- Flash
- Timer settings

When you have finished reading the manual and working through the camera settings, create a two-column list. The left side should include the settings you understood well and would be comfortable showing someone else how to use. The right side should include the settings you did not understand and would like additional explanation or help with.

Part 2

Create a cheat sheet to keep in your camera kit. This cheat sheet should fit on a 3″ × 5″ index card. Be sure to include the following in addition to any other information you find helpful (such as information you learned in Part 1 of this project):

- How to set up your camera
- An equipment checklist
- How to adjust ISO, exposure, and shutter speed
- Lighting and exposure tips
- How to transfer files from your camera to a computer or device for postprocessing

Once you become more comfortable with using your camera, you may not need to rely on the card as much. However, this is a useful tool to have when you are just starting out.

Section 3
Photography Essentials

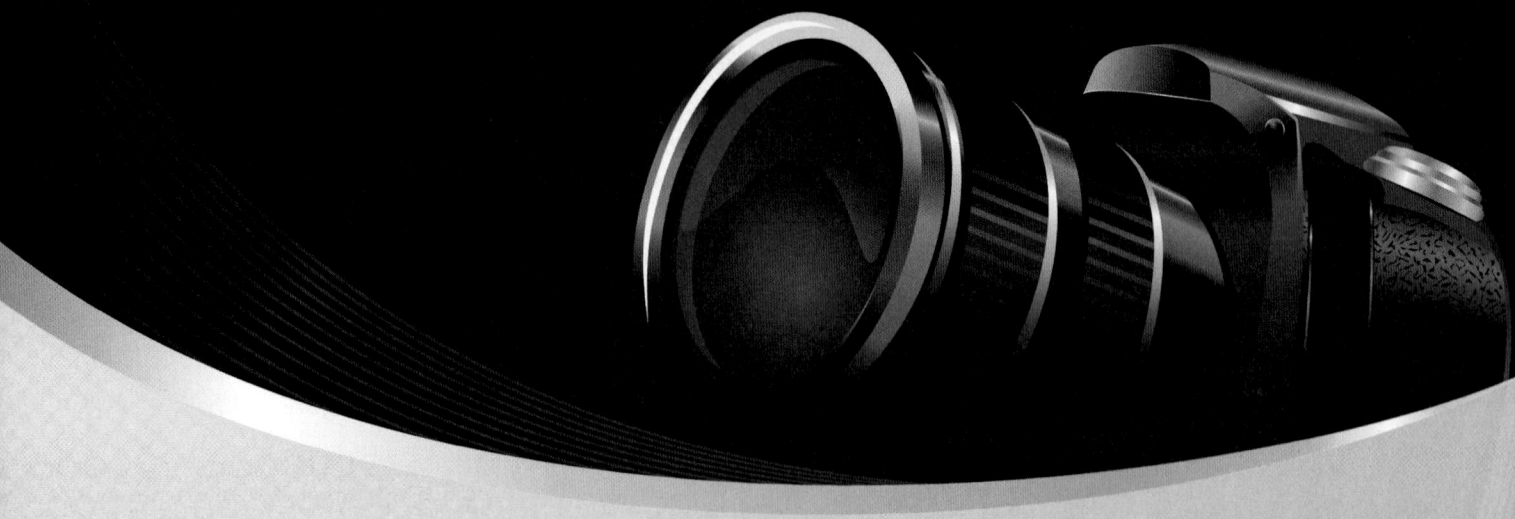

Chapter 9   Making a Picture
Chapter 10   Improving Lighting
Chapter 11   Making Exposure Decisions

In Section 2, you learned about the basic controls and functionality of a camera. Now that you understand how your camera works, you can begin tackling how to create great photos.

Section 3 will teach you how to properly utilize the elements of composition, as well as how lighting and exposure affect your final photo. Regardless of the equipment you have, the information in this section will be vital for taking great photos.

Chapter 9 explains the difference between "taking" a picture and "making" a picture. It has a heavy focus on the elements of composition. It also discusses how to focus viewer attention using various techniques and how to create visual effects while shooting.

In Chapter 10, you will learn how lighting affects your final image. This includes lighting equipment, setups, and accessories.

Chapter 11 will focus on how exposure affects your photo. Building on the previous chapter, this chapter will show you how to manipulate lighting in your photos to create specific effects.

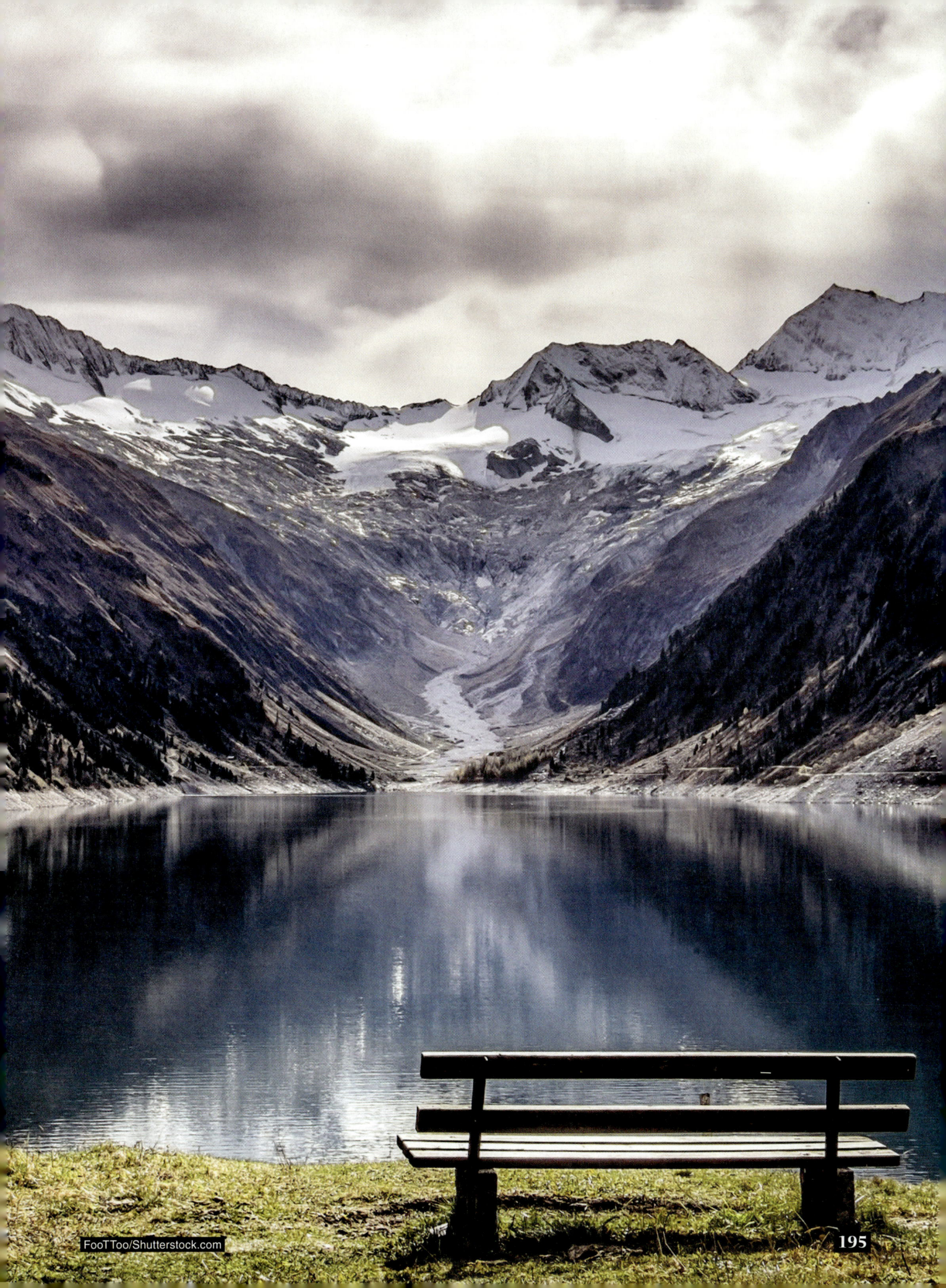

Chapter 9
Making a Picture

Learning Objectives

After completing this chapter, you will be able to:

- Understand the difference between "taking" a picture and "making" a picture.
- Recall the six traditional elements of composition.
- Understand the concept of selective framing in composition.
- Explain how the rule of thirds is used in composing a photograph.
- Identify the various methods of focusing viewer attention.
- Describe techniques that can be used while shooting to create interesting visual effects in photographs.

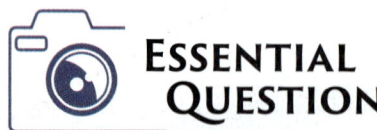

Essential Question

How do compositional elements affect a photograph?

Technical Terms

camera angle
center of interest
composition
compositional elements
contrast
convergence
depth of field (DOF) preview
emphasis
extracting
formal balance

frame
informal balance
landscape mode
leading lines
lead room
line
negative space
panning
pattern
perspective

point
portrait mode
rhythm
rule of thirds
selective focus
selective framing
shape
viewpoint
visualization
zooming

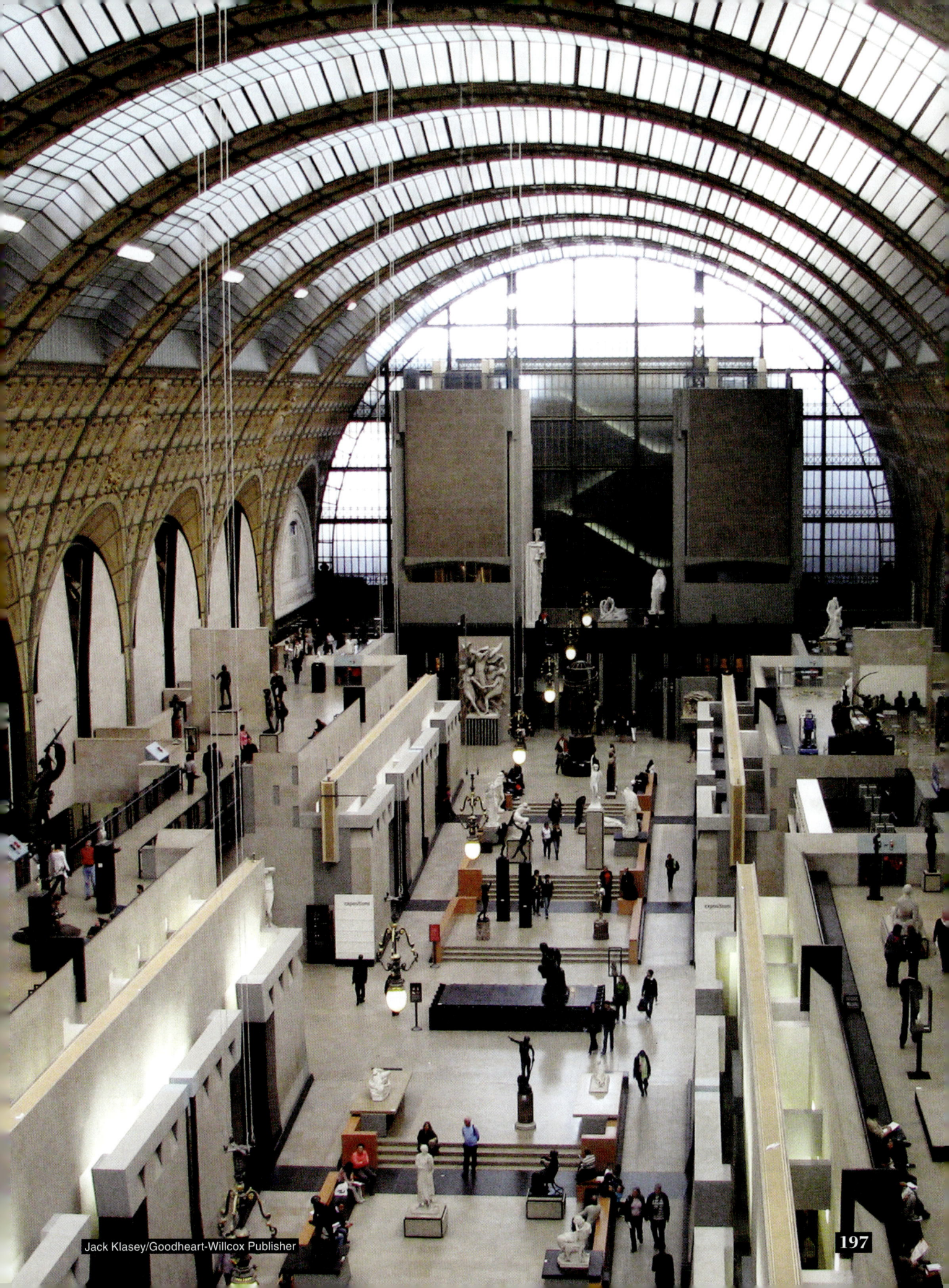

Introduction to Making a Picture

Being told that you have a "good eye" as a visual artist, especially as a photographer, is high praise. Such a person looks at a scene or a subject in a way quite different from a non-artist. Being aware of the relationship of masses and colors, the emotional content of the scene, the interplay of light and shadow, and the meaning that goes beyond the obvious and readily apparent are among the many elements of seeing photographically.

Subjects are all around us. Which ones we select to photograph depends on many factors, but as you learned in Chapter 1, *Our Visual World*, the first is personal interest. We must recognize the person, place, or thing as a possible subject, and then decide that we want to photograph it.

"Taking" a Picture vs. "Making" a Picture

The commonly used term for photographic activity is *taking a picture*. This implies a simple recording of what is in front of the camera. The vast majority of all photographs that are taken are casual snapshots. These images are simple record shots of places visited, children's activities, and family events.

More serious photographers often use the term *making a picture*, which implies conscious control of the process and the final result. Instead of merely recording what appears in the viewfinder, these photographers make choices, applying the elements and principles of art to affect what the viewer of the final image sees. For example, a photographer visiting the local farmers market might first envision a photo of two shoppers examining the bananas in a large display of fruit. Looking a bit more closely at the subject, the photographer might decide to make an image depicting the banana's shape and texture instead. See **Figure 9-1**.

To control how the finished image appears to the viewer, the photographer must visualize the final result. **Visualization** is a technique in which the photographer controls how the final product will appear to the viewer by first seeing that desired final result in their own mind. Finally, keep in mind that almost all the techniques we discuss in this chapter apply to both digital cameras and smartphone cameras. You may not have as much control over the settings for a phone's camera, but you still have the ability to control most of the important things, like exposure and focus.

Selecting the Viewpoint

To capture a visualized image, a photographer must make a series of choices. The most basic decision is selecting the subject and determining how you want to portray it. For example, an abandoned building, such as an old factory, farm structure, church, or rural schoolhouse, could be shown in many different ways.

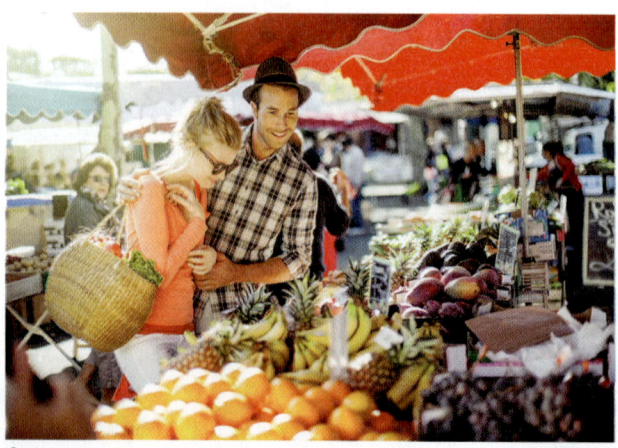

A
Jack Frog/Shutterstock.com

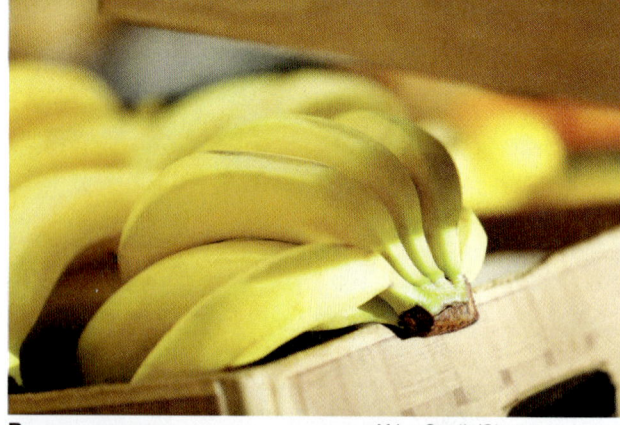

B
Africa Studio/Shutterstock.com

Figure 9-1. Taking a picture versus making a picture. A—This photo of shoppers at a farmers market, taken from standing eye level, is a competent but unexciting shot. B—To make a more interesting image, the photographer moved in closer to fill the frame, selected a different angle, and carefully exposed to bring out texture and shadow detail.

In **Figure 9-2**, each of the old church images involves a different ***viewpoint***, or the distance and angle from which the camera (and eventually, the viewer) sees the subject. **Figure 9-2A** and **Figure 9-2B** are basically eye-level exterior views from some distance away. These images show the entire structure. The pattern shot could be made from almost any distance, depending on the lens used, but includes only part of the building, **Figure 9-2C**. Texture studies are often close-up views that show an even smaller part of the subject, **Figure 9-2D**. **Figure 9-2E** is an interior view portraying the roofless, abandoned nature of the building. The interior could be shown from a number of

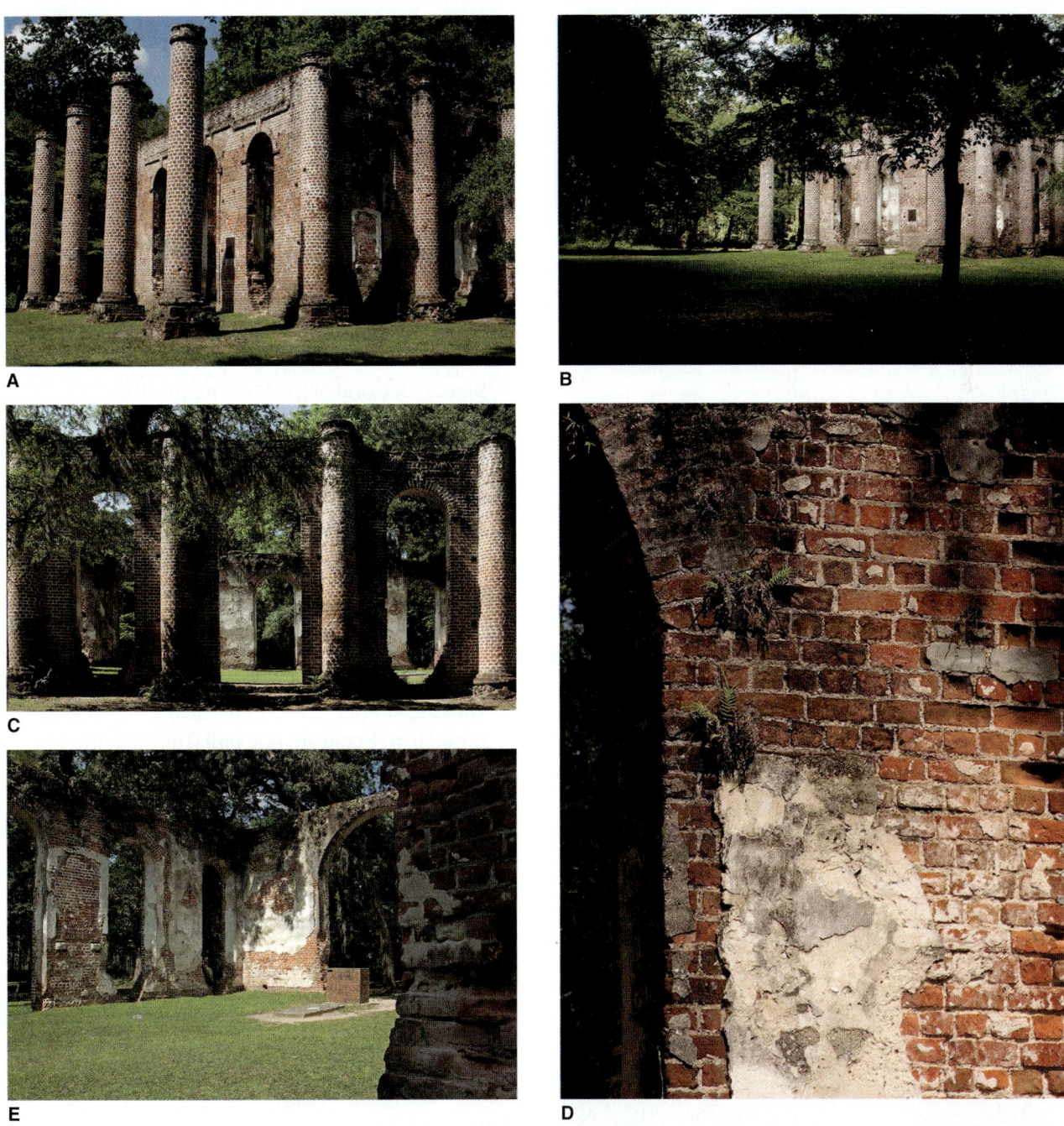

Jack Klasey/Goodheart-Willcox Publisher

Figure 9-2. An abandoned building, such as this old brick church, can be portrayed in many different ways. A—A traditional three-quarters architectural view. B—In this wider environmental view, the church ruin is a focal point. C—Repetitive arch shapes form a pattern. D—Worn brick, weathered remnants of plaster, and encroaching plants provide rich texture to an interior wall. E—The church interior, open to the elements, is a portrait of abandonment.

viewpoints (wide angle, normal, or telephoto; eye-level, low angle, or high angle).

A picture is often taken from the first possible viewpoint the photographer encounters, typically resulting in an eye-level shot that may be competent, but probably is not very exciting. Photographers who want to make a picture instead of merely taking one move around the subject to see it from as many sides and distances as practical. They also try to visualize the result of shooting from a high angle or low angle.

Two other factors that affect the choice of viewpoint are the light and the background. The strength and direction of light can make a major difference in the impact of an image. In **Figure 9-3**, the interplay of the angled shadows with the opposing diagonal lines of the fire escape provide a dramatic statement that would be absent on a cloudy day. The viewpoint—looking upward at an angle—also creates a much different composition from a straight-on shot.

What appears in your photo behind and around the subject must be taken into account. If you want to show a young couple pitching their tent in a peaceful natural setting, the viewpoint should not include a nearby line of electrical transmission towers or a factory smokestack. On the other hand, a portrait of a successful young architect might be quite effective when shot against the busy background of a construction site.

Composition Considerations

Composition is the arrangement of visual elements, such as shapes, colors, and textures, within the frame. It strongly influences the message the viewer will receive and can direct their attention toward or away from an object in the frame. For example, imagine that you have six identically sized balls and want to convey to the viewer that one of these is more important than the other five. **Figure 9-4** illustrates four compositional techniques that achieve this objective:

- **Size.** Place one of the balls nearer the camera so it appears larger. This directs your eye to the larger object, making it seem more important.
- **Focus.** Sharply focus on one ball and leave the others in soft focus. This directs your eye to the ball in sharp focus, which makes it seem more important.
- **Contrast.** Paint one of the balls a strongly contrasting color. This directs your eye to the ball that is a different color, making it seem more important. Contrast can also be shown by varying shapes, sizes, and hues.
- **Isolation.** Separate one ball from the others. This directs your eye to the ball that is isolated. Again, this makes it seem more important.

These are only a few of the many compositional techniques that experienced photographers use regularly. All techniques for composing photographs make use of a limited number of compositional elements. As visual artists, both painters and photographers make use of these same principles and elements of art. Painters can freely add, subtract, and rearrange the elements within the picture. Photographers, however, are bound by physical limitations of the scene. They must use careful framing, changes of angle, selective focus, and other techniques to achieve the desired composition, or layout, of the final photograph.

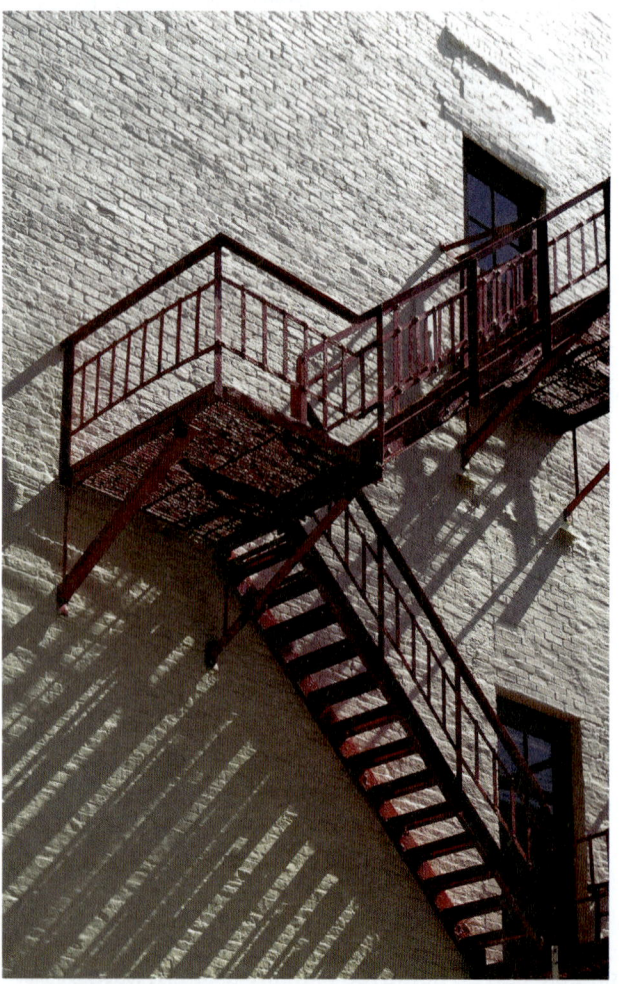

Jack Klasey/Goodheart-Willcox Publisher

Figure 9-3. Directional light and shooting upward at an angle strengthen this composition.

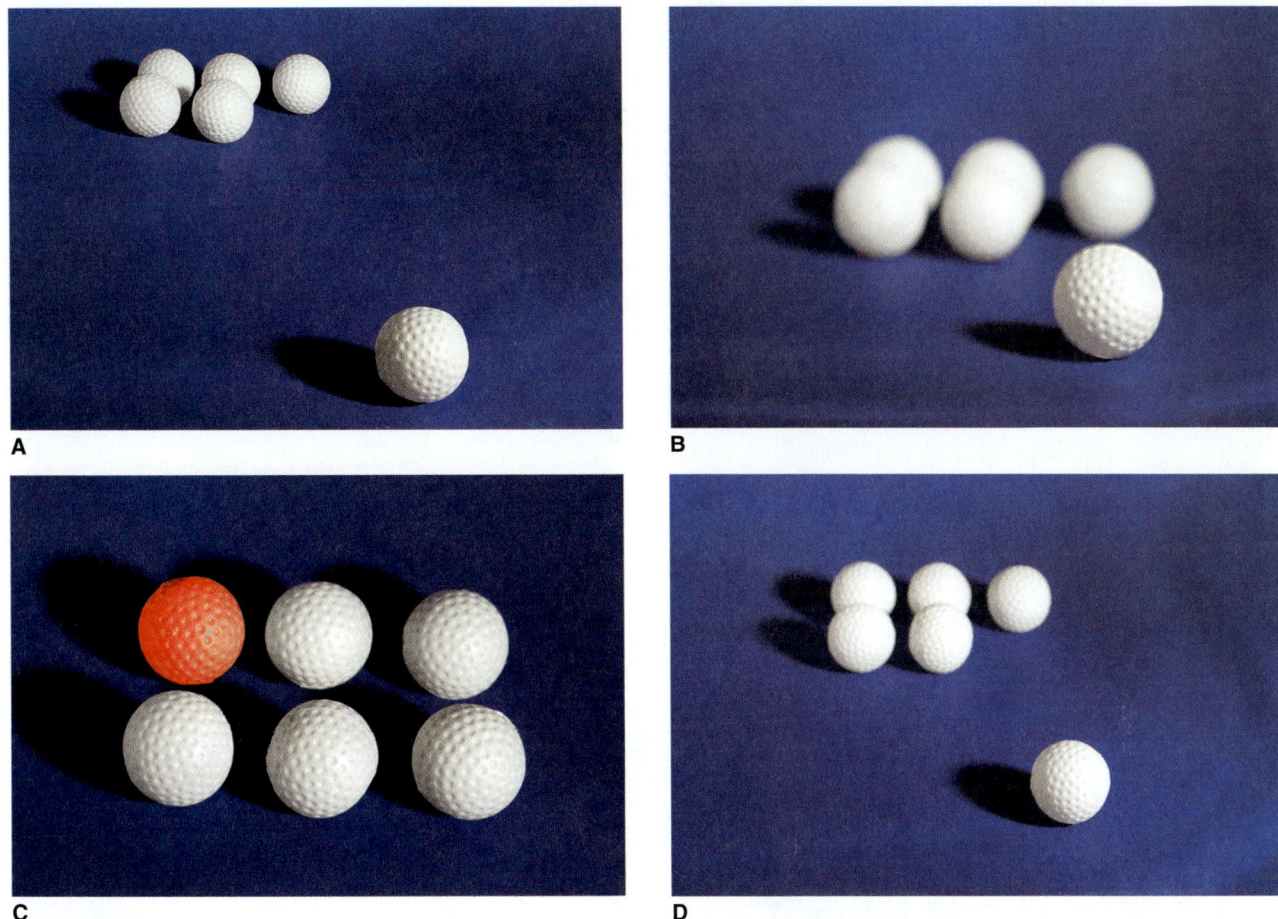

Figure 9-4. Compositional techniques. A—Apparent size. B—Focus. C—Color. D—Isolation.

Jack Klasey/Goodheart-Willcox Publisher

Traditional Elements of Composition

Compositional elements are the basic components used for effectively composing photographs. Various sources list different numbers of and names for the basic elements of composition. The traditional compositional elements consist of these six elements:

- Point
- Line
- Shape or pattern
- Balance
- Emphasis
- Contrast

The figures in the following sections each demonstrate one of the elements listed. Evaluate the figures closely to see how they convey each compositional element and take note of how you can use them in your own photos.

Point

A ***point*** is a compositional element that is a single object, typically small in size, that attracts the eye. It may serve as the focal point, or it may be a distraction that pulls the eye away from a more important object. See **Figure 9-5**.

Line

A ***line*** is a compositional element that typically draws the viewer's eye along its length, making it a useful tool for directing attention. It is a "stretched point." The orientation and shape of a line can convey certain impressions. Straight horizontal or vertical lines are static, whereas diagonal lines imply motion. Gently curved lines are considered placid and restful, while sharply curved or bent lines, as well as broken lines, convey energy or strong movement. See **Figure 9-6**.

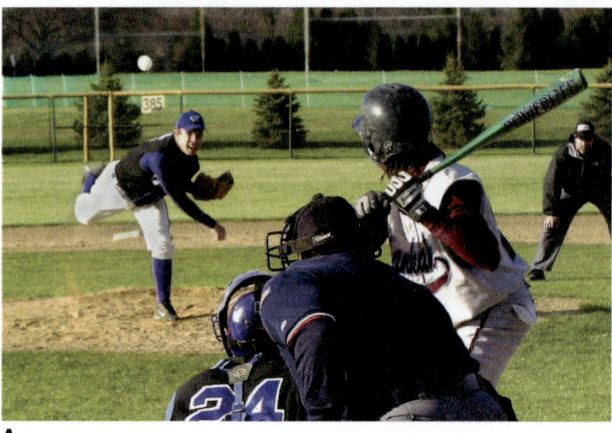
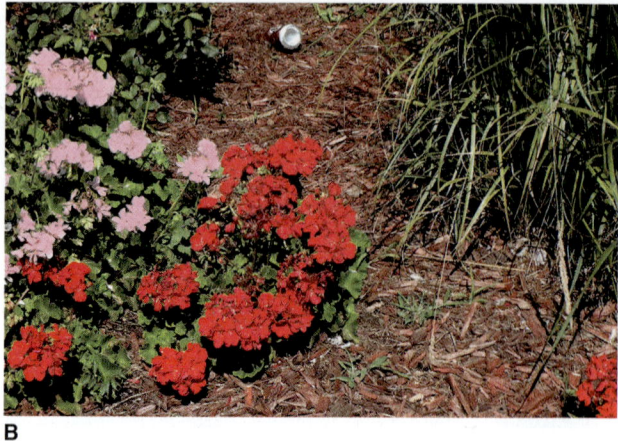

Jack Klasey/Goodheart-Willcox Publisher

Figure 9-5. Point as a compositional element. A—In this photo, the small bright spot (the baseball) is the center of interest, drawing the viewer's eye to the desired area of the photograph. B—The small bright area in this photo, a discarded soda can, draws the eye away from the intended center of interest.

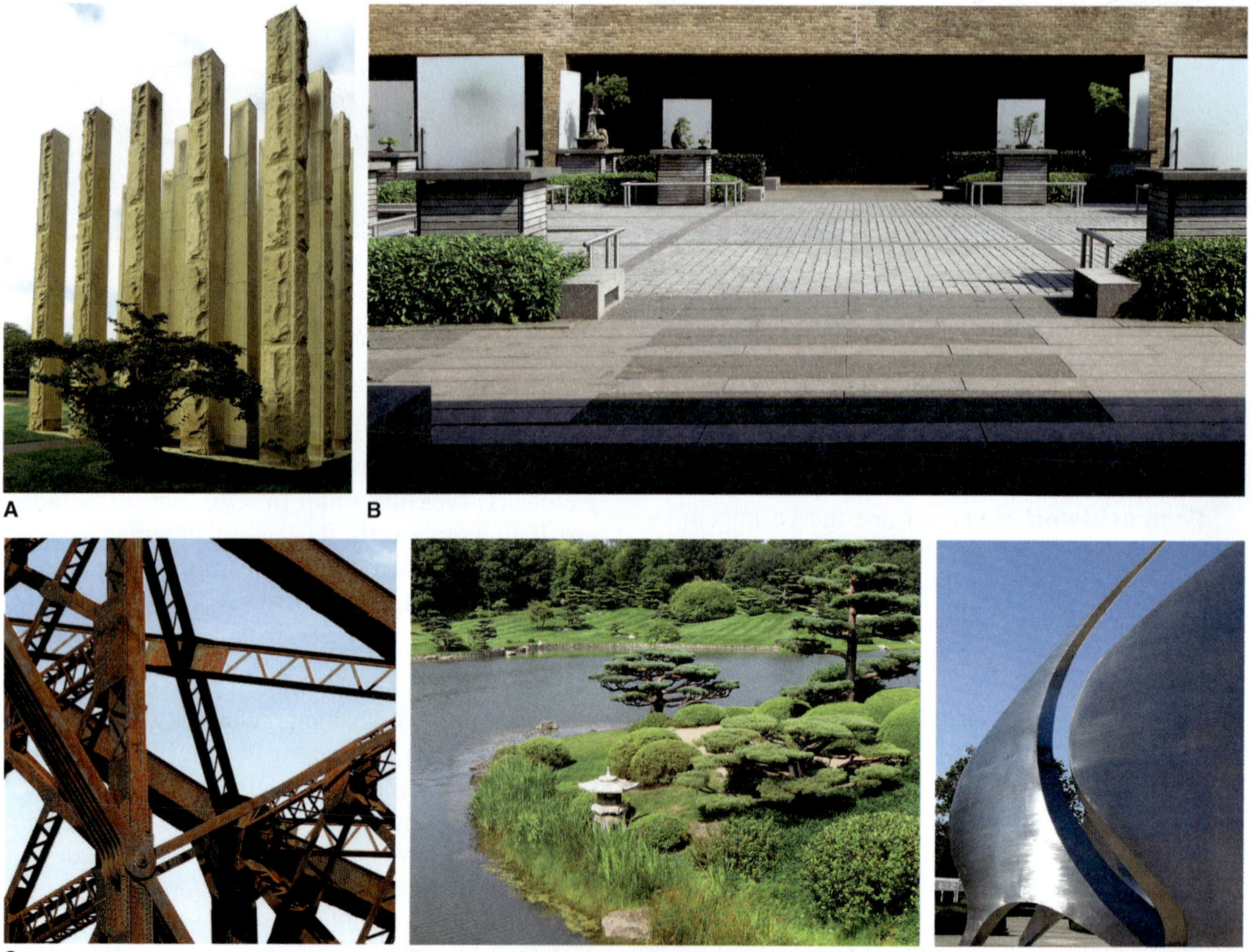

Jack Klasey/Goodheart-Willcox Publisher

Figure 9-6. Lines as compositional elements. A—Vertical lines, like those of this war memorial sculpture, are static. B—Horizontal lines are stable and restful. C—Diagonal lines, such as these bridge girders, give a sense of action and movement. D—Gentle curves, like the *S* shape of this shoreline, are placid and restful-feeling. E—Sharply curved or broken lines are energetic and have a strong feeling of movement.

202   Section 3   Photography Essentials   Copyright Goodheart-Willcox Co., Inc.

Shape or Pattern

A **shape** is a compositional element made by an individual object, and a **pattern** is a compositional element made by multiple objects. A shape may appear to be flat and two-dimensional, exhibiting only the properties of length and width. Light falling on an object creates shadows or tonal variations, adding a third dimension, the property of depth. See **Figure 9-7**. A pattern may consist of repetition of identical shapes or may have elements alternating or varying in shape, size, or color. Repeated shapes or lines establish a **rhythm** that moves the eye through the frame, **Figure 9-8**.

Balance

Overall arrangement of elements within the frame determines the compositional balance, **Figure 9-9**. **Formal balance**, also called *symmetrical balance*, is a compositional method that consists of matched halves—dividing the frame vertically or horizontally in the middle produces two mirror images. A common metaphor for formal balance is a seesaw with riders of equal weight at equal distances from the center balance point. **Informal balance**, also called *asymmetrical balance*, is a compositional method that provides a feeling of visual balance without the mirror image effect of formal balance. Using the seesaw example again, informal balance involves riders of different weights, with the larger of the two positioned closer to the balance point and the smaller rider farther from the balance point. In a photograph, informal balance may be achieved by the relative positions of two objects of different sizes or by using a smaller, brightly colored object to balance a larger dark object. Sometimes, a single large object may be balanced by several smaller objects.

Emphasis

Emphasis is a compositional element used to make some element of a picture stand out and capture the viewer's attention. By emphasizing a single element of the photo, you are making that element dominant and creating a center of interest. A **center of interest** is a single element of the photo to which all the other elements of the picture relate, and which sends a clear message to the viewer. Without a center of interest, or with more than one emphasized

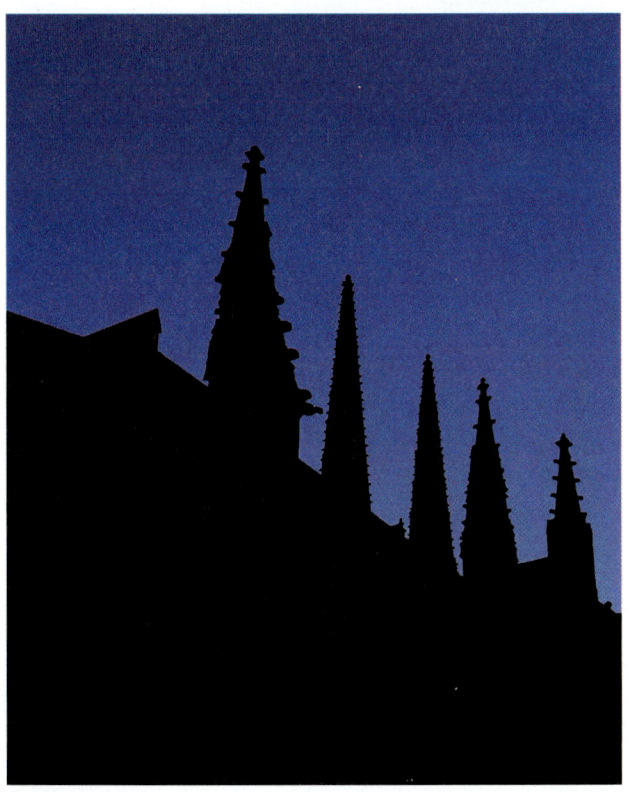
A

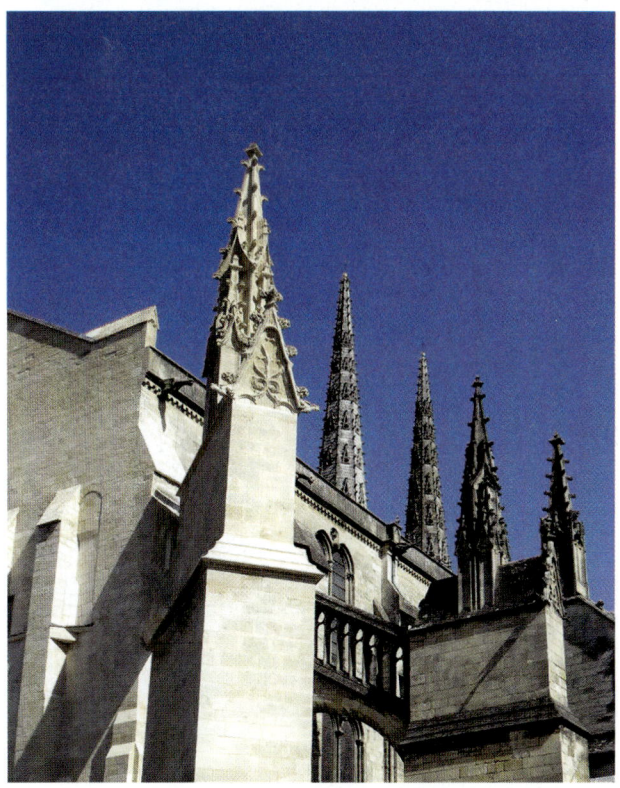
B

Jack Klasey/Goodheart-Willcox Publisher

Figure 9-7. Shape as a compositional element. A—The silhouetted church spires are two-dimensional shapes. B—Light falling on the spires creates a three-dimensional appearance through tonal variation (light and shadow).

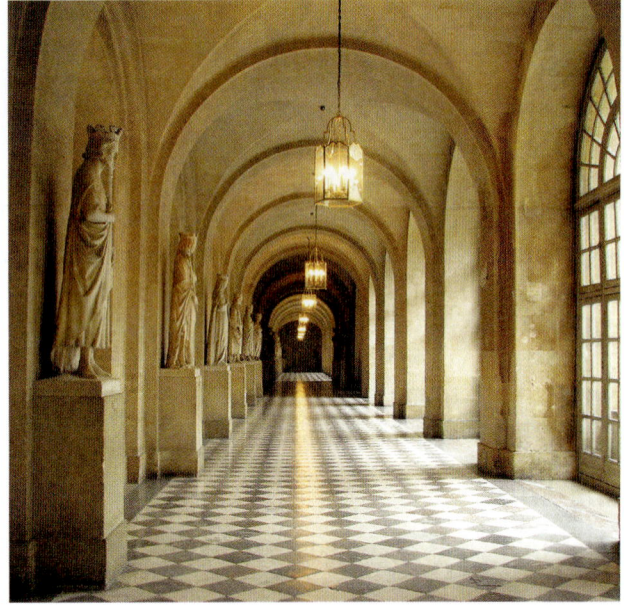

A

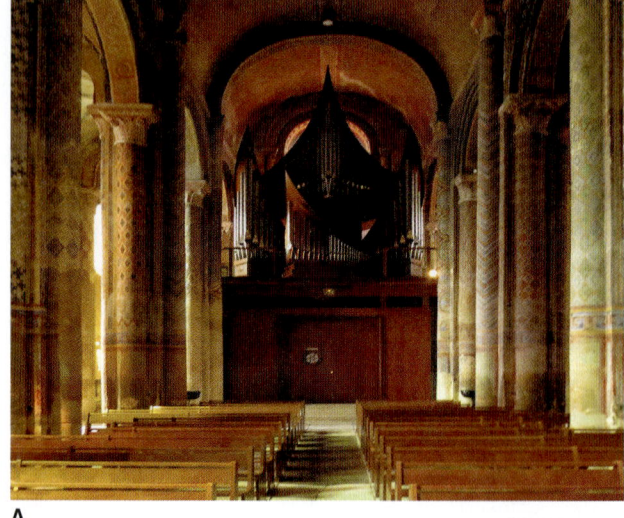

A

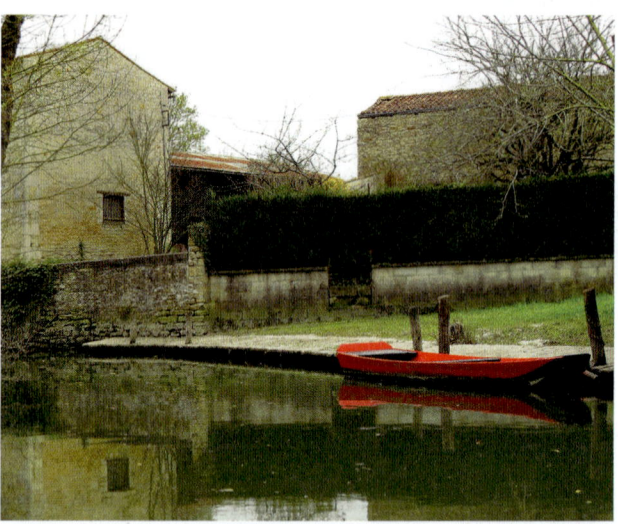

B

Jack Klasey/Goodheart-Willcox Publisher

Figure 9-9. Balance as a compositional element. A—Formal balance. B—Informal balance.

element, the photo does not send a clear message to the viewer. An old design maxim, "all emphasis is no emphasis," is illustrated in **Figure 9-10**. When every element of the photo is given equal weight, nothing stands out because the viewer receives no guidance.

Contrast

Although it is a compositional element in itself, contrast is often used to provide emphasis. **Contrast** is the relationship of shadow and highlight within a photo. It is also a noticeable difference between adjacent elements of a composition, **Figure 9-11**. These include light and shadow, large and small size, dark and light (or saturated and muted) colors, smooth and rough textures, curved and straight-edged shapes, and sharp and unsharp (soft) focus.

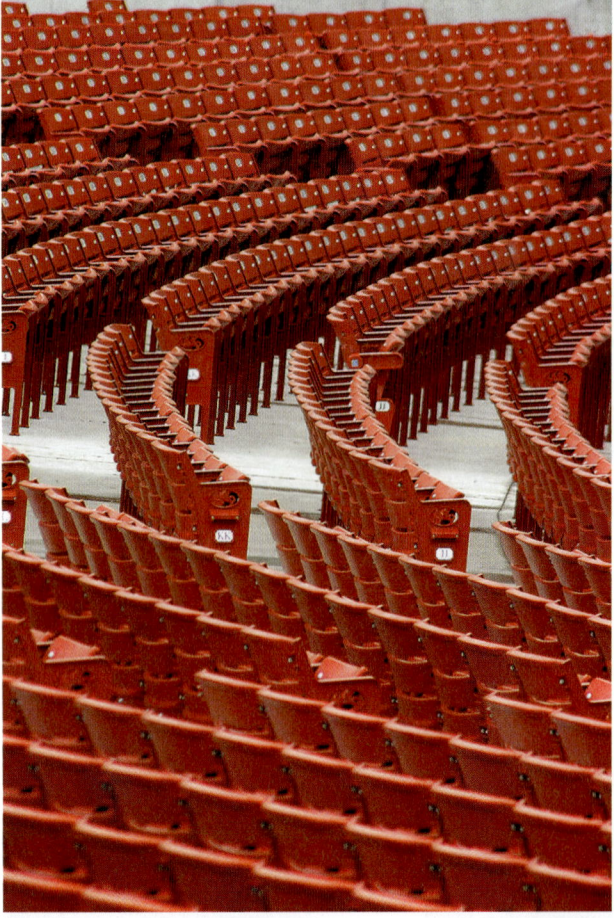

B

Jack Klasey/Goodheart-Willcox Publisher

Figure 9-8. Rhythm as a compositional device is established when a repeated shape or line leads the eye through the frame. A—Repeated arches and statues. B—Curving rows of theater seating.

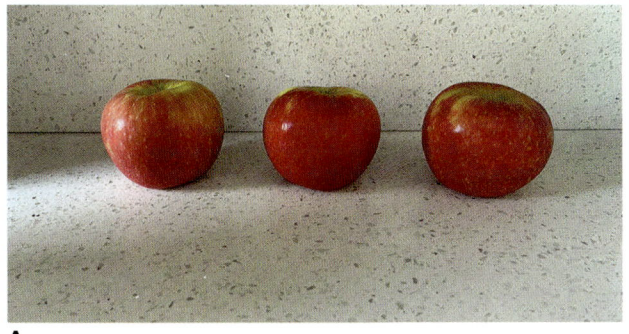
A

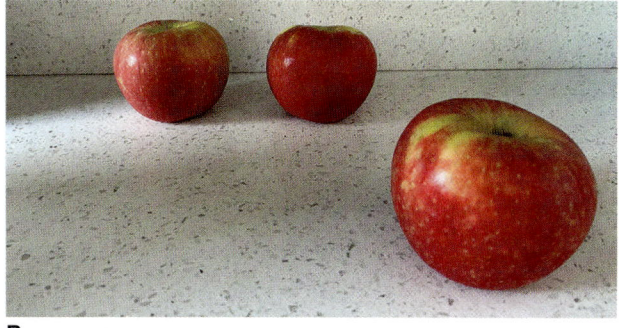
B

Goodheart-Willcox Publisher

Figure 9-10. Emphasis. A—With all objects equally emphasized, the viewer does not know where to look. B—Emphasizing one element provides a center of interest to guide the viewer.

Other Elements of Composition

In addition to the six traditional elements of composition, there are other elements that are just as important that help you properly frame and compose a photograph. The other compositional elements include perspective and harmony.

Perspective

One of the most important compositional elements a photographer must consider for their photos is perspective. **Perspective** is the relationship between objects in a photograph that can help provide a sense of depth or scale. Perspective is most often changed by altering the position of the camera itself. The three most common perspectives are bird's-eye angle, neutral angle, and worm's-eye angle:

- **Bird's-eye angle.** This angle looks down at a subject, often at a 40° angle. This perspective makes the subject seem much smaller and shorter than they are in real life, **Figure 9-12**.

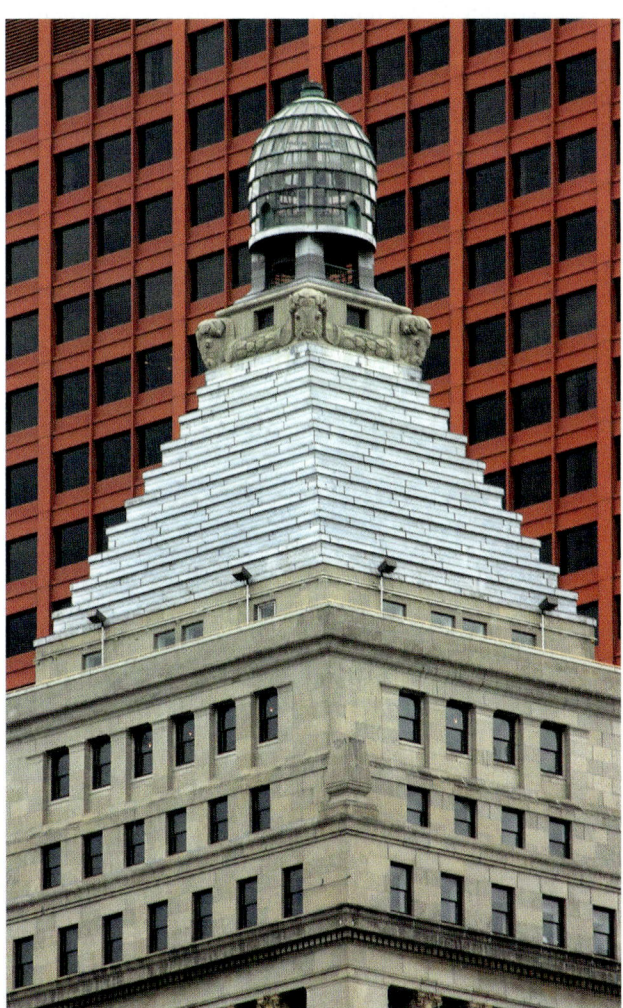

Jack Klasey/Goodheart-Willcox Publisher

Figure 9-11. This image illustrates two types of contrast—shape and color. It is also an example of formal balance.

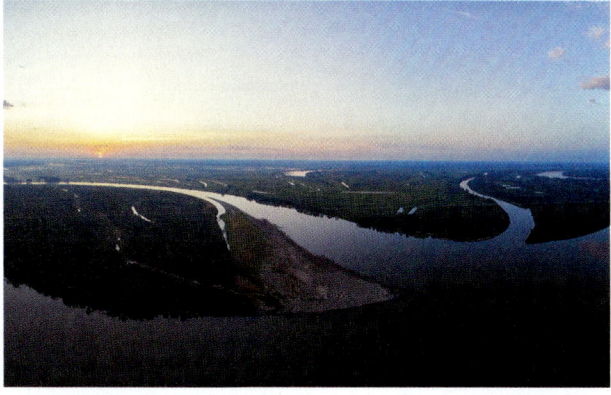

Olinchuk/Shutterstock.com

Figure 9-12. A bird's-eye angle looks down at the subject. It is commonly used in landscape photography.

Chapter 9 Making a Picture **205**

- **Neutral angle.** This angle is representative of how people view their surroundings and is often referred to as *eye-level angle*. Since this angle is close to how people see the world normally, it gives the viewer a familiar perspective. See **Figure 9-13**.
- **Worm's-eye angle.** This angle is positioned anywhere below the eyeline of a subject, filming up toward it. This perspective can help give your subject a sense of height and power, **Figure 9-14**.

Harmony

At its core, *harmony* is about creating an image that is visually interesting by combining different elements in the frame. These elements can include things like texture, shape, and color. An image is in harmony when all the elements of the photo work together to create a pleasing final composition.

In many instances, opposite elements make an image more interesting to look at and help create harmony. For example, opposite colors make one another appear stronger, such as black and white. A cool blue will also offset, but still complement, a bright red. Opposite textures can also have the same effect. A good example is when a wave is breaking on the shore and the textures of the water and the sand are contrasting, **Figure 9-15**.

Selective Framing in Composition

Selective framing is an important concept in composition. With **selective framing**, you decide what to include in the frame and what to exclude from the frame. What to include is called *inclusion*, and what to exclude is called *exclusion*. Sometimes referred to as *cropping in the camera*, selective framing produces the picture you visualized, without any extraneous elements. Depending on the situation, this may be accomplished through choice of lens (focal length), by changing angle of view, or by moving toward or away from the subject. Frequently, all three techniques may be necessary to frame the photo as you desire.

Moving in closer usually helps you create a better picture. Think of the lackluster family vacation photos you have seen, like the one in which your sibling—that tiny speck in the center of the frame—is shown at the rim of the Grand Canyon. Now think of the improved photo that would have resulted if your parent had moved in close enough so you could see your sibling's features and make out some of the details of the canyon behind them.

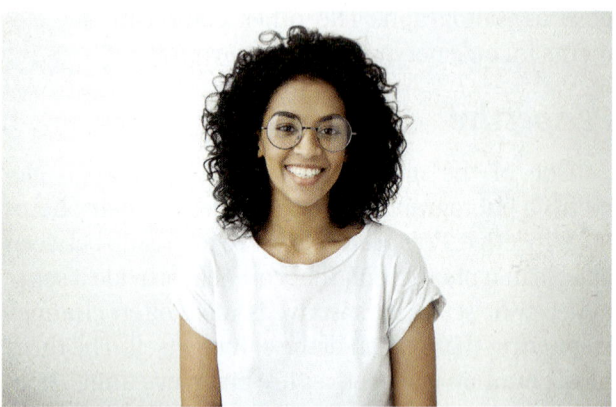

Cast Of Thousands/Shutterstock.com

Figure 9-13. A neutral angle is level with the subject. It is most common for portrait photography.

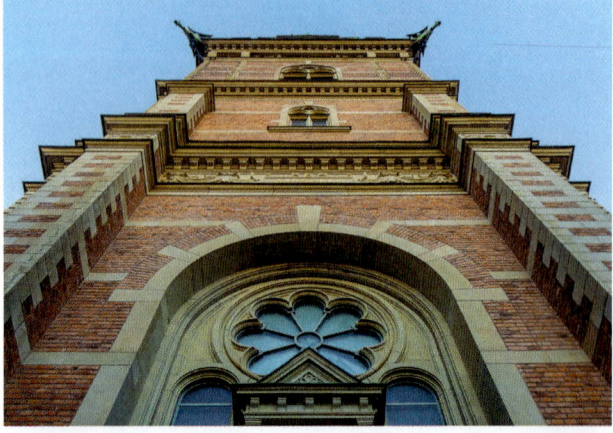

Vadim Fedotov/Shutterstock.com

Figure 9-14. A worm's-eye angle shows the height or power of the subject. It is great for architecture photography.

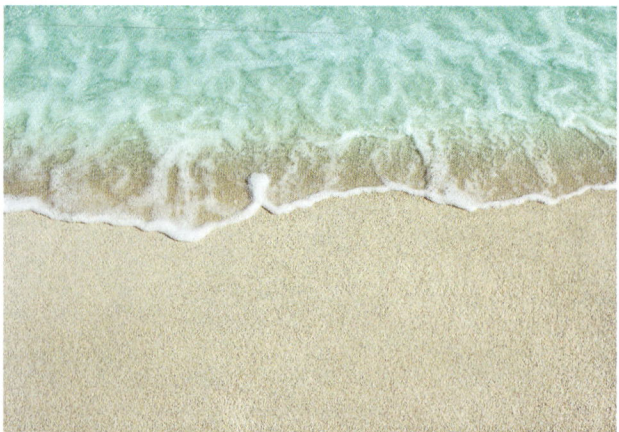

Lidiya Oleandra/Shutterstock.com

Figure 9-15. The contrasting textures of water and sand work together to achieve harmony.

As you compose your picture, check all the edges of the frame for distracting or unwanted elements, **Figure 9-16**. It is easy to focus your attention on placement of the main subject or the major elements of the composition and overlook something that is at the edge of the frame. Before pressing the shutter release, make it a habit to check the frame edges. If you find a problem, remove the distracting item if possible, or recompose to avoid it.

Also, check for the issue of **convergence**, a compositional problem in which parts of the image come together in an undesirable way. Convergence can also be referred to as *subject mergers*. A classic example of convergence is the flagpole or tree that appears to be growing out of your subject's head, **Figure 9-17A**. You can remedy this by either moving your subject or by shifting your position and taking the photo from another angle, **Figure 9-17B**. Other objects can create sometimes humorous results, but it's usually best to avoid convergence.

Seeing Pictures within the Picture

Images often contain a few, or even many, other potential images. Learning to see these pictures within a picture helps you make better-composed and more interesting photographs, **Figure 9-18**.

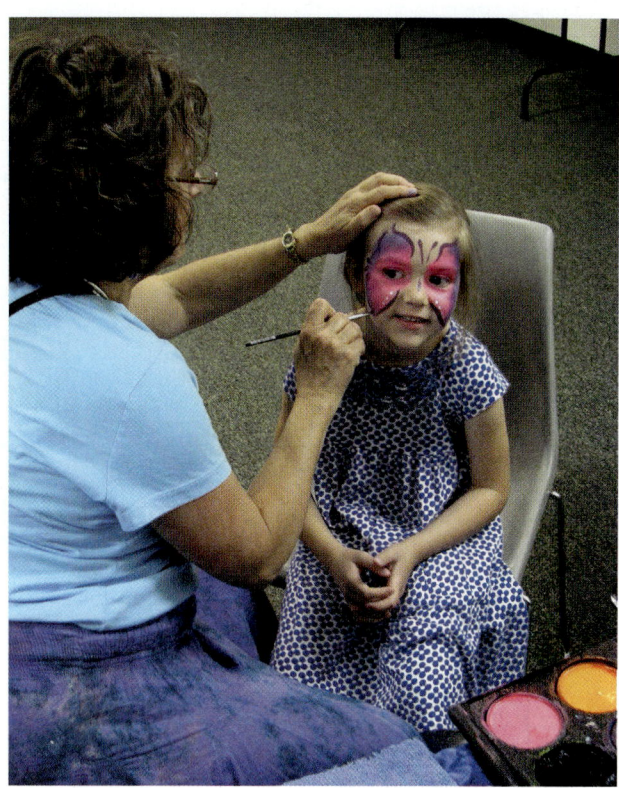

Jack Klasey/Goodheart-Willcox Publisher

Figure 9-16. The table legs in the upper-right corner draw attention away from the main subject. Eliminate them by recomposing the shot before pressing the shutter.

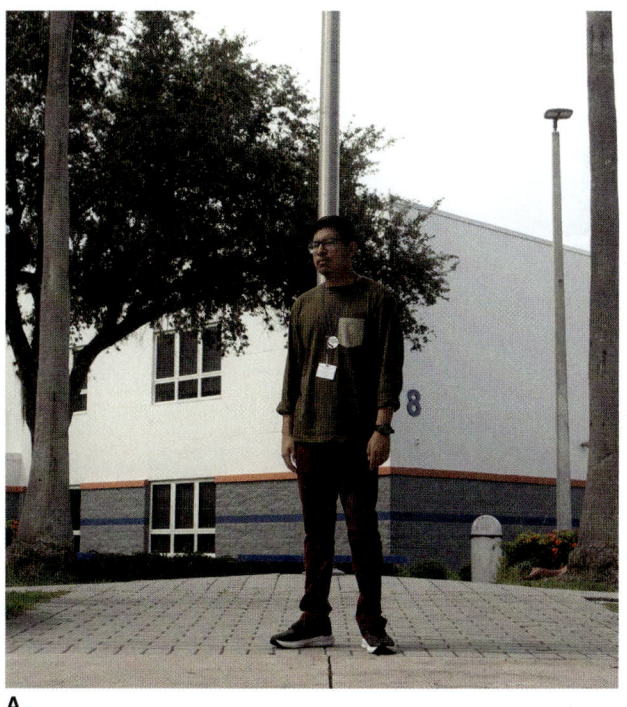

A

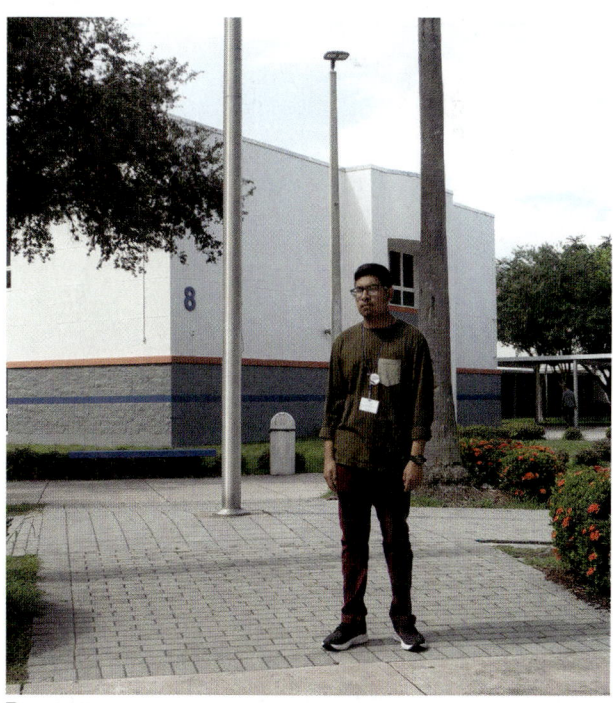

B

Goodheart-Willcox Publisher

Figure 9-17. Convergence. A—Convergence can ruin an otherwise good photo. B—Shifting position and changing the angle or moving your subject can correct convergence.

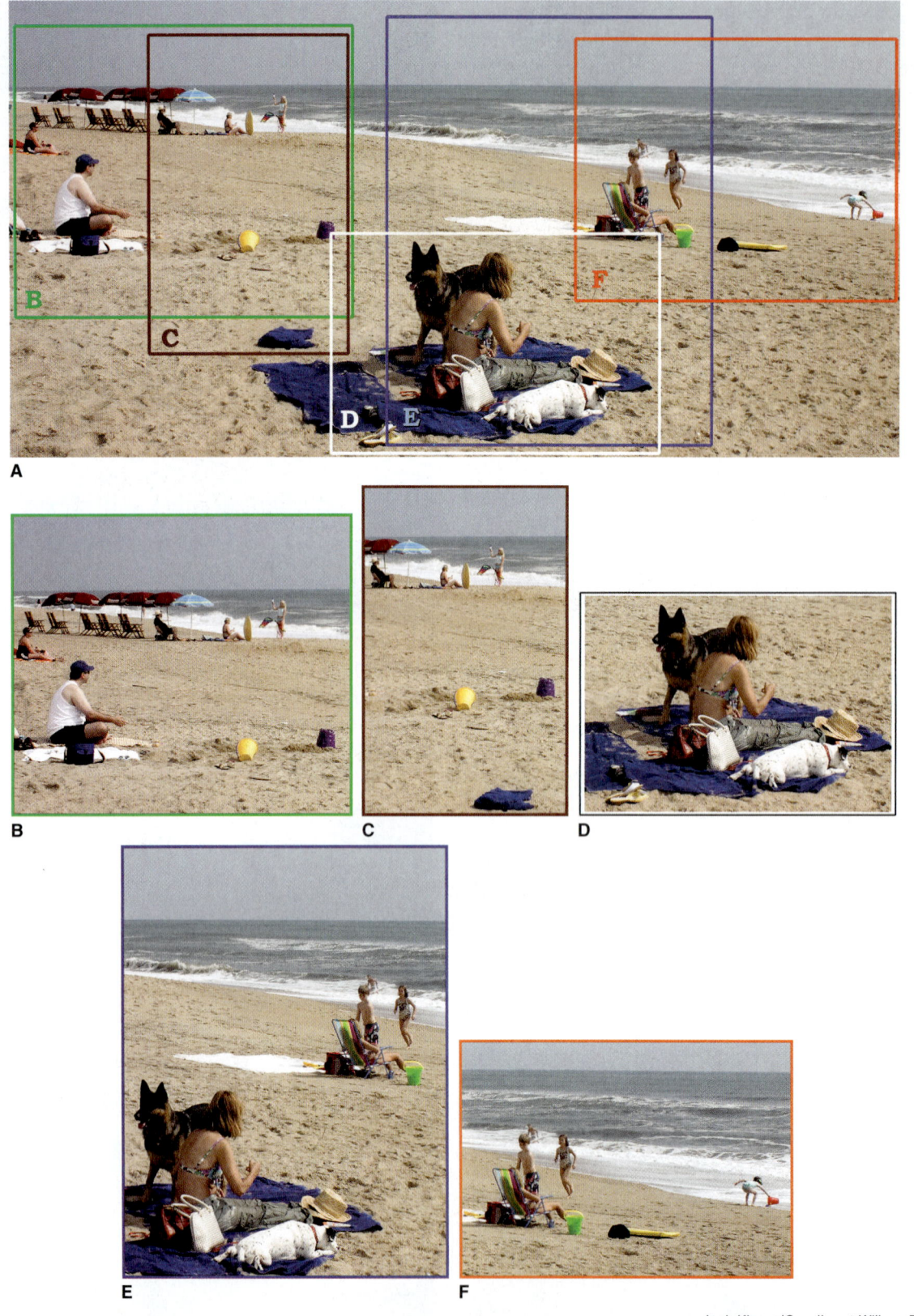

Jack Klasey/Goodheart-Willcox Publisher

Figure 9-18. Finding pictures within a picture. A—This beach scene contains many possible compositions that could be extracted. Five have been identified. B—Horizontal framing with near and distant subjects relaxing on the beach. C—A vertical scene with a family in the background and colorful foreground objects. D—A sunbather and their dogs isolated as a horizontal composition. E—The sunbather as foreground with children playing in the background. F—A horizontal view featuring the children.

With practice, you will look at a given scene and immediately begin to identify portions of that scene that could stand alone as individual shots.

Extracting (identifying and pulling out individual images from a larger scene) is most easily done with the aid of a zoom lens. While remaining in one spot, you can frame a possible image and then make necessary adjustments for good composition. If you are using a camera with a fixed focal length lens, you can still extract images from a larger scene by using the "two-legged zoom"—walking toward the subject until it is satisfactorily framed.

Choosing Vertical or Horizontal Framing

Unless you display your photos in the square format you can choose on Instagram or in your smartphone's native camera app, your images will be either landscape mode or portrait mode. *Landscape mode* is an image format that is wider than it is tall (a horizontal rectangle). *Portrait mode* is an image format that is taller than it is wide (a vertical rectangle). The frame ratio for many digital cameras is 2:3 (in landscape mode, two units high by three units wide). Some digital cameras also offer an image in a 3:4 ratio. The difference in ratios affects print proportions. A 2:3 ratio produces a standard 4″ × 6″ print using the full frame, while a 3:4 ratio yields a 4 1/2″ × 6″ image. The difference also affects display. A photo will be displayed as vertical or horizontal, depending on how the image was taken originally.

Certain subjects are suited to either landscape mode or portrait mode, **Figure 9-19**. Common subjects for landscape mode are street scenes, houses or industrial buildings, and group pictures. Portrait mode works well with subjects such as individual people, tall buildings, isolated flowers or trees, and statues.

When framing your subject, explore the possibilities by viewing both horizontal and vertical formats, possibly changing focal lengths as well to achieve a particular composition. See **Figure 9-20**. Professionals shooting for magazines strive to capture at least one striking vertical composition, since that format is required for selection as a cover image.

Using the Rule of Thirds

Since we live in a society that surrounds us with well-composed images, good composition should be almost instinctive. Unconsciously, we are disturbed

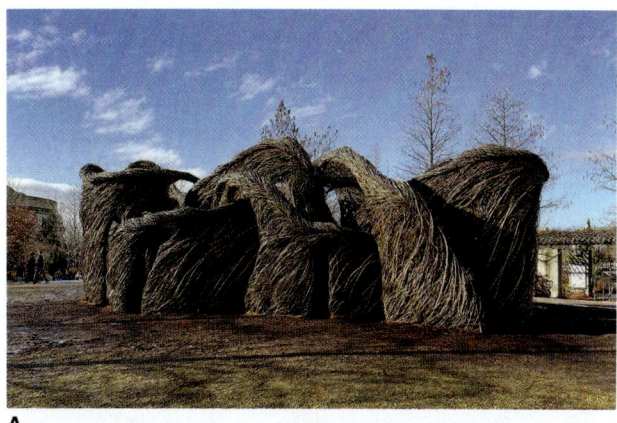

A

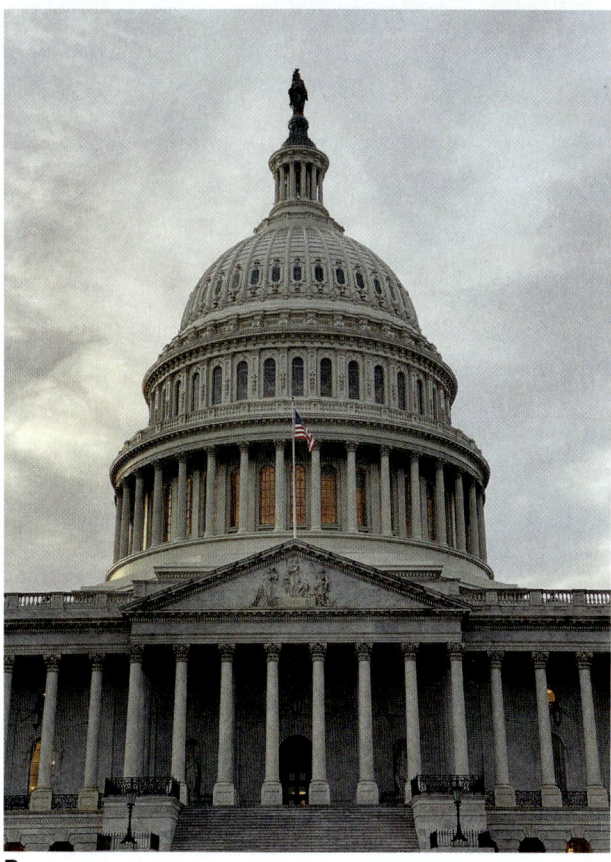

B

Goodheart-Willcox Publisher

Figure 9-19. Horizontal and vertical framing. A—The horizontal format was a natural choice for this intricate woven sculpture. B—The vertical format is ideal for portraying a tall and powerful building such as the US Capitol Building.

by a poorly composed image and pleased by a well-composed one.

The basis of any photographic composition is the frame. As you learned in Chapter 1, the *frame* is the working space within which a picture is composed. All the compositional elements are employed in

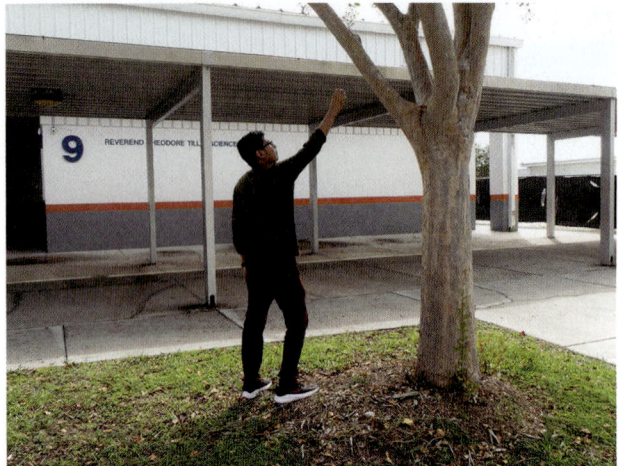

Figure 9-20. Different formats. A—Horizontal composition. B—The same subject composed as a vertical.

A well-known compositional device is the rule of thirds. The **rule of thirds** divides the frame into thirds, both horizontally and vertically, **Figure 9-21**. The four intersections created by the crossing lines are considered the most effective spots to position the center of interest, **Figure 9-22**. By mentally imposing these lines in your camera viewfinder, you can see the effects of different placement. Digital cameras and even smartphone cameras have the option of enabling this grid in the settings, so it is constantly overlaid on your images. This tic-tac-toe grid does not appear in the final composition.

The compositional tool known as **negative space** is the area within the frame surrounding the subject. When used properly, negative space isolates and emphasizes the subject. The simplest example of negative space is a silhouetted subject, like the one

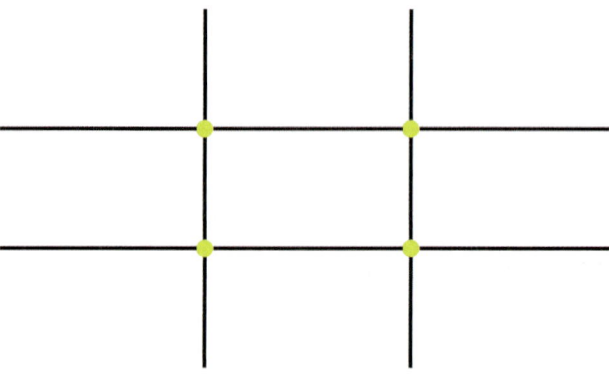

Mikhail Gnatuyk/Shutterstock.com

Figure 9-21. The rule of thirds grid will help you frame visually interesting shots. Note how the intersections are highlighted.

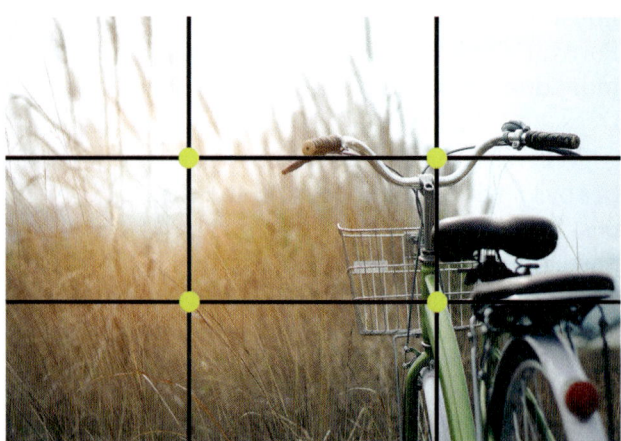

Darkroom Graphic/Shutterstock.com

Figure 9-22. Placing your center of interest at or near one of the four points where grid lines cross will make a more interesting composition than centering the subject.

relation to the frame. For example, a center of interest can be placed anywhere within the frame, but some locations are more effective than others. As a general practice, placing the center of interest in the physical center of the frame is considered rather static and boring, while placement elsewhere in the frame is usually more interesting visually.

shown in **Figure 9-7A**, but negative space may be any subdued background, such as a brick sidewalk, that helps the subject stand out.

The rule of thirds is a useful guide when your photo includes the horizon or another dominant horizontal or vertical line (such as a desert roadway or a lighthouse). Placing the horizon on or close to the top or bottom guidelines of the grid will make for a much more interesting photo than positioning it across the middle of the frame. See **Figure 9-23**.

Focusing Viewer Attention

Many different means can be used to direct the viewer's attention within a photograph. Various forms of emphasis have already been covered. You can also focus the attention of the viewer by using leading lines, different camera angles, or the elements of color, shape, and size.

Using Leading Lines

A commonly used method of directing attention is the use of **leading lines**. These pictorial elements draw the viewer's eye from one area of the photo to another, **Figure 9-24**. In an outdoor scene, a leading line might be a fence, a road, a railroad track, or even a fallen tree. In a portrait, the line of the subject's arm, a shadowed fold in clothing, or an object in the environment surrounding the subject can serve to lead the eye as intended by the photographer, **Figure 9-25**.

Try to avoid compositions that direct the viewer's attention out of the frame. This is most often a problem when photographing people or moving objects. If possible, provide some additional room on the side of the frame toward which the subject is looking or moving, **Figure 9-26**. This technique is called **lead room** or *lead space*, and it keeps the viewer's attention within the frame.

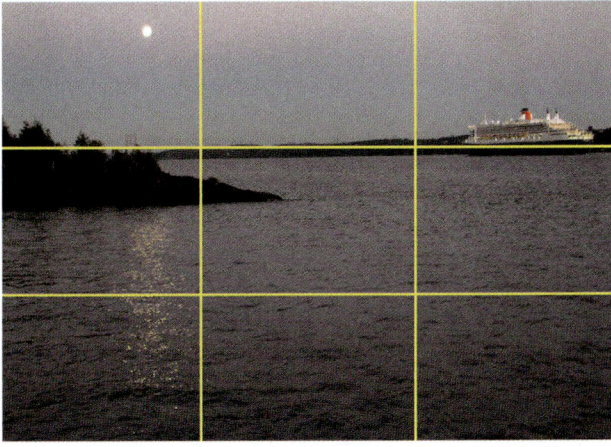
High horizon

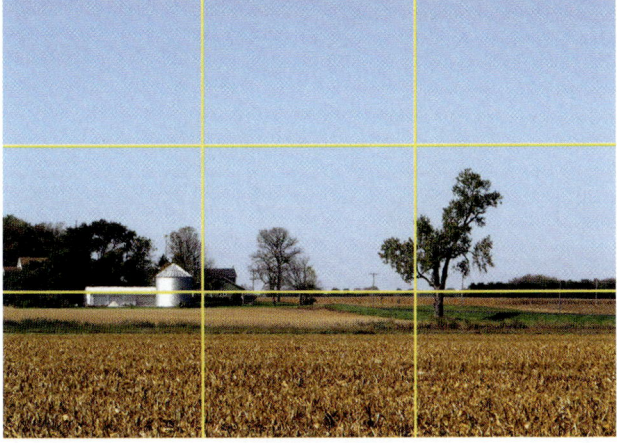
Low horizon

Jack Klasey/Goodheart-Willcox Publisher

Figure 9-23. Placing the horizon on or near one of the grid lines will result in a more effective photo.

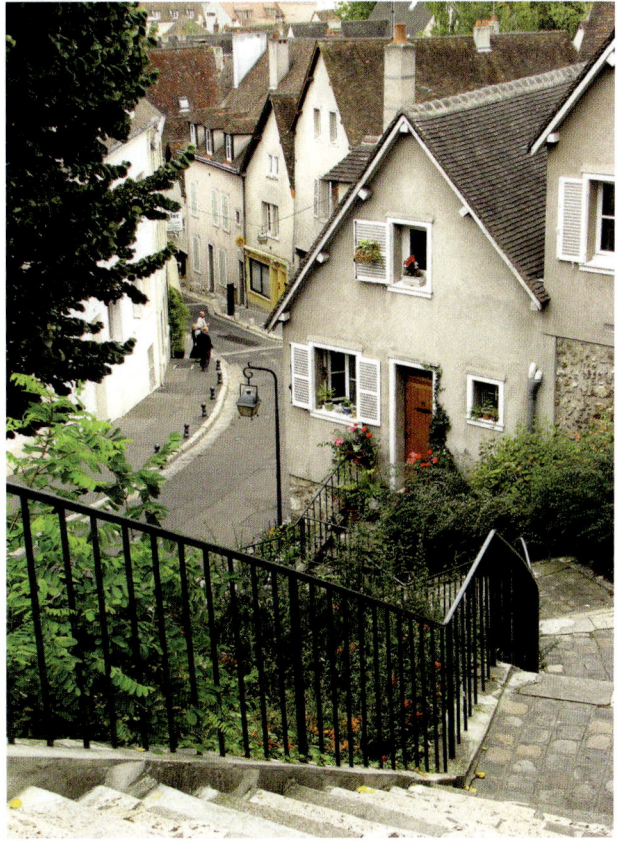

Jack Klasey/Goodheart-Willcox Publisher

Figure 9-24. Leading lines direct the viewer's attention. The railing of the stairway leads the eye to the house and then to the curving street in the quaint village of Chartres, France.

You can also have a "frame within the frame" by using a foreground object or shape to partly or fully surround your main subject. This technique directs attention into the frame, focusing it on the main subject and giving the picture a sense of depth. Although the use of an overhanging tree branch or a building archway as a frame has become a visual cliché, the concept of the frame is still valid and useful. See **Figure 9-27**.

Courtesy of the Library of Congress

Figure 9-25. The woman's arm leads the eye to her face in this classic portrait titled *Migrant Mother*, taken by Dorothea Lange in 1936. It was one of a series of photos depicting the plight of migrant farm families during the Great Depression.

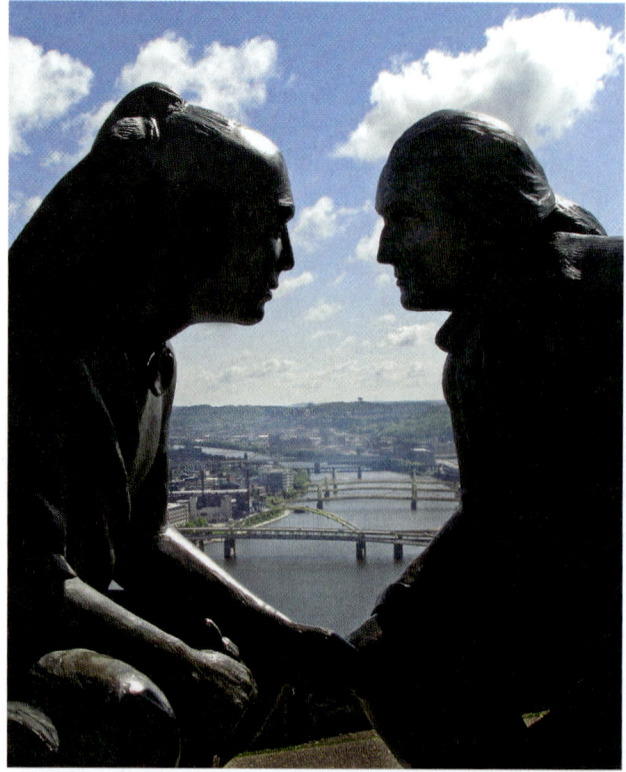

Jack Klasey/Goodheart-Willcox Publisher

Figure 9-27. A statue depicting George Washington meeting the Seneca Chief Guyasuta frames a view of the Allegheny River bridges in downtown Pittsburgh.

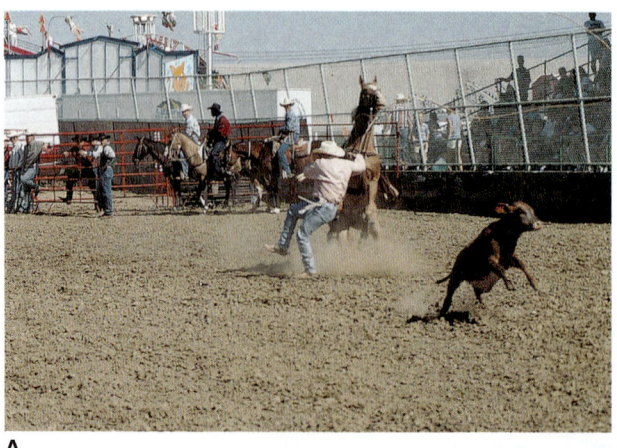
A

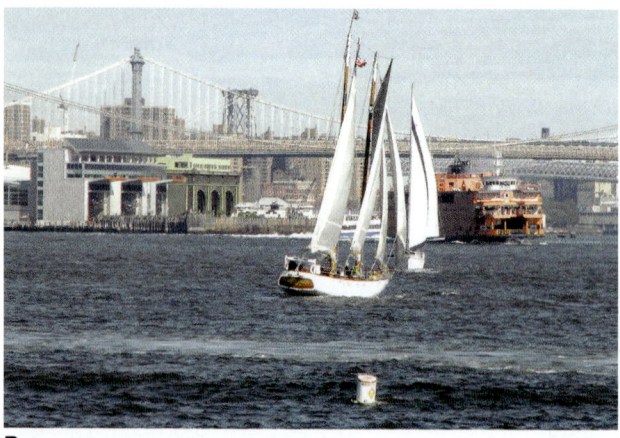
B

Goodheart-Willcox Publisher

Figure 9-26. Controlling viewer attention. A—A moving object can lead the eye out of the picture. B—Provide some space between the object(s) and the frame edge to hold attention within the frame.

Using Camera Angles

Changing your ***camera angle***, or any of the different points of view that can be used to vary a picture's composition and visual impact, can have a dramatic effect on a picture. See **Figure 9-28**. For example, an innovative way of photographing a field of flowers is to lie on your back and shoot upward through blossoms that are backlit by the sky.

Alternatively, you could stand on a chair or ladder for a high-angle approach, or even shoot from a second-story window or the roof of a building (be sure to take the proper safety measures when using a ladder or shooting from a great height). Photographing from a high angle is a good way to show patterns or to avoid a visual obstacle, such as a foreground fence. When photographing a landscape, a high angle permits you to tilt down and eliminate an uninteresting expanse of cloudless sky.

When working with children or animals, the opposite is true. Getting down to their eye level often results in a better picture than the bird's-eye view of shooting downward from an adult viewpoint. See **Figure 9-29**.

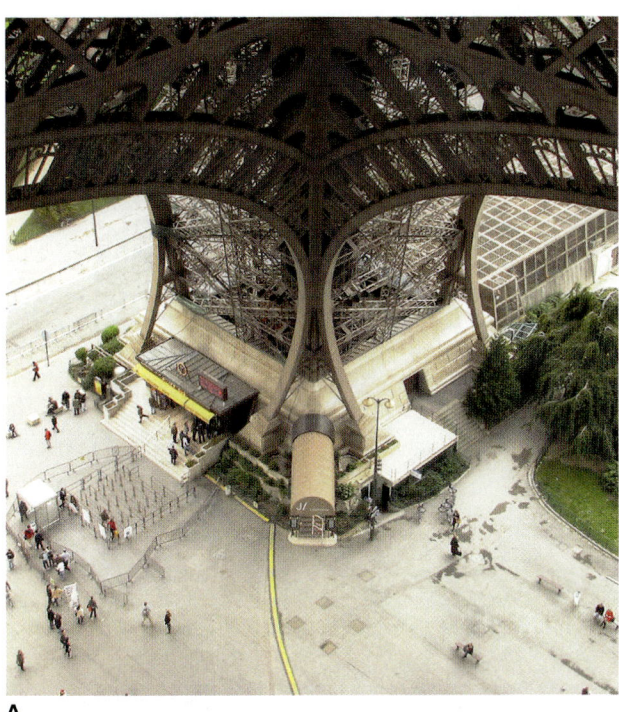

A

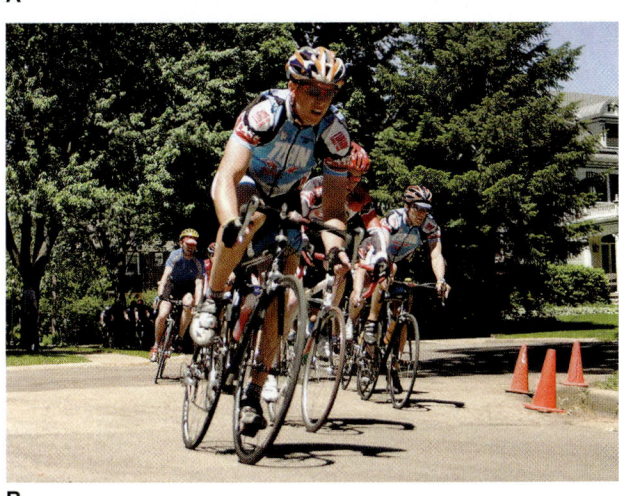

B

Jack Klasey/Goodheart-Willcox Publisher

Figure 9-28. Using camera angle to focus the viewer's attention. A—A high-angle shot taken from the first platform of the Eiffel Tower. B—This low-angle view emphasizes the movement of these bicycle racers.

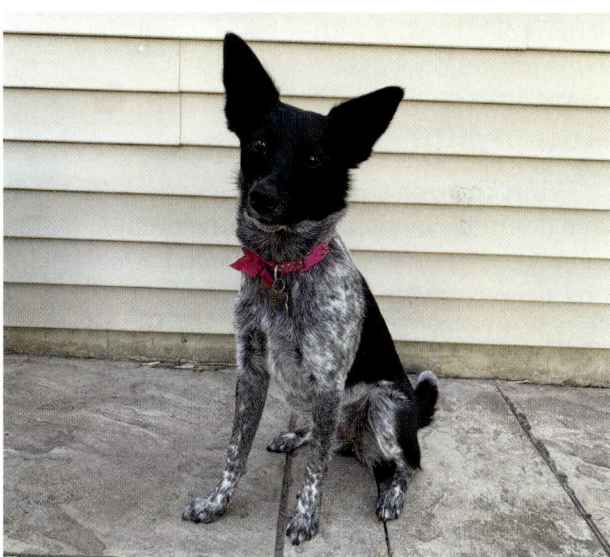

A

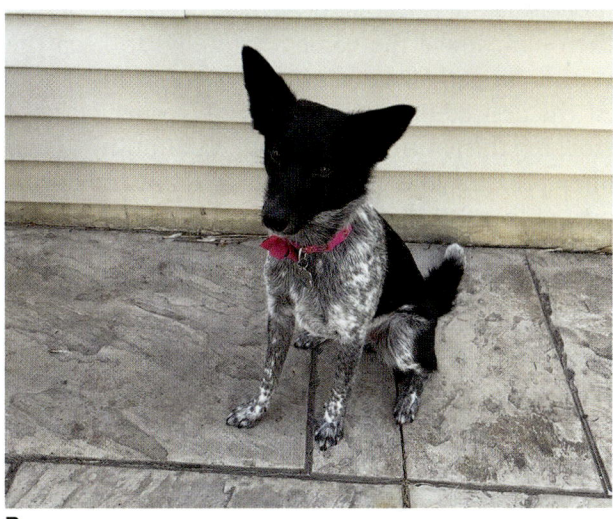

B

Goodheart-Willcox Publisher

Figure 9-29. Suit the camera angle to the subject. A—Photograph animals or children from their own eye level. B—Adult viewpoint diminishes shorter subjects.

Using Color, Shape, or Size

The viewer's eye is drawn to the brightest element in a picture. That brightest element is often white or a light color, but it also can be the most strongly saturated color visible. Shape and relative size are other tools you can use to focus viewer attention. See **Figure 9-30**.

Creating Visual Effects While Shooting

A number of techniques can be used to achieve visual effects that make your pictures more interesting or help to convey your intended meaning. Most of these effects work with both color and black-and-white images.

Motion Blur

While blurring as a result of camera shake is seldom desirable, motion blur due to movement of the subject can be used creatively. Manipulating a zoom lens during exposure can produce motion effects.

A technique called *panning* (moving the camera along with an object crossing the field of view) conveys speed and movement by streaking the background behind a sharply focused moving subject, such as when you are shooting moving vehicles. Practice and experimentation are needed to obtain acceptable results, but the concept is simple. See **Figure 9-31**. With the camera prefocused for the proper distance, frame the vehicle as it approaches, then pan (move the camera laterally) to keep the vehicle properly framed as it crosses in front of you. At the desired point, make your exposure without stopping the panning movement. Continuing to pan after pressing the shutter release is an important part of this technique. The result is a vehicle that is sharply focused against a background that is blurred and streaked horizontally to show movement.

Zooming is moving the camera's zoom lens in or out during the exposure, usually done to impart a sense of motion to a photo of a stationary subject. Striking motion effects can be achieved by using a relatively slow shutter speed and zooming out or zooming in during the exposure. Mount the camera on a tripod to hold the desired framing on the subject during the zooming action. See **Figure 9-32**. Each exposure made with this technique results in a different effect because the zooming rate and

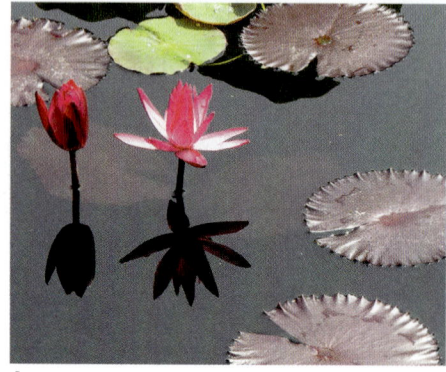

A

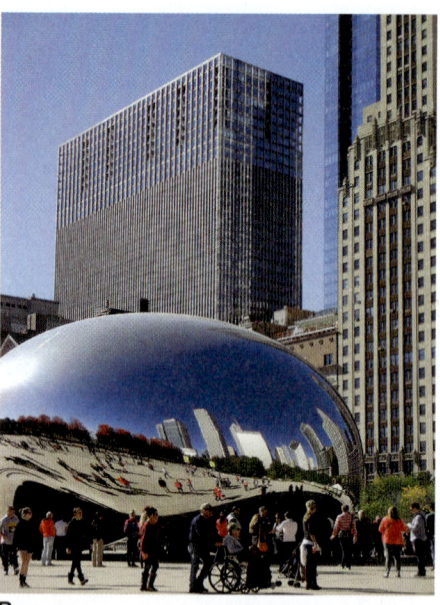

B

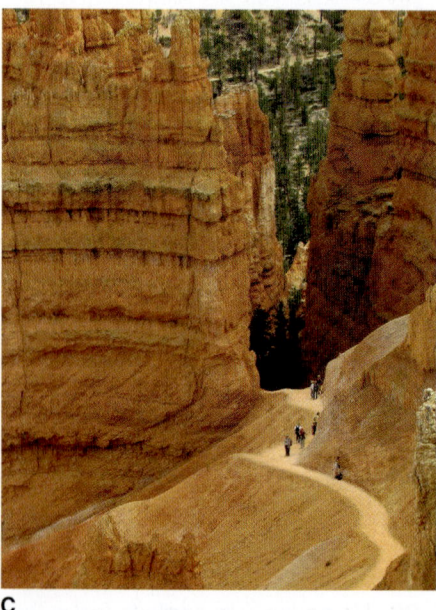

C

Jack Klasey/Goodheart-Willcox Publisher

Figure 9-30. Focusing viewer attention using different methods. A—Color. B—Shape. C—Relative size.

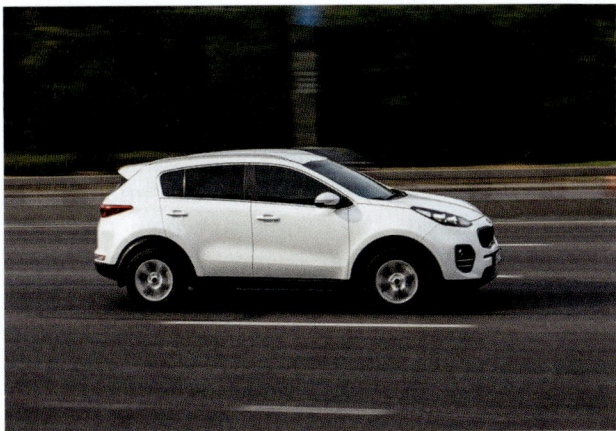

Iurii Vlasenko/Shutterstock.com

Figure 9-31. Panning the camera along with the motion of the subject conveys speed and movement.

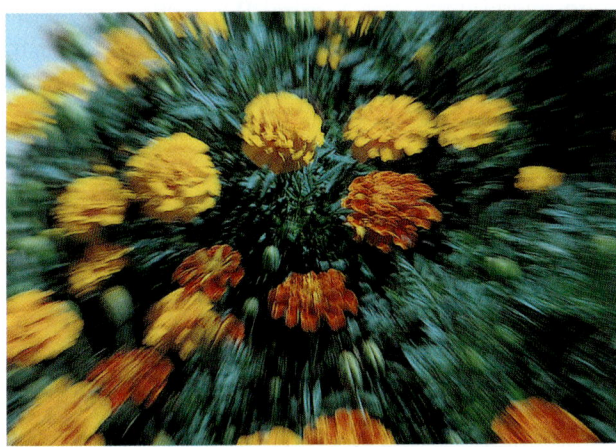

Jack Klasey/Goodheart-Willcox Publisher

Figure 9-32. Zooming creates an interesting, almost abstract effect and a strong feeling of motion.

smoothness of the motion are different each time. Zooming in produces a different effect from zooming out. Lenses with different ranges of focal lengths can be used to create different effects.

Soft Focus

Soft focus is used primarily in portrait photography because it is flattering and helps to mask any minor blemishes. The effect is subtle and is different in quality from the unsharpness caused by imprecise focusing, **Figure 9-33**. To achieve the soft-focus effect, stretch a single thickness of sheer black stocking fabric across the lens, or smear a thin coat of petroleum jelly on a clear (UV) filter. However, you should avoid potentially damaging a filter or lens and instead use an image processing program

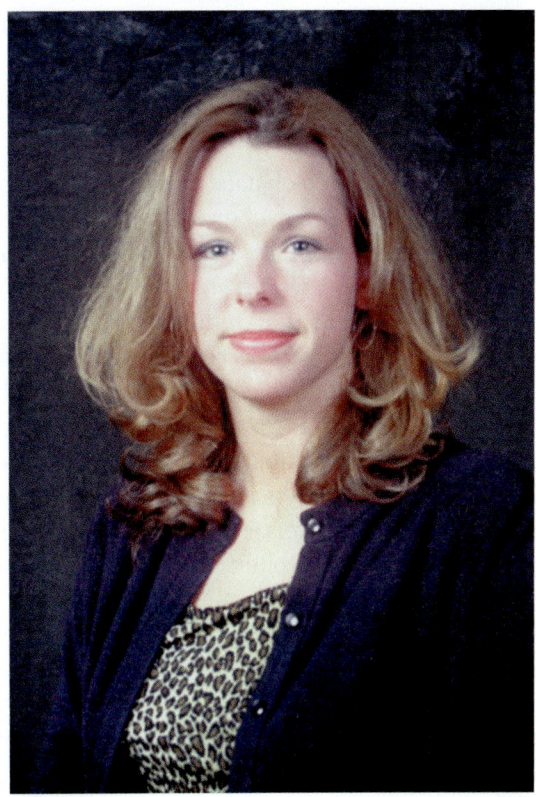

A

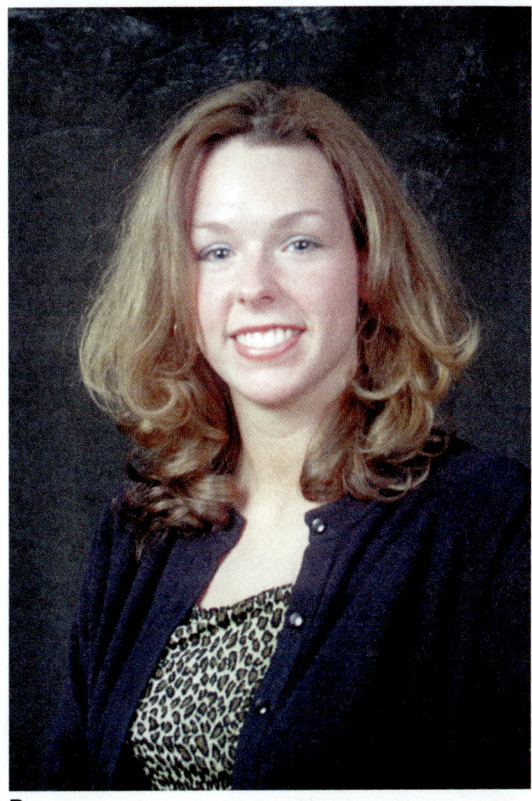

B

Goodheart-Willcox Publisher

Figure 9-33. Soft focus can be pleasing and flattering. A—Soft-focus portrait. B—The same subject in sharp focus.

to achieve the same effect. Special soft-focus filters are also available in several degrees of softness.

Selective Focus

Sharp definition of objects from the near foreground to the distant background is desirable in some photographs but less desirable in others. **Figure 9-34** shows two versions of a flower portrait. A depth of field that renders the busy background sharp enough to be recognizable distracts the eye from the main subject. A shallower depth of field that throws the background out of focus draws attention to the main subject. This *selective focus* technique is used extensively in photographing flowers and small animals, especially in natural settings. In the studio, it is often used for both product photos and portraits.

Depth of field (DOF) preview is a desirable camera feature that allows the photographer to see the scene at the desired aperture and assess the actual depth of field. It also allows the photographer to view the degree to which the background is out of focus or if one subject is emphasized and another is de-emphasized. The degree to which the background is out of focus can be judged and adjusted by shifting the plane of focus or changing to a higher or lower f-stop. Without depth of field preview, selective focus is more difficult to achieve. However, a depth of field chart or the depth of field scale found on some lenses can be used.

Multiple Exposure

Unintended multiple exposures were once a common occurrence. See **Figure 9-35**. Older cameras had separate mechanisms for advancing the film

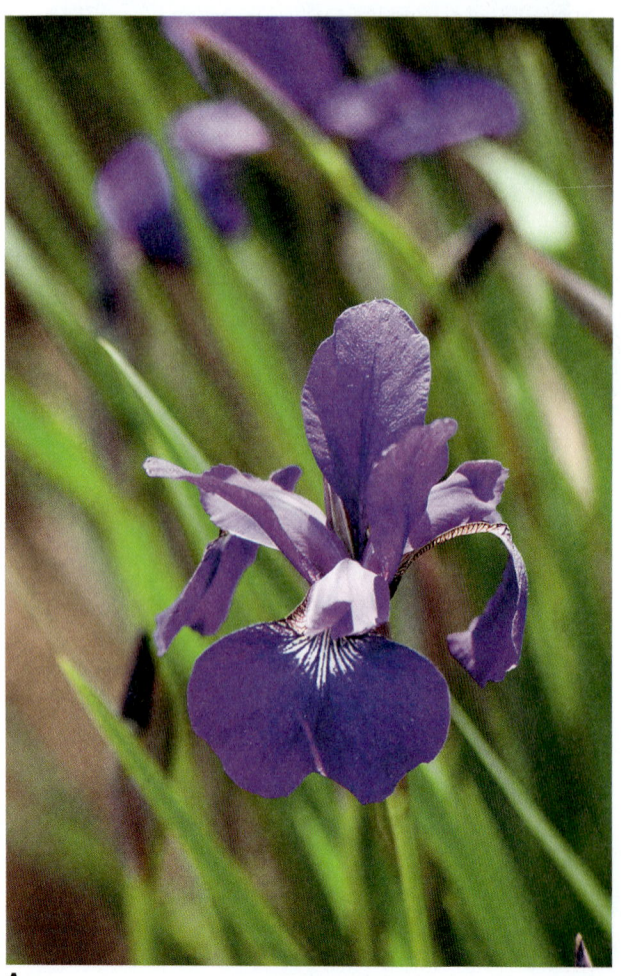
A

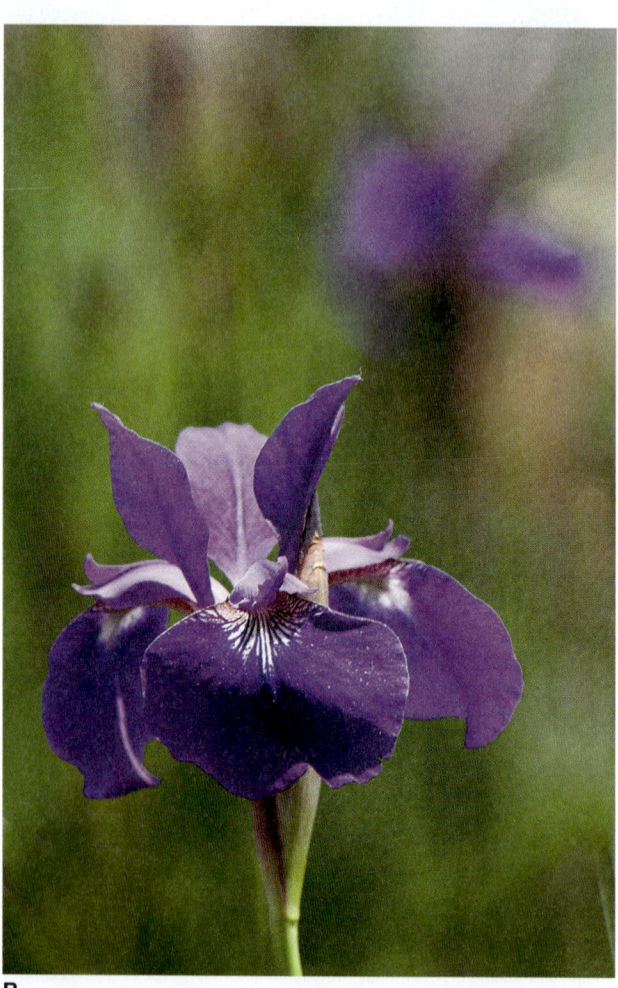
B

Jack Klasey/Goodheart-Willcox Publisher

Figure 9-34. Selective focus. A—The busy background draws attention away from the iris bloom. B—A wider aperture made the background much farther out of focus, isolating the flower.

and cocking the shutter for the next exposure. If the photographer forgot to advance to the next frame after making an exposure, it was easy to cock the shutter and make an unplanned second exposure on the same frame.

With most digital cameras today, a multiple exposure is impossible. Unlike film, which allows you to build up multiple images on the same frame, the sensor in most digital cameras is wiped clean after each exposure. Multiple exposures must be created using a computer and image editing software to combine individual files.

Technically, any image created in the computer by combining individual files is termed a *composite* rather than a multiple exposure, although the visual effect is the same. The multiple exposure photos shown in **Figure 9-36** and **Figure 9-37** were created from digital files. You should visualize the desired result, make a rough sketch if necessary, and then shoot the needed images. The techniques for creating composites are covered in Chapter 19, *Advanced Digital Postprocessing Techniques*.

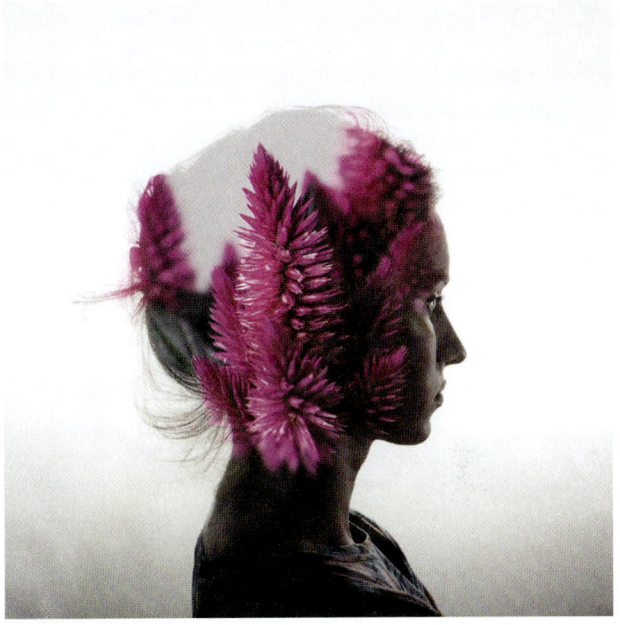

ImYanis/Shutterstock.com

Figure 9-36. This is a planned, creative double exposure. These files were taken separately and combined using postprocessing software for the photo you see here.

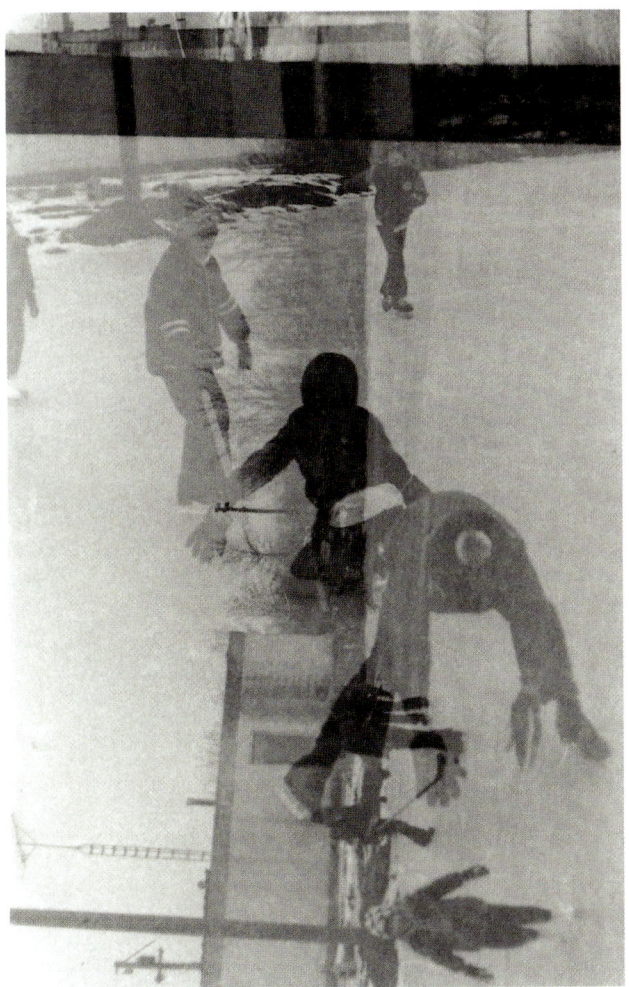

Jack Klasey/Goodheart-Willcox Publisher

Figure 9-35. This unplanned double exposure combines vertical and horizontal scenes of children skating on a neighborhood pond.

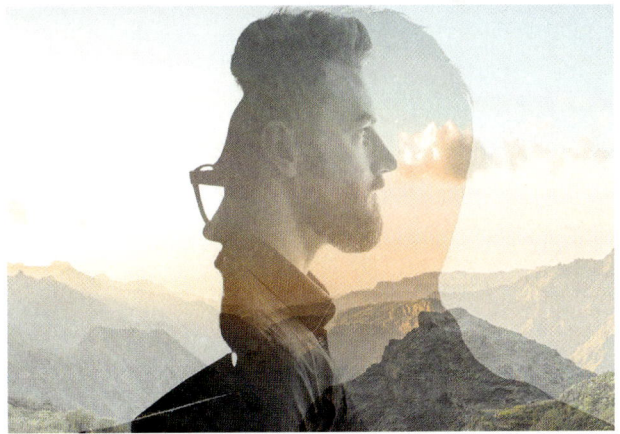

RossHelen/Shutterstock.com

Figure 9-37. Similar to **Figure 9-36**, this planned, creative triple exposure is a combination of three separate images.

PORTFOLIO ASSIGNMENT

Extracting Images

Without using a camera, practice the technique of "seeing pictures within the picture." Look at a scene and find parts of that scene you could extract as separate images. Refer to **Figure 9-18**. Once you are comfortable with the technique, try it with your camera.

1. Find an area that will give you the opportunity to find pictures within pictures, such as a classroom, a park, or a store.
2. Once you have chosen your location, frame and shoot several photos of the overall scene. Be sure to use your knowledge of compositional elements when framing your images.
3. Use your zoom lens to compose and record separate images that focus on more detail. Try to shoot at least four different subjects within your initial image. Take at least two photos for each of these subjects.

Select the best photo you shot of the overall scene, as well as the best one of each of your four different subjects. Include all five photos in your portfolio.

Chapter 9 Review

Summary

- Being aware of the relationship of masses and colors, the emotional content of the scene, the interplay of light and shadow, and the meaning that goes beyond the obvious and readily apparent are among the many elements of seeing photographically.
- The term "making a picture" implies conscious control of the process and the final result. To control how the finished image appears to the viewer, the photographer must visualize the final result.
- To capture a visualized image, a photographer must make a series of choices. The most basic decision is selecting the subject and determining how you want to portray it.
- Composition is the arrangement of visual elements, such as shapes, colors, and textures, within the frame. Four common compositional techniques are size, focus, contrast, and isolation.
- Compositional elements are the basic components used for effectively composing photographs. The traditional compositional elements consist of point, line, shape or pattern, balance, emphasis, and contrast.
- Other important elements of composition include perspective and harmony.
- Selective framing is an important concept in composition. With selective framing, you decide what to include in the frame and what to exclude from the frame.
- Images often contain a few, or even many, other potential images. Extracting (identifying and pulling out individual images from a larger scene) is most easily done with the aid of a zoom lens.
- Landscape mode is an image format that is wider than it is tall (a horizontal rectangle). Portrait mode is an image format that is taller than it is wide (a vertical rectangle). Certain subjects are suited to either landscape mode or portrait mode.
- The rule of thirds divides the frame into thirds, both horizontally and vertically. The four intersections created by the crossing lines are considered the most effective spots to position the center of interest.
- A commonly used method of directing attention is the use of leading lines. These pictorial elements draw the viewer's eye from one area of the photo to another.
- Changing your camera angle, or any of the different points of view that can be used to vary a picture's composition and visual impact, can have a dramatic effect on a picture.
- Color, shape, and relative size are other tools you can use to focus viewer attention.
- Motion blur due to movement of the subject can be used creatively. Two techniques to do this are panning and zooming.
- Soft focus is used primarily in portrait photography because it is flattering and helps to mask any minor blemishes.
- Sharp definition of objects from the near foreground to the distant background is desirable in some photographs but less desirable in others. Selective focus is used extensively in photographing flowers and small animals, especially in natural settings.
- With most digital cameras today, a double exposure is impossible. Multiple exposures must be created using a computer and image editing software to combine individual files.

Review Questions

Answer the following questions using the information provided in this chapter.

Know and Understand

1. _____ is a technique in which the photographer controls how the final product will appear to the viewer by first seeing that desired final result in their own mind.
   A. Selective focus
   B. Viewpoint
   C. Visualization
   D. Composition

2. The distance and angle from which the camera (and eventually, the viewer) sees the subject is called the _____.
   A. viewpoint
   B. camera angle
   C. center of interest
   D. frame

3. *True or False?* Composition strongly influences the message the viewer will receive and can direct their attention toward or away from an object in the frame.

4. Which of the following is *not* one of the six traditional compositional elements?
   A. Point
   B. Pattern
   C. Emphasis
   D. Color

5. A _____ is a compositional element that is a single object, typically small in size, that attracts the eye.
   A. line
   B. point
   C. shape
   D. pattern

6. *True or False?* Sharply curved lines are considered placid and restful.

7. Repeated shapes or lines establish a(n) _____ that moves the eye through the frame.
   A. formal balance
   B. rhythm
   C. informal balance
   D. emphasis

8. In a photograph, _____ may be achieved by the relative positions of two objects of different sizes or by using a smaller, brightly colored object to balance a larger dark object.
   A. informal balance
   B. formal balance
   C. center of interest
   D. rhythm

9. *True or False?* When every element of the photo is given equal weight, nothing stands out because the viewer receives no guidance.

10. _____ is a noticeable difference between adjacent elements of a composition.
    A. Emphasis
    B. Balance
    C. Contrast
    D. Pattern

11. *True or False?* A worm's-eye angle is representative of how people view their surroundings.

12. *True or False?* Inclusion is deciding what to include in the frame.

13. _____ is a compositional problem in which parts of the image come together in an undesirable way.
    A. Extracting
    B. Convergence
    C. Negative space
    D. Informal balance

14. Identifying and pulling out individual images from a larger scene is known as _____.
    A. inclusion
    B. convergence
    C. exclusion
    D. extracting

15. *True or False?* Portrait mode is an image format that is wider than it is tall.

16. The compositional tool known as _____ is the area within the frame surrounding the subject.
    A. shape
    B. size
    C. negative space
    D. focus

17. _____ is the additional room on the side of the frame toward which the subject is looking or moving.
    A. Lead room
    B. Composition
    C. Camera angle
    D. Frame

18. *True or False?* It is best to shoot photos of children and animals from a high angle.
19. *True or False?* The viewer's eye is drawn to the brightest element or most strongly saturated color in a picture.
20. _____ conveys speed and movement by streaking the background behind a sharply focused moving subject, such as when you are shooting moving vehicles.
    A. Soft focus
    B. Panning
    C. Selective focus
    D. Zooming
21. *True or False?* Soft focus is used primarily in portrait photography.
22. _____ is a technique that uses a shallow depth of field to throw the background out of focus, drawing attention to the main subject.
    A. Panning
    B. Zooming
    C. Soft focus
    D. Selective focus
23. *True or False?* Any image created in the computer by combining individual files is technically termed a composite.

Apply and Analyze

1. How is "making a picture" different from "taking a picture"?
2. List five of the six traditional compositional elements.
3. What is the rule of thirds and how is it used?
4. What does negative space do when used properly?
5. List the three common methods of focusing viewer attention.
6. Why is soft focus a technique commonly used in portrait photography?

Critical Thinking

1. Imagine you composed an image of a single colorful wildflower in the foreground, occupying about one-fourth of the frame. The space surrounding the flower is varying shades of green foliage. Do you think the space surrounding the flower can be described as negative space?
2. The rule of thirds is actually a useful technique rather than a rule. Many successful photographs have been created that do not conform to this rule. Think of some types of images that could be considered well-composed without conforming to the rule of thirds.
3. How can shadows be used in a photo to add contrast and drama to the image? Think of several different examples.

Suggested Activities

1. In small groups, examine the images in your portfolio and those belonging to the other members of your group. Discuss, analyze, and critique the compositional elements of each image. Each student should then choose three images from the portfolios and write a report. In the report, list the design elements noted and describe how those elements make the images more interesting or convey intended meaning.
2. Study the works of famous photographers. Print one image from each of three different photographers and prepare a written or oral report that discusses the composition of these images. Comment on the color, design, shape, shadow, negative space, and background shown in the images.

Communicating about Photography

1. **Speaking.** Choose one of the elements of composition (such as pattern or balance) discussed in this chapter. Prepare a visual display of three images that include this element. Explain to the class how the compositional element is used in each image.
2. **Writing and Speaking.** Working in a group, brainstorm ideas for creating classroom tools (posters, flash cards, and/or games, for example) that will help your classmates learn and remember the elements of composition. Choose the best idea(s), and then delegate responsibilities to group members for constructing the tools and presenting the final products to the class.
3. **Speaking.** In small groups, discuss the principles of design in photographic work with a focus on color. Discuss how color can be used to create contrast and focus viewer attention.

Chapter 10
Improving Lighting

Learning Objectives

After completing this chapter, you will be able to:
- Understand the importance of lighting and how it affects a photograph.
- Define the different types of lights and light qualities.
- Recall the basic goals to accomplish when creating a lighting design.
- Identify common lighting approaches.
- Explain common lighting setups and understand how to achieve them.

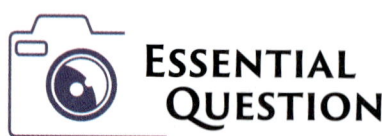

Essential Question

How does lighting affect how you view a photograph?

Technical Terms

atmosphere
background light
blocking
brightness
broad lighting
butterfly lighting
contrast
darkness
diffused light
fill light
gel
hard light
key light
lighting instrument
lighting ratio
loop lighting
mood
motivated lighting
overexposure
Rembrandt lighting
rim light
rim lighting
short lighting
soft light
specular light
split lighting
three-point lighting
tonal range
underexposure

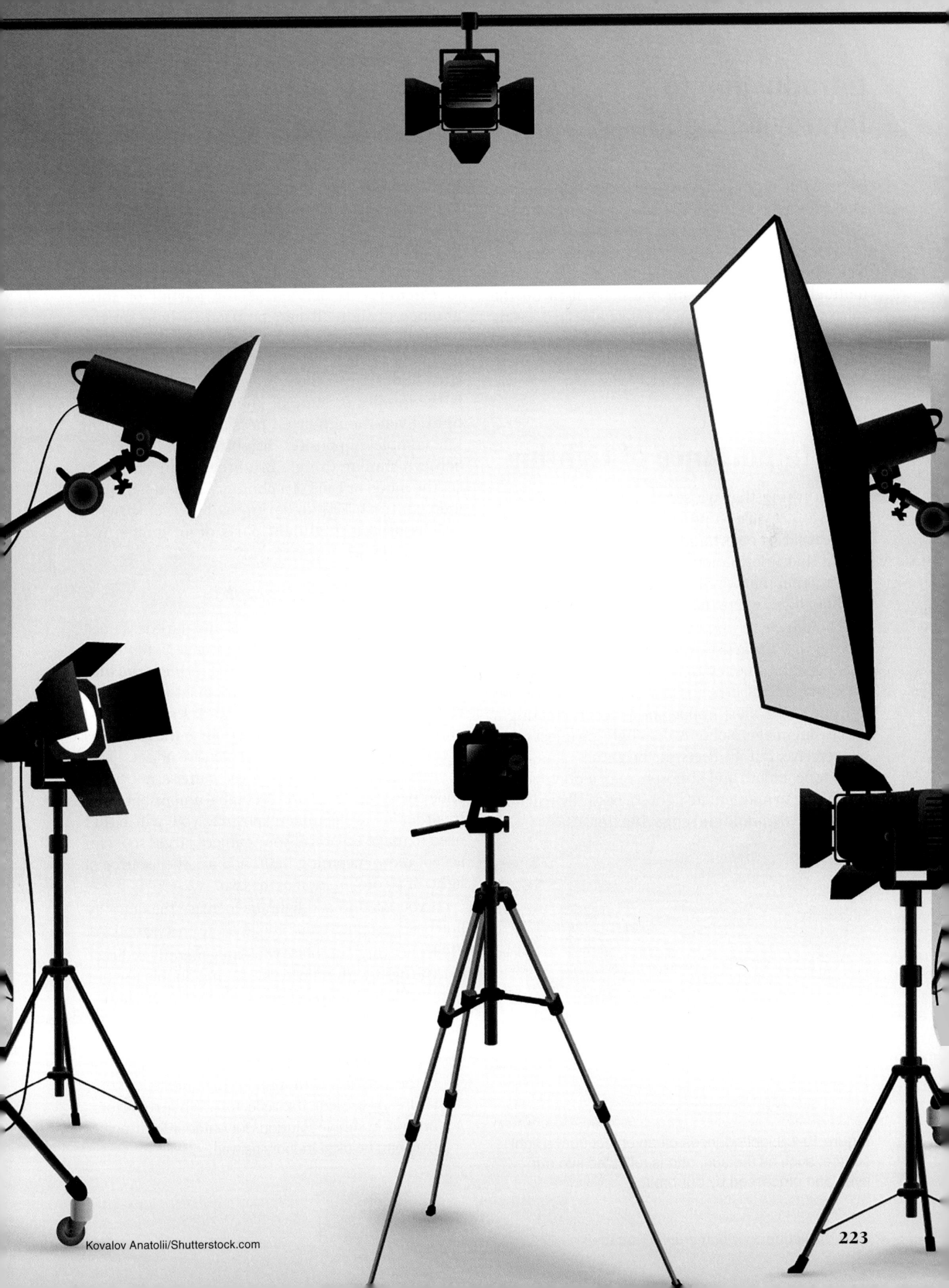

Introduction to Improving Lighting

Light is more than just a collection of wavelengths our brain processes to receive information, especially when it comes to photography. Lighting is one of the most powerful tools in photography because it has the ability to elicit emotions from people. Whether it is through the use of shadows and highlights or a setup with one main light on the subject, lighting allows you to create a desired feeling in your audience. Being able to understand and manipulate lighting will allow you to have more control over the images you create and give you more creative freedom.

The Importance of Lighting

Everything that we see is a reflection of light. Our eyes are able to process images because light bounces off an object and is reflected into our eyes, where that information is translated by our brain into a signal that we can understand, **Figure 10-1**. Without light, we would not be able to see.

Though we rely on light on a fundamental level, there is also an artistic quality to it that photographers can manipulate to achieve a desired effect in their images. In fact, some photographers claim that lighting is the most important factor in creating a successful image. Not only does lighting affect what we perceive, but it affects the brightness and darkness, tone, mood, and atmosphere of a photograph. Being able to manipulate light successfully will help you create dynamic and engaging images.

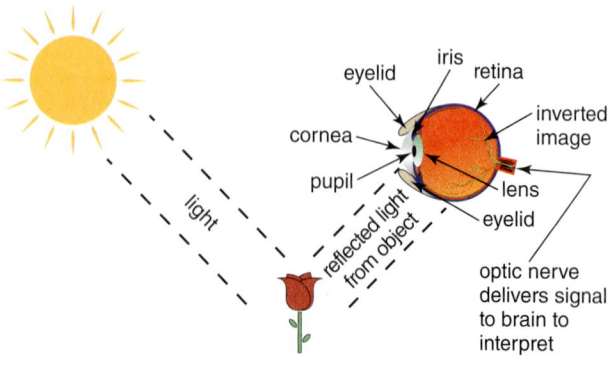

Goodheart-Willcox Publisher

Figure 10-1. Light bounces off an object from a light source, such as the sun, and is reflected into our eyes and processed by our brain.

Darkness and Brightness

When it comes to photography, darkness and brightness are equally important. You need one to successfully perceive the other. There must always be some light parts to balance the dark parts in an image, and vice versa, **Figure 10-2**. The balance you want to achieve will eventually come naturally to you as you gain more experience as a photographer and develop your personal aesthetic.

Darkness is defined as the partial or total absence of light. It can be used to help set the mood or tone of a photograph, conceal parts of an image, or help provide contrast. In direct contrast to darkness, there is brightness. **Brightness** is the quality or state of giving out or reflecting light. Even though brightness and darkness seem like complete opposites, brightness and darkness achieve similar things. Brightness can also help set the mood or tone of a photograph and help provide contrast. Unlike darkness, however, brightness is used to highlight parts of an image, not conceal them.

Underexposed Photographs

Like most things, brightness and darkness need to be used in moderation. If an image is too dark, it will be considered underexposed. **Underexposure** refers to a photo that is very dark due to an insufficient amount of light, **Figure 10-3**. Underexposed photos can be hard to decipher since the darkness of the photo hides details or even entire objects. This is often caused by the iris of the camera not being wide enough to let in an acceptable amount of light. In order to avoid underexposure, you will either need to make the iris of your camera larger so it can accept more incoming light, add another source of light, or a combination of the two.

If you need to add light, or increase the quantity (intensity) of light in your image, there are two options:

1. If shooting outdoors, you can generally redirect the light with reflectors, making double use of the illumination available. Reflectors are lighting tools that help redirect light by reflecting it off their surface.
2. If shooting indoors, you can typically add lighting to the available illumination. To redirect light that is already present, use reflectors. While reflectors are quick, simple solutions for outdoor lighting, they can be used indoors as well.

To add light to the available illumination, use one or more lighting instruments. A **lighting instrument** is a piece of lighting hardware, such

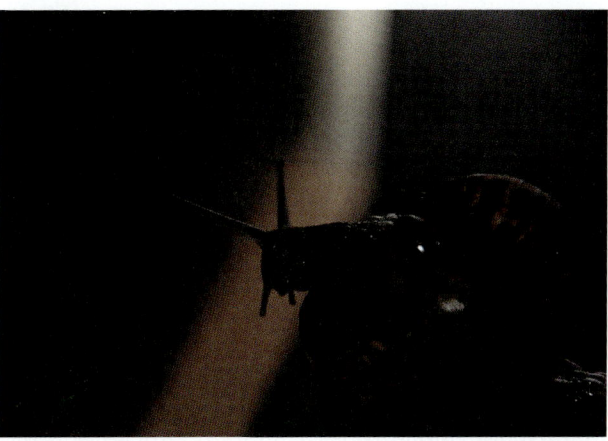

4-life-2-b/Shutterstock.com

Figure 10-3. This image is underexposed, meaning that there is not enough light to see the subject properly.

as a spotlight. Photo lighting can be as simple as an on-camera fill light, or as elaborate as a set lit with 20 instruments. In professional photography work, almost all interior locations are lit for shooting, sometimes by supplementing the light already available at the location.

There may be times when you want to intentionally create an underexposed image, but those images are often carefully planned and coordinated to achieve a specific effect. Those images do not just happen by accident. Creating an underexposed photo accidentally could ruin the photo you did have planned.

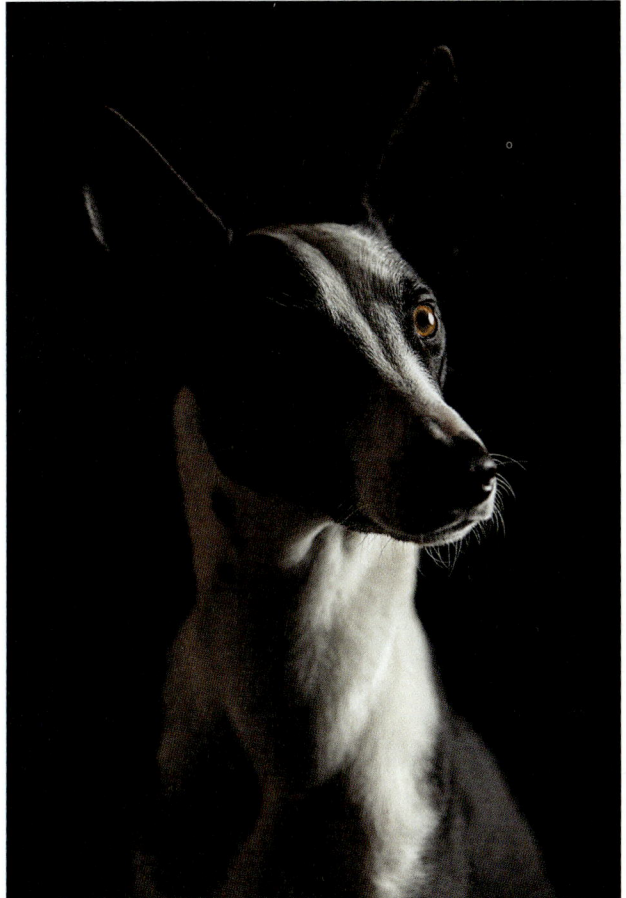

A — *Jigs jigar07/Shutterstock.com*

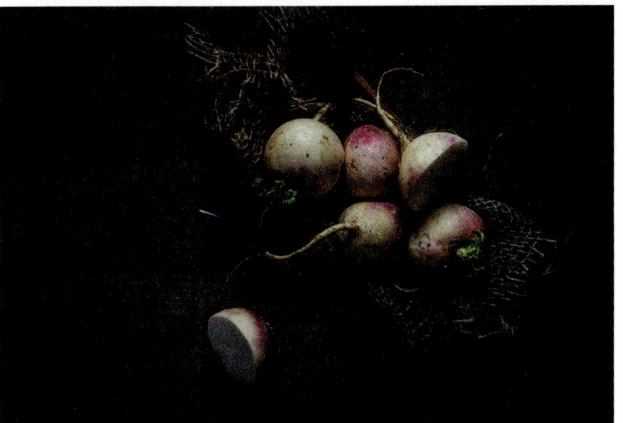

B — *JOAT/Shutterstock.com*

Figure 10-2. Photos must have a balance of brightness and darkness. A—Even though most of the dog is in shadow, the highlights in this image help us perceive the rest of the dog. B—The darkness and shadows in this image help make the highlights more vibrant.

PROCEDURE

Working with Reflectors

1. Hold a reflector opposite your key light (main light source). This allows the reflector to reflect bright light onto your subject.
2. Adjust the reflector to fill in any shadows created by your key light but avoid shining the light into your subject's eyes.
3. For softer lighting, move the reflector away from your subject. For more intense lighting, move the reflector closer to your subject.

Overexposed Photographs

Overexposed photographs are the exact opposite of underexposed photographs. If an image is too light, it will be considered overexposed. **Overexposure** refers to a photo that is very bright due to an excessive amount of light. These photos also have very little detail visible in their highlights and are often referred to as "blown out" or "washed out," **Figure 10-4**.

If your photo is overexposed, you need to decrease the amount of light your camera is taking in. When shooting outside, you will often need to control the light by reducing the quantity. You can do this by either blocking or screening the light.

To block light entirely, place an opaque shield, such as a flag (a lighting tool used to block light), between the light source and the subject. This technique works when there is enough light from other sources to illuminate the blocked area of the subject.

To screen light instead of block it, place a large, framed screen (a lighting tool used to filter light) of mesh or cloth between the light source and the subject.

Unlike underexposure, there are not many instances in which you would want to intentionally create an overexposed image. It is typically recommended to avoid overexposure because you lose a lot of detail, making it difficult for people to figure out what is in the image.

Procedure

Using Screens

1. Set up your screen (or screens) close to your subject.
2. Frame your shot so any screens are not visible. You may need to adjust the screen's position if you want to get a variety of shots.
3. Adjust the screen (or screens) as needed to achieve your desired lighting effect.

Contrast

Contrast is the difference between the lightest and darkest areas in an image. Lighting contrast is expressed as a ratio, such as 3:1. In this example, it means that the lightest areas of the image are three times as light as the darkest areas. This ratio is different in almost every photograph you take, **Figure 10-5**.

When working with contrast, you need to be careful when selecting the amount of light. If you have too little contrast, you risk your subjects appearing flat and boring, which could lead to an uninteresting photograph, **Figure 10-6**. On the

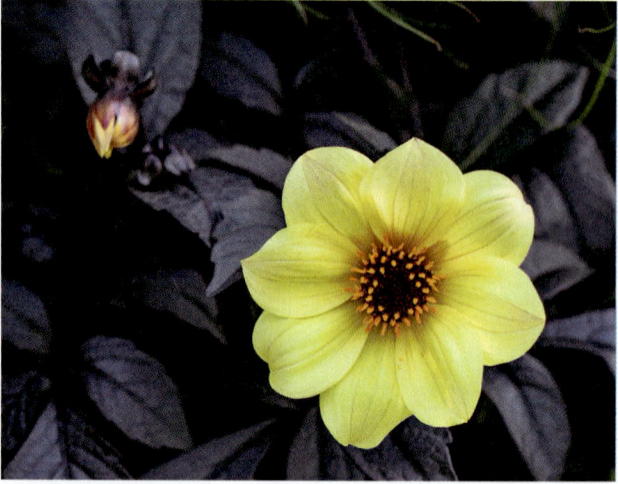

LCRP/Shutterstock.com

Figure 10-5. Contrast helps separate your subject from other objects in the image. In this photo, the bright yellow of the flower contrasts dramatically with the dark leaves.

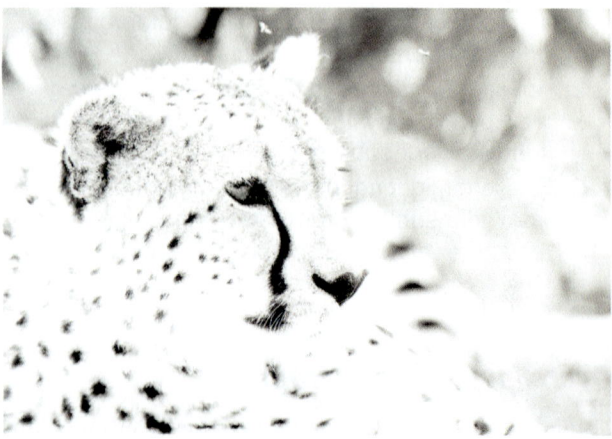

Dr. Ajay Kumar Singh/Shutterstock.com

Figure 10-4. An overexposed image lets too much light into the camera, which washes out the subject.

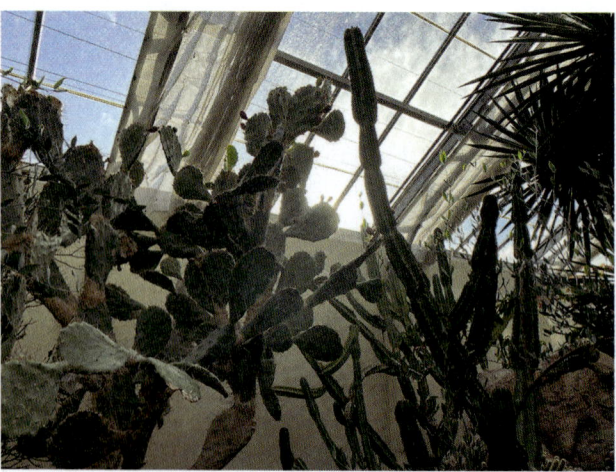

Goodheart-Willcox Publisher

Figure 10-6. This image has too little contrast, which makes it appear rather flat and dull despite the interesting subject.

other hand, too much contrast in your photo will create extreme visual differences between the light and dark areas. The lighter areas of the photo will appear as stark white, the darker areas will appear as solid black, and in more extreme cases, both may appear in the same photograph, **Figure 10-7**.

It is important to remember that no matter what type of mood or style you are trying to achieve in your photograph, a well-lit image is consistent across its range of brightness levels. Here are some qualities of an evenly lit photograph that you can use as a reference:

- True white in the lightest areas of your photo
- Details in the highlights of your image
- Varying levels of brightness in the middle range
- Shadows that still have visible details
- True black in the darkest areas of your photo

Color

To make sure you maintain a high quality of light, it is important to pay attention to the color of the light. This is typically done through setting your white balance. Ensuring your white balance is set properly will allow colors to appear accurate in your final image. However, there are times when you may want to have more selective control over the color of the lighting in your image to achieve a certain aesthetic or look. For instance, you may want an image to appear more blue than it would normally look if you were trying to create a feeling of sadness or melancholy. It is also important to remember that white balance is a function of color temperature. For a review of color temperature, refer to Chapter 7, *Light and Exposure*.

Depending on where you shoot, you may be required to mix different light sources of various color temperatures, **Figure 10-8**. For example, you may have to balance halogen lights, fluorescent lights, and the natural light from a window. You may also want to simulate naturally occurring color temperatures at unnatural times of the day. For instance, you may want to simulate the golden hour light found naturally in the 20–30 minutes before the sun rises and sets in the middle of the evening with different colored gels that help replicate a specific color. **Gels** are transparent, colored materials placed over a light source to create a specific-colored effect. No matter when or where you shoot, you must always ensure the color of your light stays properly balanced and mixed in order to maintain proper white balance in your images.

Tone

Another important lighting factor is tone. As defined in Chapter 7, **tonal range** is the spread of tones, from deepest shadows to brightest highlights, represented in a photograph, **Figure 10-9**. Brightness and darkness also play an integral role in how we perceive and measure tone in photographs. Look at **Figure 10-10**. The shadows (circled in blue) are considered dark tones, while the highlights (circled in red) are bright tones. A photograph that is made of mostly darker tones will be considered *low key*. These photos often feel heavy and dramatic,

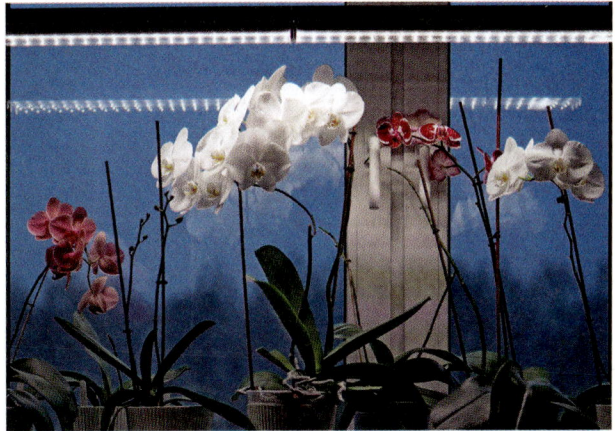

Nadya So/Shutterstock.com

Figure 10-8. There may be some instances in which you have to shoot in an environment with light sources of varying color temperatures. In this image, the photographer had to balance the outside light (which tends to be blue-tinted) with the inside grow lights (which are more neutral).

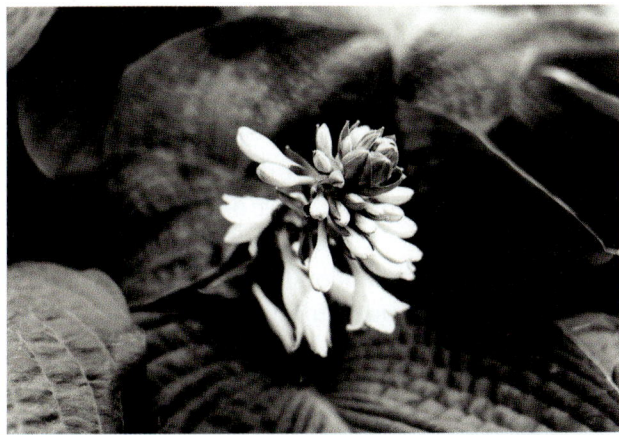

Dave Waddling/Shutterstock.com

Figure 10-7. In some cases, you will have very dark blacks and very bright whites in the same photograph.

Lower key tones   **Higher key tones**

Goodheart-Willcox Publisher

Figure 10-9. Tonal range is the spread of tones in a photograph, from the deepest shadows to the brightest highlights. This range plays an important role in how we perceive light in a photo.

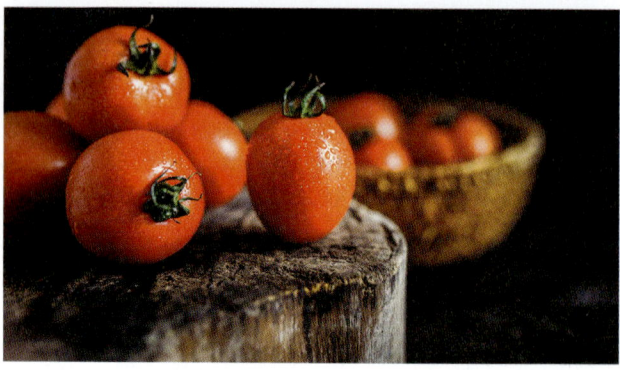

ThaiThu/Shutterstock.com

Figure 10-11. This photo consists of mostly dark tones, making it a low-key image. Low-key images tend to feel moody and dramatic.

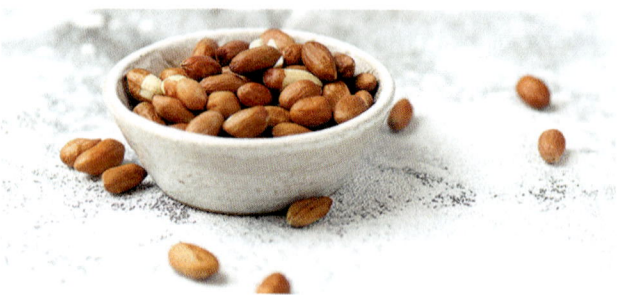

Alina Nikitaeva/Shutterstock.com

Figure 10-12. The brighter tones in this photo make it a high-key image. These photos tend to feel bright and airy.

Mood

The tone of a photograph contributes to the overall mood. While the tone focuses on the levels of brightness in a photograph, the mood relies on the lighting in the photograph. **Mood** is defined as the feeling created by the lighting in a photograph. As mentioned previously, photos with darker tones will come across as heavy and brooding, and photos with brighter tones will come across as happy and airy. Often, you are only able to achieve a specific mood in your photograph through the tone. For example, if you want to achieve a dark and brooding mood in your photo, you will most likely use darker tones. The opposite is true if you want to achieve a happy and carefree mood. You would most likely use lighter tones.

When shooting indoors, you can achieve your desired mood by manipulating your lighting. For example, turning lights off will darken your environment, **Figure 10-13A**, while turning lights on will brighten your environment, **Figure 10-13B**. You can also use windows to your advantage by using them as a light source. Another option is to bring in extra lighting equipment.

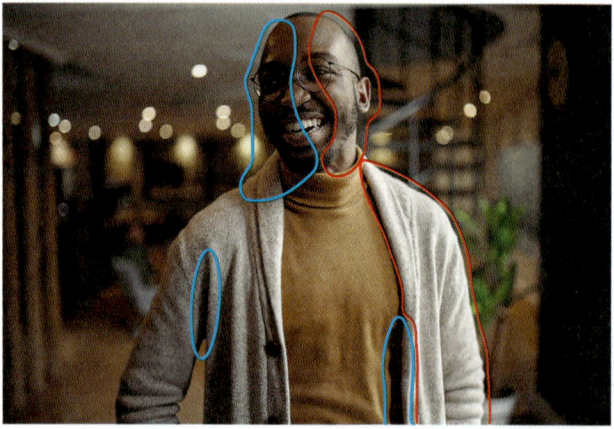

Jono Erasmus/Shutterstock.com

Figure 10-10. Shadows (circled in blue) and highlights (circled in red) help determine the key of a photo.

Figure 10-11. A photo that is made of mostly bright tones is called *high key*, and it often feels bright and airy, **Figure 10-12**.

Understanding how tone affects your image is incredibly important if you plan on taking good photographs. For example, if you are trying to capture a feeling of isolation and loneliness, you may want to take photos with a darker tone. Conversely, if you are trying to convey a more uplifting or upbeat feel, you might want to take photos with a lighter tone. The location where you take your photos will also affect your photograph's tone, as will how you process your photos in postproduction. Tone and the Zone System are discussed more thoroughly in Chapter 7.

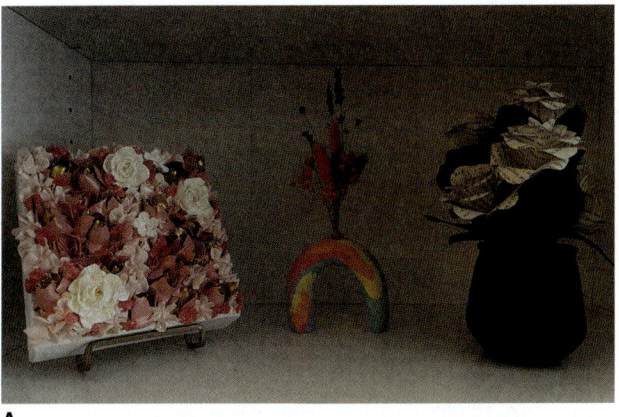
A

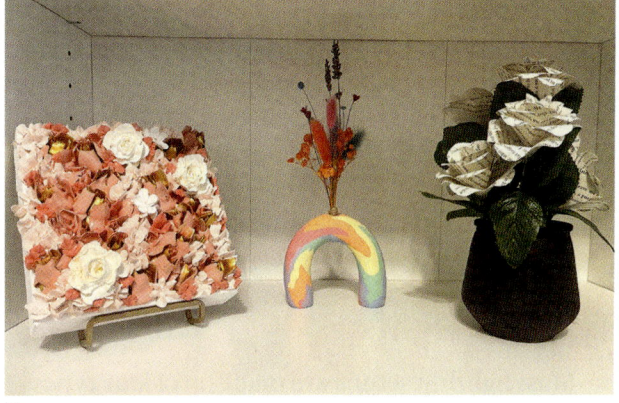
B

Goodheart-Willcox Publisher

Figure 10-13. A—Turning the lights in a room off can darken the overall lighting significantly and intensify shadows. B—Turning the lights in a room on can brighten the overall lighting significantly and intensify highlights.

When shooting outdoors, the weather will often change the mood of your photograph, with or without external lighting. Think of how you feel when it is raining or overcast versus how you feel when it is bright outside with minimal clouds. Those same feelings can and will often be the same in your photography.

If you are unsure what mood your photographs convey or how your shooting environment will affect it, a good tip is to look at the light. Look at your photograph and pay close attention to which direction the light is coming from. This will help you find the highlights in your photo and will dictate the mood. More highlights tend to create a more peaceful image, and fewer highlights tend to create a more intense image. However, it is important to keep in mind that mood can be subjective depending on your viewer's personal experiences.

Atmosphere

Out of all the qualities discussed so far, atmosphere is perhaps the most difficult to capture accurately. While tone, and even mood, have a value to them through the differences between light and dark, atmosphere is more about a feeling. Photographers have tried for years to be able to effectively capture atmosphere. The struggle often comes from the fact that atmosphere does not only rely on technical settings like tonal value, aperture, or even composition. **Atmosphere** is a quality of a photograph that projects a sense of place and time. It helps capture the essence of the environment's smells, sounds, and images so that feeling and atmosphere can be repeated whenever you look at a photograph.

Lighting drastically affects the atmosphere of an image. Typically, warm, soft lighting creates a cozier atmosphere, and cool, harsh lighting creates a businesslike atmosphere. If you are shooting outside, the weather will affect the image's atmosphere. Lighting on an overcast day is very different from lighting on a bright summer day.

Qualities that help contribute to the atmosphere of a photo include but are not limited to the following:

- **Candid photographs.** Photos that are more candid than posed help contribute to an atmosphere in your images. Imagine shooting in a coffee shop. Seeing a person relaxing in a chair while reading a book and holding a cup of coffee can create a cozy or relaxed atmosphere. If the subject in that same photo was sitting up straight and looking directly at the camera, the atmosphere would not be the same.
- **Showing the setting and environment.** Being able to place a subject in an environment can help you establish where your image is being captured. Giving your viewer context as to where your photo is taking place will not only set up the location, but make your photos stand out to your viewers.
- **Showing emotions.** Many of our most memorable photographs contain some sort of visible emotion, like big smiles or tears running down someone's face. Being able to spot and capture emotions will contribute to the atmosphere of your photo as well as contribute to the impact your photo has on someone viewing it.

Introduction to Lights

There are many different types of lights that photographers might use when shooting. It is important to know some basic information about the lights you may encounter. This information is also helpful for understanding various lighting setups, or how lights are organized to achieve a specific lighting effect.

Types of Lights

Most lighting setups are made up of four types of lights. These lights are essential and are included in nearly every lighting style and design. Understanding the use and purpose of these lights will help improve your photography:

- The *key light* is the main light on a subject, **Figure 10-14**. The key light is usually the brightest light and imitates real-world light sources, such as lights that are already present at the shooting location. You need to place your key light first before building the rest of your lighting setup.
- The *fill light* is the secondary light on a subject, **Figure 10-15**. The fill light is normally placed on the opposite side of the key light to help fill in shadows created by the key light. It softens dark shadows, decreases the contrast range of the light reflected from the subject, and helps to reveal detail in shadow areas. It is also helpful in reducing contrast.
- The *rim light* is placed behind and above the subject so it is out of frame, **Figure 10-16**. The rim light helps create a separation between the background and the subject by creating a rim of light on the subject's head and shoulders. It is often used for dramatic effect or to help separate a dark-haired subject from the background. The rim light can also be referred to as an *accent light*, *back light*, *hair light*, or *halo light*.

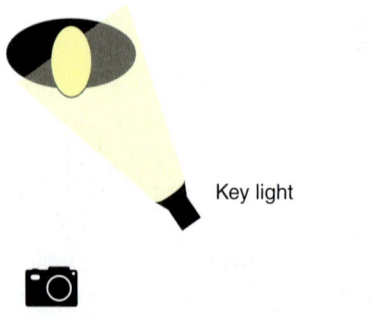

Goodheart-Willcox Publisher

Figure 10-14. The key light is the main light illuminating the subject.

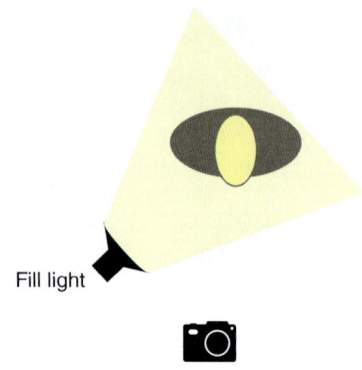

Goodheart-Willcox Publisher

Figure 10-15. The fill light helps balance out shadows created by the key light and typically sits opposite the key light.

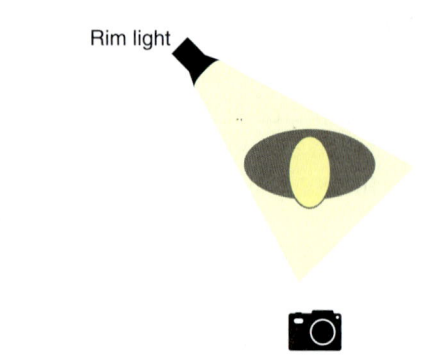

Goodheart-Willcox Publisher

Figure 10-16. The rim light is placed behind the subject and out of the frame so it is not seen. It helps create separation between the subject and the background.

- The *background light* (or lights) provides sufficient visual separation between the subject and the background and helps create visual interest in your image, **Figure 10-17**. It also helps make the background easier to see, and it can aid in adding depth to your photograph by literally shining a light on features or objects in the back part of the frame.

Light Qualities

Now that the basic types of light have been established, it is important to discuss the different qualities of light. As you can guess, lighting is more than just taking a light and aiming it at a subject. Depending on what look you are trying to achieve, you may want your light to appear different. Hard, soft, specular, and diffused light all contribute to how people perceive a photo. No matter what type

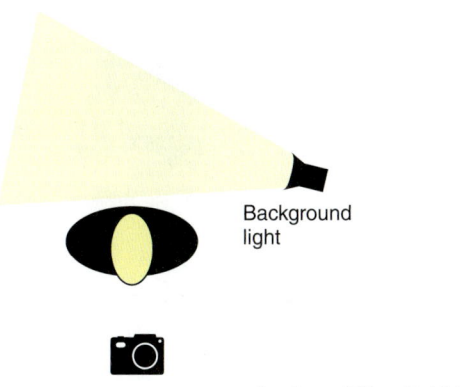

Figure 10-17. The background light provides more contrast and visual interest in a photograph.

of lighting setup or strategy you use, you can alter your setup at any point to help achieve the look you want for your image.

Hard Light

Like the name implies, **hard light** creates harsh shadows, or places with stark contrast between the highlights and the shadows. Also called *harsh lighting*, hard lighting exaggerates the planes and angles of the face, **Figure 10-18**. This can emphasize skin texture or other characteristics. In order to create hard lighting, you need to keep the key light high to create more pronounced shadows. You also want to avoid diffusing the light and over-filling the light from another angle. The contrast between the light and dark areas of the photo is also harsh and defined. Think of the light during a hot summer day. The sun is shining bright, and you can see your shadow clearly on the ground. The borders of your shadow are crisp, which is an indication that you are dealing with hard light.

Images that use hard light often come across as edgier than those without. Having hard light also gives you an opportunity to add dimension and depth to your image by capitalizing on the high contrast created with shadows. Hard light is often used in portraits to make a subject seem more serious or strong. If you only have one light available and are looking to create a harder lighting effect on your subject, moving the light closer to your subject will help create more defined shadows.

Soft Light

The opposite of hard light, soft light can create a more glamorous effect. **Soft light** creates very few harsh shadows, or places with stark contrast between the highlights and the shadows, **Figure 10-19**. Between the shadows and highlights, there is more of a smooth gradient, meaning the edges of the shadow are wider and fuzzier. Usually, there will be few to no shadows on your subject if they are lit with soft light. If there are shadows, they are not as dark or as bold as those created by hard light. Imagine how your shadow looks on an overcast day. This is a good indication of how soft light looks.

Soft light is generally more flattering than hard light and appears much more natural. Beauty portraits, fashion photography, travel photography, and food photography all tend to use soft light for their images to make them appear more realistic. Furthermore, soft light generally requires less

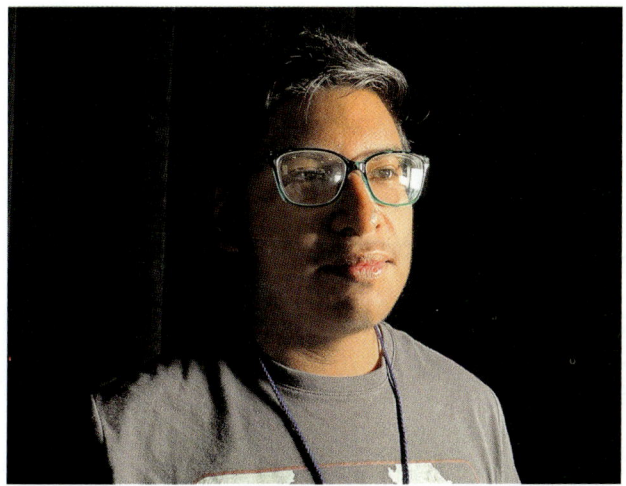

Figure 10-18. Hard light creates harsh shadows and often makes a subject appear more serious or strong.

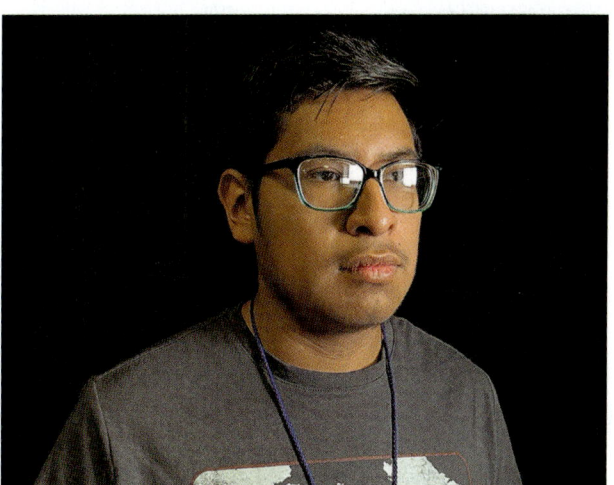

Figure 10-19. Soft light creates very few harsh shadows and is generally more flattering than hard light.

retouching, as it has the ability to smooth out any imperfections on a subject. If you only have one light available and are looking to create a softer lighting effect on your subject, you can move your light further back to help soften the shadows.

Specular Light

While hard and soft light focus on the shadows created by light, specular and diffused light focus on how the light falls on the subject. **Specular light** is light that is very concentrated in the center, but gradually seems to fade in intensity as it moves farther out from the center, **Figure 10-20**. If you picture the light created from a flashlight, the effect is nearly identical. The advantage of specular light is that it allows you to create very bright, exposed areas on your subject from a specific angle. This type of lighting is often used in interviews.

Diffused Light

Diffused light is disbursed over a wide surface for a softer effect, **Figure 10-21**. It refers to the equal distribution of light across a single light source. The light will then hit your subject from a wider angle, decreasing the overall contrast on your subject. It is worth noting that you may hear the terms *specular* and *harsh* and *diffused* and *soft* used interchangeably. While they are often used interchangeably, their effects are different.

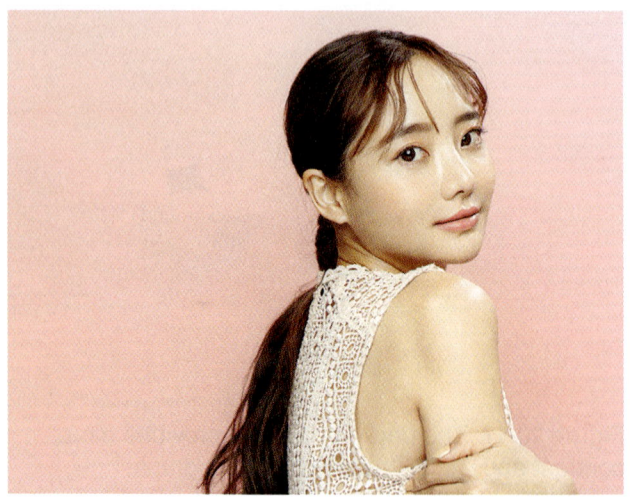

K-Angle/Shutterstock.com

Figure 10-21. Diffused light creates a softer effect and decreases the overall contrast on a subject.

Lighting Design

Understanding what the end goal for your photograph is will help you decide how to approach your lighting design. As you start the planning process for each shoot, you will need to decide what your end goals are. This includes figuring out how you want your image to look, which types of light will work best for a given situation, and whether the photo requires a high-key or low-key appearance. After you have identified all those aspects, you can begin creating your lighting design.

Identifying Basic Goals

When creating a lighting design, you typically want to accomplish three goals:

- Replicate real-world lighting within your image where possible.
- Focus on lighting your subject, not the areas around them.
- Create and enhance depth in your image.

The following sections cover several ways in which you can accomplish these goals.

Replicate Real-World Lighting

Whether they are natural or artificial, you are surrounded by light sources every day. An overcast sky, a lamp on a side table, classroom lights, neon signs, phone screens, and candles are all examples of items that can provide light, **Figure 10-22**. The main goal of **motivated lighting** is to look as real

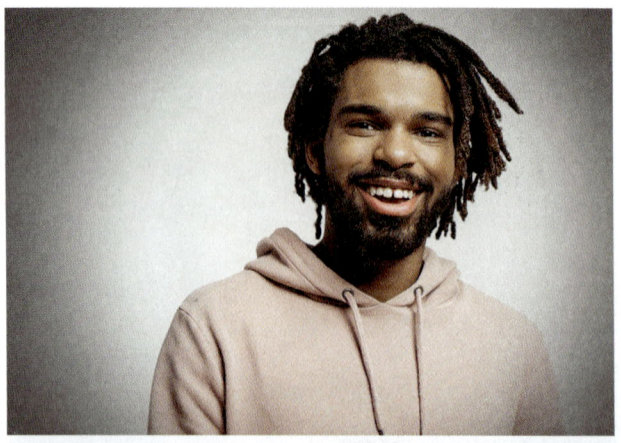

Dean Drobot/Shutterstock.com

Figure 10-20. Specular light mimics the light from a flashlight. The beam is concentrated in the center and gradually fades in intensity farther out from the center.

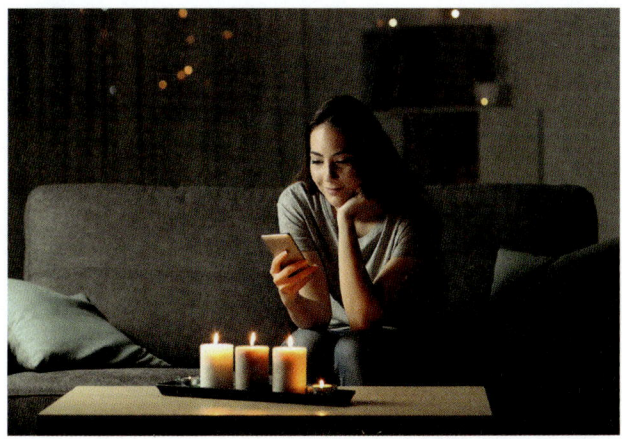

Antonio Guillem/Shutterstock.com

Figure 10-22. Replicating real-world lighting helps give photos a more realistic feel. Candles, lamps, and phone screens can all be used to create motivated lighting.

as possible. Typically, this is done by attempting to replicate light sources that you would normally find in a given environment. Remember, lighting in a house's living room will be vastly different from the lighting on a street at night. In order to properly motivate your lighting, you will need to decide what lights would usually be present and then try to replicate them with lighting instruments. In some instances, it may be useful to scout your location ahead of time and make note of what sources exist before planning your lighting setup.

Look for the Light

Because you are just starting out, you may not have access to lighting kits. This means you have to be especially reliant on motivated light when shooting. When you can (and only if it is practical), you can move subjects closer to an available light source to help add more light to your subject. Keep in mind that this is not feasible with overhead lights, but it is very easy with other light sources, such as the light coming from a window.

One of the most helpful pieces of advice for any photographer is to look for the light. Good photographers always keep an eye out for existing light, or light that may provide an interesting visual for their images.

Light the Subject

As mentioned in the beginning of this chapter, everything we see is a reflection of light. In photography, the light reflects off an object and is taken in through the lens to the camera for processing.

Because your camera only sees what you choose to frame, you only need to worry about lighting the areas that you will be photographing. This makes it much easier than trying to light every inch of your location. To light just the areas that will show in the frame, do the following:

- Block the shooting location. **Blocking** is the process of studying a subject's positions to frame and light shots properly.
- Ensure your subject is lit by directing and focusing light on them.
- Create a sense of depth and atmosphere by lighting the background of your image. This can include furniture and any floor or ceiling areas.

If you do not have a place to hide your lights so they do not show up in the frame, you may decide to light the entire area. If you choose this method, add additional lights, and adjust their positions as needed.

Create and Enhance Depth with Light

Photography is a two-dimensional art, meaning that it is perceived as flat. However, you can always create a sense of depth in your photography by using some common techniques. This can often involve adding highlights where you are shooting to provide that depth in the back of your image, **Figure 10-23**. Doing this will help guide viewers' eyes past the objects or subjects in the front of the photograph and into the back, giving that illusion of a third dimension.

In most cases, you will want to motivate the lighting, light your subject, and create/enhance depth using light. However, there may be times when you do not

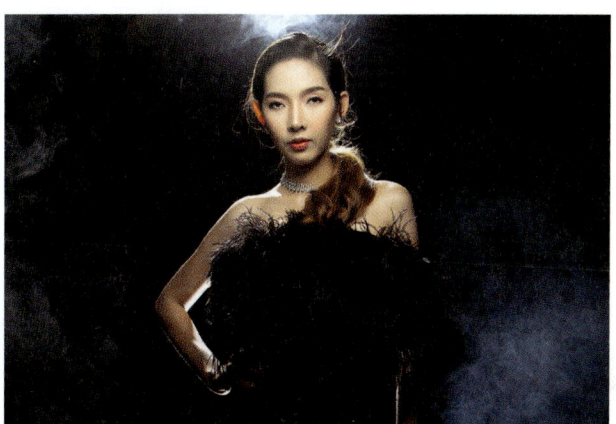

Jade ThaiCatwalk/Shutterstock.com

Figure 10-23. The bright light above and behind the subject in this photo helps provide a great sense of depth.

want to achieve all three of those lighting goals. A few exceptions include the following:

- Motivated lighting might not always be necessary or desirable for your photograph, **Figure 10-24**.
- Lighting a wide shot may prove difficult because you have so much ground to cover with just one (or even many) lights.
- Depth may not always be necessary in your photograph if you decide to purposefully create a photo that does not need depth to be effective.

Choosing a Lighting Approach

Keeping your lighting goals in mind, you can now choose a lighting approach for your photographs. Outside of a photography studio environment, you usually have three options to light your compositions:

- **Work with the available light at the location.** This prevents you from hauling around heavy equipment and gives you flexibility with the movement of your subject. If this is the method you choose, you should ensure there is plenty of lighting available, so your images come out the way you want them to.
- **Start with the available light and strengthen it with photography lights.** If you find yourself needing more light, you can use the available light as your primary light source and supplement it with additional lights. You will have to bring these lights with you, but it gives you more control over your end results than you have when you rely solely on the available light.
- **Get rid of the existing available light and use only photography lights.** This requires the most equipment out of these three options and may not be feasible for a beginning photographer. However, this gives you the most control over your lighting approach and allows you to achieve the exact effect you are trying to create.

Your decision will ultimately depend on what light is available at the location, the style you are trying to achieve, the equipment available to you, and the amount of power available.

Common Lighting Setups

The lighting setups in the following sections are commonly found in most photography studios. However, these are not the only ways to light a subject. You are encouraged to experiment with lighting as you see fit. Keep in mind that many of these lighting setups also have alternative names.

It is also worth noting that all the setups mentioned involve using one light (aside from three-point lighting). If you deem it necessary, however, you can also add a reflector or a fill light to help balance some of the shadows you create. If you do not have an additional light available, you can use a reflector to bounce light from your key light and back onto your subject. When doing this, you must understand the basics of lighting ratios. A *lighting ratio* is the comparison of the key light to the fill light expressed as a ratio, such as 1:2. The higher the ratio, the more contrast you have to deal with. Dynamic photos tend to have a high contrast ratio, **Figure 10-25**.

 REAL-WORLD PHOTOGRAPHY

Lighting Safety

When working with lights, you must follow general safety procedures. Here is a list of some best practices:

- Place properly weighed sandbags on all lighting stands to keep them stable.
- When dealing with light bulbs in any capacity, wear gloves to protect your hands and wait for them to cool down before touching them.
- Properly secure all lighting fixtures to ensure they will not fall. If you are attaching anything like a flag or a silk, make sure it is fastened properly to the lighting fixture as well.
- If a lighting fixture falls or a bulb breaks, clear the area as soon as possible and wear appropriate safety gear while cleaning up.
- For gels and any other type of lighting accessory, make sure you are using material that is specifically made to be used for lighting. Do not use any other material, such as paper or plastic.
- Ensure all cables are taped down to the floor to prevent tripping.
- Be cautious of where you place lights and what you place next to them. Lights tend to generate heat, so you do not want to place them near anything flammable.

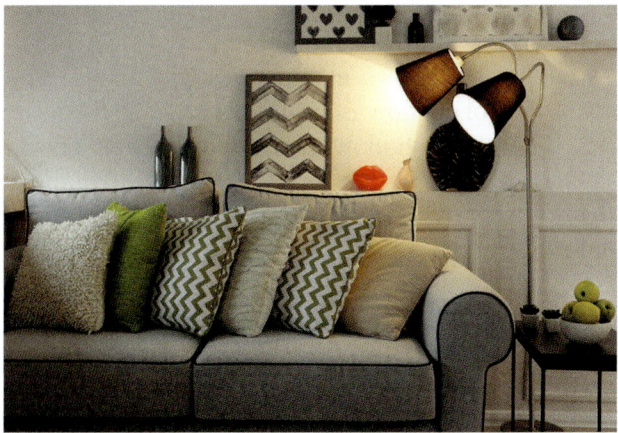

Africa Studio/Shutterstock.com

Figure 10-24. The motivated lighting in this image (the floor lamp) is not necessary and is even a bit distracting where the beam is concentrated on the back wall of the room.

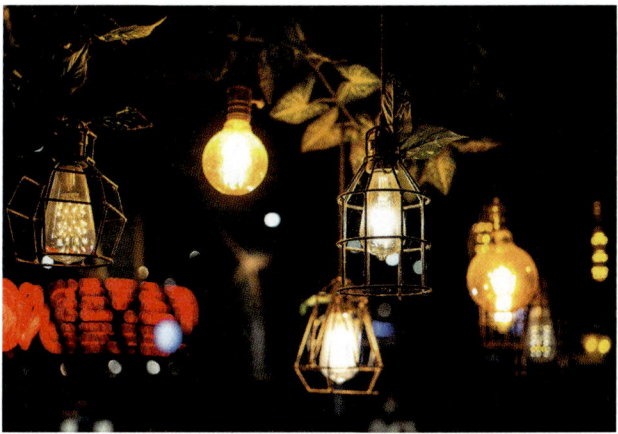

Nattawit Khomsanit/Shutterstock.com

Figure 10-25. This dynamic photo uses a high lighting ratio to help draw the viewer's eye to a specific portion of the image.

Single Lighting

Sometimes you may only have one light available to use. Depending on the type of light you are using and how far it is positioned from your subject, you can create a natural look or something a bit more dramatic, **Figure 10-26**. Single lighting can be handy for portraits when used in addition to an environment's existing light.

Three-Point Lighting

Three-point lighting is a lighting style in which three lights (typically a key, fill, and rim light) are used to light a subject. Many consider three-point lighting the standard for light in both photography

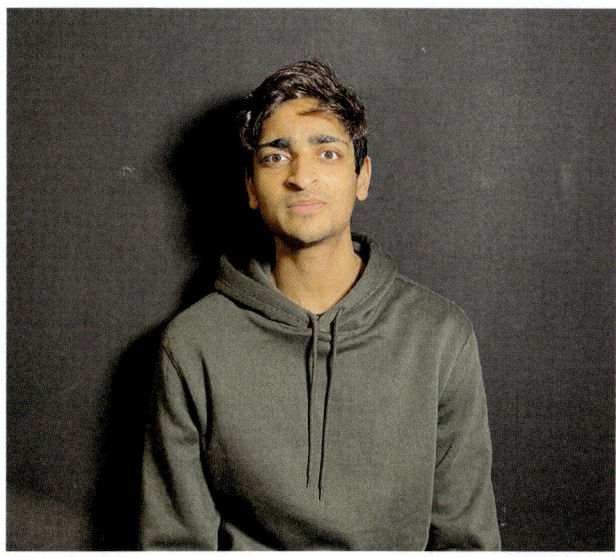

Goodheart-Willcox Publisher

Figure 10-26. You can achieve several different types of moods with just a single light. How it is positioned and where it shines on the subject helps create a specific mood.

and video. The three lights are placed in different positions, and you can change the intensity, distance, and position as you see fit to get your desired effect, **Figure 10-27**. This lighting setup is incredibly flexible, so it can be used for almost any situation.

The key light is the brightest of the three lights in this setup. It is generally set on either the left or right side of the subject at a 45° angle to create a slight

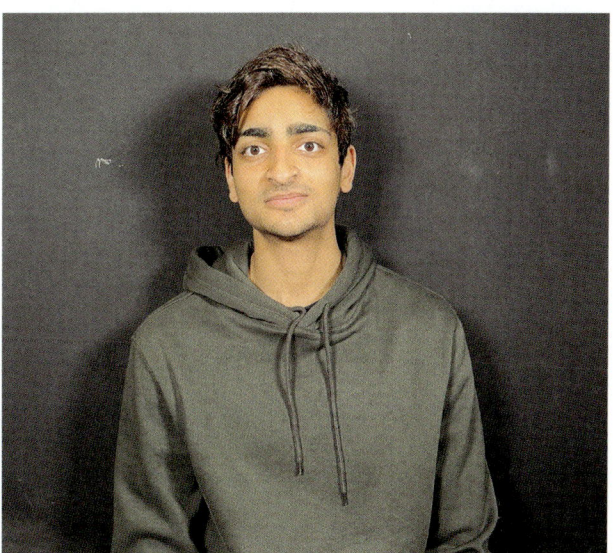

Goodheart-Willcox Publisher

Figure 10-27. Three-point lighting is highly flexible and suitable for almost any lighting situation.

Chapter 10 Improving Lighting **235**

shadow. This helps gives the subject depth and will also set the mood of the photo.

The fill light sits opposite the key light and fills in the shadows created by the key light. This light will be less bright than the key light and will also help you control the feel or mood of your image.

The third light is the rim light. This light is the least bright and is set behind the subject and aimed toward the camera. This creates a halo-like effect on the subject and helps separate them from the background. Depending on the space you have available, this light can be directly behind your subject or high enough to not be visible in the frame.

Butterfly Lighting

Also called *Paramount lighting*, **butterfly lighting** is a lighting setup that creates a distinct butterfly-shaped shadow beneath the nose of a subject. To achieve this lighting setup, place one light above and directly behind your camera, angled down at your subject. The higher the light is behind you, the longer the shadows will be on your subject. Even though there is only one light used in this setup, you will see shadows under the nose, chin, and cheeks, **Figure 10-28**. Butterfly lighting is most commonly used in portrait photography and glamour shots.

Loop Lighting

Loop lighting is a lighting style in which a small loop of shadow is created on a subject's nose, and a separate shadow is created on their cheek. This is created by placing a light slightly above the eye level of your subject at a 45° angle. It does not matter if the light is on the left or right side of your subject, but the shadow appears on the side of the face opposite the light's position. The size of the shadow that appears on your subject's face will depend on the light's position and the size of your subject's nose, **Figure 10-29**.

Loop lighting is like butterfly lighting, but it is angled to one side of the face. If you are having a difficult time positioning your light for loop lighting, you can start off with a butterfly lighting setup and then shift the light's position to the side. Loop lighting is commonly used for portrait photography.

Rembrandt Lighting

If you continue to adjust the position of your light higher, farther to the side, and at a slightly more severe angle from loop lighting, you will achieve Rembrandt lighting. Named for the Dutch painter, **Rembrandt lighting** is a lighting style in which the small loop of shadow on a subject's nose is long enough to merge with the shadow on their cheek. This leaves a small triangle of light on the cheek that is mostly in shadow, **Figure 10-30**. While also used in portraits, Rembrandt lighting can create a moody or mysterious feeling in a photograph.

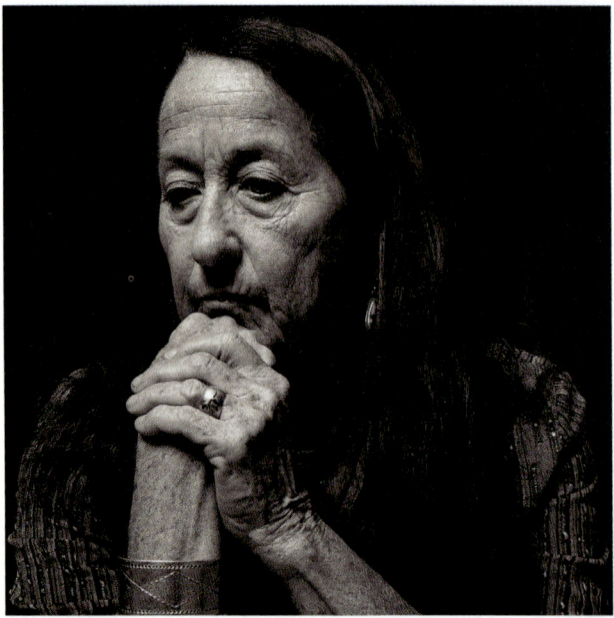

Eliece Shorten

Figure 10-28. Butterfly lighting is often used in portrait photography. It creates distinct shadows under the nose, chin, and cheeks.

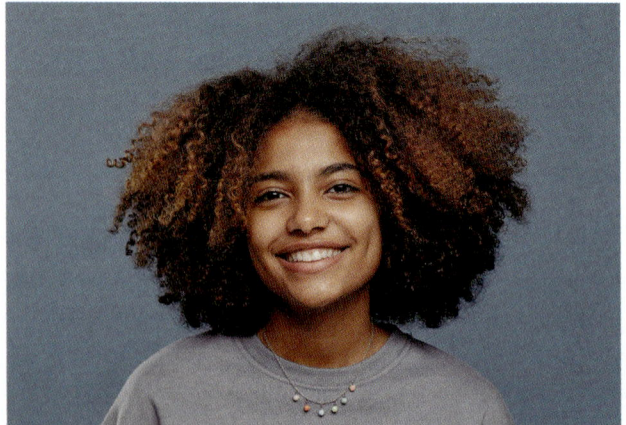

SeventyFour/Shutterstock.com

Figure 10-29. Loop lighting is commonly used for portraits. It is similar to butterfly lighting but is angled to one side of the face.

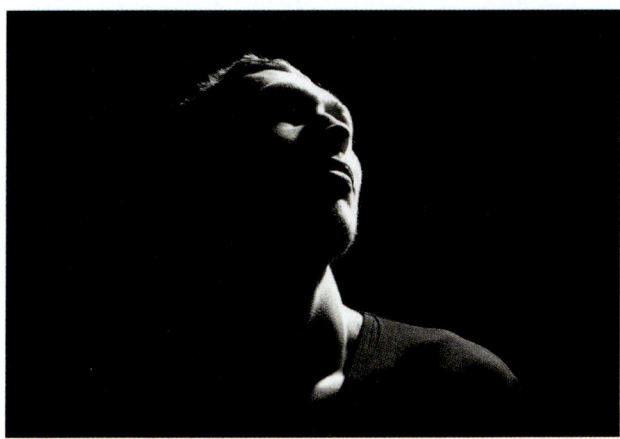

Figure 10-30. Photos lit with Rembrandt lighting appear very dramatic, moody, or mysterious.

Split Lighting

Also referred to as *side lighting* or *profile lighting*, **split lighting** is a lighting style in which half of the subject's face is lit, and the other is left in complete shadow. To achieve this dramatic style, you need to place your light at a 90° angle to your subject, **Figure 10-31**. From there, you can leave it as it is, or you can add a fill light to show more detail. If you want to show some detail, but not too much, you can use a small reflector on the side of your subject's face opposite the light. Split lighting is also commonly used for portrait photography. Note that this style will emphasize any texture on your subject's face.

Rim Lighting

Rim lighting is a lighting style in which light is placed around the edges of a subject from behind, outlining them in light. This style can be achieved both indoors and outdoors and can vary in terms of dramatic effect. In this setup, position the light directly behind your subject and aim it toward the camera. Depending on if there are any other lights present in your setup, you will get either a silhouette of your subject, or something that allows you to see more of your subject's face. This style is very common in sports portraits because it can make a subject appear strong, **Figure 10-32**.

Broad Lighting

Broad lighting is a lighting style that highlights the broad side of a subject's face, or the side that is closer to the camera, by placing light on the same side. For example, if the right side of your subject's face is closer to the camera, that is the side that is lit. It can be combined with other setups to solve specific problems, such as glare from eyeglasses. In

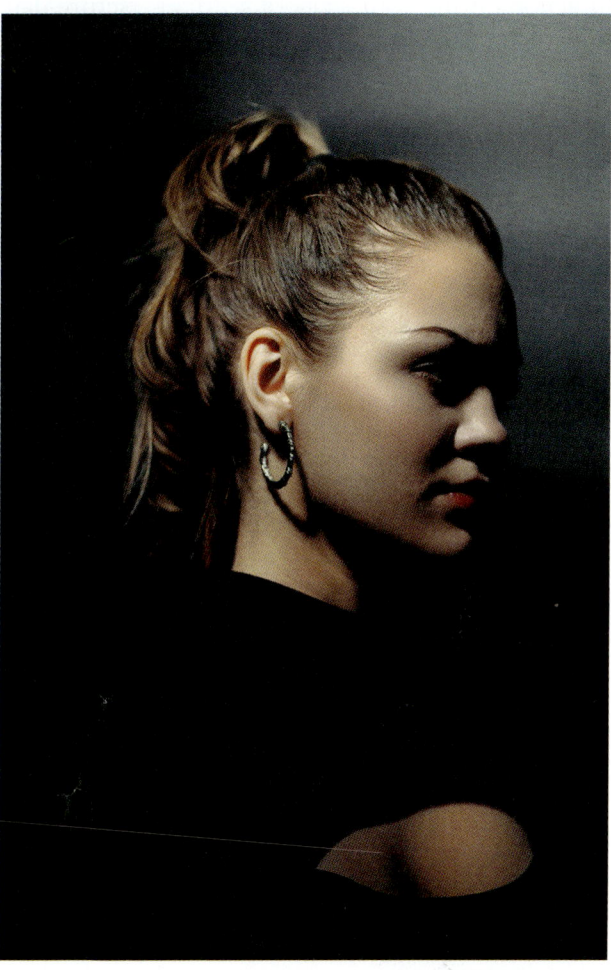

Figure 10-31. Split lighting only lights half of the subject's face. The other half is kept in shadow.

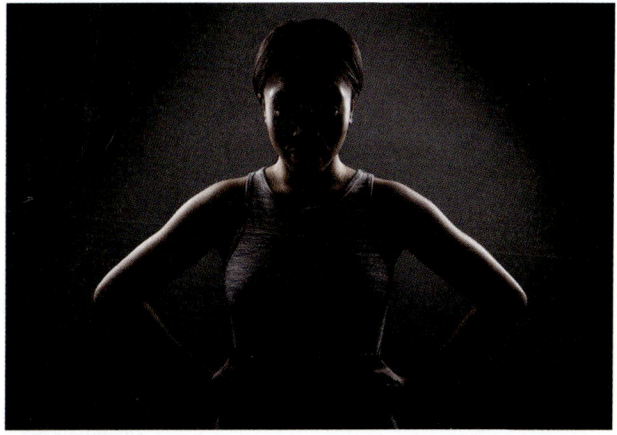

Figure 10-32. Rim lighting outlines the subject in light and often makes them appear strong.

order to set up this style, you should first have your subject sit at a slight angle, with the side of their face that is receiving the most light closest to the camera, **Figure 10-33**. You have most likely seen this setup in action during your school's yearbook picture day. In addition to school photos, it is a common setup for corporate headshots. The only drawback of this style is that it can make a face look wider than it actually is.

Short Lighting

The opposite of broad lighting, ***short lighting*** is a lighting style that highlights the short side of a subject's face, or the side that is farther away from the camera, by placing light on the same side. For example, if the left side of your subject's face is farther from the camera, that is the side that is lit, **Figure 10-34**. Similar to broad lighting, you should first have your subject sit at a slight angle, with the side of their face that is receiving the most light farthest from the camera. If you position your light properly, short lighting is great for creating definition in a face.

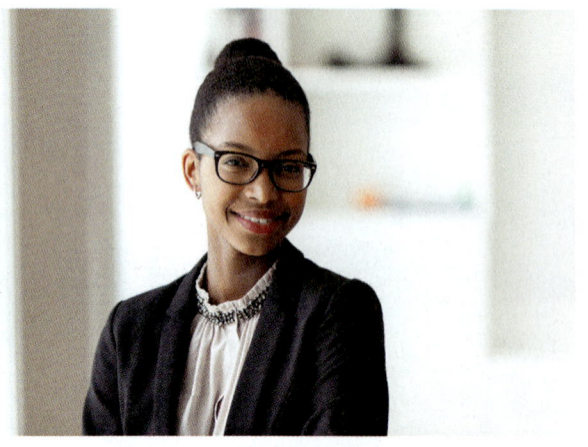

Samuel Borges Photography/Shutterstock.com

Figure 10-33. Broad lighting highlights the side of the subject's face that is closest to the camera.

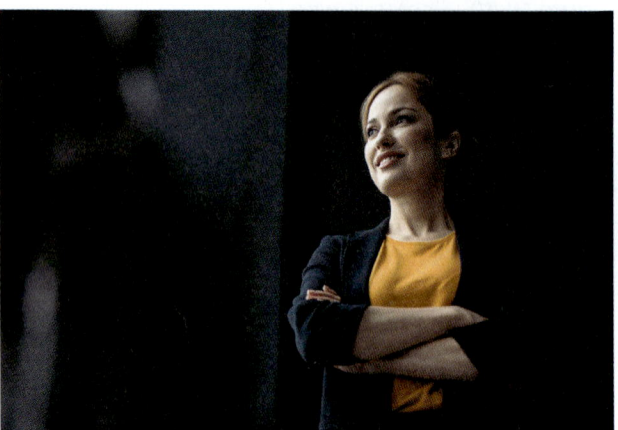

Olena Yakobchuk/Shutterstock.com

Figure 10-34. Short lighting highlights the side of the subject's face that is farther away from the camera.

PORTFOLIO ASSIGNMENT

Selecting a Mood

As a photographer, it is crucial to understand how to create different moods in a photograph. For this assignment, you will experiment with how different lighting setups can convey specific moods.

1. Identify four moods you would like to convey in a photograph. A few examples of moods you can choose are happy (**Example A**), melancholy, carefree, and brooding (**Example B**).

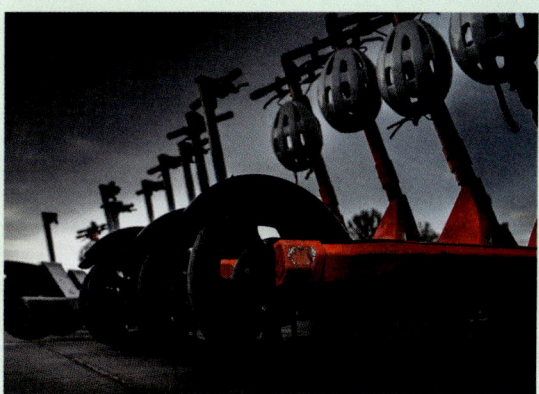

Ramon Cliff/Shutterstock.com

Example B. The dark tones in this photo help give it a brooding feel.

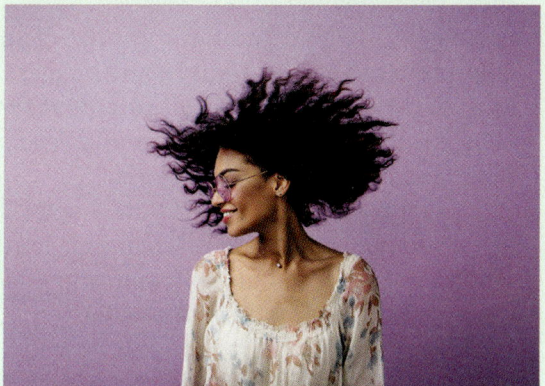

Look Studio/Shutterstock.com

Example A. The soft, bright lighting contributes to the happy mood of this photo.

2. Determine the type of lighting equipment you will need for each mood. Remember that you may be able to use the same equipment for each mood, but the difference will be in the color and intensity of the lights, as well as the positioning.
3. Set up the lights for your first mood and take at least three photos. Repeat this step until you have shot at least three photos for all four moods.

Once you have finished shooting, select the best photo from each mood. Add all four photos to your portfolio, making note of which mood you chose to convey for each photo.

Chapter 10 Review

Summary

- Being able to manipulate light successfully will help you create dynamic and engaging images.
- When it comes to photography, darkness and brightness are equally important. You need one to successfully perceive the other.
- If an image is too dark, it will be considered underexposed. If you need to add light or increase the quantity, you can redirect the light or add more lighting instruments.
- If an image is too light, it will be considered overexposed. If you need to decrease the amount of light, you can block or screen the light.
- Contrast is the difference between the lightest and darkest areas in an image. Lighting contrast is expressed as a ratio.
- Ensuring your white balance is set properly will allow colors to appear accurate in your final image.
- Tonal range is the spread of tones, from deepest shadows to brightest highlights, represented in a photograph.
- The tone of a photograph contributes to the overall mood. Mood relies on the lighting in the photograph.
- Atmosphere helps capture the essence of an environment's smells, sounds, and images.
- Most lighting setups are made up of four types of lights. They include a key light, fill light, rim light, and background light.
- The quality of the light affects how people perceive a photo. Light qualities include hard light, soft light, specular light, and diffused light.
- Understanding what the end goal for your photograph is will help you decide how to approach your lighting design. You must identify your basic goals, such as replicating real-world lighting, focusing lighting on the subject, and creating and enhancing depth, and then choose a lighting approach.
- There are many lighting setups commonly used in photography studios. Some of these setups include single lighting, three-point lighting, butterfly lighting, loop lighting, Rembrandt lighting, split lighting, rim lighting, broad lighting, and short lighting.

Review Questions

Answer the following questions using the information provided in this chapter.

Know and Understand

1. _____ is defined as the partial or total absence of light.
   A. Underexposure
   B. Darkness
   C. Brightness
   D. Overexposure

2. *True or False?* Creating an underexposed photo accidentally could ruin the photo you had planned.

3. *True or False?* If your photo is overexposed, you need to increase the amount of light your camera is taking in.

4. Which of the following is *not* a quality of an evenly lit photograph?
   A. True white in the lightest areas of the photo
   B. Shadows that still have visible details
   C. The same level of brightness in the middle range
   D. True black in the darkest areas of the photo

5. A _____ is a transparent, colored material placed over a light source to create a specific-colored effect.
   A. screen
   B. reflector
   C. flag
   D. gel

6. *True or False?* A photograph that is made of mostly darker tones is considered high key.

7. The feeling created by the lighting in a photograph is known as _____.
   A. mood
   B. atmosphere
   C. tone
   D. brightness

8. *True or False?* Atmosphere is a quality of a photograph that projects a sense of place and time.

9. The _____ light is usually the brightest light and imitates real-world light sources, such as lights that are already present at the shooting location.
   A. key
   B. background
   C. fill
   D. rim

10. The _____ light can also be referred to as a back light or a halo light.
    A. background
    B. rim
    C. key
    D. fill

11. *True or False?* Hard lighting exaggerates the planes and angles of the face.

12. _____ light is light that is very concentrated in the center, but gradually seems to fade in intensity as it moves farther out from the center.
    A. Hard
    B. Soft
    C. Specular
    D. Diffused

13. The main goal of _____ lighting is to look as real as possible.
    A. soft
    B. motivated
    C. loop
    D. specular

14. Which of the following does *not* help accomplish the goal of lighting the subject rather than the areas around them?
    A. Block the shooting location.
    B. Create a sense of depth and atmosphere by lighting the background of the image.
    C. Direct and focus light on the subject.
    D. Decide what lights would usually be present at the shooting location and try to replicate them.

15. *True or False?* The higher the lighting ratio, the more contrast you have to deal with.
16. _____ lighting is a lighting style in which three lights (typically a key, fill, and rim light) are used to light a subject.
    A. Rembrandt
    B. Three-point
    C. Broad
    D. Rim
17. To achieve a _____ lighting setup, place one light above and directly behind the camera, angled down at the subject.
    A. short
    B. broad
    C. split
    D. butterfly
18. _____ lighting is a lighting style in which the small loop of shadow on a subject's nose is long enough to merge with the shadow on their cheek.
    A. Loop
    B. Rembrandt
    C. Single
    D. Broad
19. _____ lighting is a lighting style in which light is placed around the edges of a subject from behind, outlining them in light.
    A. Three-point
    B. Short
    C. Rim
    D. Butterfly

Apply and Analyze

1. What are the three common qualities that help contribute to the atmosphere of a photo?
2. How can you create a softer lighting effect on a subject with only one light?
3. List three situations in which you may not want to achieve all three typical lighting goals.
4. Describe one of the three options for lighting compositions outside of a photography studio.
5. If you do not have an additional light available, what can you use to bounce light from the key light back onto your subject?

Critical Thinking

1. Figuring out how to expose your photographs properly is a crucial part of the photography process. However, there may be situations in which you want to achieve a specific effect. What are some situations in which you would want to intentionally underexpose or overexpose a photo?
2. Imagine you are asked to take dramatic photos for a client, but you only have one light available. Do you think you can achieve a dramatic image with just one light, or do you think you would need more lights or accessories?

Suggested Activities

1. Find a subject to photograph and set up a three-point lighting setup with a key light, fill light, and rim light. Take three photos of your subject and examine how the light affects your image. Now, keep your key light in place and substitute your fill and rim light with reflectors. You may need to recruit two classmates to hold the reflectors for you. Take three more photos. Select the best photo from each setup and compare them. What are the visible differences between the photograph with three lights and the photograph with one light and two reflectors?
2. Choose a famous photographer and study their portfolio of work. Select three of your favorite photographs and identify the following: a lighting setup or style (if any), the mood they created in the photos, and any other notes or interesting observations about how light affected the photo. Create a short presentation documenting your findings and observations.

Communicating about Photography

1. **Speaking and Writing.** Choose one of the lights discussed in this chapter (key, fill, rim, or background). In your own words, explain the type of light to the class. Talk about the effect of the light.

2. **Speaking and Listening.** In small groups, discuss with your classmates—in basic, everyday language—your knowledge of the different types of lighting setups. Take notes on the observations expressed. Then review the points discussed, factoring in your new knowledge of lighting setups. Develop a summary of what you have learned about lighting setups and present it to the class. Use the terms that you have learned in this chapter.

Chapter 11
Making Exposure Decisions

Learning Objectives

After completing this chapter, you will be able to:
- Understand how to obtain proper exposure.
- Determine proper exposure using your camera's built-in light meter.
- Make appropriate corrections to resolve exposure problems.
- Select appropriate aperture/shutter speed combinations for different situations.
- Identify the various types of lighting used in photography.

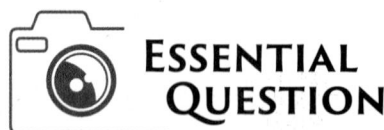

How does exposure affect how you make a picture?

Technical Terms

ambient lighting
blocked shadows
burned-out highlights
center-weighted averaging
circles of confusion
clipping
depth of field
diffusing
digital noise
equivalent exposures
evaluative metering
exposure bracketing
exposure compensation
fill flash
focusing mark
high key
histogram
hyperfocal distance
low key
metering modes
partial metering
permissible circle of confusion
plane of focus
proper exposure
sidelighted
spot metering
white balance bracketing

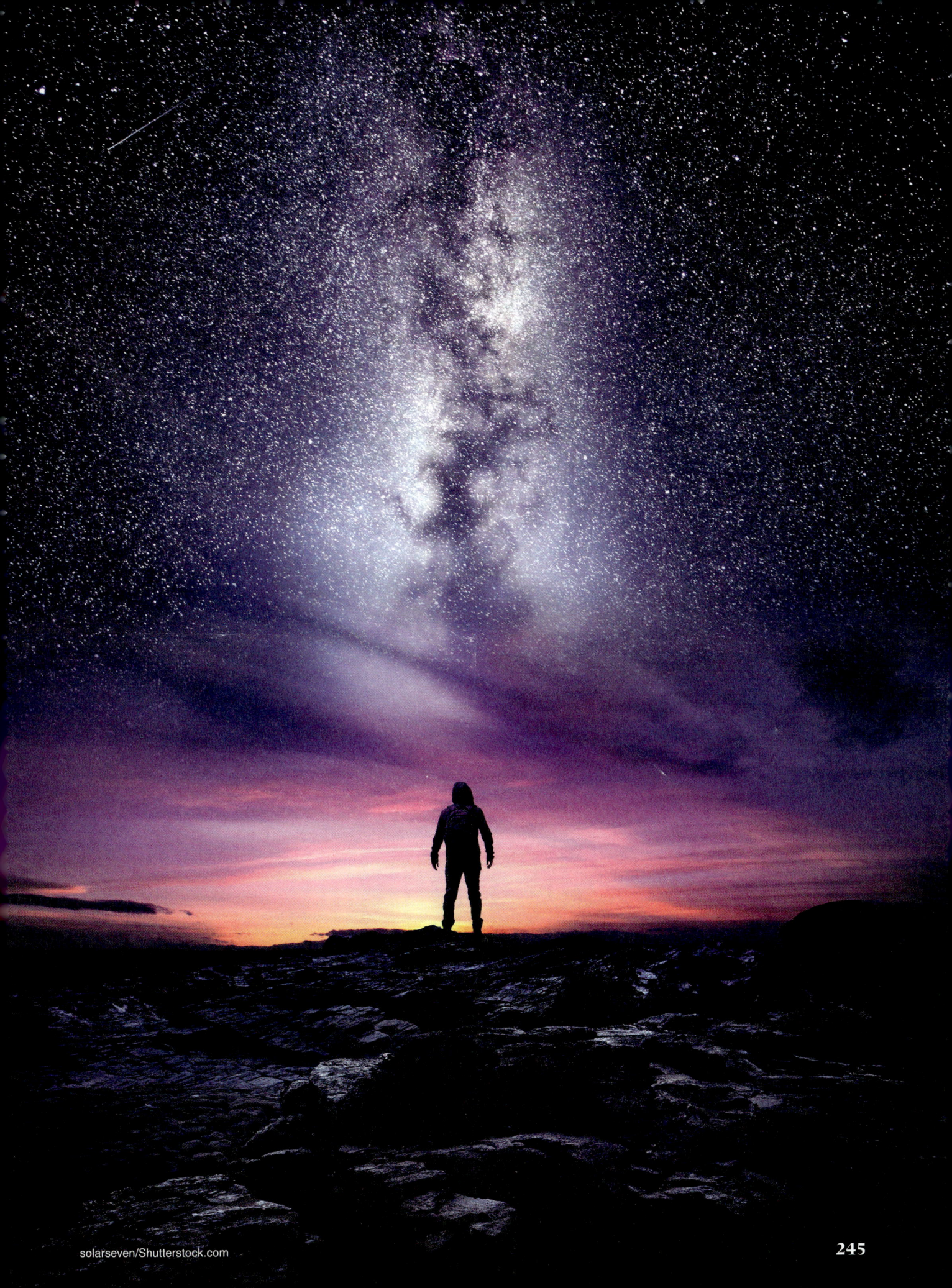

Introduction to Making Exposure Decisions

If you want to move beyond *taking* pictures and begin *making* pictures, you will be faced with many decisions. While Chapter 9, *Making a Picture*, discussed composition and other artistic considerations, this chapter concentrates on the technical decisions needed to achieve a proper exposure. In the automatic mode, your camera makes all the exposure decisions. In the manual, shutter priority, aperture priority, and Program AE modes, you must make those decisions.

Proper Exposure

What is a proper exposure? It could be described as one that is not too dark or too light, but just right. However, that description is subjective—what is too dark for one photographer might be just right for another. Furthermore, some scenes are **high key** (predominately shades of white or light tones), while others are **low key** (predominately dark tones). The technical definition for **proper exposure** is the correct combination of aperture, shutter speed, and ISO that best reflects the image that the photographer is trying to shoot.

Some characteristics of exposure are objective rather than subjective. A properly exposed photo does not display featureless white **burned-out highlights** (overexposed, featureless areas of an image that occur when the amount of light in a scene is too much for the camera's sensor to handle) or equally featureless black areas of **blocked shadows** (underexposed, featureless areas of an image that occur when there is not enough light on a subject). See **Figure 11-1**. Except in the case of high-key or low-key subjects, photographs should display a full range of tonal values from shadows through midtones to highlights, **Figure 11-2**.

For many photographers, choosing the right combination of shutter speed and aperture to make a proper exposure is a difficult decision. To complicate matters, the exposure situation keeps changing. The speed and f-stop combination suitable for one scene is often incorrect for another scene.

To find out whether their exposure choices were correct, digital photographers can assess image exposure immediately by using the camera's histogram. As defined in Chapter 4, *Camera Handling, Care, and Support*, a **histogram** is a bar graph that displays all the tonal values of an image.

There is no perfect or ideal shape for a histogram, but it should display the following, as shown in **Figure 11-3**:

- A good range of tones, spreading across most of the space on the graph
- No **clipping**, or loss of shadows or highlights in a digital file, which are indicated by tall vertical lines at the extreme left and/or right ends of the graph
- No obvious gaps (spaces) that indicate missing groups of tones

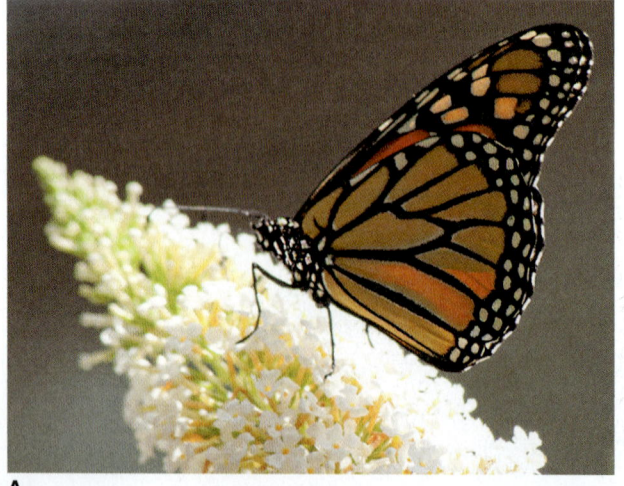

A

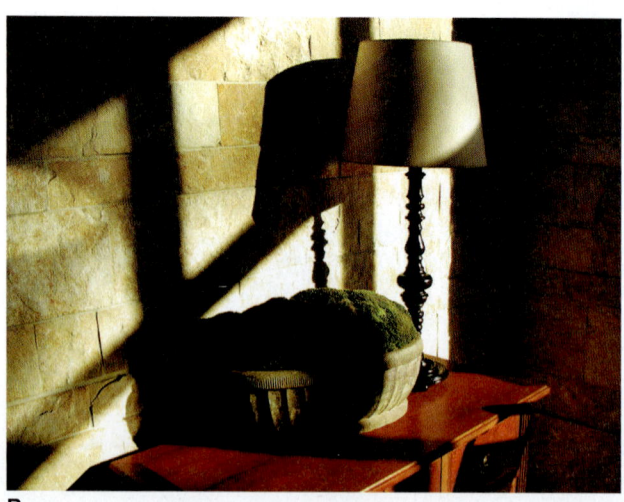

B

Jack Klasey/Goodheart-Willcox Publisher

Figure 11-1. Exposure defects. A—Highlight areas are blank, with no texture or detail. B—Blocked shadow areas are totally black, without detail or texture.

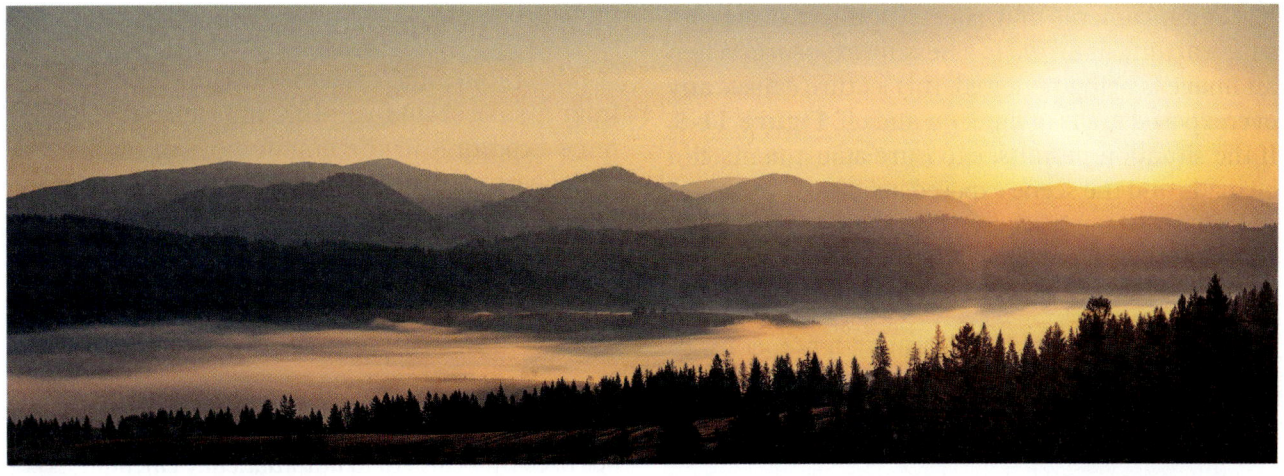

Stone36/Shutterstock.com

Figure 11-2. A wide tonal range, from deep black shadows to brilliant white highlights. A full palette of middle tones is evident.

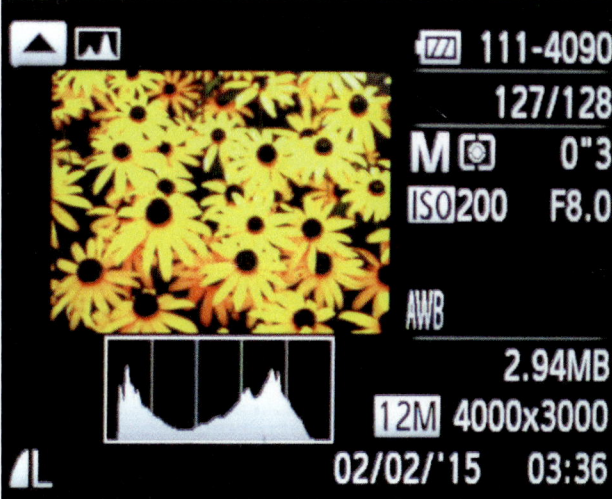

Jack Klasey/Goodheart-Willcox Publisher

Figure 11-3. A histogram displaying proper exposure, with no clipping of highlights or shadows.

The left and right ends of the histogram are the areas where problems usually appear. A graph that is weighted heavily toward the left end indicates an underexposed image. A graph that is "bunched" at the right end shows overexposure. See **Figure 11-4**.

Exposing for Highlights

Digital photographers are often advised to underexpose by 1/3 or 1/2 stop to retain highlight detail. While this approach is sometimes worthwhile, it should not be standard practice. Try to make as perfect an exposure as you can, then check the histogram and increase or decrease exposure based on what it shows.

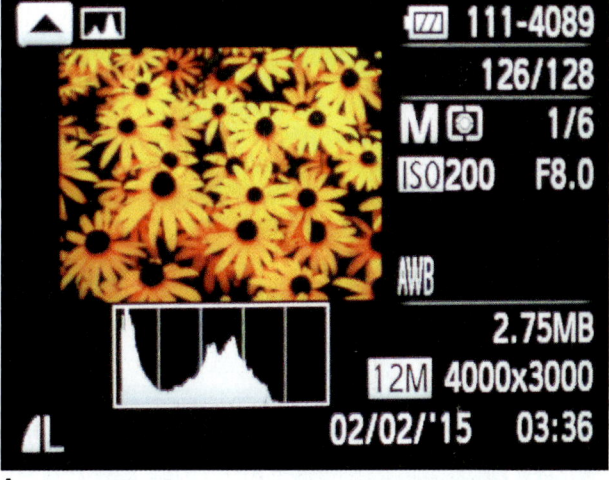

A

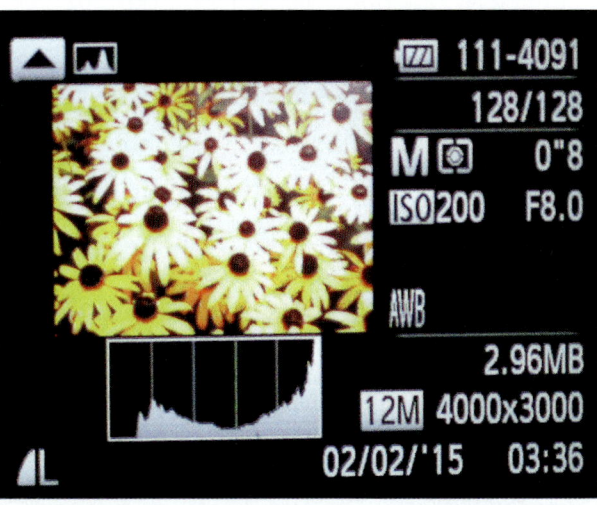

B

Jack Klasey/Goodheart-Willcox Publisher

Figure 11-4. Exposure defects shown on a histogram. A—Underexposure. B—Overexposure.

Chapter 11 Making Exposure Decisions **247**

Digital cameras may offer a highlight overexposure warning as an aid to assessing exposure. When an image is being reviewed, this feature causes any overexposed areas to blink on and off, **Figure 11-5**. If the situation permits, exposure adjustments can be made and the scene exposed again.

Determining Exposure

In the early days of photography, a proper exposure often depended on the ability to judge the particular combination of shutter speed and aperture required by a given scene. A sunny day meant a small aperture and relatively fast shutter speed. A dark day indicated a wider aperture and slower shutter speed. Today, photographers generally rely on their camera's built-in meter to determine exposure.

Using Built-in Meters

Meters built into cameras measure light reflected from a subject and use this information to determine exposure. In the automatic, shutter priority, and aperture priority shooting modes, metering information is used to set shutter speed, aperture, or both. In manual mode, the reading indicates whether chosen settings will underexpose or overexpose the image. This allows the photographer to adjust shutter and aperture settings as needed.

For use in different situations, in-camera meters offer two or more *metering modes*, or different methods used by a camera to automatically calculate exposure. See **Figure 11-6**. Advanced camera models allow the photographer to select the metering mode.

Evaluative metering is a metering mode in which light reflected from the scene is read and analyzed using a number of points spread across the

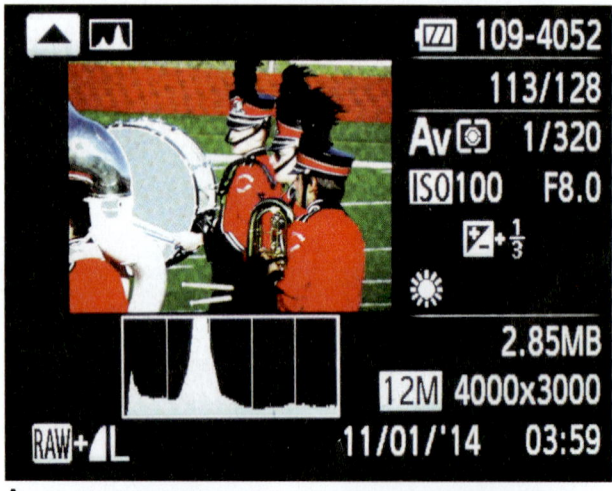

A

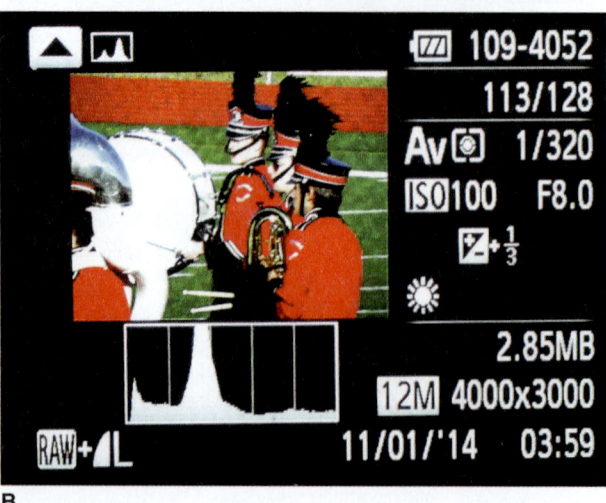

B

Jack Klasey/Goodheart-Willcox Publisher

Figure 11-5. Highlight overexposure warning. A—Blink on. B—Blink off.

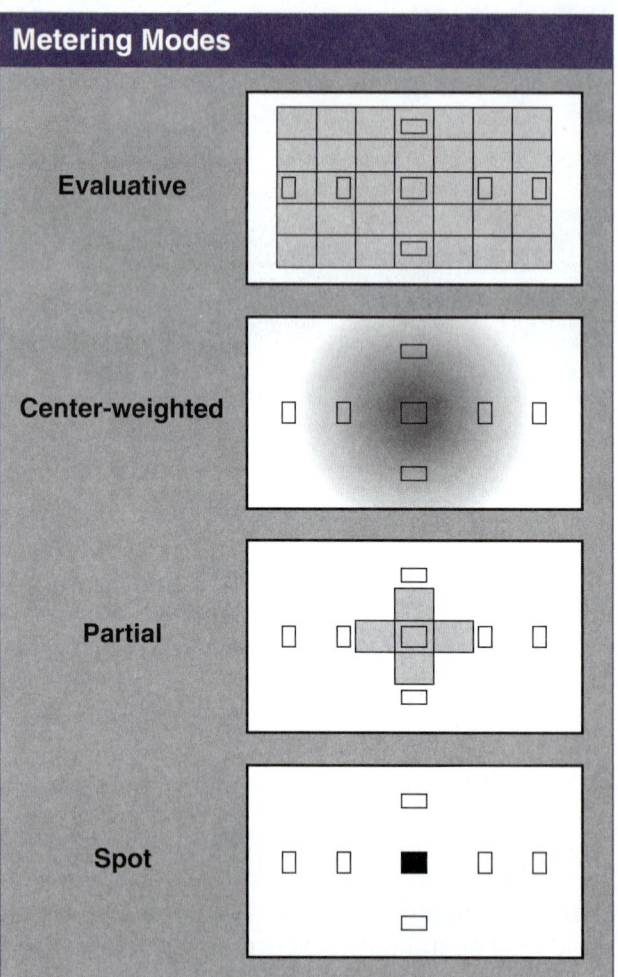

Goodheart-Willcox Publisher

Figure 11-6. Metering modes used by in-camera exposure meters.

field of view. The shadows, highlights, and midtones are evaluated to produce an averaged reading that usually results in an acceptable exposure. It is the most common mode.

Center-weighted averaging is a metering mode that gives greater importance (weight) to information from the center of the frame than to information from the edges. An average reading is then developed for the scene.

Partial metering and spot metering make exposure readings from only part of the scene, which is a particular advantage when photographing backlit subjects. ***Partial metering*** is a metering mode that reads information from a small area (usually about 10%) in the center of the frame. ***Spot metering*** is a metering mode that reads information from an even smaller area in the frame—as little as 1% in some cameras.

Meter readings produce an exposure value for middle gray, equivalent to a tone that reflects 18% of the light that falls on it. When a scene is properly exposed for its middle gray value, the darker and lighter tones in the scene will generally reproduce correctly.

Large areas of very bright or very dark subject matter create a metering problem. These areas fool the meter and result in readings that produce an underexposed or overexposed image. When the subject is very bright, such as a field of fresh snow, the meter senses too much light and returns a middle gray value to prevent overexposure. For a very dark subject, the meter does not sense enough light and returns a middle gray value to prevent underexposure.

For a very bright subject, more exposure is needed. Opening up (increasing aperture size) by 1 to 1 1/2 stops will result in snow that is white, not gray. See **Figure 11-7**. A very dark subject needs less exposure. Stopping down (decreasing aperture size) by 1 to 1 1/2 stops renders black as truly black.

Correcting Exposure Problems

To correct underexposure or overexposure, increase or decrease (respectively) the amount of light falling on the camera's sensor. This is commonly done in two ways:

- In manual shooting mode, change either the aperture or the shutter speed for a single adjustment. Alternatively, bracket the metered exposure with increased or decreased exposures.
- In Program AE, shutter priority, or aperture priority mode, use the camera's exposure compensation feature to increase or decrease exposure. As in manual mode, this can be done as a single exposure adjustment or as bracketed exposures.

Exposure Bracketing

Exposure bracketing is a method of exposure in which the scene is shot three times—once at the exposure indicated by the meter, once at a decreased exposure value, and once at an increased exposure value.

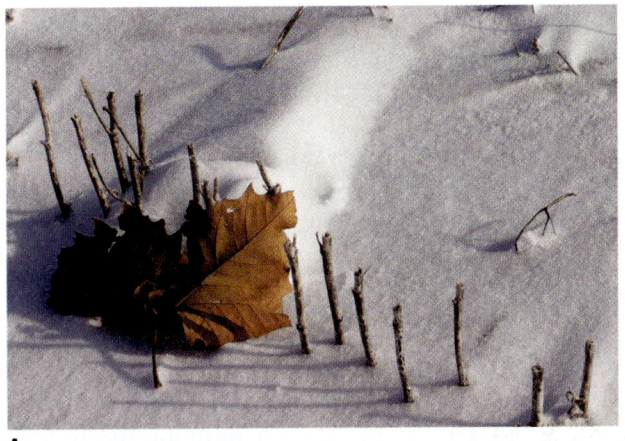
A

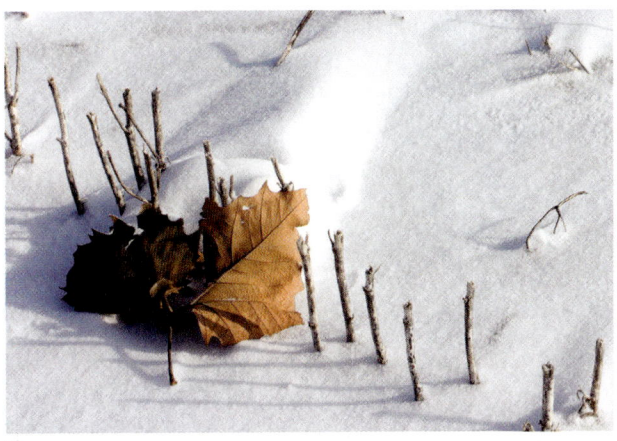
B

Jack Klasey/Goodheart-Willcox Publisher

Figure 11-7. Exposing for bright subjects. A—The metered exposure rendered the snow as gray. B—Opening up one stop renders the snow as white and presents other colors accurately.

Some digital cameras offer automatic exposure bracketing (AEB). The camera's AEB control can be set to decrease or increase exposure, usually in 1/3 stop increments, by up to two stops. Most cameras make the metered exposure first, then the decreased exposure, and finally the increased exposure. See **Figure 11-8**. You can also combine the images in Adobe Lightroom or Adobe Photoshop to achieve an average exposure, **Figure 11-9**.

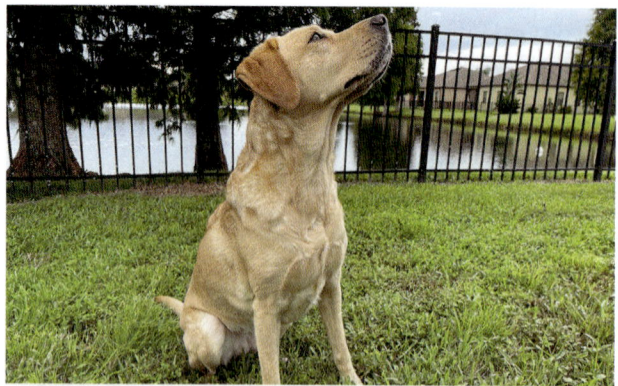

A

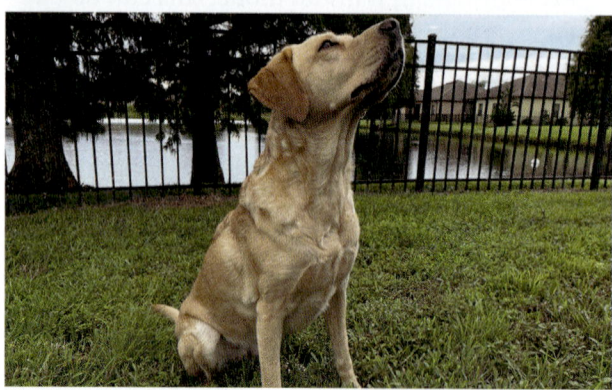

B

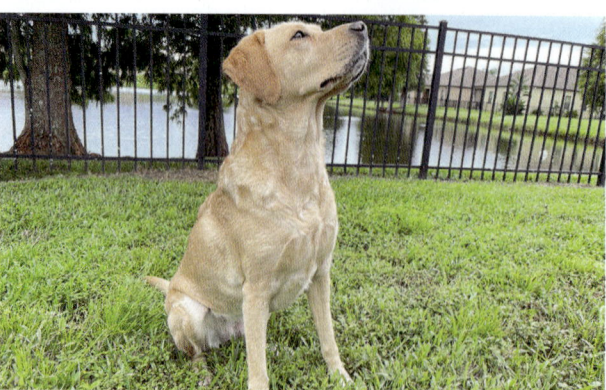

C

Goodheart-Willcox Publisher

Figure 11-8. Exposure bracketing. A—Metered exposure (1/500 second at f/5.6). B—Underexposure (1/1000 second at f/5.6). C—Overexposure (1/250 second at f/5.6).

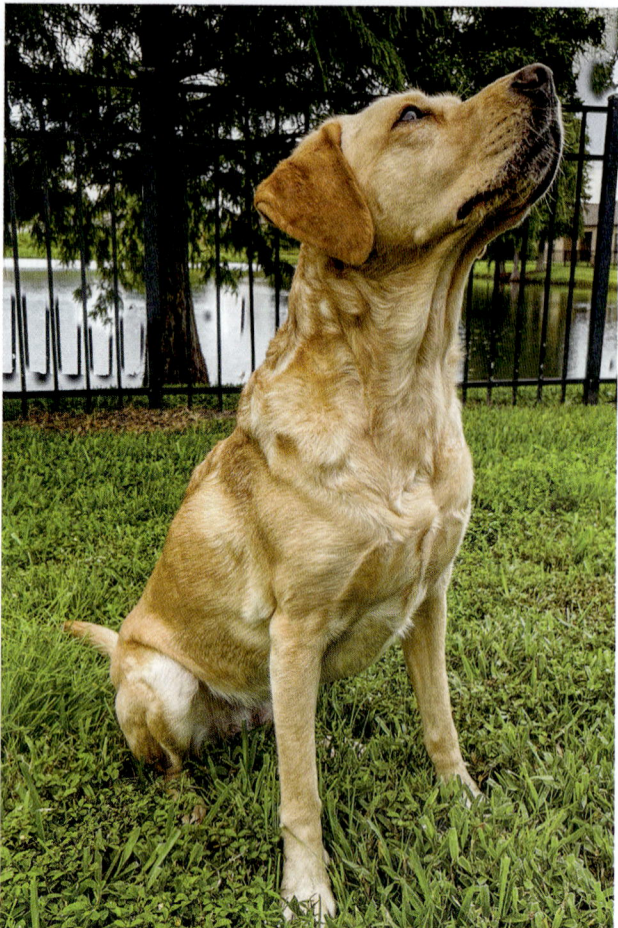

Goodheart-Willcox Publisher

Figure 11-9. An average of the images used for exposure bracketing in Adobe Lightroom.

Exposure Compensation

You may need to increase or decrease the metered exposure in special lighting situations. If you are using the camera's manual settings, you can adjust either the aperture or shutter speed to make a proper exposure. If you are shooting in shutter priority or aperture priority mode, however, you cannot override the meter reading. If you change one setting, the camera adjusts the other to allow the same amount of light to reach the sensor.

The *exposure compensation* feature on DSLRs and some advanced compact cameras allows you to increase or decrease exposure while using the shutter priority or aperture priority modes. You can select an increase or decrease of as much as three stops, typically in 1/3 stop increments. See **Figure 11-10**. A plus setting lightens the image, and a minus setting darkens it.

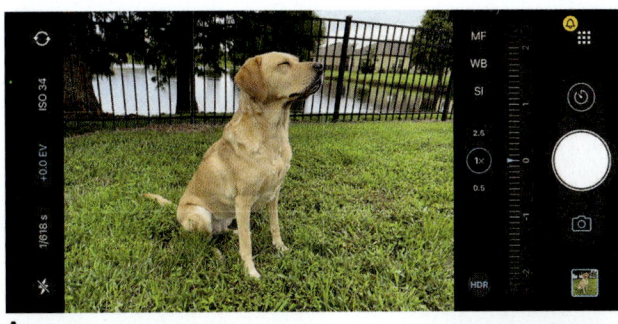

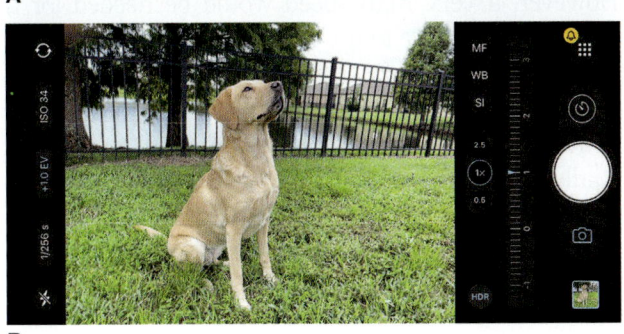

Equivalent Exposures			
f/2	1/2	f/2	1/2
f/2.8	1/4	f/2.8	1/4
f/4	1/8	f/4	1/8
f/5.6	1/15	f/5.6	1/15
f/8	1/30	f/8	1/30
f/11	1/60	f/11	1/60
f/16	1/125	f/16	1/125
f/22	1/250	f/22	1/250
f/32	1/500	f/32	1/500
f/45	1/1000	f/45	1/1000
Stop Down		**Open Up**	

Goodheart-Willcox Publisher

Goodheart-Willcox Publisher

Figure 11-10. Exposure compensation. A—Scale is set to 0 stop. B—Scale is set to +1, which changed exposure time from 1/2 second to one second, lightening the image.

Figure 11-11. Equivalent exposure examples. The metered exposure is f/11 @ 1/60. Left—Stopping down by two stops, from f/11 to f/22, moves the shutter speed two steps in the opposite direction. Right—Opening up by four stops.

Equivalent Exposures

Many different combinations of aperture and shutter speed can be used to allow the same amount of light to reach the image receiver. For example, the pairs 1/60 at f/8 and 1/250 at f/4 result in identical exposure values. Such pairs are called *equivalent exposures*. In the shutter priority, aperture priority, or Program AE modes, the camera calculates and sets an equivalent exposure if you change either the shutter speed or the aperture.

Remember that a one-stop change in aperture either doubles the amount of light reaching the image receiver or cuts it in half. The same relationships apply to changing shutter speeds. To quickly calculate equivalent exposures, count stops or shutter speed units in opposite directions. As shown in **Figure 11-11**, if you make your aperture smaller by two stops, you move two shutter speed units in the opposite direction, so the shutter is open longer.

Memorizing the sequence of f-stops and shutter speeds found on your cameras and lenses allows you to easily determine equivalent exposures.

Shutter Speed vs. Aperture Trade-offs

To achieve specific effects, you can select different shutter speed/aperture combinations. Fast shutter speeds and the resulting large apertures are typically chosen to capture action. Small apertures and the resulting slow shutter speeds achieve greater *depth of field* (the distance between the nearest and farthest objects that are in acceptably sharp focus) with stationary subjects. When capturing action, choose shutter priority. For situations where depth of field is important, select aperture priority. Some photographers favor these modes over full manual shooting, since only one variable (shutter speed or aperture) must be selected.

Using Higher Shutter Speeds to Capture Action

Selecting a shutter speed to stop the movement of a subject involves three factors:
- Speed of the subject's motion
- Direction of the subject's movement in relation to the camera
- Distance of the subject from the camera

The rate at which your subject is moving affects the choice of shutter speed. For example, stopping the motion of a motorcyclist requires a faster shutter speed than stopping the movement of a pedestrian.

The direction of the subject's movement in relation to the camera has a major effect on motion-stopping capability. See **Figure 11-12**. When the subject is moving directly toward or away from the camera, movement may be stopped by a relatively low shutter speed. A subject moving at an angle across the camera's field of view requires a somewhat faster shutter speed. The highest shutter speeds are needed to stop motion of subjects moving directly across the field of view.

A subject that is close to the camera crosses the field of view more rapidly than a subject that is far away, so a faster shutter speed is needed. A distant subject that is moving slowly toward or away from the camera is easily stopped with a relatively slow shutter speed. However, a very high speed would be needed for a subject that is close to the camera and moving rapidly across the field of view. See **Figure 11-13**.

The trade-off of using a high shutter speed to stop action is usually a shallow zone of sharp focus. The shallow depth of field results from the need to use large apertures to provide the proper exposure. This may be relieved by using a higher ISO setting. Each step upward in ISO gains one stop at a given shutter speed.

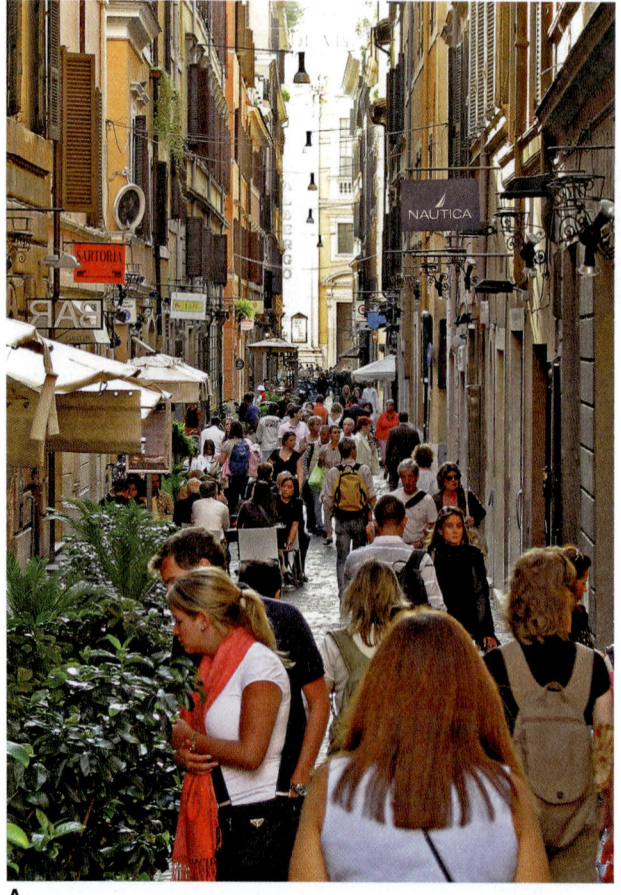

A

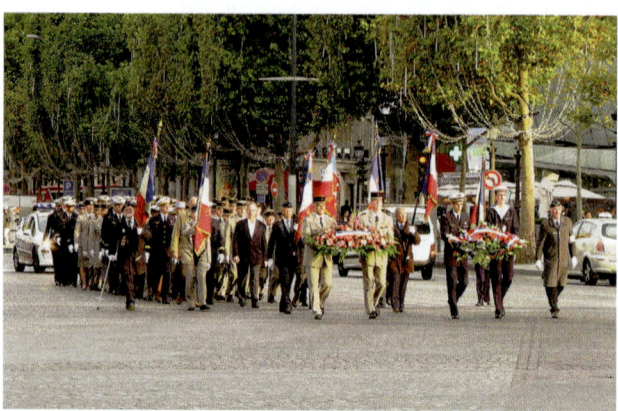

B

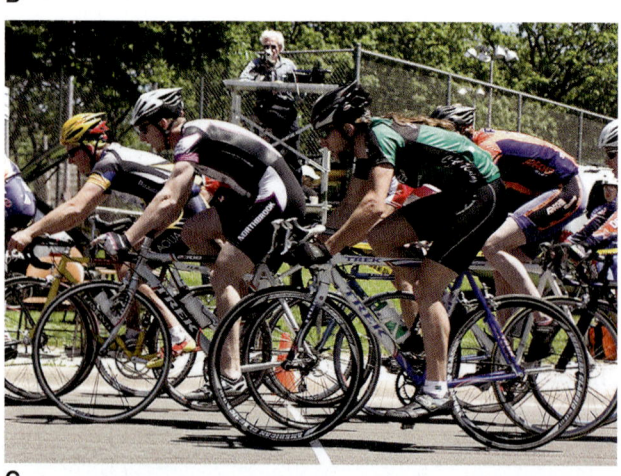

C

Jack Klasey/Goodheart-Willcox Publisher

Figure 11-12. Apparent motion. A—Moving directly toward or away from the camera. B—Diagonal movement. C—Moving across the field of view.

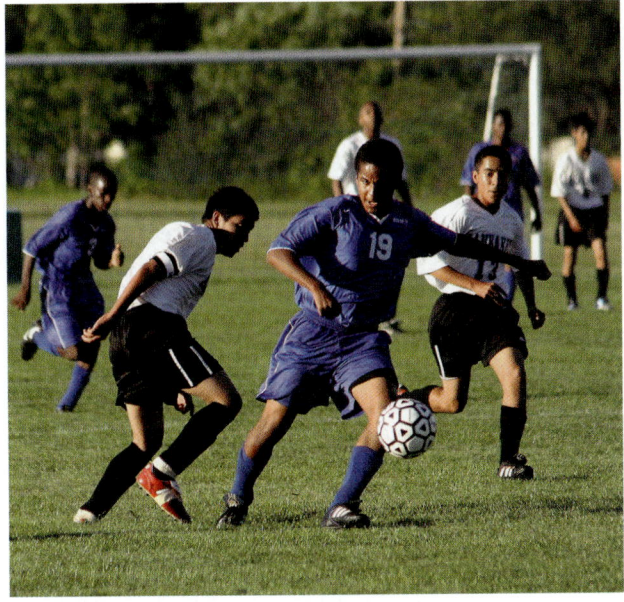

Jack Klasey/Goodheart-Willcox Publisher

Figure 11-13. Rapid movement and nearness to the camera require a high shutter speed to stop motion.

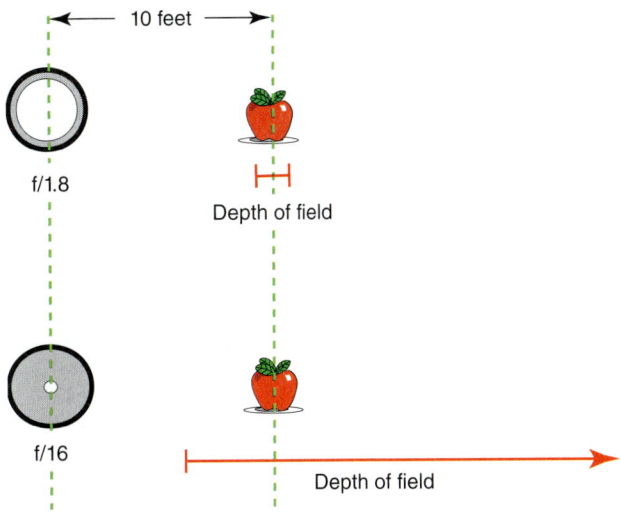

Goodheart-Willcox Publisher

Figure 11-14. With a 50 mm lens focused on an object 10′ away, depth of field at f/1.8 is measured in inches. At f/16, depth of field extends from approximately 6′ to almost 30′.

Using Smaller Apertures to Maximize Depth of Field

If motion is not a factor, aperture becomes more important than shutter speed. The size of the lens opening is the major element in controlling depth of field, or how much of the scene will be in focus. In mountain landscape photography, depth of field may be measured in miles, while in close-up flower photography, it may be in fractions of an inch. As the aperture becomes larger, depth of field decreases. Conversely, as the aperture becomes smaller, depth of field increases. See **Figure 11-14**.

Technically, only a single part of a scene, or the **plane of focus**, can be in sharp focus. Parts of the scene closer to or farther from the camera will be progressively softer or out of focus, **Figure 11-15**. The limited resolving power of the human eye finds focus to be apparently sharp in a zone extending some distance in front of and behind the plane of focus. That is why the term "appears to be in sharp focus" was used when defining depth of field.

Sharpness of focus results from the way that light rays reflected from the subject are refracted by the lens and projected onto the image receiver plane. As shown in **Figure 11-16**, each point of light reflected from the subject has a corresponding point on the plane of the image receiver. Points from the plane of focus are represented as points on the image receiver, but points in front of or behind the

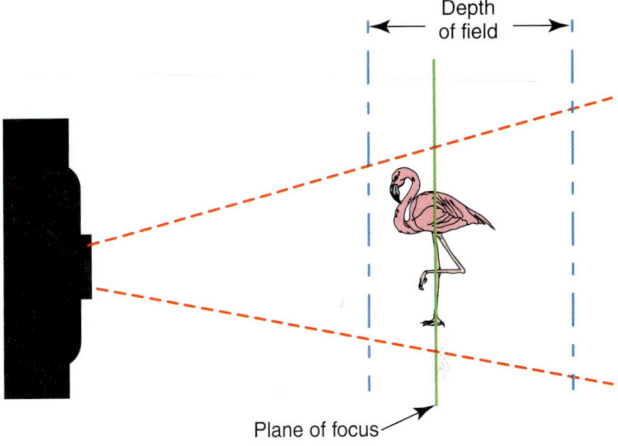

Goodheart-Willcox Publisher

Figure 11-15. The zone of acceptable sharpness is usually considered to be one-third in front of the plane of focus and two-thirds behind it.

plane of focus appear as small circles and become larger as the distance of the originating point from the plane of focus increases. These circles are called **circles of confusion**. The size of these circles determines sharpness of the image on the receiver. Up to a certain diameter, a circle is seen as a point, and thus appears to be sharp. Depending on individual eyesight and other factors, the size of the **permissible circle of confusion** (the largest diameter circle that is seen as a point and thus appears to be sharp at normal distance) varies. It is generally defined as a circle 1/100″ in diameter on a 6″ × 8″ print when viewed from a distance of 10″.

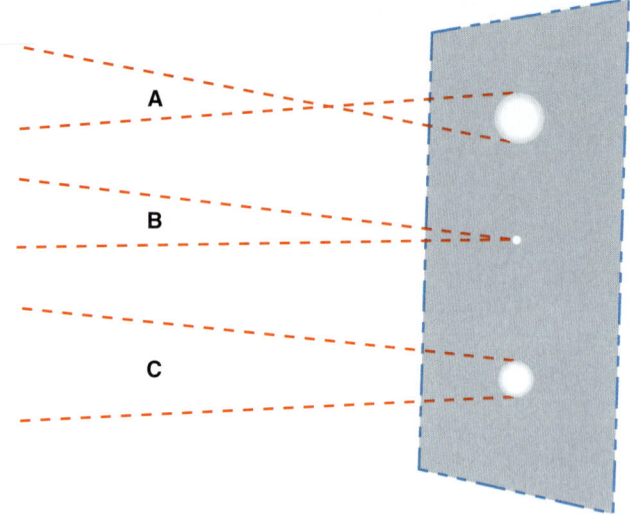

Figure 11-16. Circles of confusion. A—Light rays from an object farther away than the plane of focus. B—Light rays from an object at plane of focus. C—Light rays from an object nearer than the plane of focus.

Factors Controlling Depth of Field

How much or how little depth of field you can obtain in a specific photographic situation is governed by three factors—the distance of the subject from the camera, the f-stop used, and the focal length of the lens. You often can alter one, two, or all three factors, allowing considerable control. The ways in which these factors can be altered are as follows:

- **Subject distance.** The farther the subject is from the camera, the greater the depth of field, and vice versa. As shown in **Figure 11-17**, if you focus on a subject 5′ away from the camera, the depth of field might be from about 4′ to 7′. When you take a few steps backward, so the subject is 10′ away, and then refocus, you increase depth of field by four times. Objects in the scene now will be in acceptable focus from about 6.5′ to almost 18′ away.
- **F-stop.** This is the control factor most often used to alter depth of field. The relationship of f-stops to depth of field is the same as their relationship to exposure, but in reverse. Stopping down increases depth of field, while opening up decreases depth of field. By adjusting shutter speed to compensate, you can adjust depth of field while maintaining correct exposure. See **Figure 11-18**.
- **Focal length.** The choice of lens has a considerable effect on depth of field. Changing from a 50 mm lens to a 100 mm lens while

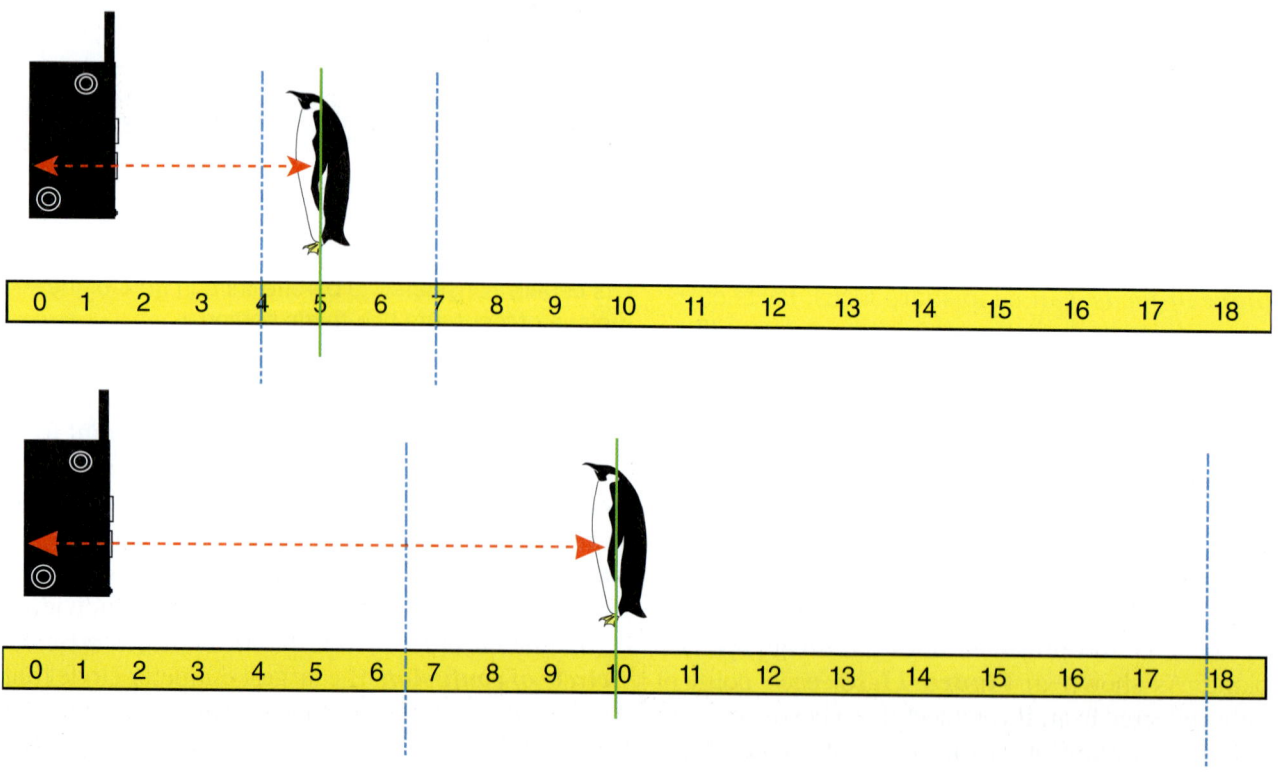

Figure 11-17. The distance of the subject from the camera is a factor in depth of field.

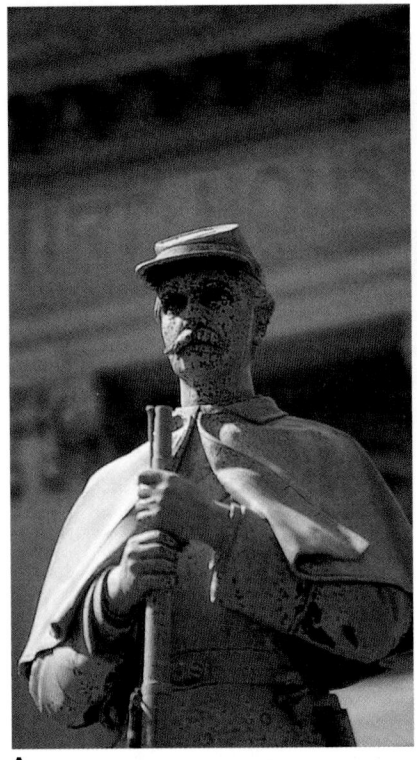 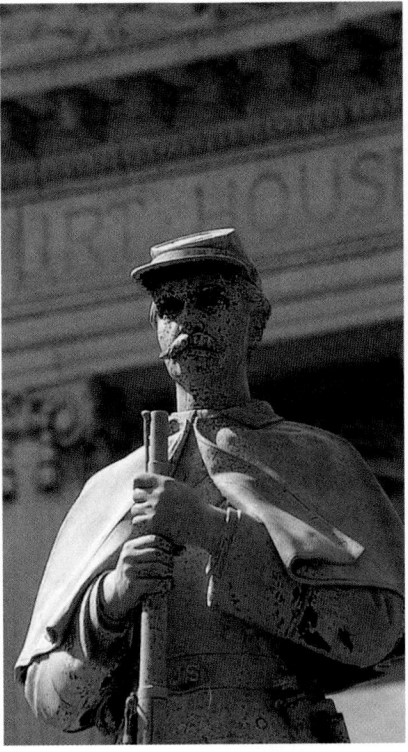 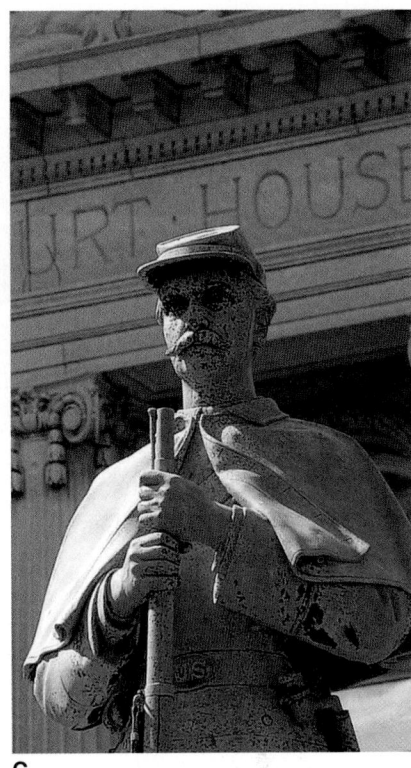

Jack Klasey/Goodheart-Willcox Publisher

Figure 11-18. Stopping down increases depth of field. A—Aperture at f/5.6. B—Aperture at f/11. C—Aperture at f/32.

maintaining the same f-stop and subject distance cuts depth of field in half. Moving from a 50 mm lens to a 24 mm lens doubles depth of field. If the camera is moved to keep the image the same size with each of the lenses, however, depth of field will be exactly the same.

To maximize depth of field, use all three control factors. Focus on a subject that is reasonably distant from the camera, use the smallest practical f-stop, and select a wide-angle lens.

Determining Depth of Field

Most older lenses include depth of field scales to permit direct reading of the distances in acceptable focus. The scale has markings for the lens apertures on either side of the focusing mark. A *focusing mark* is a short line or a dot on a manual focus lens that is used to determine the distance from the camera to the subject, **Figure 11-19A**. After focusing on the subject, you can determine the distance from the camera by noting the number on the distance scales that is aligned with the focusing mark. Distances appearing above the markings for the selected f-stop will be the nearest point in focus (left-hand mark) and the most distant point in focus (right-hand mark). Some newer lenses show depth of field on a small LCD display, **Figure 11-19B**.

For lenses without scales, a depth-of-field table must be used. Data sheets packed with a new lens and various reference books provide such tables.

Hyperfocal Distance

To obtain the greatest possible depth of field for a given lens at a specific aperture, set the lens at its *hyperfocal distance*, which is the nearest point that is in sharp focus when the lens is focused on infinity. This distance is different for each f-stop and each focal length. If the lens is set to the hyperfocal distance, focus will be sharp from one-half that distance to infinity.

To find the hyperfocal distance of a lens without a depth of field scale, a chart must be used. Finding the hyperfocal distance on a lens with a depth of field scale is simple. See **Figure 11-20**.

The hyperfocal method is useful in landscape and nature photography, as well as in street photography or similar situations where you wish to be unobtrusive. It is also helpful in sports or action photography where focusing on a rapidly changing scene would be difficult.

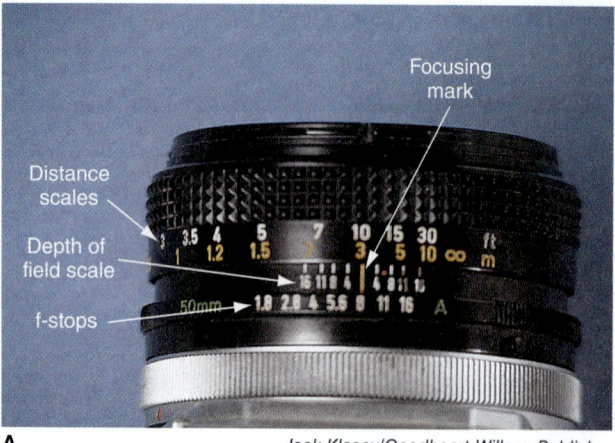
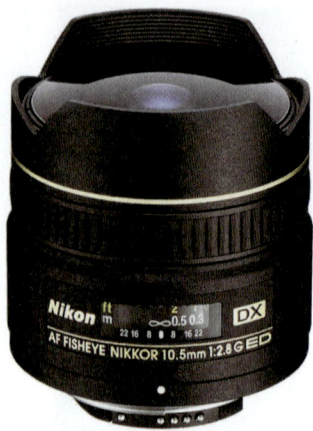

Figure 11-19. Depth of field scales. A—Physical scale used on older lens. In this example, depth of field at f/8 will be from about 8′ to almost 15′. B—Newer lens with an LCD display.

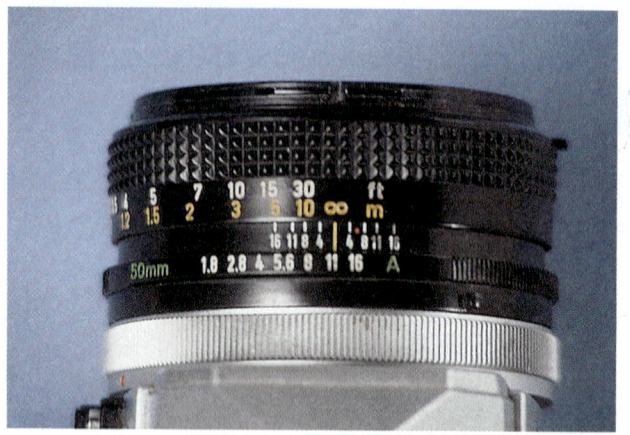
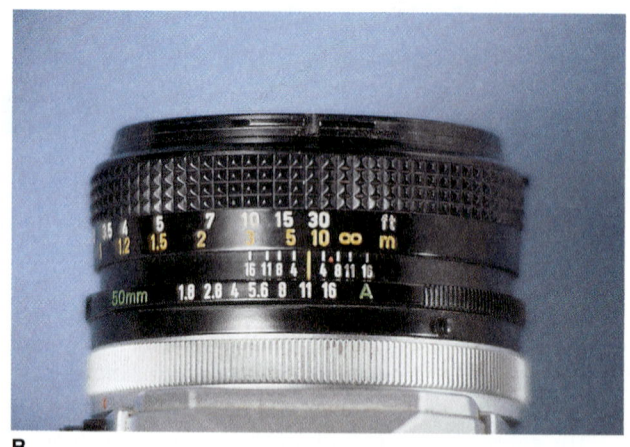

Figure 11-20. Hyperfocal focusing. A—Aligning the infinity symbol on the focusing mark. B—Aligning the hyperfocal distance with the focusing mark.

PROCEDURE

Finding the Hyperfocal Distance

1. Align the infinity symbol (∞) on the focusing mark.
2. On the left-hand scale, note the distance (in feet or meters) shown above the mark for the appropriate f-stop. This is the hyperfocal distance.
3. Rotate the focusing ring until the hyperfocal distance found in Step 2 is aligned with the focusing mark.
4. Find the distance figure above the appropriate f-stop on the left-hand scale. It will be one-half the hyperfocal distance. Everything from that point to infinity will be in focus.

Effect of ISO Settings on Exposure

You can use the range of ISO ratings, in combination with aperture and shutter speed settings, to capture usable images under a wide variety of conditions. Increasing the camera's ISO setting is especially helpful under low-light conditions where the indicated shutter speed is too low for a successful handheld exposure. For each increase in ISO rating (such as from 100 to 200), you can gain one full step in shutter speed. For example, instead of 1/30 second, you could shoot at 1/60 second and properly expose the photo.

The danger of using higher ratings (especially above ISO 400) is increased digital noise in the image. **Digital noise** is specks of various colors that are most noticeable in shadows or areas of smooth color, such as clear skies, **Figure 11-21**.

Capturing the Light

How long an exposure is needed to take a photo of a black cat in a coal mine at midnight? What if the subject were a white rabbit instead of a black cat? Since the description "in a coal mine at midnight" indicates a condition of total darkness, you would not get a picture in either case. Without light, you cannot capture a photographic image.

Under the described conditions, you must supply the necessary light to obtain a photograph. The amount of light needed can be amazingly small—with a long-enough time exposure, a tiny birthday candle would allow you to capture a picture of that black cat. See **Figure 11-22**.

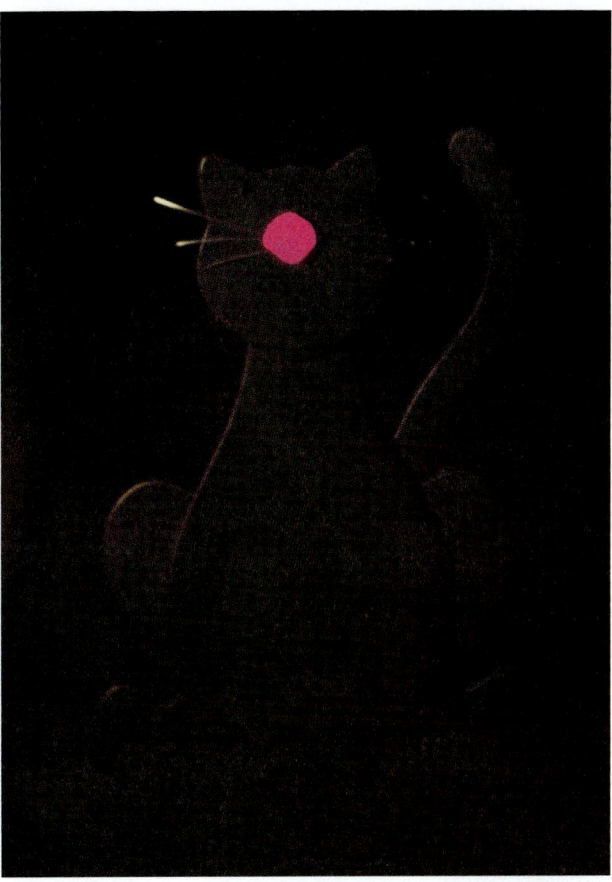

Jack Klasey/Goodheart-Willcox Publisher

Figure 11-22. A toy black cat photographed with light from a small birthday candle. Exposure was 1/30 second at f/8, with ISO set at 100.

Types of Lighting

Light necessary to make a photographic exposure can be natural, artificial, or a combination of the two. Outdoor photography usually involves working with natural light, while indoor photography is mostly done using artificial light. Natural light may be supplemented with artificial light when working outdoors, and vice versa when shooting indoors.

Natural Light

The intensity, color, and direction of natural light are all highly variable. At the beginning and end of the day, sunlight has a warm red-orange hue and a horizontal direction due to the rising or setting sun. During the rest of the day, sunlight is colder and bluer. At midday, sunlight is hardest and most intense, **Figure 11-23**. Light intensity and color are further modified by the presence of clouds. A thin layer of clouds softens, diffuses (disperses light over a

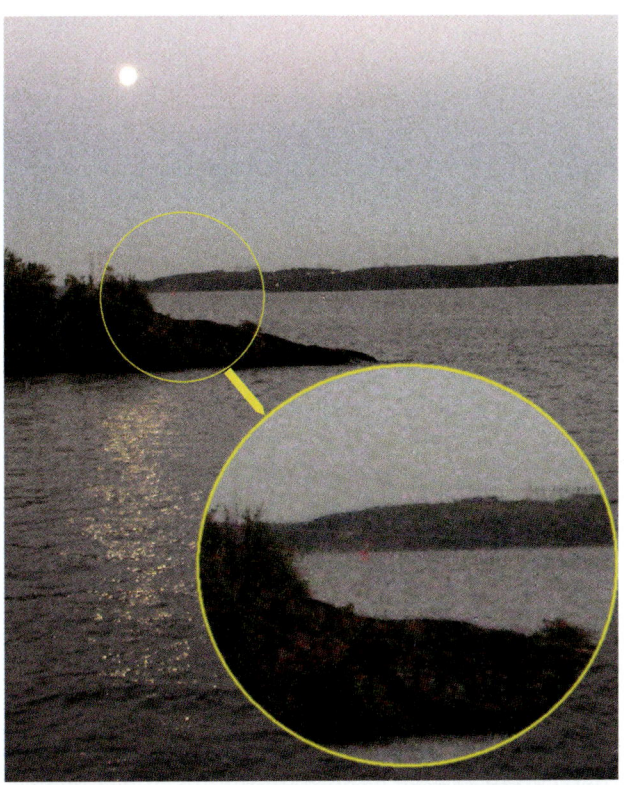

Jack Klasey/Goodheart-Willcox Publisher

Figure 11-21. An example of digital noise.

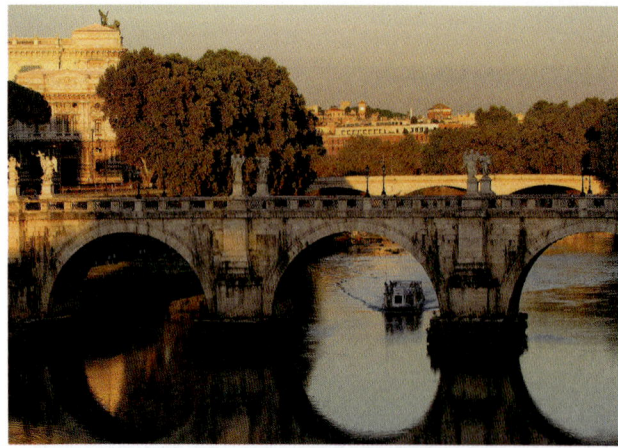

A

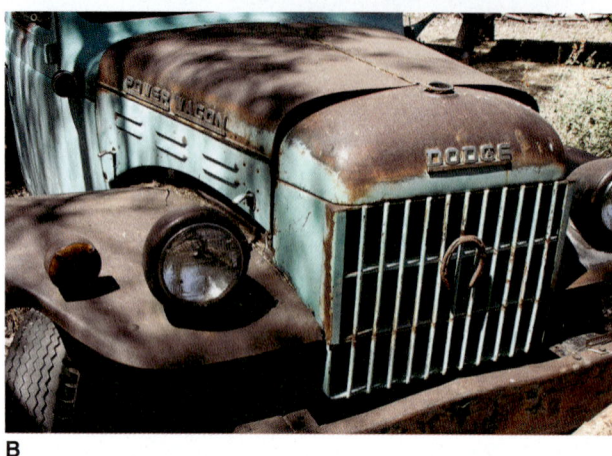

B

Jack Klasey/Goodheart-Willcox Publisher

Figure 11-23. Natural light. A—Warm, soft light from a setting sun. B—Harsh, bright midday light.

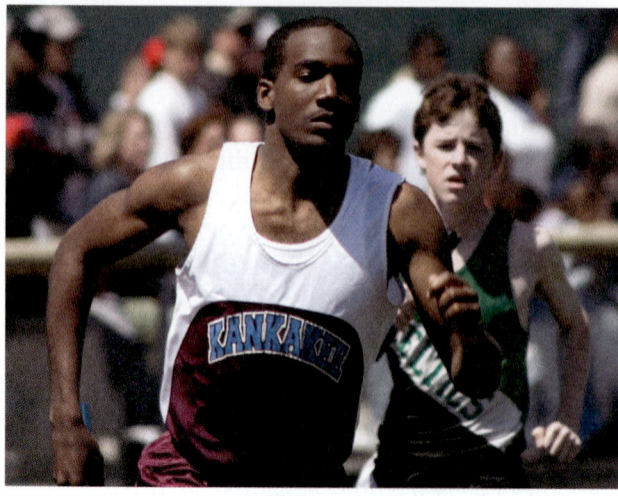

Jack Klasey/Goodheart-Willcox Publisher

Figure 11-24. Sidelighting from the sun at about a 45° angle to the horizon.

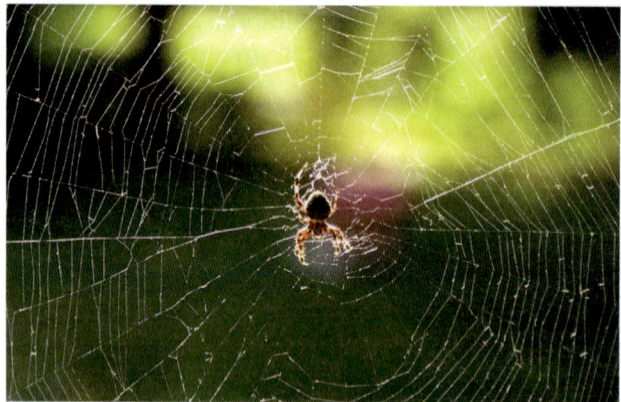

Jack Klasey/Goodheart-Willcox Publisher

Figure 11-25. A spider and a web backlit by the sun.

wide area), and slightly warms the light of the midday sun. Broken clouds present a photographic challenge since the intensity and color of the sunlight can change rapidly and unpredictably. They can also create challenges when it comes to shadows on your subject or other areas in your image.

The direction of light striking the subject must also be taken into account. A subject that is *sidelighted* (strongly lighted from one side) often exhibits strong contrast between the lighted and shadowed sides, providing a dramatic effect. See **Figure 11-24**. However, sidelighting can also result in an image with burned-out highlights or blocked and featureless shadows.

Backlighting can render a subject as a dramatic silhouette, or with more exposure, as a recognizable person or object against a bright background. Certain subjects exhibit a brightly glowing halo effect when backlit. See **Figure 11-25**.

Modifying Natural Light

Strong sunlight on a subject often produces an extreme range of contrast—highlights are too bright, and shadows are too dark. As a result, both lose detail. To remedy this problem, modify the light by reducing its intensity or by exposing for the highlights and adding light to the shadow areas.

Diffusing, or softening, the light falling on a subject decreases the range of contrast to retain detail in both shadow and highlight areas. The light can be diffused by placing a translucent material, such as tracing paper or white nylon fabric, between the light source and the subject. See **Figure 11-26**. The translucent material permits only a portion of the light to reach the subject. The image receiver can then capture detail in both highlights and shadows. Since less light is falling on the subject, an exposure adjustment is almost always necessary.

To reveal detail in the shadowed area of a side-lighted subject, additional light is needed. The simplest way to add light is to use a reflective material to bounce back some of the daylight, **Figure 11-27**. Some photographers use a simple white card, while others prefer silver or gold metallic reflectors. Silver material produces a somewhat harder light, while gold reflections are softer and warmer.

Adding artificial light to the shadowed area is also a possibility. Often, the added light is in the form of *fill flash*, light of reduced intensity used to brighten deep shadow areas to make them easier to see and appear more natural. Some cameras have a fill flash setting, while others allow you to use a separate flash at a fraction of its normal power. Some photographers leave the flash at full power setting but reduce and soften its light output by covering it with one or more layers of a white handkerchief or similar material.

Artificial Light

Photographers use three basic types of artificial lighting—ambient (room) lighting, portable (usually electronic flash) lighting, and studio lighting. Each has advantages and drawbacks, especially in terms of controllability. Ambient lighting is the least controllable, and studio lighting the most easily controlled.

Ambient Lighting

The lighting that already exists in a scene or space, without any additions, is called *ambient lighting*. Indoors, this lighting can be natural (such

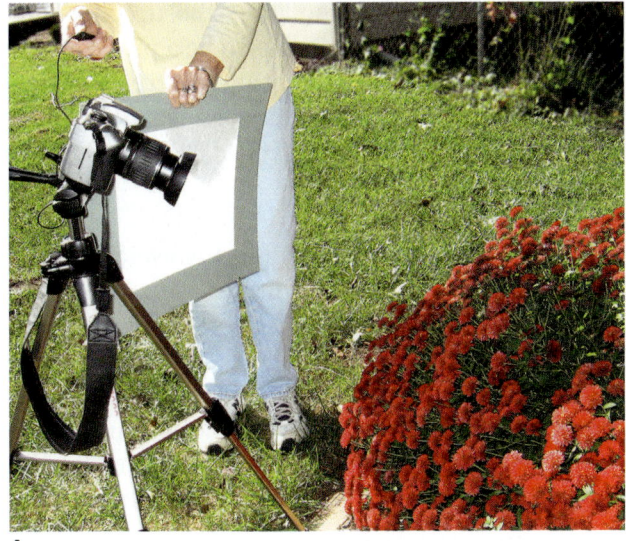

A

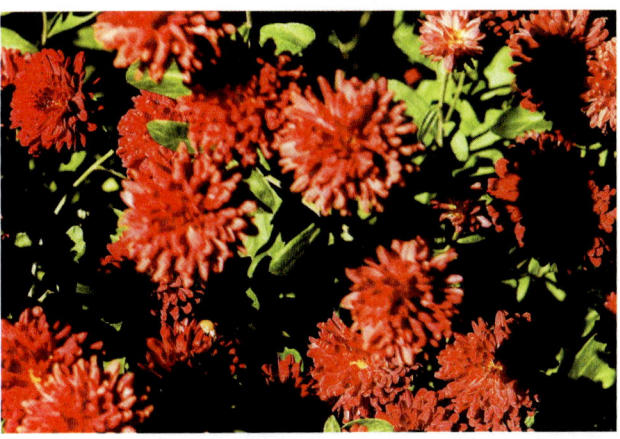

B

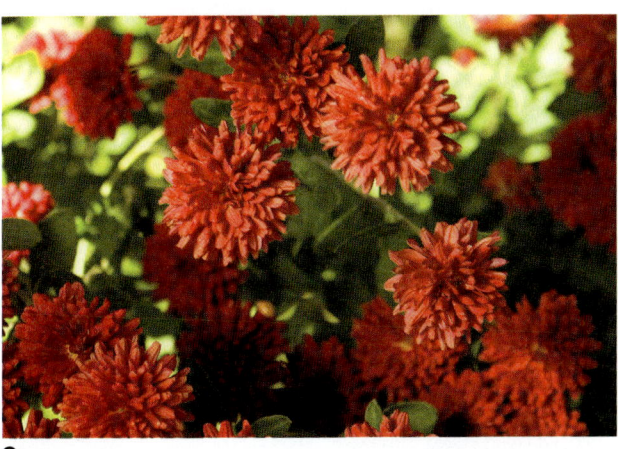

C

Jack Klasey/Goodheart-Willcox Publisher

Figure 11-26. A diffuser in use. A—Translucent material taped to a cardboard window mat makes a usable diffuser. B—No diffusion. The flower image is very contrasty, with lost highlight and shadow detail. C—Using a diffuser tames the extreme contrast.

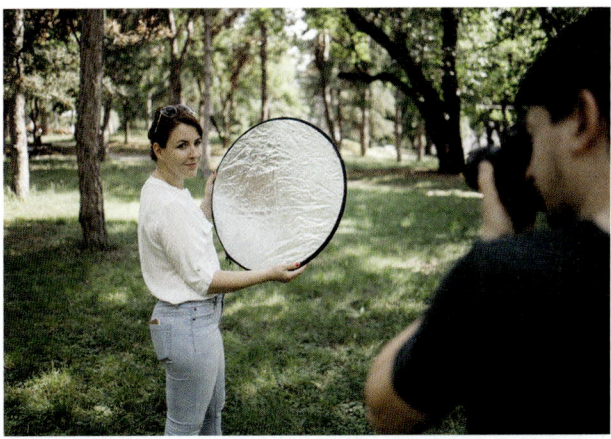

Synergic Works OU/Shutterstock.com

Figure 11-27. A silver reflector bounces light onto the shadowed side of a subject. Depending on the shot composition, the subject may be able to hold the reflector themselves.

as daylight from a window or skylight), artificial (such as electric lamps, candles, or firelight), or a mixture of both. See **Figure 11-28**.

The primary advantage of ambient lighting is that you do not need to provide any additional light to make sure your subject can be seen properly in your photos. It also can give a feeling or mood to an image that would be almost impossible to duplicate with portable flash or studio light sources, **Figure 11-29**. Using only ambient lighting also permits you to make photographs unobtrusively, an advantage in settings where use of a flash would be objectionable, such as at a concert or for candid photos.

Possible disadvantages of ambient lighting can be brightness, direction, and color. The light falling on your subject may be too strong, causing harsh shadows and washing out highlight details. On the other hand, the light could be too weak, providing low contrast and requiring long exposure at a wide aperture. Light direction can also be a problem. For example, bright overhead lighting can create unflattering deep pools of shadow in eye sockets or under the nose and chin, **Figure 11-30**.

Portable Lighting

Some photographic situations involve a mixture of artificial and natural lighting. Most often, the supplementary light source is fill flash used to add light to shadowed areas. Fill flash also brightens colors and helps separate the shapes of objects. See **Figure 11-31**. In some cases, the artificial source serves as the key light and the natural light as the fill light. Using artificial light as fill is more common, however.

Compensating for Mixed Lighting

For digital photographers, automatic white balance frequently does a good job of balancing different light sources. If the situation allows, make a second exposure with white balance set to the dominant source (such as daylight or tungsten). Some cameras also offer **white balance bracketing**. It is a camera setting that makes one exposure with the selected white balance, one with a warmer color temperature, and one with a cooler color temperature.

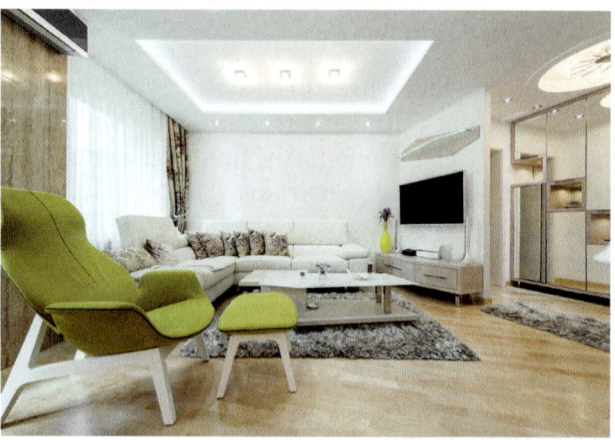

Marko Poplasen/Shutterstock.com

Figure 11-28. Ambient light from the windows and small table lamps was used to capture this interior scene.

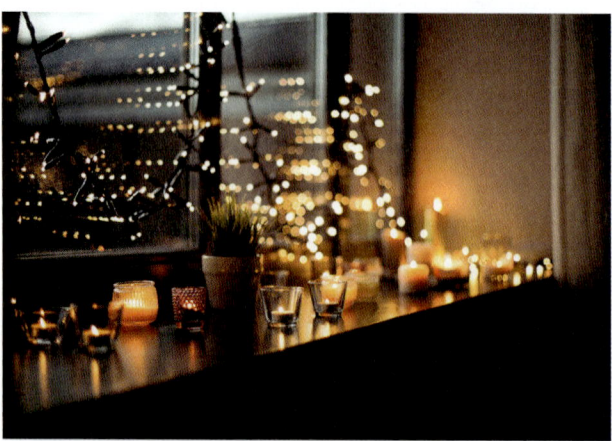

Syda Productions/Shutterstock.com

Figure 11-29. It would be difficult, if not impossible, to duplicate this photo with studio or portable flash lighting.

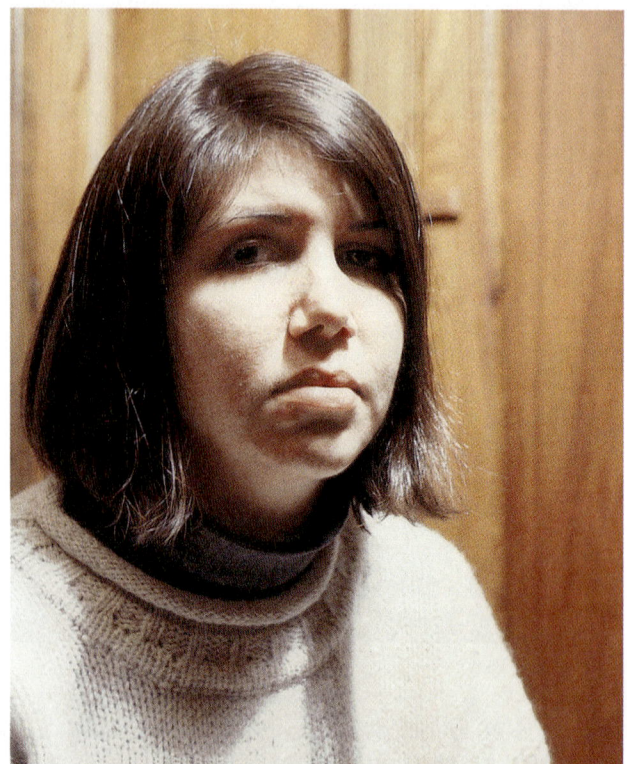

Jack Klasey/Goodheart-Willcox Publisher

Figure 11-30. A strong overhead light source is very unflattering and should be avoided whenever possible.

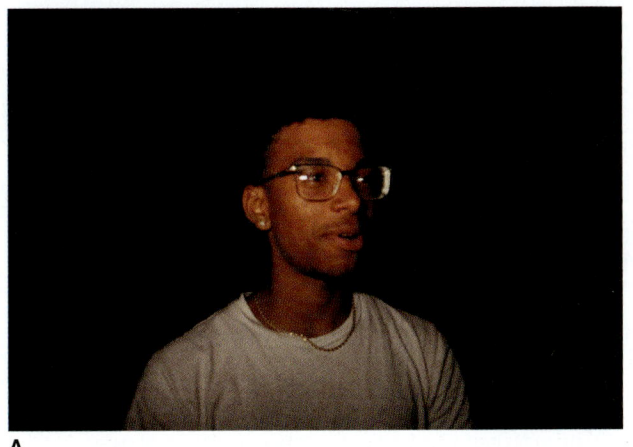
A

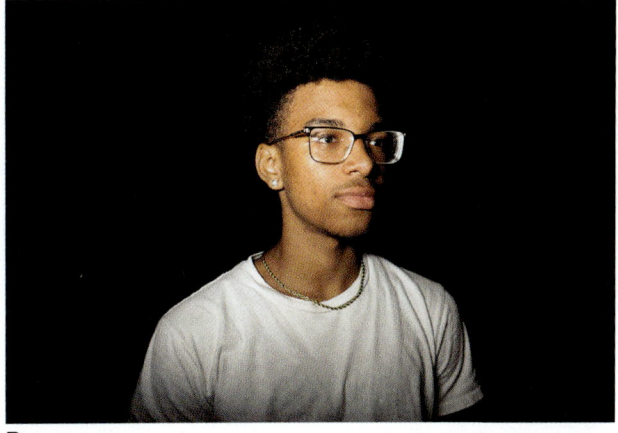
B

Goodheart-Willcox Publisher

Figure 11-31. Using fill flash. A—Only ambient light was used. B—Fill-flash light added depth and richness.

The most precise method of compensating for mixed lighting, however, is to create a custom white balance. This feature, typically offered by advanced compact and DSLR models, involves photographing a white object under the actual lighting conditions. The image is then stored and used by the camera to adjust subsequent shots under those lighting conditions. See **Figure 11-32**.

Studio Lighting

Some photographers have access to a photography studio. This allows them to control all the lighting in their photographs, which gives them a bit more creative flexibility. Many photographers consider studio lighting conditions to be ideal because the photographer sets up and controls everything themselves. When shooting with studio lights, it is recommended to start with an ISO of 1600 and adjust from there. You should also increase your shutter speed and set your aperture between f/3.5 and f/5.6. Take a few test shots to test your settings and ensure they work with what you are shooting. The advantage of studio lighting is that it will stay consistent, so once you take your test shots and determine the ideal parameters for your photo, you will not have to change them.

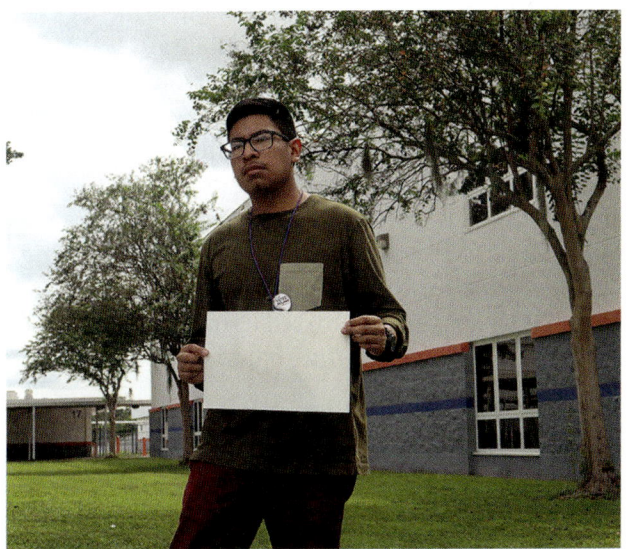

Goodheart-Willcox Publisher

Figure 11-32. Shoot a white card in mixed lighting situations to create a custom white balance.

📷 PORTFOLIO ASSIGNMENT

Minus and Plus

Choose a well-lighted subject with a good range of tones (see **Figure 11-2** for an example). Then, complete the following steps:

1. Mount your camera on a tripod and select aperture priority mode.
2. Set the ISO to 100, and then adjust the aperture to a value in the middle of the available range (probably f/8 or f/11).
3. Shoot the scene five times, using exposure compensation in this sequence: −2, −1, 0, +1, +2. Review the shots on the LCD, noting how the shutter speed selected by the camera becomes longer (slower) in regular steps as you move from −2 to +2.
4. Save the file for each of your five exposures without making any adjustments. Make a note for each image that includes the shutter speed, aperture, and exposure compensation. Compare the photos to observe the effects of exposure compensation.
5. Add the photos to your portfolio.

Chapter 11 Review

Summary

- Proper exposure is the correct combination of aperture, shutter speed, and ISO that best reflects the image that the photographer is trying to shoot.
- To expose for highlights or shadows, try to make as perfect an exposure as you can, then check the histogram and increase or decrease exposure based on what it shows.
- Today, photographers generally rely on their camera's built-in meter to determine exposure.
- Meters built into cameras measure light reflected from a subject and use this information to determine exposure. For use in different situations, in-camera meters offer two or more metering modes, or different methods used by a camera to automatically calculate exposure.
- To correct underexposure or overexposure, increase or decrease (respectively) the amount of light falling on the camera's sensor.
- Exposure bracketing is a method of exposure in which the scene is shot three times—once at the exposure indicated by the meter, once at a decreased exposure value, and once at an increased exposure value. Some digital cameras offer automatic exposure bracketing (AEB).
- You may need to increase or decrease the metered exposure in special lighting situations. The exposure compensation feature on DSLRs and some advanced compact cameras allows you to increase or decrease exposure while using the shutter priority or aperture priority modes.
- Many different combinations of aperture and shutter speed can be used to allow the same amount of light to reach the image receiver. Such pairs are called equivalent exposures.
- To achieve specific effects, you can select different shutter speed/aperture combinations. Fast shutter speeds and the resulting large apertures are typically chosen to capture action. Small apertures and the resulting slow shutter speeds are typically chosen to capture stationary objects.
- How much or how little depth of field you can obtain in a specific photographic situation is governed by three factors—the distance of the subject from the camera, the f-stop used, and the focal length of the lens.
- You can use the range of ISO ratings, in combination with aperture and shutter speed settings, to capture usable images under a wide variety of conditions.
- The intensity, color, and direction of natural light are all highly variable. You can modify natural light by diffusing the light striking the subject, adding light using a reflector, or adding artificial light to shadowed areas.
- Photographers use three basic types of artificial lighting—ambient (room) lighting, portable (usually electronic flash) lighting, and studio lighting. Each has advantages and drawbacks, especially in terms of controllability.
- Some photographic situations involve a mixture of artificial and natural lighting. Most often, the supplementary light source is fill flash used to add light to shadowed areas.
- For digital photographers, automatic white balance frequently does a good job of balancing different light sources. The most precise method of compensating for mixed lighting, however, is to create a custom white balance.

Review Questions

Answer the following questions using the information provided in this chapter.

Know and Understand

1. _____ are overexposed, featureless areas of an image that occur when the amount of light in a scene is too much for the camera's sensor to handle.
   A. Histograms
   B. Blocked shadows
   C. Burned-out highlights
   D. Clippings

2. *True or False?* A histogram weighted heavily toward the left end indicates an overexposed image.

3. _____ is a metering mode in which light reflected from the scene is read and analyzed using a number of points spread across the field of view.
   A. Evaluative metering
   B. Center-weighted averaging
   C. Partial metering
   D. Spot metering

4. _____ is a metering mode that reads information from a small area (usually about 10%) in the center of the frame.
   A. Center-weighted averaging
   B. Spot metering
   C. Evaluative metering
   D. Partial metering

5. _____ is a method of exposure in which the scene is shot three times—once at the exposure indicated by the meter, once at a decreased exposure value, and once at an increased exposure value.
   A. Exposure compensation
   B. Exposure bracketing
   C. White balance bracketing
   D. Depth of field

6. *True or False?* Exposure compensation allows you to increase or decrease exposure while using only the shutter priority mode.

7. Different combinations of aperture and shutter speed that are identical in exposure value are known as _____.
   A. equivalent exposures
   B. proper exposures
   C. digital noise
   D. exposure bracketing

8. *True or False?* For situations where depth of field is important, select aperture priority.

9. The trade-off of using a high shutter speed to stop action is usually a _____ zone of sharp focus.
   A. deep
   B. wide
   C. shallow
   D. large

10. *True or False?* As the aperture becomes larger, depth of field increases.

11. The size of the _____ determines sharpness of the image on the image receiver.
    A. depth of field
    B. circles of confusion
    C. shallow
    D. plane of focus

12. Which of the following is the control factor most often used to alter depth of field?
    A. Subject distance
    B. F-stop
    C. Focal length
    D. Plane of focus

13. _____ is the nearest point that is in sharp focus when the lens is focused on infinity.
    A. Plane of focus
    B. Depth of field
    C. Focusing mark
    D. Hyperfocal distance

14. _____ is specks of various colors that are most noticeable in shadows or areas of smooth color, such as clear skies.
    A. Diffusing
    B. Ambient lighting
    C. Digital noise
    D. Clipping

15. *True or False?* At midday, sunlight is hardest and most intense.

16. _____ is softening the light falling on a subject, usually by placing a translucent material between the light source and the subject.
    A. Fill flash
    B. Partial metering
    C. Diffusing
    D. Ambient lighting

17. The lighting that already exists in a scene or space, without any additions, is called _____.
    A. natural lighting
    B. ambient lighting
    C. artificial lighting
    D. daylight

18. Which of the following is the most precise method of compensating for mixed lighting?
    A. Use automatic white balance
    B. Use the white balance bracketing setting
    C. Add fill flash to shadowed areas
    D. Create a custom white balance

Apply and Analyze

1. What are the two ways in which you can increase or decrease the amount of light falling on the camera's sensor to correct underexposure or overexposure?
2. The metered exposure for a scene is f/8 at 1/60. To stop motion, you change the shutter speed to 1/250. For an equivalent exposure, what must you reset the aperture to?
3. Selecting a shutter speed to stop the movement of a subject involves what three factors?
4. What is a focusing mark?
5. List the three basic types of lighting photographers use.

Critical Thinking

1. Imagine you are photographing a desert scene and wish to keep everything from the foreground cactus to the distant mountains in sharp focus. Your camera, with a wide-angle lens, is mounted on a tripod. What camera setting adjustment would you make to obtain the greatest possible depth of field?
2. Think of locations in or near your community where you could photograph a high-key or a low-key image. If none come to mind, consider other places where you could make such images. Identify at least one high key possibility and one low key possibility.

Suggested Activities

1. Explore the effects of different white balance settings on a photographed scene. Choose an outdoor scene that is fairly brightly lit and exhibits a good range of colors. Make one exposure with the auto white balance (AWB) setting, and then make exposures of the same scene using each of the white balance settings offered by your camera. Make a 4″ × 6″ straight (uncorrected) print of each image. Mount your prints on a poster board, labeling each with the white balance setting used. Which setting most closely matched the auto white balance image? Display the board in your classroom.
2. Can looking directly at the sun through your DSLR's viewfinder cause damage to your vision? Research the subject on the internet and write a report. If you find that viewing the sun this way is dangerous, describe the possible effects and proper precautions. Alternatively, create a safety poster on the subject.

Communicating about Photography

1. **Writing and Speaking.** Create an informational pamphlet about the camera model of your choice. Research the camera's features, controls, and cost. Include images in your pamphlet. Present your pamphlet to the class and answer any questions the other students may have.

2. **Listening and Speaking.** Search online for photography instruction videos. Watch two or three of the videos and listen for terms that you have learned from this textbook. Write a short summary of each video, including the important terms mentioned. Be prepared to present your report to the class.

Section 3 Project
Making Photographs

For this project, you will make photographs to use for your portfolio. It is important to remember that the photos in your portfolio are meant to show off your talent and skill as a photographer. As such, you should approach these photos with that end goal in mind: showcasing what you can do. This project has three parts.

Part 1

Choose a subject to photograph several times. Your subject can be a fellow classmate, a friend, or an inanimate object. Using the camera on your phone, enable the rule of thirds grid (this will vary by phone type). Then, take the following photographs:
- The subject centered in the middle third of the grid, taken at eye level
- The subject aligned with the left-most intersections of the grid, taken at a low angle (angled up at the subject)
- The subject aligned with the right-most intersections of the grid, taken at a high angle (angled down at the subject)

Once you have taken the photos, answer the following questions:
1. Which photo appears the most neutral?
2. What effect is created by shooting up at your subject?
3. What effect is created by shooting down at your subject?

Part 2

Place your subject from Part 1 in front of a neutral background (a solid-colored wall works best). Obtain one lighting instrument, such as an LED light on a stand, and set it up so it is in front of your subject but behind the camera. Frame your subject in the middle of the frame and take the following photographs:
- The subject centered in the middle of the frame with the light shining directly in front of them
- The subject centered in the middle of the frame with the light shining on their left side
- The subject centered in the middle of the frame with the light shining on their right side
- The subject centered in the middle of the frame with the light shining directly behind them

Once you have taken the photos, answer the following questions:
1. What differences do you notice among all four photos, especially regarding shadows?
2. How does the subject's appearance differ among all four photos?
3. Do you have an aesthetic preference for one photo? Why or why not?
4. Does one photo seem more dramatic than the others? Which one, and why?

Part 3

Take one photo of your subject from Parts 1 and 2 using the following lighting techniques (if you need to review these setups, please refer to Chapter 10). Make sure your subject is centered in the middle of the frame for each photo:

- Three-point lighting
- Butterfly lighting
- Split lighting

Once you have taken each photo, answer the following questions:
1. How does the subject's appearance differ among all three photos, especially regarding shadows?
2. Do you have an aesthetic preference for one photo? Why or why not?
3. Does one photo seem more dramatic than the others? Which one, and why?
4. How does using multiple lights change your approach to photographing your subject?

After you have all your photos from each part of the project, select the best one from each part to add to your portfolio. Submit all photos to your instructor for review.

Section 4
Types of Photography

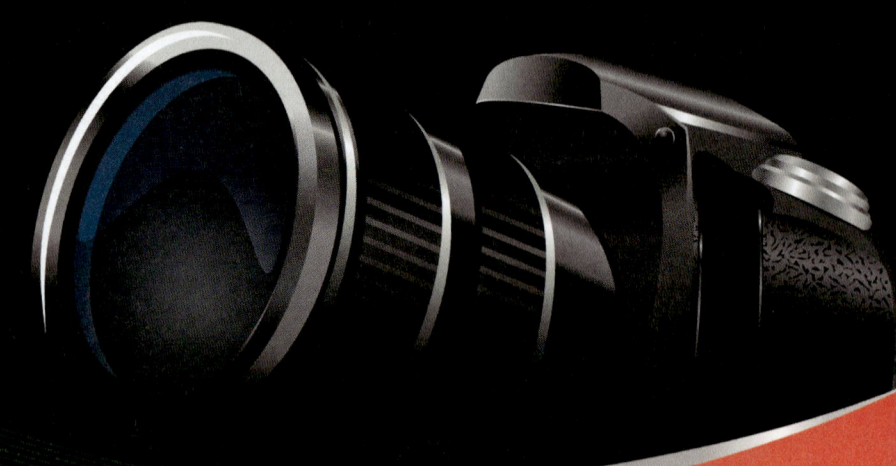

Chapter 12 Action and Event Photography
Chapter 13 Outdoor Photography
Chapter 14 Travel Photography
Chapter 15 Portrait and Studio Photography
Chapter 16 Mobile Photography

In Section 3, you learned how to make a great photo through proper composition, lighting, and exposure. Now that you know how to use your camera effectively, you can apply those skills in different settings.

Section 4 will teach you about different types of photography and how the nuances among them require slightly different approaches when shooting.

Chapter 12 covers action and event photography, which requires you to stop action and capture it as a still frame. This chapter also addresses using your camera's built-in flash and photojournalism.

In Chapter 13, you will learn about outdoor photography and evaluating how different environments affect your photography approach. It also focuses on how to photograph large landscapes and different lighting situations you may encounter outside.

Chapter 14 introduces you to travel photography. This chapter will also review what equipment is best to take when you travel since packing space may be limited.

Chapter 15 focuses on portrait and studio photography and applying existing photography knowledge to a studio setting. This chapter also explores how to control lights in a studio and the importance of flash.

Chapter 16 discusses mobile photography. In this chapter, you will learn how to maximize the photos you take with your phone's native camera application and editing on the go.

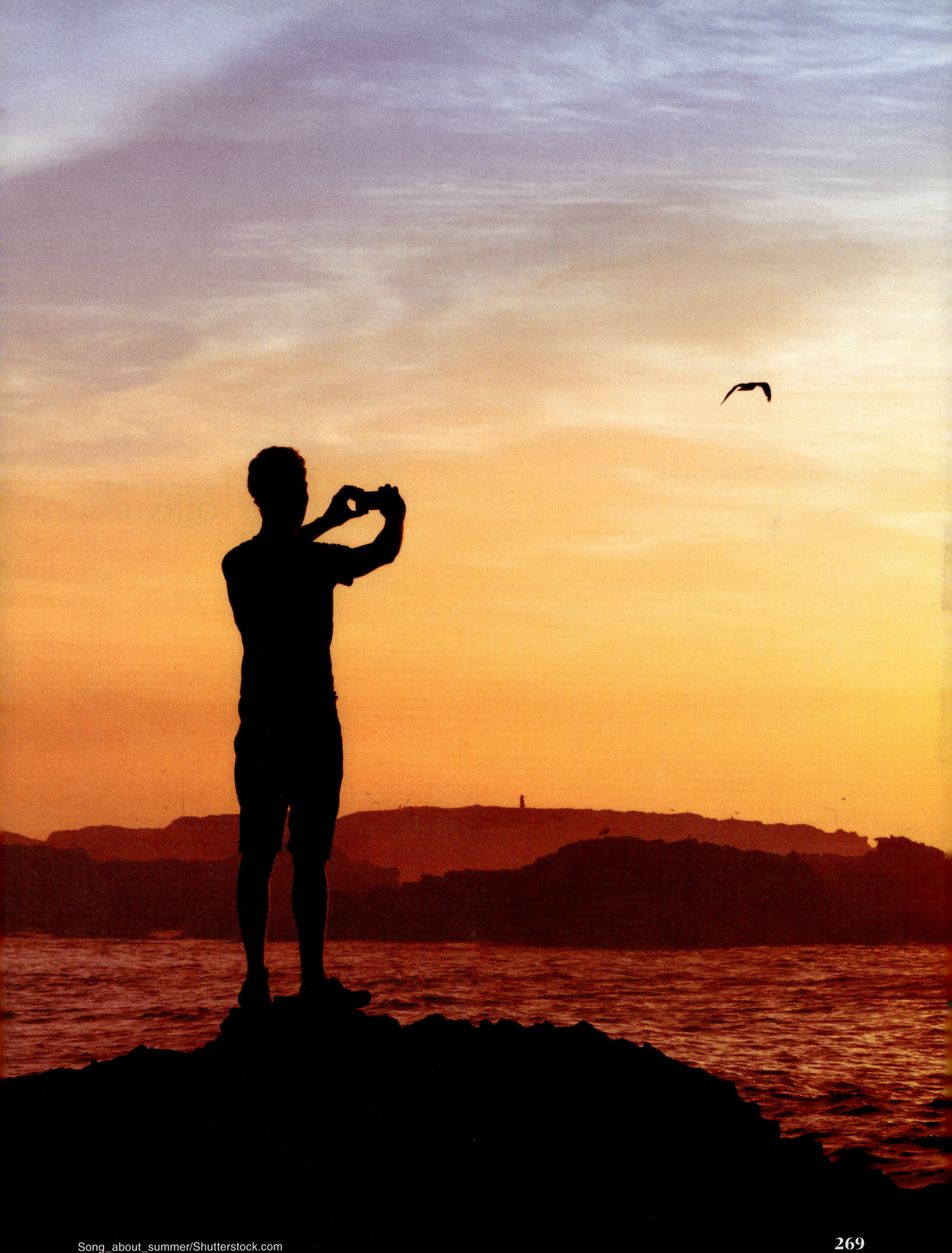

Chapter 12
Action and Event Photography

Learning Objectives

After completing this chapter, you will be able to:
- Recall the major categories of action and event photography.
- Identify the techniques used to stop motion.
- Describe the different focus techniques used in action photography.
- Explain the two types of camera motion used to induce blur to create visual interest.
- Describe the differences among the four main types of photojournalism.
- Understand how to work with flash and the differences among different types of flash units and techniques.

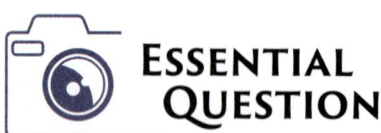

Essential Question
What differentiates action and event photography from other types of photography?

Technical Terms

bounce flash
built-in flash
capacitor
dedicated flash units
direct flash
follow focus
guide number
hard news
high-voltage power pack
hot shoe
lens collar
off-camera flash
open flash
painting with light
peak of action
photojournalism
picture story
prefocusing
rear-curtain synchronization
recycle
red eye
relative motion
self-contained flash units
slave units
soft news
zone focusing

270

Copyright Goodheart-Willcox Co., Inc.

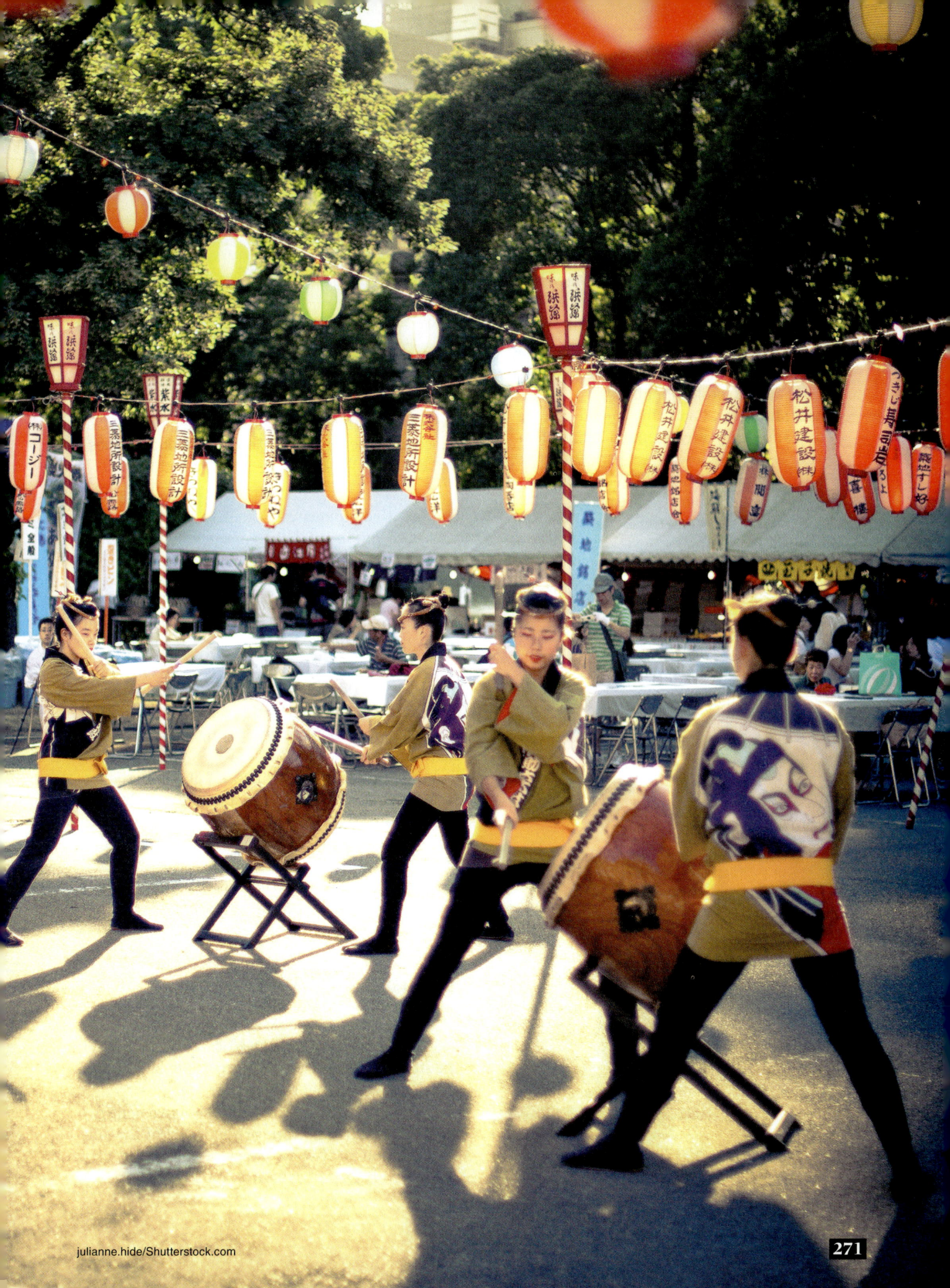

Introduction to Action and Event Photography

Virtually any picture that portrays people involved in activities—from children playing a game to the hustle and bustle of a city street—can be classified as action and event photography. Whether they are shooting fires, the effects of weather, or the doings of public officials, most assignments covered by photojournalists fall into this classification as well.

Major categories of action and event photography include the following:

- **Sports.** Portraying athletics at any level from Little League to professional.
- **Street shooting.** Capturing candid views of people and their activities, often in an urban setting.
- **Photojournalism.** Recording breaking news events of all kinds, plus feature photos to accompany articles and those shot strictly for their visual interest.
- **Performances.** Photographing all types of entertainment activities, such as concerts, stage productions, festivals, and parades.

Action and event photographs often fall in the category of *record shots* ("I was there, and this is what I saw."), **Figure 12-1**. At times, the photos convey a strong emotional or artistic impact. News photographs frequently convey emotional content, while performance photos can have an abstract artistic appearance, **Figure 12-2**.

To be successful as an action and event photographer, you must be able to respond quickly to changing conditions and often to rapidly moving subjects. You must be completely familiar with your camera's capabilities and controls, so you can make needed adjustments instinctively. You need to make technique decisions, such as freezing motion vs. motion blur, without hesitation and apply them immediately.

Alfred Eisenstaedt, a renowned photojournalist, once described his approach as "f/8 and be there." In other words, be in the right place at the right time and use the proper camera settings to capture the scene.

Although using the camera's full automatic setting is often considered an amateur's technique, professional photojournalists frequently leave their cameras set on *auto*. They do so to anticipate situations where a quick "grab shot" may be their only opportunity to capture the action. If time allows, they can then make necessary setting adjustments and keep shooting.

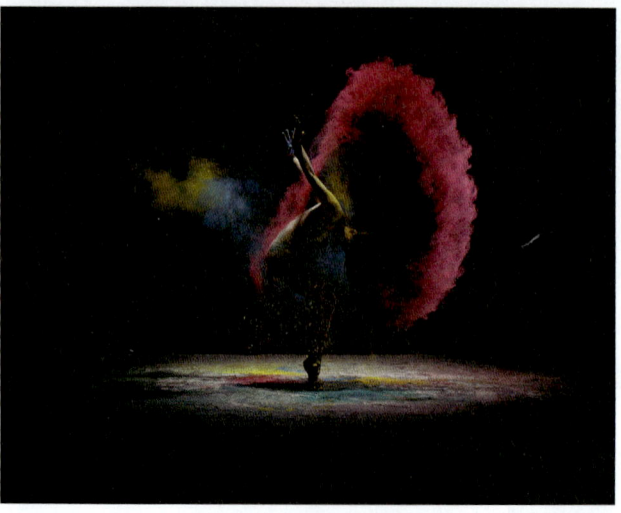

Guryanov Andrey/Shutterstock.com

Figure 12-2. The color, costumes, and motion of the dancers in a performance often provide photographs that approach the abstract.

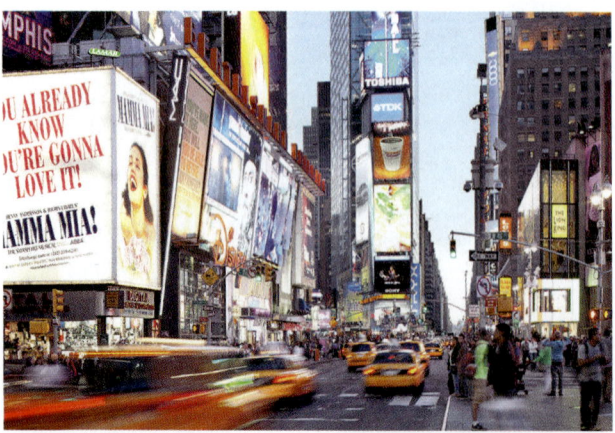

Jose Luis Stephens/Shutterstock.com

Figure 12-1. A record shot showing Times Square in New York City.

Stopping Motion

In many photographic situations, an important objective is a crisp, well-focused shot of the subject. If the subject is moving, this objective can be achieved only by stopping that subject's motion.

When you seek to fully stop the movement of a subject, **relative motion**, or the angle of the subject's motion relative to the camera's field of view or a given length of exposure, must be considered.

This means not only the speed at which the subject is moving, but the direction of movement in relation to the camera.

Effects of Relative Motion

A subject moving directly toward the camera, whether quickly or slowly, can be stopped by a relatively slow shutter speed. See **Figure 12-3**. A subject moving at an angle to the lens's axis, either toward or away from the camera, requires a higher shutter speed. If the movement is crossing your field of view, a still faster shutter speed is needed, **Figure 12-4**.

Under identical conditions, shutter speeds need to be twice as fast for each directional change. See **Figure 12-5**. For example, if 1/125 second stops movement toward or away from the camera, 1/250 second would be required to freeze a diagonal movement. Motion across the field of view would need 1/500 second. Another factor is the distance of the subject from the camera. The closer the subject, the faster it will move across the lens's field of view and the faster the shutter speed needed to stop its motion.

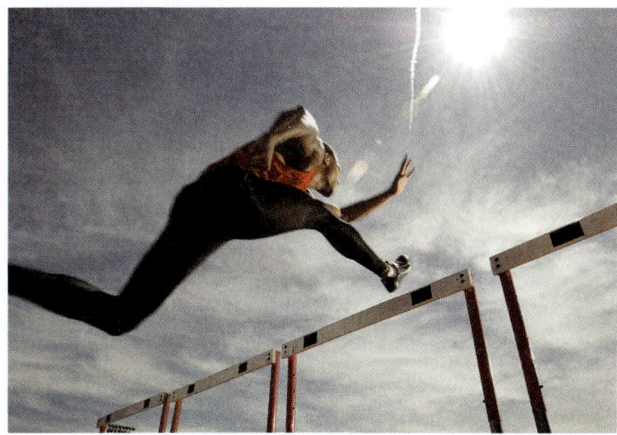

sirtravelalot/Shutterstock.com

Figure 12-4. Movement across the camera's field of view shot at 1/500 second.

The focal length of the lens you use may also require a change of shutter speed. As the focal length increases, the field of view narrows proportionately. If both a 100 mm lens and a 200 mm lens are focused on a bicycle rider 100′ away, the bicyclist would cross the field of view of the 200 mm lens twice as fast because the field of view of that lens is only half as wide. See **Figure 12-6**. The shutter speed is doubled for each doubling of the focal length. If you choose a shutter speed of 1/125 second to stop motion with the 100 mm lens, you would need a speed of 1/250 second with the 200 mm lens to achieve the same effect.

Even though today's professional DSLR cameras offer shutter speeds as brief as 1/8000 second, some action cannot be stopped by shutter speed alone. The movement may be too rapid even for a very fast shutter speed. Also, low light levels might require slower shutter speeds (even with large apertures) for proper exposure. The solution is to use electronic flash. The extremely short duration (1/10,000 second–1/50,000 second) of the light burst from the flash tube freezes the subject into stillness.

Using flash to stop motion is most effective with low levels of ambient light since the subject is isolated against a dark background. When the level of ambient light is fairly high, *ghost images* can result. As defined in Chapter 6, *Lenses*, ghost images are reflections of the pentaprism used in the viewfinder.

With older cameras, the blurred ambient light (ghost) image is in front of the subject. This occurs because the flash exposure is made the instant the shutter opens. The subject continues to move and is recorded on the film by ambient light until the shutter closes. Many newer DSLR cameras offer

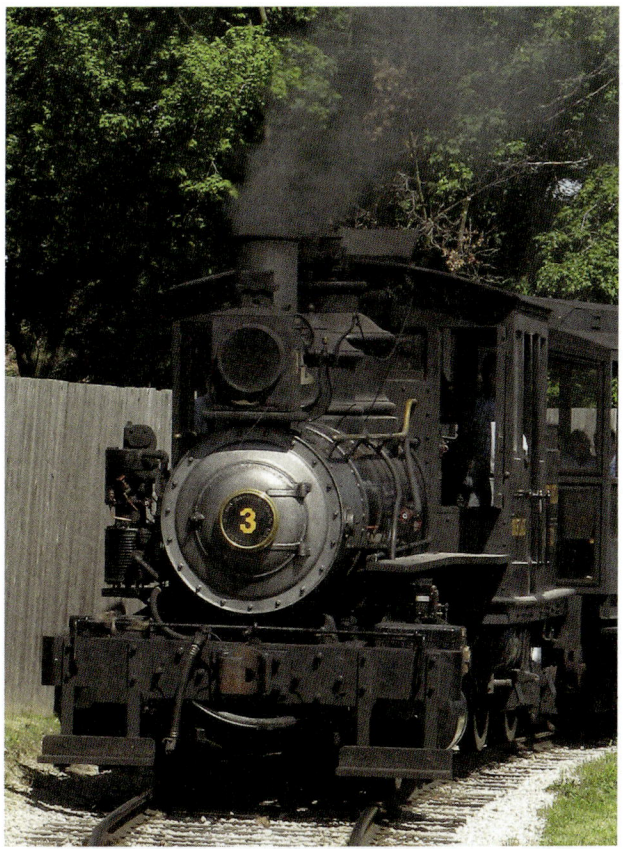

Jack Klasey/Goodheart-Willcox Publisher

Figure 12-3. Motion toward the camera shot at 1/125 second.

rear-curtain synchronization, a camera feature that delays the firing of the flash until the instant before the second curtain of the focal plane shutter begins to close. This places the ghost image behind the moving subject for a more natural appearance. See **Figure 12-7**.

Capturing the Peak of Action

Experienced action photographers, especially those covering sporting events, are often able to capture dramatic stop-action photos without the use of flash or extremely high shutter speeds. They catch

Object in Motion (or Type of Action)	Approximate Speed		Distance from Camera		Type of Movement		
	(mph)	(kph)	(feet)	(meters)	Toward/Away	Diagonal	Across
• People walking	5	8	10–12 25 50 100	4 8 16 33	1/125 1/60 1/30 1/15	1/250 1/125 1/60 1/30	1/500 1/250 1/125 1/60
• People jogging, skating, or bicycling • Children in active play	10	16	10–12 25 50 100	4 8 16 33	1/250 1/125 1/60 1/30	1/500 1/250 1/125 1/60	1/1000 1/500 1/250 1/125
• Active sports • Animals (large) running • Vehicles on city streets	25	40	10–12 25 50 100	4 8 16 33	1/500 1/250 1/125 1/60	1/1000 1/500 1/250 1/125	1/2000 1/1000 1/500 1/250
• Vehicles on highway	50	80	25 50 100 200	8 16 33 66	1/500 1/250 1/125 1/60	1/1000 1/500 1/250 1/125	1/2000 1/1000 1/500 1/250
• Racing vehicles • Other fast-moving subjects	100	160	25 50 100 200	8 16 33 66	1/1000 1/500 1/250 1/125	1/2000 1/1000 1/500 1/250	1/4000 1/2000 1/1000 1/500

Goodheart-Willcox Publisher

Figure 12-5. The effects of distance and direction of movement on shutter speeds for some typical subjects.

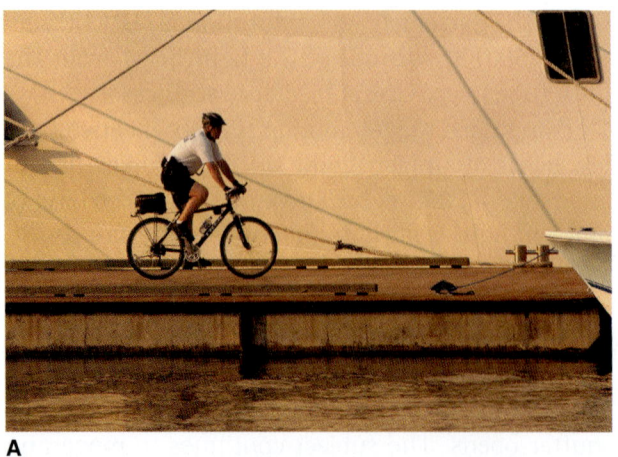

A

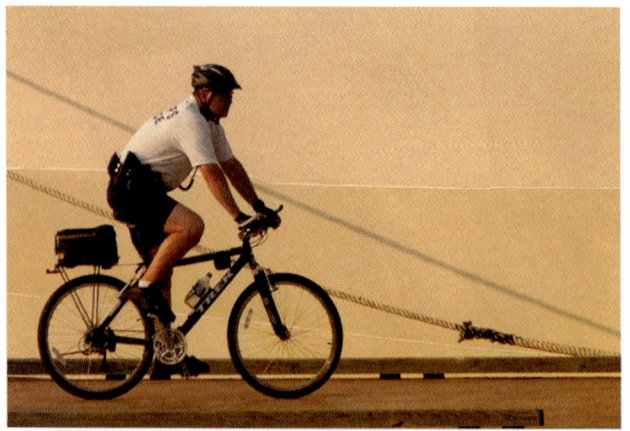

B

Jack Klasey/Goodheart-Willcox Publisher

Figure 12-6. Focal length and field of view. A—100 mm. B—200 mm.

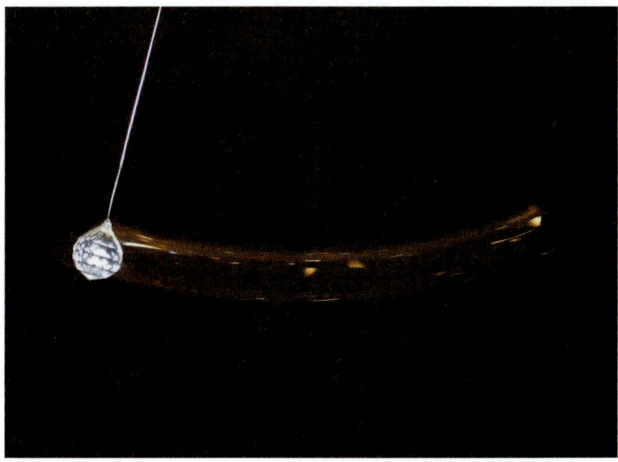

Jack Klasey/Goodheart-Willcox Publisher

Figure 12-7. Ghost image with rear-curtain flash synchronization.

their subject at the **peak of action**, or the instant when motion slows to almost a stop. A familiar example of the peak of action is the pole vaulter or high jumper who seems to hang in midair just above the bar, **Figure 12-8**. At that instant, the upward momentum of the athlete is briefly balanced with the pull of gravity. They have stopped moving upward but have not yet begun moving downward.

The key to using this technique effectively is knowing the sport (and sometimes the individual participant) well enough to anticipate when action will reach a peak. Some sports, such as the high jump or basketball, have fairly regular and predictable action peaks. Others, such as lacrosse or soccer, feature more random and unpredictable motion, making it more difficult to anticipate the peak of action. See **Figure 12-9**. Good timing is vital—the shutter must be released an instant before the peak of action takes place. If you wait to see the peak of action in your viewfinder, you will miss the shot. It takes practice plus knowledge of the sport to perfect your timing.

With older digital cameras and some current compact models, capturing the peak of action is made more difficult by *shutter lag*. This noticeable delay between the time the shutter release is pressed and the actual opening of the shutter is caused by slow operation of the camera's autofocus system. The problem often can be overcome by pressing and holding the shutter release halfway down to prefocus. To make the exposure, press the release the rest of the way.

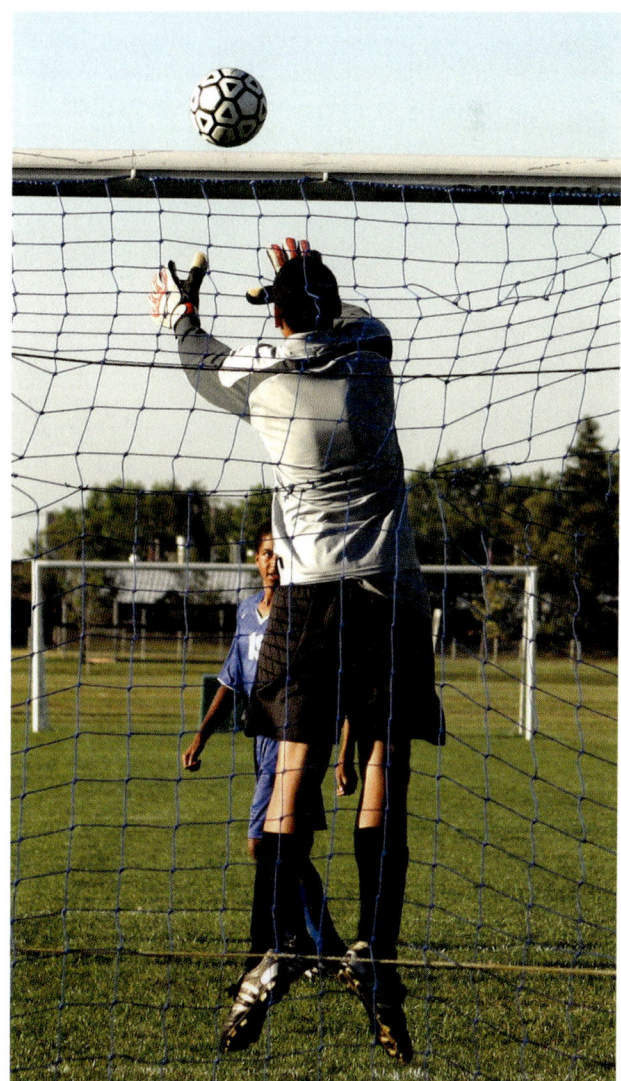

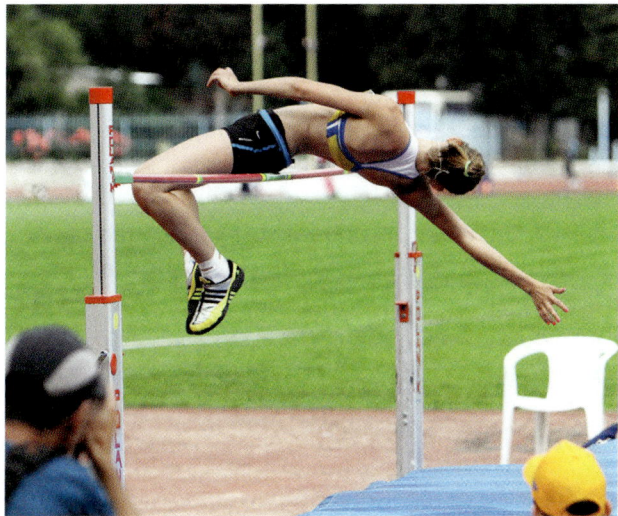

Denis Kuvaev/Shutterstock.com

Figure 12-8. This high jumper has been caught at the peak of action.

Jack Klasey/Goodheart-Willcox Publisher

Figure 12-9. In some sports, such as soccer, excellent timing is vital to capture the peak of action.

The likelihood of capturing the peak of action can be increased by careful use of the burst mode feature found on most DSLR cameras. With good timing and by making exposures in short bursts of 3–4 frames, a photographer can often get the desired shot, **Figure 12-10**.

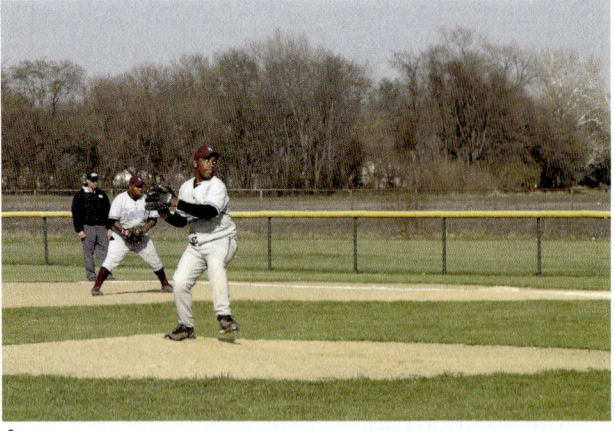

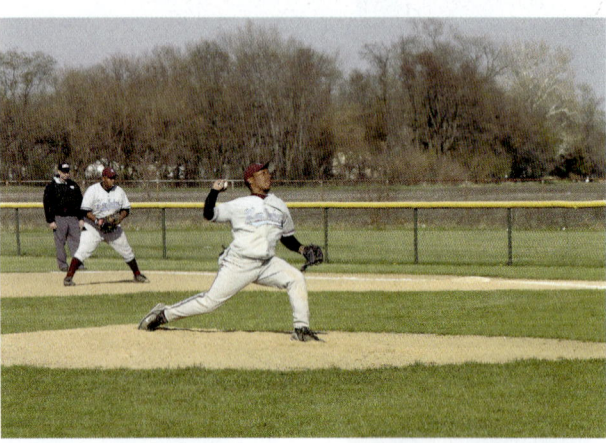

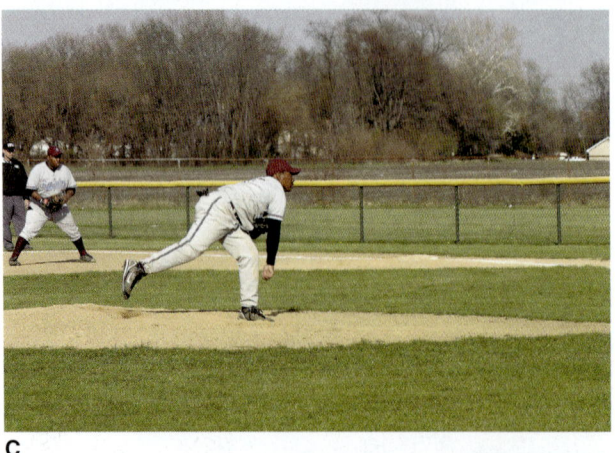

Jack Klasey/Goodheart-Willcox Publisher

Figure 12-10. A camera's motor drive or burst mode allows the photographer to capture a sequence of action. A—Windup. B—Delivery. C—Follow-through.

Focus Techniques

Cameras with predictive autofocus and similar sophisticated focusing systems have made life simpler for sports and wildlife photographers. Besides improving the percentage of well-focused shots, autofocus allows more attention to be paid to composition, timing, and other matters. There are a number of manual focusing techniques, however, that continue to be valuable photographic tools.

Follow Focus

Because some autofocus systems react too slowly for action photography, a photographer skilled in manual focusing can do the job faster and more effectively. When a moving object must be kept in focus to allow the shutter to be pressed at any time, manual focus is preferable to slow autofocus.

Follow focus is a technique in which the photographer makes continuous small focus adjustments to keep a moving subject sharp. This method permits the photographer to select the exact instant to release the shutter. The photographer usually judges the sharpness of the image on the viewfinder's ground glass rather than using the split-image or microprism portions of the viewfinder. Determining the amount of lens barrel rotation needed to keep the focus sharp requires practice. One of the many benefits of working with a digital camera is that it allows you to make a shot and immediately judge the effectiveness of your follow focus technique by being able to view your photos after you take them.

Prefocusing

A useful technique when the action follows a regular pattern or route, as it does in baseball and most types of racing, is ***prefocusing***, or focusing on a specific spot and waiting for the subject to reach that point. Prefocusing is also called *spot focusing*. Select a particular location (for example, first base or the finish line of the track), sharply focus the camera there, and wait for your subject to reach that point, **Figure 12-11**. This method works best when it is possible to use a smaller f-stop for increased depth of field.

Zone Focusing

Zone focusing, also known as *area focusing*, is a method of prefocusing on an area, making use of depth of field to provide acceptable sharpness for action within that area. It can be used to cover a

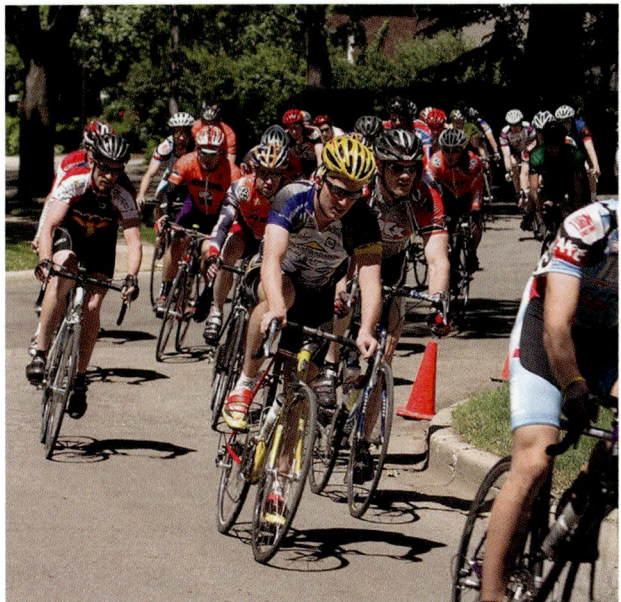

Jack Klasey/Goodheart-Willcox Publisher

Figure 12-11. In this bicycle race shot, the prefocus spot was the orange traffic cone at right.

Blurring for Visual Interest

Completely stopping a subject's motion is not always desirable. Some degree of motion blur in a photograph conveys a sense of movement.

Depending on the desired effect, the amount of blur may be very slight or almost total. As shown in **Figure 12-13**, selecting a shutter speed fast enough to stop the most important motion still allows some degree of blur to convey movement. **Figure 12-14** shows the opposite effect. A strong sense of motion is conveyed by using a shutter speed slow enough to capture streaks of colored light from moving vehicles on a city street at night.

wider area and is a good choice for less predictable activities such as football, basketball, or soccer. First, determine the pair of distances between which you wish to be able to capture action, such as 10′ and 30′. Since the area of acceptable sharpness is approximately one-third in front of and two-thirds behind the actual point of focus, your point of focus should be at approximately 17′. This is one-third the distance between 10′ and 30′. Stop the lens down to an aperture that provides acceptable sharpness from 10′ to 30′. Any action within that zone will be acceptably sharp, **Figure 12-12**.

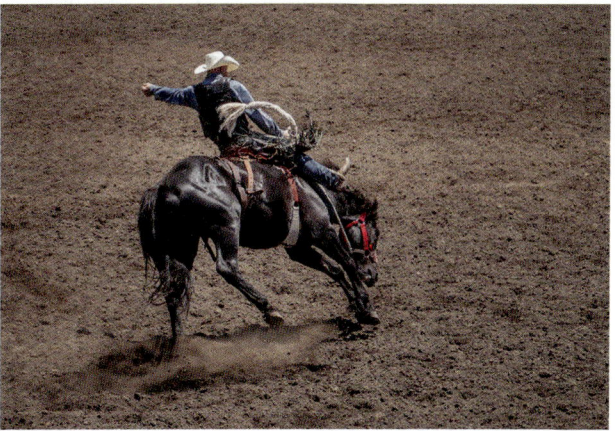

Timothy S. Allen/Shutterstock.com

Figure 12-13. The shutter speed was fast enough to preserve the movement of the horse but allowed some blurring of the horse's hooves and tail.

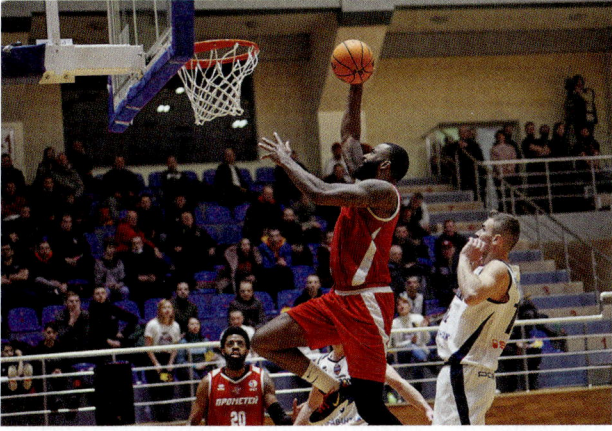

Vitalii Vitleo/Shutterstock.com

Figure 12-12. The players fighting for the rebound are in the chosen focus zone.

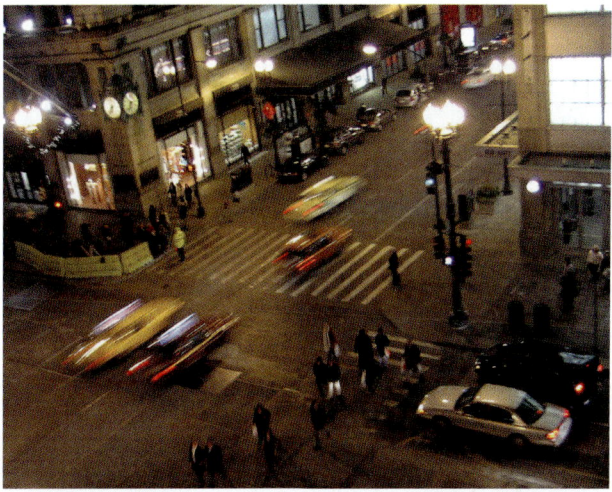

Jack Klasey/Goodheart-Willcox Publisher

Figure 12-14. A slow shutter speed was used to blur the lights of these cars in downtown Chicago into colorful streaks that show movement.

Panning and Zooming

Blurring due to movement of the camera is usually considered undesirable. However, two types of blur induced by camera motion—panning and zooming—often are used to create visual interest.

In panning, the camera is moved in an arc as the subject passes, and the shutter release is pressed at the desired point. The panning movement must continue past the point where the shutter is released. The result is a sharply focused subject, such as a runner or a vehicle, moving across a blurred background, strongly conveying the idea of rapid movement, **Figure 12-15**. A background close to the moving subject will streak more interestingly than a distant background. A tripod-mounted camera provides smoother movement than can be obtained by hand-holding, especially when a long lens is used.

Zooming is usually done to impart motion to a photo of a stationary subject. The subject is centered in the viewfinder and sharply focused, and the camera's zoom lens is moved in or out during the exposure. Tripod-mounting of the camera is vital, since a fairly long exposure time is necessary to allow zooming. A zoomed photo has a center area that is in focus and streaking that extends outward from the center to the edges of the photo. See **Figure 12-16**.

Photojournalism

In a strict sense, every photograph is an act of communication—conveying information, an idea, or an emotion. **Photojournalism** is a specialized field of photography devoted to capturing images of

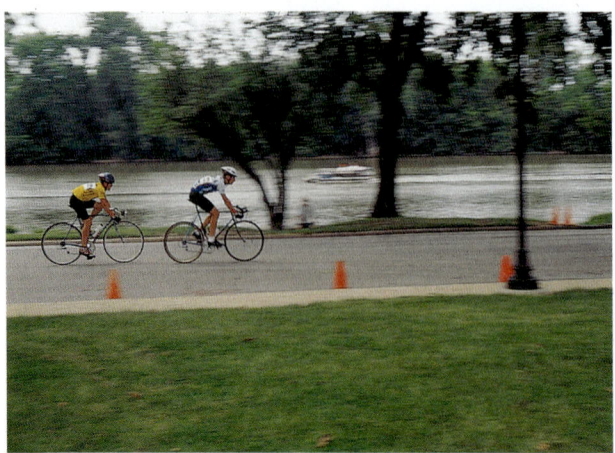

Jack Klasey/Goodheart-Willcox Publisher

Figure 12-15. Panning the camera along with the motion of the subject.

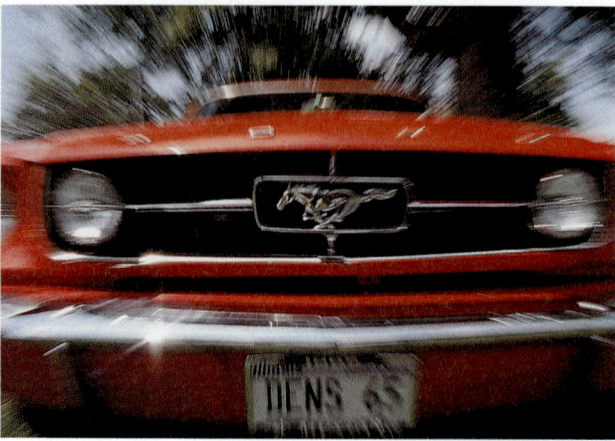

Jack Klasey/Goodheart-Willcox Publisher

Figure 12-16. Zooming creates an interesting, almost abstract effect and a strong feeling of motion.

news events and similar subjects for use in newspapers, magazines, and other print and digital media. It involves a specific kind of communication—telling a story. The story may be communicated in a single image or in a series of images called a *picture story*. Ideally, the photograph itself should be able to convey the story to the viewer. Most often, though, a writing or publishing application is used to add a caption that provides needed information. See **Figure 12-17**. Photojournalism assignments make for great additions to your portfolio because they show off your range and capabilities as a photographer. There are many different types of photojournalism with a variety of subjects, which makes for a diverse and interesting portfolio.

Types of Photojournalism

Photojournalism can be categorized in many different ways. The following four types include almost every relevant application:

- News and feature photography
- Picture stories
- School event and yearbook
- Other event photography

The categories overlap to some extent. In this section, they will be considered separately for ease of discussion.

News and Feature Photography

Most photojournalists work for newspapers, magazines, or electronic media and handle a variety of photo responsibilities. On any given day, a photojournalist may have both **hard news** assignments

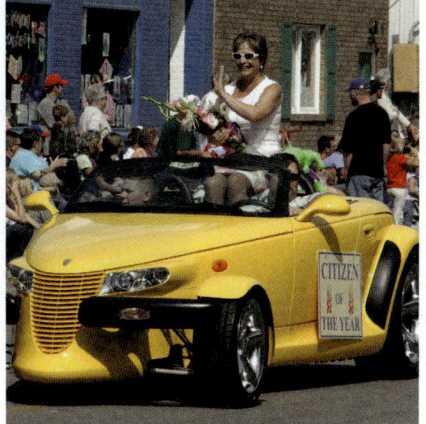

Goodheart-Willcox Publisher

Figure 12-17. The photo itself provides some information, but the caption adds necessary details.

(photojournalistic assignments such as fires, automobile or industrial accidents, or crime coverage), and **soft news** feature assignments (feature-type photo assignments such as seasonal pictures, fashion or food shots, and human interest photos). Mastery of technical skills is particularly important on the hard news assignments, where there may be no opportunity for additional shots.

Hard News Photography

Besides photographic knowledge, important skills for photojournalists are the ability to make decisions and act quickly, the determination to carry out the assignment despite obstacles, and the physical stamina to work in unpleasant and sometimes dangerous conditions. See **Figure 12-18**.

Especially in smaller news organizations, photojournalists may be on call for breaking news at any hour of the day or night, and they often work long or irregular hours. In addition, photojournalists must be able to work with people of all kinds, from political figures and government officials to distraught crime victims and antagonistic individuals. If working with a distraught or antagonistic individual, you may have to employ conflict-management skills, such as active listening and practicing empathy. Using these skills will likely help you achieve a rapport with the individual, and thus, a better photo. Furthermore, working with people

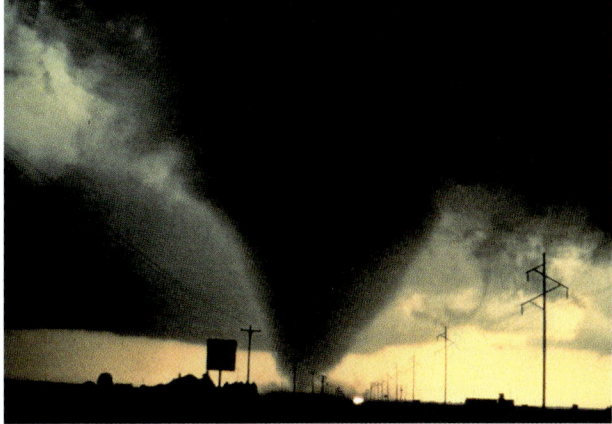

NOAA/Harald Richter

Figure 12-18. A photojournalist sometimes must work in dangerous situations, such as shooting this approaching tornado.

of all kinds also includes working with diverse individuals of various backgrounds. It is important to remember that when working in news, your job is to deliver the story without any bias. Part of this is to make sure everyone is represented fairly and accurately, which involves carefully listening to people.

Photojournalists were among the first professionals to use digital cameras because of the speed with which images could be taken, delivered, and processed. Except in the largest news organizations, the photographer is likely to shoot the photo and then use image editing software to prepare the image files for publication. The photographer does not usually select the image to be used. A member of the editorial staff typically reviews the possible images and chooses one or more to be published.

In smaller communities, photojournalists and reporters are well known to police officers and firefighters, and therefore seldom have a problem gaining access to sites where a news event is occurring. In order to control access to the scene, larger municipalities typically issue press credentials to newspeople. See **Figure 12-19**. Depending on local regulations, freelance photojournalists may also obtain credentials. The public may also send in various tips through email or social media. It is important to check your email regularly to stay on top of potential assignments.

Photojournalists are also called on to shoot a variety of civic, business, and community events. Typical assignments are civic meetings, school ceremonies, award luncheons, and groundbreaking ceremonies for new buildings, **Figure 12-20**. Assignments in which the subjects shake hands and smile for the camera are often referred to as "grip and grin" events. The challenge in such assignments is to avoid the tired photographic cliché and find a fresh approach that results in a visually interesting photo that tells a story.

Large city newspapers and television stations may have staff members who specialize in sports photography. Photographers at smaller publications handle sports assignments as well as regular news and feature pictures. Almost all outdoor sporting

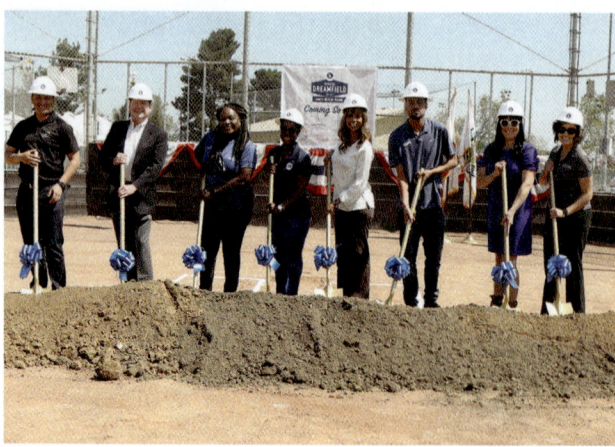

Kathy Hutchins/Shutterstock.com

Figure 12-20. Civic events are common assignments for photojournalists.

events take place on large fields, requiring use of a long telephoto lens to fill the frame with dramatic action, **Figure 12-21**. Because of their weight and physical size, such long lenses are impossible to hand-hold. Instead of a bulky tripod, sports photographers typically use a monopod for support, **Figure 12-22**. The monopod is easily repositioned and steady enough for sharp images.

Medium and long telephoto lenses are attached to a monopod or tripod with a **lens collar** rather than the tripod mounting screw on the camera body. See **Figure 12-23**. This support method prevents strain on the lens mount from the weight of the lens, as well as providing better balance for the camera/lens unit.

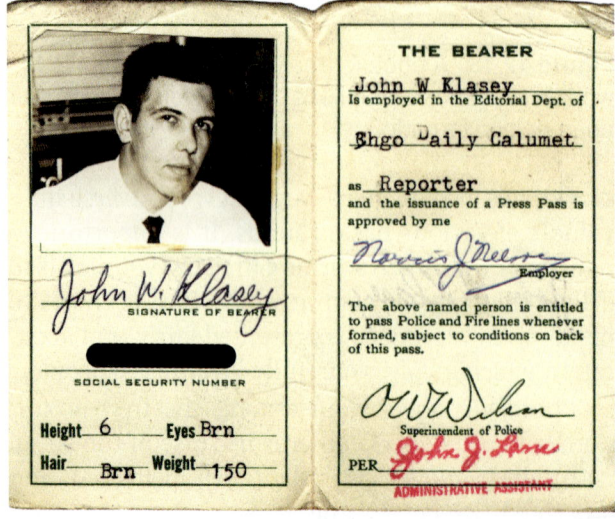

Jack Klasey/Goodheart-Willcox Publisher

Figure 12-19. Jack Klasey's Chicago press card from his early days as a photojournalist.

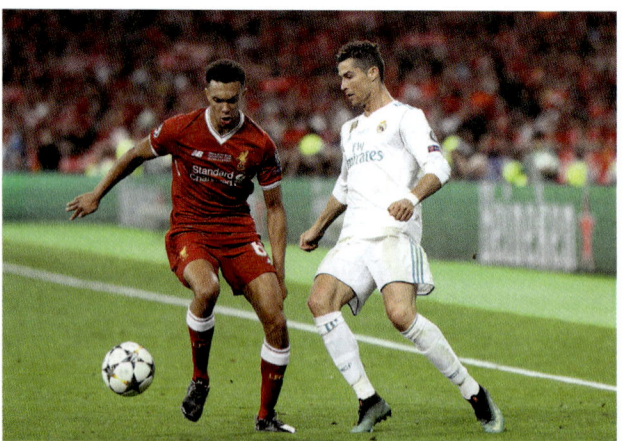

viewimage/Shutterstock.com

Figure 12-21. At outdoor sporting events, long telephoto lenses are necessary to capture action across the large playing field.

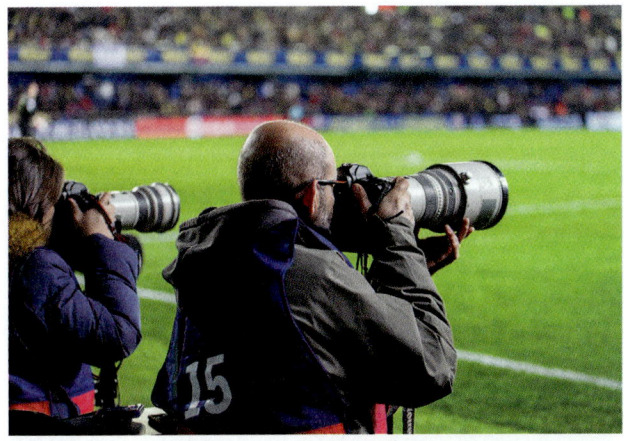

Christian Bertrand/Shutterstock.com

Figure 12-22. These sports photographers are using telephoto lenses on monopods to shoot a soccer game.

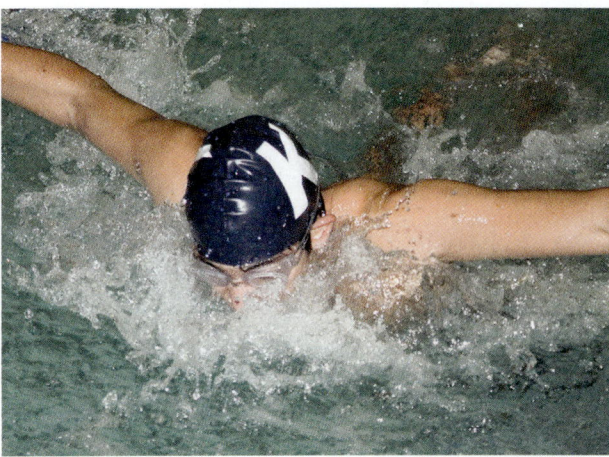

Jack Klasey/Goodheart-Willcox Publisher

Figure 12-24. Due to the low light level, a flash was necessary for this shot at a high school swim meet.

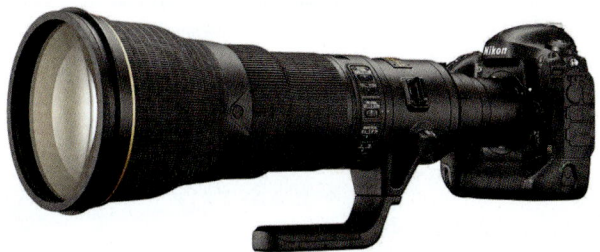

Courtesy of Nikon, Inc., Melville, New York

Figure 12-23. An 800 mm lens with an integral lens collar for tripod mounting.

Indoor sporting events usually involve a smaller playing area, so photographers are closer to the action. Offsetting the shorter distances, however, is the generally lower light level of indoor venues. A sports photographer often must supplement ambient light with a portable flash. In addition to providing enough light for proper exposure, flash may also freeze motion for dramatic effect. An example is the water droplets around the swimmer in **Figure 12-24**. Sports officials may sometimes restrict the use of flash for the safety of the athletes or in situations where the flash could adversely affect competition.

Soft News Photography

Newspapers frequently carry human interest stories about the activities of individuals or groups. An example is a feature on a person with an interesting leisure activity, such as rock climbing, **Figure 12-25**. Photo illustrations for human interest stories usually include an informal portrait of the subject, and possibly one or more illustrations of the person involved in the activity.

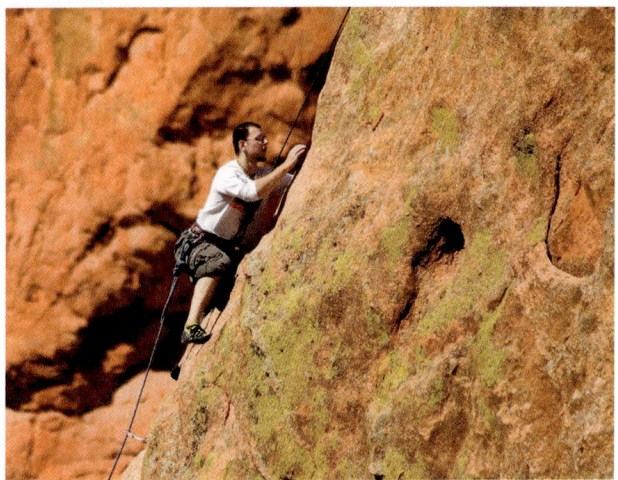

Jack Klasey/Goodheart-Willcox Publisher

Figure 12-25. This image was made to illustrate a feature story on the subject's rock climbing hobby.

Different techniques are used for the various types of illustrations. An informal portrait may be taken indoors with flash or studio-type lighting or outdoors with ambient light and fill flash to open up dark shadows. Depending on the location and lighting, photos of the subject involved in an activity can be shot with available light, possibly supplemented by flash or a reflector. If the subject is a collector, photos of the collectibles vary considerably in their requirements. Small or intricate items obviously require different lighting and shooting techniques from antique automobiles, **Figure 12-26**.

Sometimes, a photojournalist shooting a soft news assignment might be asked to keep certain information confidential. For example, a collector might show the photographer a particularly rare or valuable item but

colorful and high-interest photo opportunities, such as decorated houses, children on an Easter egg hunt, or Independence Day fireworks, **Figure 12-28**.

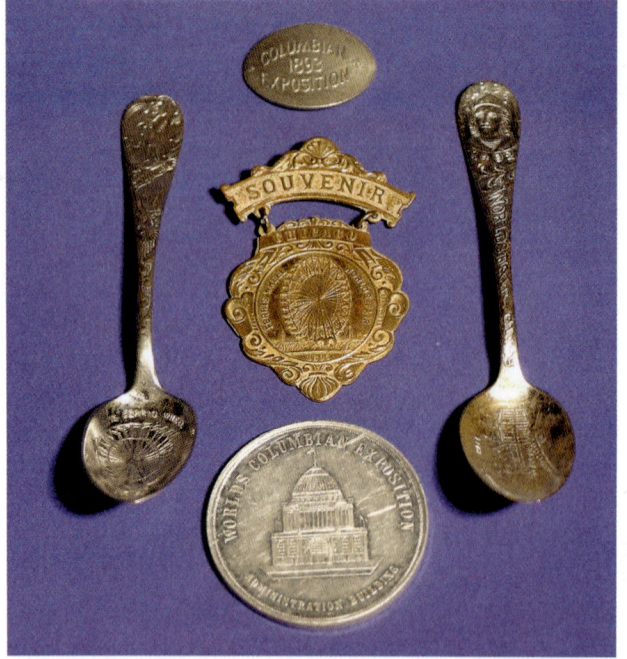

A

Jack Klasey/Goodheart-Willcox Publisher

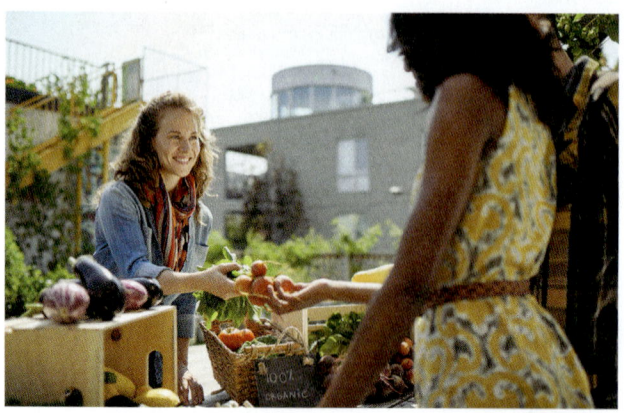

AYA images/Shutterstock.com

Figure 12-27. The interaction of buyers and sellers at a local farmers market.

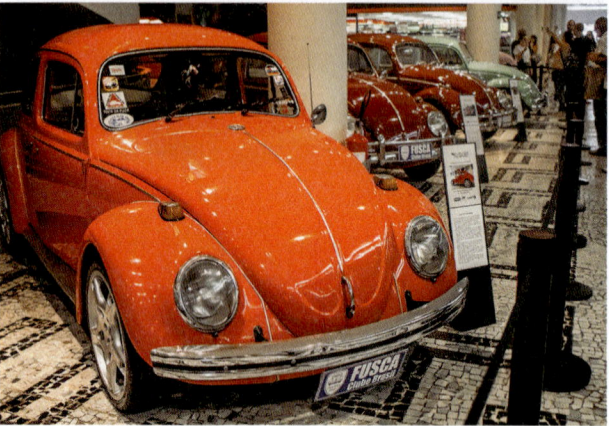

B

rafastockbr/Shutterstock.com

Figure 12-26. Illustrations for stories on collectors require different approaches. A—Souvenirs from the 1893 Columbian Exposition. B—An antique car displayed at a car show.

ask them to avoid mentioning or picturing it in the story because of concerns about theft. Such ethical questions occur more often in hard news coverage, however.

Seasonal photos are a staple item for most publications. These may be scenic shots of trees blazing with fall colors or a garden displaying spring flowers in bloom. Shoppers at the local farmers market are a popular subject, **Figure 12-27**. Holidays provide

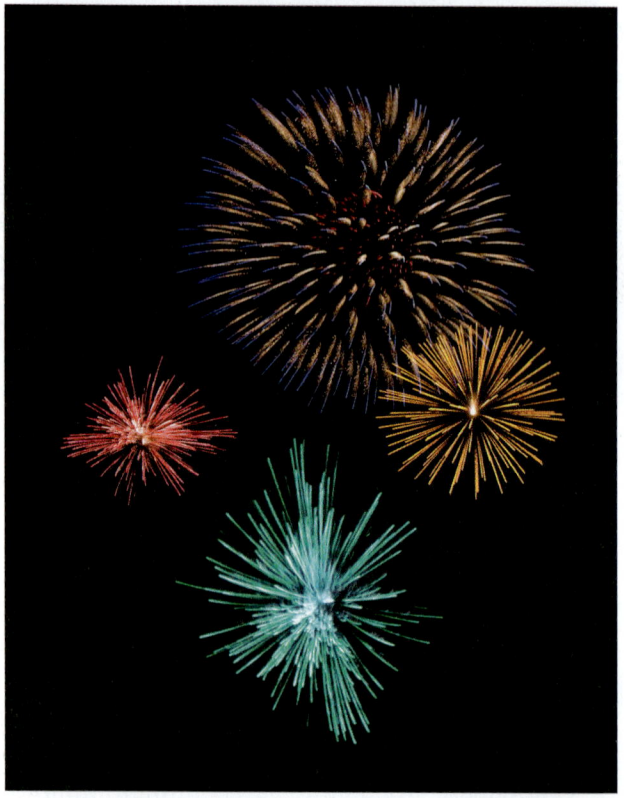

Jack Klasey/Goodheart-Willcox Publisher

Figure 12-28. Fireworks are a seasonal favorite for both photojournalists and amateur photographers.

Picture Stories

A **picture story** consists of a group of feature-type photos that carry out a theme. In purest form, a picture story, sometimes called a *photo essay*, relies on the photos and their accompanying captions to "tell the tale." While there may be an introductory paragraph or two, the emphasis is on the pictures. The heyday of the pure picture story was the mid-twentieth century, when several large format magazines were devoted to that form, **Figure 12-29**. Today, magazines use photos primarily as illustrations for written articles.

School Event and Yearbook

For a student, photojournalism opportunities usually involve shooting for the school newspaper, yearbook, website, or Facebook page. The newspaper and yearbook may be a specific class in the English or the Fine Arts department or an extracurricular activity relying on volunteers.

Activities such as assemblies or concerts provide a wealth of subject matter. For such events, a good strategy is to shoot a variety of types of shots. Examples include wide-angle overall views of the activity, medium shots of groups within the larger activity, and close-up shots of individuals taking part, **Figure 12-30**.

Yearbook photography often involves group portraits of various clubs or classes. When shooting posed groups, a tripod is recommended. This allows you to set up the shot and frame it, then make any needed adjustments before shooting. Using a tripod also permits you to make a number of exposures under identical conditions. This is useful to get the best expressions on the faces of the subjects (nobody with eyes closed, for example), as well as allowing exposure bracketing and white balance bracketing.

Covering school sports is usually an important part of student photojournalism. Although a

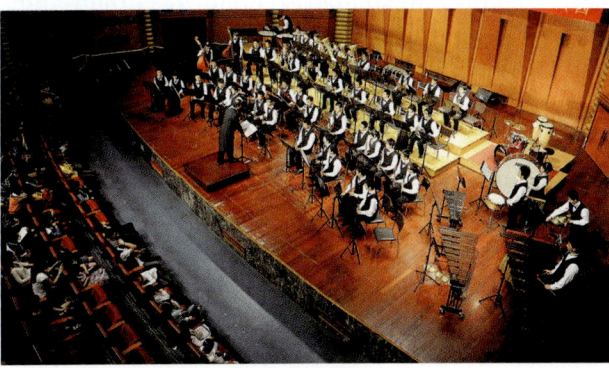

A

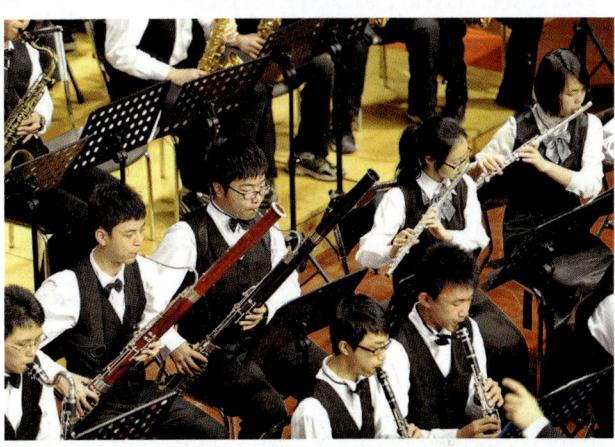

B

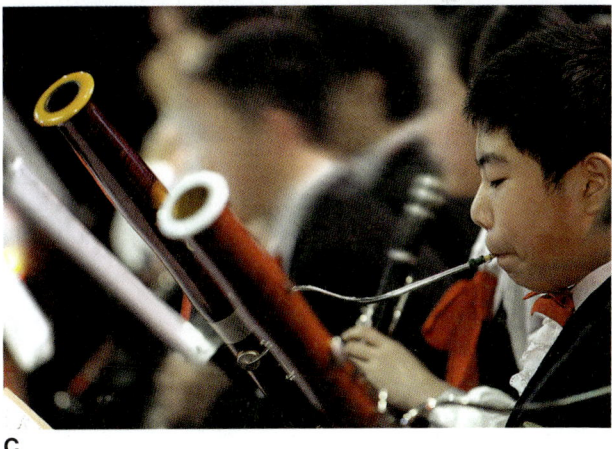

C

Jack.Q/Shutterstock.com

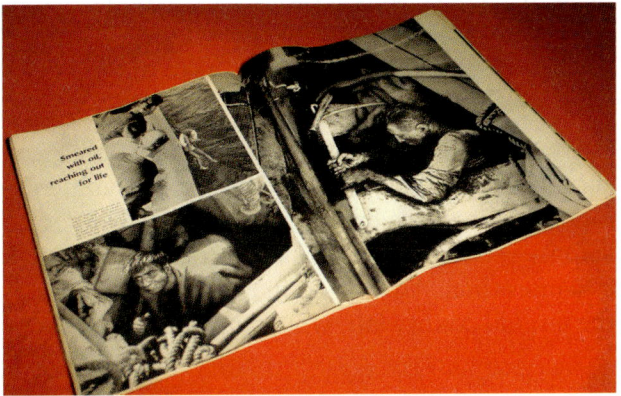

Jack Klasey/Goodheart-Willcox Publisher

Figure 12-29. Pictorial magazines filled each issue with picture stories. This 1950s spread shows shipwreck survivors being rescued.

Figure 12-30. A variety of shot types help tell the story of an event, such as a band concert. A—An overhead wide shot showing the overall activity. B—The woodwind section of the band. C—A solo performer.

good sports photo is worth using no matter whom it features, try to concentrate on members of your school's team, **Figure 12-31**. Since you are unlikely to have a very long telephoto lens, find a location close to where the action is most likely to take place—the soccer goal, the home team basket, first base, near the football sideline, at the volleyball net, or by the track finish line. Do not neglect high-angle and low-angle viewpoints to provide visual variety. Lie on the ground and shoot upward to isolate hurdlers or high jumpers against the sky or climb up in the stands for a bird's-eye view of the action, **Figure 12-32**.

Do not just shoot the action on the field or court. Look for photo opportunities like those shown in **Figure 12-33**. The yearbook or newspaper editor will appreciate the extra shots you take.

Other Event Photography

Our lives are filled with events that are worth photographing, from community activities to family celebrations. Shooting such events can be considered a form of photojournalism because you are recording activities for future reference or for the enjoyment of others who will view your prints or see your images on social media.

Be particularly careful to avoid violating the privacy of your subjects when posting images to social

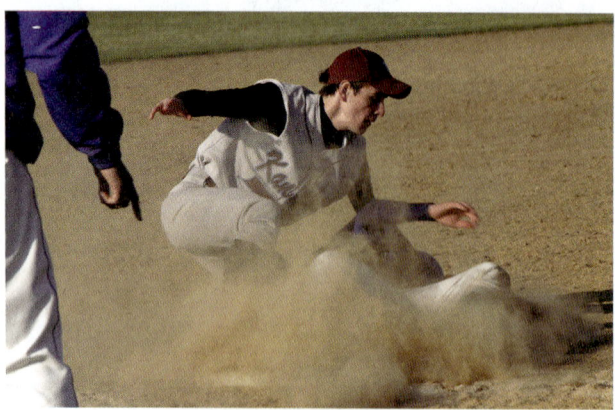

Jack Klasey/Goodheart-Willcox Publisher

Figure 12-31. When covering school sports, try to feature players from your school.

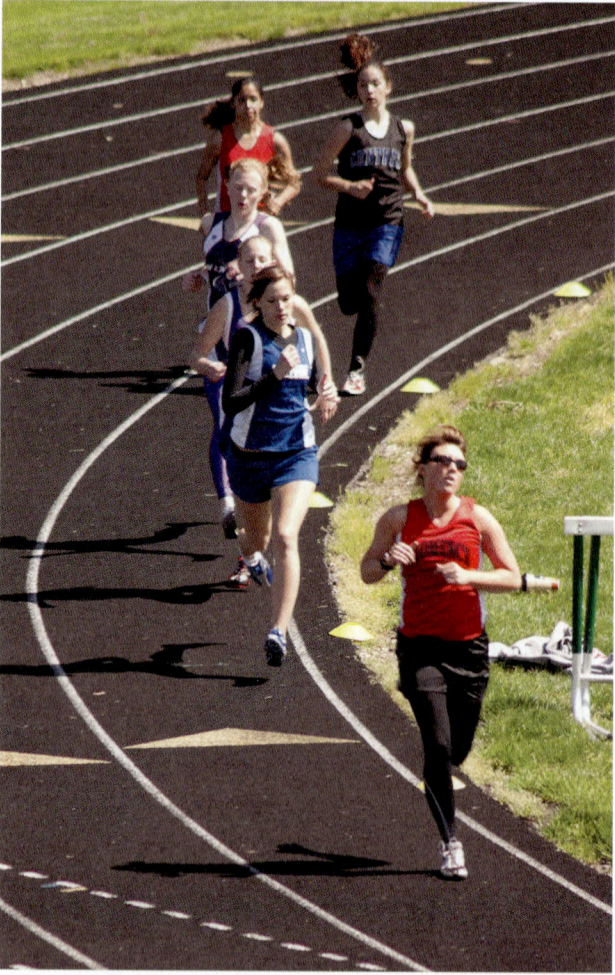

Jack Klasey/Goodheart-Willcox Publisher

Figure 12-32. Try for different viewpoints when shooting events.

media or otherwise displaying your photos. Be sensitive to the content of your photos—avoid depicting racial or gender stereotypes or showing people in embarrassing situations.

Community Events

Most communities have one or more public celebrations each year. These may be a commemoration of a historic event, a cultural festival, or an activity related to a major competitive event, such as a marathon. An important event in rural areas is the annual county fair, which includes agricultural

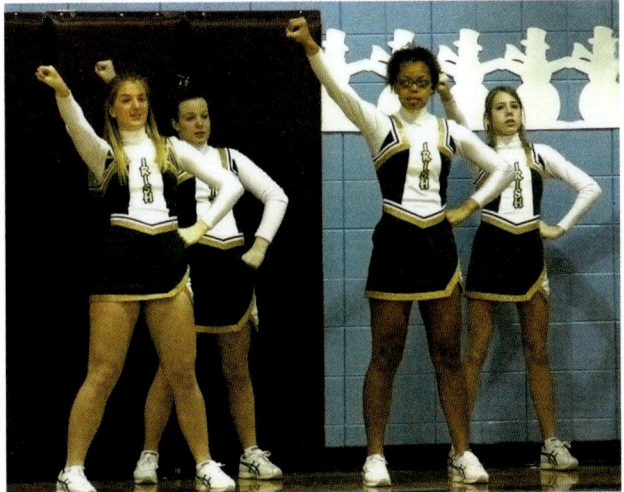
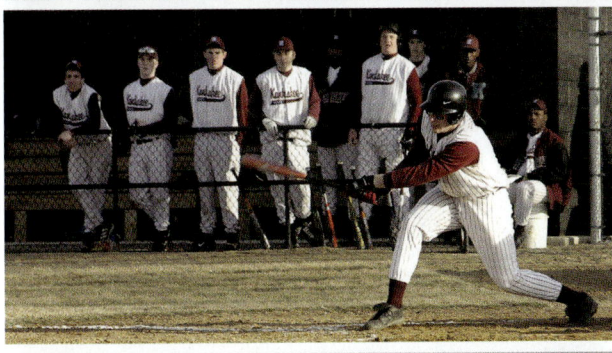
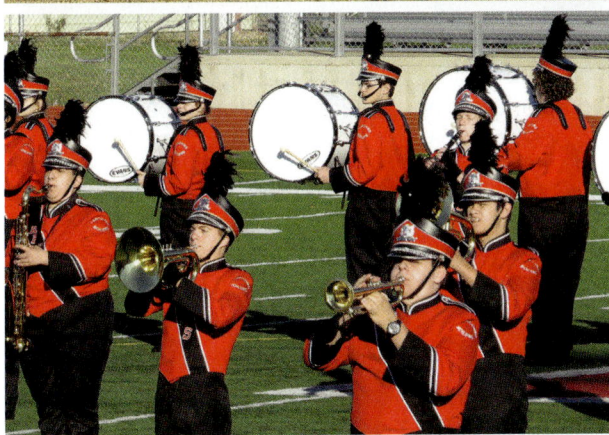
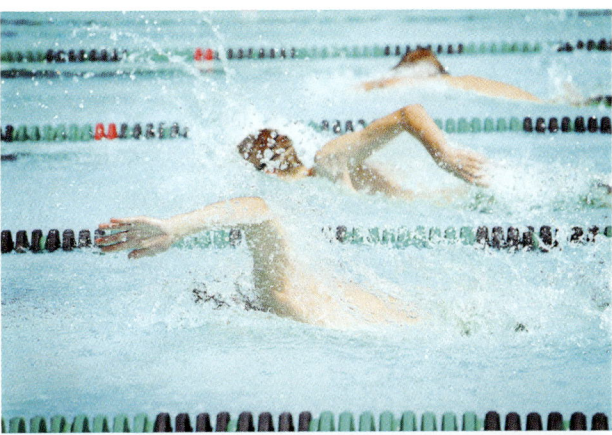
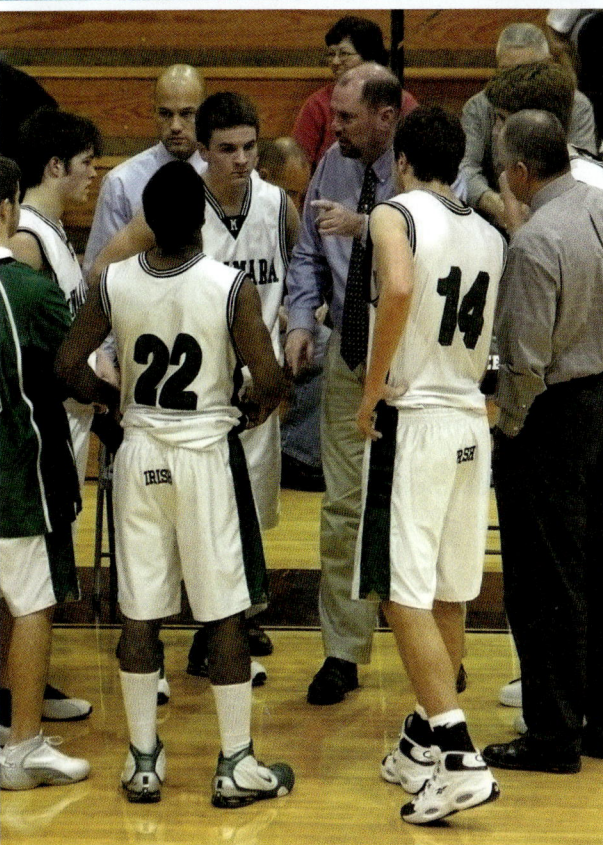

Jack Klasey/Goodheart-Willcox Publisher
Swimming picture: Suzanne Tucker/Shutterstock.com

Figure 12-33. Besides action on the field or court, sporting events provide many "photo ops" for a student photojournalist.

displays and competitions, contests of various kinds, concerts, and carnival rides, **Figure 12-34**.

These events provide opportunities to perfect your photographic skills under a variety of conditions. Parades lend themselves to various ways of recording the activity, **Figure 12-35**. Local craft fairs are good places to practice candid street photography, **Figure 12-36**.

Competitions such as auto and boat races, kite flying, cycling, and rodeo riding are colorful and allow you to perfect action-shooting techniques, **Figure 12-37**. Indoor events under stage lighting, such as dance performances and concerts, require

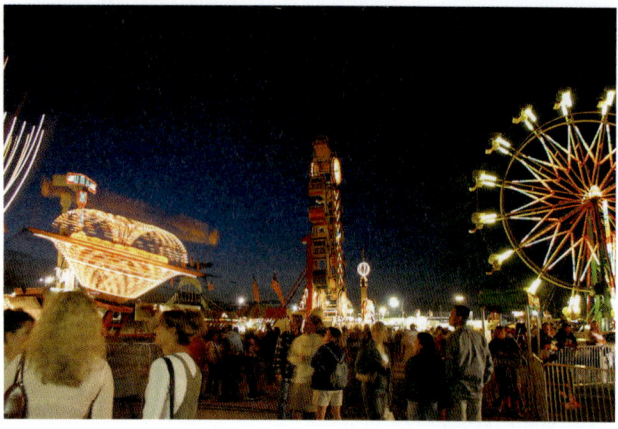

Jack Klasey/Goodheart-Willcox Publisher

Figure 12-34. When photographing a carnival scene at twilight, meter the sky near the horizon as a starting point, then bracket exposures. A 1 1/2 second exposure blurred moving rides and some of the people on the midway.

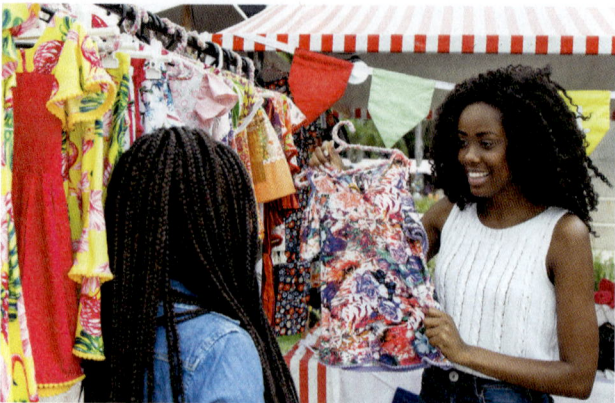

Daniel M Ernst/Shutterstock.com

Figure 12-36. Customers examine merchandise at a craft fair.

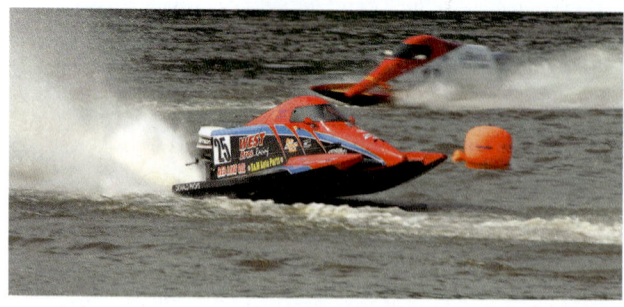

Jack Klasey/Goodheart-Willcox Publisher

Figure 12-37. Photographing competitions, like hydroplane racing, requires good timing and composition skills.

good timing, a steady hand, and the ability to shoot using only available light, **Figure 12-38**.

Family Milestones

Events such as weddings, birthday parties, and the birth of a child are usually photographed by one or more family members "for the record." If the event is indoors, flash is almost always necessary

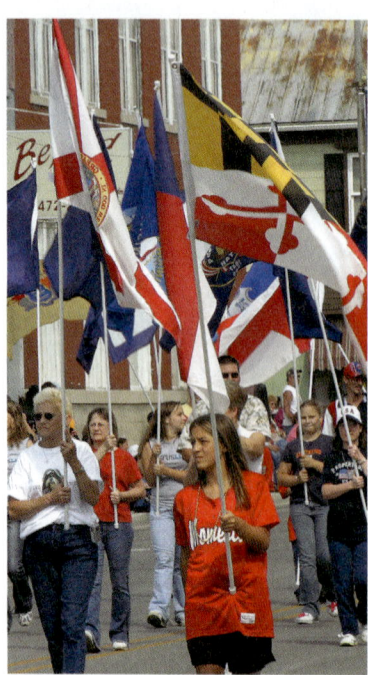
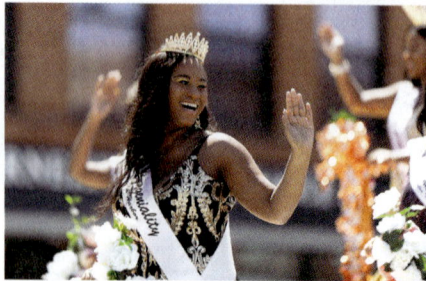
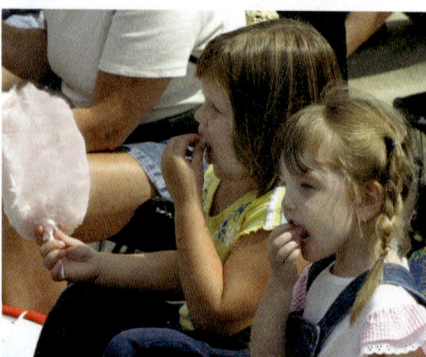
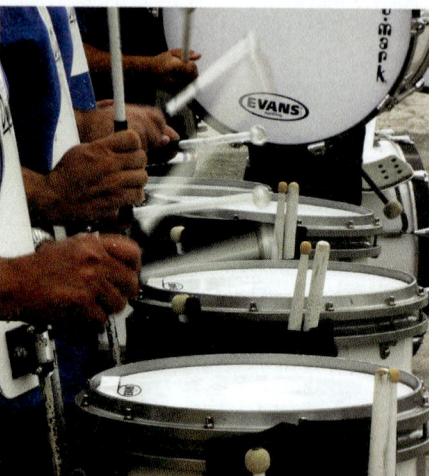

Jack Klasey/Goodheart-Willcox Publisher
Pageant winner picture: Roberto Galan/Shutterstock.com

Figure 12-35. A parade can be covered photographically in many different ways.

286 Section 4 Types of Photography

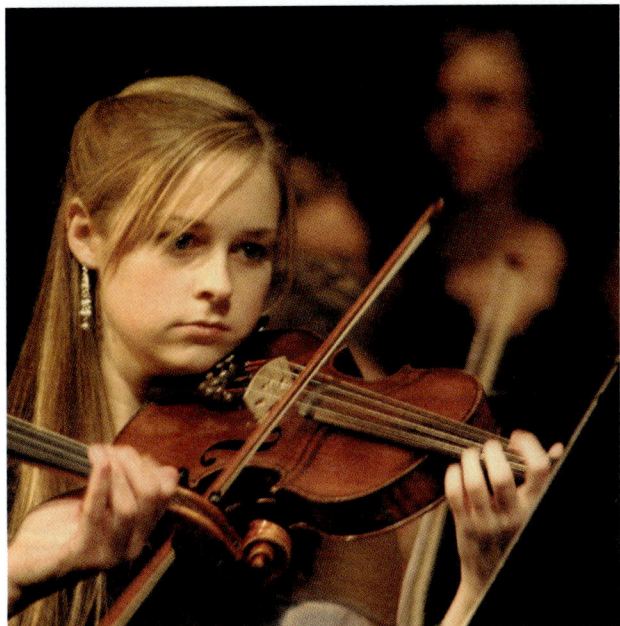

Jack Klasey/Goodheart-Willcox Publisher

Figure 12-38. The stage lighting at this concert was sufficient to capture a close-up portrait of a violinist deep in concentration on their music.

to obtain proper exposure. If flash is not permitted, shoot at the widest available aperture and lowest ISO that permits a shutter speed fast enough to avoid camera shake.

When photographing a new parent and their baby, move in to fill the frame with the subjects, since hospital backgrounds are typically cluttered and distracting. If possible, capture the infant with their eyes open (the flash will not cause any harm). See **Figure 12-39**. Today's more sophisticated digital cameras automatically adjust the duration of the flash. This results in a more natural and correctly exposed subject.

For birthdays and similar celebrations, you will likely take the traditional shots, such as blowing out the candles. You should also include as many photos as possible of friends and relatives interacting with the person being honored.

At weddings, a professional photographer is usually present to record the ceremony and its accompanying activities. Typically, a wedding photographer will use a mix of telephoto and prime lenses. This will give them plenty of options when taking candid photos (such as one of the celebrants walking down the aisle) and portrait photos (family or wedding party photos). Since the photographer was hired to produce professional results, attendees with cameras should avoid interfering with the pro, **Figure 12-40**. Some professionals are disturbed when wedding guests shadow them, copying each setup shot, while others consider it to be a minor annoyance. Be courteous to the photographer and to the couple getting married—do not act like a member of a paparazzi pack closing in on a celebrity. If you want to photograph the same scenes as the professional, such as the couple cutting the wedding cake, take your shot after they have captured the image.

Street Photography

Life on the streets of a community and showing people engaging in various activities has long been a favorite subject for photographers. Performers, **Figure 12-41**, are colorful additions to an urban

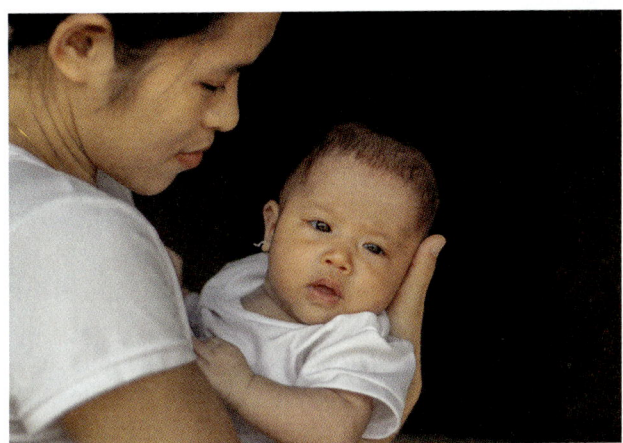

TANX/Shutterstock.com

Figure 12-39. Catching the baby with eyes open adds to the quality of this photo.

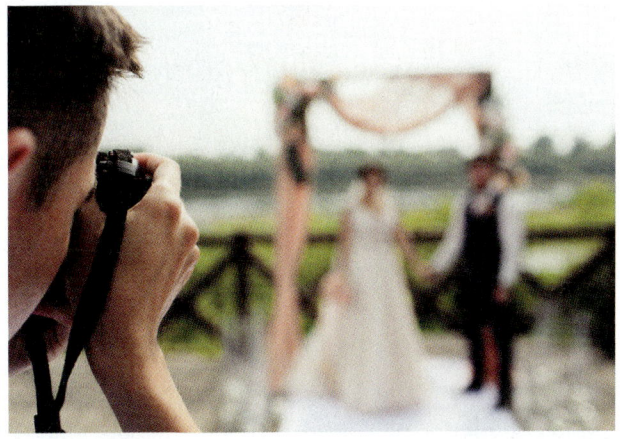

Vershinin89/Shutterstock.com

Figure 12-40. Try to find a vantage point for your shot that does not interfere with the professional hired to shoot the wedding.

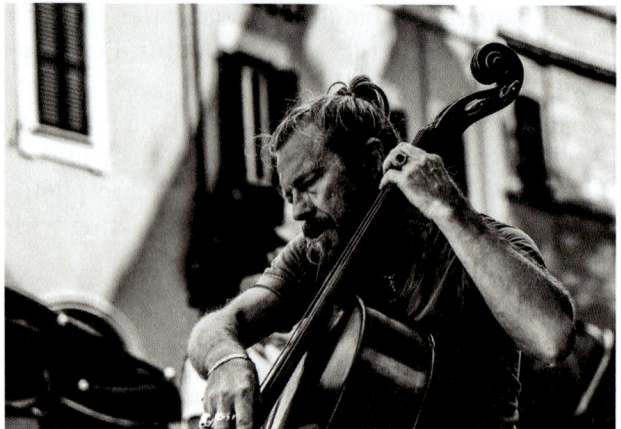

Todamo/Shutterstock.com

Figure 12-41. This cellist is performing on a street in Italy near the Pantheon.

street scene, but even a quiet view of a cat sitting outside a home tells a story about city life, **Figure 12-42**.

Street photographers use a variety of techniques to capture unposed shots of their subjects. Some work from a distance, using a telephoto lens. Others use shorter lenses while walking along the street or standing at a convenient vantage point, such as a traffic island or building doorway, **Figure 12-43**. Digital cameras with pivoting LCD viewfinders can be held at waist level to be less obtrusive or to provide a different angle.

Interesting shots can be made from a moving vehicle. However, for safety reasons, never use a camera while driving. If possible, open the window

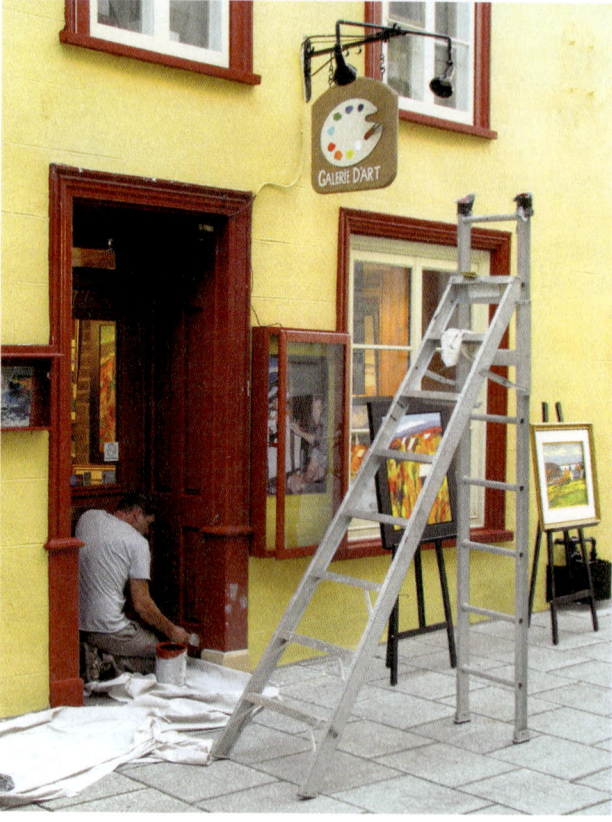

Jack Klasey/Goodheart-Willcox Publisher

Figure 12-43. A painter touches up a doorway, unaware of the photographer shooting from across the street.

and set a shutter speed high enough to compensate for the vehicle's movement. Do not support the camera by resting it or your arms on the door or windowsill of the vehicle. Vibration transmitted from the street or the engine can cause camera movement and blur. If you cannot open the window, hold the camera's lens as close as possible to the glass without touching it to prevent capturing reflections. This position also helps the camera's autofocus system avoid focusing on the window rather than the scene you are photographing. See **Figure 12-44**.

Working with Flash

Action and event photography often requires the use of a portable light source, or electronic flash unit. Flash units are the primary source of portable artificial light for most photography. They provide ease of use, greater light output, and rapid repeatability.

Electronic flash units are based on a simple circuit, **Figure 12-45**. A strong electrical charge is built up in a storage device called a ***capacitor***.

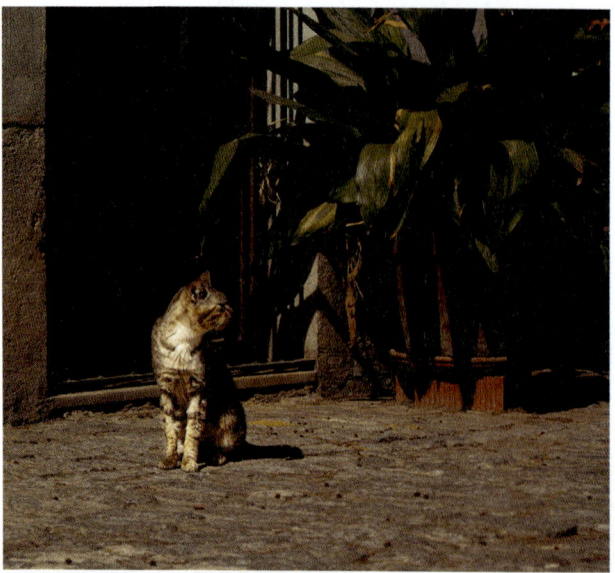

AntonioCantos/Shutterstock.com

Figure 12-42. This tranquil shot of a cat in front of a house was taken while on a casual walk outside.

When the camera's shutter release is pressed, a trigger circuit causes the accumulated electrical charge in the capacitor to discharge. An electrical pulse is released into a gas-filled flash tube, producing a burst of bright light synchronized with the opening of the camera shutter. The flash unit will then *recycle* (the process of rebuilding the capacitor's electrical charge).

Types of Flash Units

Built-in flash is a small artificial light source found in most compact digital cameras, camera phones, and many consumer-level DSLR cameras, **Figure 12-46**. While they are convenient for snapshots where you need a little extra light, they are limited in capability for serious artificial light photography.

Self-contained flash units are flash units available in a variety of sizes. They can be divided into two broad categories:

- Small units designed for mounting on a camera's hot shoe
- Larger, more powerful units attached to the camera with a removable bracket

The first type is widely used by amateur and professional photographers alike. The second type is primarily a professional tool.

Shoe-Mount Flash Units

To synchronize the shutter release and flash trigger circuit of a separate flash, a hot shoe is usually provided on top of the camera. As defined in Chapter 4, *Camera Handling, Care, and Support*, a **hot shoe** is a flash mounting terminal often located on top of a DSLR. Electrical contacts on the hot shoe mate with those on the flash unit, triggering the flash when the shutter release is pressed.

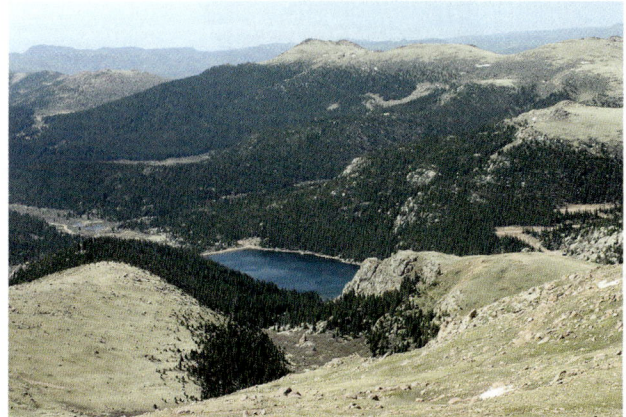
A

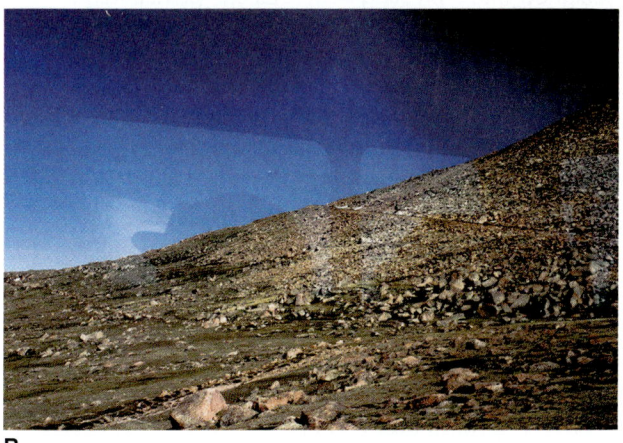
B

Jack Klasey/Goodheart-Willcox Publisher

Figure 12-44. Shooting through glass. A—Placing the lens very close to the glass of a train window eliminates reflections and allows the autofocus system to function properly. B—Moving the lens away from the window allows reflections to appear, partly obscuring the scene outside.

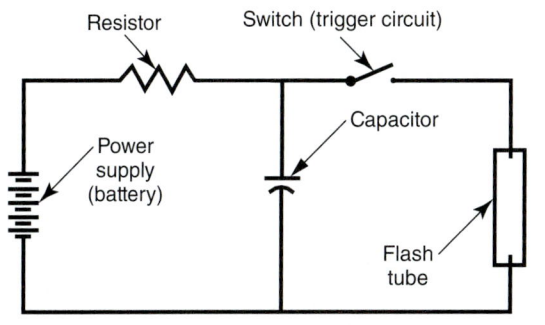

Goodheart-Willcox Publisher

Figure 12-45. An electronic flash circuit.

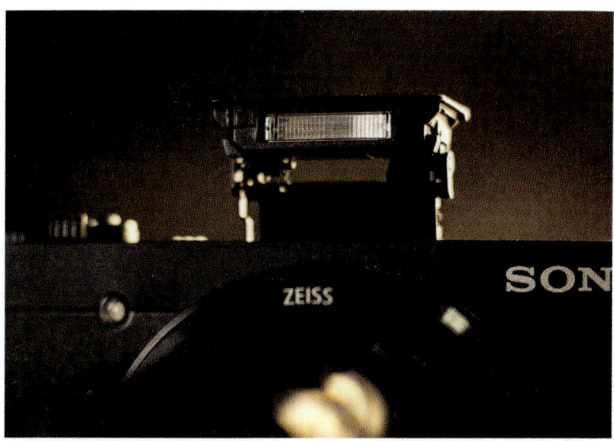

joshimerbin/Shutterstock.com

Figure 12-46. Built-in pop-up flash on a compact camera.

Shoe-mount flashes are available from camera manufacturers and from third-party equipment makers (those whose units can be used with various camera brands), **Figure 12-47**. These flashes vary in light output, physical size, mechanical design, and degree of automated operation.

Light output is measured scientifically in beam candlepower-seconds (BCPS), but from a practical photographic standpoint, the guide number is generally used. The *guide number* is a manufacturer-supplied number based on the light output of the flash and the ISO rating being used to manually determine lens aperture for proper exposure. For manual flash operation, the proper flash exposure is calculated by dividing the guide number by the flash-to-subject distance to yield the proper f-stop.

On some shoe-mount flash units, the flash head is fixed at a right angle to the body. On others, the flash head can be pivoted to point upward at an angle or even straight up, **Figure 12-48**. The pivoting head provides greater flexibility, allowing the photographer to soften the light by bouncing it off the ceiling or another surface.

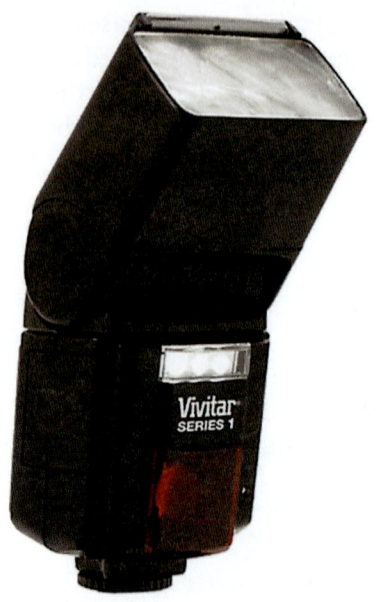

Vivitar

Figure 12-48. Many shoe-mounted flash units are designed with a pivoting head that can point straight forward, straight up, or at one or more angles in between.

A variation is the ringlight flash, which is used for close-up and macrophotography, a type of photography that is extremely close-up, usually of small subjects and details. The flash tube encircles the front of the lens to provide even, shadowless light. The flash body containing the electronic circuitry mounts on the hot shoe and is connected with a flexible cable to the flash tube.

Today's shoe-mount electronic flash units are highly sophisticated, with many automated features. The most fully featured products are the *dedicated flash units* designed for use with specific camera models or a range of models from one manufacturer. These units fully automate the process of flash photography, setting the proper aperture and shutter speed and adjusting the duration of the flash by measuring the light reaching the image receiver. Because of their metering method, such dedicated units are often referred to as through-the-lens (TTL) flash systems, **Figure 12-49**.

Dedicated flash units offer many other features, such as automatic fill flash and compensation for different zoom lens focal lengths. Most third-party flash makers offer special modules that provide dedicated operation for some of their flash units.

Handle-Mount Flash Units

Professional photographers who require high light output, durability, and the ability to use

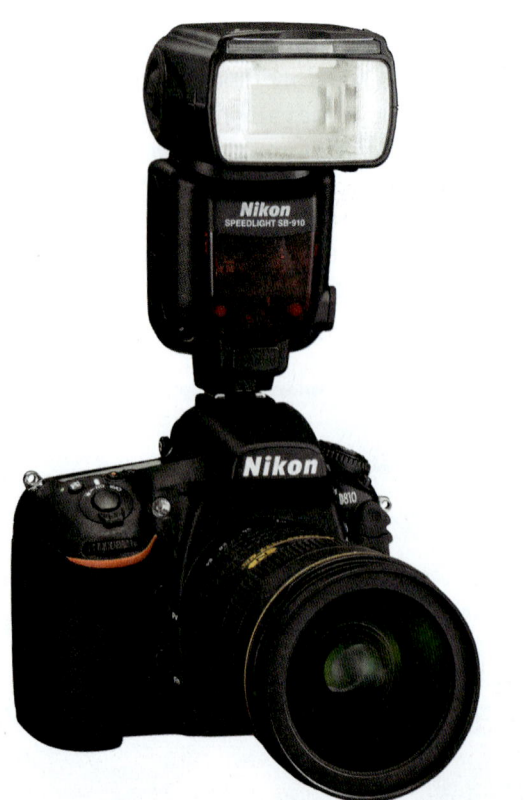

Courtesy of Nikon, Inc., Melville, New York

Figure 12-47. Small flash units are designed for mounting on a camera's hot shoe or similar camera-top locations.

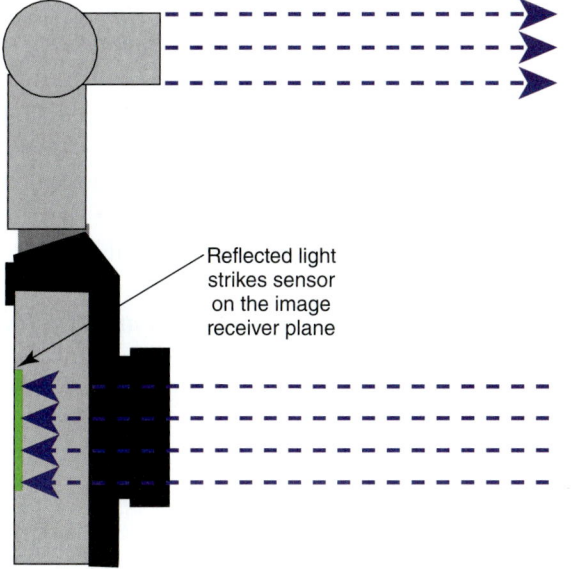

Figure 12-49. For precise control of flash exposure, TTL flash units evaluate the amount of reflected light reaching the camera's film plane. Once sufficient light has fallen on the image receiver plane sensor, the flash is cut off.

different types of power usually select a larger handle-mount flash unit, **Figure 12-50**. These units are physically much larger than shoe-mount types and are connected to the camera with a sync cord.

Wedding photographers and photojournalists need power sources that can provide numerous full-power flashes and permit fast recycling of the capacitor. Handle-mount flash units typically can be used with a number of power sources, ranging from multiple AA batteries to household current. Many photographers consider a belt-mounted **high-voltage power pack** that uses special rechargeable batteries to be most practical. Spare charged batteries can be quickly substituted as needed.

> **REAL-WORLD PHOTOGRAPHY**
>
> **Smartphone Flash**
>
> While it is ideal to take photographs with a DSLR, you may already have a great quality camera in your hands: your smartphone. Most newer smartphones have cameras that can rival some professional ones. Most of what is discussed in this chapter can also be done with your phone, as long as you have the appropriate settings.

Flash Techniques

Many amateur photographers aim the flash straight at the subject from a position directly over or right next to the lens. This **direct flash** method almost guarantees an unflattering photograph.

Direct flash creates several problems in an image, including the following:

- Harsh, flat lighting
- Unattractive shadows
- Burned-out foreground details
- Red eye

The only advantage of direct flash is ease and convenience of use—wherever the camera is pointed, the light goes as well. For people interested primarily in taking snapshots of friends, family, pets, or vacation activities, the quality of the lighting may not be an issue. From observing results of their own and friends' photography, they expect flash pictures to look that way, **Figure 12-51**.

Direct flash commonly results in a red eye appearance. **Red eye** is a problem that is caused by the light of the flash reflecting back from the retina of the subject's eye. See **Figure 12-52**. Many cameras offer a red eye reduction feature for built-in flash units. A series of short, low-power flashes occur while the camera is autofocusing in order to make the subject's pupils contract before the main flash is triggered. Since the pupil opening is smaller,

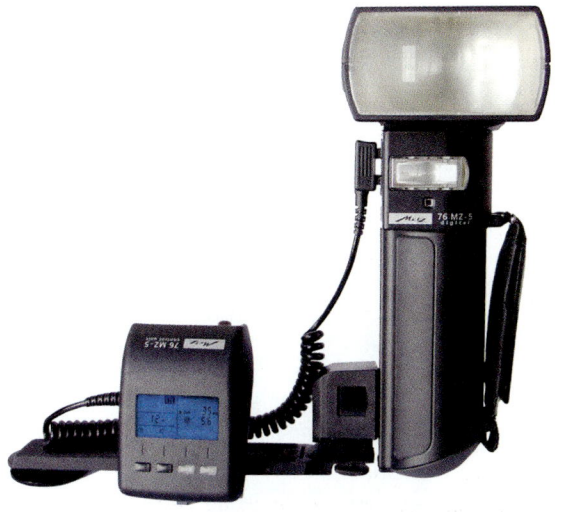

Metz

Figure 12-50. Many professionals use powerful handle-mount flash units like this one. The high light output permits photography under low-illumination conditions.

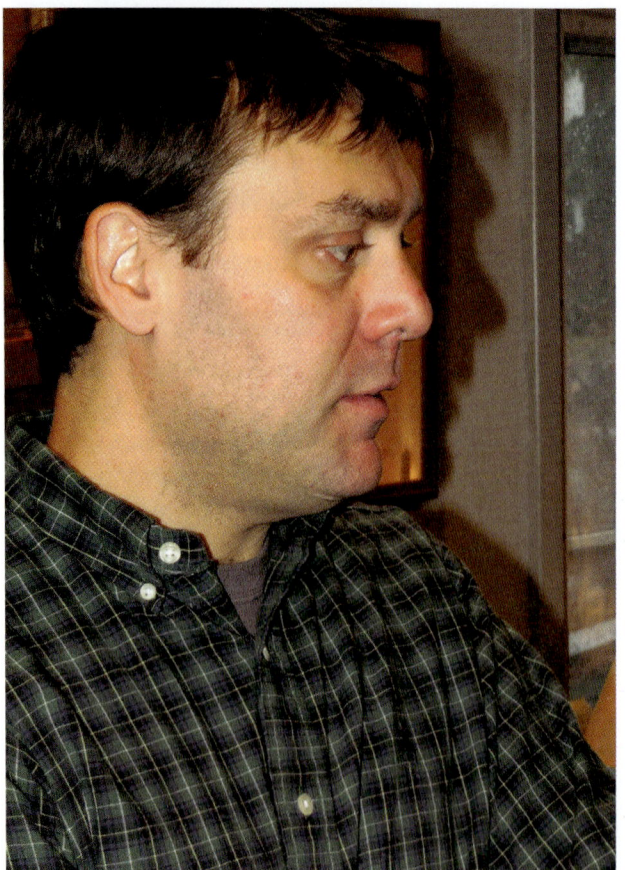

Jack Klasey/Goodheart-Willcox Publisher

Figure 12-51. Direct flash can produce harsh light and distracting shadows.

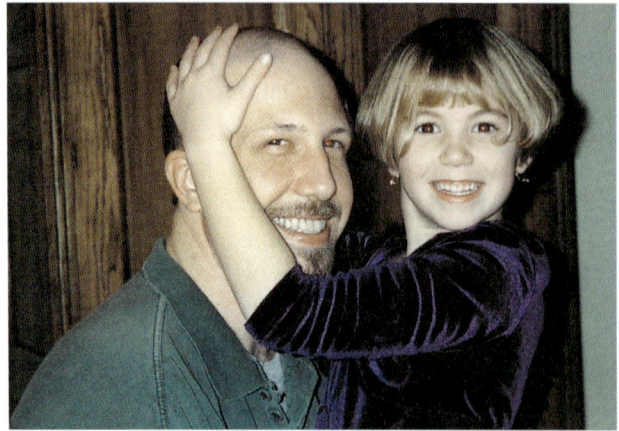

Jack Klasey/Goodheart-Willcox Publisher

Figure 12-52. Red eye is caused by flash located directly above the lens.

less red light is reflected back. This method reduces red eye but does not eliminate it.

Shoe-mount flash units can be used in a way that not only eliminates red eye but overcomes the other problems of direct flash. The simplest method for improving results with an on-camera flash is to diffuse or soften the light it produces. Diffusion is accomplished by placing a translucent material, such as a white T-shirt or frosted plastic, over the flash tube, **Figure 12-53**. This causes the light rays to scatter, eliminating the harshness of the light. The diffusion material lowers the light output, making an exposure adjustment necessary with manual flash.

A second method is the *off-camera flash* method, which involves removing the flash unit from the hot shoe and positioning it above and to one side of the camera. By using a coiled sync cord, the photographer can move the flash a foot or more to one side of the camera or raise it. Some photographers hold the flash in one hand and operate the camera with the other, while others prefer to use an L-shaped bracket, **Figure 12-54**. The off-camera flash method eliminates not only red eye but troublesome flash reflections from eyeglasses, mirrors, and metal surfaces. The higher positioning of the light also throws shadows downward behind the subject and out of sight.

Bounce Flash

A softer and more pleasing lighting effect is made possible with bounce flash. *Bounce flash* is a method of softening and diffusing flash light reaching a subject by first bouncing it off something else. For example, the light can be directed at a light-colored ceiling and reflected to the subject, becoming much more diffused and even. See **Figure 12-55**.

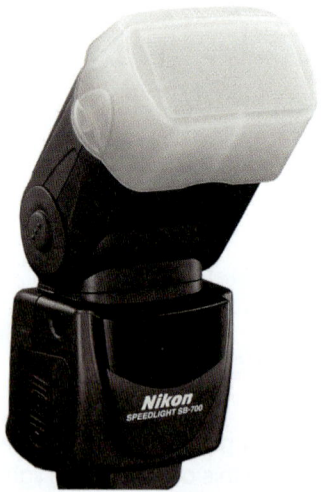

Jack Klasey/Goodheart-Willcox Publisher

Figure 12-53. A light diffuser mounted on the flash unit.

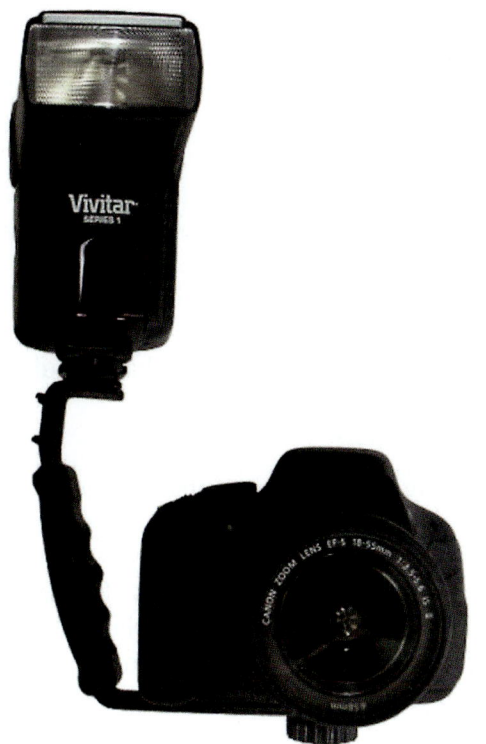

Vivitar

Figure 12-54. Moving the light source to one side of the camera will eliminate most of the problems encountered with direct on-camera flash.

Two important considerations in using bounce flash are the flash-to-subject distance and the color of the reflecting surface. Dedicated or automatic flashes compensate for the greater distance the bounced light travels, but users of manual flash units must take that factor into account. In addition to calculating the f-stop based on the increased distance, you must open up one or two stops to account for the loss of light due to scattering from the reflecting surface. To be safe, bracket exposures when using this technique.

Beware of reflecting a color cast onto your subject from a strongly colored reflecting surface. Also, avoid very dark surfaces that absorb rather than reflect much of the light.

When a suitable reflective surface is not available, you can provide your own, **Figure 12-56**.

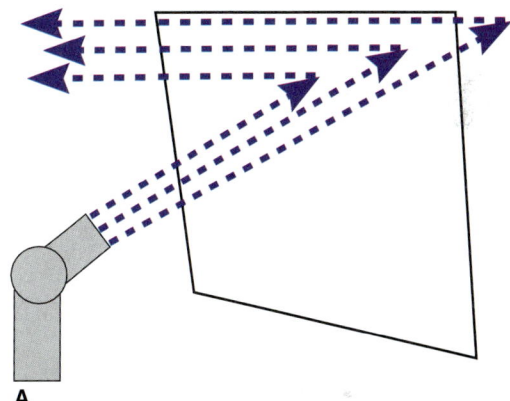

A

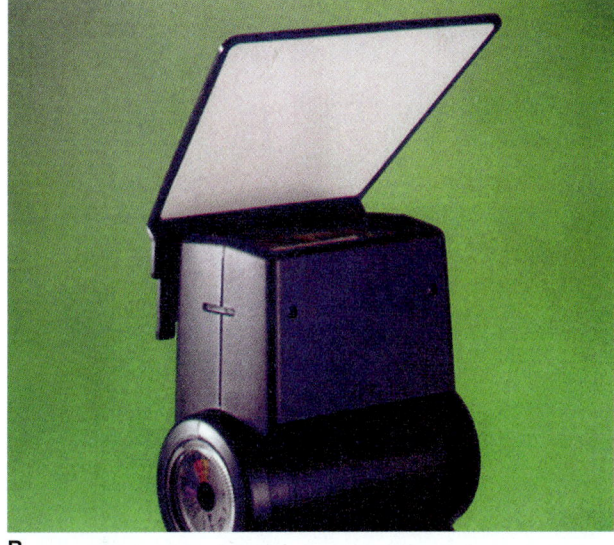

B

Porter's Camera Store

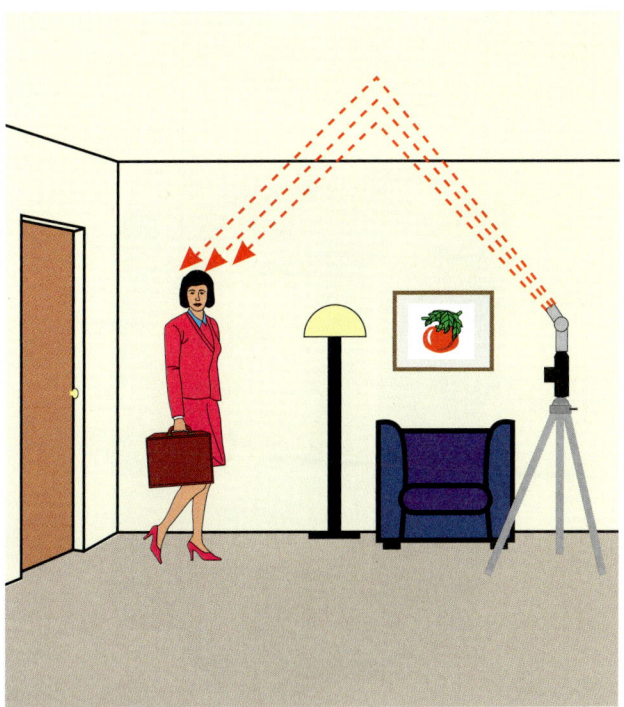

Goodheart-Willcox Publisher

Figure 12-55. Bounce flash can help light your subject evenly and avoid harsh shadows.

Figure 12-56. Alternate methods of bouncing light. A—A large square of white card can reflect light onto the subject. B—A bounce card directs most of the flash unit's light output toward the subject.

If an assistant or some form of stand is available, a piece of stiff white card several feet square can serve as a reflector. The flash unit is reversed so it points at the reflective surface rather than the subject.

A device that is simple to make is a bounce card. A small piece of white card stock is fastened to the flash head. The head is pointed straight up, and the card bent to extend over it at about a 45° angle. When the flash is triggered, most of the light bounces off the card in the direction of the subject. A rigid plastic version of the bounce card is available commercially.

Open Flash

Most flash techniques rely on synchronization to make sure the flash is triggered while the shutter is fully open. **Open flash** is a technique in which the camera's shutter is held wide open and the flash triggered manually one or more times. Because of this, it requires no synchronization. This method is most effective when there is little or no ambient light to cause additional exposure. For effect, flash and ambient light exposures may be combined. An example is a faintly moonlit scene in which a single feature, such as a plant or person, is given prominence by the use of flash exposure. See **Figure 12-57**.

Painting with light is an open flash technique typically used in large, dimly lighted spaces, such as church interiors, or for exterior photos taken at night. The basic procedure is to lock open the camera lens, and then illuminate the subject with a series of flashes. Care must be taken to avoid overlapping the different light bursts to prevent localized overexposure and to avoid silhouetting the person holding the light against the illuminated background.

Multiple Flash

Lighting a large or complex subject can also be accomplished with multiple flash units. Two or more flash units can be physically connected with sync cords to fire simultaneously. However, slave units are a more reliable and flexible method of control. **Slave units** are flash units containing a photoelectric cell that responds to the bright burst of light from a master flash that is connected to the camera. The burst of light causes the flash to fire instantaneously. A slave unit may be a small flash specifically designed for such use or an adapter connected to a conventional electronic flash, **Figure 12-58**.

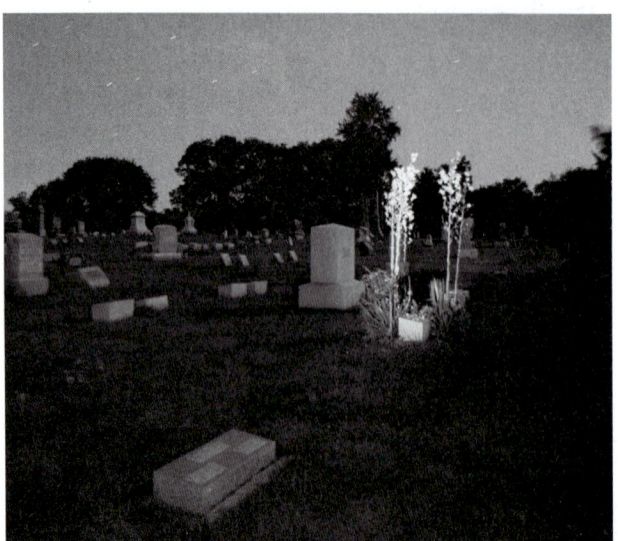

Jack Klasey/Goodheart-Willcox Publisher

Figure 12-57. The shutter was left open long enough for the overall scene to be exposed by ambient light, then a single burst of light gave the blooming yucca plants prominence.

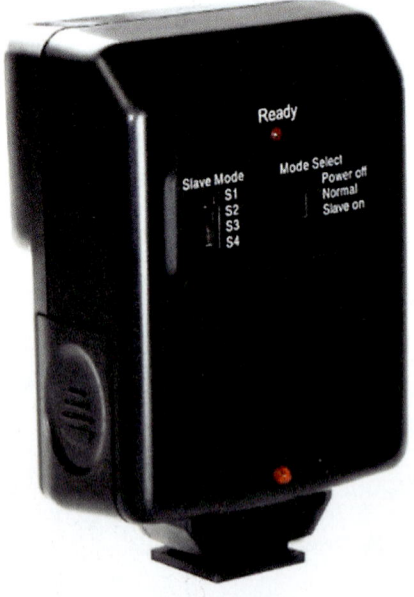

Vivitar

Figure 12-58. A small flash slave unit.

For more complex multiple flash situations, radio slaves are often used. These consist of a transmitter mounted on the camera and receivers used to trigger the flash units. See **Figure 12-59**.

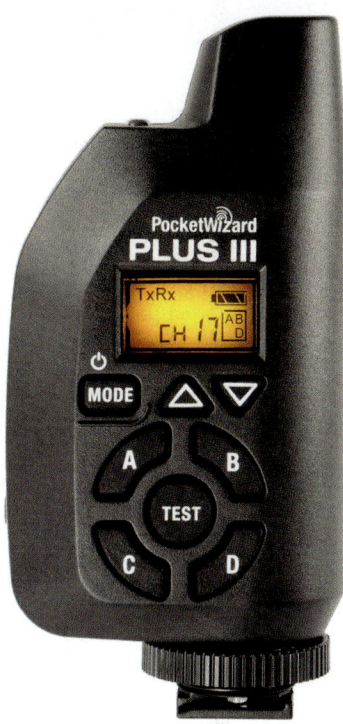

LPA Design photo by Zachary Gauthier

Figure 12-59. A radio slave transceiver that can be used as either a transmitter or a receiver attached to remote flash units.

PORTFOLIO ASSIGNMENT

Stop It!

For this assignment, you will work on stopping something in motion. Stopping motion and being able to capture clear photos is important because not every subject you take photos of will be perfectly still.

1. Depending on the season, choose an outdoor sport with subjects in motion to shoot, such as a softball pitcher, tennis player, or runner.
2. Set your camera to shutter priority mode.
3. Experiment with shutter speeds to produce varying amounts of motion blur and to completely stop motion. For example, a shutter speed of 1/250 is good for capturing a person walking, a shutter speed of 1/500 is good for capturing subjects that are running or moving a bit faster, and a shutter speed of 1/2000 is good for capturing faster motion, like cars moving or someone throwing a football.
4. Take 10 photos total, varying the shutter speed when appropriate.

Select two of your best images—one with motion blur and one with stopped motion. Note the shutter speed you used for each image and add them to your portfolio.

Chapter 12 Review

Summary

- Virtually any picture that portrays people involved in activities can be classified as action and event photography.
- When you seek to fully stop the movement of a subject, relative motion must be considered. Shutter speed and the focal length of the lens used are important factors in relative motion.
- Experienced action photographers are often able to capture dramatic stop-action photos without the use of flash or extremely high shutter speeds. They do so by capturing their subject at the peak of action.
- There are a number of manual focusing techniques that continue to be valuable photographic tools. These include follow focus, prefocusing, and zone focusing.
- Completely stopping a subject's motion is not always desirable. Some degree of motion blur in a photograph conveys a sense of movement. Panning and zooming are often used to create visual interest.
- Photojournalism is a specialized field of photography devoted to capturing images of news events and similar subjects for use in newspapers, magazines, and other print and digital media. Four of the major types include news and feature photography, picture stories, school event and yearbook, and other event photography.
- News and feature photography include both hard news assignments and soft news feature assignments.
- A picture story consists of a group of feature-type photos that carry out a theme. In purest form, a picture story relies on the photos and their accompanying captions to "tell the tale."
- For a student, photojournalism opportunities usually involve shooting for the school newspaper, yearbook, website, or Facebook page. Common events to cover include assemblies, concerts, and school sports.
- Other events commonly shot by photographers include community events, family milestones, and street photography.
- Action and event photography often requires the use of a portable light source, or electronic flash unit. Flash units are the primary source of portable artificial light for most photography.
- Types of flash units include built-in flash, self-contained flash units, shoe-mount flash units, and handle-mount flash units.
- Flash techniques include direct flash, off-camera flash, bounce flash, open flash, and multiple flash.

Review Questions

Answer the following questions using the information provided in this chapter.

Know and Understand

1. Which of the following is *not* a major category of action and event photography?
   A. Sports
   B. Portraiture
   C. Photojournalism
   D. Street shooting

2. The angle of the subject's motion relative to the camera's field of view or a given length of exposure is called _____.
   A. follow focus
   B. peak of action
   C. relative motion
   D. prefocusing

3. *True or False?* The closer the subject, the faster the shutter speed needed to stop its motion.

4. The likelihood of capturing the peak of action can be increased by careful use of the _____ feature found on most DSLR cameras.
   A. burst mode
   B. zone focusing
   C. prefocusing
   D. panning

5. _____ is a technique in which the photographer makes continuous small focus adjustments to keep a moving subject sharp.
   A. Prefocusing
   B. Panning
   C. Zone focusing
   D. Follow focus

6. *True or False?* Prefocusing is a useful technique when the action follows a regular pattern or routine.

7. _____ can be used to cover a wider area and is a good choice for less predictable activities such as football, basketball, or soccer.
   A. Follow focus
   B. Zone focusing
   C. Prefocusing
   D. Zooming

8. *True or False?* Completely stopping a subject's motion is *not* always desirable.

9. The result of _____ is a sharply focused subject, such as a runner or a vehicle, moving across a blurred background, strongly conveying the idea of rapid movement.
   A. zooming
   B. prefocusing
   C. panning
   D. zone focusing

10. Which of the following is *not* a common category of photojournalism?
    A. News and feature photography
    B. Industrial photography
    C. School event and yearbook
    D. Picture stories

11. *True or False?* Hard news assignments include feature-type photo assignments such as seasonal pictures and human interest photos.

12. A _____ is a support method used on medium and long telephoto lenses to prevent strain on the lens mount from the weight of the lens.
    A. lens collar
    B. hot shoe
    C. guide number
    D. dedicated flash unit

13. Which of the following is an example of a soft news feature assignment?
    A. Automobile accidents
    B. Crime coverage
    C. A children's Easter egg hunt
    D. Fires

14. *True or False?* A picture story consists of a group of feature-type photos that carry out a theme.

15. *True or False?* For yearbook photography, hand-holding the camera is recommended when shooting posed groups.

16. If shooting an event _____, flash is almost always necessary to obtain proper exposure.
    A. outdoors
    B. during the day
    C. with a smartphone
    D. indoors

17. To prevent capturing reflections when shooting through a window, hold the camera's lens _____ the glass without touching it.
    A. as far as possible from
    B. as close as possible to
    C. at a 90° angle to
    D. at a 45° angle to

18. A _____ is a device capable of storing an electrical charge.
    A. built-in flash
    B. hot shoe
    C. high-voltage power pack
    D. capacitor

19. _____ are flash units designed for use with a specific camera model or range of models from one manufacturer.
    A. Self-contained flash units
    B. Dedicated flash units
    C. Slave units
    D. Hot shoes

20. *True or False?* Professional photographers who require high light output typically use a handle-mount flash unit.

21. _____ is a problem that is caused by the light of the flash reflecting back from the retina of the subject's eye.
    A. Hot shoe
    B. Recycling
    C. Red eye
    D. Bounce flash

22. A method of softening and diffusing flash light reaching a subject by first bouncing it off something else is known as _____.
    A. bounce flash
    B. direct flash
    C. open flash
    D. off-camera flash

23. *True or False?* Off-camera flash is most effective when there is little or no ambient light to cause additional exposure.

24. _____ are flash units containing a photoelectric cell that responds to the bright burst of light from a master flash that is connected to the camera.
    A. Dedicated flash units
    B. Slave units
    C. Shoe-mount flash units
    D. Self-contained flash units

Apply and Analyze

1. Why is good timing vital when capturing the peak of action?
2. Describe how to use the technique of prefocusing.
3. Name the two types of camera motion used to induce blur to create visual interest.
4. List three important skills for a photojournalist besides photographic knowledge.
5. What two broad categories can self-contained flash units be divided into?

Critical Thinking

1. While reviewing photos you shot at an event for inclusion in the school yearbook, what types of sensitive content should you watch for that may make a photo unsuitable to print in the yearbook?
2. Observe a fast-moving sport, such as basketball or hockey, and think about how you would create a single image that captures the essence of the game. What viewpoint would you choose? Would you employ motion blur or freeze the action?

Suggested Activities

1. Organize and conduct a meeting of students interested in starting a newspaper at your school. Reach out to potential members through email or social media. At the meeting, set up committees to plan various aspects of the project.
2. As a small group project, plan and create a picture story entitled "One Day at Our School." Make prints and arrange them on a timeline displayed in a school hallway.
3. Dr. Harold Edgerton was a professor of Electrical Engineering at the Massachusetts Institute of Technology. What was his important contribution to photography? Do research to find out, and share your findings in an oral report to your photography class.

Communicating about Photography

1. **Speaking and Writing.** Research the National Press Photographer's Association Code of Ethics. In an oral or written report, use your own words to explain the contents of the code to the class.
2. **Speaking and Art.** Using pictures from magazines and newspapers, create a collage that helps you remember the difference between hard news and soft news photography. Show and discuss your collage in a group of four to five classmates. Are the other members of your group able to determine the difference between the two types of photography that you tried to represent?

Chapter 13
Outdoor Photography

Learning Objectives

After completing this chapter, you will be able to:

- Identify the types of subjects covered by the term *outdoor photography*.
- Explain why manual exposure, focus, and white balance controls should be used when shooting a panorama with a digital camera.
- Recall various shooting tips for successful landscape photography.
- Understand how to properly photograph smaller-scale subjects such as flowers and insects.
- Describe water photography and the various forms of water used as a subject.
- Identify key factors to consider when shooting animal photography.
- Define close-up photography.
- Compare the various types of close-up equipment and identify the most suitable use for each type.

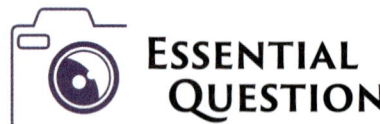

Essential Question

What techniques that you learned from other types of photography can you use to enhance your outdoor photography skills?

Technical Terms

catchlight
close-up range
flare
focusing rail
landscape photography
macro photo range
magnification rate
mirror image
nodal point
outdoor photography
panorama
photomicrography
reproduction ratio
reversing ring
windbreak
working distance

300 Copyright Goodheart-Willcox Co., Inc.

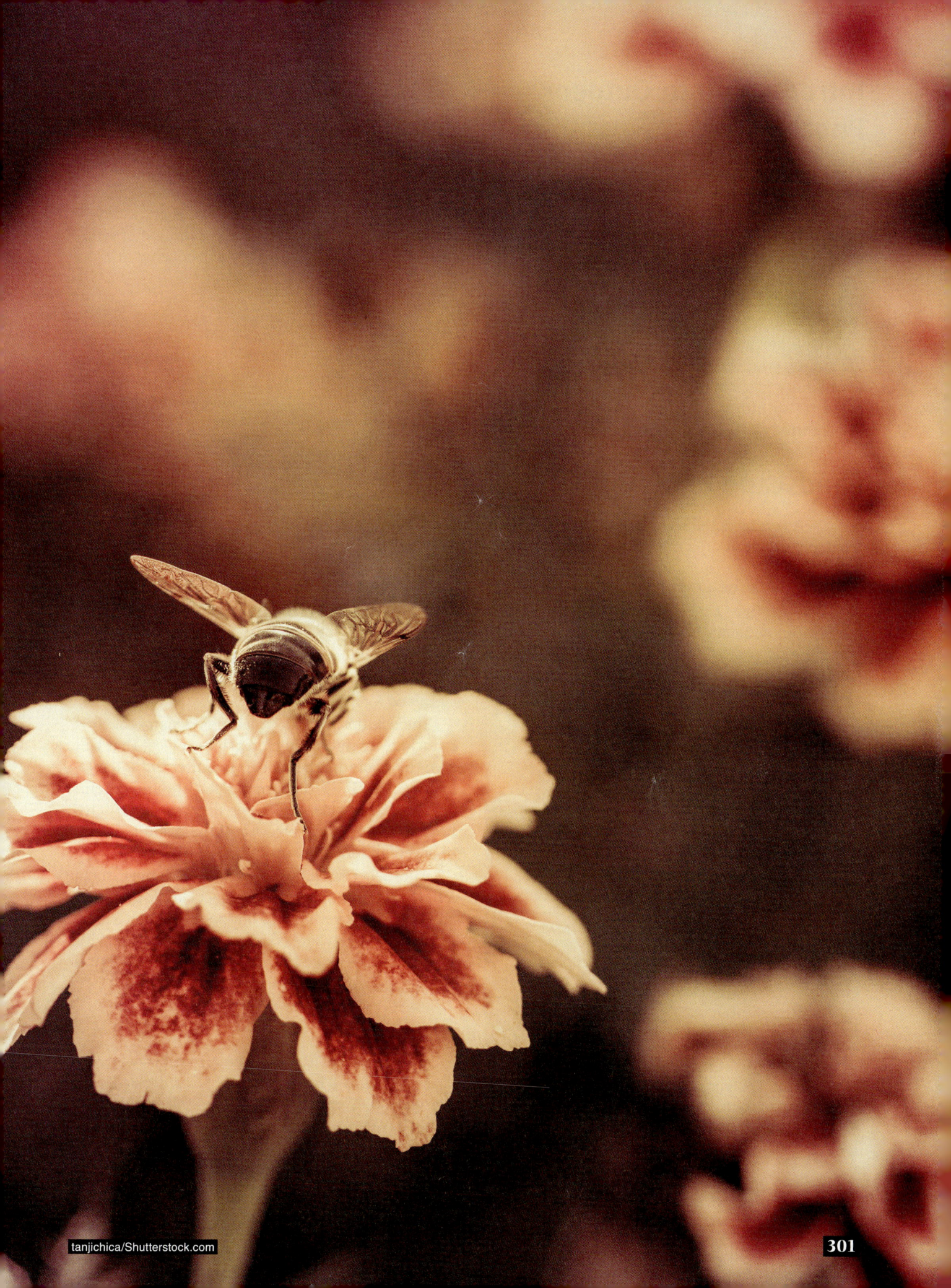

Introduction to Outdoor Photography

For most photographers, the term **outdoor photography** covers two broad areas—landscapes and wildlife. For this reason, it is also often referred to as *nature photography* because it deals with all aspects of the natural world.

Outdoor photos make fantastic additions to your portfolio. As you know, a portfolio is meant to showcase a photographer's wide range of talents. Outdoor photography is a great opportunity to show off your skills as a photographer, including your ability to shoot both small and large subjects, capture stunning colors and vistas, and overcome any lighting challenges.

Landscape Photography

When you hear the term *landscape photography*, what picture comes to mind? You probably visualize a grand vista, such as a mountain range or a river with whitewater cascading through masses of rocks, **Figure 13-1**. But what about smaller, more intimate views, such as a single windswept tree clinging to a cliff face or a pattern of bright-colored lichen on a boulder? These, too, are examples of **landscape photography**, which is defined as recorded views of the natural world in any of its aspects. While most landscape views feature the vegetable and mineral kingdoms (rocks and plants), the animal kingdom also may be represented as a part of a scene. For example, a view of peaks in the Swiss Alps that includes a mountain goat in the middle ground would be considered a landscape. If the mountain goat was the main subject, however, the image would be considered an animal or wildlife photo. Animal photography is covered later in this chapter.

Grand Vistas

Before digital technology made it possible to review an exposure on the camera's LCD screen, many photographers were disappointed when their landscape photos came back from the film processor. Their pictures seemed flat and dull, not at all like the stunning views they remembered from the scenic overlook.

The problem was most likely the focal length of the lens used to take the photo. When attempting to record a large scene, the natural tendency is to choose a wide-angle lens to "get it all in." The wide angle captures a broad, distant scene like the wind-eroded rocks of Bryce Canyon National Park, but it emphasizes the foreground rather than the more distant formations, **Figure 13-2A**. The human eye and brain process the scene differently, minimizing the bland foreground.

The solution to this wide-angle lens problem is to include an interesting foreground object that will give the photo increased depth and visual interest, **Figure 13-2B**. With a small aperture and careful focusing, the wide-angle lens allows you to have both the foreground object and the distant subject in acceptable focus.

Another possibility is to use a longer focal length to bring the distant subject closer, and then shoot several overlapping horizontal shots to form a panoramic view. It is fairly simple to do this with digital images since they can be merged in digital editing software.

Panoramic Views

A **panorama** is an extremely wide view of a scene, typically a landscape. The term, derived from ancient Greek roots, means *to see all*. Panoramic prints have been made from film for over 100 years.

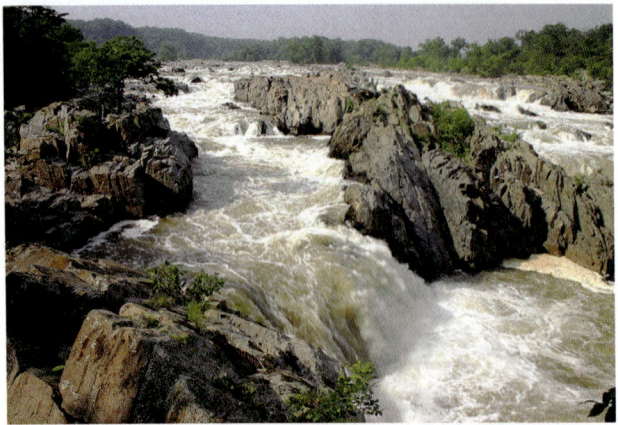

Jack Klasey/Goodheart-Willcox Publisher

Figure 13-1. This impressive expanse of whitewater and rugged rocky outcrops on the Potomac River is only a few miles upstream from Washington, D.C.

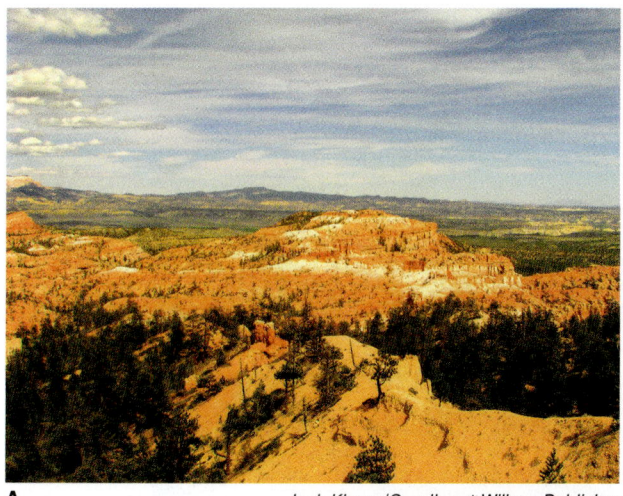
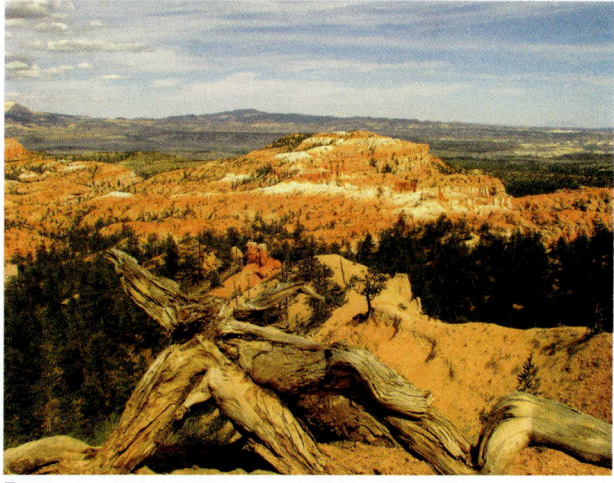

A Jack Klasey/Goodheart-Willcox Publisher B Larry Morris

Figure 13-2. Foreground improvement. A—The wide-angle lens used to record this scene emphasized the uninteresting foreground instead of the colorful rock formations. B—Including a sharply focused, visually interesting object in the foreground improves the photo by giving it a greater sense of depth.

Film Technique

The simplest way to create a panoramic view with a film camera is to shoot the desired scene with a wide-angle lens, then crop the resulting print to a long, narrow form, **Figure 13-3**. If the original is shot on 35 mm film, however, the size of the resulting print will be limited. For very large prints, a medium format or large format negative will give better results.

Digital Technique

In some instances, digital panoramas are created from individual files merged together in sequence to create the finished image. See **Figure 13-4**.

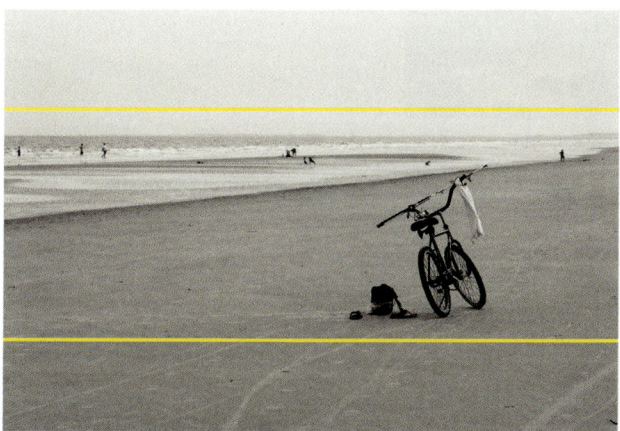

Jack Klasey/Goodheart-Willcox Publisher

Figure 13-3. Cropping to panoramic form.

Most image editing software includes a panorama-making feature, and separate stitching programs are also available. A panorama may be horizontal or vertical. The image can be taken with a lens of any focal length and can cover a scene distance measured in inches (flower close-ups) to miles (a mountain vista). Some camera phones, such as iPhone® models starting with the iOS 6 update, have the ability to capture a panorama. Simply select the Pano setting in the camera app, click the button used to take a picture, and move the phone continuously along the line.

Distant scenery panoramas are easier to create successfully than close-up views because of distortion problems. A camera's tripod socket is typically located directly below the image receiver plane. As the camera is rotated to capture the individual shots, the distance to the subject varies slightly. The extreme ends will be farther away than the center shots. The result is an alignment problem—adjacent image edges will not line up precisely. When the subject is reasonably far away, the alignment problem usually is slight. In a close-up, however, the minor difference in edge matching will stand out. To avoid this problem, the camera must be mounted so its center of rotation is beneath the **nodal point**, or optical center, of the lens. This is the point inside the lens barrel where the incoming light rays converge and turn the image upside down. Specially designed tripod mounts permit positioning the center of rotation beneath the nodal point, **Figure 13-5**.

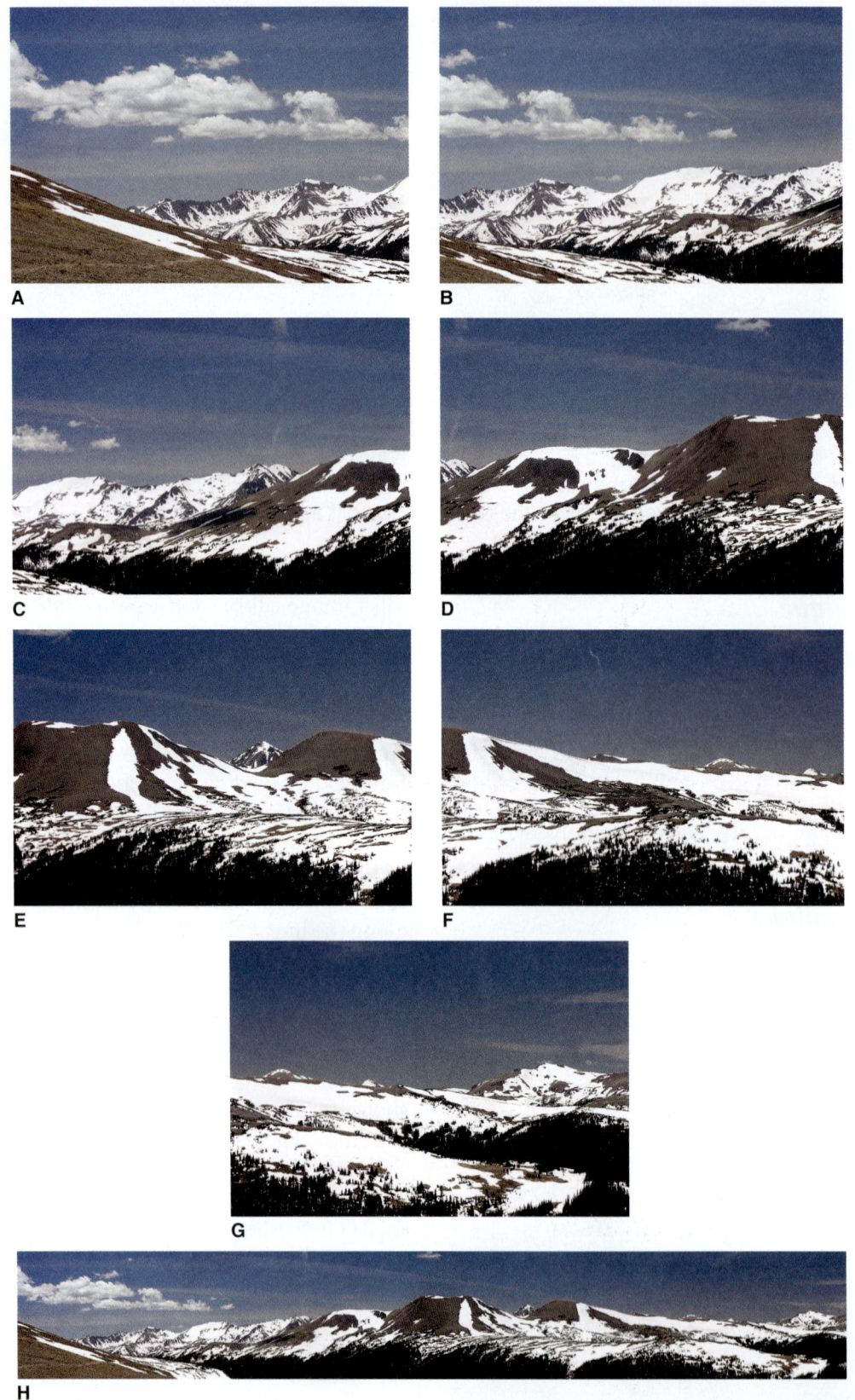

Jack Klasey/Goodheart-Willcox Publisher

Figure 13-4. A panoramic view shot in Rocky Mountain National Park. A–G—The seven individual exposures that were stitched together. The camera was mounted on a tripod and carefully leveled, and then each shot was overlapped by about one-quarter of its width. The overlapping helps the merge software achieve a smooth, seamless look. H—The resulting panorama covers a vista many miles in width.

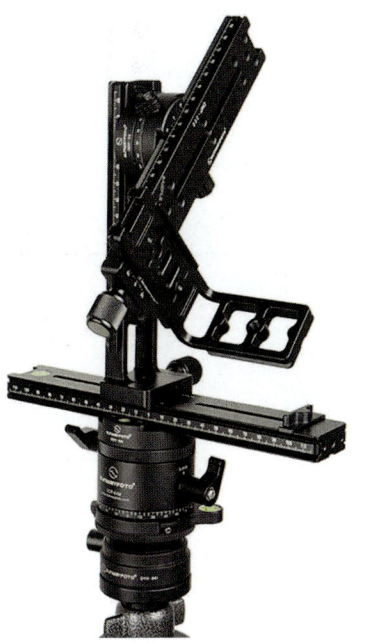

SUNWAYFOTO

Figure 13-5. A tripod mount for panoramic photography.

When shooting panoramas, follow these basic guidelines:
- Choose a subject and a composition with distinct starting and ending points and interesting subject matter in between.
- Carefully level the tripod and camera. Some tripod heads include bubble levels. A level that mounts on the camera's hot shoe also is useful. Level the setup with the camera pointed at the center of the composition, and then slowly move it through the arc that you will use when shooting. Watch the level and make any necessary adjustments.
- Select a focal length ranging from a moderate wide-angle lens to a long normal lens (between 28 mm and 75 mm is best). Wider lenses may introduce distortion, and longer lenses are more subject to sharpness-robbing vibration.
- Use your camera's autoexposure lock function to keep exposure consistent throughout the panorama. Alternatively, you may wish to turn off autoexposure and set exposure manually.
- Avoid automatic white balance (AWB) because it can shift color temperature from frame to frame. Instead, choose an appropriate white balance preset or use a custom white balance.
- Use manual focus instead of autofocus. Focus carefully for the first image, and then check focus on each succeeding image. Make minor adjustments as needed.
- Prevent an unintended shift in focal length when using a zoom lens. Use a piece of tape to lock the lens barrel.
- Overlap adjoining images between 20% and 50% so the stitching software can merge them.

If you are shooting similar material before or after your panorama, include marker frames. These blank frames make it easier to find the sequence of images. Before your first panorama shot, cover your lens and shoot a blank frame. Repeat the process after your last panorama shot. When you transfer the images to your computer for processing, it will be easy to tell which images make up the panorama.

Landscape Shooting Tips

For a landscape photographer, the angle and intensity of the light striking the subject can make the difference between a successful photograph and an unsuccessful one. The dramatic difference light direction can make is shown in **Figure 13-6**.

The color of the light can also be a strong factor in the success of your photo. On a sunny day, midday light is harsh, creating extreme contrast and adding a strong blue cast to shadows. Most photographers prefer the light of early morning and late afternoon, **Figure 13-7**. Often referred to as *magic hour* or *golden hour*, the half hour before and after either sunrise or sunset provides a warm light that makes subjects almost glow. Since magic hour is so brief, it is a good idea to use time-management skills and map out the shots you want to get *before* magic hour begins. Set up your camera ahead of time, if possible, and make sure your settings are as you want them before you start shooting.

Subjects reflecting the sun's light can be metered normally, but a different technique is necessary when the sun will be in the photo. If the sunrise or sunset itself is the subject, meter a clear area of sky near the sun, but do not include the sun in the frame. Lock in that exposure, set it manually, then reframe to include the sun.

One danger of including the sun in the frame, or positioning it just outside the field of view, is **flare**, which is the effect of stray light bouncing around inside the lens housing, causing decreased contrast. The reflections from the lens are typically visible as ghost images or bright spots obscuring parts of the picture, **Figure 13-8**. Even when ghost images are not visible, flare causes an overexposed, washed-out appearance in the photo. To prevent flare, use a lens hood or shade the lens with a hand, hat, or other object.

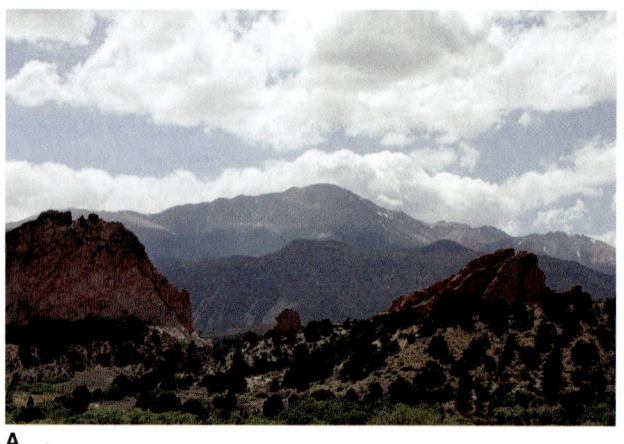 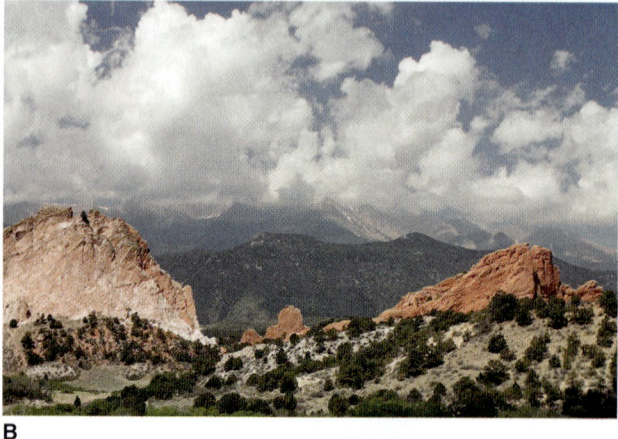

Figure 13-6. Colorado's Garden of the Gods Park. A—Early afternoon sunlight placed the foreground rocks in shadow. B—Midmorning sunlight falling on the gateway rocks brings out their full, vibrant color.

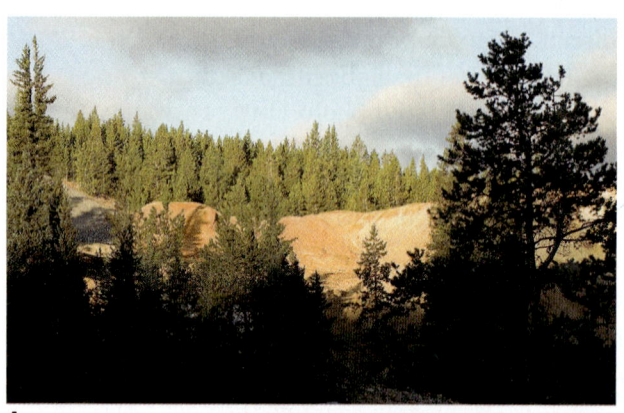 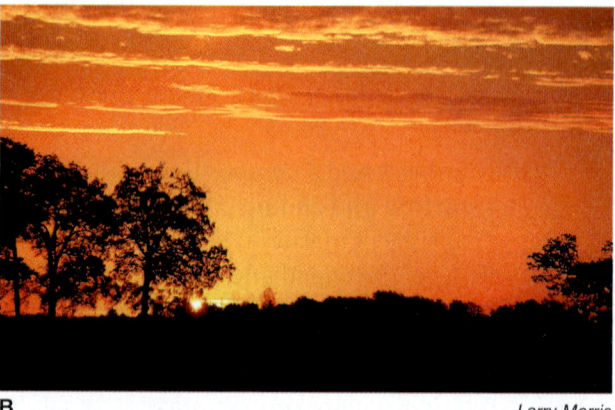

Figure 13-7. Photography in magic hour. A—Soft, warm light bathes a stand of pine trees shortly after dawn. B—Sunset and sunrise photos require careful metering to avoid overexposure.

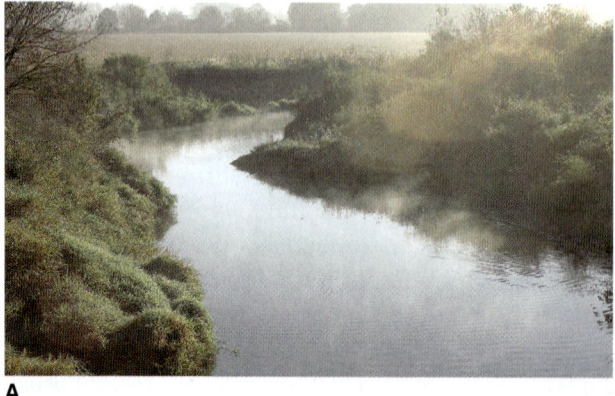 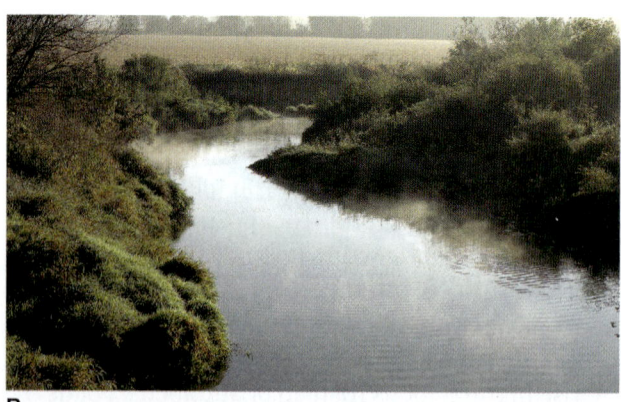

Figure 13-8. Eliminating flare. A—Flare can give a scene a washed-out appearance and create ghost images. B—Shading the lens eliminates flare.

To more dramatically render the sky during daylight hours, you can use a polarizing filter to darken the blue of the sky and increase the contrast of clouds. The filter also can improve the color saturation of foliage and other shiny surfaces by eliminating light reflections.

Whenever you shoot a scene showing the horizon, be sure that the horizon line is level in the viewfinder. When the horizon in a photo is tilted, the viewer is disoriented and made uneasy, **Figure 13-9**. Image editing software can be used to make the horizon straight, but the best practice is to be sure it appears level before pressing the shutter release.

Horizon placement in a photograph determines whether the foreground or the background is dominant. As shown in **Figure 13-10**, the horizon or other obvious dividing line may be placed high to emphasize the foreground, low to make the background more prominent, or in the center to provide a neutral, though static, appearance.

Shooting with a telephoto zoom lens allows you to locate and fine-tune a smaller composition from within a larger scene, **Figure 13-11**. When using the longer end of the telephoto zoom (for example, 300 mm), a shutter speed of at least 1/500 second is required to avoid camera shake. Whenever possible, use a tripod, even with a high shutter speed. Your chances of a sharp image greatly improve.

Smaller-Scale Subjects

Smaller-scale landscape subjects are easily accessible, whether you are in an exotic location or your own neighborhood. The size of your subject often allows you to walk around it to find a viewpoint with the best composition and lighting, **Figure 13-12**. Some photographers do this search with the naked eye, while others find it easier to do preliminary framing through the viewfinder of a

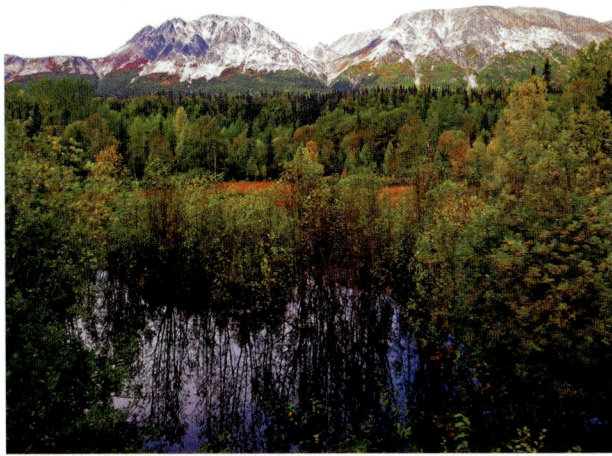

A

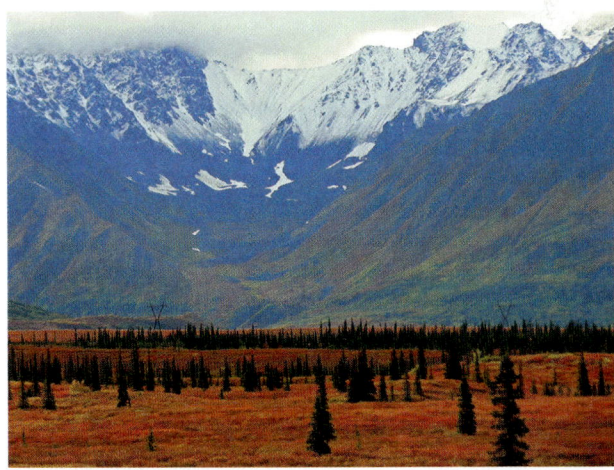

B

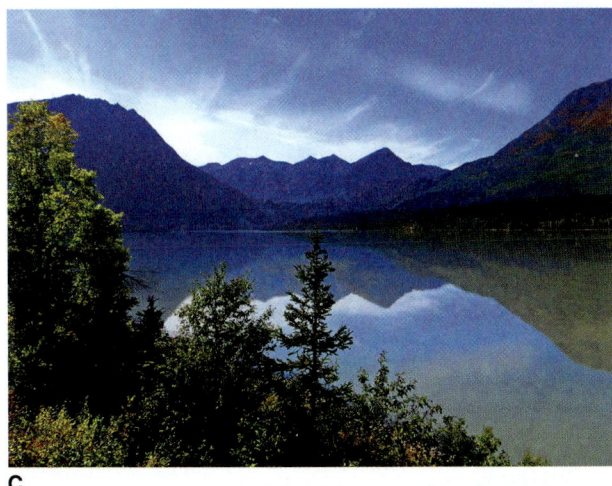

C

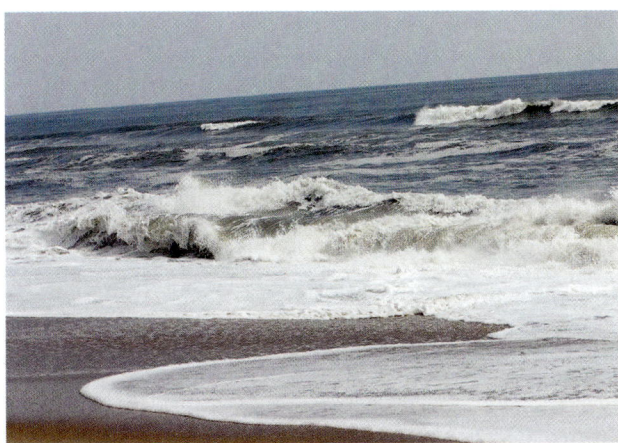

Jack Klasey/Goodheart-Willcox Publisher

Figure 13-9. With a tilted horizon line, the ocean surf appears to be flowing downhill.

Suzanne M. Silagi

Figure 13-10. Horizon placement. A—High horizon line. B—Low horizon line. C—Centered horizon line.

handheld camera. Once a viewpoint is established, the camera can be mounted on a tripod and the composition further refined.

Smaller-area subjects can usually be photographed with zoom lenses in the middle of the focal length range, typically 35 mm to 150 mm. This focal length allows you to fill your frame with a cascading woodland stream or to select a tighter view emphasizing water streaming around a boulder, **Figure 13-13**.

While grand vistas are usually shot as horizontal frames, smaller-scale subjects often lend themselves to being photographed in either horizontal or vertical formats. It is often worthwhile to shoot a subject both ways.

Flower Photography

A popular subdivision of landscape photography is shooting pictures of wildflowers and cultivated plants. Flowering plants appeal to the eye because of color, texture, shape, and structure. Another reason for their popularity as a subject is availability. Flowering plants can be found just about anywhere—from the desert to alpine tundra; in abandoned farm fields, prairie remnants, or even roadsides; and of course, in gardens both formal and informal, **Figure 13-14**.

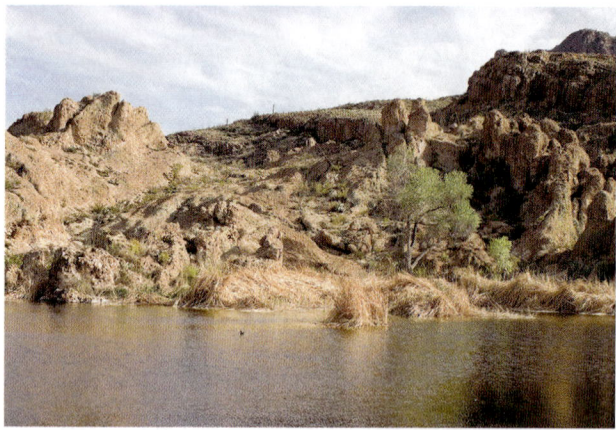

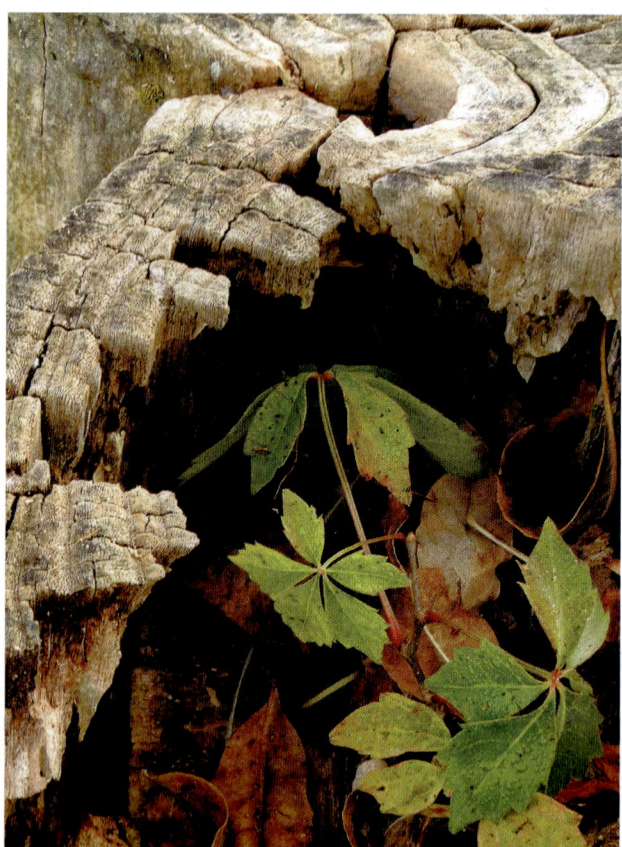

Jack Klasey/Goodheart-Willcox Publisher

Figure 13-11. Selective framing. A—A small water reservoir in the Arizona desert makes a pleasant composition. B—Zooming in and reframing provides a vertical composition with the tree as its focal point.

Jack Klasey/Goodheart-Willcox Publisher

Figure 13-12. A smaller-scale nature study of plants growing in an old, decayed tree stump. The photographer tried several different compositions and angles before settling on this one.

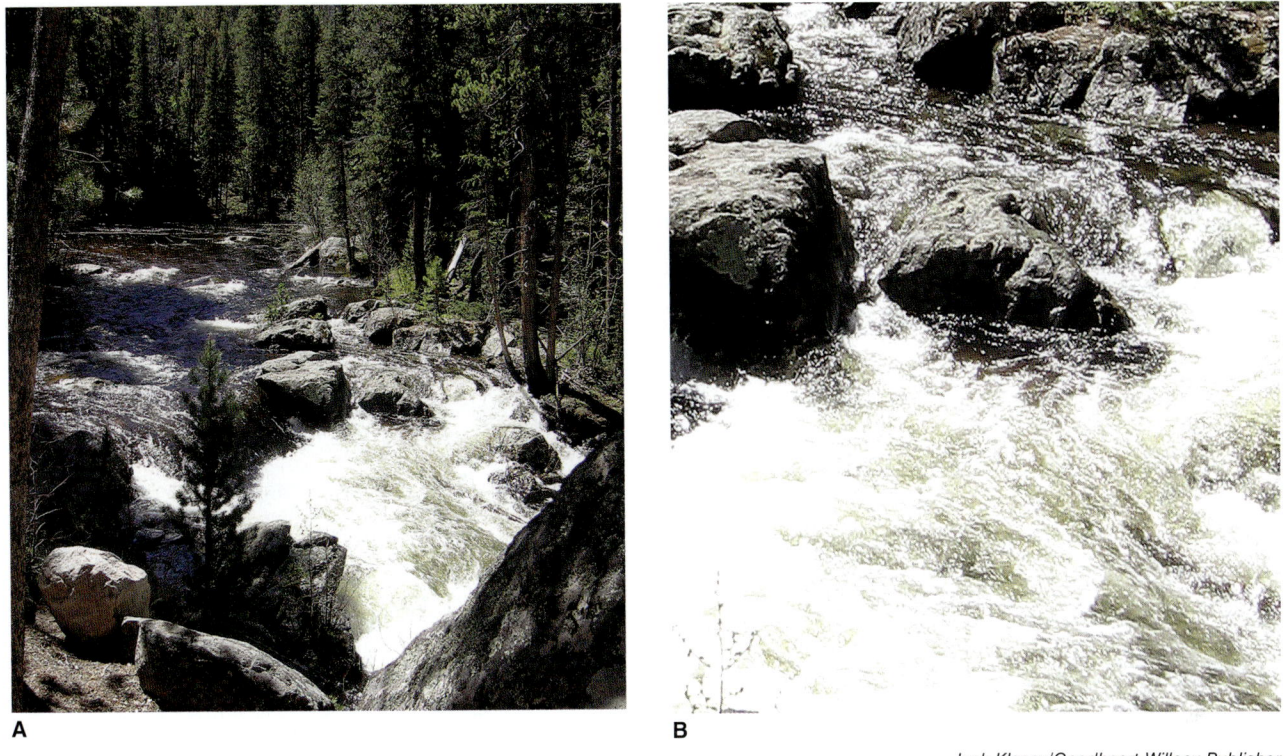

Figure 13-13. Different compositions from the same viewpoint. A—Wide view. B—Zoomed-in composition.

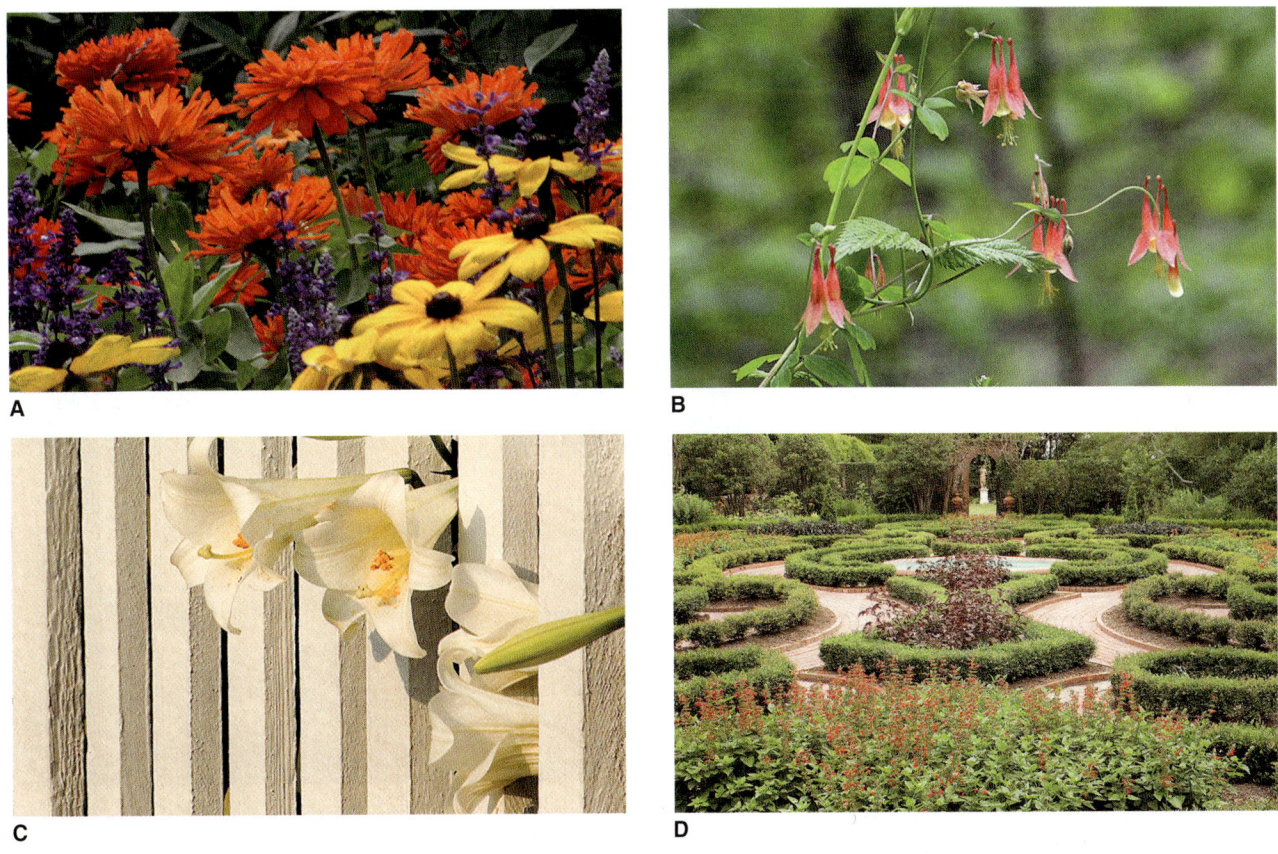

Figure 13-14. Flowers can be photographed in many settings. A—An informal garden. B—Columbines in a forest setting. C—Lilies peeking through a picket fence. D—A formal English-style garden.

Flower photography requires careful control of both exposure and focus. Bright sunlight can result in extreme contrast, with the danger of overexposing lighter areas. White flowers can be particularly difficult to shoot, even with diffused light or in a shaded area. Since the tonal variations in a white flower are very subtle, even slight overexposure loses the texture of the lightest areas, **Figure 13-15**. Bracketing in 1/3 stop increments is usually sufficient, although sometimes decreasing exposure by one stop or more may be necessary.

Controlling focus is critical to photographic success. Your camera's autofocus system can sometimes be fooled, locking on to something other than the subject you want to be in sharp focus, **Figure 13-16**. On a digital camera, you can confirm the correct focus using the LCD. Most cameras allow you to zoom in and pan to check the captured image.

Selective focus is a useful tool when photographing flowers. By choosing a large aperture, such as f/2.8, you can create a very shallow depth of field that emphasizes a single flower or even a portion of a flower. The background may be extremely out of focus, or just soft enough to be recognizable as other blossoms but not visually competitive with the sharply focused subject. See **Figure 13-17**. In some cases, you may find that the background appears unnatural in certain spots, such as a trail with markers or trash cans. In most cases, you can find shooting angles that avoid unnatural-appearing backgrounds, or you can shift your own position.

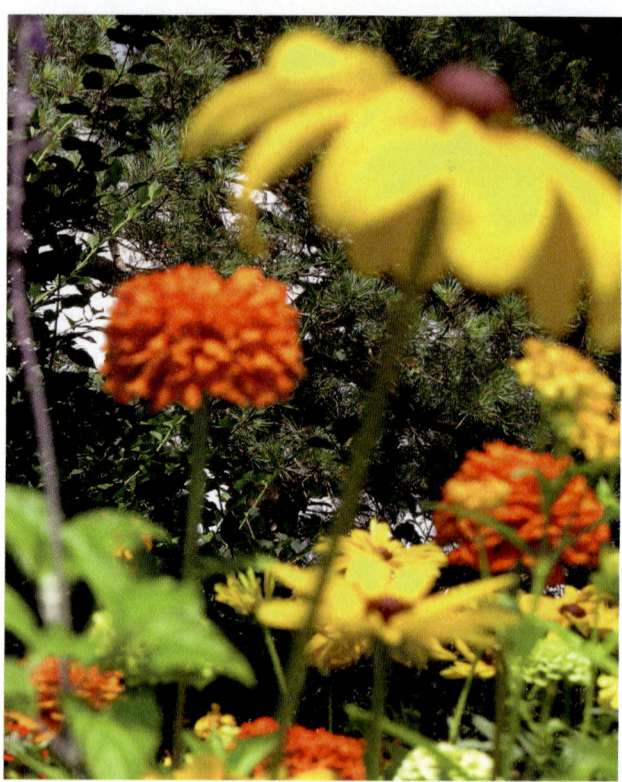

Jack Klasey/Goodheart-Willcox Publisher

Figure 13-16. Autofocus systems sometimes select a focus point different from the one you want. In this case, the background evergreens were selected instead of the flowers.

Strong emphasis is achieved when a subject is isolated from its background by lighting contrast. See **Figure 13-18**. Color can also provide visual

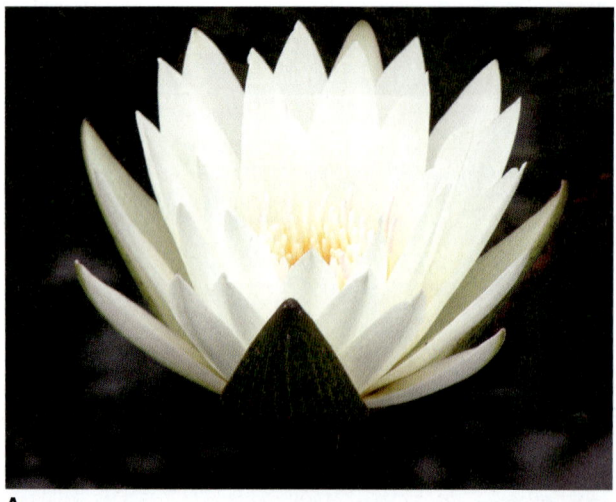
A

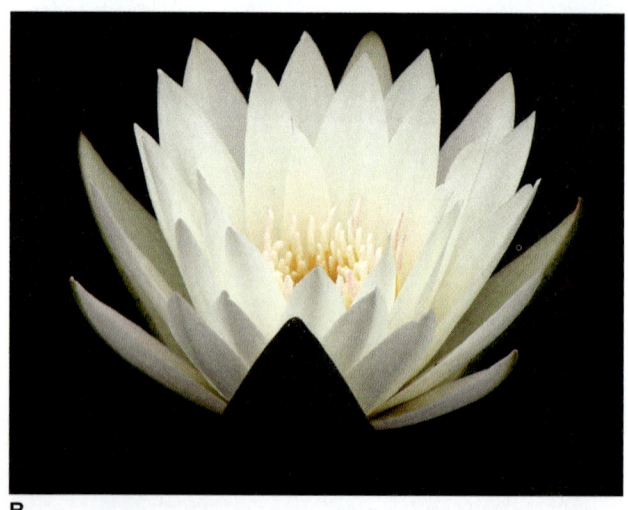
B

Jack Klasey/Goodheart-Willcox Publisher

Figure 13-15. Keeping detail in light-colored and white flowers. A—The metered exposure provided good detail in the green foreground leaf and the more-shaded petals but burned out the center and more brightly lit petals of the water lily. B—Decreasing the exposure brings out detail and texture.

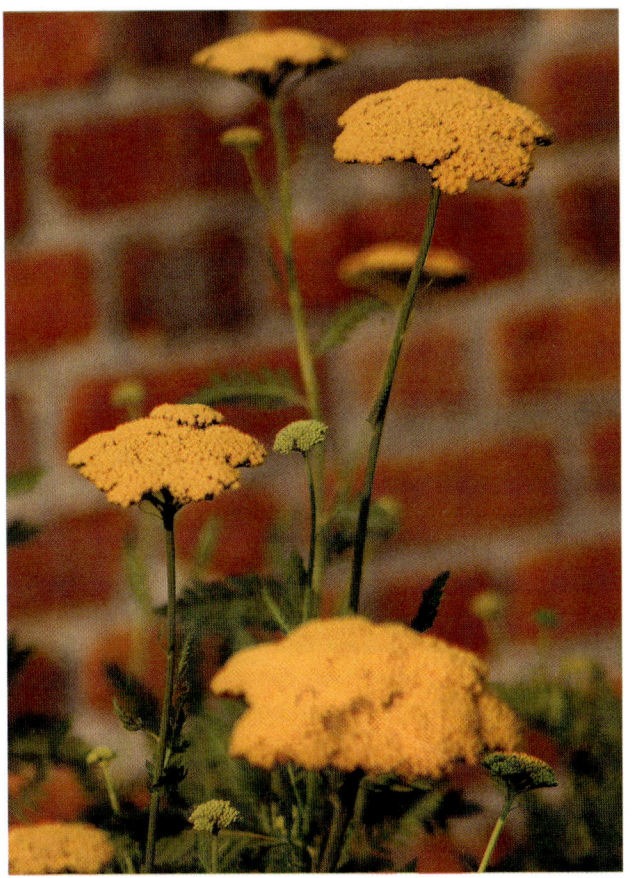
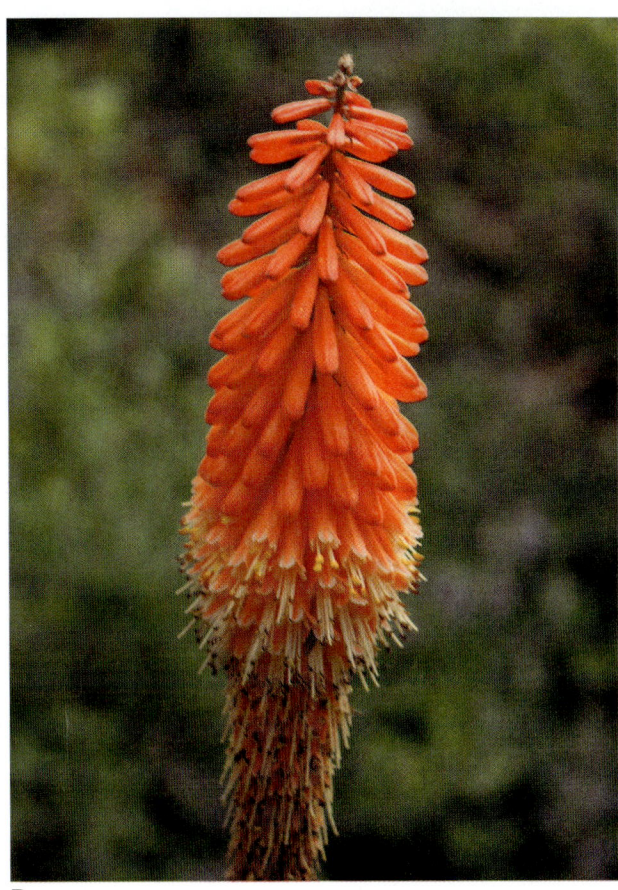

Jack Klasey/Goodheart-Willcox Publisher

Figure 13-17. Two approaches to selective focus. A—The flower in the center is sharp, while the brick wall is soft, but recognizable. B—The very soft background, along with color contrast, adds to the impact of this crisply focused flower.

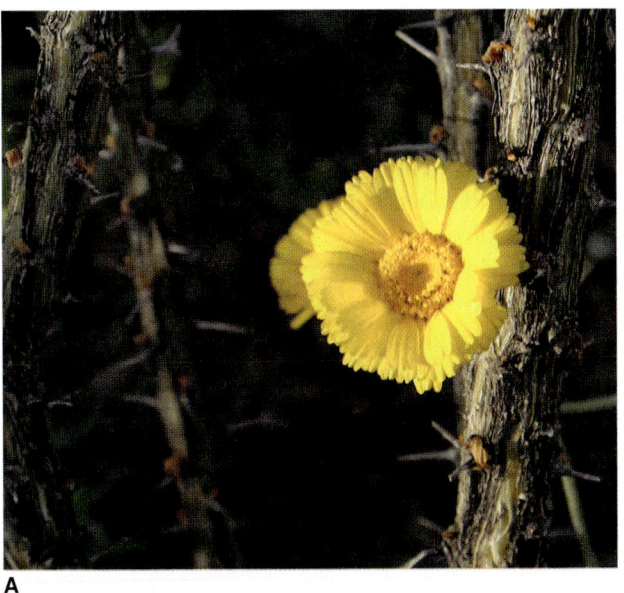
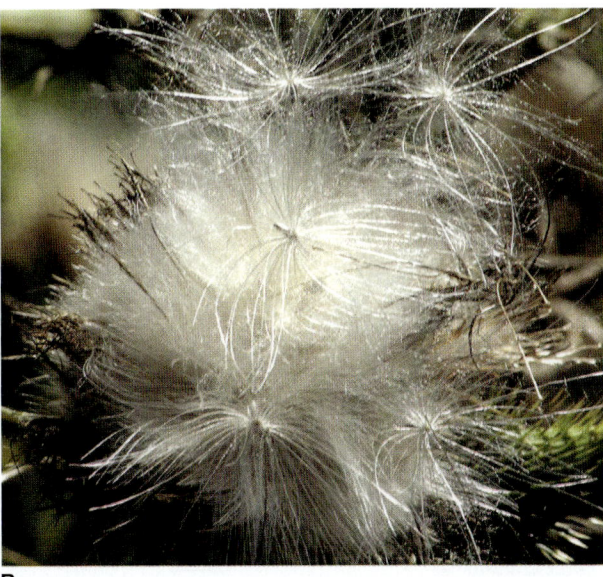

Jack Klasey/Goodheart-Willcox Publisher

Figure 13-18. Lighting contrast. A—The sunlit yellow desert flower stands out from the shadowed background of thorny stems. B—Backlighting creates a glow in the strands of milkweed seeds.

emphasis, with a bright or warm-colored subject standing out against a surrounding of cooler, more-muted colors, **Figure 13-19**.

Still another form of emphasis can be provided by physical isolation. See **Figure 13-20** and **Figure 13-21**. Repetition, the opposite of isolation, can sometimes be used to make an interesting photo. Repeated forms or plant elements create a pattern, as shown in **Figure 13-22**.

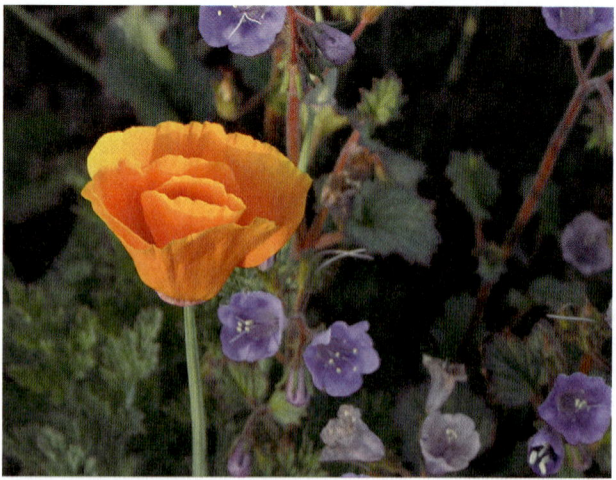

Jack Klasey/Goodheart-Willcox Publisher

Figure 13-19. Color emphasis.

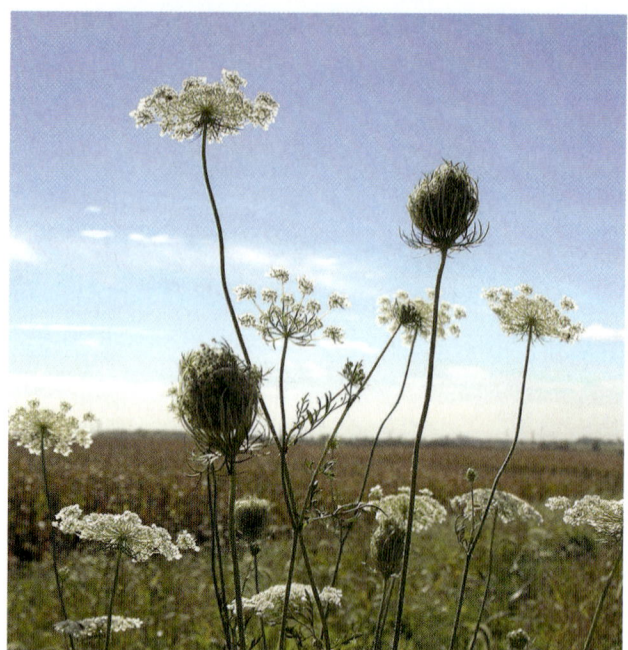

Jack Klasey/Goodheart-Willcox Publisher

Figure 13-21. Shooting from below isolates these blossoms of Queen Anne's lace against the sky.

Subject motion caused by the wind can be a problem, especially with close-ups. While some flower photography uses motion blur to good effect, close-ups are usually expected to be tack-sharp. The use of a flash can stop motion, but wildflower photographers normally prefer natural light, sometimes with a reflector for fill. If the light level is high enough, a faster shutter speed, such as 1/250 second or 1/500 second, can stop the subject's movement.

With conditions requiring lower shutter speeds, two strategies are possible—waiting for a lull or blocking the breeze. Wind seldom blows steadily for more than a few seconds. By using a tripod and waiting patiently, a photographer can make an exposure during a lull when the subject briefly remains still. A more efficient method is to block the wind. If an assistant is available, they can hold a sheet of poster board or similar material upwind of the subject and just outside camera range. If you are working alone, a **windbreak** (blocking device) creates a zone of stillness around the subject and often can be improvised from a collapsible reflector, plastic sheeting, a trash bag, or even an article of clothing.

Insects and Flowers

Flowers and some insects have a close working relationship. Two common flower visitors (and thus, the most likely photo subjects) are butterflies and

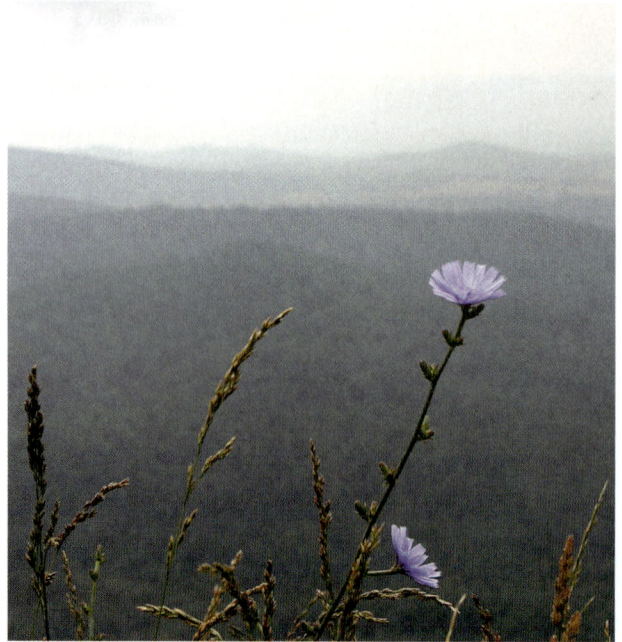

Jack Klasey/Goodheart-Willcox Publisher

Figure 13-20. Distant, misty hills form a soft backdrop to isolate the flowers and stems in the foreground.

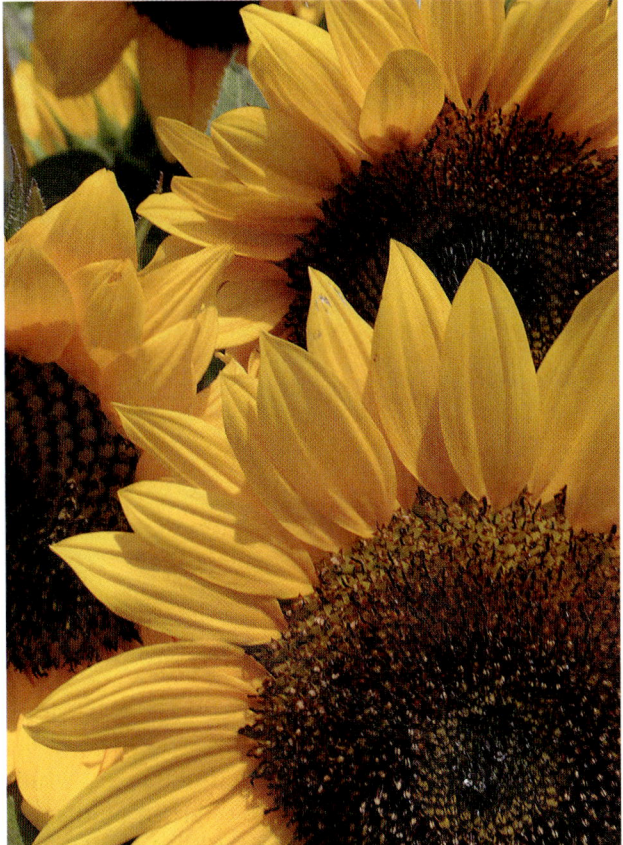
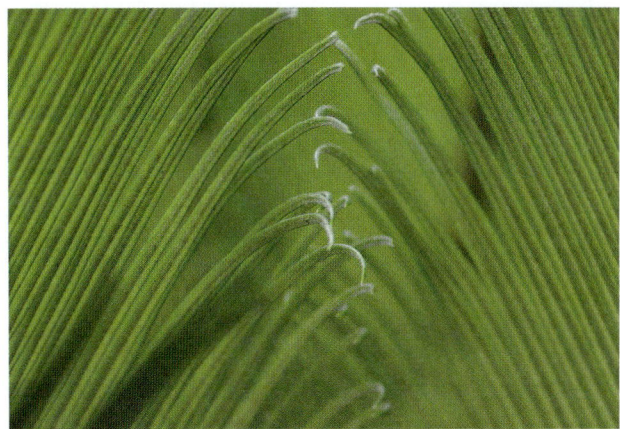
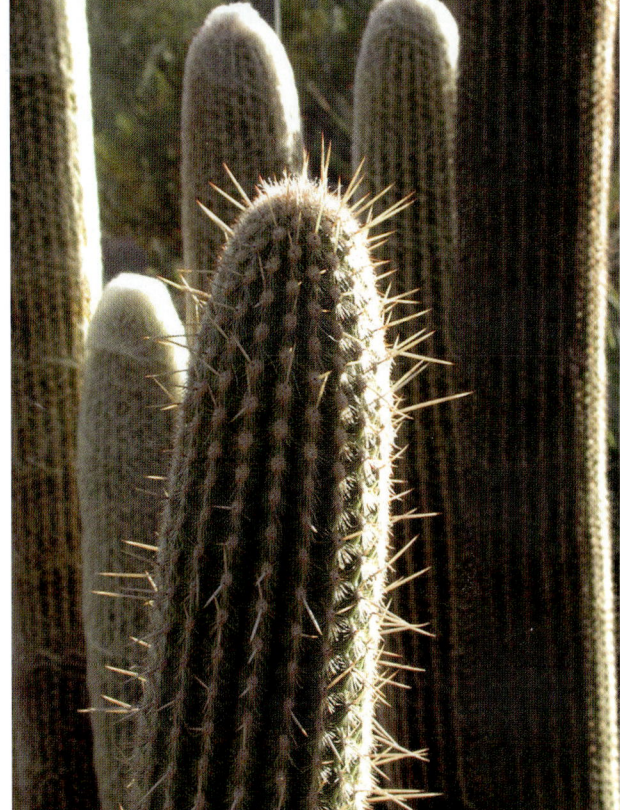

Jack Klasey/Goodheart-Willcox Publisher

Figure 13-22. Repeated shapes form visually interesting patterns.

bees, **Figure 13-23**. Most often, you would use a telephoto zoom lens to take shots of insects on flowers, since moving in too close threatens them and causes them to leave. Since insects move quickly and erratically from flower to flower, mount the camera on a monopod to provide both support and easy movement to the best vantage point. Use aperture priority to gain the desired depth of field and manual focus for the greatest possible sharpness.

Follow these environmental guidelines when photographing flowers and other plants:
- Step, kneel, or lie down carefully when composing your shot. Do not damage other plants while you are capturing your image.
- Do not uproot, prune, or break plants to improve your field of view. If necessary, use string to tie back intruding foliage, or hold it out of camera range with your free hand while releasing the shutter.

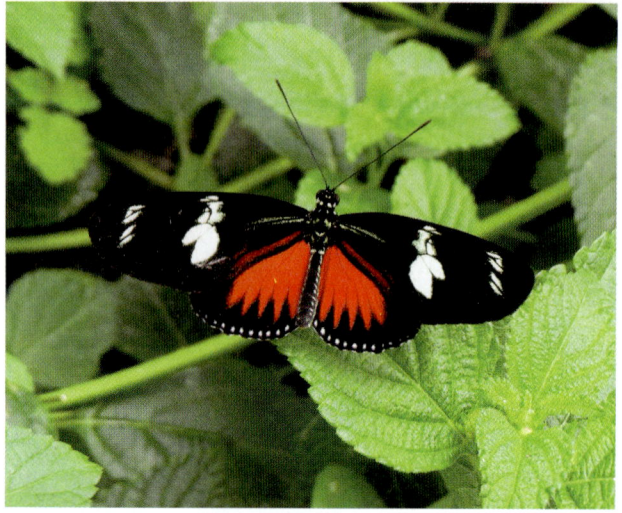
A

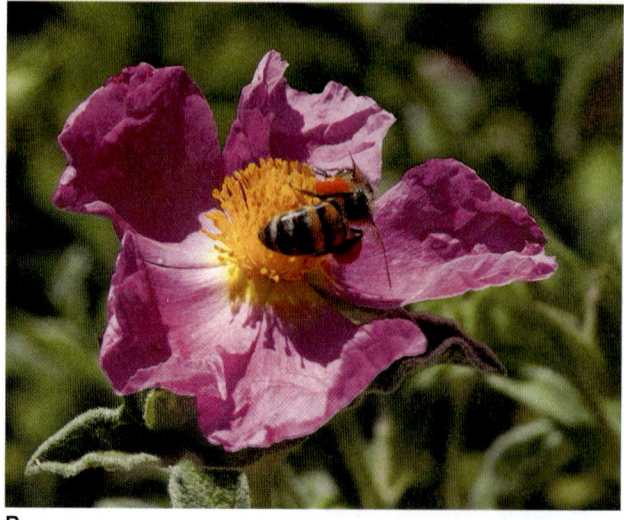
B

Jack Klasey/Goodheart-Willcox Publisher

Figure 13-23. Insects and flowers. A—A colorful butterfly stands out against green leaves. B—Honeybees are vital to the pollination of many plants.

- Do not leave behind evidence of your visit. Return a site to the state in which you found it by removing all your debris.

Infrared Photography

Striking landscape photos in which sunlit grass and tree leaves appear as bright, ghostly white objects can be produced by capturing infrared light. See **Figure 13-24**. Infrared wavelengths of light are not visible to the human eye. They can, however, be recorded on a digital sensor that has the proper sensitivity.

In a well-exposed and printed black-and-white infrared photograph, the leaves of green plants are bright white and appear to glow. Chlorophyll in the grass and leaves absorbs most of the visible light that strikes it, but it reflects most of the infrared wavelengths. As a result, the leaves and grass blades are bright reflective objects and appear white.

Most digital cameras cannot be used for infrared photography because the manufacturer has installed an infrared-blocking filter in front of the image sensor. Cameras can be modified by having the blocking filter removed, but the conversion is costly and must be done by a trained technician.

To determine whether your camera can recognize and record infrared light, you can do a simple test using your television remote control, which emits a beam of infrared light to control the TV. Most remotes use infrared technology to connect to your television and control it. To tell if your remote is infrared, you can look online or see if there is a window or knob on the top of the remote for the infrared signal to move through. If you do have an infrared remote, point it at the camera, press one of the channel-changing buttons, and take a photo. If the photo shows a bright light from the remote, your camera can detect infrared. If the light is dim or not visible at all, the camera has a blocking filter.

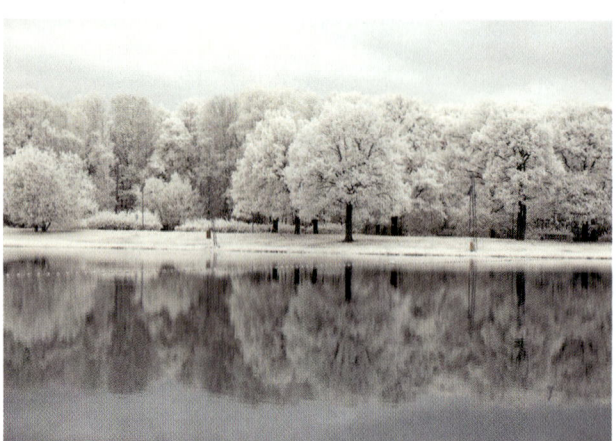

RUZvOLD/Shutterstock.com

Figure 13-24. Grass and leaves reflect almost all the infrared wavelengths, so they are recorded as strongly lighted objects—in black-and-white prints, they glow brilliant white.

Water Photography

Water may be a part of a landscape photo, or it may be the primary subject of the picture, **Figure 13-25**. Moving water—surf, streams, or waterfalls—is a favorite subject for many photographers. A mirror-like lake surface or other form of still water also can result in a memorable photo, **Figure 13-26**.

Another aspect of water as a subject is weather. A rainstorm can be captured dramatically by shooting a downpour at a relatively slow shutter speed, usually 1/60 second or less. The resulting streaks of rain convey the feeling of a storm, **Figure 13-27**. Patterns made by raindrops falling

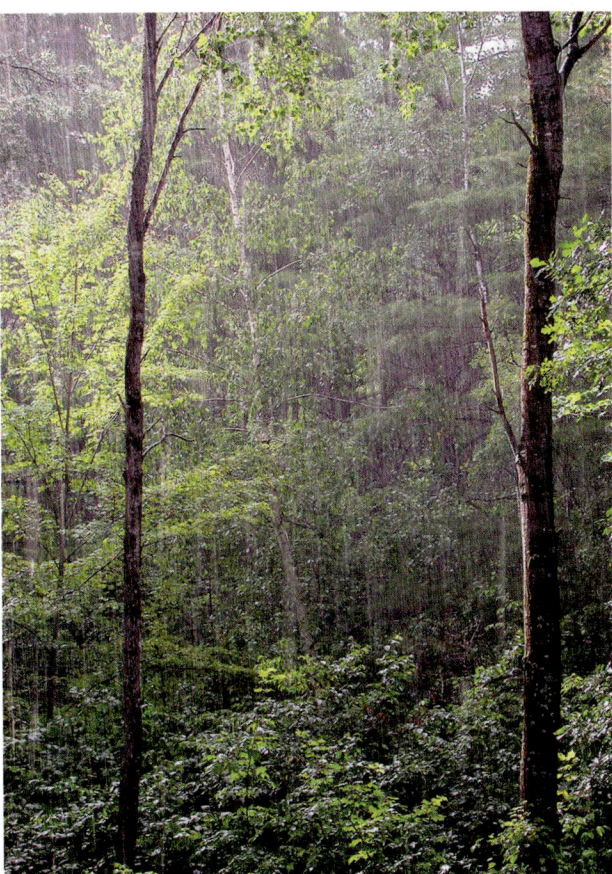

Jack Klasey/Goodheart-Willcox Publisher

Figure 13-27. This summer rainstorm was captured using a shutter speed of 1/30 second.

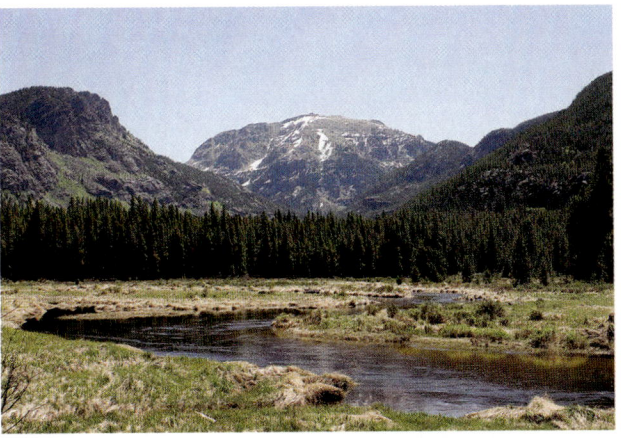

Jack Klasey/Goodheart-Willcox Publisher

Figure 13-25. A small stream meanders in an S-curve across a mountain meadow, drawing the viewer's eye into the landscape.

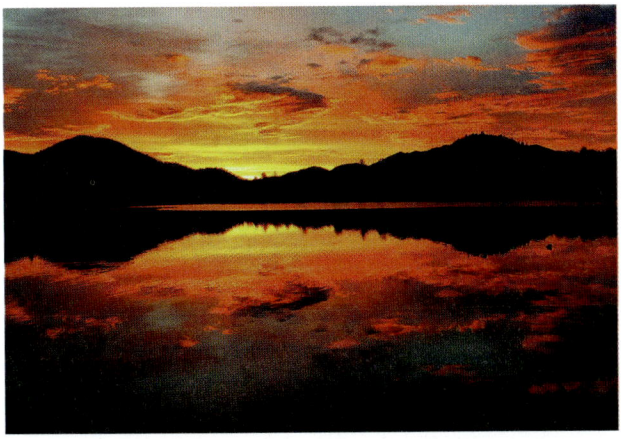

Steven Pennington/Shutterstock.com

Figure 13-26. Mirror Lake in Lake Placid, New York, is aptly named.

on a pond are also a good subject, as are the glistening drops remaining on surfaces after the rainstorm has passed, **Figure 13-28**.

Water droplets suspended in air (fog) lend a dreamlike quality, especially when photographed in early-morning light, **Figure 13-29**. In cold-weather areas, photos of water in solid form (such as ice or snow) can be dramatic and often colorful, **Figure 13-30**. Exposure must usually be increased by 1 1/2 to 2 stops from the metered value to avoid underexposure.

Water in Motion

Moving water holds a fascination for most people and poses a challenge to photographers, who must determine how best to capture the movement. Possibilities include sharply focused "stop-motion" streams and droplets, a strong-textured flow with some motion blur, and a soft, almost creamy flow.

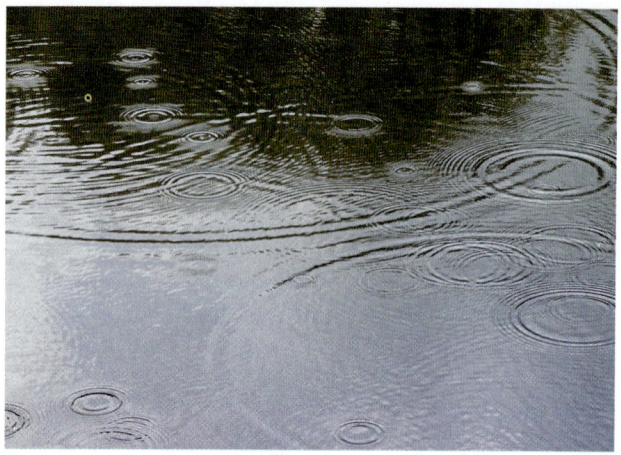

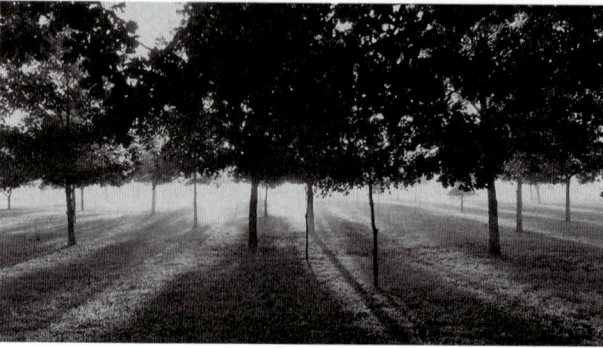

Clayton Pratt

Figure 13-29. Fog and early morning light combine for a dramatic silhouetted view of an orchard. The image was captured with a camera phone.

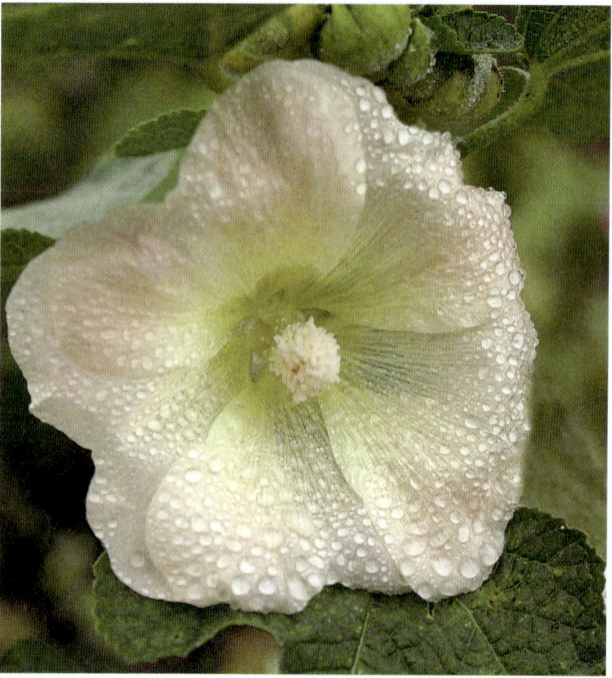

Jack Klasey/Goodheart-Willcox Publisher

Figure 13-28. Rain effects. A—Ripples from scattered raindrops form a pattern of interlocking rings on the surface of a pond. B—A blossom is beaded with raindrops, like hundreds of tiny jewels.

Each approach gives an image a different character. The degree of blurring is controlled by the choice of shutter speed. See **Figure 13-31**. Waterfalls lend themselves to wide shots, both horizontal and vertical, that convey the scope and power of the moving water. See **Figure 13-32**. A human figure can be included

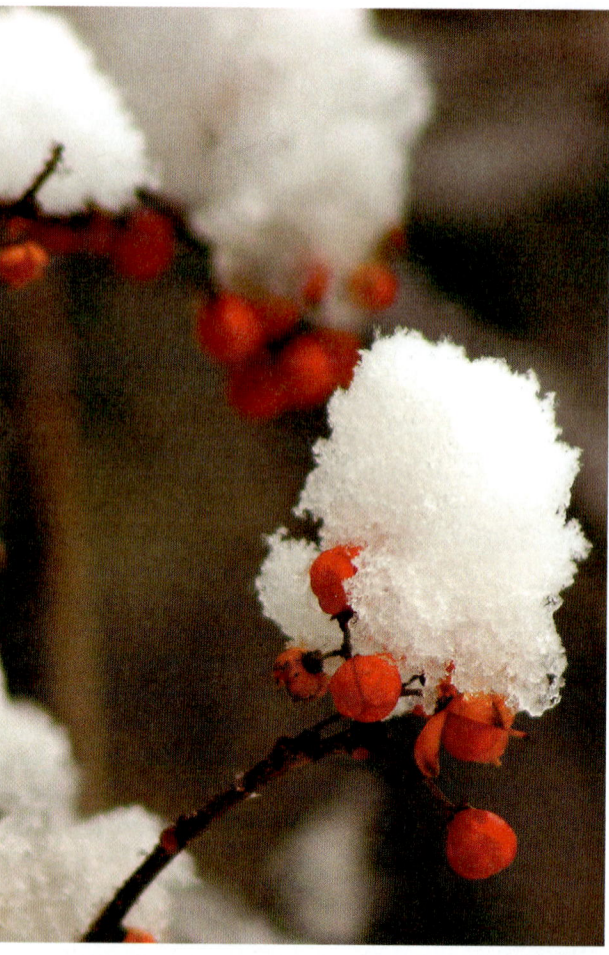

Jack Klasey/Goodheart-Willcox Publisher

Figure 13-30. White snow contrasts with the vivid red of dried bittersweet berries.

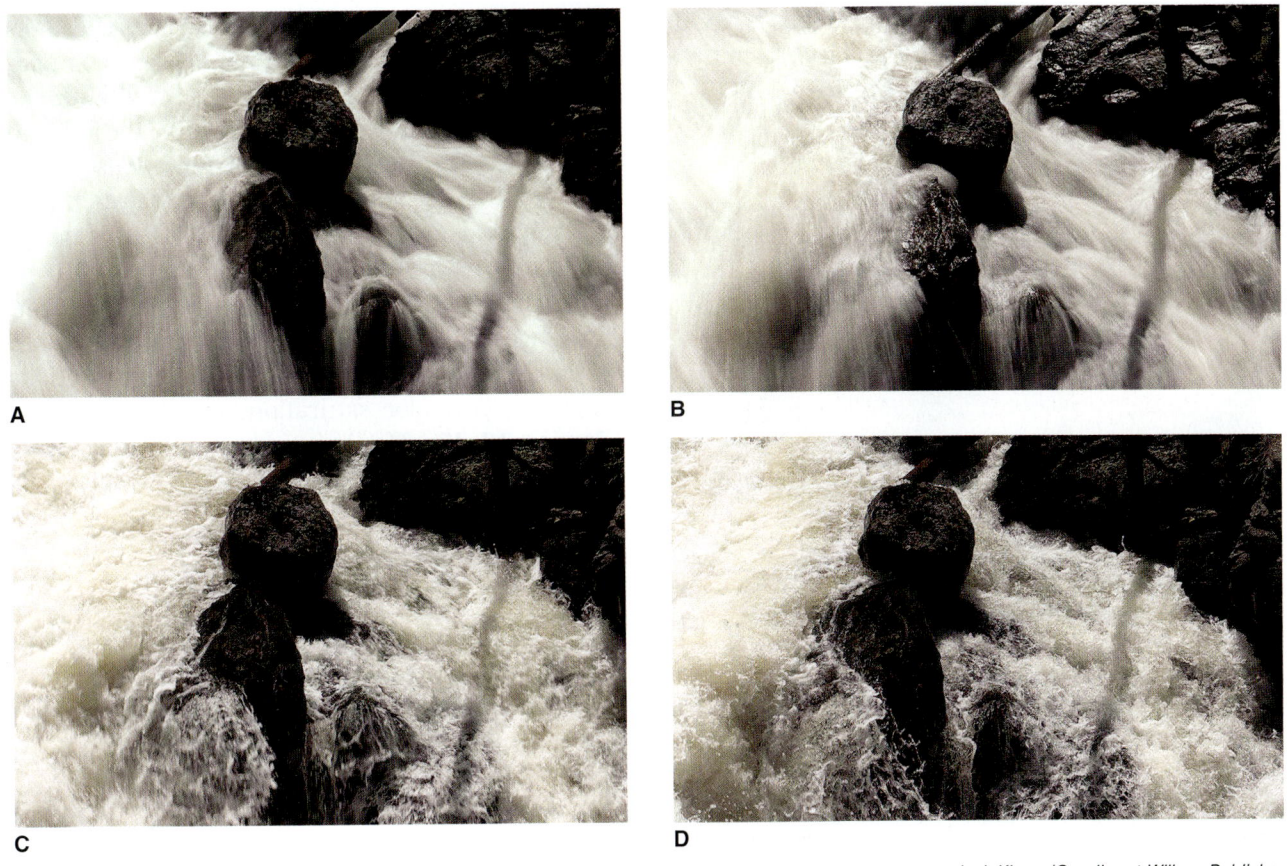

Figure 13-31. Shutter speed changes the appearance of fast-moving water. A—A very slow shutter speed (1/5 second) blurs the water into a soft, creamy flow. B—At 1/8 second, streaks of flowing water are more well defined, but the overall effect is still soft. C—The water's texture is much more sharply defined at 1/100 second. D—At 1/320 second, the water is "frozen," and individual drops can be seen. In all four shots, apertures were adjusted to provide equivalent exposures.

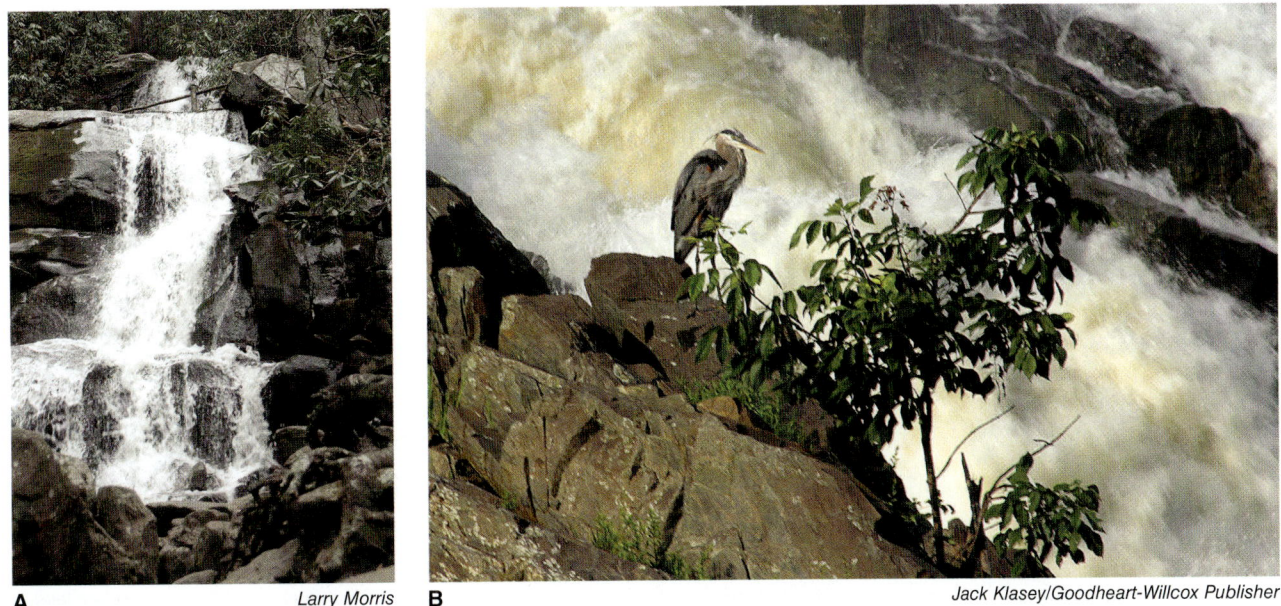

Figure 13-32. Vary format to suit the subject. A—This waterfall is a natural for a vertical format. B—The diagonal movement of water across this horizontal image is balanced by the still figure of a great blue heron.

Chapter 13 Outdoor Photography 317

in the scene to provide a sense of scale, **Figure 13-33**. Falling water is broken into tiny droplets, forming a mist that can generate a rainbow, **Figure 13-34**.

When water is still, its surface often reflects its surroundings. The most common approach to photographing reflections in water is the **mirror image**, which is an almost exact reproduction of the scene in reverse. See **Figure 13-35**. Color reflections can be captured from surfaces with only a film of water, such as beach sand, and even from moving water when the light source itself is being reflected, **Figure 13-36**.

At times, you may prefer to eliminate reflections in the water to remove distractions from the main subject. A polarizing filter both eliminates reflections and improves color saturation by reducing glare, **Figure 13-37**. Objects underwater that were obscured by reflections can be revealed as well.

Animal Photography

While some animal photography involves groups, the most striking and memorable shots are usually of an individual. In many respects, animal

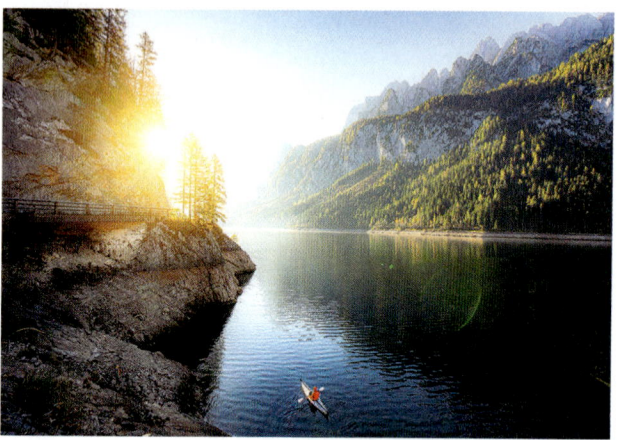

Nyokki/Shutterstock.com

Figure 13-33. The tiny figure in the kayak provides a scale reference for this Austrian scene.

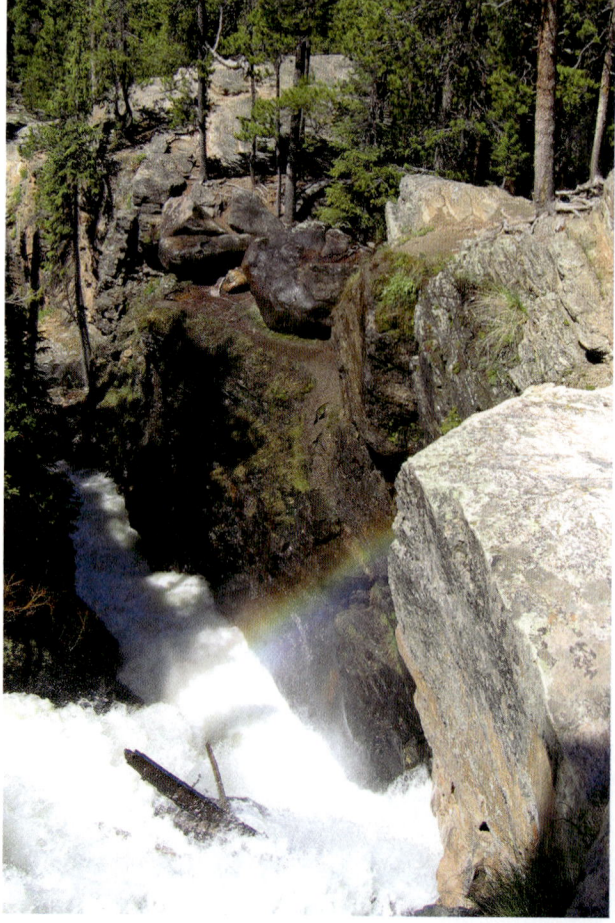

Glory Klasey

Figure 13-34. Sunlight refracted from water droplets in a churning stream forms a persistent rainbow.

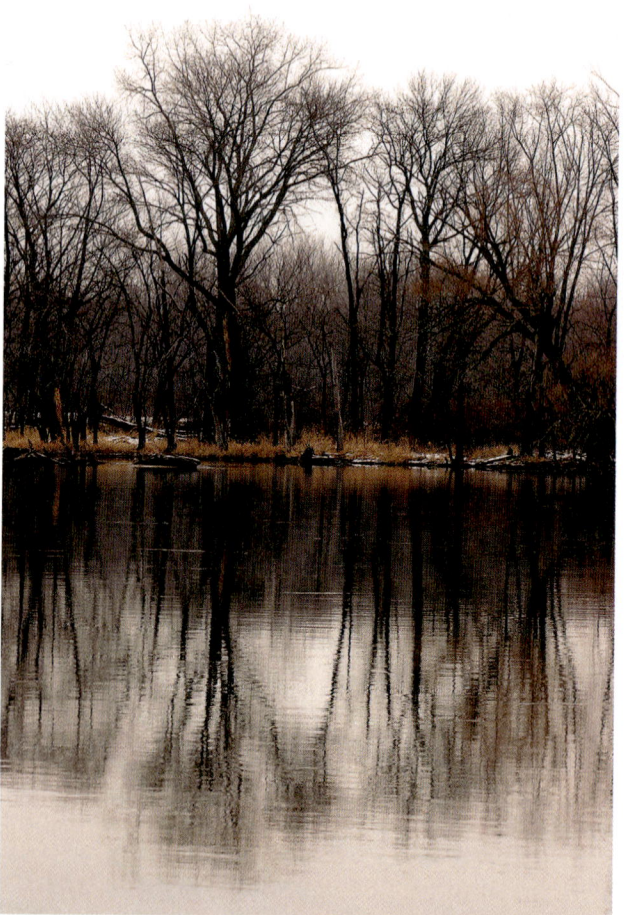

Jack Klasey/Goodheart-Willcox Publisher

Figure 13-35. On a late autumn day, a river's surface provides a mirror-image reflection of bare trees.

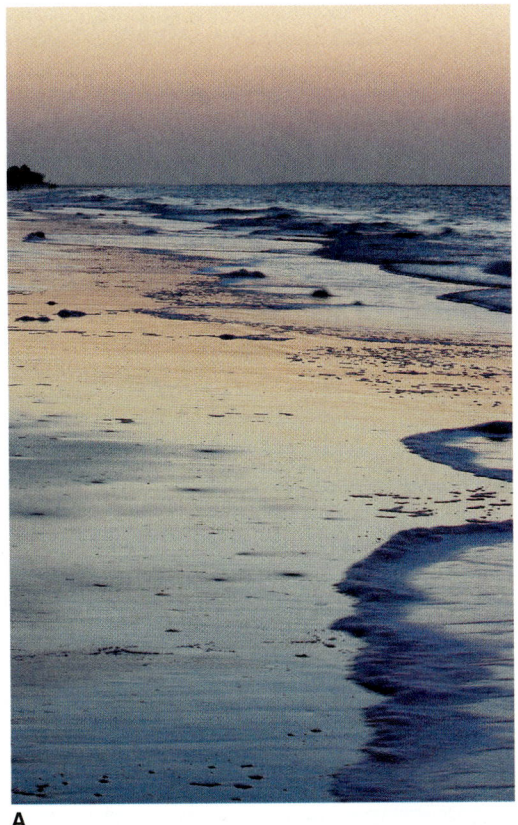
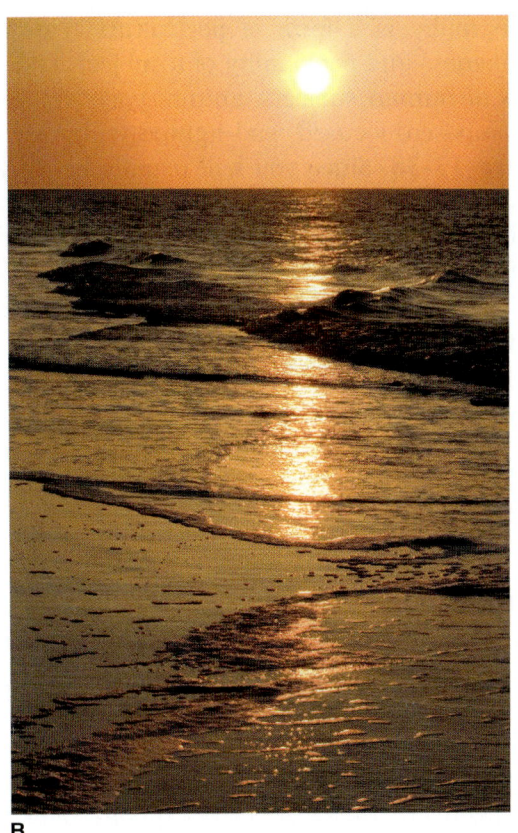

Figure 13-36. Seashore reflections. A—The colors of the predawn sky are mirrored in the film of water. B—Moving water reflects the rising sun.

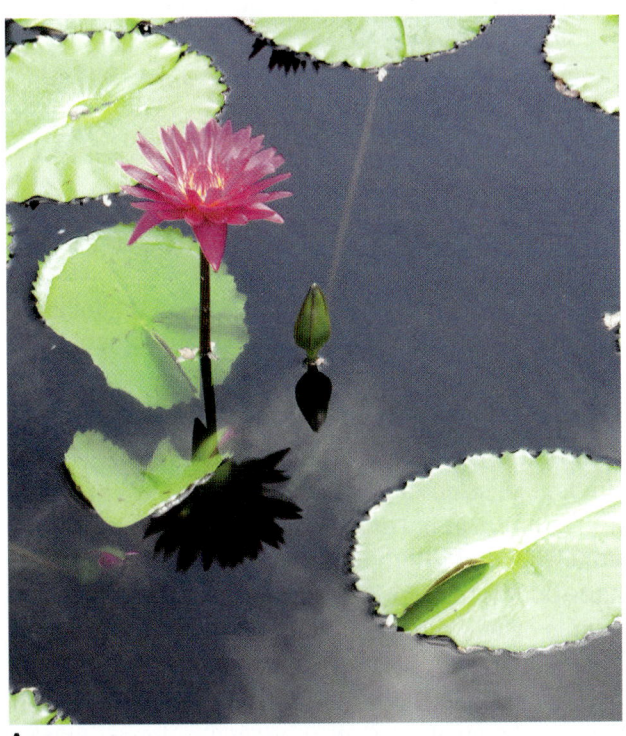
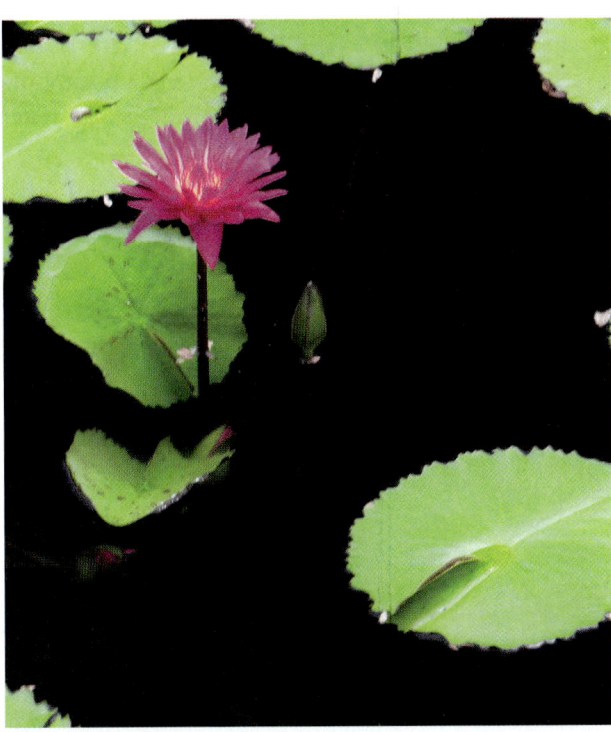

Jack Klasey/Goodheart-Willcox Publisher

Figure 13-37. Eliminating reflections. A—Without polarizing filter. B—With polarizing filter.

Chapter 13 Outdoor Photography **319**

photography is a form of portraiture, capturing the likeness and personality of a subject. Like portraits of human subjects, animal portraits should be composed, focused, and lighted with care. See **Figure 13-38**. Since you will usually be working with ambient light, try to choose a time of day and angle to the sun that provides the most effective lighting on your subject.

Compositionally, an animal's pose may be humanlike—a photographer might position a person the same way for a portrait. A key element in all types of portraiture is the subject's eyes. If visible, they must be in sharp focus and should contain a small bright reflection, called a **catchlight**, to add sparkle and liveliness.

Pet Photography

Your dog, cat, or other pet animal can be a great photographic subject and is easily accessible for practicing animal photography techniques. An advantage in photographing your own pet is your knowledge of their moods, habits, and favorite activities. There are three basic ways to photograph a pet:

- A portrait, either in a formal close-up or a wider environmental context, **Figure 13-39**.
- An action shot of the animal engaged in a favorite or typical activity, **Figure 13-40**.
- A picture of the pet interacting with another animal or a human being, **Figure 13-41**.

While many of your pet photos will be spur-of-the-moment shots, you should devote some time

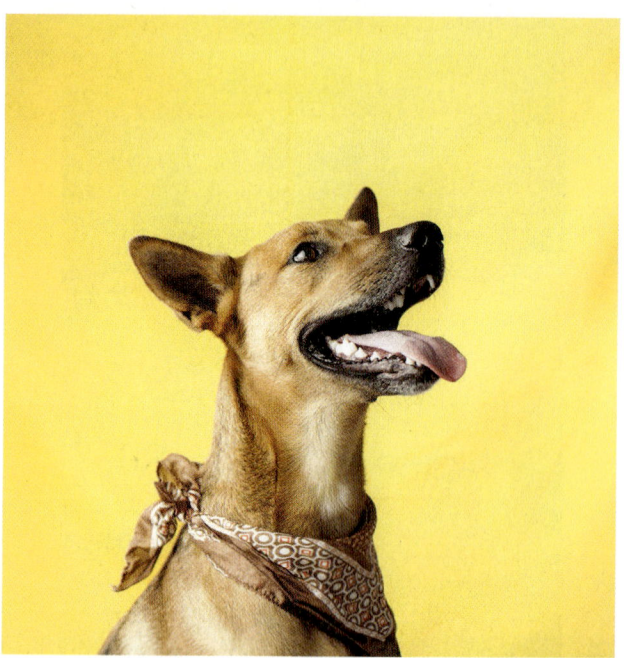

Andreina Nunez/Shutterstock.com

Figure 13-39. A portrait of a family pet is a common photo that most pet owners have.

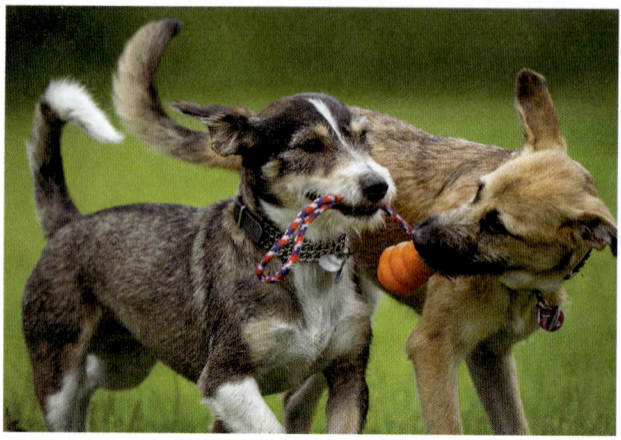

Bildagentur Zoonar GmbH/Shutterstock.com

Figure 13-40. A dog playing with a toy and another dog showcases how you can capture movement in a single image.

to making a planned photo shoot, **Figure 13-42**. If possible, select a location with good lighting and a minimum of background clutter, such as a floor area with ample light coming through a window or patio door. The location must be one that the pet frequents or will remain in long enough for you to get your shots.

Like children, pets are best photographed from their own level. Kneel or even lie down on the floor. If someone is available to act as an assistant, they can help draw the animal's attention

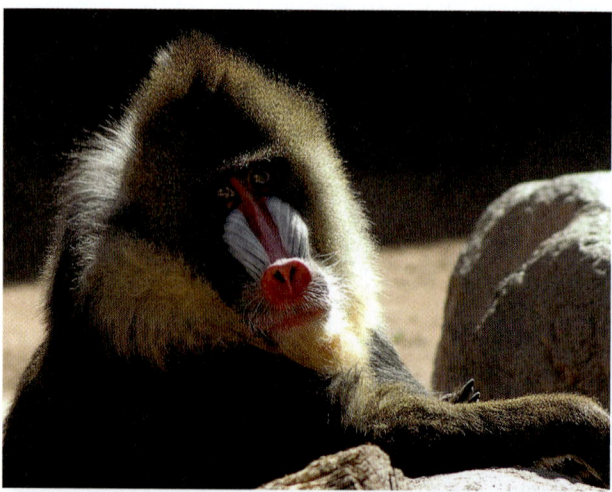

Jack Klasey/Goodheart-Willcox Publisher

Figure 13-38. This portrait of a mandrill at a Phoenix zoo would have been less striking visually with flat frontal lighting.

to a certain direction or introduce a toy or other activity. This frees you to concentrate on getting the shots you want.

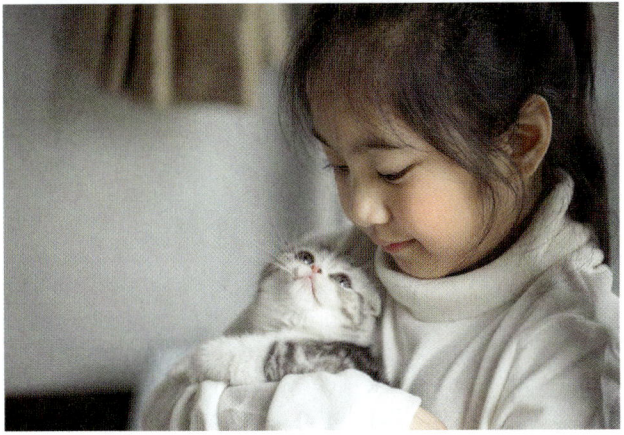

Ronnachai Palas/Shutterstock.com

Figure 13-41. Pictures of pets interacting with their owners or other members of their family make for great photographs.

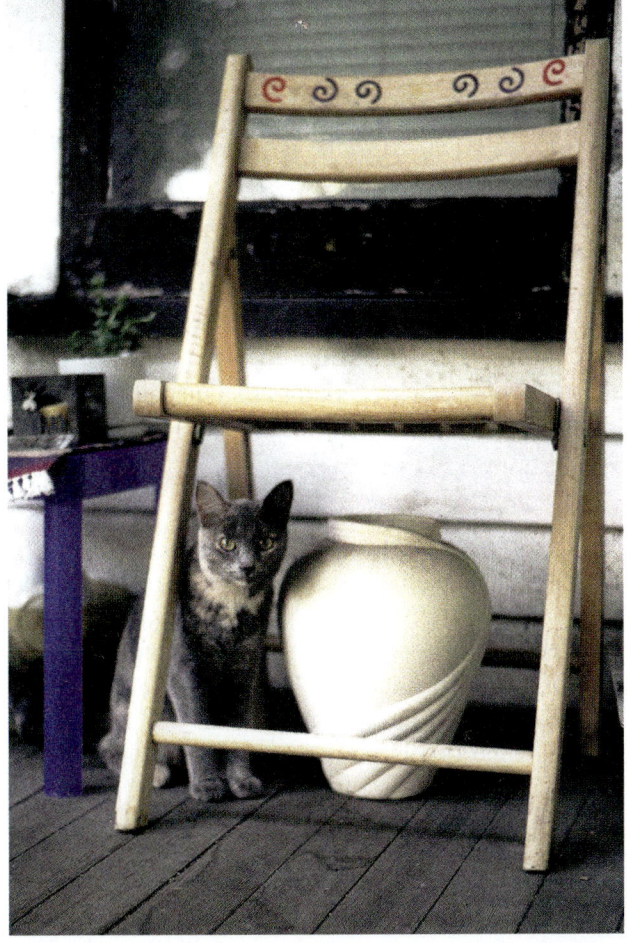

Katie Gorham

Figure 13-42. An informal pet portrait of a kitten.

Photographing in the Wild

Some photographers are fortunate enough to be able to travel to exotic locales, capturing dramatic photos of lions in Africa, penguins in Antarctica, or moose in Alaska, **Figure 13-43**. However, wildlife opportunities abound close to home, such as birds of many types, small animals of field and forest, and the denizens of swamps or deserts, **Figure 13-44**.

An acceptable wildlife photo may result from being in the right place at the right time and being prepared to shoot when a subject unexpectedly appears. See **Figure 13-45**. Wildlife photographers who are consistently successful, however, carefully study the animals they wish to photograph. They learn about the locations where they can be found, how they behave, when they are active, and how common or rare they

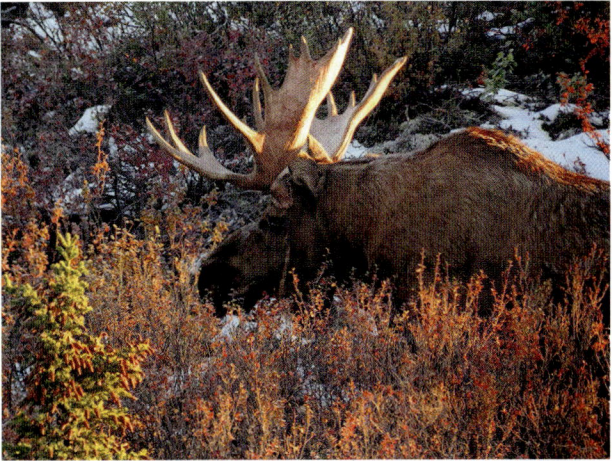

Suzanne M. Silagi

Figure 13-43. A moose browsing along a roadway in Denali National Park in Alaska.

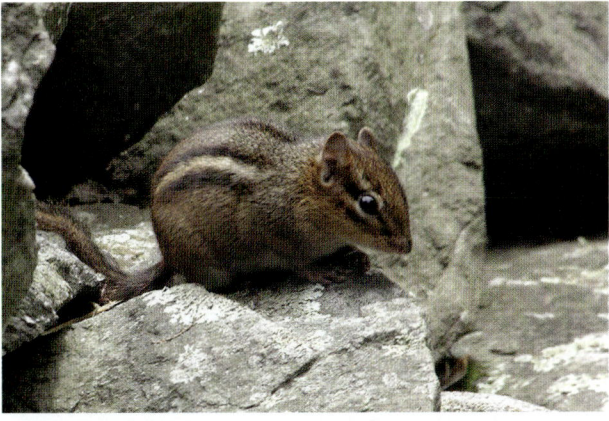

Jack Klasey/Goodheart-Willcox Publisher

Figure 13-44. Small wildlife subjects, such as this ground squirrel, usually can be found in locations close to your home (even in a city).

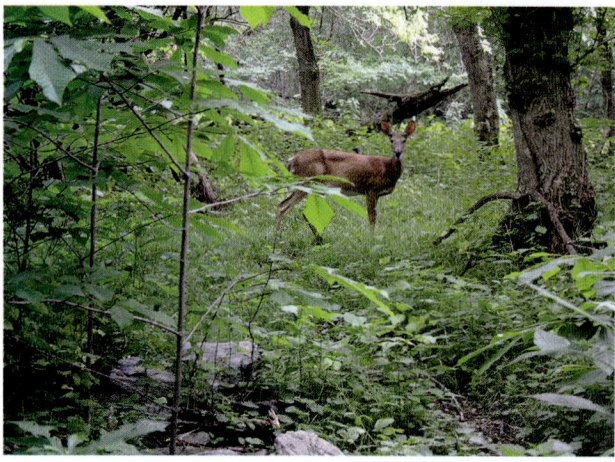

Jack Klasey/Goodheart-Willcox Publisher

Figure 13-45. This deer suddenly appeared in a clearing while the photographer was walking along a path in the woods. A wide-angle lens (35 mm), large aperture (f/5.6), and high ISO (800) resulted in a usable handheld image despite a slow (1/20 second) shutter speed.

are. With this knowledge, the photographer can plan when and where to go, what equipment to bring, and how much time to devote to the project.

The time required to obtain a desired image is often measured in days. The photographer may erect a portable blind (a small structure built to hide a photographer from sight) near the site where the animal is usually found, **Figure 13-46**. They must enter the blind when the animal is not around, and then spend many hours of patient observation before doing any shooting. Vehicles can serve as blinds since animals do not consider them a cause for alarm. A car or truck can be an effective form of concealment when photographing birds, **Figure 13-47**.

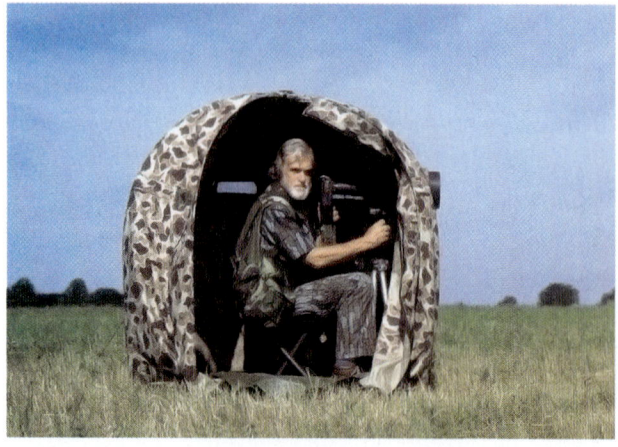

Leonard Rue Enterprises

Figure 13-46. Noted wildlife photographer Leonard Lee Rue demonstrates one type of portable shooting blind.

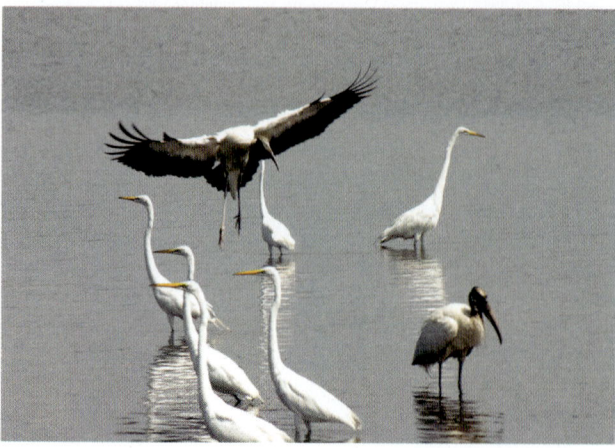

Jack Klasey/Goodheart-Willcox Publisher

Figure 13-47. The photographer got close to these birds while using a car as a blind. A road bordered the shallow area of the river where they were wading, allowing the photographer to approach close enough to use a 300 mm lens.

Most wildlife photographers consider a 500 mm lens to be the practical minimum for good animal and bird close-ups. A long lens is not as necessary, however, when the birds come to you. Providing food often attracts birds to within a reasonable distance, making them easy to photograph. See **Figure 13-48**. When birds are closer, a telephoto lens permits you to make a "head and shoulders" portrait, **Figure 13-49**.

When photographing in the wild, avoid stressing animals, especially nesting birds. Approaching too closely or making sudden movements or loud noises may cause harm to the animal, which is not worth any photograph. Be careful to avoid attracting the attention of possible predators to a nest location.

Close-up Photography

A close-up photographer is able to open the door to a strange and often beautiful world in which intricate shapes and structures emerge from everyday objects, and common insects take on the menacing appearance of prehistoric monsters. This world is conveniently located—close-up photographers can find an almost endless supply of subjects in their own backyards.

How Close Is Close?

For greater precision when discussing close-up photography, the terms *reproduction ratio* and *magnification* are commonly used. Although they present the information in different forms, both

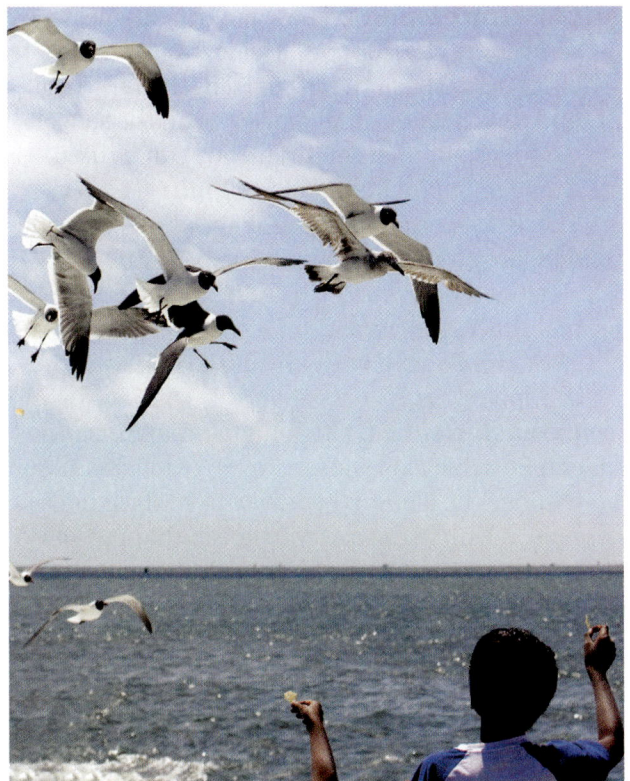

Figure 13-48. Gulls flocking behind a ferryboat to snatch food from the outstretched hands of passengers. Food will attract birds closer to your camera.

methods state the size relationship between the actual object and its recorded image.

Some people find the size relationship easiest to understand when stated as a **reproduction ratio**,

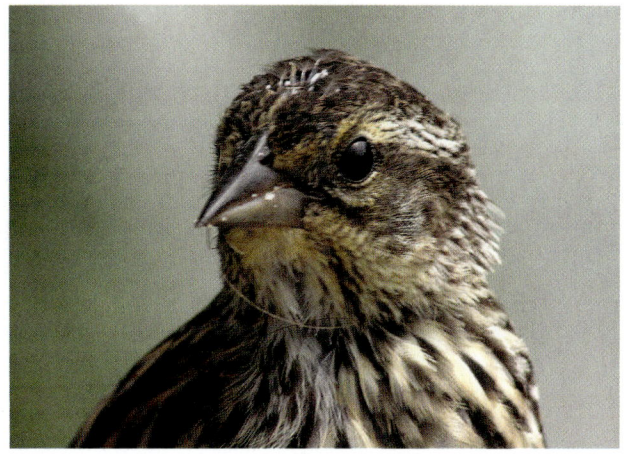

Figure 13-49. A tight close-up of a small bird made with a 300 mm lens. Note that the eye is in sharp focus and shows a small catchlight.

which is a numeric expression of size relationships, such as 1:4. The numeral before the colon represents the reproduction size, or the size of the recorded object in the digital file. The numeral after the colon represents the size of the actual object. A 1:4 ratio means that the actual object is four times larger than its representation. If the recorded image is 1″ long, then the actual object is 4″ in length.

Figure 13-50 shows examples of reproduction ratio. If a ladybug is 1/4″ long, and the recorded image is also 1/4″ long, the reproduction ratio is 1:1. The recorded image is said to be same size or life-size. If the image measures only 1/8″, the reproduction ratio is 1:2, or half life-size. The recorded image

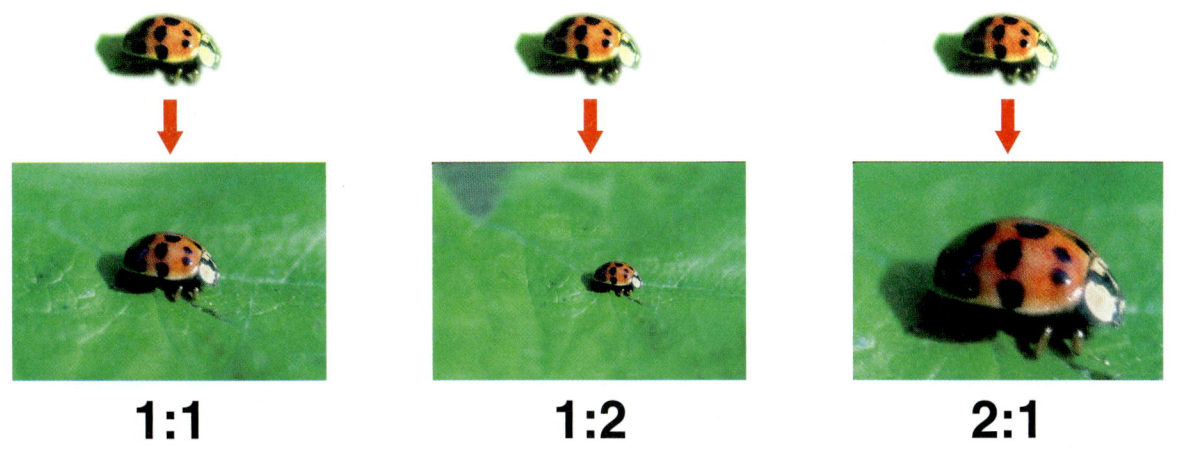

Figure 13-50. Reproduction ratio.

also may be larger than the real object. If the ladybug image measures 1/2″, it is twice as big as the real insect, so the reproduction ratio is stated as 2:1.

The *magnification rate* is a method of expressing the size relationship between the actual object and its recorded image. It provides the same information as the reproduction ratio, but in a different form. Instead of describing the size relationship as 2:1, for example, it is stated as 2×, or "two times life-size." Reproduction at less than life-size is represented by fractional magnification rates, such as 1/2× or 1/10×. Fractional rates can also be expressed in decimal form, such as 0.5× or 0.10×.

The meaning of the term *close-up* is subjective. However, three ranges of magnification can be used to help answer the question, "How close is close?" The *close-up range* is the lowest range of magnification, and it extends from about 1/20× to 1×, or 1/20 life-size to actual life-size. This degree of magnification is achieved by the use of normal-focus or close-focusing lenses alone, without employing special techniques or accessory equipment. A close-focusing lens is often referred to as a *macro* lens. The term comes from the Greek word *makros*, which means "large."

A reproduction ratio of 1:1 (life-size, or a magnification rate of 1×) is generally considered the borderline between the close-up range and the **macro photo range** which is a term used to describe photography in which the image is as large or larger than the actual object. In the macro range, various types of accessories are used to increase the magnifying power of the camera's lens.

At approximately 25×, another borderline is passed, moving into the third range of magnification. This is the highly specialized field of **photomicrography**, in which a microscope is used to achieve extremely high magnifications.

Ways of Getting Close

In the close-up range (up to life-size), macro lenses provide the advantage of simplicity and ease of use. These lenses also are versatile since they can be used for normal photography as well as close-focusing situations.

For magnifications greater than life-size, other devices must be used in combination with the camera lens. The devices and methods used to obtain greater magnification include the following:

- **Close-up diopters.** These magnifying devices screw onto the front of the camera lens. In effect, they shorten the focal length of the lens and thus increase the image size on the sensor. Usually sold in sets of three, they can be used singly or in combination. See **Figure 13-51**. These simple single-element lenses can degrade optical quality. The optically superior two-element diopters made by several camera manufacturers provide much sharper images. They can be used with any brand of lens with the appropriate filter size.
- **Extension tubes.** Much higher magnifications can be achieved by inserting an extension tube to move the lens farther away from the camera's sensor. Unlike the close-up lenses that put additional optical elements in the light path, the tubes add only distance. The tubes come in various lengths and are sometimes sold in sets, **Figure 13-52**. Tubes of different lengths can be coupled together to achieve the desired extension. To determine the extension needed for a desired magnification, multiply the focal length of the lens by the magnification. With the lens focused at infinity, adding an amount of extension equal to the focal length will produce a 1:1 reproduction ratio. Thus, to achieve a 3:1 ratio (3× magnification, or three times life-size) with a 50 mm lens, couple together tubes for a total extension of 150 mm, or about 6″.

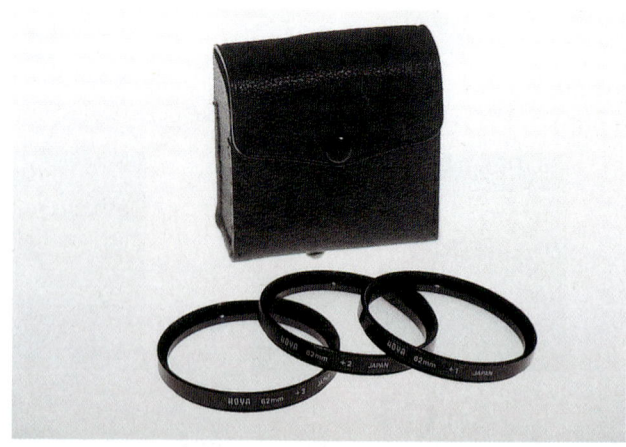

Goodheart-Willcox Publisher

Figure 13-51. A set of close-up diopters.

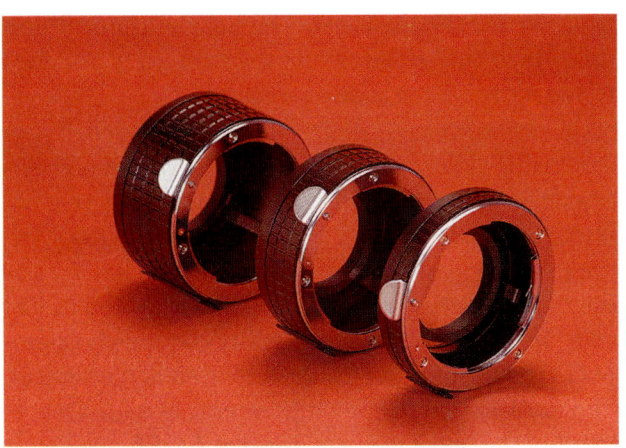

Porter's Camera Store

Figure 13-52. Extension tubes increase magnification, but they do not degrade the image.

subject. Multiply the f-stop by the focal length, and then divide the result by the extension. As an example, using the information from **Figure 13-54**,

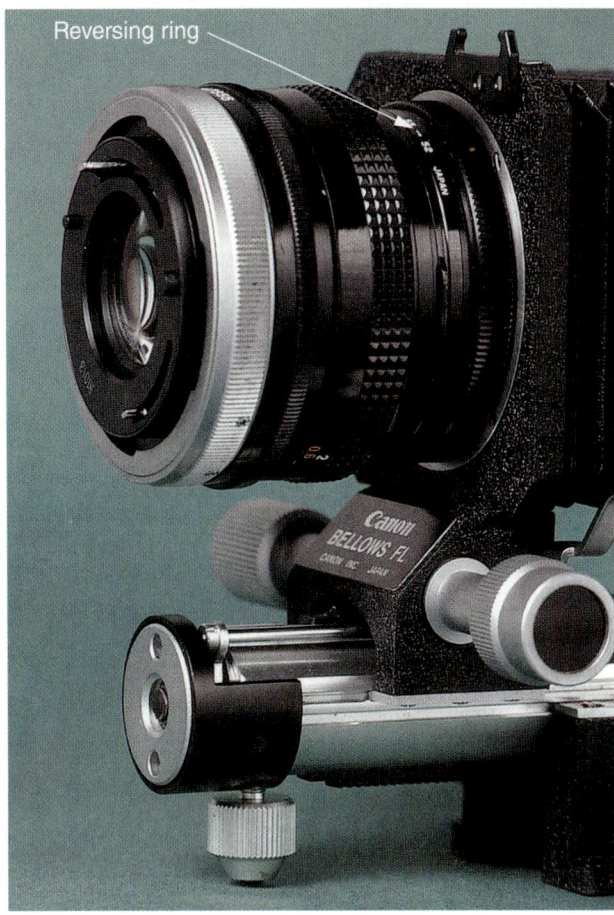

Jack Klasey/Goodheart-Willcox Publisher

Figure 13-53. A lens mounted in the reversed position on a bellows, using a reversing ring.

- **Bellows.** In effect, the bellows is a variable-length extension tube, with the camera attached to one end and a lens to the other. Due to its bulk and the fragility of the folding bellows material, this device is more commonly used in studio work than in field photography.
- **Reversed lens.** Using an accessory called a reversing ring, mounting a lens backward is one of the most effective methods of gaining higher magnifications. See **Figure 13-53**. A *reversing ring* is an accessory with filter-mounting threads on one side and a lens mount on the other, allowing a lens to be mounted backward. The lens mount connects it to the camera body, extension tubes, or a bellows. The advantages of reverse-mounting are 1× or higher magnification and increased working distance.

Exposure and Other Problems

When a bellows, extension tubes, or coupled lenses are used for close-up work, the distance that light rays must travel from the lens to the image sensor is increased. This means that less light will reach the sensor surface due to light falloff, making an exposure increase necessary. If you are using a modern camera with a built-in through-the-lens (TTL) meter, no compensation is needed. The meter reading automatically adjusts for the decreased light level.

If your camera does not have a TTL meter, a corrected exposure must be calculated. To determine the exposure change, you need three items of information—the focal length of the lens, the extension, and the exposure (f-stop) metered for the

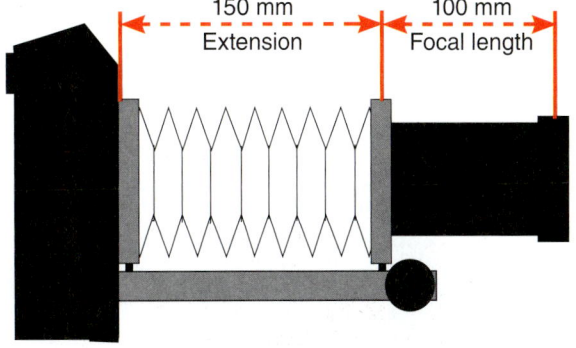

Metered exposure: f/16 @ 1/30

Goodheart-Willcox Publisher

Figure 13-54. Information needed to calculate the exposure change necessary to compensate for lens extension.

f-stop (16) × focal length (100) = 1,600 ÷ extension (150) = 10.66. Identify the nearest f-stop to this value (10.66); in this case, f/11. The corrected exposure is a one-stop increase (from f/16 to f/11).

Compensation is usually done by changing exposure time rather than aperture because opening up to change exposure would seriously decrease depth of field. Thus, the corrected exposure would be f/16 @ 1/15 second, a one-stop increase from the metered f/16 @ 1/30 second.

Depth of Field

As you increase magnification, the portion of the subject that is in acceptably sharp focus at a given f-stop decreases. The depth of field can shrink to a fraction of an inch or a few millimeters. For example, when photographing an object at twice life-size (2×), the distance from nearest to farthest sharp focus at f/8 is only 0.4 mm or 16/1000″. To increase the depth of field, stop down as you would in normal photographic situations. By using smaller apertures such as f/16, f/22, or f/32 (depending on the capability of your lens), you will obtain the greatest depth of field possible under the circumstances.

When working with a depth of field measured in units as small as tenths of a millimeter or thousandths of an inch, critical focusing and a sturdy tripod are essential. To eliminate camera movement from vibration, use a tethered shutter release and mirror lock-up, if possible. Manual focusing is almost always necessary to get the desired fineness of focus.

A *focusing rail* is a tripod-mounted accessory that permits the camera to be moved toward or away from the subject in tiny increments to achieve precise focus, **Figure 13-55**. It can be locked into position after focus is set. The base of the rail unit mounts to the tripod, while the camera is attached to the movable top slide.

A different technique can be employed if you are using lower magnification under conditions that permit hand-holding. For example, if you are photographing flowers or insects at a 0.25× (1:4) magnification and using flash or bright sunlight as illumination, your depth of field at f/16 would be just over 3/4″. In this situation, many nature photographers would focus on the desired area of the subject, and then use small body movements to adjust placement of the plane of focus, **Figure 13-56**.

Working Distance

Working distance is the amount of space between the front of the camera lens and the subject. A working distance that is too short can block natural light, placing the subject in shadow and making it virtually impossible to use artificial light. Also, animals and insects have a comfort zone—moving closer than the invisible border of that zone will cause them to flee.

The key to working distance is the focal length of the lens. The longer the focal length, the farther you can be from the subject while retaining the same magnification. The distances are proportional, **Figure 13-57**. If you fill the frame with your subject using a 50 mm lens at a lens-to-subject distance of 6″, switching to a 100 mm lens allows you to double that distance to 12″ while keeping the same image size. If the image size is kept the same and the same f-stop is used, no change in depth of field occurs

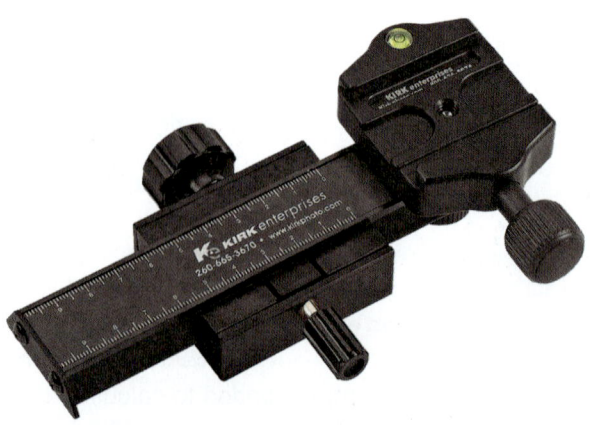

Kirk Enterprises

Figure 13-55. A focusing rail.

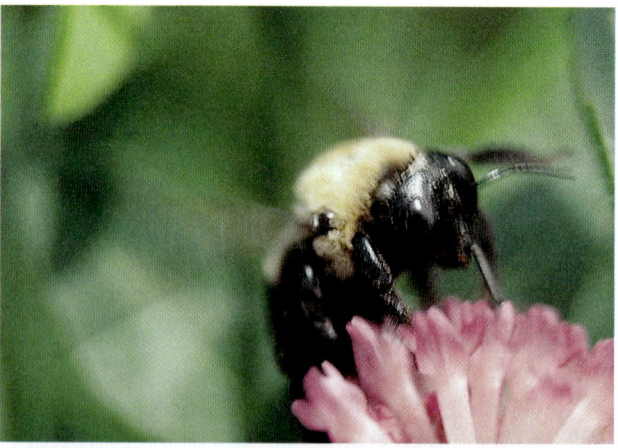

Jack Klasey/Goodheart-Willcox Publisher

Figure 13-56. To capture this close-up of a bumblebee, the photographer was able to shift the plane of focus by using body movement.

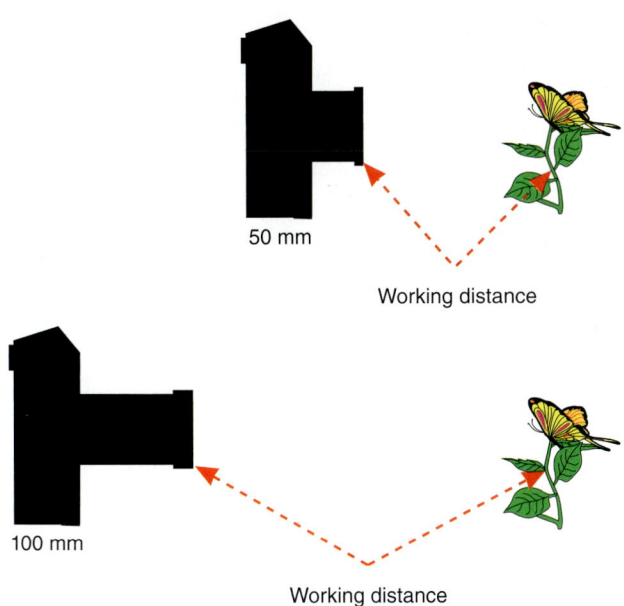

Figure 13-57. A longer focal length permits you to gain working distance while keeping the subject image the same size.

when focal length is increased to gain working distance. If the same working distance is retained, but a longer focal length lens is substituted to increase image size, the depth of field changes in inverse proportion. Doubling the focal length reduces the depth of field by one-half.

Lighting

Increased working distance makes it easier to light the subject for proper exposure. In some situations, natural light is sufficient, but more commonly, electronic flash must be used to freeze subject movement.

The use of flash illumination allows hand-holding of the camera when small animals or insects are photographed. The mobility of the subjects and the photographer's need to quickly change positions for the best composition make hand-holding a virtual necessity. While a tripod is desirable in many close-up situations, it is far too slow and cumbersome for capturing active insects or small animals. The use of flash allows the photographer to "freeze" the subject as well as achieve a good exposure.

The built-in flash found on point-and-shoot and many DSLR cameras is not suitable for close-up work. Shooting natural subjects in the field is usually done with small self-contained flash units placed on an adjustable bracket rather than the camera's hot shoe. Some photographers prefer to use a single flash positioned several inches above and just behind the front of the lens. Others employ two flashes mounted on adjustable arms positioned several inches to either side and just above the level of the lens, **Figure 13-58**. One flash serves as the main light and the other as the fill light. To an extent, it is also possible to make lighting corrections in image editing software during postprocessing.

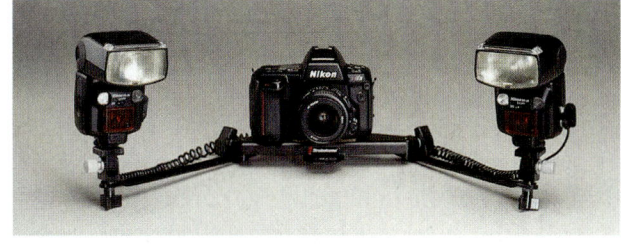

Stroboframe

Figure 13-58. Butterfly and insect photographers often use an adjustable double flash bracket.

📷 Portfolio Assignment

Photographer's Choice

Choose two of the following projects for your portfolio:
- **Create a panorama.** Look for a suitable subject (horizontal or vertical). Shoot at least four overlapping images and assemble the finished panorama using image editing software.
- **Freeze some water.** Shoot moving water, such as a waterfall, rainstorm, or even a lawn sprinkler. Use different shutter speeds (such as 1/8 second or 1/100 second) to observe the effect on motion. Choose the image you like best, noting the exposure information.
- **Capture an animal.** Photograph a pet or other animal involved in a typical activity. If the "activity" is a nap, try for an interesting or unusual angle.
- **Film a flower.** Photograph a flower or other plant. Try to capture as much detail as possible while also maintaining the clarity of your image.

Chapter 13 Review

Summary

- For most photographers, the term outdoor photography covers two broad areas—landscapes and wildlife.
- Landscape photography is defined as recorded views of the natural world in any of its aspects. While most landscape views feature the vegetable and mineral kingdoms (rocks and plants), the animal kingdom also may be represented as a part of a scene.
- When attempting to record a grand vista, the natural tendency is to choose a wide-angle lens to "get it all in." A wide-angle lens captures a broad, distant scene but emphasizes the foreground. The solution is to include an interesting foreground object that will give the photo increased depth and visual interest.
- A panorama is an extremely wide view of a scene, typically a landscape. Panoramas can be made with film or digitally.
- For a landscape photographer, the angle and intensity of the light striking the subject can make the difference between a successful photograph and an unsuccessful one. Other factors include the color of the light, using a polarizing filter, and horizon placement.
- Smaller-scale landscape subjects are easily accessible, whether you are in an exotic location or your own neighborhood.
- A popular subdivision of landscape photography is shooting pictures of wildflowers and cultivated plants. Flower photography requires careful control of both exposure and focus.
- Insects are other popular subjects. When shooting flowers and insects, be sure to follow environmental guidelines.
- Striking landscape photos in which sunlit grass and tree leaves appear as bright, ghostly white objects can be produced by capturing infrared light. They can be recorded on a digital sensor that has the proper sensitivity.
- Water may be a part of a landscape photo, or it may be the primary subject of the picture. Moving water, lakes, rain, and water in solid form are popular subjects.
- In many respects, animal photography is a form of portraiture, capturing the likeness and personality of a subject. You can take pictures of pets or wildlife.
- For greater precision when discussing close-up photography, the terms reproduction ratio and magnification are commonly used.
- A reproduction ratio is a numeric expression of size relationships. The magnification rate is a method of expressing the size relationship between the actual object and its recorded image.
- For magnifications greater than life-size, other devices must be used in combination with the camera lens. Other devices and methods include close-up diopters, extension tubes, bellows, and reversed lenses.
- Issues to consider with close-up work include exposure, depth of field, working distance, and lighting.

Review Questions

Answer the following questions using the information provided in this chapter.

Know and Understand

1. *True or False?* As long as animals are not the main subject, landscape photography can include them.
2. A _____ is an extremely wide view of a scene, typically a landscape.
   A. mirror image
   B. panorama
   C. catchlight
   D. nodal point
3. *True or False?* Distant scenery panoramas are more difficult to create successfully than close-up views.
4. _____ is the effect of stray light bouncing around inside the lens housing, causing decreased contrast or a severe washed-out appearance that mimics overexposure.
   A. Catchlight
   B. Magnification rate
   C. Flare
   D. Windbreak
5. Smaller-scale subjects can usually be photographed with _____ lenses in the middle of the focal length range, typically 35 mm to 150 mm.
   A. zoom
   B. wide-angle
   C. telephoto
   D. normal
6. Selective focus is a useful tool when photographing _____.
   A. grand vistas
   B. large animals
   C. panoramas
   D. flowers
7. A _____ lens is most often used to photograph insects on flowers because moving in too close threatens them and causes them to leave.
   A. telephoto zoom
   B. wide-angle zoom
   C. fish-eye
   D. normal
8. *True or False?* Most digital cameras can be used for infrared photography.
9. When capturing water in solid form, exposure must usually be increased by _____ stops from the metered value to avoid underexposure.
   A. 1 to 1 1/2
   B. 1 1/2 to 2
   C. 2 to 2 1/2
   D. 2 1/2 to 3
10. The most common approach to photographing reflections in water is the _____, which is an almost exact reproduction of the scene in reverse.
    A. nodal point
    B. close-up range
    C. panorama
    D. mirror image
11. *True or False?* A catchlight is a small, bright reflection in a photo subject's eyes, used to add sparkle and liveliness.
12. *True or False?* Pets are best photographed from their own level.
13. The time required to obtain a desired image of wildlife is often measured in _____.
    A. seconds
    B. minutes
    C. days
    D. years
14. *True or False?* In a reproduction ratio, the numeral before the colon represents the size of the actual object.
15. The _____ is the lowest range of magnification, and it extends from about 1/20× to 1×, or 1/20 life-size to actual life-size.
    A. macro photo range
    B. photomicrographic range
    C. magnification rate
    D. close-up range
16. Using an accessory called a(n) _____, mounting a lens backward is one of the most effective methods of gaining higher magnifications.
    A. bellows
    B. reversing ring
    C. extension tube
    D. close-up diopter

17. *True or False?* Compensation is usually done by changing exposure time rather than aperture.
18. A _____ is a tripod-mounted accessory that permits the camera to be moved toward or away from the subject in tiny increments to achieve precise focus.
    A. reversing ring
    B. windbreak
    C. focusing rail
    D. close-up diopter
19. The key to working distance is the _____.
    A. focal length of the lens
    B. aperture
    C. shutter speed
    D. exposure
20. *True or False?* Decreased working distance makes it easier to light the subject for proper exposure.

Apply and Analyze

1. List five of the eight basic guidelines to follow when shooting panoramas.
2. Define magic hour.
3. What can you use to eliminate reflections in the water?
4. What do wildlife photographers do to be consistently successful? Why does this bring them success?
5. Explain the magnification rate.

Critical Thinking

1. While photographing in a botanical garden, you find a perfect blossom that would make a spectacular photo. Unfortunately, to properly frame the shot, you would need to cut away some parts of the plant. What should you do?
2. You are capturing a four- or five-shot panorama on a partly cloudy day when the light keeps changing from sunny to cloudy. Would you expect to get better results by setting your camera's white balance to automatic, or by changing it for each shot to match the lighting? Why?

Suggested Activities

1. Use your knowledge of composition and layout to shoot the best possible "head and shoulders" animal portraits of a dog, cat, or other household pet. Take three different photos for this activity. The portraits may be of the same animal or different animals. Choose the image in which the animal looks most appealing and use it as the basis for a poster promoting a local animal shelter's pet adoption program. You may want to show the poster to the shelter and see if they would like to use it.
2. As a class project, create a calendar with nature photographs (landscapes or wildlife images). Ask each student to submit one or two images for a total of at least 24 images. Select 12 final images by voting. Use a computer program or an online or retail photo processor to produce the calendar.
3. Choose four compositional elements that are used often in outdoor photography, such as contrast or emphasis. Take five photos that showcase each element (20 photos total). Then, choose the best photo of each element. Once you have selected your four best photos, discuss with a partner how you used the compositional elements in your photographs. Offer constructive feedback to your partner and have them do the same for you. Compare your own explanations of each photo to the feedback you received from your partner in a brief paper. Submit your photos and paper to your instructor for review.

Communicating about Photography

1. **Speaking.** Select a figure in this chapter, such as Figure 13-31 or Figure 13-57. Working with a partner, tell and then retell the important information being conveyed by that figure and its caption. Through your collaboration, develop what you and your partner believe is the most interesting description of the importance of the chosen figure. Present your narration to the class.

2. **Speaking and Listening.** Divide into groups of four or five students. Each group should choose one of these topics—water photography, animal photography, flower photography, or infrared photography. Using your textbook as a starting point, research your topic and prepare a report on techniques for obtaining good photos. As a group, deliver your presentation to the rest of the class. Take notes while the other students give their reports. Ask questions about any details that you would like clarified.

Chapter 14
Travel Photography

Learning Objectives

After completing this chapter, you will be able to:
- List some of the potential uses for travel photographs taken by professional and amateur photographers.
- Recall methods of research used by photographers to prepare for both long and short trips.
- Explain the importance of bringing backup equipment, using a portable storage device for digital images, and transporting equipment safely when traveling.
- Describe various ways that buildings can be photographed to emphasize different qualities or points of view.
- Understand how to photograph people in various locations.
- Discuss the different strategies a photographer can use to cope with unfavorable weather or lighting conditions and when to move indoors.
- Demonstrate methods of supporting a camera at slow shutter speeds when a tripod cannot be used.

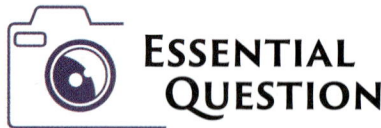

Essential Question

How does travel photography differ from other types of photography?

Technical Terms

backup copy
candid photo
recreational travel
shot list
travel guide
travel photography

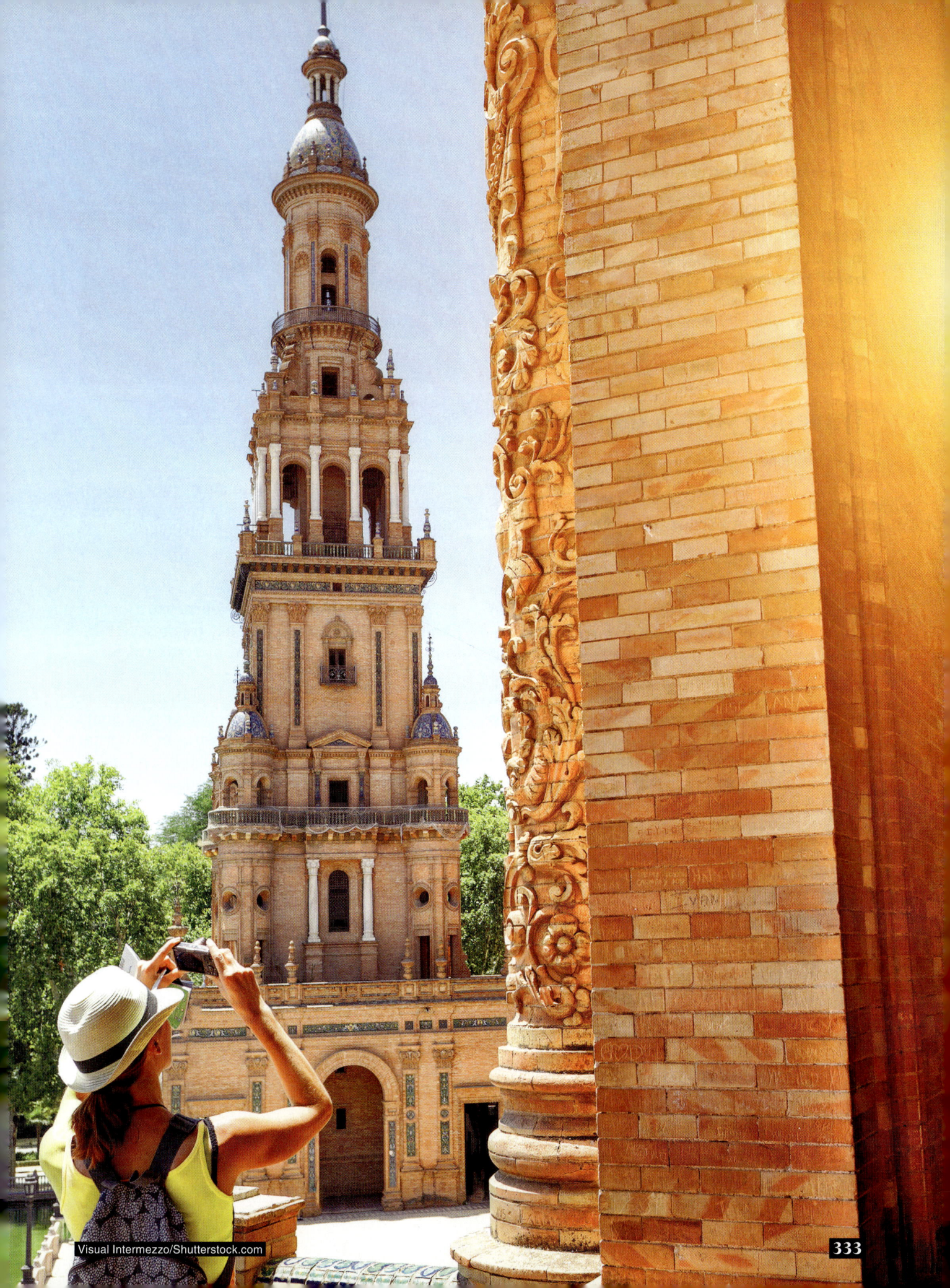

Introduction to Travel Photography

Recreational travel is defined as journeys made for leisure rather than business. It is hugely popular, and few travelers fail to bring along a camera to capture memories of the places they have visited. In addition to landscapes and other nature subjects, *travel photography* pays considerable attention to the human-made aspects of our world and to the people who inhabit it, **Figure 14-1**. While it is mostly an outdoor activity, travel photography can include a significant number of indoor locations.

Traveling with a Camera

Professionals often write magazine or newspaper travel articles illustrated by their photos. They also shoot photos for use in books and for stock photography agencies. Amateurs most often shoot vacation snapshots to share with friends and family after the trip, **Figure 14-2**. Some advanced amateurs produce high-quality travel photos rivaling those of the professionals. They may use their photos to illustrate a travel story in a local or regional publication, enter them in photo contests, sell prints at local galleries or art shows, or simply display them on their home or office walls. Most photographers, both amateur and professional, post their photos on websites and social media platforms, such as Facebook or Instagram. Travel photos also make for excellent additions to your portfolio. Shooting in a variety of locales allows for an interesting range in architecture, scenery, and candid photos of people, which greatly helps diversify your portfolio.

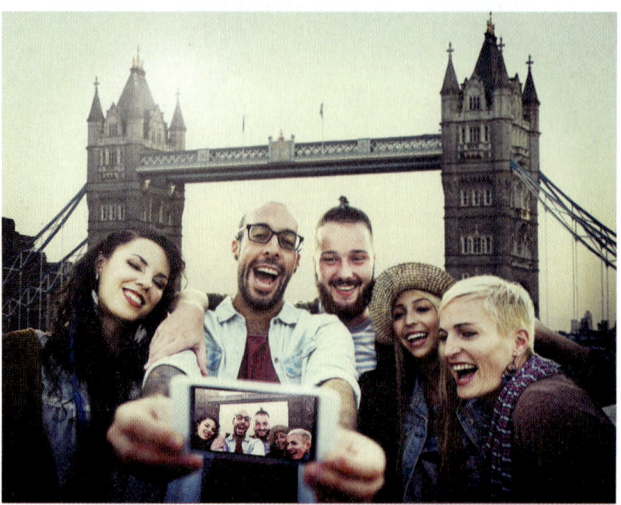

Rawpixel.com/Shutterstock.com

Figure 14-2. Friends on a visit to London capturing a selfie with a cell phone.

Researching in Advance

Whether you are planning a journey to a foreign locale, a family vacation, or a day trip, researching in advance helps you take more interesting pictures.

The internet is a great travel research tool. Before going anywhere, it is a good rule of thumb to look up what the parameters are for photography. Some locations, like the Ringling Museum in Sarasota, Florida, require photographers to obtain a permit to shoot on the grounds if they are using the area for a

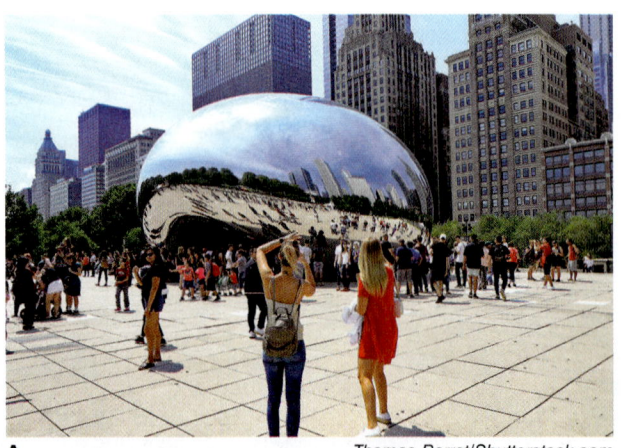

A *Thomas Barrat/Shutterstock.com*

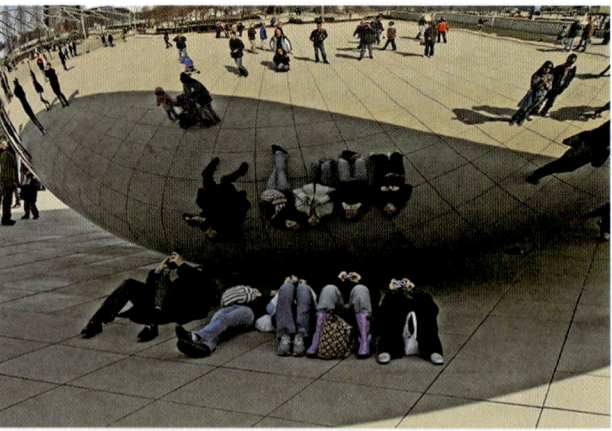

B *gary718/Shutterstock.com*

Figure 14-1. Photographing places and people. A—Chicago's reflective Cloud Gate sculpture (nicknamed "The Bean") is a popular photo subject for tourists. B—Young visitors shooting their reflections in the sculpture.

professional photoshoot, **Figure 14-3**. If this is the case for where you are shooting, you may need to reach out to the location in advance, often through email or an online form, to get permission prior to your shoot. In the event you are working in this type of environment, make sure that you are conscientious of your time at the location since other photographers may be waiting to use the same space. Use time-management skills and plan your desired shots before you get to the location. You can always add additional shots at the end of your shoot as needed.

You do not need to obtain a permit, however, if you are simply visiting the grounds to take photos to post to your Instagram account and are not making money from the photos you take. This falls under the umbrella of private, noncommercial photography, which is photography where the photographer does not sell any of the photos that they take. An internet search can also help you locate points of interest, special events, hours of operation and admission fees for attractions, and whether the facility allows you to use a tripod or a flash.

Books and travel guides are also excellent planning tools, **Figure 14-4**. Libraries have a selection of illustrated travel books on major destinations. They also are likely to have copies of *travel guides* (books or electronic publications that provide travelers with needed information about places they plan to visit) for countries or specific cities. Some are even specifically designed for photographers.

These guides are useful to take along on your trip, so you may wish to purchase the current edition of a guide at a bookstore or online. Organizations such as the American Automobile Association (AAA) offer their members maps and guidebooks

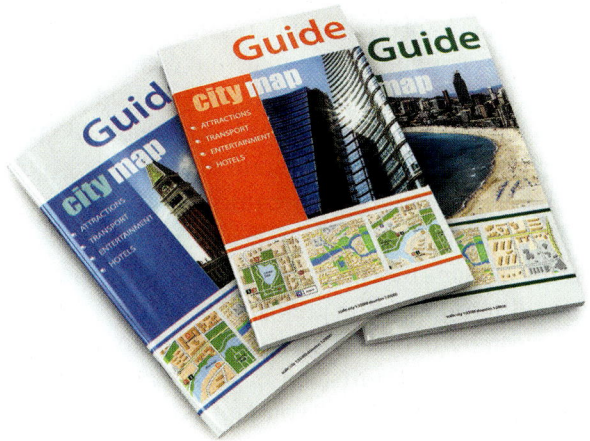

Maxx-Studio/Shutterstock.com

Figure 14-4. Travel guides are available for most major destinations.

with information on attractions, hotels, and restaurants for North American destinations. The downside of using these as resources is that some of the information may be outdated since the book has to go through the publication process. Online travel guides and books may be a better option since they are updated more easily and frequently.

For some heavily photographed areas, there are guides created specifically for photographers. An online search for *photography location guidebooks* will help you find them. You may also want to seek information from other photographers who have shot in that area. Popular shooting locations may have an online photography group or forum discussing best practices or general advice.

What Equipment Will You Need?

How much camera gear you take on your trip will vary considerably, depending on your budget, personal preferences, transportation plans, and other factors. Because of the flexibility it provides, many travel photographers prefer a camera with interchangeable lenses (DSLR or rangefinder). With two zooms—a wide-angle to short telephoto and a short-to-long telephoto—most photographic situations can be covered. Those who favor smaller, lighter equipment often choose one of the superzoom compact cameras. These cameras, typically with 16 MP sensors, provide optical zoom ranges as high as 60× (22 mm to 1200 mm).

Professionals typically carry a backup camera in case the main camera gets damaged or malfunctions while traveling. This may be a second DSLR

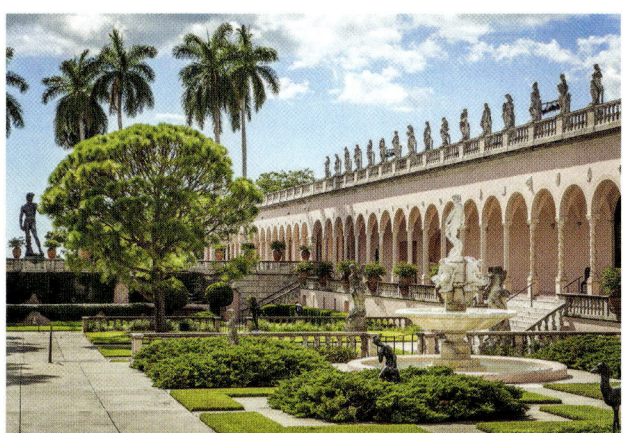

mariakray/Shutterstock.com

Figure 14-3. Some locations require a permit to take professional photos at their site.

camera body or an advanced compact camera. The advancements of phone cameras also make them an excellent secondary, or even primary, camera. If you do not have access to a DSLR, or you find yourself on an impromptu trip and did not have time to plan and pack a camera, your phone may be just as good as (if not better than) some cameras.

The development of digital cameras has made the photographer's life easier in some respects, and more difficult in others. The greatest advantage of digital photography, of course, is the ability to immediately review your photo instead of waiting until film is developed. If necessary, you can often capture the scene again. While you do not have to carry numerous rolls of film, you will need spare batteries and a charger, a supply of memory cards, and usually some type of portable storage device.

Memory Cards

Since memory cards are fairly inexpensive, some travel photographers carry enough high-capacity (64 GB or more) cards to last for the entire trip. Using high-capacity cards minimizes the need to reload the camera.

Others prefer to use a lower-capacity card (such as 4 GB or 8 GB), downloading it at the end of each day to a portable hard drive, a USB flash drive, a laptop, or cloud-based storage, **Figure 14-5**. Cards may then be reformatted to use again. This method avoids the danger of losing a large number of images if a card fails.

No matter which memory card approach they use, careful photographers make a **backup copy** to guard against possible loss of their images. Very high-capacity cards should be backed up to a portable storage device at the end of each day. If lower-capacity cards are being reused, they should be copied twice for safety. For example, copy to both a laptop and flash drive, to a laptop and portable hard drive, or to a portable hard drive and flash drive. You should also consider using a spreadsheet or database application to keep track of what you have shot, when you shot it, and which memory card it lives on. This is helpful if you are traveling among multiple locations or have multiple photography assignments at once. This way, you can easily keep track of what photographs are on which card without having to waste time searching through all of them.

Transporting Camera Equipment

While a compact camera, a spare set of batteries, and extra memory cards can often be carried in a pocket or small pouch, a sturdy camera bag is the preferred method for organizing and transporting equipment with interchangeable lenses. See **Figure 14-6**. Camera bags have compartments and dividers to hold and protect camera bodies, lenses, and other equipment and accessories.

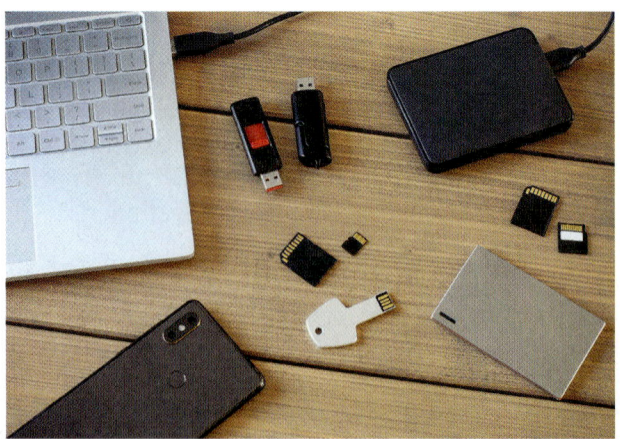

Ellyy/Shutterstock.com

Figure 14-5. A laptop or other portable storage device allows you to download images from memory cards and then reformat the cards for continued shooting.

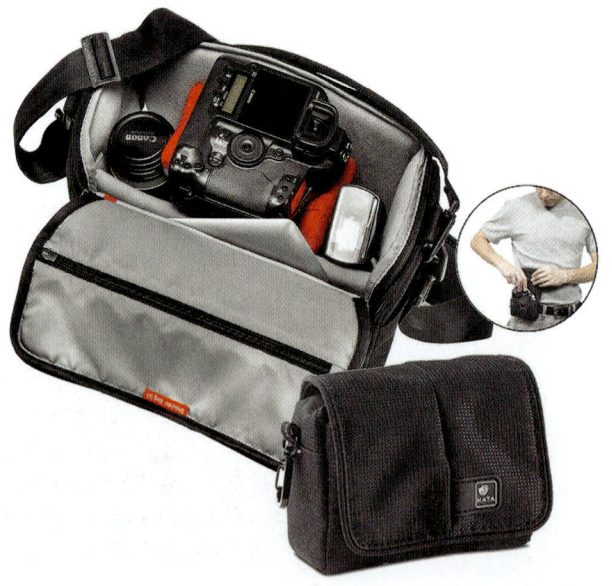

Manfrotto/Kata

Figure 14-6. Camera bags are available in various sizes.

If you travel by air, your camera bag should be treated as a carry-on, not as checked baggage, to protect it from the rough handling typical of airline baggage systems, **Figure 14-7**. You also can better protect expensive equipment from theft if you keep it in your control. If it will fit, pack a tripod in one of your suitcases. Otherwise, place it in a sturdy tube or similar container and check it as baggage.

Memory cards are not affected by the X-rays used to examine checked baggage, but film (especially 800 ISO and higher) can be fogged. Do not place film—unexposed or exposed—in your checked baggage. Instead, put it in a clear plastic bag and store the bag in a piece of carry-on luggage. The lower-dosage X-ray equipment used at passenger security checkpoints should not cause fogging, but to be perfectly safe, you can request a hand inspection of the film. This is your right under law in US airports, but security personnel at foreign airports may not honor requests for a hand inspection.

What Will You Shoot?

The answer to this question depends on your personal interests or, if you are a professional, your assignment. Professionals often work from a detailed list of photos to be taken, known as a **shot list**, and must meet strict client delivery deadlines. Some photographers concentrate on landscapes or buildings, while others focus on people and their activities, **Figure 14-8**. Most will shoot a mix of places and people.

The urban scene is typically varied, busy, and visually exciting, whereas the countryside often provides slower-paced and more restful photographic possibilities. Many of the same techniques described in Chapter 13, *Outdoor Photography*, also apply to shooting city scenes—careful composition, proper exposure, attention to focus and depth of field issues, and taking advantage of the best light.

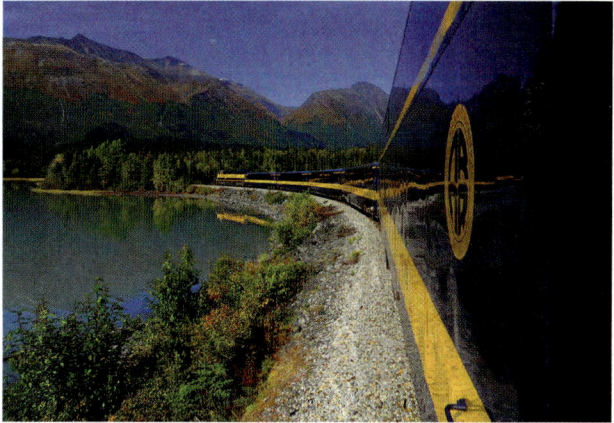

A

Suzanne M. Silagi

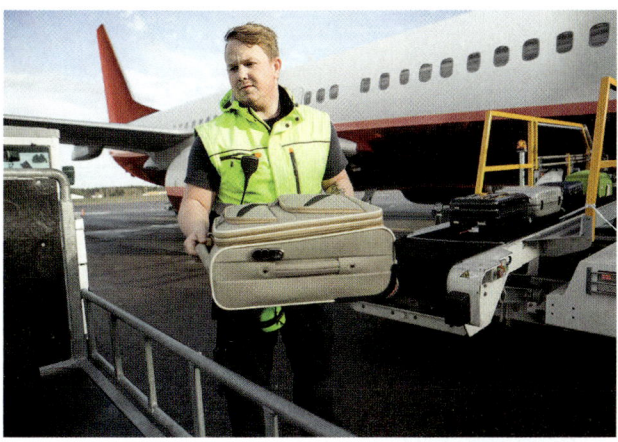

Tyler Olson/Shutterstock.com

Figure 14-7. Airline baggage is often handled roughly. To guard against damage, loss, or theft, camera bags should be treated as carry-on luggage.

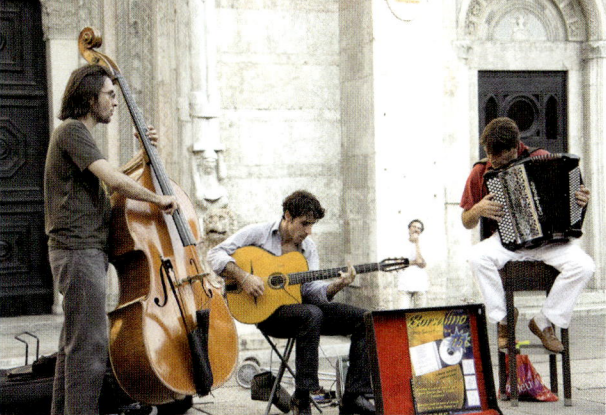

B

marino bocelli/Shutterstock.com

Figure 14-8. Travel photo subjects. A—Railroads provide access to some of Alaska's most scenic areas. B—Street artists at work are a common sight in European cities.

Photographing Buildings

When you are shooting buildings and architectural details in a city, concentrate on those aspects of the scene that are unique to the locale. A fast-food restaurant or chain store in Phoenix, Arizona, probably looks almost exactly the same as one in Toronto, Canada. Some cities have landmarks that are instantly recognizable. See **Figure 14-9**.

Buildings can be photographed in many different ways to emphasize various qualities or points of view. For example, shooting upward greatly exaggerates a tall building's height, while an elevated viewpoint can show the surrounding environment. See **Figure 14-10**. A building and its surroundings can be presented very differently when photographed

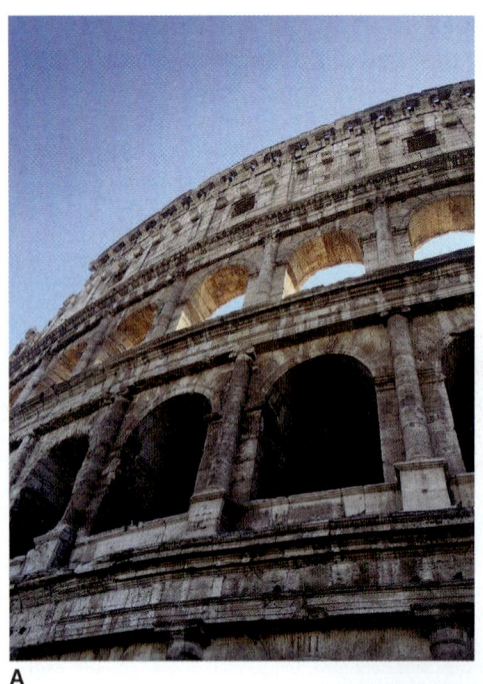

A

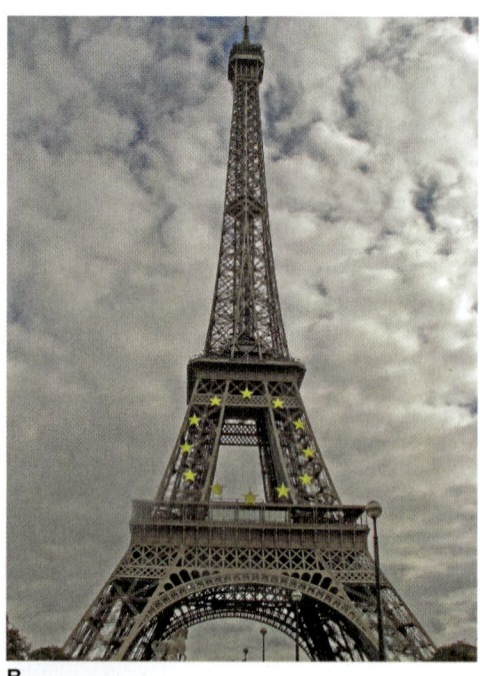

B

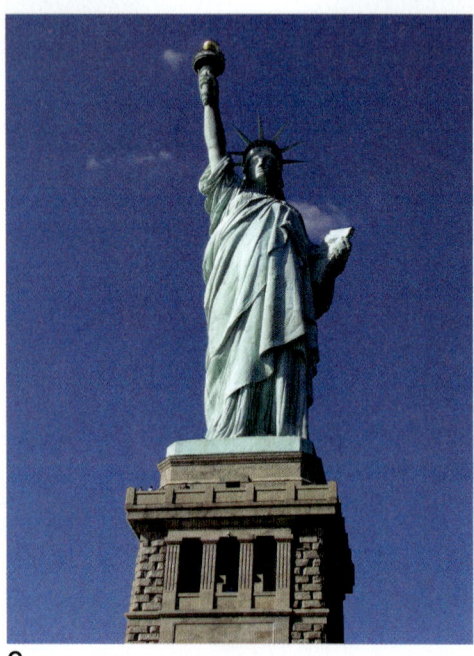

C

Jack Klasey/Goodheart-Willcox Publisher

Figure 14-9. Recognizable landmarks. A—The Colosseum in Rome. B—The Eiffel Tower in Paris. C—The Statue of Liberty in New York Harbor.

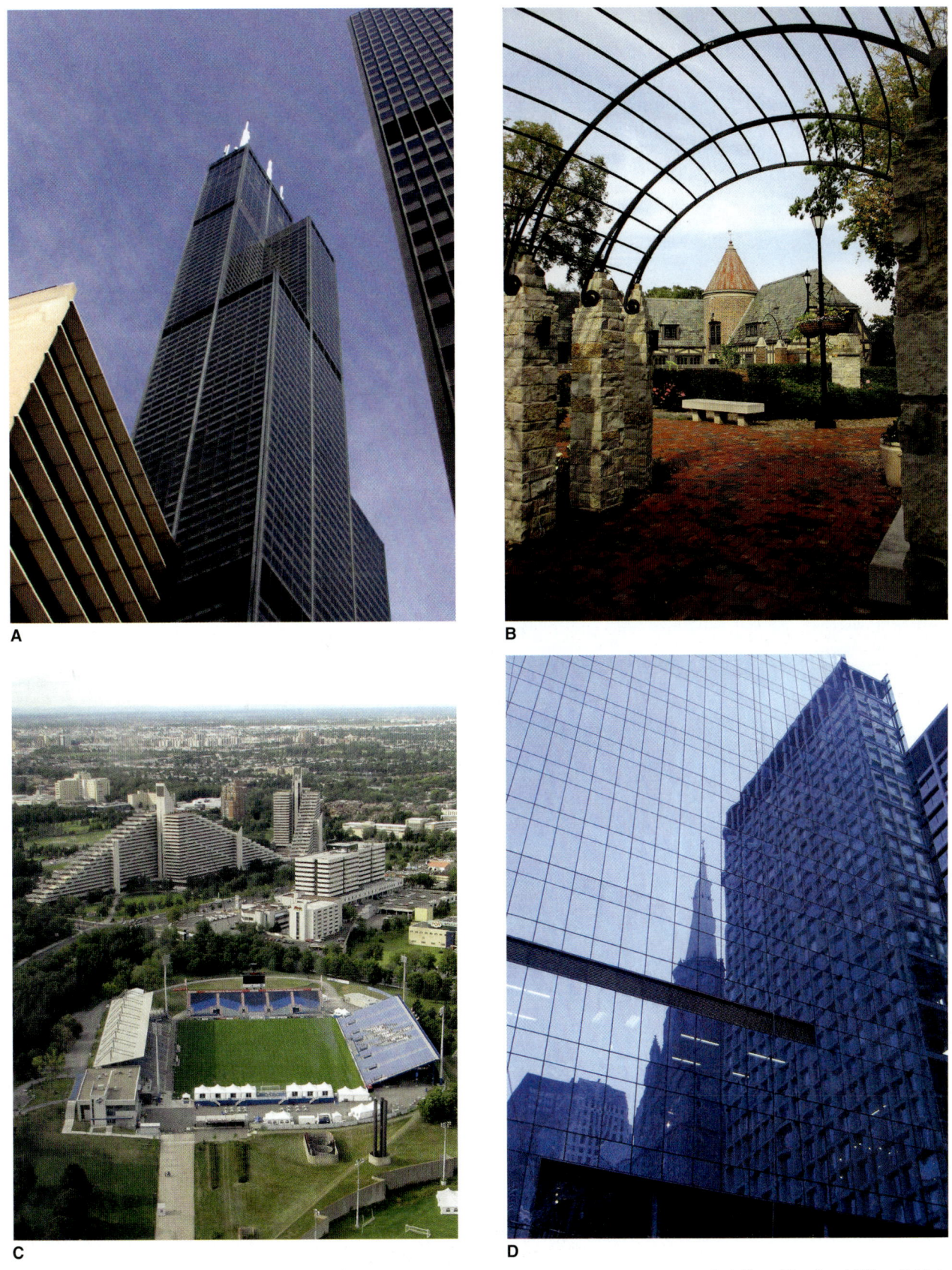

Jack Klasey/Goodheart-Willcox Publisher

Figure 14-10. Various approaches to building photography. A—Shooting upward to convey height. B—Framing a historic building with another structure. C—A high angle shot shows the building's surroundings. D—The glass wall of a downtown building reflects its neighbors.

from the same spot with wide-angle and telephoto lenses, **Figure 14-11**.

Doors, windows, carvings, textures, paint colors, shadow patterns, ornamental objects, and other details also make graphically interesting photos. See **Figure 14-12**. Some photographers have done photo essays on a single subject, such as front doors in a city or a particular neighborhood.

Photographing People

People and their activities account for a significant percentage of travel and vacation photos. Snapshots of family members are a way of saying "we were there and saw this," **Figure 14-13**. If the photographer does not pay careful attention to

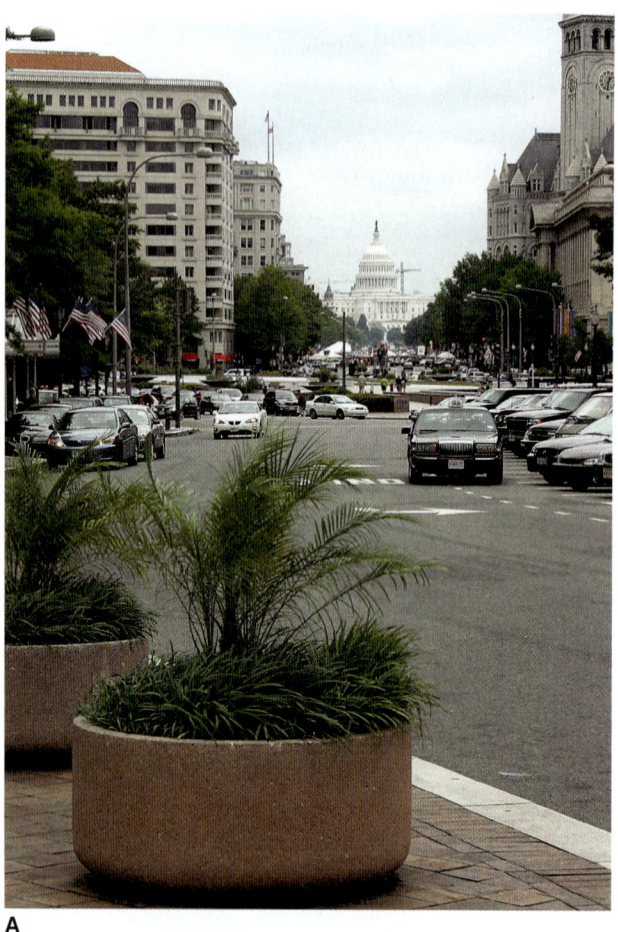
A

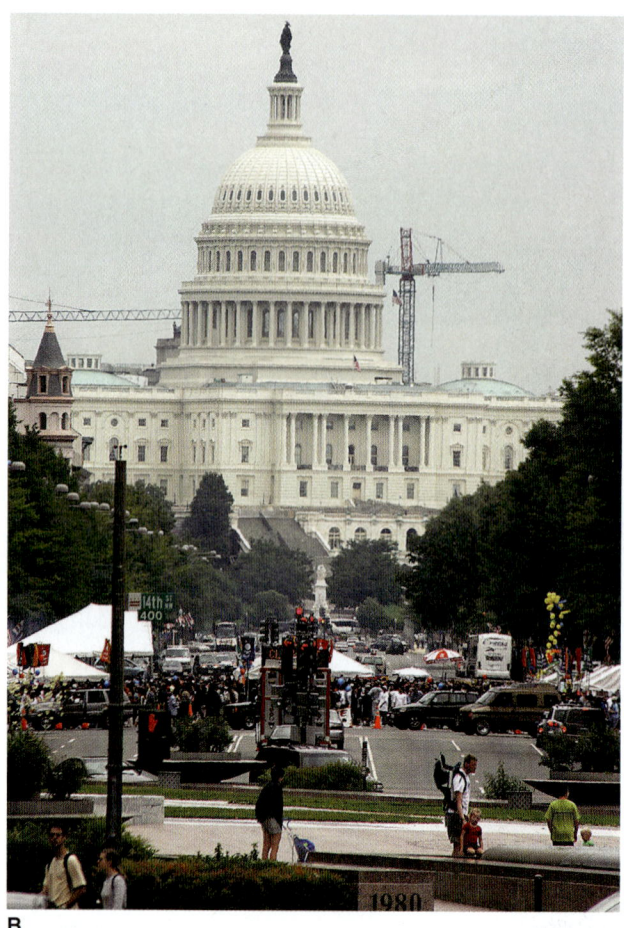
B

Jack Klasey/Goodheart-Willcox Publisher

Figure 14-11. These two views of the United States Capitol building were shot moments apart from the corner of Fifteenth Street and Pennsylvania Avenue in Washington, D.C. A—Wide-angle view down Pennsylvania Avenue. B—Telephoto view from the same position.

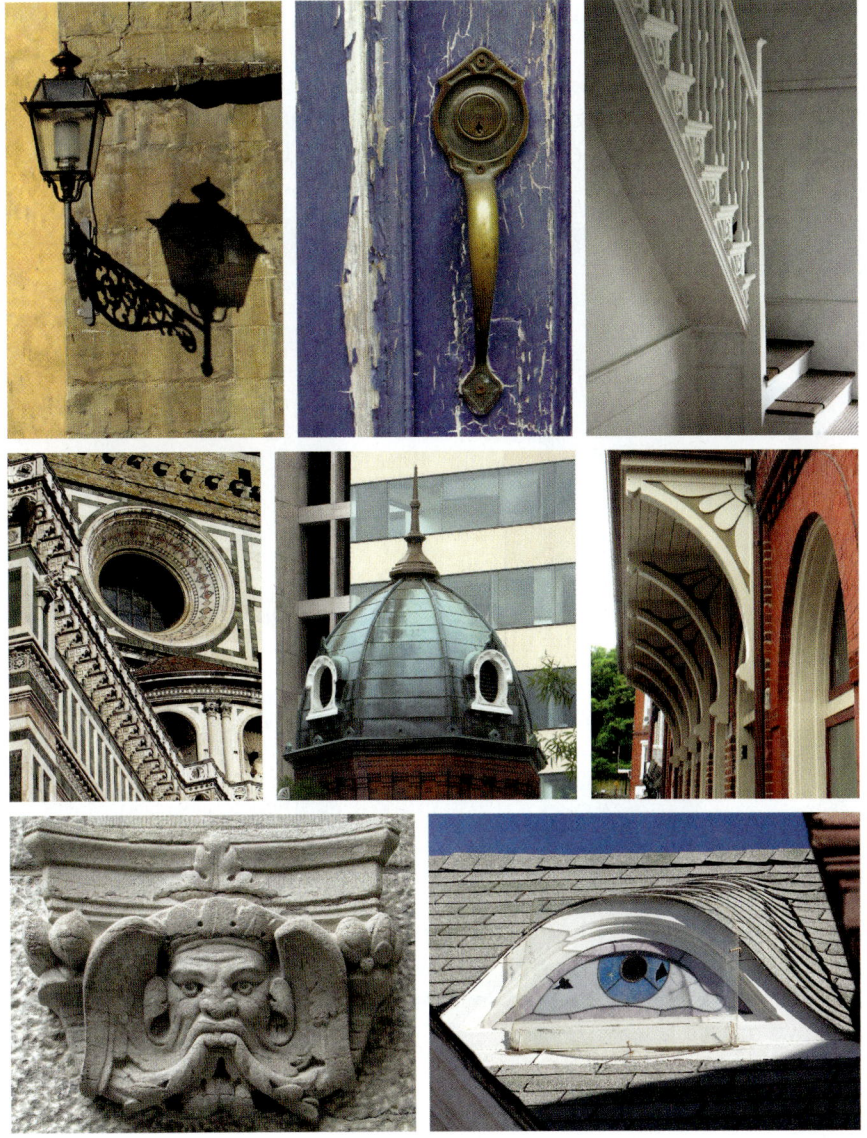

Jack Klasey/Goodheart-Willcox Publisher

Figure 14-12. Concentrating on architectural details can produce graphically strong images.

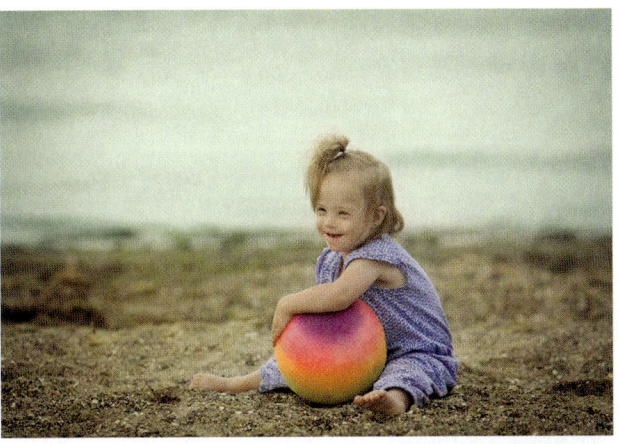

Eleonora_os/Shutterstock.com

Figure 14-13. A family vacation snapshot recording a day at the beach.

the background, such photos can sometimes have unfortunate outcomes, **Figure 14-14**.

City sidewalks, parks, shopping areas, and other areas where people gather provide numerous opportunities for *candid photos*, which are informal and unposed photographs, usually with people as the main subjects. See **Figure 14-15**. Recreational activities, such as community festivals, concerts, or fairs and carnivals, are especially rich in possible subjects. Historical sites with costumed interpreters

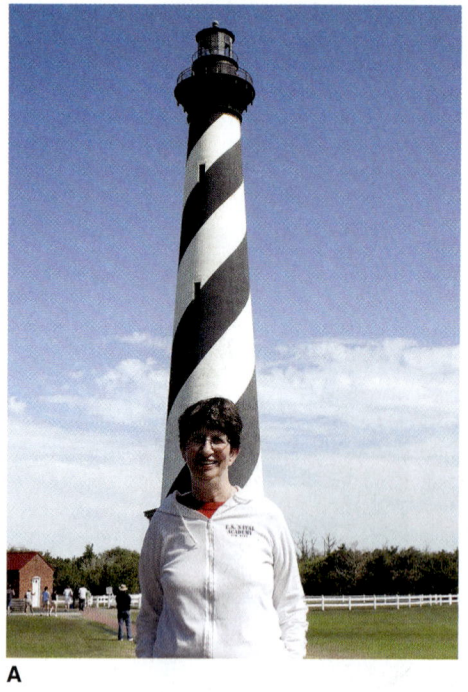 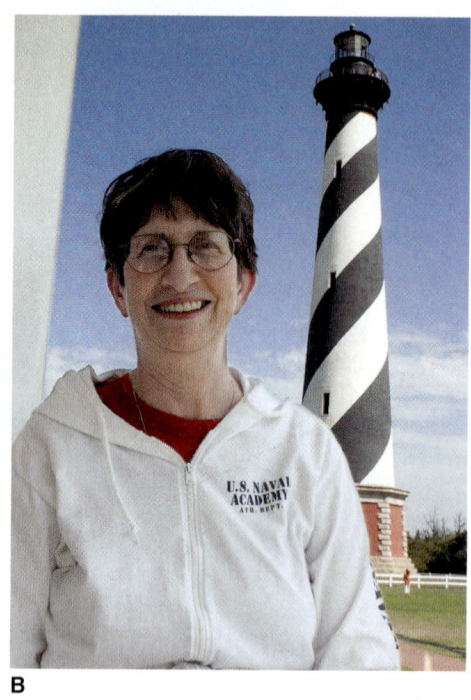

Jack Klasey/Goodheart-Willcox Publisher

Figure 14-14. Avoid unintended photographic results. A—The lighthouse appears to be sprouting from the person's shoulders. B—A better approach, with the person moved to the left and placed in the shade of an open porch to eliminate the harsh shadows on their face.

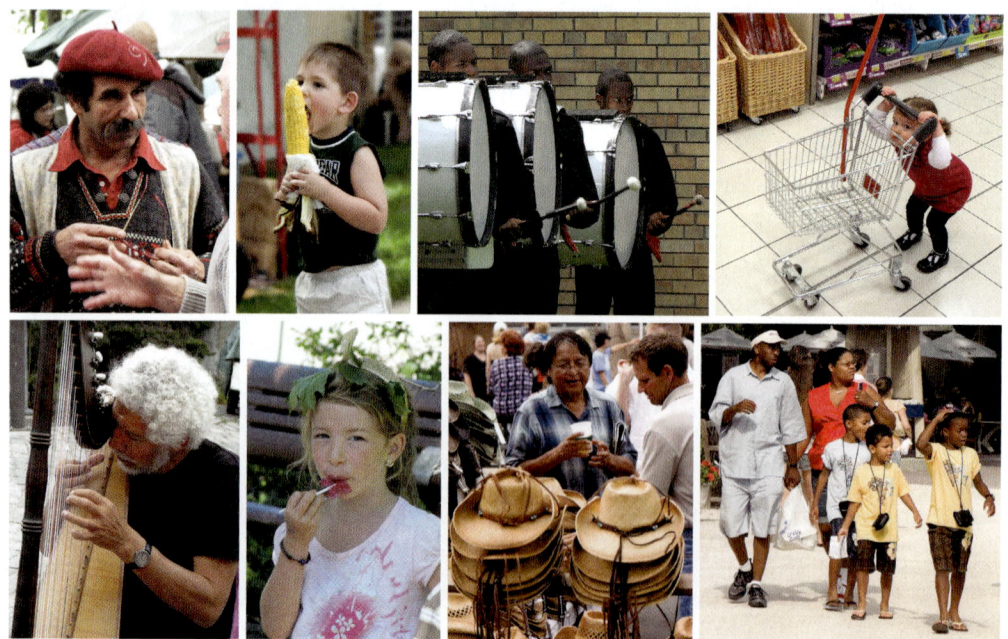

Jack Klasey/Goodheart-Willcox Publisher

Figure 14-15. On the street or in other settings, people represent an endless series of photographic possibilities.

who bring history to life also provide many photo opportunities. See **Figure 14-16**.

When Will You Shoot?

As noted in Chapter 13, most photographers prefer the warm light of magic hour, the time surrounding sunrise and sunset. The difference in mood of the same scene photographed under varied lighting conditions can be dramatic. See **Figure 14-17**.

Hand-holding the camera to shoot scenes after dark can be tricky, since long exposure times can result in blur and streaked lights from camera shake, **Figure 14-18**. Finding a means of support to steady the camera will often give acceptable results, **Figure 14-19**. Even at night, ambient light may be sufficient to allow handheld photography. See **Figure 14-20**.

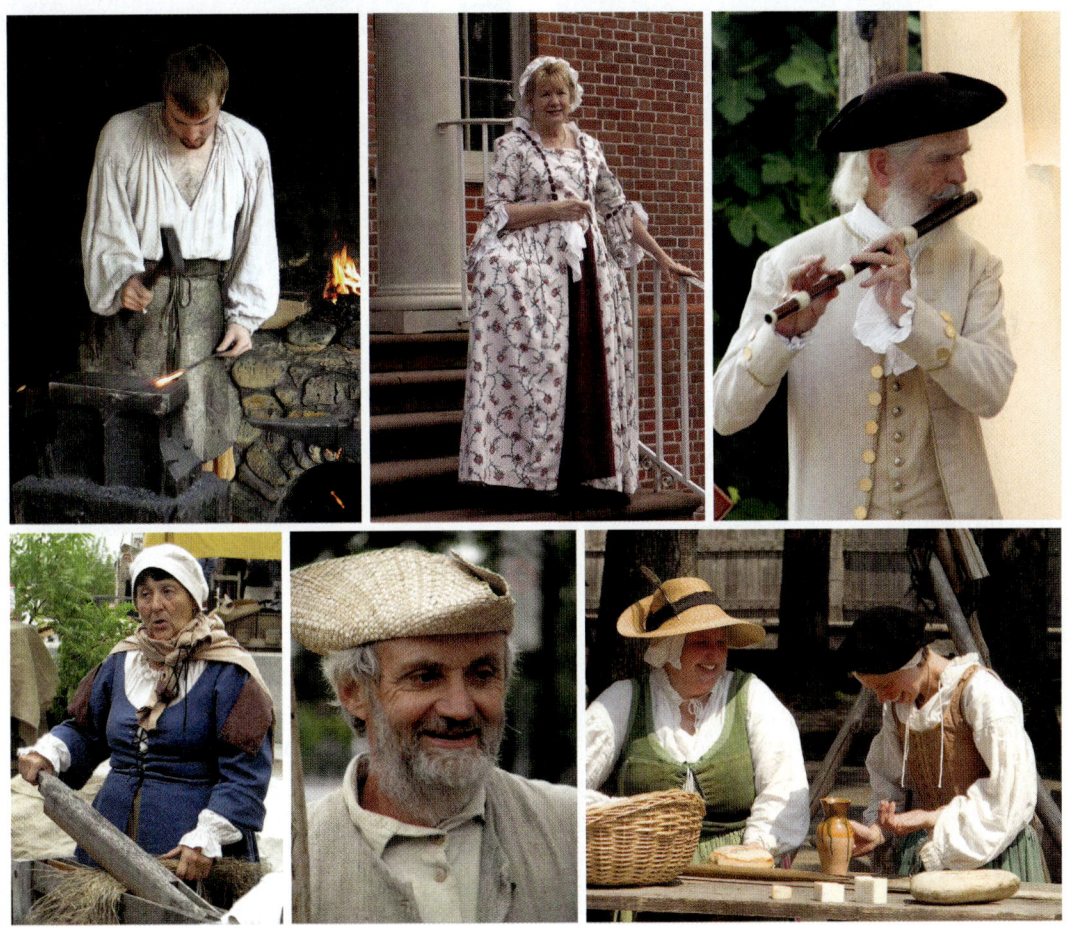

Jack Klasey/Goodheart-Willcox Publisher

Figure 14-16. Colorful period dress and visually interesting activities, such as blacksmithing, make a living history museum a rewarding photographic experience.

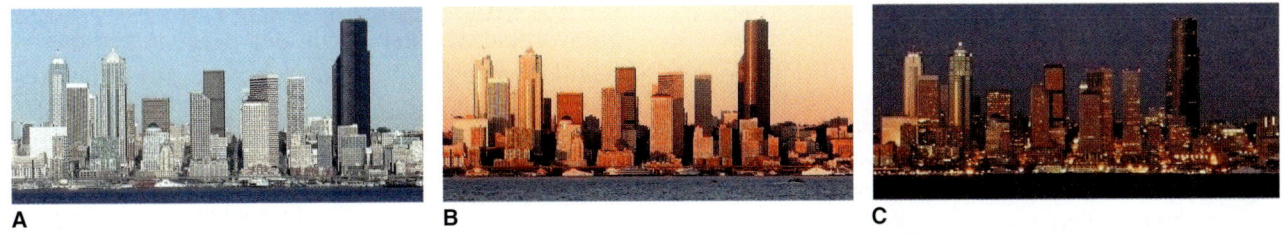

Jack Klasey/Goodheart-Willcox Publisher

Figure 14-17. Lighting strongly influences the mood of a photo. A—The Seattle skyline by day. B—Late afternoon light bathes the buildings in a warm glow. C—At dusk, the darkening sky sets off buildings illuminated by the sunset's afterglow and their own lights.

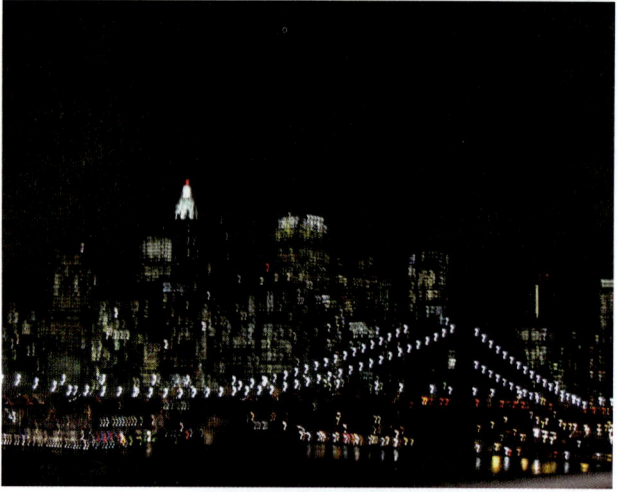

Jack Klasey/Goodheart-Willcox Publisher

Figure 14-18. Hand-holding a camera for a night shot almost always results in camera shake.

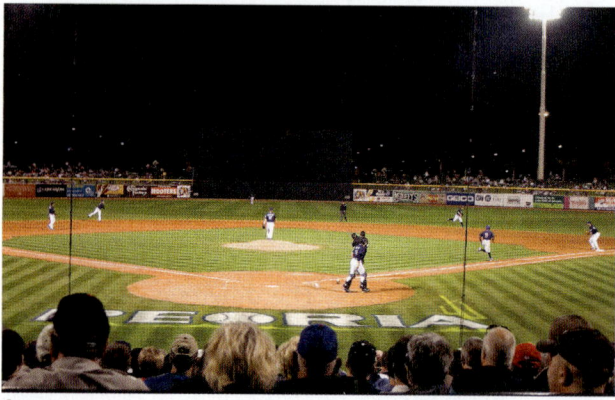

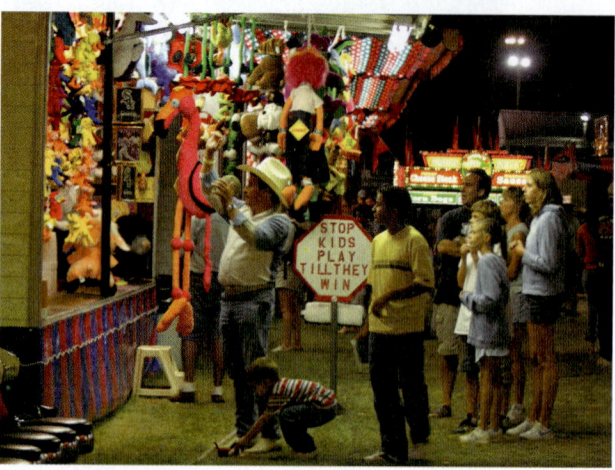

Jack Klasey/Goodheart-Willcox Publisher

Figure 14-20. Using ambient light. A—This baseball field was lit brightly enough to permit a shutter speed of 1/50 second, so that the running players were captured without motion blur. B—Lighting at this carnival booth was bright enough for an exposure of 1/15 second, with the camera steadied against a trash can.

Coping with Unfavorable Conditions

Traveling with your family or with a group can often make it difficult to photograph in the best light. Your time available at a given location may be limited to a few midday hours. Another problem may be unfavorable weather conditions that cause the cancellation of an event or make photography difficult.

A resourceful photographer copes with unfavorable conditions by changing strategies. Work around the strong, contrasting light of midday by seeking subjects sheltered from the sun. Shade from trees may be solid or dappled, **Figure 14-21**, providing different lighting effects. Photographing your subject on an open porch provides attractive, diffused light while retaining a good sunlit background. See **Figure 14-22**.

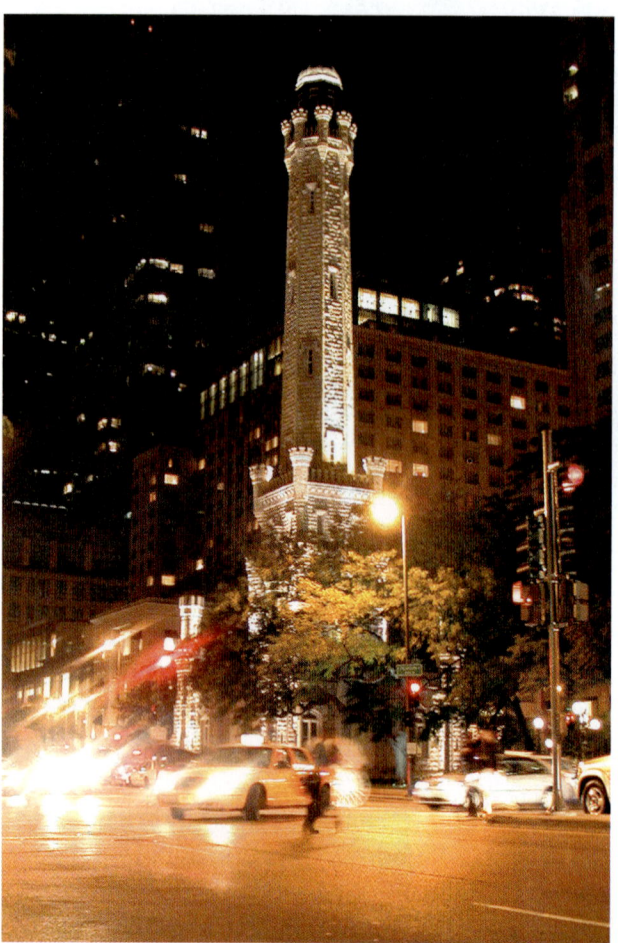

Jack Klasey/Goodheart-Willcox Publisher

Figure 14-19. The photographer steadied the camera by pressing it against a traffic light pole to take this night shot of Chicago's historic Water Tower. Because of the 1/4 second shutter speed, pedestrians and moving vehicles are motion-blurred, but the Water Tower is sufficiently sharp.

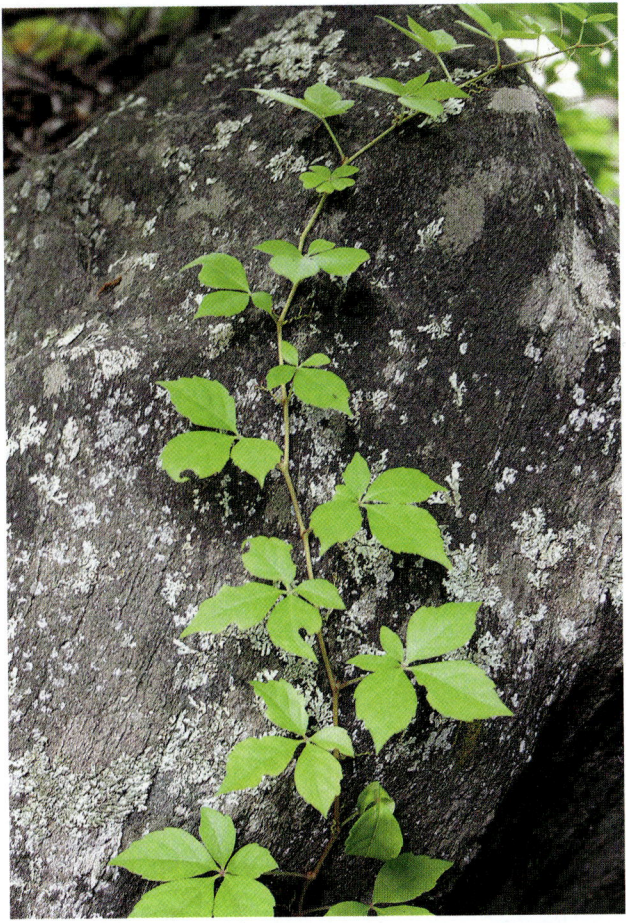
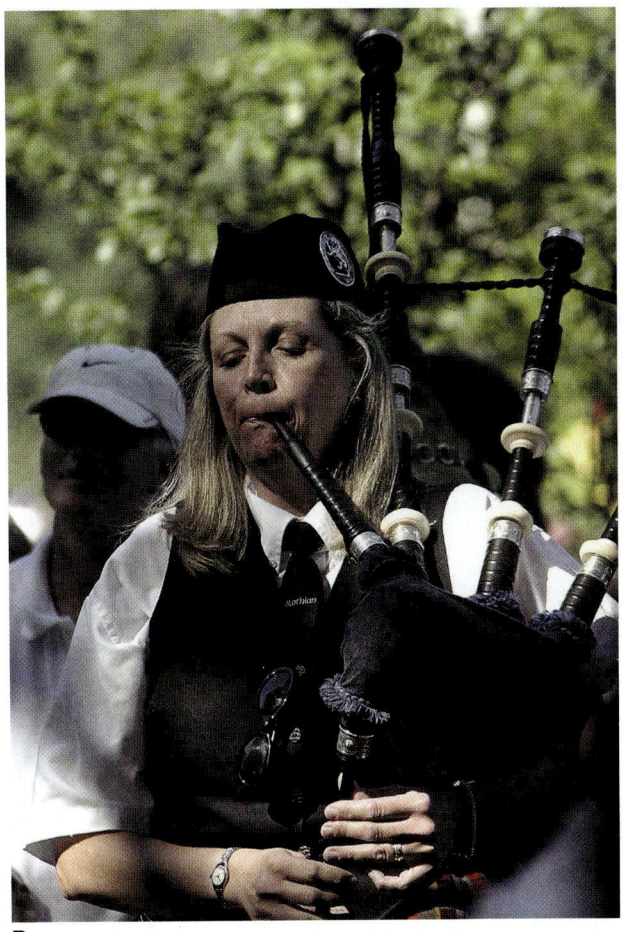

Jack Klasey/Goodheart-Willcox Publisher

Figure 14-21. Using shade to limit contrast. A—Open shade (solid but bright) provides a soft, even light for this scene. B—Dappled (broken) shade can soften light enough to avoid harsh contrast in important subject areas.

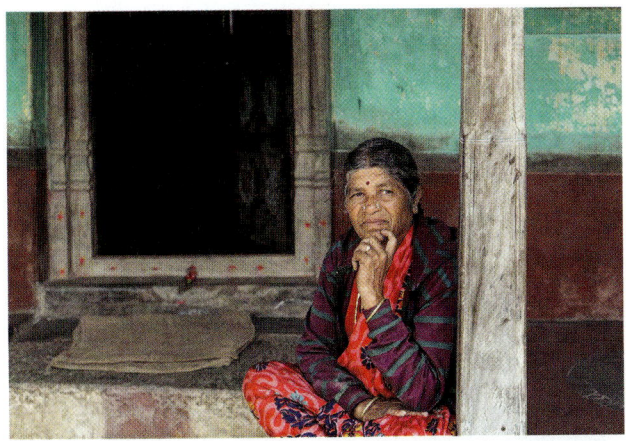

Catalin Lazar/Shutterstock.com

Figure 14-22. This softly lighted person was photographed in the shade of an open porch.

Strong, high-contrast light is actually good for certain subjects, helping to convey the feeling of heat and bright sun in a desert scene. See **Figure 14-23**. It also can be useful for spotlighting a subject against a shadowy background, **Figure 14-24**. By understanding how to use this high-contrast light to your advantage, you can create dynamic photos that make a strong impact. Furthermore, high-contrast light is great if you want to convert color photos to black-and-white down the road.

On a cloudy day with a flat, uninteresting sky, abandon the plan for broad landscape views or a sun-lit beach party scene. Instead, take advantage of the softly diffused light to capture rich, saturated colors in smaller-scale views, **Figure 14-25**. Since the sky has no color or detail, you would generally choose an angle and composition to exclude it from your shot. For example, concentrate on a portion or detail of a building instead of the whole structure. See **Figure 14-26**.

If stormy weather prevents you from carrying out plans for a sunny afternoon of photography, use the unfavorable conditions as your subject. **Figure 14-27** shows some examples of bad-weather scenes.

Moving Indoors to Shoot

To avoid unfavorable weather conditions, you can, of course, move indoors. Museums, historic

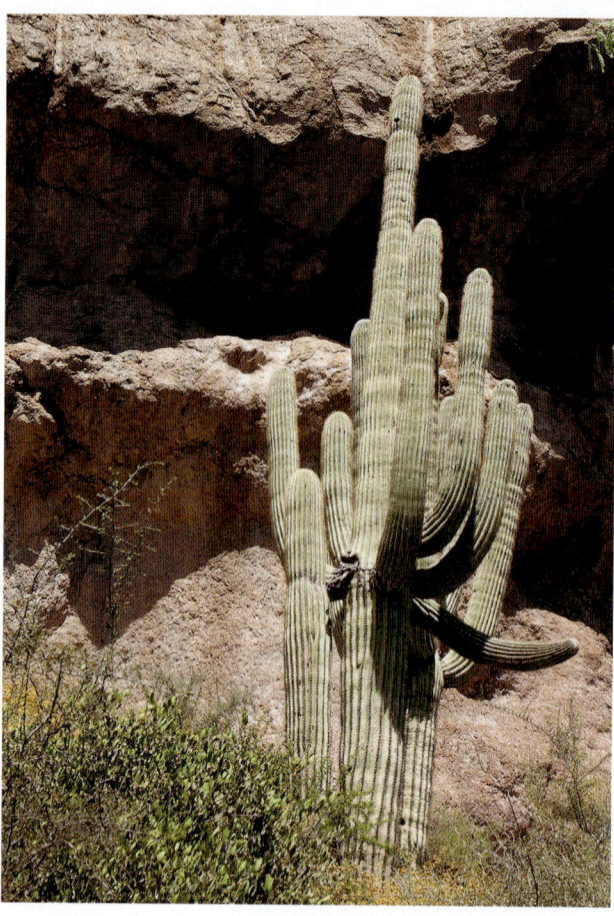

Jack Klasey/Goodheart-Willcox Publisher

Figure 14-23. Strong, midday sunlight casts deep shadows beneath the rock ledges and across this saguaro cactus.

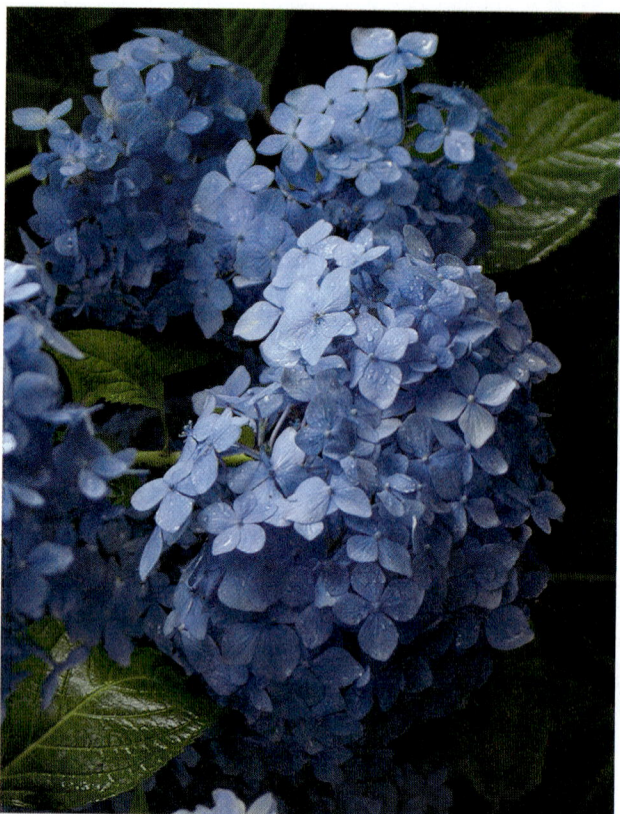

A

Jack Klasey/Goodheart-Willcox Publisher

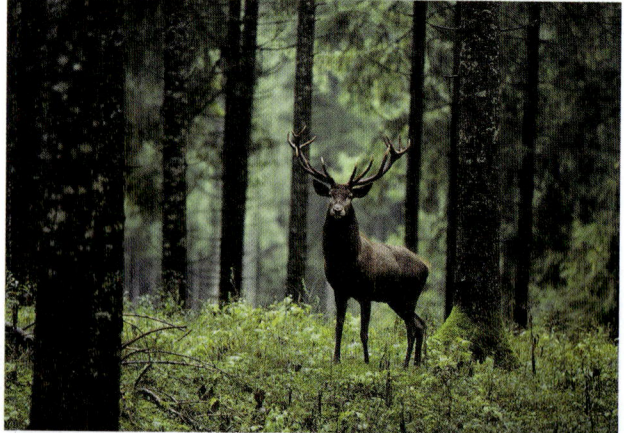

B

sirtravelalot/Shutterstock.com

Figure 14-25. Diffused light. A—Soft, even lighting brings out the rich blues and greens of a blooming hydrangea. B—Misty weather at midmorning attractively lights an elk in a forest.

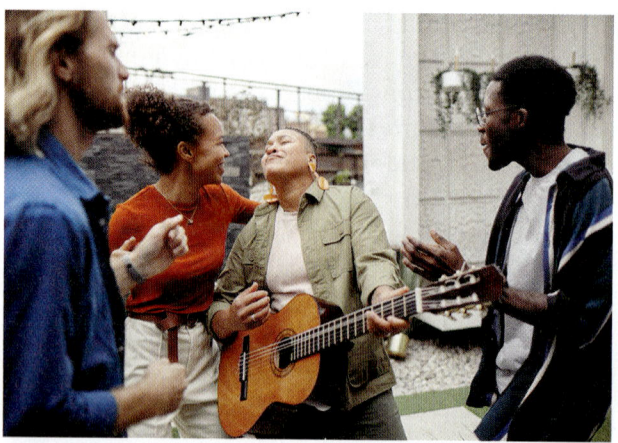

SeventyFour/Shutterstock.com

Figure 14-24. Natural spotlighting on the performer provides excellent separation from the background.

structures, public buildings, and some natural attractions allow you to photograph regardless of the weather outside. Caves such as Virginia's Luray Caverns offer visitors guided tours along paved paths to view dramatic stone formations, **Figure 14-28**. The lighting level in such caves is low enough that you usually need to select a high ISO and provide some form of support or stabilization to avoid camera shake. Since you are part of a tour group, using a tripod is not practical. However, a monopod can provide the needed support without tripping your fellow tourists.

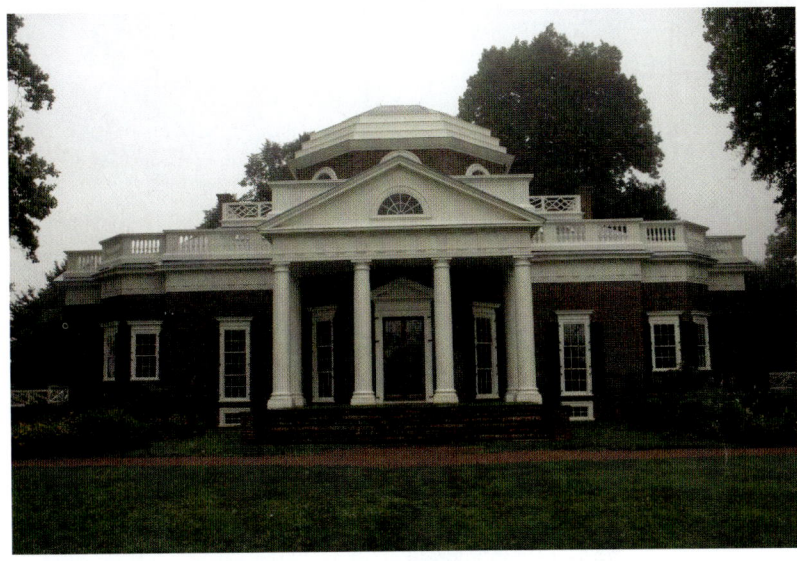
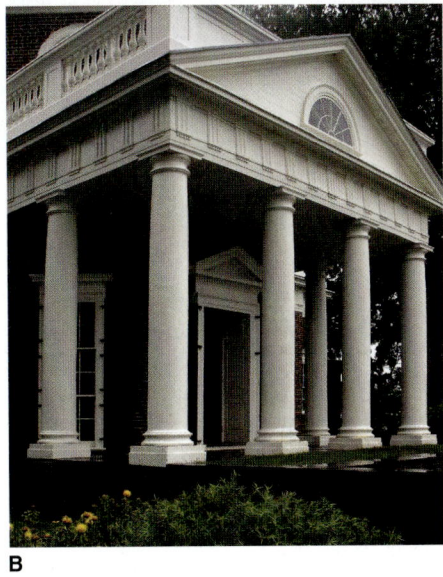

Jack Klasey/Goodheart-Willcox Publisher

Figure 14-26. Excluding a flat sky. A—The solid gray sky on a misty day adds little to this view of Monticello, Thomas Jefferson's home. B—Changing camera angle and distance eliminates the sky while retaining the character of the building.

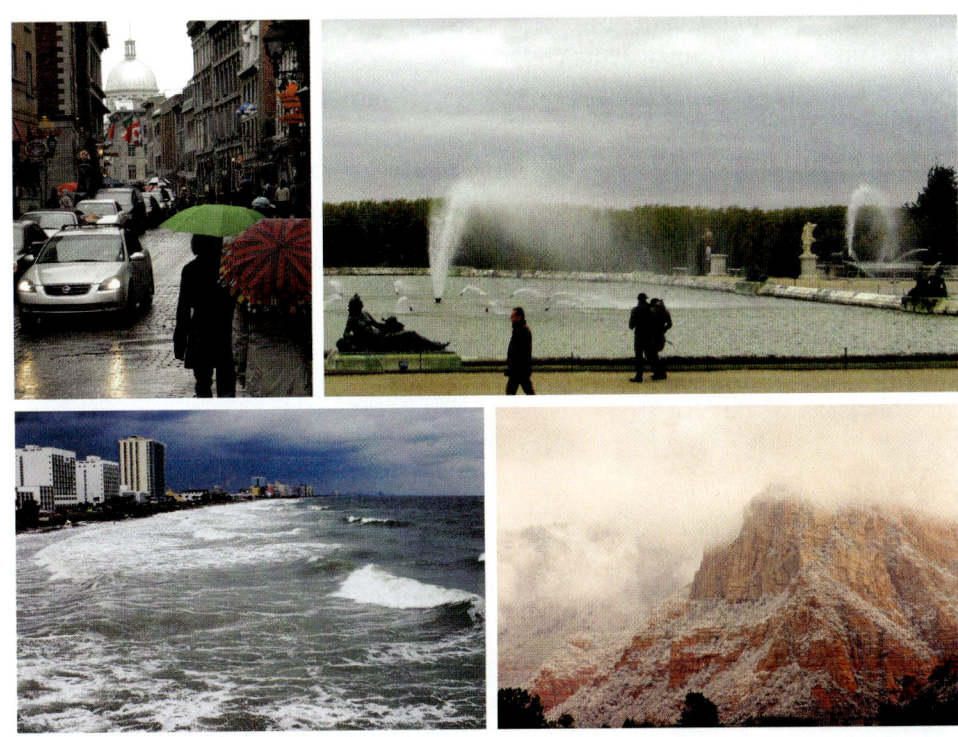

Jack Klasey/Goodheart-Willcox Publisher

Figure 14-27. Adverse weather can be a good subject.

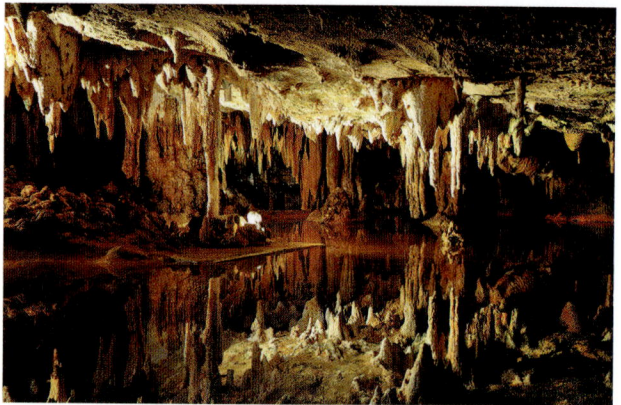

Joe Ravi/Shutterstock.com

Figure 14-28. Fantastic shapes of stalactites and their reflections at Luray Caverns in Virginia.

Tripods are almost always banned in museums because of the crowds of visitors, **Figure 14-29**. Since flash photography is usually prohibited to prevent fading of the artwork, museum shooting requires a fairly high ISO and a means of steadying the camera during longer exposures. In dimly lit church interiors, you can steady the camera on a railing or the back of a pew, **Figure 14-30**.

Period rooms in historic houses are usually dimly lit, sometimes only by natural window light. Steadying the camera on a doorframe will normally provide sufficient sharpness without use of a flash, **Figure 14-31**. Remember that in situations where you either do not have access to a tripod or are not allowed to use one, you can use your body as your stabilizer. Tuck your arms into your sides and loop the camera strap around your neck. By eliminating the natural movement of your body, you should be able to get clear, steady shots.

Even on days with favorable outdoor weather, interesting photos can be made shooting exterior scenes from indoors, using building elements to frame the shots. See **Figure 14-32**.

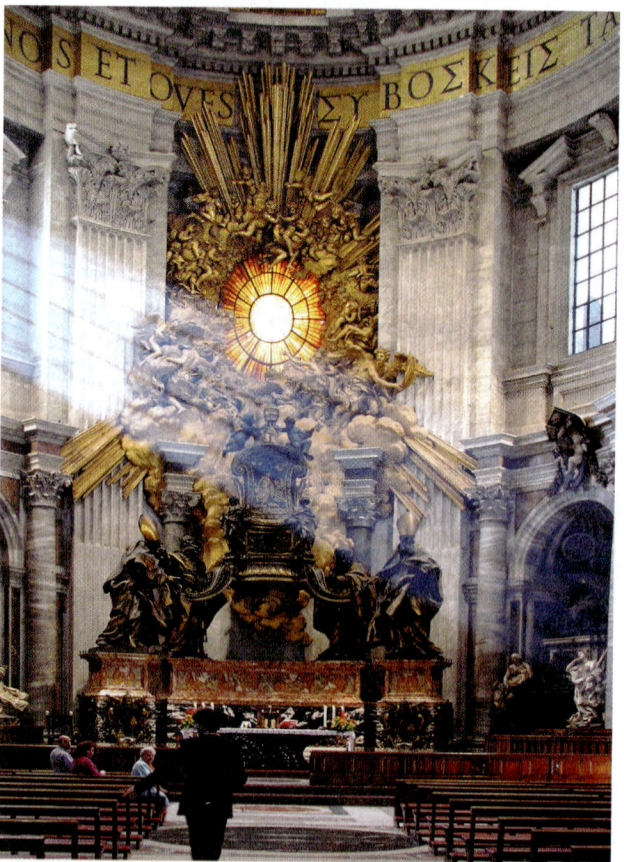

Jack Klasey/Goodheart-Willcox Publisher

Figure 14-30. The interior of St. Peter's Basilica in Rome, captured with an exposure of 1/25 second at f/2.7 with an ISO of 400.

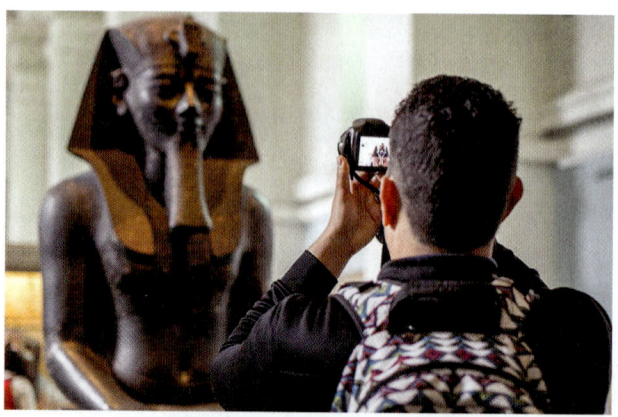

Ram Kay/Shutterstock.com

Figure 14-29. Tripods and flash photography are banned in most museums. This visitor is following the rules.

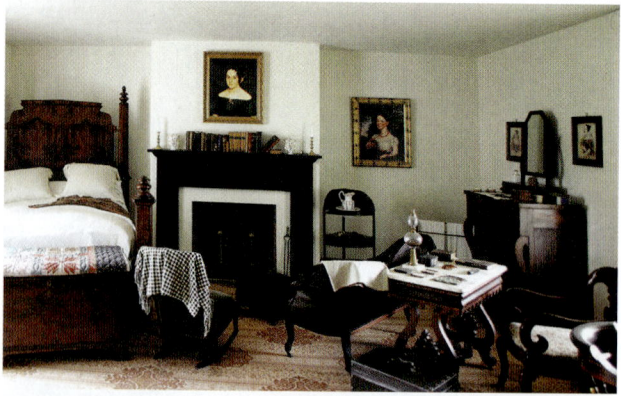

Jack Klasey/Goodheart-Willcox Publisher

Figure 14-31. This eighteenth-century period room was dimly lighted by windows on two sides. Bracing the camera on a doorframe allowed a shake-free exposure of 1/6 second.

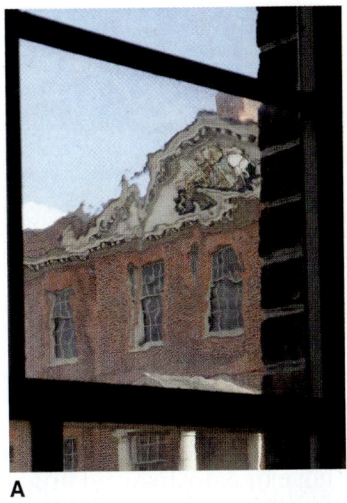
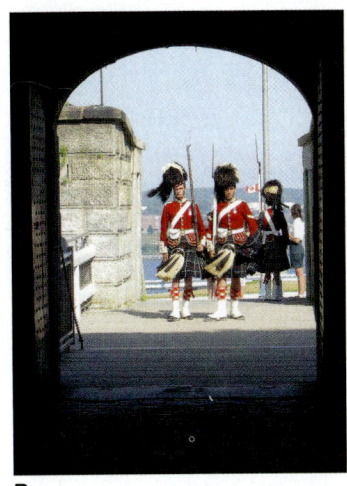
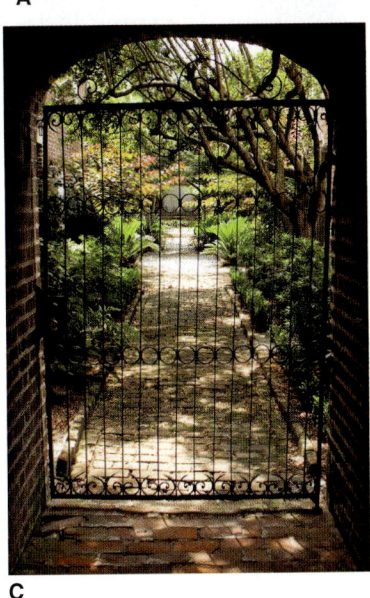

Figure 14-32. Shooting from indoors. A—The uneven, rippled quality of old window glass distorts the façade of an eighteenth-century building. B—Sentries in period uniform framed by the arched entry of a restored fortress. C—A hidden garden seen through the gate at the end of a covered passageway. D—Colorful boats in a marina framed by a restaurant window.

Jack Klasey/Goodheart-Willcox Publisher

Portfolio Assignment

Brace Yourself

Find a subject that would normally require the use of a tripod to capture without camera shake. Possible subjects include a lighted street scene at night or a dimly lit interior space. Complete the following steps:

1. Set your camera for aperture priority mode.
2. Select the widest available f-stop and set the ISO to 100.
3. Meter the scene. If the shutter speed is one second or longer, increase the ISO rating to 200 and meter again. If necessary, repeat until the shutter speed is less than one second.
4. Find a suitable support to brace your camera against and make an exposure. Check your image for blurring due to camera shake. Remember that moving subjects will blur, but stationary objects should be sharp. This shooting technique takes some practice to avoid moving the camera as you press the shutter.

Make a number of exposures until you get the desired results. Select the best image for your portfolio, noting the shutter speed, f-stop, and ISO you used.

Chapter 14 Travel Photography

Chapter 14 Review

Summary

- In addition to landscapes and other nature subjects, travel photography pays considerable attention to the human-made aspects of our world and to the people who inhabit it.
- Professionals often write magazine or newspaper travel articles illustrated by their photos. They also shoot photos for use in books and for stock photography agencies. Amateurs most often shoot vacation snapshots to share with friends and family after the trip.
- Whether you are planning a journey to a foreign locale, a family vacation, or a day trip, researching in advance helps you take more interesting pictures. Great travel research tools include the internet, books, and travel guides.
- How much camera gear you take on your trip will vary considerably, depending on your budget, personal preferences, transportation plans, and other factors. With two zooms, most photographic situations can be covered.
- Since memory cards are fairly inexpensive, some travel photographers carry enough high-capacity cards to last for the entire trip. Others prefer to use a lower-capacity card, downloading it at the end of each day to a portable hard drive, a USB flash drive, a laptop, or cloud-based storage.
- A sturdy camera bag is the preferred method for organizing and transporting equipment with interchangeable lenses.
- Professionals often work from a detailed list of photos to be taken, known as a shot list, and must meet strict client delivery deadlines. What they shoot varies by assignment, but often includes buildings and people.
- The difference in mood of the same scene photographed under varied lighting conditions can be dramatic.
- A resourceful photographer copes with unfavorable conditions by changing strategies. They work around unfavorable lighting and bad weather or use them to their advantage.
- You can move indoors to avoid unfavorable weather conditions. Museums, historic structures, public buildings, and some natural attractions allow you to photograph regardless of the weather outside.
- Even on days with favorable outdoor weather, interesting photos can be made shooting exterior scenes from indoors, using building elements to frame the shots.

Review Questions

Answer the following questions using the information provided in this chapter.

Know and Understand

1. _____ is defined as journeys made for leisure rather than business.
   A. Travel photography
   B. Professional travel
   C. Recreational travel
   D. Travel guide
2. *True or False?* Some advanced amateurs produce high-quality travel photos rivaling those of the professionals.
3. A _____ is a book or electronic publication that provides travelers with needed information about places they plan to visit.
   A. travel guide
   B. backup copy
   C. shot list
   D. recreational travel
4. *True or False?* Because of the flexibility it provides, many travel photographers prefer a camera with interchangeable lenses.

5. No matter which memory card approach they use, careful photographers make a _____ to guard against possible loss of their images.
   A. shot list
   B. guidebook
   C. travel guide
   D. backup copy
6. *True or False?* If you travel by air, your camera bag should be treated as checked baggage.
7. *True or False?* Amateurs often work from a shot list and must meet strict client delivery deadlines.
8. Which of the following is *not* a detail of a building that can make graphically interesting photos?
   A. Door
   B. Sky
   C. Ornamental object
   D. Paint color
9. *True or False?* A candid photo is informal and unposed.
10. Hand-holding the camera to shoot scenes _____ can be tricky, since long exposure times can result in blur and streaked lights from camera shake.
    A. at midday
    B. at dawn
    C. in the late afternoon
    D. after dark
11. *True or False?* Strong, high-contrast light can be useful for spotlighting a subject against a shadowy background.
12. *True or False?* Tripods are great to use in museums for steady shots.

Apply and Analyze

1. Why do you *not* need a permit if you are simply visiting a location to take pictures and will not make any money off them?
2. What two zooms can cover most photographic situations?
3. What are the two memory card approaches used by most travel photographers?
4. What is a shot list?
5. List three of the five common ways of shooting a building or urban scene.

Critical Thinking

1. After returning from a vacation to Alaska, you have been asked to deliver a short presentation to two audiences—a first-grade class and a local senior citizens' club. How could you tailor your program to the interests and needs of these very different audiences?
2. Some photographers concentrate on landscapes or buildings, while others focus on people and their activities. Which would appeal more to you? Why?

Suggested Activities

1. Work with three other students on a "Photography Rocks!" project. Each person should choose one letter (R, O, C, or K) and shoot at least six different examples of a close-up view of the letter (on a store sign, scratched in beach sand, on an alphabet block, etc.). Select four examples of each letter and make 4″ × 6″ prints. Assemble four variations of the word ROCK on a poster board with the heading "Photography Rocks!" and display it in your classroom or school hallway.
2. Research tourist attractions in the capital city of your state or province to find photographic possibilities. List five specific locations where you would shoot on a sunny day and five specific locations where you would shoot on a day with rainy or otherwise unfavorable weather. If possible, use your list on a trip to that city.
3. Look through your photos from a recent trip or vacation. Find a photo that stands out to you. First, identify what you think makes the image a good image. Then, identify how you could improve upon the existing image, especially in regard to composition and the use of compositional elements.

Communicating about Photography

1. **Reading and Speaking.** Choose a foreign country that you would like to visit. Research the culture, history, and notable features of this country. Give a short oral report to the class on the types of photos you would take to visually express the character of the country.
2. **Reading and Writing.** Partnering with another classmate, read a travel guide or photographer's guide. Make a list of the types of information found in the guide.

Chapter 15

Portrait and Studio Photography

Learning Objectives

After completing this chapter, you will be able to:
- Understand the difference between formal studio portraits and environmental portraits.
- Explain how fill flash and white balance can help modify ambient light.
- Recall the various lights used in a studio and how to work with them safely.
- Identify various lighting methods in the studio.
- Discuss the techniques for controlling light in the studio.
- Discuss the techniques for measuring light in the studio.
- Apply the basic techniques of studio lighting for both portrait and product photography.

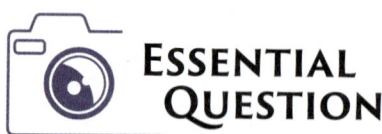

Essential Question

How has portrait photography shaped how we view photography in general?

Technical Terms

backdrop
background light
barn doors
continuous light
cookie
electronic studio flash
environmental portrait
feathering
fill light
flag

formal studio portrait
gel
gobo
grid
hard light
inverse-square law
key light
lighting ratio
monolight
pack-and-head system

photoflood
rim light
snoot
softbox
soft light
tenting
three-point lighting
tungsten-halogen bulb

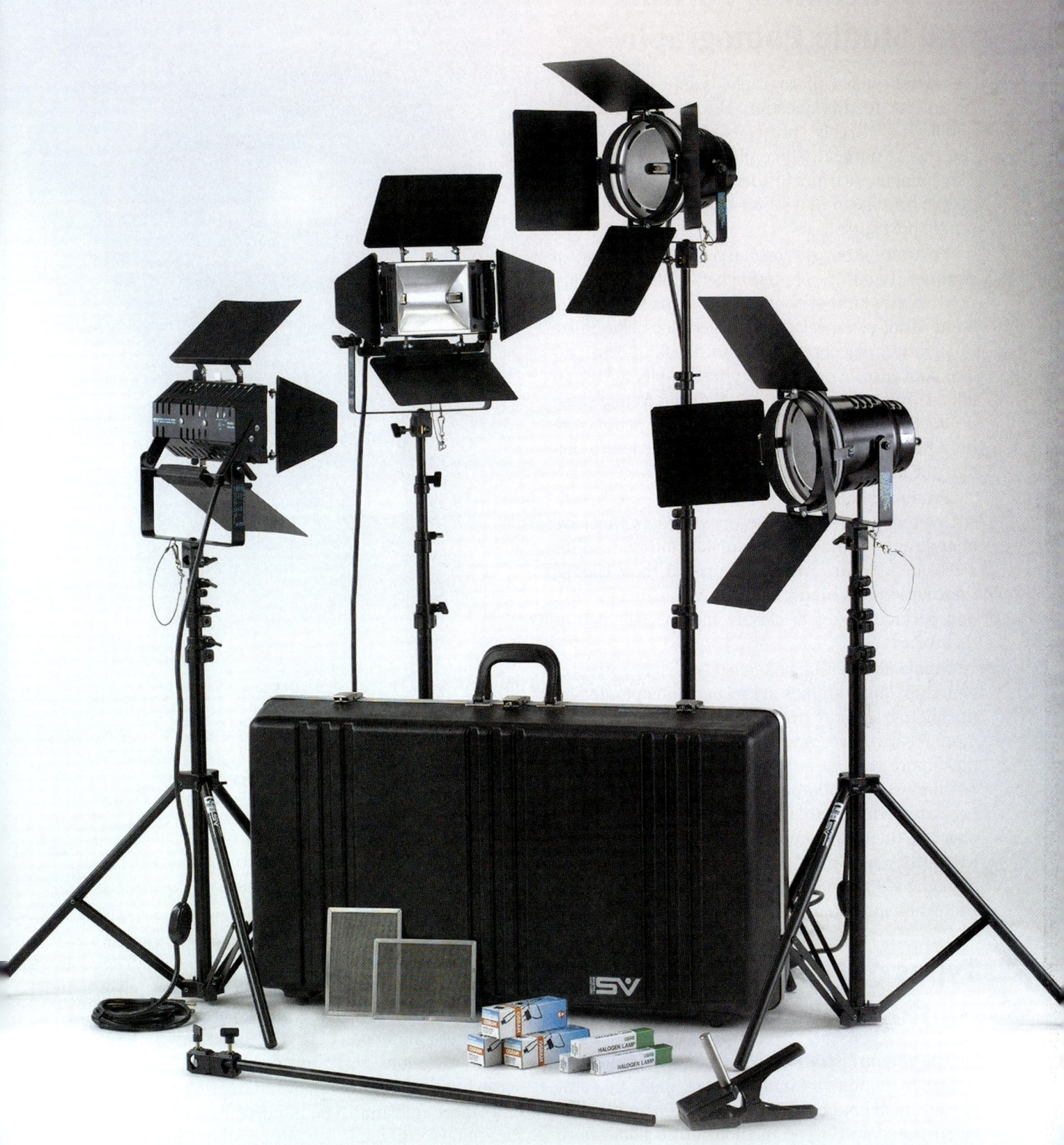

Smith-Victor Corporation

Introduction to Portrait and Studio Photography

"What type of photography is done in a studio?" In answer to this question, the great majority of people would reply "portraits." The association of the two is natural, since photo studios often display sample portraits in their windows, and many people have been in a studio to sit for individual or family portraits.

Portraits are the primary activity for most community-based photographers, but they are not the only kind of photographs made in a studio. Some studios, especially in larger cities, specialize in shooting objects rather than people. These studios concentrate on product photography for use in advertising, catalogs, and social media. While some product shots, such as clothing, involve people, the human beings are essentially props needed to display the merchandise.

Product photographers often must practice client confidentiality because the products they are photographing may not be publicly announced for weeks or months. They must protect their client's information in a highly competitive business world, and parameters for disclosure may be included in their contract.

Studio photography often lends itself to entrepreneurship. Many studios are owned and operated by the photographer themselves. While you often have more creative freedom as an entrepreneur, you also have more responsibilities, including handling the business side of photography and purchasing any necessary equipment. Even though every photographer has their own preferences for the cameras and lenses they use, most portrait photographers start off using a 35 mm lens. Other popular portrait lens choices include 50 mm lenses and 85 mm lenses.

Types of Portrait Photography

The ***formal studio portrait*** is the traditional style of individual or family portrait, made in a studio setting. It has been popular since the mid-1800s, when the slow tintype method forced subjects to hold uncomfortably stiff poses for long periods, **Figure 15-1**. Although improved technology has made portrait sessions less physically demanding,

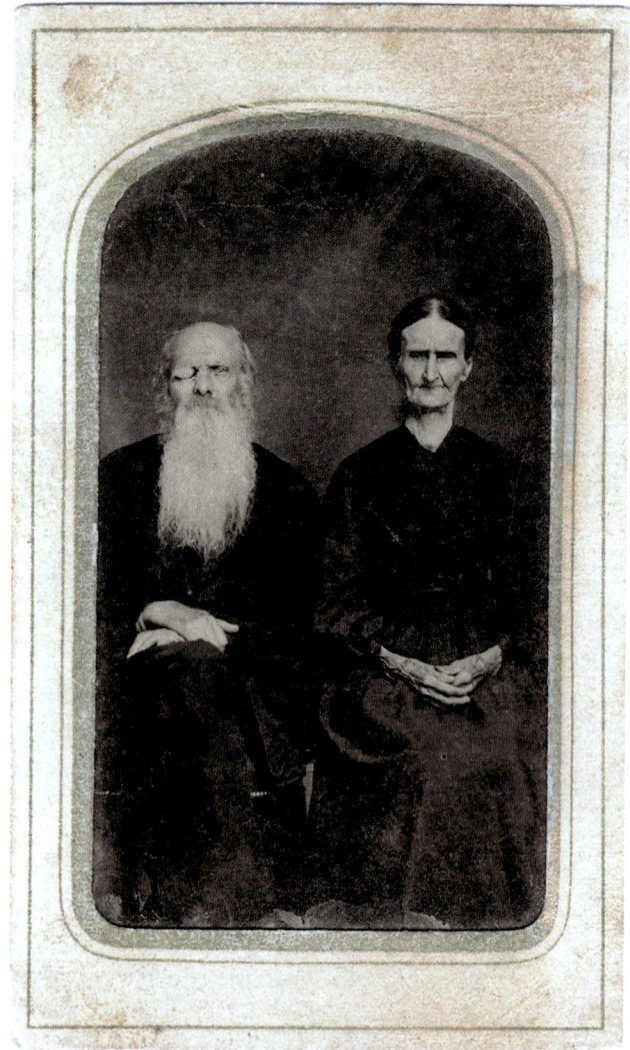

Goodheart-Willcox Publisher

Figure 15-1. Early photographic methods required long exposure times. As a result, most portrait subjects appear stiff and uncomfortable.

most studio portraits of adults remain fairly formal. This is especially true of executive portraits made for use in publications such as annual reports, **Figure 15-2**.

Studio portraits of children, on the other hand, are more spontaneous and are designed to capture the joy of childhood, **Figure 15-3**. Many parents schedule annual portraits to record their child's "growing up" years.

A more informal type of portrait, made outside the studio setting, has become popular. Often called ***environmental portraits***, these images show the subject in natural surroundings or in a setting meaningful to them. Subjects typically wear casual

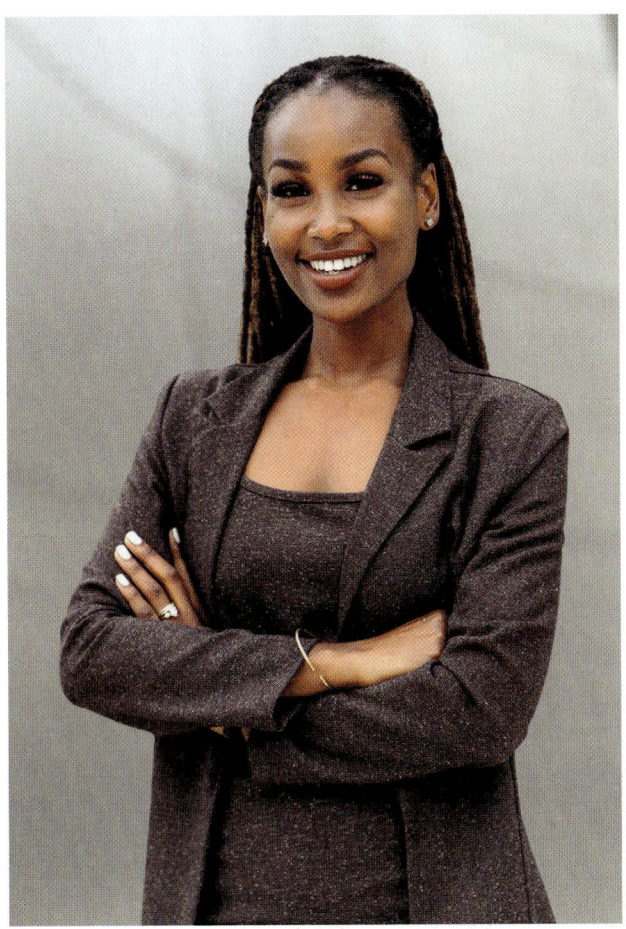

El Nariz/Shutterstock.com

Figure 15-2. Studio portraits of adults, especially businesspeople or civic leaders, are quite formal.

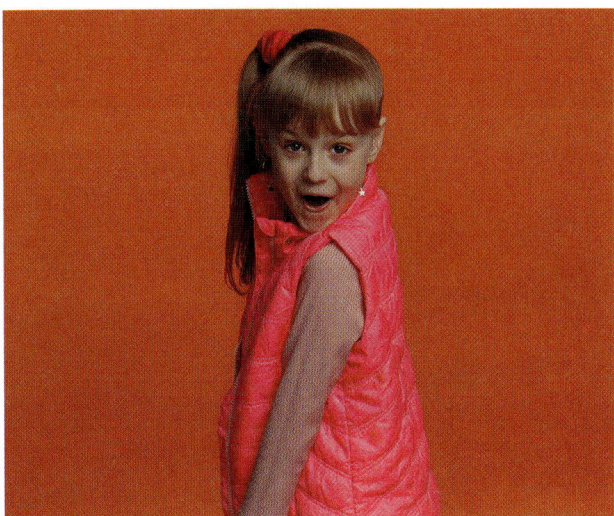

Andrii Iemelianenko/Shutterstock.com

Figure 15-3. A child's portrait session often captures delightful moments.

clothing and are posed in a much more relaxed manner than in formal studio portraits, **Figure 15-4**.

For many studios, creating environmental portraits of high school seniors is an important source of business income. To develop a reputation that will attract continuing business in a competitive local market, the photographer must carefully schedule portrait sessions and postproduction work. Good production scheduling is necessary to be able to deliver the finished product when promised.

Real-World Photography

Posing

Regardless of the type of portrait you are taking, it is important to be aware of your subject's body language and pose. The more relaxed and comfortable your subject is, the better their photos will be. If it seems like your subject is uncomfortable in front of the camera, offer them some advice or words or encouragement to help them relax. The following are a few areas to keep an eye on:

- **Shoulders.** The shoulders are typically the widest part of a person's body. If you photograph your subject's shoulders straight on, you risk making them appear square and boxy. Turning their shoulders will help with that as well as help the pose appear more natural. However, if you are trying to achieve a powerful, confident look with your subject, keep their shoulders facing forward.
- **Chin.** Many people tend to lift their chin when placed in front of a camera, which makes them appear defiant or as if they are turning their nose up at something. You can avoid this by having them push their chin forward and angle their head downward slightly. This not only helps to give them a more open and inviting appearance, but it also helps to elongate their neck.
- **Eyes.** A person's eyes are arguably the most important part of a portrait. Make sure you are capturing the irises and whites of your subject's eyes. You can still have your subject look off-lens for a specific photo, but make sure you give them a point to look at so you can control where their eyes are pointing in the photo.

Looking up some potential poses ahead of shooting can also help make you and your subject more confident. If your subject feels stuck, you can suggest a few common poses to help them feel less awkward and loosen up.

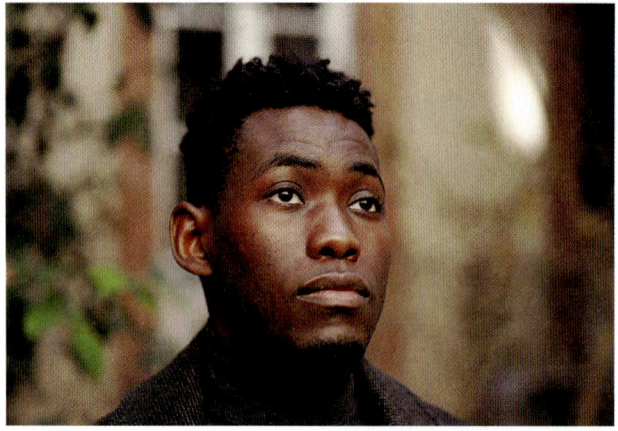 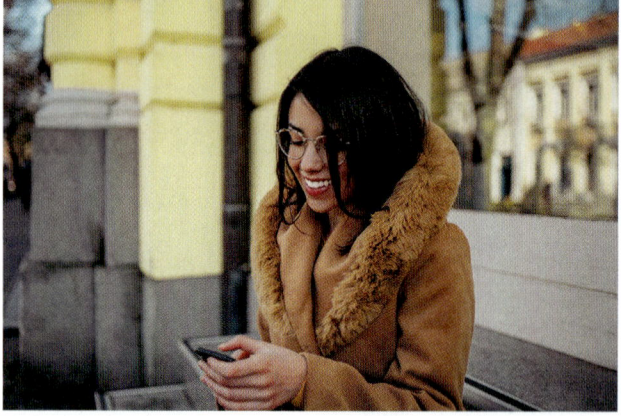

True Touch Lifestyle/Shutterstock.com   Zamrznuti tonovi/Shutterstock.com

Figure 15-4. Portraits made outside the studio, often in natural surroundings, have become increasingly popular.

Working with Ambient Light

Environmental portraits are typically made with ambient light. Outdoors, this would be sunlight or skylight. Indoor ambient light might be room lighting or a combination of room light and natural light coming through a window or door.

Ambient light often must be modified because it can be too bright, too dim, too contrasty, or too flat. The intensity of the light can be changed by strategies such as moving your subject out of harsh sunlight and into open shade or using diffusion material to soften the light. You can reduce the contrast range by using a reflector to bounce light back onto the shadowed areas or a portable flash to provide fill light.

Fill Flash

In the fill flash technique, the flash unit's output is balanced with the ambient light. Generally, the flash is set to provide approximately one-half the light that is needed for proper flash exposure. With fill flash, the lighting of the subject appears natural rather than giving the appearance of a flash picture.

Many photographers use fill flash for portraits and other outdoor situations involving people or animals. When the subject is strongly sidelighted or even partially backlit, the flash projects enough light into the shadowed areas to soften them and reveal detail, **Figure 15-5**. When subjects are evenly and softly lighted (for example, in open shade), fill flash adds a hint of directional light to better model their features.

White Balance

With a digital camera, you can affect the color of the light by changing the white balance. The camera's automatic white balance (AWB) setting usually provides good results but may render the subject too cool or too warm for your liking. By using the appropriate white balance preset (*Daylight*, *Shade*, *Cloudy*, *Flash*, etc.), you can achieve the desired mood.

For example, a photo taken in open shade may have a rather cool blue cast because of reflected skylight. Using the camera's *Cloudy* setting will compensate for the skylight and give the photo a warmer appearance. See **Figure 15-6**. If a photo taken in late afternoon appears too warm, it can be cooled down by using the *Daylight* or *Flash* settings.

Digital cameras capable of producing RAW files provide another option. RAW files are image captures with minimal in-camera processing. These files must be converted with computer software into a format such as JPEG or TIFF. As part of that processing, the photographer can preview the image with different white balance settings and choose the best appearance.

In mixed-lighting situations, such as a portrait involving both natural light and artificial light, the photographer can create a custom white balance. An image of a white card in the actual light falling on the scene is captured and then used as a reference by the camera for other images taken in that lighting situation. For detailed discussions of the modification of light color with white balance controls, refer to Chapter 7, *Light and Exposure*, and Chapter 10, *Improving Lighting*.

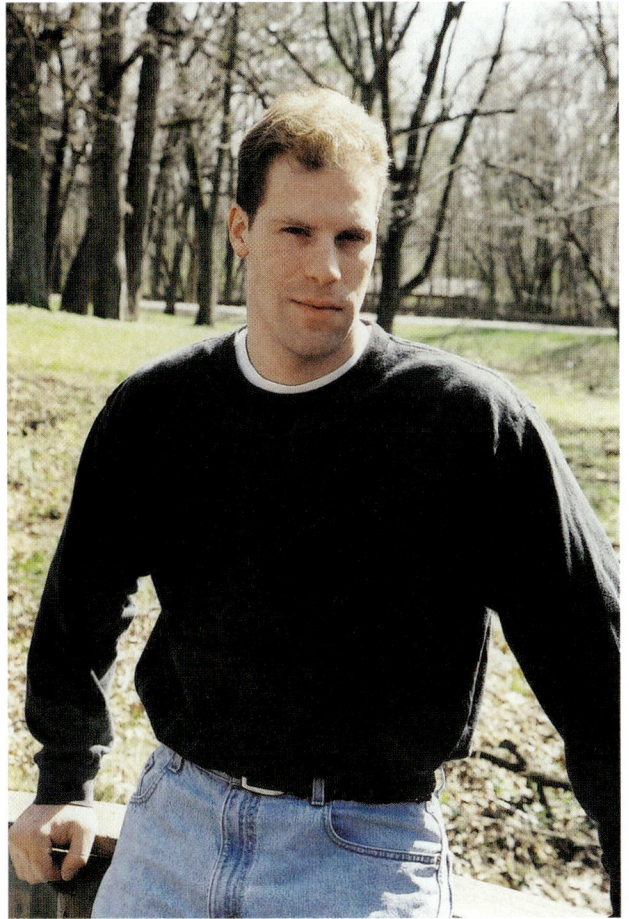
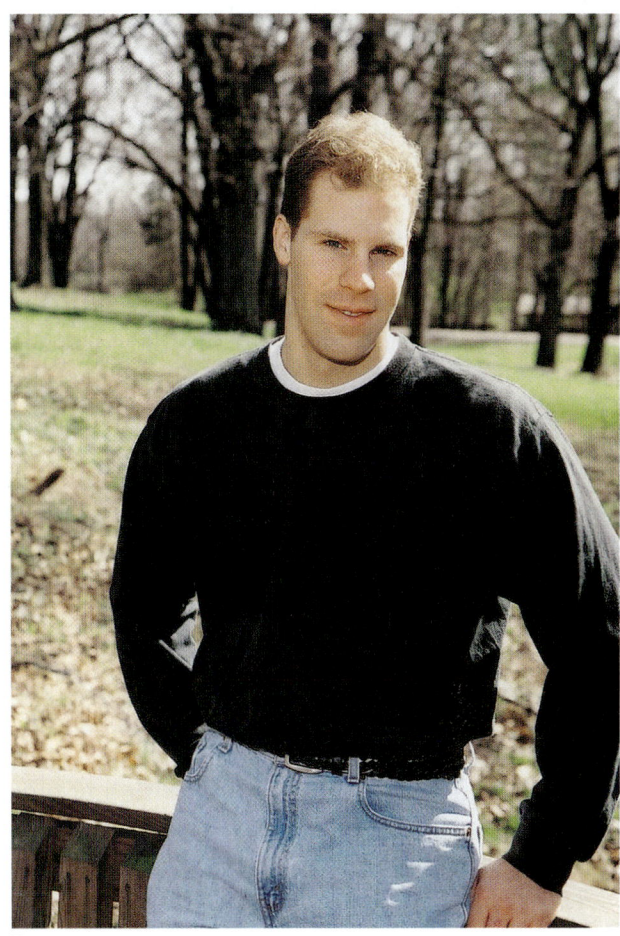

Ed Cayot

Figure 15-5. Using fill flash to balance light. A—Strong sunlight on the subject's face is too harsh and contrasty. B—Fill flash opens up the shadows for a more balanced lighting effect.

It is also worth noting that you can make both minor and significant lighting changes in postprocessing through editing software like Adobe Lightroom or Adobe Photoshop. Even though this is possible, you still need to make sure the light you capture during your photography session is good enough to work with. While you can make changes in postprocessing, bad lighting is difficult and time-consuming to correct, assuming you can fix it.

Working with Studio Lighting

The greatest amount of control over lighting can be exercised in the studio. Lighting units can be added, removed, and repositioned until the desired effect is achieved. Accessories can help control light intensity, direction, and coverage.

Always be aware of safety in the photo studio. Switch off and discharge monolights (self-contained flash units) before plugging them in or unplugging them. Use properly grounded extension cords of

Sweet-dreams 11/Shutterstock.com

Figure 15-6. Light color can be altered by changing white balance settings.

the appropriate length and rating. Avoid touching bulbs. Wear heat-resistant gloves when necessary to prevent burns from hot lights. It is also a good idea to keep a fire extinguisher handy.

Light sources for studio use are typically either continuous (remain lit) or flash, although some photographers also make use of natural light from a skylight or window in the studio. A **continuous light** remains lit and may be incandescent (often referred to as *hot lights* because of their heat output), fluorescent, or a light-emitting diode (LED) array. One of the least expensive forms of incandescent studio light is the **photoflood**, a glass bulb similar in appearance to a standard bulb but constructed for high light output. These bulbs are normally mounted in metal reflectors to direct and concentrate the light output, **Figure 15-7**.

The second form of incandescent light is the **tungsten-halogen bulb**, **Figure 15-8**. These small, extremely bright bulbs have both a higher light output (typically 600 watts) and a longer life than photoflood bulbs. Tungsten-halogen lights are very bright and extremely hot. With any type of incandescent light, be careful to prevent contact with skin or flammable materials.

In recent years, fluorescent light banks and LED light arrays have become available for studio use. These types of continuous lights overcome the problem of heat posed by incandescent lights. Continuous

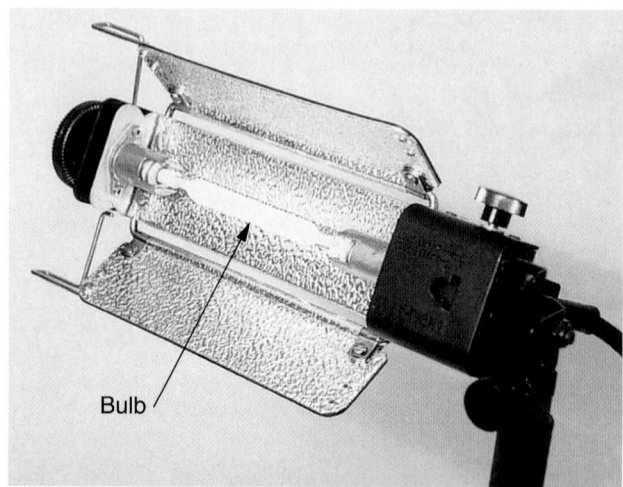

Jack Klasey/Goodheart-Willcox Publisher

Figure 15-8. Tungsten-halogen bulbs produce brilliant light but also generate considerable heat.

lights enable the photographer to directly observe the light falling on the subject. LED lights are also a very affordable option for many photographers, both amateur and professional.

A popular form of lighting, especially in studios doing product photography, is the **softbox**, **Figure 15-9**. This large source of diffused light consists of several lamps (usually fluorescent) or electronic flash units mounted inside a reflective housing. A sheet of translucent material covers the side of the housing that faces the subject. A large softbox provides a directionless light that seems to wrap around the subject.

Electronic studio flash units are the primary source of portable artificial light for photography. It is also referred to as a *strobe light* or *strobe flash*

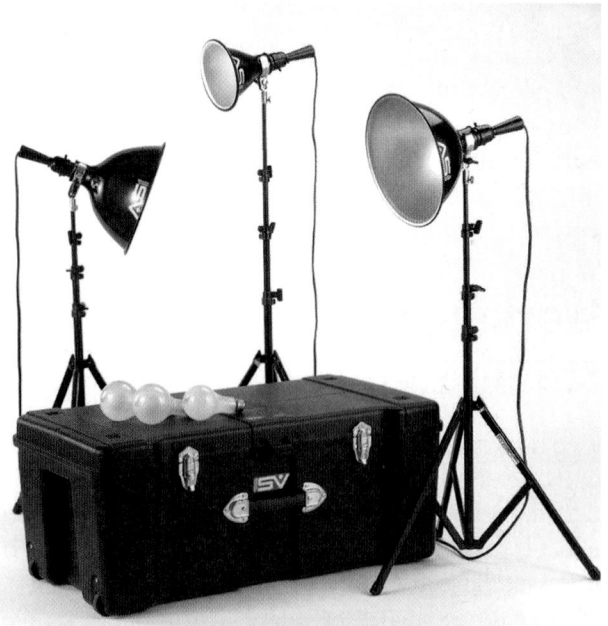

Smith-Victor Corporation

Figure 15-7. Metal reflectors are typically used with photoflood bulbs.

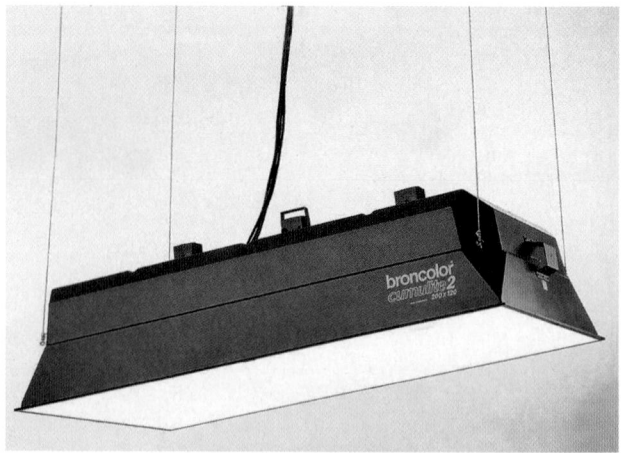

Sinar Bron Imaging

Figure 15-9. A softbox produces a very diffuse, directionless light that is ideal for product photography.

because it is synced with the camera rather than continuously lighting the subject. A strong electrical charge is built up in a storage device called a *capacitor*, then released into a gas-filled flash tube, producing a burst of bright light synchronized with the opening of the camera shutter.

Electronic studio flash units eliminate heat, the major drawback of incandescent lights. Additional advantages of electronic flash are a very short burst of light (measured in thousandths of a second) that helps freeze any slight subject movement, imitates 5500K daylight conditions, and has a steady light output that does not change as the unit ages. Many electronic units include incandescent modeling lights to help the photographer assess lighting effects.

There are two types of studio flash systems on the market—pack-and-head and self-contained, **Figure 15-10**. The **pack-and-head system** is a traditional studio flash system with a central power pack connected to separate flash heads. The power pack plugs into a wall outlet, and the separate flash heads are connected to the power pack by individual cables. The pack contains the capacitors and output controls, and the head contains only the flash tube.

Advantages of the pack-and-head system are as follows:

- The heads are less heavy than monolights.
- The output of all the heads is controlled in one place.
- Each head has only one cord.

Disadvantages of the pack-and-head system are as follows:

- If the pack malfunctions, all the lights are affected.
- The heads are not interchangeable among different brands of packs.

A **monolight**, also known as a *self-contained system*, is a combination flash head and power supply. The flash tube, controls, and capacitors are combined into a single housing. Each unit plugs into a wall outlet.

Advantages of monolights are as follows:

- If one unit fails, the others will continue to work.
- You can use monolights from multiple companies.

Disadvantages of monolights are as follows:

- Monolights are heavier than pack-and-head systems.
- Output control is done at each unit.
- A control cord and a power cord are required for each unit.

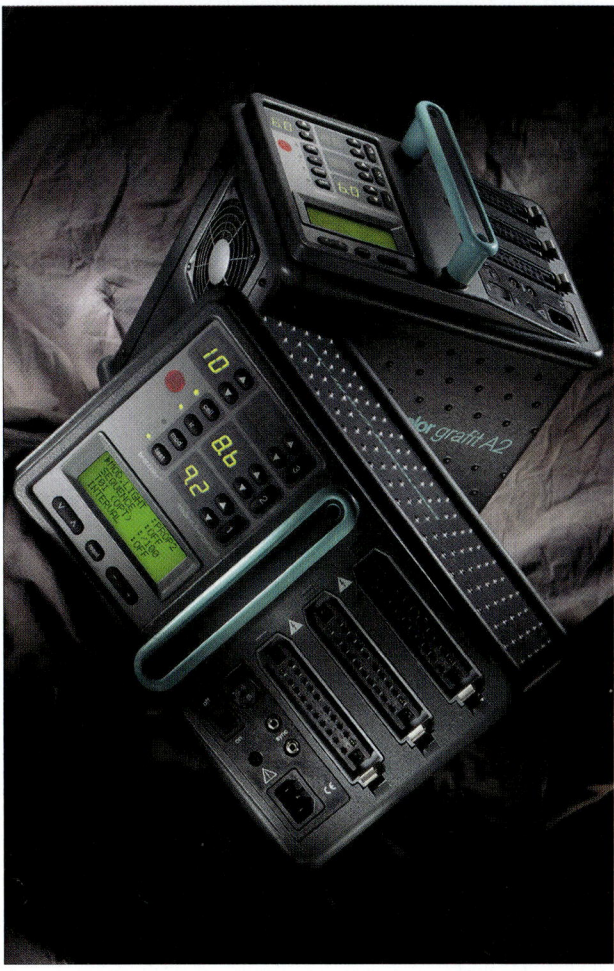

A

Sinar Bron Imaging

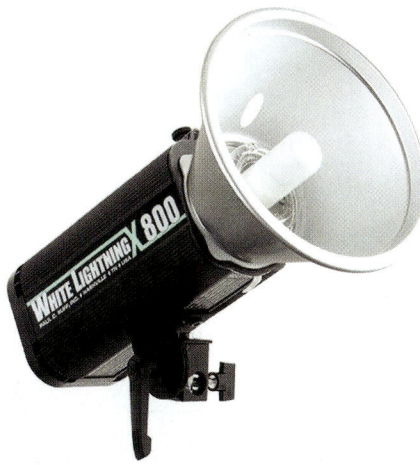

B

Paul C. Buff, Inc.

Figure 15-10. Studio flash systems. A—A pack-and-head system uses a central power pack to which a number of separate flash heads can be connected. B—Monolights combine the flash head and power pack in a single housing.

It is also important to consider what type of power you have available when selecting lighting. If there are no wall power outlets available either in your studio or on location, you will have to rely on portable power packs, which tend to be a bit pricey. Depending on the capacity of your portable power unit, you may be limited as to what lights you can use. If you do have wall power, be sure you understand the electrical load that it can handle.

Lighting Methods

Studio lighting can be as simple as a single light, or as complex as a setup involving three, four, or even more lighting instruments. The important consideration is what effect you wish to achieve, not the number of lights you use. Studio photographs, from portraits to still-life arrangements, often are made with a single light or just a light and a reflector, **Figure 15-11**.

As defined in Chapter 10, the **key light** is the main light on a subject. This light may be positioned to the left or right of the camera, at an angle of a few degrees to more than 90° to the axis of the camera lens. See **Figure 15-12**. Since we are conditioned to outdoor (sky) lighting in which the light strikes the subject from a high angle, the key light is usually raised to simulate that lighting. The light should strike the subject from an angle of 40°–65° above the horizontal.

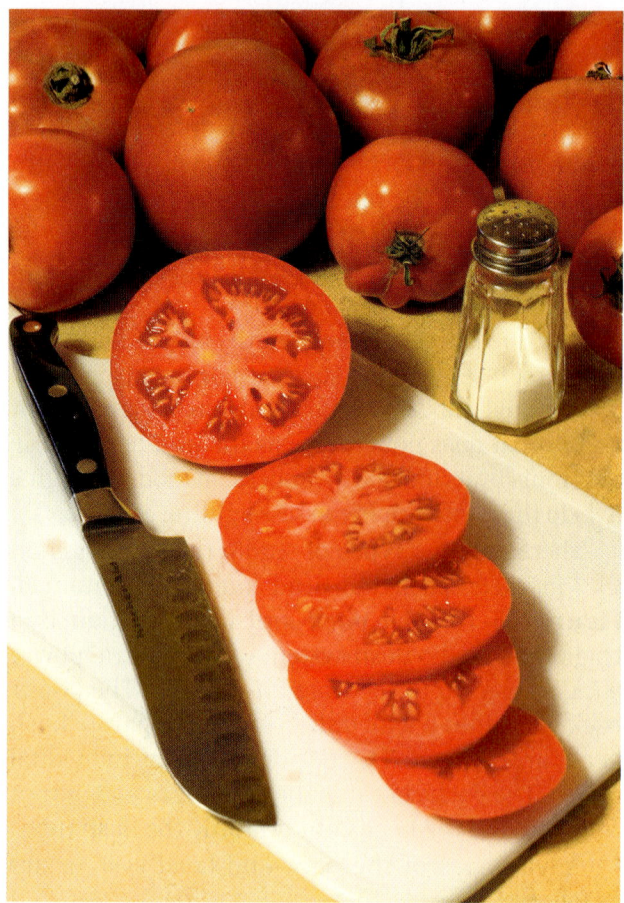

Jack Klasey/Goodheart-Willcox Publisher

Figure 15-11. A single key light was located to the left of the camera and raised to simulate conventional skylight coming through a kitchen window.

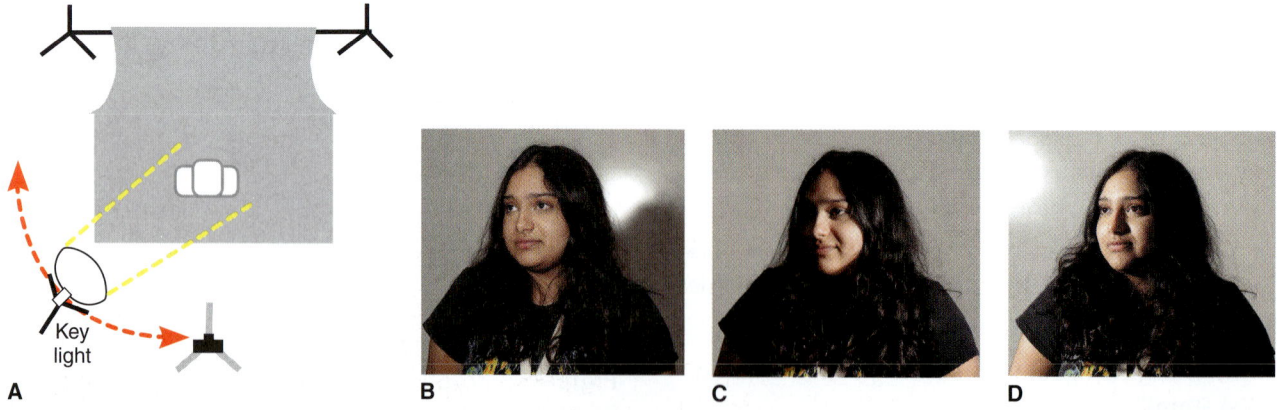

Goodheart-Willcox Publisher

Figure 15-12. The key light is the primary source of illumination falling on the subject. A—The key light may be located anywhere on the horizontal arc shown and is usually directed downward onto the subject. B—Positioning the key light just slightly off the camera lens axis provides flat frontal lighting. C—Moving the key light to strike the subject at a 45° angle to the lens axis casts shadows that provide a greater degree of modeling of the features. D—With the light at an angle of 90°, a much more dramatic appearance results because one-half of the subject's face is strongly shadowed.

Supplementary illumination of the subject can be provided by a ***fill light***, which is the secondary light on a subject. This light softens dark shadows, decreases the contrast range of the light reflected from the subject, and helps to reveal detail in shadow areas. As shown in **Figure 15-13**, a fill light is typically positioned on the opposite side of the camera from the key light. The fill light is usually placed close to the axis of the lens and set at approximately the same height as the camera. By strategically placing a fill light, a photographer can control shadows (to a degree) to help influence the mood of a photo. When using fill lighting, be sure to avoid conflicting shadows that show light coming from two directions (an unnatural situation). Alter the location or intensity of the fill light to prevent such shadows.

The ***background light*** provides sufficient visual separation between the subject and the background and helps create visual interest in an image. The background should be lighted so it is slightly less bright than the subject, **Figure 15-14**. Usually, the

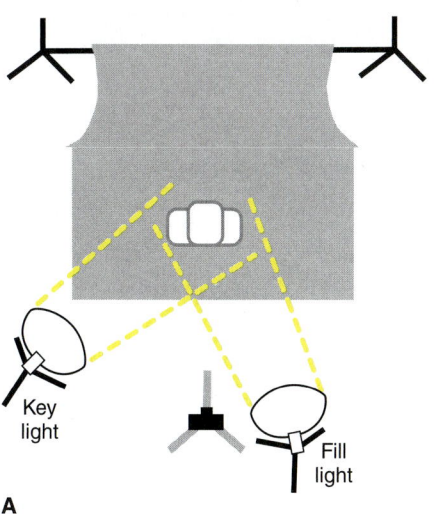
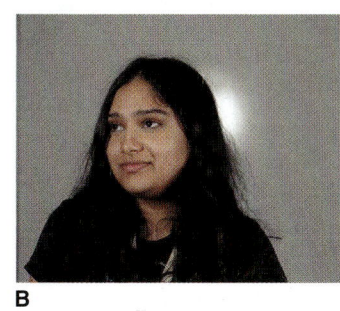
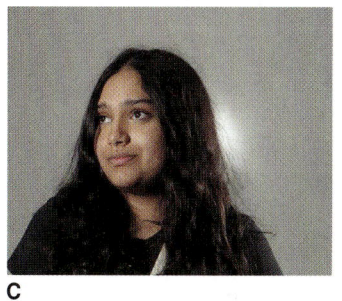

Goodheart-Willcox Publisher

Figure 15-13. The fill light supplements the key light. A—The fill light is usually located at the same height as the camera, on the side opposite the key light. B—The fill light intensity must be sufficient to soften dark shadows cast by the key light but not strong enough to create conflicting shadows. C—The combined effects of key and fill lights help to define the subject's features and avoid excessive contrast.

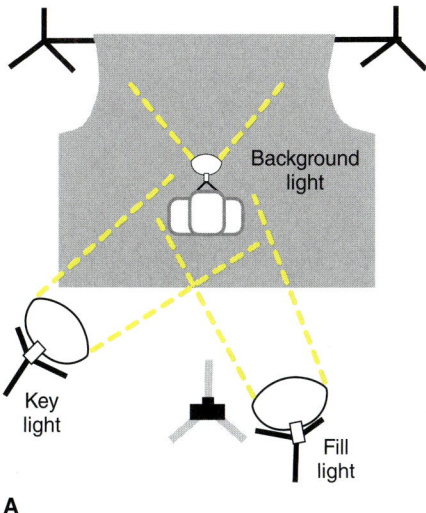
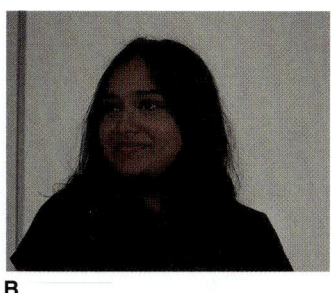
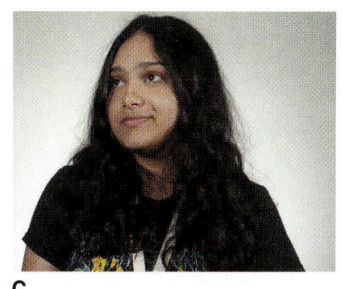

Goodheart-Willcox Publisher

Figure 15-14. A background light helps to separate a subject from its background. A—The light is pointed upward at the background. B—Placing the background light low and behind the subject hides the source from the camera. C—Lighting the background so it is somewhat less bright helps separate it from the subject.

light is placed low and behind the subject so it is hidden and gives the background a gradually shaded illumination. Sometimes, a *gel* (a transparent, colored sheet of material placed over a light source to create a specific-colored effect) is placed over the light to tint the background. A *cookie* (a patterned translucent material or an opaque cutout placed in front of a light to project textures or shadows) might also be used to add visual interest to the background.

Sometimes, additional lighting is needed for emphasis, dramatic effect, or other reasons. For example, in a catalog shoot, one of the products in a grouping may need to be highlighted to emphasize it. Use a small spotlight to place a tightly concentrated beam of light on that product. The difference in lighting intensity will make the product stand out.

In portrait photography, a *rim light*, also called an *accent light*, *back light*, *hair light*, or *halo light*, is often used both for dramatic effect and to help separate a dark-haired subject from a dark background. This light is positioned behind and to one side of the subject to provide backlighting. **Figure 15-15** shows placement of such a light. A lighting arrangement involving use of a main light, fill light, and rim light is referred to as *three-point lighting*. Three-point lighting is commonly used in various situations, not just studio photography.

Controlling Light

There are a number of ways to vary the intensity, or brightness, of the light falling on the subject. Two basic methods are changing the output of the light unit and changing the distance of the light from the subject. Many electronic studio flash units can be adjusted to change the light output over a range equivalent to several f-stops. See **Figure 15-16**.

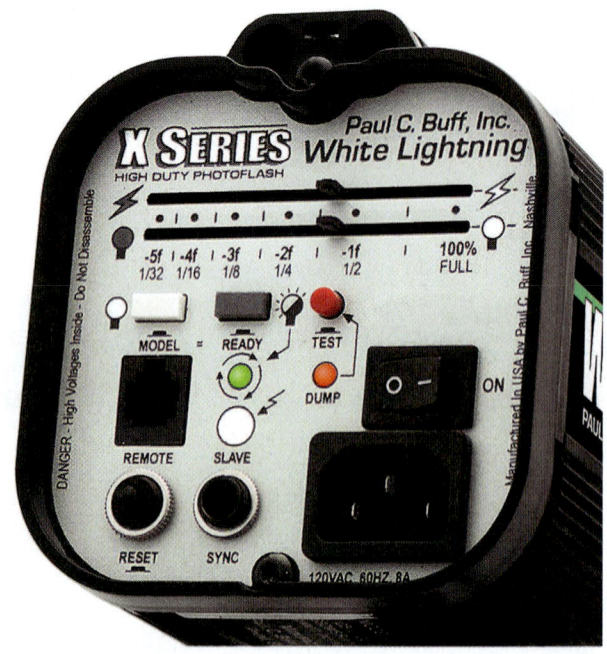

Paul C. Buff, Inc.

Figure 15-16. Controls on many electronic studio flash units allow light output to be increased or decreased.

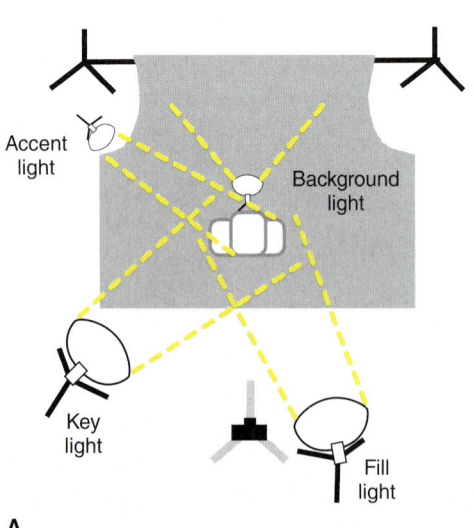

A

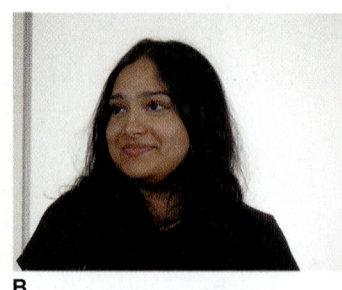

B

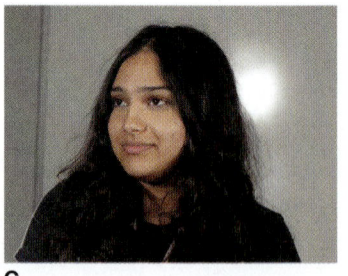

C

Goodheart-Willcox Publisher

Figure 15-15. Accent lighting can be used to emphasize certain features or parts of subjects. A—A rim light is placed behind the subject to provide backlighting. B—The rim light emphasizes the edges of the subject. C—Combined with other lights.

This allows light output to be varied while leaving the lighting unit in one spot. The most practical way to adjust the intensity of continuous lights is to move the lighting unit closer to, or farther away from, the subject.

The light's intensity may also be controlled by using special devices such as snoots or grids or a technique called *feathering*. A **snoot** is a tubular light modifier attached to a light source to direct a spot of intense light at the desired area of the subject, **Figure 15-17**. In portrait work, a snoot is often used to direct the beam of the rim light. A **grid** is a light modifier with square or hexagonal openings that align the rays of light so they are more ordered and parallel. See **Figure 15-18**. This type of light adds sparkle to a scene through increased contrast.

When a cone of light is projected from a lighting unit, the intensity is greatest at the center and falls off toward the edges. In **feathering**, the light is adjusted so the less intense outer edges of the light cone illuminate the subject. See **Figure 15-19**.

The quality of light can be termed hard or soft based on the type of shadows that are produced. Light from a small, bright source is *specular*, or made up of parallel rays. Light from a large source is *diffused*, or made up of rays scattered at various angles. **Hard light**, also known as *harsh lighting*, is a type of lighting that creates harsh shadows, or places with stark contrast between the highlights and the shadows. Conversely, **soft light** is a type of light that creates very few harsh shadows, or places with stark contrast between the highlights and the shadows. See **Figure 15-20**.

Soft light may also be obtained by the indirect or bounced light method. A reflective material, such as a matte white panel or a photographic umbrella, produces a soft, diffused light. Materials with a silver finish produce a slightly harder but still diffused light.

Reflectors can be placed opposite the key light, on the other side of the subject, to add illumination to the shadowed area. When used like this, the reflector gives results similar to a fill light. Alternatively, a piece of flat black card stock can be positioned like a reflector, but with the opposite effect—elimination of an unwanted reflection of light into shadow areas. This method is valuable when the objective is to achieve a dramatic, high-contrast photo with dense black shadows.

Light-control devices called barn doors and flags prevent light from falling in areas where it is not wanted. **Barn doors** are hinged rectangular flaps of black-painted metal attached to the front

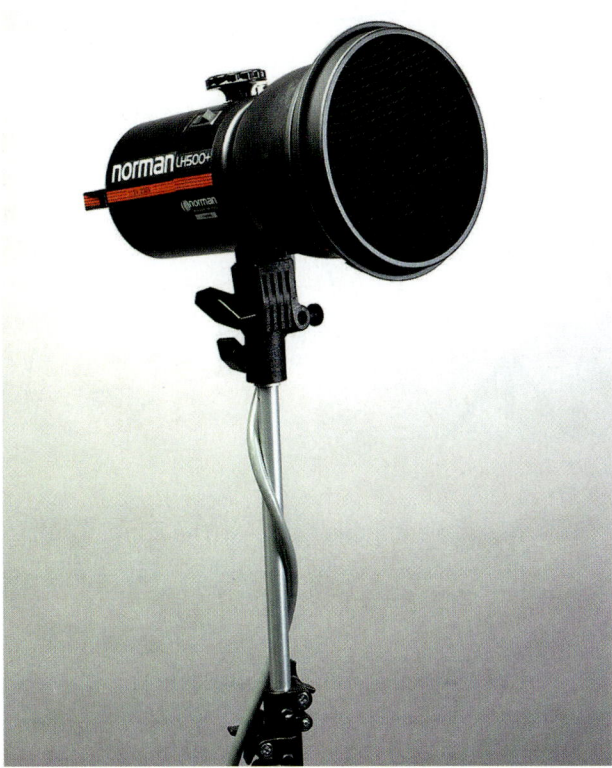

Norman Enterprises, Inc. Division of Photo Control Corporation

Figure 15-18. The square or hexagonal openings in a grid align the light rays and make them more parallel.

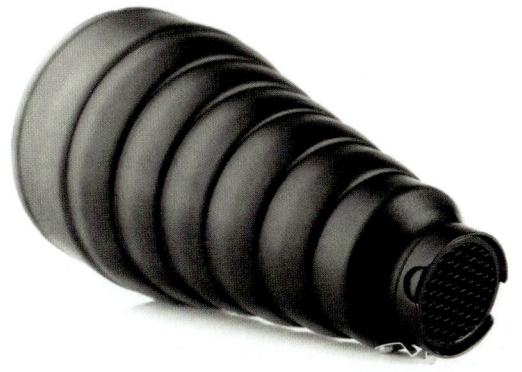

Africa Studio/Shutterstock.com

Figure 15-17. A snoot creates a small, intense spot of light.

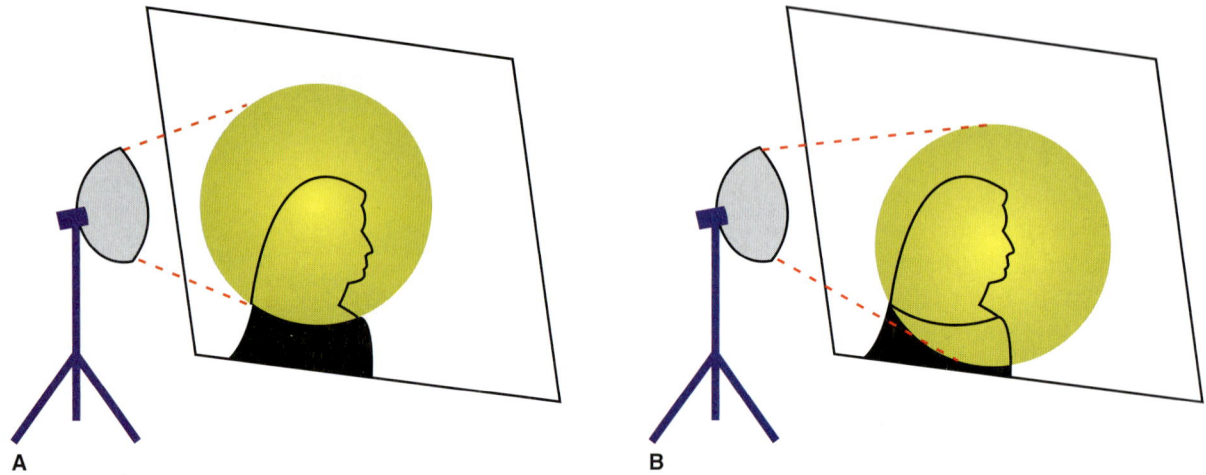

Goodheart-Willcox Publisher

Figure 15-19. Feathering light. A—The cone of light cast by a lamp is most intense in the center and decreases in intensity toward the edges. B—Intensity of light on the subject can be varied by moving the light so illumination comes from the edge of the cone.

of a lighting instrument. See **Figure 15-21**. The flaps can be adjusted to physically block a portion of the light being emitted. One reason barn doors are used is to prevent light from spilling beyond the subject onto a background.

Flags are usually smaller than barn doors. A *flag* is a shape cut from black poster board or stiff black paper attached to light stands or other fixtures to block light. A flag is often used to shade the camera lens and prevent flare from a lighting unit that is pointed toward the camera, such as when a subject is backlit.

A similar light control device is the **gobo**, a generic term for any light-control device or material that goes between the light and the area where the light is intended to fall, **Figure 15-22**. A widely used type of gobo is a cutout that places a shadow representing a multipaned window on the background. Note that these are different from cookies.

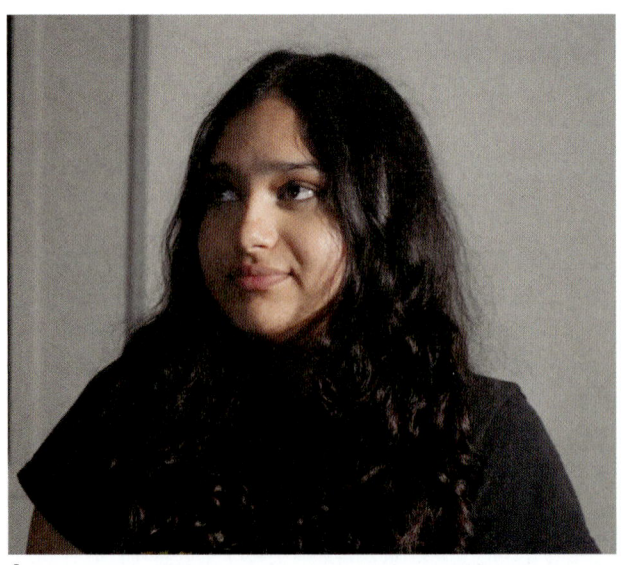
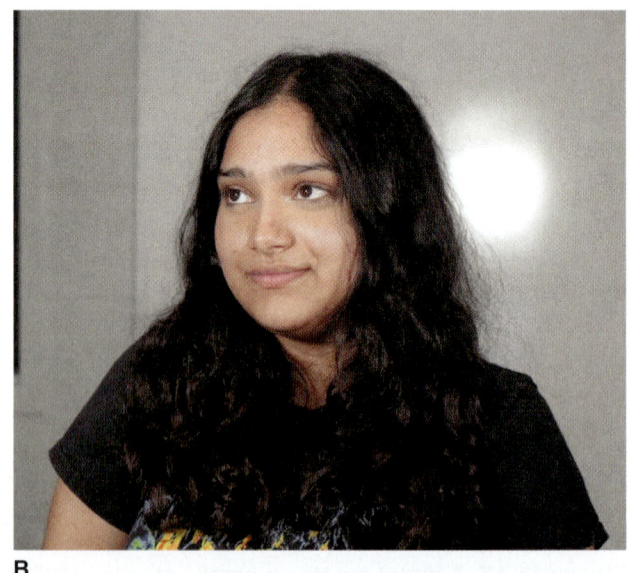

Goodheart-Willcox Publisher

Figure 15-20. Hard light vs. soft light. A—Specular hard light from a small source creates dense, well-defined shadows. B—Diffused soft light from a large source lightens shadows and makes them less defined.

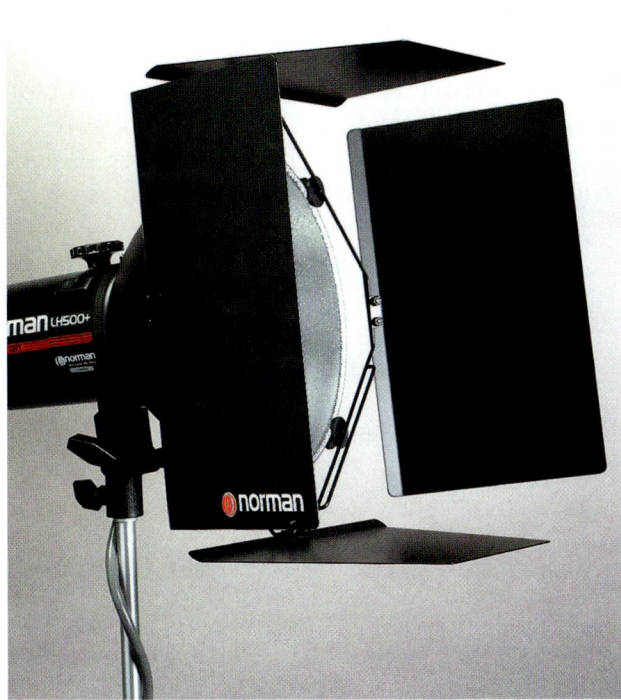

Norman Enterprises, Inc. Division of Photo Control Corporation

Figure 15-21. Barn doors are metal flaps that can be adjusted to prevent light from falling in certain areas.

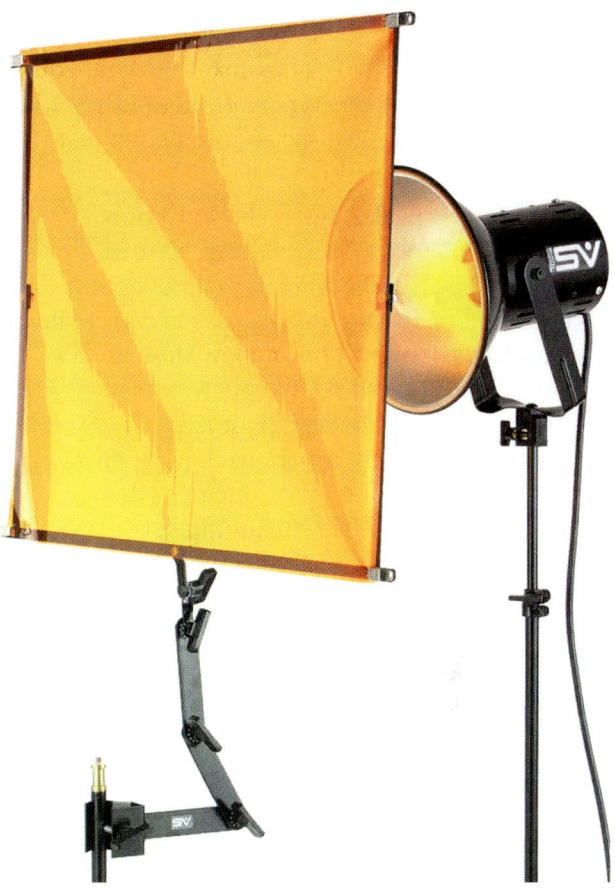

Smith-Victor Corporation

Figure 15-22. A frame like this one can be used to hold a gel or other form of gobo in front of a light source.

REAL-WORLD PHOTOGRAPHY

Photography Studio Safety

It is imperative to follow personal and workplace safety when working in a studio. The following are just a few examples of what you can do to keep yourself and your clients safe:

- **Weigh down light stands.** Sometimes the lights that are set up in a studio can be extremely heavy. By countering the weight at the top with some weight at the bottom (either with sandbags or other weighted objects), you reduce the risk of the lights falling over.
- **Widen light stand legs.** By widening the legs of a light stand, you distribute the weight more evenly and help prevent them from falling over. You can also angle the light itself to line up with one of the stand's legs to help make the stand more stable.
- **Turn off lights.** Remember that all lights—even low-energy LEDs—generate heat. Always turn them off at the end of a shoot. Never leave them unattended, and do not place any flammable materials or objects near them. If you are shooting on location, make sure the lights have a chance to cool before packing them away. It is also a good idea to wear heat-resistant gloves when handling particularly hot lights.
- **Tape down cables.** Lights need power, which means they will most likely need a cable. Taping down any cables will reduce everyone's risk of tripping in the studio.
- **Secure any backdrops.** Similar to lights, backdrops can be heavy. You want to make sure they are properly secured to their stands to prevent them from falling and potentially injuring someone.

Common Studio Lighting Equipment

Most photography studios use the same equipment regardless of the types of photos they take. Some studios may have specialized equipment, but the basics are nearly universal:

- ***Backdrops***: Backdrops are backgrounds photographers use when taking pictures, **Figure 15-23**. They vary in material, color, and scenery. In most instances, you can create a backdrop for very little money. Most studios have a backdrop stand that allows you to cycle through multiple backdrops quickly. These will almost always have a black backdrop and a white backdrop, but they can also include others.
- ***Clamps***: Clamps are useful for almost everything. Properly placed clamps can help hold a reflector in place, eliminate wrinkles in clothes or a backdrop, hold cables out of the way, and more, **Figure 15-24**. You can usually find clamps at a hardware store, but clothespins can also work in a pinch.
- *Light stands*: Nearly every light sits on a light stand. They hold lights in specific positions to give you more control over the direction of your lights, **Figure 15-25**. There are several different types of light stands, and sometimes they are specific to the type of light you are using. Make sure your stands are secure and safe to use. If you find that the light mounted to the stand is too heavy, you can reinforce the bottom with some weights or with sandbags.
- *Umbrellas and softboxes*: Even though they are slightly different, umbrellas and softboxes both allow you to achieve softer, more diffused lighting in your images. Umbrellas bounce light off the material in different directions for soft or even nonexistent shadows. Softboxes offer diffused light, but the light is more controlled and direct.

In a typical studio, you will also find light meters, various types of lights used to give the photographer added flexibility, flags, cookies, monolights, and more. If you work with others in a studio, do not hesitate to offer your help if it is needed. As you become more and more familiar with various lighting tools, you have the opportunity to mentor others if they need assistance.

Measuring Light in the Studio

Careful measurement of the light falling on the subject is important not only for establishing correct overall exposure but also for determining the relative intensities of the key and fill lights. The method used to measure studio lighting depends on the type

Kovalov Anatolii/Shutterstock.com

Figure 15-23. Backdrops come in a variety of colors, but white is perhaps the most common.

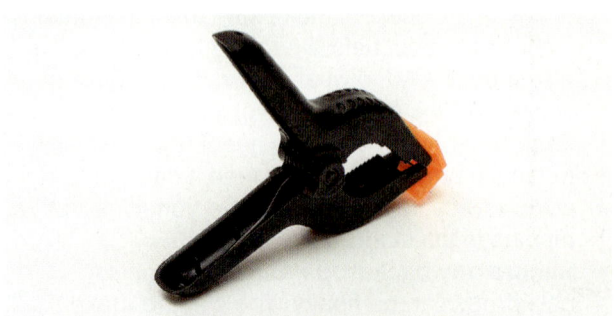

Erick ardianto w/Shutterstock.com

Figure 15-24. Clamps have a variety of uses in photography, but one of the most common is securing backdrops.

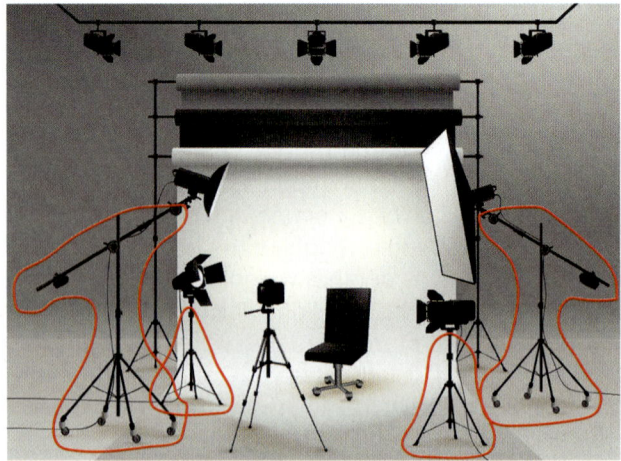

Kovalov Anatolii/Shutterstock.com

Figure 15-25. Light stands (outlined in red) help you control the positioning of your lighting instruments.

of lighting units involved. Light from continuous sources can be metered by using a camera's built-in meter or a handheld meter. There are even some apps for your smartphone that act as a digital light reader. For overall exposure, place a gray card in front of the subject and take a reflective light reading. If preferred, an incident light reading can be made by holding the meter with its diffusing dome just in front of the subject. See **Figure 15-26**.

The brief burst of light from studio electronic flash units cannot be measured with conventional handheld or in-camera meters. A special handheld flash meter allows the photographer to trigger the flash units and make an incident light reading from the subject's position. Separate flash meters are available, but the trend in recent years has been to combine the flash-reading function with the traditional reflected light and incident light capabilities of a handheld meter to create an all-in-one instrument.

Inverse-Square Law

The farther the subject is from the light source, the less brightly it is illuminated. This principle is referred to as *light falloff*. The amount of light falloff is calculated using the **inverse-square law**, which states that the illumination provided by a light source varies inversely as the square of the distance from the source. In other words, as light moves farther away from its source, it spreads out to cover a larger area and thus provides weaker illumination. See **Figure 15-27**.

Since the amount of light reaching the image receiver after reflecting from the subject is the vital factor in determining exposure, the practical importance of the inverse-square law is obvious. For example, the amount of light output by portable flash governs how distant the subject can be in order to remain properly illuminated.

Establishing the Lighting Ratio

Achieving an effective balance among the various lighting elements is important in all types of studio photography. However, the concept of **lighting ratio** is most often discussed in the context of portrait photography. As defined in Chapter 10, it is the comparison of the key light to the fill light expressed as a ratio, such as 1:2. The higher the ratio, the more contrast you have to deal with.

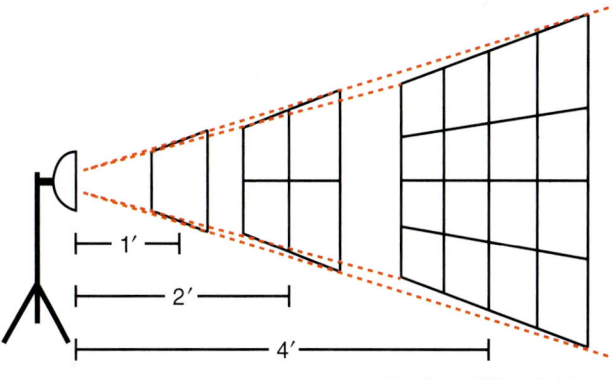

Goodheart-Willcox Publisher

Figure 15-27. Light intensity decreases as the distance from the source increases, since the light covers a larger area. As shown, a given amount of light falling on 1 ft² area at a distance of 1′ from the source spreads out to cover an area of 4 ft² at a distance of 2′ from the source. At a distance of 4′ from the source, the same amount of light covers an area of 16 ft².

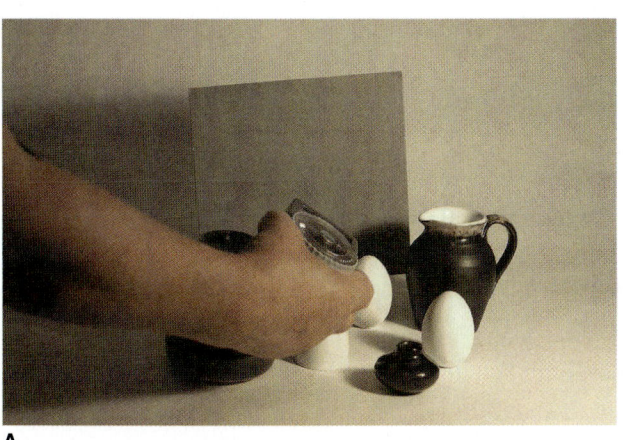
A

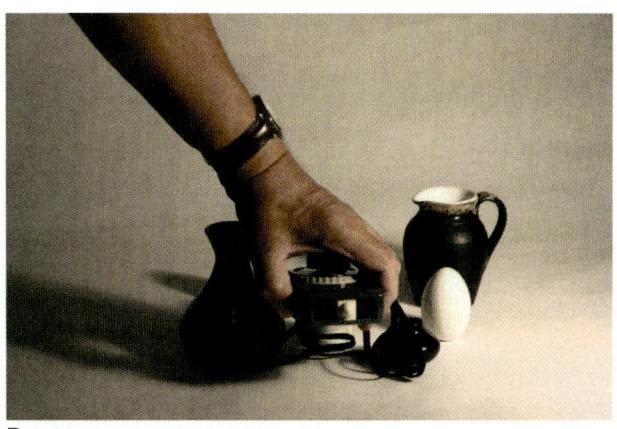
B

Jack Klasey/Goodheart-Willcox Publisher

Figure 15-26. Light readings for incandescent sources. A—Reflected light reading. B—Incident light reading.

A ratio of 1:1 means that the key light and the fill light are of equal intensity when measured at the subject position. Thinking in terms of f-stops, a 2:1 ratio indicates that the key light is one stop brighter than the fill light (i.e., twice as bright). A 4:1 ratio is a two-stop difference, an 8:1 ratio is a three-stop difference, and so on.

Traditionally, the lighting ratio for portrait work is 3:1—the highlight areas are three times (1.5 stops) brighter than the shadow areas. Low-contrast lighting ratios of 2:1 or 3:1 are preferred in some portraits because they produce flattering light for skin. Other portraits use a higher ratio of 4:1 or 5:1 for a harsher look, while more dramatically lighted portraits may use ratios of 16:1 or even higher. **Figure 15-28** shows the effects of different lighting ratios on a single subject.

The method used to establish lighting ratios differs slightly, depending on whether a reflective light meter or incident light meter is being used. The following basic techniques can be used with a normal handheld meter and incandescent lights or with a flash meter and electronic flash:

- **Reflective-reading method.** Hold a gray card at the subject's position, pointed midway between the key light and the camera. Take a reading from the card and note the exposure reading (f-stop). Shift the card so it points directly at the camera. Make a fill-light-only reading by shading the card so no illumination from the key light strikes its surface. Note this reading, and then determine the number of stops between the two readings. Refer to the table in **Figure 15-29** to convert the difference in stops to a lighting ratio.

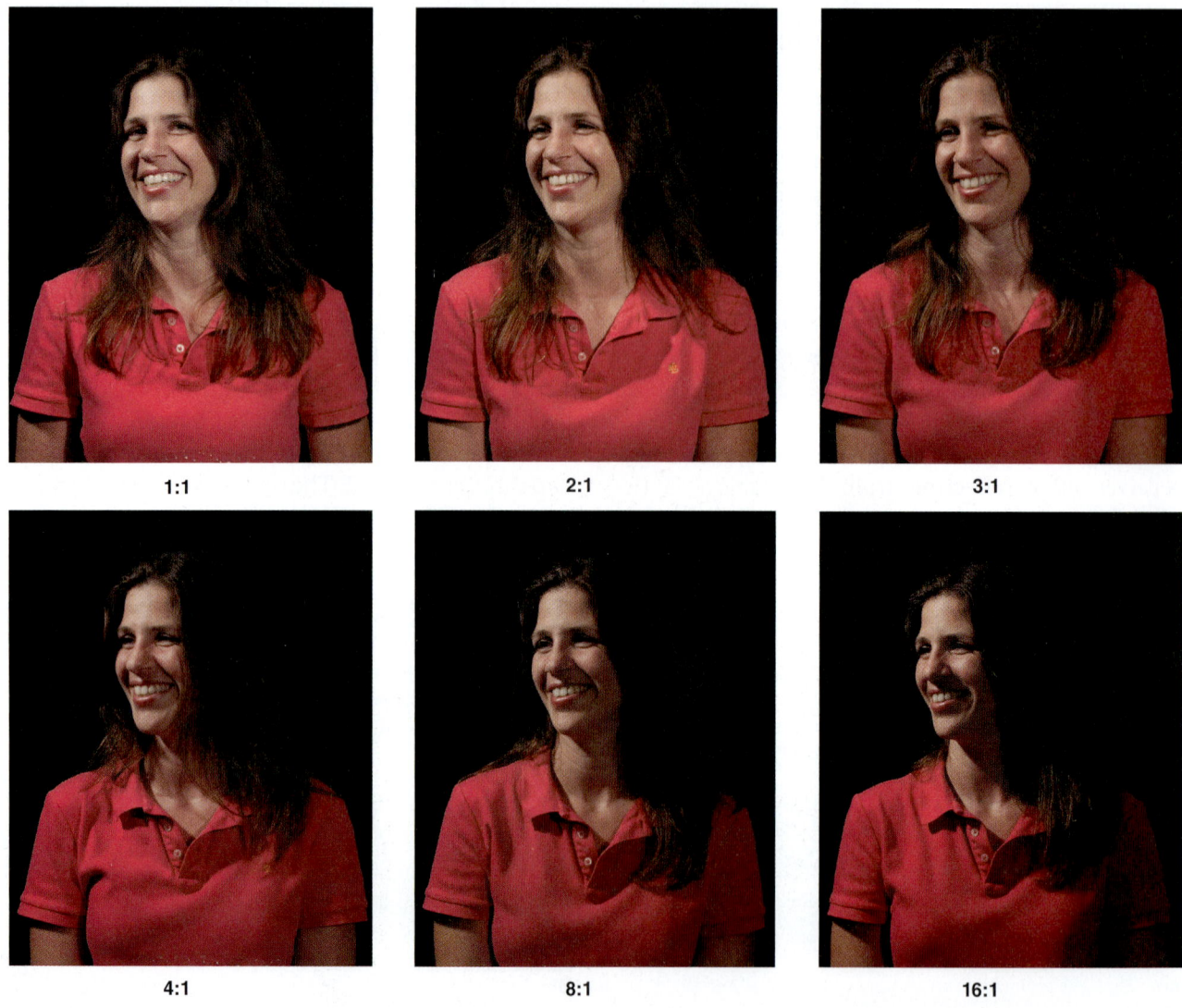

Jack Klasey/Goodheart-Willcox Publisher

Figure 15-28. Typical lighting ratios for portraiture. As ratios become higher, the lighting becomes more dramatic.

Lighting Ratios	
If the difference in f-stops is:	Then the lighting ratio is:
2/3	1.5:1
1	2:1
1 1/3	2.5:1
1 2/3	3:1
2	4:1
2 1/3	5:1
2 2/3	6:1
3	8:1
3 1/3	10:1
3 2/3	13:1
4	16:1

Goodheart-Willcox Publisher

Figure 15-29. This chart converts f-stop differences to lighting ratios.

- **Incident-reading method.** Hold the incident meter at the subject's position, aiming it directly at the key light. Note the exposure reading. Next, aim the meter at the camera. Shade the meter to prevent any key light from falling on it so you obtain a reading from just the fill light. Note the second exposure reading, determine the number of stops difference, and use the table to find the lighting ratio.

Typical Lighting Situations

Lighting methods for portrait subjects and for products have many common elements, but they also may differ in details. The following sections describe typical portrait and product lighting situations.

Portrait Photography

Basic portrait lighting can be done with a single light source, with a one light plus reflector arrangement, or with two lights (key and fill). When using only one light, avoid straight-on lighting that flattens out the subject's features. Raise the light source above the subject's head level and tilt it downward at an angle of 40°–65°. To provide some measure of sidelighting, shift the light somewhat away from the axis of the lens, as shown in **Figure 15-30**. The sidelighting casts shadows that give the face a more rounded, three-dimensional appearance. Unless a dramatic, contrasty look is desired, diffuse the light source to soften the shadows.

If the key light must be placed in a position that deeply shadows one side of the face, a second light or reflector is needed to lighten the shadows, lower the overall contrast, and reveal shadow detail. **Figure 15-31** shows how a reflector can be positioned in relation to the key light.

A two-light arrangement is used extensively for portraits because it offers considerable flexibility in creating different effects and lighting ratios. The key light is typically positioned in the same way as in the single-light method and may or may not be diffused, depending on whether hard or soft lighting is desired. The fill light is located close to the camera position, and it is usually lower than the key light, **Figure 15-32**. Normally, the fill light is diffused to provide a softer light.

The lighting ratio is established by changing the amount of fill light reaching the subject. As noted earlier, light intensity is changed by moving the light closer to or farther away from the subject or by adjusting lighting unit controls to deliver a greater or smaller amount of light. Sometimes, you need a multiple light arrangement. Adding a background light or a rim light can increase the impact of a traditional portrait. See **Figure 15-33**.

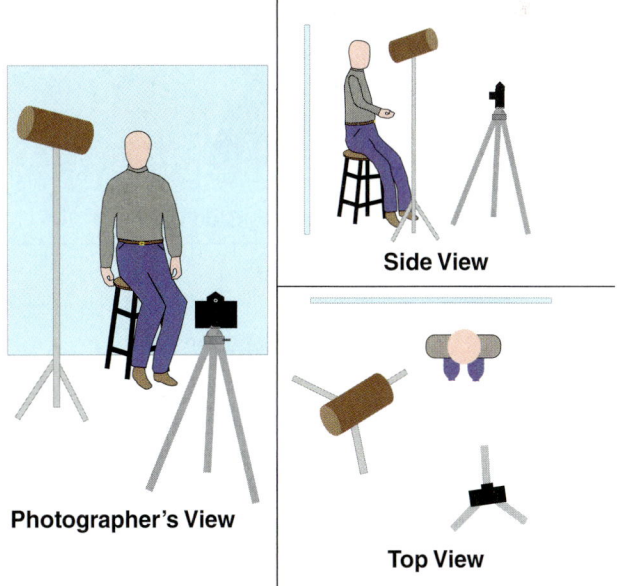

Goodheart-Willcox Publisher

Figure 15-30. In a single-light portrait setup, raise the light so it shines downward at an angle of 40°–65°. Often, the light is diffused to avoid casting dense shadows.

Product Photography

For product photography, the key light may be a softbox or similar large, diffused source to

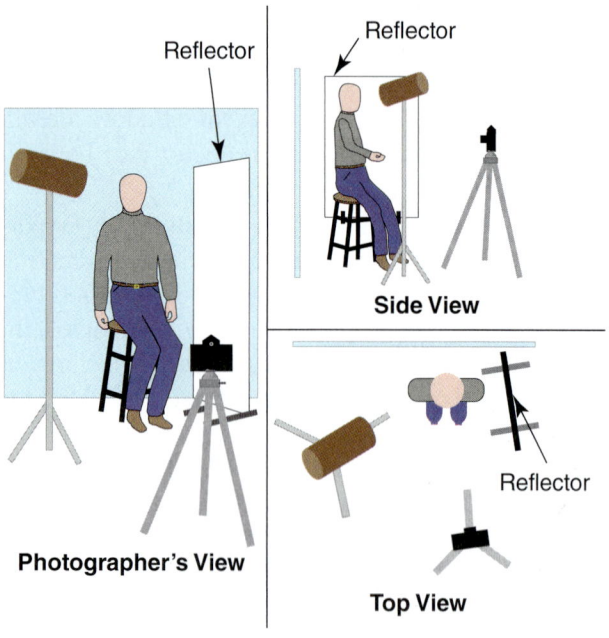

Goodheart-Willcox Publisher

Figure 15-31. A reflector can be used with a single-light setup to bounce additional illumination into shadowed areas.

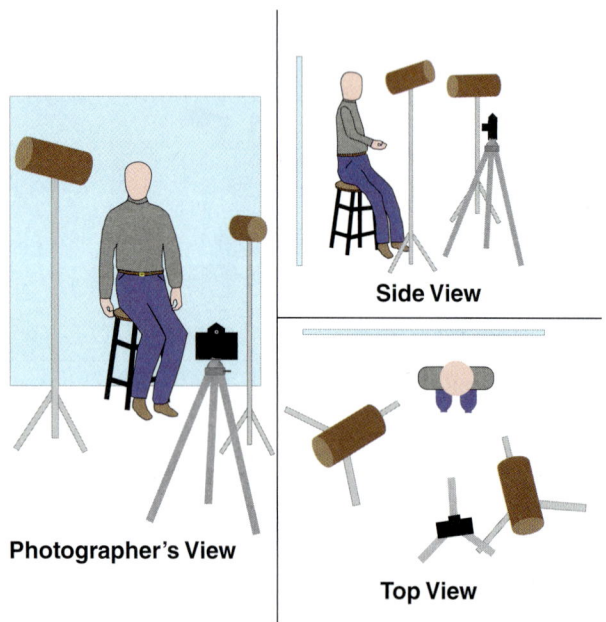

Goodheart-Willcox Publisher

Figure 15-32. The two-light arrangement is popular because of its ease of use and the flexibility it provides.

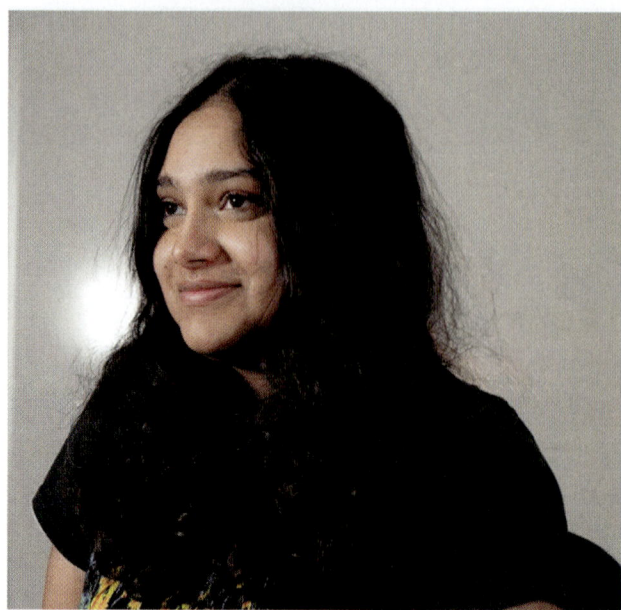

Jack Klasey/Goodheart-Willcox Publisher

Figure 15-33. To light this portrait, the photographer used three light sources. The key light was to the left of the camera and raised to direct light downward at about a 45° angle. The fill light was at head level and positioned to provide a 3:1 lighting ratio. A small spotlight provided rim lighting on the hair.

provide a soft overall lighting effect. Additional accent lights and reflectors are then positioned as necessary to create shadows and highlights. See **Figure 15-34**.

Glassware, polished metal, and other reflective objects can be difficult to light since they act as mirrors showing the light source and surrounding objects. See **Figure 15-35**. If desired, it is possible to eliminate reflections entirely by methods such as tenting the subject. **Tenting** is a lighting method in which the subject is surrounded by a cone or shell of white translucent paper or plastic, with a small hole cut in one side for the camera lens. Light thrown on the cone from the outside results in a very diffuse illumination of the subject. Although this lighting approach eliminates reflections, it tends to flatten the object. Surface texture and curvature are not conveyed very well.

Another approach, which is often used for photographing glass, is indirect or transmitted lighting. Light is bounced off the background and passes through the glass objects to the camera lens. Since

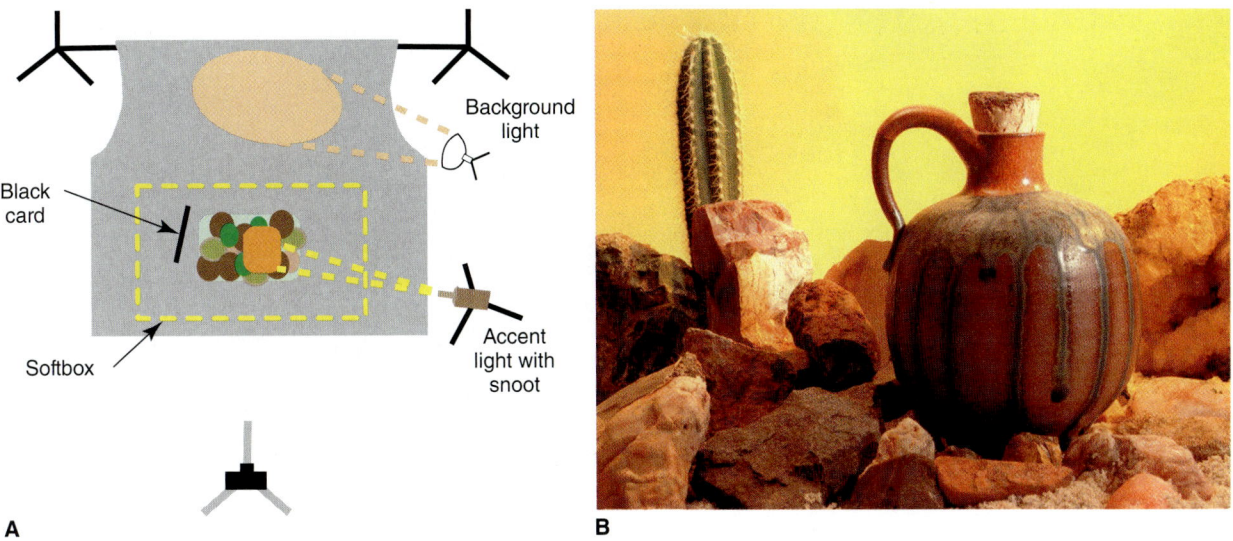

Jack Klasey/Goodheart-Willcox Publisher

Figure 15-34. A product shot using multiple light sources. A—The large softbox above the setup provided virtually directionless overall illumination. The product was given emphasis by lighting it with a small spotlight with a snoot. Positioning a black card opposite the accent light prevented lightening of the shadow areas due to reflection. A background light was placed low and directed through a colored gel. B—The final effect of the lighting setup.

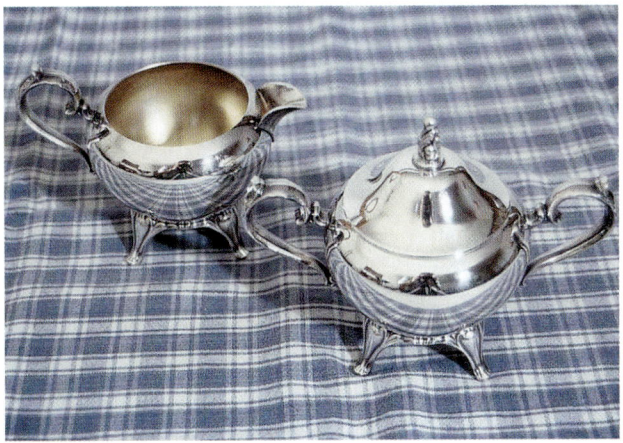

Jack Klasey/Goodheart-Willcox Publisher

Figure 15-35. Polished metal surfaces act as a mirror, showing undesirable reflections from the light source and objects in the studio. Note the reflection of the camera and photographer in these silver service pieces.

no frontal light is striking the reflective glass surface, there are no reflections. Colored backgrounds, or color gels on the lights, can be used to good effect. See **Figure 15-36**.

The key to successfully portraying most reflective subjects is controlling the reflections. Controlled reflections help to define the three-dimensional nature of the subject, convey its texture, and provide highlights that add visual interest. Reflection control involves a combination of light sources, reflectors, and black materials.

Small, bright light sources will create small specular reflections, while large, diffused light sources will result in broader and less intense reflections. To make the reflection pattern in the shiny surface more interesting, pieces of black paper or card stock may be strategically placed between the diffused light source and the object. This will break up the reflection into dark and bright areas.

Entire books have been written about the complex subject of studio lighting. Such books can provide a good grounding in the subject and many examples of different lighting treatments. Online tutorials are also a great option for learning how to work with different lighting equipment and techniques. However, the best way to learn lighting technique is practice and experimentation, **Figure 15-37**.

Use a systematic approach—start with a single key light and try various angles and distances or intensities until you are satisfied. Next, add a reflector and see the differences that result from changing angles and distances. Replace the reflector with a fill light. Turn off the key light and experiment with various fill light placements. Turn the key light on again and make any additional adjustments to the fill light. Use a meter to determine lighting ratio, and experiment with different ratios by making changes to the fill light. As you make exposures with various lighting setups, keep careful notes. Include a rough sketch of the light placement (with dimensions) and the frame or image number.

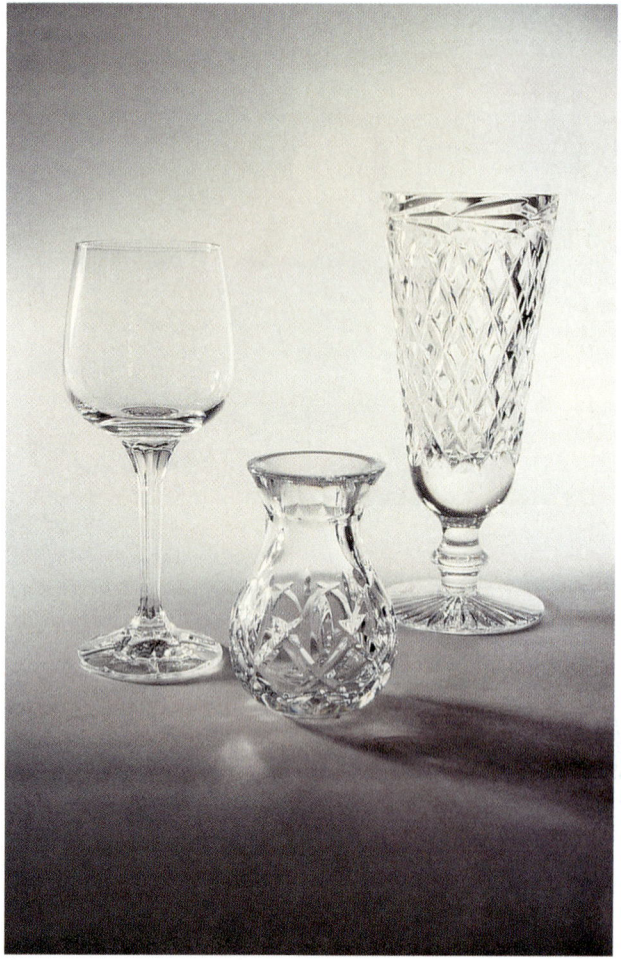

A

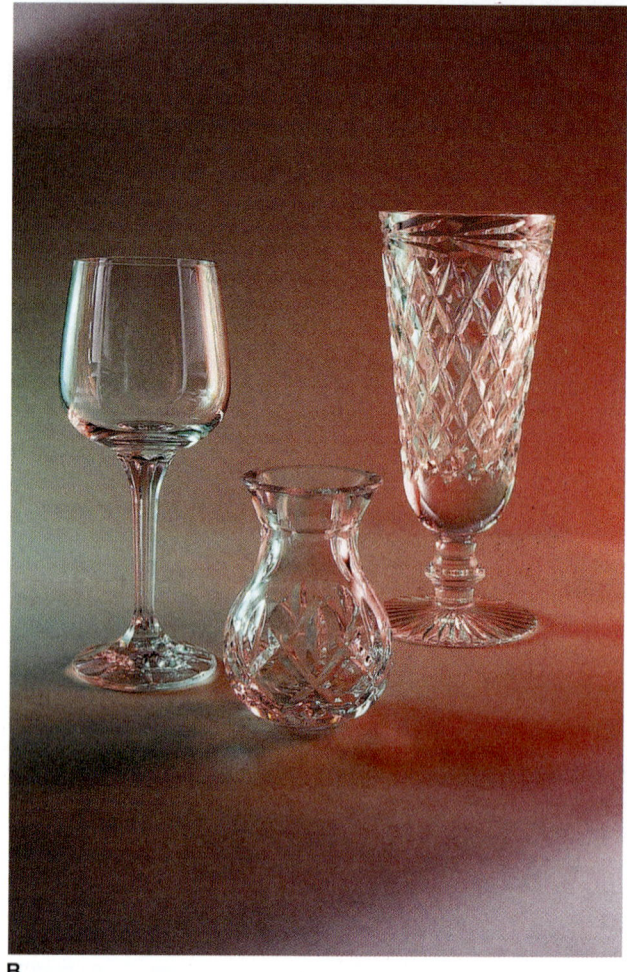

B

Jack Klasey/Goodheart-Willcox Publisher

Figure 15-36. Transmitted light can eliminate undesirable reflections when photographing glassware. A—Bouncing light off the seamless background material. B—Using a color background or adding gels to the lights.

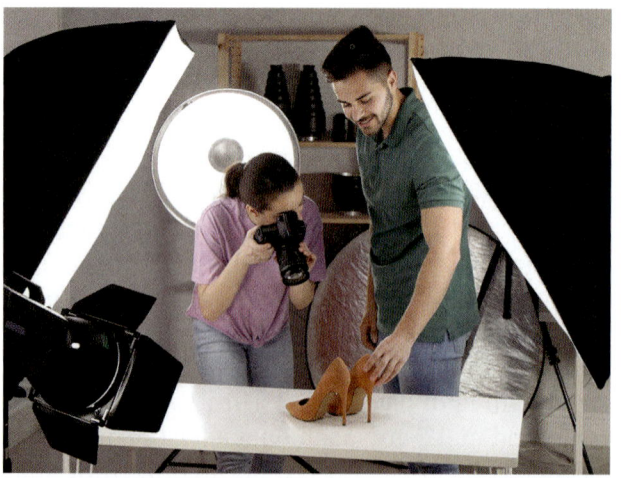

New Africa/Shutterstock.com

Figure 15-37. Experimenting with different lighting setups builds skills in the use of studio lighting.

If you are using a digital camera, the LCD screen gives you a quick general view of the lighting effect. For a more accurate assessment, view the images on your computer screen. However, do not perform any adjustments on the digital files. You want to see exactly the lighting effects your sensor is recording. Experimenting with lighting and critically studying the images allows you to learn successful techniques and discard those that do not provide the desired results.

PORTFOLIO ASSIGNMENT

Finding the Right Ratio

In this assignment, you will experiment with lighting ratios to produce a pleasing portrait. You will need a partner for this assignment to pose for your photos.

1. Find two continuous light sources, if available, or one light and a reflector. If using a reflector, make sure it stays in the same spot for consistency among your images.
2. Working with your partner, try three different key light–to–fill light ratios, such as 1:1, 2:1, and 3:1.
3. Take three photos at each ratio to get a good expression as well as a proper exposure. You should have nine photos total.

Choose the best portrait for your portfolio, noting the lighting ratio and exposure information.

Chapter 15 Review

Summary

- Portraits are the primary activity for most community-based photographers, but they are not the only kind of photographs made in a studio. Some studios, especially in larger cities, specialize in shooting objects rather than people.
- The formal studio portrait is the traditional style of individual or family portrait, made in a studio setting. A more informal type of portrait, made outside the studio setting, has become popular. Often called environmental portraits, these images show the subject in natural surroundings or in a setting meaningful to them.
- Environmental portraits are typically made with ambient light. Ambient light often must be modified because it can be too bright, too dim, too contrasty, or too flat.
- In the fill flash technique, the flash unit's output is balanced with the ambient light. Many photographers use fill flash for portraits and other outdoor situations involving people or animals.
- With a digital camera, you can affect the color of the light by changing the white balance. You can use automatic white balance, a white balance preset, or a custom white balance.
- The greatest amount of control over lighting can be exercised in the studio. Lighting units can be added, removed, and repositioned until the desired effect is achieved.
- Light sources for studio use are typically either continuous (remain lit) or flash, although some photographers also make use of natural light from a skylight or window in the studio.
- Electronic studio flash units are the primary source of portable artificial light for photography. The two types of studio flash systems on the market are pack-and-head and self-contained.
- Studio lighting can be as simple as a single light, or as complex as a setup involving three, four, or even more lighting instruments. Commonly used lights include a key light, fill light, background light, and rim light.
- There are a number of ways to vary the intensity, or brightness, of the light falling on the subject. Two basic methods are changing the output of the light unit and changing the distance of the light from the subject.
- Light intensity can be controlled by special devices such as snoots and grids and a technique known as feathering. Light quality can be hard or soft depending on the light source or device used.
- Careful measurement of the light falling on the subject is important not only for establishing correct overall exposure but also for determining the relative intensities of the key and fill lights.
- The amount of light falloff is calculated using the inverse-square law, which states that the illumination provided by a light source varies inversely as the square of the distance from the source.
- Achieving an effective balance among the various lighting elements is important in all types of studio photography. A lighting ratio is the comparison of the key light to the fill light expressed as a ratio. The higher the ratio, the more contrast you have to deal with.
- Basic portrait lighting can be done with a single light source, with a one light plus reflector arrangement, or with two lights (key and fill).
- For product photography, the key light may be a softbox or similar large, diffused source to provide a soft overall lighting effect. Additional accent lights and reflectors are then positioned as necessary to create shadows and highlights.

Review Questions

Answer the following questions using the information provided in this chapter.

Know and Understand

1. *True or False?* Good production scheduling is necessary to be able to deliver the finished product when promised.
2. When subjects are evenly and softly lighted, _____ adds a hint of directional light to better model their features.
   A. white balance
   B. ambient light
   C. fill flash
   D. photoflood
3. Which of the following white balance presets will compensate for a cool blue cast from reflected skylight and give the photo a warmer appearance?
   A. Daylight
   B. Flash
   C. Shade
   D. Cloudy
4. *True or False?* It is important to switch off and discharge monolights before plugging them in or unplugging them.
5. A(n) _____ is a glass bulb similar in appearance to a standard bulb but constructed for high light output.
   A. tungsten-halogen bulb
   B. photoflood
   C. LED array
   D. softbox
6. A(n) _____ is a large source of diffused light that consists of several lamps or electronic flash units mounted inside a reflective housing and covered with translucent material.
   A. softbox
   B. electronic studio flash
   C. gobo
   D. photoflood
7. *True or False?* In the pack-and-head system, the flash tube, controls, and capacitors are combined into a single housing.
8. Which of the following lights softens dark shadows, decreases the contrast range of the light reflected from the subject, and helps to reveal detail in shadow areas?
   A. Key
   B. Fill
   C. Background
   D. Rim
9. A _____ light is often used both for dramatic effect and to help separate a dark-haired subject from a dark background.
   A. rim
   B. key
   C. fill
   D. background
10. *True or False?* Light through a snoot adds sparkle to a scene through increased contrast.
11. A type of lighting that creates harsh shadows, or places with stark contrast between the highlights and the shadows, is called _____.
    A. soft light
    B. feathering
    C. hard light
    D. three-point lighting
12. _____ are hinged rectangular flaps of black-painted metal attached to the front of a lighting unit.
    A. Flags
    B. Gobos
    C. Barn doors
    D. Cookies
13. *True or False?* The principle of light falloff states that the farther the subject is from the light source, the less brightly it is illuminated.
14. *True or False?* Traditionally, the lighting ratio for portrait work is 3:1.
15. A two-light arrangement is used extensively for _____ because it offers considerable flexibility in creating different effects and lighting ratios.
    A. product photography
    B. three-point lighting
    C. tenting
    D. portraits

16. _____ is a lighting method in which the subject is surrounded by a cone or shell of white translucent paper or plastic, with a small hole cut in one side for the camera lens.
    A. Tenting
    B. Feathering
    C. Lighting ratio
    D. Three-point lighting

Apply and Analyze

1. What is the difference between a formal studio portrait and an environmental portrait?
2. When might a photographer create a custom white balance?
3. List three safety precautions to take when working with studio lighting.
4. Describe the reflective-reading method used to establish lighting ratios.
5. What is indirect or transmitted lighting used for?

Critical Thinking

1. You work after school in a photo studio and were present when a client's new product, a radically new type of skateboard, was photographed for a social media campaign that will be released next month. Your best friend is an avid skateboarder and blogger on skateboarding topics. What are the potential consequences of telling them about the new product?
2. Examine two social media accounts (such as Instagram or Facebook): one for a large general retail store and one for a home improvement store. Some of the photos they contain show just the product, and others contain a person. Is the balance between "product only" and "people with product" photos similar or different? Why do you think people are used in some of the photos?

Suggested Activities

1. Research the tintype photographic process popular in the late nineteenth century. Use what you learn to create a small advertisement for a tintype portrait studio that might have appeared in an 1890 newspaper.
2. In teams of two, find good locations in your school to take a portrait of a fellow student. List three locations and describe why they would be suitable for shooting a portrait of that person. Include information about the available lighting in each location.
3. In groups of two, select three compositional elements that are often used in portrait photography. This can include concepts such as composition, lighting, and posing. Once you have these elements selected, try replicating them with your partner and take at least three photos. You should each take your own photos, so be sure to swap places depending on who took their photos first. After you have both taken your photos, discuss the elements you chose to use and explain why. As you explain your photos to your partner, provide self-critiques. Your partner should then provide constructive feedback, and vice versa.

Communicating about Photography

1. **Writing and Speaking.** Working in groups of two or three students, create flash cards for the technical terms in this chapter. On the front of the card, write the term. On the back of the card, write a brief definition. Use your textbook and a dictionary for guidance. Then take turns quizzing one another on the definitions of the key terms.

2. **Reading and Speaking.** Many portrait studio websites include tips for clients regarding how to prepare for their sitting. Read through several of these lists of tips and compile your own list of top 10 tips. With another student, role-play a situation in front of the class in which you are a portrait photographer advising the client on how to prepare for the sitting. Then switch roles.

Chapter 16
Mobile Photography

Learning Objectives

After completing this chapter, you will be able to:
- Understand the difference between traditional photography and mobile photography.
- Identify various mobile camera controls and understand how to use them.
- Explain how to use traditional camera controls with a smartphone camera.
- Understand the difference between a phone's native camera app and third-party photography applications.
- Recall tips and tricks for shooting with a phone camera.

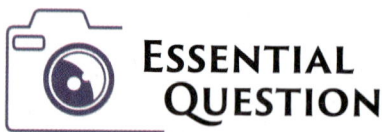

Essential Question

How does mobile photography allow you to expand your abilities as a photographer?

Technical Terms

aspect ratio
digital zoom
high dynamic range (HDR) image

mobile photography
optical zoom
traditional photography

true to color
zebras

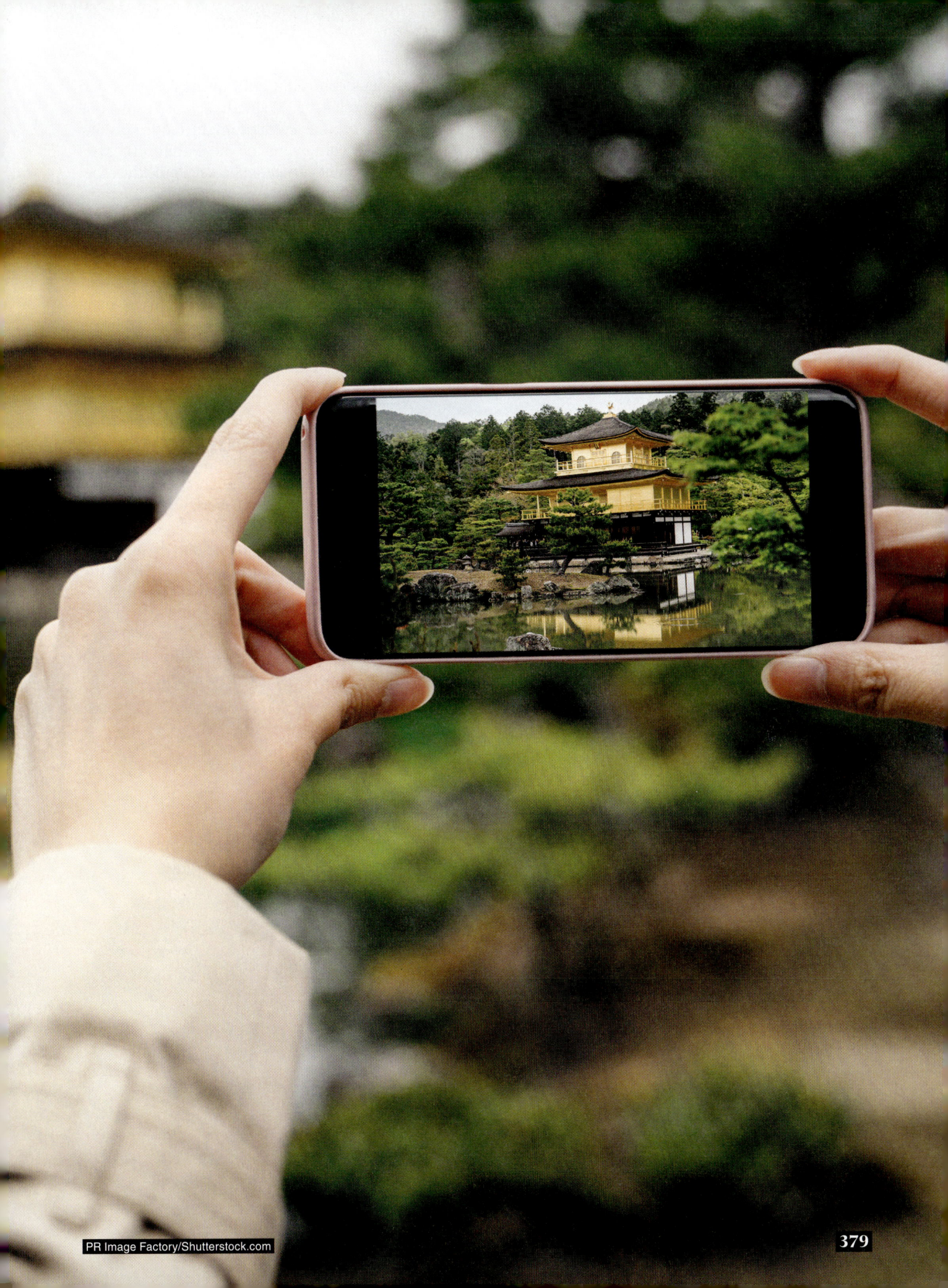
PR Image Factory/Shutterstock.com

Introduction to Mobile Photography

In recent years, cell phones have become permanent fixtures in our daily lives. They have evolved drastically since their creation and have so many incredible features, including the ability to take stunning photos. This is extremely valuable for the modern photographer. There are many times when a photo opportunity will present itself and you may not have a digital camera at your disposal. Most newer smartphones have professional-quality cameras, allowing you to capture any subject at any time.

What Is Mobile Photography?

In this book, **traditional photography** is photography taken with either a film camera or a digital camera. **Mobile photography** is photography taken with a camera phone or other mobile device, such as a tablet. When it comes to base knowledge, traditional photography and mobile photography are virtually indistinguishable. You still use the same knowledge of theory, such as the rule of thirds and other composition tools, and practical elements, such as focus and exposure. If you know how to take photos on a DSLR camera, you can take that knowledge and apply it to your phone camera.

Mobile photography became popular when smartphones became part of our everyday lives. Initially, it gave users the opportunity to take quick snapshots with their phone, but over time, it has morphed into a category of photography all its own. Mobile photography is flexible and easily accessible for most people. Furthermore, most newer phone cameras today are of exceptional quality and even rival some professional cameras. Due to their portability, they also provide the opportunity to capture nearly everything you want at a moment's notice.

Mobile Photography Supplies

Mobile photography is great for people who are frequently on the go and for people who do not want to haul around a lot of equipment. The camera you have in your pocket condenses a lot of camera equipment into one device. Your smartphone has a camera (sometimes with multiple lenses), a viewfinder, ISO and focus control, a built-in microphone, and basic editing software. Trying to achieve that same thing with a regular camera might require as few as 3 pieces of equipment, or more than 10. Also, camera equipment can get expensive quickly, especially as you buy more lenses or upgrade your camera body. Even though some smartphones are also expensive, you have the added benefit of your phone being multifunctional.

When your phone is your camera, you have a lot less equipment to gather—all you have to do is grab your phone. However, you can always bring an external battery, a small light, and a gimbal or stabilizer, but those are easy to carry in a bag or purse, **Figure 16-1**.

Mobile Camera Controls

You can achieve stunning photos using just your phone if you know how to work with what you have available. Phone cameras allow photographers greater flexibility, and it is important to use this flexibility to your advantage. In order to achieve the best photos possible, you must understand the settings in your phone's native camera app. All phones have default settings that can capture most photos just fine, but knowing what each setting does and how to adjust it can help take your images to the next level.

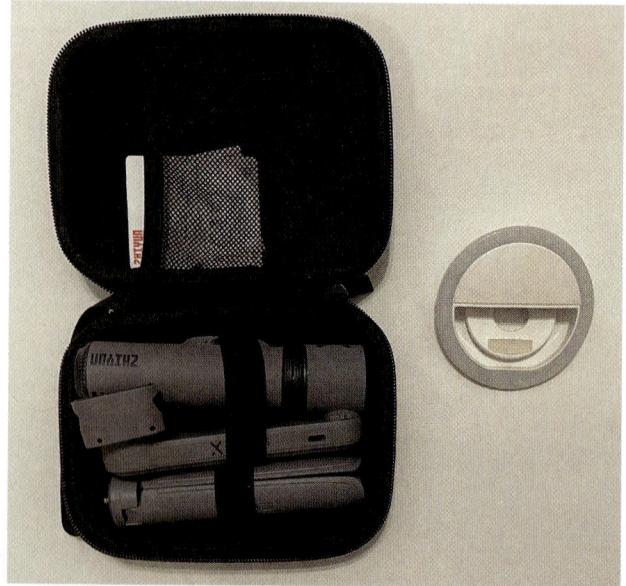

Goodheart-Willcox Publisher

Figure 16-1. A mobile shooting kit often includes a stabilizer, a spare battery or battery pack, and a light.

Enabling a Grid

One of the first things you should do before using a phone camera is enable the grid to show the rule of thirds, **Figure 16-2**. The main benefit of enabling this setting is to help you with composition. Once you become more experienced, you may be able to eyeball proper composition, but it is still helpful to have the reference available. Many professional photographers even work with the grid enabled to help them in various scenarios.

While there are grids on most smartphones, the examples in this chapter are for an iPhone®. If you do not have an iPhone, refer to your specific phone model's instructions or look for a manual online. To enable the grid on an iPhone, you need to navigate to the Settings app. From there, scroll to where the settings for the native camera app are. Once you select Camera, you will see an option to enable the grid under the Composition heading, **Figure 16-3**. When you reopen the native camera application, you should see the faint white lines overlapping the image on the screen, **Figure 16-4**. These lines will not appear in your final photos.

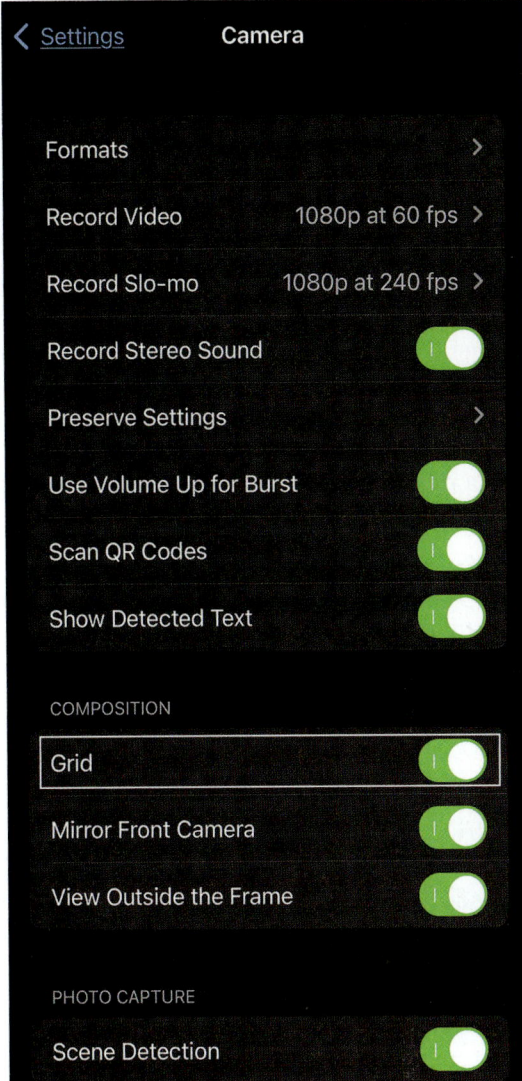

Goodheart-Willcox Publisher

Figure 16-3. You can enable the grid in your phone's settings.

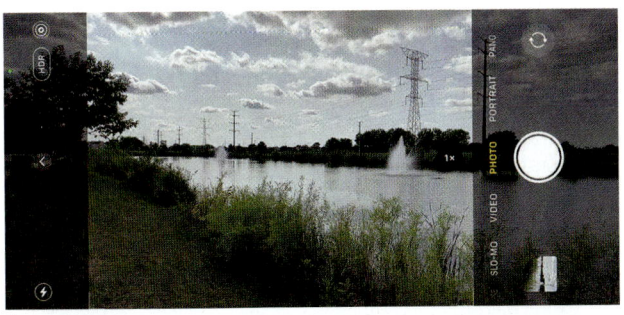

A

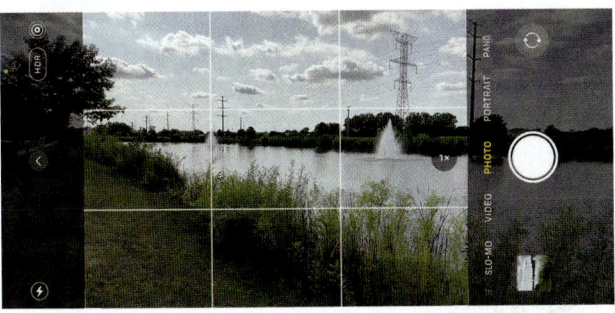

B

Goodheart-Willcox Publisher

Figure 16-2. No matter what device you have, you should enable the grid to help you with the rule of thirds. A—Taking a photo without the grid leaves room for error in your composition. B—It is much easier to frame your photos when the grid is enabled.

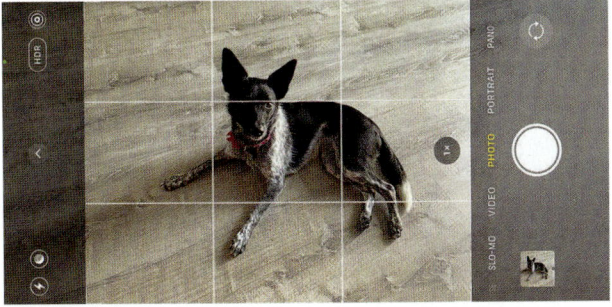

Goodheart-Willcox Publisher

Figure 16-4. Once the grid is enabled, it is laid over your image. However, it will not appear in the final photo.

Preserve Settings

If you find yourself constantly adjusting your camera's settings, you may want to enable Preserve Settings. Preserve Settings is located in the Camera settings in the Settings app. It allows you to save any changes you made to your camera when you took pictures last. There are several different features and dozens of combinations that allow for a highly customizable shooting experience. It may take some experimenting before you find what works for you. Some of the options that may be available in Preserve Settings are Camera Mode (preserves the last mode you shot in), Creative Controls (preserves the last used filter, aspect ratio, light, or depth setting), Exposure Adjustment (preserves the last exposure adjustment), Night Mode (preserves the Night Mode setting), Portrait Zoom (preserves a central area of focus), and Live Photo (preserves the Live Photo setting), **Figure 16-5**.

Formats

There are a handful of different formats you can take your photos in on a smartphone. The default file format of any iPhone photo is HEIC. As you learned in Chapter 8, *Digital Image Capture Media*, HEIC is Apple's proprietary version of the file format called HEIF, short for High-Efficiency Image File format. This format was designed to save storage space on an iPhone while maintaining the high quality of the image. HEIC photos also support a wider range of colors than most other formats.

You also have the option of saving your images as Most Compatible, which will automatically save your photos as a JPEG file. This can be adjusted in the native camera app settings, under Formats, **Figure 16-6**. Choosing the Most Compatible option presents fewer issues with compatibility between PC and Mac systems, which is often a problem when transferring files from your phone to a computer or tablet.

Different phone models also have different formats. Android cameras can take photos in JPEG, PNG (Portable Network Graphic), and AVIF (AV1 Image File Format). You will have to find what works best for you and your situation, and it may take some experimenting on your part. Deciding what works best for you will depend on how much storage you have available on your device, what types of

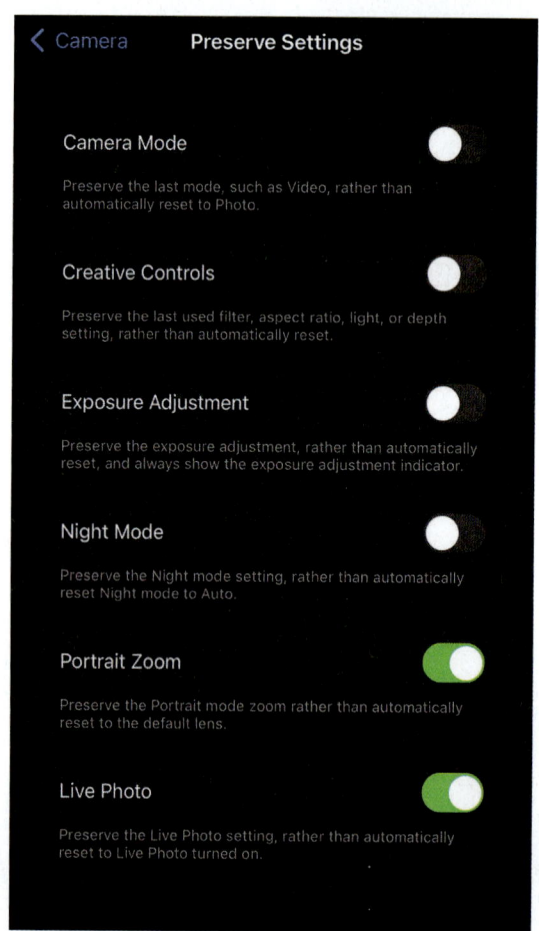

Goodheart-Willcox Publisher

Figure 16-5. Preserve Settings on an iPhone will let you save your selected settings.

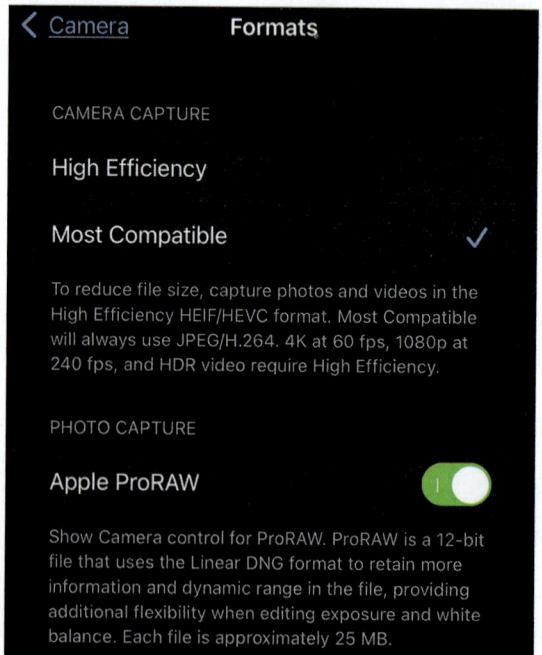

Goodheart-Willcox Publisher

Figure 16-6. You can adjust your photo format under Formats in Settings.

files are the most compatible with the image editing software you use, and what file type is the easiest to transfer, among other things.

High Dynamic Range (HDR)

A *high dynamic range (HDR) image* is a photo with a wider range between the lightest and darkest areas of a photo than a standard photo. HDR photos appear richly colored, highly contrasted, and very saturated, **Figure 16-7**. Both Android and iPhone cameras can take HDR images.

When your phone captures an HDR image, it takes several photos at different exposure levels and then combines them together to create your final image, **Figure 16-8**. While you can take these photos separately, your phone will do it automatically if you have the setting enabled, **Figure 16-9**. This is a good option for capturing photos that do not seem to be coming through true to color after you have captured the image and you are looking for more of an impact. *True to color* is the portrayal of an object's natural colors in an image.

Traditional Camera Controls

Understanding your phone camera's settings will allow you to control and manipulate them to

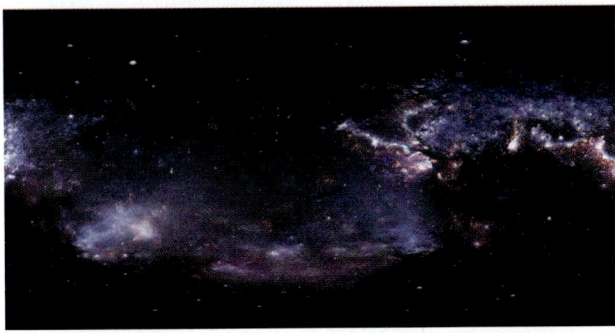

Jurik Peter/Shutterstock.com

Figure 16-7. High dynamic range (HDR) images appear richly colored and saturated.

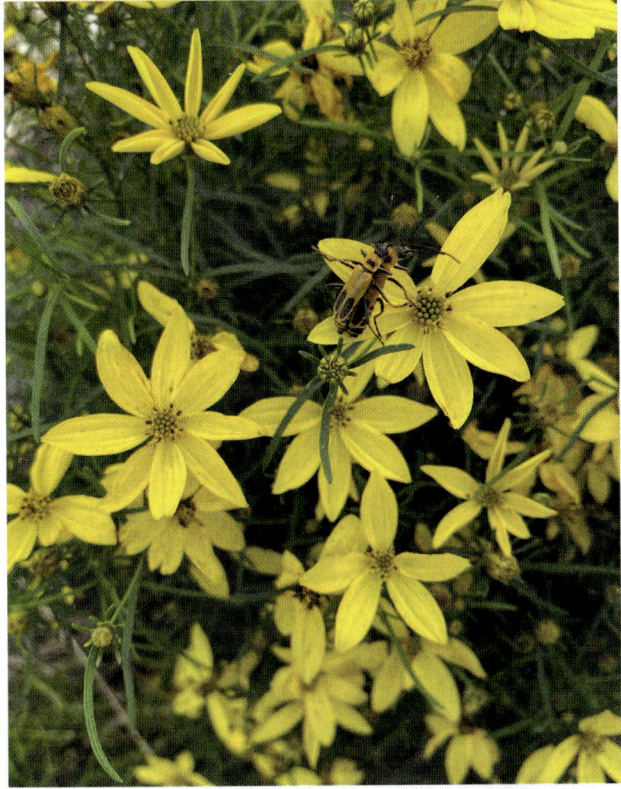

Goodheart-Willcox Publisher

Figure 16-8. An HDR image taken on an iPhone.

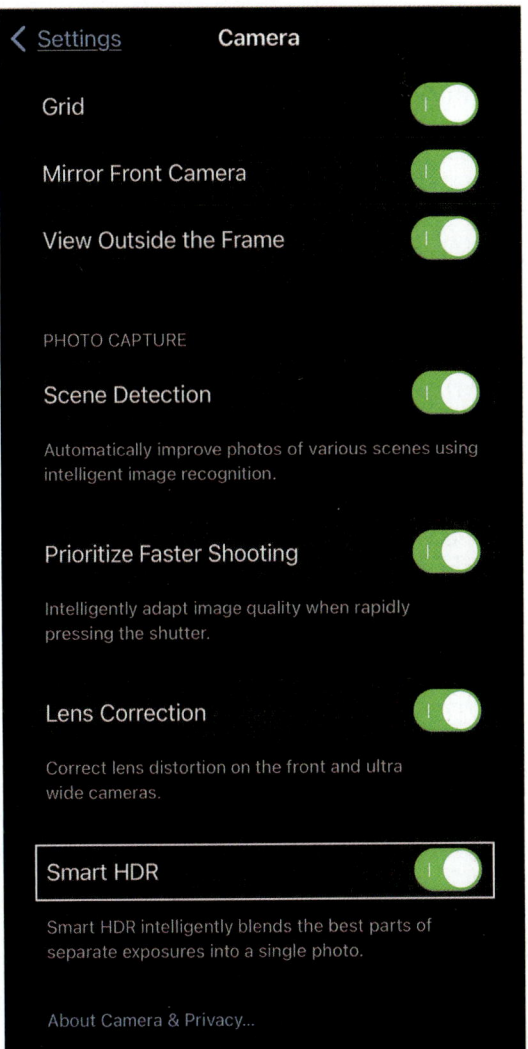

Goodheart-Willcox Publisher

Figure 16-9. Enabling the HDR setting on your phone allows you to take an HDR photo.

get professional-quality images. This section will cover several settings that you can adjust similarly to regular DSLR cameras.

Setting and Locking Focus

Setting and locking the focus on your phone camera allows you to decide what stands out to the viewer. Our eyes automatically focus on things that are crisp and clear in a photo. Determining what to clearly focus on in the photo allows the photographer to control what should be emphasized and, thus, what the viewer looks at first. Furthermore, without a focus point, your images can lack sharpness and detail.

To set the focus, open your camera app. Select the subject you want to focus on by holding your finger down over where the subject is on-screen. A small box should materialize, and shortly after, the words AE/AF Lock will appear at the top of the screen. Once those words appear, you know you have set the focus on your intended subject, **Figure 16-10**. If you want to reset the focus, simply hold your finger down over the new subject and repeat the process.

Setting and Locking Exposure

The effect of selecting the exposure is very similar to why setting focus is an effective tool for guiding your viewer's gaze. Your viewer's attention will naturally gravitate toward areas that are lighter and brighter than other areas, just like they do to areas that are in sharper focus.

To set the exposure, open your camera app. Select the area you want to change the exposure for by tapping on it where it appears on-screen. A small box should show up, this time with a small sun icon, **Figure 16-11**. Once the box is on-screen, touch the screen again and move your finger up or down at the same time. If you move your finger up, the exposure increases and makes the image brighter. If you move your finger down, the exposure decreases and makes the image darker, **Figure 16-12**. Although this will change the exposure for the entire image, selecting the specific area you want to brighten or darken will base the exposure around that area.

Flash

There are various situations in which you will need to use flash. Traditionally, using flash in photography allows you to illuminate a scene that has less than ideal lighting conditions, **Figure 16-13**. On most phones, the flash is set to automatically go off when it detects

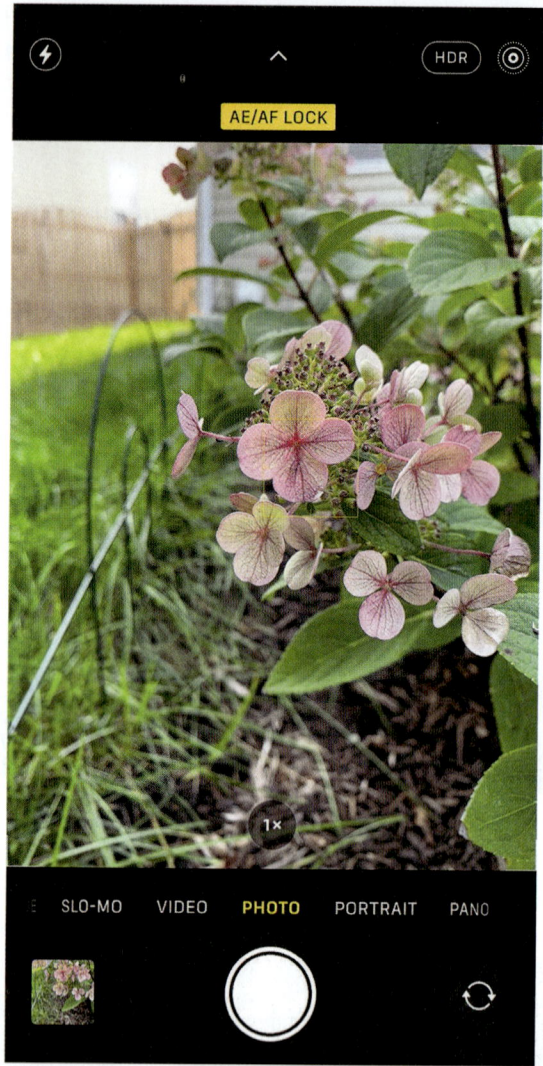

Goodheart-Willcox Publisher

Figure 16-10. A yellow box will appear around your subject to help you set the AE/AF lock. You will know it is set once the words AE/AF Lock appear at the top of the screen.

that you are taking photos that may be underexposed. Technology has come a long way for photography in the last several years, and many newer smartphones have a specific setting called Night Mode that takes well-lit photos without flash by using a longer exposure.

However, if you want the look of a flash, or if you genuinely do not have another way to illuminate a subject, you can set your phone to use the flash automatically. In the native camera app of an iPhone, look for the lightning logo in the upper left-hand corner of the screen and press it. You can also select the arrow icon in the middle of the top of the screen. You should see several options appear at the bottom of the native app that allow you to choose if the phone determines when flash should be used, if

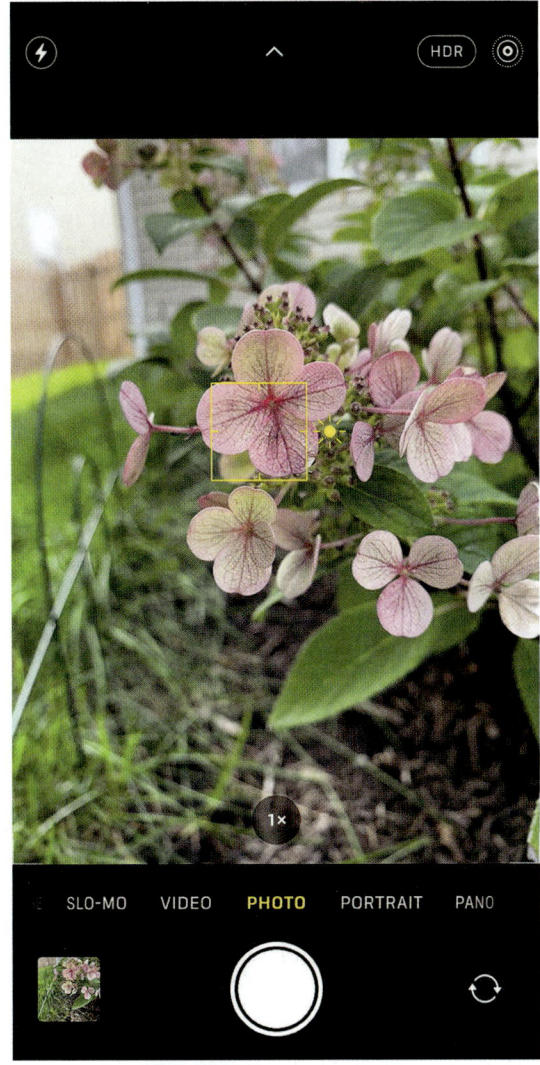

Goodheart-Willcox Publisher

Figure 16-11. A small sun icon will appear next to the yellow box to show you are working with the exposure on your phone.

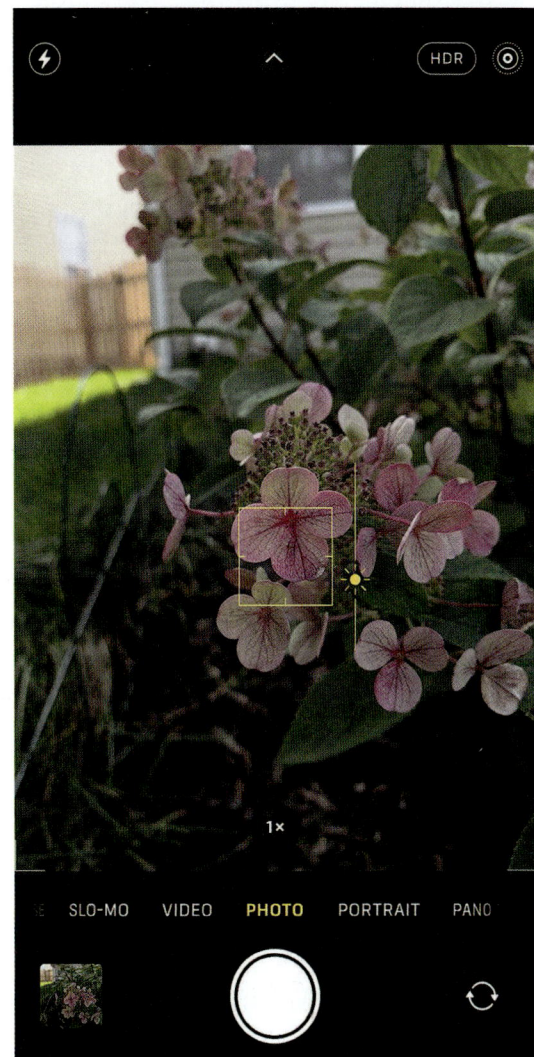

Goodheart-Willcox Publisher

Figure 16-12. Moving your finger down next to the box will decrease your image's exposure.

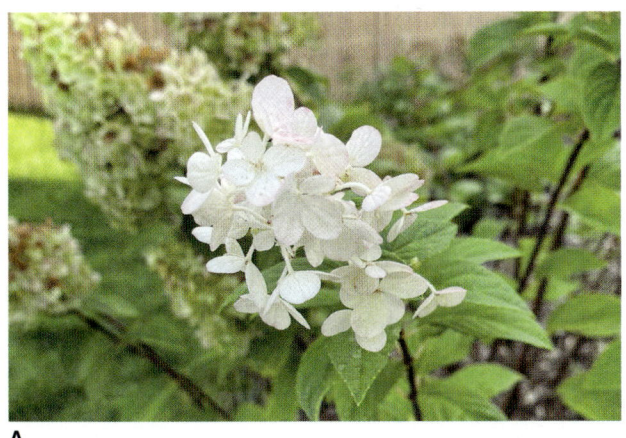

A

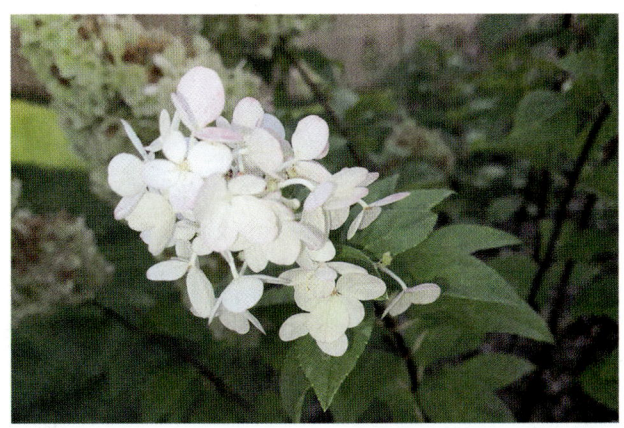

B

Goodheart-Willcox Publisher

Figure 16-13. Flash can help in less-than-ideal lighting conditions. A—A photo taken without flash. B—A photo taken with flash.

it is always on, or if it is always off, **Figure 16-14**. You can change the setting whenever you like.

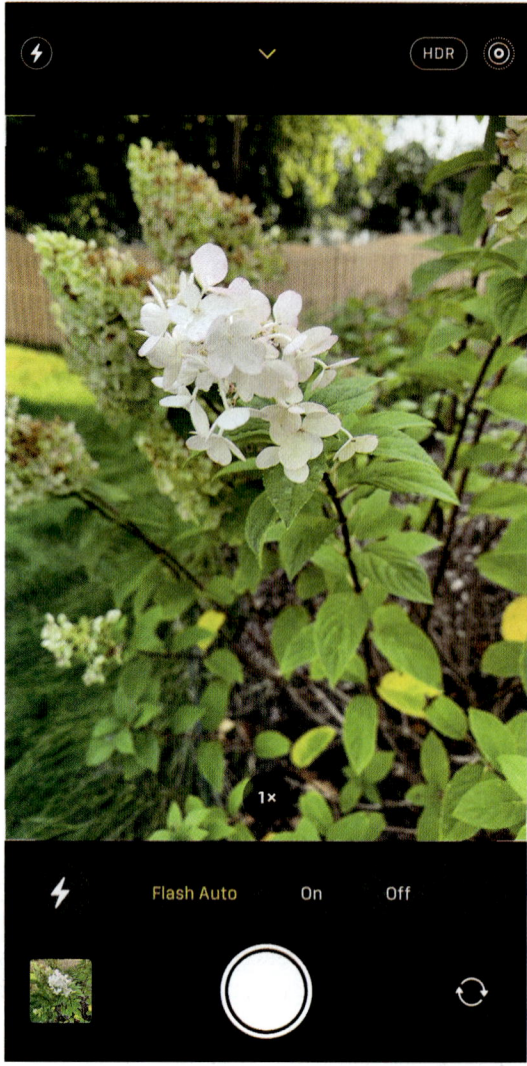

Goodheart-Willcox Publisher

Figure 16-14. You can enable the flash setting on your phone by using this icon.

REAL-WORLD PHOTOGRAPHY

Controlling Lighting with a Phone Camera

One of the things that smartphone photographers struggle with is getting the lighting right. In most cases, you will use your phone's camera outside of a studio environment with controlled lights. As such, it is essential to know how to best work with the light you have available to you:

- **Exposure in the phone app.** As mentioned earlier in this chapter, you can adjust the exposure on your smartphone. If your image is coming through too bright, decrease the exposure so your camera's sensor receives less light. If your image is too dark, increase the exposure so your camera's sensor receives more light. Thankfully, most smartphone cameras now have a feature that allows you to take great photos in darker conditions by prolonging the exposure.
- **Moving a subject.** If adjusting the exposure is not enough, or if it is not giving you the look you want, you can always move your subject. For example, if you are taking photos of someone outside and the sun is directly behind the person you are taking a picture of, you would want to move them. If you do not move them, the sun will cause your photo to be overexposed. If you are inside and the room is dark, try moving your subject toward a light or a window. When moving your subject, make sure you pay attention to shadows as well, so that they do not distract from your final picture.

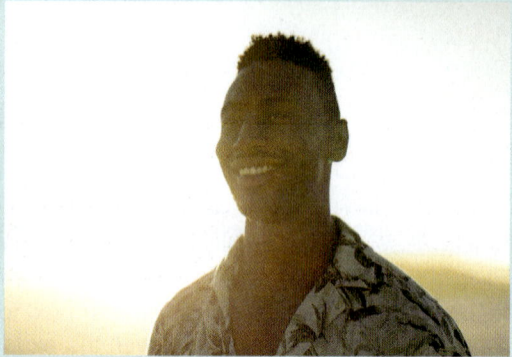

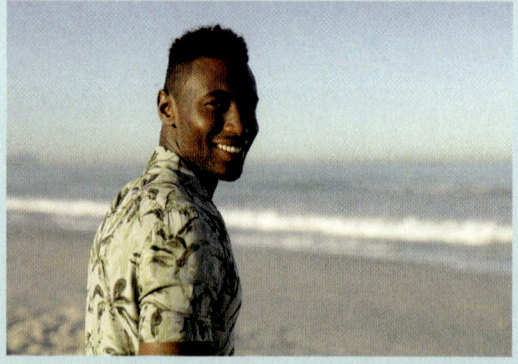

wavebreakmedia/Shutterstock.com

Moving a subject so the sun is not behind them will provide better exposure.

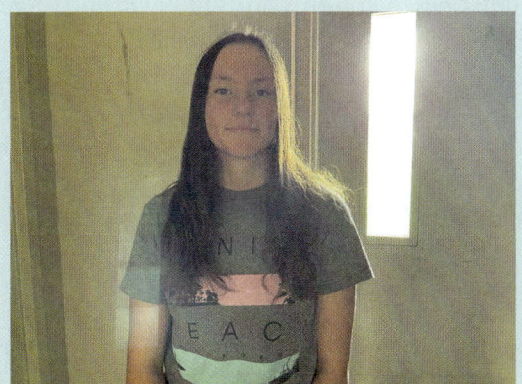

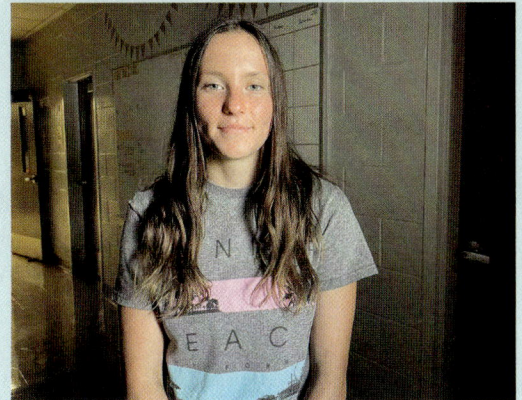

Goodheart-Willcox Publisher

Moving a subject toward a window when they are underexposed is a good solution when shooting indoors.

- **Editing photos.** You can also adjust lighting to a degree when editing your photos. Whether it is through filters or other techniques, you can edit how light appears to some extent. There are apps available that work on your mobile device, or you can import your cell phone photos to a computer and use an image editing program to have more control over the lighting in your images. This topic is covered more extensively in Chapter 21, *Mobile Postprocessing*.

Aspect Ratio

Aspect ratio is the relationship between the width and height of an image, and it is important for the proportions of your image. The most common are 1:1 (square), 4:3 (standard), and 16:9 (widescreen), **Figure 16-15**.

Aspect ratio is important for many reasons. One of the most important reasons is because it affects where your subject is positioned in the frame. Depending on your subject or environment, you could risk losing important elements that are too

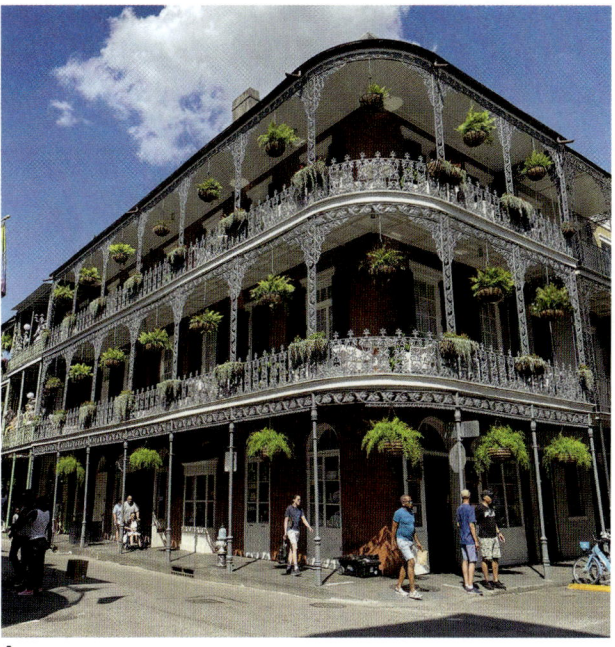

A

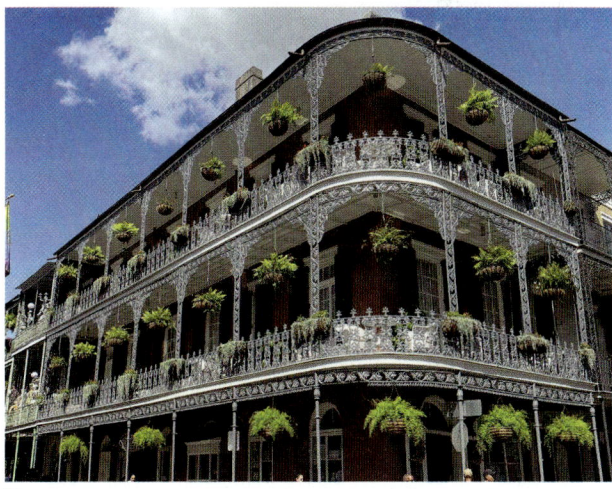

B

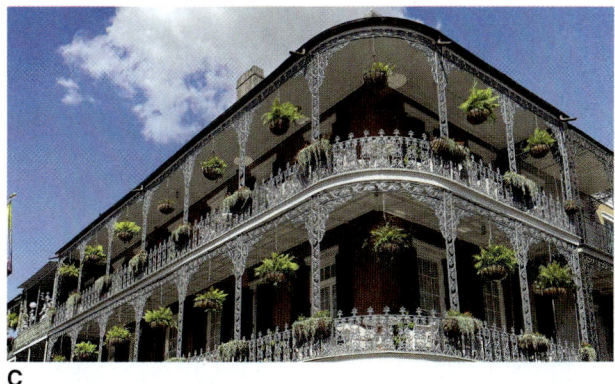

C

Goodheart-Willcox Publisher

Figure 16-15. Aspect ratios affect how your subject appears in a photo. A—1:1 square image. B—4:3 standard image. C—16:9 widescreen image.

close to the edge of the frame if you are shooting in the wrong aspect ratio. An incorrect aspect ratio can also affect how shapes appear in your photo, which will affect your composition. An incorrect aspect ratio will not change a sphere to a square, for example, but it could possibly distort the appearance of the shape itself, inhibiting all the work you put into your photograph's design and composition. To fix this potential issue, you can adjust your aspect ratio to create more room in the frame and maintain the appearance of any important elements.

Depending on your phone, the ability to change your aspect ratio will not be on the first screen in your native app since many people just default to whatever the camera opens with (in most cases, 4:3). To change your aspect ratio settings, select the arrow icon in the middle of the top of the screen, then look for the 4:3 aspect ratio button at the bottom. Clicking on this button will expand a menu that gives you the option for shooting in 1:1, 4:3, or 16:9, **Figure 16-16**. Experiment with each aspect ratio on a range of subjects to see what works best.

You also have the ability to adjust the aspect ratio once you have already taken your photo by editing the photo and adjusting the crop, **Figure 16-17**. To crop your image to a different aspect ratio after you have already taken it, go to your Photos app and select the photo in question. Once you have it selected, press the Edit button in the upper right-hand corner. From there, select the Crop icon at the bottom of the screen, **Figure 16-18**. Several new buttons will appear, including a rectangle with two smaller ones inside of it in the upper right-hand corner, **Figure 16-19**. Selecting that button enables you to choose from a wide range of aspect ratios, including Freeform (freehand crop, or moving it to your own specifications) and Square, and depending on whether you select the landscape or portrait option, 16:9 (9:16), 5:4 (4:5), 7:5 (5:7), 4:3 (3:4), 5:3 (3:5), and 3:2 (2:3).

Native Camera Apps vs. Third-Party Photography Applications

When you take photos on your phone, you have two options: using the native camera application that comes with your phone or downloading and using a separate third-party application. Many photographers are of the opinion that using a third-party app does not necessarily provide better-quality photographs than the app that comes installed on a phone. The advantage of third-party apps often lies in their functionality while taking a photo and, depending on the application, postprocessing.

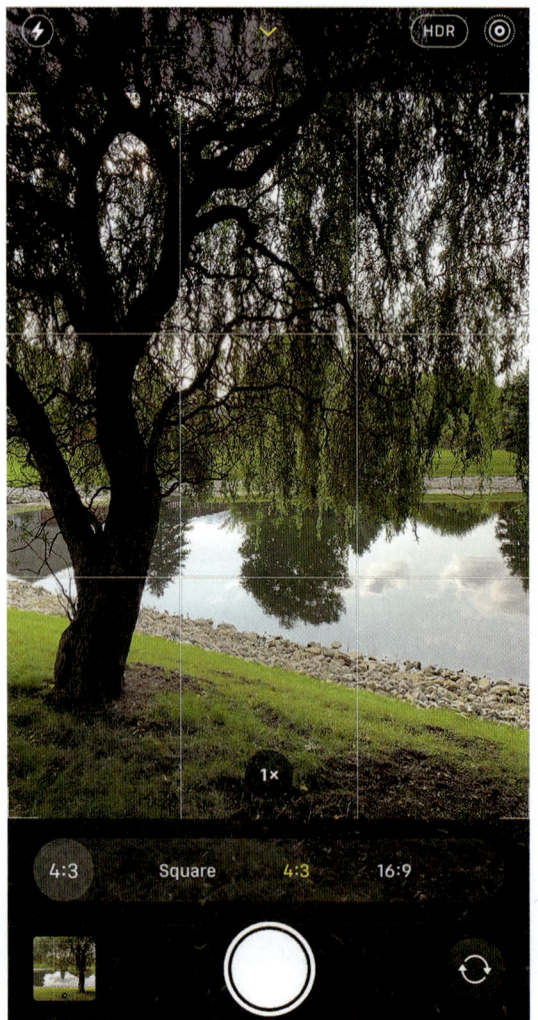

Goodheart-Willcox Publisher

Figure 16-16. An iPhone gives you the option to choose which aspect ratio you would like to shoot in.

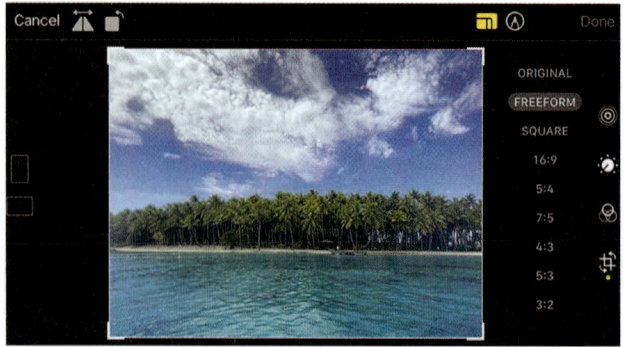

Goodheart-Willcox Publisher

Figure 16-17. You can change the aspect ratio for a photo you have already taken by adjusting the crop.

Native Camera App

The functionality of the native camera app will vary on each phone, **Figure 16-20**. However, there are some commonalities that they share. Most phones have a front-facing camera and a rear-facing camera. As technology improves, more and more lenses are added to the rear-facing camera to give users more flexibility. The iPhone® 12 Pro Max, for example, has three lenses that you can rotate through to achieve the effect that you want, **Figure 16-21**. You have access to selfies, portraits, panoramas, HDR, burst photos, and more just in the native camera app.

With each software and camera update, smartphone cameras add additional functionality. Some of the features included with the iPhone® 13 camera at the time of publication are as follows:

- Default filters that can be added to images allow users to set up their own photographic style.

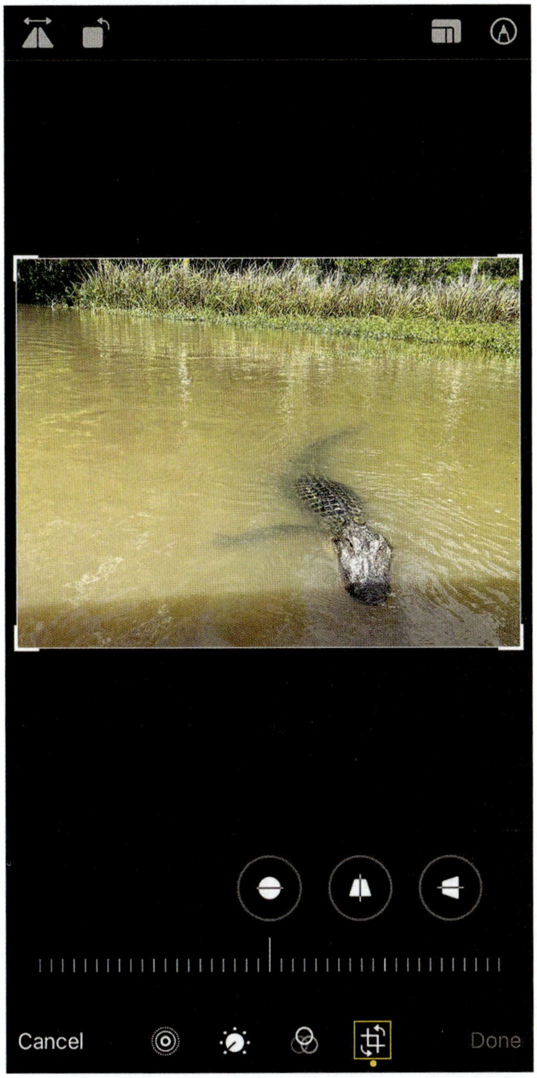

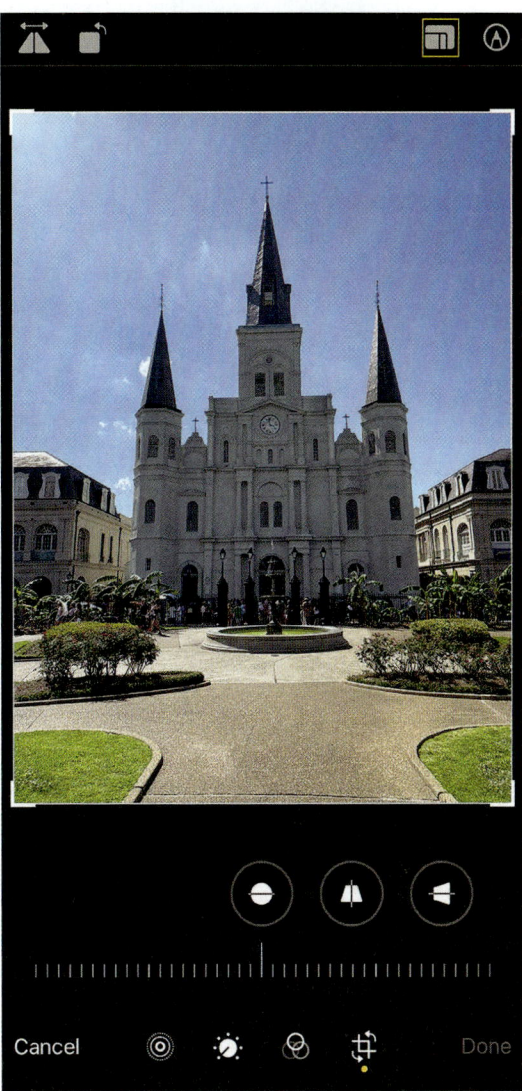

Goodheart-Willcox Publisher

Figure 16-19. This icon (highlighted in the yellow box) will allow you to change the aspect ratio of a picture you have already taken.

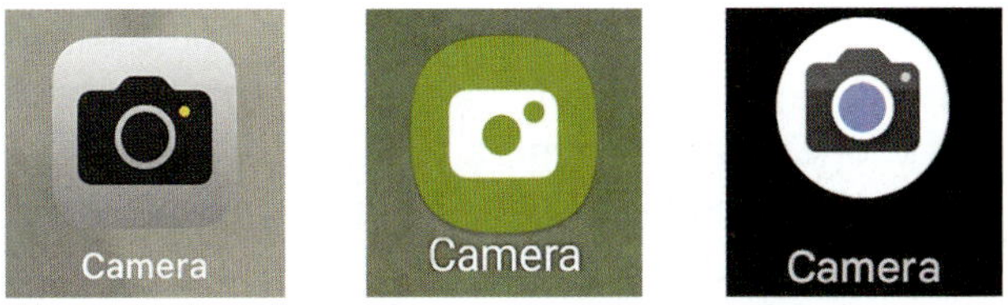

Goodheart-Willcox Publisher

Figure 16-20. The native camera app is different on each smartphone model. From left to right, the apps for the iPhone camera, Android camera, and Google Pixel camera are shown.

Goodheart-Willcox Publisher

Figure 16-18. The Crop icon (highlighted in the yellow box) is located at the bottom right of the menu.

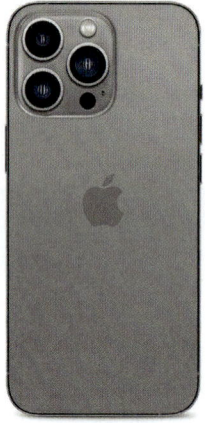

Cincila/Shutterstock.com

Figure 16-21. The three lenses on newer iPhone models give you a range to choose from to maximize your picture-taking abilities.

- Enhanced macrophotography allows users to take detailed close-up photos.
- QuickTake allows users to record quick videos without switching out of photo mode.
- Lens Correction features help photos appear more natural.

These features are all part of the native camera app and may not be accessible in third-party applications. It is important to remember that whatever photos you do take in the native camera application can also be brought into third-party editing apps for further processing.

Third-Party Photography Applications

Even though the functionality of native camera applications works for most photographers in most situations, they can sometimes leave you wanting more. Third-party applications provide different options, especially with technical features (more options to choose from when controlling the settings) and postprocessing features (adding filters or removing skin blemishes), **Figure 16-22**. While there are numerous third-party apps to choose from and experiment with, we will touch on a few of the most common.

Camera+ is regarded as one of the best third-party camera apps available for iOS. This app uses the phone's native camera to physically take the photos but gives the photographer more control over specific settings. Camera+ lets you adjust the exposure, ISO, white balance, focus lock, and image stabilization to a higher degree than the native camera app. It also allows you to track (follow) a subject, which is quite helpful when shooting moving subjects, such as at a sporting event.

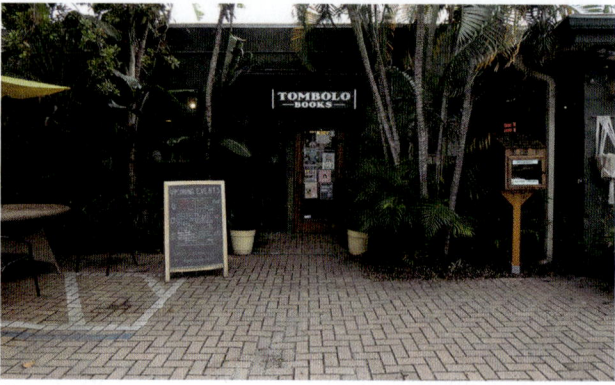

A

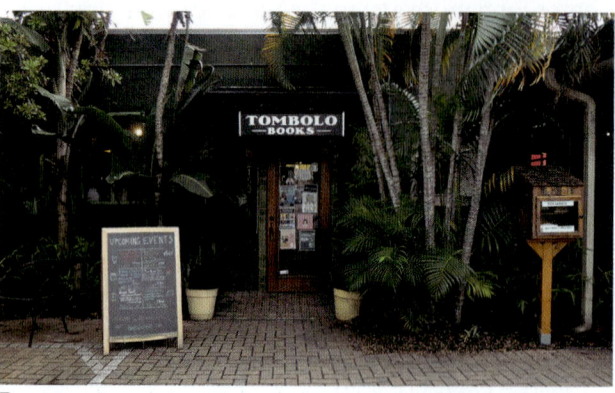

B

Goodheart-Willcox Publisher

Figure 16-22. A photo before and after editing. In the second picture you can see the following edits: cropping, increased exposure, increased shadows, and decreased brightness.

Adobe Photoshop Lightroom is available across mobile devices and computers. This app is mainly a postprocessing app that allows you to manipulate your photos after you have taken them. You can also take photos inside the app. In Lightroom, you can batch edit (edit multiple photos at once), edit RAW photos, add selective adjustments (alter only one part of an image and leave the rest untouched), and more.

ProCamera is another popular third-party app. Through ProCamera, photographers have full control over manual settings (ISO, exposure, file format, etc.). It also allows you to see *zebras*, which are highlight warning indicators that alert you if certain portions of an image are overexposed or blown out. Zebras make it easier to know when to make further adjustments.

As mentioned previously, these are not the only third-party apps available. A quick search for camera apps in your phone's app store will yield a plethora of options. Whether you want more control over your settings or to add unique and interesting effects to an image, there are hundreds of free and for-purchase options available to suit your needs.

Tips and Tricks for Shooting with a Phone

Shooting with a phone is slightly different from shooting with a digital camera. Although you still have the same basic functionality of a digital camera with your cell phone, there are some things you can do to help make your photos even better. One of the biggest tips is keeping your phone protected. If your phone has a case and a screen protector, it is more likely to survive any accidental falls that could potentially damage not only your camera, but your entire phone. Furthermore, it is important to remember that the design principles and elements of composition that apply to traditional photography apply to mobile photography as well. The biggest difference between the two is how you handle the camera, not how you compose a photograph.

Cleaning Lenses

In general, people tend to be more careless with their smartphone cameras than they are with DSLR cameras. Have you ever pulled your phone out of your back pocket or a bag and noticed it was smudged? How many times have you wiped off the front or back of your phone before taking pictures, only to drop it on accident? Being able to take good-quality photos largely comes from the cleanliness of your lens (or lenses). If there is dirt or residue from the oil on your hands on one of the camera lenses, your final photograph may look hazy or out of focus.

To get the best-quality photos possible, make sure your lenses are clean before taking a picture. If you need to clean your lenses, a microfiber cloth is the best option, **Figure 16-23**. These cloths are relatively inexpensive and can be found at most stores. Gently brush in circles on the lens until it appears clean to your eye, **Figure 16-24**. If you do not have a microfiber cloth available, you can use your shirt, depending on the material. Whatever you decide to use, it is important to ensure that it will not accidentally scratch your lens. It is possible

---

REAL-WORLD PHOTOGRAPHY

Photography Internships

A photography internship is a great way to gain experience while in high school or college. Most internships can be found by doing some online research or building connections with people in the photography community in your area. The following are some basic tips to help you potentially secure an internship:

- **Demonstrate employability.** Companies and businesses want to employ people who demonstrate positive work behaviors and personal qualities. This includes keeping a positive attitude when facing challenges, treating others with respect, meeting deadlines, dressing and acting in a professional manner, preparing for assignments, and listening to and implementing any feedback in order to improve as a photographer. It also includes being a mentor when needed. If you have more experience in something than a coworker or fellow photographer, an offer to assist is typically appreciated.
- **Understand how to work with others.** It is inevitable that you will not always get along with everyone, including the people you work with. Understanding conflict management and how to resolve a potential problem appropriately will go a long way in a work environment. When dealing with a potential conflict, it is important to stay levelheaded and communicate respectfully with everyone involved.
- **Be eager and willing to perform tasks.** An internship is an invaluable opportunity to learn a wide range of things from professionals. You may start off with small tasks, like gathering equipment or contacting clients to confirm appointments. However, if you prove you are capable of handling smaller tasks and are willing to take on more challenging tasks, you may end up assisting during photo shoots or working on assignments.

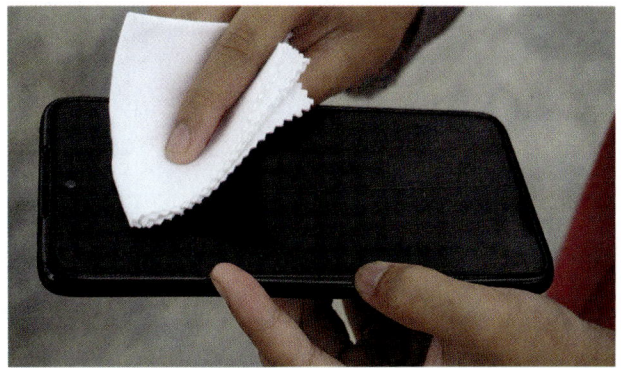

Rildik Syah/Shutterstock.com

Figure 16-23. A microfiber cloth is the best option for cleaning your lens since the cloth is soft and will not scratch the glass. It can also be used to clean the front of your phone.

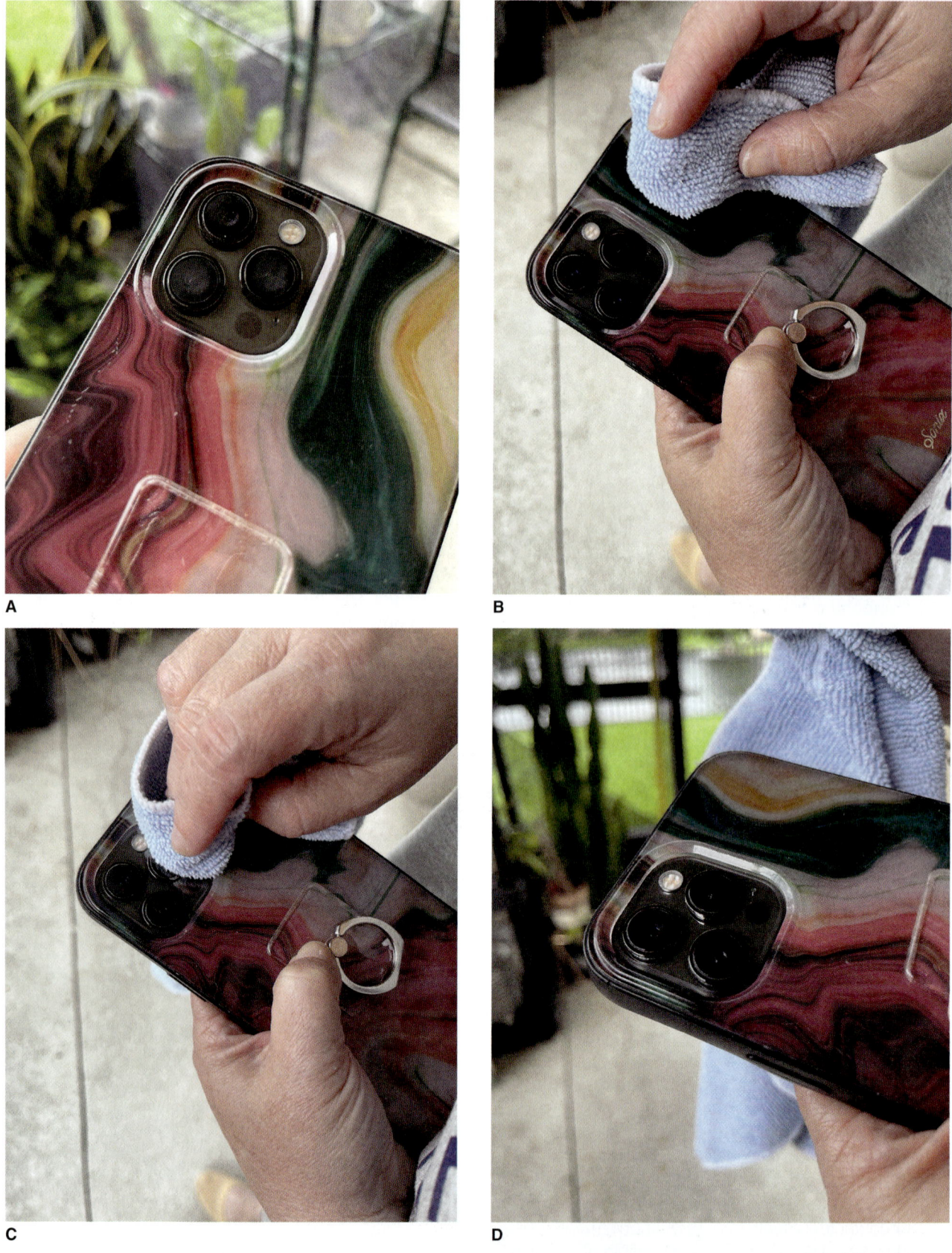

Goodheart-Willcox Publisher

Figure 16-24. How to properly clean a phone lens. A—A dirty lens. B—Holding the microfiber cloth properly is important. C—Gently clean the lens in a clockwise motion. Repeat the motion as many times as necessary to clean the lens. D—A clean, smudge-free lens.

to replace the lens of a smartphone, but it is often tedious and/or expensive.

Capturing Multiple Shots

One of the many advantages to taking digital photos is that you can (almost always) take as many photos as your phone or SD card can handle. This means that you do not have to wait for your photos to process or develop, which could take several hours or days. As soon as you take your photo, you can review it and decide to delete it or keep it. Having this ability allows you to improve your technique and gives you several potential shots to choose from.

The ability to take multiple shots is especially helpful in action photography when trying to capture moving people or objects. Most phones come with a Burst Mode setting that allows you to take several photos in a very short period of time, **Figure 16-25**. Taking photos in Burst Mode allows you to capture still shots of actions, such as people dancing or horses galloping, without missing a moment. In Burst Mode, you are also able to select individual images from the burst of photos and choose the best ones to keep.

Another way to capture multiple shots is through the Live Photos setting. Live Photos start recording 1.5 seconds before and after you press the button to take your photo. Similar to Burst Mode, this allows you to choose from a variety of images, **Figure 16-26**. You also have the option to use the Live Photo as a short video clip if desired. Simply locate the photo in your Photos app, select the Share icon in the lower left-hand corner, scroll down, and select Save as Video. It will then be added to your photo library as a video in addition to the original photo.

Avoiding Digital Zoom

While it may be tempting to rely on your phone's ability to zoom in, you should try to avoid digital zoom when possible. As you learned in Chapter 6, *Lenses*, **digital zoom** is a digital camera feature that electronically crops the image to smaller dimensions, making it appear larger but causing the image quality to deteriorate. This can be detrimental to your final picture because it reduces the number of pixels your image has, making it look blurry, **Figure 16-27**. *Optical zoom*, however, is a physical camera feature that moves the lens elements to change the angle of view, and thus, image size, without affecting the quality of the image. This helps retain your image integrity while making your subject larger, **Figure 16-28**.

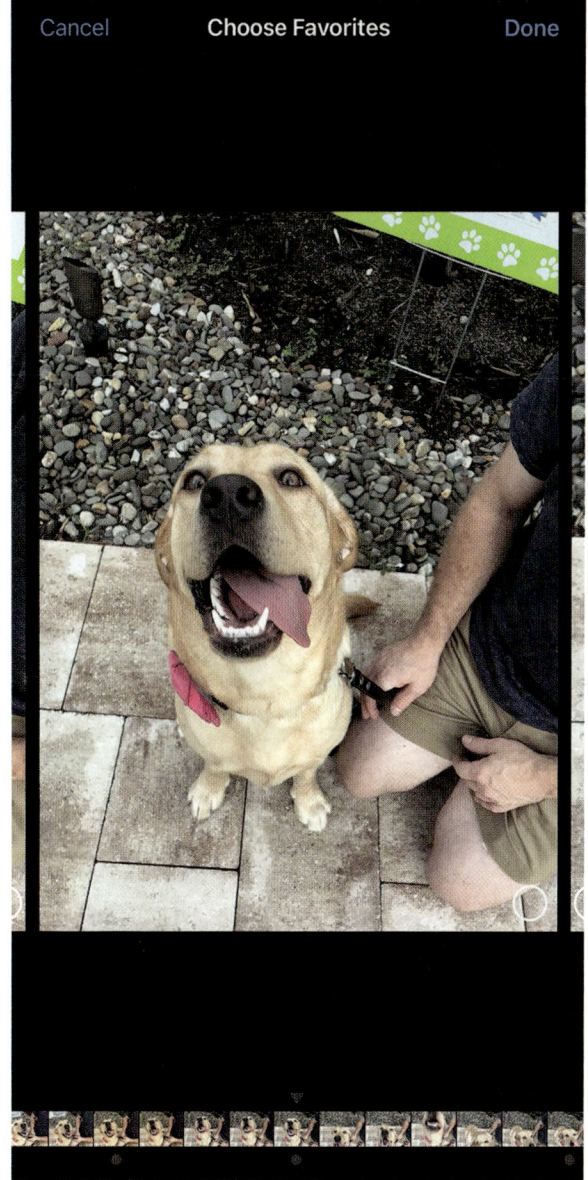

Goodheart-Willcox Publisher

Figure 16-25. Burst Mode provides several photos to choose from.

Rather than zoom in on your subject to make them appear larger in the frame, it is better to step closer to the subject if it is possible and safe to do so. Small adjustments with digital zoom will not alter the integrity of your image, but large adjustments, such as zooming in on a subject across a room, will make your picture blurry and out of focus.

Keeping the Camera Steady

One thing that many mobile photographers accidentally overlook is how to take a photo while keeping their camera stable. When shooting with

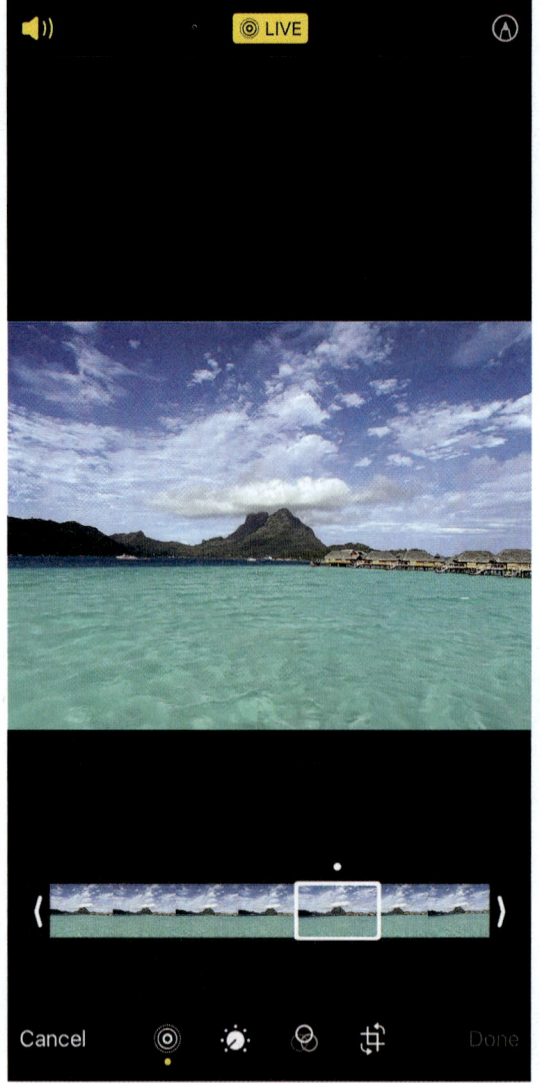

Figure 16-26. Live Photos allows you to choose a still frame that is different from the original image.

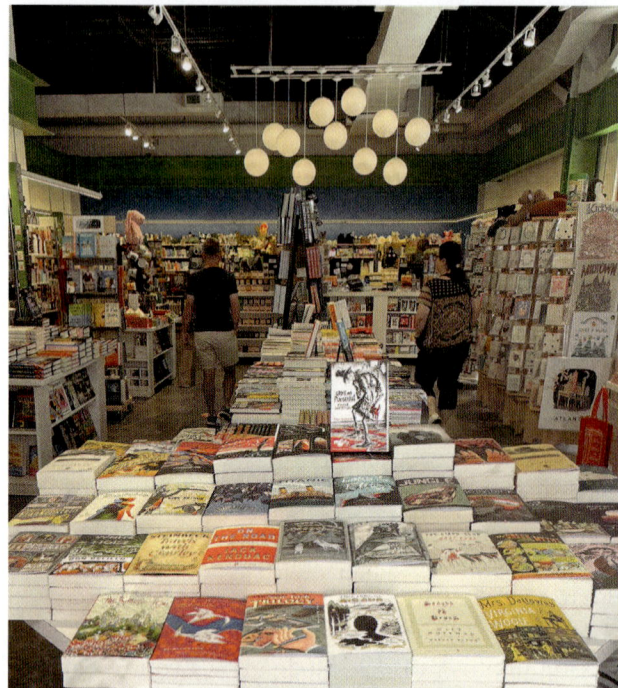

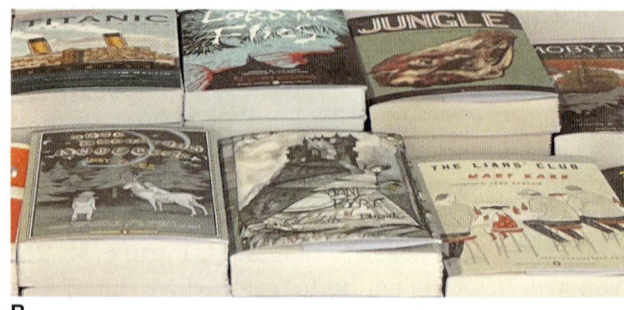

Figure 16-27. Digital zoom can make your pictures look blurry or pixelated. A—The original photo. B—The same photo, but zoomed in.

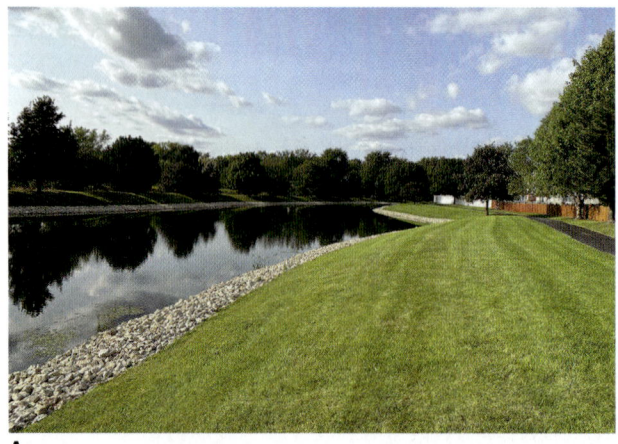

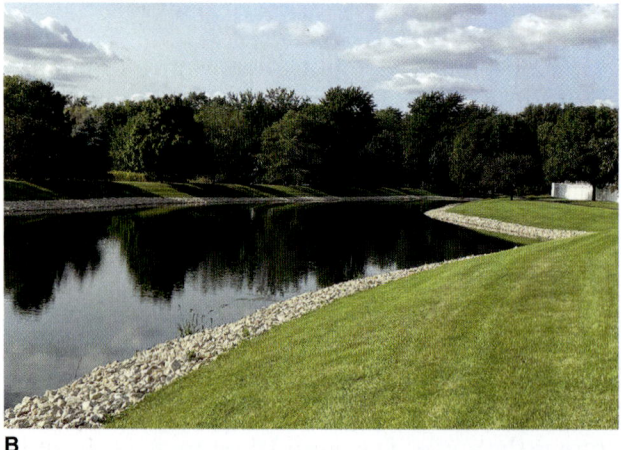

Figure 16-28. Optical zoom allows you to enlarge a subject without it becoming blurry. A—The original photo. B—The same photo zoomed in with optical zoom.

your phone, there may be situations in which you have a stabilizer available and situations in which you do not have a stabilizer available. Being able to operate your camera and take photos successfully in both situations will help you in the long run.

Using Stabilizers

There are many stabilizers for phones on the market. Tripods are the most common, but gimbals are also rising in popularity, **Figure 16-29**. There are also options for nearly every budget. The important thing is to find an option that works for you. Having a device that can help keep your phone steady when shooting is extremely helpful, especially if you are shooting an event or taking long-exposure photographs.

Hand-Holding

There will be times when you do not have access to a stabilizer. If that is the case, there are a few tips that will help you use your body as the stabilizer:
- Tuck your arms into your sides and hold out your phone. This allows you more control over your movement and stabilization of your phone, **Figure 16-30**.
- Lean against a straight and stable surface, such as a wall or a tree, **Figure 16-31**.
- Hold your phone on top of the hand that you are not shooting with, **Figure 16-32**.
- If you are sitting, balance your elbows on your thighs, **Figure 16-33**.

Finding what works best for you will take some trial and error, and how you handle stabilizing yourself may vary from situation to situation. Remember that you should never put yourself in an unsafe situation for a photo.

Taking Advantage of Flexibility

One of the biggest advantages of mobile photography is the flexibility you have when it comes to the physical camera itself. Smartphones are usually much smaller than professional digital cameras. As such, they tend to weigh less. Having to manipulate and control heavy equipment can make you tire

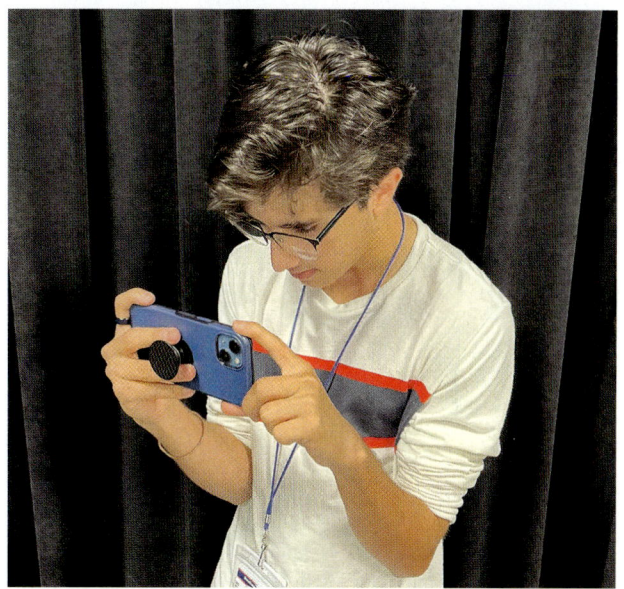

Goodheart-Willcox Publisher

Figure 16-30. Tucking your arms into your sides will help you stabilize your phone.

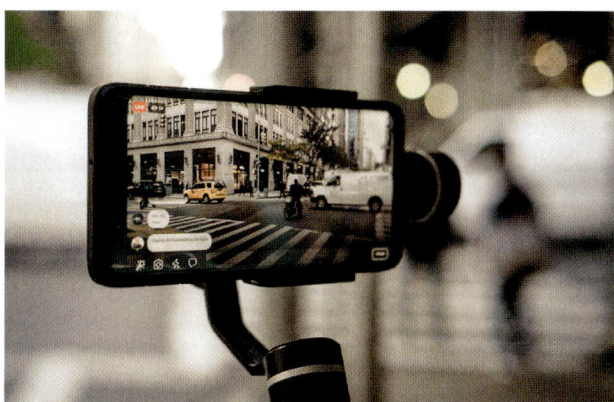

July Prokopiv/Shutterstock.com

Figure 16-29. Phone gimbals are growing increasingly popular for their ease of use and portability.

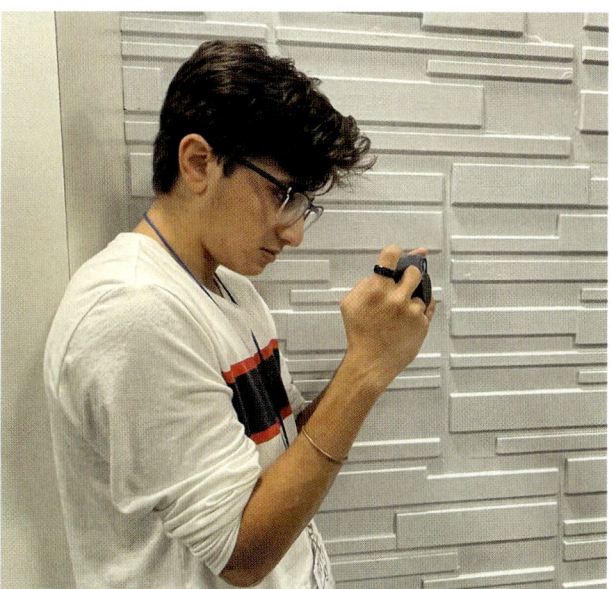

Goodheart-Willcox Publisher

Figure 16-31. Leaning against a wall will help you hold your camera steady.

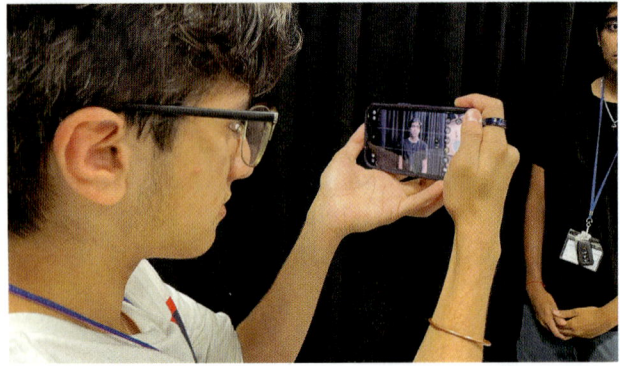

Goodheart-Willcox Publisher

Figure 16-32. You can brace your phone on top of the hand you are not shooting with for stability.

faster and make it more difficult to shoot. Using a smartphone can also make it easier to obtain specific shots you might not otherwise get with a larger camera and additional equipment.

Furthermore, because a smartphone is so portable and most people use it for reasons beyond a camera, it is incredibly convenient. Having a professional-level camera in your pocket or bag makes it much easier to capture spur-of-the-moment shots. You also do not need to worry about carrying extra equipment around. However, if you want to make the most of shooting with your phone, it is a good idea to carry a stabilizer and a portable power bank, **Figure 16-34**.

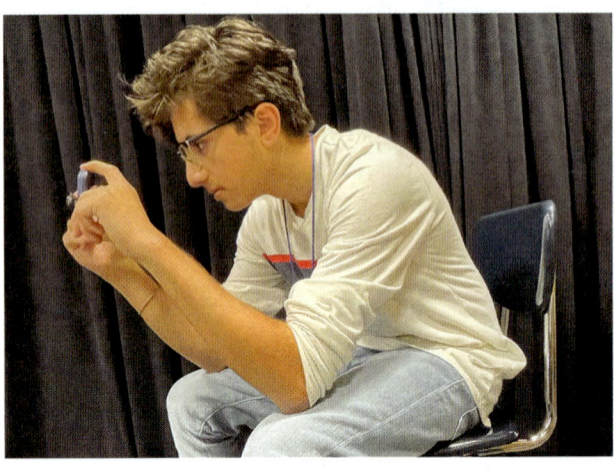

Goodheart-Willcox Publisher

Figure 16-33. Balance your elbows on your thighs to keep the camera steady when sitting.

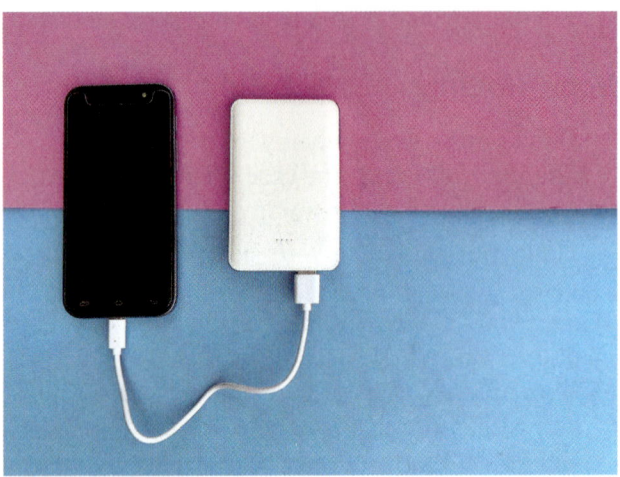

Nogwish/Shutterstock.com

Figure 16-34. A portable power bank can extend your shooting time.

Real-World Photography

Shooting for Social Media

Social media is a great way to show off your body of work and skills as a photographer. It also lends itself to entrepreneurship. If you hope to run your own photography business and build a client base, social media can help you spread awareness and advertise your services.

In addition, nearly every brand utilizes social media to help promote their company. Some businesses are even run exclusively on platforms like TikTok and Instagram. If you are employed by a company as a photographer and must take photos for their social media pages, there are a few things to keep in mind:

- **Take care of your lens(es).** Having lenses in peak condition on your smartphone is imperative when taking pictures. If they are scratched or smudged, you will lose quality in your images. Most people tend to wipe their lenses on their shirt or jacket when shooting, but to properly take care of your lenses, you must use a glass wipe or microfiber cloth. This is important because phone lenses are difficult and expensive to replace if they are permanently damaged.

- **Understand your parameters.** Different platforms use different aspect ratios for their photos. It is important to know which platform you are shooting for so you can ensure that your photos are sized appropriately. Furthermore, social media platforms occasionally change their image sizes, so if you are ever in doubt, a quick online search can help you verify the dimensions. For example, most Instagram images have a width of 1080 pixels. If you upload a photo that is larger than 1080 pixels, Instagram will resize it, which can cause the photo to lose details and quality.
- **Work with interesting angles.** Fun angles are eye-catching and can make a social media user stop scrolling to look at your post. You should always take some photos that use traditional composition so you have a backup, but do not be afraid to experiment. Certain angles can help give you the illusion of height and/or depth, which could help generate more attention.
- **Use lighting to your advantage.** Just like angles, certain lighting can help your posts stand out. You can utilize natural light, or you can set up lights as discussed in previous chapters. Regardless of what style you use, you need to make sure your subject is clear. If people cannot tell what your product or subject is, your photo is essentially useless. Additionally, keeping a consistent visual look among your photos will give your brand a cohesive look.
- **Use a stabilizer.** Whether you use a tripod or other type of phone mount, being able to keep your phone still and in the same position is a great help when taking photos. This will help you avoid camera shake, which will prevent any accidental motion blur. You can find plenty of inexpensive mounts available online, some of which are tailored to your specific device. If you do not have access to a tripod or phone mount, you can always use your body as a stabilizer.
- **Avoid digital zoom.** As mentioned in this chapter, you should avoid using digital zoom. If you need to make your subject appear larger in your photo, physically move forward rather than rely on the zoom. If you use the phone to zoom in, you risk having a pixelated or blurry photo, which looks unprofessional.

Portfolio Assignment

Smartphone Photography

For this assignment, you will practice taking photos on your smartphone and making necessary adjustments. Complete the following steps:

1. Find a partner to be your subject, and vice versa.
2. Choose three different locations that meet the following criteria: an indoor location (such as a classroom or store), an outdoor location that is in the sun (such as a park or outside someone's house), and an outdoor location that is in the shade (such as under an awning or a shady tree).
3. At the indoor location, take a photo of your subject without making any adjustments to your smartphone camera's settings.
4. At the indoor location, take four photos of your subject while adjusting the settings on your smartphone camera to achieve the best possible photo. You can alter the exposure, the focus, and/or the shutter speed.
5. Repeat Steps 3 and 4 for the sunny outdoor location and the shady outdoor location. You should have a total of 15 photos when finished.

Once you have all 15 photos, choose the best one from each location to add to your portfolio, noting the adjustments you made to each one (if any).

Chapter 16 Review

Summary

- When it comes to base knowledge, traditional photography and mobile photography are virtually indistinguishable. If you know how to take photos on a DSLR camera, you can take that knowledge and apply it to your phone camera.
- Mobile photography is great for people who are frequently on the go and for people who do not want to haul around a lot of equipment.
- In order to achieve the best photos possible, you must understand the settings in your phone's native camera app.
- One of the first things you should do before using a phone camera is enable the grid to show the rule of thirds. The main benefit of enabling this setting is to help you with composition.
- Preserve Settings allows you to save any changes you made to your camera when you took pictures last. There are several different features and dozens of combinations that allow for a highly customizable shooting experience.
- There are a handful of different formats you can take your photos in on a smartphone. The default file format of any iPhone photo is HEIC.
- A high dynamic range (HDR) image appears richly colored, highly contrasted, and very saturated. Both Android and iPhone cameras can take HDR images.
- Setting and locking the focus on your phone camera allows you to decide what stands out to the viewer. Determining what to clearly focus on in the photo allows the photographer to control what should be emphasized and, thus, what the viewer looks at first.
- Your viewer's attention will naturally gravitate toward areas that are lighter and brighter than other areas.
- On most phones, the flash is set to automatically go off when it detects that you are taking photos that may be underexposed.
- Aspect ratio is the relationship between the width and height of an image, and it is important for the proportions of your image.
- The advantage of third-party apps often lies in their functionality while taking a photo and, depending on the application, postprocessing.
- The functionality of the native camera app will vary on each phone, but there are some commonalities that they share.
- Third-party applications provide different options, especially with technical and postprocessing features. Some of the most commonly used apps are Camera+, Adobe Photoshop Lightroom, and ProCamera.
- To get the best-quality photos possible, make sure your lenses are clean before taking a picture. If you need to clean your lenses, a microfiber cloth is the best option.
- The ability to take multiple shots is especially helpful in action photography when trying to capture moving people or objects. Most phones come with a Burst Mode setting that allows you to take several photos in a very short period of time.
- Rather than zoom in on your subject to make them appear larger in the frame, it is better to step closer to the subject if it is possible and safe to do so.
- It is important to be able to keep the camera steady in all situations. You can use a stabilizer or use proper hand-holding techniques.
- One of the biggest advantages of mobile photography is the flexibility you have when it comes to the physical camera itself. Their size and portability make it easy to obtain specific shots at a moment's notice.

Review Questions

Answer the following questions using the information provided in this chapter.

Know and Understand

1. *True or False?* Traditional photography is photography taken with a camera phone or other mobile device, such as a tablet.
2. One of the first things you should do before using a phone camera is enable _____ to show the rule of thirds.
   A. Preserve Settings
   B. HDR
   C. flash
   D. the grid
3. Which of the following Preserve Settings options preserves a central area of focus?
   A. Camera Mode
   B. Portrait Zoom
   C. Creative Controls
   D. Exposure Adjustment
4. Which of the following formats supports a wider range of colors than most other formats?
   A. JPEG
   B. PNG
   C. HEIC
   D. AVIF
5. *True or False?* Both Android and iPhone cameras can take HDR images.
6. _____ allows the photographer to decide what stands out to the viewer.
   A. Setting and locking the focus
   B. Enabling the flash
   C. Setting and locking the exposure
   D. Changing the aspect ratio
7. *True or False?* Your viewer's attention will naturally gravitate to the lighter and brighter areas of your photo.
8. Many newer smartphones have a specific setting called _____ that takes well-lit photos without flash by using a longer exposure.
   A. Portrait Mode
   B. Live Photos
   C. Night Mode
   D. Burst Mode
9. Which of the following is the aspect ratio for widescreen?
   A. 1:1
   B. 4:3
   C. 5:7
   D. 16:9
10. *True or False?* Third-party applications often provide the same postprocessing options as the native camera app.
11. _____ uses the phone's native camera to physically take the photos but gives the photographer more control over specific settings.
    A. Adobe Photoshop Lightroom
    B. Camera+
    C. ProCamera
    D. The native camera app
12. *True or False?* Being able to take good-quality photos largely comes from the cleanliness of your lens (or lenses).
13. Which of the following is a setting that allows you to take several photos in a very short period of time?
    A. Preserve Settings
    B. Burst Mode
    C. Optical zoom
    D. Camera Mode

14. *True or False?* Using optical zoom can be detrimental to your final picture because it reduces the number of pixels your image has, making it look blurry.
15. Which of the following is *not* a method of keeping the camera steady?
    A. Using Preserve Settings
    B. Using a tripod
    C. Using proper hand-holding techniques
    D. Using a gimbal
16. *True or False?* One of the biggest advantages of mobile photography is the flexibility you have when it comes to the physical camera itself.

Apply and Analyze

1. When did mobile photography become popular?
2. What is a high dynamic range (HDR) image?
3. Explain how to set and lock the focus on a smartphone.
4. Describe two of the four common features included with the iPhone® 13 native camera.
5. List three of the four tips for using your body as a stabilizer.

Critical Thinking

1. Do you think smartphone cameras will ever render digital cameras obsolete? Why or why not?
2. Imagine you are taking pictures at the beach with some friends. The day starts out as very overcast, but after about 30 minutes of shooting, the bright sun comes out. How would you handle taking photos of your friends in each situation?

Suggested Activities

1. In a group of three, research the differences in specifications between a smartphone camera and a DSLR camera of your choice (such as a Canon EOS 80D). When looking at the specifications for each camera, pay special attention to the available lenses, shutter speeds, battery life, and storage capacity. Deliver an informal presentation to the class about your findings.
2. Create a digital checklist of items you might need to remember when taking photos with your smartphone. The checklist should be easy to access from your phone so you can reference it at any time. It should also be organized based on topic. Potential items to include are aspect ratio reminders, what format to choose for your photos, and what your lenses are capable of.
3. Mobile photography has been around since 1999, when the first phone camera came on the market. Research the history and evolution of mobile photography and create a short presentation to deliver to the class.

Communicating about Photography

1. **Speaking.** Choose two major smartphone companies and debate the topic of which produces the better products. Divide into two groups. Each group should gather information in support of either the *pro* argument (Company A is better) or the *con* argument (Company B is better). You will want to do further research to find expert opinions, costs associated with the smartphone camera models, and other relevant information.

2. **Speaking and Listening.** In small groups, discuss with your classmates—in basic, everyday language—your knowledge of the different types of mobile camera controls. Take notes on the observations expressed. Then review the points discussed, factoring in your new knowledge of mobile camera controls. Develop a summary of what you have learned about mobile camera controls and present it to the class. Use the terms that you have learned in this chapter.

Section 4 Project

Experimenting with Types of Photography

The goal of this project is to create photos that fit into the different categories of photography you learned about in Section 4. This project has three parts.

Part 1

For this part, you will need a digital camera and your smartphone (if you only have access to your smartphone, that is fine). Take five photos that utilize the techniques and parameters of each of the following types of photography. When shooting these images, keep the principles of design and composition in mind:

- Action and event photography
- Outdoor photography
- Travel photography (there is no need to actually travel for these photos, but you do need to shoot in a different location, such as a nature preserve or the beach)
- Portrait and studio photography (you can shoot in your classroom and set up whatever lighting instruments are available, with your instructor's permission)
- Mobile photography (while you may take your other photos with your phone, these two photos need to showcase what you can do with your phone)

When you have finished shooting, you should have 25 photos total. Do not edit these photos. You will be submitting only the best two from each category for this project.

Part 2

Answer the following questions about the photos you took for this section project:
1. For each photo you chose, explain how you achieved your photo and why it is a good example of that type of photography. Include your camera settings, the angles you chose, and any specific techniques you used.
2. Which type of photography was the most challenging for you to shoot? Why?
3. Which type of photography was the easiest for you to shoot? Why?

Part 3

Choose a classmate to partner with and swap photos. Offer constructive feedback on their photos. Constructive feedback should include both positive feedback (around two to four sentences) and something that they could improve upon (around two to four sentences) for each photo. For example, if the photo you are critiquing is well lit but not properly composed, your feedback might look something like this: *The lighting you used in your photograph is great and highlights your subject well. It also exemplifies the happy tone you were going for with your photo. Something you can improve upon is your framing. Your subject is in the center of your frame, and I think you could frame a more interesting photo by moving your subject to the left or adjusting the angle of the camera.*

When your partner has done the same for you, reflect on the feedback you received. Choose one photo from each category and explain what you would do differently based on the feedback. When you are finished, add your 10 images to your portfolio and submit them to your instructor. Be sure to include the constructive feedback you received, as well as what you would do differently.

Section 5
Postprocessing

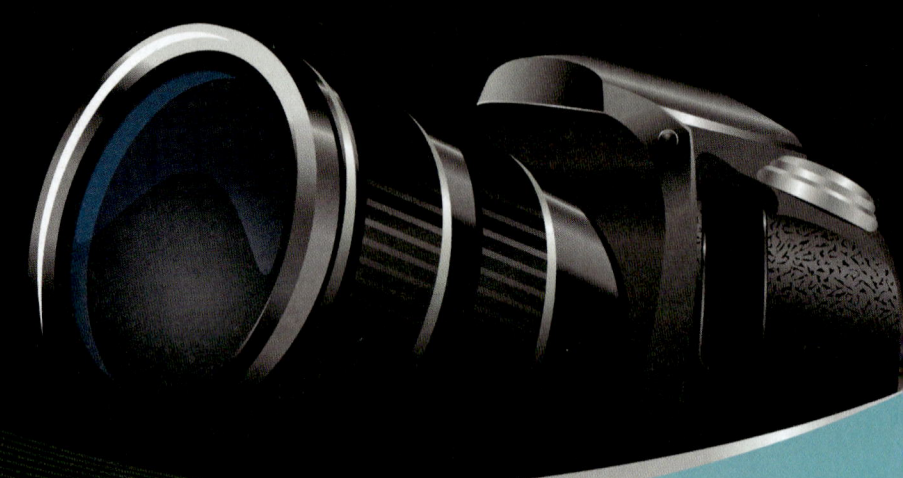

Chapter 17 Importing Images
Chapter 18 Digital Postprocessing Basics
Chapter 19 Advanced Digital Postprocessing Techniques
Chapter 20 The Finishing Touches
Chapter 21 Mobile Postprocessing

In Section 4, you learned about different types of photography and how to tailor your approach as a photographer to specific assignments. Section 5 will teach you about postprocessing, including how to import, edit, and display your final photographs.

Chapter 17 covers how to import images from a digital camera or smartphone to your computer or other storage method. This chapter will also review how important copyright laws are to the postprocessing process.

Chapter 18 will focus on digital postprocessing basics and will show you how to make beginner manipulations to your images. You will also learn the differences between processing and manipulation.

Chapter 19 discusses advanced postprocessing techniques. This chapter explores the editing process in depth and provides step-by-step instructions on how to make common edits in Adobe Photoshop.

Chapter 20 reviews the finishing touches of the photographic journey. You will learn how to choose the best printer settings for your image and how to display your photographs so they look as appealing and professional as possible.

Finally, Chapter 21 will teach you how to use your phone to edit photos on the go. This chapter includes how to use the native camera app on your phone to make basic edits, as well as how to post to various social media platforms.

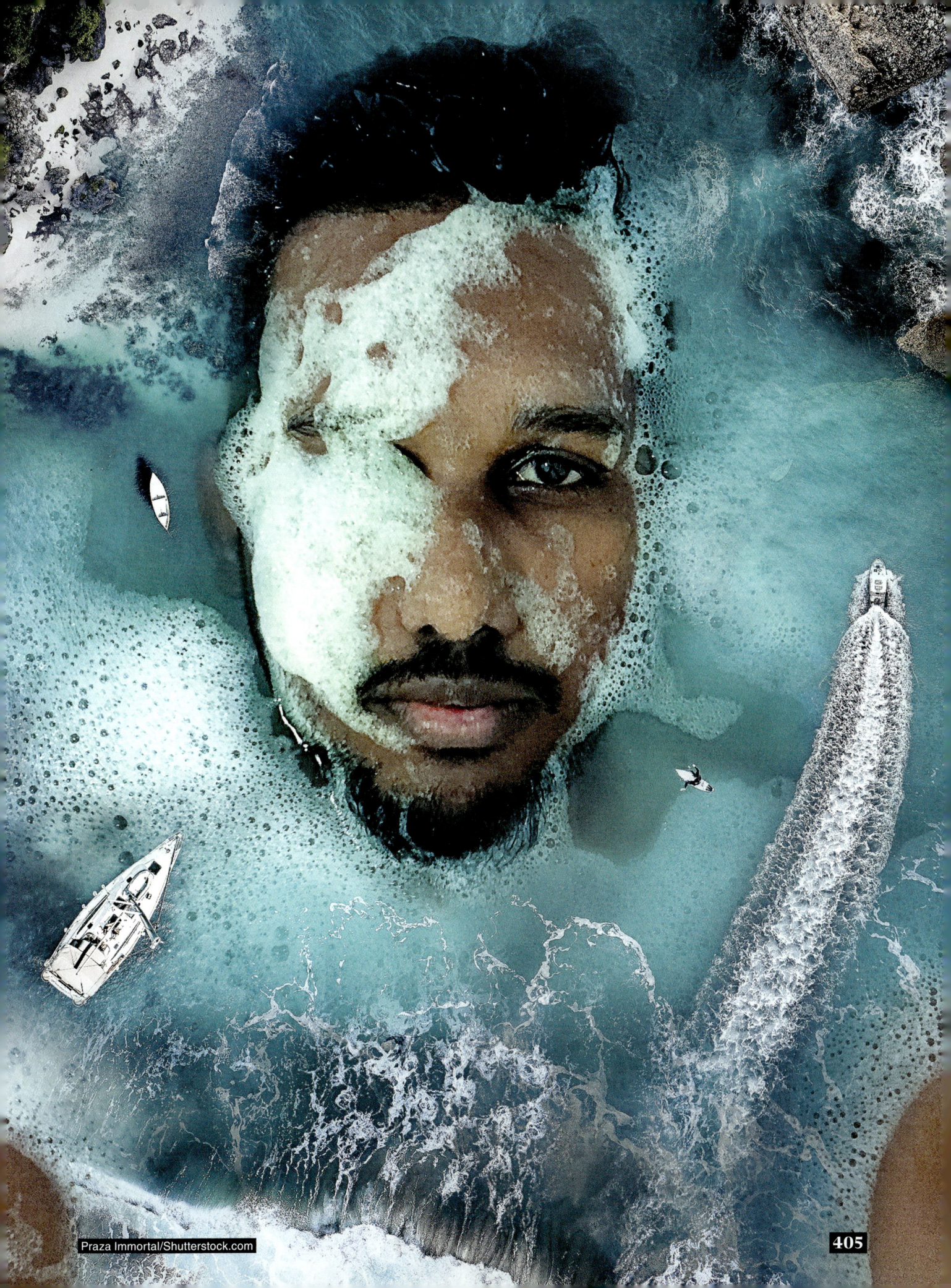

Chapter 17
Importing Images

Learning Objectives

After completing this chapter, you will be able to:
- Describe the ways files are imported from a digital camera.
- Explain how to import digital images using a scanner.
- Recall different methods of downloading digital images from the internet.
- Discuss and apply copyright laws.
- Identify the various types of online image sources.
- Understand the importance of developing a method of image management.

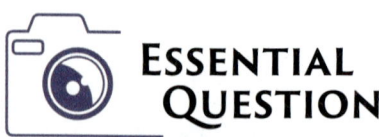

Essential Question

Why is it important to understand different types of importing and file sharing with your digital files?

Technical Terms

archival-quality disc
attribution
browsing
card reader
cataloging program
copyright
Creative Commons license
culling
database program
derivative work
digital resolution
download
EXIF (Exchangeable Image File Format)
fair use
image management
importing
infringement
keyword
metadata
online photofinishing site
optical resolution
photo sharing site
public domain
rights-managed image
royalty
royalty-free image
scanner
thumbnails
upload
watermarking

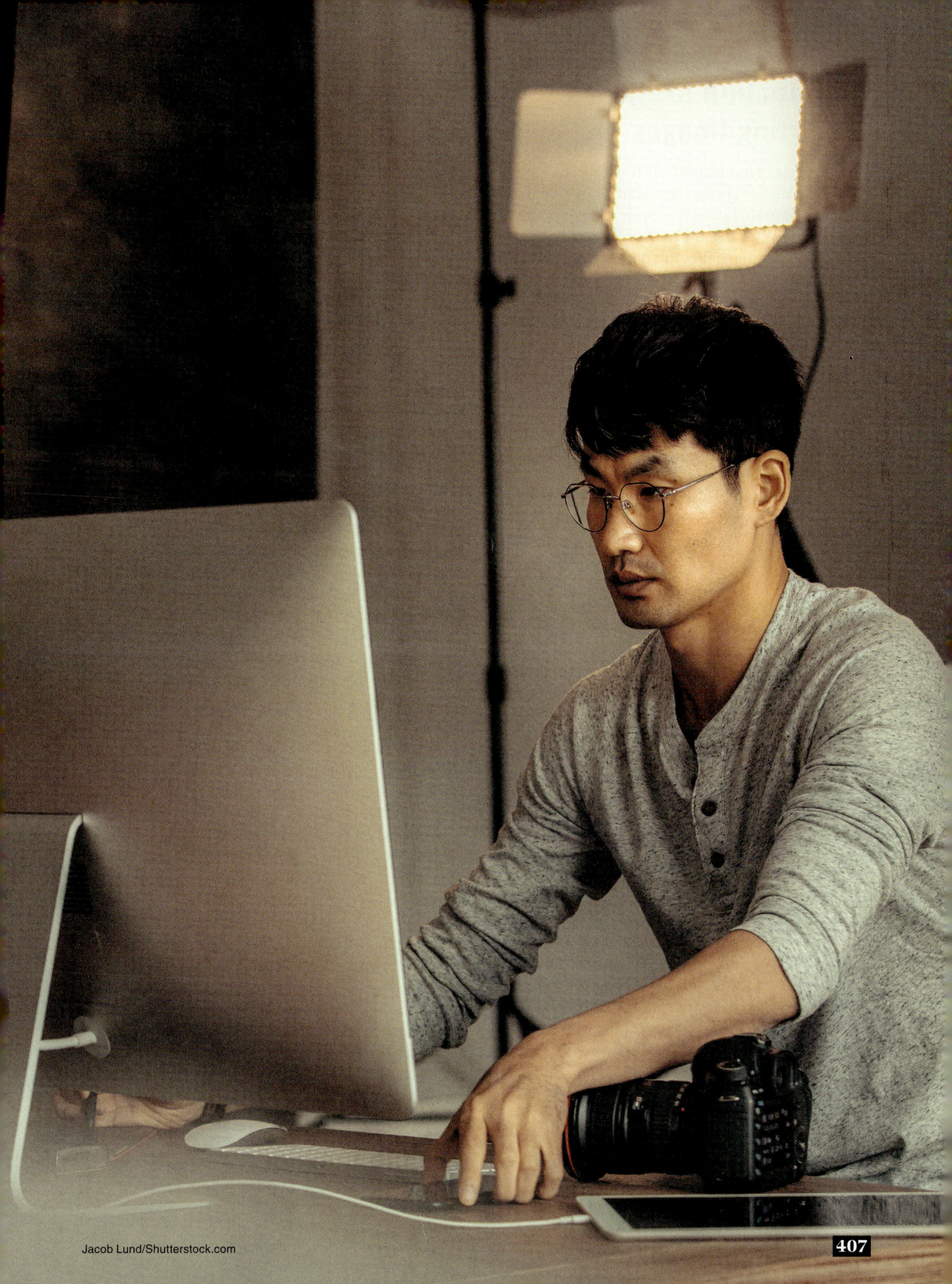

Introduction to Importing Images

After capturing images with your camera, you must take one or more additional steps to convert them to a form that can be used for display or shared with others. With a digital camera, you might need to transfer the image files to another device for processing and printing or for sharing on social media. This chapter concentrates on working with digital images and the different methods of postprocessing.

Importing Methods from a Camera

Step 1 of the postprocessing process is taking the files from your storage medium, such as a memory card or cloud-based storage, and importing them to the image editing software of your choice. **Importing**, also known as *pulling*, is the process of transferring a file from one program to another. Importing files from a digital camera typically involves sending or taking the files to a commercial processor, downloading them to a computer for processing and subsequent printing, copying to a portable storage device, or printing directly from a memory card. From a smartphone or a Wi-Fi-capable camera, images can be sent electronically directly to a printer or cloud-based storage system.

Commercial Processing

Commercial processors are most commonly used to produce prints. A major factor in the tremendous growth of digital camera use among consumers was the introduction of digital file processing by mass-market retailers. Customers can drop off a memory card or upload files online or through the retailer's smartphone app and then pick up finished prints in less than an hour. To **upload** images is to send image files from a digital device to another device or computer system via the internet. Unlike the all-or-nothing approach of film developing, customers can choose which files they want to print. It is also possible to do this with images taken on a smartphone.

Many retail photofinishing locations offer kiosks that provide quick and relatively inexpensive printing and enlargement of photos, **Figure 17-1**. The

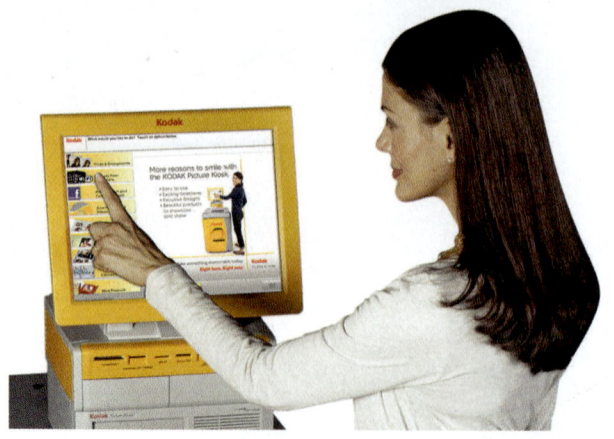

©2015 Kodak Alaris.TM: licensed from Eastman Kodak: Kodak and Kodak trade dress.

Figure 17-1. Picture kiosks are available at many photofinishing locations.

machines typically accept originals in print, negative, slide, or digital form, including images from camera phones, tablets, and social media platforms. They also offer tools for cropping and editing images. In addition to prints, the kiosks can produce photo posters, calendars, and similar products. Image files can typically be assembled and burned to a disc if desired.

Online photofinishing sites are websites that offer low-cost printing from uploaded digital files. The prints from those files are returned by mail. Common ways to upload images to these sites include from a computer, digital camera, smartphone, or tablet. Images can also be forwarded from social media platforms such as Facebook and Instagram. Large collections of images for printing can be physically sent on a DVD or a USB drive if desired.

Photo sharing sites are websites that allow people to post albums of pictures for public or private viewing, such as Flickr or Pixieset, **Figure 17-2**. To protect against unauthorized use of photos, the photographer can restrict access to the album by requiring a password. Physical prints can often be ordered for delivery by mail through these sites as well.

Professional photographers have traditionally used specialized photo processors, usually referred to as *labs*. Wedding photographers use labs to produce packages for their clients, and fine art photographers use them for individual or limited-edition prints. Advanced amateurs frequently send files to labs to obtain high-quality prints in sizes larger than they can produce on their own equipment.

KIKI MAC PHOTOGRAPHY

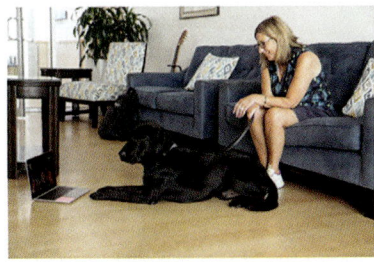
PUPPY RAISER DAY JULY 2022
JULY 23RD, 2022

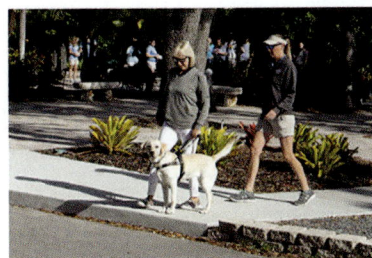
PUPPY RAISER DAY APRIL 2022
APRIL 23RD, 2022

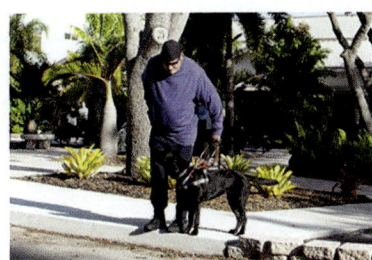
PUPPY RAISER DAY MARCH 2022
MARCH 26TH, 2022

Christy Clark

Figure 17-2. Online photo sharing sites are popular for displaying albums of photographs that can be viewed publicly or privately.

Downloading to a Computer

Photographers who want greater control of their prints typically do their own processing and printing. They **download** the images (transfer image files from the original source, such as a camera or memory card, to a computer for storage and processing), perform desired adjustments using image editing software such as Adobe Photoshop or Lightroom, and then make prints of the selected images on their own printer.

To download images, a digital camera can be connected directly to one of the computer's USB ports with a special cable. A more convenient method is the use of a **card reader**, which is a device used to transfer the contents of a memory card to a computer. See **Figure 17-3**. Card readers are relatively inexpensive and use the computer's power to operate. Many newer computers and printers have built-in card readers.

Travelers or photographers on lengthy location assignments can download memory cards to a laptop, a portable hard drive, a USB drive, or cloud-based storage, and then format the cards for reuse. At the end of the trip or assignment, the photographer transfers the stored files to a computer for processing.

> ### 📱 REAL-WORLD PHOTOGRAPHY
> **Adobe Lightroom vs. Adobe Photoshop**
> Adobe Lightroom and Adobe Photoshop are two image editing programs that many photographers use. They often work hand in hand to help you process your photos, but each program is best suited for specific needs.
> Adobe Lightroom is a one-stop shop for most photo processing needs. It is designed to help your photography workflow and assists with everything from importing photos, tagging, flagging, basic editing (light, color, perspective, sharpen, and more), and exporting photos. Lightroom uses nondestructive editing, meaning you can edit a photo without removing or replacing the original data.
> Adobe Photoshop gives the photographer more control over their photo, especially regarding image manipulation, creation, and enhancement. You can retouch photos in Photoshop as well as create incredible images through processes like compositing. Photoshop is also great for graphic designers and illustrators because it works conjointly with other Adobe products (such as Illustrator and InDesign) for a seamless experience.

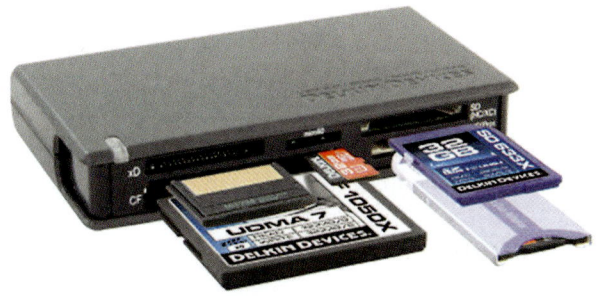
Delkin Devices

Figure 17-3. A card reader allows a photographer to download images from memory cards. This reader can be used with most types of available memory cards.

Even though Lightroom and Photoshop each have their own features, they work well together. For example, you can make basic corrections to the exposure in two different images in Lightroom and then combine them in Photoshop for a composite image. You will ultimately need to decide which program is best for your project. Postprocessing techniques are covered in more depth in Chapter 18, *Digital Postprocessing Basics*, and Chapter 19, *Advanced Digital Postprocessing Techniques*.

Wireless Transfer

Camera phone users can upload pictures electronically to their computer or printer, a social media platform, or another cell phone. With wireless networking technology, such as Wi-Fi, photos can be transferred directly from a specially equipped digital camera, **Figure 17-4**, to a computer or printer located as far as 150′ away. You can also use AirDrop® on an iPhone® or Nearby Share on Android devices to easily transfer files between devices.

Cloud-Based Storage System

Another option for transferring files is through cloud-based storage systems like Google Drive, Microsoft OneDrive, or Apple® iCloud®, **Figure 17-5**. If you shoot your images with a digital camera, you can transfer the files from your memory card to cloud-based storage by connecting it to the computer and dragging and dropping your files into a folder. Alternatively, you can upload photos directly from your phone or tablet if you have the app for that specific cloud-based storage on your device.

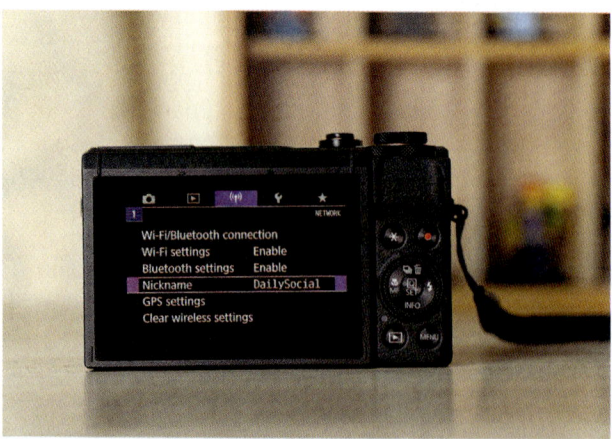

Lukmanazis/Shutterstock.com

Figure 17-4. This compact digital camera has Wi-Fi capability built in.

Left: Perfect Vectors/Shutterstock.com
Middle: Artseen/Shutterstock.com
Right: Yustin Krismada/Shutterstock.com

Figure 17-5. You can easily store and access photos online through cloud-based storage systems such as Apple® iCloud®, Google Drive, and Microsoft OneDrive.

Other Importing Methods

In addition to transfers from a digital camera or cell phone, there are other methods of acquiring digital images. These include using a scanner to create digital files from original prints or physical copies and downloading digital images from the internet.

Scanners

Scanners are mechanical/optical devices used to convert original prints or physical copies into digital form. While there are many different types of scanners, the most commonly used is the flatbed scanner.

Flatbed Scanners

The most common scanner type is the flatbed, **Figure 17-6**, which can be used to scan artwork, printed material, some three-dimensional objects, and photos.

Multipurpose devices that incorporate flatbed scanner, photocopier, and printer functions are available. The advantages of these all-in-one units are convenience and saving of desktop space.

Most flatbed scanners for home or small business use can handle originals up to 8.5″ × 11″. Some flatbed scanners can scan an area as large as 8.5″ × 14″. More expensive units intended for professional use accept originals up to 12″ × 17″ in size.

Resolution

The quality of an image produced by a scanner, like the output of a digital camera, is directly related to resolution. The higher the resolution, the more detailed the image is. Resolution is measured in

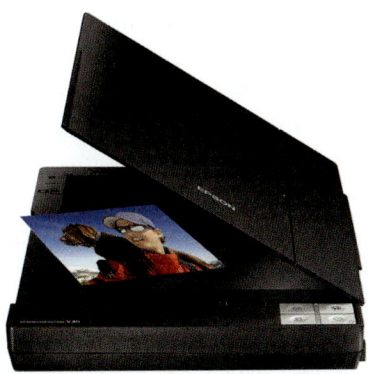

Epson Perfection V 30 Scanner

Figure 17-6. An inexpensive flatbed scanner is a popular tool for capturing digital images.

pixels per inch (ppi) and is usually stated in a form such as 1200 × 2400. The first number is the number of sensors (pixels) per inch on the scanner's trilinear array. The second is the number of distinct "steps" per inch that are made as the array moves down the length of the scanned material. See **Figure 17-7**. Typically, only the first number is used to describe a scanner's resolution (for example, a 1200 ppi scanner).

Scanner resolution may be optical or digital, and it is important to distinguish between the two. ***Optical resolution*** is the actual pixels per inch resolution—600, 1200, 2400, and so on. ***Digital resolution*** is a means of expressing scanner resolution used by some manufacturers for advertising purposes. It is achieved by using software to insert additional pixels around those actually scanned. The digital resolution figure is misleading because the resulting scan is actually lower in quality than one scanned at the comparable optical resolution.

Downloading Online Images

Many photographers set up a website to display their work or post their images in online galleries, **Figure 17-8**. For a beginning photographer, the internet provides opportunities to see a wide variety of work by others as part of the learning process.

One negative aspect of posting on the internet is the relative ease of downloading images, which can result in copyright law violations. An example is a person who downloads several images from galleries or web pages and uses them to develop a line of greeting cards for sale in local gift shops. Unless the person received permission to use the images, they have violated the owners' copyrights and have, in effect, committed theft. A method used by some photographers to help protect digital images is watermarking, **Figure 17-9**. ***Watermarking*** is an electronic method of embedding copyright information and the owner's identity in the digital file, providing a basis for identifying and prosecuting copyright violators. Photographers may also apply for a trademark, especially if they own their own business. A trademark is a type of intellectual property consisting of a recognizable symbol, design, word, or phrase that represents a product, service, or company and legally distinguishes it from others. It can be registered (providing legal protection) or unregistered (used as an identifier). Trademarks cover brands, names, designs, or expressions. The various aspects of copyright as related to photography are discussed in the following section.

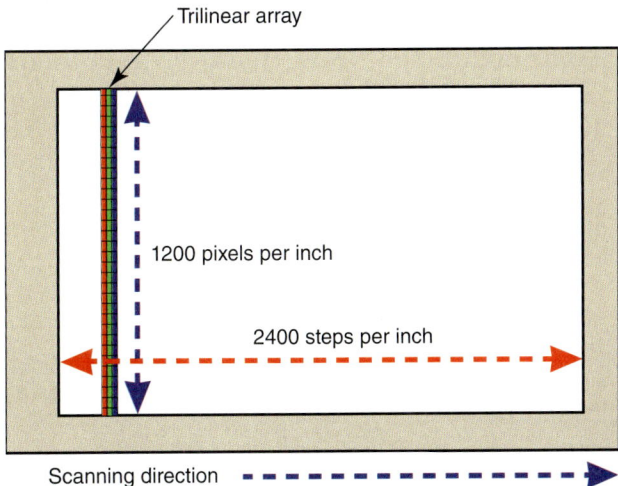

Goodheart-Willcox Publisher

Figure 17-7. The trilinear array of a flatbed scanner is parallel to the short side of the scanning area. Thus, a 1200 ppi array would have 10,200 sensors for an 8.5″ wide scanning area (1200 × 8.5). A stepper motor moves the array down the length of the scanning area, making 2400 stops per inch, or a total of 26,400 for the full 11″ scanning area.

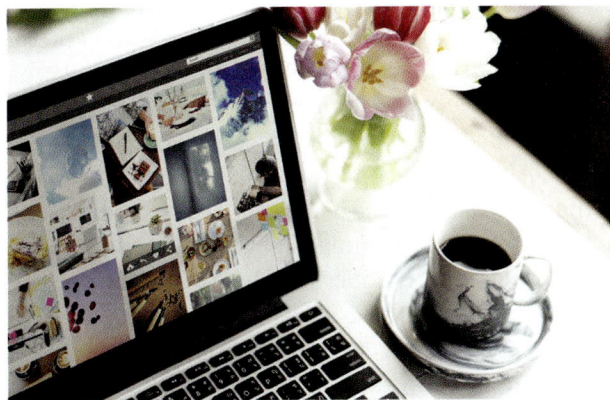

Rawpixel.com/Shutterstock.com

Figure 17-8. Many photographers use their own website to display photos or post them in an online gallery.

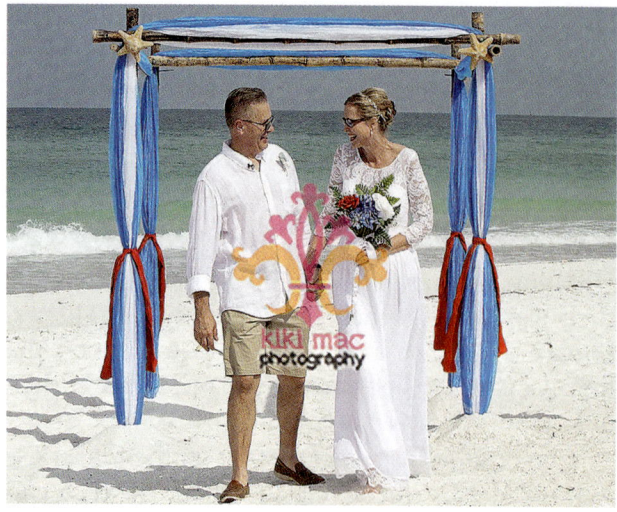

Christy Clark

Figure 17-9. Some photographers use a watermark on their digital images to protect their copyright.

Copyright and the Photographer

Copyright is a law that gives the creator of a photograph or other item of intellectual property (such as a novel, song, or computer program) the exclusive right to use and distribute that property for a specific period of time. This means that no one else can make copies or otherwise use that property without the copyright owner's express permission. Copyright protects original works, which includes everything from a poem you wrote about the beach to songs, computer programs and software, audiovisual works, visual art, text materials, pictorial and graphic works, sculpted works, illustrations and photographs, and even architecture. It also covers both published and unpublished works.

To obtain copyright for your photograph, all you have to do is press the shutter release on your camera. From the instant the image is created, it is covered by US copyright law. The law continues to provide protection for that image for your lifetime plus 70 years. Although a copyright notice, such as "©2023 Amanda Clark," can be used when the photo is printed or displayed on electronic media, it is not required by law. Displaying the notice may help discourage unauthorized copying of the image, however. If you want more protection, you can create an official copyright by registering with the US Copyright Office through the Library of Congress.

As described in Chapter 3, *Professional Photography*, a photographer can license rights for use of a photograph in specific situations. A fee is usually charged. For example, a photograph might be licensed for use in a book or magazine, on a website or billboard, or even on a T-shirt. Licenses can be limited to use in a particular geographic area or for a specific period of time.

If someone uses your photograph without obtaining permission, they are committing an **infringement** of your copyright, or violation of the copyright law by using or distributing a work without permission of the copyright owner. The infringement may appear to be an innocent error. For example, the user may have been unaware that the photo was protected by copyright. In this case, you may just demand that they stop using it. If the infringement seems deliberate, you can seek a court order to stop usage of the image and possibly sue for a financial penalty.

Fair Use

Under certain circumstances, copyrighted material can be used without seeking permission. The *fair use* provision of the copyright law allows limited use of an intellectual property by critics and reviewers, scholars and researchers, and classroom teachers.

There are no specific rules to determine whether a particular instance is fair use or an infringement, but the law provides four factors that must be considered:

- **The purpose and character of the use.** Is it a nonprofit educational use, or a commercial (for-profit) use?
- **The nature of the work.** What type of intellectual property is involved?
- **The amount of the portion used in relation to the whole work.** Is there a substantial amount of the original work used?
- **The effect of the usage on the value or potential market for the work.** Does using the original work devalue it in any way?

An example of fair use would be a photography teacher downloading an image from a website to make copies for class discussion of compositional techniques. However, downloading of the same image for reproduction on a poster that is sold on the internet would likely be considered copyright infringement.

Derivative Works

A work may be used without infringing copyright if it serves as the basis of a new creation. This is called a **derivative work**. However, the original must be substantially adapted or modified to produce what is a new and different work. For example, a photograph of a leaping ballet dancer is changed considerably by the addition of butterfly wings, cropping to a different format, and compositing with various foreground and background images.

The legal and ethical considerations of combining images from different sources, as well as manipulating those images, is discussed in Chapter 19.

> **REAL-WORLD PHOTOGRAPHY**
>
> **Copyright Ownership**
>
> When it comes to your rights as a copyright owner, there are a few things you are entitled to:
> - The distribution rights that determine how the copyrighted work is distributed
> - The right of reproduction to the copyrighted work
> - The right to create derivative works, such as spin-offs, sequels, etc.
> - The right to control the public display of your work
> - The public performance right, if applicable
> - The right of digital transmission for owners of sound recordings (such as music streaming services)

Sources of Free and Fee-Based Images

Certain websites allow images to be downloaded legally, either free or for a fee. Free images are available primarily from government websites or for promotional purposes from some corporate sites. Images available for a fee are mostly found on stock photo websites, such as Shutterstock.

Free Image Sources

The largest and most accessible source of free images that can be downloaded from the internet is the United States government. Since these images are in the **public domain** (not covered by copyright and thus available for free use by anyone), they are not subject to royalties or usage fees. The military services, the National Oceanic and Atmospheric Administration (NOAA), the National Aeronautics and Space Administration (NASA), and the Department of Agriculture all maintain huge libraries of images relating to their areas of interest.

The largest archive of images, and the most often used, is maintained by the Library of Congress. The library's website offers an incredible variety of pictures from many areas of both historic and contemporary America, **Figure 17-10**.

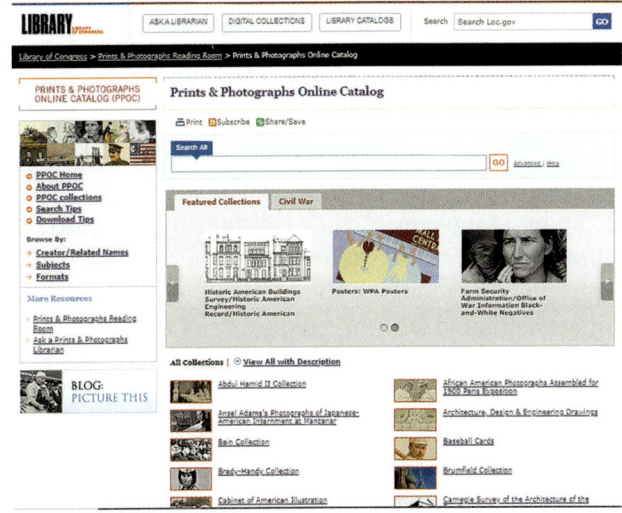

Library of Congress

Figure 17-10. The Library of Congress website offers thousands of photographs, many in high resolution, that can be downloaded for free.

Some photo sharing websites, such as Flickr, offer many images at no cost under Creative Commons licensing. Some images have usage restrictions, but most can be used freely with **attribution** (giving proper credit to the person who created the image). Creative Commons licensing is described in greater detail in the next section.

With certain restrictions on use, free images are also available from organization and company websites. Associations that promote a specific occupational area, industry, business, or charitable activity may offer images related to their area of interest. Many large companies have libraries of images showing their products or services.

Since company images are intended to be used for publicity purposes, they are usually located in a section of the website identified as *Media* or *Press*. Some sites allow access and downloading of images without registration. Others require you to provide your name and organization to obtain a password for access (some refuse access to non-journalists). Frequently, you must agree to abide by certain restrictions on the use of the images, such as not using them in a negative or demeaning context.

Creative Commons Licensing

Under copyright law, a photographer owns all rights to their image and can choose to allow others to use that image under certain circumstances, such as printing for use as a greeting card. For commercial uses, such as the greeting card, the copyright owner typically charges a fee.

Some photographers, especially those who post images on photo sharing sites, may choose to allow others to use their images (for example, by posting on a personal website) without charge. They do so by assigning certain rights using a **Creative Commons license**. These licenses permit the copyright owner to make some or all usage rights to an image available without charge. See **Figure 17-11**.

Several different licenses are available to grant or restrict different rights. Common to all the licenses is attribution, meaning that the copyright owner must be given credit for creating the image. One type of license restricts image use to noncommercial applications. For example, a photo can be shown on a charity's website but cannot be used by a company printing and selling calendars. Another type of license, called a *nonderivative license*, forbids alteration of the image, such as incorporating part of it in a composite. A *share alike license* permits the user to make changes to the image or make it the basis for a new work. The new work must be attributed to the copyright owner and licensed under the same terms as the original image.

Licenses can be combined in various ways to meet the needs of the copyright owner. A combination of attribution, noncommercial, and nonderivative licenses makes up about one-third of all Creative Commons licenses.

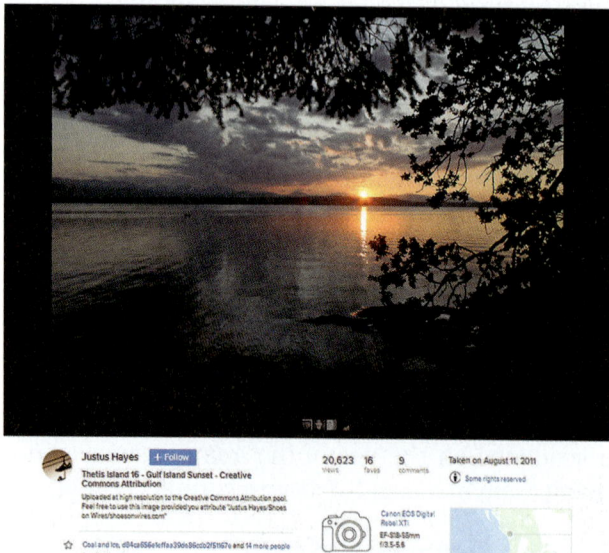

Justus Hayes/Shoes on Wires/shoesonwires.com

Figure 17-11. Photographer Justus Hayes posted this striking photo to a photo sharing site. They chose to make it available to others under a Creative Commons license requiring only attribution.

Fee-Based Image Sources

Images are also available for a wide range of fees. The most expensive images are those held in massive stock photo libraries such as Corbis. These images are known as **rights-managed images**, which are stock photos for which a fee is charged for each use, such as different editions of a book or different packaging for a family of products. Usually, these photos are used extensively in advertising, magazine work, and book publishing. Users pay a fee for each use of an image—a single advertisement, for example, or one edition of a book. The stock agency pays a royalty to the photographer or other copyright holder. A **royalty** is a percentage of the sale price paid to the author of a book, photograph, or other intellectual property by the publisher or stock photo agency. Many professional photographers "shoot for stock" to supply images to such agencies. Those whose images are popular make a significant income.

Major stock photo agencies also offer a wide selection of royalty-free images. **Royalty-free images** are stock photos that may be used multiple times without additional payment after permission has been given. Just like rights-managed images, the photographer or copyright holder receives a fee for each sale of the image.

A lower-cost option has emerged in recent years with the development of smaller stock agencies specializing in inexpensive royalty-free images. These agencies typically use a prepayment system in which customers purchase a quantity of credits, then spend them as they select images to purchase. Such agencies rely on a large number of mostly amateur or semiprofessional photographers who supply images and receive a small payment each time an image is sold. While this type of stock photography is unlikely to provide a full-time living for a photographer, it can generate a useful supplemental income.

Image Management

The more photos you shoot, the more important it becomes to develop a method of **image management**. This is the process of using a filing method or cataloging system that allows a user to quickly locate a desired image. Ideally, you should develop and begin using a system before you accumulate a large number of images. If you already have a large body of work stored on your hard drive or in cloud-based storage, the best method is to start cataloging current projects, and then gradually work backward through existing material as time allows.

One of the largest components of image management is *culling*, or the process of determining which photos to keep and which photos to delete. Inevitably, some of your photos will not come out properly or may not be what you envisioned. For instance, they may be out of focus, be timed awkwardly, or have improper white balance. Additionally, you may simply like another version of a similar photo better (such as one from a different angle or taken at a different time of day). As such, not every photo you take is worth saving. Taking some time to cull these images and determine which ones are worth keeping will help you in the long run by giving you fewer images to edit and work with.

Filing/Cataloging Methods

Depending on your needs, a cataloging system can be simple or complex. If you shoot only weddings, for example, a basic system might be to file by name and date:

Martin/Dubravec: March 2015.

Two simple lists or card files—alphabetical and year/month—make it easy to locate a particular event. For example, if files are stored on a large hard drive, the basic file folder structure could be organized by year, then by month within that year. If several weddings were shot in a given month, each would have its own folder, **Figure 17-12**. You could also have a folder for the year, and then title each subfolder with the name of the project, such as Martin/Dubravec Wedding. It is important to note that everyone's organization process is different, so you may have to try different iterations before you find what process works best for you.

Such a system works well for anyone who simply needs to locate a particular group of photos, but it is not adequate for finding a specific individual photo or similar images taken at different times and places. Travel photos filed by the group method can lead you to the 2019 Grand Canyon trip or the Florida Keys journey of 2015, but this method does not help you find images of a Cooper's hawk photographed on visits to five different locations in as many years.

Another method of organizing or culling photos is by using a rating or flagging system. Many photographers use a rating system of one to five stars to determine how much they like a photo, with five

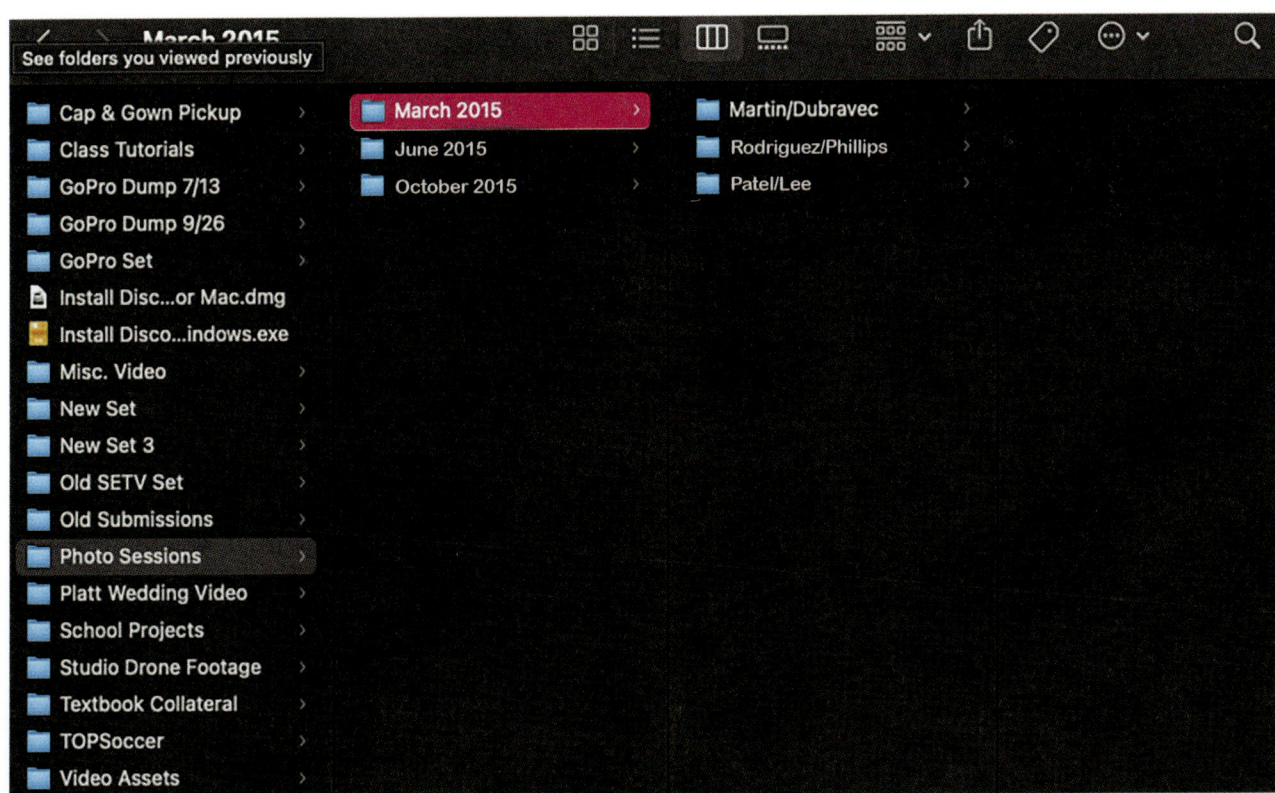

Goodheart-Willcox Publisher

Figure 17-12. A simple image filing system that might be used by a wedding photographer consists of folders for each month and a subfolder for each wedding within that month.

being the highest. By assigning one to five stars to an image after the initial culling, you will have tiers of photos that you can work with. You can decide from there how you want to move forward with postprocessing. Some photographers only work with their five-star photos, while some work with their five- and four-star photos, and others work with their five-, four-, and three-star photos. Ultimately, each photographer will develop their own system that works for them. You may try the rating system and decide it does not work for you, which is perfectly fine. You may find another system that works better with your workflow.

Database Programs

Numerous image database programs, ranging from basic to extremely complex, are on the market. A *database program* is computer software that allows a collection of files (one file for each cataloged image) to be sorted in various ways to locate desired information. The most basic programs offer a *browsing* function that allows the user to view a number of small images (*thumbnails*) on the screen at one time, **Figure 17-13**. In Lightroom, for example, a catalog is automatically created when you import your images into the program. These files

REAL-WORLD PHOTOGRAPHY

Contact Sheets

Contact sheets were originally designed to be a positive print of all the negatives from a roll of film. This allowed a photographer to see every image they shot and decide which ones they wanted to keep and have printed. Over time, the contact sheet has changed into something photographers create digitally for their reference as well as their client's reference. Adobe Lightroom offers this feature, and it is still quite useful today in both casual scenarios (such as helping a high school senior see all their photo options) and professional environments (such as providing options for a photo campaign to a client). In Lightroom, you can select the photos for a contact sheet to provide for a client, and it will include other data about the photo as well, such as the shutter speed and aperture size.

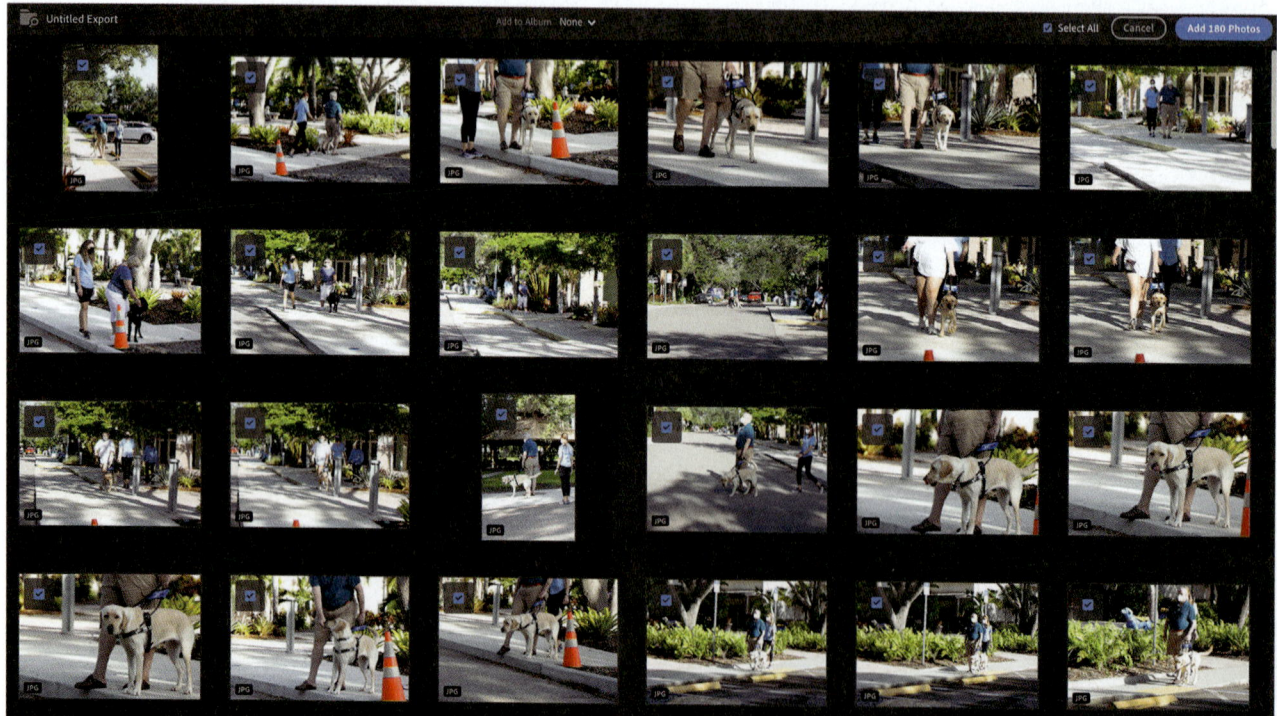

Goodheart-Willcox Publisher

Figure 17-13. Basic image database programs present stored images in thumbnail form for easy review and comparison.

are not stored in the program itself but on your computer's hard drive, and it allows you to see previews of the images in the catalog in thumbnail form. In catalogs, related images can be grouped in a labeled album or collection. Most basic programs also allow some form of ranking (for example, assigning one or more stars) for image quality or impact. Groups of images can then be sorted and displayed based on the star rankings, **Figure 17-14**.

A browsing system with ranking capability is suitable for an image collection that is relatively small and limited to such topics as family photos and vacation shots. These programs are usually designed to work strictly with images that are stored on a computer's hard drive.

Keywords

The most sophisticated and useful method of locating individual images, or groups of images on a particular topic, is the keyword technique used by advanced image database programs. A ***keyword*** is a specific descriptive word (or words) assigned to an image in a database that allows a user to search for that image. These advanced image database programs, called ***cataloging programs***, allow the use of keywords for locating files by subject, date, or other criteria.

The cataloging software reads the image files from a folder on a hard drive or in a cloud-based storage system and generates and stores both a small thumbnail image and a larger preview image for each file. Once the image files have been read, the photographer can assign keywords that describe the content of the image. Keywords can be added or deleted at any time using the program's edit function, **Figure 17-15**.

Well-chosen keywords are important in finding a desired image or images among the thousands in the database. The program's search function permits the user to be quite specific by using several keywords in combination. In the example shown in **Figure 17-16**, the first keyword is *yellow*, and the second is *lab*. Note that you can modify terms by the word *contains*. If the keyword *lab* was modified, it would find files with either *lab* or *labs* as a keyword, **Figure 17-17**. You can also tightly specify keywords. For instance, if the keyword *yellow* is tightly specified, only files that exactly match that word (not *yellows* or *yellowing*, for example) will be accepted.

Some image cataloging programs have a print feature that allows the image thumbnails to be printed out as an index print or "digital contact sheet." The photographer can scroll through the thumbnails displayed on the screen to locate the desired image or images and click on a thumbnail to examine a specific image more closely.

Metadata

Cataloging programs can display a wealth of information about any image that was made using a digital camera. This information is called ***metadata*** (loosely translated as "data about data") and is contained in a file recorded by the camera at the time of exposure. The ***EXIF (Exchangeable Image File Format)*** file is recorded by the camera at the time of exposure. It contains many image

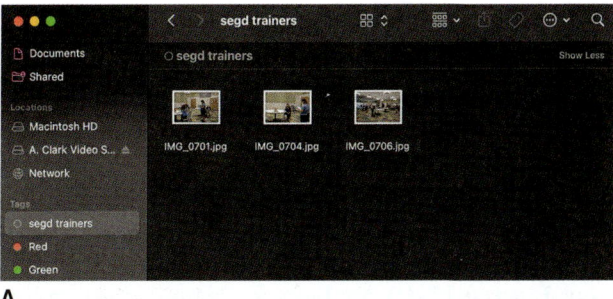

Goodheart-Willcox Publisher

Figure 17-14. Grouping photos. A—Related images can be grouped into named collections. B—Favorite shots within a collection can be identified and labeled with one or more stars for sorting.

Goodheart-Willcox Publisher

Figure 17-15. Assigning specific keywords allows identification of a given image.

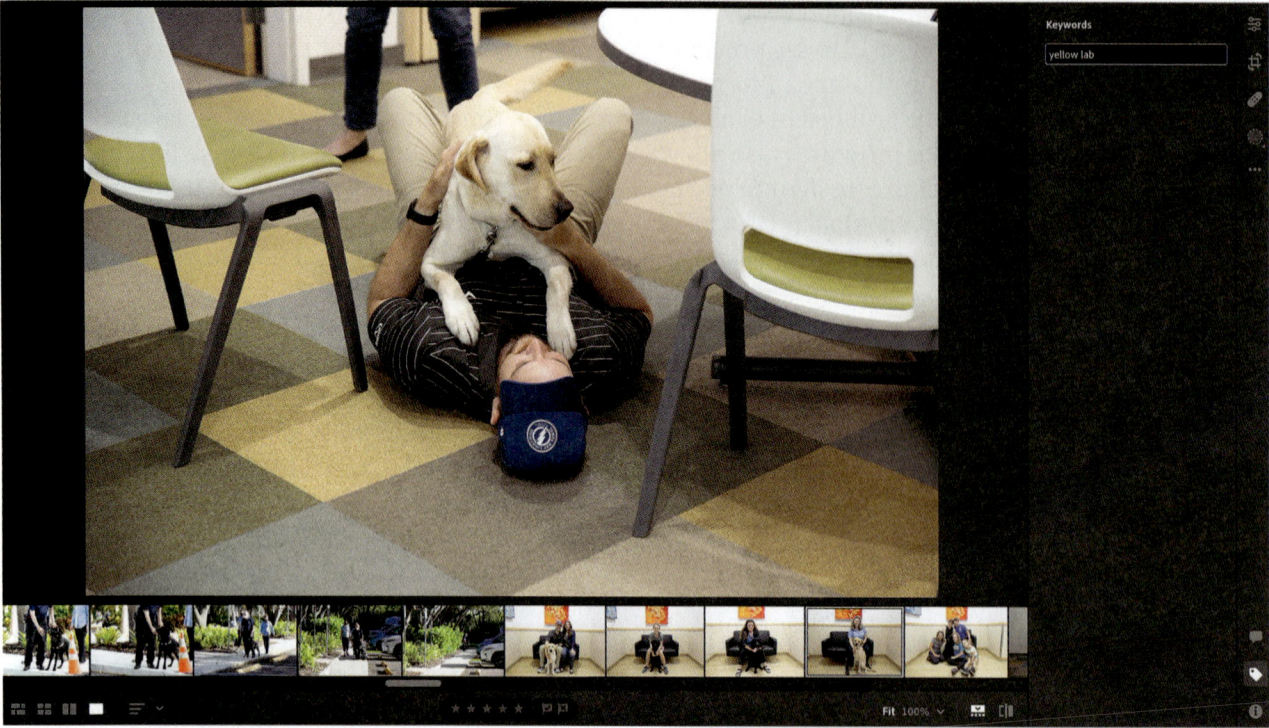

Goodheart-Willcox Publisher

Figure 17-16. Combining keywords in a search allows very specific results.

properties, including the shutter speed, aperture, ISO, and lens focal length. See **Figure 17-18**.

Once a desired image file has been identified, it can be accessed for use in an image editing program. The method for accessing the actual image file depends on its physical location as identified by the cataloging program. A file on the computer's hard drive can be opened immediately by the image editing software. A file that is located on a separate storage medium, such as a memory card, must be imported by placing the card in the computer's card reader and copying the file to the hard drive. If your computer does not have a built-in card reader, you can buy an external card reader that works with the computer's USB port.

Some photographers who shoot large numbers of images store the original files (sometimes called *digital negatives*) on CD or DVD, importing files to the computer as needed for processing. Since any storage device can fail, always make a separate backup copy of each CD or DVD on an ***archival-quality disc***, **Figure 17-19**. Such discs are made with materials designed to preserve image files for literally hundreds of years.

Large-capacity hard drives have become more affordable, making storage of large numbers of image files in the computer possible. The advantage is immediate access to files without importing them from separate storage media. Backup copies of files are stored on a second or even third hard drive (often an external unit connected via USB or FireWire cable for rapid data transfer).

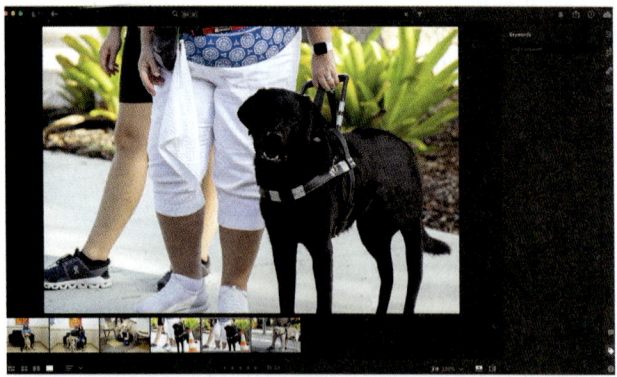

Goodheart-Willcox Publisher

Figure 17-17. The search results for *yellow* and *lab* returned some images with other lab colors visible in addition to yellow because those images included *lab* among their keywords.

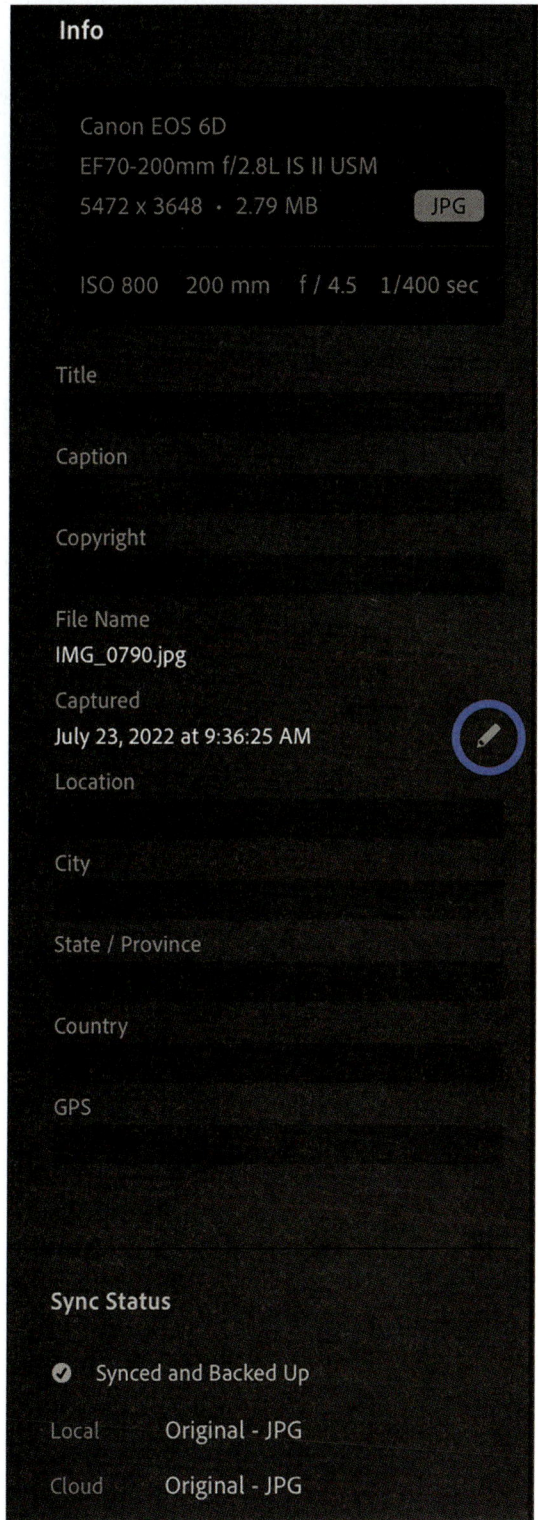

Goodheart-Willcox Publisher

Figure 17-18. The database also includes EXIF data about each image, providing the photographer with useful information for making comparisons of similar shots or analyzing exposure.

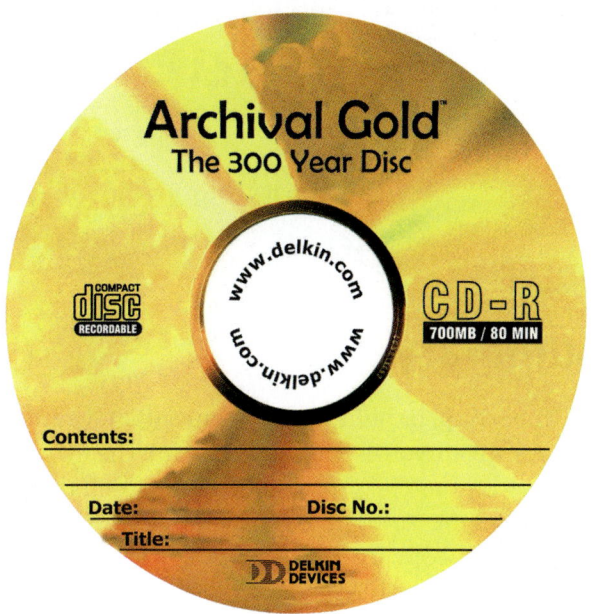

Delkin Devices

Figure 17-19. An archival-quality disc is manufactured to more rigid standards and contains higher-quality materials than standard discs.

Chapter 17   Importing Images   **419**

Chapter 17 Review

Summary

- Importing, or pulling, files from a digital camera typically involves sending or taking the files to a commercial processor, downloading them to a computer for processing and subsequent printing, copying to a portable storage device, or printing directly from a memory card.
- Commercial processors are most commonly used to produce prints. A few common options include kiosks in retail photofinishing locations, online photofinishing sites, and photo sharing sites.
- Photographers who want greater control of their prints typically do their own processing and printing. They download the images, perform desired adjustments using image editing software such as Adobe Photoshop or Lightroom, and then make prints of the selected images on their own printer. Common methods include wireless transfer and cloud-based storage.
- Other common methods of acquiring digital images include using a scanner to create digital files from original prints or physical copies and downloading digital images from the internet.
- Copyright is a law that gives the creator of a photograph or other item of intellectual property (such as a novel, song, or computer program) the exclusive right to use and distribute that property for a specific period of time.
- The fair use provision of the copyright law allows limited use of an intellectual property by critics and reviewers, scholars and researchers, and classroom teachers.
- A work may be used without infringing copyright if it serves as the basis of a new creation. However, the original must be substantially adapted or modified to produce what is a new and different work.
- Images in the public domain are not covered by copyright and are not subject to royalties or usage fees. With certain restrictions on use, free images are also available from organization and company websites.
- There are two main options for fee-based images contained in stock photo libraries: rights-managed images and royalty-free images.
- The more photos you shoot, the more important it becomes to develop a method of image management.
- Depending on your needs, a cataloging system can be simple or complex. You may have to try different iterations before you find what process works best for you.
- Numerous image database programs, ranging from basic to extremely complex, are on the market. More advanced programs use the keyword technique to locate images.

Review Questions

Answer the following questions using the information provided in this chapter.

Know and Understand

1. _____ return the prints from uploaded digital files by mail.
   A. Photo sharing sites
   B. Cataloging programs
   C. Database programs
   D. Online photofinishing sites
2. *True or False?* To download images is to send image files from a digital device to another device or computer system via the internet.
3. *True or False?* With wireless networking technology, photos can be transferred directly from a specially equipped digital camera to a computer or printer located as far as 150′ away.
4. _____ are mechanical/optical devices used to convert original prints or physical copies into digital form.
   A. Scanners
   B. Thumbnails
   C. Card readers
   D. Royalties
5. *True or False?* Optical resolution is the actual pixels per inch resolution.
6. _____ is an electronic method of embedding copyright information and the owner's identity in the digital file, providing a basis for identifying and prosecuting copyright violators.
   A. Watermarking
   B. Copyrighting
   C. Attribution
   D. Browsing
7. A(n) _____ is violation of the copyright law by using or distributing a work without permission of the copyright owner.
   A. fair use
   B. infringement
   C. derivative work
   D. attribution
8. *True or False?* A new creation from an original work does *not* have to be adapted or modified much to be considered a derivative work.
9. Giving proper credit to the person who created an image is called _____.
   A. infringement
   B. copyright
   C. attribution
   D. public domain
10. *True or False?* A nonderivative license forbids alteration of an image.
11. _____ are stock photos for which a fee is charged for each use, such as different editions of a book or different packaging for a family of products.
    A. Royalty-free images
    B. Creative Commons licenses
    C. Thumbnails
    D. Rights-managed images
12. _____ is the process of using a filing method or cataloging system that allows a user to quickly locate a desired image.
    A. Metadata
    B. Image management
    C. Uploading
    D. Downloading
13. A(n) _____ is computer software that allows a collection of files (one file for each cataloged image) to be sorted in various ways to locate desired information.
    A. image management
    B. database program
    C. cataloging program
    D. keyword
14. _____ is a function of database programs that allows the user to view a number of small images on the screen at one time.
    A. Infringement
    B. Cataloging
    C. Browsing
    D. Watermarking

15. A(n) _____ is a specific descriptive word (or words) assigned to an image in a database that allows a user to search for that image.
    A. upload
    B. metadata
    C. keyword
    D. royalty

16. *True or False?* Metadata contains information recorded by the camera at the time of exposure.

17. _____ contains many image properties, including the shutter speed, aperture, ISO, and lens focal length.
    A. Archival-quality disc
    B. Creative Commons
    C. EXIF (Exchangeable Image File Format)
    D. Image management

Apply and Analyze

1. How can you transfer files from a digital camera to cloud-based storage?
2. When flatbed scanner resolution is given in the form 1200 × 2400, what do the two numbers mean?
3. List the four factors that must be considered when determining whether a particular instance is fair use or an infringement.
4. What do Creative Commons licenses permit the copyright owner to do?
5. What is a keyword?

Critical Thinking

1. Imagine you find an old photograph showing your high school's 1940 football team. It has a stamp on the back stating "Copyright 1940 Powell Studio." Can you reproduce the photo without infringing copyright? Why or why not?
2. You are browsing the internet and find one of your images displayed on a gallery website but identified as the work of the website's owner. What course of action would you take?
3. Imagine a friend brings you a photo taken at their senior prom by a professional photographer. They say that they would like you to copy it and make ten prints because they do not want to pay what the photographer would charge for copies. What should you do, and why?
4. Think about the photos you have stored on your smartphone. How can you organize them to make it easier to find specific images?
5. Creative Commons licensing is described in this chapter. How would you find images on the internet that are available for use under this method of licensing?

Suggested Activities

1. Divide the class into two groups. One group should discuss the concept that photographs and other intellectual property posted on the internet should be freely available for use without charge. The other group should discuss the idea that creators of intellectual property should have their rights protected under the copyright law. After the discussion, each group should select a spokesperson to present its view before the class.
2. On the US Copyright Office website, search for "Copyright Law of the United States," then open Chapter 1. Locate and copy definitions for these terms—audiovisual works; computer program; copies; copyright owner; digital transmission; financial gain; pictorial, graphic, and sculptural works; work of visual art. Be prepared to explain one of the terms in your own words in class.
3. The basis of the copyright law is found in Article 1, Section 8 of the US Constitution. Read that Section and identify the paragraph that gives the US Congress the power to protect the rights to intellectual property. Report to the class how you identified the proper paragraph.
4. Browse the Library of Congress website and find a photograph you like. Download the highest-available resolution of the image to your computer. Make an inkjet print on 8.5" × 11" photo paper. Post the print in your classroom, along with information about the image.
5. Go to the Creative Commons website and explore the differences between distributing your work under the Creative Commons Attribution license and placing it in the public domain. Present your findings as a written report.

Communicating about Photography

1. **Speaking and Listening.** Compare and contrast the different types of importing methods discussed in this chapter. In what situations would the use of one type be preferable to the other (for example, downloading to a computer vs. sending to commercial processors)? Record the key points of your discussion. In a class discussion, compare your responses to those of your classmates.

2. **Speaking and Writing.** Select two different images from a student portfolio. Imagine that you are going to put these images into an image database program. Divide into groups of two or three students and, working together, develop keywords that would help locate each image in a database.

Chapter 18
Digital Postprocessing Basics

Learning Objectives

After completing this chapter, you will be able to:
- Distinguish between digital image processing and digital image manipulation.
- Understand the general procedure for using image editing software.
- Recall why it is important to create a working file for processing.
- Describe digital postprocessing techniques to adjust the size and resolution of an image.
- Determine how to work with layers.
- Explain how to adjust the overall exposure of an image.
- Understand how to alter contrast in an image.
- Determine how to correct and adjust color in an image.
- Describe different methods of converting a color image to monochrome.
- Identify when spotting is necessary and identify various methods to clean up digital images.
- Explain the process of sharpening on digital images.

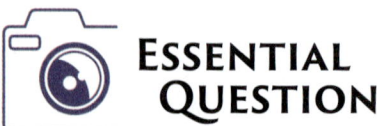

Essential Question
How is postprocessing a vital part of the photography process?

Technical Terms

active layer
additive primary colors
adjustment layer
burning in
dodging
downsampling
grayscale mode

image editor
image manipulation
image processing
interpolation
monochrome
oversharpening
RAW converter

sharpening
shortcut keys
straight photography
subtractive primary colors
upsampling
working file

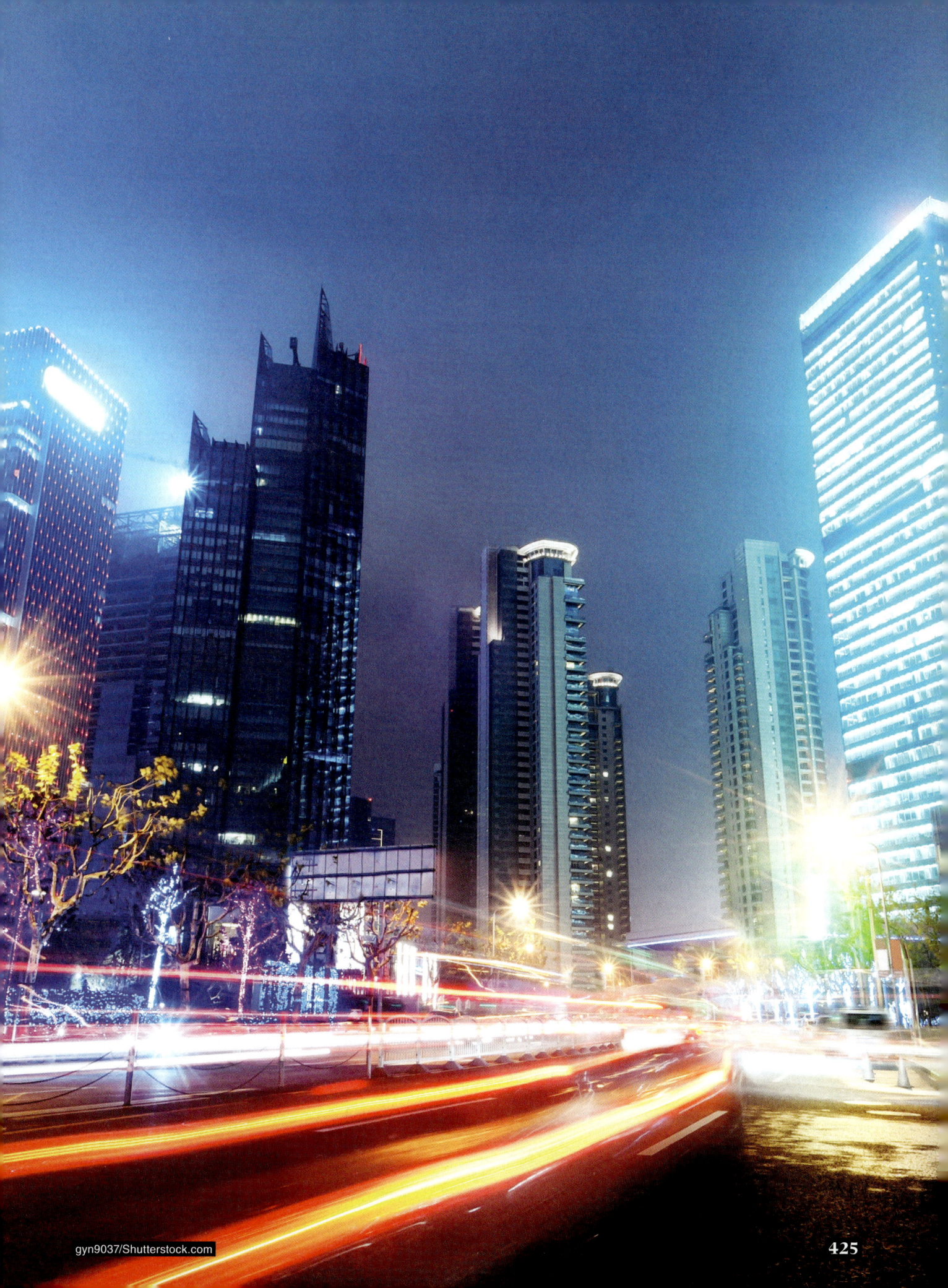

Introduction to Digital Postprocessing Basics

In this age of digital imaging, it is possible to shoot a photo, process the image, and print a color enlargement in a matter of minutes. Since postprocessing has become easily accessible, it is now a vital part of a photographer's workflow. Whether you choose to edit on a desktop computer, laptop, tablet, or smartphone, there are a number of programs that make postprocessing easy. This chapter will address the basics of digital postprocessing with examples from Adobe Photoshop and Adobe Lightroom. Both programs update nearly every year to give users the best and most seamless postprocessing experience.

Digital vs. Traditional Postprocessing

For most photographers, the advantages of working digitally are creative control, convenience, monetary savings, and time savings. Compared to a conventional darkroom (traditional postprocessing), the space required by a computer, scanner, and printer is minimal. The digital darkroom requires little setup time, and there is no need to set aside several hours to complete the work of printing, developing, fixing, washing, and drying prints.

Digital imaging also offers a great amount of flexibility. Work on a digital image can be paused, the results saved, and efforts resumed at the photographer's convenience, whereas conventional darkroom operations typically must be carried through to completion in a single session. Conventional darkroom work usually means hours of standing in a darkened room, while digital postprocessing activities are carried out in a lighted room from the comfort of a desk chair. However, despite the lack of chemicals, it is still important to follow personal and workplace safety rules and regulations when postprocessing images digitally. This includes items such as working from an ergonomically correct workstation (supportive chair, desk at the proper height for you, good lighting, etc.) and taking necessary breaks (routine standing or walking breaks as well as screen breaks).

Image Processing vs. Image Manipulation

Some photographers make a distinction between image processing and image manipulation. They consider **image processing** (changes to an image such as adjustment of exposure, color and contrast, cropping the image, and dodging and burning) to be the electronic equivalent of the work typically done in the conventional darkroom. More extreme changes to the image are considered **image manipulation**. These changes include distortion, removal of particular elements from the photo, combination of elements from one or more other sources, and radical changes of color and tone.

How much manipulation of an image is permissible depends on its intended use and the photographer's ethical standards. Most print and electronic news media maintain strict control over photo content. The photographer or other staff member can make basic processing adjustments but cannot manipulate the photo by adding or removing content.

Some changes, such as removing a distracting person in the background, might seem harmless and like an improvement to the image. However, news ethics do not permit such manipulations. The reasoning is that permitting even such minor "improvements" could lead to manipulation of photo content that would distort the meaning of the image and mislead readers or viewers.

Photographic artists are not necessarily bound by such considerations. They may use a variety of manipulation techniques to create works that distort reality to a greater or lesser extent, much like the work of impressionist or cubist painters. See **Figure 18-1**. The artist's intent is not to mislead the viewer but to convey their individual viewpoint. The work might be intended to convey a specific emotion, an idea, or a sense of altered reality.

Many photographers prefer to do what they refer to as **straight photography**, using little or no manipulation. These photographers produce prints that reflect, as accurately as possible, what they saw through the camera's viewfinder or on its LCD screen.

> ### REAL-WORLD PHOTOGRAPHY
>
> **Respecting Intellectual Property in Editing**
>
> As you learned in Chapter 17, *Importing Images*, photographs are a type of intellectual property. If you have obtained the work of another photographer legally (such as through a Creative Commons license), you are still required to show respect when editing the image. There are times when you may want to manipulate the original photo (this includes actions such as compositing or morphing) or simply apply some general edits (such as color correction or retouching). However, depending on the rights you have to the photo, this is not always possible. You should not perform any of these edits unless you have received express permission to do so. If you want to practice your editing skills, you have every right to do so with your own images.
>
> Additionally, it is important to remember who your audience is when manipulating images. For example, if you have been hired by a client to work on a campaign for a new children's toy, you would most likely want to keep your image simple and use bold and bright colors. In this instance, you could enhance the brighter tones in postprocessing and add filters to create a whimsical look. However, being able to make these adjustments does not give you the freedom to grab an image of a popular children's character to enhance your toy campaign. If a client is advocating for something like that, it is your responsibility as the photographer to communicate the legality of the situation to your client and help guide them in a new direction.

Image Editing Software

An indispensable tool for either image processing or image manipulation is an ***image editor*** or editing program. These software applications range from very simple ones that can be used for basic tasks (such as an app-based photo editor) to highly complex applications with an array of specialized features (such as Adobe Photoshop). See **Figure 18-2**. While many programs exist to help you edit your photos in a quick, seamless way, it is important to remember to manage your time. Even though you may be able to perform many tasks with just a few clicks, do not let that fool you into thinking postprocessing is always quick and easy. Remember that you may run into potential issues and may need more time to edit photos. This is especially important to consider if editing images for a client. Being able to manage your time and complete tasks by a deadline is an important skill for any photographer.

As you learned in Chapter 17, Step 1 of the image editing process is importing the image or images you will be working with. Step 2 of the image editing process may involve only a broad change or two, such as cropping the image or altering its overall brightness. Smaller adjustments may also be made, such as lightening the color of a subject's shirt.

Many different tools are available for performing actions on an image, **Figure 18-3**. Tools are typically selected and applied by using a standard computer mouse, although some users prefer a graphics tablet and pen. See **Figure 18-4**. The tablet and pen allow more precise control, especially when used to draw or retouch fine details.

Photoshop and similar full-featured programs allow the use of ***shortcut keys*** as an efficient alternative to using a mouse and menu to perform many operations. A shortcut key may be an individual key or a combination of keys, such as the **Ctrl** or **Alt** key (**Command** or **Option** key on an Apple® computer) with a letter, numeral, or punctuation mark. You can also create your own custom shortcut keys by selecting **Edit > Keyboard Shortcuts** and programming your desired function or key combinations.

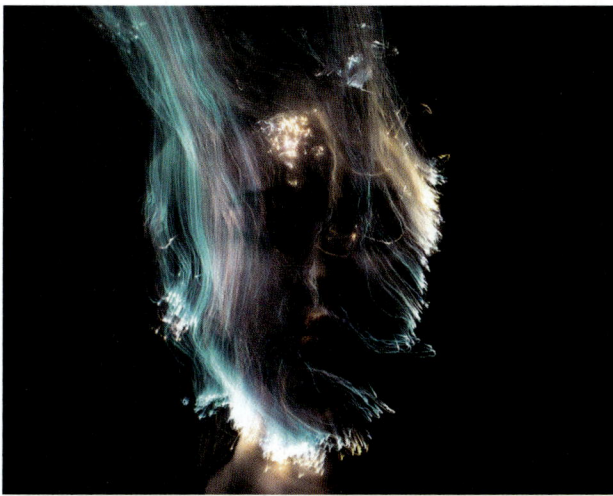

Sergiy Katyshkin/Shutterstock.com

Figure 18-1. Image manipulation techniques can produce images that distort reality.

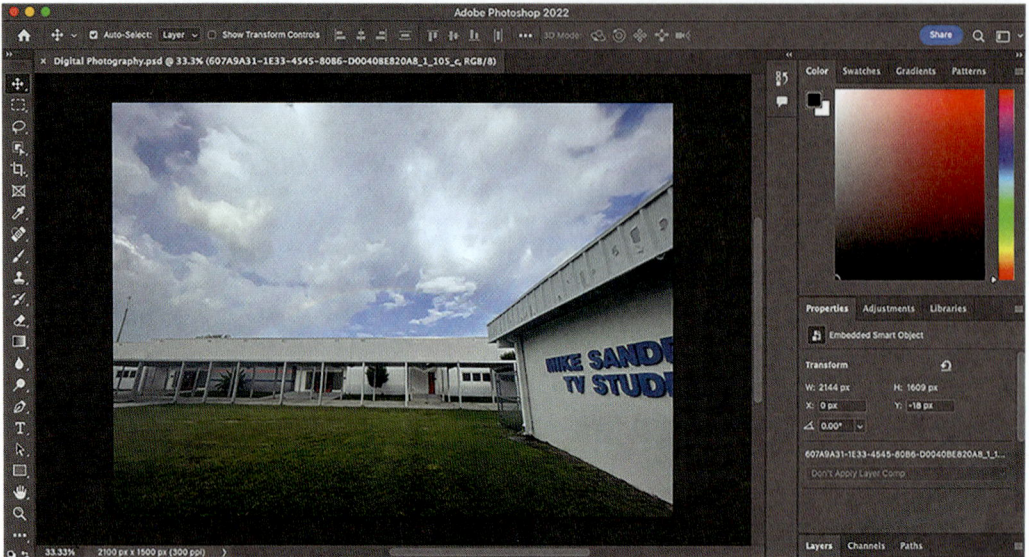

Goodheart-Willcox Publisher

Figure 18-2. Full-featured image editing programs, such as Adobe Photoshop, are more complex and require time and effort to learn.

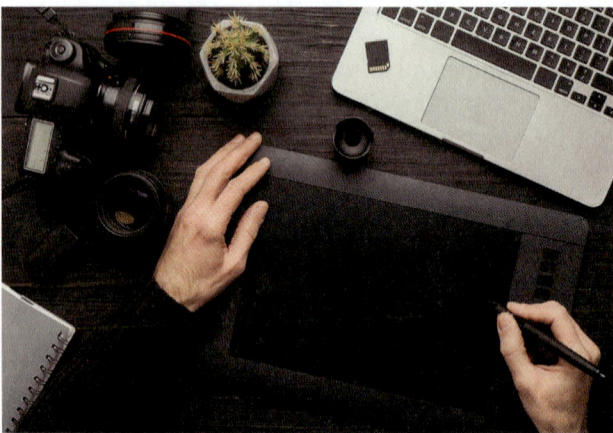

Prostock-studio/Shutterstock.com

Figure 18-4. A graphics tablet allows precise control when working on images.

The image editing window, **Figure 18-5**, varies in appearance somewhat from program to program but almost always includes the following features:

- A menu bar with drop-down menus across the top of the screen
- An options bar for configuring a chosen tool
- A toolbar displaying the available tools
- A workspace or editing area where the image is displayed
- One or more panels used for specific displays, such as color choices or brush sizes

Goodheart-Willcox Publisher

Figure 18-3. Tools available for various image editing functions are shown as icons on the toolbar.

428 Section 5 Postprocessing

Copyright Goodheart-Willcox Co., Inc.

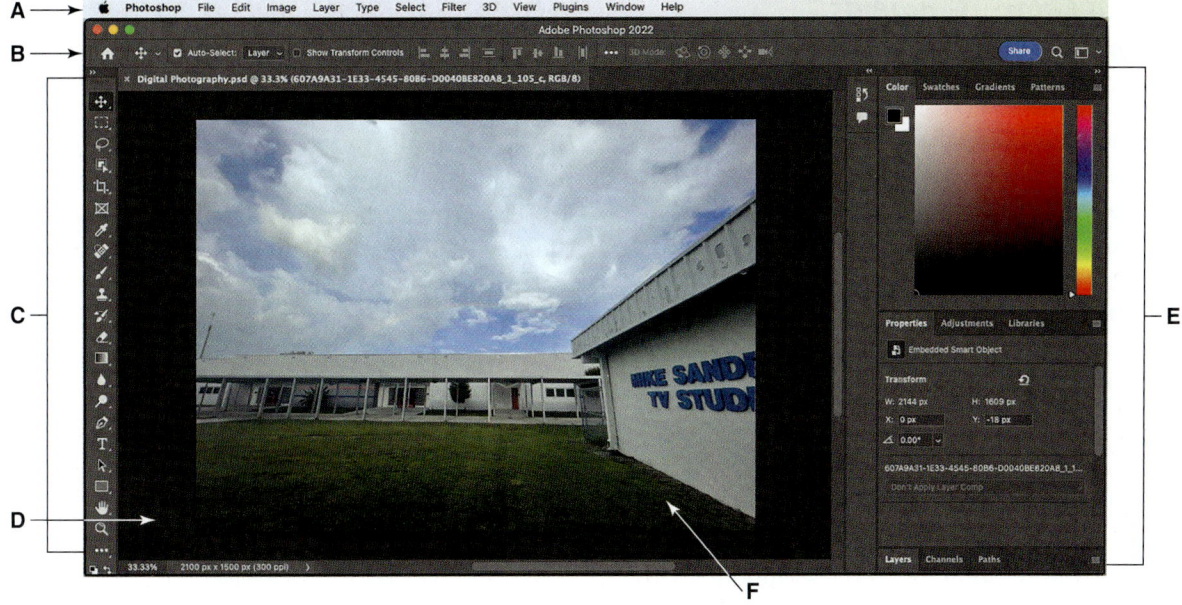

Goodheart-Willcox Publisher

Figure 18-5. The basic parts of an image editing program screen. A—Menu bar. B—Options bar (tool-specific). C—Toolbar. D—Workspace or editing area. E—Panels for specific displays. F—Displayed image.

> ## PROCEDURE
>
> ### Using Image Editing Software
> The procedure for using image editing software, in general terms, includes the following:
> 1. Open an image for editing.
> 2. Perform basic postprocessing actions, such as cropping or contrast adjustment.
> 3. Save the altered image file to preserve the changes.
> 4. Output the image to a printer or to social media.

Managing the Workspace

In Adobe Photoshop, you can customize and change your workspace to suit your needs. To rearrange your workspace, click and hold the panel you would like to move and drag it to where you need it. You also have the option to save this altered space by going to the **Window** menu bar, selecting **Workspaces**, providing a name, and selecting which properties (keyboard shortcuts, menus, toolbar, etc.) you would like to preserve.

Enabling Grids and Rulers

It may be helpful to use the built-in grids and rulers in Photoshop, especially when you are just starting out. These grids allow you to position images or elements more precisely within your workspace, and they will not appear in a printed or exported image. Grids appear as lines overlaid on your image but can also be displayed as dots. You can choose the layout of your grid. To enable a layout, navigate to **View > Show > Grid**, and then change your preference in the **Options** bar at the top of the program.

Rulers serve a similar function to grids. They appear at the top left of your workspace and reflect real-life measurements.

Managing Tools

Some helpful editing tools in Photoshop include *brushes* (allow you to paint on layers like a traditional paintbrush), *glyphs* (specialized characters such as currency numbers, letters with accents, and characters from other languages), *styles* (effects that alter the appearance of a layer), and *patterns* (repeated images within a singular image). All these tools are accessible in their own panels. If they do not automatically display in your default workspace, click on **Window** and select the item you would like to work with.

Managing Colors, Gradients, and Swatches

Colors, gradients, and swatches all have a crucial part in Photoshop. When the need to select a color arises, you can choose from the basic color palette, use the **Hex Color Picker,** or color match using the **Eyedropper** tool. You also have the option to revisit previously used colors by clicking on the **Swatches** panel and selecting **Show Recent Colors**. You can also use these options to help you create a gradient. If you want to change the style of the gradient, simply use the **Options** bar.

The Digital Postprocessing Workflow

Most of the descriptions of the tools, commands, and screen representations in this chapter are from Adobe Photoshop. Some of the descriptions of the tools, commands, and screen representations also come from Adobe Lightroom. Although they may differ in name or appearance, the corresponding tools and commands of other image editing programs accomplish similar results.

Creating a Working Copy

Always preserve an original image file without changes. Create a duplicate file, or working file, for processing. A **working file** is a copy of an original file that can be used for editing to avoid permanently altering the original file. This allows you to go back to the original and make a fresh copy at any time.

Preparing a working copy often involves a change of file type. If the original image file is a compressed JPEG (.jpg) file, the duplicate should be changed to a Tagged Image File Format (.tif) or the Photoshop file format (.psd). As described in Chapter 8, *Digital Image Capture Media*, .jpg files are lossy—they lose quality each time they are opened and resaved. The .tif and .psd file types are not lossy, but lossless. Furthermore, both .tif and .psd files support the use of layers, an important image processing feature that is covered later in this chapter. It can be helpful to use a spreadsheet or database application to keep track of your original files and your working files, especially if you change the names of the files. Taking some extra time at the beginning of a project to get organized can save you trouble down the road if you need to relocate the original or working files.

RAW Conversion

RAW is a file type but not a file format like .jpg or .tif. Essentially, a RAW file is unprocessed image information—the camera's processor does not make any adjustments to the image as it does for .jpg files. Many digital photographers prefer to shoot RAW because it allows them more precise control of their images.

Image editing programs cannot work directly on RAW files. These files must be changed to a file format that the program can handle. This is done with a **RAW converter**, software that allows the photographer to make a number of adjustments to the file data before saving the image as a .tif or .psd file. The major areas of adjustment are exposure, white balance, and contrast. See **Figure 18-6**. Photoshop and most other full-featured image

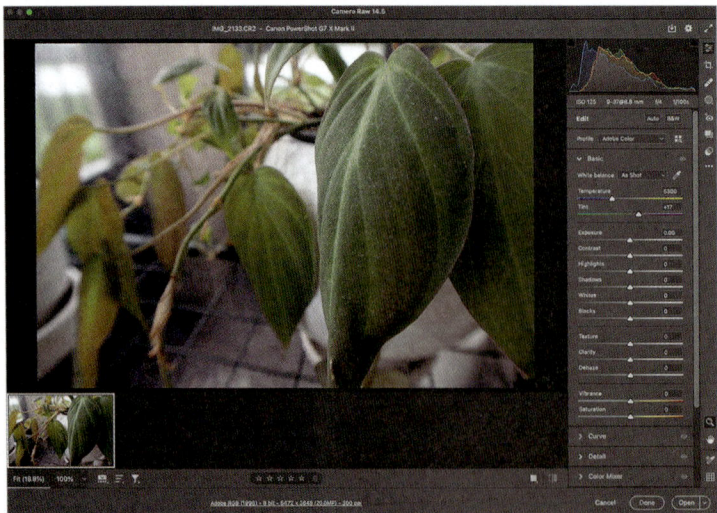

Goodheart-Willcox Publisher

Figure 18-6. RAW converter software allows the user to alter the white balance of the image to correct color casts or to simulate the effects of warming or cooling filters.

processing programs include a RAW converter. Camera manufacturers typically provide a RAW converter with their cameras as well. As technology continues to advance, we may see more integration with RAW files into other postprocessing software, such as apps for mobile postprocessing.

Cropping and Resizing Images

To bring out the best in an image, cropping is often necessary. The **Crop** tool can be used to crop an image, **Figure 18-7**. It can also help you straighten out your image or adjust the perspective of your photo. Highlight the tool on the toolbar with a mouse click, and then click on one of the intended corners of the area to be cropped. You can then adjust as needed by clicking and dragging the highlighted corners to where you wish to crop your image, **Figure 18-8**. Once you have your image cropped the way you like, press the Enter key on your keyboard, and the image will crop, **Figure 18-9**. You can also select the crop tool and highlight the area you wish to crop by clicking and dragging over the whole area.

The image also can be rotated by clicking outside one of the corners and dragging the mouse in the desired direction. This is especially useful for correcting a

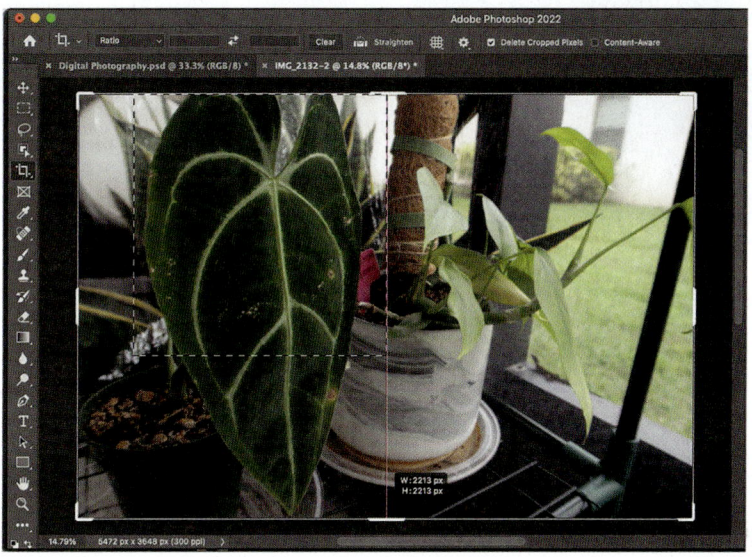

Goodheart-Willcox Publisher

Figure 18-7. Clicking and dragging create a frame to specify the desired crop.

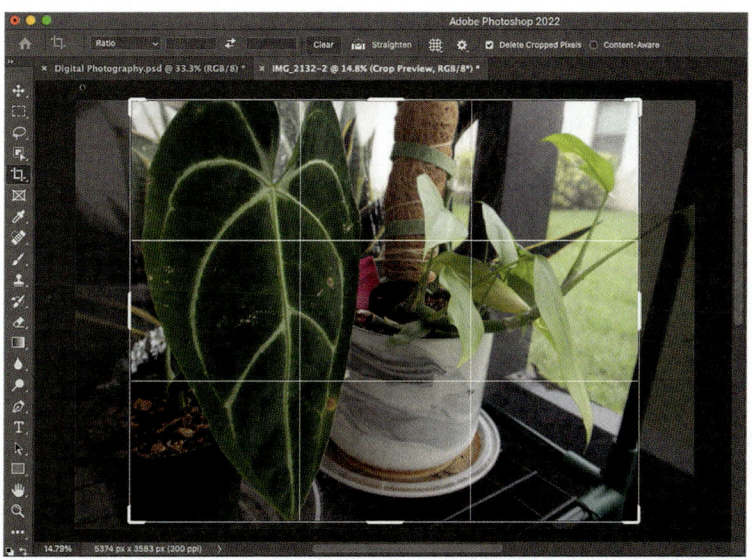

Goodheart-Willcox Publisher

Figure 18-8. Clicking and dragging the corners will allow you to choose the size of your frame.

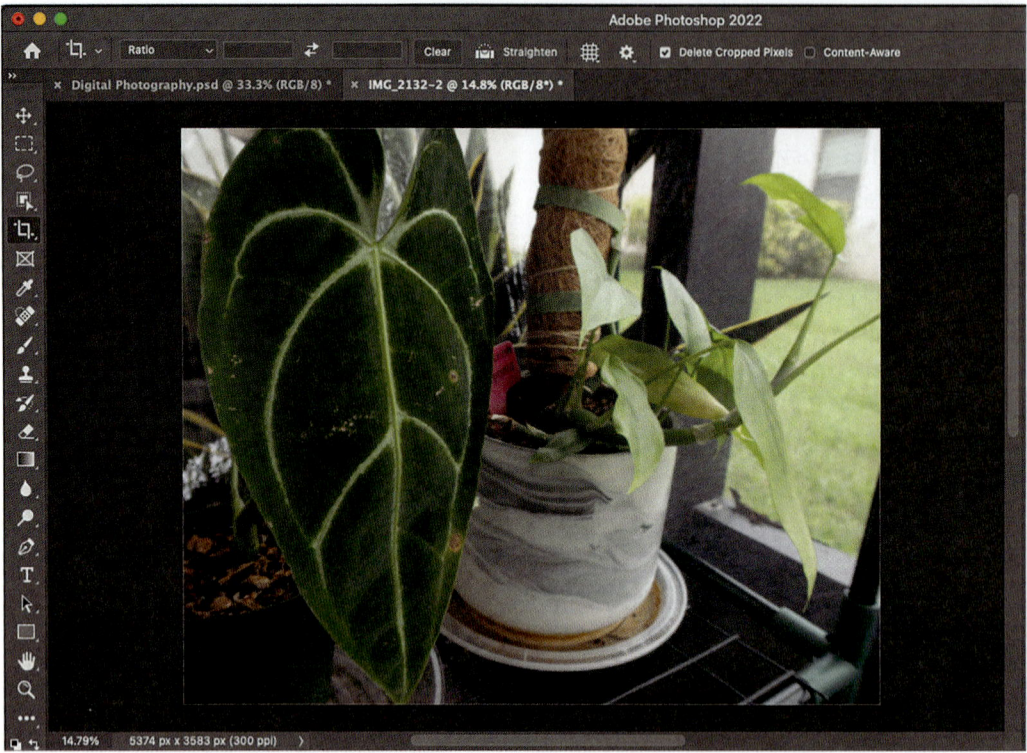

Goodheart-Willcox Publisher

Figure 18-9. Press the Enter key to crop your image to the desired size.

crooked scan or an image where the camera was tilted. The change is previewed on-screen, making it easy to determine when the proper amount of rotation has been achieved. To perform the crop, you can double-click inside the frame or merely press the Enter key.

Sometimes an image looks better if it is reversed left-to-right or even top-to-bottom. In digital postprocessing, this reversal can be done with a single mouse click. Simply go to the top toolbar and select **Image > Image Rotation > Flip Canvas Horizontal** or **Flip Canvas Vertical**, **Figure 18-10**. In addition to the **Flip Canvas Horizontal** and **Flip Canvas Vertical** choices, it is possible to rotate the entire frame in 90° increments.

Changing Image Size and Resolution

There are situations that require a higher-resolution image (such as for print or display) and situations that require a lower-resolution image (such as for file transfers or saving space). Image processing software allows you to change the size of your digital image, the resolution, or both. This is helpful when you need to alter your photo for a specific purpose, such as posting it online, having it printed, or putting it in a presentation. The physical size of your image and its resolution (calculated by multiplying the number of pixels of length and width) depends on the type of camera and the settings programmed into it by you or the camera manufacturer.

 REAL-WORLD PHOTOGRAPHY

Adobe Lightroom Develop Module

As you are aware, Adobe Lightroom is an image editing software many photographers choose to use when postprocessing their images. You can make many of the same edits with Lightroom as you can in Photoshop. Many common edits can be made using the Develop module, which is located on the right half of the screen. There are several panels available, including the **Histogram** panel, **Color Grading** panel, **Transform** panel, **Effects** panel, and more. With these options, you can perform almost any edit that you need, including resizing and cropping, retouching (adjusting red eyes, removing blemishes, etc.), straightening, and working with presets. You can also organize the subpanels as needed to maximize your workflow.

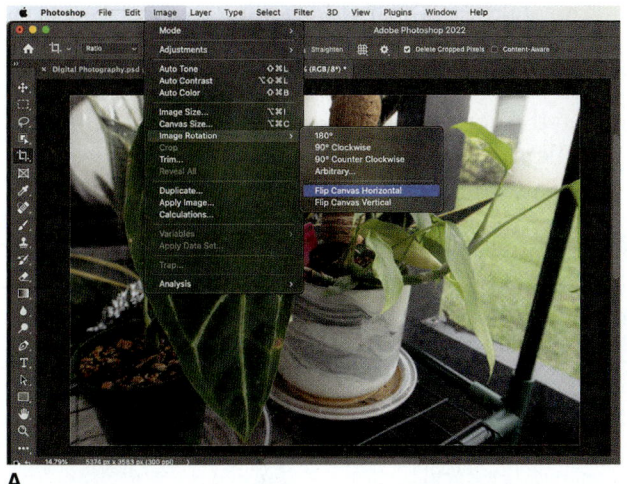
A

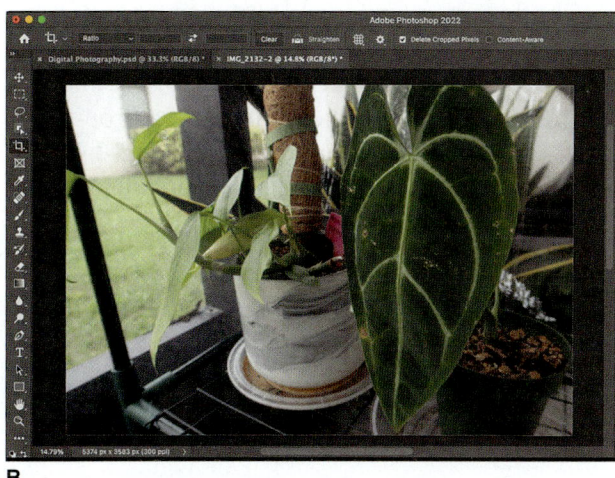
B

Goodheart-Willcox Publisher

Figure 18-10. Flipping an image. A—An image can be flipped vertically or horizontally. B—The reversed image.

If the camera's file is output at 72 ppi, as many are, the physical dimensions could be quite large. For a 16 MP camera, such a file measures 64″ × 48″. In its original state, the file is not of much use, since the dimensions are far too large for full-size display on a computer monitor, and the resolution is far too low for acceptable print quality. For a file output at 300 ppi, the dimensions are much more manageable at approximately 16″ × 12″.

In Photoshop, you can change the size or resolution with the **Image Size** dialog box (other programs have similar controls) by going to **Image > Image Size**. See **Figure 18-11**. The dialog box has three key areas:

- **Image Size/Dimensions**
- **Width/Height/Resolution**
- **Resample**

The top portion of the dialog box shows the file size in kilobytes (K) or megabytes (M), and the width and height dimensions in pixels. A drop-down menu allows changing dimensions to other measurement units, **Figure 18-12**.

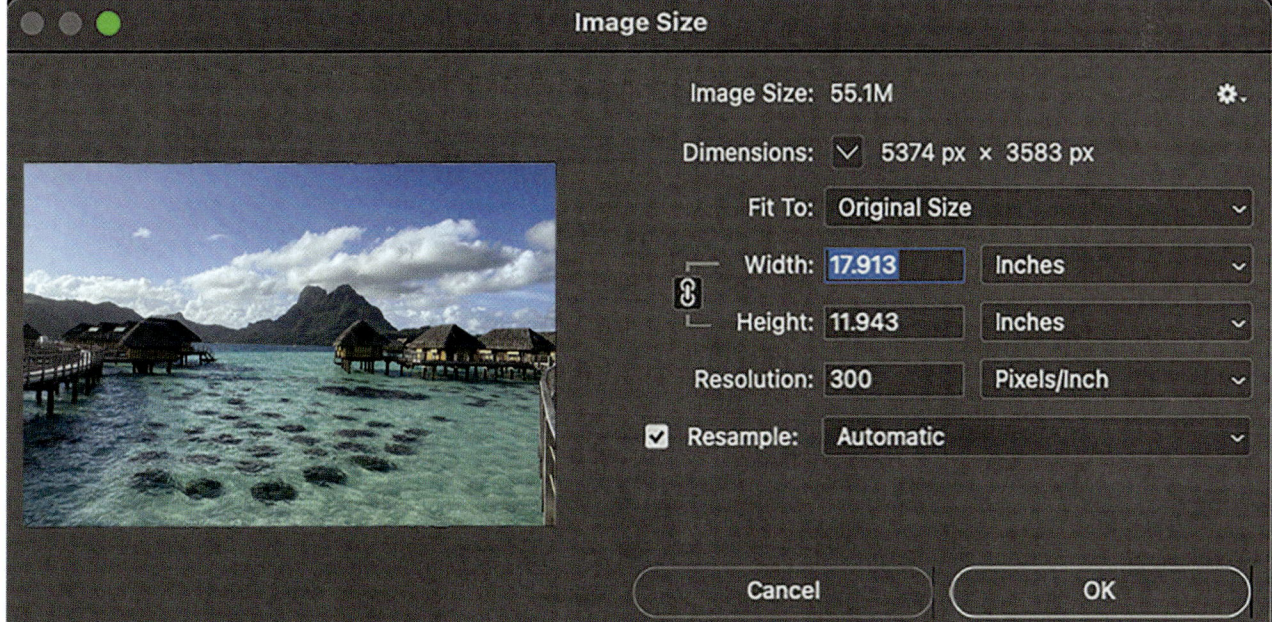

Goodheart-Willcox Publisher

Figure 18-11. The **Image Size** dialog box provides information on the current file size, image dimensions, and resolution.

The document's width, height, and resolution are shown in the center section. You can display width and height in various measurement units. Clicking on the down arrow at the right opens a drop-down menu showing the choices, **Figure 18-13**. The **Resolution** drop-down lists two choices—**pixels/inch** and **pixels/cm**.

At the bottom of the dialog box, **Resample** is checked by default. A drop-down menu displays *Automatic* but shows other resampling methods when the down arrow is clicked, **Figure 18-14**. The default **Automatic** choice is effective for most size changes. When size changes are 50% or more, some photographers prefer using **Bicubic Smoother** when

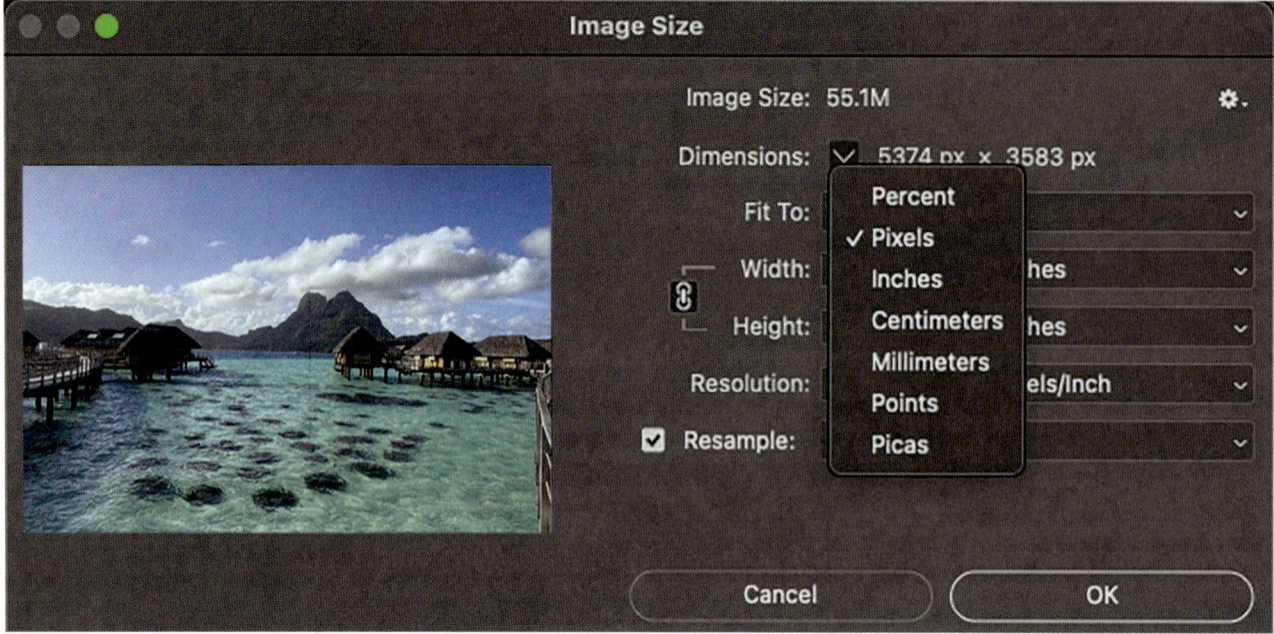

Goodheart-Willcox Publisher

Figure 18-12. You can change the size or resolution with the **Image Size** dialog box.

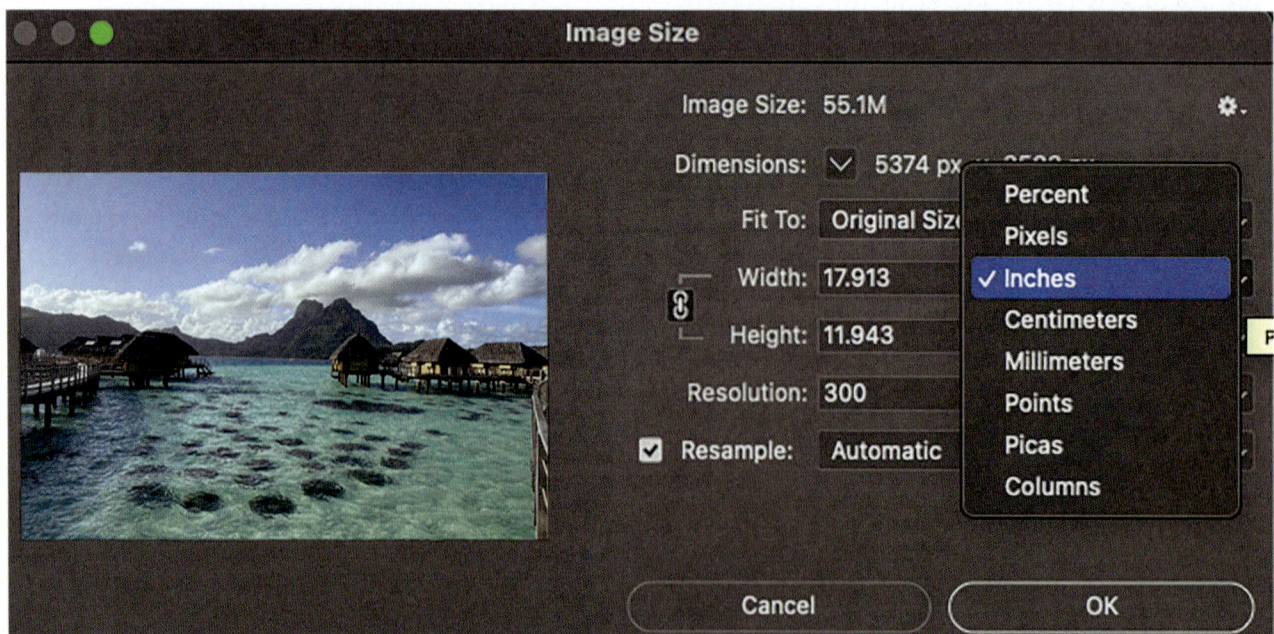

Goodheart-Willcox Publisher

Figure 18-13. A drop-down menu offers a number of choices for measurement unit displays. Pixels, inches, millimeters, or centimeters are most commonly used.

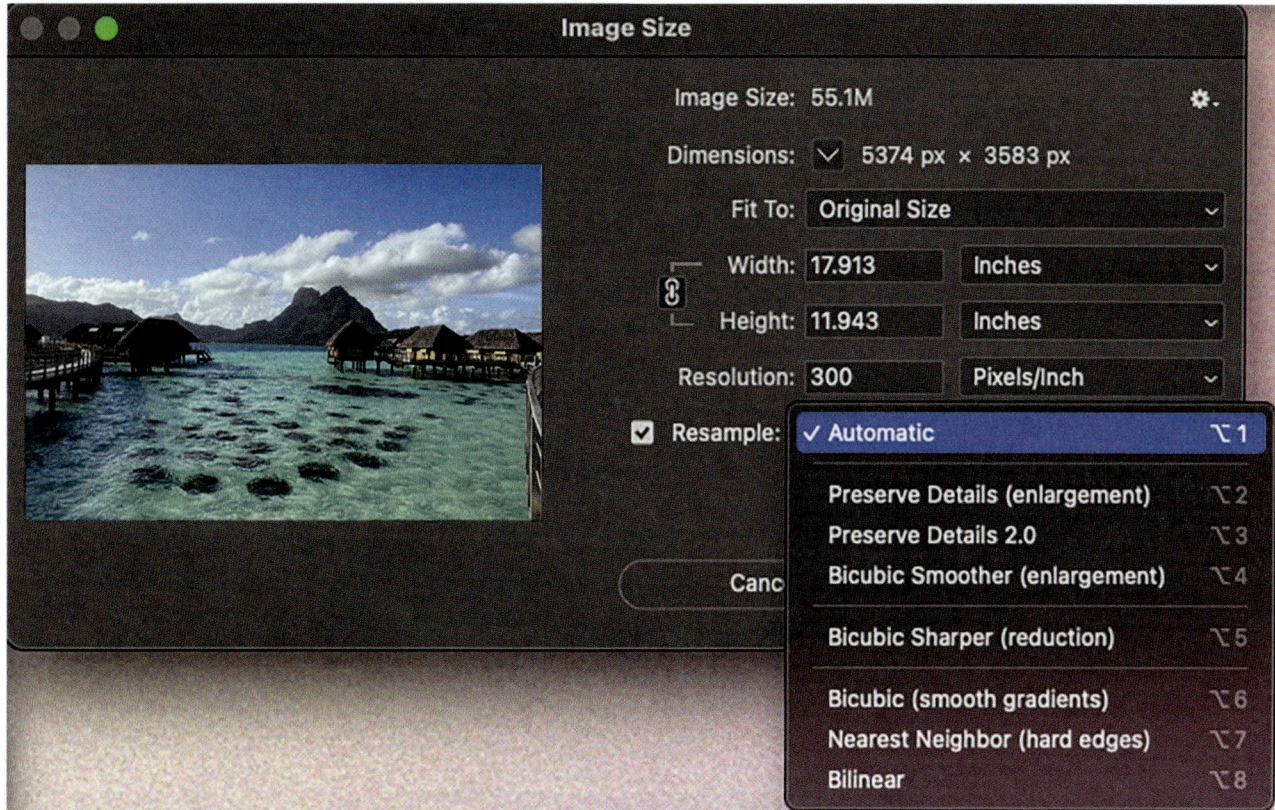

Goodheart-Willcox Publisher

Figure 18-14. The resampling method to be used when making image size changes can be selected from a drop-down menu.

increasing size or **Bicubic Sharper** when decreasing size. For extreme enlargements of 100% or more, **Preserve Details (enlargement)** or **Preserve Details 2.0** may be selected to upscale the image in multiple steps. **Preserve Details 2.0** uses artificial intelligence to detect and preserve image details without oversharpening anything else. The **Nearest Neighbor** and **Bilinear** settings are seldom used.

The **Resample** checkbox has a different effect on image size and resolution changes, depending on whether it is checked or unchecked. When the **Resample** box is checked (turned on), the following effects occur:

- A change in image dimensions does not increase or decrease the resolution.
- A change in the resolution does not increase or decrease the image dimensions.

If you decrease the image dimensions, the software selects and discards enough pixels to match the new size at the specified resolution. The same process, called ***downsampling***, is followed if you decrease resolution while keeping the dimensions the same. Downsampling generally has less effect on image quality than ***upsampling***, which occurs when image size or resolution is increased with the **Resample** box checked, **Figure 18-15**.

When you increase the dimensions, the size of the pixels remains the same (300 per inch), but the number of pixels has to increase to fill the added space. The image processing software creates new pixels to fill the gaps, a process called ***interpolation***. The new pixels are created by averaging the values of the surrounding existing pixels.

In **Figure 18-15**, note that the width and height dimensions are linked. Any change in width is accompanied by a corresponding change in height, and vice versa. This avoids any distortion of the image when it is enlarged or reduced. If you uncheck the **Constrain Proportions** lock button (chain-link symbol), you can stretch or squeeze the image by changing the dimensions independently. This capability is useful for making small adjustments in one dimension.

When the **Resample** box is unchecked (turned off), **Figure 18-16**, the following effects occur:

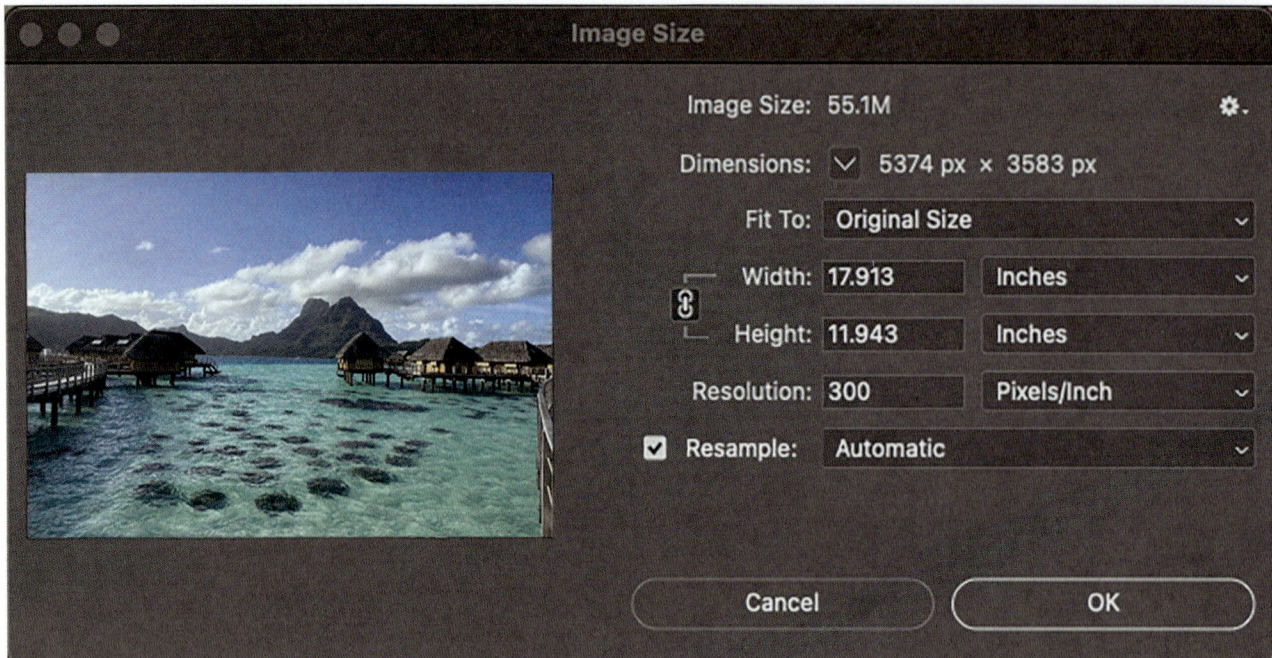

Figure 18-15. The **Resample** box checked.

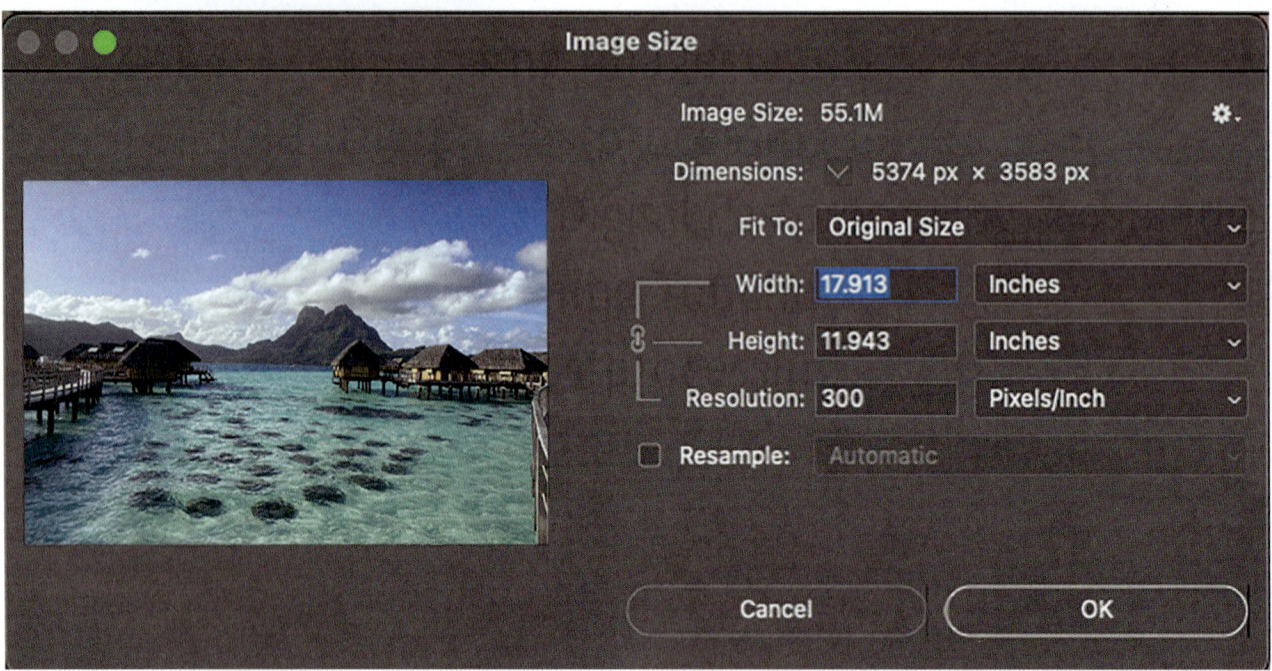

Figure 18-16. The **Resample** box unchecked.

- A change in image dimensions either increases or decreases the resolution.
- A change in the resolution either increases or decreases the image dimensions.

For example, if your original file is at a resolution of 180 ppi and you change the resolution setting to 300 ppi, the dimensions shrink by 40%. The number of pixels remains unchanged—you are just packing more of them into each inch by making them physically smaller. The result is a higher-quality image that reproduces better when printed or displayed digitally. This is a major reason why you should shoot images at the highest quality setting available on your camera. The larger the file, the more information is captured, giving you greater capabilities for image editing and manipulation.

Changing Canvas Size

If you want to increase the size of the space around your image, open the **Canvas Size** dialog box by clicking **Image > Canvas Size**. See **Figure 18-17**.

The uppermost section shows the current size of the image, while the center section has **Width** and **Height** boxes, a **Relative** checkbox, and a grid labeled **Anchor**, **Figure 18-18**.

There are two ways to specify the amount of extension:

- With the **Relative** box checked, the amount of increase (in inches or other units) can be specified for both height and width, **Figure 18-19**.

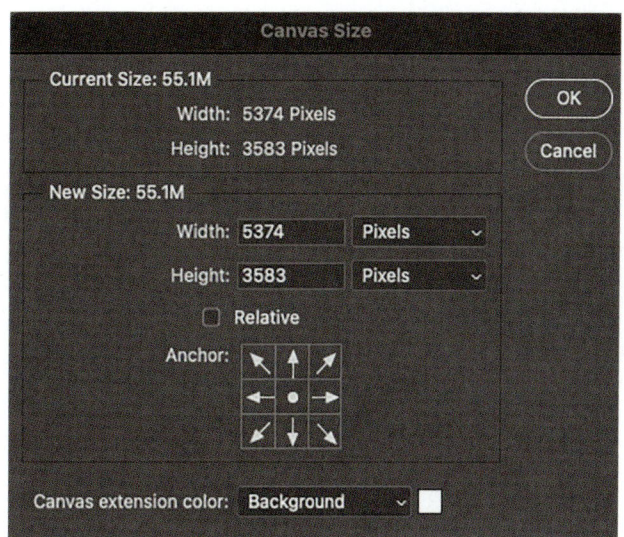

Goodheart-Willcox Publisher

Figure 18-18. The center section houses the **Width** and **Height** boxes, a **Relative** checkbox, and an **Anchor** grid.

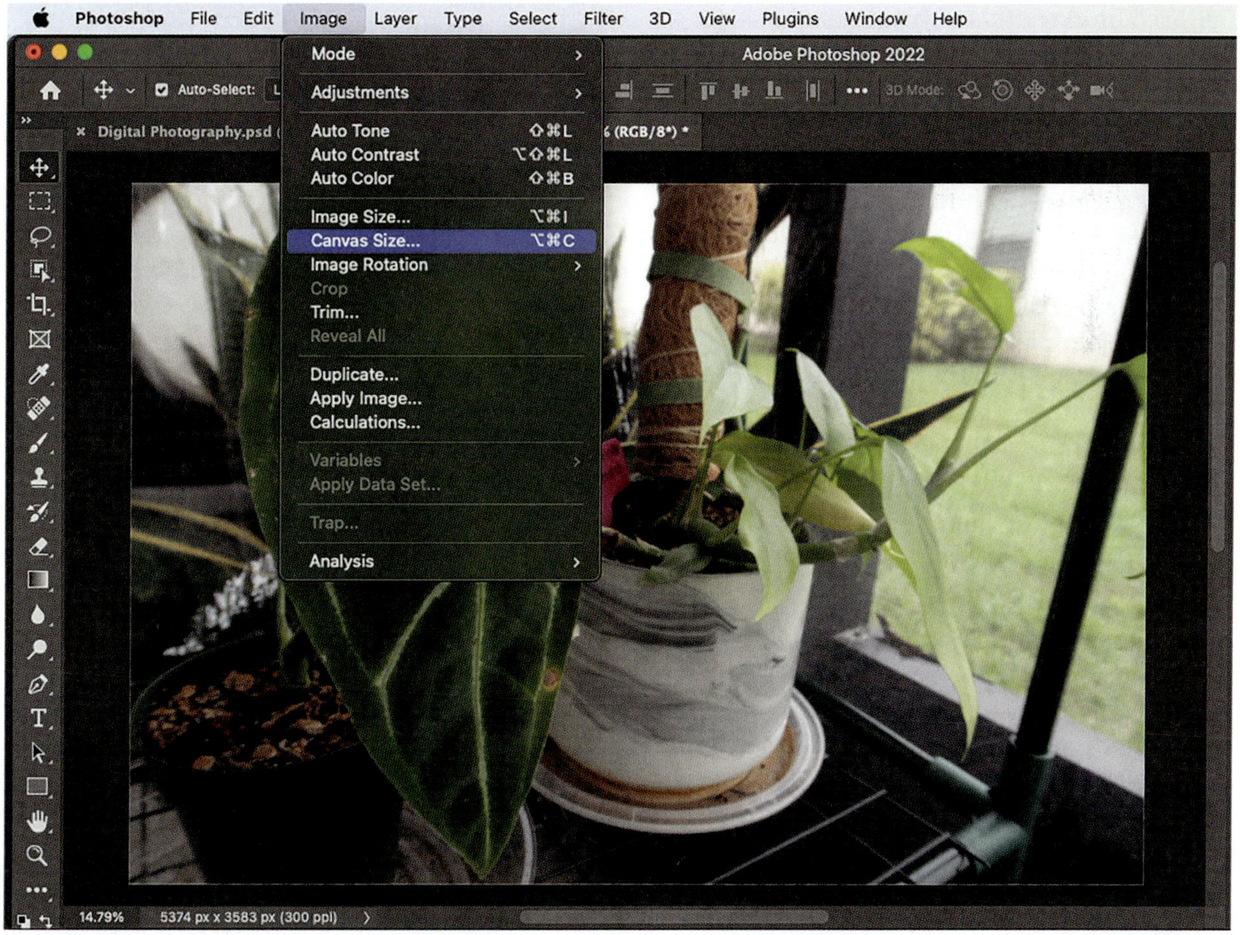

Goodheart-Willcox Publisher

Figure 18-17. Think of the canvas as the base on which your image rests. You can use the **Canvas Size** dialog box to increase the space around your image.

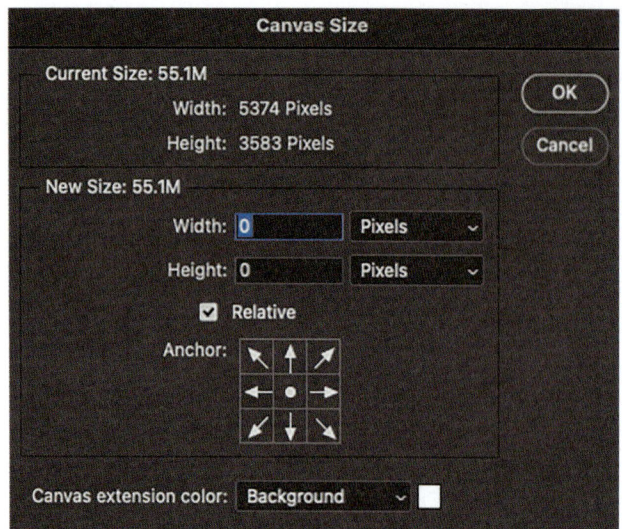

Goodheart-Willcox Publisher

Figure 18-19. To increase the canvas size by a specific amount, check the **Relative** box, and then enter the desired increase in width and height.

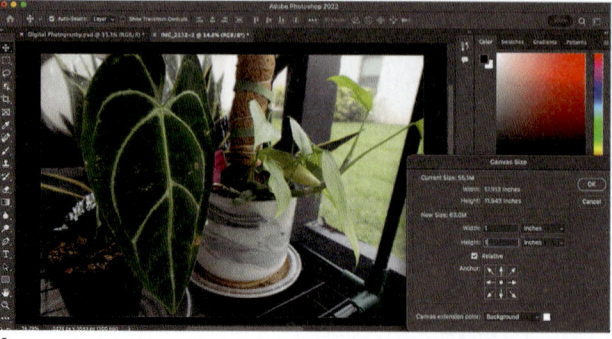

A

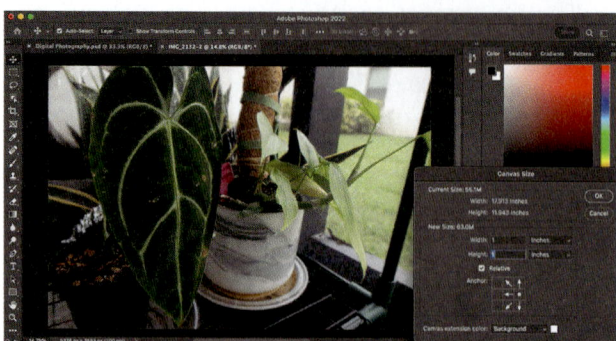

B

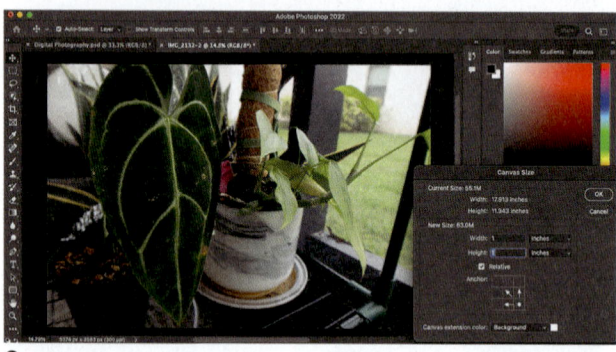

C

Goodheart-Willcox Publisher

Figure 18-20. Effects of using different anchor grid locations. A—With the dot square in the center position, the desired 1″ amount of canvas extension is split, adding 1/2″ on all four sides. B—When the dot square is moved to the left side, the canvas is extended 1/2″ on top and bottom and 1″ on the right side. C—Moving the dot square to the lower-right corner adds 1″ on the top and 1″ on the left side.

- With the **Relative** box unchecked, the desired final width and height dimensions must be entered.

If the **Anchor** grid is left in its default state (with the black dot in the center square), the canvas is extended as specified on all four sides of the image. Moving the square with the dot to one of the outside spaces distributes the canvas extension in other ways. See **Figure 18-20**.

You can select the color of the extended canvas at the bottom of the dialog box. The default is the **Background** color shown in the **Toolbar** (which is normally set to white). A drop-down menu allows you to select the **Foreground** color, white, black, gray, or a custom color.

Working with Layers

One of the most attractive features of full-featured image editing programs is the ability to create *image layers*. These layers can be thought of as separate transparent sheets attached to the base image and layered on top of the same base image. Different elements of the image can be placed on separate layers so they can be worked on independently without changing the rest of the image, which makes working with layers a great nondestructive editing technique. Material on a layer can totally block out the corresponding image area on layers below it or may be decreased in opacity to allow the underlying material to show through to some degree. Layers can be blended together for various effects, including overall darkening or lightening of the image.

When an image is first opened in the editing program, it is on a single layer called the **Background** layer. If only basic digital postprocessing tasks are to be performed on the image, the single background layer may be sufficient. As noted earlier, you should make changes on a copy of the image, preserving the original in its unchanged state for possible future use.

The background layer and any layers that you add as you work on the image appear on the **Layers** panel, **Figure 18-21**. Each layer is a separate item on the panel. An individual layer can be displayed on the monitor by itself or in combination with other layers. The visibility of each layer is indicated by an eye icon to the far left of the item. Clicking on the icon turns layer visibility on and off. Changes can be made only to the *active layer*, which is indicated by highlighting, **Figure 18-22**.

Layers can be added, deleted, or moved to a different position within the stack of items shown on the **Layers** panel. As new layers are added, they are placed on top of the stack. You can delete a layer by dragging the item to the trashcan shown at the bottom of the panel. To move a layer, drag it upward or downward in the stack. A layer also can be relocated using the **Arrange** commands from the **Layer** menu. It is also helpful to label your layers as you work with them to help keep them organized.

Creating New Layers

New layers can be created in several ways. To open a new blank layer, click on the **Create New Layer** icon at the bottom of the **Layers** panel, **Figure 18-23**, or select **Layer > New > Layer** from the drop-down menu, **Figure 18-24**.

When you have selected part of an image (selection tools are covered in detail in Chapter 19, *Advanced Digital Postprocessing Techniques*) and wish to place the selected material on a separate layer, choose **New > Layer** from the **Layer** drop-down menu. The menu choices include **Layer via Cut** and **Layer via Copy**. Either one copies the selection to a new layer, but they differ greatly in their effect on the original image layer, **Figure 18-25**.

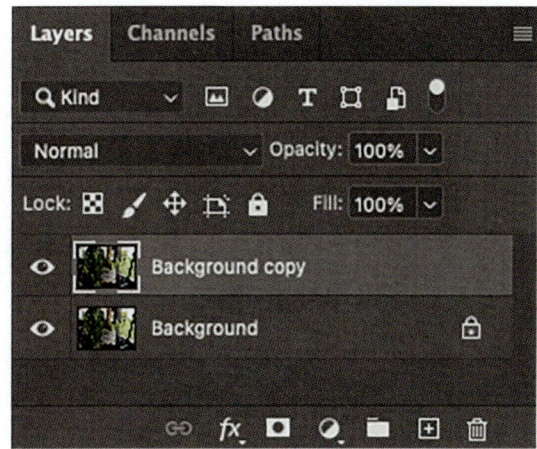

Goodheart-Willcox Publisher

Figure 18-22. The gray highlighting shows that **Background Copy Layer** is currently active. Any changes to the image are made on that layer; other layers are not affected.

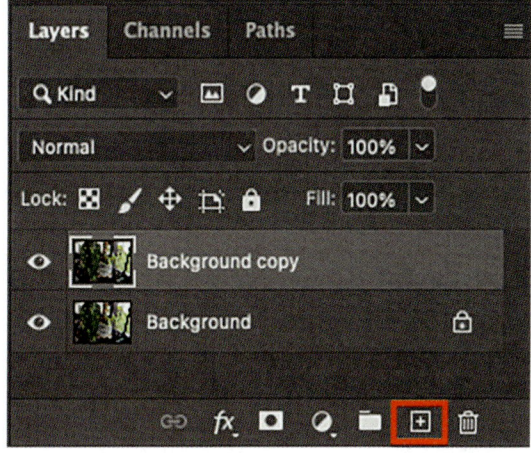

Goodheart-Willcox Publisher

Figure 18-23. You can add a new layer by navigating to the bottom of the **Layers** panel and selecting **New Layer**.

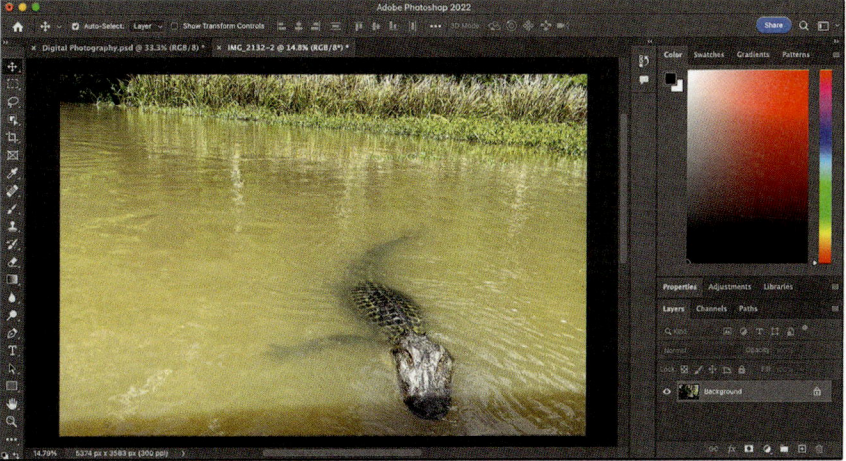

Goodheart-Willcox Publisher

Figure 18-21. All layers created for an image are shown as items on the **Layers** panel.

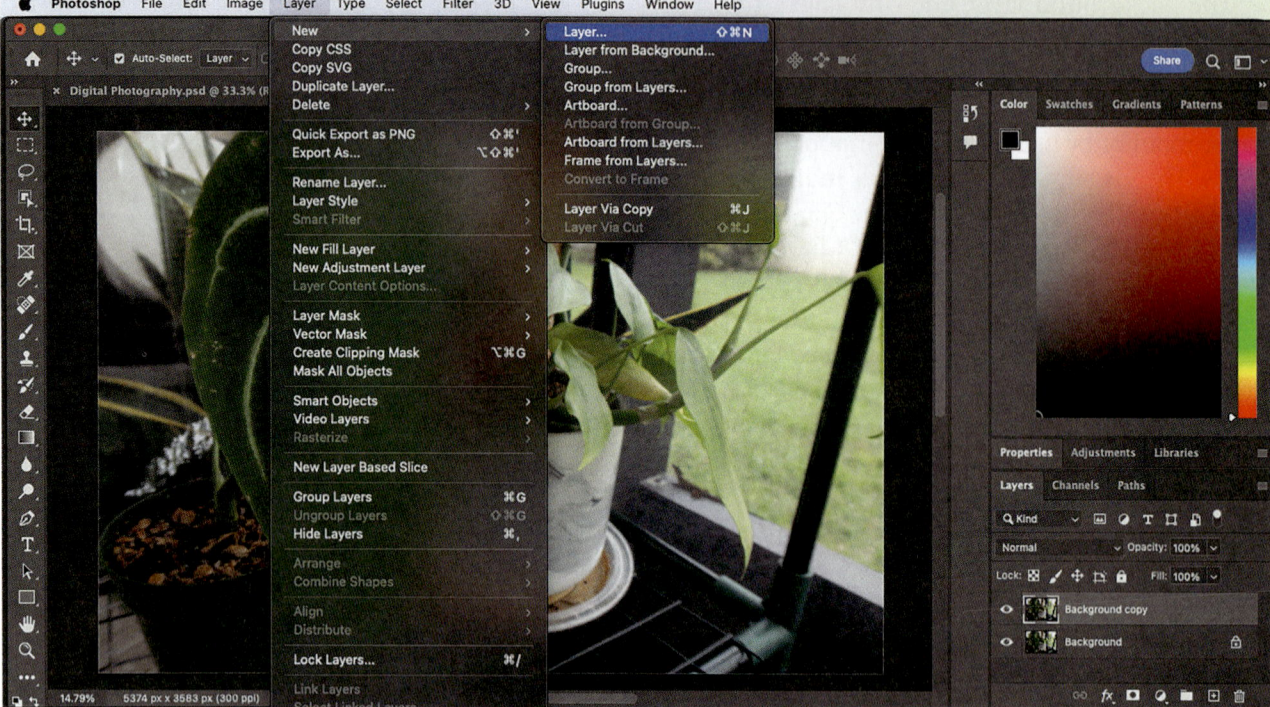

Figure 18-24. You can also add a new layer by navigating to **New > Layer** in the drop-down menu.

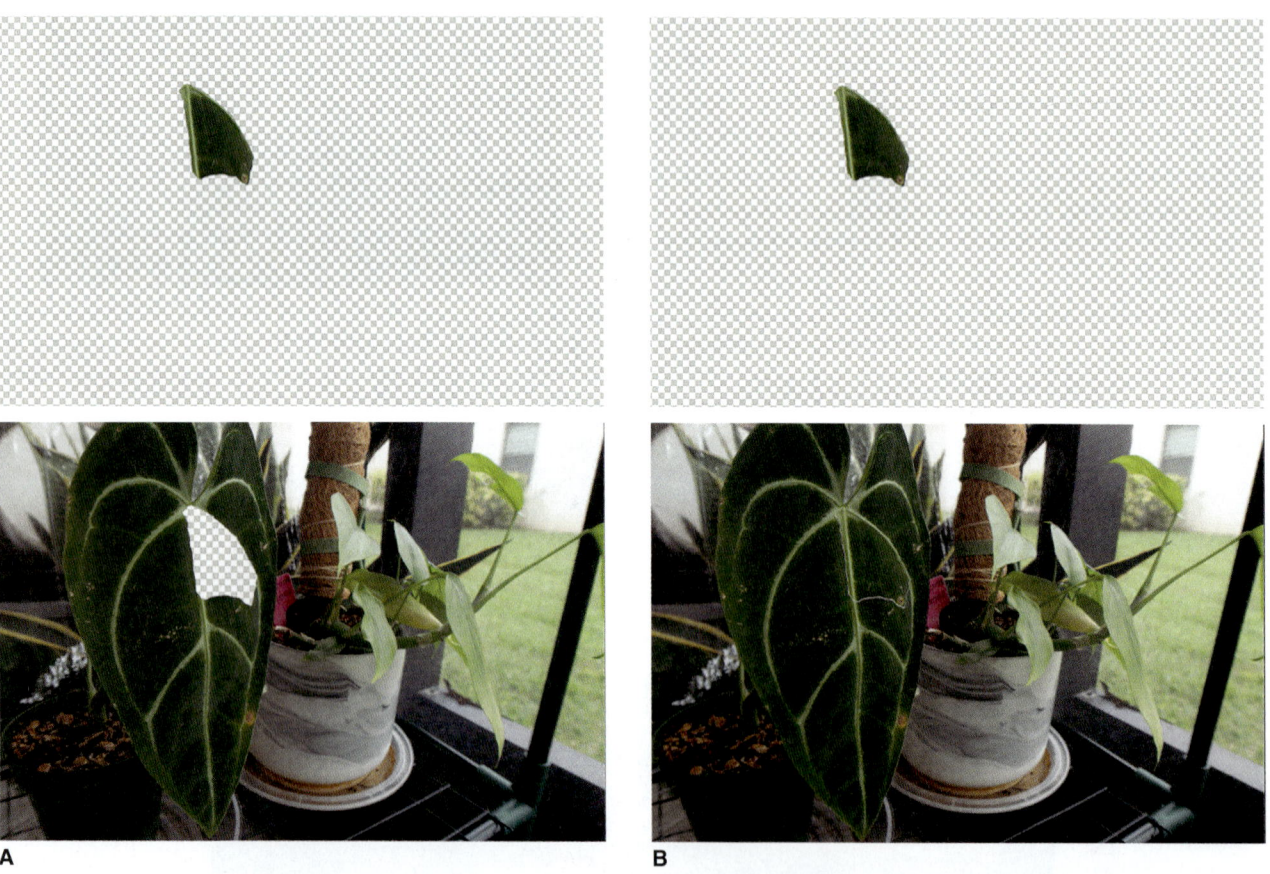

Figure 18-25. A selection can be placed on a new layer by either cutting or copying. A—The **Layer via Cut** command leaves a "hole" on the original layer. B—The **Layer via Copy** command leaves the original layer unchanged.

Layer via Cut leaves a blank area behind when the new layer is created. On a background layer, the "hole" is white. On other layers, the opening is transparent. **Layer via Copy** copies the selection onto the new layer, but the original remains intact.

You can also place a selection on a new layer in a different image, a technique commonly used to create a composite (composite creation is covered in Chapter 19). There are two different methods for moving a selection to a different image—cut-and-paste and dragging.

- **Cut-and-paste.** Click on the selection, then select **Cut** or **Copy** from the **Edit** menu. You can also use shortcut keys—Ctrl+X and Ctrl+C, respectively. Open the destination image, and then click on **Paste** from the **Edit** menu or use the shortcut, Ctrl+V. The selection is placed in the destination image as a new layer.
- **Dragging.** Both the original and destination images must be open on the monitor. Click on the **Move** tool in the toolbar, then click on the selection and drag it to the destination image. The selection is placed on a new layer in the destination image. See **Figure 18-26**. Existing layers can also be copied from one image to another by dragging. Again, both images must be open on the monitor. Click on the original image to make it active, and then click on the desired layer thumbnail on the **Layers** panel. Drag the layer to the destination image, releasing the mouse button when a black border appears around the destination image window.

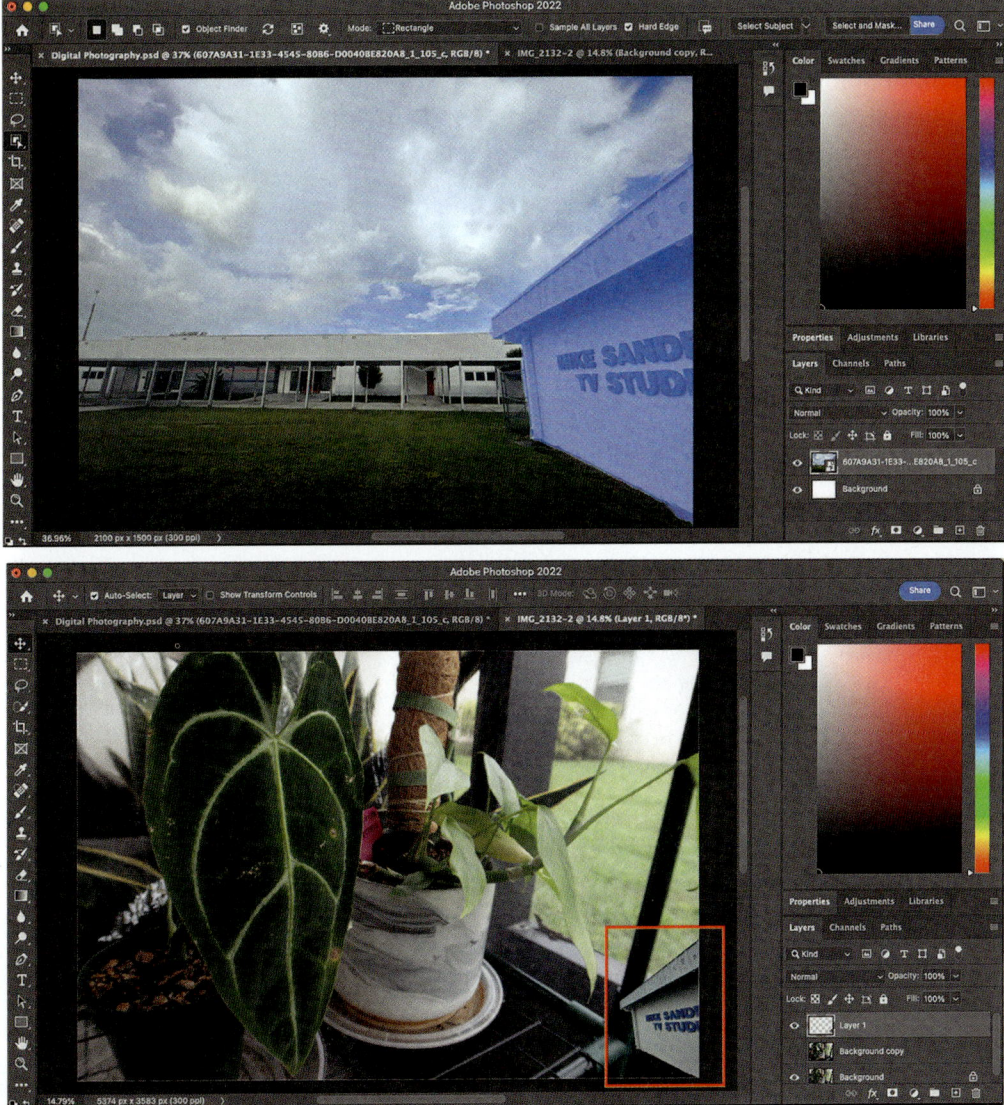

Goodheart-Willcox Publisher

Figure 18-26. Copying a selection from one image (highlighted in blue) to another with the **Move** tool. The cut-and-paste or copy-and-paste techniques can also be used.

Adjustment Layers

Adjustment layers are special-purpose layers that allow changes to be made to an image's appearance without permanently altering the original image pixels. They permit you to experiment with different effects or values while observing the changes on the display. When using a **Hue/Saturation** adjustment layer, for example, you can increase or decrease the saturation of colors in the image or change the colors themselves. See **Figure 18-27**. The use of adjustment layers is explored in greater detail in Chapter 19.

Layer Styles

A *layer style* is a collection of two or more layer effects working simultaneously to create a bigger overall look. They are similar to adjustment layers in terms of function. There are numerous layer styles preloaded into Photoshop available for use.

To choose a layer style, first select a layer in the **Layers** panel. In the **Effects** panel, choose **Layer Styles**. To apply a layer style, you can either select it and click **Apply**, double-click on it, or drag it onto your layer. These layer styles are also cumulative, meaning that many of them can be combined for a custom look. You are also able to edit a layer style's settings by selecting **Choose Layer > Layer Style > Style Settings**. Some popular layer styles are as follows:

- **Lighting Angle** specifies the lighting angle at which an effect is applied to the layer.
- **Drop Shadow** specifies the distance of a drop shadow from the layer. You can also adjust the size and opacity of drop shadows using a slider.
- **Glow (Outer)** creates a glow that comes from the outside edges of the layer. **Glow (Inner)** creates a glow that comes from the inside edges of the layer. You can adjust the opacity of the glow using a slider.
- **Bevel Size** specifies the size of beveling along the inside edge of the layer. **Bevel Direction** specifies the bevel's direction (up or down).
- **Stroke Size** allows you to choose the size of a stroke. **Stroke Opacity** allows you to adjust the opacity of a stroke.

Undo/Redo

Undo or redo is an incredibly useful tool in Photoshop, especially when working with layers. To undo a movement, you can use the shortcut Ctrl+Z or select **Edit > Undo**. To redo a movement, you can use the shortcut Shift+Ctrl+Z or select **Edit > Redo**.

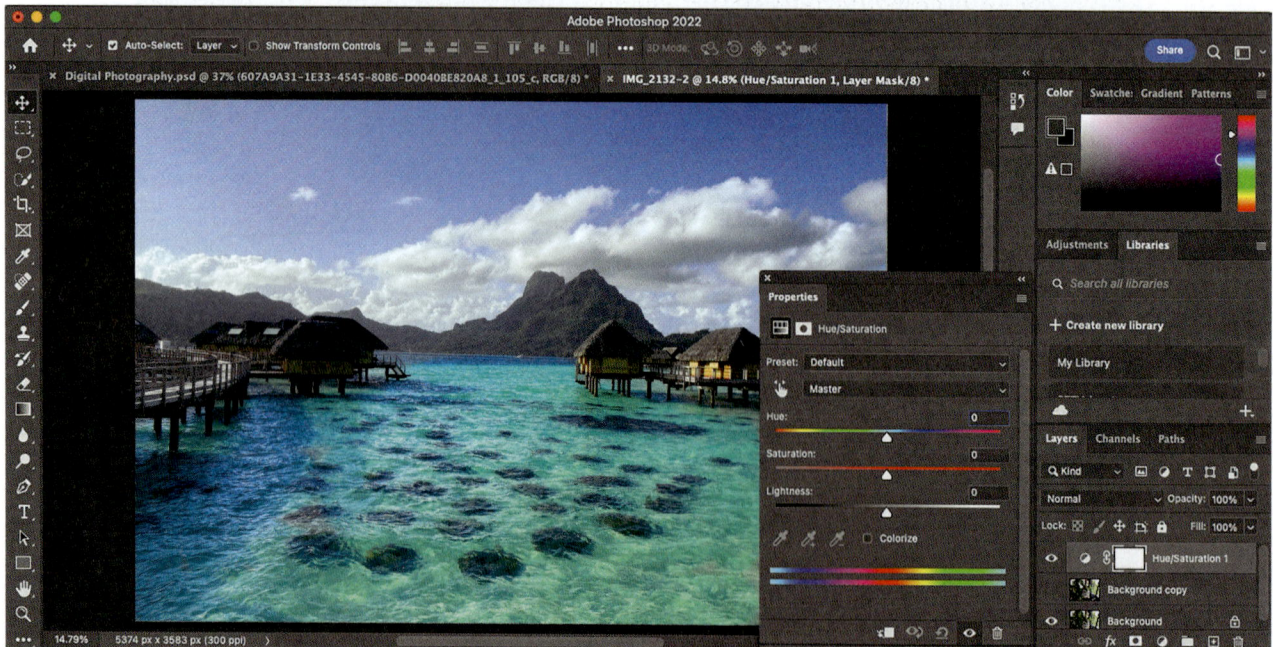

Goodheart-Willcox Publisher

Figure 18-27. Using a **Hue/Saturation** adjustment layer to emphasize the bright colors of the water and huts.

You can also use the **History** panel to return to any recent state of the image from your current working session. Each time you make an edit to your working document, that movement is saved in the **History** panel to provide easy access to a list of all recent changes. If you select a previous state, your document will revert, and you will be able to edit from that point. It defaults to the previous 20 versions, and this is adjustable in the program settings.

Adjusting Overall Exposure

Most images, even those that are generally well-exposed, require some adjustment for best appearance. The most basic image refinement is expanding the tonal range with the **Levels** adjustment command. While the **Levels** command can be used on the **Background** layer, it is preferable to make changes using an adjustment layer. To create a **Levels** adjustment layer, click on the **Levels** icon in the **Adjustments** panel. The **Levels** histogram appears, and a new layer (**Levels 1**) is shown on the **Layers** panel. See **Figure 18-28**.

The histogram is a graphic display of the number and distribution of tones in an image. The peaks and valleys represent the actual number of pixels of each shade, from 0 (pure black) at left to 255 (pure white) at right. The histogram for an image with a full range of tones shows smaller numbers of pixels at the extremes and a large number distributed through the middle tones.

A histogram that displays empty areas at either end indicates no pixels at the lowest or highest values. You can adjust the image's black point and white point to distribute tones over the full tonal range by moving the small triangular sliders below either end of the histogram. Position the sliders beneath the lowest and highest values shown,

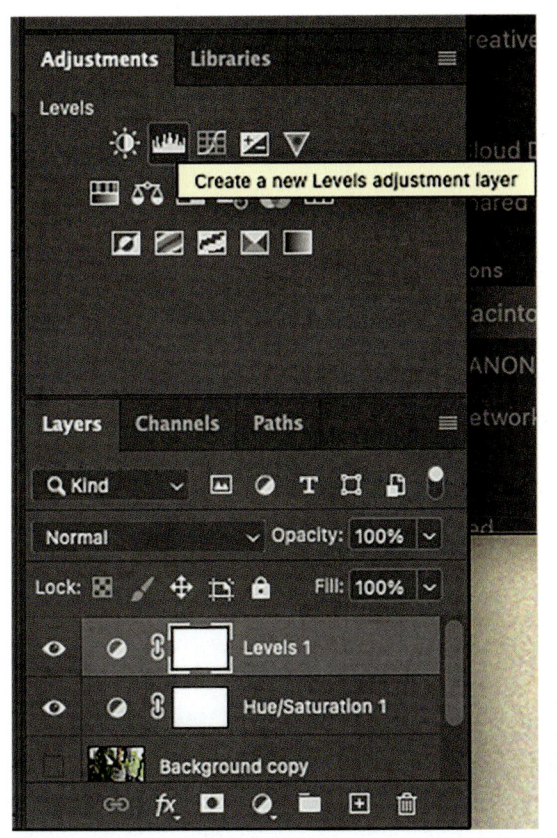
A

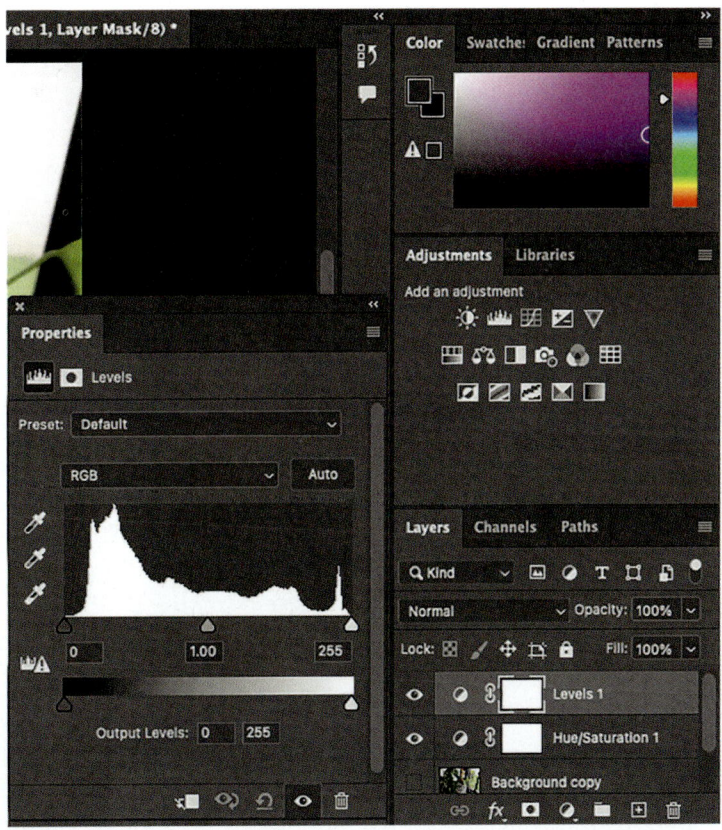
B

Goodheart-Willcox Publisher

Figure 18-28. Using the **Adjustments** panel. A—Click on the **Levels** icon to create a new adjustment layer. B—A **Levels 1** adjustment layer is shown on the **Layers** panel, and a histogram appears. The empty area at the right side of the histogram indicates that the image is dark and underexposed.

Figure 18-29. This reassigns the values of the pixels, so the darkest value becomes 0 and the lightest value becomes 255. All pixel values in the image are redistributed to provide a full tonal range.

To lighten or darken the midtones of an image, use the slider located below the center of the histogram. Moving the slider to the left lightens, while moving it to the right darkens. You can view the effects of the changes in the preview image.

Another command used to adjust the overall lightness or darkness of an image is **Brightness/Contrast**. Unlike the **Levels** command, it does not expand the tonal range—it merely shifts the histogram to the right (lighter) or to the left (darker).

An image can also be lightened or darkened overall by using **Duplicate Layer** and one of the blending modes. As shown in **Figure 18-30**, the duplicate layer appears above the **Background** layer in the **Layers** panel. To lighten the image, choose the **Screen** blending mode from the blending modes list and adjust the opacity slider until the desired degree of lightening is achieved. This is a useful method for salvaging an image that has been overexposed. To darken an underexposed image, follow the same procedure, but choose the **Multiply** blending mode.

Sometimes, using the **Levels** adjustment improves the overall brightness of the image but does not lighten the shadow areas. The **Shadows/Highlights** command, accessed by clicking **Image > Adjustments > Shadows/Highlights**, lightens the darker (shadow) areas of the image without affecting the lighter (highlight) areas. See **Figure 18-31**. The amount of shadow lightening is adjustable using a slider control. The default setting is 50%, but many photographers feel this is too light. Highlight areas can be darkened (but not lightened) using a separate slider. The **Shadows/Highlights** command cannot be used as an adjustment layer; however, it can be applied to a new duplicate background layer. By positioning the duplicate layer between the **Levels** adjustment layer and the **Background** layer, both the levels and the shadow and highlight changes are visible.

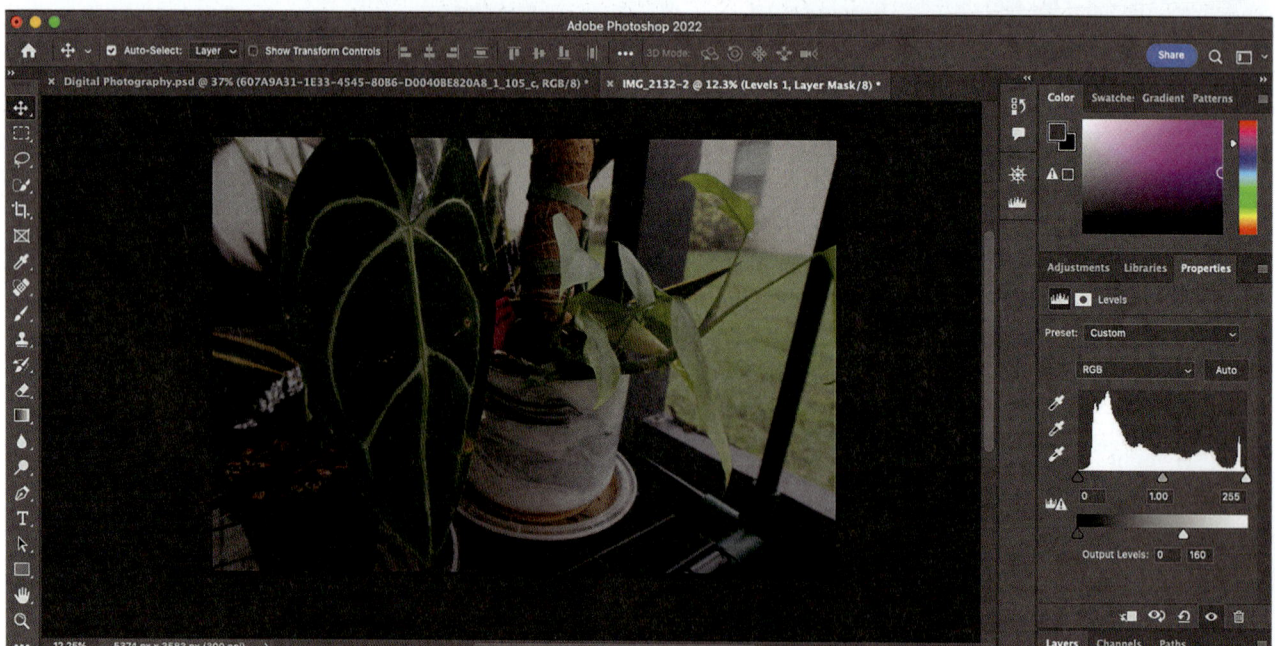

Goodheart-Willcox Publisher

Figure 18-29. Moving the slider below the right side of the histogram adjusts the white point, distributing image tones over the full tonal range.

Adjusting Local Exposure (Burning In and Dodging)

Those who have worked in a conventional darkroom are familiar with the processes of *burning in* and *dodging* in specific areas of a physical photo. In Photoshop, the toolbar contains a **Burn** tool and **Dodge** tool that serve the same purposes, **Figure 18-32**. In image editing software, **burning in** is a technique that involves applying additional

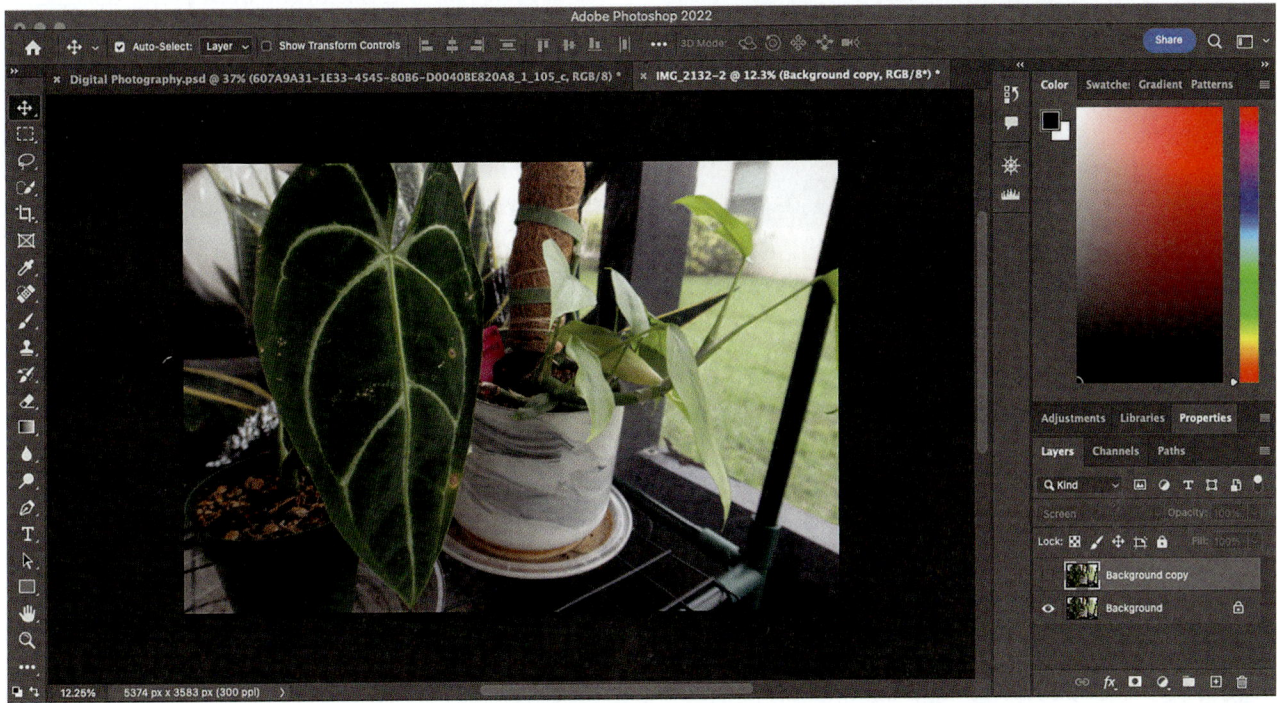

A

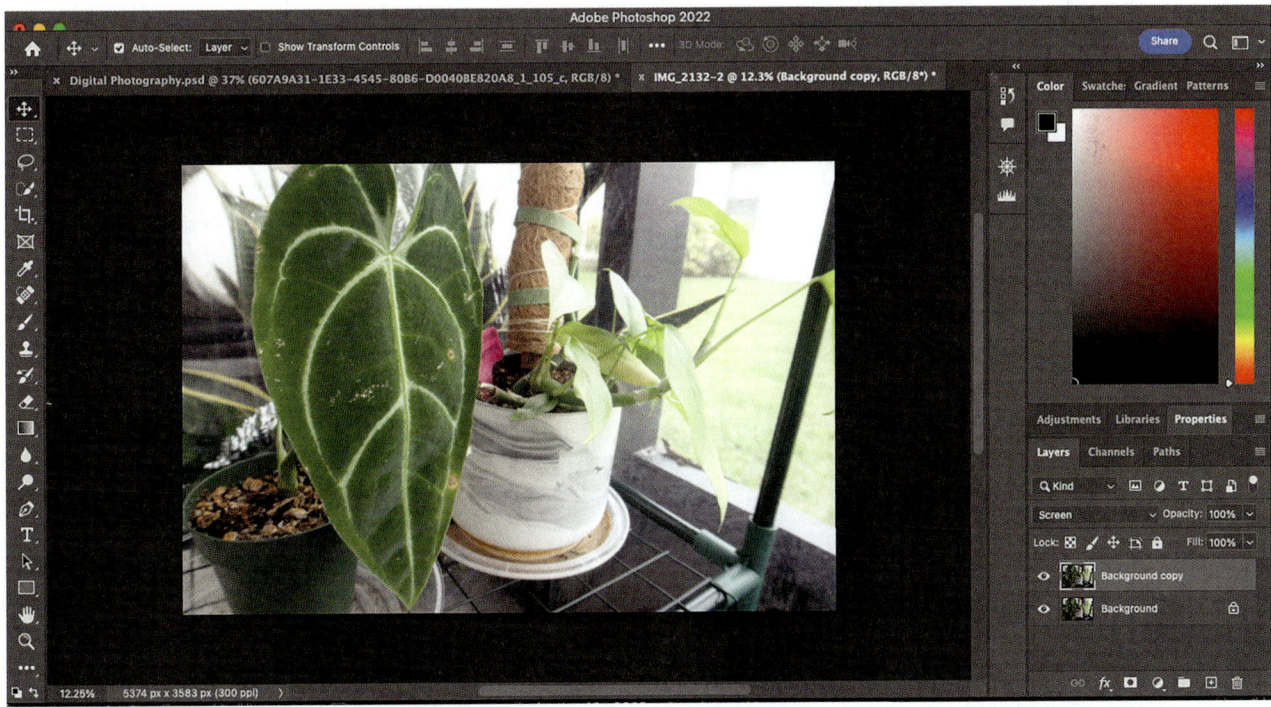

B

Goodheart-Willcox Publisher

Figure 18-30. Using blending modes. A—This image is somewhat dark. B—Adding a duplicate layer and changing the **Blending** mode to **Screen** lightens the image.

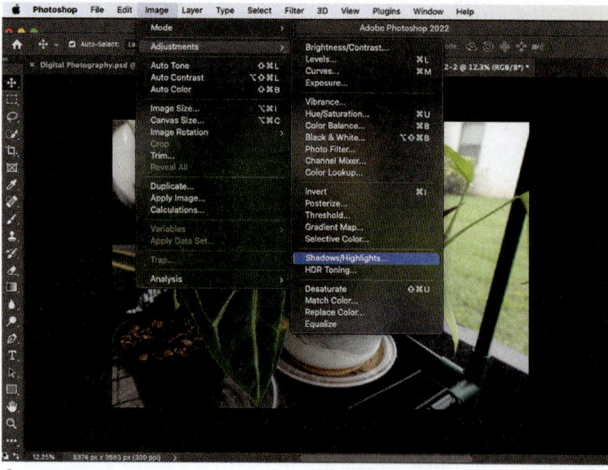

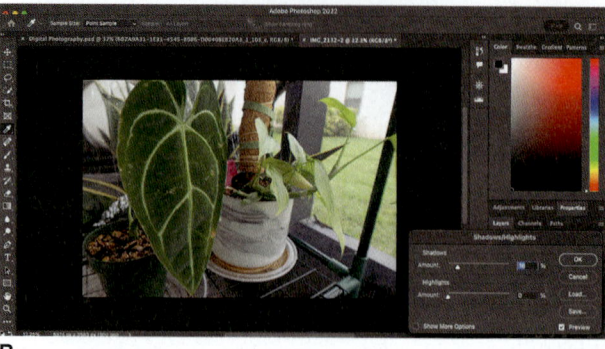

Goodheart-Willcox Publisher

Figure 18-31. Shadow/Highlight command. A—This original image is fine, but it can read a little dark. B—The shadows were increased slightly to brighten up the darker areas.

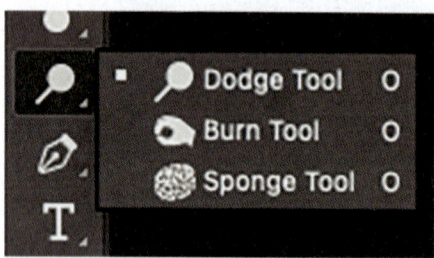

Goodheart-Willcox Publisher

Figure 18-32. The **Dodge** and **Burn** tools are available in the toolbar.

exposure to a selected area of an image. This is primarily used to darken and bring out detail in midtones and highlight areas. ***Dodging*** is a technique that involves applying additional processing to a specific area of a photo, but it is primarily used to lighten and bring out detail in an image. Both tools offer the option of being applied to shadows, midtones, or highlights. Exposure can be controlled on the options bar by typing in a value from 1 to 100 or using a slider. See **Figure 18-33**.

Once the **Dodge** tool or **Burn** tool is selected, the tool size can be chosen from the **Brushes** panel. Typically, a soft-edged brush is used to help blend the effect with surrounding image areas. Brush size depends on the size of the area being dodged or burned in. For those who use a pen and graphics tablet, the options bar has an icon to specify whether pen pressure affects the size of the brush being used.

Burning in and dodging cannot create texture and detail where none is available. If highlight areas are "blown out" to pure white by overexposure, burning in creates a featureless and unattractive gray tone. Similarly, dense black underexposed shadow areas can be lightened, but they will also be without any detail or texture.

Altering Contrast

Altering the relationship of shadow and highlight, or contrast, within a photo is a basic operation, since a straight print, or unaltered image, is seldom totally satisfactory. The tonal range may be too narrow, resulting in a flat and dull image, or too wide, producing a harsh and too-contrasty print.

Digital postprocessing permits use of an infinite range of contrast alterations. There are two basic methods for altering contrast—the **Brightness/Contrast** command and the **Curves** command. Both are available as adjustment layers, allowing them to be applied without affecting the pixels of the original image.

Brightness/Contrast is simple to use—sliders allow adjustment of contrast from 0 to 100 (increase) or 0 to –100 (decrease). Control is not precise, however, since sliders are difficult to adjust in small increments.

Curves is more versatile, **Figure 18-34**. Its tone graph is initially presented as a straight diagonal line, representing the gradation from darkest value (at lower left) to brightest value (at upper right). Using the mouse, a graph curve can be constructed that is reflected by value changes in the image. If the **Preview** box is checked (the usual configuration), changes can be observed on the monitor as adjustments are made.

For greater control when working with a color image, you can individually adjust contrast of the red, green, and blue color channels. Use the **Channel** box above the tone graph to select the desired channel. **RGB** is the default—when it is

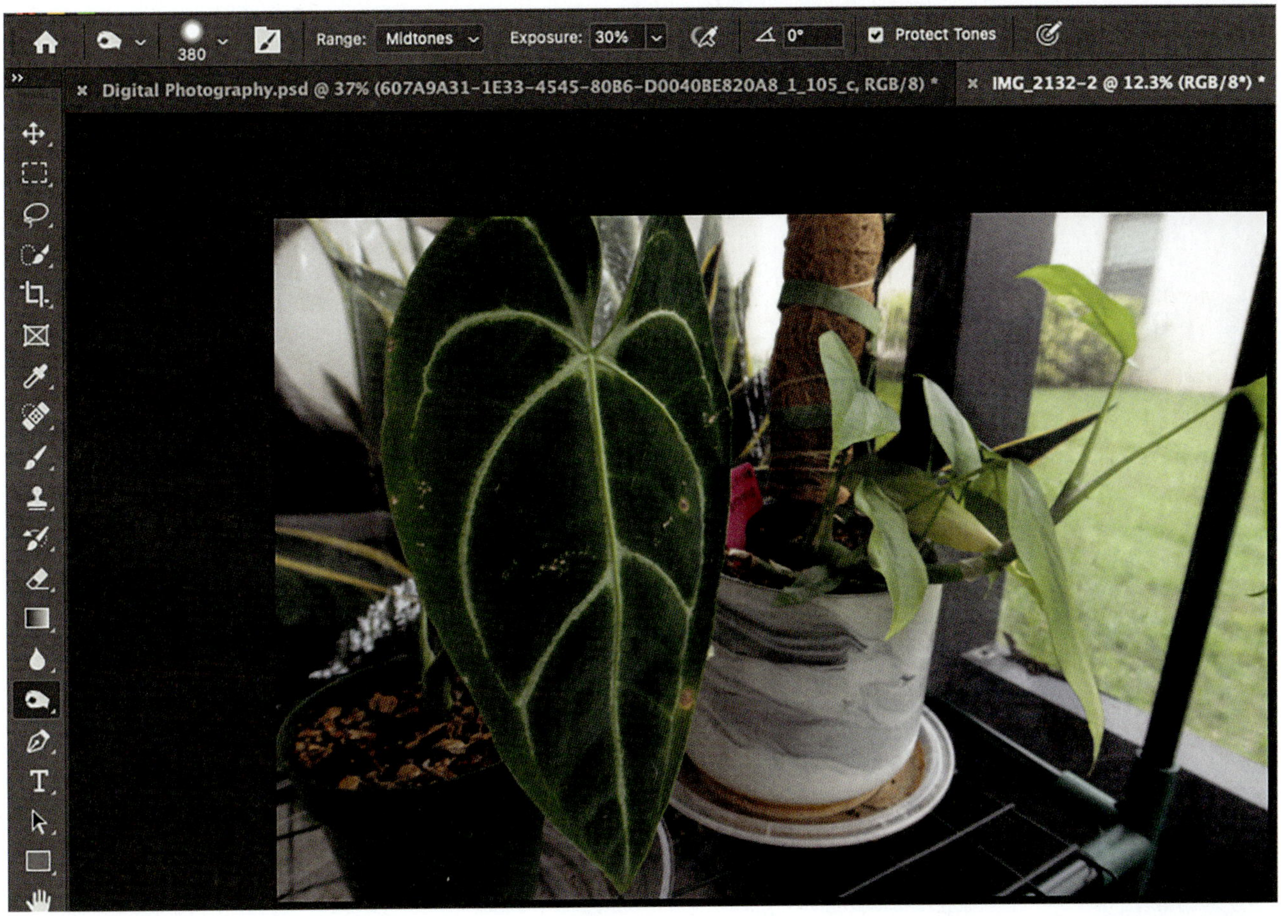

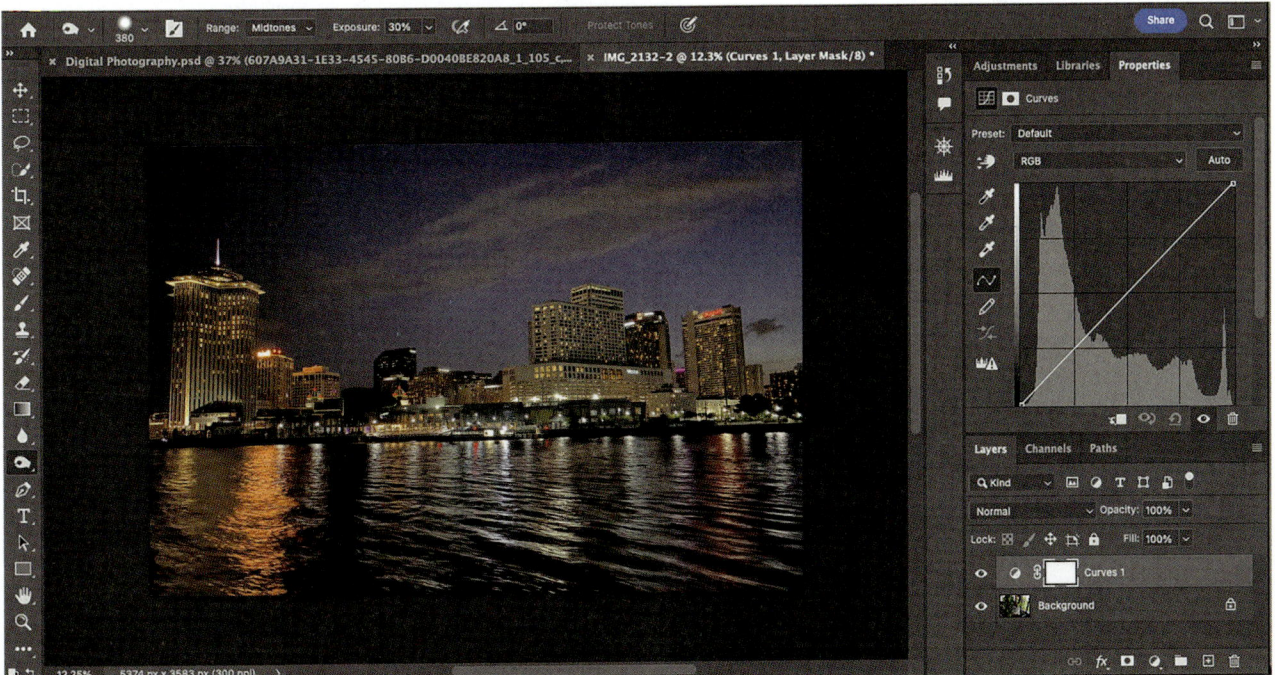

Figure 18-33. The **Burn** tool is being used at a low (30%) value to increase the midtones on the smaller leaves on the right side of the plant.

Figure 18-34. The **Curves** adjustment layer.

Chapter 18   Digital Postprocessing Basics   447

displayed, contrast adjustments are applied to all three channels simultaneously.

Contrast also can be adjusted in a selected area of the image. Such a local change might be made to bring up detail in the somewhat dark foreground of a landscape. First, make a selection, then make the contrast adjustment. The change will affect only the selected area.

PROCEDURE

Using Curves to Alter Contrast

1. With the image open, click on the **Curves** icon in the **Adjustments** panel.
2. Click on the midpoint of the diagonal line to anchor it at that point. A small black dot will appear at the center of the graph line.
3. Click on the line at a point midway between the center and the lower-left corner, then drag it a small distance diagonally down and to the right. Note that the line is now a curve from the midpoint to the lower-left corner. The line from the midpoint to the upper-right corner has assumed a matching (but opposite) curved shape, **Figure A**.
4. The image now has more contrast, with the tonal range extended. The degree of contrast change depends on the distance the point was moved. The farther the line curves away from the diagonal, the greater the change.
5. To decrease contrast, move the curve in the opposite direction, curving upward from the lower-left corner to the midpoint and downward from the midpoint to the upper-right corner. The tonal range is decreased, flattening the image.

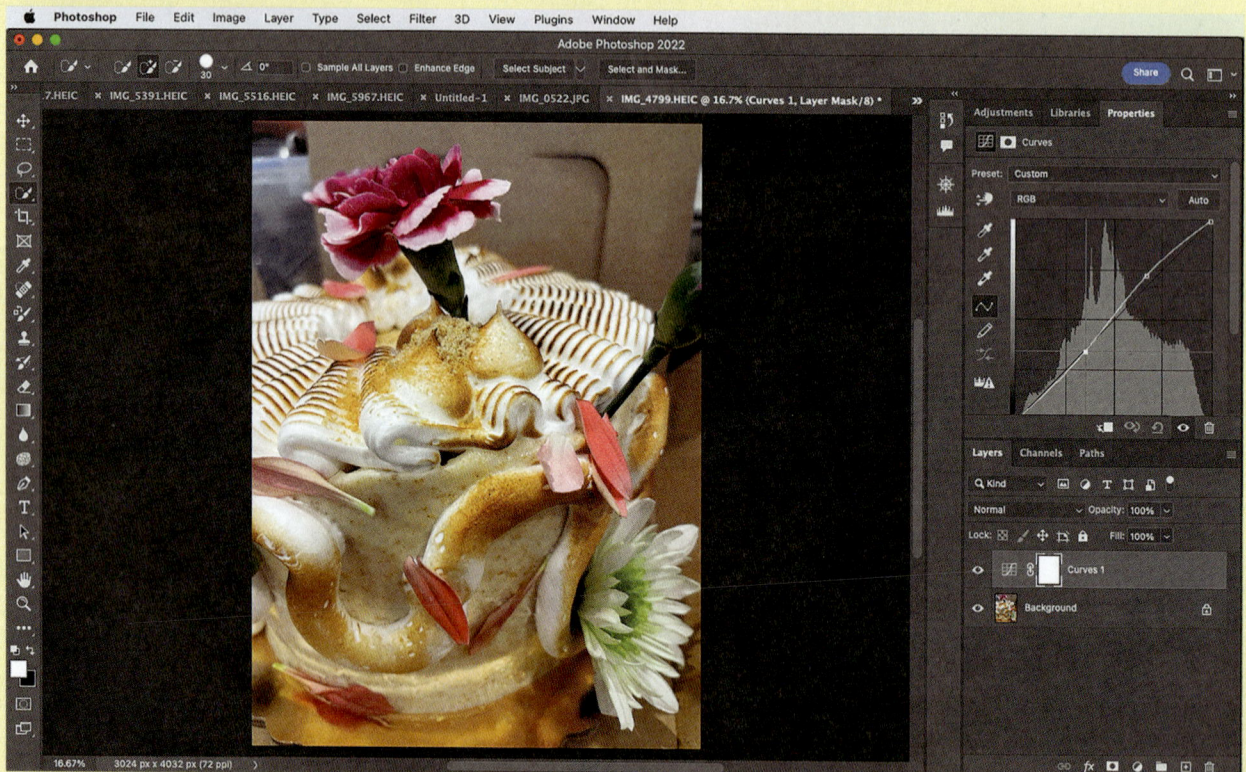

Goodheart-Willcox Publisher

Figure A. This mildly S-curved line represents a moderate increase in the contrast of the image.

448 Section 5 Postprocessing

Correcting and Adjusting Color

As compared to black-and-white images, working with color images can be considered three or four times as complicated, since color images consist of either three channels (red, blue, and green) or four channels (cyan, magenta, yellow, and black). The images displayed on your computer screen are RGB images—all the colors you see are combinations of varying amounts of red, blue, and green light. Tiny phosphor dots of red, blue, and green glow when struck by a beam of electrons, transmitting the color. Light-emitting diode displays (LEDs) and liquid crystal displays (LCDs) operate on different principles but have the same visual effect. Red, green, and blue are referred to as the ***additive primary colors***, since their light is added together to make a color.

Images that are printed on paper or another opaque base material convey colors to the eye using reflected light instead of transmitted light. Printed images make use of a different set of colors—cyan, magenta, and yellow. Each color blocks, or subtracts, a specific color and reflects others. Yellow absorbs the blue wavelengths of light but reflects red and green, magenta absorbs green but reflects red and blue, while cyan absorbs red and reflects blue and green. For this reason, these colors are called the ***subtractive primary colors***.

On the standard color wheel, **Figure 18-35**, the additive and subtractive primaries alternate and thus are paired on opposite sides—red is opposite cyan, blue is opposite yellow, and green is opposite magenta. The colors in each pair are known as *complementary colors*.

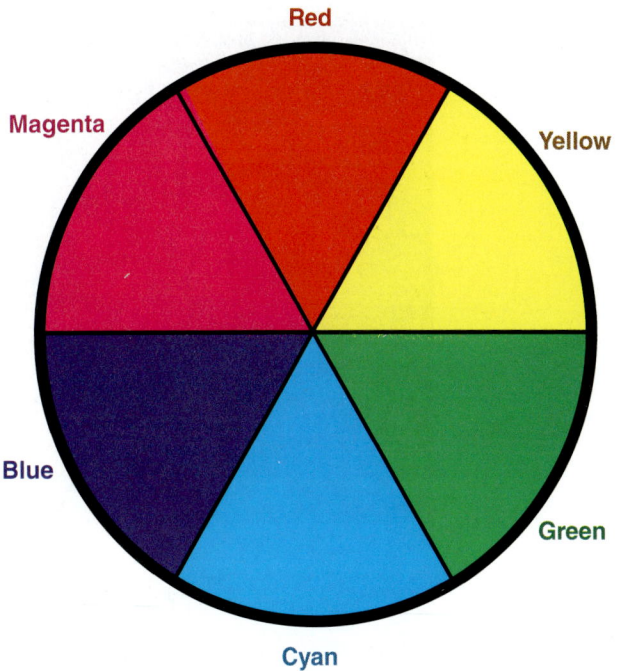

Goodheart-Willcox Publisher

Figure 18-35. A standard color wheel.

Color Correction

Being familiar with complementary color pairs is important when correcting color images using a **Curves** adjustment layer. With this method, adjustments can be made to the composite (RGB) curve, which affects all colors in the image, or to the individual color channels.

The **Color Balance** adjustment layer is less precise but easier to use than the **Curves** adjustment layer. It presents the three pairs of complementary colors, with a slider control for each pair. To make a color correction, the appropriate slider is moved toward the color that is to be increased, **Figure 18-36**. If desired, color balance can be adjusted differently in the image's shadows, midtones, and highlights.

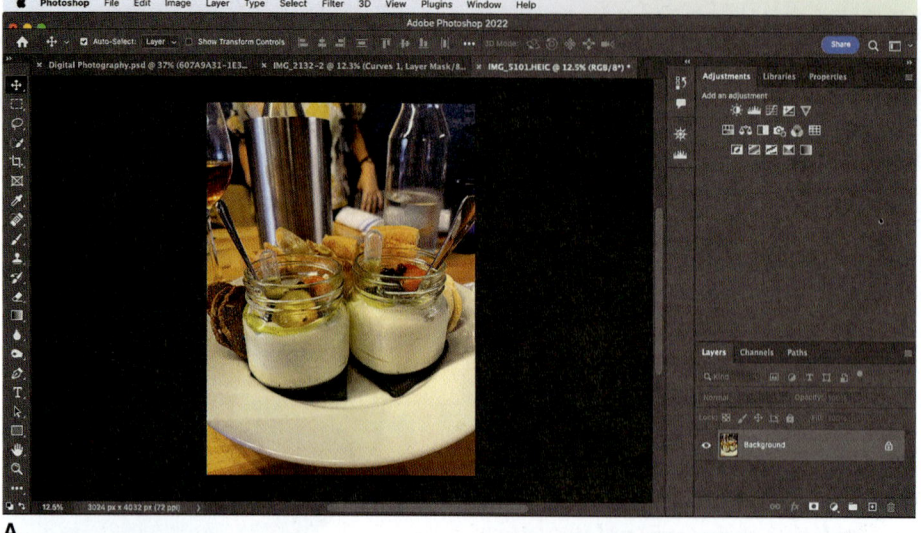

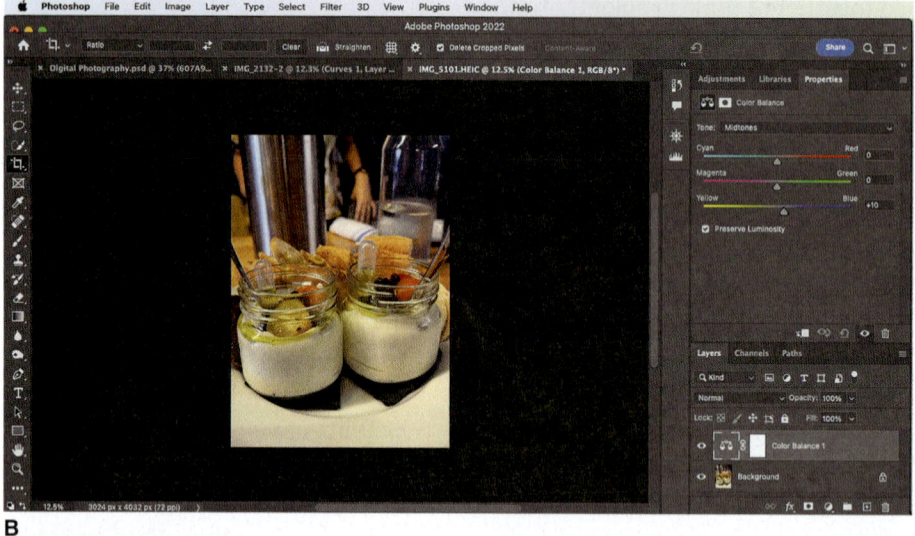

Goodheart-Willcox Publisher

Figure 18-36. Using **Color Balance**. A—This photo was taken with low incandescent light inside of a restaurant, and it is slightly too yellow. B—Using a slider to add blue and decrease yellow.

PROCEDURE

Correcting a Color Cast

Photos taken under industrial fluorescent or mercury vapor lighting often have an overall green color cast. To correct such a color cast, follow these steps:

1. Create a **Curves** adjustment layer and switch to the green channel (since green is the problem color).
2. Click on the **Target Adjustment** tool button located to the left of the channel indicator. Move the cursor (eyedropper tool) to an area where the color cast is most noticeable. A small circle appears on the diagonal line of the tone graph. The circle indicates the graph location for the pixel values being sampled.
3. Click the mouse button, and the cursor will change to the **Target Adjustment** tool (a hand and double-headed arrow). Drag the tool downward to reduce green and increase its complementary color, magenta, **Figure B**. If you drag too far, the image takes on a distinct magenta cast.
4. The curve changes may cause the image to darken somewhat. To lighten the entire image, switch to the composite (RGB) curve and pull diagonally up to the left on the midpoint of the curve, **Figure C**.

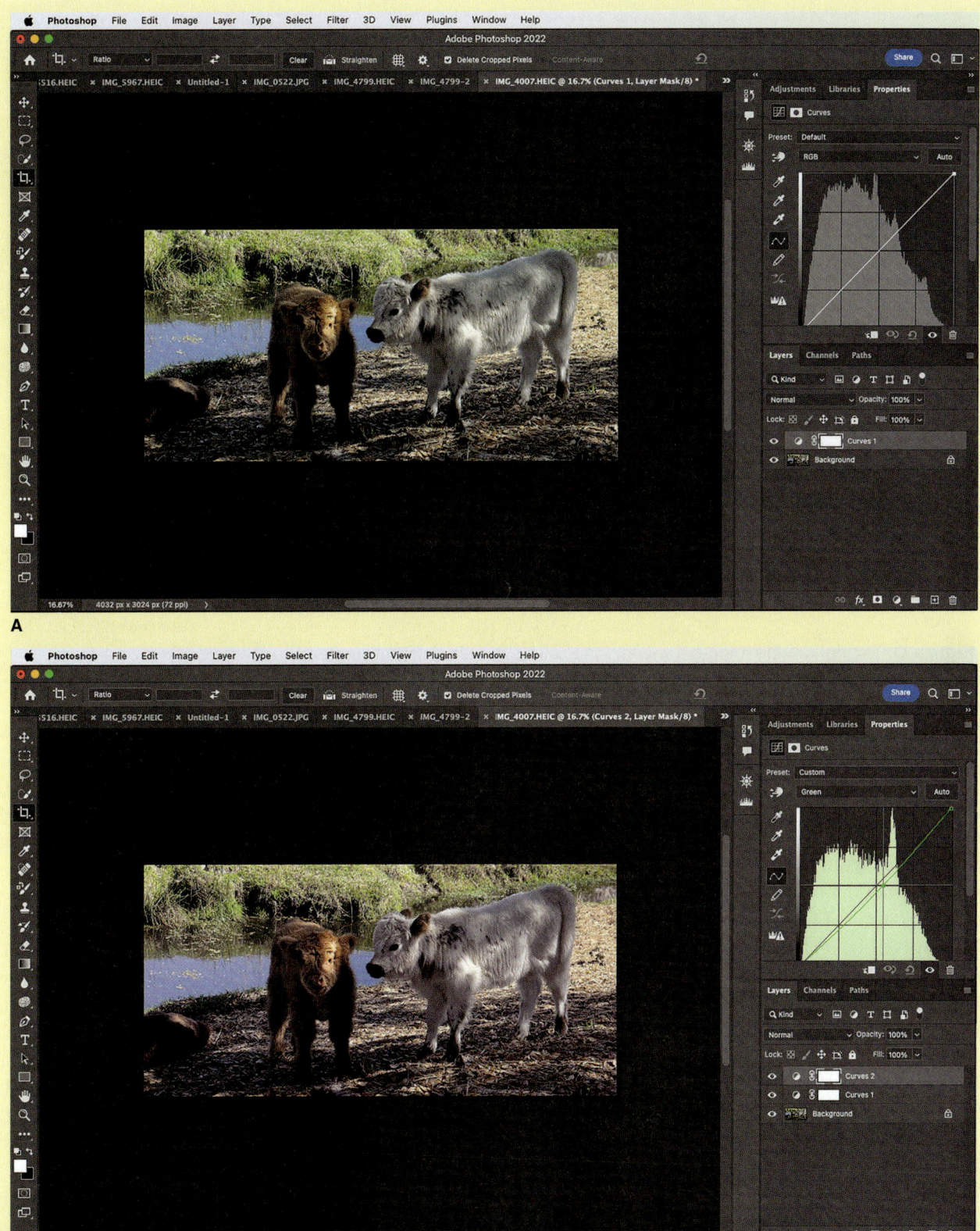

Figure B. Correcting a color cast. A— Since this photo was taken outdoors, it appears slightly blue. B— Using a **Curves** adjustment layer, green was added to correct the color.

Goodheart-Willcox Publisher

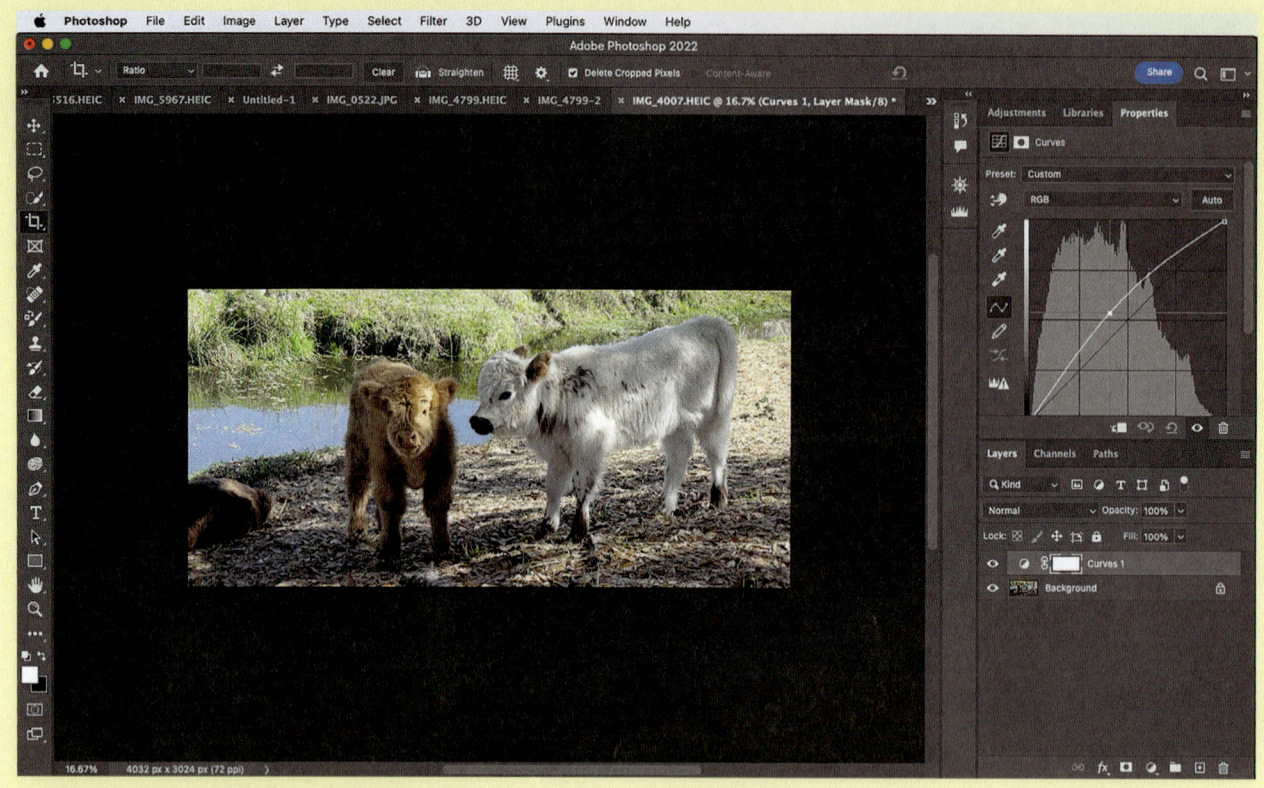

Figure C. To brighten the image, the composite curve is pulled slightly upward.

Color Adjustment

The **Hue/Saturation** adjustment layer can be used to fine-tune colors in an image. You can select any of the six primary colors in the image (red, green, blue, cyan, magenta, yellow) and adjust the hue, saturation, and brightness of the chosen color.

As shown in **Figure 18-37**, the **Hue** slider can shift a given color through shades of all the other primary colors. For example, moving the slider to the left can change a red bird's plumage to blue, while sliding to the right can make it yellow. The **Saturation** slider changes the intensity (strength) of the color, while the **Lightness** slider alters the overall brightness.

Similar changes can be made with the **Replace Color** command or the **Color Replacement** tool. The **Replace Color** command's dialog box has a preview window that shows (in white) the color selected for replacement, **Figure 18-38**. You make a selection by using an eyedropper to sample the desired area of the image. Move the **Fuzziness** slider in the dialog box to expand or contract the selection in the preview window. To replace the selected color, use the **Hue**, **Saturation**, and **Lightness** sliders.

The **Color Replacement** tool is selected from the toolbar (right-click on the **Brush** tool to see it). Once you have selected the **Color Replacement** tool, click on the foreground color in the toolbar to open a color picker. Select the desired replacement color by clicking **OK**. The **Color Replacement** tool brush appears as a circle with a crosshair in the center. Placing the crosshair over the color to be replaced and then clicking changes the color under the brush

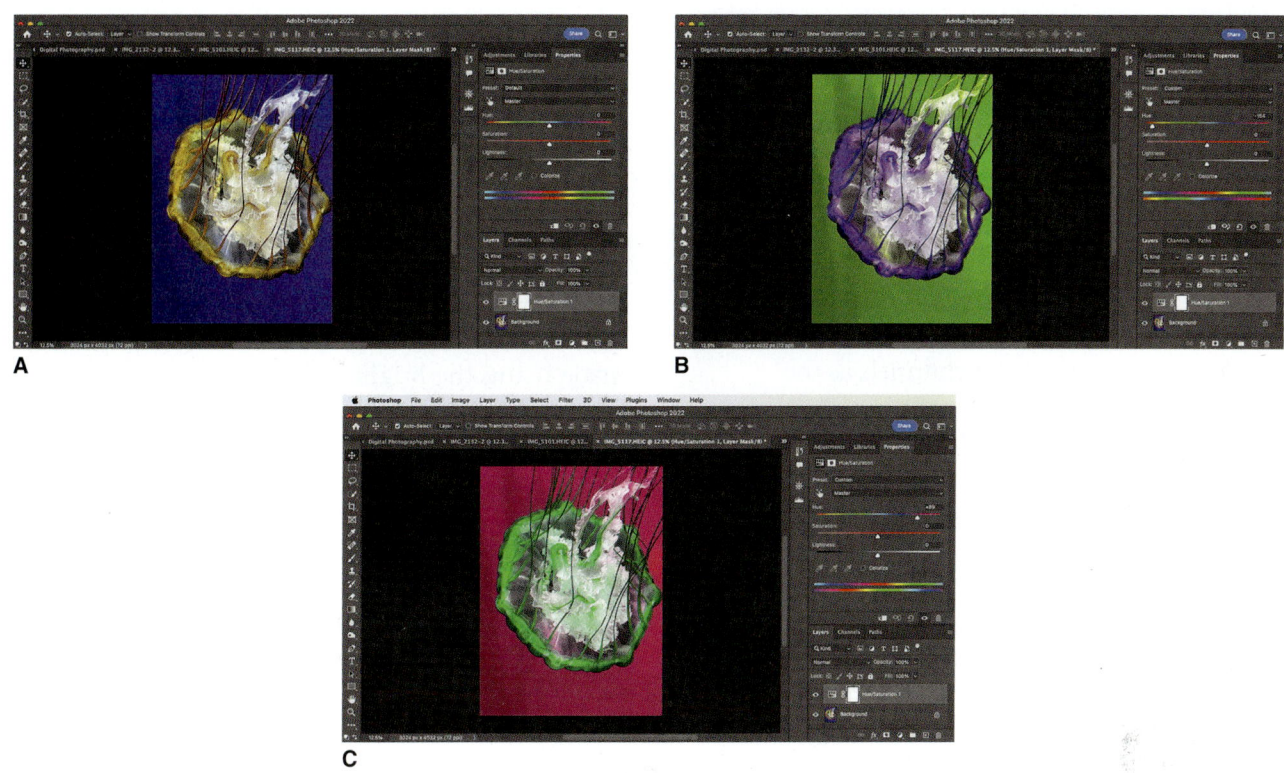

Goodheart-Willcox Publisher

Figure 18-37. Shifting color with the **Hue** slider. A—Original image of a jellyfish. B—Sliding the control to the left shifts the color of the water to green and the color of the jellyfish to purple. C—Sliding the control to the right shifts the hue of the water to a vibrant pink and the jellyfish to a bright green.

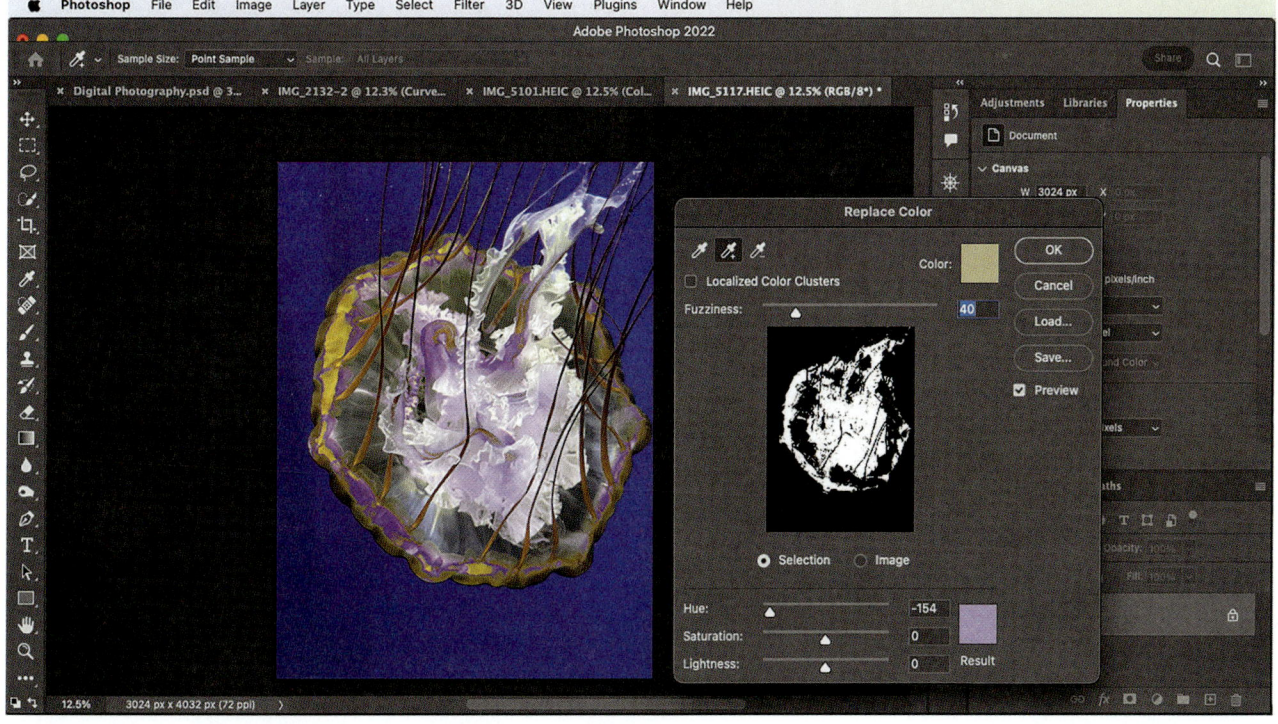

Goodheart-Willcox Publisher

Figure 18-38. **Replace Color** is being used to change some of the white inside the jellyfish to lavender. The area selected for change is shown in the preview window.

circle, **Figure 18-39**. You can change brush size and sensitivity (tolerance) on the **Options** bar.

Converting Color to Monochrome

For dramatic effect or other reasons, it may be desirable to change a color image to one that is *monochrome*, or single-color (typically black-and-white). The following are several ways to do so:

- Convert the image mode to grayscale.
- Choose one of the color channels as the grayscale source.
- Remove color (desaturate).
- Use the **Channel Mixer** command.
- Create a **Black & White** adjustment layer.

When an image is converted from a color mode to *grayscale mode* (a mode in which all picture information is conveyed by up to 256 shades of gray), all the color information is discarded. The red, green, and blue color channels are merged into a single grayscale channel. The resulting image is often flat and lacking in contrast (especially local contrast in adjoining areas of the image). This problem occurs because quite different colors, such as some shades of red and green, have very similar brightness values. When converted from color to a shade of gray, similar brightness values make it difficult to distinguish a red flower from its background of green leaves. To improve the contrast of the converted image, adjust it using **Levels** or **Curves**.

A conversion method that often gives better contrast is to review the individual color channels, which are displayed in grayscale, and select the one that looks best. The grayscale conversion will be made using the brightness values of that channel. **Figure 18-40** compares the results of the two conversion methods.

When the **Desaturate** command is used, color is removed from the image, and gray values are displayed. The image remains in the color mode, with the three color channels still intact. In this mode, possibilities for image manipulation are increased. Areas of color can be added, or some parts of the image can be restored to their original color values (see the paragraph on the **History Brush** in the section titled *Adding Color to a Monochrome Image* in Chapter 19).

To desaturate part of an image so some areas are gray and others are in color, two techniques are

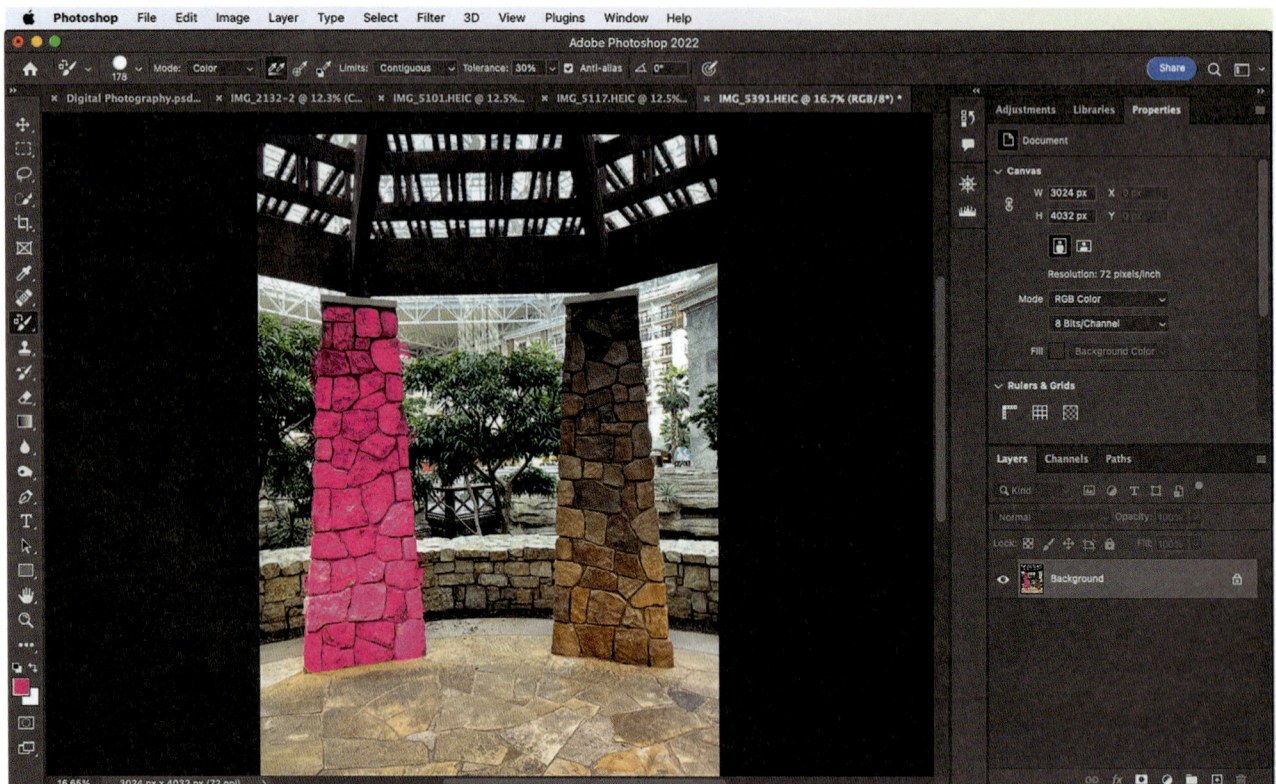

Goodheart-Willcox Publisher

Figure 18-39. The **Color Replacement** tool brush paints a new color over an object while retaining the original surface texture.

available. The **Desaturate** command can be applied after a selection is made to isolate the desired part of the image. Desaturation also can be done directly with the **Sponge** tool. This tool, located with the **Dodge** and **Burn** tools on the toolbar, is applied like a paintbrush to the desired area. Opacity can be set to 100% to remove all color or to a lower value that leaves a tint of the color. See **Figure 18-41**.

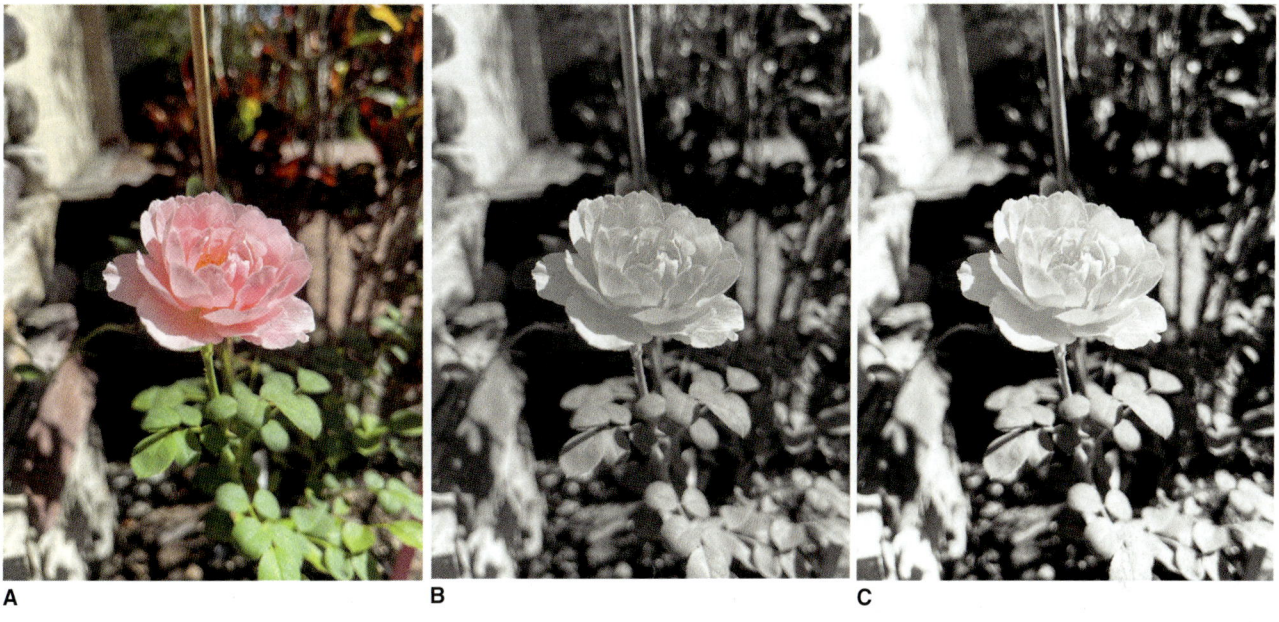

Goodheart-Willcox Publisher

Figure 18-40. Converting from color to grayscale. A—The original color image. B—A straight conversion to the grayscale mode. C—Selecting the best color channel and converting it to grayscale.

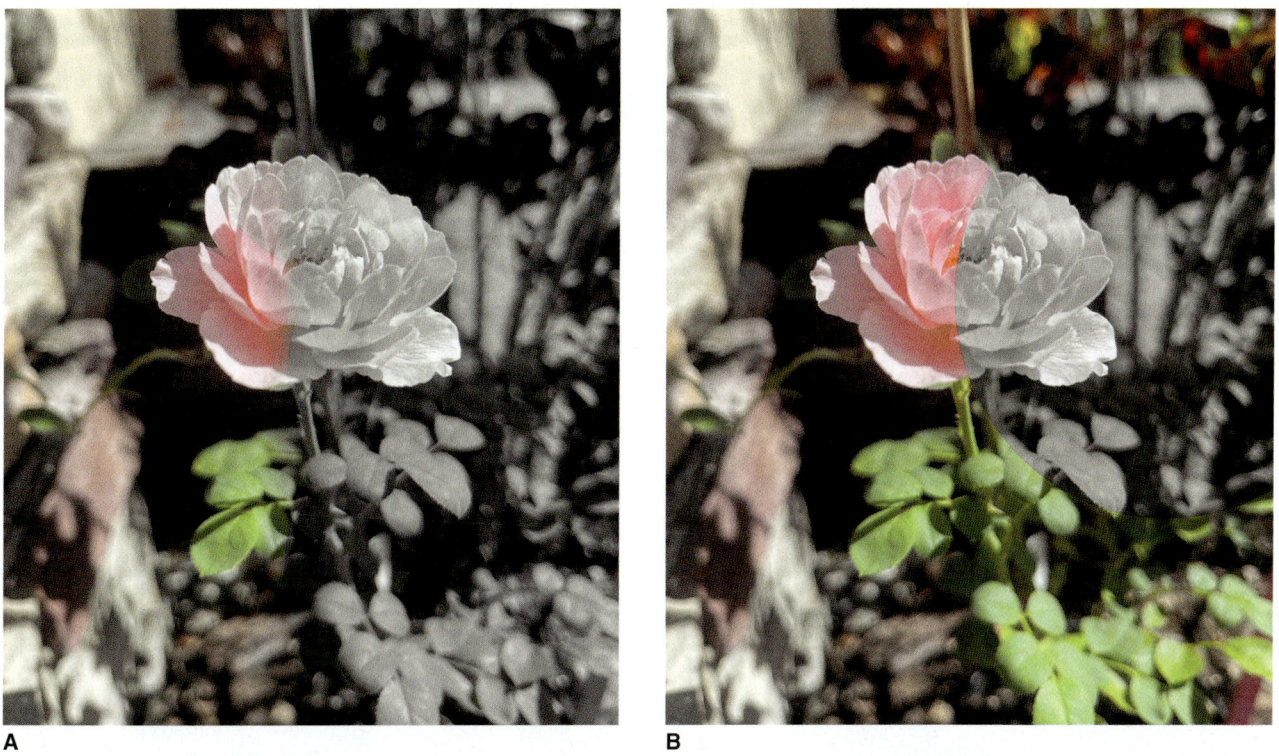

Goodheart-Willcox Publisher

Figure 18-41. Desaturation. A—The right side of this image was desaturated, while the original color was retained on the left side. B—The Sponge tool can "wipe away" color in selected areas for effect.

The **Channel Mixer** command provides a great deal of control when converting a color image to monochrome. With the **Monochrome** box checked, you can select different percentages from each of the color channels (red, green, blue) while observing, in monochrome, the effects of the changes. See **Figure 18-42**.

A drawback to using any of the preceding methods for monochrome conversion is that they are *destructive*—once the image has been saved, the change cannot be reversed. A better choice is to use the **Black & White** adjustment layer. Adjustment layers are *nondestructive*. This means the image can be saved and closed, then opened again, and the changes removed to bring the image back to its original state.

Like **Channel Mixer**, the **Black & White** adjustment layer allows you to adjust color sliders and try different combinations to find the best monochrome conversion. Instead of the three color sliders in the **Channel Mixer**, however, the **Black & White** adjustment layer has five sliders. An alternate method to the color sliders is the **Target Adjustment** tool, as described earlier in this chapter. Once you are satisfied with the conversion, save and close the image.

Procedure

Converting to Monochrome with a Black & White Adjustment Layer

1. Open the image you wish to convert.
2. Click on the **Black & White** icon on the **Adjustments** panel.
3. Try different combinations of the channel sliders while observing the effect on the monochrome image. Alternatively, use the **Target Adjustment** tool as shown in **Figure D**.
4. When you are satisfied with the changes, save and close the image.
5. If you later wish to try a different set of adjustments, reopen the file, and then click on the **Black & White** adjustment layer on the **Layers** panel.
6. Make your changes, and then resave and close the file.

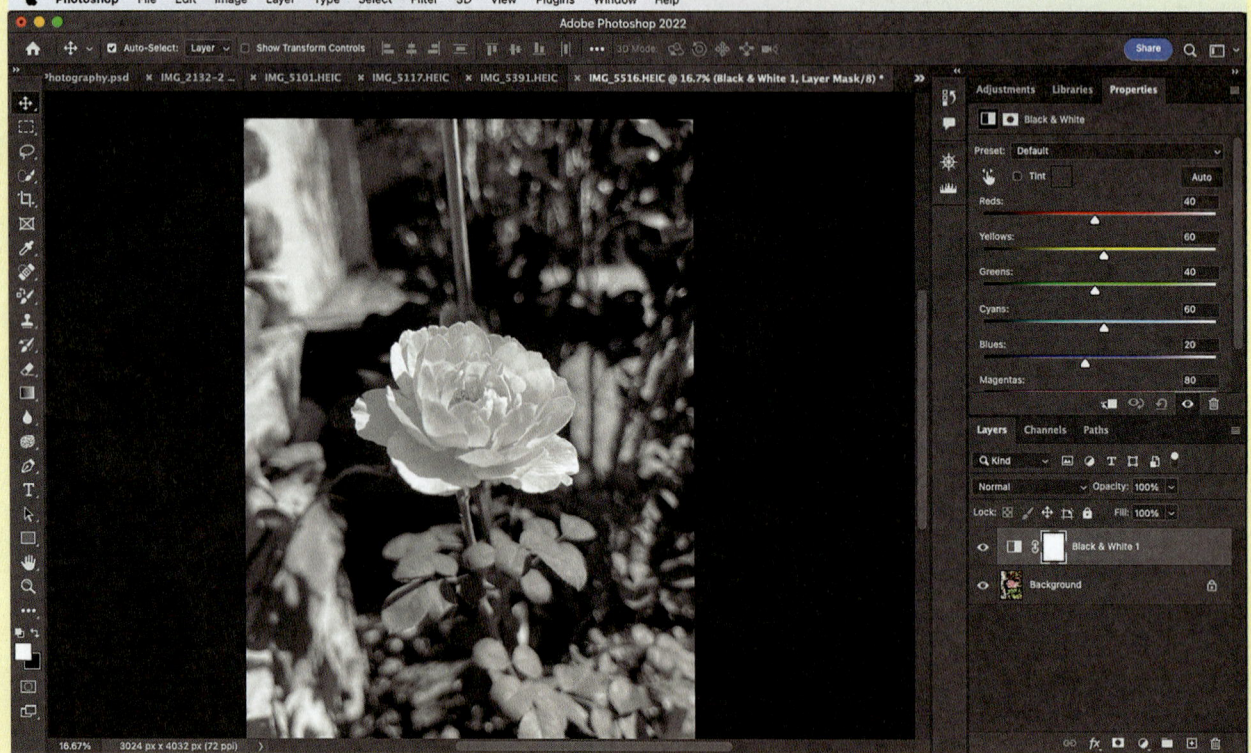

Goodheart-Willcox Publisher

Figure D. Using the **Black & White** adjustment layer's **Target Adjustment** tool to make a monochrome conversion.

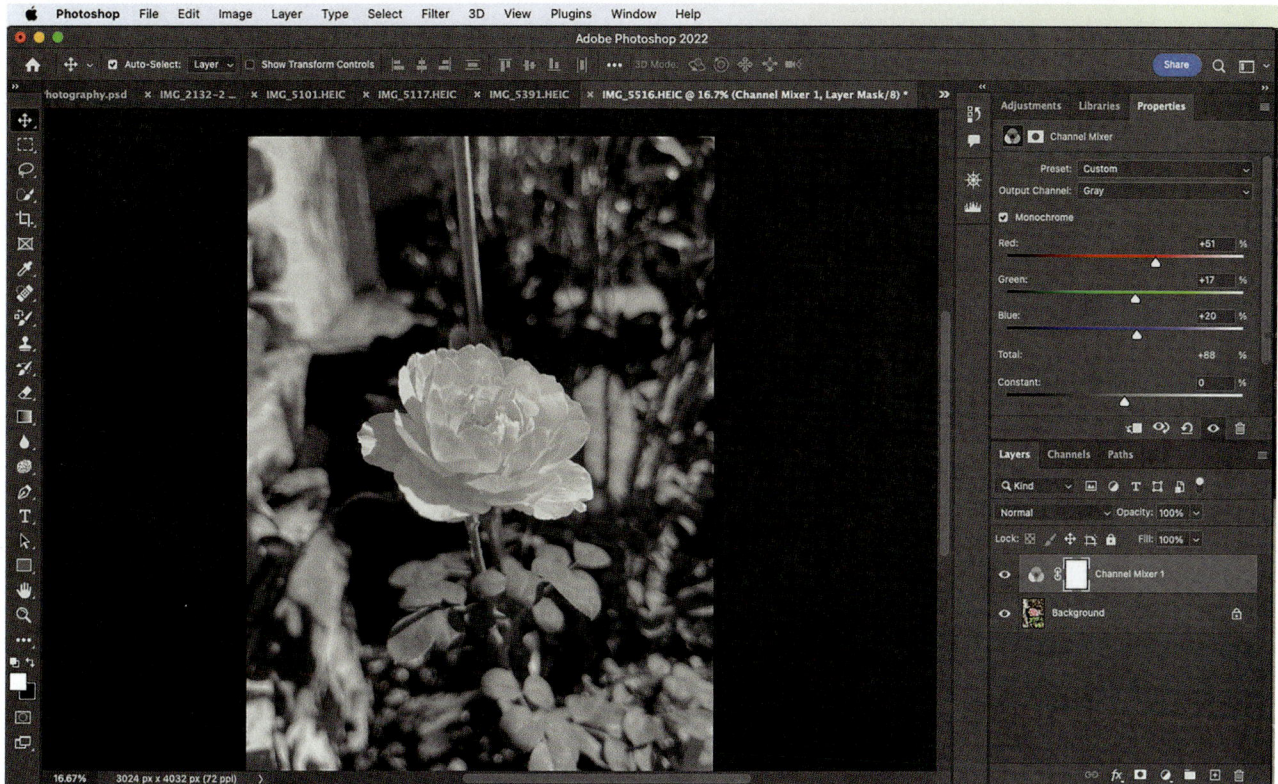

Goodheart-Willcox Publisher

Figure 18-42. Using the **Channel Mixer** command, a scene can be given a different interpretation by varying the percentages of the three channels.

Retouching the Image

Careful cleaning of scanned materials is necessary to minimize the need for **spotting** (removing small dust spots on the image). When scanning from prints, inspect the glass of the flatbed scanner and clean it if necessary.

Spotting may also be necessary on images captured with a DSLR camera. When the camera body is opened to change lenses, dust and lint particles can enter and settle on the cover plate of the sensor. The particles show up as dark spots when the image is displayed. The spots are especially noticeable in areas of light, continuous tone, such as the sky or an expanse of snow or sand.

Spotting is done with the **Clone Stamp** tool. It is used to copy (clone) a small area of the image and place it over the dust spot. Set the working size of the **Clone Stamp** tool by choosing a brush size from the **Brushes** panel. For spotting work, a fairly small, soft-edged brush is normally used.

Figure 18-43 shows a scanned antique image that requires spotting. All spotting work should be done with the image displayed at the full-size (100%) setting. This allows you to see what the image will look like when printed so even tiny defects can be identified and corrected. Spotting should be done systematically, beginning at one of the image corners and proceeding in steps until the entire image has been displayed and processed. The Page Up and Page Down keys allow you to step through the image vertically; combined with the Ctrl key, they allow horizontal stepping.

When cleaning up imperfections on human subjects or in the background of photos, the **Spot Healing** brush tool is particularly useful. See **Figure 18-44**. Select a brush size, and then place it over the imperfection to be removed to blend the repair with the color and texture of the area surrounding the imperfection. This tool works well for removing small skin imperfections in portraits since the blending makes the repair virtually invisible. It also works well to cover any inconsistencies in solid-colored backgrounds. You can also correct red eye using the **Spot Healing** brush tool. Simply select the **Red Eye** tool and navigate to the menu at the top left of the screen to adjust pupil size and darken the red areas. Click and drag the tool around the eye as needed until the red eye is corrected.

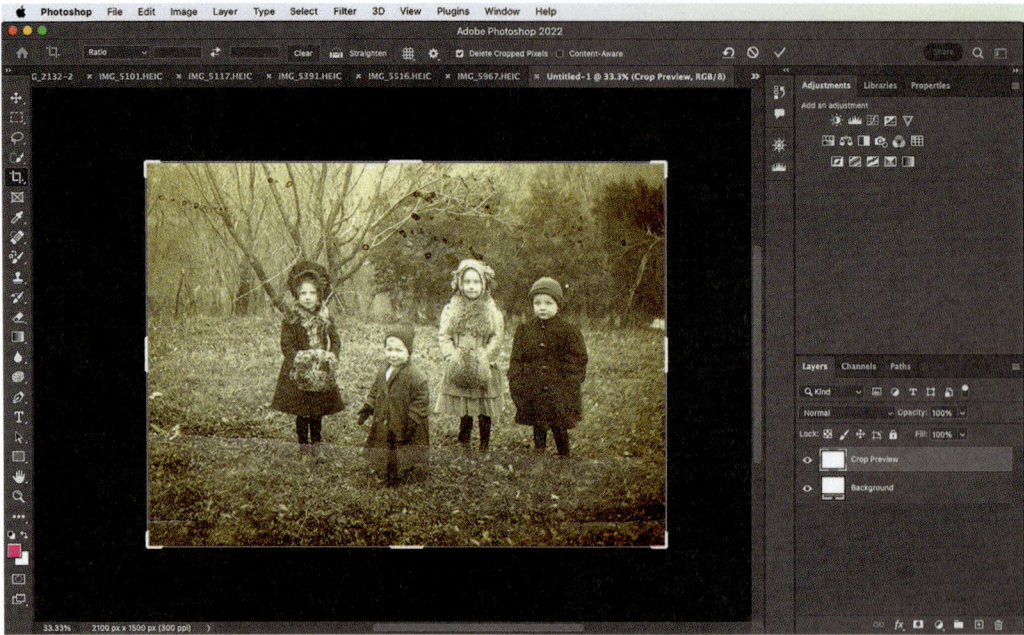

Figure 18-43. This antique image has numerous spots (both black and white) that must be cleaned up. Spotting should be done with the image displayed at 100% to make even small defects visible.

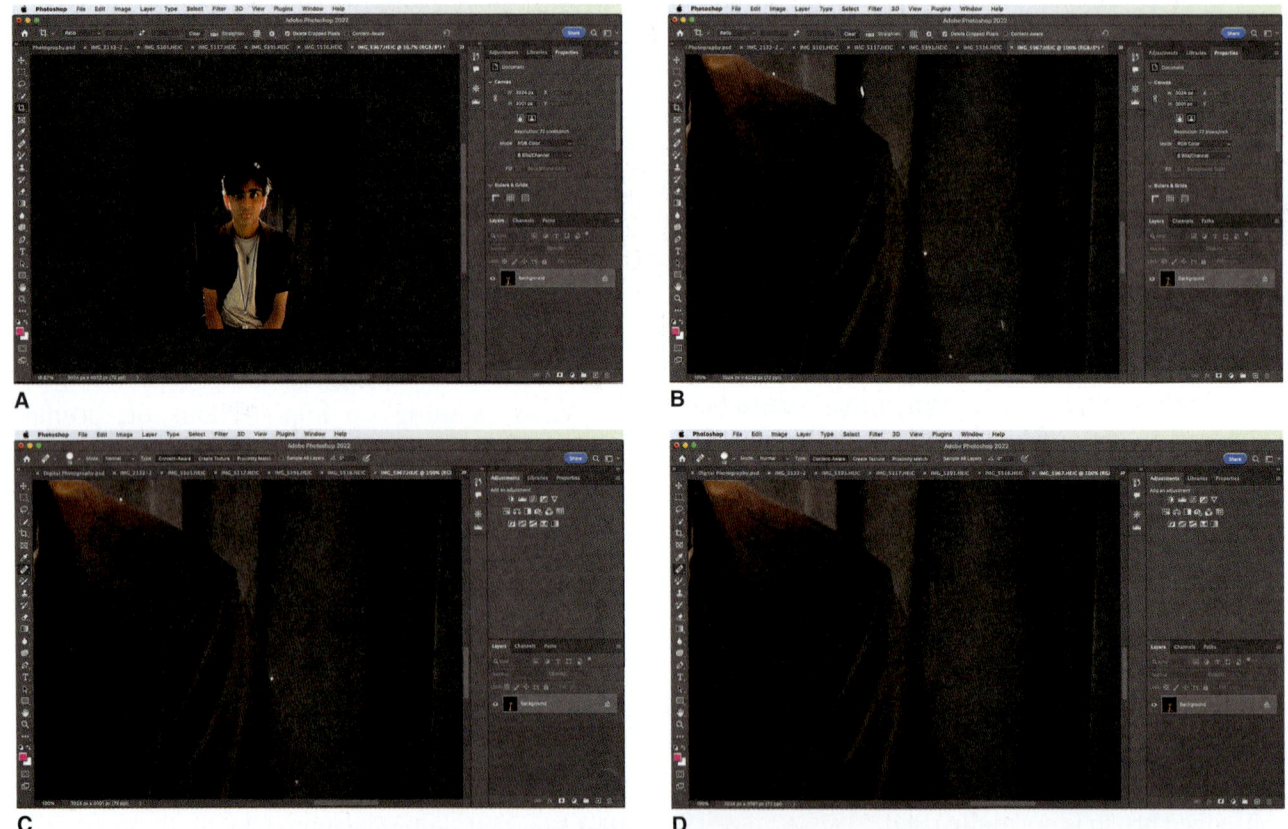

Figure 18-44. The **Spot Healing** brush works well for cleaning up imperfections in the background of photos. A—The original photo. B—A close-up of spots that need to be cleaned up. C—The **Spot Healing** brush in action. D—The spots cleaned up.

PROCEDURE

Eliminating a Spot Using the Clone Stamp Tool

1. Position the cursor (brush-size circle) on an area near the spot to be removed. See **Figure E**. The area should be as close as possible in appearance to the spot's immediate surroundings. This will make the correction less obvious.
2. Hold down the Alt key (Option on a Mac) and click with the left mouse key to select the image pixels that will be copied. Release the Alt key.
3. Reposition the cursor over the spot and press the left mouse key. The spot will be covered with the image information (pixels) you selected in Step 2. If the spot is larger than the brush size, move the cursor and press the left mouse key again. Continue moving and clicking until the spot is eliminated.
4. Larger areas can be covered by clicking and dragging (using the tool as a paintbrush), but the results are often an unsatisfactory patterned appearance. Move and click to cover the imperfection with a series of smaller cloned spots for better results.

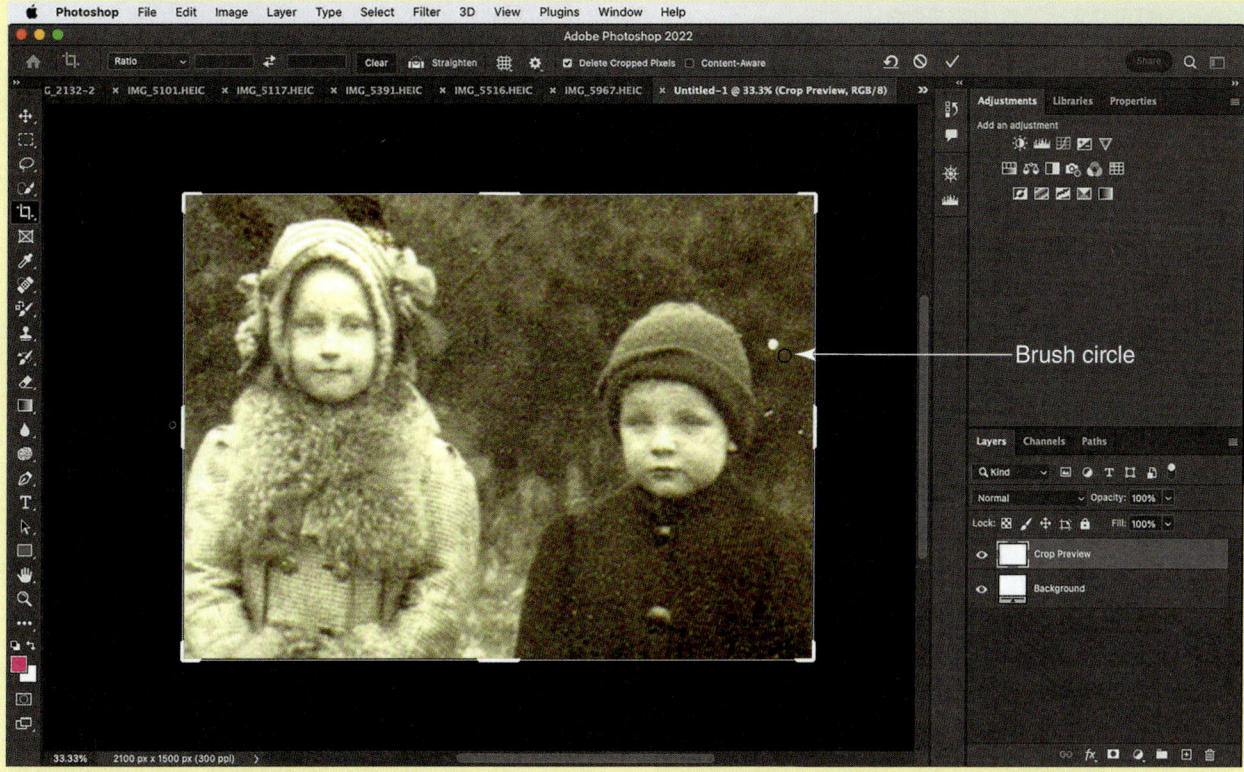

Goodheart-Willcox Publisher

Figure E. After selecting an area from which to clone image information, the brush circle is placed over the spot. A mouse click copies the selected image over the white spot. Note that the image is displayed at 100%. At that size, only a portion of it can be displayed on the screen.

Eliminating Dust Spots and Scratches

Many scanners offer a feature that automatically cleans up dust spots and scratches during the scanning process. This can be a real time-saver, especially if the original is in poor condition from improper storage.

Image editing programs offer a tool that automatically cleans up scans from images that exhibit a large number of such imperfections. In Photoshop, the tool is called the **Dust & Scratches** filter. This filter works by blurring pixels in small bright areas (which are usually dust spots or scratches), but it can cause an undesirable softening of the entire image.

Two settings in the dialog box for the **Dust & Scratches** filter allow you to select the degree of change. The *Radius* setting determines the width of the imperfection that the program will identify as a spot or scratch. The larger the number, the more blurred the image will be. The *Threshold* setting sets the filter's sensitivity—how much the color of the spot must differ from its surroundings to be considered an imperfection. If the setting is 1, the filter considers everything an imperfection and blurs the whole image. A value of 255 has the opposite effect—no imperfections are recognized, and nothing is changed. Checking the **Preview** box allows you to see the amount of blurring and spot elimination done at various settings. Because of its effect on image quality, use this filter only for images that show a very large number of imperfections. Although it can be tedious, cleaning up spots and scratches with the **Clone Stamp** tool is a better choice for preserving image quality.

Sharpening the Image

Sharpening involves enhancing edge contrast through a built-in filter to make an image appear more sharply focused by varying the filter's intensity. While it cannot correct an image that is badly out of focus, it may improve one that is slightly soft. The most common use for the sharpening technique, however, is overcoming the slight blurring that can occur when an image is resized, rotated, or otherwise processed digitally.

Sharpening is actually an optical illusion. It does not restore lost detail but increases the difference in the color of adjacent pixels, especially along edges. This tricks the eye into seeing the image as sharper and more detailed. Use this technique with care because *oversharpening* (applying a sharpening filter at too high an intensity) can give the image an unattractive, harsh, blotchy appearance. See **Figure 18-45**.

Sharpening Filters

An image editing program may offer several sharpening tools or filters. Photoshop, for example, lists six choices—**Shake Reduction**, **Sharpen**, **Sharpen Edges**, **Sharpen More**, **Smart Sharpen**, and **Unsharp Mask**. The **Unsharp Mask** tool is most often used because of the control it offers. Three of the remaining choices are all-or-nothing in their

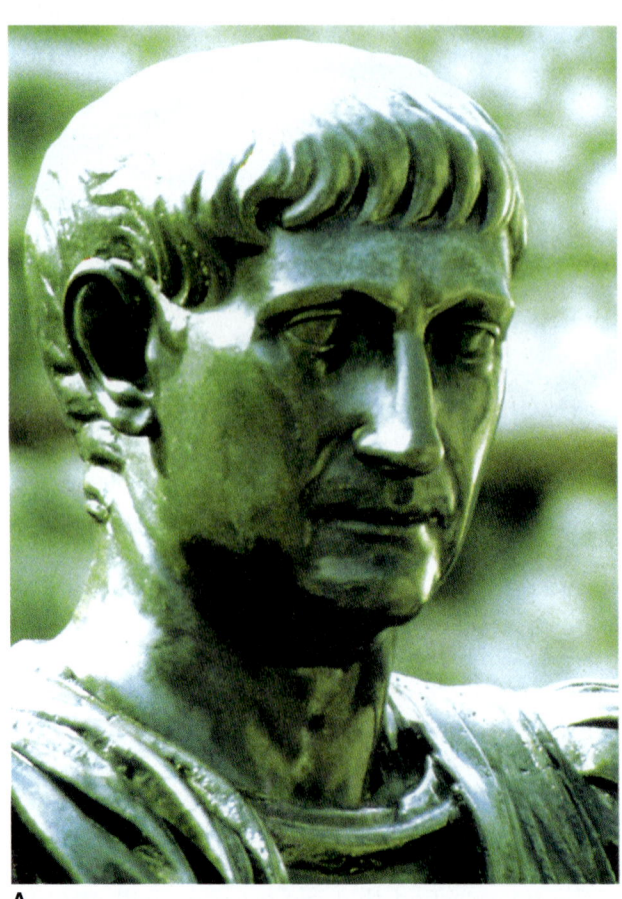
A

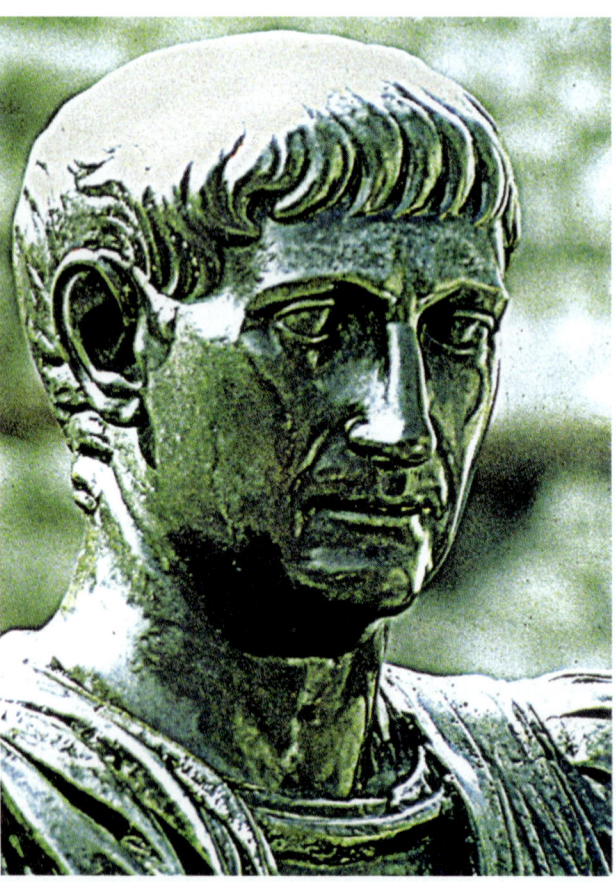
B

Jack Klasey/Goodheart-Willcox Publisher

Figure 18-45. Oversharpening can seriously degrade image quality. A—A properly sharpened image. B—The same image that has been badly oversharpened.

approach, providing a set amount of sharpening. The amount of sharpening is minimal in the case of **Sharpen** and **Sharpen Edges** and considerably greater in **Sharpen More**. The fifth choice, **Smart Sharpen**, has the same control advantage as **Unsharp Mask**, plus some additional features that make it more difficult to use. **Shake Reduction** is a complex sharpening tool that is designed to eliminate or greatly reduce the blurring caused by slight camera movement.

The **Unsharp Mask** filter creates a slightly blurred copy of the image and uses it as a mask (hence, the term *unsharp*) to determine which areas will be sharpened. When using this filter, you can control and preview the degree of sharpening. The chosen degree of sharpening is displayed on both a small detail view and the full-size screen image, **Figure 18-46**. For accurate judgment of the sharpening effect, the displayed image should be at 100%. By checking and unchecking the **Preview** box or by clicking on the detail view, you can compare the image before sharpening and with sharpening applied.

Three sliders control the effect of the filter. The amount can be adjusted from 1% to 500%, but most often it is set somewhere between 100% and 200%. Higher values are typically used with larger images that will be reproduced on inkjet or dye sublimation printers. Lower values are used for smaller images, especially if they will be reproduced by the halftone printing process (for example, in a magazine).

Radius settings can be varied from 0.1 pixels to 250 pixels. At the lower values, sharpening is confined mainly to edges within the image. Settings of 5 pixels or lower are typical. The *Threshold* setting identifies how different two pixels must be in brightness level before sharpening will be applied. The adjustment range is 1 to 255, with the number of pixels affected decreasing as the setting increases. A typical starting point for *Threshold* settings is 3 to 4.

Sharpening should be done as the final step before printing, after all other adjustments have been made to the file. If sharpening is applied earlier in the process, additional image changes could exaggerate its effects. For example, increasing file dimensions after sharpening could make the edges of objects appear to be oversharpened.

Sharpening Layered Images

If an image has more than one layer, the layers must be sharpened individually (or the image flattened to a single layer before sharpening). Only "content" layers can be sharpened, however. Sharpening has no visible effect when applied to an adjustment layer, since it has no pixel content.

Figure 18-47 shows a file with three "content" layers. Sharpening this image is a three-step process—each layer is selected and sharpened individually. An advantage of this method is the ability to independently sharpen layers or even selected portions of layers. Depending on the image content and artistic intent, different amounts of sharpening could be applied.

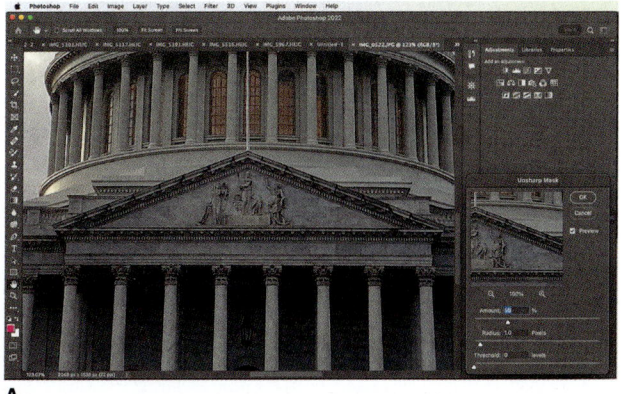
A

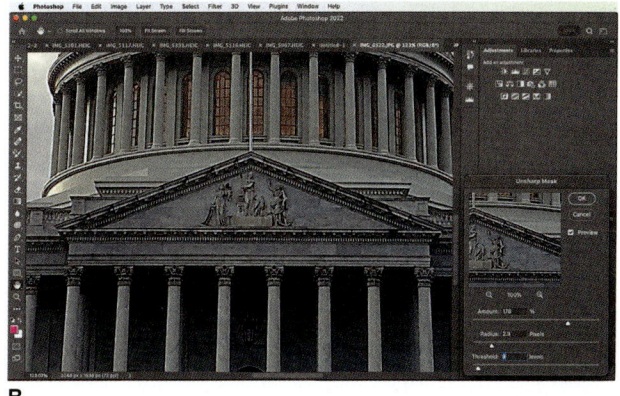
B

Goodheart-Willcox Publisher

Figure 18-46. Unsharp masking. A—A portion of an image with various textures, before applying sharpening. B—With sharpening applied, texture details are more visible.

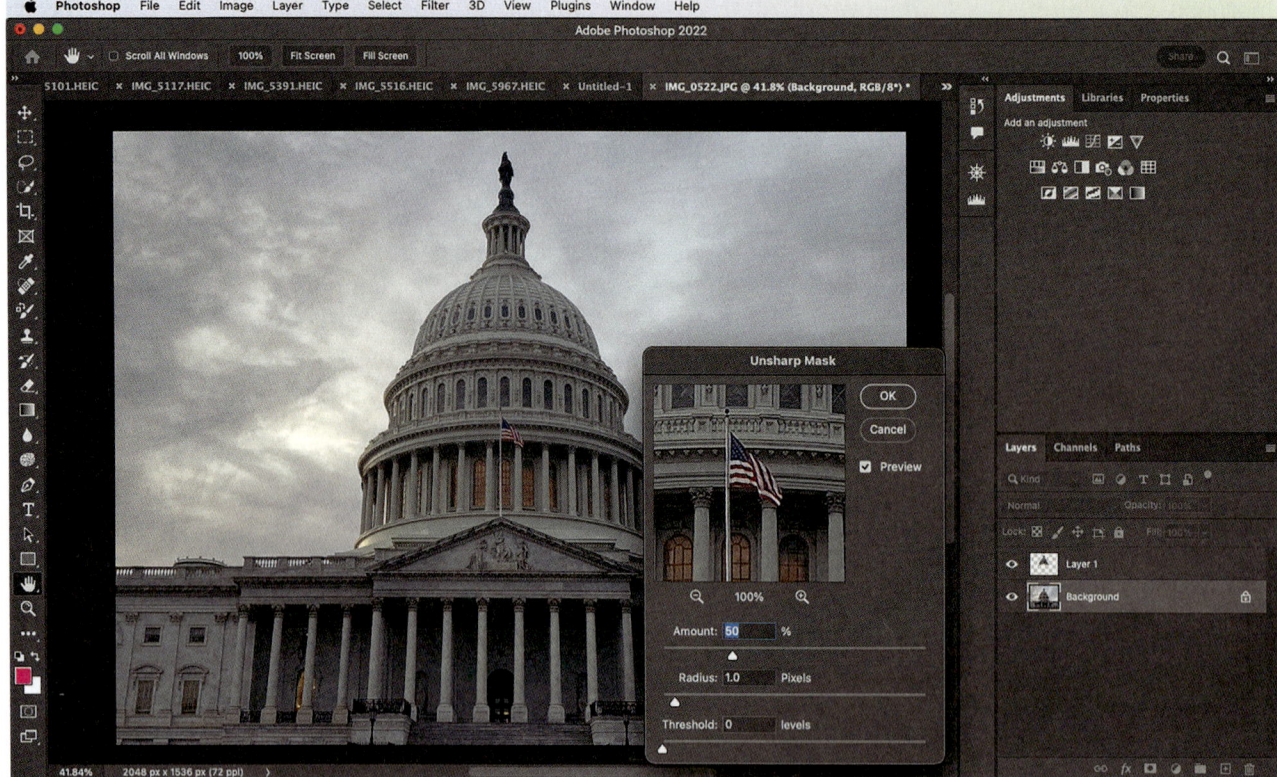

Goodheart-Willcox Publisher

Figure 18-47. Sharpening an image with several layers must be done on a layer-by-layer basis. As indicated by the highlight in the **Layers** panel, the sharpening is being applied to the **Background** layer, which is the active layer.

Portfolio Assignment

Monochrome Conversion

For this assignment, you will create a black-and-white image from a color image to add to your portfolio.

1. Choose one of your images (or shoot a new one) that you feel would make an effective black-and-white image.
2. Create a new project in Photoshop and set the dimensions to the Default Photoshop Size of 7″ × 5″ at 300 ppi.
3. Using a **Black & White** Adjustment Layer, experiment with different conversions.
4. Use the **Target Adjustment** tool or move the color bar sliders to set various combinations of percentages.

When you are satisfied with the appearance of the image, export the image as a JPEG and add it to your portfolio.

Chapter 18 Review

Summary

- For most photographers, the advantages of working digitally are creative control, convenience, monetary savings, and time savings. Digital imaging also offers a great amount of flexibility.
- Some photographers make a distinction between image processing and image manipulation. How much manipulation of an image is permissible depends on its intended use and the photographer's ethical standards.
- An indispensable tool for either image processing or image manipulation is an image editor or editing program. There are numerous programs to choose from, but most have similar features.
- Always preserve an original image file without changes. Create a duplicate file, or working file, for processing.
- To bring out the best in an image, cropping is often necessary. The image also can be rotated or reversed from left-to-right or top-to-bottom.
- Image processing software allows you to change the size of your digital image, the resolution, or both. The physical size of your image and its resolution depend on the type of camera and the settings programmed into it by you or the camera manufacturer.
- One of the most attractive features of full-featured image editing programs is the ability to create image layers. Different elements of the image can be placed on separate layers so they can be worked on independently without changing the rest of the image.
- Most images, even those that are generally well-exposed, require some adjustment for best appearance. The most basic image refinement is expanding the tonal range with the **Levels** adjustment command.
- Digital postprocessing permits use of an infinite range of contrast alterations. There are two basic methods for changing contrast—the **Brightness/Contrast** command and the **Curves** command.
- As compared to black-and-white images, working with color images can be considered three or four times as complicated, since color images consist of either three or four channels.
- Being familiar with complementary color pairs is important when correcting color images using a **Curves** adjustment layer. The **Hue/Saturation** adjustment layer can be used to fine-tune colors in an image.
- For dramatic effect or other reasons, it may be desirable to change a color image to one that is monochrome, or single-color (typically black-and-white). There are several ways to change a color image to a monochrome image.
- Spotting may be necessary on images captured with a DSLR camera. When the camera body is opened to change lenses, dust and lint particles can enter and settle on the cover plate of the sensor.
- Sharpening involves enhancing edge contrast to make an image appear more sharply focused. While it cannot correct an image that is badly out of focus, it may improve one that is slightly soft.

Review Questions

Answer the following questions using the information provided in this chapter.

Know and Understand

1. *True or False?* Despite the lack of chemicals, it is still important to follow personal and workplace safety rules and regulations when post-processing images digitally.
2. *True or False?* More extreme changes to an image are considered image manipulation.

3. _____ are individual keys or a combination of keys used to perform an operation as an alternative to a mouse and menu.
   A. Adjustment layers
   B. Shortcut keys
   C. RAW converters
   D. Image editors

4. *True or False?* You only need to create a working file if making extreme changes to an image.

5. A(n) _____ is software that allows the photographer to make a number of adjustments to the file data before saving the image as a .tif or .psd file.
   A. image editor
   B. active layer
   C. interpolation
   D. RAW converter

6. *True or False?* Cropping is often necessary to bring out the best in an image.

7. _____ occurs when image size or resolution is increased with the **Resample** box checked.
   A. Upsampling
   B. Interpolation
   C. Downsampling
   D. Burning in

8. *True or False?* In an image editing program, changes can be made only to the adjustment layer.

9. When creating new layers, **Layer via** _____ leaves a blank area behind when the new layer is created.
   A. **Copy**
   B. **Paste**
   C. **Cut**
   D. **Edit**

10. _____ layers are special-purpose layers that allow changes to be made to an image's appearance without permanently altering the original image pixels.
    A. Adjustment
    B. Active
    C. Mask
    D. Background

11. When adjusting overall exposure, the most basic image refinement is expanding the tonal range with the _____ adjustment command.
    A. **Layers**
    B. **Levels**
    C. **Adjustments**
    D. **Hue/Saturation**

12. *True or False?* Dodging is primarily used to lighten and bring out detail in an image.

13. Which of the following commands is a basic method for changing contrast?
    A. **Hue/Saturation**
    B. **Curves**
    C. **Color Balance**
    D. **Shadows/Highlights**

14. *True or False?* Red, green, and blue are referred to as the additive primaries.

15. When correcting color images, the _____ adjustment layer is less precise but easier to use than the **Curves** adjustment layer.
    A. **RGB**
    B. **Channel**
    C. **Preview**
    D. **Color Balance**

16. *True or False?* When adjusting colors in an image, the **Saturation** slider alters the overall brightness of a color.

17. *True or False?* A destructive change *cannot* be reversed once the image has been saved.

18. Spotting is done with the _____ tool.
    A. **Black & White**
    B. **Channel Mixer**
    C. **Desaturate**
    D. **Clone Stamp**

19. The most common use for _____ is overcoming the slight blurring that can occur when an image is resized, rotated, or otherwise processed digitally.
    A. sharpening
    B. spotting
    C. oversharpening
    D. dodging

20. The sharpening tool used most often is the _____ tool because of the control it offers.
    A. **Sharpen**
    B. **Sharpen Edges**
    C. **Unsharp Mask**
    D. **Sharpen More**

Apply and Analyze

1. List four of the five features included in almost all image editing program windows.
2. When changing canvas size, what are the two ways to specify the amount of extension?
3. Explain the cut-and-paste method for moving a selection on a new layer to a different image.
4. How do you create a **Levels** adjustment layer?
5. Name the two basic methods for altering contrast.
6. Describe how the **Replace Color** command works.
7. Why is using the **Black & White** adjustment layer a better choice when converting a color image to a monochrome image?
8. Explain the two settings in the dialog box for the **Dust & Scratches** filter that allow you to select the degree of change.

Critical Thinking

1. One of your photos has won first place for originality in a local photo contest. The idea for your image occurred to you when a friend showed you a similar photo they had taken. Should you give credit to your friend publicly when you accept the award, should you thank them personally at a later time, or should you do nothing?
2. Photography clubs and other organizations that sponsor competitions often require manipulated images and straight images to be judged in separate categories. What arguments can you think of in favor of permitting the two categories of images to compete in a single category? Alternatively, what reasons would you cite for keeping the categories separate?

Suggested Activities

1. Find a news photograph that includes elements that distract the viewer from the main subject. If you had captured the image and were not bound by the photojournalist's "no manipulation" rule, how would you improve the photograph? Make a copy of the image and mark it to show areas where you would make changes, such as deleting a distracting object. Discuss the final result with your instructor.
2. Select one of your images, adjust its overall exposure, and then make a full-frame print. Set the print aside, then view the image on-screen again. In what ways could you crop the image to make it more visually interesting? Create different cropped versions, saving each under a different file name. Make a print of each image. Choose the one you believe is most effective. Ask several friends to look at the full-frame print and the cropped images and select the one they think is the best photo. Do their choices match yours?
3. Shoot two identical exposures of a scene with quite a bit of detail, such as a bed of flowers or a crowd scene. Open the first image in Photoshop or a similar image editor. Make sure **Resample** is checked in the **Image Size** dialog box. Check the resolution and reset it if necessary to 72 ppi. Next, change the width of the image to 10″ and close the **Image Size** dialog box. Save the image with the name *Example 72* and make a print. Open the second image and bring up the **Image Size** dialog box. If necessary, uncheck **Resample**, and then change the resolution to 300 ppi. Note that the width and height dimensions change. Turn on **Resample**, then change the width to 10″ and close the **Image Size** dialog box. Save this image as *Example 300* and make a print. Compare the two prints. Which one looks better, especially in areas with fine detail?

Communicating about Photography

1. **Speaking.** Research the image editing apps that are available for an iPhone® and an Android phone. Locate promotional materials for a variety of apps. Analyze the data in these materials and make inferences about the apps and recommend the best ones to the class.
2. **Speaking and Listening.** In small groups, discuss with your classmates—in basic, everyday language—the types of changes that can be made to an image in an image editing program. Then discuss the tools in an image editing program that can be used to effect these changes. Summarize your discussion for the class, using the terms that you have learned in this chapter.

Chapter 19
Advanced Digital Postprocessing Techniques

Learning Objectives

After completing this chapter, you will be able to:
- Understand how image manipulation can create situations that raise ethical and legal questions for photographers.
- Describe the various types of selection tools and their uses.
- Use **Quick Mask** and the **Eraser** tools to refine selections.
- Explain how to use layers when creating composites.
- Understand the importance of using adjustment layers when altering images.
- Describe how to add a border to an image.
- Explain how to overlay type on a photo or arrange type so a photo shows through the letters.
- Apply various transformations and filters to images.
- Explain how to add color to a monochrome image.

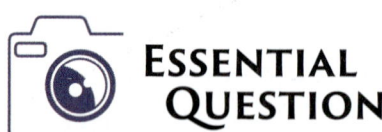

How do advanced digital postprocessing techniques differ from basic digital postprocessing techniques?

Technical Terms

anchor points
clipping mask
composite
elliptical marquee
filter
handles
layer mask
morphing
path
rectangular marquee
selection tools

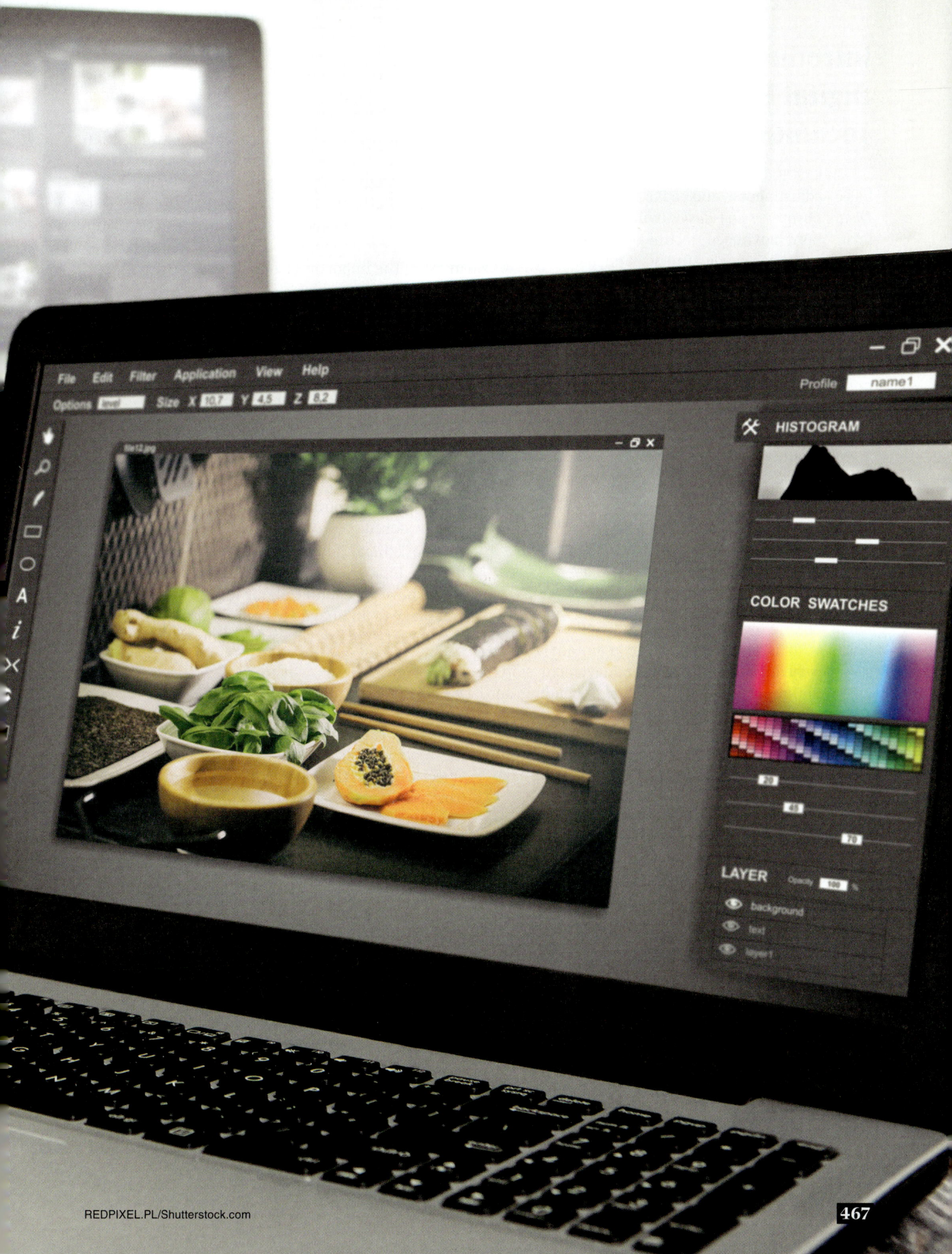

REDPIXEL.PL/Shutterstock.com

Introduction to Advanced Digital Postprocessing Techniques

Understanding and being able to perform the basic adjustments and edits from Chapter 18, *Digital Postprocessing Basics*, will enable you to perform more advanced techniques. As you move beyond the basic adjustments and techniques of digital postprocessing, you enter the realm of image manipulation, which is still part of Step 2 of the postprocessing process. The basic areas of manipulation include removing or adding picture elements; altering the shape, color, texture, or other visible attributes of the subject; changing the relationship of elements in the picture; and combining elements from two or more pictures into a single image.

While these basic and advanced techniques are great to have under your belt, there is always more to learn. There is a plethora of options for continuing education courses and online tutorials regarding digital postprocessing. There are also several certifications offered for various image editing software. Furthering your education and training, and potentially earning a certification, can help you greatly when looking for a job or hoping to gain a client's business. It is also important to maintain a consistent schedule and use time-management skills when editing, especially for clients. Depending on the deadline, you may have months to turn the photos around, or you may only have a couple weeks. Regardless of the time constraints, you must stay on task and turn photos over in a timely manner.

Ethical Conduct and Image Manipulation

While image manipulation opens many creative possibilities for the photographer, it can also create situations that raise ethical and legal questions. For example, some publications have been criticized for altering their cover photos to make the subject appear in a way that is different from how they look in real life. During political campaigns, photographs have been manipulated to discredit candidates by showing them in situations contradicting their stated beliefs, or even showing them with unflattering or inappropriate facial expressions. Even if they are created with humorous intent, manipulated images often reinforce racial, gender, and other forms of stereotyping.

Sometimes even an unmanipulated image can be used in a manner that invades a person's privacy, damaging their reputation or self-esteem. Many unflattering or embarrassing photos or videos have been posted on social media without the subject's permission. Before posting an image, keep in mind the importance of cultural sensitivity and image appropriateness.

The wide availability of images online and the relative ease of altering or combining those images can result in failure to respect intellectual property rights. As noted in Chapter 17, *Importing Images*, the person who creates an image has the exclusive right to duplicate and distribute that image. If you publish that image without permission, you are violating the creator's copyright. Although an idea cannot be copyrighted, you should always acknowledge the source of an inspiration that resulted in an image you produced.

The ethical alteration of images is a much broader topic than what we can cover in this book. If you have any doubts about whether the changes you make to an image are appropriate, conduct further research or ask your instructor.

Selecting Parts of Images

A basic skill for manipulating images is mastering the tools used to select one element of an image. Once selected, that element can be manipulated (rotated, changed in color, etc.) without affecting other portions of the image. The selected element can be copied, changed in size or shape, repositioned within the image, or moved to another image.

Selection Tools

Selection tools are tools in an image editing program that allow you to choose one element or portion of an image to work with and manipulate. In Photoshop, the selection tools include the marquee tools, the **Lasso** tools, the **Pen** tools, and the **Quick Selection** and **Magic Wand** tools. See **Figure 19-1**. Selections can also be made using the **Color Range** command, one of the choices in the **Select** drop-down menu.

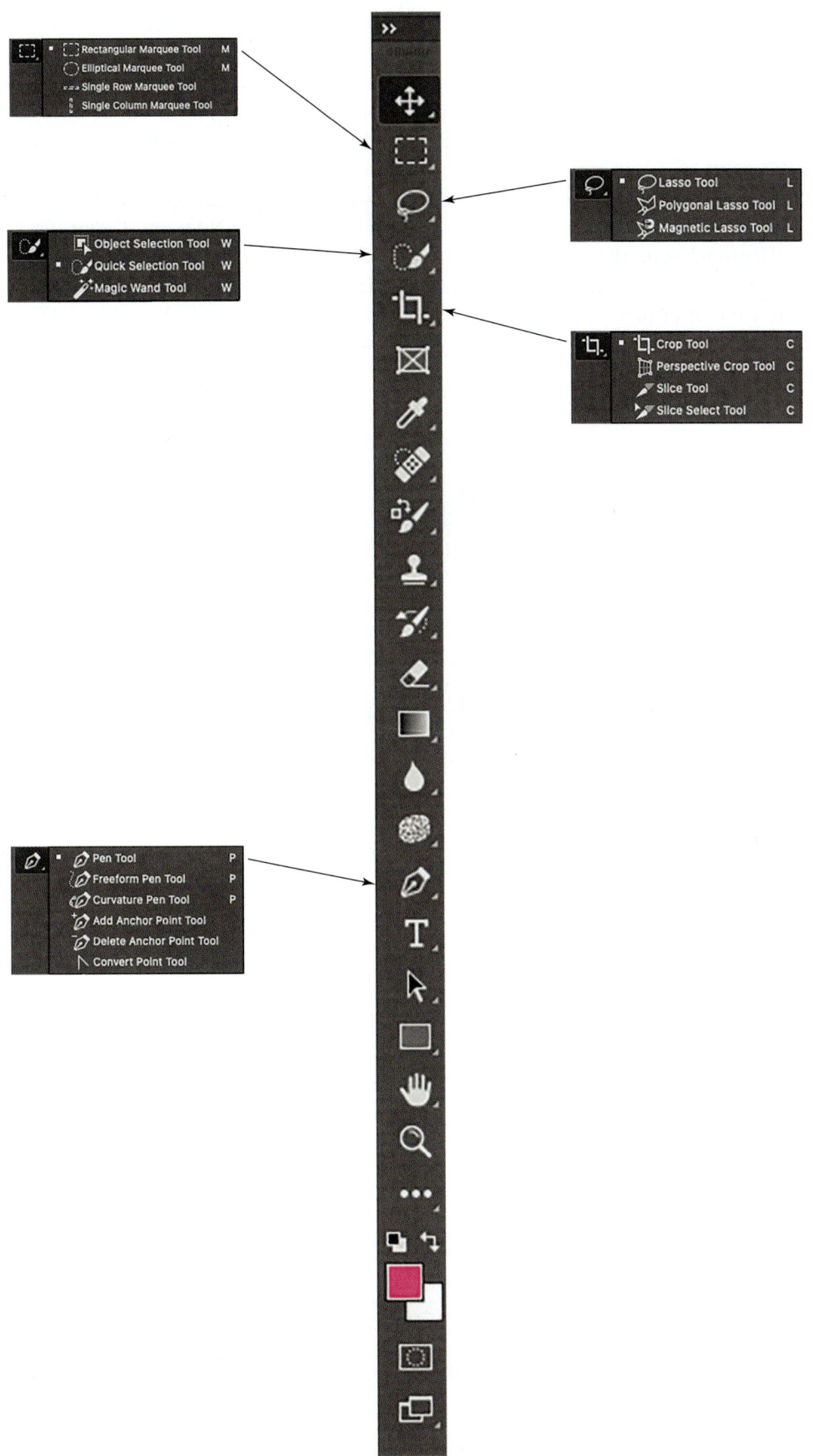

Figure 19-1. Image editing software typically offers a choice of several selection tools.

Marquee Tools

The marquee tools are quick and easy to use when the area being selected is a simple rectangular or elliptical shape. All are used by clicking with the mouse at the point of origin, then dragging to the final size and shape. The ***rectangular marquee*** tool allows the user to make a square or rectangular selection. The ***elliptical marquee*** tool allows the user to make a circular or oval selection. To constrain the rectangular marquee to a square selection, or the elliptical marquee to a circle, hold down the Shift key while selecting. Holding down the Alt (Option on a Mac) key radiates the selection outward from a center point.

The rectangular marquee can be used to crop an image, but the elliptical marquee cannot do so directly. However, an elliptical marquee selection can be used for cropping by clicking **Layer** on the menu bar, then **New** and **Layer via Copy** or **Layer via Cut**. **New Layer via Cut** creates a new layer with the selection, leaving a corresponding "hole" in the **Background** layer (original file), **Figure 19-2**. The **Background** layer can then be deleted.

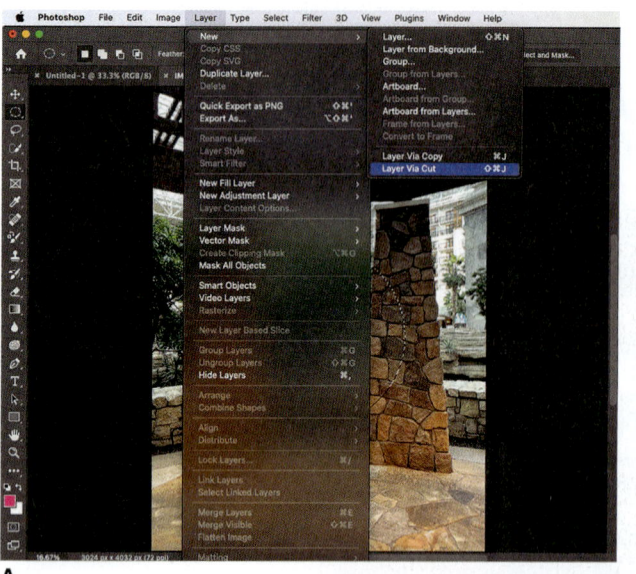
A

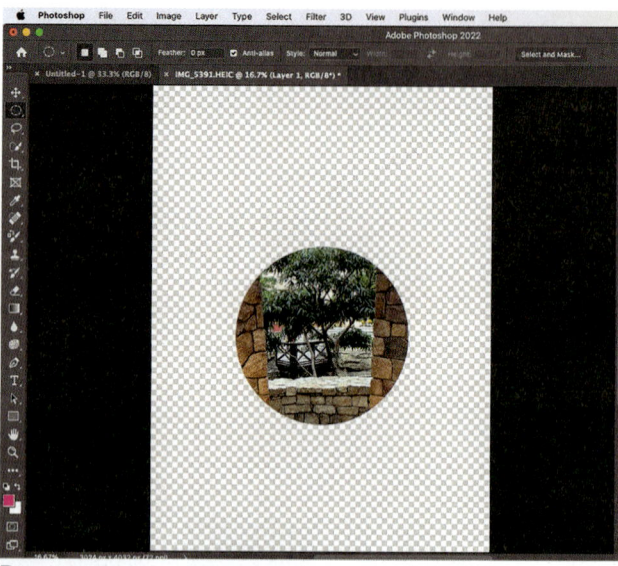
B

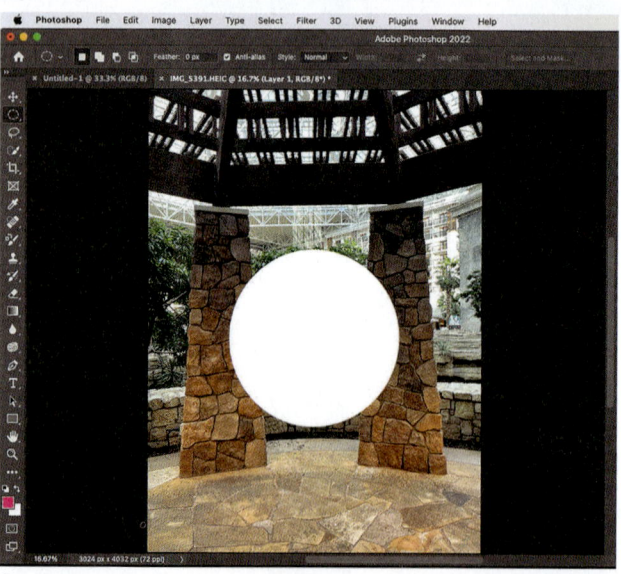
C

Goodheart-Willcox Publisher

Figure 19-2. Creating a circular crop. A—After making the selection, choose **New Layer via Cut**. B—The cropped image is extracted from the **Background** layer and displayed on a new layer. C—The **Background** layer can then be deleted.

If you need to keep the original file intact, use **New Layer via Copy**. You can then save the image with a new name (using **Save As**) and delete the background layer from the new file.

Lasso Tools

Lasso tools allow you to select irregular shapes by drawing around the desired outline with the mouse or a pen and graphics tablet. There are three lasso tools, each using a slightly different selection technique.

The basic **Lasso** tool is a freehand drawing tool used to trace around the desired outline, **Figure 19-3**. After the initial click, the mouse button is held down until tracing is completed. When the button is released back at the point of origin, the selection outline appears. This tool is often used to make a loose selection that is then refined using the **Quick Mask** overlay or one of the eraser tools, which are described later in this chapter.

The **Magnetic Lasso** tool works in a similar fashion but does not require holding down the mouse button after the initial click. This tool works best when selecting shapes with well-defined edges, since it distinguishes differences in color or brightness, **Figure 19-4**. As you trace the shape, the **Magnetic Lasso** sets fastening points to anchor the selection. If the selection strays from the edge you are trying to select, you can make a correction by moving the cursor back over the selection while pressing the **Delete** or **Backspace** key. Once back on the correct line, you can set additional fastening points by left-clicking the mouse as you move the cursor.

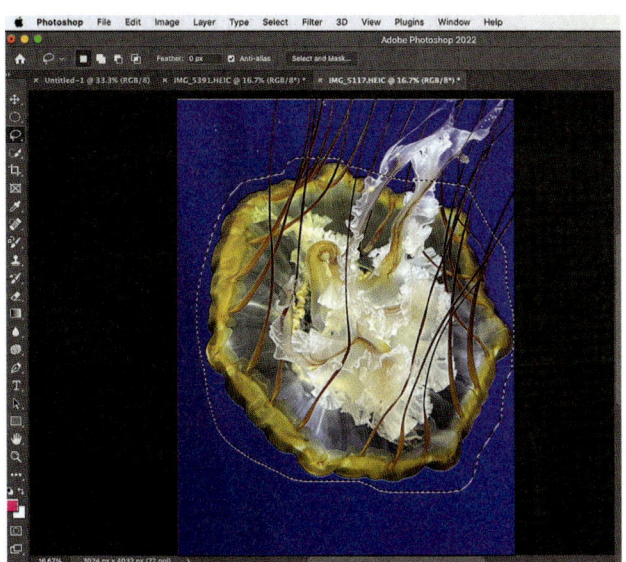

Goodheart-Willcox Publisher

Figure 19-3. A loose selection made with the **Lasso** tool.

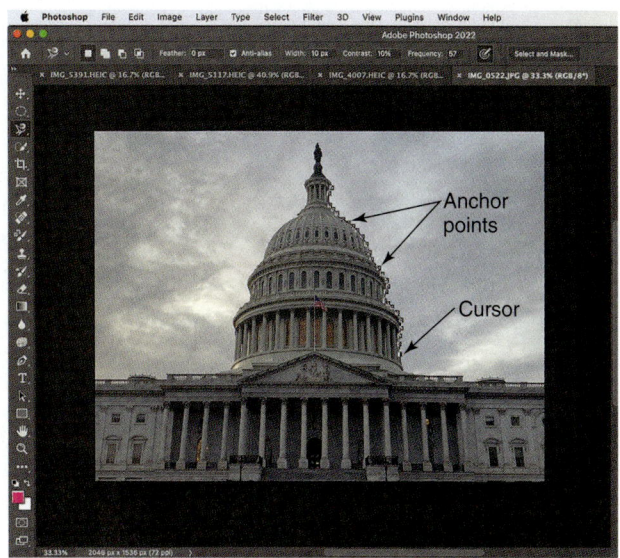

Goodheart-Willcox Publisher

Figure 19-4. A **Magnetic Lasso** selection "clings" to the edge as you move the cursor, setting anchor points as it moves.

The **Polygon Lasso** tool is useful for making selections that have straight edges. It is used by clicking the origin, then stretching the visible line (rubberbanding) to the point where the edge changes direction. Clicking sets a point to lock the first line segment in place, and the line is then stretched to the next direction change and a point placed. The process continues until the entire shape has been defined. Curved portions of a selection can be defined with many short straight-line segments, but such shapes are better selected using the **Pen** tool.

Pen Tools

The most precise of the selection tools, the **Pen** tool is used to define a ***path***, which is a line or closed figure that can be edited and altered as necessary. A closed figure can be converted to a selection. Like the **Polygon Lasso** tool, the **Pen** tool uses a "connect the dots" technique. The difference is in the nature of the points set by clicking the mouse. Single clicks set ***anchor points*** (control points set by clicking the mouse while making a selection using the **Pen** tool). When working with anchor points, you will also use ***handles***, which are control points on the **Pen** tool that can be used to curve the line segment between them. The handles allow you to select curved shapes, **Figure 19-5**.

Some people find the **Freeform Pen** tool easier to use—you click to set an origin point and then move the mouse around the desired outline. Clicking again

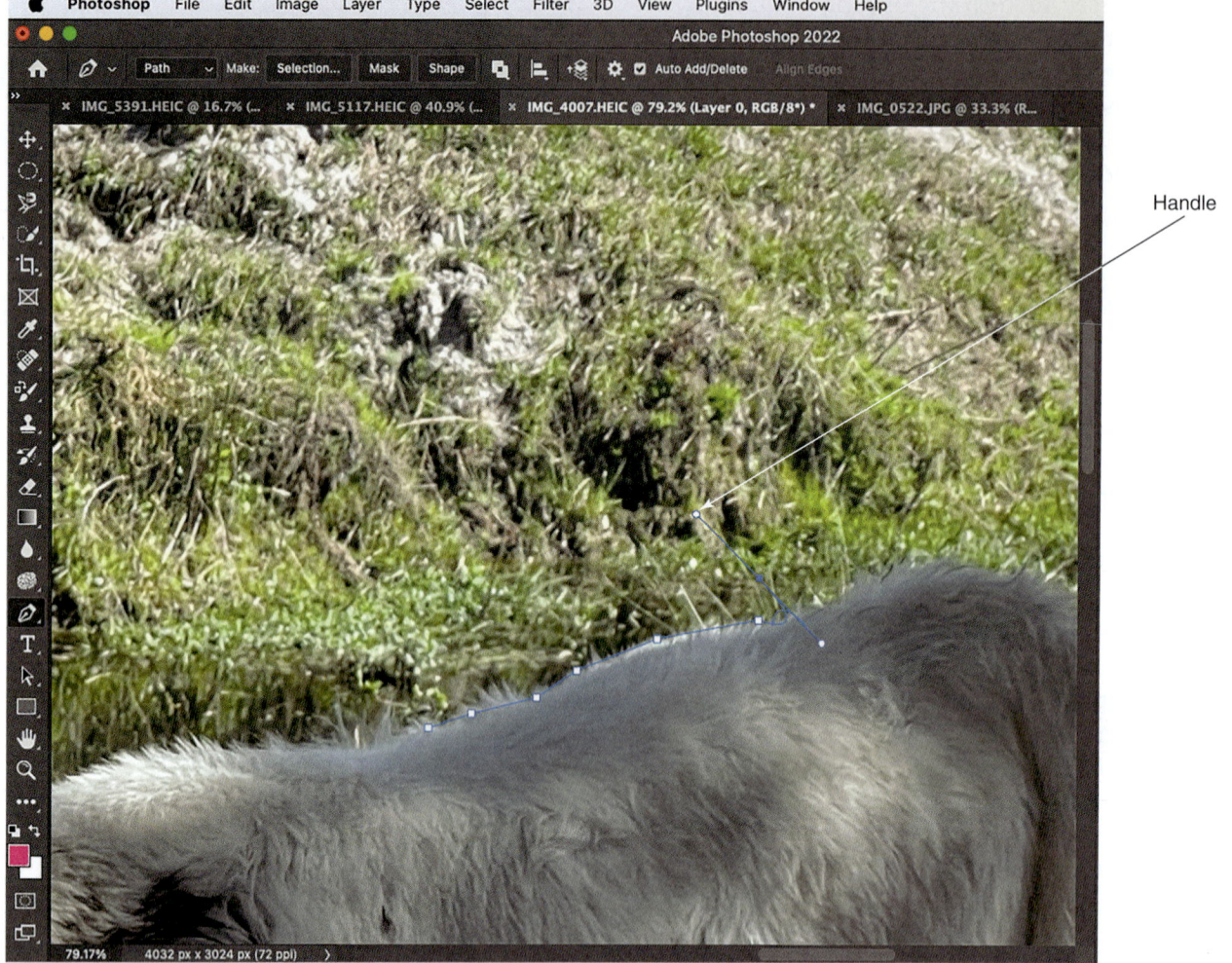

Figure 19-5. Handles on the points set by the **Pen** tool can be used to fit the line to curved shapes.

on the origin point defines the completed path. If you check the **Magnetic** box on the **Options** bar, the **Freeform Pen** tool behaves like the **Magnetic Lasso** tool. Clicking on the down arrow on the **Options** bar opens a drop-down menu, **Figure 19-6**. The higher the value entered in the **Curve Fit** box (between 0.5 and 10), the closer together anchor points are set, resulting in a smoother curve.

Once a path has been adjusted to its final contour, it can be turned into a selection. The simplest way to do so is to right-click anywhere on the image and select Make selection from the resulting menu, **Figure 19-7**.

Quick Selection and Magic Wand Tools

Making selections based on color and tone can be done with either the **Quick Selection** tool or the **Magic Wand** tool, which are somewhat similar in operation. Both allow you to quickly select areas of similar color by clicking on them. The **Magic Wand** is somewhat more complex to use than the **Quick Selection** tool. For example, **Magic Wand** requires use of the Ctrl key and additional clicks to add to a selection, while **Quick Selection** uses a simpler click-and-drag method.

472 Section 5 Postprocessing

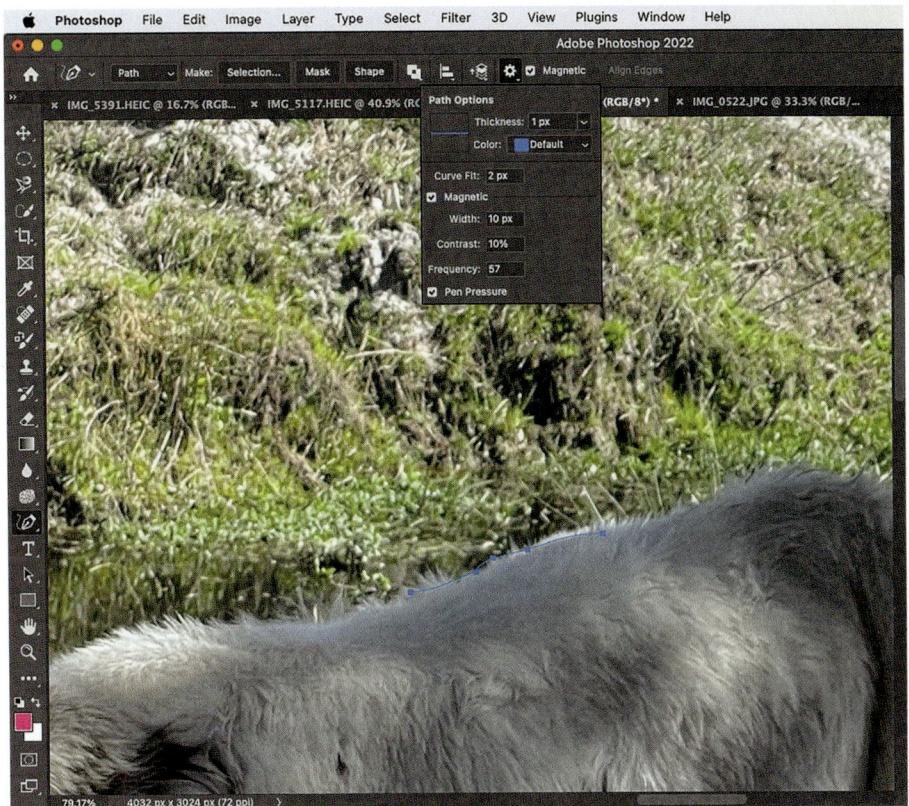

Goodheart-Willcox Publisher

Figure 19-6. The **Curve Fit** box lets you specify how close together anchor points are set along a curved path.

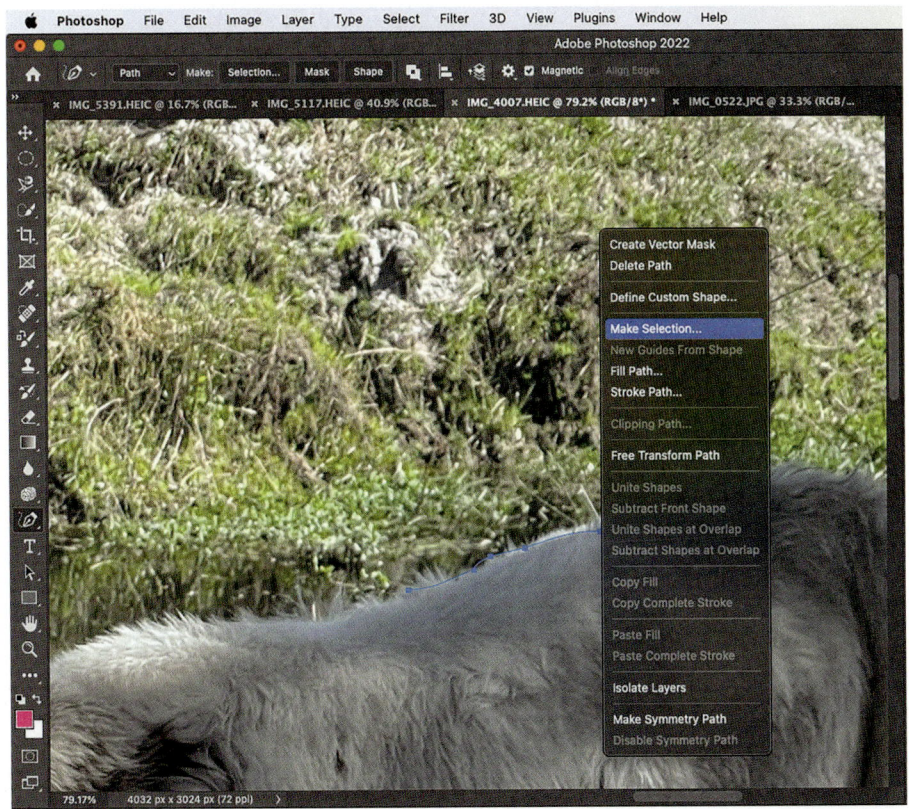

Goodheart-Willcox Publisher

Figure 19-7. Converting a path to a selection.

PROCEDURE

Using the Quick Selection Tool

1. Click on the **Quick Selection** tool icon on the toolbar.
2. Place the cursor in the image area you wish to select, then click and drag.
3. As you drag the cursor, the selection outline is displayed, **Figure A**.
4. A selection may be expanded, or additional selections made, by using the same click-and-drag method.
5. To subtract an area from a selection, press the Alt key, place the cursor, and then click and drag.
6. To better visualize the selected area, press the Q key. This displays a red overlay, or **Quick Mask**, that covers everything outside the selection, **Figure B**. (**Quick Mask** is described in detail later in this chapter.)
7. Press Q again to return to the selection.
8. Refine the selection by continuing to add or subtract.

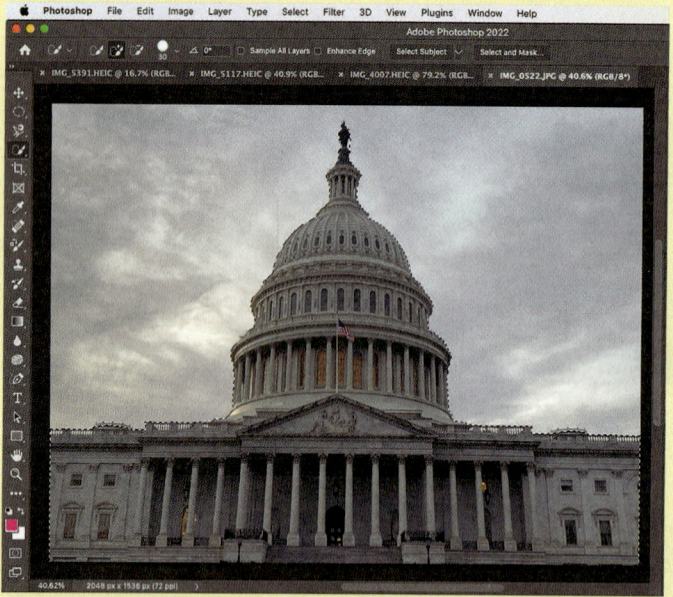

Goodheart-Willcox Publisher

Figure A. The **Quick Selection** tool is dragged across an area, such as this semi-silhouetted building, to make a selection.

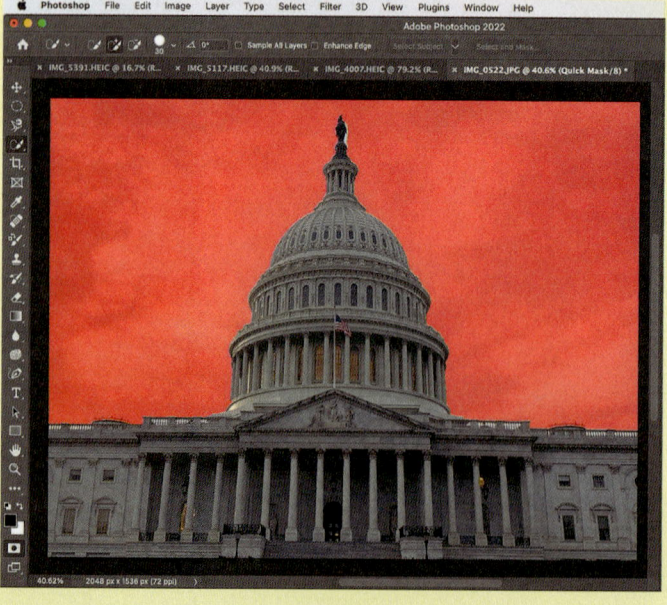

Goodheart-Willcox Publisher

Figure B. The **Quick Mask** overlay covers areas outside the selection.

Color Range

You might find the **Color Range** command easier to use than the **Quick Selection** or **Magic Wand** tools because the selections are simpler to visualize. **Color Range** is on the **Select** drop-down menu, **Figure 19-8**. It opens a dialog box with an eyedropper cursor that is used to sample a color in the image. The sampled color is shown as white or a shade of gray in the preview window, **Figure 19-9**. Expand or contract the range of shades in the sampled color with the **Fuzziness** slider—sliding right expands the range and sliding left contracts the range. The two eyedropper symbols with plus (+) and minus (−) signs are used to add or subtract sampled colors from the selection. Once you are finished sampling, click **OK** in the dialog box. The selection outline appears on the image, **Figure 19-10**.

Refining Selections

Even the most careful selection often needs some touch-up work along the edges. The **Quick Mask** mode is most commonly used to add to or delete areas from a selection. In **Quick Mask**, you use the **Brush** tool to apply or erase a semitransparent color overlay on the image. The edges of the color overlay define the selection.

Using Quick Mask

Once you have made your selection, click on the **Quick Mask** icon at the bottom of the toolbar. This generates a translucent (50% opacity) red mask over the image, **Figure 19-11**. The red color covers all the area outside the selection. If preferred, the overlay can be reversed, or inverted, to cover the selection instead.

By selecting a brush size and setting black as the foreground color, you can paint new areas onto the mask to refine the selection. Switching to the background color (white) allows you to use the brush to erase the red mask in chosen areas. For precise work, use a small brush and zoom in to 200%, 300%, or more. See **Figure 19-12**. To check the effect of mask changes on the actual selection, you can toggle (switch) back and forth between the **Quick Mask** and the selection outline by pressing the letter Q on the keyboard.

Using Eraser Tools

You can selectively delete portions of an image with one of the eraser tools in the toolbar. These tools are especially useful for cleaning up stray pixels and small areas along edges of a selection when a background is removed or after a selected portion of the image is moved to a new layer. Photoshop has three different erasers:

- **Eraser** tool
- **Background Eraser** tool
- **Magic Eraser** tool

The **Eraser** tool removes pixels much like the **Brush** tool applies color. The size and hardness of the **Eraser** tool can be changed using the **Options** bar. On the **Background** layer, the opaque (usually white) background color shows through after erasing. Other layers erase to a transparent background.

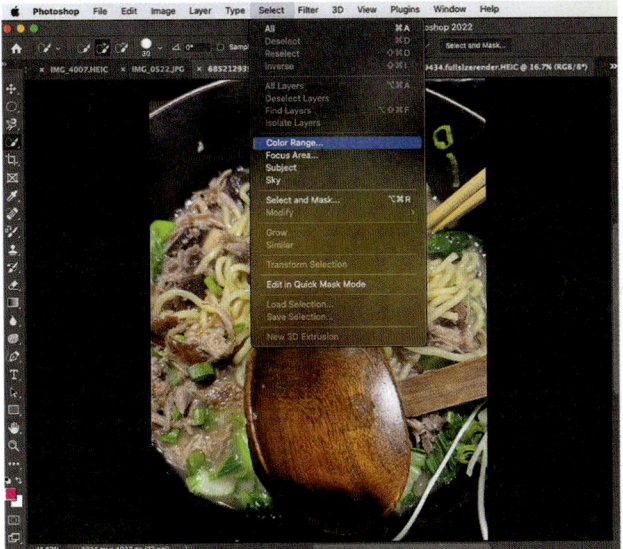

Goodheart-Willcox Publisher

Figure 19-8. The **Color Range** command is accessed from the **Select** drop-down menu.

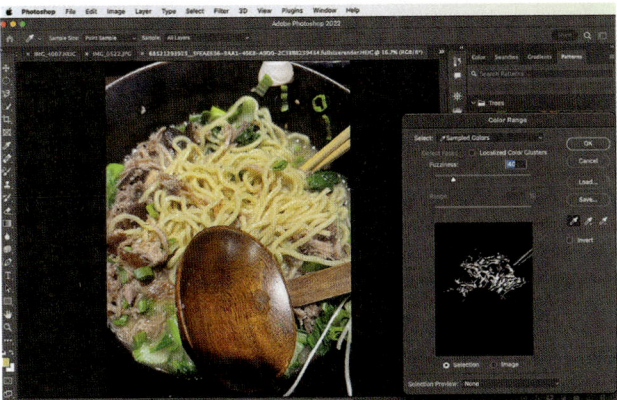

Goodheart-Willcox Publisher

Figure 19-9. A preview window in **Color Range** displays the sampled color as white against a black background.

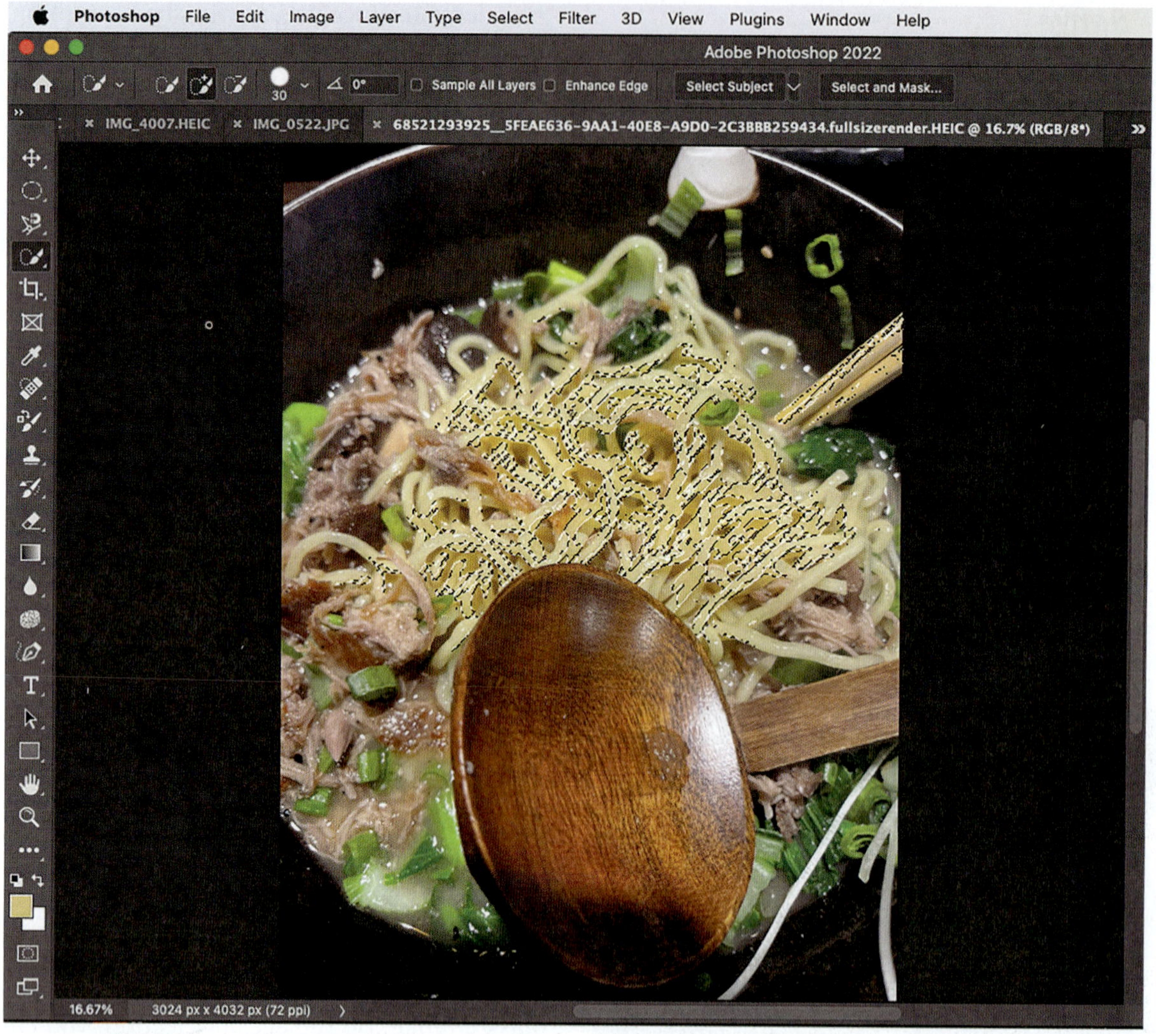

Figure 19-10. The selected area is outlined on the image.

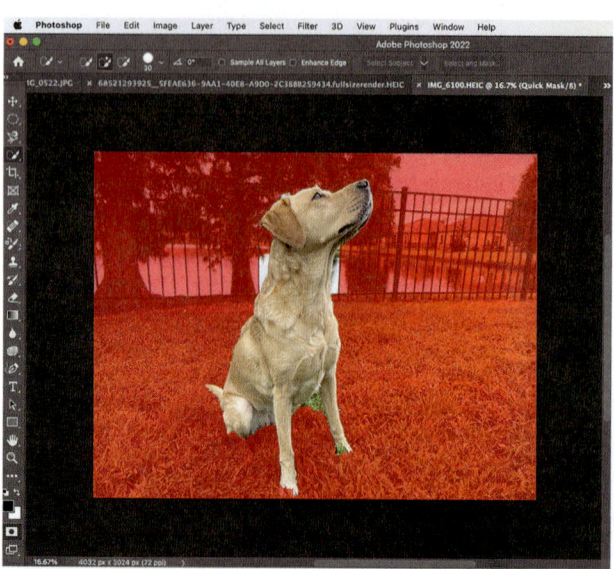

Figure 19-11. The translucent red overlay covers the area outside the selection.

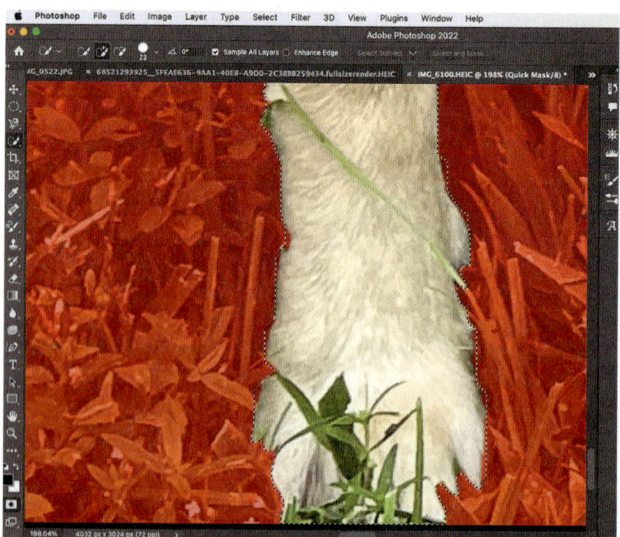

Figure 19-12. Erasing part of the mask using a small brush at high magnification.

See **Figure 19-13**. Like most image editing tools, the **Eraser** tool has a number of options. It can be used like a paintbrush, with any of the hard-edged or soft-edged brush sizes; like a pencil, with only hard-edged sizes; or like an airbrush, for very soft edge transitions. Also available is a square block eraser, which is selected by clicking on the **Mode** drop-down menu on the **Options** bar. With the image zoomed to its maximum (3200%), the block eraser can erase one pixel at a time, **Figure 19-14**. Erasers can be varied in opacity, allowing partial erasure of pixels. This can be useful for fading effects or for blending overlapping images.

The **Background Eraser** tool has a cursor with centered crosshairs (+) that is used for sampling. When you click, the sampled color within the brush diameter is erased, **Figure 19-15**. The **Background Eraser** tool has a tolerance setting that determines

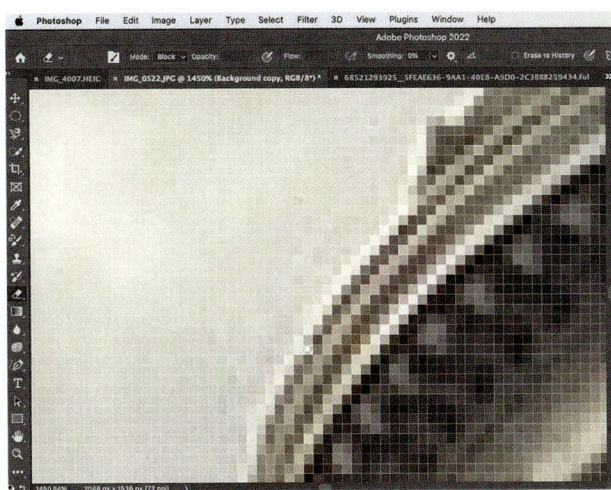

Goodheart-Willcox Publisher

Figure 19-14. The block eraser can be used to remove single pixels.

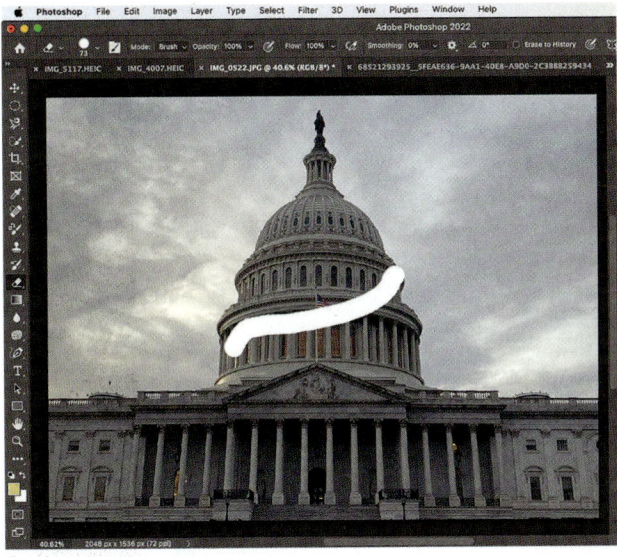
A

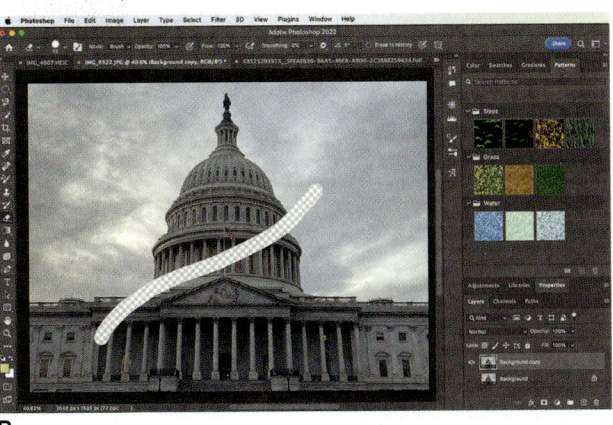
B

Goodheart-Willcox Publisher

Figure 19-13. Using the **Eraser** tool. A—On the **Background** layer. B—On other layers.

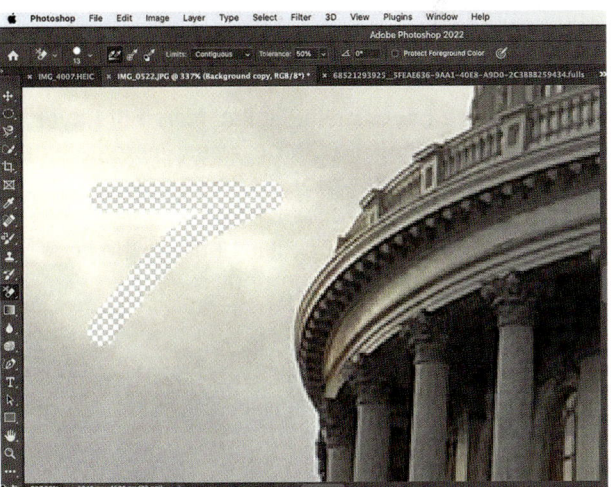

Goodheart-Willcox Publisher

Figure 19-15. The **Background Eraser** removes sampled colors within the brush diameter.

how many closely related colors are selected. You can also choose whether **Contiguous** (touching) or **Discontiguous** (separated) pixels of the sampled color are erased. A third option, **Find Edges**, works well when the foreground object has a clearly defined edge. See **Figure 19-16**.

The **Magic Eraser** is similar in function to the **Magic Wand** tool, but it both selects and erases pixels instead of merely selecting them. It has the same controls in the **Options** bar as the **Magic Wand** but also offers an **Opacity** slider. The slider allows you to leave a hint (from faint to strong) of the background instead of erasing it completely.

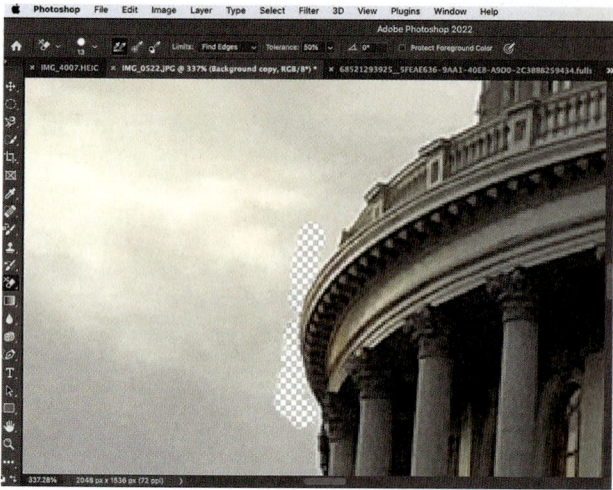

Goodheart-Willcox Publisher

Figure 19-16. Using **Find Edges**.

The **Erase to History** checkbox on the **Eraser Options** bar will allow you to restore pixels that have been erased. The **Background Eraser** and the **Magic Eraser** options bars do not have an **Erase to History** checkbox, but the feature can be accessed by switching to the **Eraser** tool, **Figure 19-17**.

Depending on the settings you use, eraser tools may miss or only partly erase some pixels in the background. These scrap pixels should be cleaned up so they do not appear in the finished image.

PROCEDURE

Making Scrap Pixels More Visible to Simplify Cleanup

1. From the **Layer** menu, select **New Fill Layer**, then choose **Solid Color**. This will create a new layer. When the **Color Picker** appears, select a bright yellow or similar light color.
2. Move the new layer so it is beneath the layer with the erased background.
3. Zoom in and look for scrap pixels, which should show up well against the bright color of the **Fill** layer, **Figure C**.
4. Make the layer with the erased background the active layer.
5. Use the **Eraser** tool to systematically clean up all the scrap pixels.
6. When finished, delete the **Fill** layer.

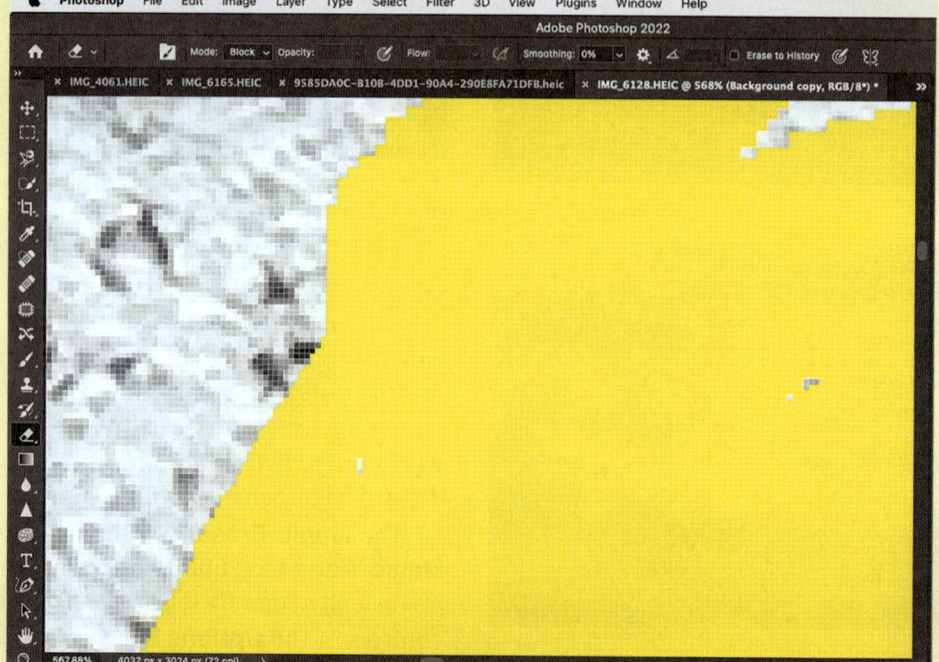

Goodheart-Willcox Publisher

Figure C. A bright-colored temporary fill layer will make obvious any scrap pixels that were missed in erasing.

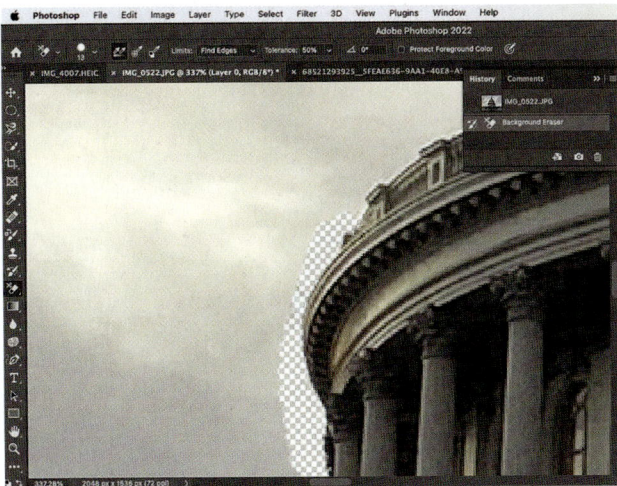

Goodheart-Willcox Publisher

Figure 19-17. Using **Erase to History** to restore the missing pixels on the edge of a building.

Combining Images

The ability to select part of one image and make it part of another is the key to creating combined images, or composites. A **composite** is an image created by combining either parts of or all of several separate images. Sometimes these combinations are strictly practical, **Figure 19-18**. Composites often are created for an artistic purpose, resulting in images ranging from the clearly fantastic to what have been called *believable lies*—scenes that might have been captured with a camera. See **Figure 19-19**.

Artistic composites may involve extensive editing and various types of manipulation. One technique is **morphing**, in which images may be merged or distorted to transform an object's appearance. An example is an age progression portrait, which depicts a child as they would look in adulthood.

Using Layers

To create a composite, you will make extensive use of layers. As described in Chapter 18, layers function like a series of sheets that can be stacked one atop another. Portions of these layers are transparent, permitting image material from lower layers to show through. The characteristics of a layer, such as its opacity, can be altered by applying blending modes and masks. These tools are described later in this section.

Adding Layers

Layers can be added to an image in various ways:
- To add a new, blank layer, click on **Layer > New**, then choose **Layer...** from the drop-down menu, or click the **New Layer** icon at the bottom of the **Layers** panel, **Figure 19-20**.
- To create a copy of the **Background** layer (or any other active layer), choose **Duplicate Layer...** from the **Layer** drop-down menu.

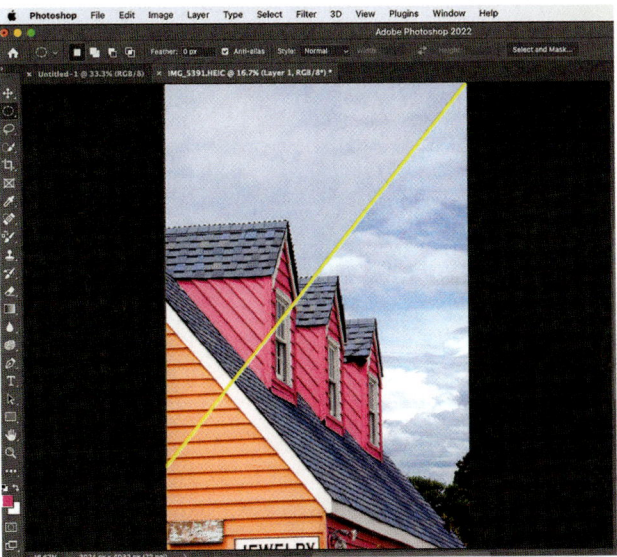

Goodheart-Willcox Publisher

Figure 19-18. Left—A dull gray sky weakened the visual impact of this colorfully painted building in a seashore community. Right—The sky area was selected, erased, and replaced with a brighter, more visually interesting sky.

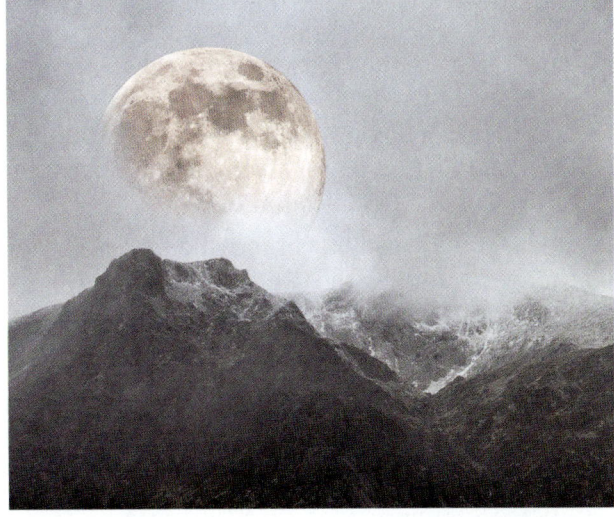

Matt Gibson/Shutterstock.com

Figure 19-19. The moon and the mountain range were photographed miles apart in distance and months apart in time.

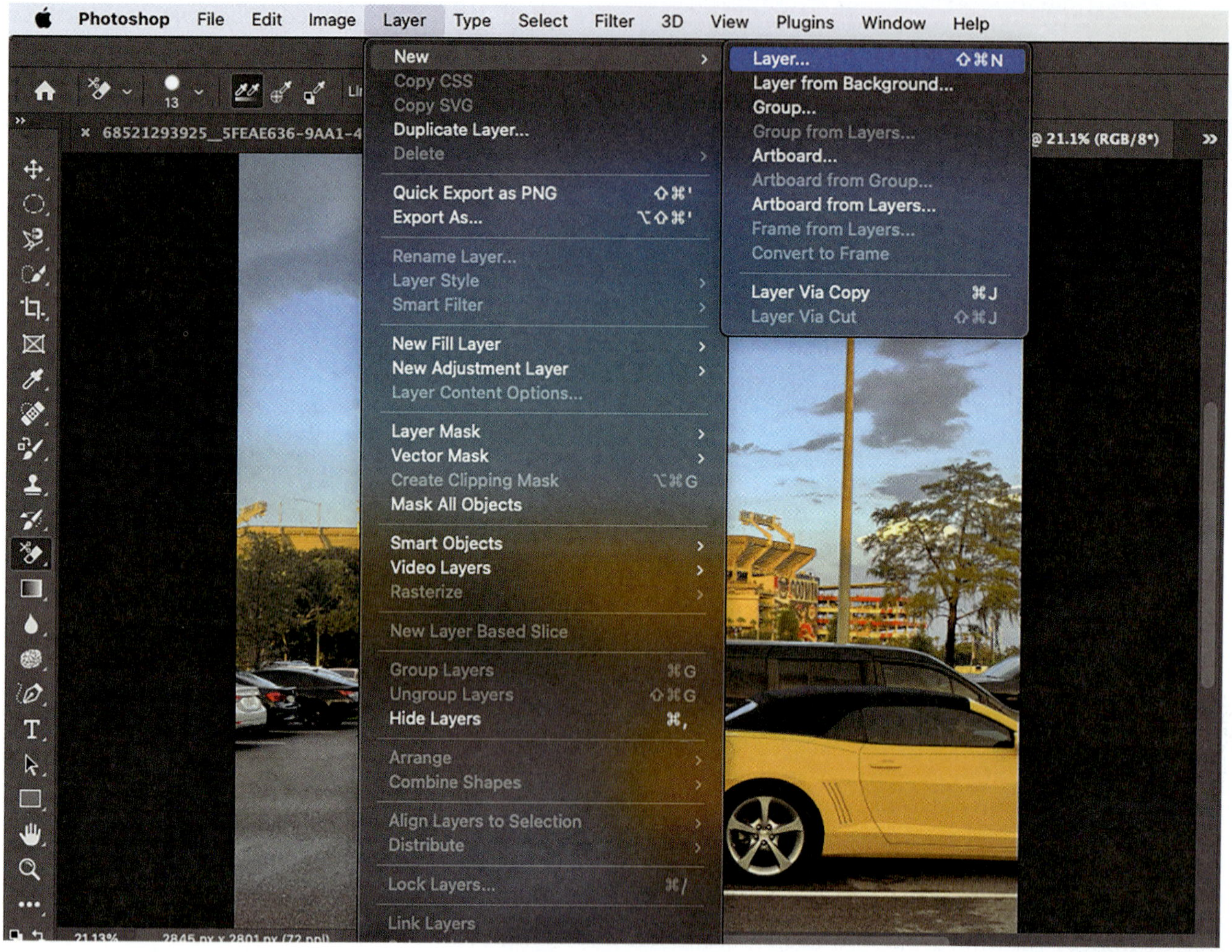

Figure 19-20. Adding a new blank layer to an image using the **Layer** drop-down menu.

- To add an **Adjustment** layer, click on the desired icon on the **Adjustments** panel.
- To make a selection from an existing layer and save it as a new layer, use **Layer > New > Layer via Copy** or **Layer via Cut**.
- To add a selection from a different image to the original image as a new layer, use the **Move** tool or the **Cut** and **Paste** commands.

When you are copying or moving material from one image to another, the two images must have the same resolution, or the size relationship changes. As shown in **Figure 19-21**, when you make a 1″ × 1″ selection from one 300 ppi image and move it to another 300 ppi document, it remains 1″ × 1″. However, when you make a 1″ × 1″ selection from a 72 ppi image and move it to a 300 ppi document, the selected material is only about 1/4″ × 1/4″.

As new layers are added, they appear at the top of the layer stack, **Figure 19-22**. New layers are created with a transparent background.

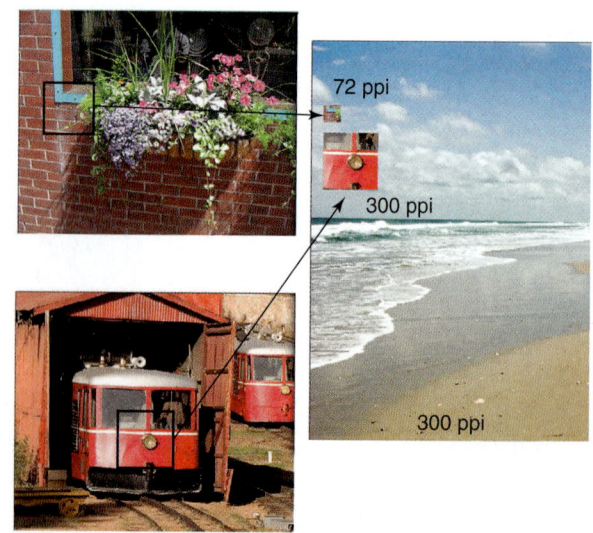

Figure 19-21. When constructing a composite, be sure that the resolutions match.

480   Section 5   Postprocessing

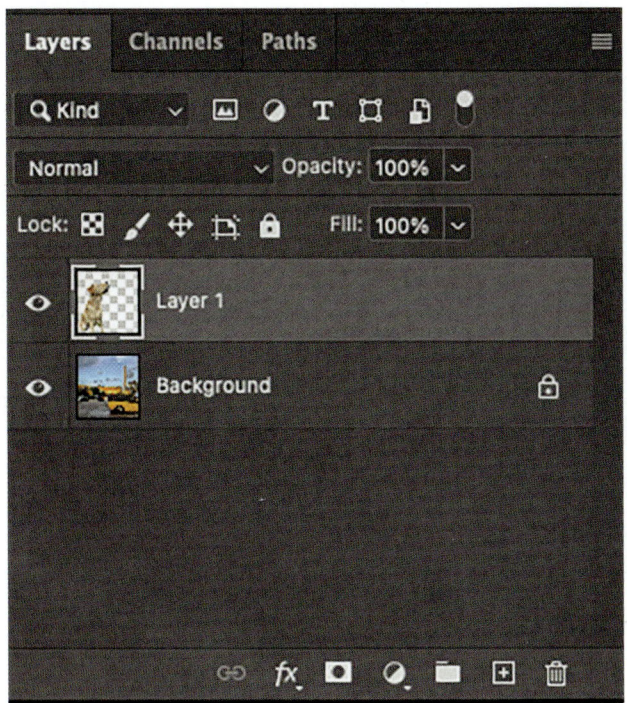

Goodheart-Willcox Publisher

Figure 19-22. New layers are added to the top of the stack on the **Layers** panel.

When creating a composite, the order of the image layers is important. Each layer obscures some or all of the layers below it, and new layers are added on top by default. You can change the ordering of layers by dragging with the cursor or by using the commands listed under **Layer > Arrange**, **Figure 19-24**. The **Bring Forward** and **Send Backward** commands move the active layer up or down in the stack by one place. The **Bring to Front** and **Send to Back** commands move the active layer to the top or bottom of the stack (if there is a **Background** layer, the moved layer will be positioned just above it).

At times, it is desirable to have the image on a lower layer show through the image on the layer above it. The upper layer image can be made more or less transparent by changing its opacity. You can use a slider control on the **Layers** panel to change the opacity of the upper layer image, making it more or less transparent. See **Figure 19-25**.

Deleting Layers

Deleting layers is very straightforward. Simply right-click on the layer you want to remove, select **Delete Layer**, and confirm the deletion in the dialog box that appears. You can also hold down the Alt or Option key on your keyboard and click on the layer you want to delete.

If an image is later placed on that layer, only the image area obscures the layer below. The transparent background allows the rest to be visible. See **Figure 19-23**. As mentioned in Chapter 18, it is a good idea to name each layer uniquely as it is created so you can keep better track of your work.

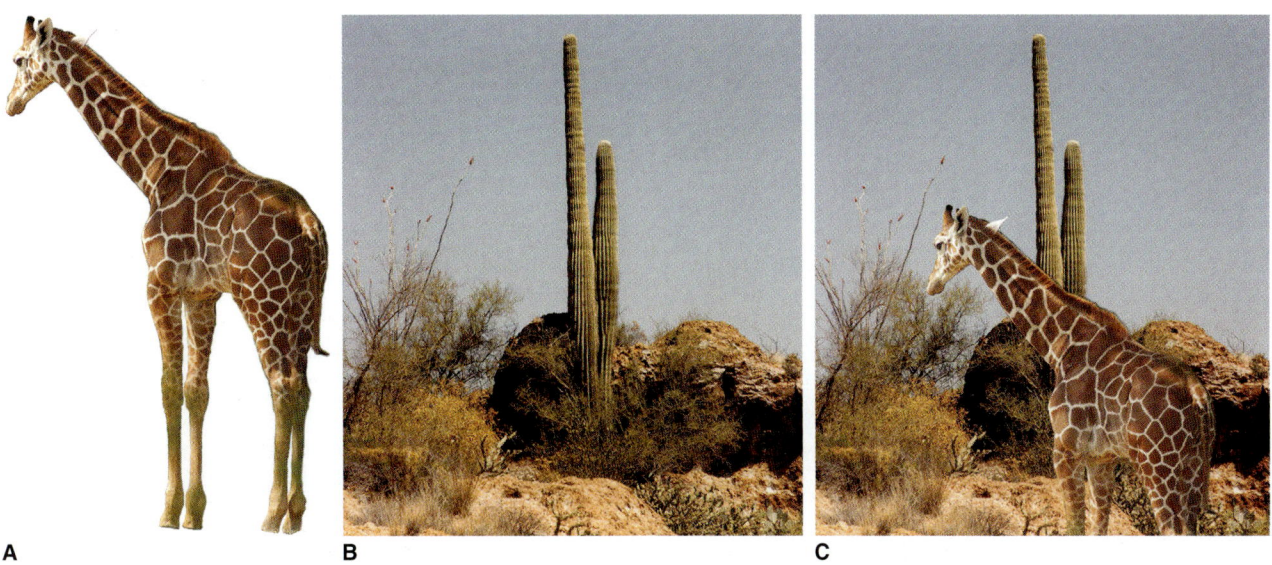

Goodheart-Willcox Publisher

Figure 19-23. In a composite, an image will obscure areas on the layer below it. A—The top layer. B—The background layer. C—The two-layer composite.

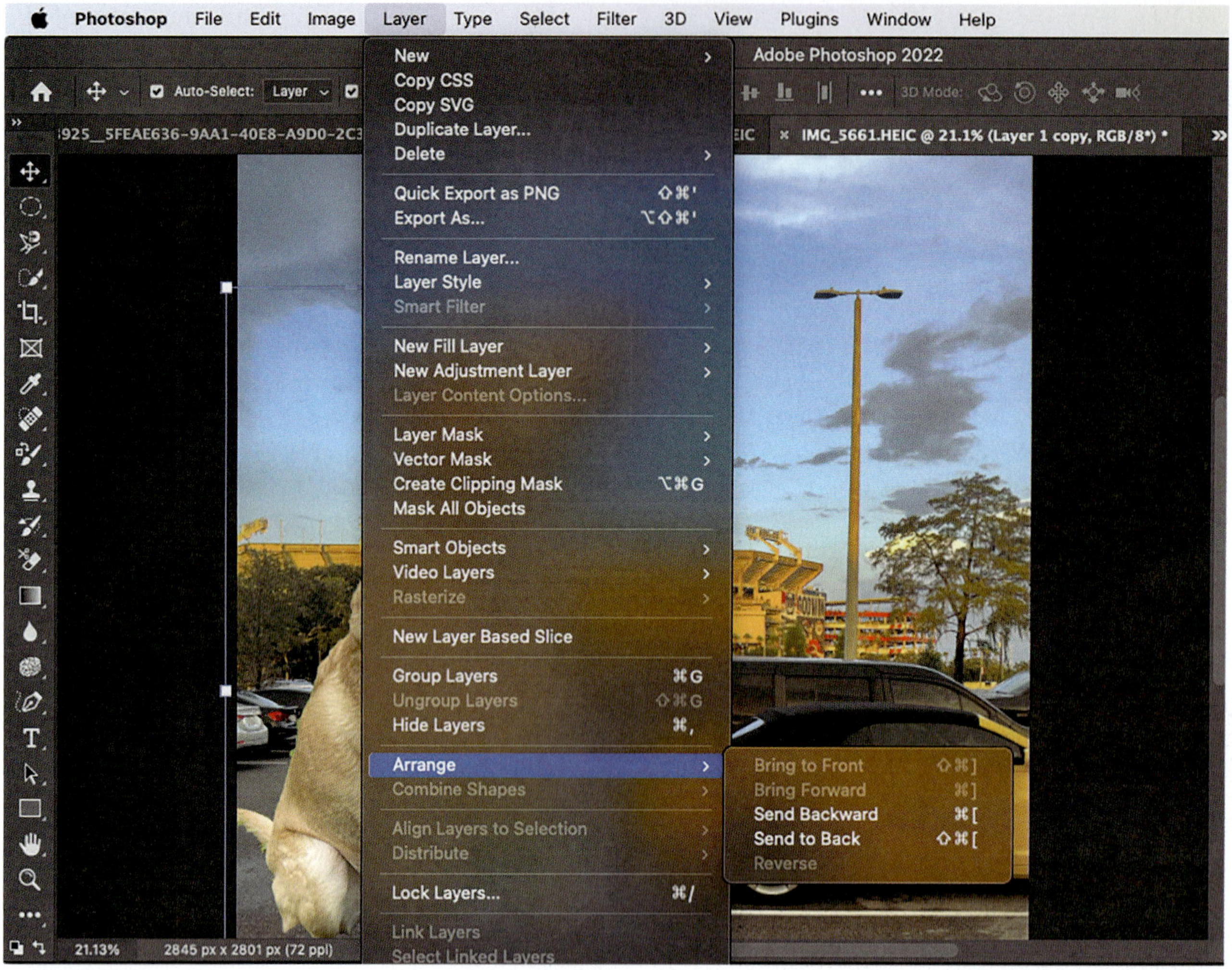

Figure 19-24. Commands for changing layer order are on the **Layer > Arrange** menu.

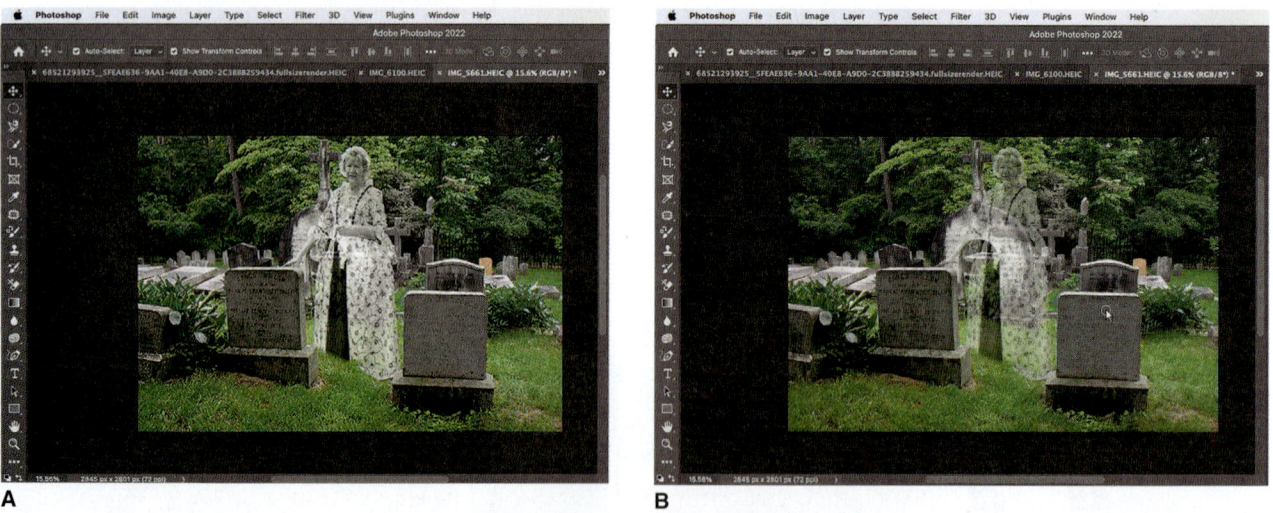

Figure 19-25. The amount of show-through from the lower layer was varied by changing the opacity of the upper layer to produce two different versions of this "ghost" in a Colonial-era graveyard. A—An opacity of 75%. B—An opacity of 45%.

Using Adjustment Layers

Whenever possible, make changes to the working file by using one or more adjustment layers. As defined in Chapter 18, an *adjustment layer* is a special-purpose layer that allows you to make changes to the appearance of an image without permanently altering the original image pixels. To add an adjustment layer to an open working file, click on the icon for the desired type of layer on the **Adjustments** panel, **Figure 19-26**. The type of adjustment layer an icon represents is displayed at the top of the panel when the cursor is placed on the icon.

When you alter a "regular" image layer by using one of the tools from the **Image** menu, the change becomes permanent when you save and close the image. You have made alterations to the image pixels themselves and you cannot restore the image to exactly what it was before the change. If you change your mind before you close the image, however, you can undo the change. The **History** panel records each change as it is made, allowing you to undo one or more changes with a single mouse click, **Figure 19-27**.

By using an adjustment layer, you can close an image and then later open it and make additional changes. For example, assume that you used a **Curves** adjustment layer to increase contrast of the

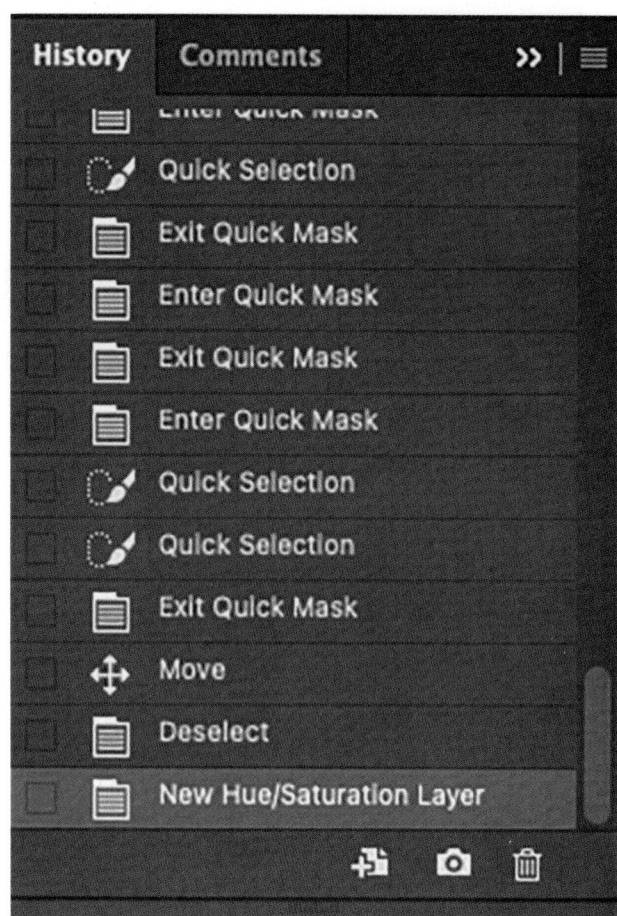

Goodheart-Willcox Publisher

Figure 19-27. Changes to an image are listed on the **History** panel.

image. After making a print from the image file, you decide that it is too contrasty. You can then reopen the file, select the **Curves 1** layer in the **Layers** panel, and adjust the curve to decrease contrast while observing the effect of the adjustment on the image. See **Figure 19-28**.

Layer Masks

Changes made using an adjustment layer can be applied to the entire image or just to a portion of it. A *layer mask* is an image manipulation tool used to protect a portion of an image from change or to permit a lower layer to show through the topmost layer. It limits the effect of the adjustment layer. A mask is typically used to protect part of the image from change.

Assume you have an image of flowers, **Figure 19-29**, and want to make one of the blossoms stand out. You can use the **Brush** tool to create a layer mask for that blossom and protect it from change as you alter the rest of the image.

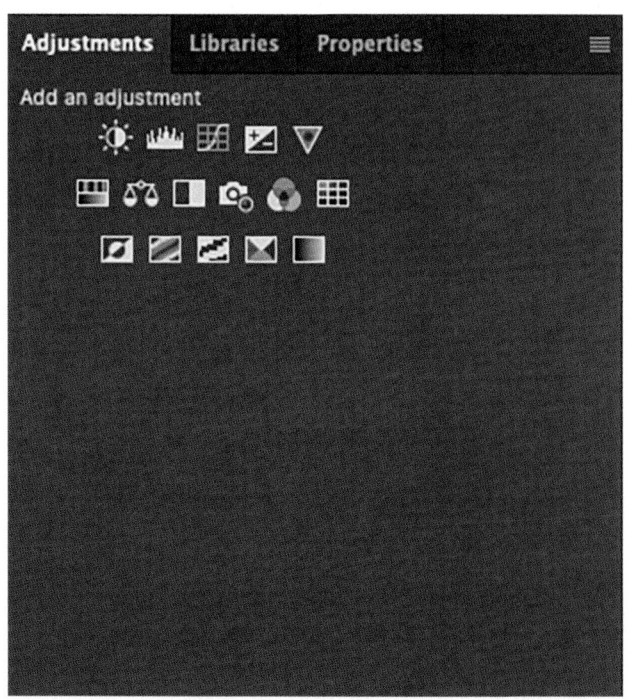

Goodheart-Willcox Publisher

Figure 19-26. An adjustment layer can be added to an image by clicking on the icon of the desired type in the **Adjustments** panel.

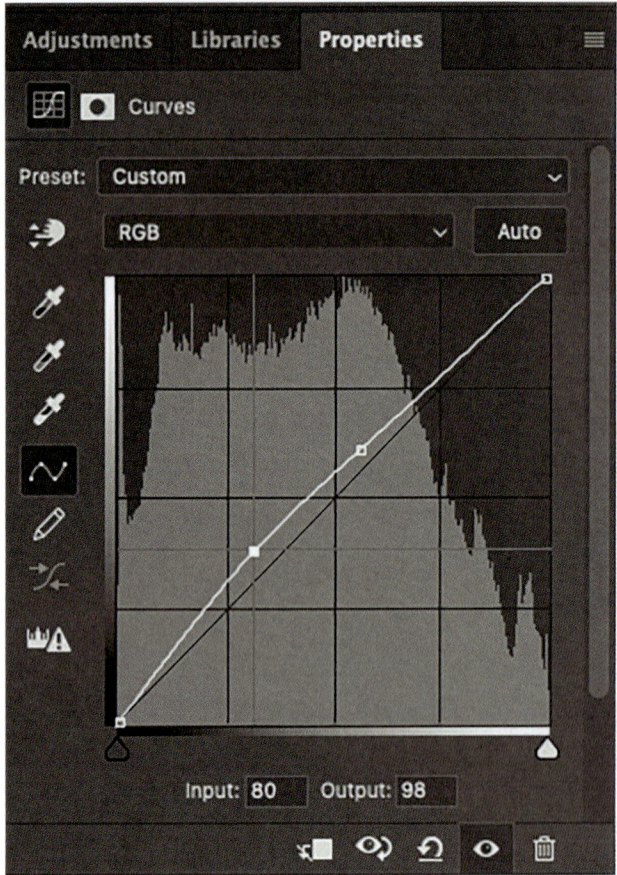

Goodheart-Willcox Publisher

Figure 19-28. An adjustment layer can be reopened to make changes to an image.

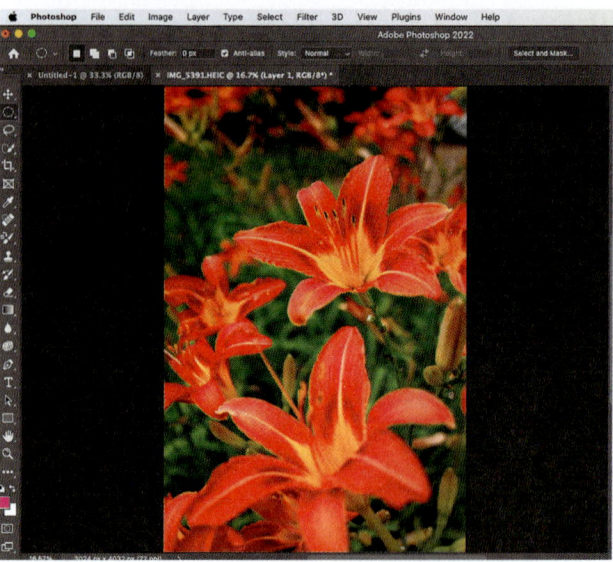

Goodheart-Willcox Publisher

Figure 19-29. A layer mask helps make one blossom stand out from this colorful bed of red-orange daylilies.

Procedure

Creating a Layer Mask

1. Add a **Hue/Saturation** adjustment layer, and then click **OK** to close the dialog box without making any changes.
2. With the adjustment layer active, double-click the white rectangle (layer mask thumbnail) in the **Layers** panel. This opens the **Layer Mask Display Options** dialog box.
3. By default, the box displays black as the mask color and 50% as the opacity for the mask. To change the masking color for better visibility, click on the color sample to open the color picker. After selecting a new color, you might also want to change the opacity. The masking color used in **Figure D** is blue at 80%.
4. Click on the **Layer Mask** thumbnail again while holding down the Shift and Alt keys. This allows you to view the mask as you paint it.
5. Select a brush size and hardness, and then begin painting. Zoom in to see detail if necessary. If you paint outside the area you wish to mask, press X on the keyboard to swap foreground and background colors. Paint over the error using the background color, which acts like an eraser rather than appearing as a color.
6. When you have completed the mask, hide it by pressing Shift+Alt while clicking on the **Layer Mask** thumbnail. This allows you to better see the changes you make with the adjustment layer.
7. Click on the **Layer** thumbnail (displayed to the left of the **Layer Mask** thumbnail). This reopens the **Hue/Saturation** dialog box.
8. Moving the **Saturation** slider all the way to the left changes the entire image, except the masked squirrel, to monochrome. See **Figure E**. If you prefer to leave some color in the image, slowly move the slider to the right until you get the look you want.

9. To make additional changes, convert the mask to a selection. Right-click on the **Layer Mask** thumbnail, and then click on **Add Layer Mask to Selection**. A selection border appears around the masked area.
10. To preserve the original pixels, create a copy of the **Background** layer to work on. Make the **Background** layer active, right-click on it, and then click **Layer > Duplicate Layer**.
11. With the **Background Copy** layer active, select **Filter > Blur > Gaussian Blur**. Move the **Radius** slider to the right until you see the desired amount of blur, then click **OK**. See **Figure F**. To hide or reveal the selection border, press Ctrl+H.

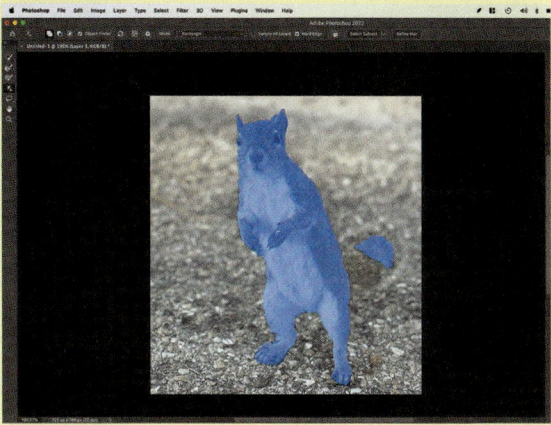

Goodheart-Willcox Publisher

Figure D. Painting a mask on the portion of the image protects it from change. Note that the mask is also displayed in the small black-and-white layer mask thumbnail as you paint it.

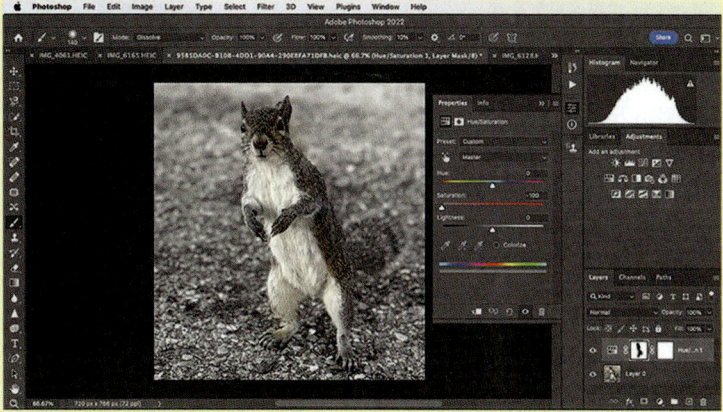

Goodheart-Willcox Publisher

Figure E. Use the **Saturation** slider to remove color from the area not protected by the mask.

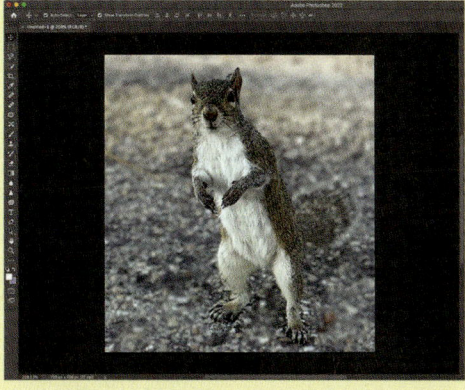

Goodheart-Willcox Publisher

Figure F. The black-and-white portion of the image can be blurred to further emphasize the squirrel. For safety, do the blurring on a copy of the **Background** layer.

Blending Modes

When an image has two or more layers, the pixels of those layers can be blended in various ways to create different effects. This is done by selecting a blending mode from a menu in the **Layers** panel, **Figure 19-30**. The colors in the topmost layer are blended with the colors in all the lower layers, changing the overall appearance.

A common reason for blending layers is to lighten or darken an image. In **Figure 19-31**, a too dark image is lightened by creating a duplicate layer and then applying the **Screen** blending mode. The amount of lightening is adjusted by using the **Opacity** slider in the **Layers** panel. To darken a light image, use the **Multiply** mode. Experiment with various blending modes, as well as different opacities, to observe the different effects on the image's appearance.

A different use of blending modes is with painting tools. These modes blend the foreground color with the color of the object or area being painted over. To protect the pixels of the original, paint on a new, blank layer—click on the **New Layer** icon at the bottom of the **Layers** panel.

In some modes (**Darken**, **Multiply**, **Color Burn**, **Linear Burn**), the result of the blending is a darker color. In other modes (**Lighten**, **Screen**, **Color Dodge**), the blended colors are lighter. See **Figure 19-32**. The **Hue** blending mode preserves shadow and highlight detail while changing the color of the object being painted over. The intensity of the color being painted over is strengthened when the **Saturation** blending mode is used. The **Color** blending mode darkens, and the **Luminosity** mode lightens.

Adding a Border

A border may be added to an image for practical or artistic reasons. Image borders can be created easily with several techniques.

For a narrow black border, **Figure 19-33**, press Ctrl+A to select the entire image. Next, click on **Edit > Stroke**. In the dialog box, fill in a pixel width for the stroke (a width of 6 to 10 pixels is often used for an 8″ × 10″ image). Select *inside* for the location. If the color shown in the **Color** box is not black, click on it to open the **Color Picker** and reset the color. Finally, click **OK** to add the border.

A similar technique can create the oval vignette often used for portraits. Make a selection of the desired size with the **Elliptical Marquee** tool, then invert the selection and apply a wide feather (40–50 pixels) to produce a soft edge. Create a new **Fill** layer and choose a color. While white is most common, the fill layer may be any color, **Figure 19-34**.

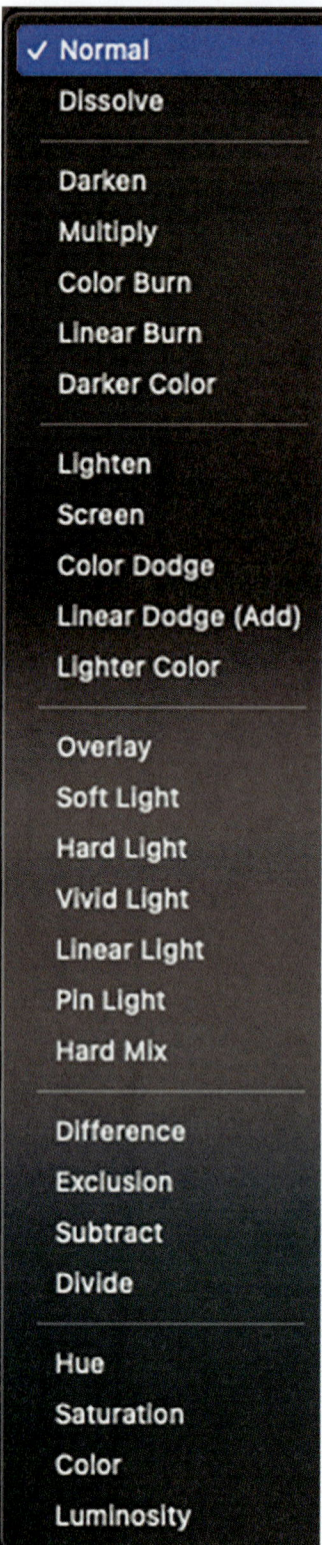

Goodheart-Willcox Publisher

Figure 19-30. Selecting a blending mode.

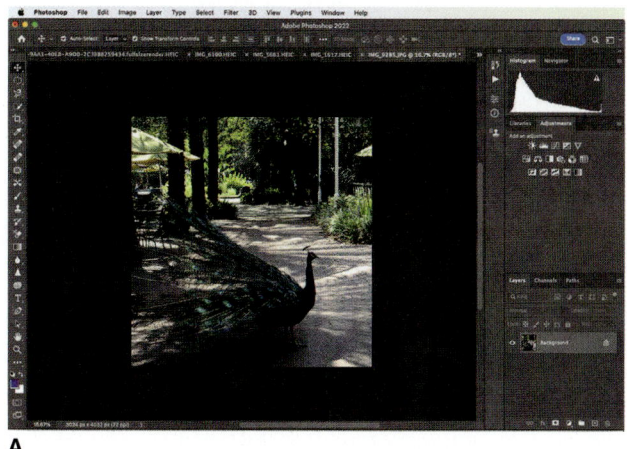
A

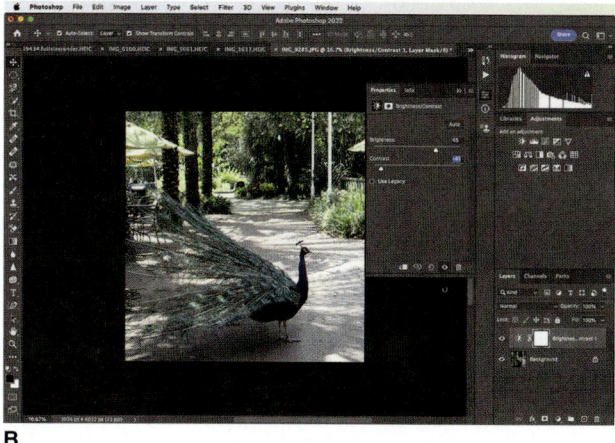
B

Goodheart-Willcox Publisher

Figure 19-31. Using a blending mode. A—The original is too dark. B—Using the **Screen** blending mode lightens the image and reveals more detail of the peacock's feathers.

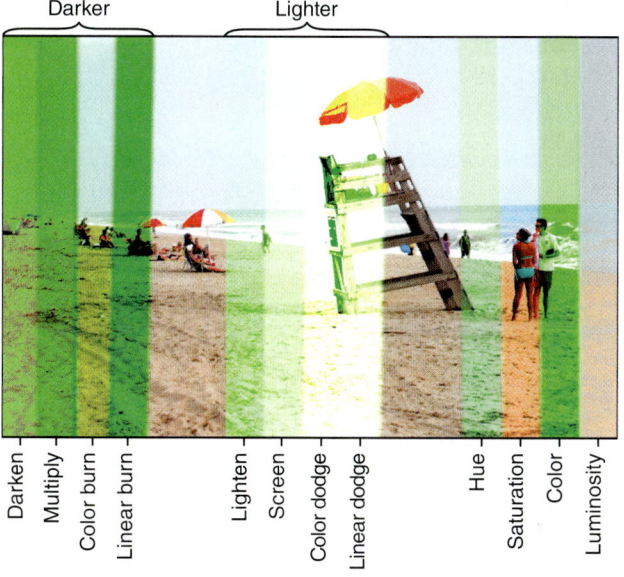

Goodheart-Willcox Publisher

Figure 19-32. Using different blending modes when applying colors with painting tools produces darker or lighter hues, depending on the selected mode. This beach scene was painted with strokes of green at 100%. The effect of the different blending modes on the color can be compared. A different color would produce a different appearance, but the effect (darkening or lightening of the blend) would be the same.

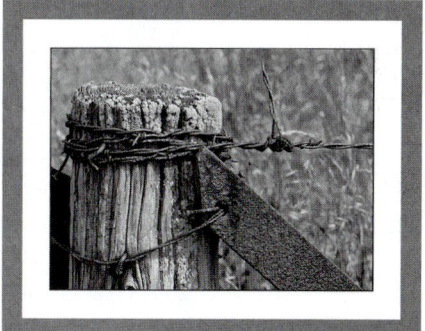

Goodheart-Willcox Publisher

Figure 19-33. A narrow black border helps separate the image from its mounting board.

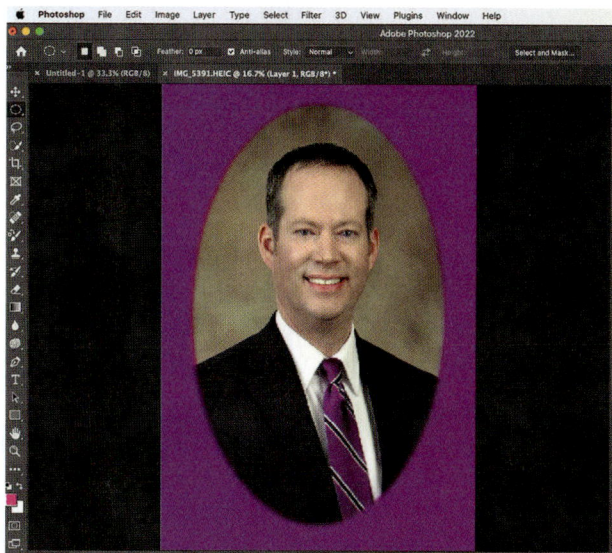

Portrait courtesy of Image Group Photography, LLC

Figure 19-34. The soft inner edge of this oval vignette was created by applying a 70-pixel feather to the selection.

Chapter 19 Advanced Digital Postprocessing Techniques 487

PROCEDURE

Creating Irregular Borders

1. Make a duplicate of the **Background** layer, and then use a marquee or other selection tool to define the area that you wish to make the border.
2. Enter the **Quick Mask** mode by pressing Q. See **Figure G**. You will modify the mask to make your border.
3. Click on **Filter > Filter Gallery**, **Figure H**. Try different effects from the **Filter** menu to see how they affect the softened (blurred) inner edges of your border. Experiment with filters in the **Texture**, **Distort**, and **Brush Strokes** categories in particular. You can click on the **New Effect Layer** button at the bottom right to "stack" the effects of the filters.
4. Once you have found a satisfactory effect, change the mask to an active selection by pressing Q.
5. Click on **Select > Inverse**.
6. Create a new **Fill** layer and select a color for the border. Click **OK** to create the border, **Figure I**.

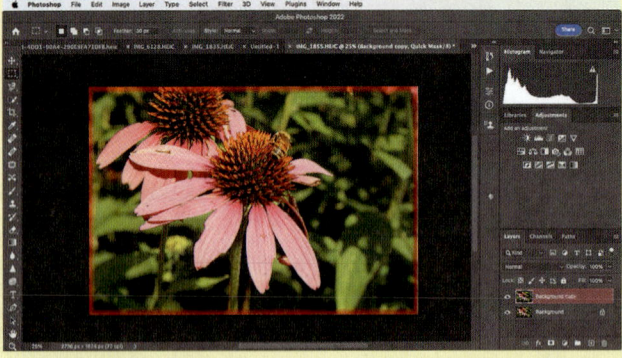

Goodheart-Willcox Publisher

Figure G. The selection outline displayed as a **Quick Mask**.

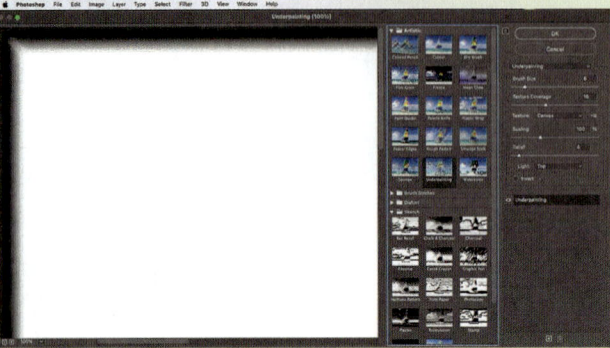

Goodheart-Willcox Publisher

Figure H. In the **Filter Gallery**, a large black-and-white preview image shows the changes as you add and modify the filters.

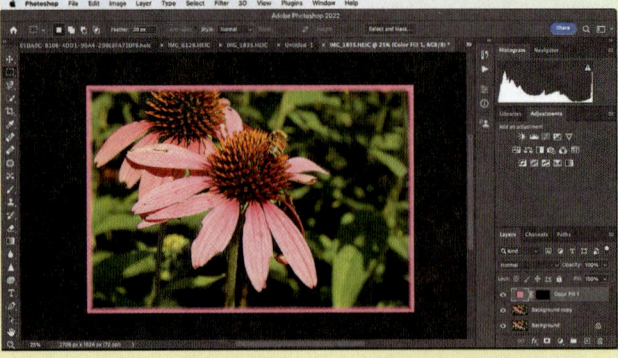

Goodheart-Willcox Publisher

Figure I. The completed border was created by using a pink **Fill** layer to complement the color of the wildflowers.

Combining Type with Photos

You can overlay type on a photo or arrange type so a photo shows through the letters. In the first case, the type is added to the image as a layer. It can be treated like any other layer, with the color, opacity, and other characteristics changed as necessary. With white or light-colored type, you can adjust the opacity of the type layer to allow the underlying image to show through to a greater or lesser degree.

To fill type with a background image, various methods may be used. One that works well is creating a *clipping mask*, which is a blocking method that allows some of the content of a lower layer to be masked out by the upper layer. It is often used to create type that is filled by a photographic subject. It results in letters that are on a transparent background and filled with the desired image. The filled letters can then be moved as a layer to a new document that will provide a solid color or other background.

PROCEDURE

Creating a Clipping Mask That Fills Type with an Image

1. Open the image that you wish to have showing through the letters. Note the dimensions of the image.
2. Set the background color in the toolbar to the desired hue (the color that will surround the type in your final image).
3. Open a new, blank image with the same dimensions and resolution as the first image. Select **Background Color** in the dialog box.
4. Make your photo image the active image again, and then select the **Horizontal Type** tool from the toolbar.
5. From the typeface drop-down menu, select the desired type. The type should have thick, bold letter strokes. Choose a point size appropriate to the size of your image and set the text color to white.
6. Click an insertion point (the spot where you want the first letter to appear) on the image, then key in the desired letters, **Figure J(A)**. When all letters have been keyed in, press Ctrl+Enter.
7. The type is now on its own layer. The type can be moved using the **Move** tool or manipulated using a transformation (such as **Scale**) from the **Edit** menu. Position the type and resize it, if necessary, **Figure J(B)**.
8. Convert the **Background** layer to a regular layer so it can be moved. To do so, double-click the **Background** layer in the **Layers** panel, then click **OK** in the **New Layer** dialog box, **Figure K**. The layer is now named **Layer 0**.
9. Drag **Layer 0** upward in the **Layers** panel so it is above the **Type** layer.
10. With **Layer 0** as the active layer, click on **Layer > Create Clipping Mask**. The result is image-filled type on a transparent background, **Figure L**.
11. Link the two layers of the image so they can be moved together. Press Ctrl and click on the **Type** layer to select both layers, and then click on the **Link** (chain) icon at the bottom of the **Layers** panel.
12. Click on the type image you have created and drag it to the open image with the color background, **Figure M**. If necessary, use the **Move** tool to position it, then click on **Layer > Flatten Image**.

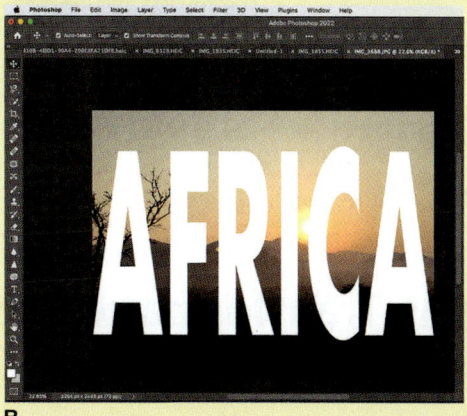

Goodheart-Willcox Publisher

Figure J. Create the **Type** layer. A—Select the desired typeface and size, and then key in the letters. B—Scale and move the type to fill the frame.

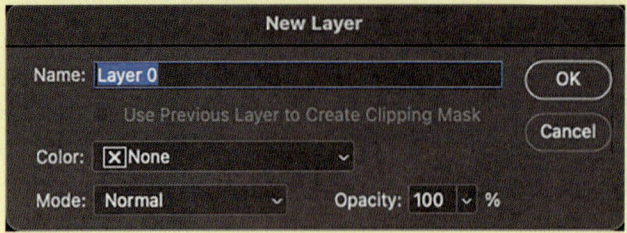

Goodheart-Willcox Publisher

Figure K. Convert the **Background** layer using the **Layers** panel.

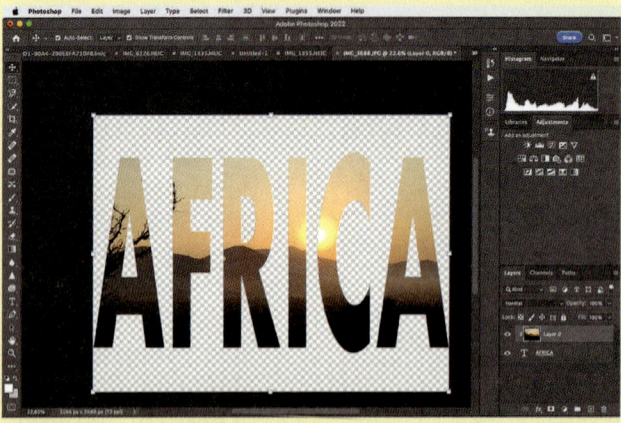

Goodheart-Willcox Publisher

Figure L. The clipping mask fills the type with the image on a transparent background.

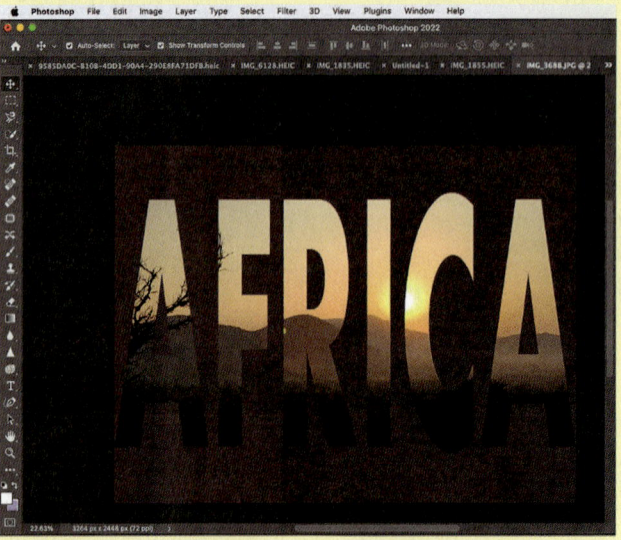

Goodheart-Willcox Publisher

Figure M. The final, combined image.

Applying Transformations and Filters

The **Edit** drop-down menu provides access to a number of tools for changing the size, shape, and orientation of an image or a selection. The **Transform** section of that menu offers tools for scaling the image to a larger or smaller size, rotating it a specified amount, skewing or distorting it in different directions, or altering its perspective.

Transformations

A transformation can be applied only to a selection made on a layer (usually the entire layer). To select an entire layer or the entire image, press Ctrl+A. One often-used type of transformation is a slight rotation to correct a tilted horizon. See **Figure 19-35**.

Another commonly used transformation is the correction of converging lines (perspective). Select the entire image, and then click on **Edit > Transform > Perspective**. As shown in **Figure 19-36**, dragging one of the corner handles outward adjusts both sides of the image, correcting the convergence. Perspective correction and cropping also can be done with the **Perspective Crop** tool. This tool can be selected from the menu that appears when you click on the **Crop** tool in the toolbar. You can also use the **Transform** tool to scale, skew, flip, and distort an image.

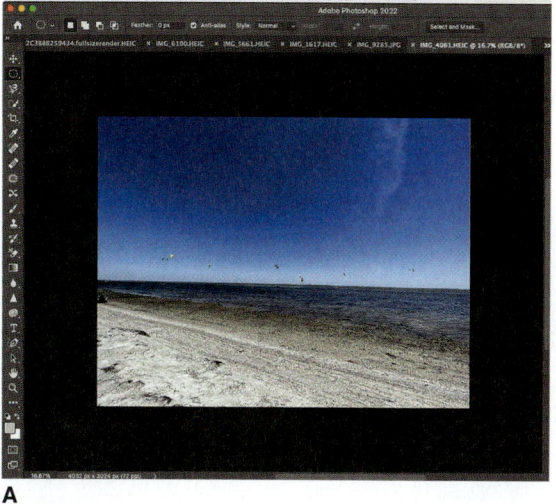

A

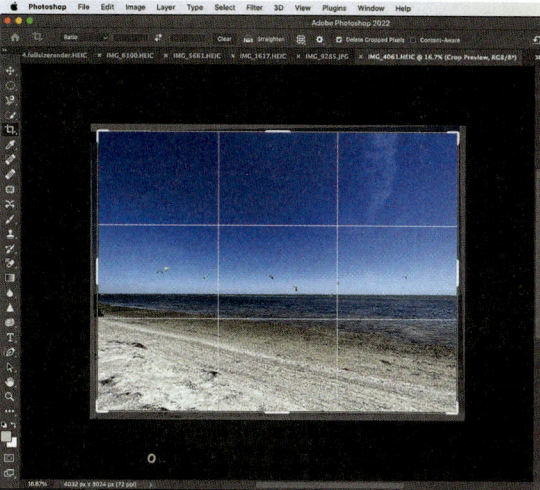

B

> ## 🛈 Procedure
>
> ### Correcting a Tilted Horizon
>
> 1. Select the entire image and adjust the window so you can see the edges of the image.
> 2. Click on **Edit > Transform > Rotate**. Move the cursor outside the image at one of the corners. The cursor becomes a curved, double-headed arrow.
> 3. Move the cursor to rotate the image until the horizon is level. Press Enter to complete the transformation.
> 4. After rotating the image, you usually have to crop to restore the rectangular format. You can use the **Rectangular Marquee** tool, but the **Crop** tool is easier to adjust. (Since the **Crop** tool can also rotate an image, some photographers prefer to use it for both the rotation and cropping steps.)
> 5. Alternatively, you can correct a tilted horizon with the **Ruler** tool. This method has the advantage of straightening and cropping in a single step.
> 6. Click on the **Eyedropper** in the toolbar and select the **Ruler** tool from the menu that appears.
> 7. Click and drag from one end of the horizon to the other.
> 8. Release the mouse button.
> 9. In the **Options** bar for the **Ruler** tool, click the **Straighten** button.

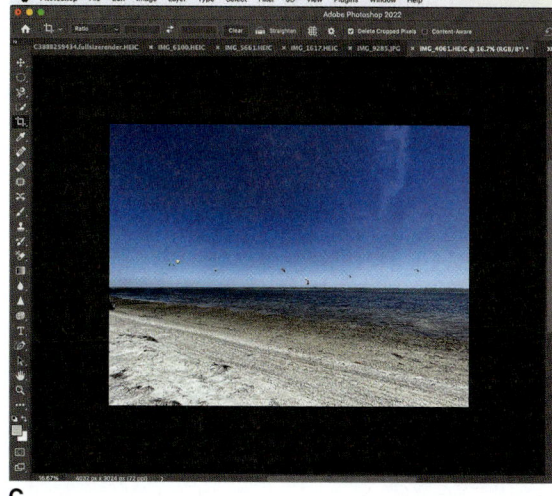

C

Goodheart-Willcox Publisher

Figure 19-35. Correcting horizon tilt. A—The entire frame is selected with Ctrl+A. B—Rotating the image counterclockwise corrects the tilt. C—Cropping restores the rectangular format.

Filters

Changes ranging from mild to extreme are achieved by using *filters*, which are special effects that can be applied to all or part of an image to change its appearance. See **Figure 19-37**. The more dramatic filters, which radically alter image appearance, often are best applied to an entire image to

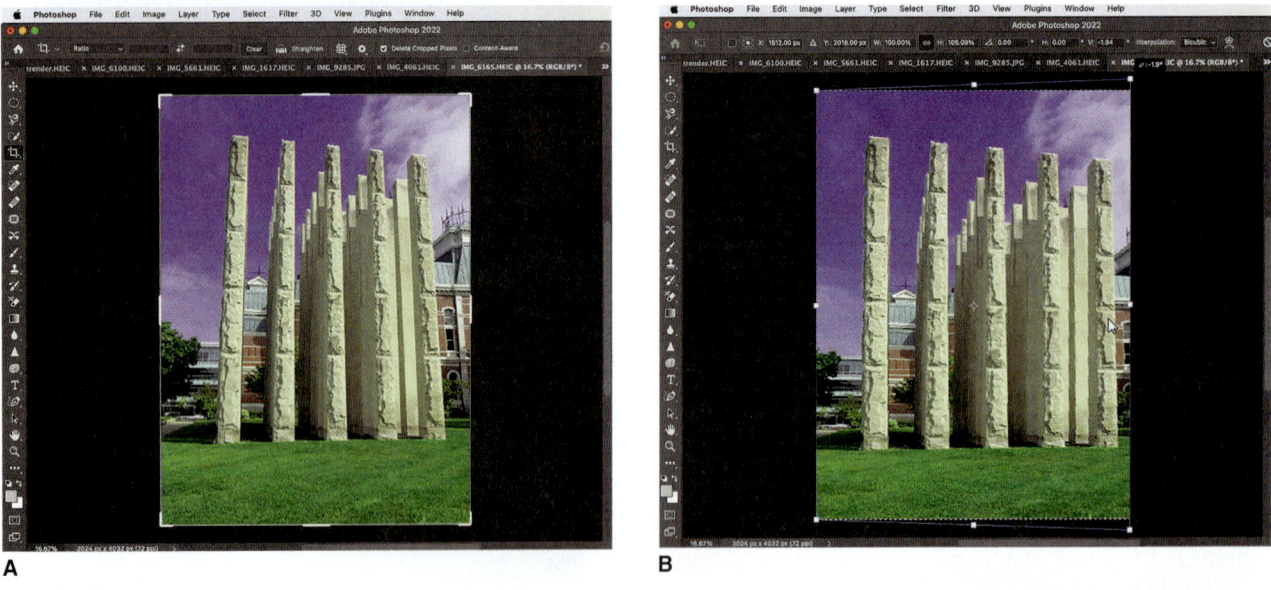

Goodheart-Willcox Publisher

Figure 19-36. Perspective correction. A—The tall columns of this war memorial sculpture appear to be tilting inward. B—Moving the **Perspective** tool outward returns the columns to the perpendicular.

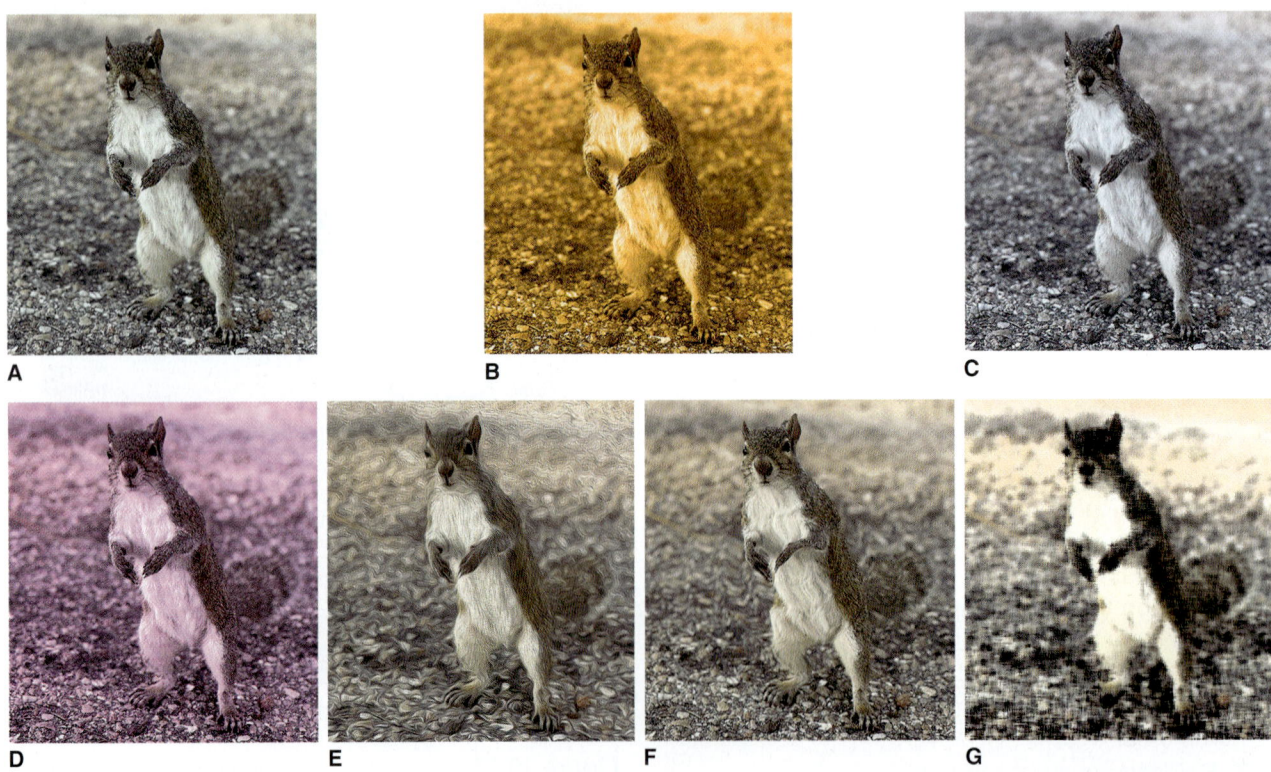

Goodheart-Willcox Publisher

Figure 19-37. A sampling of filter effects. A—The original image before filtering. B—**Warming** filter. C—**Cooling** filter. D—**Violet** filter. E—**Oil Painting** filter. F—**Zigzag** filter. G—**Water Paper** filter.

492 Section 5 Postprocessing

serve as a background. Applying them to only part of an image, however, can make a strong visual statement, **Figure 19-38**.

Warming, cooling, and color filters are accessed by clicking **Image > Adjustment > Photo Filter**. The strength of the filter effect can be previewed while adjusting it with the **Density** slider. **Figure 19-39** shows use of a warming filter.

The **Lens Blur** filter can simulate the effect of a shallow depth of field. To create this effect, choose a suitable image (one with a fairly prominent foreground object works well). See **Figure 19-40**.

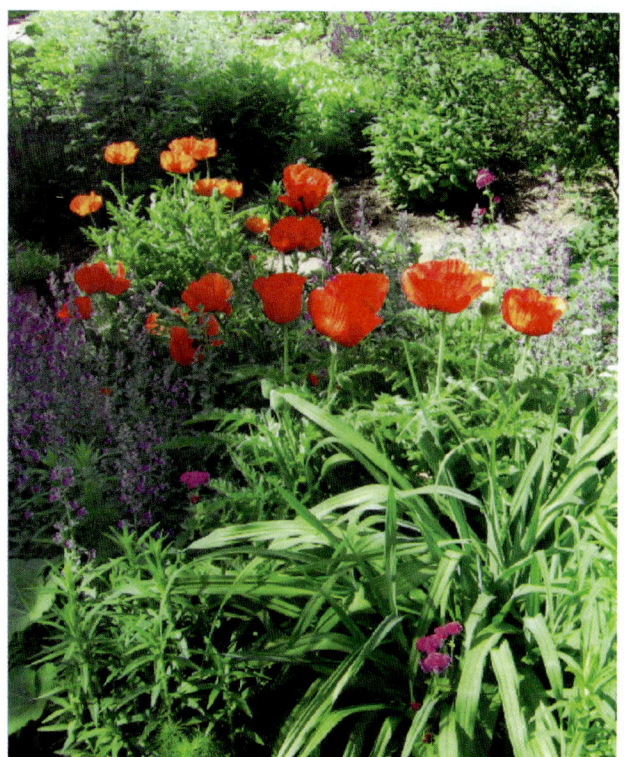

Goodheart-Willcox Publisher

Figure 19-40. This image of a bed of poppies currently has good depth of field.

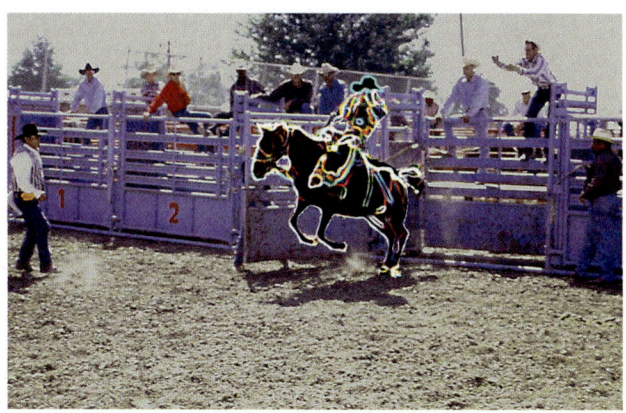

Goodheart-Willcox Publisher

Figure 19-38. The neon cowboy image was created by selecting the rodeo rider and horse and applying the **Glowing Edges** filter. The rest of the scene was shifted in hue and lowered in saturation to further emphasize the cowboy.

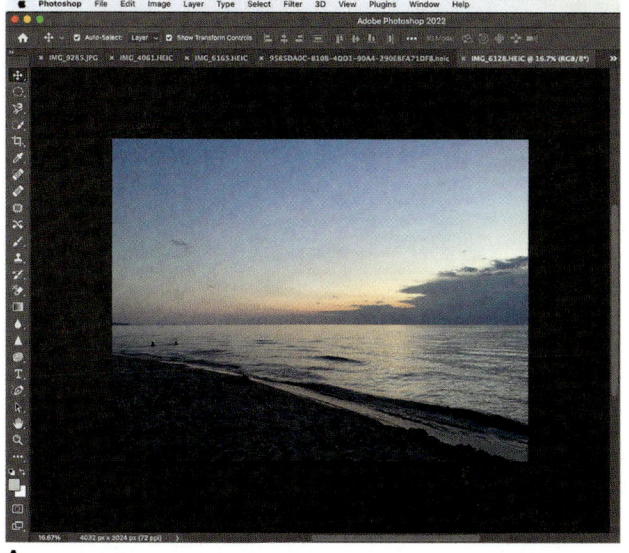
A

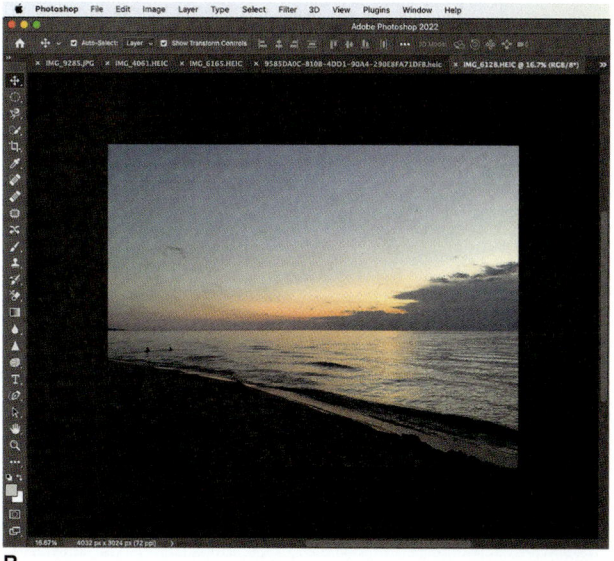
B

Goodheart-Willcox Publisher

Figure 19-39. Warming filter. A—This beach scene was taken just after sunrise. Despite the color of the sky, the overall light is cool and blue in tone. B—Applying a warming filter at 60% provides a much warmer appearance.

Procedure

Using the Lens Blur Filter to Reduce Depth of Field

1. Click on the **Channels** tab in the **Layers** panel, then click on the **Create New Channel** icon at the bottom of the panel.
2. A channel named **Alpha 1** is created and appears as a black fill obscuring your image.
3. Select the **Gradient** tool in the toolbar and choose the black-to-white gradient in the **Options** bar. The foreground color should be set to black and the background color to white.
4. Click at the bottom of the image and drag the cursor straight upward to the top to create the gradient, **Figure N**.
5. Click on the **RGB Channel** to make it active, and then click on the **Layers** tab.
6. Click on **Filter > Blur > Lens Blur**. In the dialog box, **Alpha 1** should be shown in the **Depth Map Source** box. If not, click and select it from the drop-down menu.
7. On the large preview image, click on the point you wish to display as the plane of sharpest focus. Note that areas in front of and behind that plane are increasingly blurred the farther they are from it. See **Figure O**. If desired, set a different focal plane by clicking on a different point in the preview image.
8. To alter the degree of blur, experiment with the **Radius** slider in the **Iris** section of the dialog box. You may also want to see the effect of trying different iris shapes.
9. When you are satisfied with the effect, click **OK**.

Goodheart-Willcox Publisher

Figure N. Creating a black-to-white gradient to serve as a mask on the Alpha 1 channel.

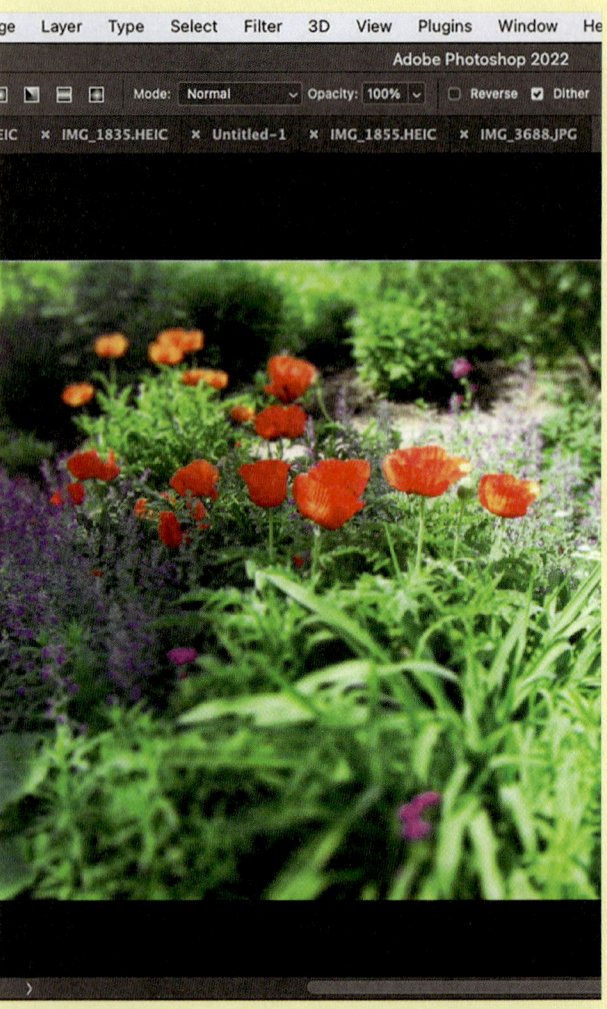

Goodheart-Willcox Publisher

Figure O. Compare the blurred foreground and background in this image with the original in Figure 19-40.

Adding Color to a Monochrome Image

While striking by itself, a black-and-white image can sometimes be made even more dramatic by the addition of color. The process of hand-coloring black-and-white conventional prints with oils or pencils, popular in the days before color films, achieved a distinctive look that can be duplicated with digital techniques. Another approach makes use of a strategically placed spot or two of vivid color in a monochrome image.

To create either effect digitally, the image must be in a color mode. If the original is a grayscale image, convert it to RGB mode. An image that is already in color can be desaturated to display grayscale values while remaining in a color mode.

If you want to achieve the appearance of a hand-colored photograph, avoid highly saturated colors and apply your hues at low opacity settings, as shown in **Figure 19-41**. The most effective coloration of this type is closer to tinting than applying solid color. The details of the photograph show through the color.

Photoshop's **History Brush** tool is another method for adding color to a desaturated (monochrome) image. This tool allows you to "paint in" details from the full-color version of an image, resulting in a grayscale image with areas or spots of the original color. See **Figure 19-42**. To use this technique most dramatically, select a single element—preferably with a strong color—to which you want to draw the viewer's attention.

Applying an overall color (toning) can make an image stronger or help it communicate a period feeling. Digital toning can be done quite easily with a **Hue/Saturation** adjustment layer. Click on the **Colorize** checkbox and then use the **Hue** slider to cycle through the entire color wheel to find the desired color. Use the **Saturation** and **Lightness** sliders to refine the appearance of the image on the monitor. **Figure 19-43** shows examples of images that have been colorized.

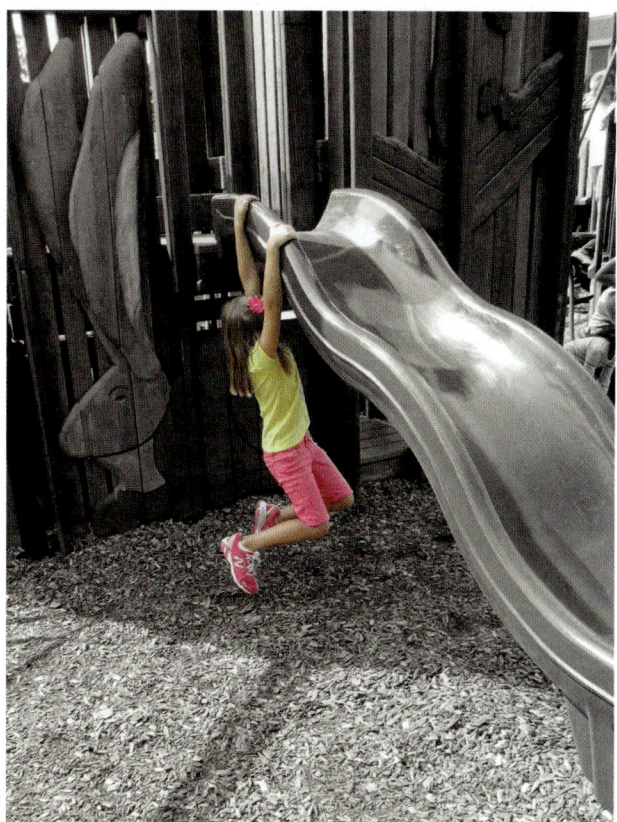

Jack Klasey/Goodheart-Willcox Publisher

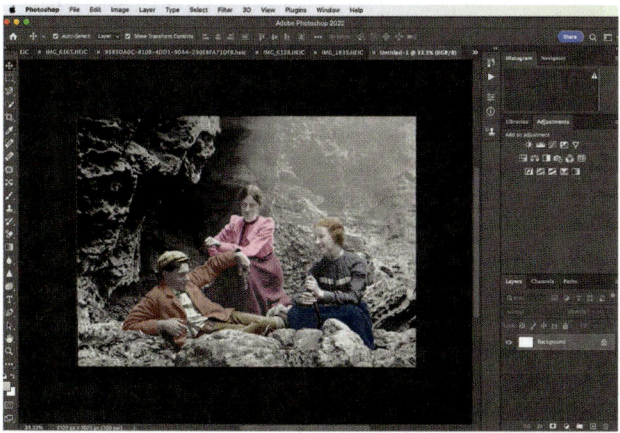

Kankakee County Museum archives

Figure 19-41. Applying color to a black-and-white image at a low opacity provides a soft tinting effect that lets the image details show through.

Figure 19-42. After converting this playground image to monochrome, the **History Brush** was used to "paint in" the child from the original color image.

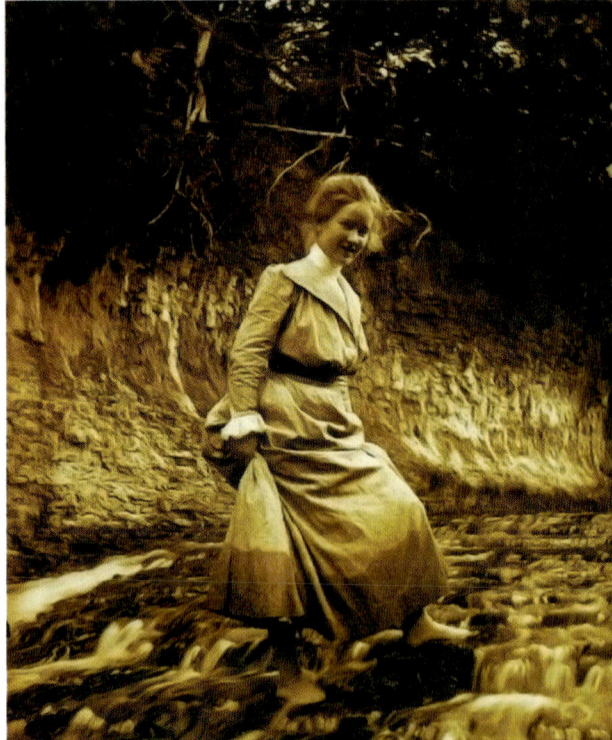

A

Kankakee County Museum archives

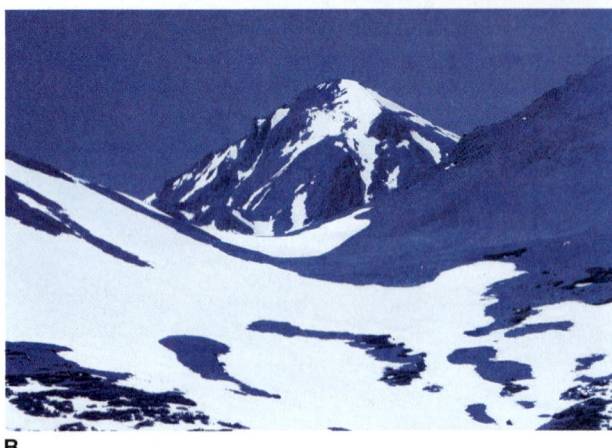

B

Goodheart-Willcox Publisher

Figure 19-43. Applying overall color to a monochrome image. A—A sepia tone is appropriate for this image of a person taken over a century ago. B—A deep blue tone was chosen to convey the cold, stark nature of this mountain scene.

PROCEDURE

Creating a Vector Image

Vector images are a great option for photographers or designers that may need to alter the size of their image after the initial delivery. A vector image is scalable without negatively affecting the quality of the image. This Procedure details how to vectorize an image, but this can also work for creating things such as logos, icons, or buttons:

1. Create a **New Project** and open an image you wish to vectorize in the workspace.
2. Press the Ctrl key and click on the image in the **Layers** panel. This will select the entirety of the image, and you will see your selection outlined, **Figure P**.
3. Select the **Selection** tool and right-click on your image. Select **Make Work Path** from the menu that appears, **Figure Q**. You can adjust the **Tolerance** or keep it at the default.
4. Navigate to the **Layer** menu and select **Vector Mask**. From the second menu that appears, select **Current Path**, **Figure R**.
5. The vector mask is now reflected in the **Layers** panel, **Figure S**. It is now scalable inside Photoshop and other software.
6. Save your vector image by selecting **Save As** and choosing your desired file type, **Figure T**.

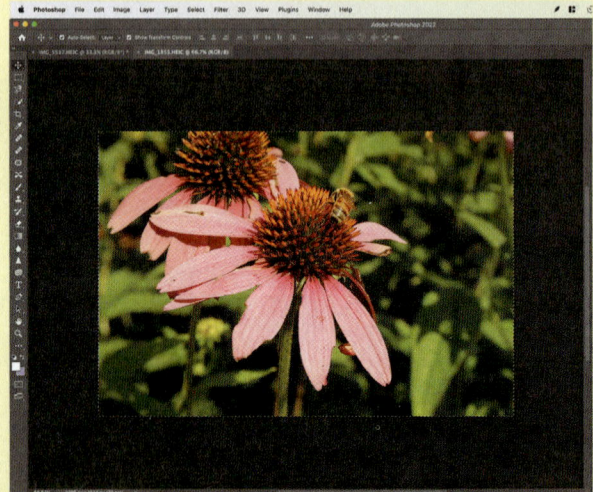

Goodheart-Willcox Publisher

Figure P. Your selection will be outlined with marching ants. These will move around the selection, even though they appear stationary in this image.

496 Section 5 Postprocessing

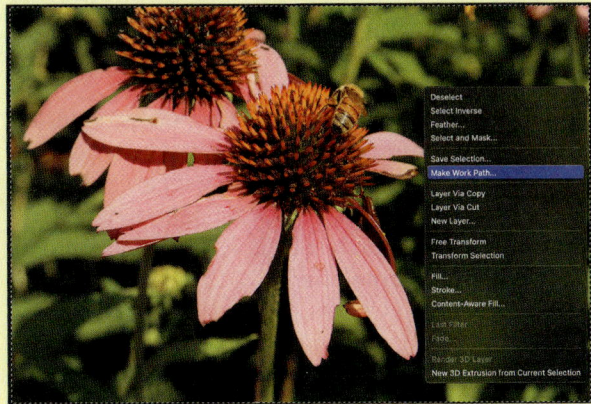

Goodheart-Willcox Publisher

Figure Q. Right-click and select **Make Work Path** or use the **Type** menu and select **Create Work Path**.

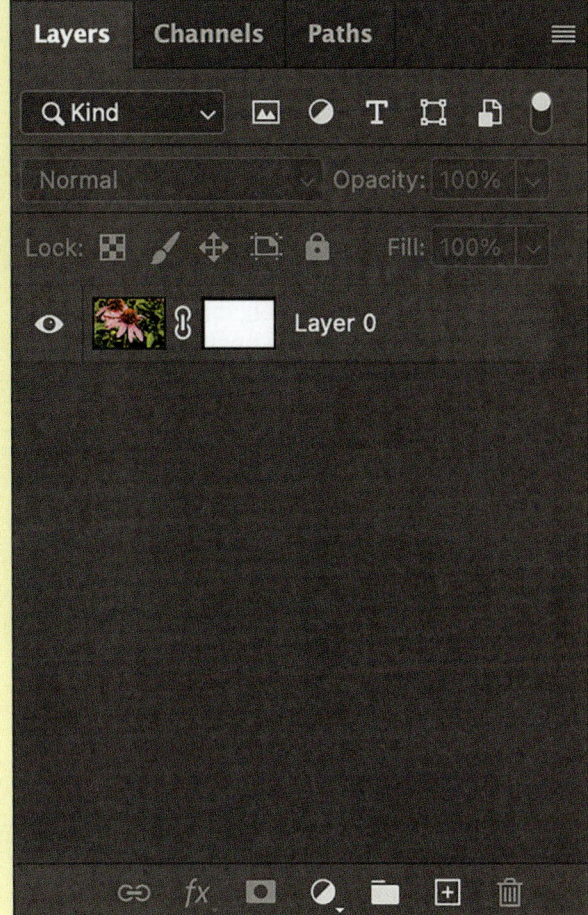

Goodheart-Willcox Publisher

Figure S. The vector mask will appear in the **Layers** panel.

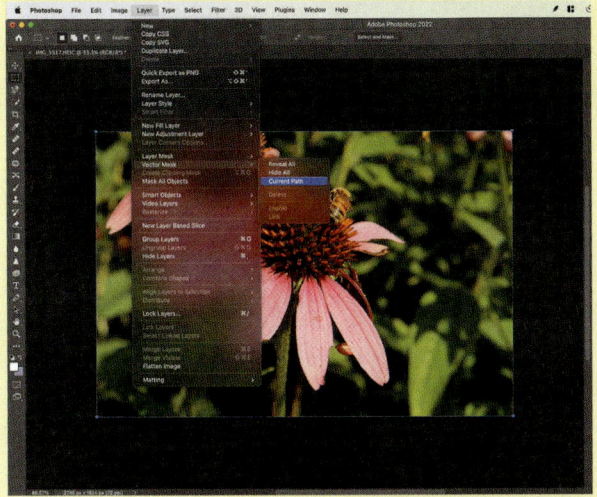

Goodheart-Willcox Publisher

Figure R. Right-click in the selection and click on **Current Path**.

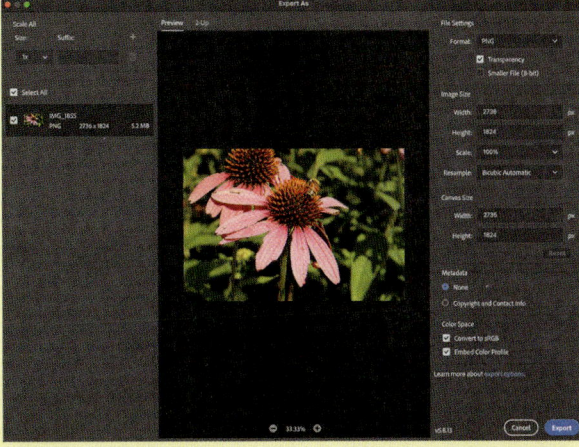

Goodheart-Willcox Publisher

Figure T. For best results, export your image as a PNG or a JPG.

Chapter 19 Advanced Digital Postprocessing Techniques 497

PORTFOLIO ASSIGNMENT

Edit It!

For this assignment, you will create a promotional picture for your school that will appear through type.

1. Take several photos of significant places in and around your school. This might include the football field, gym, auditorium, or library.
2. Once you have your photos, import them to your computer. Select the best one to use for this assignment.
3. Create a new Photoshop document. Name it "[Your School's Name]_Edit It PA" to locate it easily later.
4. Prepare the photo you chose by following the steps in the Procedure feature titled *Creating a Clipping Mask That Fills Type with an Image*. When typing the name of your school, make sure it is in all capitals (SOUTHEAST instead of Southeast). Remember to keep your font type legible. A loopy, cursive font would not work as well as a bold, sans serif font.
5. Adjust the placement and appearance of the text and photo until you are satisfied with how it looks.

Once you are satisfied, save the file as a JPEG and submit it to your instructor for review before adding it to your portfolio.

Chapter 19 Review

Summary

- While image manipulation opens many creative possibilities for the photographer, it can also create situations that raise ethical and legal questions.
- Selection tools are tools in an image editing program that allow you to choose one element or portion of an image to work with and manipulate. In Photoshop, the selection tools include the marquee tools, the **Lasso** tools, the **Pen** tools, the **Quick Selection** and **Magic Wand** tools, and the **Color Range** command.
- Even the most careful selection often needs some touch-up work along the edges. The **Quick Mask** mode and **Eraser** tools are common refining selections.
- The ability to select part of one image and make it part of another is the key to creating combined images, or composites.
- To create a composite, you will make extensive use of layers. The characteristics of a layer, such as its opacity, can be altered by applying blending modes and masks.
- Layers can be added to an image in various ways. As new layers are added, they appear at the top of the layer stack.
- Whenever possible, make changes to the working file by using one or more adjustment layers. By using an adjustment layer, you can close an image and then later open it and make additional changes.
- Changes made using an adjustment layer can be applied to the entire image or just to a portion of it. A layer mask is used to protect a portion of an image from change or to permit a lower layer to show through the topmost layer.
- When an image has two or more layers, the pixels of those layers can be blended in various ways to create different effects. This is done by selecting a blending mode from a menu in the **Layers** panel.
- A border may be added to an image for practical or artistic reasons. Image borders can be created easily with several techniques.
- You can overlay type on a photo or arrange type so a photo shows through the letters.
- A transformation can be applied only to a selection made on a layer. Commonly used transformations include a slight rotation to correct a tilted horizon and the correction of converging lines.
- Changes ranging from mild to extreme are achieved by using filters, which are special effects that can be applied to all or part of an image to change its appearance.
- While striking by itself, a black-and-white image can sometimes be made even more dramatic by the addition of color. There are two common approaches to this.

Review Questions

Answer the following questions using the information provided in this chapter.

Know and Understand

1. *True or False?* Although an idea cannot be copyrighted, you should always acknowledge the source of an inspiration that resulted in an image you produced.

2. *True or False?* The **Magic Eraser** tool is an example of a selection tool.

3. The _____ tool allows the user to make a circular or oval selection.
   A. elliptical marquee
   B. magic wand
   C. lasso
   D. rectangular marquee

4. The _____ tool is useful for making selections that have straight edges.
   A. basic **Lasso**
   B. elliptical marquee
   C. **Magnetic Lasso**
   D. **Polygon Lasso**

5. Anchor points are control points set by clicking the mouse while making a selection using the _____ tool.
   A. **Magic Wand**
   B. **Lasso**
   C. **Pen**
   D. **Quick Selection**

6. *True or False?* The **Quick Selection** tool is somewhat more complex to use than the **Magic Wand** tool.

7. *True or False?* The **Quick Mask** mode is most commonly used to add to or delete areas from a selection.

8. Which of the following eraser tools has the same controls in the **Options** bar as the **Magic Wand** but also offers an **Opacity** slider?
   A. **Erase to History**
   B. **Magic Eraser**
   C. **Eraser**
   D. **Background Eraser**

9. Which of the following is an example of morphing?
   A. Replacing a dull gray sky with a brighter, more visually interesting sky
   B. Depicting a child as they would look in adulthood through an age progression portrait
   C. Adding fireworks into the background of a photo
   D. Changing the color of a bird's plumage from red to blue

10. *True or False?* As new layers are added, they appear at the bottom of the layer stack.

11. A(n) _____ is an image manipulation tool used to protect a portion of an image from change or to permit a lower layer to show through the topmost layer.
    A. layer mask
    B. adjustment layer
    C. clipping mask
    D. anchor point

12. A common reason for _____ layers is to lighten or darken an image.
    A. adding
    B. morphing
    C. compositing
    D. blending

13. A(n) _____ is often used to create type that is filled by a photographic subject.
    A. adjustment layer
    B. handle
    C. layer mask
    D. clipping mask

14. The _____ section of the **Edit** drop-down menu offers tools for scaling the image to a larger or smaller size, rotating it a specified amount, skewing or distorting it in different directions, or altering its perspective.
    A. **Transform**
    B. **Distort**
    C. **New Layer**
    D. **Saturation**

15. *True or False?* A transformation can be applied only to a selection made on a layer.

16. *True or False?* The **Density** filter can simulate the effect of a shallow depth of field.

17. Applying an overall color (toning) to an image can be done quite easily with a _____ adjustment layer.
    A. **Curves**
    B. **Hue/Saturation**
    C. **Gradient**
    D. **Colorize**

Apply and Analyze

1. How might an unmanipulated image be considered unethical?
2. Describe how to use the **Color Range** command when making selections.
3. What should you do for precise work when using the **Quick Mask** mode?
4. Explain how to add a new, blank layer.

5. How do you add a narrow black border to an image?
6. What is the **History Brush** tool used for?

Critical Thinking

1. The selection tools are important in any image editing software. Which tool (or tools) would work best when trying to select a person's shirt to edit?
2. After converting an image to grayscale mode and saving it, you decide to recover the color in a foreground clump of flowers. Since you have already saved the image as grayscale, you cannot use the **History Brush** tool. What options do you have to obtain the color effect you visualize?

Suggested Activities

1. Using the techniques described in this chapter, make a composite combining a word of up to six letters (your name, a hobby, the name of a color, etc.) with an appropriate photo. The photo should show through the letters of the word. Include the composite photo in your portfolio.
2. Select one of your images and apply different filters to it, one at a time. Choose the six most interesting filter effects and make 4″ × 6″ prints of your image, each with a different filter applied. Mount the prints on a sheet of poster board, add the title "Filter Effects," and display it in your classroom.
3. Download a copy of artist Grant Wood's *American Gothic* painting. Working with two other students, brainstorm ways that you could manipulate this image and combine it with one or more other images to create a derivative work (a new work of art that is based on an existing work). Create and display your derivative work. Be sure to acknowledge that it is "based on a painting by Grant Wood."

Communicating about Photography

1. **Speaking.** Working in a group, brainstorm ideas for creating classroom tools (posters, flash cards, and/or games, for example) that will help your classmates learn and remember the different tools in Adobe Photoshop. Choose the best idea(s), and then delegate responsibilities to group members for constructing the tools and presenting the final products to the class.
2. **Writing and Speaking.** Create an informational pamphlet on recoloring black-and-white photos. Select a black-and-white photo you have shot (or shoot one to use as an example) and list the steps you would take to recolor it. Present your pamphlet to the class.

Chapter 20
The Finishing Touches

Learning Objectives

After completing this chapter, you will be able to:
- Recall common ways to display digital images.
- Describe the types of printers used for digital images.
- Explain methods used for monitor calibration.
- Select appropriate mounting materials.
- Identify the most suitable mounting method for a print.
- Understand the reasons for using different types of overmats.

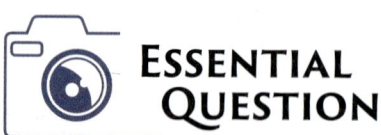

Essential Question

How does preparing an image for presentation affect how the image is perceived by the viewer?

Technical Terms

archival quality
buffered
calibrate
CMYK
coated paper
cold-adhesive mounting
colorimeter
conservation board
dry mounting
dye sublimation printer
edge mounting
flush mount
foam board
giclée
inkjet printer
large-format inkjet printer
mat board
metamerism
museum board
online gallery
overmat
pH
pigment-based ink
pressure-sensitive adhesive material
profile
quad-tone ink set
sublimate

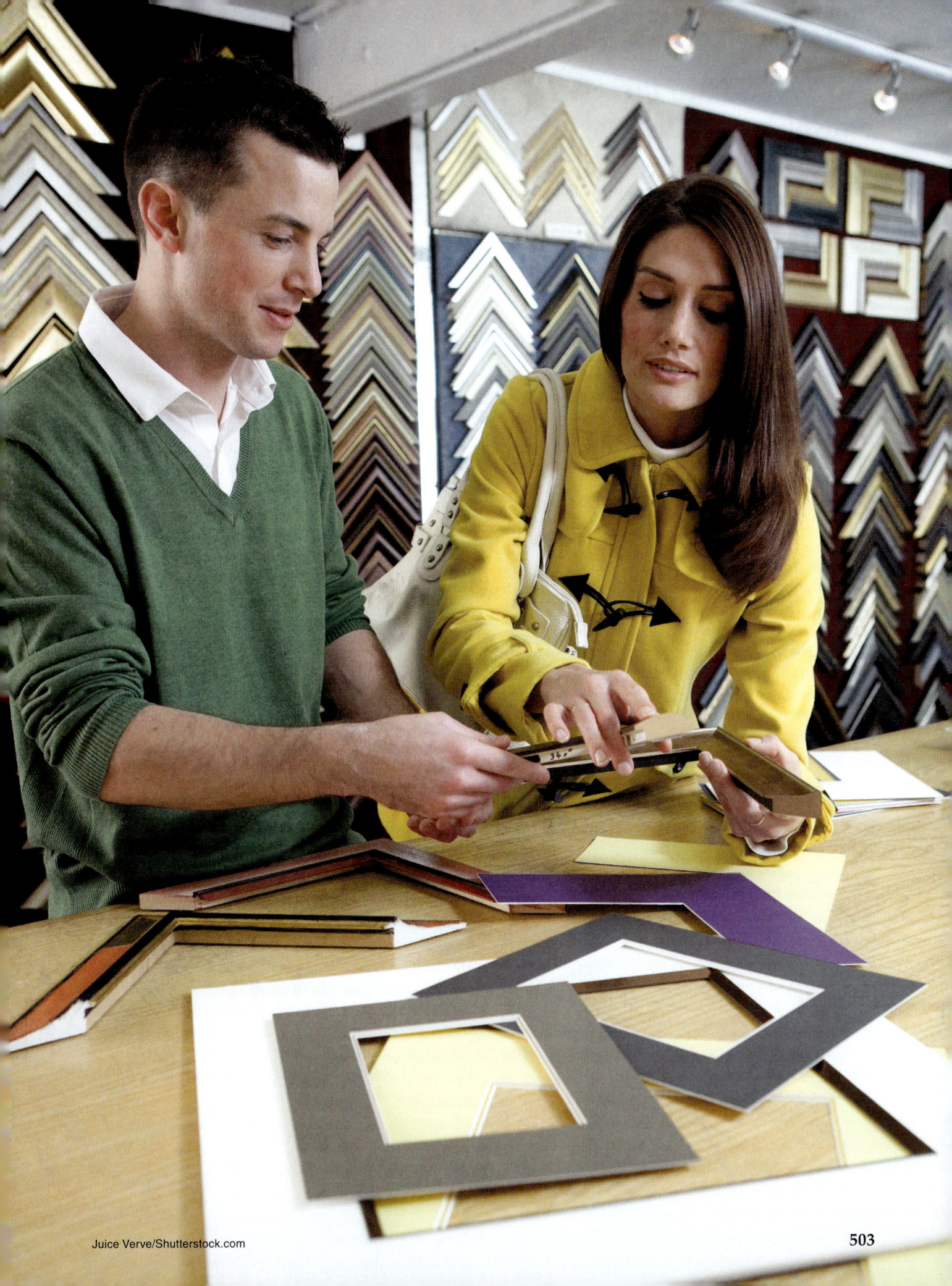

Introduction to the Finishing Touches

Once you have captured digital images, it is natural to want to share those images with others. Sharing methods include but are not limited to posting images to an online digital portfolio, posting them to social media, and making physical prints. This is the final step of the image editing process.

Electronic Display

Once an image has been captured or scanned into digital form, it can be displayed in a number of electronic venues. Many photographers use a favorite image as the wallpaper on their smartphone, tablet, or computer monitor, **Figure 20-1**, or display a series of images as a screen saver.

Pictures can be posted on a number of online sites and social media platforms, such as Facebook, Flickr, and Instagram, for the enjoyment of friends, family, and others, **Figure 20-2**. Aimed at more serious photographers, a similar approach is the **online gallery**. These websites are often maintained by schools or organizations such as photo clubs, **Figure 20-3**, and access may be restricted to members of the organization. Others are available for public viewing. Many amateur and professional photographers maintain personal websites to display their work. These range from simple, single-page sites to elaborate, professionally developed sites displaying numerous images with accompanying information and biographical/personal data about the photographer.

File Compression

When preparing to share or display your digital images, you must keep file compression in mind (the squeezing of an electronic file to reduce its size) since some platforms will not be able to handle a photo at full resolution. Oftentimes when you are exporting an image, you will have a choice of the following types of lossy compression (reduction of image size by removing bits of data in your image):

- **Extra fine.** Also referred to as *superfine*, this is the least compressed, or highest-quality, exporting option that you have available. This means that there is less noise, or *artifacts*, in your photo, but the file size is larger than the other options. This compression type is not ideal for specific scenarios, such as posting online.
- **Fine.** Also referred to as *basic*, this compression type uses more compression than extra fine. This means that the image quality is not as good, and the chance of having noticeable artifacts in your image is increased. However, the file size is smaller, which allows you to store more images in the same place, like on your SD card or in archive storage.
- **Normal.** This is the most compressed option, which means there will be a noticeable loss of image quality. You will most likely have artifacts in this type of compression, but you will be able to store numerous photos as well as post several at a time since the file size is so small.

Remember that because these types of compression are considered lossy, some data will be lost in your image. If you want to avoid losing data, and therefore quality, in your photos, you should work in a lossless format, such as RAW camera files. Furthermore, remember that resolution impacts quality. For example, photos with high resolution (at least 300 ppi) are best suited for physical presentation and not suited for digital formats (such as email and photo sharing). Photos with low resolution (less than 300 ppi) are ideal for online presentation and not ideal for physical presentation.

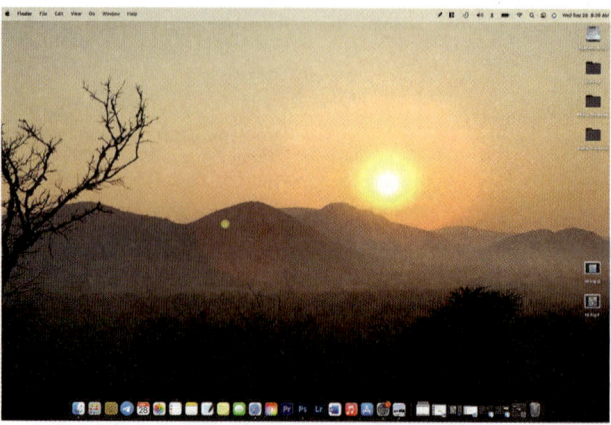

Goodheart-Willcox Publisher

Figure 20-1. A digital image displayed as the wallpaper on a computer desktop.

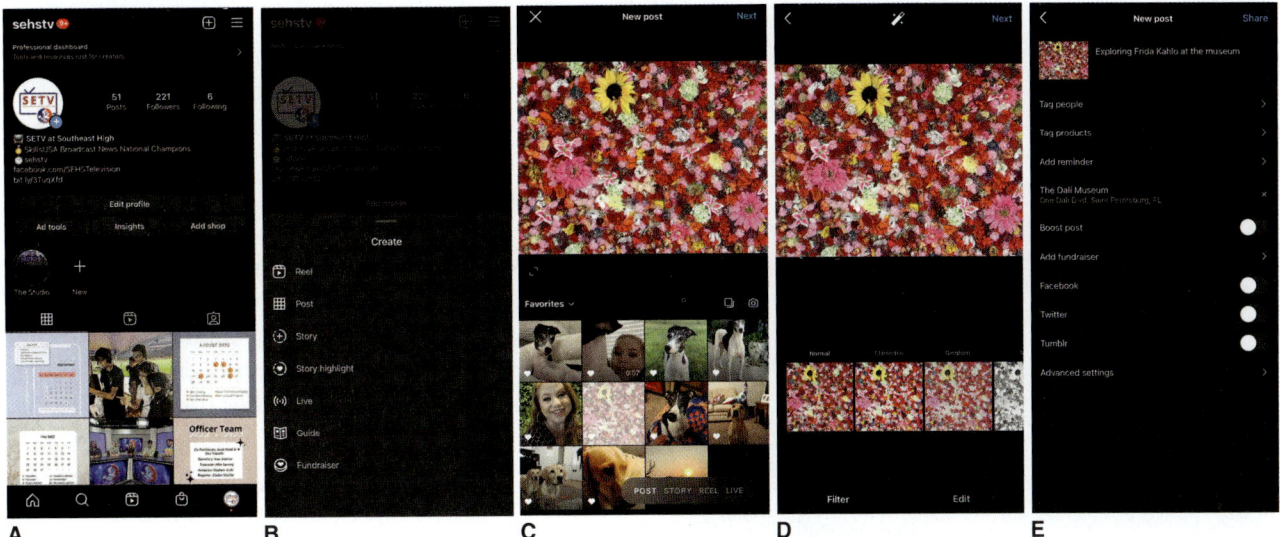

A   B   C   D   E

Goodheart-Willcox Publisher

Figure 20-2. Using a smartphone to post a photo to Instagram. A—Navigate to your profile. B—Select the plus icon at the top of your profile to create a post. A new menu will pop up. C—Select the photo you want to post. D—Make any edits to the photo if you wish to do so. E—Add a caption and any hashtags you want to post along with the photo. Then, press the *Share* button.

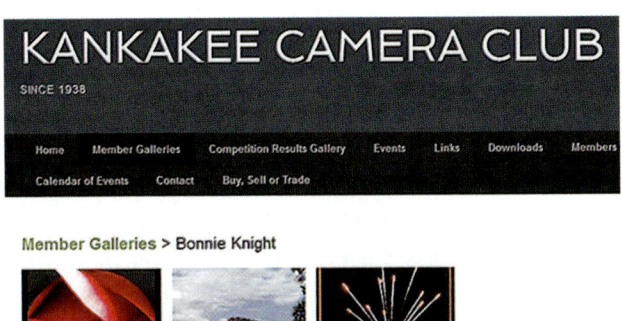

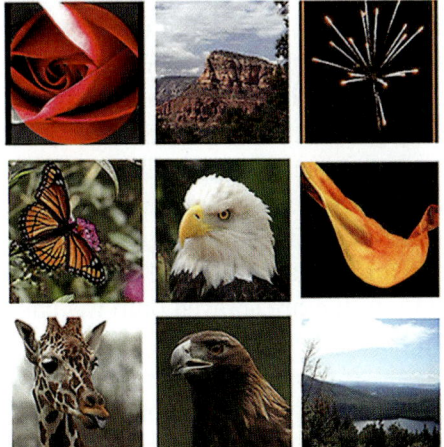

Bonnie Knight/Kankakee Camera Club

Figure 20-3. A member's gallery on a photo club website.

> ### REAL-WORLD PHOTOGRAPHY
> **Exporting from Lightroom**
>
> When working in Lightroom, exporting an image is quite easy. Once you have finished editing your photo, simply perform the following:
> 1. Navigate to **File > Export**.
> 2. Select your settings for export, including image type, dimensions, quality, and the name of the image.
> 3. Select **Export Photo**, identify your exporting location, and press **Export**. Your edited image should be named and stored properly in the desired location.

Display Devices

Digital photo frames were developed in response to the rapid growth in digital photography, **Figure 20-4**. These devices, available in a number of sizes, can display a changing series of images.

An LCD projector is the electronic equivalent of the traditional slide projector. When connected to a computer, the device can be used to display digital

Chapter 20   The Finishing Touches   **505**

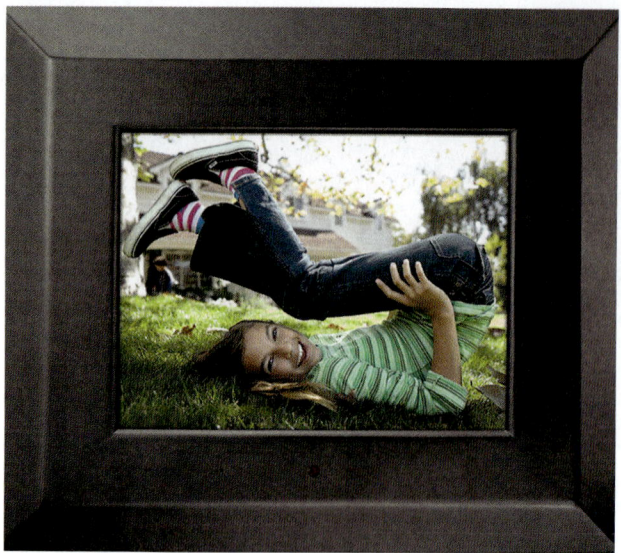

Eastman Kodak Company

Figure 20-4. A digital photo frame is an LCD display small enough to fit on a desktop or bookshelf.

images on a large screen for group viewing. See **Figure 20-5**. Due to their cost, most of these devices are currently owned by businesses, schools, or organizations.

You can also display photos from your phone or a computer straight to a television screen. Most computers have an HDMI port that will connect with an HDMI cable so you can display your photos on a TV screen. Some phones also have the capability to stream to a TV over a local Wi-Fi network.

Making Prints

One of the most common forms of image display is the photographic print. Each year, millions of snapshots are printed to allow photographers to share experiences and events with others. Many retail locations offer fast and relatively inexpensive printing from digital image files. Customers bring image files into the store on a memory card or flash drive or upload them online for printing. Larger-size prints may be made at do-it-yourself print kiosks at retail locations. These kiosks allow cropping and some control of print color and other characteristics.

Prints and enlargements can also be obtained by uploading files to an online photofinishing site, which returns the finished prints by mail. Some of these sites have a gallery or album feature that allows the photographer's friends or family members to view the images and order their own prints.

Many photographers print their digital images on a printer they have at home. There are at least five different types of color printers on the market, but only two—the inkjet printer and the dye sublimation printer—are used for serious photographic output.

Inkjet Printers

The **inkjet printer** is a type of printer that works by depositing a fine spray of tiny ink dots on paper. It was originally intended to provide color printing capability to home computers for applications such as word processing and simple art programs. Thus, it was well established by the time consumer-level digital cameras came on the scene. Even earlier, photographers and graphic designers had begun experimenting with the inkjet as an output device. In the early 1990s, the French term **giclée** (meaning spray or squirt) was adopted by fine art photographers to characterize the prints they were producing on high-quality commercial inkjet printers.

Several printer manufacturers identified the emerging consumer market for photo-quality reproduction and began producing inkjet printing papers that would provide the look and feel of photographic papers, **Figure 20-6**. An inkjet image is formed by very small droplets of liquid ink that are sprayed onto the paper. On an uncoated paper, the ink droplets soak into the surface. This ink spread produces a soft image with flat color. **Coated papers** resist the spread of ink droplets. Instead, the drops retain their shape and color brilliance as they bond to the paper surface. This is a desirable trait for images that must be sharp. The high gloss of the paper makes printed materials shinier and brighter and reinforces the photo-like appearance. Photo-quality inkjet papers are offered in glossy, semi-glossy (luster or pearl), and matte finishes. Sizes range from 4″ × 6″ to 13″ × 19″. Some papers are also available in long rolls and various widths.

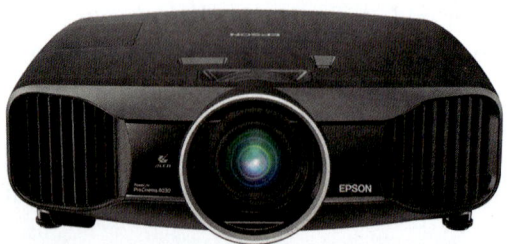

Epson Pro Cinema 4030 2D/3D 1080p 3LCD Projector

Figure 20-5. An LCD projector can be used to present digital images to an audience.

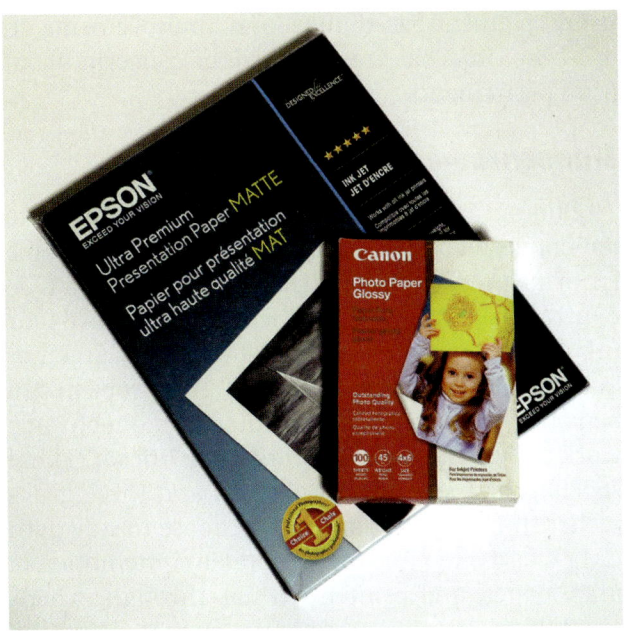

Goodheart-Willcox Publisher

Figure 20-6. Coated papers for photo reproduction allow inkjet printers to produce output that rivals traditional photographic prints.

Printer Sizes

The two basic formats of desktop inkjet printers are letter-size and wide-format. A letter-size printer accepts standard 8 1/2″ × 11″ paper. Although veteran photographers still refer to the output as an "eight by ten," most photo papers for inkjet printing are the standard letter-size.

Wide-format printers accept paper up to 13″ in width, allowing the photographer to make larger prints. Most of these printers also accept paper in rolls, which may be used for making multiple prints (usually snapshot-size) or panoramic prints up to several feet long. See **Figure 20-7**.

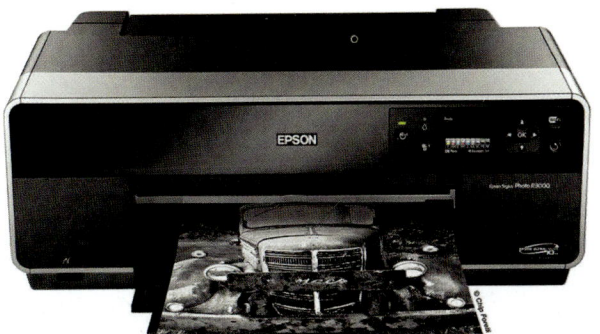

Epson Stylus R3000

Figure 20-7. Wide-format printers are popular with photographers who want to produce larger prints. Most wide-format printers accept paper 13″ in width.

Normally operated by commercial printing houses or service bureaus, *large-format inkjet printers* are used to produce large fine art prints, posters, banners, billboard sheets, and similar products. These units accept paper and other media as large as 6′ in width with virtually no length restriction. See **Figure 20-8**.

Ink Colors

Originally, all inkjet printers used a four-ink set—the traditional **CMYK**, or cyan, magenta, yellow, and black. As color photo printing became more popular, however, manufacturers introduced ink sets consisting of eight or more inks, **Figure 20-9**. In addition to the basic CMYK inks, these ink sets typically include at least two different black inks—one for matte photo paper and one for glossy papers. Other inks that may be included are light magenta

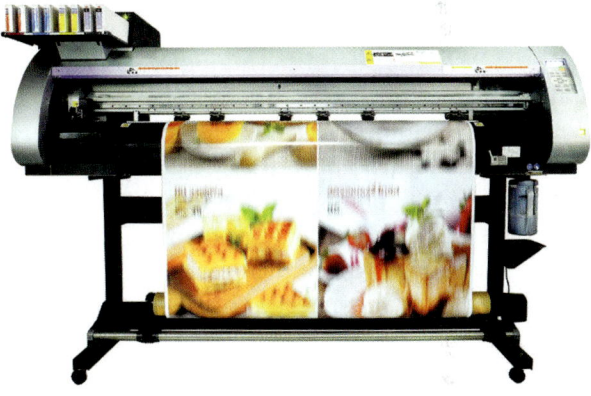

KOKTARO/Shutterstock.com

Figure 20-8. Large-format inkjet printers produce big images, such as banners and posters.

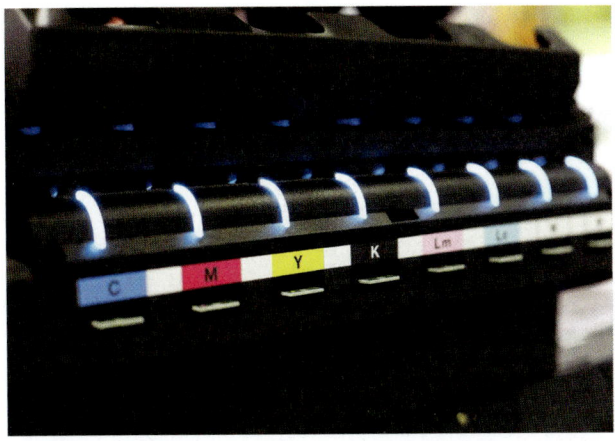

Genkur/Shutterstock.com

Figure 20-9. This wide-format inkjet printer uses eight ink cartridges.

and light cyan, red and blue, red and green, or shades of gray. A clear gloss enhancer may be included to produce a very high-gloss coating on a print.

Ink Types

All inkjet printers originally used inks based on liquid color dyes. These dye-based inks provided rich, vivid colors on photographic paper but tended to fade and show color shifts when exposed to ultraviolet light sources (especially sunlight) and high humidity.

The print fading problem led to the development of **pigment-based inks**. These consist of solid color pigments ground into extremely fine particles and suspended in a liquid. Pigment-based inks resist fading much better than the early dye-based inks. When used with compatible papers, they produce prints capable of lasting for 100 years or more without fading.

Archival Quality

The question of print permanence, or archival quality, has long been a concern of photographers using inkjet printers. **Archival quality** is a term applied to photographic prints that are processed with the intent of achieving very long life. In addition to concern about their work being preserved for future generations, these photographers are motivated by an ethical concern. They maintain that a museum or individual purchasing one of their works has a right to expect it will not deteriorate in a reasonable period of time and thus lose both its artistic and monetary value. The availability of printers using pigment-based inks and improvements in dye-based inks has greatly eased the concerns about print permanence.

Monochrome Printing

Photographers who work in black-and-white (or convert color digital images to monochrome for printing) face the challenge of producing a true neutral gray. When printed with the standard four ink colors, images often exhibit a slightly green or magenta cast. See **Figure 20-10**. This problem can be solved by dedicating a printer to monochrome work and using a special **quad-tone ink set**. These specialty ink sets consist of black and three grays rather than CMYK. Those who choose to stay with CMYK can often find an acceptable combination of inks, paper, and printer settings through experimentation. This is especially true when using the newer printers with ink sets that include two or more black inks.

Dye Sublimation Printers

Archival quality and brilliant color have always been a selling point for **dye sublimation printers**. These printers have a print head with many tiny, precisely controlled heating elements, and the print head works in conjunction with a wide plastic transfer ribbon carrying CMYK dyes. The print head causes the dyes to vaporize, or **sublimate** (change state from solid to gas without an intermediate liquid state), and deposit as tiny color spots on specially coated paper, **Figure 20-11**. Dye sublimation prints are not subject to fading.

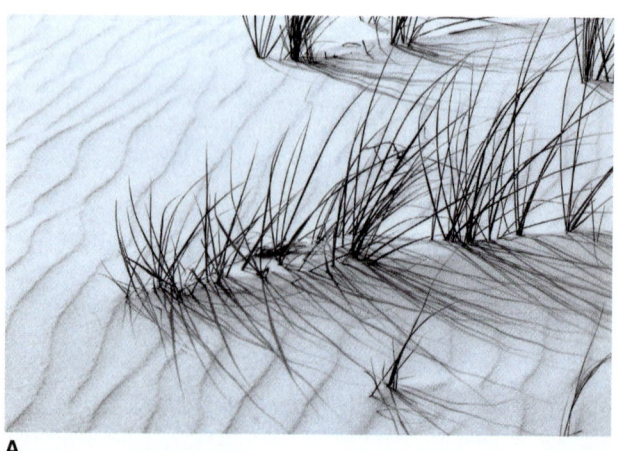
A

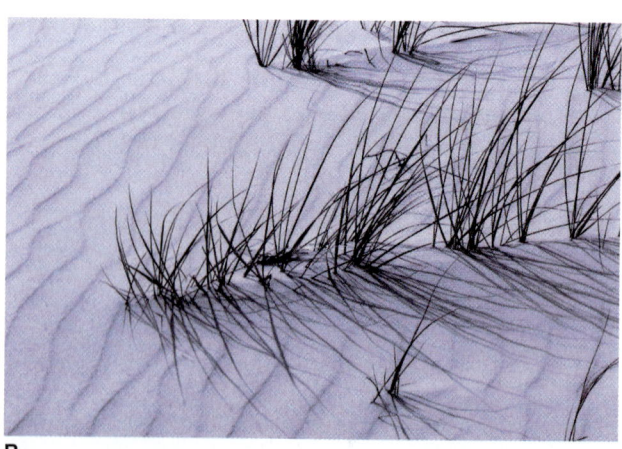
B

Jack Klasey/Goodheart-Willcox Publisher

Figure 20-10. Standard color inks can produce a color cast when used to make a monochrome print. A—Neutral gray monochrome print. B—Monochrome print with a magenta color cast.

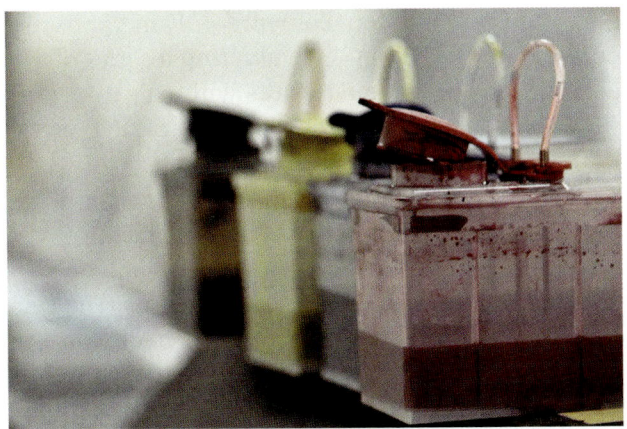

Joanna Grzybowska/Shutterstock.com

Figure 20-11. Ink for dye sublimation printers comes like this rather than in the traditional printer cartridges.

At least one manufacturer offers snapshot-type cameras with a built-in printer producing $2'' \times 3''$ prints, **Figure 20-13**. The developing process makes use of paper with embedded dye crystals that are activated by heat.

With the rise of phone photography, some manufacturers like Canon and Polaroid have created small portable printers that connect directly to a smartphone and fit in a camera bag or purse, **Figure 20-14**. Once you have the small dye sublimation printer attached to your phone (either physically or through

The drawback has been the high cost for models capable of printing sizes up to $8'' \times 10''$. In recent years, however, small dye sublimation printers for making snapshot-sized prints have become popular. See **Figure 20-12**. These printers typically produce a $4'' \times 6''$ print in 30 seconds or less. The printers are stand-alone units that do not have to be connected to a computer and are small enough to be easily portable. Some models can run on battery power, and a few are equipped to receive and print images sent wirelessly from a Wi-Fi–equipped camera or a cell phone.

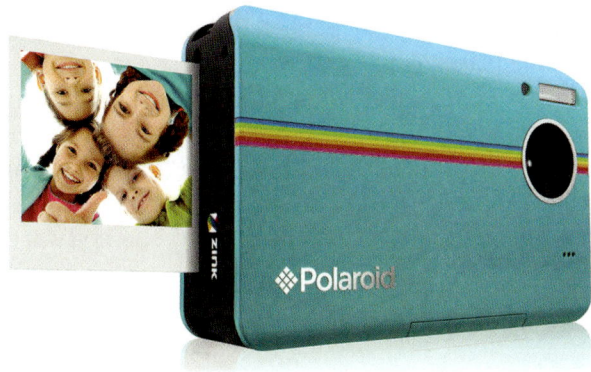

Polaroid Corporation

Figure 20-13. Small photo prints can be produced directly from this camera.

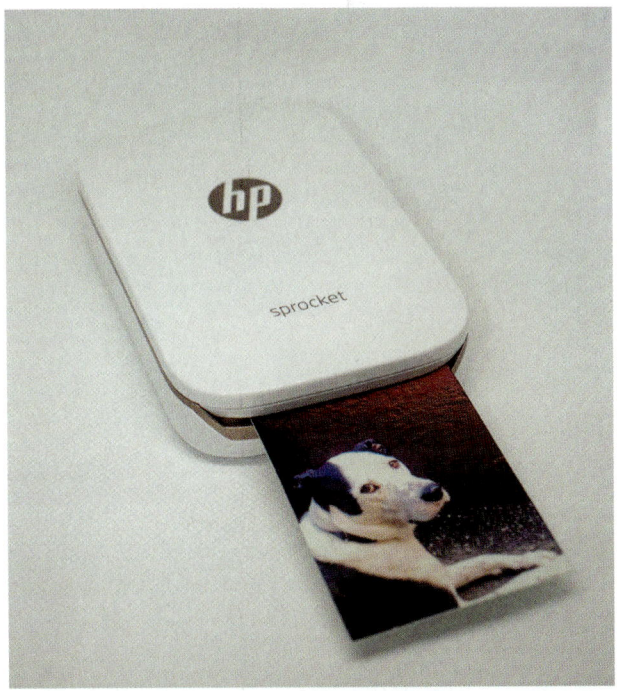

Epson PictureMate MP-400

Figure 20-12. Small dye sublimation printers are popular for making quick, high-quality, snapshot-size prints.

Random NZ Photography/Shutterstock.com

Figure 20-14. Printers that are made for phones are becoming more popular.

Bluetooth), you can print your photos almost instantly without having to find a place to print your photos, **Figure 20-15**.

Making Quality Prints

The most difficult aspect of printing—especially when using an inkjet printer—is making a print that reflects exactly the image displayed on your computer monitor. It is possible through trial and error to develop a method that provides acceptable results for a specific paper and ink combination. However, this approach requires making numerous test prints to find the right settings.

The best way to achieve consistent and predictable prints is to *calibrate* (adjust a device so it displays colors accurately and consistently) your monitor so it truly reflects the colors you are working with. You will also need to test and find the appropriate profile for your printer and paper. The two calibration methods are software only and software/hardware combination. Software-only methods rely on the user's judgment in evaluating a series of test patterns on the screen. Results will vary from person to person, but software-only calibration is better than no calibration.

Software/hardware systems use a *colorimeter*, **Figure 20-16**. This device reads color values from the monitor screen so the accompanying calibration software can make the necessary adjustments. The calibrated monitor accurately displays the color values in an image file. This allows the photographer to see the effect of changes made with image editing software and to determine how the final print will appear.

A *profile* is a program that tells a printer how to handle a particular paper so the final print accurately reproduces the color values of the image file. When a monitor is calibrated and the correct profile is used, the print should be a close match to the monitor image. The two never match precisely because a print is a reflected-light image while the monitor image is seen by transmitted light.

The software installed with the printer includes a set of profiles for the papers offered by the printer manufacturer. Profiles for other papers, such as fine art papers from a number of companies, can often be downloaded from the paper company's website and installed on a computer.

When preparing to print, the type of paper being used is selected from a drop-down menu, **Figure 20-17**. This tells the printer which profile to apply when printing. Depending on the printer make and model, you also may be prompted to choose a quality level for the print. The quality levels represent changes in the resolution (dots per inch, or dpi) of the finished print. The higher the resolution,

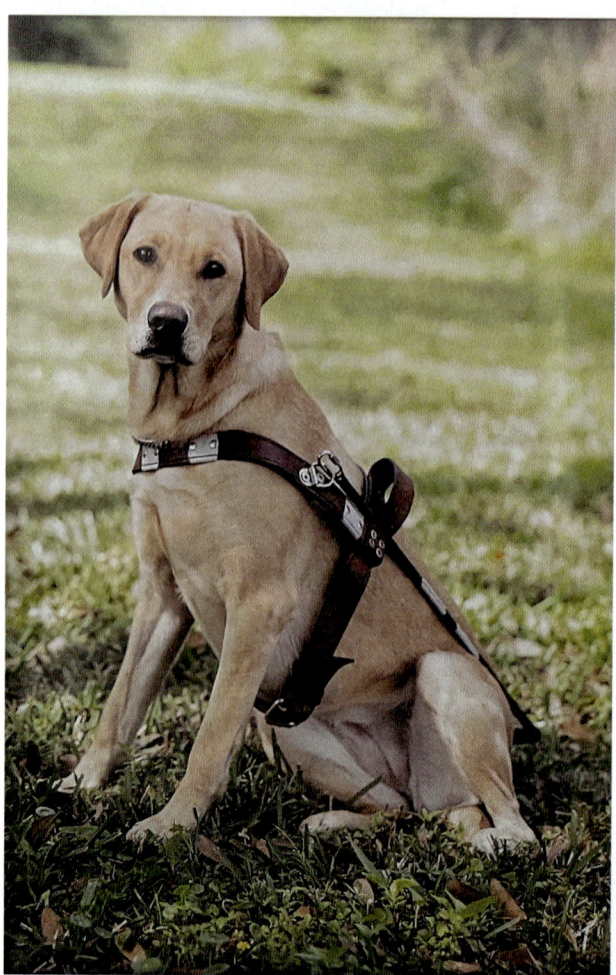

Goodheart-Willcox Publisher

Figure 20-15. A photo printed from a portable printer.

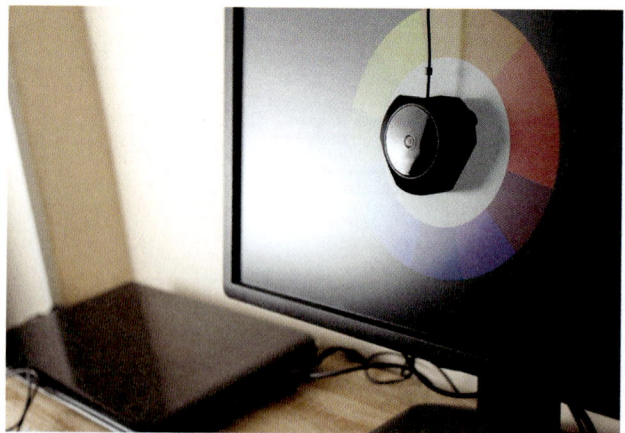

maRRitch/Shutterstock.com

Figure 20-16. A colorimeter is used with appropriate software to calibrate a monitor.

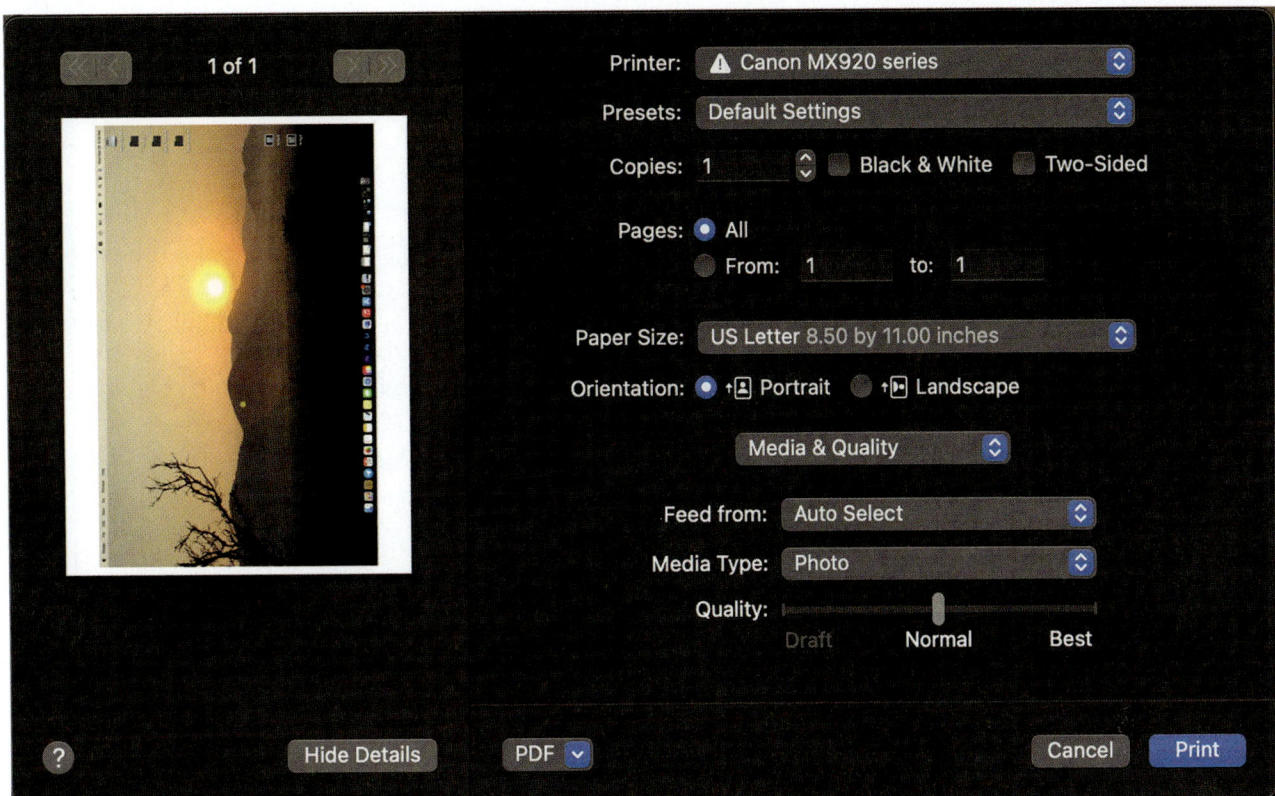

Figure 20-17. Selecting the desired paper type from a drop-down menu will tell the printer which profile to apply.

Goodheart-Willcox Publisher

the finer the detail exhibited by the print. For inkjet prints, a resolution of 300 dpi or 350 dpi is typically used. Lower resolutions, such as the 72 dpi or 96 dpi normally used for website or other electronic displays, would produce a much lower quality, less detailed print. The price for higher quality, however, is a longer printing time. Print size also affects printing time. A 4″ × 6″ print will be completed more quickly than an 8″ × 10″.

Prints made with modern inks and papers also have a lesser tendency to exhibit **metamerism**, which is a color shift that is noticeable when a print is viewed under different lighting conditions, such as tungsten and daylight. This problem was most common with prints made by printers using the early pigment-based ink formulations.

Print Mounting and Matting

Something interesting happens when a photographic print is mounted, overmatted, and framed—it becomes *art*. Whether or not a critic might agree to that label, the viewer's perception of a photo is different when it is presented in unmounted and mounted forms. See **Figure 20-18**. The wide border formed by the mounting board or overmat eliminates distracting surroundings, helping the viewer concentrate on the photo itself. An **overmat**, also known as a *window mat*, is a sheet of mat board with a hole or window cut in it to display and help protect a print. The mat is hinged to the mounting board.

Preparation for Mounting

Two basic decisions must be made before starting the mounting process. You must select the surface (substrate) and determine which mounting method is appropriate to the situation. Photographers usually do not make these decisions each time they mount prints but settle on a basic substrate and method and use it for most work. Changes in substrate or method are then made as necessary.

To avoid possible print contamination by skin oils, many photographers wear lint-free white cotton gloves whenever they handle photographic prints. Others find the gloves cumbersome and minimize skin contact through handling prints by the edges.

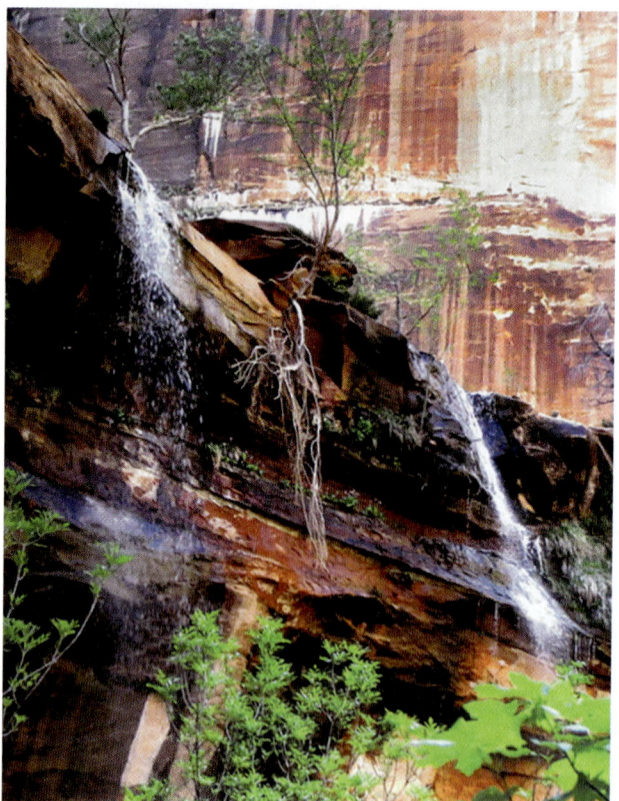
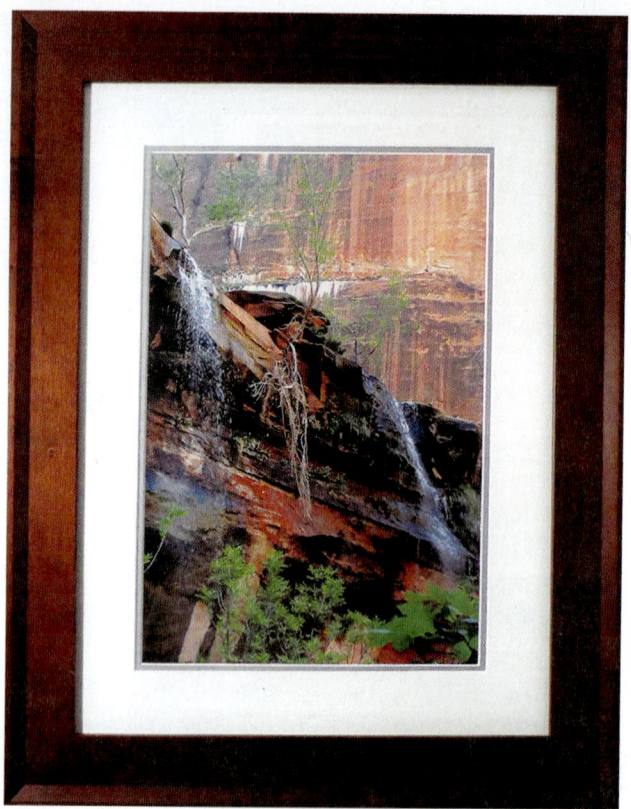

Jack Klasey/Goodheart-Willcox Publisher

Figure 20-18. Compare the unmounted print (left) with the same print that has been mounted, overmatted, and framed (right).

The workspace for print mounting should be a table or counter with an area that holds the mounting equipment and still leaves a clear surface area large enough for the biggest mat board that will be used. A hard, easily cleaned surface such as a plastic laminate is preferred.

Selecting a Mounting Surface

The vast majority of mounted photographic prints are placed on *board*, the general term for a stiff, paper-faced material that supports the print and keeps it flat for display. The two basic types are **mat board**, which is mounting material composed of two or more layers of cellulose fiber, and **foam board**, which is mounting material made with a paper facing on a rigid core of plastic foam. See **Figure 20-19**.

When selecting a board for mounting a photograph, consider the following:
- Composition
- Weight/thickness
- Color
- Size

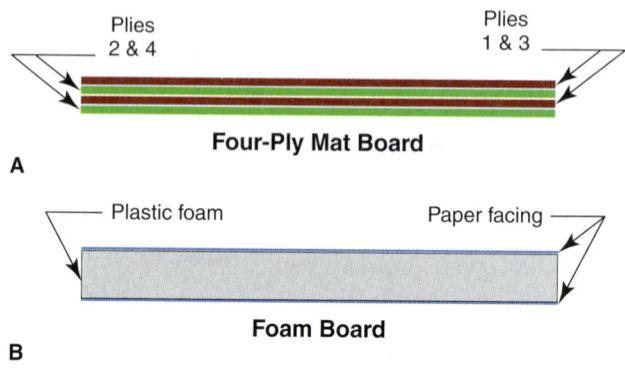

Goodheart-Willcox Publisher

Figure 20-19. Board for mounting. A—Mat board is made up of two or more layers, called *plies*, of cellulose fiber. B—Foam board has a core of rigid plastic foam with paper facing on each side.

Composition

Composition is the material from which the board is made. Board composition is important when permanence is a consideration. Common mat boards, made with cellulose fibers derived from wood pulp, are slightly acidic. Over time, the acids can combine with airborne moisture and attack the photograph, causing it to yellow and deteriorate. When archival-quality prints are being produced, *museum board* or *conservation board* should be used. These boards are made using acid-free fibers. **Conservation board** is a type of mat board made with fibers derived from specially processed wood pulp. It is typically less expensive than **museum board**, which is an acid-free archival mounting board made with fibers from cotton. An acid-free board has a neutral **pH** (a scale that is used to determine acid/alkaline balance).

Conservation boards and some museum boards are **buffered**, or made slightly alkaline to counter the long-term effects of weak airborne acids. The choice of buffered or nonbuffered board depends on the material being mounted. Black-and-white prints should be mounted on a buffered board to take advantage of the additional protection offered. Color prints, especially dye-based inkjet prints, should be placed on nonbuffered board because the prints themselves contain acidic dyes. The dyes could react with the alkaline buffering and cause a color shift. Foam board typically has an acid-free, buffered-paper facing on both sides. The core material is a chemically inert polystyrene foam.

Thickness

The weight or thickness of mat board is measured in the number of layers or plies that have been glued together. Boards are available with 1-, 2-, 4-, or 8-ply construction. For prints up to 8″ × 10″, a 2-ply board is stiff enough to stand alone for display. 4-ply should be used for larger items. If an overmat will be used, a common combination is 2-ply for mounting and 4-ply for the mat, **Figure 20-20**.

Foam board is available in various thicknesses from 1/8″ to 1/2″ or more. It combines very high rigidity with light weight and is often used for mounting mural-sized prints for applications such as trade show displays.

Color

Selecting the most appropriate mat color is somewhat a matter of personal taste, although there are traditional choices. Photographers working in black-and-white usually mount their work on a white mat. If used, an overmat is normally white or black, depending on the photo. A high-key photo with its predominately white or light gray tones would be set off most dramatically by a black overmat. A dark, low-key photo might benefit from a white overmat. See **Figure 20-21**.

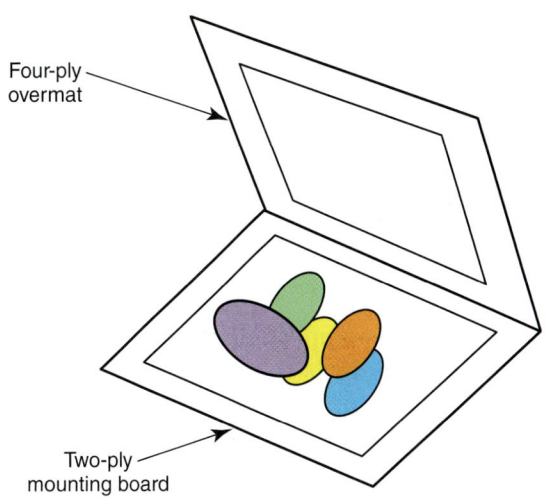

Goodheart-Willcox Publisher

Figure 20-20. Mounting on a 2-ply board with a 4-ply overmat will provide sufficient rigidity and protection for the print.

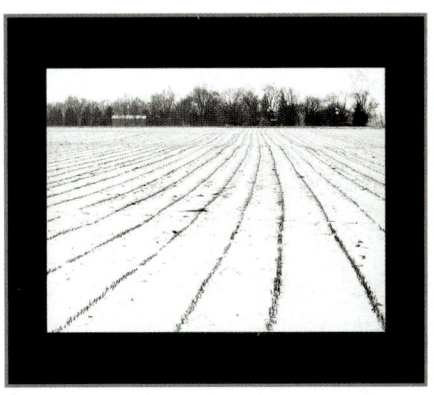

A

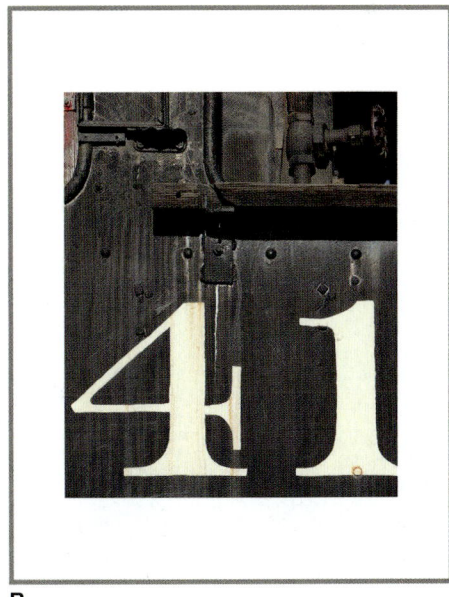

B

Jack Klasey/Goodheart-Willcox Publisher

Figure 20-21. Selecting overmat colors. A—Light-toned image with black. B—Dark-toned image with white.

For framed display in a home or office, a colored overmat may be selected. The mat color for a black-and-white print may be selected to match or complement a room's color scheme. If a color print is being displayed, mat color is often selected to emphasize or contrast with the dominant color in the photo, **Figure 20-22**.

Size

One of the most important reasons for mounting and matting a print is to provide visual isolation, which removes distractions and allows the viewer to focus on the photo. To achieve this isolation, a relatively wide border is needed on all sides of the print.

The rule of thumb is to make the mat size for a given print equal to the next-larger print size. Thus, an 8″ × 10″ print would be mounted on an 11″ × 14″ mat, an 11″ × 14″ print on a 16″ × 20″ mat, and so on. For dramatic effect, proportionally larger mats may be used. Avoid proportionally smaller mats because a too-narrow border around the print is cramped-looking and fails to provide the desired visual isolation. Prints with atypical proportions may be mounted on standard-size mats or effectively displayed on mats proportioned to their dimensions. See **Figure 20-23**.

Other Substrates

In addition to the traditional boards, photos may be mounted for display on a wide variety of other substrates, such as composition board, wood, metal, glass, or plastic. Most of these provide a hard, smooth finish and good dimensional stability

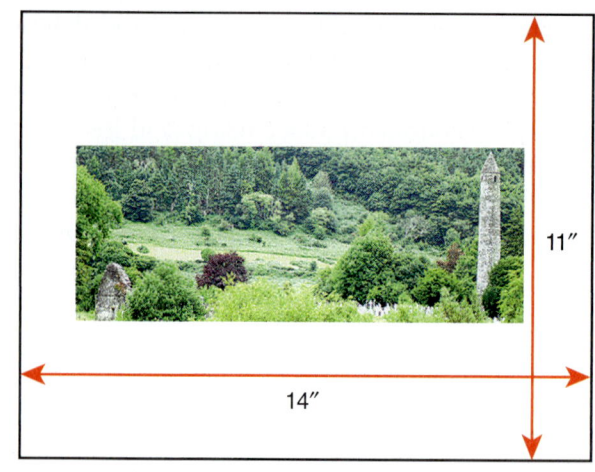

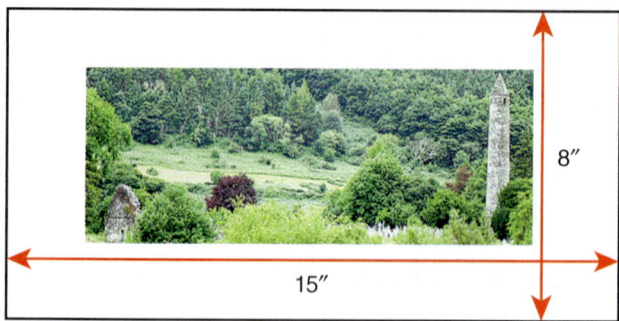

Goodheart-Willcox Publisher

Figure 20-23. A photo with nonstandard proportions, such as 4″ × 11″, can be effectively displayed with a standard 11″ × 14″ mat, or with a more proportional 8″ × 15″ mat.

(they do not expand or shrink excessively). However, they may not provide the permanence available from mounting on archival, acid-free boards.

Selecting a Mounting Method

Factors influencing the selection of a mounting method include permanence, convenience, time and cost, and the availability of needed materials and equipment. Mounting methods can be grouped into the following three categories:

- Edge or "loose" mounting
- Cold-adhesive mounting
- Dry (heated-adhesive) mounting

Edge Mounting

Edge mounting is a loose mounting method in which the photographic print is held by its corners or by hinges made from easily removed acid-free paper tape. Museum curators and others concerned with maximum archival preservation of photos favor this approach.

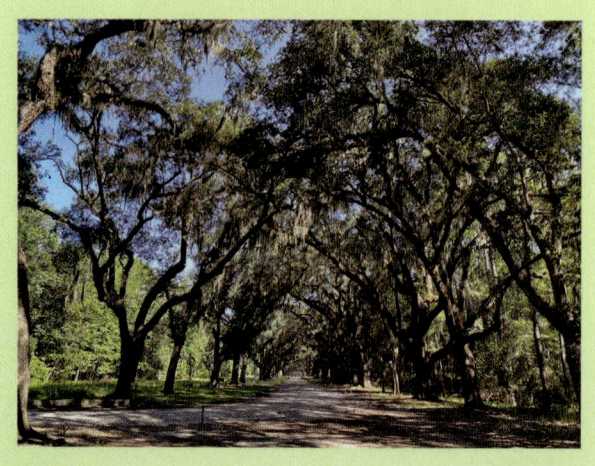

Goodheart-Willcox Publisher

Figure 20-22. Overmatting in a color to emphasize a key hue in the image.

Corners are available from commercial sources in polyester or paper form. They also can be easily formed from strips of acid-free paper. As shown in **Figure 20-24**, the corners are positioned and fastened to the mat, and then the print is slipped into place. Corners are used when the print has a sufficiently wide border so the corners can be concealed by the overmat. The loose mounting allows the print to be removed and rematted if necessary.

There are two types of hinges formed from acid-free tape and used for archival mounting, **Figure 20-25**. The hinging material can be removed, if necessary, without damaging the print.

A T hinge is formed by adhering a piece of tape to the back of the print with half its width extending above the edge. The print is then positioned on the mat and a second piece of tape is adhered to the extended part of the first piece and to the mat. This hinge is used when the edges of the print will be covered by an overmat.

If the edges will be exposed, a V hinge must be formed. The first piece of tape is positioned in the same way as the T hinge, but the part of the tape extending above the print edge is then bent downward. Viewed from the end of the print, the tape forms an inverted V, with the point just below the print's top edge. The print is positioned on the mat, and then rotated or flipped along its top edge. The bent-over portions of the hinge are dampened and adhered to the mat. For additional security, a second piece of tape is adhered to the mat over the first piece. The print is then folded down into position, hiding the hinges.

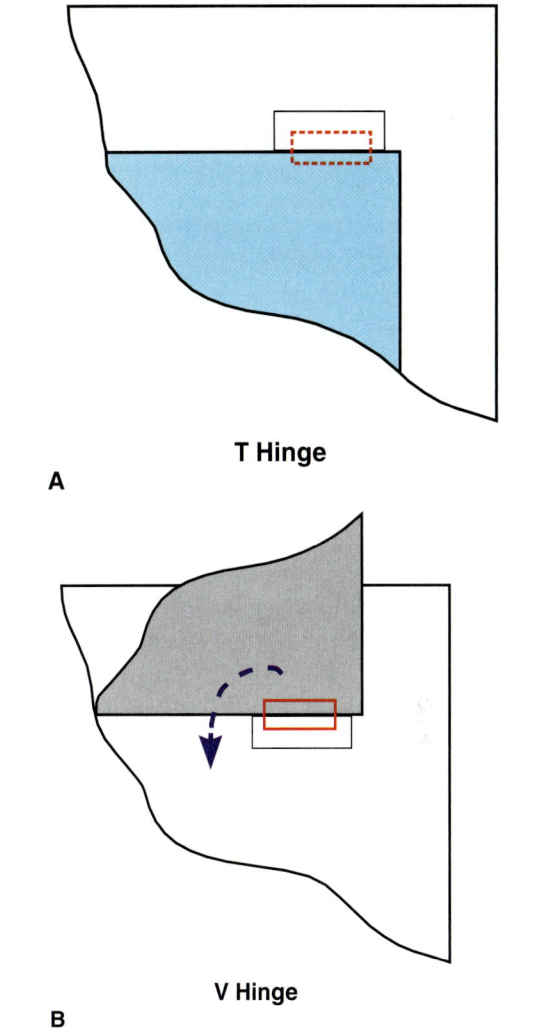

Goodheart-Willcox Publisher

Figure 20-25. Hinging methods. A—The T hinge. B—The V hinge.

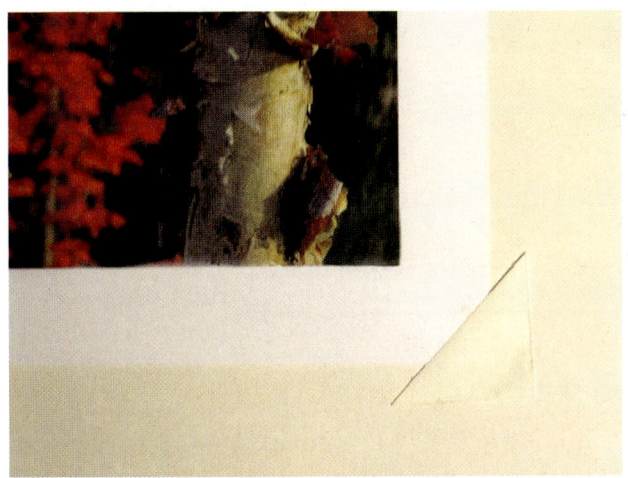

Goodheart-Willcox Publisher

Figure 20-24. Corners of acid-free material hold a print firmly in position on the mat but allow it to be removed when necessary. An overmat will cover the corners.

The major disadvantage of loose mounting methods is that they leave the print free to expand or contract with changing humidity levels. This often results in some degree of curling or rippling.

Cold-Adhesive Mounting

Cold-adhesive mounting is a mounting method that uses an adhesive that does not require heat to activate to bond the print to the substrate. Adhesive mounting methods bind the print tightly to the substrate, and they are generally considered permanent. As compared to heated-adhesive mounting, the greatest advantage of cold-adhesive mounting is convenience, particularly when only one or a few photos need to be mounted. There is no need to set up or prepare equipment, and the mounting usually can be done in a more limited amount of space.

Chapter 20 The Finishing Touches 515

There are two methods of mounting with cold adhesive. Pressure-sensitive adhesives may be supplied in sheet form or already applied to a substrate. Alternatively, an adhesive can be applied to the print or the mount by spraying, brushing, or applying with a roll-on applicator.

Pressure-sensitive adhesive material comes in sheets or rolls coated with a sticky material that is activated by applying pressure with a squeegee or roller. See **Figure 20-26**. The material is positioned between the print and substrate, and pressure is applied with the squeegee or roller. This activates the adhesive, forming a permanent bond. An advantage of this material is the ability to reposition the print, if necessary, before applying pressure to activate the adhesive.

Foam board with an already-applied adhesive can be purchased and used for *flush mounts* (mounts in which the photo extends to the edge of the mount, with no border). See **Figure 20-27**. To mount a photo, a sheet of protective paper is peeled away from the adhesive and the print is carefully aligned with the mount edges. The print is then burnished (rubbed with a tool for smoothing) to assure a good bond.

Applied cold adhesives are not as popular as they once were. Rubber cement, the oldest form of brush-on adhesive, is no longer recommended because the solvent in the cement often causes discoloration of the mounted material. A water-based acrylic adhesive that allows repositioning and alignment of the print is a more acceptable form of brush-on material. The print is not bonded to the substrate until pressure is applied with a roller or burnisher.

A spray-on adhesive can be applied quickly but is messy to use. Adjacent areas must be protected from overspray, and good ventilation must be provided.

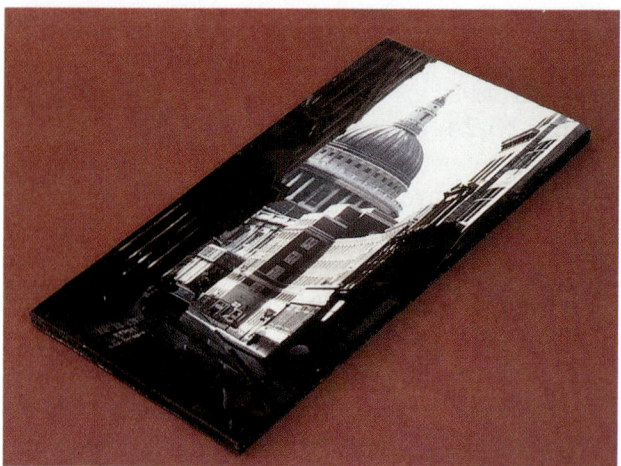

Goodheart-Willcox Publisher

Figure 20-27. This print has been flush-mounted on a piece of foam board with an already-applied adhesive.

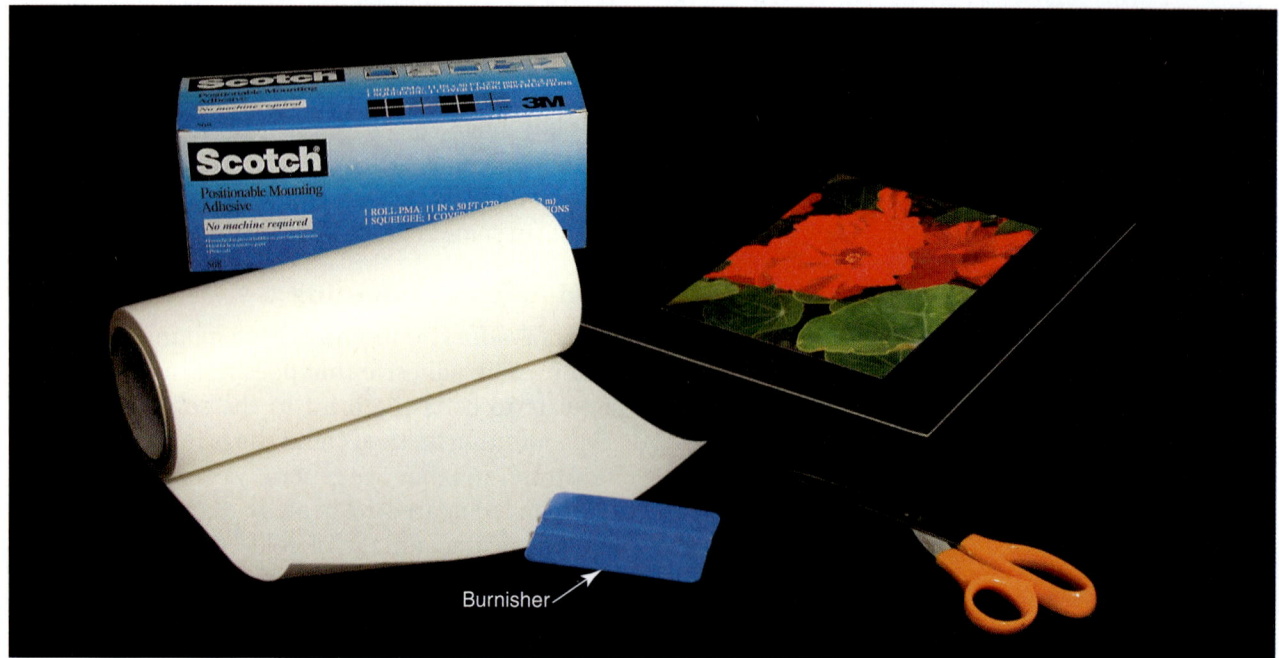

Goodheart-Willcox Publisher

Figure 20-26. Mounting with pressure-sensitive adhesive material requires a knife or scissors and a burnisher.

Several types of roll-on adhesive applicators are marketed. The liquid adhesive forms a pressure-sensitive bond, allowing the photo to be repositioned until burnished down.

Dry (Heated-Adhesive) Mounting

Dry mounting, a mounting method that uses heat and pressure to bond the print to the substrate, is most widely used by professional studios and framing shops. It is also known as *heated-adhesive mounting*. The heat-activated adhesive material, called *mounting tissue*, is generally sold in sheet form. Various types are available for different applications. One type is intended strictly for use with porous materials, such as fiber-based photo paper. Another is used for either porous or nonporous materials. Both form permanent bonds. A special archival mounting tissue allows reversal of the bonding action—reheating a mounted print allows it to be removed from the mount without damage.

Heated-adhesive mounting is done using a dry-mount press, which has an electrically heated platen (a large, heavy metal plate) that is clamped down to apply both heat and pressure, **Figure 20-28**. Dry-mount presses range in size from home units capable of mounting an 11″ × 14″ print to large commercial presses able to handle material up to 52″ in width.

Overmatting a Print

An overmat with a window cut into it to allow the print to show through has two primary functions—appearance and protection. The color (and sometimes texture and pattern) of the mat can help to show the photo to its best advantage. Protection, however, is equally important. When a mounted photo is framed and displayed behind glass or plastic, the mat provides spacing to prevent the photo from touching the glazing material. If a mat is not used, moisture in the air may discolor and warp the print or cause the emulsion to stick to the glazing material.

Overmat Types

The most common form of overmat is one with a beveled-edge opening that slightly overlaps the print borders. Multiple-opening mats are widely used for displaying a collection of school or family-member portraits. Double- or even triple-layer window mats are available in most framing and art supply stores. Special die cut shapes are also popular. Framers often create mats to meet customer desires by adhering various fabrics, papers, or other coverings to mat board.

A less common form of window mat is cut with an opening somewhat larger than the print. Sometimes referred to as a *reveal mat*, this larger version is most popular among fine-art photographers and museum curators. Curators like this style of mat for its archival preservation quality—it protects the print like a standard window mat, but it does not actually touch the print (minimizing sources of possible contamination or chemical reaction).

Fine art photographers also like the fact that a reveal mat does not overlap the edges of the print, so the entire photo is revealed to the viewer. A reveal mat, if cut sufficiently oversize, also allows room for the copyright date, photographer's signature, and edition numbering. See **Figure 20-29**.

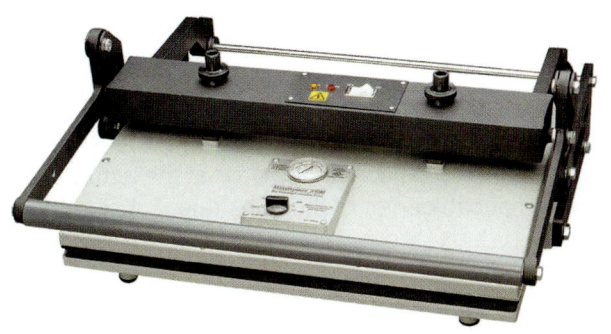

Seal/Bienfang

Figure 20-28. A dry-mount press for heated-adhesive mounting.

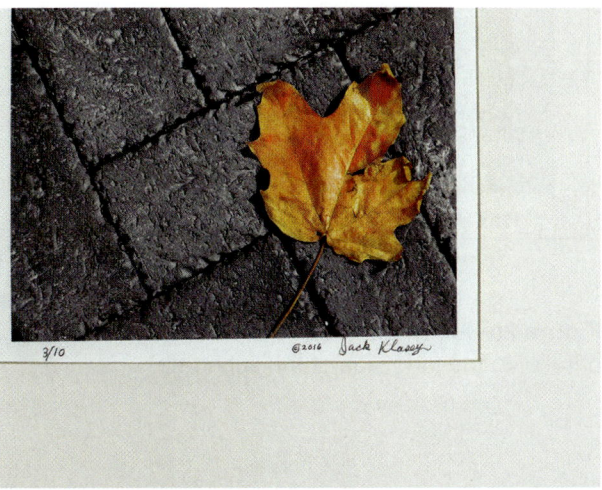

Jack Klasey/Goodheart-Willcox Publisher

Figure 20-29. The reveal mat allows room for the photographer's signature and other information.

Positioning the Print

No matter which mounting method you select, you must position your print carefully and accurately on the substrate to show it to its best advantage. A basic rule of print positioning is that the print's long axis should be parallel with the long axis of the board. For example, if you have an 8″ × 10″ print, the 10″ side should be parallel with the 14″ side of the 11″ × 14″ board. This is true whether you have a horizontal or a vertical print, **Figure 20-30**.

There are two slightly different ways of positioning the print on the board, depending on whether you plan to use a precut overmat. When the print will be displayed without an overmat or with a custom-cut overmat, the preferred mounting method places the print at the optical center of the board. This means that the print has equal amounts of space on either side, but unequal amounts above and below. Since the space below the print is somewhat greater than the space above, the center of the print will be slightly higher than the center of the mounting board. If you are mounting a horizontal 8″ × 10″ print on an 11″ × 14″ board, the margins at each side would be 2″, the bottom margin would be 1 3/4″, and the top margin would be 1 1/4″. See **Figure 20-31**.

If you are using a precut window mat like those available from art supply stores, the print position must match the window. This generally requires the print to be centered on the mounting board at top and bottom as well as from side to side. In this case, the side margins are 2″, but both top and bottom margins are 1 1/2″, **Figure 20-32**. The opening in the precut mat is slightly smaller than 8″ × 10″ so the edges of the mounted print will be hidden.

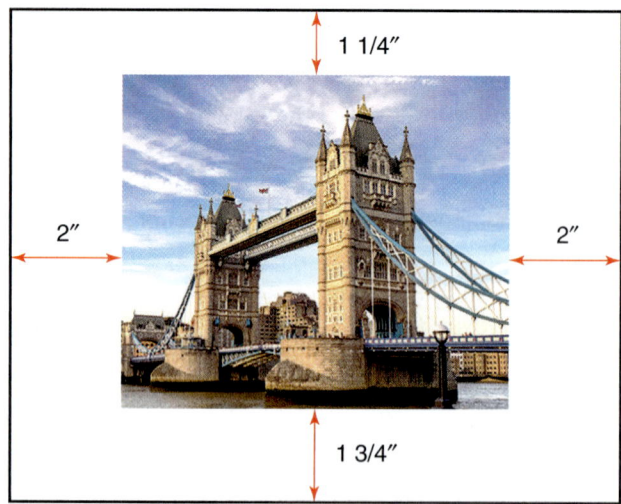

Tower Bridge image: alberto cervantes/Shutterstock.com
Diagram: Goodheart-Willcox Publisher

Figure 20-31. Positioning the print at the optical center of the substrate.

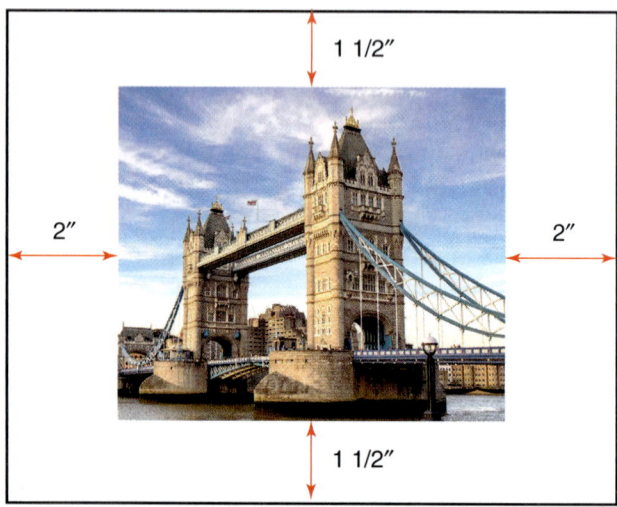

Tower Bridge image: alberto cervantes/Shutterstock.com
Diagram: Goodheart-Willcox Publisher

Figure 20-32. Positioning the print at the actual (mathematical) center of the substrate.

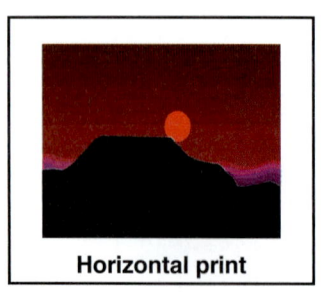 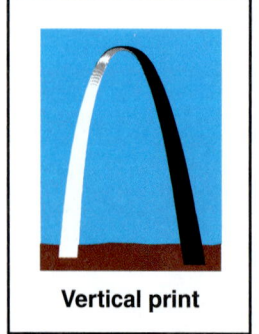

Goodheart-Willcox Publisher

Figure 20-30. Orient the print so its long side is parallel to the long side of the substrate.

PORTFOLIO ASSIGNMENT

Framing and Matting

Selecting the right frame and overmat for a photograph can help elevate it from a great photo to a work of art. For this portfolio assignment, you will review the photos you have taken for your portfolio thus far and select a few of your favorites to frame and mat. This assignment will help prepare you for framing and matting these photos in the future.

1. Select three images from your portfolio. They can be of any subject matter (though it is preferable to show a variety) and can be in black-and-white or color.
2. After you have selected your images, begin planning how you would like to frame and mat them. Research framing and matting options online, taking the following into consideration:

- Desired color and size of the frame (as well as the thickness and finish)
- Desired color and size of the overmat (as well as the material or if you do not want an overmat)
- Price of desired frame and overmat
- How your choices best complement each of your photos

Compile your final choices in a chart that includes a description of the photo you are framing and matting, the frame details, the overmat details, and an explanation for your choices. Submit your chart to your instructor for review and feedback.

Chapter 20 Review

Summary

- Once an image has been captured or scanned into digital form, it can be displayed in a number of electronic venues, such as a wallpaper or screen saver on an electronic device or posted to online sites and social media platforms.
- Digital photo frames and LCD projectors are great ways to display digital images.
- One of the most common forms of image display is the photographic print. Photographers can have them printed at retail locations, through online photofinishing sites, or on a home printer.
- The inkjet printer is a type of printer that works by depositing a fine spray of tiny ink dots on paper. The two basic formats of desktop inkjet printers are letter-size and wide-format.
- Originally, all inkjet printers used a four-ink set (the traditional CMYK), but as color photo printing became more popular, manufacturers introduced ink sets consisting of eight or more inks. The types of inks used today are typically pigment-based inks. Specialty ink sets are used for monochrome printing.
- Archival quality and brilliant color have always been a selling point for dye sublimation printers. The drawback has been the high cost for models capable of printing sizes up to 8″ × 10″.
- The most difficult aspect of printing is making a print that reflects exactly the image displayed on your computer monitor. The best way to achieve consistent and predictable prints is to calibrate your monitor so it truly reflects the colors you are working with.
- Two basic decisions must be made before starting the mounting process. You must select the surface (substrate) and determine which mounting method is appropriate to the situation.
- The vast majority of mounted photographic prints are placed on board. The two basic types are mat board and foam board. When selecting a board for mounting a photograph, you should consider composition, weight/thickness, color, and size.
- Factors influencing the selection of a mounting method include permanence, convenience, time and cost, and the availability of needed materials and equipment. Mounting methods can be grouped into three categories: edge mounting, cold-adhesive mounting, and dry (heated-adhesive) mounting.
- An overmat with a window cut into it to allow the print to show through has two primary functions—appearance and protection. The most common form of overmat is one with a beveled-edge opening that slightly overlaps the print borders.
- No matter which mounting method you select, you must position your print carefully and accurately on the substrate to show it to its best advantage. A basic rule of print positioning is that the print's long axis should be parallel with the long axis of the board.

Review Questions

Answer the following questions using the information provided in this chapter.

Know and Understand

1. *True or False?* Displaying photos in an online gallery is aimed at amateur photographers.
2. The _____ printer is a type of printer that works by depositing a fine spray of tiny ink dots on paper.
   A. giclée
   B. inkjet
   C. dye sublimation
   D. buffered
3. *True or False?* Coated papers resist the spread of ink droplets.
4. Which of the following is *not* one of the colors used in a traditional CMYK ink set?
   A. Yellow
   B. Black
   C. Red
   D. Magenta
5. *True or False?* Pigment-based inks resist fading much better than early dye-based inks.
6. _____ is a term applied to photographic prints that are processed with the intent of achieving very long life.
   A. Archival quality
   B. Metamerism
   C. Sublimate
   D. Flush mount
7. A _____ consists of black and three grays rather than CMYK.
   A. pigment-based ink
   B. quad-tone ink set
   C. dye-based ink
   D. monochrome ink set
8. *True or False?* Dye sublimation prints are subject to fading.
9. A _____ is a device that reads color values from the monitor screen so the accompanying calibration software can make the necessary adjustments.
   A. conservation board
   B. buffer
   C. profile
   D. colorimeter
10. _____ board is mounting material made with a paper facing on a rigid core of plastic foam.
    A. Mat
    B. Conservation
    C. Foam
    D. Museum
11. *True or False?* A board that is buffered is made slightly alkaline to counter the long-term effects of weak airborne acids.
12. For prints up to 8″ × 10″, a _____ board is stiff enough to stand alone for display.
    A. 1-ply
    B. 2-ply
    C. 4-ply
    D. 8-ply
13. *True or False?* A white overmat is best for a high-key photo.
14. An 11″ × 14″ print should normally be mounted on a mat that is at least _____ in size.
    A. 4″ × 6″
    B. 8″ × 10″
    C. 11″ × 14″
    D. 16″ × 20″
15. Museum curators and others concerned with maximum archival preservation of photos favor _____ mounting.
    A. edge
    B. cold-adhesive
    C. heated-adhesive
    D. dry

16. _____ mounting is a mounting method that uses an adhesive that does not require heat to activate to bond the print to the substrate.
    A. Edge
    B. Cold-adhesive
    C. Heated-adhesive
    D. Dry

17. _____ mounting is a mounting method that uses heat and pressure to bond the print to the substrate.
    A. Archival
    B. Dry
    C. Edge
    D. Cold-adhesive

18. *True or False?* A photo that is optically centered on the substrate has equal amounts of space on either side, but unequal amounts of space above and below.

Apply and Analyze

1. List the two basic formats of desktop inkjet printers.
2. Describe the basic difference between museum board and conservation board.
3. What is an advantage of using pressure-sensitive adhesive material?
4. Why is rubber cement *not* recommended for mounting prints?
5. Why should an overmat be used when a photo is framed and displayed behind glass or plastic?

Critical Thinking

1. Imagine you have taken a gorgeous landscape photo that you would like to have printed and hung up on your wall. You perform some basic editing to the photo on your computer and print the photo. When you look at the printed photo, the colors appear off from what you saw in your camera. What are two possible causes of this and how can you fix it?
2. You have made a dramatic print of an image with deep black shadows and brilliant white highlights. How would you mount, overmat, and frame the print to display it on your wall most effectively?

Suggested Activities

1. Find three to five examples of effective mountings, either around your house, classroom, in an art museum or gallery, or online. Create a brief PowerPoint presentation to deliver to your class explaining why the mountings are effective. If you think they could be improved, explain what you would do differently and why.
2. Compare the results of printing an image on different types of paper. Choose a color image with a good range of tones and make a 5″ × 7″ print on plain white copier paper. Next, make a print of the same image on glossy photo paper. If matte finish and semi-glossy (luster) papers are available, make prints on them as well. Mount the prints side by side and label each type of paper. Compare the prints and decide which type of paper produced the best results.

3. Make a print on 8.5″ × 11″ photo paper and mount it on an 11″ × 14″ board. Use the cold-adhesive mounting method. Position the print so you can use an overmat with an 8″ × 10″ precut window. Choose a suitable color overmat and hinge it to the mounting board. If desired, frame your mounted and matted print for display.

Communicating about Photography

1. **Speaking and Writing.** Working in pairs, create flash cards for the technical terms that you find challenging in this chapter. Each student should choose six technical terms and make flash cards for those terms. Using your textbook and a dictionary, write the term on the front of the card and the pronunciation and definition on the back. Quiz each other on the pronunciations and definitions of the terms.

2. **Listening and Speaking.** Survey several people you know about how they display their photos physically and electronically. Be sure to get a range of ages to see clear differences among age groups. When surveying each person, adapt your language as necessary to aid in understanding. Report your findings to the class, giving reasons why you would or would not want to display your own photos in those ways.

Chapter 21
Mobile Postprocessing

Learning Objectives

After completing this chapter, you will be able to:
- Understand and apply the various edits possible through a mobile device's native camera app.
- Identify edits possible through third-party editing apps.
- Recognize how to maximize reach on different social media platforms.
- Recall ways in which to print mobile photographs.
- Define the types of paper used to print mobile photographs.

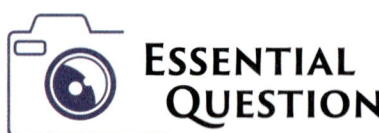

Essential Question

What techniques can you bring from traditional postprocessing to mobile postprocessing?

Technical Terms

black point
brightness
brilliance
definition
mobile postprocessing
noise reduction
reach
saturation
sharpness
tint
vibrance
vignette
warmth

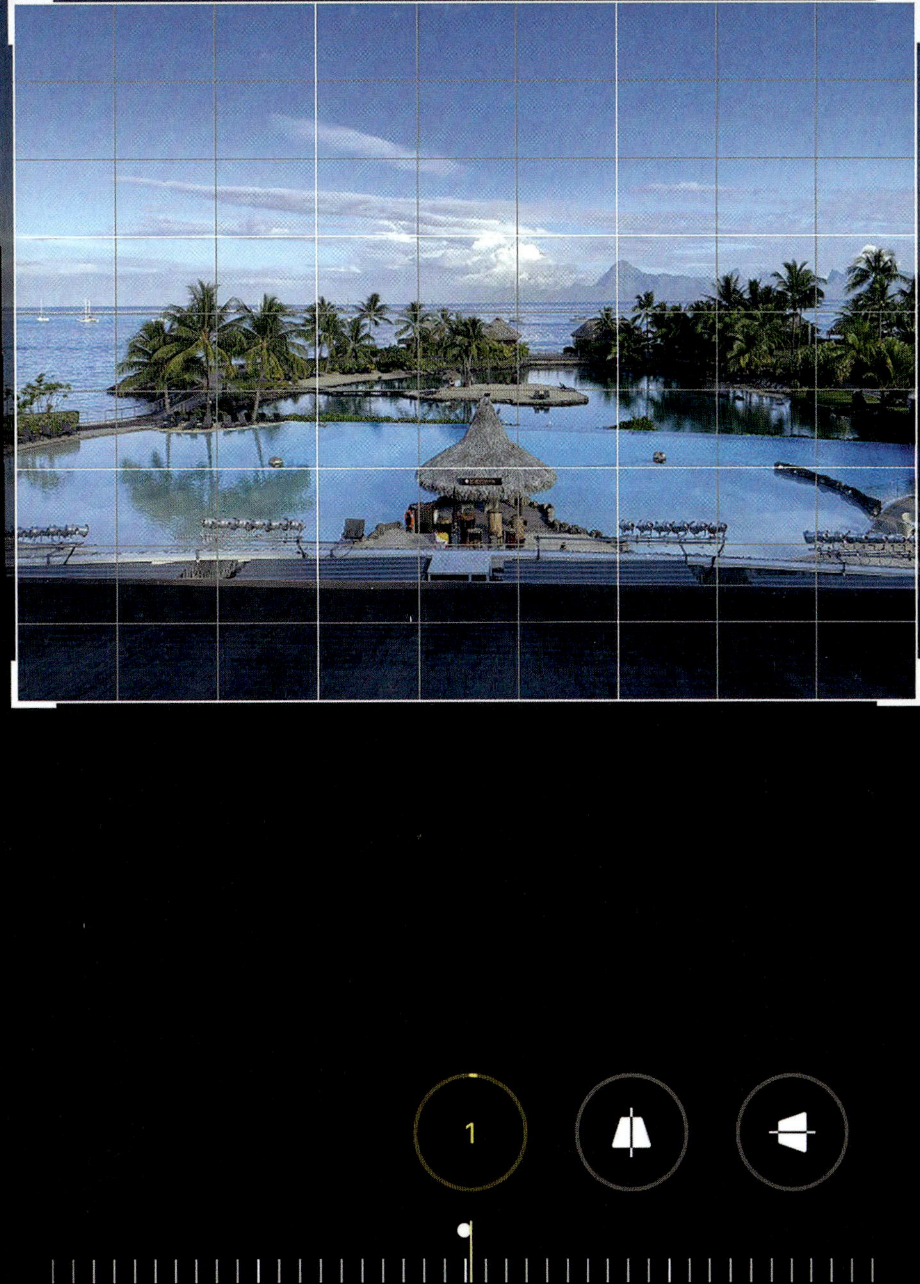

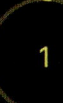

Introduction to Mobile Postprocessing

It is becoming more and more common for photographers to shoot images primarily with their smartphone or other type of mobile device, **Figure 21-1**. As such, it is important to have plenty of options when it comes to editing. This chapter will discuss how to edit photos on a mobile device. The editing process on a mobile device is very similar to the editing process on a typical computer.

What Is Mobile Postprocessing?

Mobile postprocessing is the process of editing photographs on a mobile device. It allows you to edit nearly anywhere and reduces the need for a desktop computer or laptop. It is worth noting that mobile editing programs can only get you so far, and for more advanced edits, you may have to work on a computer. However, for many of the more basic edits most photographers perform (such as editing lighting or cropping), a phone- or tablet-based app should suffice.

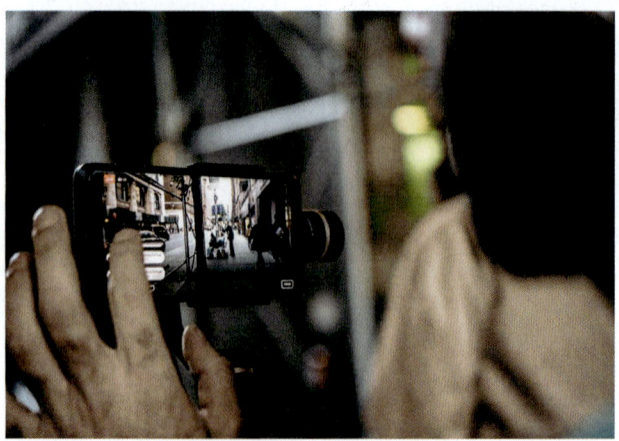

July Prokopiv/Shutterstock.com

Figure 21-1. Mobile phones are a go-to option for many photographers.

There are dozens, if not hundreds, of programs to choose from for mobile postprocessing. New editing apps are released constantly, and older apps are updated on a regular basis to keep up with changes or advancements in editing. Finding the program that works best for you as a photographer is often done through trial and error.

Editing in the Native Camera App

If the plethora of image editing apps is overwhelming, you can always start with the basic functionality of the editor built into your device's native camera. Many of these edits are stackable, meaning that you can perform multiple edits on a single image. The following sections provide a broad overview of the major editing features available in the native camera app of an iPhone®. Since technology is constantly changing and evolving, editing capabilities will continue to expand and adjust.

Note that you can always toggle between the edited version and the original version of your photo by clicking on the icon for the adjustment you made. For example, if you are adjusting an image's brilliance and want to compare the original photo with the edited version, simply click on the icon for brilliance and it will revert to the original or toggle back to the edited version, **Figure 21-2**. You can also click on the image itself, which will revert it to the original very briefly.

Straightening an Image

Straightening an image is one of the most basic edits you can perform using the native camera app, and it is something you will probably do quite frequently. Even with the assistance of a tripod, gimbal, or other stabilizing device, it can be difficult to take a picture that is completely straight. Thankfully, it is incredibly easy to straighten a photo with just a few small adjustments.

First, select the Edit option in the upper right-hand corner of the screen, **Figure 21-3**. Next, select the Crop icon at the bottom middle of the screen, **Figure 21-4**. From there, you will have the ability

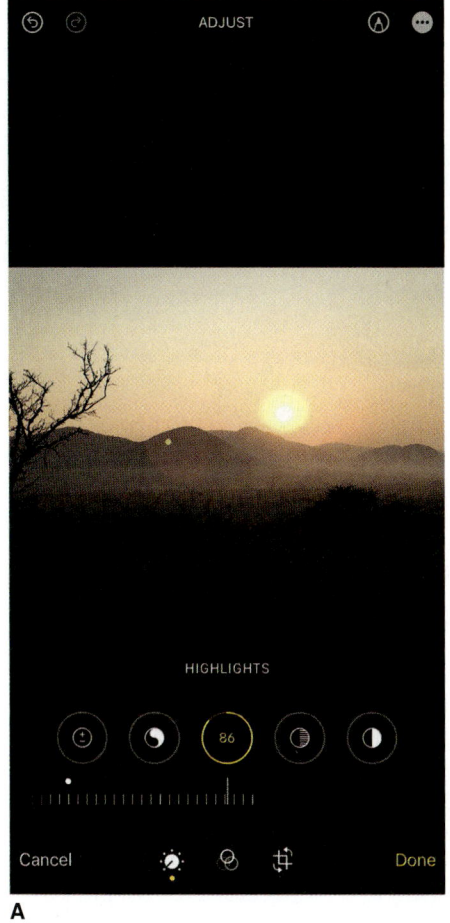
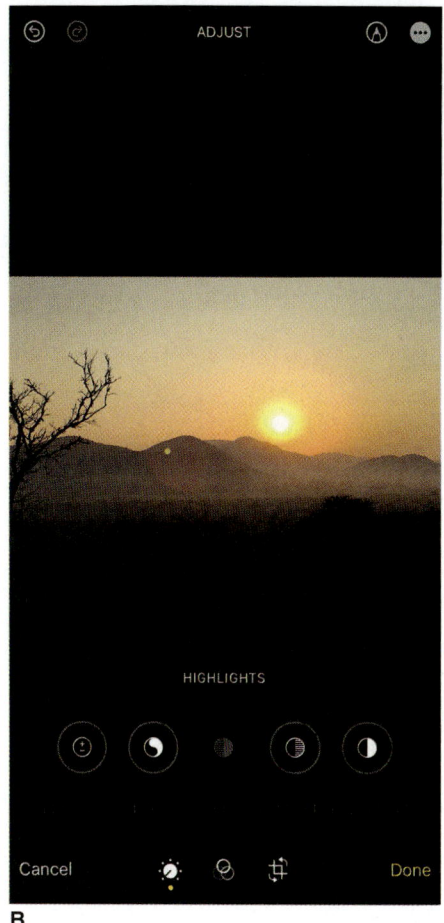

Goodheart-Willcox Publisher

Figure 21-2. You can always toggle your adjustments on or off by pressing on the icon for that adjustment. A—Highlight adjustment on. B—Highlight adjustment off.

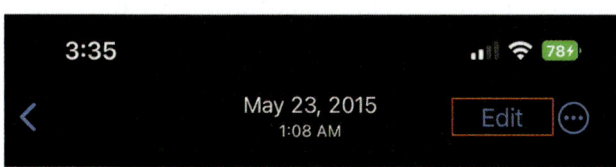

Goodheart-Willcox Publisher

Figure 21-3. To access all the editing options discussed in this chapter, select the Edit option in the upper right corner of the screen.

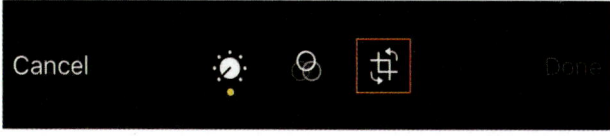

Goodheart-Willcox Publisher

Figure 21-4. This icon opens the crop editing feature.

to rotate your image slightly to the left or to the right using the hashed line at the bottom of the screen, **Figure 21-5**. To adjust your picture until it appears straight, move your finger along the line. Notice that as you make the straightening adjustment, the image will zoom in to compensate for any empty space created by the adjustment. Because of this, your final image will appear slightly larger than it was originally. If you do not like the changes, you can always select Reset, and your image will return to its original state, **Figure 21-6**.

Crop

Crop is another basic edit used quite frequently. Crop is commonly used to focus on a specific area in a photo, to exclude unnecessary items in the frame, or to fit a photo to specific proportions.

As with straightening an image, first select the Edit option and then the Crop icon. You will notice that a white border with thicker white corners will

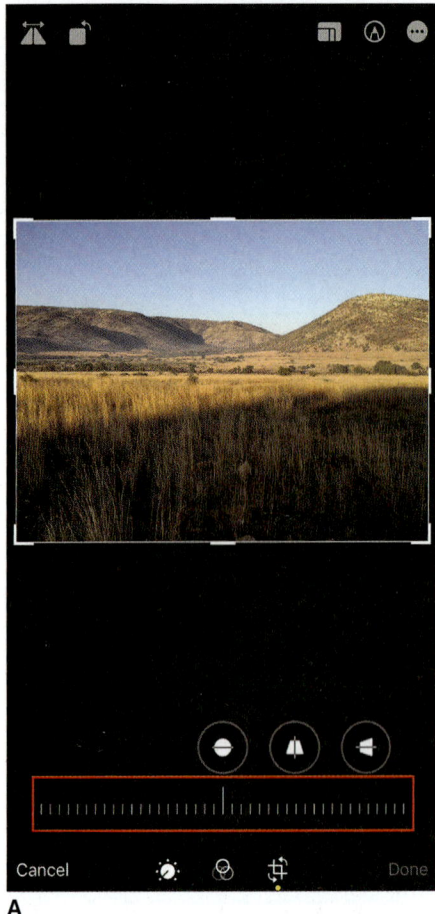
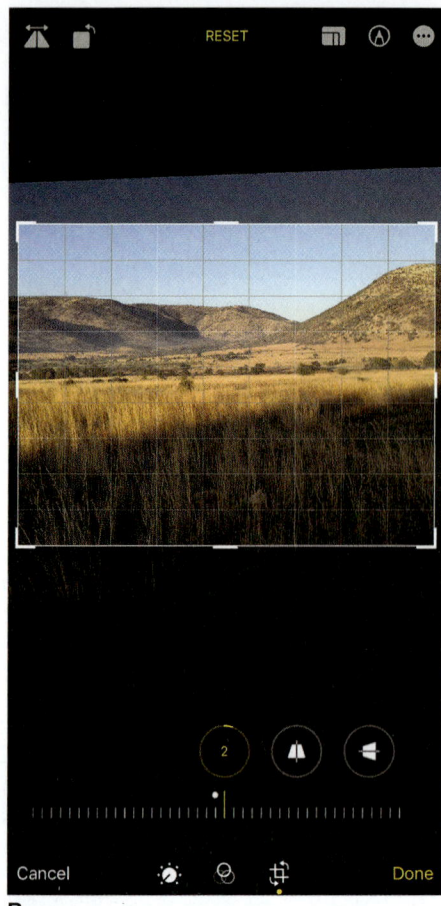

Figure 21-5. Straightening an image. A—Use the slider at the bottom of the screen to adjust the rotation of your image. B—Notice that the image will zoom in slightly to compensate for the adjustment.

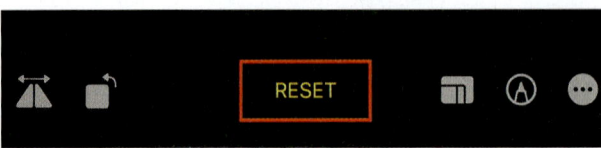

Goodheart-Willcox Publisher

Figure 21-6. The Reset button will return your photo to its original state.

appear around the image, **Figure 21-7**. You can drag either the corners or the edges of the border to crop the image how you want, **Figure 21-8**.

When you move the borders, you will see the rule of thirds grid appear, and the portion of the photo you crop out will become desaturated, leaving you

with the final cropped image, **Figure 21-9**. You can adjust the crop as many times as you need. When you are satisfied with how you cropped the image, select Done at the lower right-hand corner of the screen, **Figure 21-10**. The newly cropped image will save in place of the original. If you find you are no longer satisfied with the crop, simply select Edit again, click on Revert at the lower right-hand corner of the screen, and select Revert to Original once it pops up.

Height and Depth

You can also change the height and depth of your photos to make the perspective change slightly. This is helpful if your camera was tilted forward, backward, up, or down when you were taking photos

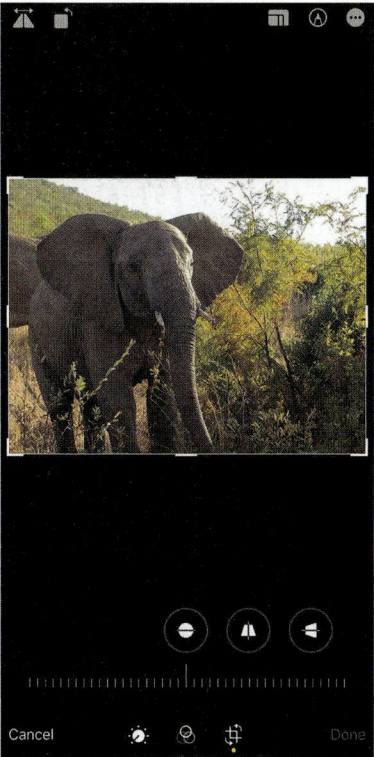

Goodheart-Willcox Publisher

Figure 21-7. When Crop is selected, white borders appear that you can use to adjust your image.

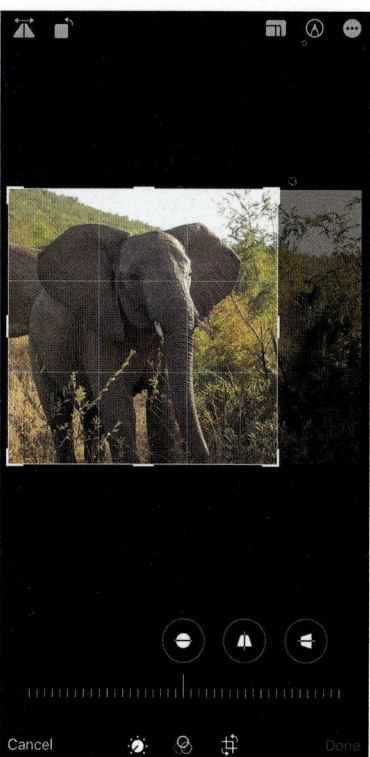

Goodheart-Willcox Publisher

Figure 21-9. When cropping an image, everything outside the white border will be desaturated and the rule of thirds grid will appear.

and you need to adjust the perspective. This is the digital equivalent of adjusting the camera's position when taking photos. Since this is a function of cropping, you will find the ability to adjust these when you select the Crop icon, **Figure 21-11**. Remember that you will lose parts of your image with these adjustments to compensate for the change in perspective, so adjust accordingly, **Figure 21-12**.

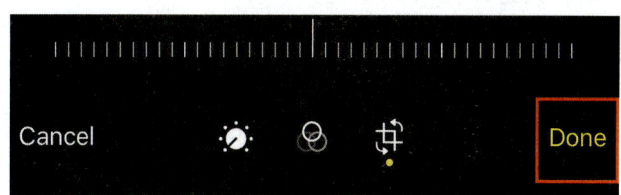

Goodheart-Willcox Publisher

Figure 21-10. Whenever you are finished editing your photos, make sure to press Done to save your changes.

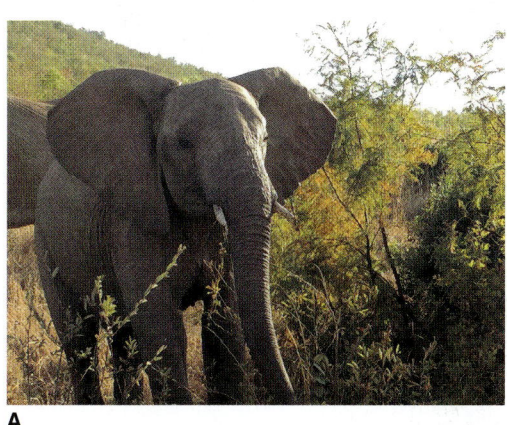
A

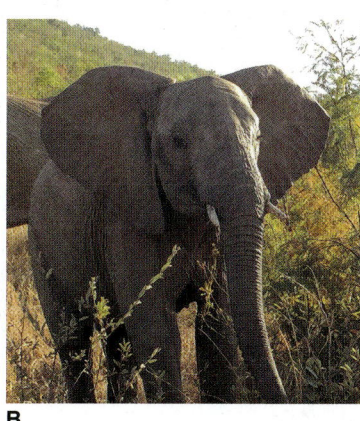
B

Goodheart-Willcox Publisher

Figure 21-8. A—An image before cropping. B—An image after cropping.

Chapter 21   Mobile Postprocessing   **529**

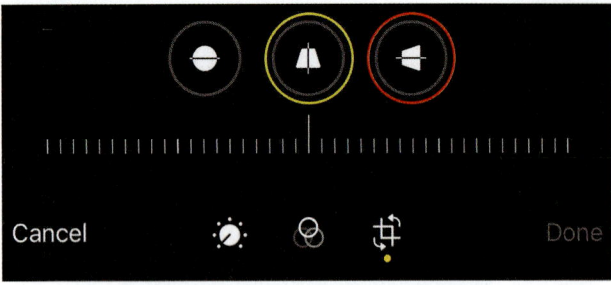

Figure 21-11. The ability to change an image's height or depth is in the crop editing feature. The icon in the middle (circled in yellow) is for adjusting height. The icon on the right (circled in red) is for adjusting depth.

Adding Filters

Similar to the filters you can add to photos and videos on Instagram and TikTok, you can add filters to your photos directly in the native camera app on your phone. While the options are much more limited than the ones available in a separate app or platform, you can choose from an array of colored and monochrome filters, **Figure 21-13**.

To add a filter to an image, first select Edit. Then, select the three concentric circles at the bottom middle of the screen, **Figure 21-14**. This will pull up all the available filters that you have to choose from. You can also adjust the intensity of your filter with the slider that appears at the bottom, giving you even more control over postprocessing, **Figure 21-15**.

Auto

iPhone camera editors come with a feature called Auto. This feature applies various adjustments to an image to improve how it looks. To use the auto adjustment, choose the photo you wish to edit from your gallery, select Edit, and then select the Auto icon, **Figure 21-16**. Generally, this boosts the contrast and saturation, as well as a few other values. The goal of the auto adjustment is to make an image appear more like it does

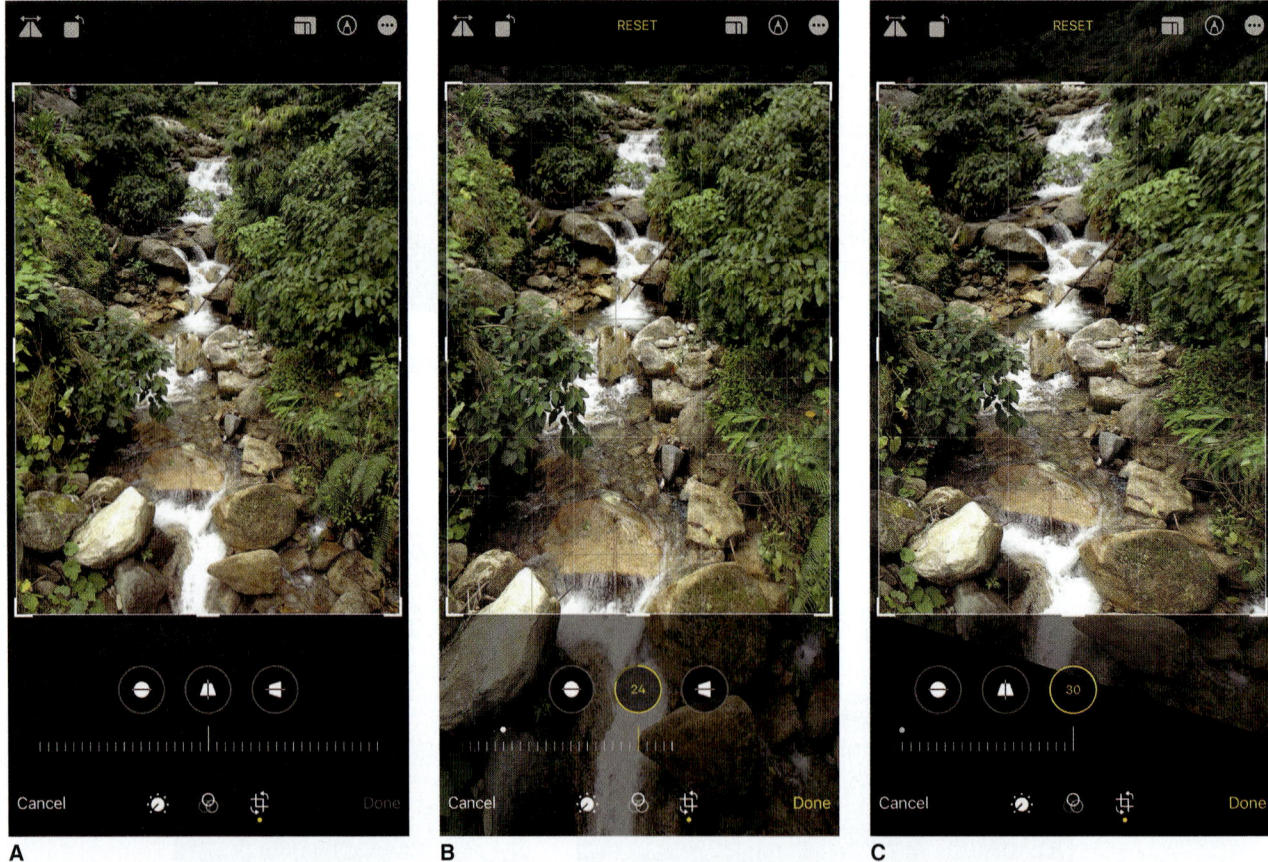

Figure 21-12. Editing an image's height or depth will help change perspective, but you will lose other parts of the photo. A—Original image. B—Change in an image's height. C—Change in an image's depth.

to your eye naturally rather than how it appears through a camera lens, **Figure 21-17**. While this works for some photos, it does not work for all. If you want to achieve a specific edit, it is better to adjust values separately.

Exposure

Adjusting the exposure in a photo affects all tones, but it affects highlights the most. Editing exposure is helpful if your image is too dark or too bright. To adjust exposure, choose the photo you

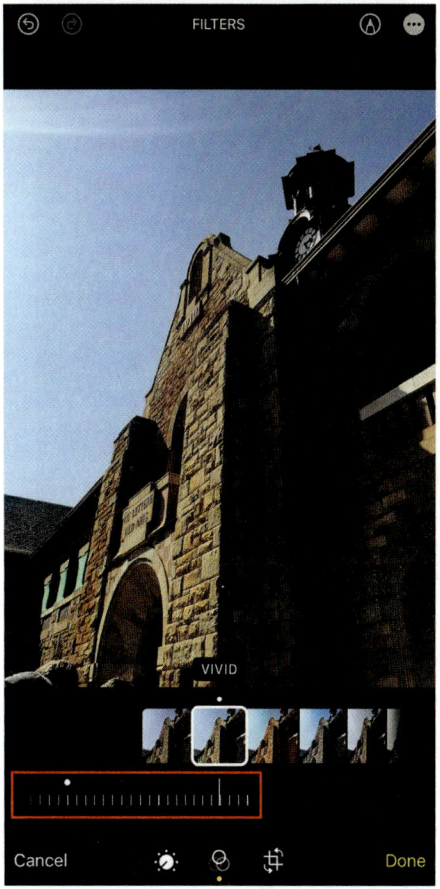

Goodheart-Willcox Publisher

Figure 21-15. You can vary the intensity of the filters by using the slider.

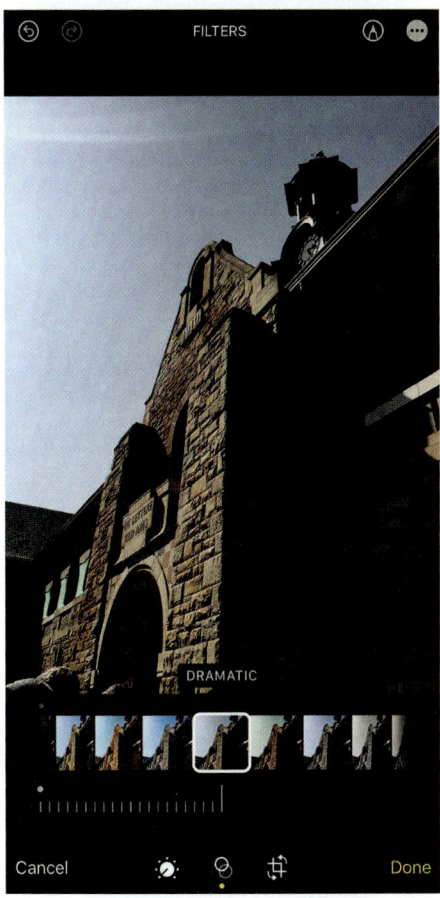

Goodheart-Willcox Publisher

Figure 21-13. The editor built into the native camera of an iPhone comes with an array of built-in filters to use.

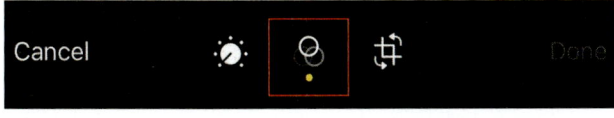

Goodheart-Willcox Publisher

Figure 21-14. You can access the available filters by pressing this button at the bottom of the screen.

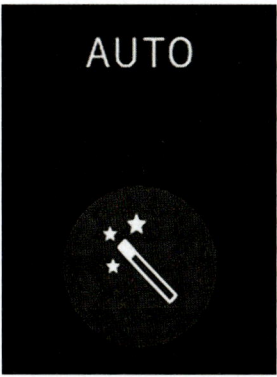

Goodheart-Willcox Publisher

Figure 21-16. The Auto icon resembles a magic wand.

Chapter 21　Mobile Postprocessing　531

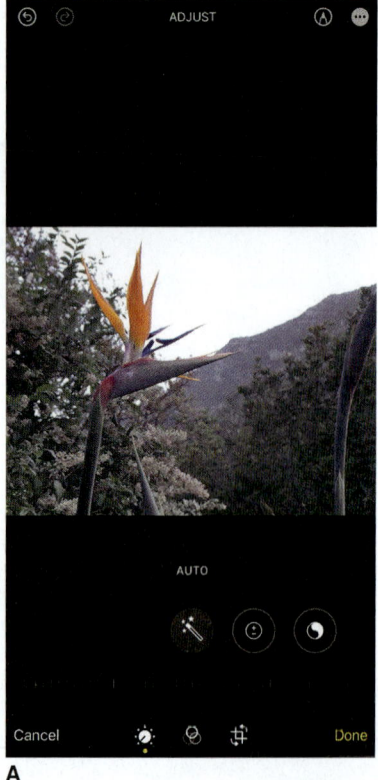 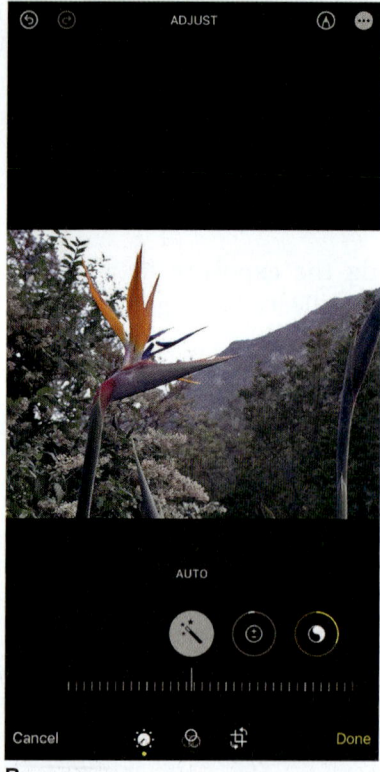

Figure 21-17. The Auto adjustment feature automatically senses what changes should be made to an image. A—Original image. B—Image with Auto adjustments.

Goodheart-Willcox Publisher

wish to edit from your gallery, select Edit, and then select the Exposure icon, **Figure 21-18**. Once this is selected, you can adjust the slider below it to increase or decrease the image's exposure, **Figure 21-19**. Note that you may have to adjust other settings, such as the highlights, brightness, saturation, or contrast, to finish adjusting your image to prevent it from becoming underexposed or overexposed.

Brilliance

Brilliance is an editing tool that brightens shadows, adjusts contrast, and tones down highlights to help make an image appear more vibrant or rich. This is because the additional contrast can reveal hidden details in your photo. Because of this altered contrast, the colors in the photo may appear more vivid. Editing brilliance is useful if you want a photo to appear more radiant. An example of when you may want to use it is to enhance a picture of a flower in a garden.

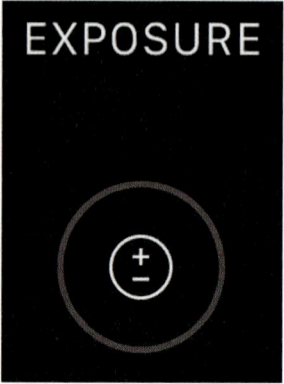

Goodheart-Willcox Publisher

Figure 21-18. The Exposure icon is a circle with a plus sign over a minus sign inside it.

To edit brilliance, choose the photo you wish to edit from your gallery, select Edit, and then select the Brilliance icon, **Figure 21-20**. Adjust the slider

532 Section 5 Postprocessing

Copyright Goodheart-Willcox Co., Inc.

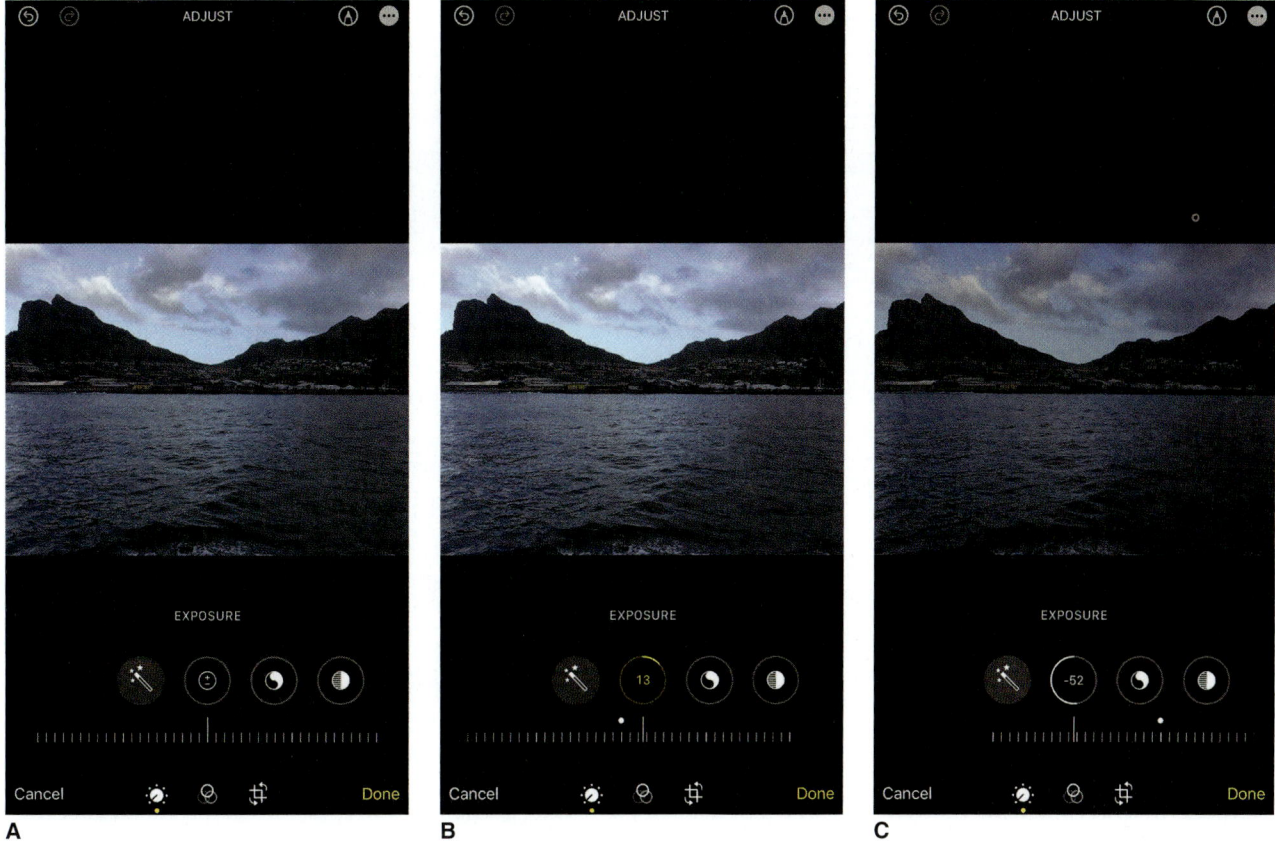

Figure 21-19. Adjusting exposure is ideal for images that are too dark or too bright. A—Original image. B—Image with increased exposure. C—Image with decreased exposure.

until you are satisfied, and then save the changes to your image, **Figure 21-21**.

Highlights and Shadows

Although editing highlights and shadows are two separate adjustments in your phone's editor, they often work hand in hand. The highlights option allows you to increase or decrease highlights in a photo, and the shadows option adjusts the details that appear in the shadows of a photo. Adjusting the highlights in your photo is great if you want a certain section to stand out from the rest, while adjusting the shadows works well if you want to create more contrast and darken portions of your photo.

To edit highlights, choose the photo you wish to edit from your gallery, select Edit, and then select the Highlights icon, **Figure 21-22A**. To edit shadows, choose the photo you wish to edit from your

Goodheart-Willcox Publisher

Figure 21-20. The Brilliance icon resembles the yin-yang symbol.

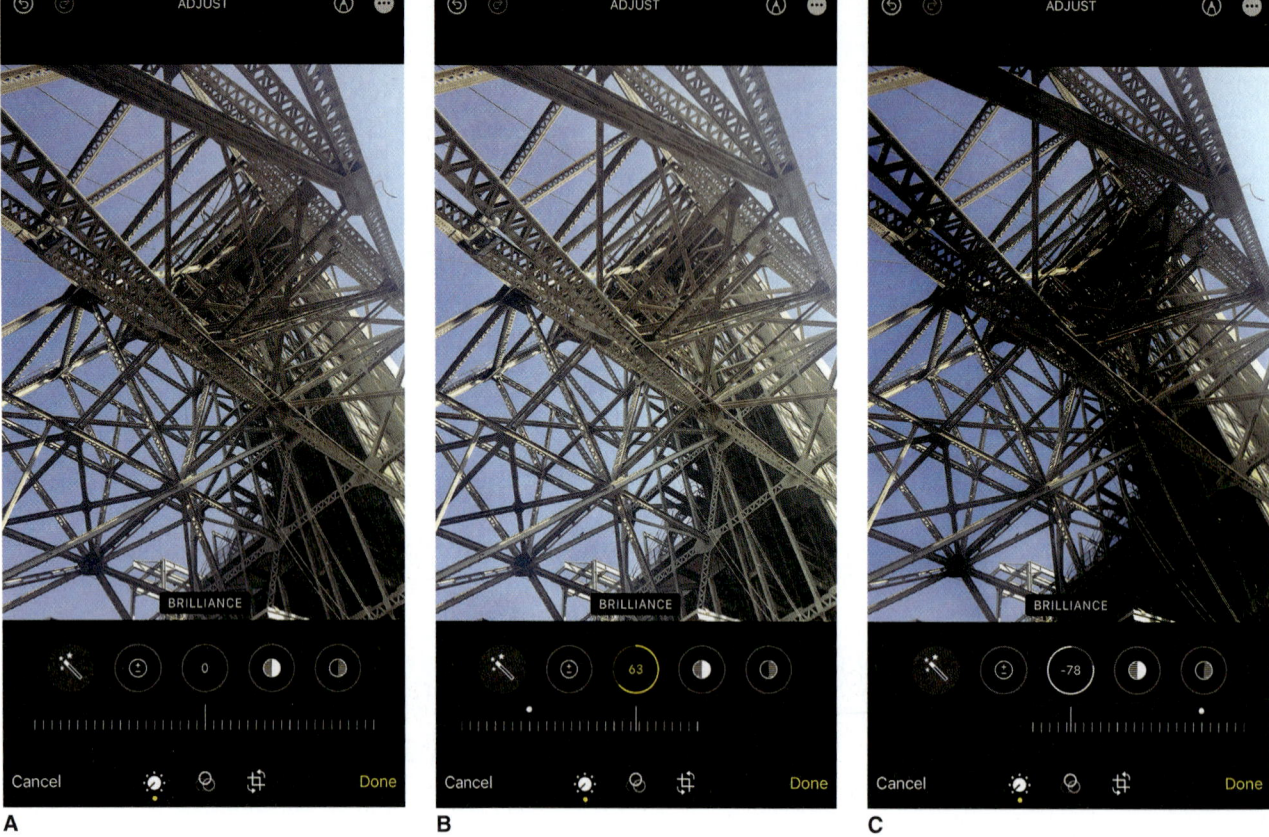

Figure 21-21. Editing brilliance can reveal previously hidden details in a photo. A—Original image. B—Image with increased brilliance. C—Image with decreased brilliance.

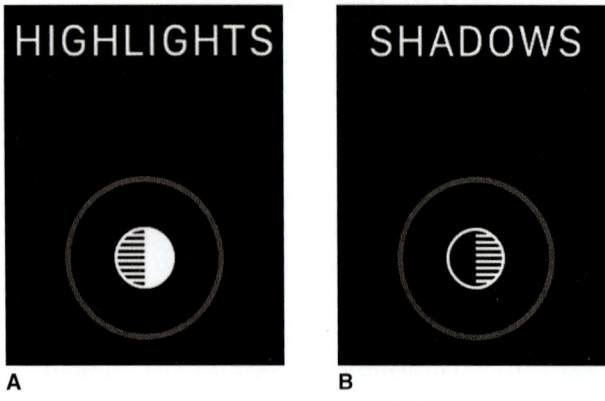

Figure 21-22. A—The Highlights icon is a circle with the left half filled with white horizontal hashed lines and the right half completely filled in. B—The Shadows icon is a circle with the left half completely open and the right half filled with white horizontal hashed lines.

gallery, select Edit, and then select the Shadows icon, **Figure 21-22B**. Adjust the slider to increase or decrease the highlights, **Figure 21-23**, and/or shadows, **Figure 21-24**, in your image.

Contrast

As you learned in Chapter 9, *Making a Picture*, *contrast* is the relationship of shadow and highlight within a photo. Increasing the contrast makes the bright areas brighter and the dark areas darker. Decreasing contrast reduces the difference between the bright and dark areas. Remember that contrast determines the range of shades in a photo. A high-contrast image can sometimes look surreal or cartoonlike since areas of detail can be lost if there are graduated tones. A photo with normal contrast looks crisp with a typical amount of detail, and a low-contrast image looks softer and shows less detail.

To adjust contrast, choose the photo you wish to edit from your gallery, select Edit, and then

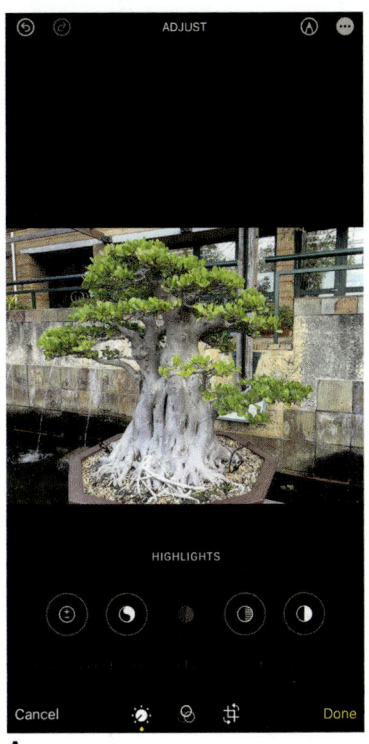 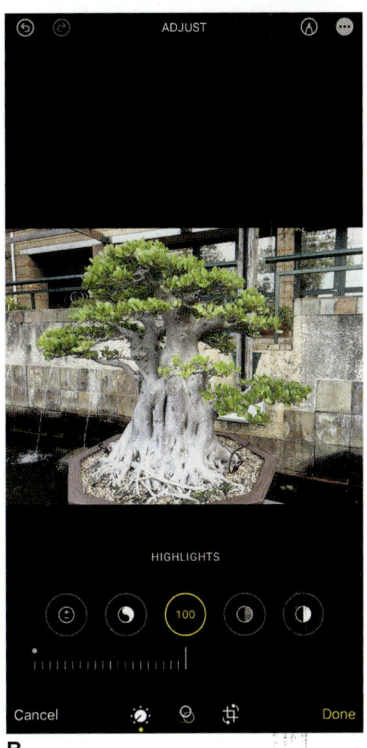 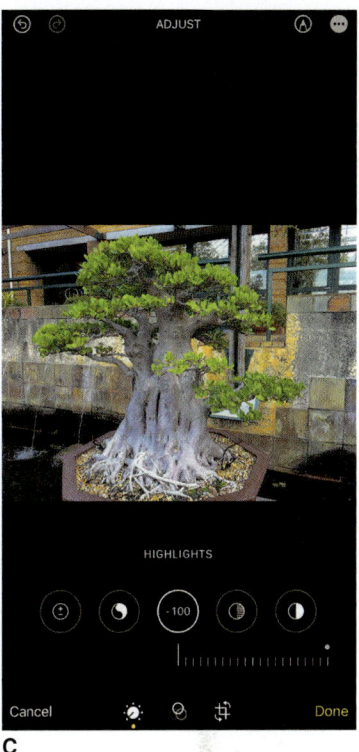

Goodheart-Willcox Publisher

Figure 21-23. Adjusting highlights helps specific parts of a picture stand out. A—Original image. B—Image with lighter highlights. C—Image with darker highlights.

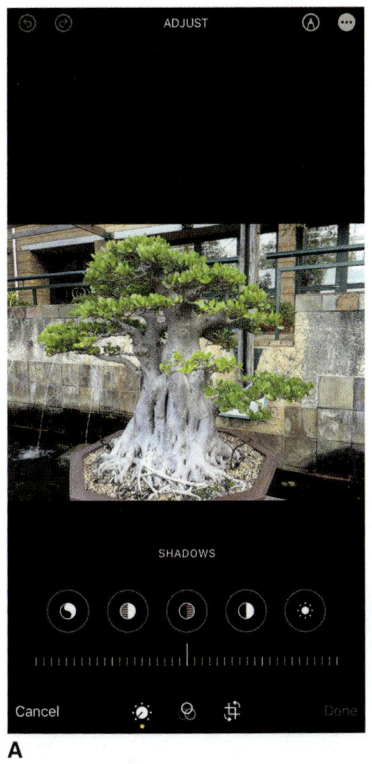 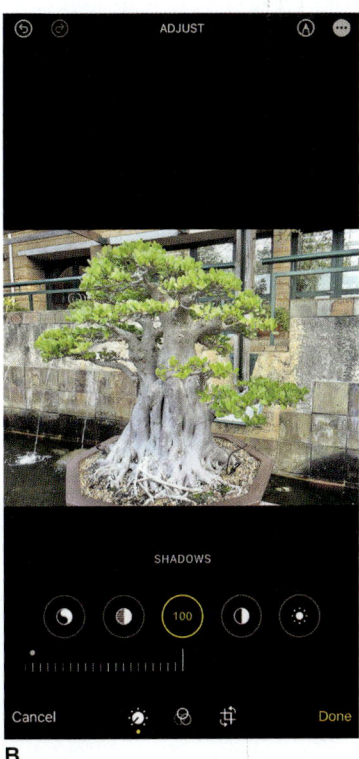 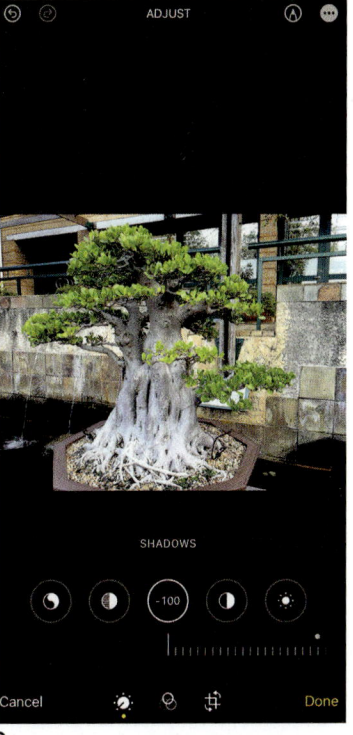

Goodheart-Willcox Publisher

Figure 21-24. Adjusting shadows helps darken specific parts of a picture. A—Original image. B—Image with lighter shadows. C—Image with darker shadows.

select the Contrast icon, **Figure 21-25**. Moving the slider to the right increases the contrast, and moving the slider to the left decreases the contrast, **Figure 21-26**. It may be necessary to pair this edit with another one in the editor for best results, such as adjusting shadows or brilliance.

Brightness

Brightness is an editing tool that adjusts how light an image appears. It is similar to exposure in that they both adjust the lightness of the image. However, unlike exposure, brightness affects all tones in the image equally. The process for adjusting an image's brightness is nearly identical to adjusting the exposure. Choose the photo you wish to edit from your gallery, select Edit, and then select the Brightness icon, **Figure 21-27**. Adjust the brightness by dragging the slider to the right to increase it, or to the left to decrease it, **Figure 21-28**. You would use this to enhance the brightest parts of your image and draw your viewer's eye.

Black Point

The **black point** is the darkest part of an image, at which black areas of your image become completely black and no details can be seen. Adjusting the black point determines the image's tonal range and impacts contrast, brightness, and other tone-related values. Decreasing the black point (making

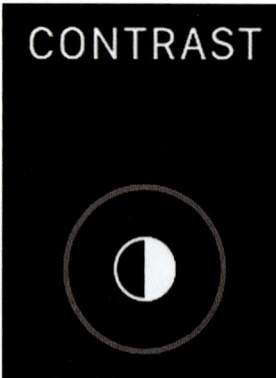

Goodheart-Willcox Publisher

Figure 21-25. The Contrast icon is a circle with the left half completely open and the right half completely filled in.

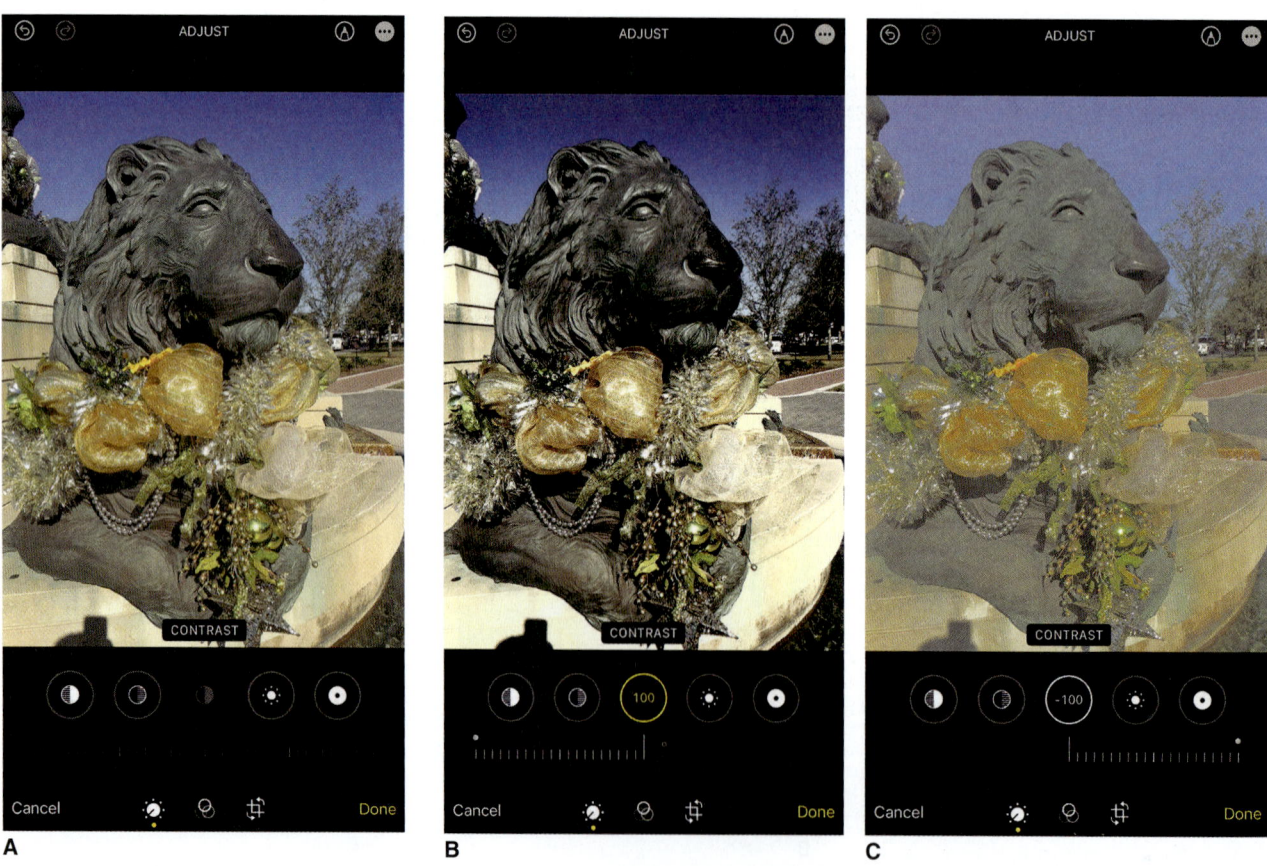

Goodheart-Willcox Publisher

Figure 21-26. Editing contrast can brighten or darken areas of a photo depending on whether you increase or decrease it. A—Original image. B—Image with increased contrast. C—Image with decreased contrast.

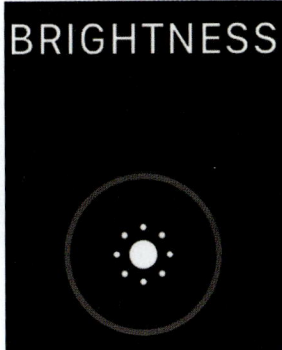

Figure 21-27. The Brightness icon resembles the sun.

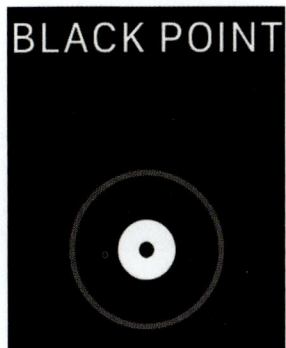

Figure 21-29. The Black Point icon is a white circle with a small black circle in the center.

values lighter) can give your image a more romantic feel, while increasing the black point (making values darker) can add drama.

To adjust the black point in an image, choose the photo you wish to edit from your gallery, select Edit, and then select the Black Point icon, **Figure 21-29**. Move the slider to the right to increase the black point, or move it to the left to decrease the black point, **Figure 21-30**.

Saturation

Saturation is an editing tool that changes the intensity of all the colors present in an image equally. Using this appropriately can help photos avoid appearing washed out as well as provide a bit of liveliness. However, it is easy to oversaturate your images, so make saturation adjustments in small increments.

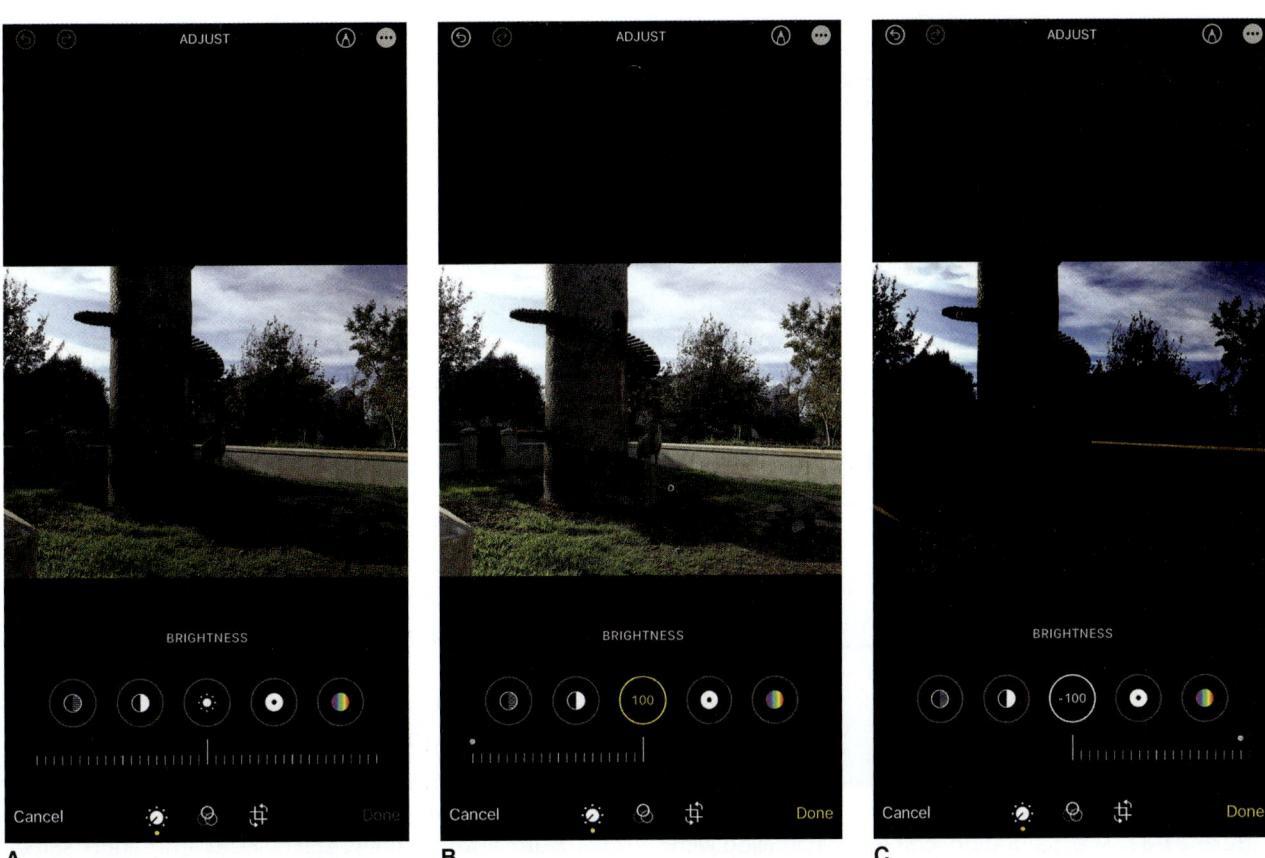

Figure 21-28. Brightness affects all tones in a photo equally. A—Original image. B—Image with increased brightness. C—Image with decreased brightness.

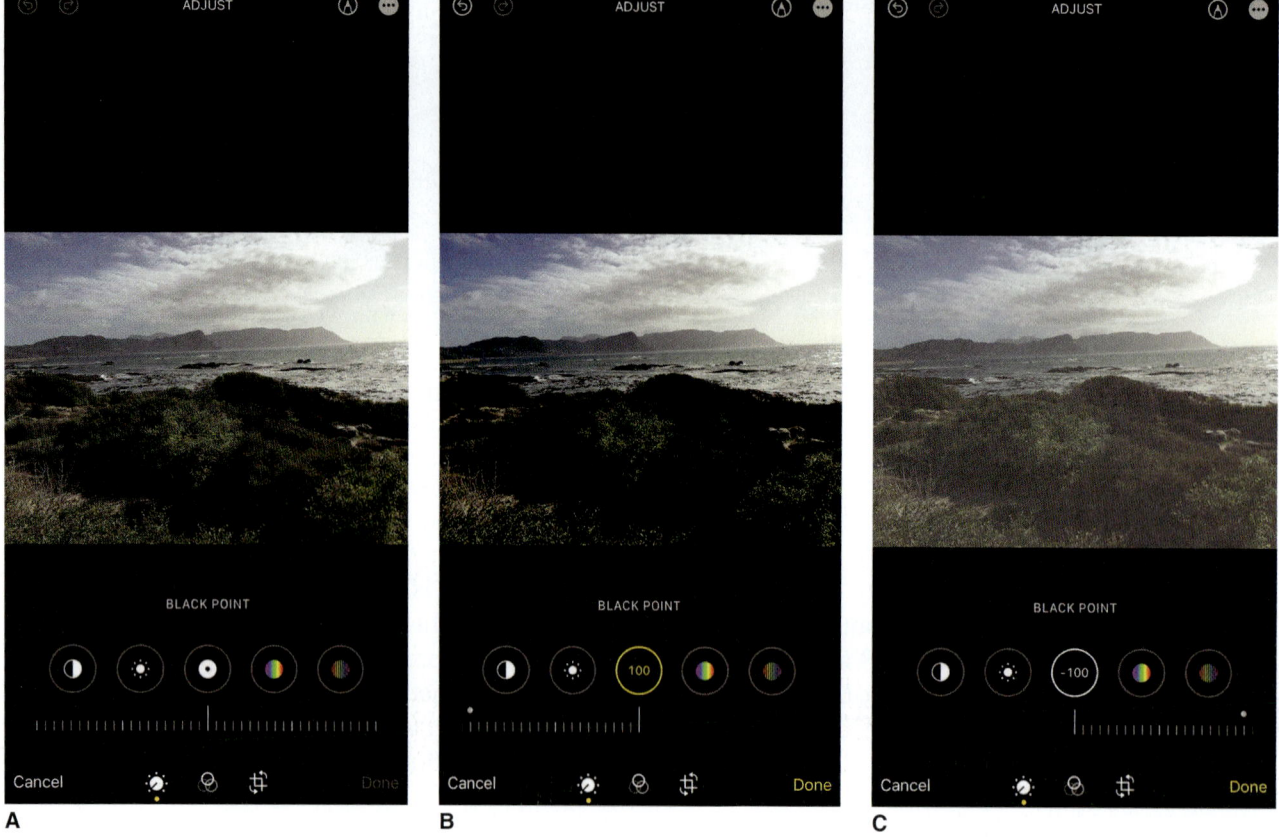

Goodheart-Willcox Publisher

Figure 21-30. Editing the black point can affect the mood of a photo. A—Original image. B—Image with a higher black point. C—Image with a lower black point.

To edit saturation, choose the photo you wish to edit from your gallery, select Edit, and then select the Saturation icon, **Figure 21-31**. Drag the slider to the right to increase the saturation and to the left to decrease the saturation, **Figure 21-32**. As with other adjustments, editing saturation can and often should be paired with other edits to maximize the effect.

Vibrance

Vibrance is an editing tool that increases the intensity or vibrancy of a muted color while leaving saturated colors unaffected. However, vibrance prevents the oversaturation of skin tones. Since this pairs with saturation, you may want to develop the habit of evaluating your photo's vibrance whenever you adjust the saturation to make sure your photo is still visually appealing. Editing vibrance is helpful when only some tones in your image need extra adjustments. If something in an image is too saturated, it tends to look fake and odd. Adjusting the vibrance gives more intensity only to the muted areas rather than the whole image.

To edit vibrance, choose the photo you wish to edit from your gallery, select Edit, and then select the Vibrance icon, **Figure 21-33**. Dragging the

Goodheart-Willcox Publisher

Figure 21-31. The Saturation icon is a circle filled with a rainbow gradient.

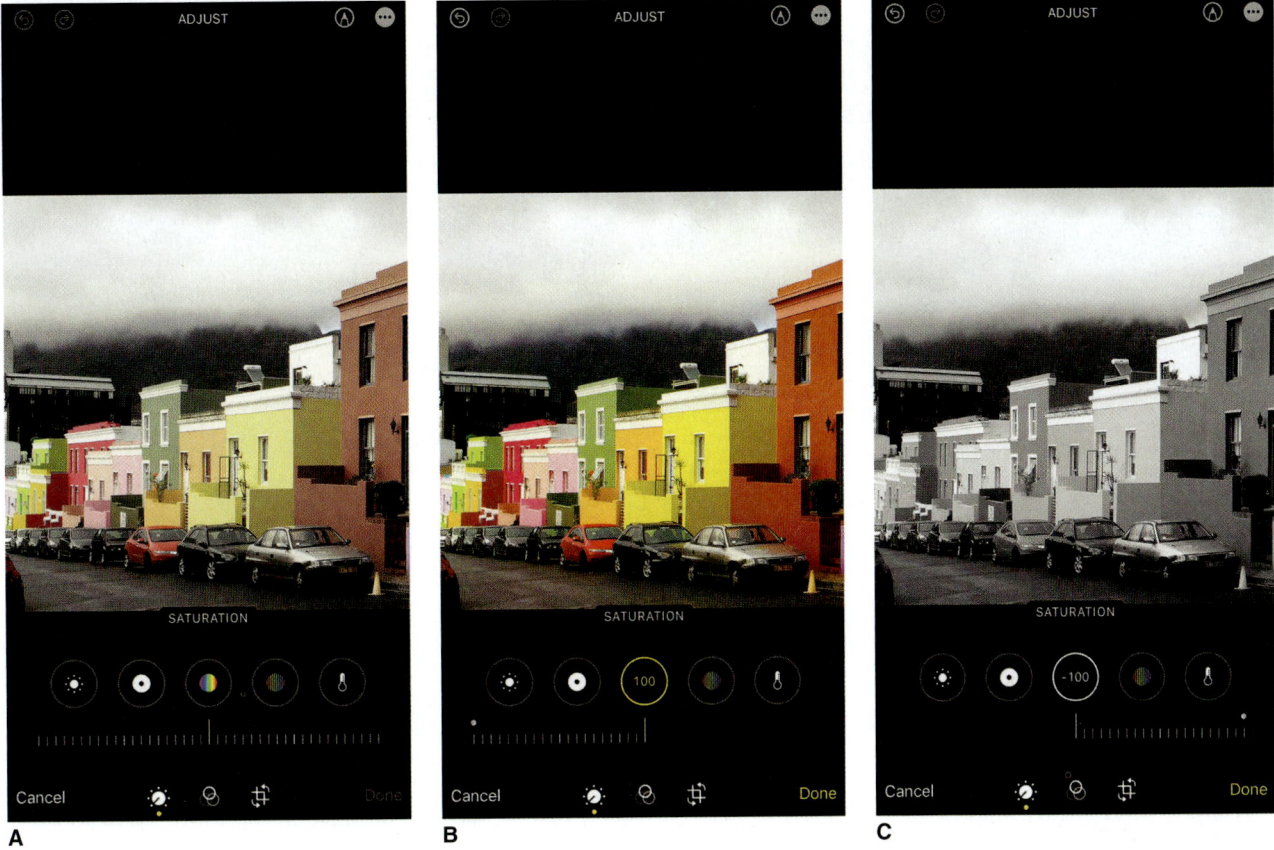

Goodheart-Willcox Publisher

Figure 21-32. Editing saturation can help an image pop. A—Original image. B—Image with increased saturation. C—Image with decreased saturation.

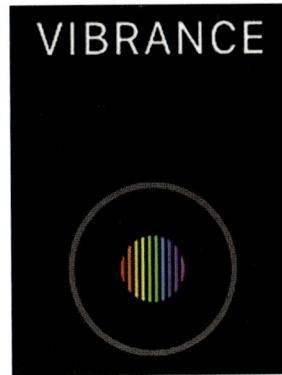

Goodheart-Willcox Publisher

Figure 21-33. The Vibrance icon is a circle filled with a hashed rainbow gradient.

slider to the right will increase the vibrance, which makes the more muted tones in your photo richer; dragging the slider to the left will decrease the vibrance, which makes the more muted tones in your photo less vivid, **Figure 21-34**.

Warmth

Warmth is an editing tool that boosts the red, orange, and yellow tones in an image while decreasing the blue tones. This can often help correct an improperly white balanced image or if an image looks too blue or too yellow. For example, if your phone's white balance did not adjust properly when going from indoors to outdoors, you can adjust the warmth to help make that correction.

To adjust the warmth of a photo, choose the photo you wish to edit from your gallery, select Edit, and then select the Warmth icon, **Figure 21-35**. Dragging the slider to the right will increase the warmth,

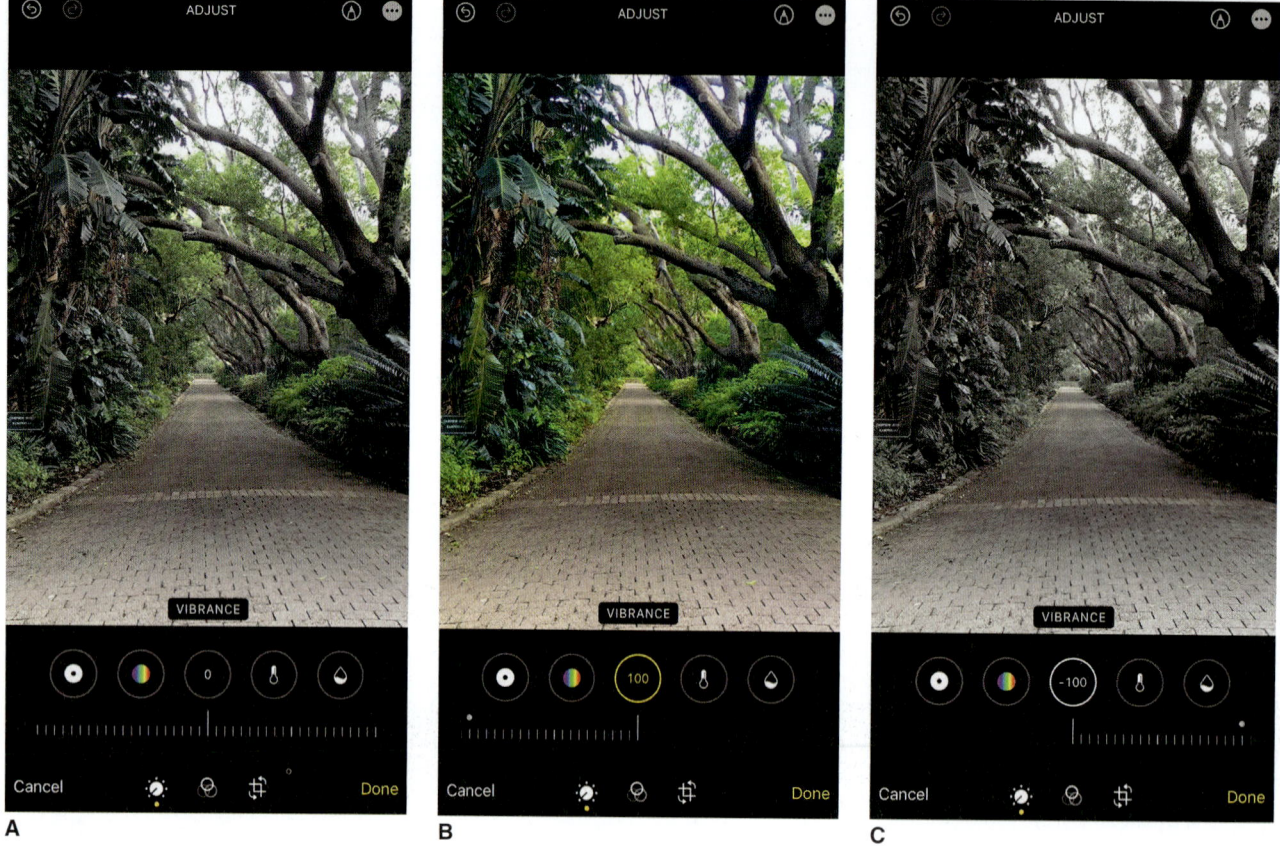

Goodheart-Willcox Publisher

Figure 21-34. Editing vibrance can provide liveliness to muted areas in a photo. A—Original image. B—Image with increased vibrance. C—Image with decreased vibrance.

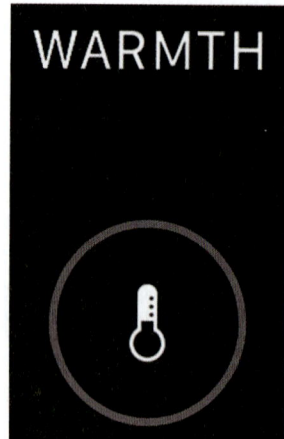

Goodheart-Willcox Publisher

Figure 21-35. The Warmth icon resembles an old-school thermometer.

and dragging the slider to the left will decrease the warmth, **Figure 21-36**.

Tint

Also referred to as *hue*, **tint** is an editing tool that adds a hint of color across an entire image. It can give photos a slight color cast, which is often blue, green, or red. This is only for slight adjustments, such as boosting the blues in a picture of the ocean. Any major tint additions or corrections should be done in other editing software.

To adjust the tint of an image, choose the photo you wish to edit from your gallery, select Edit, and then select the Tint icon, **Figure 21-37**. Moving the slider to the right will add more of a warm, reddish tint to the image, and moving the slider to the

540   Section 5   Postprocessing

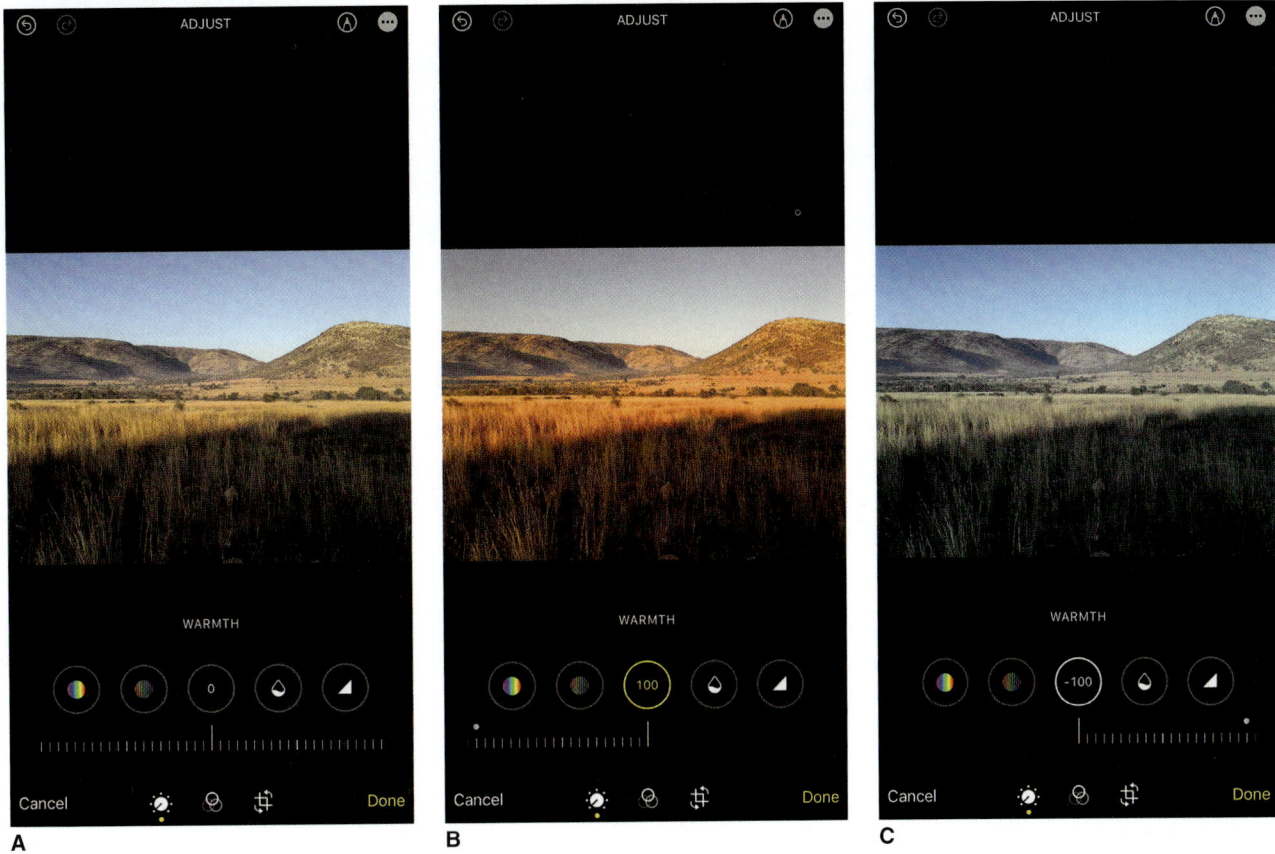

Figure 21-36. Editing warmth can often help correct an improperly white balanced photo. A—Original image. B—Image with increased warmth. C—Image with decreased warmth.

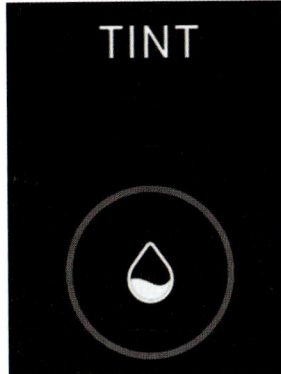

Goodheart-Willcox Publisher

Figure 21-37. The Tint icon looks like a raindrop, with half of it filled in and the other half open.

left will add more of a cool, blue tint to the image, **Figure 21-38**. Editing the tint of a photo often partners with editing the warmth.

Sharpness

Sharpness is an editing tool that adjusts the clarity of detail in a photo. It can also be used to emphasize texture. Sharpness adjusts the contrast between dark and light pixels along the edges of the subject in a picture. This then leads to highlighting the edges to make them stand out more. This is a useful edit if you want to separate your subject from any surrounding elements, such as the background.

To edit sharpness, choose the photo you wish to edit from your gallery, select Edit, and then select the Sharpness icon, **Figure 21-39**. Unlike other adjustments, you can only increase a photo's sharpness

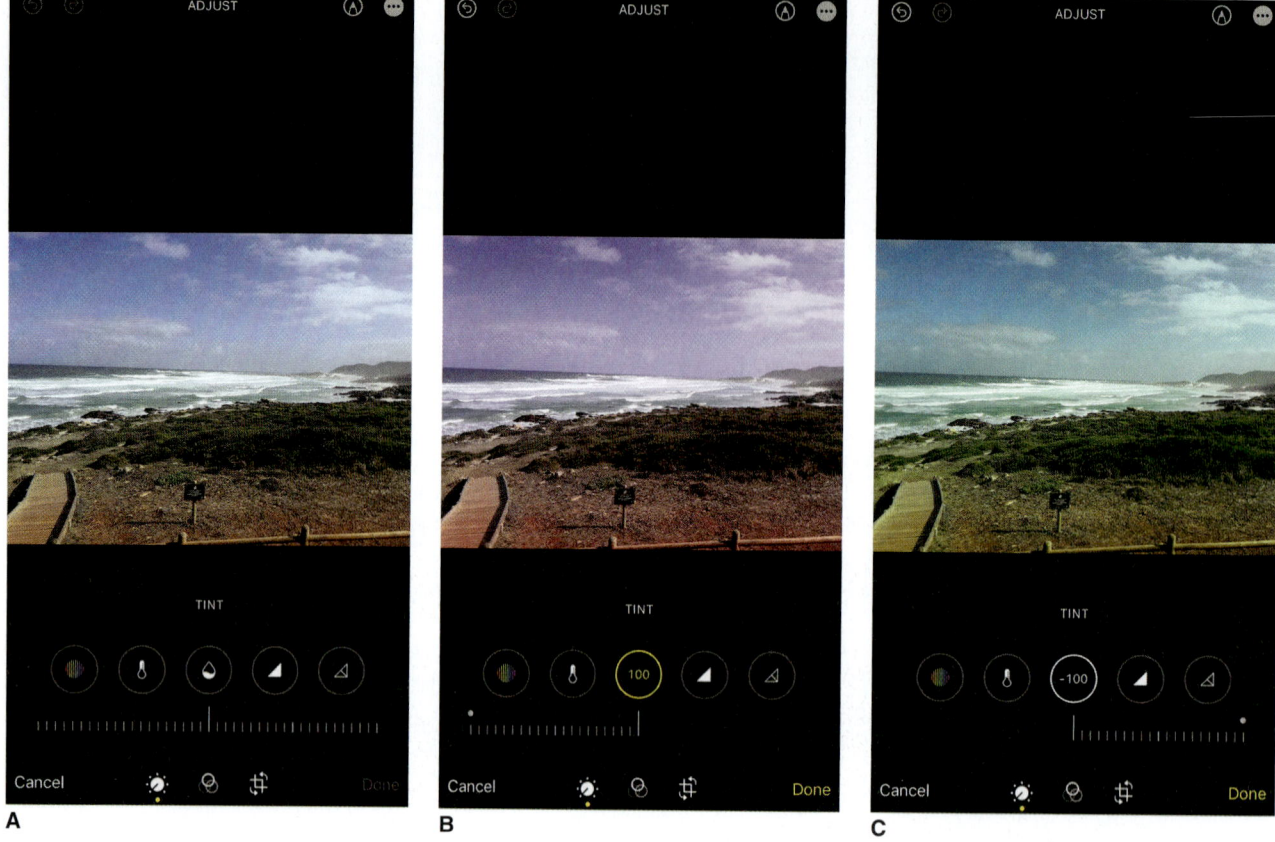

Figure 21-38. Editing tint is great for slight adjustments. A—Original image. B—Image with a warm, reddish tint. C—Image with a cool, blue tint.

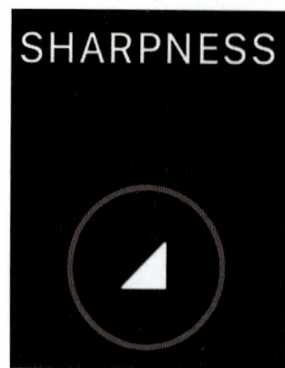

Figure 21-39. The Sharpness icon is a white right triangle.

(you cannot decrease it), **Figure 21-40**. Use caution when increasing sharpness, as oversharpening an image can make it look fake or overprocessed.

Definition

Definition is an editing tool that helps an image appear clearer by removing layers of haze. This could make the colors more saturated and slightly increase the contrast. This is great for providing a bit of extra clarity in your image.

To adjust the definition of an image, choose the photo you wish to edit from your gallery, select Edit, and then select the Definition icon, **Figure 21-41**. Like the sharpness adjustment, you can only increase the definition in your image, not decrease

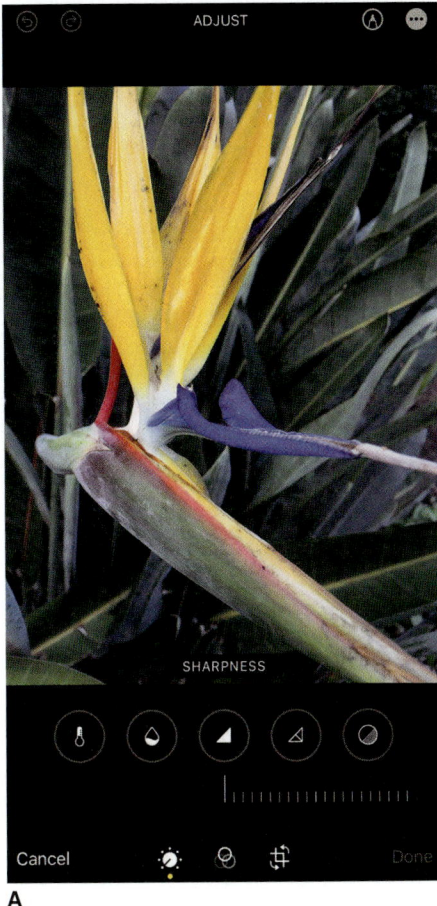 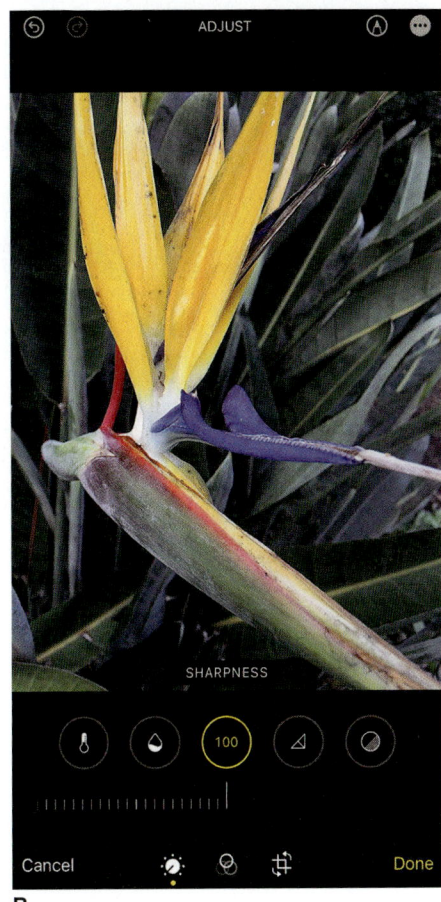

Goodheart-Willcox Publisher

Figure 21-40. Editing sharpness can help a subject stand out from the background better. A—Original image. B—Image with increased sharpness.

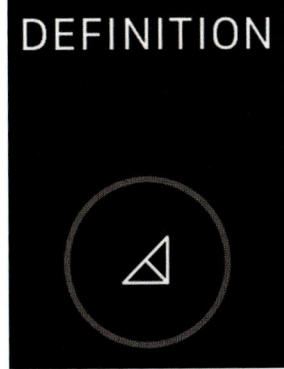

Goodheart-Willcox Publisher

Figure 21-41. The Definition icon is a right triangle with a white diagonal line drawn through it.

it, **Figure 21-42**. Definition is often adjusted when sharpness is adjusted.

Noise Reduction

Noise reduction is an algorithm used to decrease the *digital noise* (tiny light-colored spots especially noticeable in shadow areas of an image) in a photo, but it could over-soften other details if you are not careful. It is helpful when taking photos with low light and high ISO settings to help them appear less grainy.

To adjust noise reduction, choose the photo you wish to edit from your gallery, select Edit, and then select the Noise Reduction icon, **Figure 21-43**. Like sharpness and definition, it is only possible to increase the noise reduction value, not decrease it.

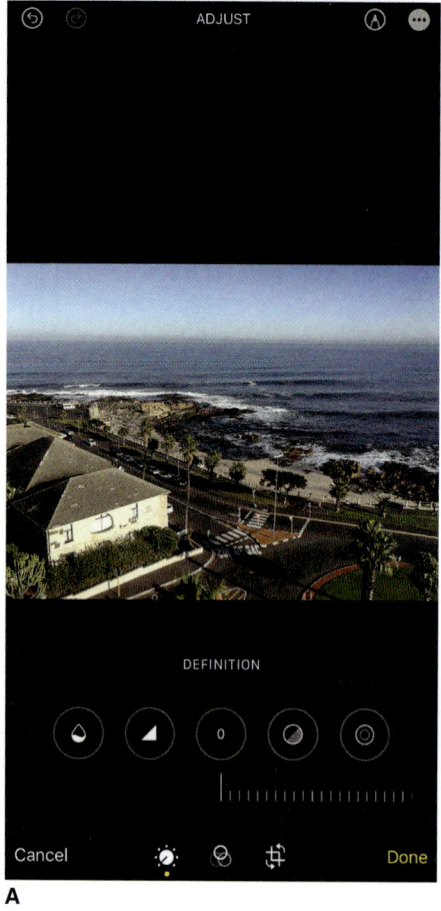
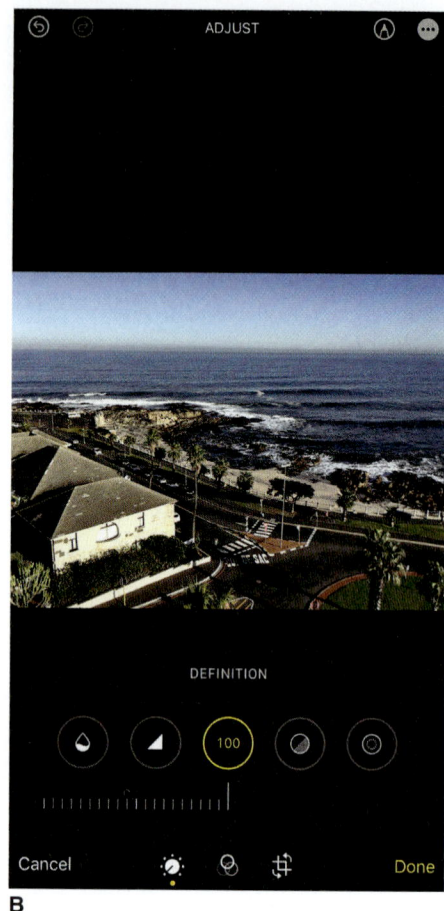

Figure 21-42. Definition can only be increased in a photo. A—Original image. B—Image with increased definition.

Goodheart-Willcox Publisher

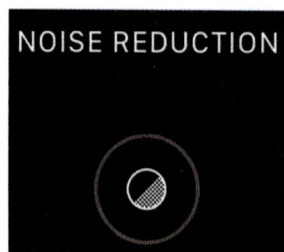

Goodheart-Willcox Publisher

Figure 21-43. The Noise Reduction icon is a circle cut in half diagonally. The left half is completely open, and the right half is filled with white crisscrossed lines.

Adjust as needed to help clarify your image but be careful not to overdo it so you do not accidentally lose details, **Figure 21-44**.

Vignette

A **vignette** is a dark border around the edge of a photo that can be used to draw a viewer's attention to a specific part of the photo. Vignettes darken the edges of a photo while leaving the center portion bright. This can often give photos a vintage look and/or direct viewers' attention to the brighter center.

To adjust vignette, choose the photo you wish to edit from your gallery, select Edit, and then select the Vignette icon, **Figure 21-45**. With the vignette

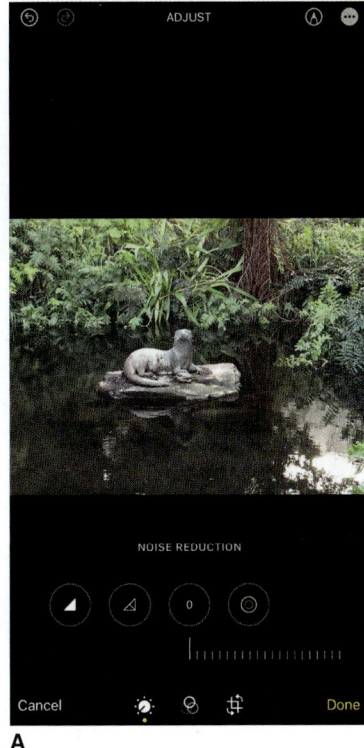
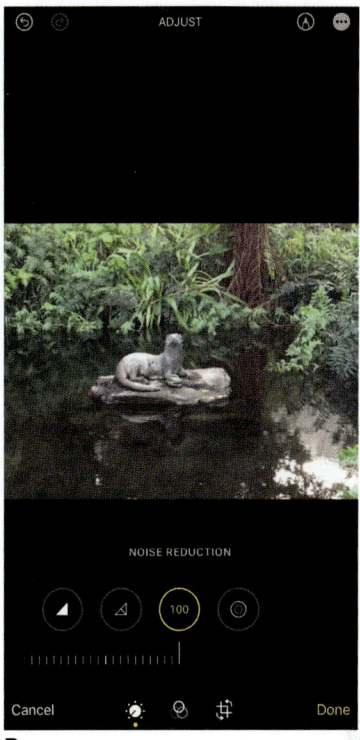

Goodheart-Willcox Publisher

Figure 21-44. Editing noise reduction can help decrease digital noise in a photo. A—Original image. B—Image with increased noise reduction.

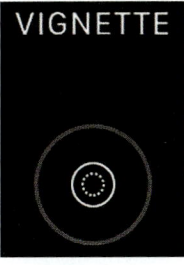

Goodheart-Willcox Publisher

Figure 21-45. The Vignette icon is a circle with a smaller, dotted circle inside it.

adjustment, **Figure 21-46A**, you can adjust the corners of your image to make them brighter or make them darker. To create a darker border for your image (like a traditional vignette), drag the slider to the right, **Figure 21-46B**. To brighten up the edges of your image, drag the slider to the left, **Figure 21-46C**.

Editing Using Third-Party Apps

Occasionally, there may be times when what you want to achieve in your photos is not possible by using your camera's native editor. If that is the case, there is a wide range of third-party apps that you can use to perform more precise or specific edits.

This section discusses how to use Adobe Lightroom for mobile, the phone version of the Lightroom editing software discussed previously in this book. They share the same functions, but some of the buttons are in different places in order to be more compatible with a mobile device. It is important to remember that you can sync your work across devices by using Adobe Creative Cloud. In other words, if you start editing a photo in Lightroom on your phone, you can open the same image in the same program on your computer to continue your work.

Basic Edits in Lightroom for Mobile

Lightroom for mobile offers the same functionality as Lightroom for desktop, which makes it easy to transfer your knowledge of the computer version to the mobile version. The first step is to import the photo you want to work on into the app itself. Once you allow the app access to the photos on your device, you can select which ones to import. To import a photo, click on the Add Photo icon at the bottom right of your screen, **Figure 21-47**, and select how you want to import your photos. Once your image is imported, you can begin editing it as you see fit. The following sections outline how to perform a few basic edits.

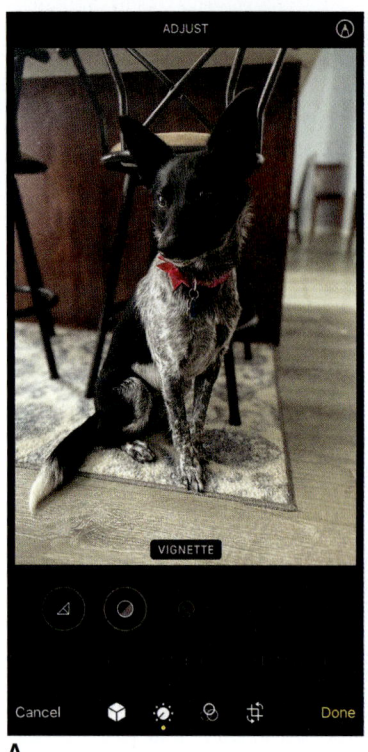 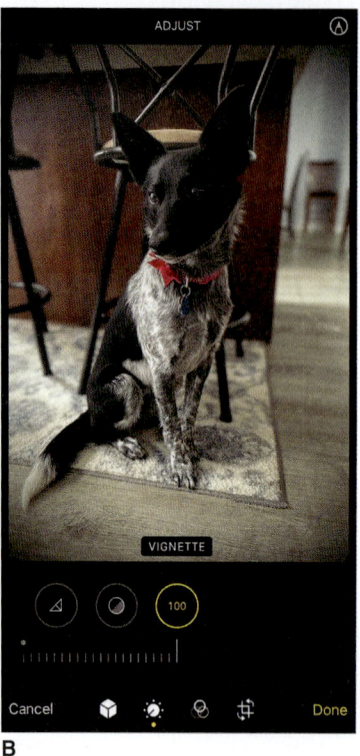 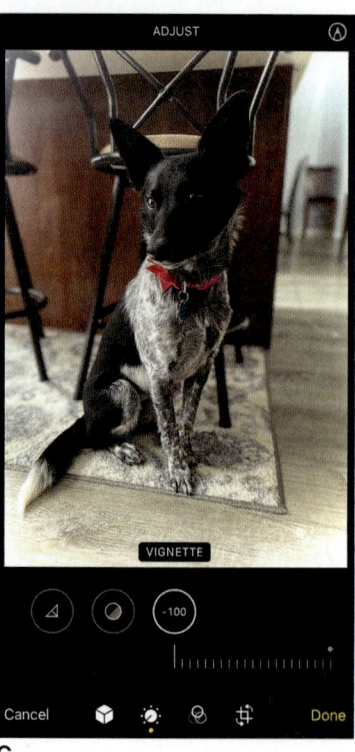

Goodheart-Willcox Publisher

Figure 21-46. A—Original image. B—Dragging the slider to the right will increase the dark vignette along the photo's borders, drawing the viewer's attention to the center. C—Dragging the slider to the left will create lighter edges on your photo.

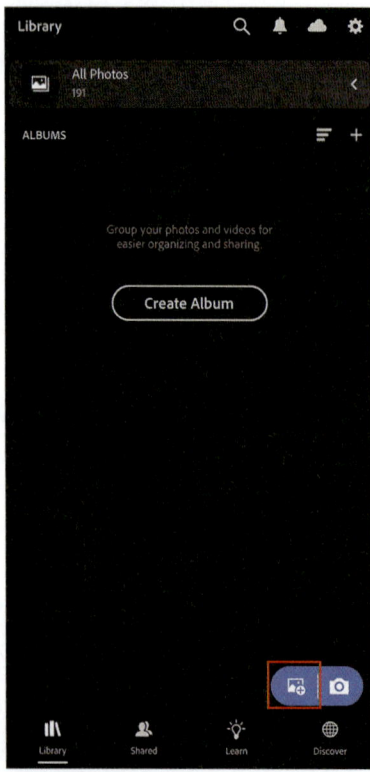 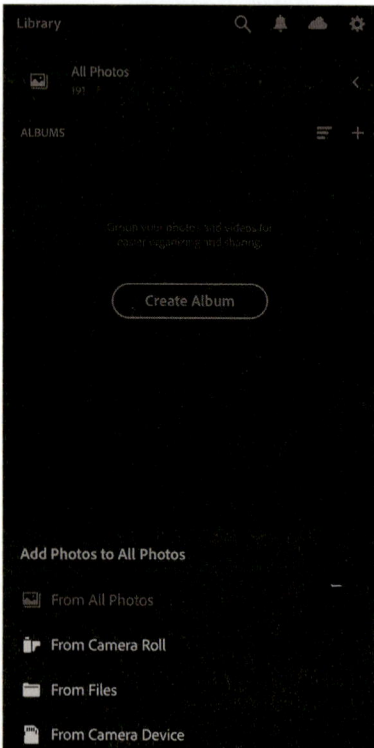

Goodheart-Willcox Publisher

Figure 21-47. To import a photo, select the icon at the bottom right of the screen and allow the app access to your camera roll. Select the photo or photos you want to edit.

546 Section 5 Postprocessing

Crop/Straighten

To crop or straighten an image, select the Crop icon at the bottom of the screen, **Figure 21-48**. Crop corners will appear at all corners of the photo and a level will appear at the bottom of the photo to help you straighten the image if needed, **Figure 21-49**.

Drag the corners to your desired placement. Notice that the cropped areas turn a light gray, leaving only your selection in full color, **Figure 21-50**.

To straighten an image, use your finger to slide along the level at the bottom until you are satisfied with what you see, **Figure 21-51**. If you are happy with your edits thus far, press the check mark at the bottom right of the screen. To discard the edits you have made, press the X at the bottom left of the screen, **Figure 21-52**.

If at any point you are unhappy with any of the edits you have made, you can always undo them using the back arrow at the top right of the screen, **Figure 21-53**.

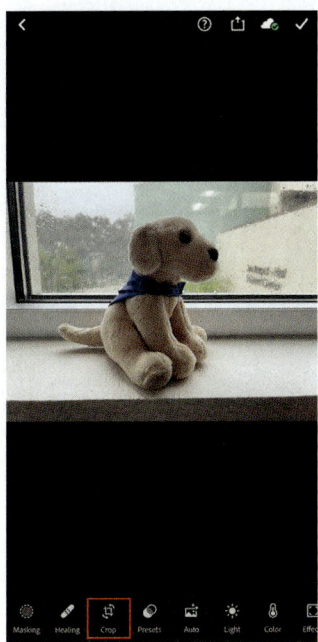

Goodheart-Willcox Publisher

Figure 21-48. Select the Crop icon at the bottom of the screen to crop or straighten your photo.

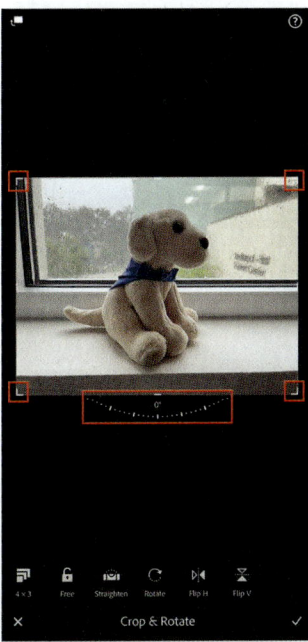

Goodheart-Willcox Publisher

Figure 21-49. Crop corners and a level will help guide you when cropping or straightening an image.

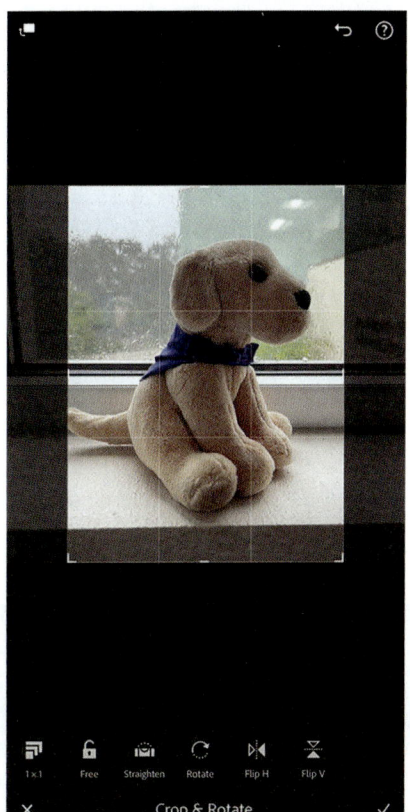

Goodheart-Willcox Publisher

Figure 21-50. Adjust the crop until you are happy with the result.

Lighting

Another basic edit you can do in Lightroom for mobile is adjust the lighting. To access this, select the Light option at the bottom of the screen, **Figure 21-54**. Options for adjusting Exposure, Contrast, Highlights, Shadows, Whites, and Blacks

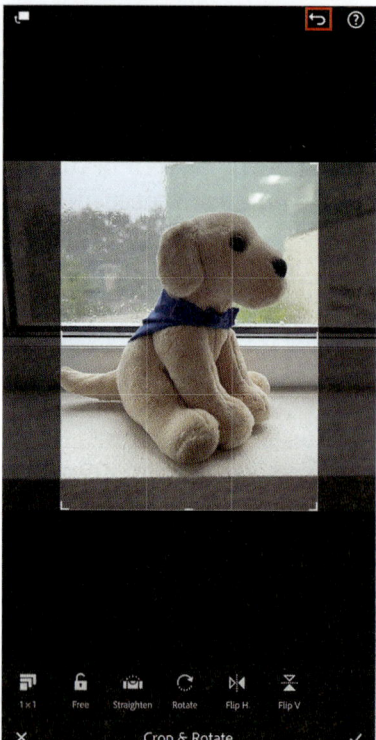

Goodheart-Willcox Publisher

Figure 21-53. The back arrow at the top right of the screen will undo whatever edit you just performed.

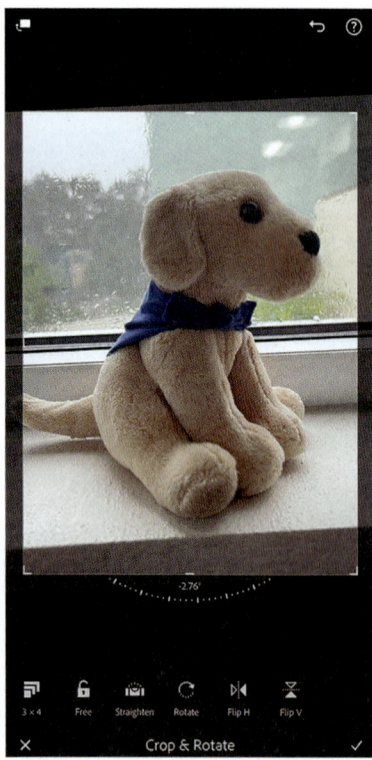

Goodheart-Willcox Publisher

Figure 21-51. To straighten your image, move your finger along the bottom level.

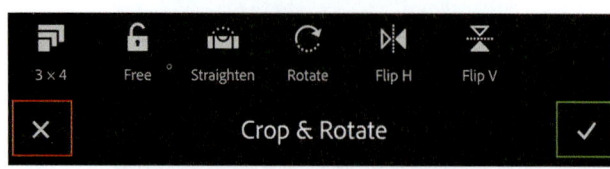

Goodheart-Willcox Publisher

Figure 21-52. To approve any edits, press the check mark at the bottom right of the screen (outlined in the green box). To reject any edits, press the X at the bottom left of the screen (outlined in the red box).

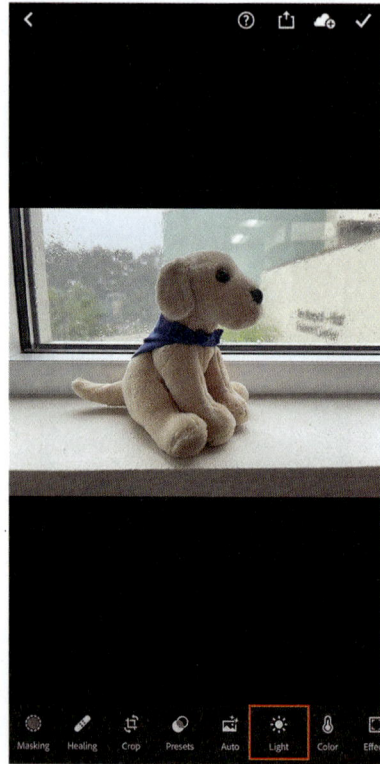

Goodheart-Willcox Publisher

Figure 21-54. To access the lighting adjustments, press the Light icon at the bottom of the screen.

548 Section 5 Postprocessing

with sliders will appear, **Figure 21-55**. To increase any of these values, slide the dot to the right; to decrease any of these values, slide the dot to the left, **Figure 21-56**. You also can use Curves to edit lighting in this app, **Figure 21-57**.

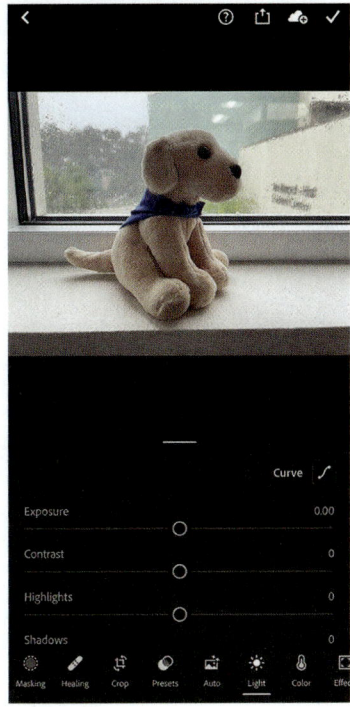 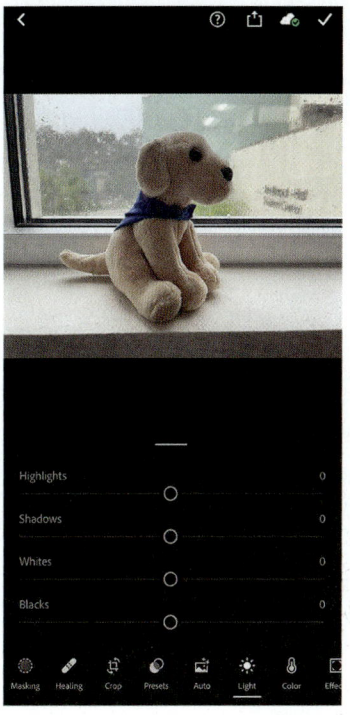

Goodheart-Willcox Publisher

Figure 21-55. You can adjust Exposure, Contrast, Highlights, Shadows, Whites, and Blacks by using sliders.

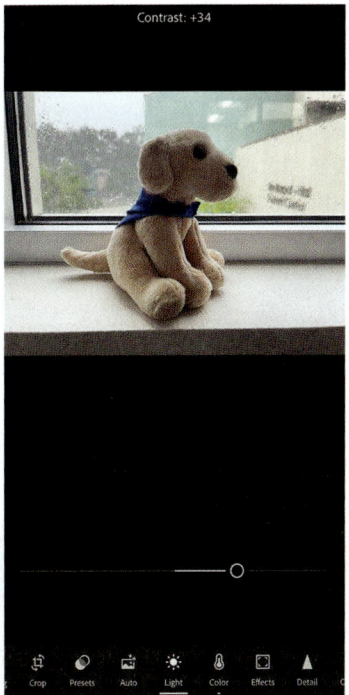

Goodheart-Willcox Publisher

Figure 21-56. To increase values, drag the slider to the right. To decrease values, drag the slider to the left.

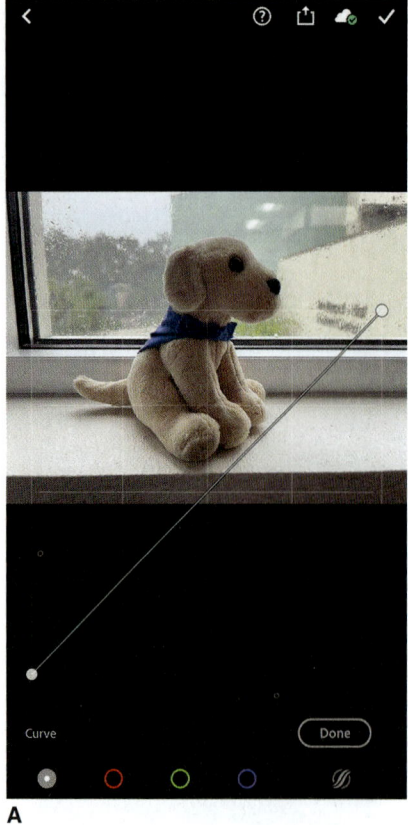
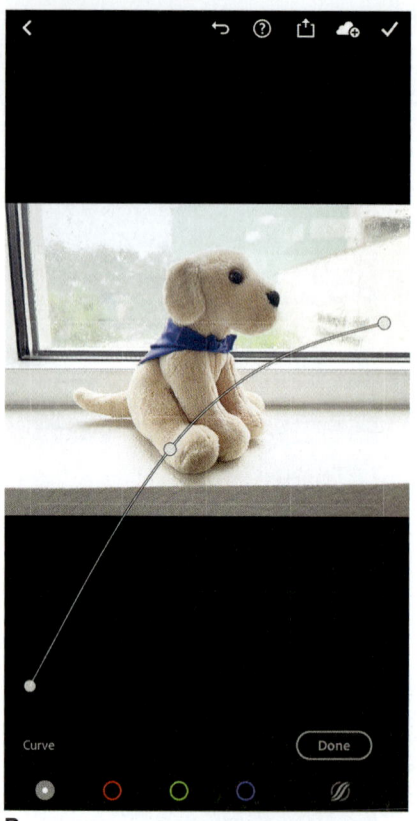

Goodheart-Willcox Publisher

Figure 21-57. You can adjust Curves in Lightroom for mobile. A—The default Curves for any image. B—Adjusting Curves to increase exposure.

PROCEDURE

Exporting for Presentation

Once you have finished editing a photo, the next step is to export it. Exporting in Lightroom for mobile is very straightforward and only takes a few steps:

1. Locate the Export icon at the top of the screen, **Figure A**.

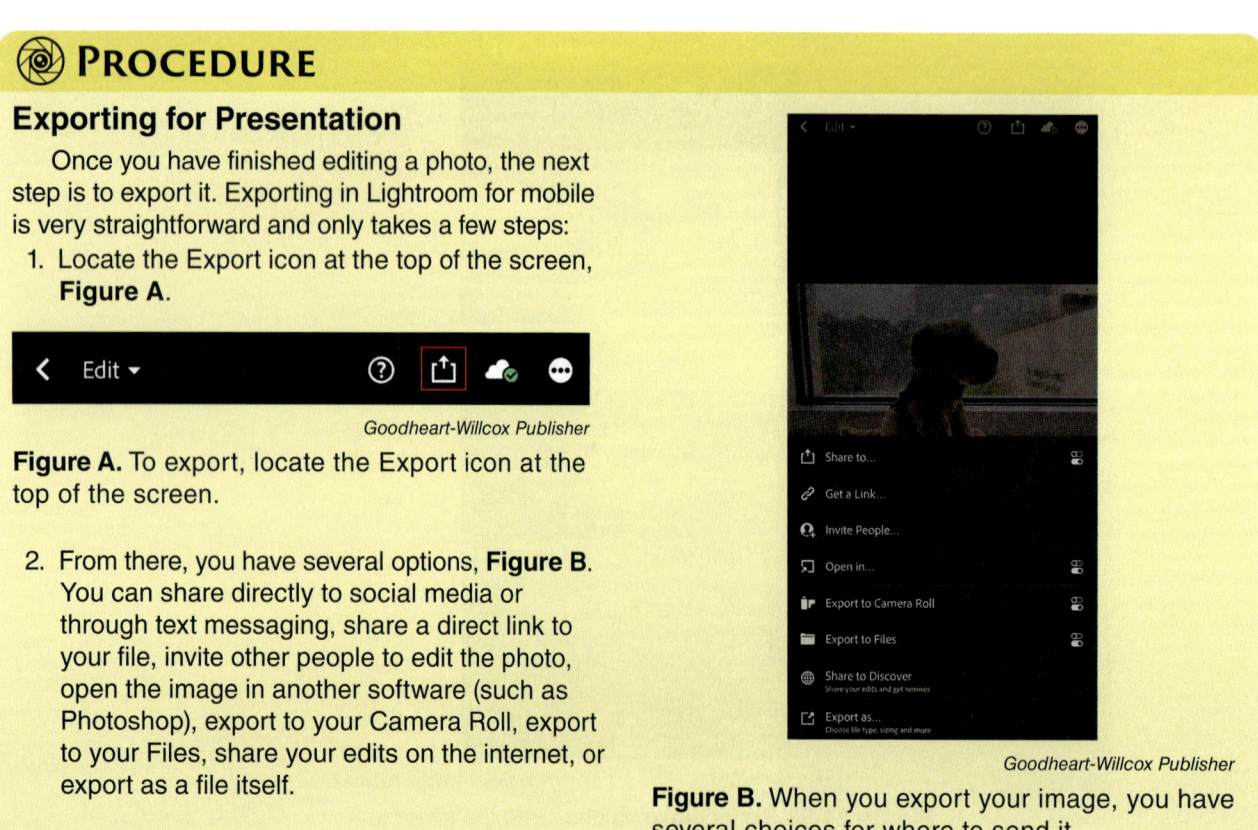

Goodheart-Willcox Publisher

Figure A. To export, locate the Export icon at the top of the screen.

2. From there, you have several options, **Figure B**. You can share directly to social media or through text messaging, share a direct link to your file, invite other people to edit the photo, open the image in another software (such as Photoshop), export to your Camera Roll, export to your Files, share your edits on the internet, or export as a file itself.

Goodheart-Willcox Publisher

Figure B. When you export your image, you have several choices for where to send it.

3. If you opt to export the image as a file, you will need to select a file type from the dropdown menu. You can choose the original format, JPG, TIF, or DNG, **Figure C**.

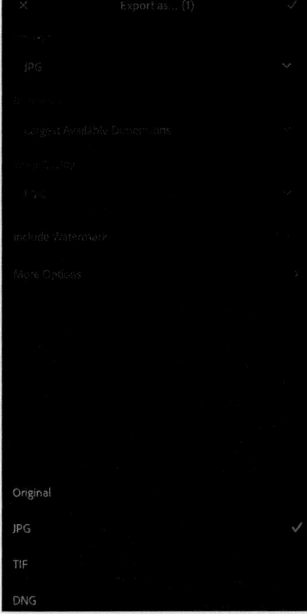

Goodheart-Willcox Publisher

Figure C. Select the file type for export from the resulting dropdown menu.

4. Next, adjust the dimensions, **Figure D**, and choose the image quality, **Figure E**.

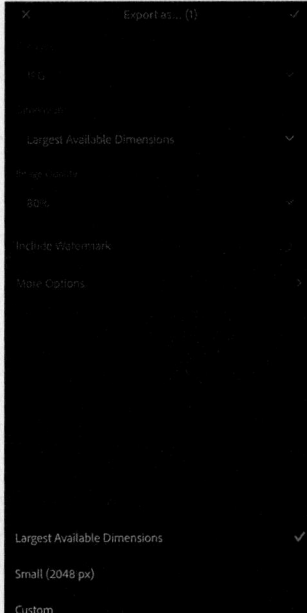

Goodheart-Willcox Publisher

Figure D. Adjust the dimensions to your specifications.

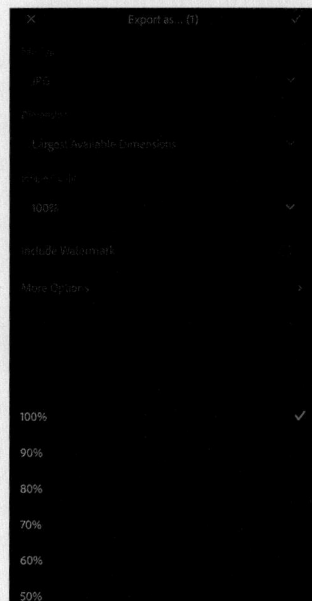

Goodheart-Willcox Publisher

Figure E. Select the image quality.

5. In More Options, you can include metadata, camera and camera raw information, location information, adjust the name of the file itself, adjust the output sharpening, and adjust the color space. It is up to you if you decide to adjust any of those values, **Figure F**.

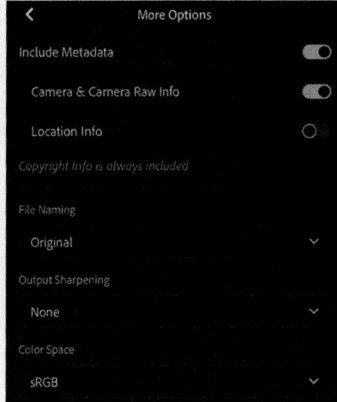

Goodheart-Willcox Publisher

Figure F. You can adjust any extra information as needed.

Once you have all these options set, select the check mark at the top right of the screen, **Figure G**. Your photo will render to export, and you have a choice of where to send your final file.

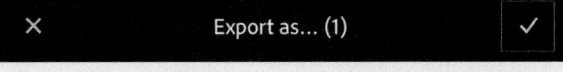

Goodheart-Willcox Publisher

Figure G. To export your final image, select the check mark at the top right of the screen.

Other Third-Party Editing Apps

Depending on your desired look, you may decide to download another third-party editing app that can meet your needs. Other popular third-party apps include ProCamera Raw, Picsart, and VSCO. These apps are free to download but often come with premium upgrades that you must pay for.

> **REAL-WORLD PHOTOGRAPHY**
>
> **Mobile Postprocessing Tips**
>
> While traditional digital postprocessing on a computer and mobile postprocessing on a smartphone have similar functionalities, they also have some fundamental differences. The following are some helpful tips that can help you when postprocessing your photos on a mobile device:
>
> - **Less is more.** Even though today's mobile cameras are far superior to early models, you are still relatively limited by the amount of light your camera can take in because of the sensors in your mobile phone. Because of this, there is only so much editing you can do to your image before it starts to lose its quality. A good example of this is cropping a photo. If you have your original image as a 16:9 aspect ratio and then edit it to a 4:3 aspect ratio, your image will be larger, but you will lose some of the quality. Additionally, if you start adjusting the exposure in your photos, you may end up washing out and losing details in your image.
> - **Save an original.** It is imperative that you save an original copy of your photo before you start editing. If you find mistakes later or if you simply do not like how your edits look after reviewing them more closely, you can always go back to the original and adjust from scratch.
> - **Back up your photos.** Whether it is on a computer, an SD card, or in some sort of cloud storage, you want to make sure you back up your photos. Once you lose a photo, it can be nearly impossible to recover. By having backups of your photos, you always have them in a safe place and have access to originals.

Posting to Social Media

A large part of taking and editing photos on your smartphone is the ability to post them online quickly and easily. You can edit your photos on a computer if you want, but many photographers find it more convenient to do it all on a mobile device since you do not have to worry about transferring files back and forth between devices.

Maximizing Reach on Popular Platforms

In many instances, social media platforms can be considered third-party editors because each platform offers different customizations. For instance, Instagram allows you to apply Instagram-only filters in varying degrees when posting a photo or video from your camera roll, in addition to making color corrections, crop edits, and other adjustments. Facebook allows you to add effects and adjust the brightness on photos you add to a status update. Other platforms have other options, so you must decide which one suits your needs best. These editing options can help you maximize your **reach**, or the total number of people who see your content.

If you edit in a third-party app and post the same image to all platforms, you can do that as well. Most photographers end up doing this or share their post from one platform to another. **Figure 21-58** provides a brief overview of a few of the most popular social media platforms and how you can maximize your reach.

> **REAL-WORLD PHOTOGRAPHY**
>
> **Ethical Implications of Editing Photos**
>
> Editing photos effectively is an art and takes a lot of practice. However, there are some ethical questions about the amount of editing that can or should be done to a photo. In some spheres (such as the art community), it is completely normal, if not encouraged, to edit photos to evoke a certain emotion or to achieve a specific aesthetic. In other areas (such as photojournalism), too much editing can be seen as deceptive because it alters the viewer's perception of what happened in a photograph. Other concerns revolve around altering a person's appearance, such as photoshopping physical attributes to make them look different from how they do in real life.
>
> If you decide to edit your photo in any capacity, you must be aware of the effects those edits might have on viewers or their perception of the photo. It is important not to intentionally misrepresent any individual or event through editing. Remember, you only have the right to manipulate and edit your own images since you own the intellectual

property to whatever images you take. If you are using someone else's work as inspiration for your own work, or even editing someone else's creation, you must obtain explicit consent. If you do not, you risk running into potential legal issues. Even if you are using bits and pieces of other people's photos to morph into a collage or as a template for your own work, remember that the intellectual property rights for the original image do not belong to you.

Printing Mobile Photos

Since the cameras on smartphones often rival those of digital cameras, you may want to have some images printed rather than keep them contained to your phone. There are a couple of options available for printing out mobile photos.

Personal Printer

Many people who enjoy mobile photography invest in small personal printers, **Figure 21-59**. They range in price from around $70 to $200 and are often small enough to fit in a bag. The trade-off with this is that the prints are often small because of the size of the printer. Not all small printers are the same, however. Some are significantly better in quality, so it is important to research different types before buying one.

Sending Off for Printing

If you do not mind waiting for your photos and/or prefer larger prints or other items (such as a canvas or mug), you may want to consider sending them off for printing. As discussed in Chapter 17, *Importing Images*, you can choose to send your photos to a commercial processor or online photofinishing site. It is incredibly convenient to send your mobile photos to these retailers through their specific apps available for download on your device.

Choosing the Right Paper

Like any other photo, mobile photos can be printed on different types of paper. The following are some of the most popular types:

- **Matte finish.** This choice is popular among professional photographers and those who want to elevate their photography. This paper maintains a texture that many photographers find desirable, and it reduces glare, which makes photos printed on this paper easy to display in a frame.

Social Media for Photography		
Platform	Potential Uses	Strategies for Maximizing Reach
Facebook	Building a business page Interacting with an audience	Consistent posting Interacting with other accounts/users Adding links to a portfolio or website
Instagram	Sharing photos and short videos Interacting with an audience Creating a visual feed	Consistent posting Using hashtags Determining your personal style
Twitter	Creating a brand identity Directing users toward a portfolio	Consistent posting Interacting with other accounts/users

Goodheart-Willcox Publisher

Figure 21-58. This table provides a brief overview of a few of the most popular social media platforms and strategies to maximize reach.

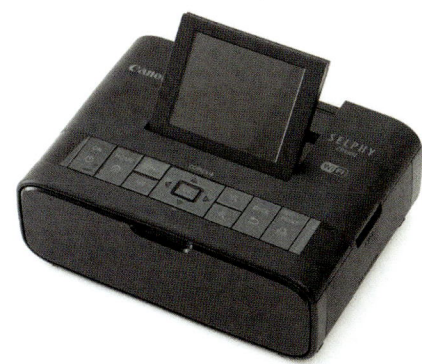

gd_project/Shutterstock.com

Figure 21-59. Small personal printers are relatively affordable and a great option for printing out mobile photos.

- **Glossy finish.** This paper creates a bright, shiny finish, and it provides great color and detail. Most photos that are printed out are printed on glossy paper by default, but they are prone to glare, especially when put in a frame.
- **Semi-matte finish.** Also referred to as *satin finish*, this is a popular option for many photographers. This provides the same color and detail as a glossy print, but it retains some texture and decreases the shininess of your photo, like a matte finish.
- **Luster finish.** Also known as *pearl finish*, this paper helps make the colors in your photo appear vibrant while retaining some texture. Many wedding photographers use this type of paper for prints.

It is also possible, and often desirable, to mat and frame printed mobile photos. You can mat and frame printed mobile photos just as you would photos taken with more traditional cameras. You may need to find specific materials depending on the size of the photo, but conventions are often the same.

PORTFOLIO ASSIGNMENT

On-the-Go Edits

For this assignment, you will edit three photos taken with a smartphone camera so they are display ready. You can use photos you already have in your camera roll, or you can take new ones for this assignment. The photos must meet the following criteria:

- One photo of scenery or a landscape
- One photo of an inanimate object
- One photo of a person

Once you have your photos, edit them using your phone camera's native photo editor. On every photo, you will need to perform the following basic edits:

1. Straighten the photos (if necessary).
2. Crop out any unnecessary elements in the photos.
3. Adjust the exposure in the photos.

After you have completed these edits, perform one of the following edits on each photo (one edit per photo):

1. Adjust the depth or height of one photo.
2. Adjust the brilliance of one photo.
3. Perform the Auto adjustment on one photo.

Once you have finished editing all three photos, write a sentence for each photo explaining why the specific edits made improved the photo overall. Add the photos and explanations to your portfolio.

Chapter 21 Review

Summary

- Mobile postprocessing is the process of editing photographs on a mobile device. It allows you to edit nearly anywhere and reduces the need for a desktop computer or laptop.
- If the plethora of image editing apps is overwhelming, you can always start with the basic functionality of the editor built into your device's native camera.
- Straightening an image is one of the most basic edits you can perform using the native camera app, and it is something you will probably do quite frequently.
- Crop is another basic edit used frequently. It is commonly used to focus on a specific area in a photo, to exclude unnecessary items in the frame, or to fit a photo to specific proportions.
- You can add filters to your photos directly in the native camera app on your phone. While the options are much more limited than the ones available in a separate app or platform, you can choose from an array of colored and monochrome filters.
- iPhone camera editors come with a feature called Auto. This feature applies various adjustments to an image to improve how it looks.
- Other common basic editing tools available in a phone's native editor include exposure, brilliance, highlights, shadows, contrast, brightness, black point, saturation, vibrance, warmth, tint, sharpness, definition, noise reduction, and vignette.
- There is a wide range of third-party apps that you can use to perform more precise or specific edits.
- Lightroom for mobile offers the same functionality as Lightroom for desktop, which makes it easy to transfer your knowledge of the computer version to the mobile version. Basic edits include cropping, straightening, and adjusting lighting.
- In many instances, social media can be considered a third-party editor since each platform offers different customizations.
- Since the cameras on smartphones often rival those of digital cameras, you may want to have some images printed rather than keep them contained to your phone.
- You can choose to print out your images yourself or send them to a commercial processor or online photofinishing site for printing.
- Like any other photo, mobile photos can be printed on different types of paper. It is important to choose the right type depending on your needs.

Review Questions

Answer the following questions using the information provided in this chapter.

Know and Understand

1. *True or False?* Mobile editing programs work well for more advanced edits.
2. *True or False?* You can toggle between the edited version and the original version of your photo when editing in the editor built into your device's native camera.
3. _____ is commonly used to focus on a specific area in a photo, to exclude unnecessary items in the frame, or to fit a photo to specific proportions.
    A. Straighten
    B. Crop
    C. Contrast
    D. Definition
4. The goal of the _____ adjustment is to make an image appear more like it does to your eye naturally rather than how it appears through a camera lens.
    A. auto
    B. exposure
    C. black point
    D. sharpness
5. *True or False?* Adjusting the exposure in a photo affects all tones, but it affects highlights the most.
6. Editing which of the following is great if you want to create more contrast and darken portions of your photo?
    A. Exposure
    B. Black point
    C. Vignette
    D. Shadows
7. _____ affects all tones in an image equally.
    A. Saturation
    B. Highlights
    C. Brightness
    D. Tint
8. *True or False?* Editing saturation is helpful when only some tones in your image need extra adjustments.
9. _____ is an editing tool that boosts the red, orange, and yellow tones in an image while decreasing the blue tones.
    A. Warmth
    B. Brilliance
    C. Vibrance
    D. Tint
10. *True or False?* Tint should only be used for slight adjustments.
11. _____ can be used to emphasize texture.
    A. Definition
    B. Sharpness
    C. Noise reduction
    D. Black point
12. A _____ is a dark border around the edge of a photo that can be used to draw a viewer's attention to a specific part of the photo.
    A. black point
    B. tint
    C. vignette
    D. filter
13. *True or False?* Lightroom for mobile offers the same functionality as Lightroom for desktop.
14. *True or False?* It is *not* possible to undo any of the edits you make in Lightroom for mobile.
15. _____ is the total number of people who see your content.
    A. Mobile postprocessing
    B. Posting
    C. Social media
    D. Reach
16. *True or False?* The trade-off with using personal printers is that the prints are often small because of the size of the printer.
17. Which type of paper is prone to glare, especially when put in a frame?
    A. Semi-matte finish
    B. Matte finish
    C. Glossy finish
    D. Luster finish
18. Which type of paper helps make the colors in your photo appear vibrant while retaining some texture?
    A. Matte finish
    B. Luster finish
    C. Glossy finish
    D. Semi-matte finish

Apply and Analyze

1. What is the difference between editing exposure and editing brightness?
2. What two issues can editing warmth help correct?
3. List the six items you can adjust in the More Options menu of Lightroom for mobile.
4. Why can social media platforms be considered third-party editors?
5. What are two main reasons why matte finish paper is popular among professional photographers?

Critical Thinking

1. How has our ability to take mobile photos affected society as a whole? Consider the implications of always having a camera within reach and the advent of social media.
2. With a group of three other students, think about ways in which specialty third-party photo editing apps expand your ability to edit mobile photos. Is there a significant difference between your native app editor and a third-party app?

Suggested Activities

1. Working in groups of three or four, imagine you are shooting with a DSLR camera when the battery dies, but you do not have a backup battery or place to charge the one you have. How would you proceed to take high-quality photos on your phone and edit them? Be sure to think through general composition and lighting, as well as how to overcome any limitations. If there are any conflicting ideas/disagreements while completing this activity, remember to use conflict-management skills to help get the group back on track.
2. Use the information in this chapter to do one of the following:
    A. Create a three-image photo carousel for Instagram that shows off your photography style. Include a caption and hashtags that will help maximize your reach.
    B. Write a plan to create a Facebook page that showcases your photography business. Think through how often you should post and what you should post to bring in clients.
    C. Compose a 280-character tweet for Twitter to help promote your need for models for an upcoming photo shoot.

Communicating about Photography

1. **Speaking.** Working in a group, brainstorm ideas for creating classroom tools (posters, flash cards, and/or games, for example) that will help your classmates learn and remember the different editing features in the native camera app on a smartphone. Choose the best idea(s), and then delegate responsibilities to group members for constructing the tools and presenting the final products to the class.
2. **Speaking and Listening.** In groups of three students, choose an edit you can perform using the native camera app, such as adding filters, brilliance, saturation, or tint. Explain the edit in a PowerPoint presentation to the class. Take notes while other students give their presentations. Ask questions about any details that you would like clarified.

Section 5 Project

Postprocessing and Displaying Photos

In this final section project, you will edit a few of the images you have taken for the Section 4 project. You will import your photos to edit them in either Adobe Photoshop or Lightroom, export them to post on a social media platform of your choosing, and include them in your portfolio. These photos should also be ready to put on display, either in a home or in a gallery. This project has three parts.

Part 1

Choose three of the final photos you submitted for the Section 4 project. Import the three photos you selected into an image editing software of your choosing, such as Photoshop or Lightroom.

On each photo, you will perform general edits before moving on to more transformative edits. Perform the following on each image:

- Crop and straighten as necessary
- Adjust the exposure and contrast
- Adjust the white balance
- Remove any imperfections (if present)
- Sharpen the image by adjusting the color and clarity

After you have made your general edits, perform each of the following more complex edits:

- Convert one photo to black-and-white
- Leave one photo with the general edits performed previously
- Remove one element from one photo that is not your main subject (such as removing a person from the background or a tree from the foreground)

Part 2

Once you have edited each photo, think about how they should be presented. Consider the following questions:
- Should they be displayed in a frame or posted online?
- If they should be printed, how should they be printed? As a standard print or on a specific type of material (such as canvas or metal)?
- Would the photos work best individually or as a collage?

With these questions in mind, describe how each photo should be displayed. For any framed photo, be sure to include the type of frame, the color, and any matting should you choose to use it.

Part 3

Review the photos that are part of your portfolio. Choose three to submit for a display in an art gallery for your class. Submit these to your instructor with your plans for mounting, matting (if applicable), and framing, so they can help choose the best one to submit for display.

Appendix
Film Basics and Safety

Introduction to Film Basics and Safety

Most photography today has shifted into the digital realm, but there is still a significant group of photographers, both professional and hobbyist, that choose to use film for their photography. Some photographers shoot with film for aesthetic reasons, and others shoot with film because they enjoy it as a hobby and take pleasure in the development process. While working with film can be fun, it comes with a need for safety procedures because the development of film photographs involves chemicals that are potentially harmful or dangerous.

Basic Film Safety

When it comes to developing film, there is a myriad of toxic chemicals that you need to be careful with when working with them. While these chemicals are perfect for bringing out film photos, they can be harmful if they get on your skin or in your eyes. It is essential to familiarize yourself with darkroom safety procedures as well as how to follow emergency procedures so you can minimize any side effects if you do happen to get a harmful chemical on your skin or in your eyes. Some of these include wearing specialized gloves, storing chemicals in proper containers and at proper temperatures, and having access to a water source to help wash your skin or flush your eyes if exposed.

Working with Chemicals

Large-scale users of photographic chemicals, such as commercial developing labs, must dispose of chemical wastes under Environmental Protection Agency (EPA) regulations. Home darkrooms are not subject to these regulations, but local governments often have regulations that apply to any material being discharged into the sewer system.

The key to proper disposal of home darkroom chemicals is dilution. Most photographic solutions are nontoxic in the concentrations normally used, and further diluting them with plenty of water makes them even less likely to cause harm. Once all the solution has been poured out and the container rinsed, let the water continue to flow for a minute or so to clear any residue out of the sink trap.

When working with photographic chemicals, follow proper chemical handling procedures and wear appropriate protective equipment. When mixing any acid with water to make a dilute solution, always pour acid into water; never pour water into acid. This eliminates the possibility of a violent reaction that could splatter acid onto your skin or into your eyes.

If a photographic chemical is splashed in your eyes, immediately flush your eyes with clean, lukewarm tap water. Continue flushing for at least 20 minutes. Do not rub your eyes. If you wear contact lenses, they may be flushed out by the water. If not, remove them. Then, thoroughly wash and rinse your hands to remove any chemical residue. Seek medical attention as soon as possible after flushing your eyes. Tell medical personnel the name of the chemical or bring the chemical container with you.

Chemical Spills

A major chemical spill is an emergency and must be handled immediately and appropriately. A major chemical spill is defined as a spill where one or more of the following is true: a large amount of chemical was spilled, an uncontrolled reaction occurred (such as a fire), an unknown or unidentified chemical was spilled, a small amount of a high-hazard chemical was spilled, or you or another person were seriously injured. If this happens, you must evacuate the area as soon as possible and report the spill to the proper authorities. You will need to detail what happened, including where it happened, the materials that were spilled, how much was spilled, what you did immediately after the spill, and if there were any injuries.

Special Printing Techniques

Many approaches to printing can be taken with technique, materials, or both. Two examples will be discussed in the following sections.

Bleaching

Selective bleaching chemically alters prints. A dilute solution of a reducing agent is applied to areas of the print, lightening them for emphasis or for better balancing of tones. Usually, a 1:10 dilution (1 part of solution and 10 parts of water) provides good control of the bleaching action. While you are working with the bleaching solution, make sure to wear safety goggles and safety gloves. The gloves need to be nitrile gloves, not latex gloves, because latex gloves do not provide consistent protection. Ensure that the gloves do not have any holes in them before use. You will also need tongs and a face mask to prevent inhalation of chemicals.

If you manage to get bleach in your eyes while working with your diluted solution, follow the proper procedure for flushing out your eyes that was detailed previously. Make sure to wash your eyes thoroughly and then seek medical attention to prevent any damage to your eyes.

Toning

Toning is a chemical process that changes or intensifies the color of a black-and-white print. The most common toning colors are a yellowish-tan to brown color called *sepia*, blue, and the slightly purple tone that results from selenium toner.

When performing toning work, pay special attention to ventilation and to avoiding contact with the solutions. Many toning chemicals produce gases with unpleasant odors; these gases are potentially dangerous in a confined space without sufficient ventilation. Some toning materials, especially selenium, can be toxic if absorbed through the skin. Always wear rubber gloves or use tongs to handle prints while toning. Wear goggles or safety glasses with side shields to protect the eyes against splashes. Since toning solutions stain clothing, a plastic or rubber apron is recommended. As with other chemicals, if you manage to get any of the solution on your skin, wash yourself quickly and thoroughly, and seek medical attention if necessary.

Selecting a Printing Paper

Even though most photos today are kept in a digital format, there will be photos you take that you want to display in your home or submit to a gallery. One of the most important aspects of printing a photo for display is selecting the paper on which it is printed. Different papers have different textures and finishes that can alter the way a photo looks. While you have several different choices available to you at a professional lab, you can also make prints on your own as long as you have the right paper and the right printer.

Printers

If you want to print your photos yourself, it is a good idea to invest in a photographic printer. These printers are specifically geared toward making quality photo prints. They are usually, but not always, inkjet printers. They are also able to support a wide range of sizes for photo paper and print in a wide range of colors. This is because they have more color cartridges, meaning the ink can be mixed to create a larger range of colors. Numerous cartridges also give the printer the ability to provide depth to black-and-white photos.

Finish

One of the most important considerations when selecting a printing paper is the surface finish of the paper. Before you choose a paper, you must decide how you want your final photo to look. Do you want it to have a matte appearance, or do you want it to appear glossy?

Matte paper is the most like traditional art papers and prints, and some even have texture to them that can add to the appearance of your printed photo. Additionally, matte photos do not show fingerprints or other marks from handling. Papers with a glossy finish are the most common when it comes to photographic prints. The glossy paper can show off saturated blacks and vibrant colors to make your photos stand out and make them appear crisp to the viewer. Luster paper is a hybrid between matte and glossy. It typically has a light reflexivity to it and has a little bit of texture. Like glossy papers, luster paper can show off dark blacks and bright colors and has the texture to show off elements in the picture. It also lacks the glare that is common among glossy prints, and it does not lack contrast like some matte prints. Many photographers prefer luster paper for their prints for these reasons.

Materials and Coatings

When selecting a printing paper for photographic prints, you must also consider the material and coating of the paper. You may hear several different terms, and this can make choosing the right paper more difficult. Different paper materials can affect the finish of your print, and coatings affect how the ink adheres to the paper you choose. The following are some materials you may come across:

- **Alpha cellulose.** One of the most used materials, this is a less expensive alternative to cotton rag. It is made from high-quality wood pulp and can provide similar results to its more expensive counterpart. Most photographers will choose alpha cellulose if they want to make high-quality prints to display in a more relaxed setting, such as their home.
- **Cotton rag.** Considered a higher grade, cotton rag is similar to alpha cellulose. However, it is more expensive. Cotton rag, also known as *cotton fiber*, is a popular choice when printing photos for display in a gallery or selling them.
- **Canvas.** Considered a classic choice, canvas helps give prints a unique look. Canvas is most often used for gallery displays because it can outlast paper, and the material itself is very durable. However, the texture of the canvas has the potential to detract from the image printed on it.
- **Rice.** Similar to canvas, rice paper creates a unique look for your prints. It can make a photo seem nostalgic due to the way the texture absorbs the colors of the print.

The following are some coatings you may come across:

- **Baryta.** Baryta is used to replicate traditional darkroom prints because of the color intensity that it gives to the image even though it is typically used for monochrome photos. Baryta coating gives a photo richer blacks and highlights details in the photo. This coating is made of barium sulphate and is applied before the paper is coated with other chemicals. Typically, this is applied to cotton rag or alpha cellulose papers to be used in an inkjet printer.
- **Metallic.** Metallic coatings add a shiny, metallic sheen to papers and can help make prints appear bright. This is great if you want to add a subtle brilliance to your printed photos.

Other Considerations

There are various other factors that go into the appearance of printing papers. They are as follows:

- **Weight.** Weight is defined as the heft of paper, often expressed in grams per square meter (gsm). A paper's weight does not influence the overall quality of the printed image. A heavier paper has a higher gsm and is less prone to deterioration or defects over time, so it tends to be used for prints that need to last for a long time. Lighter paper does not necessarily deteriorate over time, but since it is not as sturdy as heavier paper, it is more prone to damage. However, it is typically less expensive than heavier paper.
- **Thickness.** Thickness is defined as how thick a sheet of paper is, expressed in mils (thousandths of an inch). The thicker a paper is, the more rigid and sturdy it is. This is generally a representation of how dense a piece of paper is, which may be an important factor if you want to make prints that will last a long time and can sustain some minor damage.

- **Brightness.** The brightest part of an image is affected by the overall brightness of the selected paper. It also affects the dynamic range of a photo. Paper brightness is measured on a scale of 0 to 100 and determines how much light is reflected off the surface of the paper. The higher the number, the brighter the paper.
- **Whiteness.** Whiteness is the amount of red, blue, and green reflectance that your eyes can see when viewing a piece of paper. It can be warmer if the paper reflects more red tones (a lower percentage) and cooler if it reflects more blue tones (a higher percentage). The overall color of a printed image is determined by the whiteness of the paper itself.
- **Opacity.** Opacity is defined as how much light shows through a sheet of paper. Most photographic paper is opaque to prevent details from showing through, especially when printed on.

Glossary

A

abstractionism. A school of photographic thought that places strong emphasis on forms and their relationships. (1)

active autofocus. A focusing system in which a beam of infrared light is emitted to bounce off the subject. The system times the interval between the departing and returning burst of light, calculates the distance, and focuses the camera to that distance. (5)

active layer. In an image editing program, the layer to which changes can be made. (18)

additive color process. A color reproduction method used with transmitted light in which the additive primaries (red, blue, and green) interact to create all other colors. (7)

additive primary colors. The colors red, green, and blue. When added together in equal parts, they create the color white. (18)

adjustment layer. In an image editing program, a special-purpose layer that allows changes to be made to an image's appearance without permanently altering the original image pixels. (18)

Adobe RGB. A color space that was developed by the manufacturer of Photoshop and other graphics software. (4)

advanced compact digital camera. A camera that has many of the same features as SLR cameras, except for interchangeable lenses. Cameras in this category have extended zoom ranges and often include image stabilization to counteract camera shake. (5)

ambient lighting. The lighting that already exists in a scene or space, without any additions. (11)

ambrotype. A glass negative placed over a black backing material that changed the appearance of the negative into a positive so it resembled a daguerreotype. (2)

analog signal. A continuous signal in which the electrical charges vary in strength. (8)

anchor points. Control points set by clicking the mouse while making a selection using the **Pen** tool. (19)

angle of view. How much of an image in front of the camera and its lens will be captured by the camera's sensor. (6)

aperture. The size of the opening through which light passes to strike the camera's image receiver. (5, 7)

aperture priority. An exposure mode in which the photographer selects the aperture setting, and the camera sets a shutter speed based on its meter reading. (4)

APS-C size sensor. A sensor approximately 24 mm × 16 mm, used in most digital compact, mirrorless, and prosumer DSLRs. (5)

archival quality. A term applied to photographic prints that are processed with the intent of achieving very long life. (20)

archival-quality disc. A CD or DVD made with materials designed to preserve image files for literally hundreds of years. (17)

area array. A grid made up of rows and columns of electronic sensors. (8)

aspect ratio. The relationship between the width and height of an image. (16)

astigmatism. The inability of a lens to bring horizontal and vertical lines of the subject into sharp focus at the same time. (6)

atmosphere. A quality of a photograph that projects a sense of place and time. (10)

attribution. Giving proper credit to the person who created an image. (17)

Note: The number in parentheses following each definition indicates the chapter in which the term can be found.

Autochrome process. The first practical form of color photography, in which fine grains of colored potato starch were applied to a plate covered with wet varnish. The plate was then coated with varnish for a second time, another layer of starch was added, and then the plate was coated with an emulsion. After exposure and development, it produced a viewable color image. (2)

B

backdrop. A background photographers use when taking pictures. They vary in material, color, and scenery. (15)

back focus. The distance from the rear element of the lens to the image receiver. (6)

background light. The light that provides sufficient visual separation between the subject and the background and helps create visual interest in an image. (10, 15)

backlit. A descriptive term for a subject that has most of the light coming from behind it. (7)

backup copy. A duplicate set of image files downloaded to a flash drive, portable hard drive, laptop, or cloud-based storage system to guard against possible loss of the originals. (14)

ball head. A tripod head that uses a single control to lock the camera in position. (4)

barn doors. Hinged rectangular flaps of black-painted metal attached to the front of a lighting instrument. The flaps can be adjusted to physically block a portion of the light being emitted. (15)

barrel distortion. A type of distortion in which a rectangular image has outward-bulging sides. (6)

bit depth. A numeric expression of the number of shades of gray a pixel is capable of displaying. (8)

black point. The darkest part of an image, at which black areas of an image become completely black and no details can be seen. (21)

blocked shadows. Underexposed, featureless areas of an image that occur when there is not enough light on a subject. (11)

blocking. The process of studying a subject's positions to frame and light shots properly. (10)

bounce flash. A method of softening and diffusing flash light reaching a subject by first bouncing it off something else, such as a ceiling or wall. (12)

brightness. 1. The quality or state of giving out or reflecting light. 2. An editing tool that adjusts how light an image appears. (10, 21)

brilliance. An editing tool that brightens shadows, adjusts contrast, and tones down highlights to help make an image appear more vibrant or rich. (21)

broad lighting. A lighting style that highlights the broad side of a subject's face, or the side that is closer to the camera, by placing light on the same side. (10)

browsing. A function of database programs that allows the user to view a number of small images (thumbnails) on the screen at one time. (17)

buffer. Internal memory in a camera that functions as a holding tank for image information that has been processed but not yet transferred to a memory card. (8)

buffered. A descriptive term for mounting boards that are made slightly alkaline to counter the long-term effects of weak airborne acids. (20)

built-in flash. A small artificial light source found in most compact digital cameras, camera phones, and many consumer-level DSLR cameras. (12)

burned-out highlights. Overexposed, featureless areas of an image that occur when the amount of light in a scene is too much for the camera's sensor to handle. (11)

burning in. A technique that involves applying additional exposure to a selected area of an image. It is primarily used to darken and bring out detail in midtones and highlight areas. (18)

burst mode. A continuous shooting mode in which the number of possible exposures ranges from two to eight or more per second. (4)

business plan. A document that describes a proposed business in detail and lays out a roadmap for its growth over a period of up to five years. (3)

butterfly lighting. A lighting setup that creates a distinct butterfly-shaped shadow beneath the nose of a subject. Also known as *Paramount lighting.* (10)

C

cadmium sulfide (CdS) cell meter. An exposure meter that measures the electrical resistance caused by light striking the CdS cell. The intensity of the light causes a change in electrical resistance, which is directly reflected as a change in the current flowing through the circuit. The changing current is translated into exposure values indicated on a scale or a display. (7)

calibrate. To adjust a device (usually a monitor) so it displays colors accurately and consistently. (20)

calotype. An early version of the negative/positive system that used treated paper as the negative material. (2)

camera. A device used to capture a photographic image. (5)

camera angle. Any of the different points of view that can be used to vary a picture's composition and visual impact. (9)

camera lucida. A tracing aid consisting of a prism mounted on a stand that projects a scene at a right angle onto a piece of paper, which could then be traced onto the paper. (2)

camera obscura. An enclosed space with a pinhole opening (later a lens) on one side through which an image of the scene outside is projected onto a movable screen or wall, where it could be traced onto paper or canvas. Means *dark chamber* or *dark room*. (2)

camera phone. A cell phone that includes a photographic device. (2)

camera shake. The involuntary movement of a camera during exposure that causes a blurred picture. (5)

candid photo. An informal and unposed photograph, usually with people as the main subjects. (14)

capacitor. A storage device capable of storing an electrical charge. (12)

card reader. A device used to transfer the contents of a memory card to a computer. (17)

card speed. A measure of how rapidly image files can be transferred from a camera to a memory card. (8)

cataloging program. An advanced image database program that allows the use of keywords for locating files by subject, date, or other criteria. (17)

catchlight. A small, bright reflection in a photo subject's eyes, used to add sparkle and liveliness. (13)

cellulose nitrate. A highly flammable plastic used as the clear base for early roll films, later replaced by the more stable cellulose acetate. Also known as *celluloid*. (2)

center of interest. A single element of the photo to which all the other elements of the picture relate, and which sends a clear message to the viewer. (9)

center-weighted averaging. A metering mode that gives greater importance (weight) to information from the center of the frame than to information from the edges. An average reading is then developed for the scene. (11)

charge-coupled device (CCD). An electronic sensor that has an array of light-sensitive elements that captures images by converting photons to electrons. (5, 8)

chromatic aberration. An optical problem in which different wavelengths (colors) of light focus at slightly different distances behind the lens. (6)

circles of confusion. Points in front of or behind the plane of focus that appear as small circles on the image receiver and become larger as the distance of the originating point from the plane of focus increases. The size of the circles determines sharpness of the image on the image receiver. (11)

clipping. Loss of shadows or highlights in a digital file, indicated by tall vertical lines at the extreme left or right ends of the histogram. (11)

clipping mask. A blocking method that allows some of the content of a lower layer to be masked out by the upper layer. It is often used to create type that is filled by a photographic subject. (19)

close-up range. The lowest range of magnification, from about 1/20 life-size to actual life-size, achieved by the use of normal-focus or close-focusing lenses alone. (13)

CMYK. The original four-ink set for inkjet printers. Abbreviation for cyan, magenta, yellow, and black. (20)

coated paper. A type of paper used in inkjet printers to produce photographic prints. The coating material resists the spread of ink droplets and instead allows them to retain their shape and color brilliance as they bond to the paper surface. (20)

cold-adhesive mounting. A mounting method that uses an adhesive that does not require heat to activate to bond the print to the substrate. (20)

collodion. A viscous liquid that dries to form a clear, tough layer. (2)

color cast. An unwanted color shift across an entire image caused by light temperature or other elements in an image. (7)

colorimeter. A device that reads color values from the monitor screen so the accompanying calibration software can make the necessary adjustments. (20)

color temperature. A measurement of the color of light, expressed in units called degrees kelvin (K). (7)

coma. A lens aberration that occurs when light rays that are not parallel to the lens axis create a series of overlapping circles of decreasing size. (6)

compact digital camera. A camera that is small enough to carry in a pocket, usually with zoom lenses and built-in flash. They are the most common point-and-shoot class of digital cameras. (5)

complementary metal oxide semiconductor (CMOS). An electronic sensor that converts light into images in a digital camera. (5, 8)

composite. An image created by combining part or all of other images. (19)

composition. The arrangement of visual elements, such as shapes, colors, and textures, within the frame. (1, 9)

compositional elements. The basic components used for effectively composing photographs. The traditional compositional elements consist of point, line, shape or pattern, balance, emphasis, and contrast. (9)

compression. The squeezing of an electronic file to reduce its size. (4, 8)

concave. A lens shape that is curved inward. (6)

conservation board. A type of mat board made with fibers derived from specially processed wood pulp. (20)

continuous light. An incandescent, fluorescent, or light-emitting diode (LED) array that remains lit. (15)

contract. A legal document that specifies the responsibilities of both the photographer and the client and spells out every detail of the arrangement. (3)

contrast. 1. The relationship of shadow and highlight within a photo. 2. A noticeable difference between adjacent elements of a composition. 3. The difference between the lightest and darkest areas in an image, expressed as a ratio. (9, 10)

contrast filter. A filter that is made in either deep shades of red, green, or blue. Each transmits light of its own color and absorbs light of the other two colors. (7)

converge. To come together, as in light rays passing through a convex lens. (6)

convergence. A compositional problem in which parts of the image come together in an undesirable way. Also known as *subject mergers*. (9)

convex. A lens shape that is curved outward. (6)

cookie. A patterned translucent material or an opaque cutout placed in front of a light to project textures or shadows. (15)

cooling filter. A light blue filter used to make the coloration of a scene a bit less yellow. (7)

copyright. A law that gives the creator of a photograph or other item of intellectual property (such as a novel, song, or computer program) the exclusive right to use and distribute that property for a specific period of time. (17)

corporation. A form of business organization in which investors or shareholders purchase ownership in the form of shares of stock. A board of directors appoints or hires the people who operate the corporation. (3)

Creative Commons license. A license that permits the copyright owner to make some or all usage rights to an image available without charge. (17)

creative control. The ability to affect image appearance through choice of shutter speed, aperture, white balance, and other camera settings. (7)

creative effects lens. An accessory lens that permits manipulation of the area of sharp focus in an image. (6)

culling. The process of determining which photos to keep and which photos to delete. (17)

curvature of field. A failure of light rays to focus at a common point. The projected image is either in focus at the center and out of focus at the edges, or vice versa, depending on which focal point is chosen. (6)

D

daguerreotype. The first widely available form of permanent photography, in which the image was recorded on a silver plate. (2)

darkness. The partial or total absence of light. (10)

database program. Computer software that allows a collection of files (one file for each cataloged image) to be sorted in various ways to locate desired information. (17)

dedicated flash units. Flash units designed for use with a specific camera model or range of models from one manufacturer. (12)

definition. An editing tool that helps an image appear clearer by removing layers of haze. (21)

depth of field. The distance between the nearest and farthest objects that are in acceptably sharp focus. (4, 11)

depth of field (DOF) preview. A camera feature that allows the photographer to see the scene at the desired aperture and assess the actual depth of field. (4, 9)

derivative work. A work that may be used without infringing copyright because it serves as the basis of a new creation. (17)

developing-out paper. A photographic paper that requires the use of a developer to bring out the latent image. (2)

diffused light. Light that is disbursed over a wide surface for a softer effect. (10)

diffusing. Softening the light falling on a subject, usually by placing a translucent material between the light source and the subject. (11)

digital back. A digital capture device that can be attached to a medium format or large format camera. (2)

digital noise. 1. Tiny light-colored spots especially noticeable in shadow areas of an image. 2. Specks of various colors that are most noticeable in shadows or areas of smooth color, such as clear skies. (7, 11)

digital photography. The process of using electronic devices to capture, create, edit, and share digital images. (2)

digital resolution. A means of expressing scanner resolution used by some manufacturers for advertising purposes. It is achieved by using software to insert additional pixels around those actually scanned. (17)

digital signal. A signal in which image information is encoded as a series of on/off states (usually represented by 1 and 0) rather than varying continuously. (8)

digital zoom. A digital camera feature that electronically crops the image to smaller dimensions, making it appear larger but causing the image quality to deteriorate. (6, 16)

direct flash. A method of aiming the flash straight at the subject from a position directly over or right next to the lens. (12)

distortion. A change in the shape of a rectangular image projected by a lens. (6)

diverge. To be spread apart, as in light rays passing through a concave lens. (6)

documentation. Photography that records what a photographer saw, such as a scene, event, person, or object. (1)

dodging. A technique that involves applying additional processing to a specific area of a photo. It is primarily used to lighten and bring out detail in an image. (18)

download. To transfer image files from the original source, such as a camera or memory card, to a computer for storage and processing. (17)

downsampling. Decreasing the dimensions or resolution of an image with the **Resample** box checked. (18)

dry mounting. A mounting method that uses heat and pressure to bond the print to the substrate. Also known as *heated-adhesive mounting*. (20)

dry plate process. A photographic system in which a glass plate was coated with a gelatin-based photosensitive emulsion. Plates could be prepared and stored for months before being exposed, and development could be delayed until convenient. (2)

dye sublimation printer. A type of printer that contains a print head with many tiny, precisely controlled heating elements. The print head works in conjunction with a wide plastic transfer ribbon carrying CMYK dyes. The print head causes the dyes to vaporize, or *sublimate* (change state from solid to a vapor), and deposit as tiny color spots on specially coated paper. (20)

E

e-commerce capability. A feature of a website that allows clients to view images and order prints or other products. (3)

edge mounting. A loose mounting method in which the photographic print is held by its corners or by hinges made from easily removed acid-free paper tape. (20)

electronic studio flash. The primary source of portable artificial light for photography. A strong electrical charge is built up in a storage device called a capacitor, then released into a gas-filled flash tube, producing a burst of bright light synchronized with the opening of the camera shutter. Also known as a *strobe light* or *strobe flash*. (15)

electronic viewfinder. A small LCD screen that shows the image that the camera will produce after receiving information from the camera's sensor. (5)

elliptical marquee. A selection tool in an image editing program that allows the user to make a circular or oval selection. (19)

emphasis. A compositional element used to make some element of a picture stand out and capture the viewer's attention. (9)

entrepreneurship. The process of starting a business. (3)

environmental portrait. An informal portrait made outside the studio setting, usually designed to show the subject in natural surroundings or in a setting meaningful to them. (15)

equivalent exposures. Different combinations of aperture and shutter speed that are identical in exposure value. (11)

evaluative metering. A metering mode in which light reflected from the scene is read and analyzed using a number of points spread across the field of view. The shadows, highlights, and midtones are evaluated to produce an averaged reading that usually results in an acceptable exposure. (11)

EXIF (Exchangeable Image File Format). A file recorded by the camera at the time of exposure. It contains many image properties, including the shutter speed, aperture, ISO, and lens focal length. (17)

exposure. The amount of light reflected from a scene that reaches the camera's image receiver. (7)

exposure bracketing. A method of exposure in which the scene is shot three times—once at the exposure indicated by the meter, once at a decreased exposure value, and once at an increased exposure value. (11)

exposure compensation. A feature on DSLRs and some advanced compact cameras that allows you to increase or decrease exposure while using the shutter priority or aperture priority modes. (11)

exposure lock. A function that allows the photographer to reframe a shot while keeping the current exposure reading the same. Also known as *AE lock*. (4)

extracting. Identifying and pulling out individual images from a larger scene. (9)

F

fair use. A provision of copyright law that allows limited use of an intellectual property by critics and reviewers, scholars and researchers, and classroom teachers. (17)

feathering. Adjusting the light source so the less intense outer edges of the light cone illuminate the subject. (15)

ferrotype. The formal name for the tintype process. (2)

file formats. Different modes of saving image data, such as JPEG or TIFF. (8)

fill flash. Light of reduced intensity used to brighten deep shadow areas to make them easier to see and appear more natural. (11)

fill light. The secondary light on a subject used to soften dark shadows, decrease the contrast range of the light reflected from the subject, and help to reveal detail in shadow areas. (10, 15)

filter. A special effect that can be applied to all or part of an image to change its appearance. (19)

firmware. The built-in program found in a digital camera or similar device. (8)

fish-eye lens. A lens with an angle of view greater than 180° that produces a round image with considerable spherical distortion. (6)

fixing. The chemical process of treating a developed photographic image to prevent further darkening of the silver by exposure to light. (2)

flag. A shape cut from black poster board or stiff black paper attached to light stands or other fixtures to block light. (15)

flare. The effect of stray light bouncing around inside the lens housing, causing decreased contrast or a severe washed-out appearance that mimics overexposure. (13)

flush mount. A type of mount in which the photo extends to the edge of the mount, with no border. (20)

foam board. Mounting material made with a paper facing on a rigid core of plastic foam. (20)

focal length. The distance from the optical center of the lens to the point where the light rays converge (the image receiver plane). (6)

focal plane shutter. A type of shutter that is located in the camera body, just in front of the image receiver. (5)

focal point. The common point at which converging light rays meet. (6)

focusing mark. A short line or a dot on a manual focus lens that is used to determine the distance from the camera to the subject. Numbers on a distance scale align with the focusing mark to show the distance to the subject being focused on. (11)

focusing rail. A tripod-mounted accessory that permits the camera to be moved toward or away from the subject in tiny increments to achieve precise focus. (13)

focus lock. A function that allows the photographer to set and maintain focus on a specific point in a shot and then recompose the shot while holding the focus on the previously selected point. Also known as *AF lock*. (4)

follow focus. A technique in which the photographer makes continuous small focus adjustments to keep a moving subject sharp. It permits the photographer to select the exact instant to release the shutter. (12)

formal balance. A compositional method that consists of matched halves. Also known as *symmetrical balance*. (9)

formal studio portrait. The traditional style of individual or family portrait, made in a studio setting. (15)

frame. The working space within which a picture is composed. (1, 9)

freelancer. A self-employed photographer, especially one without a physical studio, who actively seeks business from many sources and takes on various types of photographic assignments. (1)

frequency. A measure of the number of waves (cycles) passing a given point in one second, measured in hertz (Hz). (7)

front-focusing. A telephoto lens design in which the front element group has a converging design, and the rear element group has a diverging design. This shortens the light path, making a larger image possible at the focal plane with less physical distance between the front lens element and the image receiver. (6)

f-stop. A unit of measure that represents the size of a specific aperture. The standard f-stop designations are f/0.7, f/1, f/1.4, f/2, f/2.8, f/4, f/5.6, f/8, f/11, f/16, f/22, f/32, f/45, and f/64. (7)

full-frame. A term describing digital camera sensors that are 24 mm x 36 mm, corresponding to the 35 mm film frame. (8)

G

gel. A transparent, colored material placed over a light source to create a specific-colored effect. (10, 15)

giclée. A French term meaning spray or squirt. It was adopted in the early 1990s by fine art photographers to characterize the prints they were producing on high-quality commercial inkjet printers. (20)

gobo. A generic term for any light-control device or material that goes between the light and the area where the light is intended to fall. (15)

gray levels. The distinct steps between pure white and pure black. (8)

grayscale mode. A mode in which all picture information is conveyed by up to 256 shades of gray. (18)

grid. A light modifier with square or hexagonal openings that align the rays of light so they are more ordered and parallel. This type of light adds sparkle to a scene through increased contrast. (15)

guide number. A manufacturer-supplied number based on the light output of the flash and the ISO rating being used to manually determine lens aperture for proper exposure. (12)

H

handles. Control points on the **Pen** tool that can be used to curve the line segment between anchor points, allowing the selection of curved shapes. (19)

hard light. A type of lighting that creates harsh shadows, or places with stark contrast between the highlights and the shadows. Also known as *harsh lighting*. (10, 15)

hard news. Photojournalistic assignments such as fires, automobile or industrial accidents, or crime coverage. (12)

HEIC. Apple's proprietary version of the file format HEIF, short for High-Efficiency Image File format. It allows small image files to retain high quality. (8)

high dynamic range (HDR) image. A photo with a wider range between the lightest and darkest areas of a photo than a standard photo. (16)

high key. Term describing a photograph in which shades of white or light tones are predominate. (11)

high-voltage power pack. A belt-mounted power supply for flash units that uses special rechargeable batteries. (12)

histogram. A bar graph that displays all the tonal values of an image. (4, 11)

hot shoe. A flash mounting terminal often located on top of a DSLR. Its electrical contacts mate with those on the flash unit, triggering the flash when the shutter release is pressed. (4, 12)

hyperfocal distance. The nearest point that is in sharp focus when the lens is focused on infinity. This distance is different for each f-stop and each focal length. (11)

I

image editor. A software application considered an indispensable tool for either image processing or image manipulation. (18)

image file. An individual digital image that can be stored, transferred, or manipulated. (8)

image management. The process of using a filing method or cataloging system that allows a user to quickly locate a desired image. (17)

image manipulation. Changes to an image that are more extreme than those done in image processing. These changes include distortion, removal of particular elements from the photo, combination of elements from one or more other sources, or radical changes of color and tone. (18)

image processing. Changes to an image such as adjustment of exposure, color and contrast, cropping the image, and dodging and burning. (18)

image receiver system. A camera system designed to place a light-sensitive medium at the point where light rays converge after passing through the lens. Depending on the camera type, it consists of either film and the means to hold it in place or a digital sensor and related electronic circuits. (5)

importing. The process of transferring a file from one program to another. Also known as *pulling*. (17)

incident light reading. A light reading that measures the intensity of the light falling on a subject. (7)

informal balance. A compositional method that provides a feeling of visual balance without the mirror image effect of formal balance. Also known as *asymmetrical balance*. (9)

infringement. Violation of the copyright law by using or distributing a work without permission of the copyright owner. (17)

inkjet printer. A type of printer that works by depositing a fine spray of tiny ink dots on paper. (20)

intellectual property. A one-of-a-kind work, such as an artistic or musical work, that is protected by law. (3)

internship. A position that provides a student or trainee experience in a working environment. It is normally done for academic credit and may be paid or unpaid. (3)

interpolation. The creation of new image pixels by averaging the values of the surrounding existing pixels in image processing software. (18)

inverse-square law. A scientific formula for calculating the amount of light falloff that states that the illumination provided by a light source varies inversely as the square of the distance from the source. (15)

invoice. A detailed list of the fees for a photographer's services and any expenses or other charges. (3)

iris. A variable-aperture device consisting of an assembly of thin, overlapping metal blades. Also known as a *diaphragm*. (5)

ISO. The camera image receiver's sensitivity to light. (4)

ISO rating. A numerical designation indicating the light sensitivity of an image receiver, with higher numbers indicating greater sensitivity. It is an international standard that was originally developed to ensure consistency in films from different manufacturers and has since been adapted for use with digital cameras. (7)

J

JPEG. The most common compressed file format and the only compression choice offered on many cameras. The amount of compression can be small or large. Also known as *JPG*. (8)

K

key light. The main light on a subject. (10, 15)
keyword. A specific descriptive word (or words) assigned to an image in a database that allows a user to search for that image. (17)

L

landscape mode. An image format that is wider than it is tall (a horizontal rectangle). (9)
landscape photography. Recorded views of the natural world in any of its aspects. Most views feature the vegetable and mineral kingdoms (plants and rocks), but the animal kingdom also may be represented as a part of a scene. (13)
large format camera. A camera that uses image receivers around 100 mm × 130 mm. (5)
large-format inkjet printer. A type of printer used to produce large fine art prints, posters, banners, billboard sheets, and similar products. It accepts paper and other media as large as 6′ in width with virtually no length restriction. (20)
latent image. A photographic image that does not develop (become visible) until exposed to developing chemicals. (2)
layer mask. An image manipulation tool used to protect a portion of an image from change or to permit a lower layer to show through the topmost layer. (19)
leading lines. Pictorial elements that draw the viewer's eye from one area of the photo to another. (9)
lead room. The additional room provided on the side of the frame toward which a subject is looking or moving. Also known as *lead space*. (9)
lens. An optical lens or assembly of lenses that work together with a camera body to bring light to a fixed focal point that is processed by the camera to create an image. (6)
lens collar. A support method used on medium and long telephoto lenses to prevent strain on the lens mount from the weight of the lens. (12)
lens elements. Pieces of glass that are part of a lens and bend light in specific ways. (6)
light. A form of electromagnetic radiation, or radiant energy, that is visible to the human eye. (7)
lighting instrument. A piece of lighting hardware, such as a spotlight. (10)
lighting ratio. The comparison of the key light to the fill light expressed as a ratio, such as 1:2. The higher the ratio, the more contrast you have to deal with. (10, 15)
limited liability company (LLC). A hybrid form of business organization that combines some of the advantages of a corporation with some of the advantages of a sole proprietorship or a partnership. (3)
line. A compositional element that typically draws the viewer's eye along its length, making it a useful tool for directing attention. (9)
loop lighting. A lighting style in which a small loop of shadow is created on a subject's nose, and a separate shadow is created on their cheek. (10)
low key. Term describing a photograph in which dark tones are predominate. (11)
luminances. Percentages of reflected light. (7)

M

macro lens. A lens that can focus more closely than a typical lens of the same focal length, providing a larger image of an object on the image receiver. Short for *macro-focusing lens*. (6)
macro photo range. A term used to describe photography in which the image is as large or larger than the actual object. (13)
magnification rate. A method of expressing the size relationship between the actual object and its recorded image. An example is 2×, or "two times life-size." (13)
manual exposure. An exposure mode in which the photographer chooses the aperture, shutter speed, and ISO. (4)
marketing. Everything a businessperson does to acquire clients and establish an ongoing relationship with them. (3)
mass marketing. Marketing aimed at a wide range of people. (3)
mat board. Mounting material composed of two or more layers of cellulose fiber. (20)

medium format camera. A camera that uses image receivers larger than 24 mm × 36 mm but smaller than 100 mm × 130 mm. (5)

medium format digital camera. A digital camera equipped with a sensor similar in size to the frame of 120-size film. (5)

memory card. A digital storage device used in digital cameras. Commonly referred to as an *SD card*. (8)

meniscus lens. The first lens developed specifically as a camera lens. It was designed to improve the image projected by the camera obscura. (6)

metadata. Information contained in a file recorded by the camera at the time of exposure. Loosely translated as "data about data." (17)

metamerism. A color shift that is noticeable when a print is viewed under different lighting conditions, such as tungsten and daylight. (20)

metering. The process of using an in-camera or handheld exposure meter to determine the amount of light being reflected from the subject. (7)

metering modes. Different methods used by a camera to automatically calculate exposure. See *center-weighted averaging*, *evaluative metering*, *partial metering*, and *spot metering*. (11)

middle gray. An exposure value equivalent to a tone that reflects 18% of the light that falls on it. (7)

mirror image. A reflection in water that is an almost exact reproduction, in reverse, of a scene. (13)

mirrorless camera. An interchangeable-lens camera that is smaller and lighter than a traditional SLR interchangeable lens camera because it does away with the mirror assembly and pentaprism. (5)

mobile photography. Photography taken with a camera phone or other mobile device, such as a tablet. (16)

mobile postprocessing. The process of editing photographs on a mobile device. (21)

monochrome. Single-color, typically black-and-white. (18)

monolight. A combination flash head and power supply. The flash tube, controls, and capacitors are combined into a single housing. Also known as a *self-contained system*. (15)

monopod. A one-legged camera support that combines improved camera support with good mobility, especially when using telephoto lenses. (4)

mood. The feeling created by the lighting in a photograph. (10)

morphing. An editing technique in which images may be merged or distorted to transform an object's appearance. (19)

motivated lighting. A type of lighting in which the main goal is to look as real as possible. (10)

museum board. An acid-free archival mounting board made with fibers from cotton. (20)

N

nanometer. The unit of measure for wavelength, which is equal to one-billionth of a meter (0.000000001 m = 1 nm). (7)

negative. An image made on film that is reversed in light, shade, tone, and orientation. (2)

negative/positive system. The basis of chemical-based photographic printing, in which the original is a negative image that can be used to print any number of duplicate positive images. (2)

negative space. The area within the frame surrounding the subject. This area can isolate and emphasize the subject when used properly. (9)

neutral density (ND) filter. A type of filter that attaches to the front of a camera's lens to reduce the quantity of light reaching the image receiver without altering the light's color. (7)

nodal point. The optical center of a lens. This is the point inside the lens barrel where the incoming light rays converge and turn the image upside down. (13)

noise reduction. An algorithm used to decrease the digital noise in a photo. Noise reduction could over-soften other details if not careful. (21)

normal lens. A lens that provides an angle of view and a perspective close to that of the unaided human eye. Also known as a *standard lens*. (6)

O

off-camera flash. A method of removing the flash unit from the hot shoe and positioning it above and to one side of the camera to eliminate red eye, reflections from eyeglasses and other surfaces, and some shadow problems. (12)

online gallery. A website for photo display, intended for more serious photographers and often maintained by organizations or schools. (20)

online photofinishing site. A website that offers low-cost printing from uploaded digital files. The prints from those files are returned by mail. (17)

open flash. A technique in which the camera's shutter is held wide open and the flash triggered manually one or more times. (12)

optical resolution. The actual pixels per inch resolution, such as 600, 1200, or 2400. (17)

optical zoom. A physical camera feature that moves the lens elements to change the angle of view, and thus, image size, without affecting the quality of the image. (6, 16)

outdoor photography. A type of photography that encompasses the broad areas of landscape and wildlife. Also known as *nature photography*. (13)

overexposure. A photo that is very bright due to an excessive amount of light. (7, 10)

overmat. A sheet of mat board with a hole or window cut in it to display and help protect a print. The mat is hinged to the mounting board. Also known as a *window mat*. (20)

oversharpening. Applying a sharpening filter at too high an intensity, giving the image an unattractive, harsh, blotchy appearance. (18)

P

pack-and-head system. A traditional studio flash system with a central power pack connected to separate flash heads. (15)

painting with light. An open flash technique typically used in large, dimly lighted spaces or for exterior photos taken at night. The camera shutter is held open, and the flash is moved around to illuminate different sections of the subject. (12)

pan head. A tripod head that allows the camera to move in either two or three axes. (4)

panning. Moving the camera along with an object crossing the field of view, conveying speed and movement by streaking the background behind a sharply focused moving subject. (9)

panorama. An extremely wide view of a scene, typically a landscape. (13)

parallax error. A mismatch in what the photographer sees through the viewfinder and what the camera's taking lens sees. The slight difference can result in cutting off part of a subject. (5)

partial metering. A metering mode that reads information from a small area (usually about 10%) in the center of the frame. (11)

partnership. A form of business organization in which two or more individuals join together to operate a business. (3)

passive autofocus. A focusing system that evaluates incoming light and makes focusing adjustments automatically. (5)

path. A line or closed figure, defined with an image editing program's **Pen** tool, which can then be edited and altered as necessary. A closed figure can be converted to a selection. (19)

pattern. A compositional element made by multiple objects. A pattern may consist of repetition of identical shapes or may have elements alternating or varying in shape, size, or color. (9)

peak of action. The instant when motion slows to almost a stop. (12)

permissible circle of confusion. The largest diameter circle that is seen as a point and thus appears to be sharp at normal distance. (11)

perspective. 1. The relative size of objects in a scene and how they are aligned. 2. The relationship between objects in a photograph that can help provide a sense of depth or scale. (6, 9)

pH. A scale that is used to determine acid/alkaline balance. (20)

photoelectric light meter. An exposure meter that uses electrical changes caused by different light intensities to indicate various levels of illumination. These indications, in turn, can be used to determine the exposure needed for a scene. (7)

photoflood. A glass bulb similar in appearance to a standard bulb but constructed for high light output. (15)

photogram. A stencil-like photographic image created by placing opaque objects on treated paper that is then exposed to light. (2)

photographic daylight. The light produced by the midday sun on a clear and cloudless day, with a color temperature of 5500 K. (7)

photography. The act of "drawing with light," or capturing reflected light to form an image. (1)

photography assistant. A person who aids a photographer with a variety of tasks in the studio and on location. (3)

photojournalism. A specialized field of photography devoted to capturing images of news events and similar subjects for use in newspapers, magazines, and other print and digital media. (12)

photojournalist. A photographer who produces still pictures or videos for use in various forms of print and digital media to tell a story. (1)

photomicrography. A highly specialized field in which a microscope is used to achieve extremely high magnifications. (13)

photo sharing site. A website that allows people to post albums of pictures for public or private viewing. (17)

photosite. A light-sensitive picture element found in a digital camera's sensor. (5)

picture story. A group of feature-type photos that carry out a theme. In purest form, it relies on the photos and their accompanying captions to "tell the tale." Also known as a *photo essay*. (12)

pigment-based ink. A type of ink used to print photos that resists fading. It consists of solid color pigments ground into extremely fine particles and suspended in a liquid. (20)

pincushion distortion. A type of distortion in which a rectangular image has sides that are pushed inward. (6)

pixel. An abbreviation of the term *picture element*. Digital cameras are often classified by the number of picture elements contained in their CCD array. (5)

plane of focus. The single part of a scene in sharp focus. Parts of the scene closer to or farther from the camera are progressively more out of focus. (11)

point. A compositional element that is a single object, typically small in size, that attracts the eye. (9)

polarizing filter. A photographic filter used to deepen the color of a blue sky, improve the color saturation of natural objects by reducing glare, and reduce or eliminate reflections from glass, water, and similar surfaces. (7)

Polaroid process. A process that developed a picture one minute after exposure by incorporating a small packet of chemicals in each sheet of film. (2)

portfolio. A physical or digital collection of a photographer's best work used to show potential clients or employers their skills and abilities. (1)

portrait mode. An image format that is taller than it is wide (a vertical rectangle). (9)

portrait photography. Photography of individuals or groups of people. Also known as *portraiture*. (1)

positive. An image that shows the light, shade, tone, and orientation as it appears in the original scene. (2)

prefocusing. Focusing on a specific spot and waiting for the subject to reach that point. Also known as *spot focusing*. (12)

pressure-sensitive adhesive material. Sheets or rolls coated with a sticky material that is activated by applying pressure with a squeegee or roller. (20)

prime lens. A lens with a fixed focal length. (6)

printing-out paper. A photographic paper on which an image appears without the use of a chemical developer. (2)

product photography. Photography that involves taking pictures of products in a way that makes them stand out to consumers in order to drive sales. Also known as *advertising photography*. (1)

professional photographer. A photographer who makes all or most of their living from photographic work. (1)

professional photography. An occupation in which photographic skills are used to create images in exchange for payment. (3)

profile. A program that tells a printer how to handle a particular paper so the final print accurately reproduces the color values of the image file. (20)

profit. The amount of money left after paying all the expenses for a business. (3)

Program AE. An exposure mode in which the camera's processor selects exposure settings based on the meter reading, but the photographer can change either the shutter speed or aperture. (4)

proper exposure. The correct combination of aperture, shutter speed, and ISO that best reflects the image that the photographer is trying to shoot. (11)

prosumer. A marketing term used to identify cameras that bridge the gap between amateur and professional equipment. Blending of the terms *professional* and *consumer*. (2)

public domain. A term used to describe intellectual property not covered by copyright and thus available for free use by anyone. (17)

Q

quad-tone ink set. A specialty ink set used with a dedicated inkjet printer for black-and-white reproduction. Consists of black and three grays rather than CMYK. (20)

R

RAW. The basic image information captured by the camera's sensor and saved with minimal processing by the camera's computer. (8)

RAW converter. Software that allows the photographer to make a number of adjustments to the file data before saving the image as a .tif or .psd file. (18)

reach. The total number of people who see your content. (21)

rear-curtain synchronization. A camera feature that delays the firing of the flash until the instant before the second curtain of the focal plane shutter begins to close. (12)

reciprocity law. The theory that a one-stop increase in aperture is equivalent to the shutter duration doubling. Both increase light by one stop. (7)

recreational travel. Journeys made for leisure rather than business. (14)

rectangular marquee. A selection tool in an image editing program that allows the user to make a square or rectangular selection. It can also be used to crop an image. (19)

recycle. The process of rebuilding the electrical charge in a flash unit's capacitor. (12)

red eye. A problem that is caused by the light of the flash reflecting back from the retina of the subject's eye. (12)

reflective light reading. A light reading made by pointing the meter at the main subject. Also known as an *averaged reading*. (7)

refraction. The bending of light rays that takes place in a lens because of the differing densities of glass and air. (6)

relative motion. The angle of the subject's motion relative to the camera's field of view or a given length of exposure. (12)

release. A legal document granting permission to include people, places, and objects in a photograph. (3)

Rembrandt lighting. A lighting style named for the Dutch painter in which the small loop of shadow on a subject's nose is long enough to merge with the shadow on their cheek. (10)

reproduction ratio. A numeric expression of size relationships, such as 1:4. The numeral before the colon represents the reproduction size, or the size of the recorded object in the digital file. The numeral after the colon represents the size of the actual object. (6, 13)

retrofocus. A type of wide-angle lens design that combines negative and positive lens elements to "stretch" the light path within the lens. This provides sufficient back focus for mirror clearance while maintaining the focal length of the lens. (6)

reversing ring. An accessory with filter-mounting threads on one side and a lens mount on the other, allowing a lens to be mounted backward for greater magnification. (13)

rhythm. An element of the compositional element pattern that consists of repeated shapes or lines that move the eye through the frame. (9)

rights-managed image. A stock photo for which a fee is charged for each use, such as different editions of a book or different packaging for a family of products. (17)

rim light. A light positioned behind and to one side of the subject for dramatic effect or to help separate a dark-haired subject from the background. Also known as an *accent light*, *back light*, *hair light*, or *halo light*. (10, 15)

rim lighting. A lighting style in which light is placed around the edges of a subject from behind, outlining them in light. (10)

royalty. A percentage of the sale price paid to the author of a book, photograph, or other intellectual property by the publisher or stock photo agency. (17)

royalty-free image. A stock photo that may be used multiple times without additional payment after permission has been given. (17)

rule of thirds. A compositional device that divides the frame into thirds, both horizontally and vertically. The four intersections created by the crossing lines are considered the most effective spots to position the center of interest. (9)

S

saturation. An editing tool that changes the intensity of all the colors present in an image equally. (21)

scanner. A mechanical/optical device used to convert original prints or physical copies into digital form. (17)

selection tools. Tools in an image editing program that allow you to choose one element or portion of an image to work with and manipulate. (19)

selective focus. A technique that uses a shallow depth of field to throw the background out of focus, drawing attention to the main subject. (9)

selective framing. Deciding what to include in the frame and what to exclude from the frame. Also known as *cropping in the camera*. (9)

selenium cell meter. An exposure meter that measures photoelectric light and is used to generate or control an electric current. (7)

self-contained flash units. Flash units available in a variety of sizes and types, either for mounting on the camera's hot shoe or on a separate bracket. (12)

sensor. An array of light-sensitive picture elements that serves as the image receiver in digital cameras. (5)

separate viewfinder. A small viewing window found on cameras ranging from simple, inexpensive cameras to rangefinder models and twin-lens reflex (TLR) cameras. It does not present a "through the lens" view of the subject. (5)

shape. A compositional element made by an individual object. A shape may appear to be flat and two-dimensional, exhibiting only the properties of length and width. (9)

sharpening. Enhancing edge contrast through a built-in filter to make an image appear more sharply focused by varying the filter's intensity. (18)

sharpness. An editing tool that adjusts the clarity of detail in a photo. It can also be used to emphasize texture. (21)

shortcut keys. Individual keys or a combination of keys used to perform an operation as an alternative to a mouse and menu. (18)

short lighting. A lighting style that highlights the short side of a subject's face, or the side that is farther away from the camera, by placing light on the same side. (10)

shot list. A detailed list of photos to be taken for a professional assignment. (14)

shutter. A device that opens and closes to control the flow of light to the camera's image receiver. (5, 7)

shutter lag. A delay between pressing the shutter button and the actual opening of the shutter. (4)

shutter priority. An exposure mode in which the photographer selects the shutter speed, and the camera chooses an aperture based on its meter reading. (4)

shutter speed. How long the shutter remains open (in combination with the size of the aperture). (7)

sidelighted. Description of a subject lighted strongly from one side. Such lighting often exhibits strong contrast between the lighted and shadowed sides, providing a dramatic effect. (11)

slave units. Flash units containing a photoelectric cell that responds to the bright burst of light from a master flash that is connected to the camera. The burst of light causes the flash to fire instantaneously. (12)

small format camera. A camera that uses image receivers in 35 mm size or smaller. (5)

snapshot. A photo taken to record an event, activity, or location, often with a point-and-shoot camera or camera phone. (4)

snoot. A tubular light modifier attached to a light source to direct a spot of intense light at the desired area of the subject. (15)

softbox. A large source of diffused light that consists of several lamps or electronic flash units mounted inside a reflective housing and covered with translucent material. (15)

soft light. A type of light that creates very few harsh shadows, or places with stark contrast between the highlights and the shadows. (10, 15)

soft news. Feature-type photo assignments such as seasonal pictures, fashion or food shots, and human interest photos. (12)

sole proprietor. A person who owns an unincorporated business by themselves. (3)

solid-state. A term describing a device that has no moving parts. (8)

specular light. Light that is very concentrated in the center, but gradually seems to fade in intensity as it moves farther out from the center. (10)

specular reflection. Bright points of light bounced back from smooth polished surfaces. The rays are reflected in an orderly and concentrated manner. (7)

spherical aberration. An optical problem in which the light rays entering the outer edges of a lens are bent more sharply than those entering closer to the center. The outer rays come to a focus at a point closer to the lens, which results in an overall softness of focus or fuzziness of the image. (6)

split lighting. A lighting style in which half of the subject's face is lit, and the other is left in complete shadow Also known as *side lighting* or *profile lighting*. (10)

spot metering. A metering mode that reads information from a small area in the frame (as little as 1% in some cameras). (11)

spotting. Removing small dust spots on an image. (18)

sRGB. A color space (standard Red, Green, Blue) that was defined by the computer industry for consistent display of colors on monitors. (4)

stabilizing systems. Methods used to control camera shake that causes blurry photos. Some stabilizing systems are specific to camera bodies, while others are specific to interchangeable lenses. (4)

straight photography. Photography with little or no manipulation. (18)

subject blur. An out-of-focus condition that occurs when a person or object is moving too fast for the selected shutter speed to stop its motion. (5)

subject brightness range (SBR). Luminances present in the scene, from brightest to darkest, expressed in stops. Also known as *dynamic range*. (7)

sublimate. To change state from solid to gas without an intermediate liquid state. (20)

subtractive color process. A color reproduction method used with reflected light, in which the subtractive primaries (cyan, magenta, and yellow) subtract or block specific colors from the white light that is used to view an image. Cyan absorbs red light and passes blue and green; magenta absorbs green light and passes blue and red; yellow absorbs blue light and passes red and green. (7)

subtractive primary colors. The colors cyan, magenta, and yellow. Each color absorbs one of the additive primary colors. Adding two subtractive primary colors together will create one of the additive primary colors. (18)

superzoom. A type of advanced compact digital camera with exceptionally wide zoom ranges, from as wide as 21 mm to as long as 1365 mm. (6)

sync speed. The fastest speed at which a camera's image sensor can be open to light. (7)

T

targeted marketing. Marketing aimed at a specific group of people. (3)

teleconverter. An accessory lens that is mounted between the camera body and a telephoto lens to increase focal length by 1.4× or 2×. (6)

telephoto lens. A lens with an angle of view roughly 25° or smaller. (6)

tenting. A lighting method in which the subject is surrounded by a cone or shell of white translucent paper or plastic, with a small hole cut in one side for the camera lens. Light thrown on the cone from the outside results in a very diffuse illumination of the subject and eliminates reflections. (15)

tethered shutter release. A wired remote trigger that enables the camera's shutter release. (4)

three-point lighting. A lighting style in which three lights (typically a key, fill, and rim light) are used to light a subject. (10, 15)

through-the-lens (TTL) metering. A feature of a camera where the intensity of light reflected from the scene is measured through the camera's lens as opposed to using a separate light meter. (7)

through-the-lens viewing system. A composing and focusing method in which the viewfinder image is the scene viewed through the camera's taking lens. (5)

thumbnails. Small images displayed in database programs to help the photographer locate a desired file. (17)

TIFF. A file format that retains all the image information through the processing steps performed by the camera's computer. Short for Tagged Image File Format. (8)

tint. An editing tool that adds a hint of color across an entire image. Also referred to as *hue*. (21)

tintype. The process in which a wet collodion emulsion was applied to a thin iron plate that had been painted with a black or brown enamel. Also known as *ferrotype*. (2)

tonal range. The spread of tones, from deepest shadows to brightest highlights, represented in a photograph. (7, 10)

traditional photography. Photography taken with either a film camera or a digital camera. (16)

travel guide. A book or electronic publication that provides travelers with needed information about places they plan to visit. Some are specifically designed for photographers. (14)

travel photography. Photography that focuses on landscapes and other nature subjects, as well as paying considerable attention to the human-made aspects of our world and to the people who inhabit it. (14)

trilinear array. A bar containing three rows of sensors that is moved across the image receiver area, permitting image capture in a single pass. (5)

tripod. A three-legged camera support in which each leg's length is independently adjustable, allowing it to be firmly set in place on almost any kind of terrain. (4)

true to color. The portrayal of an object's natural colors in an image. (16)

tungsten-halogen bulb. A small, extremely bright bulb with a higher light output and a longer life than a photoflood bulb. (15)

U

ultraviolet (UV) filter. A virtually clear filter that is screwed into place on the front of the lens to protect the front lens element from dust, salt spray, and bumps against hard objects. Also known as a *haze filter* or *skylight filter*. (4)

underexposure. A photo that is very dark due to an insufficient amount of light. (7, 10)

untethered shutter release. A wireless remote trigger that enables the camera's shutter release. (4)

upload. Send image files from a digital device to another device or computer system via the internet. (17)

upsampling. Increasing the dimensions or resolution of an image with the **Resample** box checked. (18)

V

vibrance. An editing tool that increases the intensity or vibrancy of a muted color while leaving saturated colors unaffected. (21)

view camera. A camera that accepts individual sheets of film, uses a ground-glass back for composition and focusing, and offers a variety of mechanical adjustments for control of perspective and depth of field. It can be fitted with a scanning back for digital image capture. (5)

viewfinder. A small viewing screen on the back side of a digital camera that allows review of each image immediately after it is exposed. (4)

viewpoint. The distance and angle from which the camera (and eventually, the viewer) sees the subject. (9)

vignette. A dark border around the edge of a photo that can be used to draw a viewer's attention to a specific part of the photo. (21)

visible spectrum. The tiny portion of the electromagnetic spectrum that can be seen by the human eye. It consists of waves with wavelengths ranging from about 400 nm to about 700 nm. (7)

visualization. A technique in which the photographer controls how the final product will appear to the viewer by first seeing that desired final result in their own mind. (9)

W

warming filter. A yellowish filter that will absorb some of the blue light, warming the scene. (7)

warmth. An editing tool that boosts the red, orange, and yellow tones in an image while decreasing the blue tones. (21)

watermarking. An electronic method of embedding copyright information and the owner's identity in the digital file, providing a basis for identifying and prosecuting copyright violators. (17)

wavelength. The distance from the crest (top) of one wave to the crest of the next. (7)

wet-plate collodion process. A photographic system in which a glass plate was coated with a liquid emulsion and then exposed and developed while the emulsion was still wet. (2)

white balance. A method of adjusting how the camera sees a white object. (4)

white balance bracketing. A camera setting that makes one exposure with the selected white balance, one with a warmer color temperature, and one with a cooler color temperature. (11)

white light. Light composed of red, green, and blue wavelengths in approximately equal proportions. (7)

wide-angle lens. A lens with an angle of view from about 55° to as much as 180°. (6)

windbreak. A blocking device, such as a piece of cardboard, used by nature photographers to keep a flower or similar subject from being moved by a breeze. (13)

working distance. The amount of space between the front of the camera lens and the subject. (13)

working file. A copy of an original file that can be used for editing to avoid permanently altering the original file. (18)

Z

zebras. Highlight warning indicators that alert you if certain portions of an image are overexposed or blown out. Also known as a *zebra pattern*. (7, 16)

zone focusing. A method of prefocusing on an area, making use of depth of field to provide acceptable sharpness for action within that area. Also known as *area focusing*. (12)

Zone System. A photographic method designed to produce consistent, predictable results through careful control of exposure, film development, and printing. It uses a 10-step scale of image values (tones) from pure black to pure white to allow precise description and control. (7)

zooming. Moving the camera's zoom lens in or out during the exposure, usually done to impart a sense of motion to a photo of a stationary subject. (9)

zoom lens. A lens that has a variable focal length, allowing a photographer to use a range of focal lengths in a single lens. (6)

zoom range. The classification of a zoom lens by the spread from its shortest focal length to its longest focal length, such as 100 mm–300 mm. (6)

Index

A

abstractionism, 10
action and event photography, 272–295
    blurring, 277–278
    flash, 288–295
    focus techniques, 276–277
    panning and zooming, 278
    photojournalism, 278–288
    stopping motion, 272–276
active autofocus, 111
active layer, 439
additive color process, 151
additive primary colors, 449
adjustment layer, 442, 483
Adobe RGB, 84
advanced compact digital camera, 118
ambient light, 356–357
    fill flash, 356
    white balance, 356–357
ambient lighting, 259–260
ambrotype, 29
analog signal, 181
anchor points, 471
angle of view, 132
animal photography, 318–322
    pet photography, 320–321
    wild animals, 321–322
aperture, 112–113, 160–162
aperture priority, 79
applications, 388–390
    native camera, 389–390
    third-party, 390
APS-C size sensor, 116
archival quality, 508

archival-quality disc, 418
area array, 181
aspect ratio, 387–388
astigmatism, 130
atmosphere, 229
attribution, 413
Autochrome process, 32

B

backdrop, 366
back focus, 136
background light, 230, 361
backlit, 167
backup copy, 334
ball head, 99
barn doors, 363
barrel distortion, 131
bit depth, 182
black point, 536
blocked shadows, 246
blocking, 233
blurring, 277–278
borders, 486–488
bounce flash, 292
brightness, 224, 536
brilliance, 532
broad lighting, 237–238
browsing, 416
buffer, 187
buffered, 513
built-in flash, 289
burned-out highlights, 246
burning in, 445

Note: Page numbers followed by *f* indicate figures.

burst mode, 83
business
    building, 56–60
    financing, 52–53
    generating income, 53–54
    operation, 52–56
    paperwork, 55–56
    setup, 49–52
    staffing, 54–55
business plan, 53
butterfly lighting, 236

C

cadmium sulfide (CdS) cell meter, 163
calibrate, 510
calotype, 28
camera angle, 213
camera care, 85–90
    body cleaning and maintenance, 87–88
    dust protection, 85–87
    storage and transportation, 88–90
    wet-weather protection, 85
camera controls, 380–383
    aspect ratio, 387–388
    exposure, 384
    flash, 384–387
    focus, 384
    formats, 382–383
    grid, 381
    high dynamic range (HDR), 383
    preserve settings, 382
    traditional, 383–388
camera lucida, 26
camera obscura, 26
camera phone, 36
cameras, 74–101, 108–121
    carrying methods, 90–91
    definition, 108
    digital controls and features, 79–85
    image receiver system, 115–117
    light control system, 112–115
    physical attributes and controls, 75–79
    physical care, 85–90
    support methods, 91–101
    types, 117–121
    viewing/focusing system, 108–111
camera shake, 114
camera support methods, 91–101
    devices, 94–96
    hand-holding, 91–94
    tripods, 96–101
camera types
    mirrorless cameras, 121
    rangefinder cameras, 120
    reflex cameras, 120–121
    simple cameras, 117–120
    view cameras, 121
candid photo, 340
capacitor, 288
card reader, 409
card speed, 187
careers, 10–15
    professional field, 11
    requirements, 11–12
cataloging methods, 415–416
cataloging program, 417
catchlight, 320
cellulose nitrate, 31
center of interest, 203
center-weighted averaging, 249
charge-coupled device (CCD), 116, 180
chemical safety, 560–561
chromatic aberration, 130
circles of confusion, 253
clipping, 246
clipping mask, 489
close-up photography, 322–327
    exposure, 325–327
    methods, 324–325
    range, 322–234
close-up range, 324
CMYK, 507
coated paper, 506
cold-adhesive mounting, 515

collodion, 28
color, 149, 151–152, 154–156
    correction, 449–454
    monochrome, 454–456
color cast, 153
colorimeter, 510
color temperature, 149
coma, 130
commercial processing, 408
compact digital camera, 118
complementary metal oxide semiconductor (CMOS), 116, 180
composite, 479
composition, 17, 198–218
    considerations, 200–214
    focusing viewer attention, 211–214
    perspective and harmony, 204–206
    selective framing, 206–211
    traditional elements, 200–204
    viewpoint, 198–200
    visual effects, 214–217
compositional elements, 201
compression, 83, 187
concave, 128
conservation board, 513
continuous light, 358
contract, 55
contrast, 153, 204, 226–227, 446–448
contrast filter, 153
converge, 128
convergence, 207
convex, 128
cookie, 362
cooling filter, 157
copyright, 412–414
    derivative works, 412–413
    fair use, 412
    sources of images, 413–414
corporation, 50
Creative Commons license, 414
creative control, 160
creative effects lens, 140
cropping images, 431–438

culling, 415
curvature of field, 130

D

daguerreotype, 27
darkness, 224
database programs, 416–419
dedicated flash units, 290
definition, 542
depth of field, 80, 251
depth of field (DOF) preview, 82, 216
derivative works, 412–413
developing-out paper, 28
diffused light, 232
diffusing, 258
digital back, 34
digital cameras, controls and features, 79–85
digital image capture media, 180–188
    digital imaging process, 181–188
    film, 180–181
    gray and color, 182
    image storage, 184–188
    post-shoot storage, 188
    sensor sizes, 183
    studio cameras, 183–184
digital noise, 169, 257
digital photography, 34
digital postprocessing, 426–462
    advanced techniques, 468–497
    borders, 486–488
    combining images, 479–490
    ethics, 468
    filters, 491–494
    imaging editing software, 427–462
    layers, 479–486
    monochrome, 495–497
    photos with type, 489
    selecting parts, 468–478
    traditional, 426–427
    transformations, 490–491
digital resolution, 411

digital sensor, 115–117
digital signal, 182
digital zoom, 138, 393
direct flash, 291
display
    electronic, 504–506
        making prints, 506–511
        print mounting and matting, 511–518
distortion, 131
diverge, 128
documentation, 8
dodging, 446
download, 409
downsampling, 435
dry mounting, 517
dry plate process, 29
dye sublimation printers, 508–510

E

e-commerce capability, 57
edge mounting, 514
electronic display, 504–506
    devices, 505–506
    file compression, 504–505
electronic studio flash, 358
electronic viewfinder, 109
elliptical marquee, 470
emphasis, 156–157, 203
entrepreneurship, 48–49
environmental portrait, 354
equivalent exposures, 251
ethics, 468
evaluative metering, 248
event photography. *See* action and event photography
EXIF (Exchangeable Image File Format), 417
exposure, 160, 246–261, 443–446
    aperture, 160–162, 253
    bracketing, 249–250
    built-in meters, 248–249
    capturing light, 257–261
    compensation, 250

    correcting problems, 249–250
    depth of field, 254–255
    determining, 248–249
    equivalent, 251–257
    highlights, 247–248
    ISO rating, 162–163
    ISO settings, 256–257
    shutter speed, 162, 252
exposure bracketing, 249–250
exposure compensation, 250
exposure lock, 78
extracting, 209

F

fair use, 412
feathering, 363
ferrotype, 29
file compression, 504–505
file formats, 187
filing methods, 415–416
fill flash, 259, 356
fill light, 230, 361
film basics, 560–563
    printing paper, 561–563
    safety, 560–561
filters, 153–159, 492
    contrast, 153
    emphasis, 156–157
    reduce light, 153–154
    reflection and color saturation, 154–156
    special effects, 157–159
firmware, 182
fish-eye lens, 136
fixing, 27
flag, 364
flare, 305
flash, 288–295
    techniques, 291–295
    types of units, 289–291
flush mount, 516
foam board, 512

focal length, 131–134
focal plane shutter, 113
focal point, 128
focus, 276–277
    follow, 276
    prefocusing, 276
    zone focusing, 276–277
focusing mark, 255
focusing rail, 326
focus lock, 78
follow focus, 276
formal balance, 203
formal studio portrait, 354
frame, 16, 209
freelancer, 8
frequency, 148
front-focusing, 136
f-stop, 160
full-frame, 183

G

gel, 227, 362
giclée, 506
gobo, 365
grand vistas, 302
gray levels, 182
grayscale mode, 454
grid, 363
guide number, 290

H

handles, 471
hard light, 231, 363
hard news, 278–281
HEIC, 188
high dynamic range (HDR) image, 383
high key, 246
high-voltage power pack, 291
histogram, 77, 246
history, 26–39
    color photography, 32–34
    digital photography, 35–37
    first permanent image, 27–28
    negative discovery, 28
    plate-based photography, 28–30
    roll film, 30–32
hot shoe, 78, 289
hyperfocal distance, 255

I

image editing software, 427–462
    color correction, 449–454
    color to monochrome, 454–456
    contrast, 446–448
    cropping and resizing, 431–438
    digital postprocessing, 430
    exposure, 443–446
    layers, 438–443
    retouching images, 457–460
    sharpening images, 460–462
    working copy, 430–431
    workspace, 429–430
image editor, 427
image file, 181
image management, 414–419
    database programs, 416–419
    filing/cataloging methods, 415–416
image manipulation, 426, 468
image processing, 426
image receiver system, 115–117
    digital sensor, 115–117
images
    combining, 479–490
    importing, 408–419
    retouching, 457–460
    sharpening, 460–462
image storage, 184–188
importing, 408
importing images, 408–419
    commercial processing, 408
    copyright, 412–414

downloading online, 411
   downloading to computers, 409–410
   image management, 414–419
   methods, 408–410
   scanners, 410–411
incident light reading, 166
informal balance, 203
infrared photography, 314
infringement, 412
inkjet printers, 506–508
intellectual property, 53
internship, 47
interpolation, 435
inverse-square law, 367
invoice, 56
iris, 112
ISO, 79
ISO rating, 162–163

J

JPEG, 188

K

key light, 230, 360
keyword, 417

L

landscape mode, 209
landscape photography, 302–314
   definition, 302
   grand vistas, 302
   infrared, 314
   panoramic views, 302–305
   shooting tips, 305–307
   smaller-scale subjects, 307–314
large format camera, 117
large-format inkjet printer, 507
latent image, 27
layer mask, 483

layers, 438–443, 479–486
leading lines, 211
lead room, 211
lens collar, 280
lens elements, 129
lenses, 128–141
   aberrations, 129–131
   coatings, 131
   definition, 128
   focal length, 131–134
   mobile, 391–393
   normal, 135
   shapes and light, 128
   specialty, 139–141
   telephoto, 136
   wide-angle, 135–136
   zoom, 136–138
light
   capturing, 257–261
   definition, 148
   exposure meters, 163–165
   making reading, 165–169
   measuring, 163–169
light absorption and reflection, 149–150
light and exposure, 148–172
   basic light theory, 148–153
   controlling exposure, 160–163
   filters, 153–159
   measuring light, 163–169
   Zone System, 169–172
light control system, 112–115
   aperture, 112–113
   shutter, 113–115
lighting, 224–239
   artificial, 259–261
   atmosphere, 229
   choosing approach, 234
   common setups, 234–238
   darkness and brightness, 224–227
   design, 232–234
   importance, 224–229
   lights, 230–232
   mood, 228–229

    natural, 257–259
    studio, 357–372
    tone, 227–228
lighting design, 232–234
lighting instrument, 225
lighting ratio, 234, 367
lighting setups, 234–238
    broad, 237–238
    butterfly, 236
    loop, 236
    Rembrandt, 236
    rim, 237
    short, 238
    single, 235
    split, 237
    three-point, 235–236
light movement, 148
light reduction, 153–154
Lightroom for mobile, 545–551
lights, 230–232
    qualities, 230–232
    types, 230
light theory, 148–153
    absorption and reflection, 149–150
    additive and subtractive color, 151–152
    color, 149
    movement, 148
    visible spectrum, 148–149
    white balance, 152–153
limited liability company (LLC), 50–51
line, 201
loop lighting, 236
low key, 246
luminances, 169

M

macro lens, 139
macro photo range, 324
magnification rate, 324
manual exposure, 81
marketing, 46

mass marketing, 56
mat board, 512
media, 180–188
medium format camera, 117
medium format digital camera, 116
memory card, 184
meniscus lens, 128
metadata, 417
metamerism, 511
metering, 165
metering modes, 248
middle gray, 166
mirror image, 318
mirrorless camera, 121
mobile photography, 380–397
    apps, 388–390
    camera controls, 380–383
    cleaning lenses, 391–393
    definition, 380
    digital zoom, 393
    flexibility advantage, 395–396
    multiple shots, 393
    stabilizing, 393–395
    supplies, 380
mobile postprocessing, 526–554
    definition, 526
    native camera app, 526–545
    posting to social media, 552–553
    printing, 553–554
    third-party apps, 545–552
monochrome, 454, 497
monolight, 359
monopod, 94
mood, 228–229
morphing, 479
motion, 272–276
    capturing action peak, 274–276
    effects, 273–274
motion blur, 214–215
motivated lighting, 232
mounting, 511–517
multiple exposure, 216–217
museum board, 513

N

nanometer, 148
native camera app, 526–545
    auto, 530–531
    black point, 536–537
    brightness, 536
    brilliance, 532–533
    contrast, 534–536
    crop, 527–529
    definition, 542–543
    exposure, 531–532
    filters, 530
    highlights and shadows, 533–534
    noise reduction, 543–544
    saturation, 537–538
    sharpness, 541–542
    straightening images, 526–527
    tint, 540–541
    vibrance, 538–539
    vignette, 544–545
    warmth, 539–540
negative, 28
negative/positive system, 28
negative space, 210
neutral density (ND) filter, 153
nodal point, 303
noise reduction, 543
normal lenses, 135

O

off-camera flash, 292
online gallery, 504
online photofinishing site, 408
open flash, 294
optical resolution, 411
optical zoom, 138, 393
outdoor photography, 302–327
    animal, 318–322
    close-up, 322–327
    definition, 302
    landscape, 302–314
    water, 315–318
overexposure, 166, 225
overmat, 511
overmatting, 517
oversharpening, 460

P

pack-and-head system, 359
painting with light, 294
pan head, 98
panning, 214
panorama, 302
panoramic views, 302–305
parallax error, 108
partial metering, 249
partnership, 49
passive autofocus, 111
path, 471
pattern, 203
peak of action, 275
permissible circle of confusion, 253
perspective, 134, 205
pH, 513
photoelectric light meter, 163
photoflood, 358
photogram, 26
photographic daylight, 149
photographs
    composing, 16–18
    selecting, 15
photography
    action and event, 272–295
    art, 10
    definition, 6
    display, 504–518
    documentation, 8–9
    entertainment, 9
    history, 26–39
    milestones, 38–39f
    mobile, 380–397

organizations, 62–63
outdoor, 302–327
portrait, 7
portrait and studio, 354–372
product, 7
professional, 46–63
scientific and technical, 9
society, 6–10
travel, 332–347
workshops, 63
photography assistant, 47
photojournalism, 278–288
community, 284–286
definition, 278
family milestones, 286–287
news and feature, 278–282
picture, 283
school event and yearbook, 283–284
street photography, 287–288
photojournalist, 8
photomicrography, 324
photo sharing site, 408
photosite, 115
picture story, 283
pigment-based ink, 508
pincushion distortion, 131
pixel, 115
plane of focus, 253
point, 201
polarizing filter, 154
Polaroid process, 33
portfolio, 19–20
digital, 20
physical, 19–20
portrait and studio photography, 354–372
ambient light, 356–357
studio lighting, 357–372
types, 354–355
portrait mode, 209
portrait photography, 7
positioning prints, 518
positive, 28

prefocusing, 276
pressure-sensitive adhesive material, 516
prime lens, 132
printing-out paper, 28
printing paper, 561–563
finish, 561–562
materials and coatings, 562
mobile photos, 553–554
printers, 561
prints, 506–511
dye sublimation printers, 508–510
inkjet printers, 506–508
quality, 510–511
product photography, 7
professional photographer, 11
professional photography, 46–63
assistant, 47–48
business operation, 52–56
business setup, 49–52
clients, 61
corporation, 50
definition, 46
entering field, 47–49
entrepreneurship, 48–49
limited liability company (LLC), 50–51
marketing, 56–60
partnership, 49–50
professional growth, 62–63
sole proprietorship, 49
team, 61–62
working with people, 60–62
profile, 510
profit, 52
Program AE, 79
proper exposure, 246
prosumer, 35
public domain, 413

Q

quad-tone ink set, 508

R

rangefinder cameras, 120
RAW, 188
RAW converter, 430
reach, 552
rear-curtain synchronization, 274
reciprocity law, 168
recreational travel, 332
rectangular marquee, 470
recycle, 289
red eye, 291
reflection, 154–156
reflective light reading, 166
reflex cameras, 120–121
refraction, 128
relative motion, 272
release, 55
Rembrandt lighting, 236
reproduction ratio, 139, 323
retouching, 457–460
retrofocus, 136
reversing ring, 325
rhythm, 203
rights-managed image, 414
rim light, 230, 362
rim lighting, 237
royalty, 414
royalty-free image, 414
rule of thirds, 210

S

safety, 560–561
    chemicals, 560–561
saturation, 537
scanner, 410
school event photography, 283–284
selection refinement, 475–478
selection tools, 468–475
selective focus, 216
selective framing, 206
selenium cell meter, 163
self-contained flash units, 289
sensor, 115
sensor sizes, 183
separate viewfinder, 108
shape, 203
sharpening, 460–462
sharpness, 541
shortcut keys, 427
short lighting, 238
shot list, 335
shutter, 113–115, 162
shutter lag, 76
shutter priority, 80
shutter speed, 162
sidelighted, 258
simple cameras, 117–120
slave units, 294
smaller-scale subjects, 307–314
small format camera, 117
snapshot, 74
snoot, 363
softbox, 358
soft focus, 215–216
soft light, 231, 363
soft news, 279, 281–282
sole proprietor, 49
solid-state, 184
special effects, 157–159
specialty lenses, 139–141
specular light, 232
specular reflection, 150
spherical aberration, 129
split lighting, 237
spot metering, 249
spotting, 457
sRGB, 84
stabilizing systems, 93
straight photography, 426
studio cameras, 183–184
studio lighting, 357–372
    controlling light, 362–366
    measuring light, 366–369

methods, 360–362
portrait photography, 369
product photography, 370–372
studio photography. *See* portrait and studio photography
subject blur, 114
subject brightness range (SBR), 170
sublimate, 508
subtractive color process, 151
subtractive primary colors, 449
superzoom, 132
sync speed, 162

T

targeted marketing, 56
teleconverter, 139
telephoto lens, 136
tenting, 370
tethered shutter release, 75
third-party apps, 545–552
Lightroom for mobile, 545–551
three-point lighting, 235–236, 362
through-the-lens (TTL) metering, 163
through-the-lens viewing system, 108
thumbnails, 416
TIFF, 188
tint, 540
tintype, 29
tonal range, 166, 227–228
traditional photography, 380
traditional processing, 426–427
travel guide, 333
travel photography, 332–347
definition, 332
equipment, 333–335
research, 332–333
subjects, 335–341
timing and locations, 341–347
trilinear array, 116
tripod, 96–101
true to color, 383
tungsten-halogen bulb, 358

U

ultraviolet (UV) filter, 86
underexposure, 166, 224
untethered shutter release, 75
upload, 408
upsampling, 435

V

vibrance, 538
view camera, 121
viewfinder, 76
viewing/focusing system, 108–111
focusing methods, 109–111
viewing methods, 108–109
viewpoint, 199
vignette, 544
visible spectrum, 148–149
visual effects, 214–217
motion blur, 214–215
multiple exposure, 216–217
selective focus, 216
soft focus, 215–216
visualization, 15–18, 198

W

warming filter, 156
warmth, 539
water photography, 315–318
watermarking, 411
wavelength, 148
wet-plate collodion process, 28
white balance, 83, 356–357
white balance bracketing, 260
white light, 149
wide-angle lenses, 135–136
windbreak, 312
working distance, 326
working file, 430

Y

yearbook photography, 283–284

Z

zebras, 167, 390
zone focusing, 276–277
Zone System, 169–172
    digital cameras, 172
    exposure value, 170
    simplified exposure method, 170–172
    value scale, 169–170
zooming, 214
zoom lens, 131, 136–138
zoom range, 138